Discovering Computers

Tools, Apps, Devices, and the Impact of Technology

Dedication

With heartfelt thanks to my husband, Bill, and children, Jackie and Ricky ... for their endless support, devotion, assistance, understanding, and patience during my work on this and all other projects throughout my career. I love you all dearly.

Thanks also to Sue, Steve, Jennifer, and Mark. It's a pleasure to work with such a dedicated team.

— *Misty E. Vermaat*

Thanks to my family and friends for their support, encouragement, and patience. Special acknowledgement goes to my mother, Mandy, and to my professors at Purdue University, especially James Quasney, Ralph Webb, and Daniel Yovich, who taught me that keeping a positive mental attitude and striving for excellence are the keys to success.

— *Susan L. Sebok*

For my wife, Traci, and my children, Maddy and Sam, whose support and love are incredibly motivating. Thanks to my parents for their endless encouragement, and to Linda Linardos, who was instrumental in starting my writing career.

— *Steven M. Freund*

I would like to thank Mike, Emma, and Lucy for their support and inspiration, and Maggie for providing welcome distractions. Special thanks to my parents for being terrific role models.

— *Jennifer T. Campbell*

Thanks to my family and friends for their encouragement, and to my colleagues and students at Bentley University for their helpful feedback, which guided my contributions to this book. Thanks to Bentley University for providing me with an environment to learn and teach new technology.

— *Mark Frydenberg*

The author team also would like to thank our developmental editor, Lyn Markowicz, whose patience, attention to detail, and determination contributed in so many meaningful ways to this project.

We dedicate this book to the memory of Thomas J. Cashman (4/29/32 – 1/7/15). As one of the founders of the Shelly Cashman Series, Tom partnered with Gary Shelly to write and publish their first computer education textbook in 1969, revolutionizing the introductory computing course and changing the path of computing course materials. From 1969 through his retirement in 2008, Tom served as educator, author, leader, and inspiration to his fellow authors and Shelly Cashman Series team members. His mark on the series and the introductory computing market is indelible and he will be both remembered and missed.

SHELLY CASHMAN SERIES®

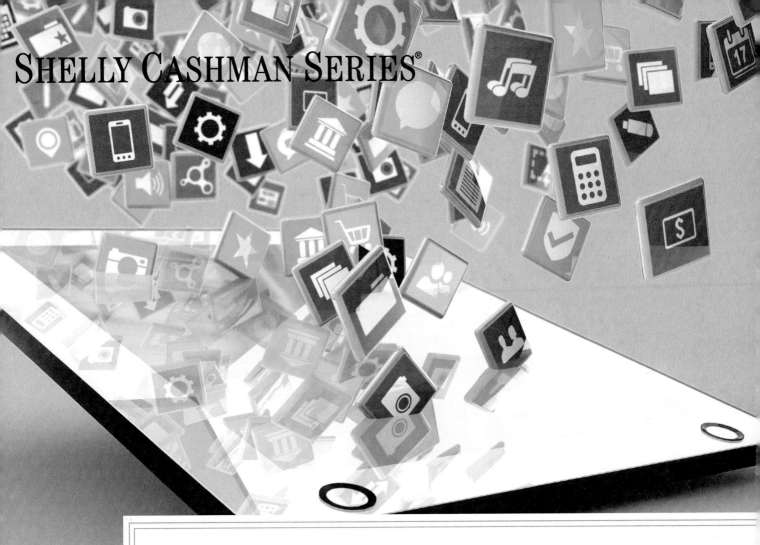

Discovering
Tools, Apps, Devices, and
the Impact of Technology
Computers 2016

VERMAAT | SEBOK | FREUND | CAMPBELL | FRYDENBERG

Shelly Cashman Series®

CENGAGE
Learning·

Australia · Brazil · Mexico · Singapore · United Kingdom · United States

Discovering Computers: Tools, Apps, Devices, and the Impact of Technology
Misty E. Vermaat
Susan L. Sebok
Steven M. Freund
Jennifer T. Campbell
Mark Frydenberg

Product Director: Kathleen McMahon

Product Manager: Amanda Lyons

Managing Developer: Emma Newsom

Associate Content Developer:
Crystal Parenteau

Marketing Manager: Kristie Clark

Marketing Coordinator: William Guiliani

Manufacturing Planner: Julio Esperas

Senior Content Project Manager:
Matthew Hutchinson

Development Editor: Lyn Markowicz

Researcher: F. William Vermaat

Management Services: Lumina Datamatics, Inc.

Art Director: Jackie Bates, GEX

Text Design: Joel Sadagursky

Cover Design: Lisa Kuhn, Curio Press, LLC

Cover Photo: © iStock.com/audioundwerbung

Illustrator: Lumina Datamatics, Inc.

Compositor: Lumina Datamatics, Inc.

Printer: RRD Menasha

For product information and technology assistance, contact us at
Cengage Learning Customer & Sales Support, 1-800-354-9706

For permission to use material from this text or product,
submit all requests online at **cengage.com/permissions**
Further permissions questions can be emailed to
permissionrequest@cengage.com

Library of Congress Control Number: 2014955985

ISBN-13: 978-1-305-39185-7

Cengage Learning
20 Channel Center Street
Boston, MA 02210
USA

Cengage Learning is a leading provider of customized learning solutions with office locations around the globe, including Singapore, the United Kingdom, Australia, Mexico, Brazil and Japan. Locate your local office at:
international.cengage.com/region

Cengage Learning products are represented in Canada by Nelson Education, Ltd.

Purchase any of our products at your local college bookstore or at our preferred online store at **www.cengagebrain.com**

Printed in the United States of America
Print Number: 01   Print Year: 2015

Discovering Computers
Tools, Apps, Devices, and the Impact of Technology

Table of Contents at a Glance

Intro Chapter
**Succeeding in this Course:
Tips and Pointers** I-1

Chapter **1**
**Introducing Today's Technologies:
Computers, Devices, and the Web** 1

Chapter **2**
**Connecting and Communicating
Online: The Internet, Websites,
and Media** 55

Chapter **3**
**Computers and Mobile Devices:
Evaluating Options for Home
and Work** 107

Chapter **4**
**Programs and Apps: Productivity,
Graphics, Security, and
Other Tools** 157

Chapter **5**
**Digital Security, Ethics, and
Privacy: Threats, Issues,
and Defenses** 211

Technology Timeline 261

Chapter **6**
**Computing Components: Processors,
Memory, the Cloud, and More** 275

Chapter **7**
**Input and Output: Extending
Capabilities of Computers
and Mobile Devices** 317

Chapter **8**
**Digital Storage: Preserving
Content Locally and on the Cloud** 367

Chapter **9**
**Operating Systems: Managing,
Coordinating, and Monitoring
Resources** 409

Chapter **10**
**Communicating Digital Content:
Wired and Wireless Networks
and Devices** 449

Chapter **11**
**Building Solutions: Database,
System, and Application
Development Tools** 497

Chapter **12**
**Working in The Enterprise: Systems,
Certifications, and Careers** 551

**Appendix A: Technology
Acronyms** . . . . APP 1

**Appendix B: Troubleshooting
Computer and Mobile
Device Problems** . . . . . . APP 5

Index . . . . IND 1

Discovering Computers
Tools, Apps, Devices, and the Impact of Technology

Table of Contents

INTRO CHAPTER

Succeeding in this Course: Tips and Pointers   I-1

INTRODUCTION I-1
   Browsing the Web I-1
   Book and Online Content.............................. I-2
PURCHASING THE RIGHT COMPUTER I-5
   Step 1: Choose the Computer Type I-5
   Step 2: Choose the Operating System I-7
   Step 3: Choose Configuration Options................ I-10
   Step 4: Choose the Purchasing Option................ I-11
STUDENT ASSIGNMENTS: • How To: Your Turn
   • Internet Research .... I-12 – I-14

CHAPTER 1

Introducing Today's Technologies: Computers, Devices, and the Web   1

TODAY'S TECHNOLOGY 2
COMPUTERS.. 4
   Laptops 4
   Tablets 4
   Desktops and All-in-Ones............................. 6
   Servers 6
MOBILE AND GAME DEVICES........................... 7
   Smartphones 7
   Digital Cameras 8
   Portable and Digital Media Players 8
   E-Book Readers 9
   Wearable Devices..................................... 9
   Game Devices 10
DATA AND INFORMATION 12
   Input 12
   Output 14
   Memory and Storage 16
THE WEB 20
   Web Searching.. 22
   Online Social Networks 23
   Internet Communications.............................. 24
DIGITAL SECURITY AND PRIVACY....................... 24
   Viruses and Other Malware 24
   Privacy 24
   Health Concerns...................................... 26
   Environmental Issues................................. 26
PROGRAMS AND APPS.................................. 26
   Operating Systems.................................... 27
   Applications... 27

Installing and Running Programs....................... 28
Developing Programs and Apps......................... 29
COMMUNICATIONS AND NETWORKS 30
   Wired and Wireless Communications.................... 31
   Networks 32
TECHNOLOGY USES.................................... 35
   Government 36
   Finance.. 36
   Retail 36
   Entertainment 38
   Health Care 38
   Science.. 38
   Travel 39
   Publishing 39
   Manufacturing.. 40
TECHNOLOGY USERS................................... 41
CHAPTER SUMMARY.................................... 43
STUDENT ASSIGNMENTS: Study Guide • Key Terms • Checkpoint
   • Problem Solving • How To: Your Turn • Internet Research
   • Critical Thinking .... 44 – 54

CHAPTER 2

Connecting and Communicating Online: The Internet, Websites, and Media   55

THE INTERNET 56
   Evolution of the Internet 56
CONNECTING TO THE INTERNET 58
   Internet Service Providers 61
   How Data Travels the Internet 62
   IP Addresses and Domain Names........................ 62
THE WORLD WIDE WEB 65
   Navigating the Web 65
   Web Addresses.. 68
   Web Apps and Mobile Apps............................. 69
TYPES OF WEBSITES................................... 71
   Search Engines....................................... 71
   Informational and Research........................... 74
   Media Sharing 75
   Bookmarking 75
   News, Weather, Sports, and Other Mass Media 76
   Educational 77
   Business, Governmental, and Organizational........... 77
   Blogs 78
   Wikis and Collaboration.............................. 78
   Health and Fitness 79
   Science.. 79

Entertainment 79
Banking and Finance 79
Travel and Tourism 80
Mapping 80
Retail and Auctions 81
Careers and Employment 82
E-Commerce 82
Portals 82
Content Aggregation 83
Website Creation and Management 84
DIGITAL MEDIA ON THE WEB **85**
Graphics 85
Audio 86
Video 87
Plug-Ins 88
OTHER INTERNET SERVICES **88**
Email 88
Email Lists 90
Internet Messaging 90
Chat Rooms 91
Online Discussions 91
VoIP 92
FTP 92
NETIQUETTE **94**
CHAPTER SUMMARY **95**
STUDENT ASSIGNMENTS: Study Guide • Key Terms • Checkpoint
• Problem Solving • How To: Your Turn • Internet Research
• Critical Thinking . . . . 96 – 106

Port Replicators and Docking Stations 136
Wireless Device Connections 137
PROTECTING HARDWARE **139**
Hardware Theft and Vandalism 139
Hardware Failure 139
HEALTH CONCERNS OF USING TECHNOLOGY **142**
Repetitive Strain Injuries 142
Other Physical Risks 143
Behavioral Health Risks 144
CHAPTER SUMMARY **145**
STUDENT ASSIGNMENTS: Study Guide • Key Terms • Checkpoint
• Problem Solving • How To: Your Turn • Internet Research
• Critical Thinking . . . . 146 – 156

CHAPTER **3**

Computers and Mobile Devices: Evaluating Options for Home and Work — **107**

COMPUTERS AND MOBILE DEVICES **108**
MOBILE COMPUTERS AND DESKTOPS **108**
Laptops, Tablets, and Other Mobile Computers 111
Handheld Computers 112
Desktops and All-in-Ones 114
SERVERS **116**
TERMINALS **117**
Point-of-Sale Terminals 118
ATMs 118
Self-Service Kiosks 119
SUPERCOMPUTERS **120**
CLOUD COMPUTING **121**
MOBILE DEVICES **122**
Smartphones 123
Digital Cameras 125
Portable and Digital Media Players 127
E-Book Readers 129
Wearable Devices 130
GAME DEVICES **131**
EMBEDDED COMPUTERS **132**
PUTTING IT ALL TOGETHER **134**
PORTS AND CONNECTIONS **134**
USB Ports 136

CHAPTER **4**

Programs and Apps: Productivity, Graphics, Security, and Other Tools — **157**

PROGRAMS AND APPS **158**
Role of the Operating System 158
Obtaining Software 161
Installing Software 162
Categories of Programs and Apps 163
PRODUCTIVITY APPLICATIONS **165**
Developing Projects 165
Word Processing 167
Presentation 168
Spreadsheet 168
Database 170
Note Taking 171
Calendar and Contact Management 171
Software Suite 172
Project Management 172
Accounting 173
Personal Finance 174
Legal 175
Tax Preparation 176
Document Management 176
Enterprise Computing 177
GRAPHICS AND MEDIA APPLICATIONS **179**
Computer-Aided Design 180
Desktop Publishing 180
Paint/Image Editing 181
Photo Editing and Photo Management 181
Video and Audio Editing 183
Multimedia and Website Authoring 184
Media Player 185
Disc Burning 185
PERSONAL INTEREST APPLICATIONS **185**
COMMUNICATIONS APPLICATIONS **188**
SECURITY TOOLS **189**
Personal Firewall 189
Antivirus Programs 191
Spyware, Adware, and Other Malware Removers 192
Internet Filters 193
FILE, DISK, AND SYSTEM MANAGEMENT TOOLS **194**
File Manager 194

Search 195
Image Viewer 195
Uninstaller 195
Disk Cleanup 196
Disk Defragmenter 197
Screen Saver 197
File Compression 198
PC Maintenance 198
Backup and Restore 198
CHAPTER SUMMARY **199**
STUDENT ASSIGNMENTS: Study Guide • Key Terms • Checkpoint
• Problem Solving • How To: Your Turn • Internet Research
• Critical Thinking . . . . 200 – 210

CHAPTER **5**

Digital Security, Ethics, and Privacy: Threats, Issues, and Defenses   211

DIGITAL SECURITY RISKS **212**
Cybercrime 212
INTERNET AND NETWORK ATTACKS **215**
Malware 215
Botnets 216
Denial of Service Attacks 217
Back Doors 217
Spoofing 217
Safeguards against Internet and Network Attacks 218
Firewalls 219
UNAUTHORIZED ACCESS AND USE **221**
Safeguards against Unauthorized Access and Use 221
Access Controls 222
User Names and Passwords 222
Possessed Objects 224
Biometric Devices 224
Two-Step Verification 226
Digital Forensics 227
SOFTWARE THEFT **228**
Safeguards against Software Theft 228
INFORMATION THEFT **229**
Safeguards against Information Theft 229
Encryption 229
Digital Signatures and Certificates 231
HARDWARE THEFT, VANDALISM, AND FAILURE . . . **233**
BACKING UP — THE ULTIMATE SAFEGUARD **233**
WIRELESS SECURITY **236**
ETHICS AND SOCIETY **238**
Information Accuracy 239
Intellectual Property Rights 240
Codes of Conduct 241
Green Computing 241
INFORMATION PRIVACY **242**
Electronic Profiles 242
Cookies 243
Phishing 244
Spyware and Adware 245
Social Engineering 245
Privacy Laws 246
Employee Monitoring 247
Content Filtering 247

CHAPTER SUMMARY **249**
STUDENT ASSIGNMENTS: Study Guide • Key Terms • Checkpoint
• Problem Solving • How To: Your Turn • Internet Research
• Critical Thinking . . . . 250 – 260
TECHNOLOGY TIMELINE **261**

CHAPTER **6**

Computing Components: Processors, Memory, the Cloud, and More   275

INSIDE THE CASE **276**
The Motherboard 278
PROCESSORS **280**
The Control Unit 281
The Arithmetic Logic Unit 281
Machine Cycle 281
Registers 282
The System Clock 282
Personal Computer and Mobile Device Processors 283
Processor Cooling 284
Mini Feature 6-1: The Internet of Things 284
CLOUD COMPUTING **287**
Mini Feature 6-2: Cloud Computing Services 287
DATA REPRESENTATION **288**
Bits and Bytes 288
Coding Schemes 289
MEMORY **290**
Bytes and Addressable Memory 290
Types of Memory 290
RAM 290
Cache 293
ROM 294
Flash Memory 295
CMOS 296
Memory Access Times 296
ADAPTERS **297**
Adapter Cards 297
USB Adapters 298
BUSES **299**
Bus Width 300
Types of Buses 300
POWER SUPPLY AND BATTERIES **301**
Mini Feature 6-3: Proper Care for Computers
and Mobile Devices 302
CHAPTER SUMMARY **305**
STUDENT ASSIGNMENTS: Study Guide • Key Terms • Checkpoint
• Problem Solving • How To: Your Turn • Internet Research
• Critical Thinking . . . . 306 – 316

CHAPTER **7**

Input and Output: Extending Capabilities of Computers and Mobile Devices   317

WHAT IS INPUT? **318**
KEYBOARDS **320**
Types of Keyboards 321

POINTING DEVICES **322**
    Mouse 322
    Touchpad 323
    Trackball..................................... 324
TOUCH SCREENS **324**
    Mini Feature 7-1: Touch Input 324
PEN INPUT **326**
    Stylus 326
    Digital Pen 327
    Graphics Tablet............................... 328
MOTION, VOICE, AND VIDEO INPUT **328**
    Mini Feature 7-2: Motion Input 328
    Voice and Audio Input 330
    Mini Feature 7-3: Digital Video Technology 330
    Webcams and Integrated DV Cameras........... 332
SCANNERS AND READING DEVICES................. **334**
    Optical Scanners 334
    Optical Readers 335
    Bar Code Readers............................. 335
    RFID Readers 336
    Magstripe Readers 337
    MICR Readers 338
    Data Collection Devices 338
WHAT IS OUTPUT? **339**
DISPLAYS **340**
    Display Technologies 341
    Display Quality............................... 342
    DTVs and Smart TVs.......................... 343
PRINTERS **344**
    Nonimpact Printers 345
    Ink-Jet Printers 345
    Photo Printers 347
    Laser Printers 348
    All-in-One Printers 349
    3-D Printers 349
    Thermal Printers.............................. 349
    Mobile Printers............................... 350
    Label Printers 350
    Plotters and Large-Format Printers.............. 350
    Impact Printers 351
OTHER OUTPUT DEVICES **351**
    Speakers..................................... 351
    Headphones and Earbuds 352
    Data Projectors 352
    Interactive Whiteboards....................... 353
    Force-Feedback Game Controllers and Tactile Output 353
ASSISTIVE TECHNOLOGY INPUT AND OUTPUT................. **353**
CHAPTER SUMMARY................................ **355**
STUDENT ASSIGNMENTS: Study Guide • Key Terms • Checkpoint
    • Problem Solving • How To: Your Turn • Internet Research
    • Critical Thinking .... 356 – 366

Storage Access Times 371
Mini Feature 8-1: Media Sharing 371
HARD DRIVES...................................... **373**
    Hard Disk 373
    SSDs.. 376
    External Hard Drives 378
    RAID.. 380
PORTABLE FLASH MEMORY STORAGE **381**
    Memory Cards 381
    USB Flash Drives 382
CLOUD STORAGE **383**
    Mini Feature 8-2: Services Offered by Cloud Storage Providers ... 384
OPTICAL DISCS **386**
    Characteristics of Optical Discs 386
    CDs 388
    DVDs 388
ENTERPRISE STORAGE.............................. **389**
    RAID.. 390
    NAS and SAN................................ 390
    Magnetic Tape 392
OTHER TYPES OF STORAGE **392**
    Magnetic Stripe Cards 393
    Smart Cards 393
    RFID Tags 394
    NFC Chips and Tags 394
    Mini Feature 8-3: Backup Plans 395
CHAPTER SUMMARY................................ **397**
STUDENT ASSIGNMENTS: Study Guide • Key Terms • Checkpoint
    • Problem Solving • How To: Your Turn • Internet Research
    • Critical Thinking .... 398 – 408

CHAPTER **9**

OPERATING SYSTEMS: Managing, Coordinating, and Monitoring Resources   409

OPERATING SYSTEMS **410**
OPERATING SYSTEM FUNCTIONS......................... **412**
    Starting Computers and Mobile Devices 412
    Shutting Down Computers and Mobile Devices.............. 413
    Providing a User Interface 414
    Managing Programs.................................. 415
    Managing Memory 416
    Coordinating Tasks.................................. 418
    Configuring Devices.................................. 419
    Monitoring Performance 420
    Establishing an Internet Connection 420
    Updating Operating System Software 421
    Providing File, Disk, and System Management Tools 422
    Controlling a Network 423
    Administering Security................................ 423
TYPES OF OPERATING SYSTEMS **425**
DESKTOP OPERATING SYSTEMS.......................... **426**
    Windows/Mini Feature 9-1.............................. 426
    Mac OS/Mini Feature 9-2.............................. 427
UNIX **429**
    Linux 429
    Chrome OS... 430
    Running Multiple Desktop Operating Systems.............. 431

CHAPTER **8**

DIGITAL STORAGE: Preserving Content Locally and on the Cloud   367

STORAGE **368**
    Storage Capacity 370
    Storage versus Memory 370

SERVER OPERATING SYSTEMS................................ 432
MOBILE OPERATING SYSTEMS.............................. 433
    Android 434
    iOS 434
    Windows Phone...................................... 435
    Mini Feature 9-3: Mobile versus Desktop Operating Systems 435
CHAPTER SUMMARY...................................... 437
STUDENT ASSIGNMENTS: Study Guide • Key Terms • Checkpoint
    • Problem Solving • How To: Your Turn • Internet Research
    • Critical Thinking .... 438 – 448

CHAPTER **10**

Communicating Digital Content: Wired and Wireless Networks and Devices **449**

COMMUNICATIONS 450
NETWORKS 452
    LANs, MANs, WANs, and PANs........................ 453
    Network Architectures 456
COMMUNICATIONS SOFTWARE........................... 457
    Mini Feature 10-1: Mobile Communications 457
NETWORK COMMUNICATIONS STANDARDS AND PROTOCOLS 459
    Ethernet... 460
    Token Ring 460
    TCP/IP 461
    Wi-Fi.. 462
    LTE 462
    Bluetooth/Mini Feature 10-2 463
    UWB... 464
    IrDA 465
    RFID 465
    NFC 466
COMMUNICATIONS LINES 466
    Cable 466
    DSL... 467
    ISDN.. 467
    FTTP.. 467
    T-Carrier... 468
    ATM 468
COMMUNICATIONS DEVICES.............................. 468
    Digital Modems: Cable, DSL, and ISDN............... 468
    Wireless Modems..................................... 469
    Wireless Access Points 470
    Routers... 471
    Network Cards.. 472
    Hubs and Switches................................... 473
HOME NETWORKS 473
    Mini Feature 10-3: Planning and Designing Your
    Home Network...................................... 474
TRANSMISSION MEDIA 476
PHYSICAL TRANSMISSION MEDIA 477
    Twisted-Pair Cable 477
    Coaxial Cable.. 478
    Fiber-Optic Cable 478
WIRELESS TRANSMISSION MEDIA 478
    Infrared 479
    Broadcast Radio...................................... 479
    Cellular Radio.. 480
    Microwaves 482

    Communications Satellite 482
CHAPTER SUMMARY...................................... 485
STUDENT ASSIGNMENTS: Study Guide • Key Terms • Checkpoint
    • Problem Solving • How To: Your Turn • Internet Research
    • Critical Thinking .... 486 – 496

CHAPTER **11**

Building Solutions: Database, System, and Application Development Tools **497**

DATABASES, DATA, AND INFORMATION...................... 498
    The Hierarchy of Data 500
    File Maintenance 502
    Validating Data 503
FILE PROCESSING SYSTEMS AND DATABASES.................. 504
    File Processing Systems 504
    The Database Approach............................... 504
    Mini Feature 11-1: Web Databases 506
    Types of Databases 508
    Mini Feature 11-2: Big Data.......................... 508
DATABASE MANAGEMENT SYSTEMS........................ 510
    Data Dictionary 510
    File Retrieval and Maintenance 511
    Data Security 513
    Backup and Recovery................................ 515
SYSTEM DEVELOPMENT................................... 515
    System Development Guidelines 517
    Who Participates in System Development? 517
    Project Management 517
    Feasibility Assessment 519
    Documentation 519
    Data and Information Gathering Techniques 520
    Planning Phase 521
    Analysis Phase....................................... 521
    Design Phase 523
    Implementation Phase................................ 525
    Support and Security Phase 526
APPLICATION DEVELOPMENT LANGUAGES AND TOOLS 527
Procedural Languages 528
Object-Oriented Programming Languages and Application
Development Tools... 530
Other Languages and Application Development Tools 532
Web Development 534
Mini Feature 11-3: Web Application Development................. 536
CHAPTER SUMMARY...................................... 539
STUDENT ASSIGNMENTS: Study Guide • Key Terms • Checkpoint
    • Problem Solving • How To: Your Turn • Internet Research
    • Critical Thinking .... 540 – 550

CHAPTER **12**

Working in the Enterprise: Systems, Certifications, and Careers **551**

THE TECHNOLOGY INDUSTRY 552
INFORMATION SYSTEMS IN THE ENTERPRISE 554

Functional Units 554
Enterprise Resource Planning 555
Document Management Systems 556
Content Management Systems 557
Other Enterprise-Wide Information Systems 557
Mini Feature 12-1: Information Literacy 560
TECHNOLOGY CAREERS **562**
General Business and Government Organizations
and Their IT Departments 562
Technology Equipment 564
Software and Apps 564
Technology Service and Repair 565
Technology Sales 566
Technology Education, Training, and Support 567
IT Consulting 568
Putting It All Together — Job Titles and Descriptions 568
Mini Feature 12-2: Mobile App Development 570
TECHNOLOGY CERTIFICATIONS **572**
Application Software Certifications 572

Data Analysis and Database Certifications 573
Hardware Certifications 573
Networking Certifications 573
Operating System Certifications 574
Programmer/Developer Certifications 574
Security Certifications 575
JOB SEARCHING AND CAREER PLANNING **576**
Mini Feature 12-3: Creating a Professional Online
Presence 577
CHAPTER SUMMARY **579**
STUDENT ASSIGNMENTS: Study Guide • Key Terms • Checkpoint
• Problem Solving • How To: Your Turn • Internet Research
• Critical Thinking . . . . 580 – 590

APPENDIX A: Technology Acronyms . . . . **APP 1**
APPENDIX B: Troubleshooting Computer and Mobile
Device Problems . . . . **APP 5**
INDEX . . . . **IND 1**

Table of Boxed Elements

ETHICS & ISSUES BOXES

Chapter 1

1-1: Should It Be Legal to Use a Hands-Free Device while Driving? 8
1-2: Should You Be Required to Obtain Permission before
   Posting Photos of Others? 23
1-3: Would You Connect to an Unsecured Network? 33
1-4: Should Wikis Be Allowed as Valid Sources
   for Academic Research? 40
1-5: Should Employees Be Held Accountable for Their
   Online Social Network Posts? 41

Chapter 2

2-1: Should Cybersquatters Be Prosecuted? 64
2-2: Should Apps Be Allowed to Track Your Location? 70
2-3: Is it Ethical to Use a Fake Name or ID on a Website? 77
2-4: Who Is Responsible for Monitoring Cyberbullying? 94

Chapter 3

3-1: What Punishment for Webcam Spying Is Appropriate? 111
3-2: Should Recycling of Electronics Be Made Easier? 122
3-3: Are Fitness Video Games and Apps Qualified
   to Provide Medical Advice? 132
3-4: Does In-Vehicle Technology Foster a False Sense of Security? 133

Chapter 4

4-1: What Can Schools and Employers Do to Prevent
   Internet Plagiarism? 165
4-2: Should an Attorney Review Documents Created
   with Legal Software? 175
4-3: Is It Ethical to Alter Digital Photos? 183
4-4: Should Your Email Provider Be Allowed
   to Read or Scan Your Email? 189

Chapter 5

5-1: How Should Cybercriminals Be Punished? 214
5-2: Who Is Responsible for Data Left on the Cloud? 233
5-3: Do You Have the Right to be Digitally Forgotten? 247
5-4: Does Content Filtering in a Public Library Violate
   First Amendment Rights? 248

Chapter 6

6-1: Does the Internet of Things Discriminate? 286
6-2: Should Companies Reveal Which Products They Manufacture
   Using Fair Trade Practices? 295
6-3: Should Manufacturers Eliminate Proprietary Connectors? 299
6-4: Should Businesses Be Allowed to Make Policies Regarding Customer
   Mobile Phone Use? 302

Chapter 7

7-1: Should a Vehicle Be Able to Prevent User Input on a Mobile
   Device while the Vehicle is in Motion? 326
7-2: Is It More Efficient to Take Notes by Hand or with a Digital Device? 327
7-3: Should We Be Concerned with Hardware Radiation? 344
7-4: Who Should Pay for Assistive Technologies? 354

Chapter 8

8-1: Is Government Search and Seizure of Computers Ethical? 374
8-2: Are Businesses Vulnerable when Employees Use Their Own
   Devices to Access Company Data? 389
8-3: Should Manufacturers Be Required to Close Back Doors
   after Product Development? 393
8-4: How Much Data Should Companies Be Required to Keep? 396

Chapter 9

9-1: Should Manufacturers Include Extra Programs in Operating
   Systems for Computers and Mobile Devices? 421
9-2: Should Operating System Manufacturers Be Liable for
   Breaches Due to Security Flaws? 424
9-3: Should You Be an Early Adopter of a New Technology? 425
9-4: Should Text Messages Sent by Employees Be Private? 433

Chapter 10

10-1: Would You Use a BAN to Monitor Medical Data? 456
10-2: Do the Benefits of Telemedicine Outweigh the Risks? 459
10-3: Should ISPs Be Allowed to Control Your Internet Usage? 477
10-4: Should Phone Companies Be Allowed to Force Customers
   to Switch from Landlines to Mobile Phones? 481

Chapter 11

11-1: Should Companies Inform Consumers about How
   Collected Data Is Used? 502
11-2: Does the Use of Criminal Databases Help or Hinder Investigations? 505
11-3: What Should the Consequences Be If a User Accidentally
   Accesses Confidential Data? 514
11-4: Should Colleges Teach Hacking? 528

Chapter 12

12-1: Is Telecommuting Good or Bad for Business? 563
12-2: Can You Trust Data Recovery or Computer Repair Services? 566
12-3: Is Outsourcing Jobs Wrong? 568
12-4: How Can Social Media Help Your Job Search? 578

HOW TO BOXES

Chapter 1

1-1: Interact with a Touch Screen 5
1-2: Protect Your Hearing when Using Earbuds or Headphones 16
1-3: Perform a Basic Web Search 22
1-4: Locate, Install, and Run Programs and Mobile Apps 29

Chapter 2

2-1: Register a Domain Name 63
2-2: Tag Digital Content 76
2-3: Download Digital Media from Online Services 87
2-4: Set Up a Personal VoIP Service and Make a Call 92

Chapter 3

3-1: Pair Bluetooth Devices 137
3-2: Connect Your Phone to a Wi-Fi Network
   to Save Data Charges. 138

3-3: Evaluate Surge Protectors and UPSs 141
3-4: Evaluate Earbuds and Headphones 143

Chapter 4

4-1: Manage a Project Using Project Management Software 173
4-2: Edit and Share Photos 182
4-3: Use Features in Voice Command Personal Assistant
and Mobile Search Apps 186
4-4: Uninstall a Program or Remove an App 196

Chapter 5

5-1: Determine If an Email Message Has Been Spoofed 218
5-2: Set Up a Personal Firewall 221
5-3: Secure Your Wireless Network. 236
5-4: Protect against a Phishing Scam 245

Chapter 6

6-1: Select the Right Processor. 283
6-2: Determine Memory Requirements 292
6-3: Install Memory Modules 293
6-4: Determine Which Ports You Need on a Computer or
Mobile Device. 297
6-5: Protect and Replace Screens. 304

Chapter 7

7-1: Set Up and Use Webcams and Integrated DV Cameras. 332
7-2: Connect a Laptop to an External Display 341
7-3: Show Media on a Smart TV from Your Computer or Device 343
7-4: Print from a Smartphone or Tablet 347

Chapter 8

8-1: Defragment a Hard Disk 376
8-2: Transfer Files from One Internal Hard Drive to Another. 377
8-3: Select a Cloud Storage Provider and Decide What to
Upload to the Cloud 385
8-4: Clean an Optical Disc and Fix Scratches 387

Chapter 9

9-1: Remove a Program or App 416
9-2: Find the Latest Drivers for Devices 419
9-3: Set Up and Use a Virtual Machine 431
9-4: Use Boot Camp to Install the Windows Operating System
on a Mac. 432

Chapter 10

10-1: Add a Computer or Mobile Device to a Wi-Fi Network 455
10-2: Use Your Phone as a Mobile Hot Spot. 470
10-3: Strengthen Your Wireless Signal 471
10-4: Create a Home Network 475
10-5: Add a Wireless Printer to a Home/Small Office Network. 479

Chapter 11

11-1: Import Spreadsheet Data into a Database and Export Database
Data to a Spreadsheet 511
11-2: Secure and Maintain a Database 513
11-3: Determine Which Object-Oriented Programming
Language or Application Development Tool to Use. 530
11-4: Publish a Webpage 534

Chapter 12

12-1: Set Up Your Home Office for Telecommuting. 563
12-2: Evaluate Extended Warranty Options 567
12-3: Start Your Job Search Online. 576
12-4: Create a Professional Presence on LinkedIn 578

HOW TO: YOUR TURN ASSIGNMENTS

Intro Chapter

I-1: Get the Most out of Your Book. I-12
I-2: Access This Book's Free Resources I-13
I-3: Sign Up for a Microsoft Account. I-13

Chapter 1

1-1: Create a Facebook Account, Find the Discovering
Computers Facebook Page, and Like It. 49
1-2: Create a Twitter Account, Find the Discovering
Computers Twitter Account, and Follow It 49
1-3: Connect to a Wireless Network 50
1-4: Manage Your Calendar. 50
1-5: Back Up Photos from a Phone or Tablet 51

Chapter 2

2-1: Determine Your IP (Internet Protocol) Address 101
2-2: Participate in an Online Auction 101
2-3: View and Manage Data Usage 102
2-4: Search for a Job Online 102
2-5: Send Email Messages Using Various Email
Programs and Web Apps 103

Chapter 3

3-1: Synchronize a Device 151
3-2: Find, Download, and Read an E-Book on an
E-Book Reader. 151
3-3: Manage Power for Mobile Computers and Devices. 152
3-4: Use Your Mobile Device Ergonomically 153
3-5: Transfer Media from a Mobile Device to
a Computer. 153

Chapter 4

4-1: Obtain Help about Programs and Apps 205
4-2: Compress/Uncompress Files and Folders 205
4-3: View Current Virus Threats 206
4-4: Back Up Your Computer 206
4-5: Share your Online Calendar 207

Chapter 5

5-1: Evaluating Your Electronic Profile 255
5-2: Update Virus Definitions. 256
5-3: Determine Whether a Computer or Mobile Device
Is Secured Properly 256
5-4: Clear Your Browsing History 257
5-5: Configure a Browser's Cookie Settings 257

Chapter 6

6-1: Conserve Battery Life of Mobile Computers and Devices 311
6-2: Locate a Lost Mobile Computer or Device. 311
6-3: Run Diagnostic Tools and Check for Computer Hardware Errors. 312

6-4: Determine How Much Memory Is Being Used on Your
Computer or Mobile Device 313
6-5: Check Your Computer's Hardware Configuration 313

Chapter 7

7-1: Work with QR Codes. 361
7-2: Record and Edit a Video 361
7-3: Save as or Print to a PDF File 362
7-4: Take Screenshots. 362
7-5: Share a Photo or Video from Your Mobile Device with
an Online Social Network 363

Chapter 8

8-1: Determine Your Device's Storage Capacity 403
8-2: Organize Files on a Storage Device Using Folders. 403
8-3: Copy Individual Files to Another Storage Device, and
Copy Files to Cloud Storage 404
8-4: Manage Space on a Storage Device 405

Chapter 9

9-1: Determine Your Operating System Version 443
9-2: Search for Files on a Computer 443
9-3: Personalize Your Operating Environment 444
9-4: Configure Accessibility Settings 444
9-5: Add Users to an Operating System 445

Chapter 10

10-1: Evaluate Internet Access Plans 491
10-2: Locate Hot Spots. 491
10-3: Test Your Internet Speed 492
10-4: Connect Your Computer and Mobile Device via Bluetooth
and Exchange Files 493

Chapter 11

11-1: Obtain and Verify the Accuracy of a Credit Report 545
11-2: Use a Research Database 545
11-3: Protect Your Data If Your Device Is Lost or Stolen 546
11-4: Create and View a Text File 547

Chapter 12

12-1: Conduct an Effective Interview 585
12-2: Create a Video Resume. 586
12-3: Create an Online Survey 587

SECURE IT BOXES

Chapter 1

1-1: Backing Up Computers and Mobile Devices 19
1-2: Protection from Viruses and Other Malware. 25
1-3: Creating Strong Passwords 25
1-4: Shopping Safely Online 37

Chapter 2

2-1: Using Public Wi-Fi Hot Spots Safely 59
2-2: Safe Browsing Techniques 66
2-3: Privacy and Security Risks with Online Social Networks 74
2-4: Protecting Yourself from Identity Theft. 80

Chapter 3

3-1: Avoid Malware Infections. 110
3-2: ATM Safety 119
3-3: Safe Mobile Device Use in Public Areas 125
3-4: Public USB Charging Stations — Safe or Not? 136

Chapter 4

4-1: Safe Downloading Websites 162
4-2: Using Personal Finance Apps Safely. .174
4-3: Avoiding Risks Using Payment Apps .179
4-4: Recognizing Virus Hoaxes. 192
4-5: Malware Risks to Mobile Devices 193

Chapter 5

5-1: Play It Safe to Avoid Online Gaming Risks 216
5-2: Protection from Viruses and Other Malware. 219
5-3: Safely Use a Password Manager 223
5-4: Risks Associated with Inaccurate Data. 240

Chapter 6

6-1: Securing Computers and Mobile Devices 279
6-2: Chip Implants Secure Animals' Identity. 280
6-3: Does the Internet of Things Encroach on Privacy? 286
6-4: Wiping Mobile Phone Memory 295
6-5: Plug and Play Security Flaws. 298

Chapter 7

7-1: Keyboard Monitoring 321
7-2: Digital Video Security 333
7-3: Safely Scanning QR Codes 336
7-4: Protecting Credit Cards from Scanning Devices 337

Chapter 8

8-1: Encrypting Data and Files on Storage Devices 379
8-2: Safely Remove Media 383
8-3: Using Credit Cards Safely 394
8-4: Keeping NFC Transactions Safe 395

Chapter 9

9-1: Automatic Updates — Safe or Not? 422
9-2: Using and Evaluating an Operating System's
Built-In Security Tools 423
9-3: Open Source or Closed Source — Which Is More Secure? 430
9-4: BYOD Security Issues 433

Chapter 10

10-1: Monitoring Network Traffic. 462
10-2: Preventing Bluebugging 464
10-3: Detecting an Intruder Accessing Your Wireless Home Network. . . . 474
10-4: Fake Cell Towers Are Tracking Devices. 480

Chapter 11

11-1: Recovering from Identity Theft 514
11-2: Security Issues Arising from Outsourcing 522
11-3: Technology Security Plan Components 527
11-4: Protection from Macro Viruses 534

Chapter **12**

12-1: How Secure Are Content Management Systems?. 557
12-2: Using Unlicensed Software Is a Crime. 565
12-3: Risks of Jailbreaking and Rooting. 574
12-4: Protecting Customer Data. 575

TECHNOLOGY @ WORK BOXES

Chapter 1: Health Care 43
Chapter 2: Transportation 95
Chapter 3: Energy Management 145
Chapter 4: Entertainment 199
Chapter 5: National and Local Security. 249
Chapter 6: Publishing. 305
Chapter 7: Finance 355
Chapter 8: Automotive. 397
Chapter 9: Meteorology 437
Chapter 10: Agriculture 485
Chapter 11: Sports 539
Chapter 12: Architecture and Design 579

DISCOVER MORE ONLINE WITH THESE FREE RESOURCES

HIGH-TECH TALK ARTICLES

Chapter 1: Neural Networks • Triangulation
Chapter 2: DNS Servers • IP Addresses
Chapter 3: Touch Screen Technology • Voice Recognition Technology
Chapter 4: Compression Algorithms • Filtering Data
Chapter 5: Digital Forensics • Encryption Algorithms
Chapter 6: Coding Schemes and Number Systems • How Data Is
          Written To RAM
Chapter 7: Biometric Input • How 3-D Printers Work
Chapter 8: How Data Is Recovered • RAID Levels
Chapter 9: Benchmarking • Virtualization
Chapter 10: Network Topologies: Star, Bus, Ring • OSI Reference Model
Chapter 11: Types of Databases, Database Design, and the Normalization
          Process • Process and Object Modeling • Programming Logic
Chapter 12: 3-D Graphics • Bioinformatics

HOW TO: YOUR TURN ASSIGNMENTS – APP ADVENTURES

Chapter 1: Health • Fitness
Chapter 2: Messaging Apps
Chapter 3: News • Sports • Weather
Chapter 4: Office (Email, Calendar, To-Do Lists)
Chapter 5: Retail
Chapter 6: Media Sharing
Chapter 7: Travel and Tourism
Chapter 8: Reference and Information
Chapter 9: Mapping
Chapter 10: Streaming Audio and Video
Chapter 11: Scanning
Chapter 12: Banking and Finance

TECHNOLOGY INNOVATOR

Chapter 1: Apple • Facebook • Microsoft • Twitter
Chapter 2: Arianna Huffington • LinkedIn • Tim Berners-Lee • Yahoo!
Chapter 3: Dell/Michael Dell • Nintendo • Samsung • Sony
Chapter 4: Adobe Systems • Dan Bricklin • eBay/PayPal • Google/Sergey Brin/
          Larry Page
Chapter 5: AVG • Intel Security • LoJack • Symantec
Chapter 6: Intel and Gordon Moore • AMD • Nvidia • VMWare
Chapter 7: Logitech • QR Code Inventors • HP
Chapter 8: Pinterest/Ben Silbermann • Seagate/Al Shugart • SanDisk •
          Amazon/Jeff Bezos
Chapter 9: Linus Torvalds • Red Hat • Sun • IBM
Chapter 10: Robert Metcalfe • AT&T and Verizon • Cisco
Chapter 11: E. F. Codd • Oracle/Larry Ellison • Lenovo •
          Electronic Arts
Chapter 12: Wikimedia Foundation/Jimmy Wales • Ray Kurzweil •
          Meg Whitman • Salesforce

TECHNOLOGY TREND

Chapter 1: MOOCs • QR Codes in the Medical Field
Chapter 2: Responsive Web Design • Uses of Bookmarking Sites
Chapter 3: Bitcoin • Volunteer Computing
Chapter 4: Evernote • Instagram • iTunes U
Chapter 5: Cloud Security • Uses of Face Recognition Technology
Chapter 6: Medical Robotics • Self-Driving Cars
Chapter 7: Drones • Assistive Technologies
Chapter 8: Digitizing Nondigital Media • Digitizing Media with RECAPTCHAs
Chapter 9: Linux Powering the Internet of Things • Mobile versus Desktop
          Operating System Usage
Chapter 10: Wireless Charging • Geocaching
Chapter 11: Forensic Databases • Custom Crime Fighting Software •
          Programs behind Mars Rover
Chapter 12: Crowd Sourcing • Monitoring Health Status

Preface

The Shelly Cashman Series® offers the finest textbooks in computer education. We are proud of the fact that the previous seventeen editions of this textbook have been the most widely used in computer education. With this edition of *Discovering Computers*, we have implemented significant improvements based on current computer trends and comments made by instructors and students. *Discovering Computers: Tools, Apps, Devices, and the Impact of Technology* continues with the innovation, quality, and reliability you have come to expect from the Shelly Cashman Series.

In *Discovering Computers: Tools, Apps, Devices, and the Impact of Technology* you will find an educationally sound, highly visual, interactive, and easy-to-follow pedagogy that, with the help of animated figures, relevant video, and interactive activities in the e-book, presents an in-depth treatment of introductory computer subjects. Readers will finish the course with a solid understanding of computers, how to use computers, and how to access information on the web.

Objectives of This Text, eReader, and CourseMate Web site

Discovering Computers: Tools, Apps, Devices, and the Impact of Technology is intended for use as a stand-alone solution or in combination with an applications, Internet, or programming textbook in a full-semester introductory technology course. No experience with computers is assumed. The objectives of this offering are to:

- Present the most-up-to-date technology in an ever-changing discipline
- Give readers an in-depth understanding of why computers are essential in business and society
- Teach the fundamentals of and terms associated with computers and mobile devices, the Internet, programs and apps, and digital safety and security
- Present the material in a visually appealing, interactive, and exciting manner that motivates readers to learn
- Provide exercises, assignments, and interactive learning activities that allow readers to learn by actually using computers, mobile devices, and the Internet
- Present strategies for purchasing desktop computers, mobile computers, and mobile devices
- Provide additional learning materials and reinforcement online
- Offer distance-education providers a textbook with a meaningful and exercise-rich digital learning experience

Hallmarks of Discovering Computers

To date, more than six million readers have learned about computers using *Discovering Computers*. With the online integration and interactivity, step-by-step visual drawings and photographs, unparalleled currency, and the Shelly and Cashman touch, this book will make your computer concepts course exciting and dynamic. Hallmarks of Shelly Cashman Series *Discovering Computers* include:

A Proven Pedagogy

Careful explanations of complex concepts, educationally-sound elements, and reinforcement highlight this proven method of presentation.

A Visually Appealing Book that Maintains Student Interest

The latest technology, photos, drawings, and text are combined artfully to produce a visually appealing and easy-to-understand book. Many of the figures include a step-by-step presentation, which simplifies the more complex technology concepts. Pictures and drawings reflect the latest trends in computer technology.

Latest Technologies and Terms

The technologies and terms readers see in *Discovering Computers* are those they will encounter when they start using computers and mobile devices personally and professionally. Only the latest applications are shown throughout the book.

Web Integrated

This book uses the web as a major learning tool. The purpose of integrating the web into the book is to (1) offer students additional information and currency on important topics; (2) use its interactive capabilities to offer creative reinforcement; (3) make available alternative learning techniques with games and quizzes;

Distinguishing Features

Discovering Computers: Tools, Apps, Devices, and the Impact of Technology includes a variety of compelling features, certain to engage and challenge students, making learning with *Discovering Computers* an enriched experience. These compelling features include:

NEW!
- **Introducing Today's Technologies.** This new introductory chapter details how to succeed in this course by setting the stage for the rich resources available in the text and online to support learning.

NEW!
- **Technology Timeline.** This engaging visual provides milestones in technology history.

NEW!
- **Cloud and Skills Coverage.** An integrated approach to cloud computing and search skills appears throughout the text shows how to apply these concepts to learning.

NEW!
- **Career Coverage.** Career information is covered, including using social media to jumpstart your technology career.

NEW!
- **Discover More Online.** Free resources and premium content include currency updates and additional detailed topical content.

- **Strong Content.** Based on market research, assessment of organization of each chapter's content, *Discovering Computers* has been restructured and reorganized to improve retention of material and promote transference of knowledge. The text's visually engaging presentation showcases current technology as well as course fundamentals in order to reinforce classroom and real-world applications.

- **Balanced Presentation.** The print book provides students with what they need to know to be successful digital citizens in the classroom and beyond. Online resources address timely content and expand on the print text with content appropriate for Information Technology majors. Readers can choose to utilize this digital-only content, empowering each to fit the content to their specific needs and goals for the course.

- **Thematic Approach.** Chapter boxes, marginal elements, and accompanying online content are linked by common themes to facilitate class discussions and help students make connections. These connections shed light on the integral role technology plays in business and society.

- **Media Engagement.** Enrichment content is available online to enhance student knowledge and understanding through additional free resources and premium content. Developed by the authors, this content provides deeper understanding and encourages learning by doing, as well as offering practical skill development.

- **Reinforcement and Support.** End-of-chapter student assignments, along with the accompanying CourseMate website, offer students an exceptional learning solution in addition to significant practice opportunities in the form of study guide materials, flash cards, practice tests and critical thinking opportunities.

(4) underscore the relevance of the web as a fundamental information tool that can be used in all facets of society; (5) introduce students to web-based research; and (6) offer instructors the opportunity to organize and administer their traditional campus-based or distance-education-based courses on the web using various learning management systems.

Extensive End-of-Chapter Student Assignments

A notable strength of *Discovering Computers* is the extensive student assignments and activities at the end of each chapter. Well-structured student assignments can make the difference between students merely participating in a class and students retaining the information they learn. End-of-chapter student assignments include the following:

- Study Guide exercises reinforce material for the exams
- Key Terms page reviews chapter terms
- Checkpoint exercises test knowledge of chapter concepts
- How To: Your Turn exercises require that students learn new practical skills
- Problem Solving exercises require that students seek solutions to practical technology problems
- Internet Research exercises require that students search for information on the web
- Critical Thinking exercises challenge student assessment and decision-making skills

Instructor Resources

The Instructor Resources include both teaching and testing aids.

Instructor's Manual Includes lecture notes summarizing the chapter sections, figures and boxed elements found in every chapter, teacher tips, classroom activities, lab activities, and quick quizzes in Microsoft Word files.

Syllabus Customizable sample syllabi that cover policies, assignments, exams, and other course information.

Solutions to Exercises Includes solutions for all end-of-chapter student assignments.

PowerPoint Presentations A one-click-per-slide presentation system that provides PowerPoint slides for every subject in each chapter.

Test Bank and Test Engine Cengage Learning Testing Powered by Cognero is a flexible, online system that allows you to author, edit, and manage test bank content from multiple Cengage Learning solutions and to create multiple test versions. It works on any operating system or browser with no special installs or downloads needed, allowing you to create tests from anywhere with Internet access. Multi-language support, an equation editor and unlimited metadata help ensure your tests are complete and compliant, and it enables you to import and export content into other systems. The *Discovering Computers* Test Bank includes multiple for every chapter, featuring objective-based and critical thinking question types, and including page number references and figure references as appropriate.

Free Resources Available on the student companion website accessed via www.cengagebrain.com, additional free resources for each chapter allow students to discover more materials and deeper content online to enrich learning.

Computer Concepts CourseMate

The Computer Concepts CourseMate for *Discovering Computers* is the most expansive digital website for any computer concepts text in the market today. The content in the CourseMate solution is integrated into each page of the text, giving students easy access to current information on important topics, reinforcements activities, and alternative learning techniques.

These interactive activities are captured within the CourseMate EngagementTracker, making it easy to assess students' retention of concepts.

MindTap

Typical courses often require students to juggle a variety of print and digital resources, as well as an array of platforms, access codes, logins, and homework systems. Now all of those resources are available in one personal learning experience called MindTap. MindTap is a cloud-based, interactive, customizable, and complete online course. More than an e-book, and different than a learning management system, each MindTap course is built upon authoritative Cengage Learning content, accessible anytime, anywhere.

Additional Online Material

SAM: Skills Assessment Manager

Get workplace-ready with SAM, the market-leading proficiency-based assessment and training solution for Microsoft Office! SAM's active, hands-on environment helps students master Microsoft Office skills and computer concepts that are essential to academic and career success, delivering the most comprehensive online learning solution for your course.

Through skill-based assessments, interactive trainings, business-centric projects, and comprehensive remediation, SAM engages students in mastering the latest Microsoft Office programs on their own, giving instructors more time to focus on teaching. Computer concepts labs supplement instruction of important technology-related topics and issues through engaging simulations and interactive, auto-graded assessments. With enhancements, including streamlined course setup, more robust grading and reporting features, and the integration of fully interactive MindTap Readers containing Cengage Learning's premier textbook content, SAM provides the best teaching and learning solution for your course.

CourseCasts: Learning on the Go

Always available... always relevant Our fast-paced world is driven by technology. You know because you are an active participant — always on the go, always keeping up with technological trends, and always learning new ways to embrace technology to power your life. Let CourseCasts, hosted by Ken Baldauf of Florida State University, be your guide to weekly updates in this ever-changing space. These timely, relevant podcasts are produced weekly and are available for download at http://coursecasts.course.com or directly from iTunes (search by CourseCasts). CourseCasts are a perfect solution to getting students (and even instructors) to learn on the go!

Visual Walkthrough of the Book

Current. Relevant. Innovative.

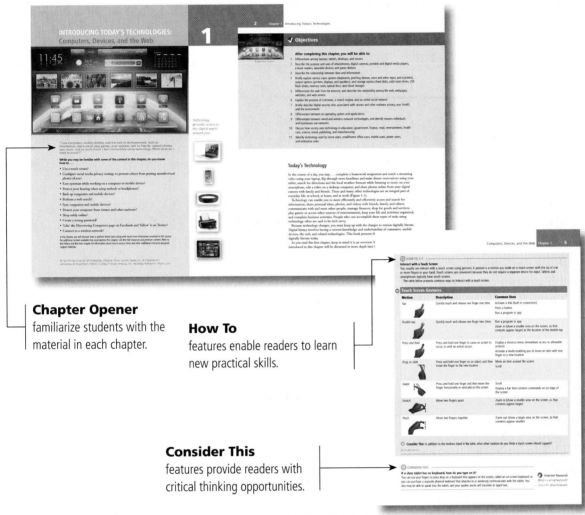

Chapter Opener
familiarize students with the material in each chapter.

How To
features enable readers to learn new practical skills.

Consider This
features provide readers with critical thinking opportunities.

Mini Features
throughout the text explore various real world topics to deepen concept understanding.

Secure IT
features allow students to broaden their knowledge with details regarding security issues they will face.

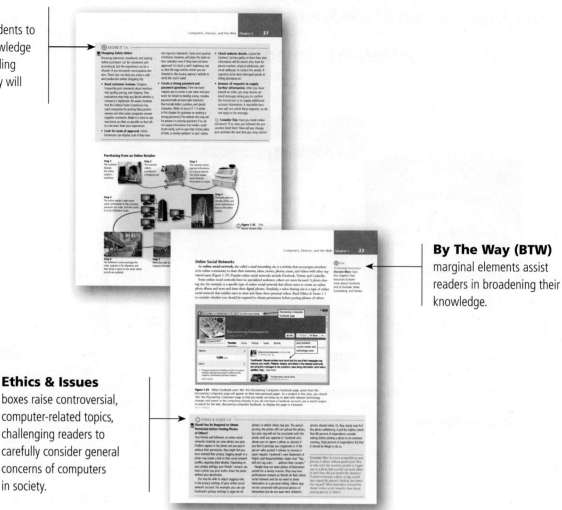

By The Way (BTW)
marginal elements assist readers in broadening their knowledge.

Ethics & Issues
boxes raise controversial, computer-related topics, challenging readers to carefully consider general concerns of computers in society.

Now You Should Know
feature provides assessment opportunity and integrates directly to chapter learning objectives to assess learning outcomes.

Chapter Summary
allows another review of materials presented in the chapter to reinforce learning and provide additional self-assessment opportunities.

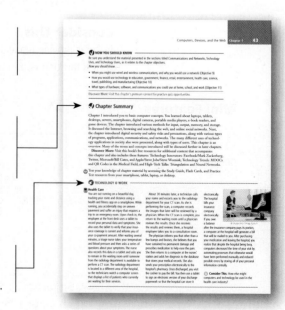

Technology @ Work
features put chapter information to practical use and provide context within students' lives.

End-of-Chapter Student Assignments

Study Guide
materials reinforce chapter content.

Checkpoint
activities provide multiple-choice, true/false, matching, and consider this exercises to reinforce understanding of the topics presented in the chapter.

Problem Solving
activities call on students to relate concepts to their own lives, both personally and professionally, as well as provide a collaboration opportunity.

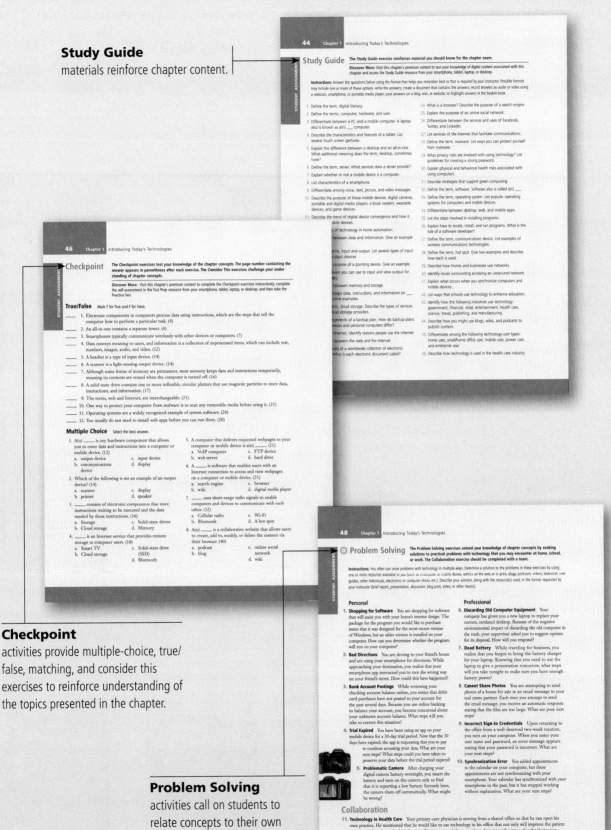

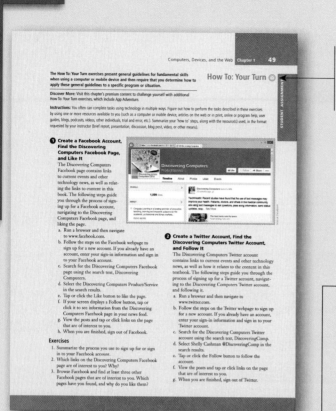

How To: Your Turn

activities enable readers to learn and to reinforce new practical skills with personally meaningful and applicable exercises.

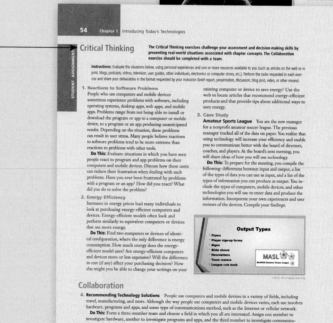

Internet Research

exercises require follow-up research on the web and suggest writing a short article or presenting the findings of the research to the class.

Critical Thinking

activities provide opportunities for creative solutions to these thought-provoking activities presented in each chapter. The Critical Thinking exercises are constructed for class discussion, presentation, and independent research. The Collaboration exercise is designed for a team environment.

Visual Walkthrough of the Computer Concepts CourseMate, MindTap, and Free Resources

CourseMate

Introduce the most current technology into the classroom with the Computer Concepts CourseMate. An integrated MindTap eReader and a wide range of online learning games, quizzes, practice tests, and web links expand on the topics covered in the text with hands-on reinforcement. Visit www .cengagebrain.com to register your access code and access your course and the premium resources assigned by your instructor.

Engagement Tracker

Engagement Tracker makes assessing students easy by tracking student progress on the interactive activities. Clear and visual reports illustrate the class progress as a whole.

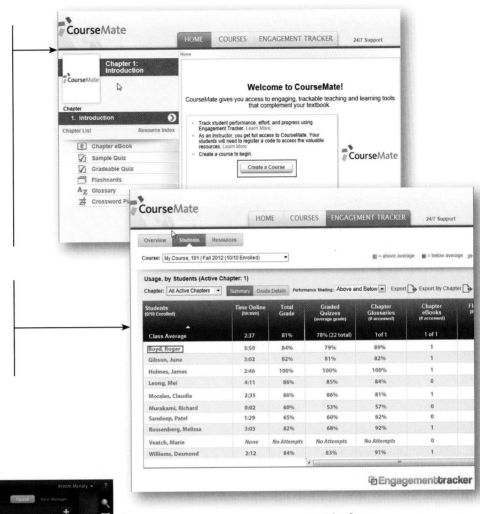

MindTap

MindTap is a personalized teaching experience with relevant assignments that guide students to analyze, apply, and improve thinking, allowing you to measure skills and outcomes with ease.

Free Resources on CengageBrain

Start with locating *Discovering Computers* on www.cengagebrain .com in order to access the free resources found on the student resources page.

You can improve your digital literacy by reading this book and accessing its associated online content.

Introduction

This introductory chapter is designed to prepare you to succeed in this course. It begins with a discussion of browsing the web, followed by overview of the book and its associated additional online content, which familiarizes you with the meanings of references and symbols that appear throughout the book. Next is a brief buyer's guide that you can use to purchase a desktop, laptop, or tablet for use during the semester. Finally is an abbreviated set of exercises designed to acquaint you with the resources you will be expected to use in Chapter 1.

Keep in mind that this chapter uses a variety of terms that are described in more depth in Chapter 1 and throughout the book. These terms also are defined in this book's index. If you need additional information about a particular topic, refer to the appropriate chapter.

Browsing the Web

Each chapter in this book contains topics, elements, and assignments that presume you already know how to use a browser. As you may know, a browser is software that enables you to access and view webpages on a computer or mobile device that has an Internet connection. Some widely used browsers include Internet Explorer, Firefox, Safari, and Chrome. Read How To 1 for instructions about using a browser to display a webpage on a computer or mobile device.

✺ HOW TO 1

Use a Browser to Display a Webpage
The following steps describe how to use a browser to display a webpage on a computer or mobile device:

1. Run a browser. (Chapter 1 discusses running programs and apps.)

2. If necessary, tap or click the address bar to select it and any previously displayed web address it may contain. (A web address is a unique address that identifies a webpage.)

3. In the address bar, type the web address of the webpage you want to visit and then press the ENTER key or tap or click the Go (or similar) button to display the webpage. For example, www.cengagebrain.com is a valid web address, which displays the CengageBrain webpage shown in the figure below. (Chapter 2 discusses the components of a web address.)

4. If necessary, scroll to view the entire webpage. You can scroll either by sliding your finger across a touch screen or by using a pointing device, such as a mouse, to drag the scroll bar.

5. Tap or click links on the webpage to navigate to the link's destination.

✺ **Consider This:** What should you do if the web address you enter does not display a webpage or you receive an error message?

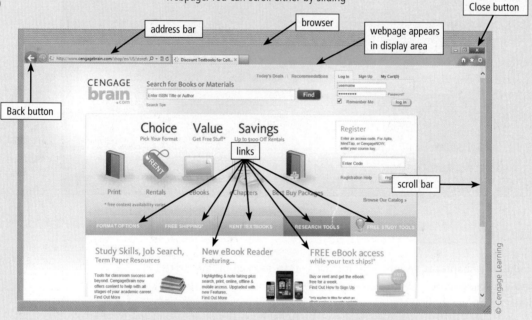

© Cengage Learning

✺ CONSIDER THIS

What does the ✺ icon mean that appears in the book?
This icon denotes that the questions or exercises that follow require critical thinking. Your instructor may assign or expect you to discuss in class any of these questions that appear throughout the chapters.

Book and Online Content

As a student in this course, you should be aware that the material located in the pages of this book includes content you should know to be successful as a student and as a digital citizen. Other content is available online only as free resources or premium content. The free resources are available at no additional cost with your book purchase, whereas the premium content may or may not have been included with your purchase, as determined by your instructor. Please see the preface or your instructor for details related to the location of the free resources and the premium content, as well as information about purchasing the premium content, if desired.

Free Resources   The free resources, which are available online, present (1) up-to-date content including current statistics, trends, models, products, programs, apps, etc., (2) content that elaborates on essential material in the book, or (3) content required for those students majoring in the information technology or computer science fields. When free resources are available for a topic in this book, they will be identified in one of two ways:

(a) Free resources icon (📄): These icons precede chapter boxed elements to indicate that additional material is available in the free resources. The chapter boxed elements that may have associated free resources include the following (Figure 1):

- Ethics & Issues
- How To
- Secure IT
- Technology @ Work

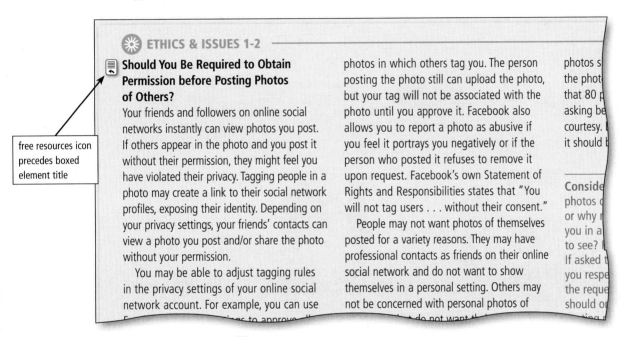

free resources icon precedes boxed element title

ETHICS & ISSUES 1-2

📄 **Should You Be Required to Obtain Permission before Posting Photos of Others?**

Your friends and followers on online social networks instantly can view photos you post. If others appear in the photo and you post it without their permission, they might feel you have violated their privacy. Tagging people in a photo may create a link to their social network profiles, exposing their identity. Depending on your privacy settings, your friends' contacts can view a photo you post and/or share the photo without your permission.

You may be able to adjust tagging rules in the privacy settings of your online social network account. For example, you can use

photos in which others tag you. The person posting the photo still can upload the photo, but your tag will not be associated with the photo until you approve it. Facebook also allows you to report a photo as abusive if you feel it portrays you negatively or if the person who posted it refuses to remove it upon request. Facebook's own Statement of Rights and Responsibilities states that "You will not tag users . . . without their consent."

People may not want photos of themselves posted for a variety reasons. They may have professional contacts as friends on their online social network and do not want to show themselves in a personal setting. Others may not be concerned with personal photos of

photos s the phot that 80 asking be courtesy. it should

Conside photos or why you in a to see? If asked you respe the reque should o

Figure 1   When you see the 📄 icon to the left of a boxed element title or the phrase, it means you can find additional related online material in the free resources.

(b) **Discover More** reference: These references within the text and in the margins briefly identify the type of material you will find in the free resources. The Discover More references appear within the paragraphs of text in the chapter (Figure 2). The marginal elements that may have associated free resources include the following:

- High-Tech Talk
- Technology Innovator
- Technology Trend

⚙ BTW

Table of Boxed Elements
For a complete list of every print and online boxed element in this book, see the Table of Boxed Elements in the preface.

to help you locate the information. A **search engine** is software that finds websites, webpages, images, videos, news, maps, and other information related to a specific topic. Read How To 1-3 for instructions about how to perform a basic web search using a search engine on a computer or mobile device.

Discover More reference

Discover More: Visit this chapter's free resources to learn more about search engines.

Figure 2   When you see the **Discover More** reference, it means you can find additional, related online content that will direct you either to material in the free resources or premium content.

Premium Content The premium content, which is available online, includes interactive activities, additional exercises, and other resources designed to enhance your learning experience, reinforce and test your knowledge of chapter concepts, or challenge you with additional assignments. When premium content is available for a topic in this book, it will be identified in one of two ways:

(a) Premium content icon ( ): These icons precede chapter figures and other elements to indicate that additional resources are available as premium content. The chapter elements with associated premium content include the following (Figure 3):

- Animation videos: View these animations to better understand some of the more complex figures in the book.
- Drag-and-drop activities: Practice these interactive activities to test your knowledge of a concept in a table or figure.
- Study Guide, Flash Cards, and Practice Test resources: Prepare for quizzes and exams by viewing the material from your smartphone, tablet, laptop, or desktop.

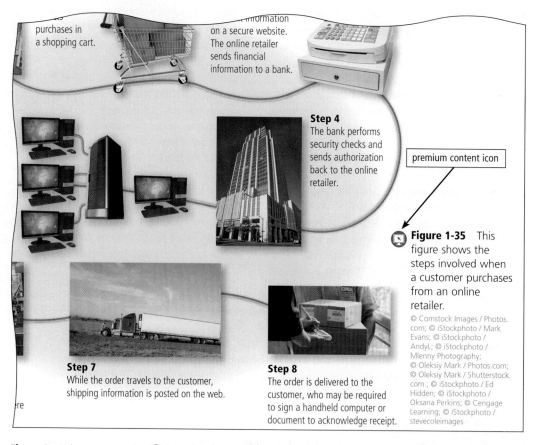

purchases in a shopping cart.

...information on a secure website. The online retailer sends financial information to a bank.

Step 4
The bank performs security checks and sends authorization back to the online retailer.

premium content icon

 Figure 1-35 This figure shows the steps involved when a customer purchases from an online retailer.

© Comstock Images / Photos.com; © iStockphoto / Mark Evans; © iStockphoto / AndyL; © iStockphoto / Mlenny Photography; © Oleksiy Mark / Photos.com; © Oleksiy Mark / Shutterstock.com.; © iStockphoto / Ed Hidden; © iStockphoto / Oksana Perkins; © Cengage Learning; © iStockphoto / stevecoleimages

Step 7
While the order travels to the customer, shipping information is posted on the web.

Step 8
The order is delivered to the customer, who may be required to sign a handheld computer or document to acknowledge receipt.

Figure 3 When you see the icon, it means you can find additional, related online chapter resources in the premium content.

(b) **Discover More** reference: These references within the text briefly identify the type of material you will find in the premium content. Resources available as premium content include practice quizzes, study guide questions for material presented in the free resources, Key Terms and Checkpoint activities, additional How To: Your Turn and Internet Research exercises, and more.

Purchasing the Right Computer

As a student in a technology course, you might be thinking of purchasing a desktop, laptop, or tablet to help you with this course and future courses in your academic career. In addition to the information in this section, consider speaking with your instructors, as well as an academic advisor, to see if they have any specific recommendations for computers or mobile devices you might use in the courses you plan to take. If your academic institution has a store that sells computers, it also might have specific computer or mobile device recommendations, as well as a student discount program. Make sure the computer or mobile device you purchase is capable of running the software that you will need for your classes.

Step 1: Choose the Computer Type

Laptops, tablets, and desktops each serve a different purpose. It is important that you choose the type of computer best suited to your needs. This section briefly describes and identifies some of the pros and cons associated with each type of computer. See Chapter 3 for a more thorough discussion of computer types.

Laptops   A laptop is a thin, lightweight mobile computer with a screen in its lid and a keyboard in its base (Figure 4). Users who need or want to be able carry a computer from place to place may choose a laptop.

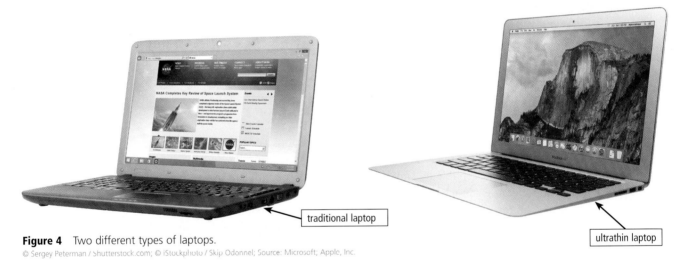

traditional laptop

ultrathin laptop

Figure 4   Two different types of laptops.
© Sergey Peterman / Shutterstock.com; © iStockphoto / Skip Odonnel; Source: Microsoft; Apple, Inc.

PROS

- Portable
- Uses less electricity than a desktop
- Contains a battery that can last at least several hours without being plugged in to an external power source
- Often more powerful than a tablet
- Contains several different types of ports
- All required components housed in a single unit (i.e., compact keyboard, touchpad, screen, speakers, etc.)
- Can support more types of external devices than tablets (i.e., full-sized keyboard, mouse, microphone, monitor, printer, scanner, webcam, speakers, etc.)
- Supports programs and apps specifically designed for desktops and laptops
- Can connect to a large monitor

CONS

• Might not be as powerful as high-end desktops
• May not support as much memory and hard drive space as desktops
• Contains fewer ports than desktops
• May support fewer external devices than desktops
• Not as easy for a user to upgrade or repair as desktops
• May not be as portable as tablets

Tablets   A tablet is a thin, lightweight mobile computer that has a touch screen (Figure 5). Users who do not need the power of a laptop but require a portable computer for basic tasks may choose a tablet.

Figure 5   One type of tablet.
© iStockphoto / franckreporter

PROS

• More portable than laptops
• Lightweight (most tablets weigh less than two pounds)
• Use less electricity than a desktop
• Battery life often is superior to laptops
• All required components housed in a single unit (touch screen, speakers, etc.)
• Can connect a removable keyboard
• Use thousands of free and fee-based apps
• Often are easier to use than desktops and laptops
• Built-in memory card slots can increase storage capacity

CONS

• Not as powerful as desktops and laptops
• Hardware cannot be upgraded
• Typically do not support the same types of apps as desktops and laptops
• Have limited multitasking capabilities
• More susceptible to damage because they frequently are moved from place to place
• Because a touch screen is the primary form of input, it may be difficult to enter large amounts of text on a tablet (unless an external keyboard is connected)
• Lack surface to rest wrists and arms, so ergonomic problems may develop

Desktops   A desktop is a computer designed to be in a stationary location, where all of its components fit on or under a desk or table (Figure 6). Users who may prefer desktops include those with basic home or office computing needs who do not require the portability of a mobile computer or those with high-end computing needs, such as 3-D gaming or HD video editing.

desktop with tower

all-in-one

Figure 6   Two different types of desktops.
© iStockphoto / Oleksiy Mark; Source: Microsoft; © iStockphoto / hocus-focus; Apple, Inc.

PROS

- Often more powerful than laptops and tablets
- Can connect to one or more large monitor(s)
- Contain several different types of ports or multiple duplicate ports
- Can accommodate more types of external devices than laptops and tablets (i.e., keyboard, mouse, microphone, monitor, printer, scanner, webcam, speakers, etc.)
- Often support more memory and hard drive capacity than laptops and tablets
- Support programs and apps specifically designed for desktops and laptops
- Relatively easy for a user to upgrade and repair

CONS

- Require several external, separate components, such as a keyboard, mouse, speakers, and sometimes the monitor
- High-end models can be more expensive than laptops and tablets
- Cannot run apps designed for mobile device operating systems, such as Android and iOS

Most students will find that a laptop or desktop is most suitable for their coursework or for gaming. In addition, they might choose a tablet to carry with them at other times because tablets are ideal for everyday tasks, such as searching the web, checking email messages, participating in video calls, and reading e-books.

Step 2: Choose the Operating System

An operating system is software (a program) that coordinates all the activities among computer components. Multiple operating systems exist for each type of device (Table 1). Deciding which operating system is best for you will be the next step in determining the specific brand of computer that ultimately meets your needs.

Certain courses may require specific applications (apps), and those applications may be available only on a specific operating system. For example, a course that teaches digital media might require an application that is available only for Mac OS. Table 2 illustrates the various categories of programs and apps. This section outlines the more common operating systems for each type of device. See Chapter 4 for a more thorough discussion of an operating system.

Table 1	Examples of Operating Systems by Category
Category	**Name**
Desktop	Windows
	OS X
	UNIX
	Linux
	Chrome OS
Mobile	Google Android
	Apple iOS
	Windows Phone

Table 2   Categories of Programs and Apps

Category	Sample Uses for Students
Communications	View course websites. Communicate via email with instructors and other students. Send and receive files. Facilitate and participate in online meetings with instructors and other students.
File, Disk, and System Management	Organize personal and school-related files. Copy and move files. Search for files.
Graphics and Media	Create digital media, such as images and movies. View multimedia course content, such as online lectures.
Personal Interest	Perform research using content from dictionaries, encyclopedias, etc. Learn through tutors and prepare for tests.
Productivity	Create research papers and other documents. Develop presentations to use in classes. Organize your academic and personal schedule.
Security	Protect your computer and schoolwork from viruses and other malicious software.

Laptops and Desktops   The two primary operating systems available on laptops and desktops are Windows (shown in Figure 7) and Mac OS (shown in Figure 8). While other operating systems, such as UNIX, Linux, and Chrome OS also are available, Windows and Mac OS are the most common. Some computers can run multiple operating systems. For example, Apple computers can run Windows and Linux in addition to Mac OS. Windows and Mac OS each offer a unique user experience; the best way to determine which one you are most comfortable with is to try using each one. Most stores that sell laptops and desktops will have some working models that you can evaluate. Make sure the operating system you decide to use also is capable of running the programs and apps required for your courses.

Figure 7   Windows operating system.
Source: Microsoft

Figure 8 Mac OS operating system.
Source: Apple, Inc.

Tablets   Tablets often include one of three operating systems: Android (Figure 9), iOS (Figure 10), or Windows (Figure 11). While Android and iOS are the most popular operating systems on tablets, the Windows operating system is increasing in popularity. Determine the types of apps you wish to use on the tablet and then determine which operating systems support those apps.

If you want your tablet to synchronize seamlessly with other computers and devices, such as a laptop, desktop, or smartphone, consider an operating system that is compatible with your other computer or device. For example, if you have an Android phone, you might prefer the Android operating system for your tablet. If you use an iPhone or iPod Touch, you might prefer the iOS operating system for your tablet.

Figure 9 Tablet running Android operating system.
© iStockphoto / PetkoDanov

Figure 10 Tablet running iOS operating system.
© iStockphoto / Hocus Focus Studio

Figure 11 Tablet running Windows operating system.
© Pieter Beens / Shutterstock.com

Step 3: Choose Configuration Options

The final step in choosing the best laptop, tablet, or desktop to meet your needs is to choose the specific configuration details. For example, you may have to choose the size of the display, amount of memory, storage capacity, and processor speed.

Display Screen Size Display screens for computers are available in a variety of sizes (Figure 12). A laptop's screen typically can range from 11 to 17 inches, and a tablet's screen generally is between 7 and 12 inches. If you purchase a laptop or tablet, a smaller screen size will make the device lighter and more portable. For example, laptops with screens exceeding 15 inches typically are much heavier, which makes them less convenient to transport. Desktops often use a monitor as their display, with the size of screens on these monitors ranging from 13 inches to more than 30 inches.

If you primarily will be sending and receiving email messages, creating and editing documents using a word processing app, and browsing the web, a device with a smaller screen should meet your needs. If you require a larger screen to work with large documents or display multiple windows simultaneously, or if you want to experience less eyestrain with the contents appearing larger on the screen, consider a desktop or laptop display with a larger screen size. If you require touch functionality (and the operating system you plan to use supports it), purchase a screen that supports touch input. In addition, if you decide to purchase a laptop or desktop, you usually can connect a second monitor.

monitor display

laptop display

digital camera display

Figure 12 A variety of displays.
© cobalt88 / Shutterstock.com;
© Pawel Gaul / Photos.com

Memory The amount of memory (RAM) installed in your laptop, tablet, or desktop will help determine the types of programs and apps that can run on the computer, as well as how many programs and apps can run simultaneously (Figure 13). If you are purchasing a laptop or desktop, review the system requirements for the programs and apps you plan to use, and make sure to purchase a computer with enough memory to meet those system requirements. For example, if the operating system you plan to use requires at least 4 GB (gigabytes) of memory, and you plan to use a word processing app that requires 4 GB of memory, you should purchase a laptop or desktop with at least 8 GB of memory. It is recommended that you purchase a computer with slightly more memory than you need at the present time. This enables you to use multiple programs and apps simultaneously and also accommodates programs and apps you might install and use at a later time.

Figure 13 Memory modules contain memory chips.
© TerryM / Shutterstock.com

Storage Capacity and Media   Laptops, tablets, desktops are available with various storage capacities. The higher the storage capacity, the more data and information you can keep on the computer or device. To determine the ideal storage capacity, add together the amount of storage space required for all the programs and apps you want to use. In addition, estimate the amount of space you might need to store the files you create. If you are planning to store digital media, such as audio, photos, and videos, make sure the storage device has sufficient space for those files as well. Try not to purchase a device with exactly the amount of storage space you anticipate needing. Always purchase more than you need so that you do not risk running out of space.

In addition to determining sufficient storage capacity for your needs, two main types of primary storage devices from which you may be able to choose include a hard disk (also called a hard drive) or an SSD (solid-state drive) (Figure 14). Hard disks use magnetic particles to store data, instructions, and information on one or more inflexible, circular platters. SSDs are flash memory storage devices that contain their own processors to manage their storage. Hard disks often are less expensive than SSDs and offer greater storage capacities. SSDs, however, are faster than hard disks and may be less susceptible to failure.

Figure 14   Two different types of storage devices.
© Andresr / Shutterstock.com; © roadk / Shutterstock.com

Processor Speed   If you are purchasing a laptop or desktop, you probably will have to determine the processor that will best meet your needs. Many different brands and models of processors are available (Figure 15). Review the system requirements for the programs and apps you want to run to determine the processor best suited to your needs. Because a variety of brands and models of processors exist, you may find it difficult to decide which one to purchase. When you are shopping for your laptop, tablet, or desktop, ask a sales associate to explain the differences among the various processors so that you can make an informed decision.

Step 4: Choose the Purchasing Option

You can purchase new computers and mobile devices in physical stores as well as from online retailers. Each purchasing option has advantages and disadvantages, and it is important to consider these before making a purchasing decision. If, after reading this section, you still do not have a strong preference to purchase from a physical store or an online retailer, compare costs from each for a computer with an identical or similar configuration.

Figure 15   Processor that might be found in a computer or device.
Courtesy of Intel Corporation

Physical Stores   A variety of computers and mobile devices are available for sale at physical stores. While physical stores offer the convenience of being able to shop for and bring home a computer or mobile device the same day, they have a limited inventory and available configuration options. Computers and mobile devices in retail stores are prebuilt and often cannot be customized at the store. For example, if you evaluate the various computers at a physical store and see a laptop you are considering, that laptop may be available in only one configuration. If you want to make changes to the hardware configuration (such as adding a larger hard drive), that would need to be done by a third party after you make the purchase. Some computer and mobile device manufacturers may void their warranty if a third party upgrades your computer or mobile device after the purchase has been made, so be sure to purchase a computer that adequately meets your needs.

Online Retailers Unlike physical stores, online retailers may offer greater configuration options for a computer or mobile device you are considering purchasing. For example, you may be able to completely customize a computer by choosing the exact processor, memory, and hard drive capacity. Online retailers also may offer prebuilt options, so consider the cost difference between purchasing a prebuilt computer and a customized computer with similar specifications. You may find that purchasing a prebuilt computer with a configuration slightly better than one you customized is less expensive. Prebuilt computers often may be less expensive because they are mass produced. If you purchase a computer from an online retailer, however, you will not be able to see the computer and evaluate it before purchase. In addition, it may take several days to several weeks before computers and mobile devices purchased from online retailers may arrive on your doorstep. If you receive the computer or mobile device and do not like it, returning or exchanging it may not be as easy as if you were to purchase it in a physical store.

✴ How To: Your Turn

The How To: Your Turn exercises present general guidelines for fundamental skills when using a computer or mobile device and then require that you determine how to apply these general guidelines to a specific program or situation.

Instructions: You often can complete tasks using technology in multiple ways. Figure out how to perform the tasks described in these exercises by using one or more resources available to you (such as a computer or mobile device, articles on the web or in print, online or program help, user guides, blogs, podcasts, videos, other individuals, trial and error, etc.). Summarize your 'how to' steps, along with the resource(s) used, in the format requested by your instructor (brief report, presentation, discussion, blog post, video, or other means).

❶ Get the Most out of Your Book

Unlike many traditional textbooks, this book contains a variety of elements to help enrich your understanding of the concepts taught in the text. These elements include steps that teach you how to perform real-world tasks, current issues related to technology, and a variety of information to keep you secure while interacting with computers and mobile devices. The following steps guide you through the process of navigating this book and getting the most out of it.

a. Locate and read a How To box in Chapter 1 (or other chapter of your choice). How To boxes appear in shaded boxes with orange borders at the top and bottom. These boxes teach you how to perform real-world tasks that are related to the surrounding chapter content. Answer the question(s) at the bottom of the How To box.

b. Locate and read a Consider This box in Chapter 1 (or other chapter of your choice). Consider This boxes are identified by a green border at the top and bottom. These boxes contain common questions and answers that are related to the surrounding chapter content and often promote critical thinking.

c. Locate and read a Secure IT box in Chapter 1 (or other chapter of your choice). Secure IT boxes

appear in shaded boxes with orange borders at the top and bottom. These boxes contain information about security concerns and helpful safety and security tips that are related to the surrounding chapter content. Answer the question(s) at the bottom of the Secure IT box.

d. Locate and read an Ethics & Issues box in Chapter 1 (or other chapter of your choice). Ethics & Issues boxes appear in shaded boxes with orange borders at the top and bottom. These boxes contain information about current, relative ethical issues and present multiple sides of the issue. Answer the question(s) at the bottom of the Ethics & Issues box.

e. Locate and read a Mini Feature in Chapter 1 (or other chapter of your choice). Mini Features are one page in length and present interesting concepts that are related to the surrounding chapter text. Answer the question(s) at the bottom of the Mini Feature.

f. Locate and read a BTW element (BTW stands for "by the way"). BTW elements provide extra tidbits of information related to the chapter text and also may reference additional online content.

g. Locate and read an Internet Research element. These elements provide suggested search keywords to help you use a search engine to locate current information about the surrounding chapter text.

How To: Your Turn

h. Locate and read the Technology @ Work box in Chapter 1 (or other chapter of your choice). Technology @ Work boxes are identified by purple borders at the top and bottom and provide information about how technology is used in various industries. Answer the question(s) at the bottom of the Technology @ Work box.

Exercises

1. What type of box or element described above is your favorite? Why? Which one is your least favorite? Why?
2. Describe ways that each type of box and element in the chapter can help enhance your understanding of the chapter contents.
3. Review the topics of the boxes in Chapter 1 (or other chapter of your choice). Which one is of most interest to you? Why?

❷ Access This Book's Free Resources

This book's free resources contain a wealth of information that extends beyond what you learn by reading this book. The free resources also contain additional information about current technology developments and content required for those students majoring in the information technology or computer science fields.

You can access the free resources at the web address of www.cengagebrain.com. Once the book's free resources are displayed, select Chapter 1 to view the resources associated with that chapter. View the resources available with another chapter and notice the similarities between the types of content offered in Chapter 1 and the other chapter you chose.

Exercises

1. What exact steps did you take to access the free resources?
2. List and describe the different types of content present in the Chapter 1 free resources.

3. Do you feel the free resources will be useful to you and further enhance your understanding of computers and other technology? Why or why not?

❸ Sign Up for a Microsoft Account

A Microsoft account provides access to resources to several Microsoft services. These services include access to resources, such as a free email account, cloud storage, a location to store information about your contacts, and an online calendar. You will need a Microsoft account to complete some of the exercises in this book. The following steps guide you through the process of signing up for a Microsoft account.

a. Run a browser and navigate to www.outlook.com.
b. Tap or click the link and then follow the on-screen instructions to sign up for a free Microsoft account.
c. Browse the resources available to you in your Microsoft account.
d. If assigned by your instructor, compose and send a new email message from your Microsoft account to your instructor stating that you have signed up for a Microsoft account successfully.
e. Add your instructor's contact information. Next, add contact information for at least three more people.
f. Add your birthday to the calendar.
g. Edit your Microsoft account profile to add more contact and work information.

Exercises

1. If necessary, navigate to and view your new outlook .com email account. What are some ways to prevent junk email messages using the mail settings? What is junk email?
2. What is OneDrive? How much space do you have available on OneDrive to post files?
3. How can you see yourself using the various features in your newly created Microsoft account?

✳ Internet Research

The Internet Research exercises broaden your understanding of chapter concepts by requiring that you search for information on the web.

Instructions: Use a search engine or another search tool to locate the information requested or answers to questions presented in the exercises. Describe your findings, along with the search term(s) you used and your web source(s), in the format requested by your instructor (brief report, presentation, discussion, blog post, video, or other means).

❶ Social Media

You likely have heard and seen the phrases, "Like us on Facebook" and "Follow us on Twitter." Facebook and Twitter are two websites that advertisers, organizations, celebrities, and many groups use to promote and share their products, causes, events, and interests. Millions of people have accounts on Facebook, Twitter, and many other websites known collectively as online social networks. You will learn about social media throughout this book and, in Chapter 1, will learn how to create Facebook and Twitter accounts. You then will view information on these websites and realize that social media can engage and connect the online social network community members effectively.

Research This: If you are signed in to your Facebook account, sign out. Run a browser and then navigate to www.facebook.com. What information is required to sign up for an account? Why does Facebook require a birthdate? Locate and then tap or click the About link. How many 'likes' does Facebook have? What is the content of the first post on this page? How many people 'liked' this first post, and how many people replied to it?

If you are signed in to your Twitter account, sign out. Navigate to www.twitter.com. Describe the contents of the cover photos. Tap or click the About link at the bottom of the page and read the information. What is the content of the three most recent Tweets?

❷ Search Skills

Searching in an E-Book

One advantage that e-books have over printed books is that you can search the text to locate specific content easily. To search within an e-book, locate its search box, often identified by a 'Search inside this book' (or similar) label. Type the word or phrase for which to search, and tap or click a search button. The search button usually contains the word Search or the word Go, or displays a magnifying glass icon. The reader will highlight or provide a list of occurrences where the search text appears within the e-book. You often can jump directly to the page where the word or phrase appears or tap or click buttons labeled Next or Previous (or displaying forward- and backward-pointing arrow icons) to navigate through the occurrences. Within the text, the key words appear highlighted.

A search box also may include options for narrowing down search results, such as limiting search results to a particular chapter. When you type a page number in a search box, some e-book readers will navigate to the location in the e-book corresponding to that page in the printed book.

Research This: Select any e-book to display on your computer or mobile device. Type a significant word from the title as your search text. Use the e-book reader's search feature to answer these questions: (1) Where on the screen, and in what format, does the e-book reader display search results? (2) What information do search results include to help you find the result you are seeking? (3) How do you navigate from one occurrence of the search term to the next? (3) How does the e-book display your search text within the book so that you can locate it easily?

If you are reading the *Discovering Computers* e-book, display it on your computer or mobile device. Enter appropriate search text into the search box for the *Discovering Computers* e-book reader to search for answers to each of these questions: (1) How many times does the word, Twitter, appear in Chapter 1? (2) Complete the sentence in Chapter 1 that begins, "Most e-book reader models have…" (3) What sentence contains the first occurrence of the word, laptop, in Chapter 1?

If you read both the *Discovering Computers* e-book and another e-book, compare the experience using both e-book readers. Which features are common to both? What differences did you notice?

❸ Security

The buyer's guide in this introductory chapter provides information you can use to purchase a laptop, tablet, or desktop. No matter which operating system you choose and how you configure the computer or device, you need to protect your investment from security risks. You will learn about these unwelcome intrusions, called malware, in Chapter 1 and throughout this book, but it is important to obtain malware protection when, or soon after, you purchase the computer or mobile device. You also should install the latest updates.

Research This: Visit a physical electronics store or view online retailers' websites to learn about software that helps prevent malware from infecting computers. Read the packaging or the product details or talk to employees to determine the names of three programs recommended or rated highly. What protections against Internet threats are offered? For example, do they safeguard your photos, music, and financial data, include updates and backup tasks, and offer parental controls? What is the cost, if any, of these programs and the updates? Do computer or mobile device manufacturers include this software with the original purchase? Which operating system is required? How much memory is required?

Technology provides access to the digital world around you.

"I use computers, mobile devices, and the web to do homework, look up information, check email, play games, post updates, talk to friends, upload photos, sync music, and so much more! I feel comfortable using technology. What more do I need to know?"

While you may be familiar with some of the content in this chapter, do you know how to . . .

- Use a touch screen?
- Configure social media privacy settings to prevent others from posting unauthorized photos of you?
- Ease eyestrain while working on a computer or mobile device?
- Protect your hearing when using earbuds or headphones?
- Back up computers and mobile devices?
- Perform a web search?
- Sync computers and mobile devices?
- Protect your computer from viruses and other malware?
- Shop safely online?
- Create a strong password?
- 'Like' the Discovering Computers page on Facebook and 'follow' it on Twitter?
- Connect to a wireless network?

In this chapter, you will discover how to perform these tasks along with much more information essential to this course. For additional content available that accompanies this chapter, visit the free resources and premium content. Refer to the Preface and the Intro chapter for information about how to access these and other additional instructor-assigned support materials.

✔ Objectives

After completing this chapter, you will be able to:

1 Differentiate among laptops, tablets, desktops, and servers

2 Describe the purpose and uses of smartphones, digital cameras, portable and digital media players, e-book readers, wearable devices, and game devices

3 Describe the relationship between data and information

4 Briefly explain various input options (keyboards, pointing devices, voice and video input, and scanners), output options (printers, displays, and speakers), and storage options (hard disks, solid-state drives, USB flash drives, memory cards, optical discs, and cloud storage)

5 Differentiate the web from the Internet, and describe the relationship among the web, webpages, websites, and web servers

6 Explain the purpose of a browser, a search engine, and an online social network

7 Briefly describe digital security risks associated with viruses and other malware, privacy, your health, and the environment

8 Differentiate between an operating system and applications

9 Differentiate between wired and wireless network technologies, and identify reasons individuals and businesses use networks

10 Discuss how society uses technology in education, government, finance, retail, entertainment, health care, science, travel, publishing, and manufacturing

11 Identify technology used by home users, small/home office users, mobile users, power users, and enterprise users

Today's Technology

In the course of a day, you may . . . complete a homework assignment and watch a streaming video using your laptop, flip through news headlines and make dinner reservations using your tablet, search for directions and the local weather forecast while listening to music on your smartphone, edit a video on a desktop computer, and share photos online from your digital camera with family and friends. These and many other technologies are an integral part of everyday life: at school, at home, and at work (Figure 1-1).

Technology can enable you to more efficiently and effectively access and search for information; share personal ideas, photos, and videos with friends, family, and others; communicate with and meet other people; manage finances; shop for goods and services; play games or access other sources of entertainment; keep your life and activities organized; and complete business activities. People who can accomplish these types of tasks using technology often are said to be tech savvy.

Because technology changes, you must keep up with the changes to remain digitally literate. *Digital literacy* involves having a current knowledge and understanding of computers, mobile devices, the web, and related technologies. This book presents the knowledge you need to be digitally literate today.

As you read this first chapter, keep in mind it is an overview. Most of the terms and concepts introduced in this chapter will be discussed in more depth later in the book.

Figure 1-1 People use a variety of computers, mobile devices, and apps everyday.
© iStockPhoto / bo1982; © iStockPhoto / michaeljung; © iStockPhoto / vgajic; © Fotolia / vadymvdrobot; © iStockPhoto / PeopleImages

Computers

A **computer** is an electronic device, operating under the control of instructions stored in its own memory, that can accept data (*input*), process the data according to specified rules, produce information (*output*), and store the information for future use. Computers contain many electric, electronic, and mechanical components known as *hardware*.

Electronic components in computers process data using instructions, which are the steps that tell the computer how to perform a particular task. A collection of related instructions organized for a common purpose is referred to as software or a program. Using software, you can complete a variety of activities, such as search for information, type a paper, balance a budget, create a presentation, or play a game.

One popular category of computer is the personal computer. A *personal computer* (PC) is a computer that can perform all of its input, processing, output, and storage activities by itself and is intended to be used by one person at a time. Most personal computers today also can communicate with other computers and devices.

Types of personal computers include laptops, tablets, and desktops, with the first two sometimes called mobile computers. A *mobile computer* is a portable personal computer, designed so that a user can carry it from place to place. A *user* is anyone who interacts with a computer or mobile device, or utilizes the information it generates.

Discover More: Visit this chapter's free resources to learn more about electronic components and circuitry of a computer.

Laptops

A **laptop**, also called a *notebook computer*, is a thin, lightweight mobile computer with a screen in its lid and a keyboard in its base (Figure 1-2). Designed to fit on your lap and for easy transport, most laptops weigh up to 7 pounds (varying by manufacturer and specifications). A laptop that is less than one inch thick and weighs about three pounds or less sometimes is referred to as an ultrathin laptop. Most laptops can operate on batteries or a power supply or both.

screen

keyboard

hinges

Figure 1-2   A typical laptop has a keyboard in the base and a screen in the lid, with the lid attaching to the base with hinges.
© iStockphoto / Stephen Krow

Tablets

Usually smaller than a laptop but larger than a phone, a **tablet** is a thin, lighter-weight mobile computer that has a touch screen (read How To 1-1 for ways to interact with a touch screen). A popular style of tablet is the slate, which does not contain a physical keyboard (Figure 1-3). Like laptops, tablets run on batteries or a power supply or both; however, batteries in a tablet typically last longer than those in laptops.

Figure 1-3   A slate tablet.
© iStockphoto / franckreporter

Computers, Devices, and the Web   **Chapter 1**   **5**

 HOW TO 1-1

Interact with a Touch Screen

You usually can interact with a touch screen using gestures. A *gesture* is a motion you make on a touch screen with the tip of one or more fingers or your hand. Touch screens are convenient because they do not require a separate device for input. Tablets and smartphones typically have touch screens.

The table below presents common ways to interact with a touch screen.

 Touch Screen Gestures

Motion	Description	Common Uses
Tap 	Quickly touch and release one finger one time	Activate a link (built-in connection) Press a button Run a program or app
Double-tap	Quickly touch and release one finger two times	Run a program or app Zoom in (show a smaller area on the screen, so that contents appear larger) at the location of the double-tap
Press and hold	Press and hold one finger to cause an action to occur, or until an action occurs	Display a shortcut menu (immediate access to allowable actions) Activate a mode enabling you to move an item with one finger to a new location
Drag, or *slide*	Press and hold one finger on an object and then move the finger to the new location	Move an item around the screen Scroll
Swipe	Press and hold one finger and then move the finger horizontally or vertically on the screen	Scroll Display a bar that contains commands on an edge of the screen
Stretch	Move two fingers apart	Zoom in (show a smaller area on the screen, so that contents appear larger)
Pinch	Move two fingers together	Zoom out (show a larger area on the screen, so that contents appear smaller)

 Consider This: In addition to the motions listed in the table, what other motions do you think a touch screen should support?

© Cengage Learning

 CONSIDER THIS

If a slate tablet has no keyboard, how do you type on it?

You can use your fingers to press keys on a keyboard that appears on the screen, called an *on-screen keyboard*, or you can purchase a separate physical keyboard that attaches to or wirelessly communicates with the tablet. You also may be able to speak into the tablet, and your spoken words will translate to typed text.

 **Internet Research**

What is a virtual keyboard?

Search for: virtual keyboard

Desktops and All-in-Ones

A **desktop**, or desktop computer, is a personal computer designed to be in a stationary location, where all of its components fit on or under a desk or table. On many desktops, the screen is housed in a display device (or simply display) that is separate from a tower, which is a case that contains the processing circuitry (Figure 1-4a). Another type of desktop called an **all-in-one** does not contain a tower and instead uses the same case to house the display and the processing circuitry (Figure 1-4b). Some desktops and all-in-ones have displays that support touch.

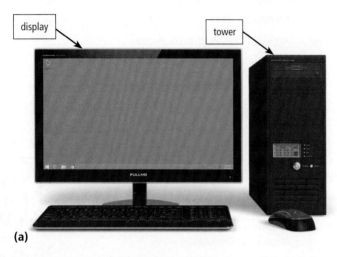

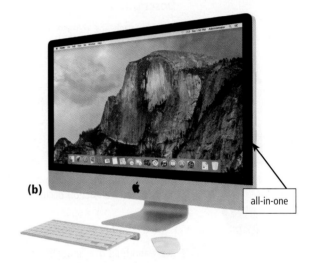

Figure 1-4   Some desktops have a separate tower; all-in-ones do not.
© iStockphoto / Oleksiy Mark; Source: Microsoft; © iStockphoto / hocus-focus; Apple, Inc.

 CONSIDER THIS

Which type of computer — laptop, tablet, or desktop — is best?

It depends on your needs. Because laptops can be as powerful as the average desktop, more people today choose laptops over desktops so that they have the added benefit of portability. Tablets are ideal for those not needing the power of a laptop or for searching for information, communicating with others, and taking notes in lectures, at meetings, conferences, and other forums where a laptop is not practical. Desktops and all-in-ones often have larger displays than laptops or tablets, which make them well suited for developing software, editing large documents, or creating images and videos.

Figure 1-5   A server provides services to other computers or devices on a network.
© iStockPhoto / GuidoVrola

Servers

A **server** is a computer dedicated to providing one or more services to other computers or devices on a network. A network is a collection of computers and devices connected together, often wirelessly. Services provided by servers include storing content and controlling access to hardware, software, and other resources on a network.

A server can support from two to several thousand connected computers and devices at the same time. Servers are available in a variety of sizes and types for both small and large business applications (Figure 1-5). Smaller applications, such as at home, sometimes use a high-end desktop as a server. Larger corporate, government, and web applications use powerful, expensive servers to support their daily operations.

Mobile and Game Devices

A *mobile device* is a computing device small enough to hold in your hand. Because of their reduced size, the screens on mobile devices are small — often between 3 and 5 inches.

Some mobile devices are Internet capable, meaning that they can connect to the Internet wirelessly. You often can exchange information between the Internet and a mobile device or between a computer or network and a mobile device. Popular types of mobile devices are smartphones, digital cameras, portable and digital media players, e-book readers, and wearable devices.

 CONSIDER THIS

Are mobile devices computers?
The mobile devices discussed in this section can be categorized as computers because they operate under the control of instructions stored in their own memory, can accept data, process the data according to specified rules, produce or display information, and store the information for future use.

Smartphones

A **smartphone** is an Internet-capable phone that usually also includes a calendar, an address book, a calculator, a notepad, games, and several other apps (which are programs on the smartphone). Other apps are available through an app store that typically is associated with the phone.

Smartphones typically communicate wirelessly with other devices or computers. With most smartphone models, you also can listen to music, take photos, and record videos.

Many smartphones have touch screens. Instead of or in addition to a touch screen, some smartphones have a keyboard that slides in and out from behind the phone (Figure 1-6). Others have built-in mini keyboards or keypads that contain both numbers and letters. Some are called a *phablet* because they combine the features of a smartphone with a tablet.

 Internet Research
What are some app stores?
Search for: popular app stores

touch screen

slide out keyboard

 Figure 1-6
Smartphones may have a touch screen and/or a slide out keyboard.
© iStockphoto / Moncherie;
© iStockPhoto / scanrail

Instead of calling someone's phone to talk, you can send messages to others by pressing images on an on-screen keyboard on the phone, keys on the phone's mini keyboard, or buttons on the phone's keypad. Four popular types of messages that you can send with smartphones include voice messages, text messages, picture messages, and video messages.

- A *voice mail message* is a short audio recording sent to or from a smartphone or other mobile device.
- A *text message* is a short note, typically fewer than 300 characters, sent to or from a smartphone or other mobile device.
- A *picture message* is a photo or other image, sometimes along with sound and text, sent to or from a smartphone or other mobile device.
- A *video message* is a short video clip, usually about 30 seconds, sent to or from a smartphone or other mobile device.

BTW

Messaging Services
Mobile service providers may charge additional fees for sending text, picture, or video messages, depending on the messaging plan.

Read Ethics & Issues 1-1 to consider whether it should be legal to use a hands-free device, such as a smartphone, while driving.

 ETHICS & ISSUES 1-1 ——————————————————————————————

Should It Be Legal to Use a Hands-Free Device while Driving?
Your new vehicle includes a sophisticated hands-free system that enables you to connect a mobile device to the vehicle's sound system. In addition to making phone calls without holding your device, you also can use this technology to read and respond to email messages or to update your Facebook status using speech-to-text, which converts your spoken words to text. Is this technology safe to use?

The debate about hands-free device safety elicits different points of view from vehicle insurance companies, consumer safety groups, and the telecommunications industry. AAA (American Automobile Association) conducted a study to measure the mental effect of using hands-free devices while driving. The conclusions indicated that drivers using hands-free devices are distracted, miss visual clues, and have slower reaction times. The report also stated that 3000 fatalities occur each year due to the use of hands-free devices.

Critics say that using a hands-free device gives people a false sense of security. Others claim that drivers can be just as easily distracted if they are discussing business or emotional matters with passengers in the vehicle. Some states have outlawed any use of mobile phones while driving; others require drivers to use hands-free devices while driving. Lawmakers are attempting to regulate "distracted driving" caused by using hands-free devices. One issue that remains unclear is whether law enforcement has a right to look at a user's devices to determine whether they were used illegally.

Consider This: Do you think the government should be able to establish rules about hands-free device usage while driving? Why or why not? Do you believe you are distracted if you use hands-free devices while driving? Why or why not? Do you think auto manufacturers should continue to put hands-free device technology in vehicles? Why or why not?

Digital Cameras

A **digital camera** is a device that allows you to take photos and store the photographed images digitally (Figure 1-7). A smart digital camera also can communicate wirelessly with other devices and include apps similar to those on a smartphone. Many mobile computers and devices, such as tablets and smartphones, include at least one integrated digital camera.

Digital cameras typically allow you to review, and sometimes modify, images while they are in the camera. You also can transfer images from a digital camera to a computer or device, so that you can review, modify, share, organize, or print the images. Digital cameras often can connect to or communicate wirelessly with a computer, a Smart TV (discussed later in the chapter), a printer, or the Internet, enabling

Figure 1-7 With a digital camera, you can view photographed images immediately through a small screen on the camera to see if the photo is worth keeping.
Source: Samsung

Internet Research
What is a digital SLR camera?

Search for: digital slr camera

you to access the photos on the camera without using a cable. Some also can record videos. Many digital cameras also have built-in GPS (discussed later in this chapter), giving them the capability to record the exact location where a photo was taken and store these details with the photo.

Portable and Digital Media Players

A **portable media player** is a mobile device on which you can store, organize, and play or view digital media (Figure 1-8). *Digital media* includes music, photos, and videos. Thus, portable media players enable you to listen to music, view photos, and watch videos, movies, and television shows. With most, you transfer the digital media from a computer or the web, if the device is Internet capable, to the portable media player. Some enable you to play the media while it streams, that is, while it transfers to the player.

Portable media players usually require a set of *earbuds*, which are small speakers that rest inside each ear canal. Some portable media player models have a touch screen, while others have a pad that you operate with a thumb or finger, so that you can navigate through digital media, adjust volume, and customize settings. Some portable media players also offer a calendar, address book, games, and other apps (discussed later in this chapter).

Portable media players are a mobile type of digital media player. A *digital media player* or *streaming media player* is a device, typically used in a home, that streams digital media from a computer or network to a television, projector, or some other entertainment device.

Internet Research

What are popular digital media players?

Search for: digital media players

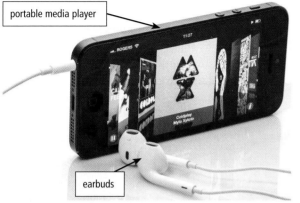

portable media player

earbuds

digital media player

Figure 1-8 Portable media players, such as the iPod shown here, typically include a set of earbuds. Digital media players stream media to a home entertainment device.
© iStockphoto / Sebastien Cote; © iStockPhoto / marvinh

E-Book Readers

An **e-book reader** (short for electronic book reader), or *e-reader*, is a mobile device that is used primarily for reading e-books (Figure 1-9). An *e-book*, or digital book, is an electronic version of a printed book, readable on computers and other digital devices. In addition to books, you typically can purchase and read other forms of digital media such as newspapers and magazines.

Most e-book reader models have a touch screen, and some are Internet capable. These devices usually are smaller than tablets but larger than smartphones.

Wearable Devices

A **wearable device** or *wearable* is a small, mobile computing consumer device designed to be worn (Figure 1-10). These devices often communicate with a mobile device or computer.

Wearable devices include activity trackers, smartwatches, and smartglasses. Activity trackers monitor heart rate, measure pulse, count steps, and track sleep patterns. In addition to keeping time, a smartwatch can communicate with a smartphone to make and answer phone calls, read and send messages, access the web, play music, work with apps, such as fitness trackers and GPS, and more. With smartglasses, a user looks into an eyeglass-type device to view information or take photos and videos that are projected to a miniature screen in the user's field of vision.

Figure 1-9 An e-book reader.
© iStockPhoto

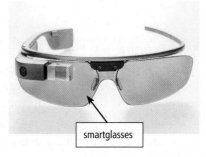

activity tracker

smartwatch

smartglasses

Figure 1-10 Activity trackers, smartwatches, and smartglasses are popular types of wearable devices.
© iStockPhoto / MileA;
© iStockPhoto / scanrail;
© iStockPhoto / ferrantraite

Game Devices

A **game console** is a mobile computing device designed for single-player or multiplayer video games. Gamers often connect the game console to a television so that they can view their gameplay on the television's screen (Figure 1-11). Many game console models are Internet capable and also allow you to listen to music and watch movies or view photos. Typically weighing between three and eleven pounds, the compact size of game consoles makes them easy to use at home, in the car, in a hotel, or any location that has an electrical outlet and a television screen.

A handheld game device is small enough to fit in one hand, making it more portable than the game console. Because of their reduced size, the screens are small — similar in size to some smartphone screens. Some handheld game device models are Internet capable and also can communicate wirelessly with other similar devices for multiplayer gaming.

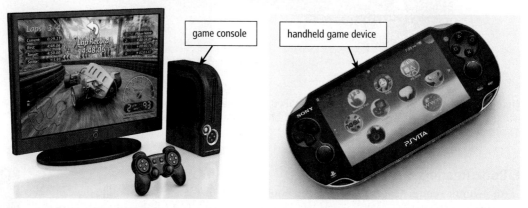

game console

handheld game device

Figure 1-11 Game consoles often connect to a television; handheld game devices contain a built-in screen.
© iStockPhoto / pagadesign; © iStockPhoto / AnthonyRosenberg

✸ CONSIDER THIS

Are digital cameras, portable media players, e-book readers, and handheld game devices becoming obsolete because more and more smartphones and tablets include their functionality?

Many smartphones and tablets enable you to take and store photos; store, organize, and play or view your digital media; read e-books; and play games. This trend of computers and devices with technologies that overlap, called **digital device convergence**, means that consumers may need fewer devices for the functionality that they require.

Still, consumers may purchase separate stand-alone devices (i.e., a separate digital camera, portable media player, etc.) for a variety of reasons. The stand-alone device (i.e., a digital camera) may have more features and functionality than the combined device offers (i.e., a smartphone). You might want to be able to use both devices at the same time; for example, you might send text messages on the phone while reading a book on an e-book reader. Or, you might want protection if your combined device (i.e., smartphone) breaks. For example, you still can listen to music on a portable media player if your smartphone becomes nonfunctional.

Mini Feature 1-1: Living Digitally — Gaming and Digital Home

Technology has made homes entertaining, efficient, and safe. Read Mini Feature 1-1 to learn how game devices provide entertainment and education, and home automation offers convenience and significant cost savings.

MINI FEATURE 1-1

Gaming and Digital Home

Academic researchers developed the first video games in the 1950s as part of their studies of artificial intelligence and simulations, and their work was applied and expanded commercially to early home consoles and arcade games. The concept of home automation can be traced back to 1898 when Nikola Tesla invented the first remote control. The following sections describe how these two technologies are used today.

Gaming

Video gamers spend billions of dollars each year making the most of their downtime with game consoles and devices, with an estimated 5 billion people worldwide playing at least 45 hours per week. The popularity is due, in large part, to the social aspect of gathering families and friends to play together as a group or online with each other and those around the world. The wide variety of categories offers a gaming experience for practically everyone in genres such as adventure, education, fitness, puzzles, sports, role-playing, and simulation.

- **Obtaining Games:** Gamers have several options available for locating games. For tablets and smartphones, they can download games from an app store to a mobile computer or device. For game consoles, they can purchase or rent discs or other media that contain games; download or transfer them from online stores; or sign up for cloud services that stream or transfer games on demand.

- **Accessories and Input Techniques:** The more popular game consoles work with a wide variety of accessories and input techniques for directing movements and actions of on-screen players and objects. They include gamepads, voice commands, and fitness accessories, some of which are shown here. Although many games are played using a controller, several systems operate by allowing the player to be the controller.

© iStockphoto / Florea Marius Catalin; © iStockphoto / Brandon Alms; © iStockphoto / Lee Pettet; © iStockphoto / Craig Veltri; © Courtesy of DDR Game

Home Automation

New home builders and existing homeowners are integrating features that automate a wide variety of tasks, save time and money, and enhance the overall at-home environment.

- **Lighting:** Controlling lighting is one of the more common uses of technology in the home. Remotes turn light fixtures on and off, and motion sensors turn on lights when a car or a visitor approaches the driveway or walkway.

- **Thermostats**: Programmable thermostats adjust to seasonal needs and can be set to control temperatures in individual rooms. Homeowners can use their smartphones to monitor heating and cooling systems, adjust temperatures, and manage energy consumption.

- **Appliances:** Smart appliances, such as dishwashers, can be programmed to run at nonpeak electrical times. Coffeemakers can turn on at set times and shut off if an overheating coffeepot has been left on accidentally. Refrigerators can track expiration dates and create shopping lists.

- **Security:** Security systems can detect break-ins at doors and heat from fires, and they can send text and email messages to alert a homeowner when someone has entered or left the home. Surveillance cameras keep a watchful eye on the premises and interior rooms; homeowners can view the images on televisions and computers within the house or on a webpage when they are away from home, as shown in the figure.

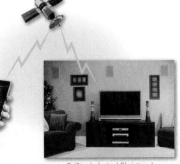

© DavidEwingPhotography / Shutterstock.com; © Poulsons Photography / Shutterstock.com; © Anthony Berenyi / Shutterstock.com

- **Remotes:** Many people are turning to using their smartphones and tablets to control all the devices in the room. Users enjoy the convenience of customizing apps to operate their television, DVR, and security system and to perform other functions anywhere in the home.

  Discover More: Visit this chapter's free resources to learn more about game genres, game controllers, remotes, programmable thermostats, smart appliances, security systems, and vacuum systems.

© iStockphoto / Christian J. Stewart; © Mmaxer / Shutterstock. com; © iStockphoto / Nastco; © ESPN; © Cengage Learning

✳ **Consider This:** How has your life become more efficient, safe, and enjoyable by using home automation and entertainment features? What are the advantages of playing games, and do they outweigh the disadvantages?

Data and Information

Computers process data (input) into information (output) and often store the data and resulting information for future use. *Data* is a collection of unprocessed items, which can include text, numbers, images, audio, and video. *Information* conveys meaning to users. Both business and home users can make well-informed decisions because they have instant access to information from anywhere in the world.

Many daily activities either involve the use of or depend on information from a computer. For example, as shown in Figure 1-12, computers process several data items to print information in the form of a cash register receipt.

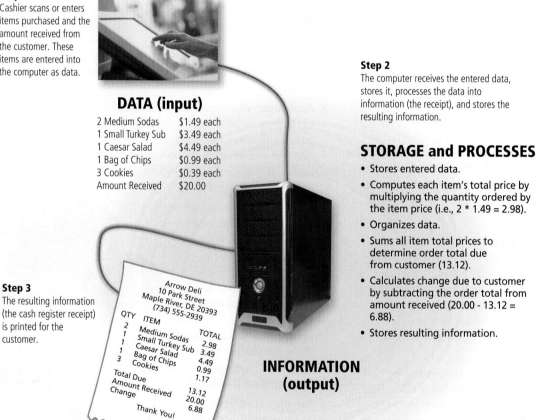

Step 1
Cashier scans or enters items purchased and the amount received from the customer. These items are entered into the computer as data.

DATA (input)

2 Medium Sodas	$1.49 each
1 Small Turkey Sub	$3.49 each
1 Caesar Salad	$4.49 each
1 Bag of Chips	$0.99 each
3 Cookies	$0.39 each
Amount Received	$20.00

Step 2
The computer receives the entered data, stores it, processes the data into information (the receipt), and stores the resulting information.

STORAGE and PROCESSES

- Stores entered data.
- Computes each item's total price by multiplying the quantity ordered by the item price (i.e., 2 * 1.49 = 2.98).
- Organizes data.
- Sums all item total prices to determine order total due from customer (13.12).
- Calculates change due to customer by subtracting the order total from amount received (20.00 - 13.12 = 6.88).
- Stores resulting information.

Step 3
The resulting information (the cash register receipt) is printed for the customer.

Arrow Deli
10 Park Street
Maple River, DE 20393
(734) 555-2939

QTY	ITEM	TOTAL
2	Medium Sodas	2.98
1	Small Turkey Sub	3.49
1	Caesar Salad	4.49
1	Bag of Chips	0.99
3	Cookies	1.17

Total Due	13.12
Amount Received	20.00
Change	6.88

Thank You!

INFORMATION (output)

 Figure 1-12 A computer processes data into information. In this simplified example, the item ordered, item price, quantity ordered, and amount received all represent data (input). The computer processes the data to produce the cash register receipt (information, or output).
© Cengage Learning; © iStockphoto / Norman Chan; © bikeriderlondon / Shutterstock

 BTW

Mobile Computer Input
If you prefer a full-sized keyboard to a laptop's keyboard or a tablet's on-screen keyboard, you can use a full-sized keyboard with your mobile computer. Likewise, if you prefer using a mouse instead of a touchpad, you can use a mouse with your mobile computer.

CONSIDER THIS

Can you give another example of data and its corresponding information?
Your name, address, term, course names, course sections, course grades, and course credits all represent data that is processed to generate your semester grade report. Other information on the grade report includes results of calculations such as total semester hours, grade point average, and total credits.

Input

Users have a variety of input options for entering data into a computer, many of which involve using an input device. An **input device** is any hardware component that allows you to enter data and instructions into a computer or mobile device. The following sections discuss common input methods.

Keyboards A *keyboard* contains keys you press to enter data and instructions into a computer or mobile device (Figure 1-13). All desktop keyboards have a typing area that includes letters of the alphabet, numbers, punctuation marks, and other basic keys. Some users prefer a wireless keyboard because it eliminates the clutter of a cord.

Keyboards for desktops contain more keys than keyboards on mobile computers and devices. To provide the same functionality as a desktop keyboard, many of the keys on mobile computers and devices serve two or three purposes. On a laptop, for example, you often use the same keys to type numbers and to show various areas on a screen, switching a key's purpose by pressing a separate key first.

Instead of a physical keyboard, users also can enter data via an on-screen keyboard or a virtual keyboard, which is a keyboard that projects from a device to a flat surface.

desktop keyboard

laptop keyboard

 Figure 1-13 Users have a variety of options for entering typed text.
© skyfotostock / Shutterstock.com;
© Africa Studio / Shutterstock.com;
© iStockphoto /
kycstudio; © iStockphoto /
MorePixels; Courtesy of Virtek, Inc.

on-screen keyboard

mini keyboard

virtual keyboard

Pointing Devices A pointing device is an input device that allows a user to control a small symbol on a screen, called the pointer. Desktops typically use a mouse as their pointing device, and laptops use a touchpad (Figure 1-14).

A *mouse* is a pointing device that fits under the palm of your hand comfortably. With the mouse, you control movement of the pointer and send instructions to the computer or mobile device. Table 1-1 identifies some of the common mouse operations. Like keyboards, some users prefer working with a wireless mouse.

A *touchpad* is a small, flat, rectangular pointing device that is sensitive to pressure and motion. To control the pointer with a touchpad, slide your fingertip across the surface of the pad. On most touchpads, you also can tap the pad's surface to imitate mouse operations, such as clicking.

Figure 1-14 A mouse and a touchpad.
© iStockphoto / PhotoTalk;
© iStockphoto / Michael Bodmann

mouse

touchpad

Table 1-1 Mouse Operations

Operation	Description	Common Uses
Point	Move the mouse until the pointer is positioned on the item of choice.	Position the pointer on the screen.
Click	Press and release the primary mouse button, which usually is the left mouse button.	Select or deselect items on the screen or start a program or feature.
Right-click	Press and release the secondary mouse button, which usually is the right mouse button.	Display a shortcut menu.
Double-click	Quickly press and release the primary mouse button twice without moving the mouse.	Start a program or program feature.
Drag	Point to an item, hold down the primary mouse button, move the item to the desired location on the screen, and then release the mouse button.	Move an object from one location to another or draw pictures.

Voice and Video Input   Some mobile devices and computers enable you to speak data instructions using voice input and to capture live full-motion images using video input. With your smartphone, for example, you may be able to use your voice to send a text message, schedule an appointment, and dial a phone number. Or, you may opt for video calling instead of a voice phone call, so that you and the person you called can see each other as you chat on a computer or mobile device. As in this example, video input usually works in conjunction with voice input. For voice input, you use a microphone, and for video input you use a webcam (Figure 1-15).

A *microphone* is an input device that enables you to speak into a computer or mobile device. Many computers and most mobile devices contain built-in microphones. You also can talk into a *headset*, which contains both a microphone and a speaker. Many headsets can communicate wirelessly with the computer or mobile device. A *webcam* is a digital video (DV) camera that allows you to capture video and usually audio input for your computer or mobile device.

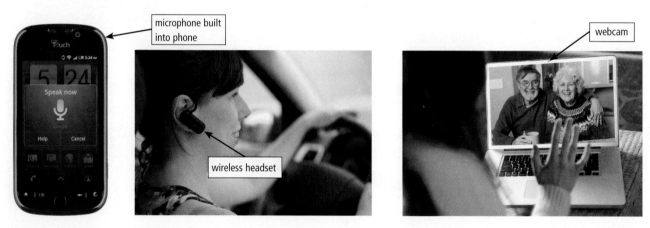

Figure 1-15   You can speak instructions into a microphone or wireless headset and capture live video on a webcam for a video call.
© iStockphoto / Stephen Krow; © iStockphoto / pierrephoto; © iStockphoto / Suprijono Suharjoto

Figure 1-16   A scanner.
© iStockphoto / Edgaras Marozas

Scanners   A *scanner* is a light-sensing input device that converts printed text and images into a form the computer can process (Figure 1-16). A popular type of scanner works in a manner similar to a copy machine, except that instead of creating a paper copy of the document or photo, it stores the scanned document or photo electronically.

Output

Users have a variety of output options to convey text, graphics, audio, and video — many of which involve using an output device. An **output device** is any hardware component that conveys information from a computer or mobile device to one or more people. The following sections discuss common output methods.

Printers   A **printer** is an output device that produces text and graphics on a physical medium, such as paper or other material (Figure 1-17). Printed content sometimes is referred to as a *hard copy* or *printout*. Most printers today print text and graphics in both black-and-white and color on a variety of paper types with many capable of printing lab-quality photos. A variety of printers support wireless printing, where a computer or other device communicates wirelessly with the printer.

A *3-D printer* can print solid objects, such as clothing, prosthetics, eyewear, implants, toys, parts, prototypes, and more. 3-D printers use a plastic substance that prints in layers to create a 3-D (three-dimensional) model.

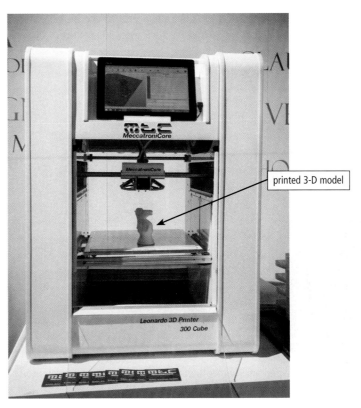

printed 3-D model

printed photo

Figure 1-17 A printer can produce a variety of printed output including photos and 3-D solid objects.
Courtesy of Epson America, Inc.; © iStockPhoto / Stefano Tinti

Displays A display is an output device that visually conveys text, graphics, and video information. Displays consist of a screen and the components that produce the information on the screen. The display for a desktop typically is a monitor, which is a separate, physical device. Mobile computers and devices typically integrate the display in their same physical case (Figure 1-18). Some displays have touch screens.

Home users sometimes use a digital television or a Smart TV as a display. A *Smart TV* is an Internet-enabled high-definition television (HDTV) from which you can use the Internet to watch video, listen to the radio, play games, and communicate with others — all while watching a television show.

smartphone
display

digital camera display

tablet display

laptop display

monitor display

Figure 1-18 Displays vary depending on the computer or mobile device.
© iStockphoto / Sebastien Cote; © David Lentz / Photos.com; © Dmitry Rukhlenko / Photos.com; © Mrallen / Dreamstime.com; © Pakhnyushcha / Shutterstock.com

CONSIDER THIS

What can you do to ease eyestrain while using a computer or mobile device?
Position the display about 20 degrees below eye level. Clean the screen regularly. Blink your eyes every five seconds. Adjust the room lighting. Face into an open space beyond the screen. Use larger fonts or zoom the display. Take an eye break every 30 minutes. If you wear glasses, ask your doctor about computer glasses.

headphones

Figure 1-19 In a crowded environment where speakers are not practical, users can wear headphones to hear music, voice, and other sounds.
© iStockphoto / Photo_Alto

Speakers, Earbuds, and Headphones

Speakers allow you to hear audio, that is, music, voice, and other sounds. Most personal computers and mobile devices have a small internal speaker. Many users attach higher-quality speakers to their computers and mobile devices, including game consoles.

So that only you can hear sound, you can listen through earbuds (shown earlier in this chapter in Figure 1-8) or headphones, which cover or are placed outside of the ear (Figure 1-19). Both earbuds and headphones usually include noise-cancelling technology to reduce the interference of sounds from the surrounding environment. To eliminate the clutter of cords, users can opt for wireless speakers or wireless headphones. Read How To 1-2 to learn how to protect your hearing when using earbuds or headphones.

 HOW TO 1-2

Protect Your Hearing when Using Earbuds or Headphones
Using earbuds and headphones improperly can lead to permanent hearing loss. The following tips describe some ways to protect your hearing when using earbuds or headphones:

- If people standing next to you can hear the sound being transmitted through the earbuds or headphones you are wearing, decrease the volume until they no longer can hear it. The quieter the sounds, the less damage you will incur.

- If you intend to listen to music through earbuds or headphones for hours at a time, consider listening at only 30 percent maximum volume. Listening for extended periods of time at a high volume may be unsafe for your ears.

- Consider using a high-quality set of headphones. These headphones reduce your risk of developing hearing loss because the sound quality often is better and does not require you to turn up the volume as loud. Also, their design is better, allowing a closer fit and thus

reducing the necessary volume required for optimal listening.

- Consider using a set of earbuds or headphones that reduce outside noise. When the earbuds or headphones eliminate the external noise effectively, they can reduce the volume level needed. The lower the volume levels, the less potential hearing damage.

 Consider This: Do you prefer earbuds or headphones? Why? Do you think you turn the volume up too loud while listening to music through earbuds or headphones?

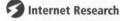 **Internet Research**

What types of headphones are available?

Search for: headphone reviews

Memory and Storage

Memory consists of electronic components that store instructions waiting to be executed and the data needed by those instructions. Although some forms of memory are permanent, most memory keeps data and instructions temporarily, which means its contents are erased when the computer is shut off.

Storage, by contrast, holds data, instructions, and information for future use. For example, computers can store hundreds or millions of student names and addresses permanently.

A computer keeps data, instructions, and information on **storage media**. Examples of local storage media includes hard disks, solid-state drives, USB (universal serial bus) flash drives, memory cards, and optical discs. The amount of storage for each type of storage media varies, but hard disks, solid-state drives, and optical discs usually hold more than USB flash drives and memory cards. Some storage media are portable, meaning you can remove the medium from one computer and carry it to another computer.

A **storage device** records (writes) and/or retrieves (reads) items to and from storage media. Storage devices often also function as a source of input and output because they transfer items from storage to memory and vice versa. Drives and readers/writers, which are types of storage devices, accept a specific kind of storage media. For example, a DVD drive (storage device) accepts a DVD (storage media).

Discover More: Visit this chapter's free resources to learn more about media storage capacity.

Hard Disks

A *hard disk* is a storage device that contains one or more inflexible, circular platters that use magnetic particles to store data, instructions, and information. The entire device is enclosed in an airtight, sealed case to protect it from contamination. Laptops and desktops often contain at least one hard disk that is mounted inside the computer's case (Figure 1-20).

hard disk is positioned in base of laptop

Figure 1-20 A hard disk mounted inside a laptop's case.
© iStockphoto / Brian Balster

Solid-State Drives

A *solid-state drive* (SSD) is a storage device that typically uses flash memory to store data, instructions, and information. Flash memory contains no moving parts, making it more durable and shock resistant than other types of media. For this reason, some manufacturers are using SSDs instead of hard disks in their laptops, tablets, and desktops (Figure 1-21).

SSD contains no moving parts

hard disk contains moving parts

Figure 1-21 A solid-state drive (SSD) is about the same size as a laptop hard disk.
© iStockphoto / Ludovit Repko

✳ **CONSIDER THIS** ────────────────────────────

What is an external hard drive?
An external hard drive is a separate, portable, freestanding hard disk or SSD that usually connect to the computer with a cable (Figure 1-22). As with an internal hard disk or SSD, the entire external hard drive is enclosed in an airtight, sealed case.

external hard drive connected to laptop

Figure 1-22 A external hard drive is a separate, freestanding storage device.
© iStockphoto / murat sarica

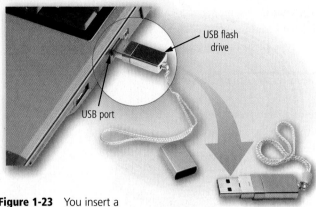

USB flash drive

USB port

Figure 1-23   You insert a USB flash drive in a USB port on a computer.
© Pakhnyushcha / Shutterstock.com

USB Flash Drives   A *USB flash drive* is a portable flash memory storage device that you plug in a USB port, which is a special, easily accessible opening on a computer or mobile device (Figure 1-23). USB flash drives are convenient for mobile users because they are small and lightweight enough to be transported on a keychain or in a pocket.

Memory Cards   A *memory card* is removable flash memory, usually no bigger than 1.5 inches in height or width, that you insert in and remove from a slot in a computer, mobile device, or card reader/writer (Figure 1-24). With a card reader/writer, you can transfer the stored items, such as digital photos, from a memory card to a computer or printer that does not have a built-in card slot.

Figure 1-24
Computers and mobile devices use a variety of styles of memory cards to store documents, photos, and other items.
© Verisakeet / Fotolia;
© Sonar / Fotolia; Courtesy of Mark Frydenberg;
© uwimages / Fotolia

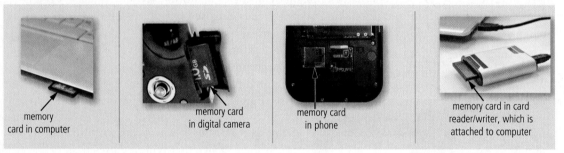

memory card in computer

memory card in digital camera

memory card in phone

memory card in card reader/writer, which is attached to computer

✳ **CONSIDER THIS**

What is the general use for each type of local storage media?
Hard disks and SSDs store software and all types of user files. A *file* is a named collection of stored data, instructions, or information and can contain text, images, audio, and video. Memory cards and USB flash drives store files you intend to transport from one location to another, such as a homework assignment or photos. Optical discs generally store software, photos, movies, and music.

DVD

DVD drive

Figure 1-25   You can insert a DVD in a DVD drive on a computer.
© iStockphoto / Hanquan Chen

Optical Discs   An *optical disc* is a type of storage media that consists of a flat, round, portable metal disc made of metal, plastic, and lacquer that is written and read by a laser. CDs (compact discs) and DVDs (digital versatile discs) are two types of optical discs (Figure 1-25).

Cloud Storage   Instead of storing data, instructions, and information locally on a hard drive or other media, some users opt for cloud storage. **Cloud storage** is an Internet service that provides remote storage to computer users. For example, Figure 1-26 shows JustCloud, which provides cloud storage solutions to home and business users.

Types of services offered by cloud storage providers vary. Some provide storage for specific types of media, such as photos, whereas others store any content and provide backup services. A **backup** is a duplicate of content on a storage medium that you can use in case the original is lost, damaged, or destroyed. Read Secure IT 1-1 for suggestions for backing up your computers and mobile devices.

Figure 1-26 JustCloud is an example of a website that provides cloud storage solutions to home and business users.

Source: JustCloud.com

⚙ SECURE IT 1-1

📄 Backing Up Computers and Mobile Devices

Power outages, hardware failure, theft, and many other factors can cause loss of data, instructions, or information on a computer or mobile device. To protect against loss, you should back up the contents of storage media regularly. Backing up can provide peace of mind and save hours of work attempting to recover important material in the event of a mishap.

A backup plan for laptop and desktop computers could include the following:

• Use a backup program, either included with your computer's operating system or one that you purchased separately, to copy the contents of your entire hard drive to a separate device.

• Regularly copy music, photos, videos, documents, and other important items to an external hard drive, a USB flash drive, or a DVD.

• Subscribe to a cloud storage provider.

• Schedule your files to be backed up regularly.

Backup plans for mobile devices are less specific. Apps for backing up your smartphone or tablet's content are available. You also can back up a mobile device to your computer's hard drive using synchronization software that runs on your computer (synchronization software is discussed later in this chapter). Some mobile device manufacturers, such as Apple, provide cloud storage solutions to owners of their devices. Other services allow subscribers to use another computer as a backup storage location. Overall, the best advice is to back up often using a variety of methods.

☀ **Consider This:** Do you back up files regularly? If not, why not? What would you do if you had no backup and then discovered that your computer or mobile device had failed?

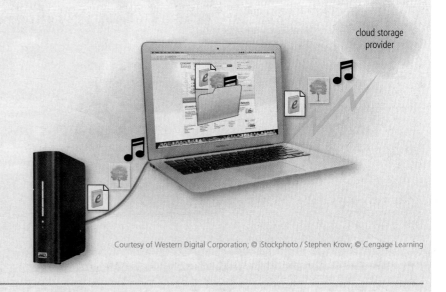

cloud storage provider

Courtesy of Western Digital Corporation; © iStockphoto / Stephen Krow; © Cengage Learning

NOW YOU SHOULD KNOW

Be sure you understand the material presented in the sections titled Today's Technology, Computers, Mobile and Game Devices, and Data and Information, as it relates to the chapter objectives.
Now you should know . . .

- Which type of computer might be suited to your needs (Objective 1)

- Why you would use a smartphone, digital camera, portable or digital media player, e-book reader, or wearable device, and which game software/apps you find interesting (Objective 2)

- How to recognize the difference between data and information (Objective 3)

- When you might use the various methods of input, output, and storage (Objective 4)

Discover More: Visit this chapter's premium content for practice quiz opportunities.

The Web

The World Wide Web (or web, for short) is a global library of information available to anyone connected to the Internet. The **Internet** is a worldwide collection of computer networks that connects millions of businesses, government agencies, educational institutions, and individuals (Figure 1-27).

CONSIDER THIS

How do I access the Internet?
Businesses, called Internet service providers (ISPs), offer users and organizations access to the Internet free or for a fee. By subscribing to an ISP, you can connect to the Internet through your computers and mobile devices.

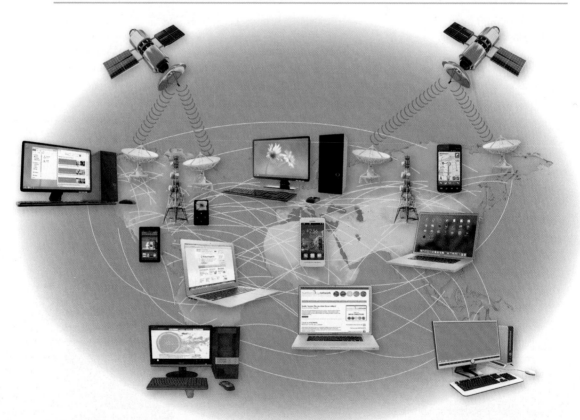

Figure 1-27　The Internet is the largest computer network, connecting millions of computers and devices around the world.

 **CONSIDER THIS** ⎯⎯⎯⎯⎯⎯⎯⎯⎯⎯⎯⎯⎯⎯⎯⎯⎯⎯⎯⎯⎯⎯⎯⎯⎯⎯⎯⎯⎯⎯⎯⎯⎯

Are the web and Internet the same?
No. The Internet provides more than three billion home and business users around the world access to a variety of services. The World Wide Web is one of the widely used services of the Internet. Other popular services include email, instant messaging, VoIP, and FTP (all discussed later in this chapter).

People around the world access the web to accomplish the following types of online tasks:

- Search for information
- Conduct research
- Communicate with and meet other people
- Share information, photos, and videos with others
- Access news, weather, and sports
- Participate in online training

- Shop for goods and services
- Play games with others
- Download or listen to music
- Watch videos
- Download or read books
- Make reservations

BTW

Downloading
Downloading is the process of transferring content from a server on the Internet to a computer or mobile device.

The **web** consists of a worldwide collection of electronic documents. Each electronic document on the web is called a **webpage**, which can contain text, graphics, audio, and video (Figure 1-28). A **website** is a collection of related webpages, which are stored on a web server. A **web server** is a computer that delivers requested webpages to your computer or mobile device.

Webpages often contain links. A *link*, short for *hyperlink*, is a built-in connection to other documents, graphics, audio files, videos, webpages, or websites. To activate an item associated with a link, you tap or click the link. In Figure 1-27, for example, tapping or clicking the audio link connects to a live radio show so that you can hear the broadcast. A text link often changes color after you tap or click it to remind you visually that you previously have visited the webpage or downloaded the content associated with the link.

Links allow you to obtain information in a nonlinear way. That is, instead of accessing topics in a specified order, you move directly to a topic of interest. Some people use the phrase *surfing the web* to refer to the activity of using links to explore the web.

A **browser** is software that enables users with an Internet connection to access and view webpages on a computer or mobile device. Some widely used browsers include Internet Explorer, Firefox, Safari, and Google Chrome. Read How To 1 in the Succeeding in this Course chapter at the beginning of this book for instructions about using a browser to display a webpage on a computer or mobile device.

Figure 1-28 Webpages, such as the one shown here, can display text, graphics, audio, and video on a computer or mobile device. Pointing to a link on the screen typically changes the shape of the pointer to a small hand with a pointing index finger.
Source: WTMJ

Web Searching

A primary reason that people use the web is to search for specific information, including text, photos, music, and videos. The first step in successful searching is to identify the main idea or concept in the topic about which you are seeking information. Determine any synonyms, alternate spellings, or variant word forms for the topic. Then, use a search engine, such as Google, to help you locate the information. A **search engine** is software that finds websites, webpages, images, videos, news, maps, and other information related to a specific topic. Read How To 1-3 for instructions about how to perform a basic web search using a search engine on a computer or mobile device.

Discover More: Visit this chapter's free resources to learn more about search engines.

 HOW TO 1-3

Perform a Basic Web Search
The following steps describe how to use a search engine on a computer or mobile device to perform a basic web search:

1. Run a browser. (For instructions on running programs and apps, see How To 1-4 later in this chapter.)

2. Display the search engine's webpage on the screen by entering its web address in the address bar. For example, you could type google.com to access the Google search engine, bing.com to access the

Bing search engine, or yahoo.com to access the Yahoo! search engine.

3. Tap or click the Search box and then type the desired search text in the Search box. The more descriptive the search text, the easier it will be to locate the desired search results. As the figure shows, the search engine may provide search text suggestions as you type search text in the Search box.

4. To display search results based on your typed search text, press the ENTER key or tap or click the Search button. To display search results based on one of the suggestions provided

by the search engine, tap or click the desired search text suggestion.

5. Scroll through the search results and then tap or click a search result to display the corresponding webpage.

6. To return to the search results, tap or click the Back button in your browser or on your mobile device, which typically looks like a left-pointing arrow.

✹ **Consider This:** What search text would you enter to locate the admission criteria for your school?

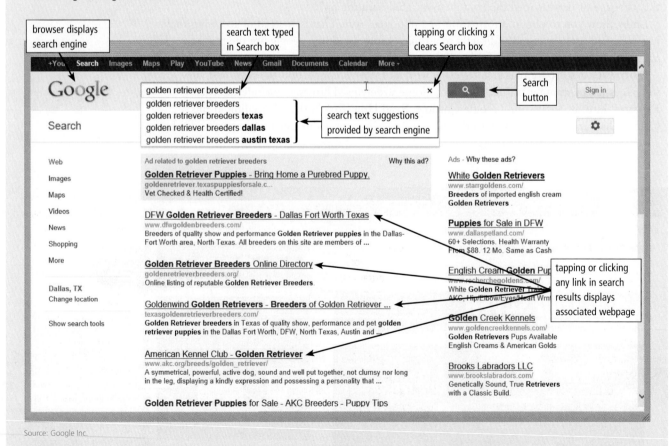

Source: Google Inc.

Online Social Networks

An **online social network**, also called a *social networking site*, is a website that encourages members in its online community to share their interests, ideas, stories, photos, music, and videos with other registered users (Figure 1-29). Popular online social networks include Facebook, Twitter, and LinkedIn.

Some online social networks have no specialized audience; others are more focused. A photo sharing site, for example, is a specific type of online social network that allows users to create an online photo album and store and share their digital photos. Similarly, a video sharing site is a type of online social network that enables users to store and share their personal videos. Read Ethics & Issues 1-2 to consider whether you should be required to obtain permission before posting photos of others.

 BTW

Technology Innovators
Discover More: Visit this chapter's free resources to learn more about Facebook and its founder, Mark Zuckerberg, and Twitter.

Figure 1-29 When Facebook users 'like' this Discovering Computers Facebook page, posts from the Discovering Computers page will appear on their own personal pages. As a student in this class, you should 'like' the Discovering Computers page so that you easily can keep up to date with relevant technology changes and events in the computing industry. If you do not have a Facebook account, use a search engine to search for the text, discovering computers facebook, to display the page in a browser.
Source: Facebook

⚜ ETHICS & ISSUES 1-2

Should You Be Required to Obtain Permission before Posting Photos of Others?

Your friends and followers on online social networks instantly can view photos you post. If others appear in the photo and you post it without their permission, they might feel you have violated their privacy. Tagging people in a photo may create a link to their social network profiles, exposing their identity. Depending on your privacy settings, your friends' contacts can view a photo you post and/or share the photo without your permission.

You may be able to adjust tagging rules in the privacy settings of your online social network account. For example, you can use Facebook's privacy settings to approve all

photos in which others tag you. The person posting the photo still can upload the photo, but your tag will not be associated with the photo until you approve it. Facebook also allows you to report a photo as abusive if you feel it portrays you negatively or if the person who posted it refuses to remove it upon request. Facebook's own Statement of Rights and Responsibilities states that "You will not tag users . . . without their consent."

People may not want photos of themselves posted for a variety reasons. They may have professional contacts as friends on their online social network and do not want to show themselves in a personal setting. Others may not be concerned with personal photos of themselves but do not want their children's

photos shared online. Or, they simply may find the photo unflattering. A poll by Sophos stated that 80 percent of respondents consider asking before posting a photo to be common courtesy. Eight percent of respondents felt that it should be illegal to do so.

Consider This: Is it ever acceptable to post photos of others without permission? Why or why not? Has someone posted or tagged you in a photo that you did not want others to see? How did you handle the situation? If asked to remove a photo or tag, would you respect the person's feelings and honor the request? What restrictions and policies should online social networks have about posting photos of others?

BTW

Blogs
Posts on Twitter also form a blog, because of its journal format with the most recent entry at the top.

 CONSIDER THIS

How do Facebook, Twitter, and LinkedIn differ?
With Facebook, you share messages, interests, activities, events, photos, and other personal information — called posts — with family and friends. You also can 'like' pages of celebrities, companies, products, etc., so that posts from others who like the same items will appear along with your other activities on Facebook. With Twitter, you 'follow' people, companies, and organizations in which you have an interest. Twitter enables you to stay current with the daily activities of those you are following via their Tweets, which are short posts (messages) that Twitter users broadcast for all their followers.

On LinkedIn, you share professional interests, education, and employment history, and add colleagues or coworkers to your list of contacts. You can include recommendations from people who know you professionally. Many employers post jobs using LinkedIn and consider information in your profile as your online resume.

Internet Communications

As mentioned earlier, the web is only one of the services on the Internet. Other services on the Internet facilitate communications among users, including the following:

- Email allows you to send messages to and receive messages and files from other users via a computer network.
- With messaging services, you can have a real-time typed conversation with another connected user (real-time means that both of you are online at the same time).
- VoIP (Voice over Internet Protocol) enables users to speak to other users over the Internet (discussed further in later chapters).
- With FTP (File Transfer Protocol), users can transfer items to and from other computers on the Internet (discussed further in later chapters).

Digital Security and Privacy

People rely on computers to create, store, and manage their information. To safeguard this information, it is important that users protect their computers and mobile devices. Users also should be aware of health risks and environmental issues associated with using computers and mobile devices.

 **BTW**

Malware
A leading maker of security software claims its software blocked more than five billion malware attacks in a single year.

Viruses and Other Malware

Malware, short for malicious software, is software that acts without a user's knowledge and deliberately alters the computer's or mobile device's operations. Examples of malware include viruses, worms, trojan horses, rootkits, spyware, adware, and zombies. Each of these types of malware attacks your computer or mobile device differently. Some are harmless pranks that temporarily freeze, play sounds, or display messages on your computer or mobile device. Others destroy or corrupt data, instructions, and information stored on the infected computer or mobile device. If you notice any unusual changes in the performance of your computer or mobile device, it may be infected with malware. Read Secure IT 1-2 for ways to protect computers from viruses and other malware.

Privacy

Nearly every life event is stored in a computer somewhere . . . in medical records, credit reports, tax records, etc. In many instances, where personal and confidential records were not protected properly, individuals have found their privacy violated and identities stolen. Some techniques you can use to protect yourself from identity theft include shredding financial documents before discarding them, never tapping or clicking links in unsolicited email messages, and enrolling in a credit monitoring service.

Adults, teens, and children around the world are using online social networks to share their photos, videos, journals, music, and other personal information publicly. Some of these unsuspecting, innocent computer users have fallen victim to crimes committed by dangerous strangers.

 **Internet Research**

What are other techniques that deter identity theft?
Search for: prevent identity theft

SECURE IT 1-2

Protection from Viruses and Other Malware

It is impossible to ensure a virus or malware never will attack a computer, but you can take steps to protect your computer by following these practices:

- **Use virus protection software.** Install a reputable antivirus program and then scan the entire computer to be certain it is free of viruses and other malware. Update the antivirus program and the virus signatures (known specific patterns of viruses) regularly.

- **Use a firewall.** Set up a hardware firewall or install a software firewall that protects your network's resources from outside intrusions.

- **Be suspicious of all unsolicited email and text messages.** Never open an email message unless you are expecting it, *and* it is from a trusted source. When in doubt, ask the sender to confirm the message is

legitimate before you open it. Be especially cautious when deciding whether to tap or click links in email and text messages or to open attachments.

- **Disconnect your computer from the Internet.** If you do not need Internet access, disconnect the computer from the Internet. Some security experts recommend disconnecting from the computer network before opening email attachments.

- **Download software with caution.** Download programs or apps only from websites you trust, especially those with music and video sharing software.

- **Close spyware windows.** If you suspect a pop-up window (a rectangular area that suddenly appears on your screen) may be spyware, close the window. Never tap or click an Agree or OK button in a suspicious window.

- **Before using any removable media, scan it for malware.** Follow this procedure even for shrink-wrapped software from major developers. Some commercial software has been infected and distributed to unsuspecting users. Never start a computer with removable media inserted in the computer unless you are certain the media are uninfected.

- **Keep current.** Install the latest updates for your computer software. Stay informed about new virus alerts and virus hoaxes.

- **Back up regularly.** In the event your computer becomes unusable due to a virus attack or other malware, you will be able to restore operations if you have a clean (uninfected) backup.

Consider This: What precautions do you take to prevent viruses and other malware from infecting your computer? What new steps will you take to attempt to protect your computer?

Protect yourself and your dependents from these criminals by being cautious in email messages and on websites. For example, do not share information that would allow others to identify or locate you, and do not disclose identification numbers, user names, passwords, or other personal security details. A user name is a unique combination of characters, such as letters of the alphabet or numbers, that identifies one specific user. A password is a private combination of characters associated with a user name. Read Secure IT 1-3 for tips on creating strong passwords.

 SECURE IT 1-3

Creating Strong Passwords

A good password is easy for you to remember but difficult for criminals and password-breaking software to guess. Use these guidelines to create effective, strong passwords:

- **Personal information:** Avoid using any part of your first or last name, your family members' or pets' names, phone number, street address, license plate number, Social Security number, or birth date.

- **Length:** Use at least eight characters.

- **Difficulty:** Use a variety of uppercase and lowercase letters, numbers, punctuation marks, and symbols. Select characters located on different parts of the keyboard, not the ones you commonly use or that are adjacent to each other. Criminals often use software that converts common words to symbols, so their program might generate the passwords

GoToSleep and Go2Sleep as possibilities to guess.

- **Modify:** Change your password frequently, at least every three months.

- **Variation:** Do not use the same password for all websites you access. Once criminals have stolen a password, they attempt to use that password for other accounts they find on your computer or mobile device, especially banking websites.

- **Passphrase:** A passphrase, which is similar to a password, consists of several words separated by spaces. Security experts recommend misspelling a few of the words and adding several numerals. For example, the phrase, "Create a strong password," could become the passphrase, "Creat a strang pasword42."

- **Common sequences:** Avoid numbers or letters in easily recognized patterns, such

as "asdfjkl;," "12345678," "09870987," or "abcdefg." Also, do not spell words backwards, use common abbreviations, or repeat strings of letters or numbers.

- **Manage:** Do not keep your passwords in your wallet, on a sheet of paper near your computer, or in a text file on your computer or mobile device. Memorize all of your passwords, or store them securely using a password management app on your computer or mobile device. Additional information about password management software is provided in Secure IT 5-3 in Chapter 5.

- **Test:** Use online tools to evaluate password strength.

Consider This: How strong are your passwords? How will you modify your passwords using some of these guidelines?

Health Concerns

Prolonged or improper computer and mobile device use can lead to injuries or disorders of the hands, wrists, elbows, eyes, neck, and back. Computer and mobile device users can protect themselves from these health risks through proper workplace design, good posture while at the computer, and appropriately spaced work breaks.

With the growing use of earbuds and headphones, some users are experiencing hearing loss. Ways to protect your hearing when using these devices were presented in How To 1-2 earlier in this chapter.

Two behavioral health risks are technology addiction and technology overload. Technology addiction occurs when someone becomes obsessed with using technology. Individuals suffering from technology overload feel distressed when deprived of computers and mobile devices. Once recognized, both technology addiction and technology overload are treatable disorders.

Environmental Issues

Manufacturing processes for computers and mobile devices along with *e-waste*, or discarded computers and mobile devices, are depleting natural resources and polluting the environment. When computers and mobile devices are stored in basements or other locations, disposed of in landfills, or burned in incinerators, they can release toxic materials and potentially dangerous levels of lead, mercury, and flame retardants.

Green computing involves reducing the electricity consumed and environmental waste generated when using a computer. Strategies that support green computing include recycling, using energy efficient hardware and energy saving features, regulating manufacturing processes, extending the life of computers, and immediately donating or properly disposing of replaced computers. When you purchase a new computer, some retailers offer to dispose of your old computer properly.

Discover More: Visit this book's premium content for the Internet Research: Green Computing exercise for each chapter in this book.

 BTW

Technology Innovators
Discover More: Visit this chapter's free resources to learn about Microsoft and its founder, Bill Gates, Apple, and its cofounders, Steve Jobs and Steve Wozniak.

 CONSIDER THIS ⎯⎯⎯⎯⎯⎯⎯⎯⎯⎯⎯⎯⎯⎯⎯

How can you contribute to green computing?
Some habits you can alter that will help reduce the environmental impact of computing include the following:

1. Do not leave a computer or device running overnight.
2. Turn off your monitor, printer, and other devices when you are not using them.
3. Use energy efficient hardware.
4. Use paperless methods to communicate.
5. Recycle paper and buy recycled paper.
6. Recycle toner, computers, mobile devices, printers, and other devices.
7. Telecommute.
8. Use videoconferencing and VoIP for meetings.

Programs and Apps

Software, also called a **program**, consists of a series of related instructions, organized for a common purpose, that tells the computer what tasks to perform and how to perform them.

Two categories of software are system software and application software (or applications). System software consists of the programs that control or maintain the operations of the computer and its devices. Operating systems are a widely recognized example of system software. Other types of system software, sometimes called tools, enable you to perform maintenance-type tasks usually related to managing devices, media, and programs used by computers and mobile devices. The next sections discuss operating systems and applications.

Operating Systems

An *operating system* is a set of programs that coordinates all the activities among computer or mobile device hardware. It provides a means for users to communicate with the computer or mobile device and other software. Many of today's computers and mobile devices use a version of Microsoft's Windows, Apple's Mac OS, Apple's iOS, or Google's Android (Figure 1-30).

To use an application, your computer or mobile device must be running an operating system.

Applications

An **application** (or **app** for short) consists of programs designed to make users more productive and/or assist them with personal tasks. Browsers, discussed in an earlier section, are an example of an application that enables users with an Internet connection to access and view webpages. Table 1-2 identifies the categories of applications with samples of ones commonly used in each category.

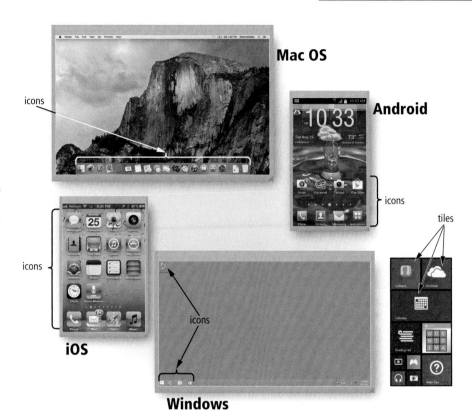

Figure 1-30 Shown here are the Mac OS and Windows operating systems for laptops and desktops and the Android and iOS operating systems for smartphones. You interact with these operating system interfaces by tapping or clicking their icons or tiles.
Sources: Apple Inc.; Apple Inc.; Google Inc.; Microsoft.

Table 1-2 Categories of Applications

Category	Sample Applications	Sample Uses
Productivity	Word Processing	Create letters, reports, and other documents.
	Presentation	Create visual aids for presentations.
	Schedule and Contact Management	Organize appointments and contact lists.
	Personal Finance	Balance checkbook, pay bills, and track income and expenses.
Graphics and Media	Photo Editing	Modify digital photos, i.e., crop, remove red-eye, etc.
	Video and Audio Editing	Modify recorded movie clips, add music, etc.
	Media Player	View images, listen to audio/music, watch videos.
Personal Interest	Travel, Mapping, and Navigation	View maps, obtain route directions, locate points of interest.
	Reference	Look up material in dictionaries, encyclopedias, etc.
	Educational	Learn through tutors and prepare for tests.
	Entertainment	Receive entertainment news alerts, check movie times and reviews, play games.

(Continued)

Table 1-2   *Continued*

Category	Sample Applications	Sample Uses
Communications	Browser	Access and view webpages.
	Email	Send and receive messages.
	VoIP	Speak to other users over the Internet.
	FTP	Transfer items to and from other computers on the Internet.
Security	Antivirus	Protect a computer against viruses.
	Personal Firewall	Detect and protect against unauthorized intrusions.
	Spyware, Adware, and other Malware Removers	Detect and delete spyware, adware, and other malware.
File, System, and Disk Management	File Manager	Display and organize files on storage media.
	Search	Locate files and other items on storage media.
	Image Viewer	Display, copy, and print contents of graphics files.
	Screen Saver	Shows moving image or blank screen if no keyboard or mouse activity occurs.

© Cengage Learning; Courtesy of NCH Software; Source: Apple Inc.; Source: Google Inc.; Courtesy of AVG Technologies; Source: Microsoft

Discover More: Visit this chapter's free resources for an expanded Categories of Applications table.

Applications include programs stored on a computer, as well as those on a mobile device or delivered to your device over the Internet.

- A *desktop app* is an application stored on a computer.
- A *web app* is an application stored on a web server that you access through a browser.
- A *mobile app* is an application you download from a mobile device's app store or other location on the Internet to a smartphone or other mobile device.

Some applications are available as both a web app and a mobile app. In this case, you typically can sync (or match) the data and activity between the web app and the mobile app, which is discussed later in this chapter.

Discover More: Visit this book's premium content for the How To: Your Turn – App Adventure exercise for each chapter in this book.

Installing and Running Programs

Installing a program is the process of setting up the program to work with a computer or mobile device, printer, and/or other hardware. When you buy a computer or mobile device, it usually has some software, such as an operating system, preinstalled on its internal media so that you can use the computer or mobile device the first time you turn it on.

Installed operating systems often include applications such as a browser, media player, and calculator. To use additional desktop apps on a computer, you usually need to install the software. Mobile apps typically install automatically after you transfer the app's files to your mobile device from its website. You usually do not need to install web apps before you can run them.

Once installed, you run a program so that you can interact with it. When you instruct a computer or mobile device to run a program, the computer or mobile device *loads* it, which means the program's instructions are copied from storage to memory. Once in memory, the computer or mobile device can carry out, or execute, the instructions in the program so that you can use it.

You interact with a program through its user interface. The *user interface* controls how you enter data and instructions and how information is displayed on the screen. Often, you work with icons or tiles (shown in Figure 1-30 earlier in the chapter), which are miniature images that link to programs, media, documents, or other objects. Read How To 1-4 for instructions about locating, installing, and running programs and mobile apps.

 HOW TO 1-4

Locate, Install, and Run Programs and Mobile Apps

The following steps describe how to locate, install, and run programs and mobile apps:

Locate the Program or Mobile App

- Locate the program or mobile app to install. Programs are available from retail stores, websites, and from other online services such as Apple's App Store or Google Play. Mobile apps are available from your device's app store.

Download and/or Install the Program or Mobile App

- If you are installing a program on your computer from physical media such as a CD or DVD, insert the media in your computer. If the installation process does not start automatically, locate the installation program on the media and then double-tap or double-click the installation program.

- If the program or mobile app is available from a website or online store, download the application to your computer or mobile device. Once the download is complete, if the installation process does not start automatically, locate and then double-tap or double-click the downloaded file to begin the installation.

Run the Program or Mobile App

- You have various options for running a program or mobile app:
  - If you are using a computer, tap or click the program's tile or double-tap or double-click the program's icon in the desktop.

- Display a list of all programs and apps on your computer or mobile device and then tap or click the icon representing the program to run (some computers may require you to double-tap or double-click the icon).

- Use the search feature in the operating system to locate the newly installed program or app and then tap or click the search result to run the program or app.

 Consider This: After installing a mobile app, where are some locations you might look to find the new app's icon or tile?

 CONSIDER THIS ────────────────────────────────

How do you know if a program will run on your computer?
When you buy a computer, you can find a list of the computer's specifications on the box, the manufacturer's website, or the order summary. Similarly, when you buy software, the box or the product's website will list specifications and minimum requirements for memory, speed, and more. Your computer's specifications should be the same as or greater than the software specifications. Ensure the software will run on your computer before making a purchase, because many retailers will not allow you to return software.

Developing Programs and Apps

A *software developer*, sometimes called a developer or programmer, is someone who develops programs and apps or writes the instructions that direct the computer or mobile device to process data into information. When writing instructions, a developer must be sure the program or app works properly so that the computer or mobile device generates the desired results. Complex programs can require thousands to millions of instructions.

Software developers use a programming language or application development tool to create programs and apps. Popular programming languages include C++, Java, JavaScript, Visual C#, and Visual Basic. Figure 1-31 shows some of the Visual Basic instructions a software developer may write to create a simple payroll program.

Figure 1-31 A software developer writes instructions using Visual Basic (a) to create the Payroll Information window shown here (b).
Source: © Cengage Learning

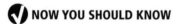

NOW YOU SHOULD KNOW ────────────────────────────────────

Be sure you understand the material presented in the sections titled The Web, Digital Security and Privacy, and Programs and Apps, as it relates to the chapter objectives.
Now you should know . . .

- Why webpages use links (Objective 5)
- How to perform a basic web search (Objective 6)
- What risks you are exposed to as a result of your technology use and how you can minimize those risks (Objective 7)
- How to recognize an operating system and which programs and apps you might find useful (Objective 8)

Discover More: Visit this chapter's premium content for practice quiz opportunities.

Communications and Networks

Communications technologies are everywhere. Many require that you subscribe to an Internet service provider. With others, an organization such as a business or school provides communications services to employees, students, or customers.

In the course of a day, it is likely you use, or use information generated by, one or more of the communications technologies in Table 1-3.

Table 1-3 Uses of Communications Technologies

Type	Brief Description
Chat rooms	Real-time typed conversation among two or more people on a computers or mobile devices connected to a network
Email	Transmission of messages and files via a computer network
Fax	Transmission and receipt of documents over telephone lines
FTP	Permits users to transfer files to and from servers on the Internet
GPS	Navigation system that assists users with determining their location, ascertaining directions, and more
Instant messaging	Real-time typed conversation with another connected user where you also can exchange photos, videos, and other content
Internet	Worldwide collection of networks that links millions of businesses, government agencies, educational institutions, and individuals
Newsgroups	Online areas in which users have written discussions about a particular subject
RSS	Specification that enables web content to be distributed to subscribers
Videoconference	Real-time meeting between two or more geographically separated people who use a network to transmit audio and video
Voice mail	Allows users to leave a voice message for one or more people
VoIP	Conversation that takes place over the Internet using a telephone connected to a computer, mobile device, or other device
Wireless Internet access points	Enables users with computers and mobile devices to connect to the Internet wirelessly
Wireless messaging services	Send and receive wireless messages to and from smartphones, mobile phones, handheld game devices, and other mobile devices using text messaging and picture/video messaging

© Cengage Learning

Wired and Wireless Communications

Computer communications describes a process in which two or more computers or devices transfer (send and receive) data, instructions, and information over transmission media via a communications device(s). A **communications device** is hardware capable of transferring items from computers and devices to transmission media and vice versa. Examples of communications devices are modems, wireless access points, and routers. As shown in Figure 1-32, some communications involve cables and wires; others are sent wirelessly through the air.

Wired communications often use some form of telephone wiring, coaxial cable, or fiber-optic cables to send communications signals. The typically are used within buildings or underground between buildings.

Because it is more convenient than installing wires and cables, many users opt for wireless communications, which sends signals through the air or space. Examples of wireless communications technologies include Wi-Fi, Bluetooth, and cellular radio, which are discussed below:

- **Wi-Fi** uses radio signals to provide high-speed Internet and network connections to computers and devices capable of communicating via Wi-Fi.

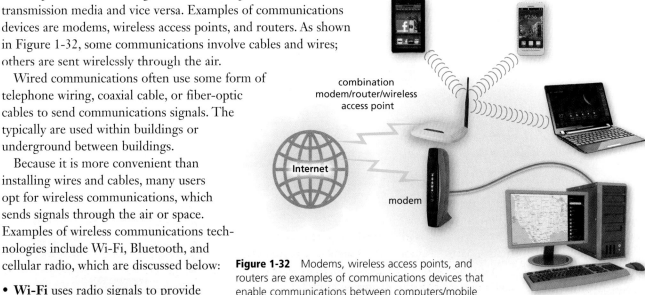

Figure 1-32 Modems, wireless access points, and routers are examples of communications devices that enable communications between computers/mobile devices and the Internet. Notice that some computers and devices communicate via wires, and others communicate wirelessly.

© Cengage Learning; © iStockphoto / Petar Chernaev; © iStockphoto / Oleksiy Mark; © Patryk Kosmider / Shutterstock.com.; © Pablo Eder / Shutterstock.com; © iStockphoto / 123render.; Source: Microsoft; © iStockphoto / aquarius83men

Most computers and many mobile devices, such as smartphones and portable media players, can connect to a Wi-Fi network.

- **Bluetooth** uses short-range radio signals to enable Bluetooth-enabled computers and devices to communicate with each other. For example, Bluetooth headsets allow you to connect a Bluetooth-enabled phone to a headset wirelessly.
- Cellular radio uses the cellular network to enable high-speed Internet connections to devices with built-in compatible technology, such as smartphones. Cellular network providers use the categories 3G, 4G, and 5G to denote cellular transmission speeds, with 5G being the fastest.

Wi-Fi and Bluetooth are both hot spot technologies. A *hot spot* is a wireless network that provides Internet connections to mobile computers and devices. Wi-Fi hot spots provide wireless network connections to users in public locations, such as airports and airplanes, train stations, hotels, convention centers, schools, campgrounds, marinas, shopping malls, bookstores, libraries, restaurants, coffee shops, and more. Bluetooth hot spots provide location-based services, such as sending coupons or menus, to users whose Bluetooth-enabled devices enter the coverage range.

Discover More: Visit this chapter's free resources to learn more about cellular transmissions.

Networks

A **network** is a collection of computers and devices connected together, often wirelessly, via communications devices and transmission media. Networks allow computers to share *resources*, such as hardware, software, data, and information. Sharing resources saves time and money. In many networks, one or more computers act as a server. The server controls access to the resources on a network. The other computers on the network, each called a client, request resources from the server (Figure 1-33). The major differences between the server and client computers are that the server typically has more power, more storage space, and expanded communications capabilities.

Many homes and most businesses and schools network their computers and devices. Most allow users to connect their computers wirelessly to the network. Users often are required to sign in to, or log on, a network, which means they enter a user name and password (or other credentials) to access the network and its resources. Read Ethics & Issues 1-3 to consider issues associated with unsecured networks.

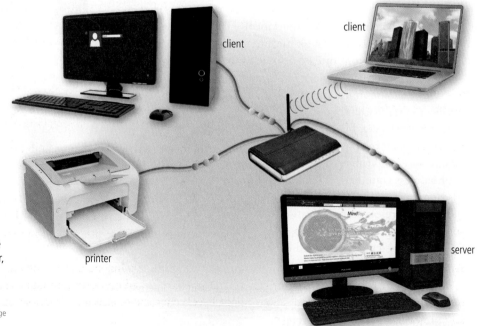

Figure 1-33 A server manages the resources on a network, and clients access the resources on the server. This network enables three separate computers to share the same printer, one wirelessly.

BTW

The Internet
The world's largest computer network is the Internet.

ETHICS & ISSUES 1-3

Would You Connect to an Unsecured Network?

If you turn on your laptop and notice that you can connect to a nearby home or business's wireless network and access the Internet without a password, for free, you may find yourself in an ethical dilemma. Because they do not know how to secure a wireless network, many home and business users leave their networks open for use by anybody in their signal's range. Experts estimate that up to 35 percent of wireless connections are unsecured, leaving them open to hackers. (A hacker is someone who accesses a computer or network illegally.)

Criminals sometimes use unsecured wireless networks to cover up technology-related crimes. Others may steal connections to avoid the costs of Internet service. In other cases, a user's laptop or mobile device may connect automatically to an open wireless network, without the user's authorization or knowledge. If you are using an unsecured wireless network, hackers may be able to capture your passwords, hijack your accounts, or send spam or a virus.

The Electronic Communications Privacy Act (ECPA) states that it is not illegal "to intercept or access an electronic communication made through an electronic communication system that is configured so that such electronic communication is readily accessible to the general public." It is unclear whether this law refers to an unsecured home network or whether it pertains only to public hot spots, such as restaurants and libraries. Some lawmakers even support punishing those who leave their networks unsecured.

Consider This: Would you use your neighbor's unsecured wireless home network without permission? Why or why not? What would you do if you found out that someone was using your wireless home network without your permission? How should legal authorities address such abuse? What punishment should violators receive? Should those leaving their networks unsecured receive punishment, too? Why or why not?

Home Networks   Home networks save the home user money and provide many conveniences. Each networked computer or mobile device on a home network has the following capabilities:

- Connect to the Internet at the same time
- Share a single high-speed Internet connection
- Access photos, music, videos, and other content on computers and devices throughout the house
- Share devices such as a printer, scanner, or external hard drive
- Play multiplayer games with players on other computers and mobile devices in the house
- Connect game consoles to the Internet
- Subscribe to and use VoIP
- Interact with other devices in a smart home (such as thermostats, lighting controls, etc.)

Home networks usually are small, existing within a single structure, and use wireless technologies such as those shown previously in Figure 1-30. You do not need extensive knowledge of networks to set up a home network. You will need a communications device, such as a router, which usually includes setup instructions. Most operating systems also provide tools enabling you easily to connect all the computers and devices in your house.

Business Networks   Business and school networks can be small, such as in a room or building, or widespread, connecting computers and devices across a city, country, or the globe. Some reasons that businesses network their computers and devices together include the following:

- **Facilitate communications.** Using a network, employees and customers communicate efficiently and easily via email, messaging services, blogs, online social networks, video calls, online meetings, videoconferencing, VoIP, and more.
- **Share hardware.** In a networked environment, each computer on the network can access the hardware on the network, instead of providing each user with the same piece of hardware. For example, computer and mobile device users can access the laser printer on the network, as they need it.
- **Share data, information, and software.** In a networked environment, any authorized computer user can access data, information, and software stored on other computers on the network. A large company, for example, might have a database of customer information that any authorized user can access.

Mini Feature 1-2: Staying in Sync

If you use multiple computers and mobile devices throughout the day, keeping track of common files may be difficult. Read Mini Feature 1-2 to learn how to keep your computers and devices in sync with each other.

 MINI FEATURE 1-2

Staying in Sync

Assume that each morning you begin the day by checking your appointment calendar on your home or office computer. That same calendar appears on your smartphone, so that you can view your schedule throughout the day. If you add, change, or delete appointments using the smartphone, however, you may need to update the calendar on your computer to reflect these edits. When you **synchronize**, or **sync**, computers and mobile devices, you match the files in two or more locations with each other, as shown in the figure below. Along with appointments, other commonly synced files from a smartphone are photos, email messages, music, apps, contacts, calendars, and ringtones.

Syncing can be a one-way or a two-way process. With a one-way sync, also called mirroring, you add, change, or delete files in a destination location, called the *target*, without altering the same files in the original location, called the *source*. For example, you may have a large collection of music stored on your home computer (the source), and you often copy some of these songs to your mobile device (the target). If you add or delete songs from your computer, you also will want to add or change these songs on your mobile device. If, however, you add or change the songs on your mobile device, you would not want to make these changes on your computer.

In two-way sync, any change made in one location also is made in any other sync location. For example,

you and your friends may be working together to create one document reflecting your combined ideas. This document could be stored on a network or on cloud storage on the Internet. Your collaboration efforts should reflect the latest edits each person has made to the file.

You can use wired or wireless methods to sync. In a wired setup, cables connect one device to another, which allows for reliable data transfer. While wireless syncing offers convenience and automation, possible issues include battery drain and low signal strength when the devices are not close to each other. Strategies for keeping your files in sync include the following:

- **Use a cable and software.** Syncing photos from a camera or a smartphone to a computer frees up memory on the mobile device and creates a backup of these files. You easily can transfer photos using a data sync cable and synchronization software. Be certain not to disconnect the mobile device from the computer until the sync is complete. You also can copy your photos and documents from the computer to a smartphone, an external hard drive, a USB flash drive, or some other portable storage device.

- **Use cloud storage.** Cloud storage can provide a convenient method of syncing files stored on multiple computers and accessing them from most devices with Internet access. Several cloud storage providers offer a small amount of storage space at no cost and additional storage for a nominal fee per month or per year. Each provider has specific features, but most allow users to share files with other users, preview file contents, set passwords, and control who has permission to edit the files.

- **Use web apps.** By using web apps for email, contacts, and calendars, your information is stored online, so that it is accessible anywhere you have an Internet connection and can sync with multiple devices.

  Discover More: Visit this chapter's free resources to learn more about wired setups, wireless syncing, and cloud storage providers.

  Consider This: Synchronization is an effective method of organizing and sharing common files. What files have you synced, such as photos, music, and email? Which sync method did you use?

© iStockphoto / 123render; Source: Microsoft; © iStockphoto / Moncherie;
© iStockphoto / Ivan Stevanovic; Courtesy of Western Digital Corporation

Technology Uses

Technology has changed society today as much as the industrial revolution changed society in the eighteenth and nineteenth centuries. People interact directly with technology in fields such as education, government, finance, retail, entertainment, health care, science, travel, publishing, and manufacturing.

Education/Mini Feature 1-3: Digital School

Educators and teaching institutions use technology to assist with education. Most equip labs and classrooms with laptops or desktops. Some even provide computers or mobile devices to students. Many require students to have a mobile computer or mobile device to access the school's network or Internet wirelessly, or to access digital-only content provided by a textbook publisher. To promote the use of technology in education, vendors often offer substantial student discounts on hardware and software.

Educators may use a course management system, sometimes called a learning management system, which is software that contains tools for class preparation, distribution, and management. For example, through the course management system, students access course materials, grades, assessments, and a variety of collaboration tools.

Many schools offer distance learning classes, where the delivery of education occurs at one place while the learning occurs at other locations. Distance learning courses provide time, distance, and place advantages for students who live far from a campus or work full time. A few schools offer entire degrees online. National and international companies offer distance learning training because it eliminates the costs of airfare, hotels, and meals for centralized training sessions.

Read Mini Feature 1-3 to learn about additional technologies integrated in the classroom.

 BTW
Technology @ Work
For more information about how technology is used in a variety of fields, read the Technology @ Work feature at the end of each chapter in this book.

 BTW
Technology Trend
Discover More: Visit this chapter's free resources to learn about massive open online courses (MOOCs).

 **Internet Research**
How do educators use iTunes U?
Search for: itunes u

 MINI FEATURE 1-3

Digital School

Technology and education intersect in today's classrooms. Students can use a variety of devices, apps, and websites to collaborate and obtain content while teachers can share information in most content areas to engage students and enhance the learning process. Digital technology offers flexibility and a revised classroom setting.

- **Mobile devices and tablets:** Schools are updating their computer labs by eliminating rows of desktops and allowing students to bring their own devices into the room and also into their classrooms, a practice often referred to as *BYOD* (bring your own device). They connect their laptops and mobile devices to power and data; they then they use educational apps, store and share files, read digital books, and create content without leaving their desks.

- **Virtual field trips:** Virtual tours of museums, ancient sites, and galleries allow audiences to see exhibits, examine paintings, and explore historical objects. After viewing 360-degree panoramas of such places as Colonial Williamsburg and Machu Picchu, students can interact with experts via Twitter and videoconferencing.

- **Games and simulations:** Game design theory can help engage students and reinforce key

concepts. When students master one set of objectives in a particular topic, they can progress to more advanced levels. They can receive instant feedback and recognition for their accomplishments, collaborate with teammates, repeat play to achieve higher scores, and document their experiences. Researchers claim that students are more likely to pursue challenging subject matter when it is offered in a gaming setting.

- **Interactive whiteboards:** Teachers and students can write directly on an interactive display, shown in the figure, which is a touch-sensitive device resembling a dry-erase board. It displays images on a connected computer screen. Touch gestures are used to zoom, erase, and annotate displayed content.

- **Share projects:** Effective movies can bring the words in a textbook to life. Students can create scripts and then use animation software or a video camera to tell stories that apply the concepts they have learned

Used with permission of SMART Technologies ULC (www.smarttech.com). SMART Board and the SMART logo are trademarks of SMART Technologies ULC and may be registered in the European Union, Canada, the United States and other countries.

(*continued*)

and upload them to media sharing websites. They also can write blogs, design graphics, and conduct interviews to apply and share the concepts they have learned in the classroom.

- **3-D printers:** Low-cost 3-D printers created for the classroom and libraries are becoming popular, especially in science and engineering classes. Geology students can create topography models, biology students can examine cross sections of

organs, architecture students can print prototypes of their designs, and history students can create artifacts.

Discover More: Visit this chapter's free resources to learn more about the digital school.

✹ **Consider This:** Which digital technologies have you used in your classrooms? Did they help you learn and retain information presented? If so, how?

Government

Most government offices have websites to provide citizens with up-to-date information. People in the United States access government websites to view census data, file taxes, apply for permits and licenses, pay parking tickets, buy stamps, report crimes, apply for financial aid, and renew vehicle registrations and driver's licenses.

Employees of government agencies use computers as part of their daily routine. North American 911 call centers use computers to dispatch calls for fire, police, and medical assistance. Military and other agency officials use the U.S. Department of Homeland Security's network of information about domestic security threats to help protect against terrorist attacks. Law enforcement officers have online access to the FBI's National Crime Information Center (NCIC) through in-vehicle laptops, fingerprint readers, and mobile devices (Figure 1-34). The NCIC contains more than 15 million missing persons and criminal records, including names, fingerprints, parole/probation records, mug shots, and other information.

Figure 1-34 Law enforcement officials use computers and mobile devices to access emergency, missing person, and criminal records in computer networks in local, state, and federal agencies.
© iStockPhoto / jacomstephens

Finance

Many people and companies use online banking or finance software to pay bills, track personal income and expenses, manage investments, and evaluate financial plans. The difference between using a financial institutions' website versus finance software on your computer is that all your account information is stored on the bank's computer instead of your computer. The advantage is you can access your financial records from anywhere in the world.

Investors often use online investing to buy and sell stocks and bonds — without using a broker. With online investing, the transaction fee for each trade usually is much less than when trading through a broker.

Discover More: Visit this chapter's free resources to learn more about online investing.

Retail

You can purchase just about any product or service on the web, including groceries, flowers, books, computers and mobile devices, music, movies, airline tickets, and concert tickets. To purchase from an online retailer, a customer visits the business's storefront, which contains product descriptions, images, and a shopping cart. The shopping cart allows the customer to collect purchases. When ready to complete the sale, the customer enters personal data and the method of payment, which should be through a secure Internet connection. Figure 1-35 illustrates the steps involved when a customer purchases from an online retailer.

Many mobile apps make your shopping experience more convenient. Some enable you to manage rewards, use coupons, locate stores, or pay for goods and services directly from your phone or other mobile device. Other mobile apps will check a product's price and availability at stores in your local area or online. Read Secure IT 1-4 for tips about shopping safely online.

Discover More: Visit this chapter's free resources to learn more about mobile payments.

SECURE IT 1-4

Shopping Safely Online

Browsing electronic storefronts and making online purchases can be convenient and economical, but the experience can be a disaster if you encounter unscrupulous vendors. These tips can help you enjoy a safe and productive online shopping trip.

- **Read customer reviews.** Shoppers frequently post comments about merchandise quality, pricing, and shipping. Their evaluations may help you decide whether a company is legitimate. Be aware, however, that the Federal Trade Commission has sued companies for posting false positive reviews and that some companies remove negative comments. Make it a habit to rate merchants as often as possible so that others can learn from your experiences.

- **Look for seals of approval.** Online businesses can display seals if they have

met rigorous standards. Some unscrupulous merchants, however, will place the seals on their websites even if they have not been approved. To check a seal's legitimacy, tap or click the logo and be certain you are directed to the issuing agency's website to verify the seal is valid.

- **Create a strong password and password questions.** If the merchant requires you to create a user name and password, be certain to develop a long, complex password with at least eight characters that include letters, numbers, and special characters. (Refer to Secure IT 1-3 earlier in this chapter for guidance on creating a strong password.) The website also may ask for answers to security questions; if so, do not supply information that hackers could locate easily, such as your high school, place of birth, or family members' or pets' names.

- **Check website details.** Locate the business's privacy policy to learn how your information will be stored. Also, look for phone numbers, physical addresses, and email addresses to contact the vendor if questions arise about damaged goods or billing discrepancies.

- **Beware of requests to supply further information.** After you have placed an order, you may receive an email message asking you to confirm the transaction or to supply additional account information. A reputable business will not solicit these requests, so do not reply to the message.

Consider This: Have you made online purchases? If so, have you followed the precautions listed here? How will you change your activities the next time you shop online?

Purchasing from an Online Retailer

Step 1
The customer displays the online retailer's storefront.

Step 2
The customer collects purchases in a shopping cart.

Step 3
The customer enters payment information on a secure website. The online retailer sends financial information to a bank.

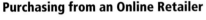

Step 5
The online retailer's web server sends confirmation to the customer, processes the order, and then sends it to the fulfillment center.

Step 4
The bank performs security checks and sends authorization back to the online retailer.

Figure 1-35 This figure shows the steps involved when a customer purchases from an online retailer.
© Comstock Images / Photos.com; © iStockphoto / Mark Evans; © iStockphoto / AndyL; © iStockphoto / Mlenny Photography; © Oleksiy Mark / Photos.com; © Oleksiy Mark / Shutterstock.com; © iStockphoto / Ed Hidden; © iStockphoto / Oksana Perkins; © Cengage Learning; © iStockphoto / stevecoleimages

Step 6
The fulfillment center packages the order, prepares it for shipment, and then sends a report to the server where records are updated.

Step 7
While the order travels to the customer, shipping information is posted on the web.

Step 8
The order is delivered to the customer, who may be required to sign a handheld computer or document to acknowledge receipt.

Entertainment

You can use computers and mobile devices to listen to audio clips or live audio; watch video clips, television shows, or live performances and events; read a book, magazine, or newspaper; and play a myriad of games individually or with others. In some cases, you download the media from the web to a computer or mobile device so that you can watch, listen to, view, or play later. Some websites support *streaming*, where you access the media content while it downloads. For example, radio and television broadcasts often use streaming media to broadcast music, interviews, talk shows, sporting events, news, and other segments so that you can listen to the audio or view the video as it downloads to your computer. You also can create videos, take photos, or record audio and upload (transfer) your media content to the web to share with others, such as on an online social network.

 CONSIDER THIS ————————————————————————

Can I make copies of songs or other media that I have purchased and downloaded from a legitimate website, such as iTunes?

You typically can make a copy as a personal backup, but you cannot share the copy with others in any format unless you have legal permission from the copyright owner to do so. That is, you cannot give someone a CD copy, nor can you share a digital file by posting it on the web or sending it as an email message.

 BTW

Technology Trend

Discover More: Visit this chapter's free resources to learn what is meant by a QR code and how QR codes are used in the medical field.

Health Care

Nearly every area of health care today uses computers. Whether you are visiting a family doctor for a regular checkup, having lab work or an outpatient test, filling a prescription, or being rushed in for emergency surgery, the medical staff around you will be using computers for various purposes:

- Hospitals and doctors use computers and mobile devices to maintain and access patient records (Figure 1-36).
- Computers and mobile devices monitor patients' vital signs in hospital rooms and at home; patients use computers to manage health conditions, such as diabetes.
- Robots deliver medication to nurses' stations in hospitals.
- Computers and computerized devices assist doctors, nurses, and technicians with medical tests.

- Doctors use the web and medical software to assist with researching and diagnosing health conditions.
- Doctors use email, text messaging, and other communications services to correspond with patients.
- Patients use computers and mobile devices to refill prescriptions, and pharmacists use computers to file insurance claims and provide customers with vital information about their medications.
- Surgeons implant computerized devices, such as pacemakers, that allow patients to live longer.
- Surgeons use computer-controlled devices to provide them with greater precision during operations, such as for laser eye surgery and robot-assisted heart surgery.
- Medical staff create labels for medicine, hospital ID bracelets, and more, enabling staff to verify dosage and access patient records by scanning the label.

Figure 1-36 Doctors, nurses, technicians, and other medical staff use computers and computerized devices to assist with medical tests.
© iStockPhoto / Neustockimage

Science

All branches of science, from biology to astronomy to meteorology, use computers to assist them with collecting, analyzing, and modeling data. Scientists also use the Internet to communicate with colleagues around the world. Breakthroughs in surgery, medicine, and treatments often result from scientists' use of computers. Tiny computers now imitate functions of the central nervous system, retina of the eye, and cochlea of the ear. A cochlear implant allows a deaf person to distinguish sounds. Electrodes implanted in the brain stop tremors associated with Parkinson's disease.

A *neural network* is a system that attempts to imitate the behavior of the human brain. Scientists create neural networks by connecting thousands of processors together much like the neurons in the brain are connected. The capability of a personal computer to recognize spoken words is a direct result of scientific experimentation with neural networks.

Travel

Whether traveling by car or plane, your goal is to arrive safely at your destination. As you make the journey, you may interact with a navigation system or GPS, which uses satellite signals to determine a geographic location. GPS technology also assists people with creating maps, determining the best route between two points, locating a lost person or stolen object, monitoring a person's or object's movement, determining altitude, calculating speed, and finding points of interest. Vehicles manufactured today typically include some type of onboard navigation system (Figure 1-37). Many mobile devices, such as smartphones, also have built-in navigation systems.

In preparing for a trip, you may need to reserve a car, hotel, or flight. Many websites offer these services to the public where you can search for and compare flights and prices, order airline tickets, or reserve a rental car. You also can print driving directions and maps from the web.

Publishing

Many publishers of books, magazines, newspapers, music, film, and video make their works available online. Organizations and individuals publish their thoughts and ideas using a blog, podcast, or wiki.

- A *blog* is an informal website consisting of time-stamped articles (posts) in a diary or journal format, usually listed in reverse chronological order. Posts can contain text, photos, links, and more. For example, Figure 1-38 shows the Nutrition Blog Network, in which registered

Figure 1-37 Many vehicles include an onboard navigation system.
© kaczor58 / Shutterstock.com

blog posts

Figure 1-38 Any group or individual can create a blog, so that they can share thoughts and ideas.
Source: Nutrition Blog Network

Internet Research

How can you create a blog?

Search for: create a blog

dietitians post articles about nutrition. As others read articles in your blog, you can enable them to reply with their own thoughts. A blog that contains video is called a video blog.

- Podcasts are a popular way to distribute audio or video on the web. A *podcast* is recorded media that users can download or stream to a computer or portable media player. Examples of podcasts include lectures, political messages, radio shows, and commentaries. Podcasters register their podcasts so that subscribers can select content to automatically download when they are connected.

- A *wiki* is a collaborative website that allows users to create, add to, modify, or delete the content via their browser. Many wikis are open to modification by the general public. The difference between a wiki and a blog is that users cannot modify original posts made by a blogger. Read Ethics & Issues 1-4 for an issue related to using wikis as a source for research.

✺ ETHICS & ISSUES 1-4

Should Wikis Be Allowed as Valid Sources for Academic Research?

As wikis have grown in number, size, and popularity, many educators and librarians have shunned them as valid sources of research. While some wikis are tightly controlled with a limited number of contributors and expert editors, these wikis usually focus on narrowly defined, specialized topics. Most large, multi-topic online wikis, such as Wikipedia, often involve thousands of editors, many of whom remain anonymous.

Critics of wikis cite the lack of certified academic credentials by the editors, as well as potential political or gender bias by contributors. Wikis also are subject to vandalism. Vandals' motives vary; some

enter false information to discredit the wiki, and others for humorous results. On occasion, rival political factions have falsified or embellished wiki entries in an attempt to give their candidate an advantage. Some wiki supporters argue that most wikis provide adequate controls to correct false or misleading content quickly and to punish those who submit it. One popular wiki now requires an experienced editor to verify changes made to certain types of articles. Other wiki protection methods include locking articles from editing, creating a list of recently edited articles, enabling readers to report vandalism, and allowing people to be notified about changes to a wiki page that

they have edited or that is about them. Some proponents propose that people should use wikis as a starting point for researching a fact, but that they should verify the fact using traditional sources.

Consider This: Should instructors allow wikis as valid sources for academic research? Why or why not? Would you submit a paper to your instructor that cites a wiki as a source? Why or why not? What policies might wikis enforce that could garner more confidence from the public? If a wiki provided verification of the credentials of the author, would you trust the wiki more? Why or why not?

Figure 1-39   Automotive factories use industrial robots to weld car bodies.
© Small Town Studio / Shutterstock.com

Manufacturing

Computer-aided manufacturing (CAM) refers to the use of computers to assist with manufacturing processes, such as fabrication and assembly. Industries use CAM to reduce product development costs, shorten a product's time to market, and stay ahead of the competition. Often, robots carry out processes in a CAM environment. CAM is used by a variety of industries, including oil drilling, power generation, food production, and automobile manufacturing. Automobile plants, for example, have an entire line of industrial robots that assemble a car (Figure 1-39).

Special computers on the shop floor record actual labor, material, machine, and computer time used to manufacture a particular product. The computers process this data and automatically update inventory, production, payroll, and accounting records on the company's network.

Technology Users

Every day, people around the world use various technologies at home, at work, and at school. Depending on the hardware, software, and communications requirements, these users generally can be classified in one of five categories. Keep in mind that a single user may fall into more than one category.

- A *home user* is any person who spends time using technology at home. Parents, children, teenagers, grandparents, singles, couples, etc., are all examples of home users.
- A *small/home office user* includes employees of companies with fewer than 50 employees, as well as the self-employed who work from home. Small offices include local law practices, accounting offices, travel agencies, and florists.
- A *mobile user* includes any person who works with computers or mobile devices while away from a main office, home, or school. Examples of mobile users are sales representatives, real estate agents, insurance agents, meter readers, package delivery people, journalists, consultants, and students.
- A *power user* is a user who requires the capabilities of a powerful computer. Examples of power users include engineers, scientists, architects, desktop publishers, and graphic artists.
- An enterprise has hundreds or thousands of employees or customers who work in or do business with offices across a region, the country, or the world. Each employee or customer who uses computers, mobile devices, and other technology in the enterprise is an *enterprise user*. Read Ethics & Issues 1-5 to consider whether employees should be held accountable for their online social network posts.

✸ ETHICS & ISSUES 1-5

Should Employees Be Held Accountable for Their Online Social Network Posts?

In addition to looking at your resume and scheduling an interview, a potential employer may search the web to find out information about you. A recent Career Builder survey found that 39 percent of employers look at applicants' use of online social networks, and 43 percent of those found information that caused them not to hire the applicant.

Once employed, your manager still may track your online activity. Companies are concerned about damaged reputations, or even lawsuits. Employee actions that worry their employers include discussing company sales activity, griping about their managers or customers, or posting photos that show them taking part in unethical, illegal, or unsavory activities.

Social network-related firings have raised the question of whether companies should monitor employees' online social network activity. Accessing an employee's or a potential employee's social network profile also could have consequences for the company. If a company realizes that a person is a member of a minority group or has a disability, the company could face discrimination charges if it does not hire or later fires the employee. Privacy experts state that your online social network posts are your own business. Debate about what falls under free speech is ongoing. Remember that you cannot delete easily what you post online. Whether or not you currently are searching for employment, online posts you make now can damage your future job prospects.

Consider This: What are the results when you search for yourself online? What steps can you take to clean up and protect your online reputation? Would you share social networking accounts or passwords with an employer or potential employer? Why or why not? Should companies monitor employees' accounts? Why or why not?

Table 1-4 illustrates the range of hardware, programs/apps, and communications forms used in each of these categories.

Table 1-4 Categories of Users

User	Sample Hardware	Sample Desktop Apps	Sample Mobile or Web Apps	Forms of Communications
All Users	– Smartphone – Digital camera – Printer	– Word processing – Schedule and contact management – Browser – Security	– Alarm clock – Calculator – News, weather, sports – Reference – Finance	– Email – Online social networks – Blogs
Home User	– Laptop, tablet, or desktop – Portable media player and earbuds or headphones – Game console – E-book reader – Wearable device – Webcam – Headset	– Personal finance – Photo and video editing – Media player – Educational – Entertainment	– Banking – Travel – Mapping – Navigation – Health and fitness – Retail – Media sharing – Educational	– Messaging – VoIP
Small/Home Office User	– Desktop(s) or laptop(s) – Server – Webcam – Scanner	– Spreadsheet – Database – Accounting	– Travel – Mapping	– Messaging – VoIP – FTP
Mobile User	– Laptop or tablet – Video projector – Wireless headset	– Note taking – Presentation – Educational – Entertainment	– Travel – Mapping – Navigation – Retail – Educational	
Power User	– Desktop – Scanner	– Desktop publishing – Multimedia authoring – Computer-aided design – Photo, audio, video editing		– FTP – Videoconferencing
Enterprise User	– Server – Desktop(s) or laptop(s) – Industry-specific handheld computer – Webcam – Scanner	– Spreadsheet – Database – Accounting	– Travel – Mapping – Navigation	– Messaging – VoIP – FTP – Videoconferencing

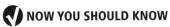

NOW YOU SHOULD KNOW

Be sure you understand the material presented in the sections titled Communications and Networks, Technology Uses, and Technology Users, as it relates to the chapter objectives.
Now you should know . . .

- When you might use wired and wireless communications, and why you would use a network (Objective 9)
- How you would use technology in education, government, finance, retail, entertainment, health care, science, travel, publishing, and manufacturing (Objective 10)
- What types of hardware, software, and communications you could use at home, school, and work (Objective 11)

Discover More: Visit this chapter's premium content for practice quiz opportunities.

🖤 Chapter Summary

Chapter 1 introduced you to basic computer concepts. You learned about laptops, tablets, desktops, servers, smartphones, digital cameras, portable media players, e-book readers, and game devices. The chapter introduced various methods for input, output, memory, and storage. It discussed the Internet, browsing and searching the web, and online social networks. Next, the chapter introduced digital security and safety risks and precautions, along with various types of programs, applications, communications, and networks. The many different uses of technology applications in society also were presented, along with types of users. This chapter is an overview. Many of the terms and concepts introduced will be discussed further in later chapters.

Discover More: Visit this book's free resources for additional content that accompanies this chapter and also includes these features: Technology Innovators: Facebook/Mark Zuckerberg, Twitter, Microsoft/Bill Gates, and Apple/Steve Jobs/Steve Wozniak; Technology Trends: MOOCs and QR Codes in the Medical Field; and High-Tech Talks: Triangulation and Neural Networks.

Test your knowledge of chapter material by accessing the Study Guide, Flash Cards, and Practice Test resources from your smartphone, tablet, laptop, or desktop.

🔧 TECHNOLOGY @ WORK

📖 Health Care

You are out running on a beautiful day, tracking your route and distance using a health and fitness app on a smartphone. While running, you accidentally step on uneven pavement and suffer an injury that requires a trip to an emergency room. Upon check-in, the employee at the front desk uses a tablet to record your personal data and symptoms. She also uses the tablet to verify that your insurance coverage is current and informs you of your co-payment amount. After waiting several minutes, a triage nurse takes your temperature and blood pressure and then asks a series of questions about your symptoms. The nurse also records this data in a tablet and asks you to remain in the waiting room until someone from the radiology department is available to perform a CT scan. The radiology department is located in a different area of the hospital, so the technicians watch a computer screen that displays a list of patients who currently are waiting for their services.

About 30 minutes later, a technician calls your name and escorts you to the radiology department for your CT scan. As she is performing the scan, a computer records the images that later will be reviewed by a physician. When the CT scan is complete, you return to the waiting room until a physician reviews the results. Once she receives the results and reviews them, a hospital employee takes you to a consultation room.

The physician informs you that other than a few bumps and bruises, she believes that you have sustained no permanent damage and prescribes medication to help ease the pain. She then returns to a computer at the nurses' station and adds her diagnosis to the database that stores your medical records. She also sends your prescription electronically to the hospital's pharmacy. Once discharged, you visit the cashier to pay the bill. You then use a tablet to sign an electronic version of your discharge paperwork so that the hospital can store it

electronically. The hospital bills your insurance company electronically. If you owe a balance

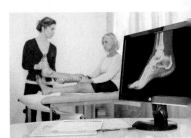
© Shutterstock / Image Point Fr

after the insurance company pays its portion, a computer at the hospital will generate a bill that will be mailed to you. After purchasing your medication and leaving the hospital, you realize that despite the hospital being busy, computers decreased the time of your visit by automating processes that otherwise would have been performed manually and reduced possible errors by storing all of your personal information centrally.

Consider This: How else might computers and technology be used in the health care industry?

Study Guide

The Study Guide exercise reinforces material you should know for the chapter exam.

Discover More: Visit this chapter's premium content to test your knowledge of digital content associated with this chapter and access the Study Guide resource from your smartphone, tablet, laptop, or desktop.

Instructions: Answer the questions below using the format that helps you remember best or that is required by your instructor. Possible formats may include one or more of these options: write the answers; create a document that contains the answers; record answers as audio or video using a webcam, smartphone, or portable media player; post answers on a blog, wiki, or website; or highlight answers in the book/e-book.

1. Define the term, digital literacy.

2. Define the terms, computer, hardware, and user.

3. Differentiate between a PC and a mobile computer. A laptop also is known as a(n) ___ computer.

4. Describe the characteristics and features of a tablet. List several touch screen gestures.

5. Explain the difference between a desktop and an all-in-one. What additional meaning does the term, desktop, sometimes have?

6. Define the term, server. What services does a server provide?

7. Explain whether or not a mobile device is a computer.

8. List characteristics of a smartphone.

9. Differentiate among voice, text, picture, and video messages.

10. Describe the purpose of these mobile devices: digital cameras, portable and digital media players, e-book readers, wearable devices, and game devices.

11. Describe the trend of digital device convergence and how it applies to mobile devices.

12. Describe uses of technology in home automation.

13. Differentiate between data and information. Give an example of each.

14. Define the terms, input and output. List several types of input devices and output devices.

15. Describe the purpose of a pointing device. Give an example.

16. List the hardware you can use to input and view output for voice and video.

17. Differentiate between memory and storage.

18. A computer keeps data, instructions, and information on ___ media. Give some examples.

19. Define the term, cloud storage. Describe the types of services offered by cloud storage providers.

20. Describe components of a backup plan. How do backup plans for mobile devices and personal computers differ?

21. Describe the Internet. Identify reasons people use the Internet.

22. Differentiate between the web and the Internet.

23. The ___ consists of a worldwide collection of electronic documents. What is each electronic document called?

24. What is a browser? Describe the purpose of a search engine.

25. Explain the purpose of an online social network.

26. Differentiate between the services and uses of Facebook, Twitter, and LinkedIn.

27. List services of the Internet that facilitate communications.

28. Define the term, malware. List ways you can protect yourself from malware.

29. What privacy risks are involved with using technology? List guidelines for creating a strong password.

30. Explain physical and behavioral health risks associated with using computers.

31. Describe strategies that support green computing.

32. Define the term, software. Software also is called a(n) ___.

33. Define the term, operating system. List popular operating systems for computers and mobile devices.

34. Differentiate between desktop, web, and mobile apps.

35. List the steps involved in installing programs.

36. Explain how to locate, install, and run programs. What is the role of a software developer?

37. Define the term, communications device. List examples of wireless communications technologies.

38. Define the term, hot spot. Give two examples and describe how each is used.

39. Describe how homes and businesses use networks.

40. Identify issues surrounding accessing an unsecured network.

41. Explain what occurs when you synchronize computers and mobile devices.

42. List ways that schools use technology to enhance education.

43. Identify how the following industries use technology: government, financial, retail, entertainment, health care, science, travel, publishing, and manufacturing.

44. Describe how you might use blogs, wikis, and podcasts to publish content.

45. Differentiate among the following technology user types: home user, small/home office user, mobile user, power user, and enterprise user.

46. Describe how technology is used in the health care industry.

You should be able to define the Primary Terms and be familiar with the Secondary Terms listed below.

Key Terms

Discover More: Visit this chapter's premium content to view definitions for each term and access the Flash Cards resource from your smartphone, tablet, laptop, or desktop.

Primary Terms (shown in **bold-black** characters in the chapter)

all-in-one (6)
app (27)
application (27)
backup (18)
browser (21)
Bluetooth (32)
cloud storage (18)
communications
  device (31)
computer (4)
desktop (6)

digital camera (8)
digital device
  convergence (10)
e-book reader (9)
game console (10)
green computing (26)
hard drive (17)
input device (12)
Internet (20)
laptop (4)
memory (16)

network (32)
online social network (23)
output device (14)
portable media player (8)
printer (14)
program (26)
search engine (22)
server (6)
smartphone (7)
software (26)
storage device (17)

storage media (17)
sync (34)
synchronize (34)
tablet (4)
wearable device (9)
web (21)
web server (21)
webpage (21)
website (21)
Wi-Fi (31)

Secondary Terms (shown in *italic* characters in the chapter)

3-D printer (15)
blog (39)
BYOD (35)
click (13)
computer-aided manufacturing (40)
data (12)
desktop app (28)
digital literacy (2)
digital media (8)
digital media player (9)
double-click (13)
double-tap (5)
downloading (21)
drag (5, 13)
earbuds (8)
e-book (9)
enterprise user (41)
e-reader (9)
e-waste (26)
file (18)
gesture (5)
hard copy (14)
hard disk (17)
hardware (4)
headset (14)
home user (41)

hot spot (32)
hyperlink (21)
information (12)
input (4)
keyboard (13)
link (21)
loads (28)
malware (24)
memory card (18)
microphone (14)
mobile app (28)
mobile computer (4)
mobile device (7)
mobile user (41)
mouse (13)
neural network (39)
notebook computer (4)
on-screen keyboard (5)
operating system (27)
optical disc (18)
output (4)
personal computer (4)
phablet (7)
picture message (7)
pinch (5)
podcast (40)

point (13)
power user (41)
press and hold (5)
printout (14)
resources (32)
right-click (13)
scanner (14)
slide (5)
small/home office user (41)
Smart TV (15)
social networking site (23)
software developer (29)
solid-state drive (17)
source (34)
streaming (38)
streaming media player (9)

stretch (5)
surfing the web (21)
swipe (5)
tap (5)
target (34)
text message (7)
touchpad (13)
USB flash drive (18)
user (4)
user interface (29)
video message (7)
voice mail message (7)
wearable (9)
web app (28)
webcam (14)
wiki (40)

all-in-one (6)

Checkpoint

The Checkpoint exercises test your knowledge of the chapter concepts. The page number containing the answer appears in parentheses after each exercise. The Consider This exercises challenge your understanding of chapter concepts.

Discover More: Visit this chapter's premium content to complete the Checkpoint exercises interactively; complete the self-assessment in the Test Prep resource from your smartphone, tablet, laptop, or desktop; and then take the Practice Test.

True/False   Mark T for True and F for False.

_____ 1. Electronic components in computers process data using instructions, which are the steps that tell the computer how to perform a particular task. (4)

_____ 2. An all-in-one contains a separate tower. (6)

_____ 3. Smartphones typically communicate wirelessly with other devices or computers. (7)

_____ 4. Data conveys meaning to users, and information is a collection of unprocessed items, which can include text, numbers, images, audio, and video. (12)

_____ 5. A headset is a type of input device. (14)

_____ 6. A scanner is a light-sensing output device. (14)

_____ 7. Although some forms of memory are permanent, most memory keeps data and instructions temporarily, meaning its contents are erased when the computer is turned off. (16)

_____ 8. A solid-state drive contains one or more inflexible, circular platters that use magnetic particles to store data, instructions, and information. (17)

_____ 9. The terms, web and Internet, are interchangeable. (21)

_____ 10. One way to protect your computer from malware is to scan any removable media before using it. (25)

_____ 11. Operating systems are a widely recognized example of system software. (26)

_____ 12. You usually do not need to install web apps before you can run them. (28)

Multiple Choice   Select the best answer.

1. A(n) _____ is any hardware component that allows you to enter data and instructions into a computer or mobile device. (12)
   a. output device
   b. communications device
   c. input device
   d. display

2. Which of the following is *not* an example of an output device? (14)
   a. scanner
   b. printer
   c. display
   d. speaker

3. _____ consists of electronic components that store instructions waiting to be executed and the data needed by those instructions. (16)
   a. Storage
   b. Cloud storage
   c. Solid-state drives
   d. Memory

4. _____ is an Internet service that provides remote storage to computer users. (18)
   a. Smart TV
   b. Cloud storage
   c. Solid-state drive (SSD)
   d. Bluetooth

5. A computer that delivers requested webpages to your computer or mobile device is a(n) _____. (21)
   a. VoIP computer
   b. web server
   c. FTP device
   d. hard drive

6. A _____ is software that enables users with an Internet connection to access and view webpages on a computer or mobile device. (21)
   a. search engine
   b. wiki
   c. browser
   d. digital media player

7. _____ uses short-range radio signals to enable computers and devices to communicate with each other. (32)
   a. Cellular radio
   b. Bluetooth
   c. Wi-Fi
   d. A hot spot

8. A(n) _____ is a collaborative website that allows users to create, add to, modify, or delete the content via their browser. (40)
   a. podcast
   b. blog
   c. online social network
   d. wiki

Checkpoint

Matching   Match the terms with their definitions.

_____ 1. all-in-one (6)

_____ 2. server (6)

_____ 3. phablet (7)

_____ 4. digital device convergence (10)

_____ 5. touchpad (13)

_____ 6. storage device (17)

_____ 7. solid-state drive (17)

_____ 8. file (18)

_____ 9. software (26)

_____ 10. operating system (27)

a. term that describes the trend of computers and devices with technologies that overlap

b. mobile device that combines features of a smartphone and a tablet

c. storage device that typically uses flash memory to store data, instructions, and information

d. small, flat, rectangular pointing device that is sensitive to pressure and motion

e. set of programs that coordinates all the activities among computer or mobile device hardware

f. named collection of stored data, instructions, or information

g. type of desktop computer that does not contain a tower and instead uses the same case to house the display and the processing circuitry

h. series of related instructions, organized for a common purpose, that tells the computer what tasks to perform and how to perform them

i. computer that is dedicated to providing one or more services to other computers or devices on a network

j. component that records and/or retrieves items to and from storage media

✳ Consider This   Answer the following questions in the format specified by your instructor.

1. Answer the critical thinking questions posed at the end of these elements in this chapter: Ethics & Issues (8, 23, 33, 40, 41), How To (5, 16, 22, 29), Mini Features (11, 34, 35), Secure IT (19, 25, 25, 37), and Technology @ Work (43).

2. What does it mean to be digitally literate, and why is it important? (2)

3. What are the different touch screen gestures and the actions they may cause to occur? (5)

4. What types of keyboards are available for smartphones and tablets? (5, 7)

5. In addition to books, what other digital media can be read on an e-book reader? (9)

6. In addition to keeping time, how might you use a smartwatch? (9)

7. Why might a consumer purchase separate stand-alone devices, such as smartphones, digital cameras, portable media players? (10)

8. How can you ease eyestrain while using a computer or mobile device? (16)

9. What types of files might you choose to store on a memory card or USB flash drive, rather than on a hard drive? (18)

10. What steps might you include in a backup plan? (19)

11. Why might you choose to use LinkedIn rather than Facebook? (24)

12. How might you know if your computer or mobile device is infected with malware? (24)

13. What types of software protect a computer from viruses and other malware? (25)

14. Why should you use a different password for all websites you access? (25)

15. How might you know if you are addicted to computers or suffer from technology overload? (26)

16. Why is green computing important? (26)

17. What steps can you take to contribute to green computing? (26)

18. What is the difference between system and application software? (26)

19. What are some examples of popular operating systems? (27)

20. How do desktop apps, web apps, and mobile apps differ? (28)

21. Where can you obtain programs or apps? (29)

22. What does a user interface control? (29)

23. What are some popular programming languages? (29)

24. Why might you opt for wireless communications? (31)

25. In a network, what is the major difference between a server and a client? (32)

26. When should you use a one-way sync or a two-way sync? (34)

27. What type of industries use computer-aided manufacturing (CAM)? (40)

✸ Problem Solving

The Problem Solving exercises extend your knowledge of chapter concepts by seeking solutions to practical problems with technology that you may encounter at home, school, or work. The Collaboration exercise should be completed with a team.

Instructions: You often can solve problems with technology in multiple ways. Determine a solution to the problems in these exercises by using one or more resources available to you (such as a computer or mobile device, articles on the web or in print, blogs, podcasts, videos, television, user guides, other individuals, electronics or computer stores, etc.). Describe your solution, along with the resource(s) used, in the format requested by your instructor (brief report, presentation, discussion, blog post, video, or other means).

Personal

1. **Shopping for Software** You are shopping for software that will assist you with your home's interior design. The package for the program you would like to purchase states that it was designed for the most recent version of Windows, but an older version is installed on your computer. How can you determine whether the program will run on your computer?

2. **Bad Directions** You are driving to your friend's house and are using your smartphone for directions. While approaching your destination, you realize that your smartphone app instructed you to turn the wrong way on your friend's street. How could this have happened?

3. **Bank Account Postings** While reviewing your checking account balance online, you notice that debit card purchases have not posted to your account for the past several days. Because you use online banking to balance your account, you become concerned about your unknown account balance. What steps will you take to correct this situation?

4. **Trial Expired** You have been using an app on your mobile device for a 30-day trial period. Now that the 30 days have expired, the app is requesting that you to pay to continue accessing your data. What are your next steps? What steps could you have taken to preserve your data before the trial period expired?

5. **Problematic Camera** After charging your digital camera battery overnight, you insert the battery and turn on the camera only to find that it is reporting a low battery. Seconds later, the camera shuts off automatically. What might be wrong?

Professional

6. **Discarding Old Computer Equipment** Your company has given you a new laptop to replace your current, outdated desktop. Because of the negative environmental impact of discarding the old computer in the trash, your supervisor asked you to suggest options for its disposal. How will you respond?

7. **Dead Battery** While traveling for business, you realize that you forgot to bring the battery charger for your laptop. Knowing that you need to use the laptop to give a presentation tomorrow, what steps will you take tonight to make sure you have enough battery power?

8. **Cannot Share Photos** You are attempting to send photos of a house for sale in an email message to your real estate partner. Each time you attempt to send the email message, you receive an automatic response stating that the files are too large. What are your next steps?

9. **Incorrect Sign-In Credentials** Upon returning to the office from a well-deserved two-week vacation, you turn on your computer. When you enter your user name and password, an error message appears stating that your password is incorrect. What are your next steps?

10. **Synchronization Error** You added appointments to the calendar on your computer, but these appointments are not synchronizing with your smartphone. Your calendar has synchronized with your smartphone in the past, but it has stopped working without explanation. What are your next steps?

Collaboration

11. **Technology in Health Care** Your primary care physician is moving from a shared office so that he can open his own practice. He mentioned that he would like to use technology in his office that not only will improve the patient experience, but also make his job easier. Form a team of three people to determine the types of technology your doctor can use in his new office. One team member should research ways that technology can help improve patient check-in and billing. Another team member should research the types of technology your doctor can use while he is working with patients, and the third team member should research any additional technology that can be used in the office to improve the patient experience. Compile your findings in a report and submit it to your instructor.

The How To: Your Turn exercises present general guidelines for fundamental skills when using a computer or mobile device and then require that you determine how to apply these general guidelines to a specific program or situation.

How To: Your Turn

STUDENT ASSIGNMENTS

Discover More: Visit this chapter's premium content to challenge yourself with additional How To: Your Turn exercises, which include App Adventure.

Instructions: You often can complete tasks using technology in multiple ways. Figure out how to perform the tasks described in these exercises by using one or more resources available to you (such as a computer or mobile device, articles on the web or in print, online or program help, user guides, blogs, podcasts, videos, other individuals, trial and error, etc.). Summarize your 'how to' steps, along with the resource(s) used, in the format requested by your instructor (brief report, presentation, discussion, blog post, video, or other means).

❶ Create a Facebook Account, Find the Discovering Computers Facebook Page, and Like It

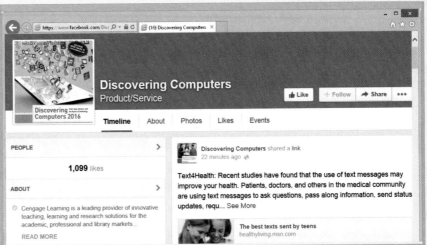

Source: Facebook

The Discovering Computers Facebook page contains links to current events and other technology news, as well as relating the links to content in this book. The following steps guide you through the process of signing up for a Facebook account, navigating to the Discovering Computers Facebook page, and liking the page.

a. Run a browser and then navigate to www.facebook.com.

b. Follow the steps on the Facebook webpage to sign up for a new account. If you already have an account, enter your sign-in information and sign in to your Facebook account.

c. Search for the Discovering Computers Facebook page using the search text, Discovering Computers.

d. Select the Discovering Computers Product/Service in the search results.

e. Tap or click the Like button to like the page.

f. If your screen displays a Follow button, tap or click it to see information from the Discovering Computers Facebook page in your news feed.

g. View the posts and tap or click links on the page that are of interest to you.

h. When you are finished, sign out of Facebook.

Exercises

1. Summarize the process you use to sign up for or sign in to your Facebook account.

2. Which links on the Discovering Computers Facebook page are of interest to you? Why?

3. Browse Facebook and find at least three other Facebook pages that are of interest to you. Which pages have you found, and why do you like them?

❷ Create a Twitter Account, Find the Discovering Computers Twitter Account, and Follow It

The Discovering Computers Twitter account contains links to current events and other technology news, as well as how it relates to the content in this textbook. The following steps guide you through the process of signing up for a Twitter account, navigating to the Discovering Computers Twitter account, and following it.

a. Run a browser and then navigate to www.twitter.com.

b. Follow the steps on the Twitter webpage to sign up for a new account. If you already have an account, enter your sign-in information and sign in to your Twitter account.

c. Search for the Discovering Computers Twitter account using the search text, DiscoveringComp.

d. Select Shelly Cashman @DiscoveringComp in the search results.

e. Tap or click the Follow button to follow the account.

f. View the posts and tap or click links on the page that are of interest to you.

g. When you are finished, sign out of Twitter.

✺ How To: Your Turn

Exercises

1. Summarize the process you use to sign up for or sign in to your Twitter account.
2. How is the Discovering Computers Twitter account similar to the Discovering Computers Facebook page? How are they different?
3. Browse Twitter and find at least three other Twitter accounts to follow. Which ones have you found, and why do you like them?

❸ Connect to a Wireless Network

Wireless networks are available in many homes and businesses. Connecting to a wireless network can provide you with high-speed access to the Internet and other network resources. The following steps guide you through the process of connecting to a wireless network from a computer or mobile device.

a. If necessary, turn on your computer or mobile device and make sure wireless functionality is enabled.
b. Obtain the name of the wireless network to which you want to connect. **Note:** *You should connect only to wireless networks for which you have permission.*
c. On your computer or mobile device, view the list of available wireless networks.
d. Select the wireless network to which you want to connect.

e. If necessary, enter the requested security information, such as an encryption key or a password.
f. Run a browser to test your connection to the wireless network.

Exercises

1. Why should you not connect to a wireless network unless you have permission?
2. What is the name of the wireless network to which you connected?
3. Why might you connect to a wireless network on your smartphone instead of using your mobile data plan?

❹ Manage Your Calendar

Individuals are choosing to use calendars on computers and mobile devices to keep track of events in their personal and professional lives more easily. In addition, students might use calendars to keep track of their class schedules. The following steps guide you through the process of managing your computer or mobile device's calendar.

a. Run the calendar app (usually by tapping or clicking its icon or tile on the home screen).
b. To add a new appointment, tap or click the Add or New Appointment button or icon and then enter the title or subject of the appointment, its date, time, location, and other information. Tap or click the Save button or icon on the New Appointment screen to save the information to your calendar.
c. Specify repeating information for appointments that occur at the same time over multiple occurrences, such as a class that meets every Tuesday from 10:00 a.m. to 11:00 a.m.
d. View your appointments on a daily, weekly, or monthly calendar by tapping or clicking the appropriate choice in the calendar app.
e. To edit an appointment, meeting, or event on your calendar, open the item by tapping or clicking it, make the necessary changes and then save the changes.

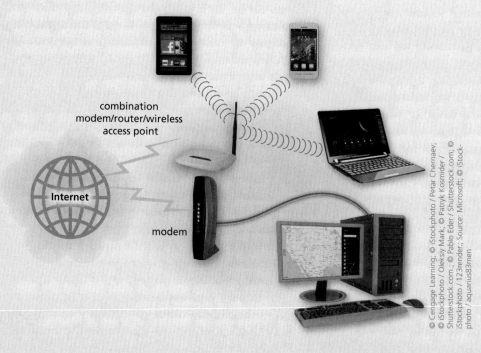

combination modem/router/wireless access point

Internet

modem

© Cengage Learning; © iStockphoto / Petar Chernaev; © iStockphoto / Oleksiy Mark; © Patryk Kosmider / Shutterstock.com; © Pablo Eder / Shutterstock.com; © iStockphoto / 123render; Source: Microsoft; © iStockphoto / aquarius83men

f. To delete an appointment, meeting, or event on your calendar, open the item by tapping or clicking it, and then tap or click the button to delete it. If necessary, confirm the deletion. If you are attempting to delete a recurring item on the calendar, the calendar app may ask whether you want to delete the one occurrence, or the entire series of appointments, meetings, or events.

Exercises

1. In addition to your class schedule, what other recurring appointments might you add to your calendar?
2. Many calendar apps have a feature that can remind you of upcoming appointments in advance. How far in advance do you think you should be reminded of upcoming appointments?
3. How can you synchronize the calendar on your mobile device with the calendar on your home computer?

❺ Back Up Photos from a Phone or Tablet

Many individuals take photos using mobile devices such as phones and tablets. Many, however, neglect to realize the importance of backing up these memories. A backup of the photos will be useful if you lose your mobile device, upgrade it to a newer model, or the device becomes damaged. While many mobile devices have built-in capabilities to back up photos to the cloud or to a desktop or laptop, it is important to make sure these features are configured properly. The following steps guide you through the process of backing up photos from a phone or tablet.

Backing Up to the Cloud

a. If necessary, install and sign in to an app on a phone or tablet that can back up photos to the cloud. Make sure the service you use gives you enough storage space for the photos you intend to upload.
b. Follow the instructions in the app and configure it to back up the photos at an interval of your choosing. Some options might include:
   • Back up all photos at certain intervals (such as one time per day or one time per week)
   • Back up photos as you take them
   • Back up photos stored in specific folders
c. If you are using a mobile device with a data plan, consider specifying whether you want the backup to occur only when you are connected to

Wi-Fi. Backing up using your phone or tablet's data plan may result in additional charges if you inadvertently exceed your quota.
d. Verify all photos have been backed up to the cloud service.

Backing Up to a Computer

a. Use the USB cable that came with your phone or tablet to connect it to the computer to which you want to back up the photos.
b. After the computer has recognized that a phone or tablet is connected, navigate to the drive on the computer representing the phone or tablet and then navigate to the folder containing the photos. If your phone or tablet stores pictures on both internal storage and a memory card, remember to back up your photos from both locations.
c. Drag the photos from the location on your phone or tablet to a folder on your computer that will store the backed up files.
d. When the files have finished backing up to the computer, close all open folder windows on the computer and then safely disconnect the phone or tablet from the computer.

Exercises

1. How often do you think you should back up your photos? Why?
2. When backing up photos, why might it be better to connect your phone or tablet to the computer using a cable instead of inserting the memory card from the phone or tablet into the computer?
3. Compare and contrast three apps or services that can back up photos from your phone or tablet to the cloud. Which one would you choose, and why?

✳ Internet Research

The Internet Research exercises broaden your understanding of chapter concepts by requiring that you search for information on the web.

Discover More: Visit this chapter's premium content to challenge yourself with additional Internet Research exercises, which include Search Sleuth, Green Computing, Ethics in Action, You Review It, and Exploring Technology Careers.

Instructions: Use a search engine or another search tool to locate the information requested or answers to questions presented in the exercises. Describe your findings, along with the search term(s) you used and your web source(s), in the format requested by your instructor (brief report, presentation, discussion, blog post, video, or other means).

❶ Making Use of the Web
Informational and Research

Informational and research websites contain factual information and include reference works such as libraries, encyclopedias, dictionaries, directories, and guides. More than 2.4 billion people worldwide use the Internet, and Google is one of the websites they visit most often. Google reports that people perform more than 100 billion searches every month using its Google Search. In How To 1 in the Succeeding in this Course chapter at the beginning of this book and How To 1-3 in this chapter, you learned how to use a browser to display a webpage on a computer or mobile device and to perform a basic web search using a search engine.

Research This: Using a browser and search engine, find the answers to the following questions. (1) Search for the top five informational websites and top five research websites. What types of information or research does each present? What search text did you use? (2) Visit Google's website and locate the company's early philosophy: "Ten things we know to be true." What are five of these values? What is the goal of the "Made with Code" initiative? (3) Visit the Engadget website and read at least three reviews of tablets. Create a table listing the product name, price, battery life, pros, and cons. (4) Locate articles about using hands-free devices for conversations while driving. Which states have passed legislation to restrict drivers' use of hands-free devices while driving? Describe the features found in the sophisticated hands-free system of one of this year's vehicles.

Google's mission is to organize the world's information and make it universally accessible and useful.

Products · Company · Management

things we know to be true

Source: Google Inc.

❷ Social Media

Online social networks are a central communications tool and the primary source of news and information for many people. Historians place the birth of online social networking with the BBS (Bulletin Board System), where users communicated with a central computer and sent messages to other BBS members and also downloaded files and games. The next phase of online social networks evolved when CompuServe, AOL (America Online), and Prodigy were among the services linking people with similar interests. Today's online social networks share many of the same basic principles by allowing members to communicate common interests, play games, and share photos, videos, and music. Some of these online social networks are for personal use, while others are for entrepreneurs, business owners, and professionals to share job-related topics.

Research This: Compare the features of the top personal online social networks, and create a table listing the number of active members in the United States and worldwide, the number of years the sites have existed, the more popular features, and the amount of content, such as photos, news stories, and links, that is shared each month. What types of advertisements are featured in each of these sites? Which sites are marketed toward younger and older users? Then, research the online social networks used for business. How does their content differ from that found on the personal online social networks? How many companies use these sites as a recruiting tool? How many native languages are supported? How are professionals using these websites to find potential clients and business partners?

❸ Search Skills
Selecting Search Terms

Search text that you send to a search engine, such as Google, Bing, or Yahoo!, impacts the quality of your search results. Rather than typing a long question in the search box, you may improve your results if you select the question's most important words as your search text. For example, instead of typing the

Internet Research ✹

entire question "How many users currently are on Facebook?" as your search text, type the following as your search text: facebook users current. Many search engines consider common words — such as how, are, and on — as stop words, or words that a search engine ignores when performing a search.

Place the most specific or important word (facebook) first in your search text and then follow it with additional words to narrow the results. To see if rearranging the order of the words yields different results, type current users facebook. Some search results from both queries likely will overlap. Many search engines assist you by automatically completing terms as you type them and will display a list of popular alternatives from which you can select. Sometimes, replacing a search term with a synonym will improve your results. For example, try using the search text, facebook users, followed by the current year instead of the using the word, current. Most search engines are not case sensitive. (They do not distinguish between uppercase and lowercase characters.)

| WEB | IMAGES | VIDEOS | MAPS | NEWS | MORE |

> bing   facebook users

facebook users
facebook users **2016**
facebook users **statistics**
facebook users **statistics**
facebook users **by country**
facebook users **by age**
facebook users **guide**
facebook users **in the world**

Source: Microsoft

Research This: Create search text using the techniques described above, and type it into a search engine to find answers to these questions. (1) What English words are stop words for Google? (2) What is the largest solid-state drive available? (3) How many hours per day on average do teens spend playing video games? (4) When is the next update to the Android mobile operating system expected to be released?

❹ Security

Secure IT 1-3 in this chapter offers advice about creating secure passwords when registering for websites. Despite suggestions and constant reminders from security experts to develop and then periodically change passwords, users continue to create weak passwords.

These common passwords are broken easily and, therefore, never should be used. For many years, the most common passwords have been the word, password, and the number sequences 123456 and 12345678.

Research This: Use a search engine to locate at least 2 different companies' lists of the 10 or 20 more common passwords in the past two years. Which passwords appear on both lists? Find a password-strength checking website and type three passwords to determine how easy or difficult they are to crack. Why do consumers continue to use these passwords despite repeated warnings to avoid them? Do you have accounts using one or more of these passwords? What advice is given for developing strong passwords, such as using the lyrics to the first line of a favorite song? How do the companies gather data to determine common passwords?

❺ Cloud Services

Cloud Storage (Iaas)

Cloud storage providers offer online access to hardware for storing files, and web and mobile apps to access, back up, and manage files. Cloud storage is an example of IaaS (infrastructure as a service), a service of cloud computing that allows individuals and businesses to use a vendor's hardware to manage their computing needs.

Cloud storage providers offer both free and paid service plans based on the amount of free storage, and some allow users to earn additional storage by recommending friends to use their services or by participating in promotional campaigns. Many cloud storage providers enable users to synchronize files across multiple devices, access files via mobile or web apps, share files with team members, and maintain previous versions of files. Some provide built-in access to web-based productivity software or integrate with third-party web and mobile apps.

Research This: (1) Use a search engine to find three popular cloud storage providers. Create accounts and try each for a period specified by your instructor. In a table, summarize their features, including amount of free storage available (offered or earned), restrictions on file sizes you can upload, ease of use of web and mobile apps, operating systems or devices supported, cost of paid plans, and additional services provided for a fee. (2) Many cloud storage providers offer several gigabytes of free storage to their users. What is the largest amount of free storage you can find? Who is the provider? Can you identify any drawbacks to using this service?

Critical Thinking

The Critical Thinking exercises challenge your assessment and decision-making skills by presenting real-world situations associated with chapter concepts. The Collaboration exercise should be completed with a team.

Instructions: Evaluate the situations below, using personal experiences and one or more resources available to you (such as articles on the web or in print, blogs, podcasts, videos, television, user guides, other individuals, electronics or computer stores, etc.). Perform the tasks requested in each exercise and share your deliverables in the format requested by your instructor (brief report, presentation, discussion, blog post, video, or other means).

1. Reactions to Software Problems

People who use computers and mobile devices sometimes experience problems with software, including operating systems, desktop apps, web apps, and mobile apps. Problems range from not being able to install or download the program or app to a computer or mobile device, to a program or an app producing unanticipated results. Depending on the situation, these problems can result in user stress. Many people believe reactions to software problems tend to be more extreme than reactions to problems with other tools.

Do This: Evaluate situations in which you have seen people react to program and app problems on their computers and mobile devices. Discuss how these users can reduce their frustration when dealing with such problems. Have you ever been frustrated by problems with a program or an app? How did you react? What did you do to solve the problem?

2. Energy Efficiency

Increases in energy prices lead many individuals to look at purchasing energy-efficient computers and devices. Energy-efficient models often look and perform similarly to equivalent computers or devices that use more energy.

Do This: Find two computers or devices of identical configuration, where the only difference is energy consumption. How much energy does the energy-efficient model save? Are energy-efficient computers and devices more or less expensive? Will the difference in cost (if any) affect your purchasing decision? How else might you be able to change your settings on your

existing computer or device to save energy? Use the web to locate articles that recommend energy-efficient products and that provide tips about additional ways to save energy.

3. Case Study

Amateur Sports League You are the new manager for a nonprofit amateur soccer league. The previous manager tracked all of the data on paper. You realize that using technology will increase your efficiency and enable you to communicate better with the board of directors, coaches, and players. At the board's next meeting, you will share ideas of how you will use technology.

Do This: To prepare for the meeting, you compile the following: differences between input and output, a list of the types of data you can use as input, and a list of the types of information you can produce as output. You include the types of computers, mobile devices, and other technologies you will use to enter data and produce the information. Incorporate your own experiences and user reviews of the devices. Compile your findings.

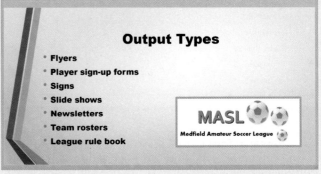

Output Types

- Flyers
- Player sign-up forms
- Signs
- Slide shows
- Newsletters
- Team rosters
- League rule book

MASL
Medfield Amateur Soccer League

Source: © Cengage Learning

Collaboration

4. Recommending Technology Solutions
People use computers and mobile devices in a variety of fields, including travel, manufacturing, and more. Although the way people use computers and mobile devices varies, each use involves hardware, programs and apps, and some type of communications method, such as the Internet or cellular network.

Do This: Form a three-member team and choose a field in which you all are interested. Assign one member to investigate hardware, another to investigate programs and apps, and the third member to investigate communications methods used in the field. Locate user reviews and articles by industry experts. Each team member should develop a list of related items that may be used. After the investigation, create a hypothetical business or organization in the field. Recommend specific hardware, programs or apps, and communications capabilities that would be best for the network or organization. Include comparisons of specific items, as well as costs. Be sure to summarize your investigations, describe the hypothetical business or organization, and outline and support your recommendations.

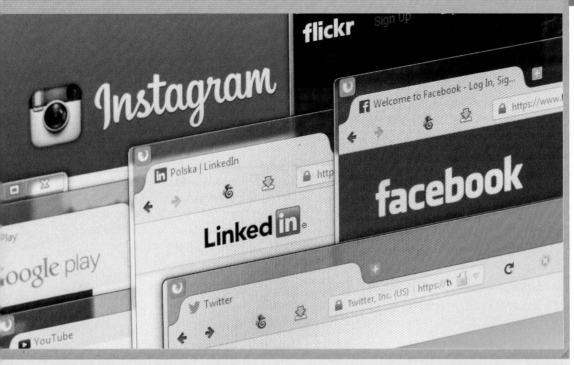

The Internet provides a variety of ways to communicate online.

"I use the Internet and web to shop for bargains, browse Google for all sorts of information, manage my fantasy sports teams, download music, check email on my phone, and so much more! What more could I gain from using the Internet?"

While you may be familiar with some of the content in this chapter, do you know how to . . .

- Use a public Wi-Fi hot spot safely?
- Register a domain name?
- Identify a cybersquatter?
- Browse the web safely?
- Tag digital content?
- Protect yourself from identity theft?
- Improve search results?
- Publish a website?
- Download digital media from online services?
- Set up a personal VoIP service?
- Combat cyberbullying?
- Determine your IP address?
- Search for a job online?

In this chapter, you will discover how to perform these tasks along with much more information essential to this course. For additional content available that accompanies this chapter, visit the free resources and premium content. Refer to the Preface and the Intro chapter for information about how to access these and other additional instructor-assigned support materials.

✔ Objectives

After completing this chapter, you will be able to:

1 Discuss the evolution of the Internet

2 Briefly describe various broadband Internet connections

3 Describe the purpose of an IP address and its relationship to a domain name

4 Describe features of browsers and identify the components of a web address

5 Describe ways to compose effective search text

6 Explain benefits and risks of using online social networks

7 Describe uses of various types of websites: search engines; online social networks; informational and research; media sharing; bookmarking; news, weather, sports, and other mass media; educational; business, governmental, and organizational; blogs; wikis and collaboration; health and fitness; science; entertainment; banking and finance; travel and tourism; mapping; retail and auctions; careers and employment; e-commerce; portals; content aggregation; and website creation and management

8 Explain how the web uses graphics, animation, audio, video, and virtual reality

9 Explain how email, email lists, Internet messaging, chat rooms, online discussions, VoIP, and FTP work

10 Identify the rules of netiquette

The Internet

One of the major reasons business, home, and other users purchase computers and mobile devices is for Internet access. The **Internet** is a worldwide collection of networks that connects millions of businesses, government agencies, educational institutions, and individuals. Each of the networks on the Internet provides resources that add to the abundance of goods, services, and information accessible via the Internet.

Today, billions of home and business users around the world access a variety of services on the Internet using computers and mobile devices. The web, messaging, and video communications are some of the more widely used Internet services (Figure 2-1). Other Internet services include chat rooms, discussion forums, and file transfer. To enhance your understanding of Internet services, the chapter begins by discussing the history of the Internet and how the Internet works and then explains each of these services.

Evolution of the Internet

The Internet has its roots in a networking project started by the Pentagon's Advanced Research Projects Agency (ARPA), an agency of the U.S. Department of Defense. ARPA's goal was to build a network that (1) allowed scientists at different physical locations to share information and work together on military and scientific projects and (2) could function even if part of the network were disabled or destroyed by a disaster such as a nuclear attack. That network, called *ARPANET*, became functional in September 1969, linking scientific and academic researchers across the United States.

The original ARPANET consisted of four main computers, one each located at the University of California at Los Angeles, the University of California at Santa Barbara, the Stanford Research Institute, and the University of Utah. Each of these computers served as a host on the network. A *host*, more commonly known today as a server, is any computer that provides services and connections to other computers on a network. Hosts often use high-speed communications to transfer data and messages over a network. By 1984, ARPANET had more than 1,000 individual computers linked as hosts. Today, millions of hosts connect to this network, which now is known as the Internet.

Figure 2-1   People around the world use the Internet in daily activities, such as accessing information, sending or posting messages, and conversing with others from their computers and mobile devices.

The Internet consists of many local, regional, national, and international networks. Both public and private organizations own networks on the Internet. These networks, along with phone companies, cable and satellite companies, and the government, all contribute toward the internal structure of the Internet.

Discover More: Visit this chapter's free resources to learn about Internet2.

 ✳ **CONSIDER THIS**

 Internet Research

Which organizations are members of the World Wide Web Consortium?

Search for: w3c members

Who owns the Internet?

No single person, company, institution, or government agency owns the Internet. Each organization on the Internet is responsible only for maintaining its own network.

The World Wide Web Consortium (*W3C*), however, oversees research and sets standards and guidelines for many areas of the Internet. The mission of the W3C is to ensure the continued growth of the web. Nearly 400 organizations from around the world are members of the W3C, advising, defining standards, and addressing other issues.

Connecting to the Internet

Users can connect their computers and mobile devices to the Internet through wired or wireless technology and then access its services free or for a fee. With wired connections, a computer or device physically attaches via a cable or wire to a communications device, such as a modem, that transmits data and other items over transmission media to the Internet. For wireless connections, many mobile computers and devices include the necessary built-in technology so that they can transmit data and other items wirelessly. Computers without this capability can use a wireless modem or other communications device that enables wireless connectivity. A *wireless modem*, for example, uses a wireless communications technology (such as cellular radio, satellite, or Wi-Fi) to connect to the Internet. Figure 2-2 shows examples of modems. The wireless modem shown in the figure is known as a *dongle*, which is a small device that connects to a computer and enables additional functions when attached.

Today, users often connect to the Internet via *broadband* Internet service because of its fast data transfer speeds and its always-on connection. Through broadband Internet service, users can download webpages quickly, play online games, communicate in real time with others, and more. Table 2-1 shows examples of popular wired and wireless broadband Internet service technologies for home and small business users.

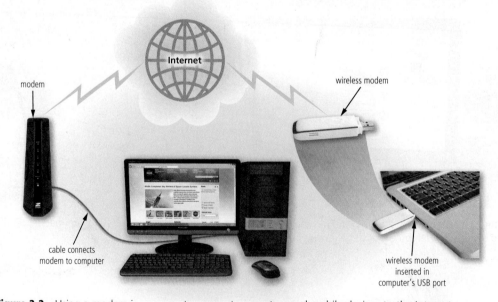

Figure 2-2   Using a modem is one way to connect computers and mobile devices to the Internet.

Courtesy of Zoom Telephonics Inc; © Oleksiy Mark / Shutterstock.com; Source: Microsoft; © Kristina Postnikova / Shutterstock.com; Kristina Postnikova / Shutterstock.com; © Cengage Learning; © DR / Fotolia

Table 2-1   Popular Broadband Internet Service Technologies

	Technology	Description
Wired	Cable Internet service	Provides high-speed Internet access through the cable television network via a cable modem
	DSL (digital subscriber line)	Provides high-speed Internet connections through the telephone network via a DSL modem
	Fiber to the Premises (FTTP)	Uses fiber-optic cable to provide high-speed Internet access via a modem
Wireless	**Wi-Fi** (wireless fidelity)	Uses radio signals to provide high-speed Internet connections to computers and devices with built-in Wi-Fi capability or a communications device that enables Wi-Fi connectivity
	Mobile broadband	Offers high-speed Internet connections over the cellular radio network to computers and devices with built-in compatible technology (such as 3G, 4G, or 5G) or a wireless modem or other communications device
	Fixed wireless	Provides high-speed Internet connections using a dish-shaped antenna on a building, such as a house or business, to communicate with a tower location via radio signals
	Satellite Internet service	Provides high-speed Internet connections via satellite to a satellite dish that communicates with a satellite modem

© Cengage Learning

Many public locations, such as shopping malls, coffee shops, restaurants, schools, airports, hotels, and city parks have Wi-Fi hot spots. Recall that a **hot spot** is a wireless network that provides Internet connections to mobile computers and devices. Although most hot spots enable unrestricted or open access, some require that users agree to terms of service, obtain a password (for example, from the hotel's front desk), or perform some other action in order to connect to the Internet. Read Secure IT 2-1 for ways to use a public Wi-Fi hot spot safely.

SECURE IT 2-1

Using Public Wi-Fi Hot Spots Safely

Connecting wirelessly to a public hot spot at your local coffee shop or at the airport can be convenient and practical. Using this free service can be risky, however, because cyber-criminals may lurk in public Wi-Fi hot spots, hoping to gain access to confidential information on your computer or mobile device. Follow these guidelines for a safer browsing experience:

- **Avoid typing passwords and financial information.** Identity thieves are on the lookout for people who sign in to accounts, enter their credit card account numbers in shopping websites, or conduct online banking transactions. If you must type this personal information, be certain the website's web address begins with "https," signifying a secure connection. If the website's web address changes to "http," indicating an unsecure connection,

sign out to end your Internet session immediately.

- **Sign out of websites.** When finished using an account, sign out of it and close the window.

- **Disable your wireless connection.** If you have finished working online but still need to use the computer, disconnect from the wireless connection.

- **Do not leave your computer or mobile device unattended.** It may seem obvious, but always stay with your computer or mobile device. Turning your back to talk with a friend or to refill your coffee gives thieves a few seconds to steal sensitive information that may be displayed on the screen.

- **Beware of over-the-shoulder snoopers.** The person sitting behind you may be watching or using a camera

phone to record your keystrokes, read your email messages and online social network posts, and view your photos and videos.

Consider This: How will you apply these precautions the next time you use a public Wi-Fi hot spot? Should businesses post signs alerting customers about Wi-Fi security issues?

Home and small business users can share and provide wireless Internet connections by creating their own Wi-Fi hot spot through a communications device in the home or business that is connected to broadband Internet service. Instead of a stationary Wi-Fi hot spot, some users opt to create mobile hot spots through mobile broadband Internet service via a separate communications device or a tethered Internet-capable device (Figure 2-3). *Tethering* transforms a smartphone or Internet-capable tablet into a portable communications device that shares its Internet access with other computers and devices wirelessly. Users may pay additional fees for mobile hot spot and tethering services.

Internet Research

What is a MiFi device?

Search for: mifi

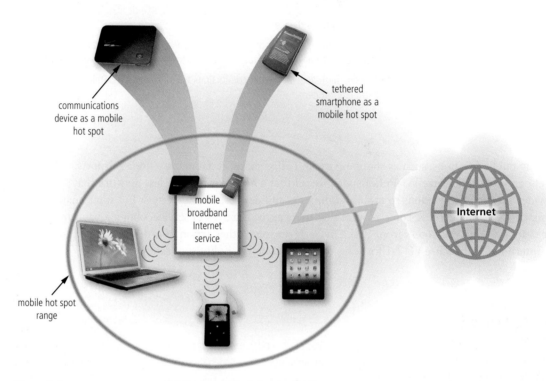

communications device as a mobile hot spot

tethered smartphone as a mobile hot spot

mobile broadband Internet service

Internet

mobile hot spot range

Figure 2-3 You can create a mobile hot spot using a communications device or by tethering a smartphone.
Courtesy of Verizon Wireless; © figarro / Can Stock Photo; © iStockphoto / Dane Wirtzfeld; © amfoto / Shutterstock.com; © Alex Staroseltsev / Shutterstock.com; Source: Microsoft; © Cengage Learning

Employees and students typically connect their computers and mobile devices to the Internet wirelessly through a business or school network, which, in turn, usually connects to a high-speed Internet service. When away from the office, home, or school, mobile users often access the Internet using Wi-Fi, mobile hot spots, or tethering services. Hotels and airports often provide wireless Internet connections as a free service to travelers. Many hotels have computers in their lobbies for customers to check email, browse the web, or print travel documents. Customers often bring their laptops or tablets to coffee shops, restaurants, libraries, hotels, and malls that offer free Wi-Fi as a service to their patrons.

✹ CONSIDER THIS

Does everyone use broadband Internet?

No. Some home users connect computers and devices to the Internet via slower-speed dial-up access because of its lower cost or because broadband access is not available where they live. Dial-up access takes place when a modem in a computer connects to the Internet via a standard telephone line that transmits data and information using an *analog* (continuous wave pattern) signal.

Internet Service Providers

An **Internet service provider** (**ISP**), sometimes called an Internet access provider, is a business that provides individuals and organizations access to the Internet free or for a fee. ISPs often charge a fixed amount for an Internet connection, offering customers a variety of plans based on desired speeds, bandwidth, and services. In addition to Internet access, ISPs may include additional services, such as email and online storage.

Bandwidth represents the amount of data that travels over a network. A higher bandwidth means more data transmits. Data sizes typically are stated in terms of megabytes and gigabytes. A *megabyte* (**MB**) is equal to approximately one million characters, and a *gigabyte* (**GB**) is equal to approximately one billion characters. Table 2-2 shows approximate data usage for various Internet activities.

BTW

Byte
A byte is the basic storage unit on a computer or mobile device and represents a single character.

Table 2-2	Data Usage Examples	
Activity	**Quantity**	**Approximate Data Usage**
Send and receive email messages (with no attachments)	100 messages	3–6 MB
Post on online social networks (text only)	100 posts	25–50 MB
Upload or download photos	50 photos	50 MB
Send and receive email messages (with attachments)	100 messages	0.75–1 GB
Visit webpages	200 visits	1 GB
Talk with others using VoIP (without video)	1 hour	1.25 GB
Listen to streaming music	1 hour	1–2 GB
Play online games	1 hour	1.75 GB
Watch smaller, standard-quality streaming video	1 hour	2–5 GB
Download apps, games, music, e-books	25 downloads	3 GB
Talk with others using VoIP (with video)	1 hour	5–7.5 GB
Watch HD streaming video	1 hour	5–20 GB

© Cengage Learning

Internet Research
Can I check the speed of my Internet connection?
Search for: internet speed test

 **CONSIDER THIS**

Does the term data have multiple meanings?
In the technology field, as discussed in Chapter 1, data can refer to unprocessed items that computers often process into information. Data also refers to the content that is stored on media or transmitted over a network. For example, when you select a data plan for your smartphone, the mobile service provider typically limits the amount of data (number of bytes) you can transfer each month depending on the plan you selected.

Wi-Fi networks often provide free Internet access, while some charge a daily or per use fee. Instead of locating a hot spot, some users prefer to subscribe to a mobile service provider, such as Verizon Wireless, so that they can access the Internet wherever they have mobile phone access. A **mobile service provider**, sometimes called a wireless data provider, is an ISP that offers wireless Internet access to computers and mobile devices with the necessary built-in wireless capability (such as Wi-Fi), wireless modems, or other communications devices that enable wireless connectivity. An antenna on or built into the computer or device, wireless modem, or communications device typically sends signals through the airwaves to communicate with a mobile service provider.

Discover More: Visit this chapter's free resources to learn more about Internet service providers.

How Data Travels the Internet

Computers and devices connected to the Internet work together to transfer data around the world using servers and clients and various wired and wireless transmission media. On the Internet, your computer or device is a client that can access data and services on a variety of servers. Wired transmission media includes phone line, coaxial cable, and fiber-optic cable. Wireless transmission media includes radio waves and satellite signals.

The inner structure of the Internet works much like a transportation system. Just as interstate highways connect major cities and carry the bulk of the automotive traffic across the country, several main transmission media carry the heaviest amount of **traffic**, or communications activity, on the Internet. These major carriers of network traffic are known collectively as the *Internet backbone*.

In the United States, the transmission media that make up the Internet backbone exchange data at several different major cities across the country. That is, they transfer data from one network to another until reaching the final destination (Figure 2-4).

How a Home User's Request for a Webpage Might Travel the Internet Using Cable Internet Service

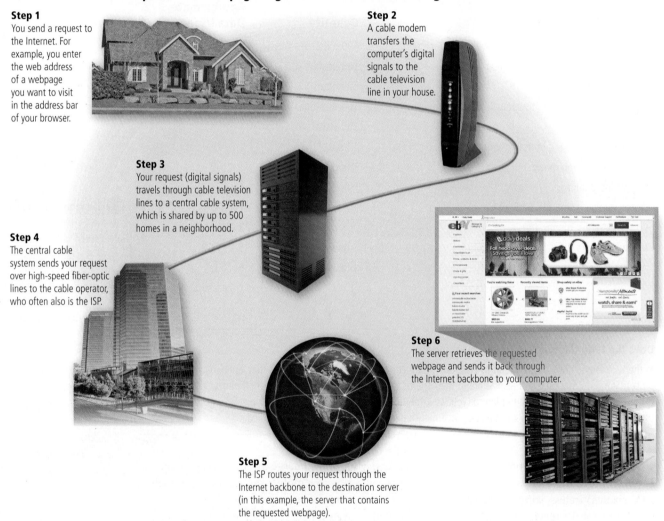

Step 1
You send a request to the Internet. For example, you enter the web address of a webpage you want to visit in the address bar of your browser.

Step 2
A cable modem transfers the computer's digital signals to the cable television line in your house.

Step 3
Your request (digital signals) travels through cable television lines to a central cable system, which is shared by up to 500 homes in a neighborhood.

Step 4
The central cable system sends your request over high-speed fiber-optic lines to the cable operator, who often also is the ISP.

Step 5
The ISP routes your request through the Internet backbone to the destination server (in this example, the server that contains the requested webpage).

Step 6
The server retrieves the requested webpage and sends it back through the Internet backbone to your computer.

Figure 2-4   This figure shows how a home user's request for eBay's webpage might travel the Internet using cable Internet service.
© romakoma / Shutterstock.com; © Pablo Eder / Shutterstock.com; © dotshock / Shutterstock.com; © TonyV3112 / Shutterstock.com; © iStockPhoto / loops7; © iStockphoto / luismmolina; Source: eBay

IP Addresses and Domain Names

The Internet relies on an addressing system much like the postal service to send data to a computer or device at a specific destination. An **IP address**, short for Internet Protocol address, is a sequence of numbers that uniquely identifies the location of each computer or device connected to the Internet.

The Internet uses two IP addressing schemes: IPv4 and IPv6. Due to the growth of the Internet, the original IPv4 addresses began dwindling in availability. The IPv6 scheme increased the available number of IP addresses exponentially. Because lengthy IP addresses can be difficult to remember, the Internet supports domain names. A **domain name** is a text-based name that corresponds to the IP address of a server that hosts a website (Figure 2-5). A domain name is part of the web address that you type in a browser's address bar to access a website.

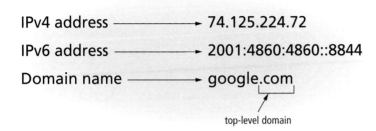

IPv4 address ⟶ 74.125.224.72

IPv6 address ⟶ 2001:4860:4860::8844

Domain name ⟶ google.com

top-level domain

Figure 2-5 The IPv4 and IPv6 addresses, along with the domain name for Google's website.
© Cengage Learning

The suffix of the domain name, called the *top-level domain* (*TLD*), identifies the type of organization associated with the domain. In Figure 2-5, for example, the .com is the TLD. Table 2-3 lists some of the original TLDs. New TLDs are being introduced to give individuals and businesses flexibility and creativity when purchasing domain names. For example, .museum, .technology, .name, and .biz have been introduced as TLDs within recent years.

The organization that approves and controls TLDs is called *ICANN* (pronounced EYE-can), which stands for Internet Corporation for Assigned Names and Numbers. For websites outside the United States, the suffix of the domain name may include a country code TLD (*ccTLD*), which is a two-letter country code, such as au for Australia. For example, www.philips.com.au is the domain name for Philips Australia. Read How To 2-1 to learn how to register a domain name.

Table 2-3	Original TLDs
TLD	**Intended Purpose**
.com	Commercial organizations, businesses, and companies
.edu	Educational institutions
.gov	Government agencies
.mil	Military organizations
.net	Network providers or commercial companies
.org	Nonprofit organizations

Discover More: Visit this chapter's free resources for an expanded table of popular TLDs.
© Cengage Learning

 HOW TO 2-1

Register a Domain Name
Individuals and companies register domain names so that people can find their websites easily using a browser. You register a domain name through a *registrar*, which is an organization that sells and manages domain names. When creating a website to post online, register a domain name that is easy to remember so that visitors can navigate to your website quickly. The following steps describe how to register a domain name.

1. Run a browser.
2. Use a search engine to locate a domain name registrar and then navigate to the website. You may want to evaluate several domain name registrars before deciding which one to use. Domain name registrars often offer various pricing models for registering domain names.

3. Perform a search on the domain name registrar's website for the domain name you wish to register. If the domain name is not available or costs too much, continue searching for a domain name that is available and within your price range, or explore various TLDs. For example, if the domain name you wish to register is not available or too expensive with the ".com" TLD, consider using another TLD such as ".net" or ".org."

4. Follow the steps on the domain name registrar's website to select and complete the purchase and registration of the desired domain name.

Consider This: What domain name based on your name would you register for your personal website? If your preferred domain name is not available, what are three alternative domain names you would consider?

BTW

High-Tech Talk

Discover More: Visit this chapter's free resources to learn more about DNS servers.

The *domain name system* (DNS) is the method that the Internet uses to store domain names and their corresponding IP addresses. When you enter a domain name (i.e., google.com) in a browser, a DNS server translates the domain name to its associated IP address so that the request can be routed to the correct computer (Figure 2-6). A *DNS server* is a server on the Internet that usually is associated with an ISP. Read Ethics & Issues 2-1 to consider issues related those who purchase unused or lapsed domain names for nefarious purposes.

How a Browser Displays a Requested Webpage

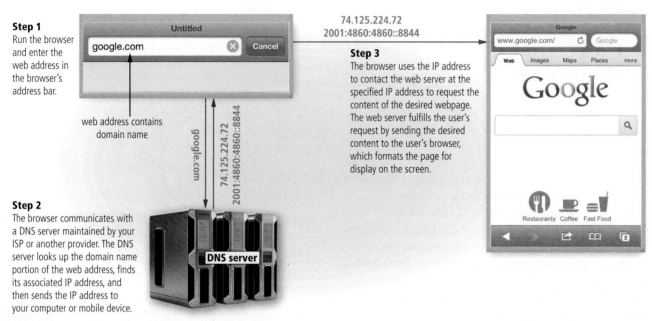

Step 1
Run the browser and enter the web address in the browser's address bar.

web address contains domain name

Step 2
The browser communicates with a DNS server maintained by your ISP or another provider. The DNS server looks up the domain name portion of the web address, finds its associated IP address, and then sends the IP address to your computer or mobile device.

Step 3
The browser uses the IP address to contact the web server at the specified IP address to request the content of the desired webpage. The web server fulfills the user's request by sending the desired content to the user's browser, which formats the page for display on the screen.

Figure 2-6 This figure shows how a user's entered domain name (google.com) uses a DNS server to display a webpage (Google, in this case).

Apple Inc.; © Cengage Learning; © Cengage Learning; © Sashkin / Shutterstock.com; Source: Google Inc.

ETHICS & ISSUES 2-1

Should Cybersquatters Be Prosecuted?
You learn from a registrar that a domain name containing your company name is not available. When you enter the web address in a browser, a webpage appears that contains ads, false content, or a notice that the domain is available for purchase, likely by a cyber-squatter. Cybersquatters purchase unused or lapsed domain names so that they can profit from selling them. Cybersquatters sometimes will sell you the domain name, but some take advantage of people trying to reach a more popular website to promote their own busi-ness or needs. One example is when a politi-cian registered several domain names that included his opponent's names and redirected them to his own campaign website.

Website owners periodically must renew domain names. Cybersquatters look for out-of-date registrations and buy them so that the original website owner must buy them back. Cybersquatters often purchase domain names with common words, alternate spellings of trademarked terms, or celebrity names. With the constant increase of new TLDs, cybersquatting cases are on the rise. Experts recommend purchasing your domain name with as many TLDs as you can afford, as well as to register your own name and that of your children.

More than 15 years ago, lawmakers enacted the *Anticybersquatting Consumer Protection Act* (ACPA). The ACPA's goal is to protect trademark owners from having

to pay a cybersquatter for a domain name that includes their trademark. To win a case against a cybersquatter, the owners must prove that the cybersquatters acted in bad faith, meaning they tried knowingly to profit from purchasing a domain name with a trademarked term, or a common misspelling or nickname of a trademarked term. Critics say that the ACPA prohibits free speech and free market.

Consider This: Should cybersquatting be illegal? Why or why not? Is it ethical to profit from cybersquatting? Why or why not? How should companies protect their brands when registering for domain names?

The World Wide Web

While the Internet was developed in the late 1960s, the World Wide Web emerged in the early 1990s as an easier way to access online information using a browser. Since then, it has grown phenomenally to become one of the more widely used services on the Internet.

As discussed in Chapter 1, the **World Wide Web** (**WWW**), or **web**, consists of a worldwide collection of electronic documents. Each electronic document on the web is called a **webpage**, which can contain text, graphics, animation, audio, and video. Some webpages are static (fixed); others are dynamic (changing). Visitors to a *static webpage* all see the same content each time they view the webpage. With a *dynamic webpage*, by contrast, the content of the webpage generates each time a user displays it. Dynamic webpages may contain customized content, such as the current date and time of day, desired stock quotes, weather for a region, or ticket availability for flights. The time required to download a webpage varies depending on the speed of your Internet connection and the amount of graphics and other media involved.

A **website** is a collection of related webpages and associated items, such as documents and photos, stored on a web server. A **web server** is a computer that delivers requested webpages to your computer or mobile device. The same web server can store multiple websites.

As web technologies matured in the mid-2000s, industry experts introduced the term *Web 2.0* to refer to websites that provide a means for users to share personal information (such as online social networks), allow users to modify website content (such as wikis), and provide applications through a browser (such as web apps).

Navigating the Web

Recall from Chapter 1 that a **browser** is an application that enables users with an Internet connection to access and view webpages on a computer or mobile device. Internet-capable mobile devices such as smartphones use a special type of browser, called a *mobile browser*, which is designed for their smaller screens and limited computing power. Many websites can detect if you are accessing their content on a mobile device (Figure 2-7).

 BTW

Web vs. Internet
Recall that the terms web and Internet should not be used interchangeably. The World Wide Web is a service of the Internet.

BTW

Technology Innovator
Discover More: Visit this chapter's free resources to learn about Tim Berners-Lee (creator of the World Wide Web).

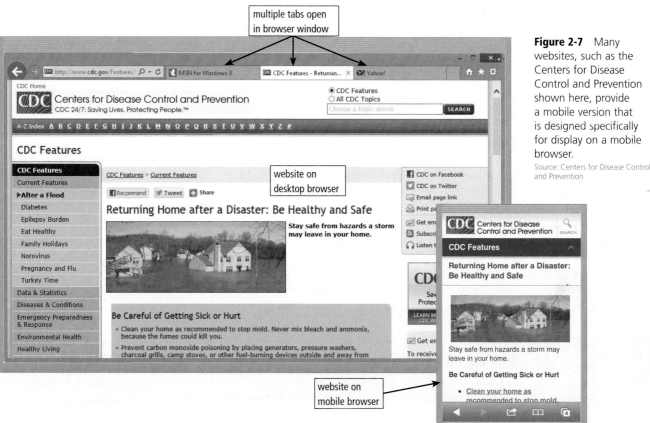

Figure 2-7 Many websites, such as the Centers for Disease Control and Prevention shown here, provide a mobile version that is designed specifically for display on a mobile browser.

Source: Centers for Disease Control and Prevention

When you run a browser, it may retrieve and display a starting webpage, sometimes called a home page. The initial home page that is displayed is specified in the browser. You can change your browser's home page at any time through its settings, options, or similar commands.

Internet Research

How do I change my browser's home page?

Search for: change browser home page

Another use of the term, **home page**, refers to the first page that is displayed on a website. Similar to a book cover or a table of contents, a website's home page provides information about its purpose and content. Many websites allow you to personalize the home page so that it contains areas of interest to you.

Current browsers typically support **tabbed browsing**, where the top of the browser shows a tab (similar to a file folder tab) for each webpage you display (shown in Figure 2-7). To move from one displayed webpage to another, you tap or click the tab in the browser. Tabbed browsing allows users to have multiple home pages that automatically are displayed when the browser runs. You also can organize tabs in a group, called a tab group, and save the group as a favorite, so that at any time you can display all tabs at once.

Because some websites attempt to track your browsing habits or gather personal information, current browsers usually include a feature that allows you to disable and/or more tightly control the dissemination of your browsing habits and personal information. Read Secure IT 2-2 for safe browsing tips.

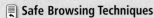 **SECURE IT 2-2**

Safe Browsing Techniques

Browsing the web is similar to crossing a busy street: you need to exercise caution and look carefully for unexpected traffic. Cybercriminals are on the lookout to prey upon unsuspecting users, so you should follow these guidelines when browsing:

- **Verify the website is safe.** Type the website address of your email, banking, online social network, and other personal accounts directly in a browser; never visit these websites merely by tapping or clicking links found in email messages. Before you sign in, double-check the web address to verify it is correct. Most browsers change the color of the address bar to verify the website is legitimate. Also, check that the web address begins with https instead of the less secure http, and look for a closed padlock symbol beside it.

- **Turn off location sharing.** At times, you may want allow *location sharing*, which gives websites access to your current location. This feature is handy when you want to obtain current weather conditions or use a navigation app. This information could be misused by dishonest individuals, however, so it is recommended you turn off location sharing.

- **Clear your browsing history.** A copy of every website you visit is stored in the browser's *cache* (pronounced cash) folder. If you perform online banking or view your credit card transactions, the cache could contain personal information, such as passwords and account numbers. You can specify to clear cache automatically each time you close a browser.

- **Never store passwords.** Many browsers can store your passwords so that you do not need to type them each time you visit the same websites. Although you may consider this feature a convenience, keep in mind that anyone who accesses your computer can view these secure websites easily using your account information.

- **Use a phishing filter.** *Phishing* is a scam in which a perpetrator attempts to obtain your personal and/or financial information. Many browsers include a *phishing filter*, which is a program that warns or blocks you from potentially fraudulent or suspicious websites.

- **Enable a pop-up or pop-under blocker.** Malicious software creators can develop a *pop-up ad or pop-under ad*, which are Internet advertisements that suddenly appear in a new window on top of or behind a webpage displayed in a browser. A **pop-up blocker** is a filtering program that stops pop-up ads from displaying on webpages; similarly a **pop-under blocker** stops pop-under ads. Many browsers include these blockers. You also can download them from the web at no cost.

- **Use private browsing.** Prevent people using your computer or mobile device from seeing the websites you viewed or searches you conducted by using *private browsing*. The browser discards passwords, temporary Internet files, data entered into forms, and other information when you exit the browser.

- **Use a proxy server.** To protect your online identity, use a *proxy server*, which is another computer that screens all your incoming and outgoing messages. The proxy server will prevent your browsing history, passwords, user names, and other personal information from being revealed.

Consider This: Which pop-ups have you encountered while browsing? What new techniques will you use to browse the web safely?

Internet Research

Does the browser war have a winner?

Search for: browser wars

Mini Feature 2-1: Browsers

The decision of which browser to use is a topic of discussion among computer experts and novices alike. Read Mini Feature 2-1 to learn about features of specific browsers.

MINI FEATURE 2-1

Browsers

All browsers can retrieve and display webpages, but their features and ease of use vary. Many factors can affect the decision to choose the browser that best fits your needs.

Configuring Options

Users can customize some settings to improve their browsing experience, such as those listed below.

- **Favorites**, also called *bookmarks*, are links to preferred websites. When you add a website to the list of favorites, you can visit that website simply by tapping or clicking its name in a list instead of typing its web address. Favorites can be organized into folders, alphabetized, and sorted by date or how frequently you view the websites.

- Security features, such as filters and secure connections, help protect you from fraudulent and malicious websites that might attempt to steal your identity and personal information. These features also can block websites you do not want to be displayed and can instruct the browser to save passwords.

- Privacy features help prevent thieves from accessing information about your browsing history, such as websites you have visited, data about your browsing session, and content you have seen on specific webpages.

Obtaining Browsers

A browser often is included in the operating system of a computer or mobile device. For example, many computer manufacturers include Internet Explorer when they install Windows and include Safari when they install Mac OS. Use a search engine to locate the browser you want to install, and visit its website to download the most recent version. Most browsers are available for download at no cost. Keep your browser up to date to prevent security holes. You can set your browser to perform updates automatically.

Making a Decision

Selecting the best browser for your needs involves some careful thought. You may decide to install several and then use each one for specific needs. Perform some research to compare browsers and then consider the following factors:

- How old is your computer or mobile device? A newer browser may not work properly on older hardware.

- How much memory is in your computer or mobile device? Some browsers work best with a lot of memory.

- Which operating system are you using? Some browsers are available for specific operating systems. For example, Internet Explorer is available only for Windows operating systems.

- What do you want the browser to do? Some browsers are best suited for performing simple searches, while others excel when running websites containing media.

Specific Browsers

- **Chrome:** Google's Chrome is one of the newer browser offerings, first released in 2008. This free browser is available for Windows and Mac OS and must be downloaded and installed. It includes a large number of security features. Chrome has independent tabbed browsing; if one tab develops a problem, the other tabs continue to function.

- **Firefox:** Developed by the Mozilla Corporation for computers running Windows, Mac OS, and Linux, Firefox is recognized for its extensive array of plug-ins (discussed later in the chapter). This free general-purpose browser was first released in 2004 and must be downloaded and installed. It has enhanced privacy and security features, a spelling checker, tabbed browsing, and a password manager.

- **Internet Explorer:** Microsoft's free browser, Internet Explorer, is available primarily for Microsoft Windows and comes preinstalled. First released in 1995, the browser features the capability to rearrange tabs, protection against phishing and malware, and settings to delete information about searches performed and webpages visited.

- **Opera:** This second-oldest browser is free, fast, and small. Used on both computers and mobile devices, Opera must be downloaded and installed. It began as a research project in Norway in 1994 and introduced several features found on most of today's browsers.

- **Safari:** Preinstalled on Apple computers and mobile devices, Safari has been the default browser for Mac OS since 2003 and is relatively new to Windows. The browser is recognized for its sleek design, built-in sharing with online social networks, fast performance, parental controls, and ease of use.

Mobile Browsers

Many browsers are included by default with some mobile devices and smartphones. Their features vary greatly. Some allow users to zoom and use keyboard shortcuts with most websites, while others display only websites optimized for mobile devices. The more popular mobile browsers are Chrome, Firefox, Internet Explorer, Safari, and Opera Mini.

Discover More: Visit this chapter's free resources to learn more about filters and secure connections, shareware websites, research to compare browsers, and specific browsers.

Consider This: Which browser or browsers have you used? Why did you use that browser? Would you consider using another browser? Why or why not? When browsers were first invented, their only function was to browse the web. What other capabilities do current browsers provide? Can you recommend a more descriptive name for today's browsers?

Chrome

Firefox

Internet Explorer

Opera

Safari

 **Internet Research**
What is the Silk browser?
Search for: silk browser

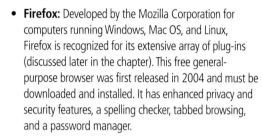

Web Addresses

A webpage has a unique address, called a **web address** or *URL* (Uniform Resource Locator). For example, the web address of http://www.nps.gov identifies the U.S. Department of the Interior National Park Service home page. A browser retrieves a webpage using its web address.

If you know the web address of a webpage, you can type it in the address bar of the browser. For example, if you type the address http://www.nps.gov/history/places.htm in the address bar and then press the ENTER key or tap or click the Search, Go, or similar button, the browser downloads and displays the associated webpage (Figure 2-8). The path, history/places.htm, in this web address identifies a webpage that is specified in a file named places.htm, which is located in a folder named history on the server that hosts the nps.gov website. When you enter this web address, after obtaining the IP address for the nps.gov domain name, the browser sends a request to the web server to retrieve the webpage named places.htm, and delivers it to your browser to be displayed.

✳ CONSIDER THIS ────────────────────────────

Although you entered the web address correctly, your screen does not match Figure 2-8. Why?
Organizations may update or redesign their websites, which may cause your screens to look different from those shown in this book.

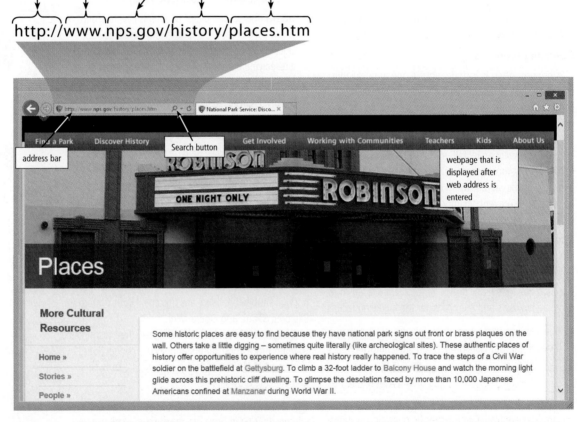

Figure 2-8 After entering http://www.nps.gov/history/places.htm in the address bar and then pressing the ENTER key or tapping or clicking the Search, Go, or similar button in a browser, the U.S. Department of the Interior National Park Service home page is displayed.
Source: National Park Service U.S. Department of the Interior

A web address consists of a protocol, domain name, and sometimes the host name, path to a specific webpage, or file name of the webpage. The *http*, which stands for Hypertext Transfer Protocol, is a set of rules that defines how webpages transfer on the Internet. Many web addresses begin with http:// as the protocol. The text between the protocol and the domain name, called the host name, identifies the type of Internet server or the name of the web server. The www, for example, indicates a web server.

 CONSIDER THIS

Do you need to type the protocol and host name in a web address?
Many browsers and websites do not require that you enter the http:// or the host name www in the web address. For example, you could enter nps.gov instead of http://www.nps.gov. As you begin typing a web address or if you enter an incorrect web address, browsers often display a list of similar addresses or related websites from which you can select. If, however, the host name is not www, you will need to type the host name as part of the web address. For example, the web address of schools.nyc.gov for the New York City schools website does not contain a www and thus requires entry of the entire web address.

When you enter a web address in a browser, you request, or pull, information from a web server. Another way users can pull content is by subscribing to a *web feed*, which contains content that has changed on a website. Mass media, blogs, and online social networks often provide web feeds, saving users the time spent checking the websites for updated content. Most browsers contain the capability to read web feeds.

Discover More: Visit this chapter's free resources to learn about Internet protocols.

 **Internet Research**
How do I read web feeds?
Search for: rss reader

Web Apps and Mobile Apps

Recall from Chapter 1 that a *web app* is an application stored on a web server that you access through a browser. Users typically interact with web apps directly on a website, sometimes referred to as the host. Web app hosts usually provide storage for users' data and information on their servers, known as *cloud storage*.

Many web app hosts provide free access to their software. Others offer part of their web app free and charge for access to a more comprehensive program. Many include advertisements in the free version and charge for an advertisement-free version. Some allow you to use the web app free and pay a fee when a certain action occurs. For example, you can prepare your tax return for free, but if you elect to print it or file it electronically, you pay a minimal fee.

A *mobile app* is an application you download from a mobile device's app store or other location on the Internet to a smartphone or other mobile device. Mobile apps often take advantage of features of the device, such as touch screens, digital cameras, microphones, and embedded GPS receivers, to enable you to enter and capture data.

 CONSIDER THIS

What are GPS receivers?
GPS (global positioning system) is a navigation system that consists of one or more earth-based receivers that accept and analyze signals sent by satellites in order to determine the receiver's geographic location. A **GPS receiver** is a handheld, mountable, or embedded device that contains an antenna, a radio receiver, and a processor. Most smartphones include embedded GPS receivers so that users can determine their location, obtain directions, and locate points of interest. Read Ethics & Issues 2-2 to consider issues related to apps that track your location.
   GPS receivers determine their location on Earth by analyzing at least 3 separate satellite signals from 24 satellites in orbit.
   Discover More: Visit the High-Tech Talk in Chapter 1's free resources to learn about how GPS receivers use triangulation.

ETHICS & ISSUES 2-2

Should Apps Be Allowed to Track Your Location?

When you install an app on your smartphone, you unintentionally may be allowing the app to send personal data. Apps can transmit your location, as well as the time you spend using the app. Apps also can collect personal information, including gender and birth year, if you access the app through an online social network profile. Although apps often present an option to review their security policies, some track user data without permission, or require you to enable tracking before you can use the app. You may see the results of tracking in the ads you see when browsing the web or using an app. Other

apps may track your location without your knowledge, such as apps that parents use to pinpoint a child's whereabouts.

If you search for driving directions, coupons, or restaurant tips based on your current location or past activities, you might be using apps that openly use this type of tracking. For example, a check-in app posts your location to online social networks, and another app enables you to locate friends by tracking their Bluetooth signals. Even when you opt to share data, use of these types of apps is not without risk. When people use location-tracking apps, for instance, they run the risk of someone stalking or robbing them. One positive use of location-tracking apps is with emergency

services. Lawmakers have struggled with whether law enforcement officials can use location-tracking without a user's knowledge. The U.S. Supreme Court recently ruled that police must get a warrant before searching a user's phone or reading text messages.

Consider This: Should app makers be able to require you to enable tracking or track your activity without your knowledge? Why or why not? Should the police be able to track GPS data without warrants? Why or why not? Would you use apps that post your location to your online social network profile or otherwise alert others of your whereabouts? Why or why not?

Internet Research

What are popular mobile apps?

Search for: top mobile apps

Web apps and mobile apps often work together (Figure 2-9). You might access your cloud storage website from a laptop or desktop. The cloud storage website hosts web apps to upload, download, browse, organize, and view files. The website also may provide a mobile app that you install on a smartphone so that you can access the same information or perform the same tasks from a mobile device. Because the data and information for each app is stored on cloud storage, all data is synchronized and accessible from anywhere you have an Internet connection, regardless of the computer or device used. The functionality of the app across computers and devices generally is the same, although the mobile app sometimes has fewer features. Some tasks may be easier to accomplish on one device or the other. For example, if a lot of typing is required, you may opt to use the web app on a laptop so that you can use a standard keyboard.

Discover More: Visit this chapter's free resources to learn more about mobile device app stores.

web app on Smart TV

web app on browser window

mobile app on tablet

mobile app on smartphone

Figure 2-9 Web and mobile apps often work together, enabling you to access your content from a variety of computers and devices.
Courtesy of Microsoft Corporation

⚙ NOW YOU SHOULD KNOW ───────────────────────────────

Be sure you understand the material presented in the sections titled The Internet, Connecting to the Internet, and The World Wide Web, as it relates to the chapter objectives.

Now you should know…

- Why you interact with hosts and networks on the Internet (Objective 1)

- Which broadband Internet service and ISP is best suited to your needs (Objective 2)

- How a browser works with domain names and IP addresses when you enter a web address (Objectives 3 and 4)

- Which browser(s) you would use and why (Objective 4)

──

Discover More: Visit this chapter's premium content for practice quiz opportunities.

══

Types of Websites

The web contains several types of websites: search engines; online social networks; informational and research; media sharing; bookmarking; news, weather, sports, and other mass media; educational; business, governmental, and organizational; blogs; wikis and collaboration; health and fitness; science; entertainment; banking and finance; travel and tourism; mapping; retail and auctions; careers and employment; e-commerce; portals; content aggregation; and website creation and management. Many websites fall into more than one of these types. All of these websites can be accessed from computers or mobile devices but often are formatted differently and may have fewer features on mobile devices.

Search Engines

A web **search engine** is software that finds websites, webpages, images, videos, news, maps, and other information related to a specific topic. You also can use a search engine to solve mathematical equations, define words, and more.

Thousands of search engines are available. Some search engines, such as Bing, Google, and Yahoo!, are helpful in locating information on the web for which you do not know an exact web address or are not seeking a specific website. Those that work with GPS devices or services are location based, meaning they display results related to the device's current geographical position. For example, your smartphone may be able to display all gas stations within a certain distance of your current location. Some search engines restrict searches to a specific type of information, such as jobs or recipes.

Search engines typically allow you to search for one or more of the following items:

- Images: photos, diagrams, and drawings
- Videos: home videos, music videos, television programs, and movie clips
- Maps: maps of a business or address, or driving directions to a destination
- Audio: music, songs, recordings, and sounds
- Publications: news articles, journals, and books
- People or Businesses: addresses and phone numbers
- Blogs: specific opinions and ideas of others

Search engines require that you enter a word or phrase, called *search text*, to describe the item you want to find. Search text can be broad, such as spring break destinations, or more specific, such as walt disney world. If you misspell search text, search engines typically correct the misspelling or identify alternative search text. Some also provide suggested search text, links, and/or images as you type your search text.

Depending on your search text, search engines may respond with thousands to billions of search results, sometimes called *hits*. The content of the search results varies depending on the type of information you are seeking and your search text. Some search results contain links to webpages or articles; others are media, such as images or videos. Most search engines sequence the search results based on how close the words in the search text are to one another in the titles and descriptions of the results. Thus, the first few links probably contain more relevant information.

If you enter a phrase with spaces between the words in search text, most search engines display results that include all of the keywords. Because keywords describe content, search

BTW
Technology Innovators
Discover More: Visit this chapter's free resources to learn about Yahoo! and Google.

Internet Research
What is a natural language search engine?
Search for: natural language search

Internet Research
What is a search engine spider?
Search for: search engine spider

results exclude articles, conjunctions, and other similar words (e.g., to, the, and). Table 2-4 lists some operators you can use in search text to refine searches. Instead of working with operators to refine search text, many search engines provide an advanced search feature or search tools that assist with limiting search results based on items such as date, TLD, language, etc.

Table 2-4 Search Engine Operators

Operator	Description	Examples	Explanation
Space or +	Display search results that include specific words.	art + music art music	Results have both words, art and music, in any order,
OR	Display search results that include only one word from a list.	dog OR puppy	Results have either the word, dog, or the word, puppy.
		dog OR puppy OR canine	Results have the word, dog, or the word, puppy, or the word, canine.
( )	Combine search results that include specific words with those that include only one word from a list.	Kalamazoo Michigan (pizza OR subs)	Results include both words, Kalamazoo Michigan, and either the word, pizza, or the word, subs.
–	Exclude a word from search results.	automobile-convertible	Results include the word, automobile, but do not include the word, convertible.
" "	Search for an exact phrase in a certain order.	"19th century literature"	Results include the exact phrase, 19th century literature.
*	Substitute characters in place of the asterisk.	writer*	Results include any word that begins with the text, writer (e.g., writer, writers, writer's)

© Cengage Learning

✳ CONSIDER THIS

How can you improve search results?
You may find that many items listed in the search results have little or no bearing on the item you are seeking. You can eliminate superfluous items in search results by carefully crafting search text and use search operators to limit search results. Other techniques you can use to improve your searches include the following:
- Use specific nouns.
- Put the most important terms first in the search text.
- List all possible spellings, for example, email, e-mail.
- Before using a search engine, read its Help information.
- If the search is unsuccessful with one search engine, try another.
- Practice search techniques by performing the Internet Research: Search Skills exercise in each chapter of this book.

Subject Directories A *subject directory* classifies webpages in an organized set of categories, such as sports or shopping, and related subcategories. A subject directory provides categorized lists of links arranged by subject. Using a subject directory, you locate a particular topic by tapping or clicking links through different levels, moving from the general to the specific. A disadvantage with a subject directory is that users sometimes have difficulty deciding which categories to choose as they work through the menus of links presented.

Discover More: Visit this chapter's free resources to learn more about search engines and subject directories.

Mini-Feature 2-2: Online Social Networks

Recall from Chapter 1 that an **online social network**, or *social networking site*, is a website that encourages members in its online community to share their interests, ideas, stories, photos, music, and videos with other registered users. Some online social networks also enable users to communicate through text, voice, and video chat, and play games together online. You interact with an online social network through a browser or mobile app on your computer or mobile device. Read Mini Feature 2-2 for features and uses of popular online social networks.

MINI FEATURE 2-2

Online Social Networks

People you know through personal and professional circles form your social networks. You share common interests, work or spend leisure time together, and know many of one another's friends. Online social networks allow you to manage your social networks online.

Your account on an online social network includes profile information, such as your name, location, photos, and personal and professional interests. You might create accounts on several online social networks to separate your personal and professional activities. Online social networks allow you to view the profiles of other users and designate them as your *friends* or contacts. Some sites, such as Facebook and LinkedIn, require friends to confirm a friendship, while others, such as Twitter and Google+, allow users to follow one another without confirmation.

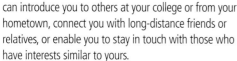

© iStockphoto / temizyurek

You can expand your online social network by viewing your friends' friends and then, in turn, designating some of them as your friends. Friends of your friends and their friends form your *extended contacts*.

- Extended contacts on a personal online social network such as Facebook can introduce you to others at your college or from your hometown, connect you with long-distance friends or relatives, or enable you to stay in touch with those who have interests similar to yours.

- Extended contacts on a professional online social network such as LinkedIn can introduce you to people who work at companies where you might be seeking employment. You can share employment history and skills in your profile, enabling potential employers who look at your profile to learn about your specific skills.

Read Secure IT 2-3 for tips about securing your privacy when using online social networks.

Personal Uses

Personal uses of online social networks include sharing photos and videos, greetings, or status updates.

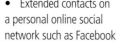

© iStockphoto / Lentz Photography

A *status update* informs friends about what you are doing. You can *like*, or show appreciation for, online content such as photos or videos

on online social networks such as Facebook and Google+. When you do, people who see the same content will know that you liked it, and the person who posted it is notified. All of your updates, likes, posts, and events appear in the activity stream associated with your account. Activity updates from friends may appear on a separate page associated with your account, often called a *news feed*.

On many online social networks, updates can include hashtags to identify their topics. A *hashtag* is a word(s) preceded by a # symbol that describes or categorizes a post. Users can search for posts on a topic by searching for a hashtag. Some online social networks list trending topics based on popular hashtags. Many television broadcasts, advertisements, and businesses post hashtags to encourage viewers and customers to share comments on Twitter or Facebook.

When accessing an online social network with a GPS-enabled mobile device, the location where you check in may be revealed as part of a status update. An online social network's mobile app can share your location with friends, find others nearby, and alert you to promotional deals from local businesses.

Follow button

© iStockphoto / hocus-focus

Business Uses

Businesses use online social networks to connect with their customers, provide promotional offers, and offer targeted advertising. For example, users who recommend online content about travel services may see travel-related advertising on their online social network's webpage.

Businesses also use data from online social networks to better connect with and understand customers. They can review comments from customers about their experiences using companies' products or services. Monitoring these feeds continuously gives companies immediate feedback from customers.

Nonprofit organizations use online social networks to promote activities and causes, accept donations, and allow volunteers to contact one another online.

Discover More: Visit this book's chapter's free resources to learn more about specific online social network websites and mobile apps.

Consider This: How can businesses and individuals use online social networks to bring people together in support of a common goal? What benefits and risks are involved when using online social networks?

⚜ SECURE IT 2-3

📄 Privacy and Security Risks with Online Social Networks

Online social networks can be excellent places to share messages, photos, and videos. They can, however, be risky places to divulge personal information. Follow these tips to help protect against thieves who are following the network traffic and attempting to invade private facets of your life.

- **Register with caution.** During the registration process, provide only necessary information. Do not disclose your birthdate, age, place of birth, or the city where you currently are living. If an email address is required, consider using a new address so that the online social network cannot access your email address book. Online social networks occasionally ask users to enter their email address and password to determine if their friends also are members of the network. In turn, the network obtains access to contacts in your address book and can send spam (unsolicited email messages) to your friends.
- **Manage your profile.** Check for privacy settings, usually found on the Settings or Options tabs, to set permissions so that you

can control who can review your profile and photos, determine how people can search for you and make comments, and if desired, block certain people from viewing your page. Be aware that online social networks may change privacy settings. Periodically check your settings to ensure you have the most up-to-date settings.

- **Choose friends carefully.** You may receive a friend request that appears to be from someone you know. In reality, this message may originate from an identity thief who created a fake profile in an attempt to obtain your personal information. Confirm with the sender that the request is legitimate.
- **Limit friends.** While many online social networks encourage the practice, do not try to gather too many friends in your social network. Some experts believe that a functional online social network should not exceed 150 people. Occasionally review what your friends are posting about you.
- **Divulge only relevant information.** Write details about yourself that are relevant to the reasons you are participating in an online social network. When posting

information, be aware that the message may be accessible publicly and associated with your identity permanently. Do not post anything you would not want to be made public.

- **Be leery of urgent requests for help.** Avoid responding to emergency pleas for financial assistance from alleged family members. In addition, do not reply to messages concerning lotteries you did not enter and fabulous deals that sound too good to be true.
- **Read the privacy policy.** Evaluate the website's privacy policy, which describes how it uses your personal information. For example, if you watch a video while signed in to your account, an external website or app may have access to this information and post this activity as an entry in both your activity stream and your friends' news feeds.

⚜ **Consider This:** Should online social networks do a better job of telling their users what information is safe or unsafe to share? What role should parents play in overseeing their child's involvement in online social networks?

Informational and Research

An informational and research website contains factual information. Examples include libraries, encyclopedias, dictionaries, directories, guides (Figure 2-10), and other types of reference. You can find guides on numerous topics, such as health and medicine, research paper documentation styles, and grammar rules. Many of the other types of websites identified in this section also are used to research information.

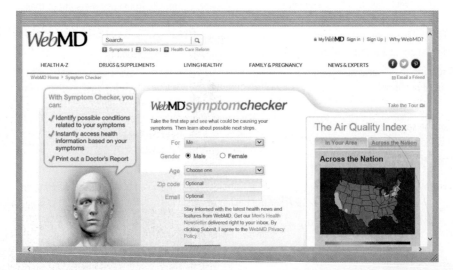

Figure 2-10   You can research health conditions from your symptoms on a medical website, such as WebMD.
Source: WebMD, LLC

Media Sharing

A *media sharing site* is a website that enables members to manage and share media such as photos, videos, and music. These websites are sometimes called photo sharing sites, video sharing sites (Figure 2-11), and music sharing sites, respectively. Media sharing sites, which may be free or charge a fee, provide a quick and efficient way to upload, organize, store, share, and download media.

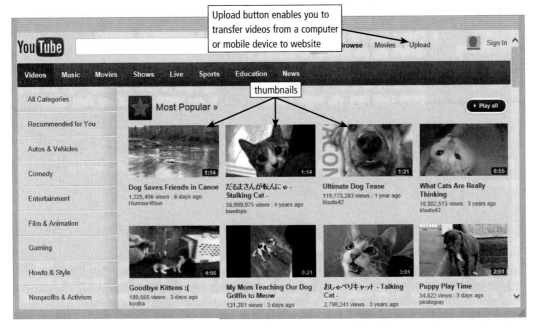

Figure 2-11 YouTube is an example of a video sharing site. You tap or click the thumbnail to view the video.
Source: YouTube, Inc.

✳ CONSIDER THIS

Why would you use a media sharing site instead of an online social network?
Although the lines between media sharing sites and online social networks are becoming blurred, some users chose a traditional media sharing site if they simply want to post photos, videos, or music to share with others and do not require the full functionality of an online social network. Before you allow someone to take your photo or record video of you, however, remember that the photo or video may be posted on a media sharing site. These photos or videos may be accessible publicly and associated with your identity for a long time. Also, once posted, you may be giving up certain rights to the media. Further, do not post photos or videos that are protected by copyright.

⚙ **BTW**
Technology Trend
Discover More: Visit this chapter's free resources to learn more about uses of bookmarking sites.

Bookmarking

A *bookmarking site* is a website that enables members to organize, tag, and share links to media and other online content (Figure 2-12). A **tag** is a short descriptive label that you assign to webpages, photos, videos, blog posts, email messages, and other digital content so that it is easier locate at a later time. Many websites and web apps support tagging, which enables users to organize their online content. Read How To 2-2 to learn how to tag digital content.

Figure 2-12 Pinterest is an example of a bookmarking site.

HOW TO 2-2

Tag Digital Content

When you post digital content online, it is a good idea to tag the content so that it is easy for you and others to locate and organize. After you have uploaded digital content to a media sharing site, follow the instructions on the website to apply tags to the digital content you uploaded. Consider the following suggestions when tagging digital content:

• Apply tags to all digital media, such as photos, music, and videos.

• If you are using multiple tags to identify one file, separate each tag with a separator. The website to which you are posting will inform you how to separate multiple tags (such as a space, comma, or semicolon).

• Choose tags that are descriptive of the content you are posting. For example, if you are posting a photo from a recent family vacation to Hammonasset Beach State Park, you might choose

"Hammonasset" and "vacation" as two of your tags for this photo.

• After you have tagged the digital content, perform a search on the media sharing site for your content, using the tags as your search criteria, to verify your content is displayed as intended.

Consider This: Why else is it important to tag digital content? What tags might you assign to your favorite song in your music library?

Discover More: Visit this chapter's free resources to learn more about websites that support tagging.

 CONSIDER THIS

What are the various kinds of social media?

Social media consists of content that users create and share online, such as photos, videos, music, links, blog posts, Tweets, wiki entries, podcasts, and status updates. Social media websites facilitate the creation or publishing of social media online and include media sharing sites (for photo, video, and audio files), bookmarking sites, blogs and microblogs, wikis, podcasts, online social networks, and online gaming sites.

News, Weather, Sports, and Other Mass Media

News, weather, sports, and other mass media websites contain newsworthy material, including stories and articles relating to current events, life, money, politics, weather (Figure 2-13), and sports. You often can customize these websites so that you can receive local news or news about specific topics. Some provide a means to send you alerts, such as weather updates or sporting event scores, via text or email messages.

News on the web is not replacing the newspaper but enhancing it and reaching different populations. Although some exist solely online, many magazines and newspapers sponsor websites that provide summaries of printed articles, as well as articles not included in the printed versions. Newspapers, magazines, and television and radio stations often have corresponding news, weather, or sports websites and mobile apps. Read Ethics & Issues 2-3 to consider the issues related to using fake names on websites.

Figure 2-13 Forecasts, radar, and other weather conditions are available on the WEATHER webpage on USA TODAY's website.
Source: Gannett

Is It Ethical to Use a Fake Name or ID on a Website?

You are signing up for an account on an online social network, an online dating website, or a news website that enables you to post comments. Should you use your real name?

Many argue that it is harmless to protect your anonymity by using a fake name but believe that it is not right to create a fake profile to mislead others or leave malicious comments on a website. The latter has become so prevalent that terms have emerged to describe this behavior. For example, *catfishing* is when someone creates a fake online social network or online dating profile and forms relationships with unsuspecting users. A *troll* is a user who

posts negative, inflammatory comments on a blog post or article with the intent of inciting other users.

One website creates very thorough, but completely fake, personas, which include email addresses, Social Security numbers, phone numbers, and more. Although law enforcement has raised concerns over the potential misuses of fake profiles, it technically is legal, even though the names and personas are not real. Legitimate uses for fake name generators include testers of large databases, such as ones for hospitals.

Facebook currently requires members to use their real names. Twitter's policy is that anyone can create a fake account, but it has a verification process to identify the official account of a celebrity or public

figure. Most fake Twitter accounts are harmless, and often are flattering. Although some argue that creating a fake account constitutes identity theft, unless the intent is to harm or embarrass the real person, it is not unethical or illegal. When a journalist created a fake account for a politician and posted discriminatory quotes and Tweets in the politician's name, many considered it an ethics violation, because journalists are supposed to report the truth.

Consider This: Is it ever acceptable to use a fake name online? Why or why not? Is it unethical to create fake personas for others to use? Why or why not? Should websites require you to use a real name, or have a verification process? Why or why not?

Educational

An educational website offers exciting, challenging avenues for formal and informal teaching and learning. The web contains thousands of tutorials from learning how to fly airplanes to learning how to cook a meal. For a more structured learning experience, companies provide online training to employees, and colleges offer online classes and degrees. Instructors often use the web to enhance classroom teaching by publishing course materials, grades, and other pertinent class information.

Business, Governmental, and Organizational

A business website contains content that increases brand awareness, provides company background or other information, and/or promotes or sells products or services. Nearly every enterprise has a business website. Examples include Allstate Insurance Company, Apple Inc., General Motors Corporation, Kraft Foods Inc., and Walt Disney Company.

Most United States government agencies have websites providing citizens with information, such as census data, or assistance, such as filing taxes (Figure 2-14). Many other types of organizations use the web for a variety of reasons. For example, nonprofit organizations raise funds for a cause and advocacy groups present their views or opinions.

Figure 2-14
Government agencies, such as the IRS webpage shown here, have websites providing assistance and information to citizens.
Source: IRS

Tweets present current events and technology news

Figure 2-15 When you 'follow' @DiscoveringComp on Twitter, you will see Tweets such as those shown here posted by the Discovering Computers user "Shelly Cashman", in your account's timeline, along with Tweets from others whom you are following. As a student in this class, you should 'follow' @DiscoveringComp so that you easily can keep current with relevant technology changes and events in the computing industry.
Source: Twitter

Blogs

As described in Chapter 1, a **blog** (short for weblog) is an informal website consisting of time-stamped articles, or posts, in a diary or journal format, usually listed in reverse chronological order. The term *blogosphere* refers to the worldwide collection of blogs. A blog that contains video sometimes is called a video blog, or vlog. A *microblog* allows users to publish short messages usually between 100 and 200 characters, for others to read. The collection of a user's Tweets, or posts on Twitter, for example, forms a microblog (Figure 2-15).

✱ CONSIDER THIS

How can you locate Tweets about certain topics?
When searching Twitter, you can use hashtags to find related posts. Similarly, you can tag any word(s) in your Tweets by typing it as a hashtag, such as #election.

Similar to an editorial section in a newspaper, blogs reflect the interests, opinions, and personalities of the author, called the **blogger**, and sometimes website visitors. Blogs have become an important means of worldwide communications. Businesses create blogs to communicate with employees, customers, and vendors. They may post announcements of new information on a corporate blog. Teachers create blogs to collaborate with other teachers and students. Home users create blogs to share aspects of their personal lives with family, friends, and others.

Wikis and Collaboration

Whereas blogs are a tool for publishing and sharing messages, wikis enable users to organize, edit, and share information. A **wiki** is a type of collaborative website that allows users to create, add, modify, or delete the website content via a browser. Wikis can include articles, documents, photos, or videos. Some wikis are public, accessible to everyone (Figure 2-16). Others are private so that content is accessible only to certain individuals or groups. Many companies, for example, set up wikis as an intranet for employees to collaborate on projects or access information, procedures, and documents. (An *intranet* is an internal network that uses Internet technologies.)

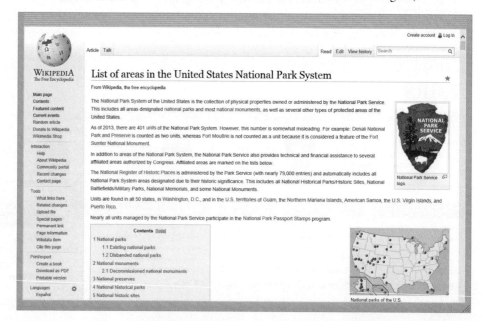

Figure 2-16 Wikipedia is a popular public wiki.
Source: Wikimedia Foundation

Contributors to a wiki typically must register before they can edit content or add comments. Wikis usually hold edits on a webpage until an editor or website manager can review them for accuracy. Unregistered users typically can review the content but cannot edit it or add comments.

Other types of collaboration sites enable users to share and edit any type of project — including documents, photos, videos, designs, prototypes, schedules, and more, often at the same time. On these websites, comments or edits are seen by other connected users. Most of these websites also enable users to communicate via chat windows, and some provide a whiteboard.

Discover More: Visit this chapter's free resources to learn more about public wikis and other collaboration websites.

Health and Fitness

Many websites provide up-to-date medical, fitness, nutrition, or exercise information for public access. Some offer users the capability of listening to health-related seminars and discussions. Consumers, however, should verify the online information they read with a personal physician. Health service organizations store your personal health history, including prescriptions, lab test results, doctor visits, allergies, and immunizations. Doctors use the web to assist with researching and diagnosing health conditions.

Science

Several websites contain information about space exploration, astronomy, physics, earth sciences, microgravity, robotics, and other branches of science. Scientists use online social networks to collaborate on the web. Nonprofit science organizations use the web to seek public donations to support research.

Entertainment

An entertainment website offers music, videos, shows, performances, events, sports, games, and more in an interactive and engaging environment. Many entertainment websites support streaming media. **Streaming** is the process of transferring data in a continuous and even flow, which allows users to access and use a file while it is transmitting. You can listen to streaming audio or watch streaming video, such as a live performance or broadcast, as it downloads to your computer, mobile device, or an Internet-connected television.

Sophisticated entertainment websites often partner with other technologies. For example, you can cast your vote on a television show via your phone or online social network account.

Banking and Finance

Online banking and online trading enable users to access their financial records from anywhere in the world, as long as they have an Internet connection. Using online banking, users can access accounts, pay bills, transfer funds, calculate mortgage payments, and manage other financial activities from their computer or mobile device (Figure 2-17). With online trading, users can invest in stocks, options, bonds, treasuries, certificates of deposit, money market accounts, annuities, mutual funds, and so on, without using a broker. Read Secure IT 2-4 for tips about protecting your bank accounts and other personal information from identity theft.

Internet Research
Have errors been found in Wikipedia?
Search for: wikipedia factual errors

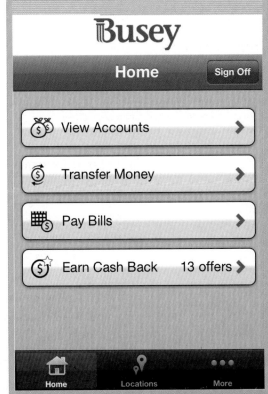

Figure 2-17 Many banks, such as Busey shown here, provide mobile versions of their online banking website so that users can manage financial accounts from their smartphones.
Source: First Busey Corporation

 **SECURE IT 2-4**

Protecting Yourself from Identity Theft

The fastest growing crime in the United States is identity theft. More than nine million people fall victim each year, with the unauthorized use of an existing credit card accounting for much of the problem. The National Crime Victimization Survey reports that household identity theft losses amount to more than $13 billion each year, and that figure does not account for the aggravation and time required to repair the accounts. Practice these techniques to thwart attempts to steal your personal data:

- Do not tap or click links in or reply to spam for any reason.
- Install a personal firewall (software that protects network resources from outside intrusions).
- Clear or disable web cookies (small text files that web servers store on a computer) in your browser. This action might prevent some cookie-based websites from functioning, but you will be able to decide which cookies to accept or reject.
- Turn off file and printer sharing on your Internet connection.
- Set up a free email account. Use this email address for merchant forms.

- Sign up for email filtering through your ISP or use an anti-spam program.
- Shred financial documents before you discard them.
- Provide only the required information on website forms.
- Avoid checking your email or performing banking activities on public computers. These computers are notorious for running *keyloggers*, which record keystrokes in a hidden file, and other tracking software. If you must use a public computer for critical activities, be certain to sign out of any password-protected website and to clear the browser's cache.
- Request a free copy of your medical records each year from the Medical Information Bureau.
- Obtain your credit report once a year from each of the three major credit reporting agencies and correct any errors. Enroll in a credit monitoring service.
- Request, in writing, to be removed from mailing lists.
- Place your phone number on the National Do Not Call Registry.
- Avoid shopping club and buyer cards.

- Do not write your phone number on charge or credit receipts. Ask merchants not to write this number or any other personal information, especially your Social Security number and driver's license number, on the back of your personal checks.
- Do not preprint your phone number or Social Security number on personal checks.
- Fill in only the required information on rebate, warranty, and registration forms.
- Learn how to block your phone number from displaying on the receiver's system.

If your identity has been stolen, immediately change any passwords that may have been compromised. If you have disclosed your debit or credit card numbers, contact your financial institutions. You also should visit the Federal Trade Commission website or call the FTC help line.

Consider This: Do you know anyone who has been a victim of identity theft? What steps will you take to protect your identity using some of these guidelines?

Travel and Tourism

Travel and tourism websites enable users to research travel options and make travel arrangements. On these websites, you typically can read travel reviews, search for and compare flights and prices, order airline tickets, book a room, or reserve a rental car.

Discover More: Visit this chapter's free resources to learn more about travel websites.

Mapping

Several mapping website and web apps exist that enable you to display up-to-date maps by searching for an address, postal code, phone number, or point of interest (such as an airport, lodging, or historical site). The maps can be displayed in a variety of views, including terrain, aerial, maps, streets, buildings, traffic, and weather. These websites also provide directions when a user enters a starting and destination point (Figure 2-18). Many work with GPS to determine where a user is located, eliminating the need for a user to enter the starting point and enabling the website to recommend nearby points of interest.

Discover More: Visit this chapter's free resources to learn more about mapping web apps.

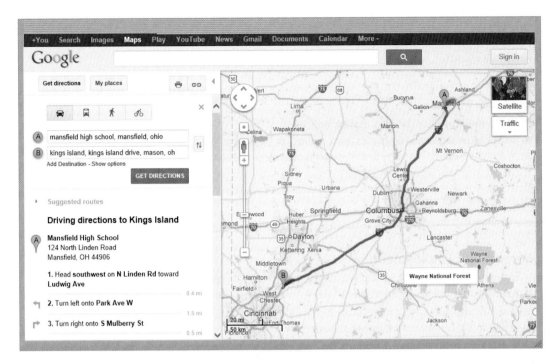

Figure 2-18 Using mapping web apps, such as Google Maps shown here, you can obtain driving directions from one destination to another.
Source: Google Inc.

Retail and Auctions

You can purchase just about any product or service on the web, a process that sometimes is called *e-retail* (short for electronic retail). To purchase online, the customer visits the business's *electronic storefront*, which contains product descriptions, images, and a shopping cart (Figure 2-19). The *shopping cart* allows the customer to collect purchases. When ready to complete the sale, the customer enters personal data and the method of payment, which should be through a secure Internet connection.

Figure 2-19 Shown here is Amazon's storefront for Professional and Technical Books.
Source: Amazon.com, Inc.

With an **online auction**, users bid on an item being sold by someone else. The highest bidder at the end of the bidding period purchases the item. eBay is one of the more popular online auction websites.

 CONSIDER THIS

Is it safe to enter financial information online?
As an alternative to entering credit card, bank account, or other financial information online, some shopping and auction websites allow consumers to use an online payment service such as PayPal. To use an online payment service, you create an account that is linked to your credit card or funds at a financial institution. When you make a purchase, you use your online payment service account, which transfers money for you without revealing your financial information.

BTW
Technology Innovator
Discover More: Visit this chapter's free resources to learn about LinkedIn (a business-oriented online social network).

Careers and Employment

You can search the web for career information and job openings. Job search websites list thousands of openings in hundreds of fields, companies, and locations. This information may include required training and education, salary data, working conditions, job descriptions, and more. In addition, many organizations advertise careers on their websites.

When a company contacts you for an interview, learn as much about the company and the industry as possible before the interview. Many have websites with detailed company profiles.

Discover More: Visit this chapter's free resources to learn more about job search websites.

E-Commerce

E-commerce, short for electronic commerce, is a business transaction that occurs over an electronic network, such as the Internet. Anyone with access to a computer or mobile device, an Internet connection, and a means to pay for purchased goods or services can participate in e-commerce. Some people use the term *m-commerce* (mobile commerce) to identify e-commerce that takes place using mobile devices. Popular uses of e-commerce by consumers include shopping and auctions, finance, travel, entertainment, and health.

Three types of e-commerce websites are business-to-consumer, consumer-to-consumer, and business-to-business.

- *Business-to-consumer (B2C) e-commerce* consists of the sale of goods and services to the general public, such as at a shopping website.
- *Consumer-to-consumer (C2C) e-commerce* occurs when one consumer sells directly to another, such as in an online auction.
- *Business-to-business (B2B) e-commerce* occurs when businesses provide goods and services to other businesses, such as online advertising, recruiting, credit, sales, market research, technical support, and training.

Portals

A **portal** is a website that offers a variety of Internet services from a single, convenient location (Figure 2-20). A wireless portal is a portal designed for Internet-capable mobile devices. Most portals offer these free services: search engine; news, sports, and weather; web publishing; yellow pages; stock quotes; maps; shopping; and email and other communications services.

Discover More: Visit this chapter's free resources to learn more about portals.

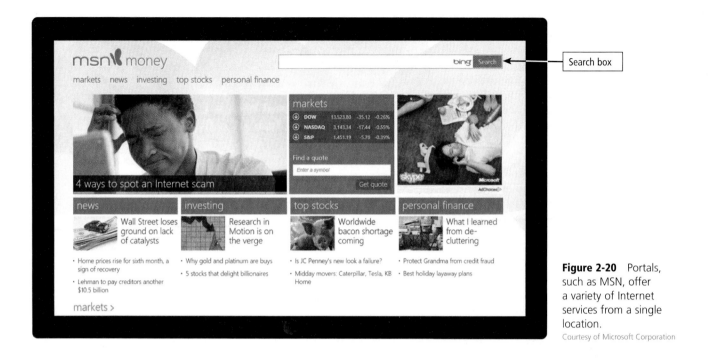

Figure 2-20   Portals, such as MSN, offer a variety of Internet services from a single location.
Courtesy of Microsoft Corporation

Content Aggregation

A **content aggregation** website or web app, sometimes called a *curation website*, allows users to collect and compile content from a variety of websites about a particular topic or theme (Figure 2-21). Types of content that may be compiled includes news, reviews, images, videos, podcasts (discussed later in this chapter), and blogs. Content aggregation websites save users time because they need to visit only one website (the content aggregation website) instead of visiting multiple websites to obtain information.

Discover More: Visit this chapter's free resources to learn more about content aggregation websites.

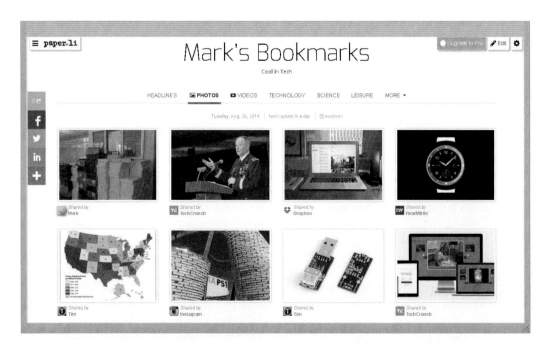

Figure 2-21   A content aggregation web app that compiles news from a variety of online sources.
Source: SmallRivers

Website Creation and Management

By creating their own websites, businesses and individuals can convey information to billions of people. The content of the webpages ranges from news stories to product information to blogs to surveys. Web creation and management sites provide tools that support the steps in **web publishing**, which is the creation and maintenance of websites. To create a website, you do not have to be a computer programmer. For the small business or home user, web publishing is fairly easy as long as you have the proper tools. Table 2-5 outlines the five main steps in web publishing.

Table 2-5   Steps in Web Publishing

Step	Description
1. Plan the website.	Identify the purpose of the website and the characteristics of the people you want to visit the website.
	Determine ways to differentiate your website from other similar ones.
	Decide how visitors will navigate the website.
	Register the desired domain name.
2. Design the website.	Design the appearance and layout of elements on the website.
	Decide colors and formats.
	Determine content for links, text, graphics, animation, audio, video, virtual reality, and blogs.
	You may need specific hardware, such as a digital camera, webcam, video camera, scanner, and/or audio recorder.
	You also may need software that enables you to create images or edit photos, audio, and video.
3. Create the website.	To create a website, you have several options:
	a. Use the features of a word processing program that enable you to create basic webpages from documents containing text and graphics.
	b. Use a *content management system*, which is a tool that assists users with creating, editing, and hosting content on a website.
	c. Use website authoring software to create more sophisticated websites that include text, graphics, animation, audio, video, special effects, and links.
	d. More advanced users create sophisticated websites by using a special type of software, called a text editor, to enter codes that instruct the browser how to display the text, images, and links on a webpage.
	e. For advanced features, such as managing users, passwords, chat rooms, and email, you may need to purchase specialized website management software.
4. Host the website.	Options for transferring the webpages from your computer to a web server include the following:
	a. A *web hosting service* provides storage space on a web server for a reasonable monthly fee.
	b. Many ISPs offer web hosting services to their customers for free or for a monthly fee.
	c. Online content management systems usually include hosting services for free or for a fee, depending on features and amount of storage used.
5. Maintain the website.	Visit the website regularly to ensure its contents are current and all links work properly.
	Create surveys on the website to test user satisfaction and solicit feedback.
	Run analytics to track visitors to the website and measure statistics about its usage.

BTW

Technology Trend
Discover More: Visit this chapter's free resources to learn more about responsive web design.

Some websites are dedicated to one portion of web publishing; others provide a variety of web publishing tools, including website design, content management, web hosting, website marketing, website analytics, survey development, and more. Because users view websites on a variety of computers and devices, many website developers use an approach called **responsive web design** (RWD) that adapts the layout of the website to fit the screen on which it is being displayed.

Discover More: Visit this chapter's free resources to learn more about website creation and management.

 CONSIDER THIS ——————————————————————

Can you assume that content on a website is correct and accurate?
No. Any person, company, or organization can publish a webpage on the Internet. No one oversees the content of these webpages.

Use the criteria below to evaluate a website or webpage before relying on its content.

- Affiliation: A reputable institution should support the website without bias in the information.
- Audience: The website should be written at an appropriate level.
- Authority: The website should list the author and the appropriate credentials.
- Content: The website should be well organized and the links should work.
- Currency: The information on the webpage should be current.
- Design: The pages at the website should download quickly, be visually pleasing, and be easy to navigate.
- Objectivity: The website should contain little advertising and be free of bias.

🕐 **NOW YOU SHOULD KNOW** ——————————————————————

Be sure you understand the material presented in the section titled Types of Websites as it relates to the chapter objectives. *Now you should know …*

- How to enter search text and improve your search results (Objective 5)
- How you can benefit from online social networks (Objective 6)
- When you would use specific types of websites (Objective 7)
- How you can publish your own website (Objective 7)

Discover More: Visit this chapter's premium content for practice quiz opportunities.

Digital Media on the Web

Most webpages include *multimedia*, which refers to any application that combines text with media. Media includes graphics, animation, audio, video, and/or virtual reality. The sections that follow discuss how the web uses these types of media.

Graphics

A **graphic** is a visual representation of nontext information, such as a drawing, chart, or photo. Many webpages use colorful graphics to convey messages (Figure 2-22). As shown in the figure, some websites use thumbnails on their pages because larger graphics can be time-consuming to display. A *thumbnail* is a small version of a larger image. You usually can tap or click a thumbnail to display the image in full size.

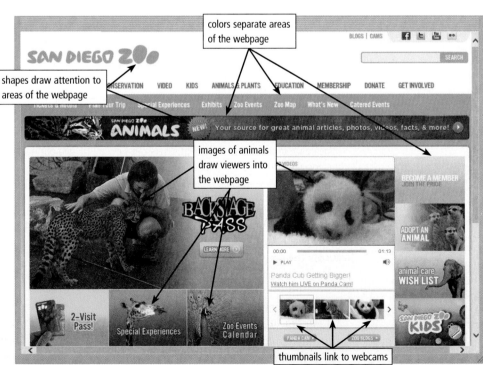

Figure 2-22 Many webpages use colorful graphics to convey messages. For example, the variety of colors, images, shapes, and thumbnails on the San Diego Zoo webpage visually separate and draw attention to areas of the webpage, making the webpage more dynamic and enticing.
Source: Zoological Society of San Diego

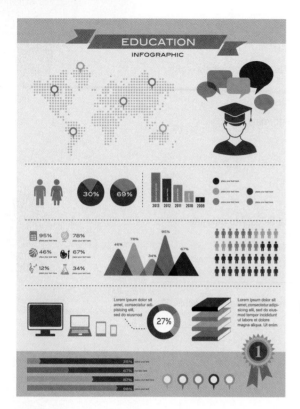

Figure 2-23 An infographic presents complex concepts at a glance.
© Marish / Shutterstock

The web often uses infographics to present concepts, products, and news. An *infographic* (short for information graphic) is a visual representation of data or information, designed to communicate quickly, simplify complex concepts, or present patterns or trends (Figure 2-23). Many forms of infographics exist: maps, signs, charts, and diagrams.

Of the graphics formats for displaying images on the web (Table 2-6), the JPEG and PNG formats are more common. *JPEG* (pronounced JAY-peg) is a compressed graphics format that attempts to reach a balance between image quality and file size. With JPG files, the more compressed the file, the smaller the image and the lower the quality. *PNG* (pronounced ping) is a patent-free compressed graphics format that restores all image details when the file is viewed. That is, the PNG format does not lose image quality during compression.

 Table 2-6   Graphics Formats Used on the Web

Abbreviation	Name	Uses
BMP	Bitmap	Desktop backgrounds Scanned images
GIF	Graphics Interchange Format	Images with few colors Simple diagrams Shapes
JPEG	Joint Photographic Experts Group	Digital camera photos Game screenshots Movie still shots
PNG	Portable Network Graphics	Comic-style drawings Line art Web graphics
TIFF	Tagged Image File Format	Photos used in printing industry

© Cengage Learning

⊞ **CONSIDER THIS**

What is a PDF file?
PDF, which stands for Portable Document Format, is an electronic image format by Adobe Systems that mirrors the appearance of an original document. Users can view a PDF without needing the software that originally created the document.

Animation   Many webpages use *animation*, which is the appearance of motion created by displaying a series of still images in sequence. For example, text that animates by scrolling across the screen can serve as a ticker to display stock updates, news, sports scores, weather, or other information. Web-based games often use animation.

Audio

On the web, you can listen to audio clips and live audio. *Audio* includes music, speech, or any other sound. Simple applications consist of individual audio files available for download to a computer or device. Once downloaded, you can play (listen to) the content of these files. Read How To 2-3 for instructions about downloading digital media from online services. Other applications use streaming audio so that you can listen to the audio while it downloads.

HOW TO 2-3

Download Digital Media from Online Services

Online services make various forms of digital media available, such as books, music, movies, and apps. You typically can use a program, such as iTunes, or an app, such as the Google Play Store, to access digital media. Digital media also may be available from these services' websites. The following steps describe how to download digital media from online services when you know the name or keyword(s) for the digital media you want to find.

1. On a computer or mobile device, run the program or app from which the digital media is available. If a program or app is not accessible easily, navigate to the online service using a browser.

2. Enter the name or keyword(s) in the Search box.

3. Tap or click the Search button to perform the search.

4. Navigate through the search results and then tap or click the search result for the item you want to download.

5. Locate and then tap or click the Download button or link to download the digital media to your computer or mobile device.

The following steps describe how to browse for and download digital media.

1. On your computer or mobile device, run the program or app from which the digital media is available. If a program or app is not accessible easily, navigate to the online service using a browser.

2. Tap or click the category corresponding to the type of digital media you want to browse. Common categories include music, movies, books, and apps.

3. Browse the items in the category.

4. When you find an item you want to download, tap or click the item to display additional information.

5. Look for and then tap or click the Download button or link to download the digital media to your computer or mobile device.

✸ **Consider This:** In addition to the online services listed in this box, what are three additional resources from which you can download digital media?

Audio files are compressed to reduce their file sizes. For example, the *MP3* format reduces an audio file to about one-tenth its original size, while preserving much of the original quality of the sound.

To listen to an audio file on your computer, you need special software called a *media player*. Most current operating systems contain a media player; for example, the Windows operating system includes Windows Media Player (Figure 2-24). Some audio files, however, might require you to download a media player. Media players available for download include iTunes and RealPlayer. You can download media players free from the web.

Discover More: Visit this chapter's free resources to learn more about audio file formats.

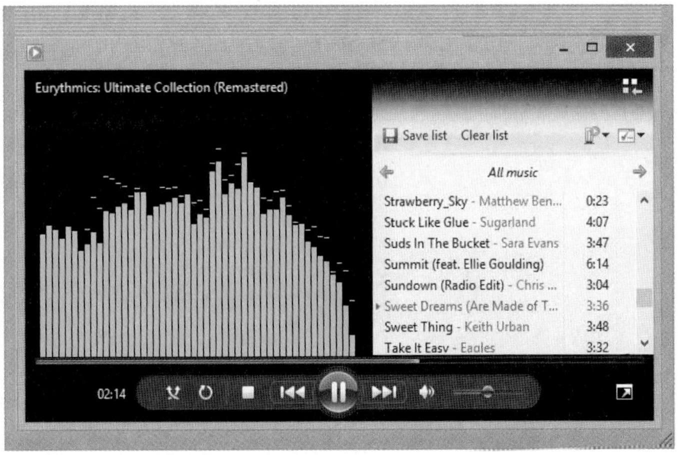

Figure 2-24 Windows Media Player is a popular media player, through which you can listen to music and watch video.
Source: Microsoft Corporation

Video

On the web, you can view video clips or watch live video. *Video* consists of images displayed in motion. Most video also has accompanying audio. You also can upload, share, or view video clips at a video sharing site. Educators, politicians, and businesses use video blogs and video podcasts to engage students, voters, and consumers.

Simple video applications on the web consist of individual video files, such as movie or television clips, that you must download completely before you can play them on a computer or mobile device. Video files often are compressed because they are quite large in size. Videos posted to the web often are short in length, usually less than 10 minutes, because they can take a long time to download. As with streaming audio files, streaming video files allows you to view longer or live videos by playing them as they download to your computer.

Discover More: Visit this chapter's free resources to learn more about video file formats.

Internet Research
What is a Smart TV?
Search for: smart tv

Virtual Reality   **Virtual reality** (VR) is the use of computers to simulate a real or imagined environment that appears as a three-dimensional (3-D) space. VR involves the display of 3-D images that users explore and manipulate interactively. Using special VR software, a developer

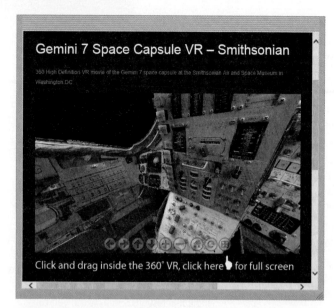

Click and drag inside the 360° VR, click here ☝ for full screen

Figure 2-25 Users can explore a VR world using a touch screen or their input device. For example, users can explore the inside of the Gemini 7 space capsule, located at the Smithsonian Air and Space Museum in Washington, D.C., from their computer or mobile device.
Source: World VR

 **Internet Research**

What is HTML5?

Search for: html5

creates an entire 3-D environment that contains infinite space and depth, called a VR world (Figure 2-25). A VR world on the web, for example, might show a house for sale where potential buyers walk through rooms in the VR house by sliding their finger on a touch screen or moving an input device forward, backward, or to the side.

In addition to games and simulations, many practical applications of VR also exist. Science educators create VR models of molecules, organisms, and other structures for students to examine. Companies use VR to showcase products or create advertisements. Architects create VR models of buildings and rooms so that clients can see how a completed construction project will look before it is built.

Plug-Ins

Most browsers have the capability of displaying basic multimedia elements on a webpage. Sometimes, however, a browser requires an additional program, called a plug-in, to display multimedia. A *plug-in*, or add-on, is a program that extends the capability of a browser. For example, your browser may require Adobe Reader to view and print PDF files. You typically can download plug-ins at no cost from various websites. Some plug-ins run on all sizes of computers and mobile devices; others have special versions for mobile devices.

Some mobile devices and browsers, however, do not support plug-ins. For this reason, web designers are using newer technologies to create websites that display correctly in both desktop and mobile browsers; these technologies generally do not require the use of plug-ins to display media.

Discover More: Visit this chapter's free resources to learn more about plug-ins.

Other Internet Services

As previously mentioned, the web is only one of the many services on the Internet. Other Internet services include the following: email, email lists, Internet messaging, chat rooms, online discussions, VoIP (Voice over IP), and FTP (File Transfer Protocol).

Email

Email (short for electronic mail) is the transmission of messages and files via a computer network. Email was one of the original services on the Internet, enabling scientists and researchers working on government-sponsored projects to communicate with colleagues at other locations.

You use an **email program** to create, send, receive, forward, store, print, and delete email messages. Email programs are available as desktop apps, web apps, and mobile apps. An email message can be simple text or can include an attachment such as a document, a graphic, an audio clip, or a video clip.

Just as you address a letter when using the postal system, you address an email message with the email address of your intended recipient. Likewise, when someone sends you a message, he or she must have your email address.

An *email address* is a combination of a user name and a domain name that identifies a user so that he or she can receive Internet email. A **user name** is a unique combination of characters, such as letters of the alphabet and/or numbers, that identifies a specific user. Your user name must be different from the other user names in the same domain. For example, a user named Rick Claremont whose server has a domain name of esite.com might want to select rclaremont as his user name. If esite.com already has an rclaremont (for Rita Claremont) user name, then Rick will have to select a different user name, such as rick.claremont or rclaremont2.

Sometimes, organizations decide the format of user names for new users so that the user names are consistent across the company. In many cases, however, users select their own user names, often selecting a nickname or any other combination of characters for their user name. Many users select a combination of their first and last names so that others can remember it easily.

In an Internet email address, an @ (pronounced at) symbol separates the user name from the domain name. Your service provider supplies the domain name. A possible email address for Rick Claremont would be rclaremont@esite.com, which would be read as follows: R Claremont at e site dot com. Most email programs allow you to create a *contacts folder*, which contains a list of names, addresses, phone numbers, email addresses, and other details about people with whom you communicate.

Figure 2-26 illustrates how an email message may travel from a sender to a receiver. When you send an email message, an outgoing mail server determines how to route the message through the Internet and then sends the message. As you receive email messages, an incoming mail server holds the messages in your mailbox until you use your email program to retrieve them. Most email programs have a mail notification alert that informs you via a message and/or sound when you receive a new email message(s).

Discover More: Visit this chapter's free resources to learn more about email programs.

 **CONSIDER THIS** ───────────────────────

What are good practices to follow when using email?

1. Keep messages brief.
2. Respond to messages promptly.
3. Use proper grammar, spelling, and punctuation.
4. Never respond to unsolicited messages.
5. Use meaningful subject lines.
6. Read the message before you send it.
7. Use email when you want a permanent record of a communication.

How an Email Message May Travel from a Sender to a Receiver

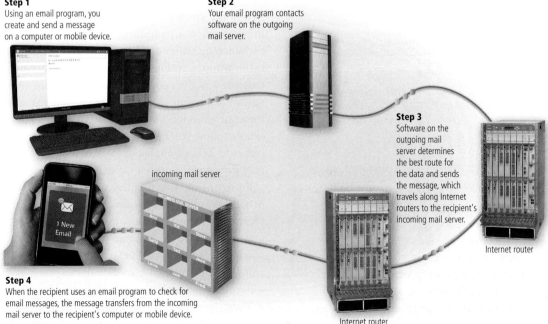

Step 1
Using an email program, you create and send a message on a computer or mobile device.

Step 2
Your email program contacts software on the outgoing mail server.

Step 3
Software on the outgoing mail server determines the best route for the data and sends the message, which travels along Internet routers to the recipient's incoming mail server.

incoming mail server

1 New Email

Internet router

Step 4
When the recipient uses an email program to check for email messages, the message transfers from the incoming mail server to the recipient's computer or mobile device.

Internet router

 Figure 2-26 This figure shows how an email message may travel from a sender to a receiver.

Email Lists

An **email list**, or electronic mailing list, is a group of email addresses used for mass distribution of a message. When a message is sent to an email list, each person on the list receives a copy of the message in his or her mailbox. You *subscribe* to an email list by adding your email address to the mailing list, which is stored on a list server. To remove your name, you *unsubscribe* from the mailing list.

The original use of email lists, such as *LISTSERV*, allowed any subscriber to send a message, which created a discussion-type forum among all subscribers via email. Many mailing lists today, such as in Figure 2-27, however, are one-way communications and do not allow subscribers to send messages.

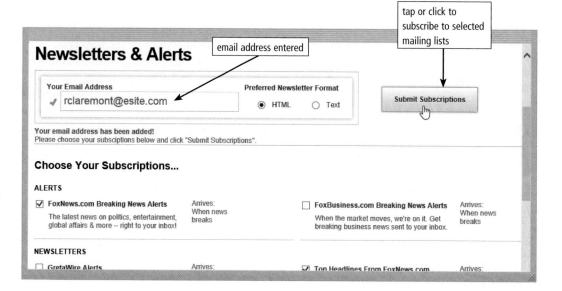

Figure 2-27 When you subscribe to a mailing list, you and all others in the list receive messages from the website. Shown here is a user who receives newsletters and alerts from FoxNews.com.
Source: FOX News Network, LLC

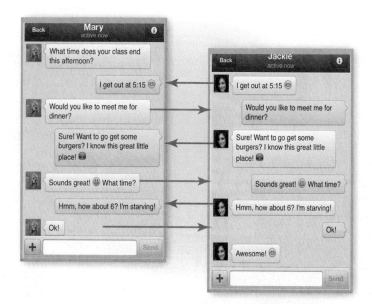

Figure 2-28 With Internet messaging services, you and the person(s) with whom you are conversing are online at the same time. The conversation appears on all parties' screens at the same time. Shown here is Facebook messenger.
© iStockphoto / Petar Chernaev; © Cengage Learning; © iStockphoto / Oleksiy Mark; © Cengage Learning

Internet Messaging

Internet messaging services, which often occur in real-time, are communications services that notify you when one or more of your established contacts are online and then allows you to exchange messages or files or join a private chat room with them (Figure 2-28). *Real time* means that you and the people with whom you are conversing are online at the same time. Some Internet messaging services support voice and video conversations, allow you to send photos or other documents to a recipient, listen to streaming music, and play games with another online contact.

For real-time Internet messaging to work, both parties must be online at the same time. Also, the receiver of a message must be willing to accept messages. To use an Internet messaging service, you may have to install messenger software or an app on the computer or mobile device, such as a smartphone, you plan to use.

Many online social networks include a messaging feature. To ensure successful communications, all individuals on the friend list need to use the same or a compatible messenger.

Discover More: Visit this chapter's free resources to learn more about Internet messaging services.

Chat Rooms

A **chat** is a real-time typed conversation that takes place on a computer or mobile device with many other online users. A **chat room** is a website or application that permits users to chat with others who are online at the same time. A server echoes the user's message to everyone in the chat room. Anyone in the chat room can participate in the conversation, which usually is specific to a particular topic. Businesses sometimes use chat rooms to communicate with customers.

As you type on your keyboard, others connected to the same chat room server also see what you have typed (Figure 2-29). Some chat rooms support voice chats and

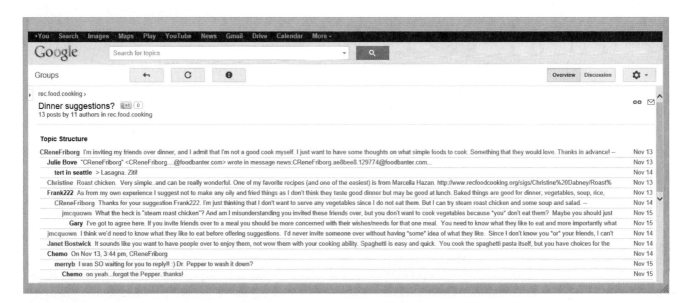

Figure 2-29 As you type, others in the same chat room see what you have typed.
Attribution: © ARENA Creative / Shutterstock.com; © Cengage Learning; © topseller / Shutterstock.com; © Alex Staroseltsev / Shutterstock.com; © Oleksiy Mark / Shutterstock.com; © Oleksiy Mark / Shutterstock.com; © Tom Wang / Shutterstock.com; © vlad_star / Shutterstock.com; © artjazz / Shutterstock.com

video chats, in which people hear or see each other as they chat. Most browsers today include the capability to connect to a chat server.

Online Discussions

An **online discussion**, or *discussion forum*, is an online area in which users have written discussions about a particular subject (Figure 2-30). To participate in a discussion, a user posts a message, called an article, and other users read and reply to the message. A *thread*, or threaded discussion, consists of the original article and all subsequent related replies.

Some discussion forums require that you enter a user name and password to participate in the discussion. For example, an online discussion for students taking a college course may require a user name and password to access the discussion. This ensures that only students in the course

Figure 2-30 Users in an online discussion read and reply to other users' messages.
Source: Google Inc.

participate in the discussion. Posts in an online discussion usually are stored for a certain amount of time, such as a semester, in this example.

VoIP

VoIP, short for Voice over IP (Internet Protocol), enables users to speak to other users via their Internet connection. That is, VoIP uses the Internet (instead of the public switched telephone network) to connect a calling party to one or more local or long-distance called parties.

To place an Internet phone call, you need a broadband Internet connection, a microphone and speaker, both of which are included with a standard computer or mobile device, and VoIP software, such as Skype. Some VoIP services require that you purchase a separate phone and VoIP router, and subscribe to their service. Others offer certain services free and require a subscription for additional services. Read How To 2-4 for instructions about how to set up a personal VoIP service and make a call.

⚙ **HOW TO 2-4**

📘 **Set Up a Personal VoIP Service and Make a Call**

VoIP services enable you to make free video or voice calls to others around the world. In many cases, the person you are calling also must use the same VoIP service. The following steps describe how to set up a VoIP service and make a call.

1. If you do not know the VoIP service you want to use, search for a program or app that enables you to place and receive VoIP calls.

2. If necessary, download the program or app for the VoIP service you will use.

3. Most VoIP services require you to have an account with their service before you can place or receive a call. When you start the VoIP program or app, search for the button or link to create a new account.

Follow the steps in the program or app to finish creating the account.

4. Once the account has been created, if necessary, sign in to the VoIP service with your user name and password.

5. Make sure the person you are calling also has an account with the same VoIP service. You should know at least one person using this service to successfully place a call. VoIP services typically allow you to locate and call someone by entering their user name or adding them to your list of contacts. If necessary, add the person you want to call to your list of contacts.

6. On the list of contacts, select the person you want to call and then tap or click the appropriate button to place the call.

7. When the other person answers, you can start your voice or video call.

8. When you are ready to end the call, tap or click the button to end the call.

9. When you are finished using the VoIP service, you should sign out of and exit the VoIP program or app.

✴ **Consider This:** Survey your friends and family to see if they use a VoIP service. If so, which service is the most popular among them?

Source: Microsoft

FTP

FTP (File Transfer Protocol) is an Internet standard that permits file uploading and downloading to and from other computers on the Internet. *Uploading* is the process of transferring files from your computer or mobile device to a server on the Internet. Recall that downloading is the process of transferring files from a server on the Internet to your computer or mobile device. Webpage developers, for example, often use FTP to upload their webpages to a web server.

Many operating systems include FTP capabilities. If yours does not, you can download FTP programs from the web, usually for a small fee.

An *FTP server* is a computer that allows users to upload and/or download files using FTP. An FTP site is a collection of files that reside on an FTP server. Many FTP sites have *anonymous FTP*, whereby anyone can transfer some, if not all, available files. Some FTP sites restrict file transfers to those who have authorized accounts (user names and passwords) on the FTP server.

Discover More: Visit this chapter's free resources to learn more about FTP programs.

Mini Feature 2-3: Digital Communications

Home users, small/home office users, mobile users, power users, and enterprise users interact with technology for many reasons, including communication, productivity, and information. Read Mini Feature 2-3 for examples of how a home user might interact with digital communications.

 MINI FEATURE 2-3

Digital Communications

This scenario, which assumes you are a home user with a busy family, presents situations and questions regarding technology use during a single day.

7:30 a.m. You notice a leaky pipe under the kitchen sink. Your regular plumber recently has retired. On your smartphone, you run an app that enables you to use search criteria, GPS, and user reviews. You find a local plumber who has many positive reviews and tap the phone number on the smartphone touch screen to place the call. You leave a message explaining the problem and asking the plumber to call you back.
✸ How can you evaluate reviews for authenticity and bias? How might an app provider use your location information in ways you have not authorized?

8:45 a.m. The plumber calls you back to schedule an appointment time. You open your laptop and use the electronic calendar web app your entire family uses to keep track of appointments. You find a time that works for both of you and update the electronic calendar.
✸ What features enable multiple people, such as a family or small business, to use an electronic calendar? What issues may occur from using a shared calendar?

10:00 a.m. You have a freelance job blogging for a local florist. You are required to post twice weekly to the florist's blog about agreed-upon topics. You use a wiki to confirm the symbolic meaning of different types of roses so that you can include that in your next blog post. You sign in to the blog's content management system and submit your post to the blog.
✸ What responsibility do bloggers have to post accurate, verified information? Should users rely on wikis to verify content?

 **11:00 a.m.** While you are driving to a doctor's appointment, you receive several text messages on your smartphone. You use your Bluetooth headset and your smartphone's speech-to-text feature to respond to the text messages without taking your eyes off of the road.
✸ Is it legal in your state to use hands-free devices while driving? What, if any, are the consequences of noncompliance?

1:00 p.m. Back at home, you flip through today's mail. You received a bill for your monthly mortgage payment. Using your laptop, you navigate to your bank's website and schedule a recurring payment for the mortgage to ensure you never will be late on a payment.
✸ What precautions should you take when accessing financial information and authorizing payments on the web?

5:30 p.m. Unsure of what to make for dinner, you use your tablet to view recipes you bookmarked on a bookmarking site. You verify that you have the ingredients on hand and follow the recipe on your tablet as you prepare dinner.
✸ Who owns the content posted to social networking or bookmarking sites? What risks are involved with using these types of websites?

8:30 p.m. While helping your daughter with her math homework, you discover a website that includes the answers to questions asked in her textbook. You have a discussion with your daughter about ethical issues surrounding posting and using that type of content.
✸ Should students receive punishment for using answers they find on a website?

9:00 p.m. You sit down to watch your favorite vocal competition reality show, streaming live through your Smart TV. The show enables you to send a text message to vote for your favorite contestant. You debate between two popular singers, then finally send your vote via text message.
✸ How else do TV, movie, and other entertainment websites use the Internet to interact with viewers or listeners?

10:30 p.m. You use the calendar app on your smartphone to confirm your schedule for tomorrow and then head to bed.
✸ How does technology enhance the daily life of a home user?

Discover More: Visit this chapter's free resources for additional scenarios for small/home office users, mobile users, power users, and enterprise users.

Netiquette

Netiquette, which is short for Internet etiquette, is the code of acceptable behaviors users should follow while on the Internet; that is, it is the conduct expected of individuals while online. Netiquette includes rules for all aspects of the Internet, including the web, social media, Internet messaging, chat rooms, online discussions, and FTP. Figure 2-31 outlines some of the rules of netiquette, with respect to online communications. Read Ethics & Issues 2-4 to consider issues related to an extreme misuse of online communications — online bullying.

Discover More: Visit this chapter's free resources to learn more about emoticons.

Netiquette Guidelines for Online Communications
Golden Rule: Treat others as you would like them to treat you.

Be polite. Avoid offensive language.

Avoid sending or posting *flames*, which are abusive or insulting messages. Do not participate in *flame wars*, which are exchanges of flames.

Be careful when using sarcasm and humor, as it might be misinterpreted.

Do not use all capital letters, which is the equivalent of SHOUTING!

Use **emoticons** to express emotion. Popular emoticons include:

:) Smile   :| Indifference   :o Surprised   :(Frown   :\ Undecided   ;) Wink

Use abbreviations and acronyms for phrases:

BTW	by the way	IMHO	in my humble opinion	FWIW	for what it's worth
FYI	for your information	TTFN	ta ta for now	TYVM	thank you very much

Clearly identify a *spoiler*, which is a message that reveals an outcome to a game or ending to a movie or program.

Be forgiving of other's mistakes.

Read the *FAQ* (frequently asked questions), if one exists.

Figure 2-31 Some of the rules of netiquette, with respect to online communications.
© Cengage Learning

❀ ETHICS & ISSUES 2-4

Who Is Responsible for Monitoring Cyberbullying?
Sending or forwarding threatening text messages, posting embarrassing or altered pictures of someone without his or her permission, or setting up a fake online social network page where others make cruel comments and spread rumors about someone all are examples of cyberbullying. *Cyberbullying* is harassment using technology, often involving teens and preteens. Unlike verbal bullying, the perpetrators can hide behind the anonymity of the Internet and can reach a wide audience quickly. Victims cannot just walk away or ignore bullying that comes in the form of text messages, email, or online social network posts.

Cyberbullying often takes place outside of school hours on personal devices or computers not owned or monitored by a school. Yet the ramifications affect the victim at school. Schools struggle to come up with policies. Many schools are adopting policies that include consequences for any form of student-to-student bullying, even using nonschool resources, if it contributes to a hostile environment for any student or group of students. Some schools specify that students who retaliate against anyone who reports instances of bullying or cyberbullying will receive punishment.

Anti-bullying laws vary from state to state and often do not include specific language about cyberbullying. One argument against criminalizing cyberbullying is the protection of free speech. Awareness campaigns, school policies, and parent monitoring of technology use are some ways to attempt to prevent cyberbullying. These methods are not always effective. The impact on the victim can lead to poor grades, health issues, mental health concerns, and even suicide.

Consider This: Should schools be responsible for punishing students who cyberbully other students outside of school? Why or why not? What role can parents play in reducing cyberbullying? What are the positive and negative aspects of the freedom to be anonymous on the Internet?

NOW YOU SHOULD KNOW

Be sure you understand the material presented in the sections titled Digital Media on the Web, Other Internet Services, and Netiquette as it relates to the chapter objectives.

Now you should know ...

- Why you use media on the web (Objective 8)

- How you can benefit from using email, email lists, Internet messaging, chat rooms, discussion forums, VoIP, and FTP (Objective 9)

- What rules you should follow in online communications (Objective 10)

Discover More: Visit this chapter's premium content for practice quiz opportunities.

Chapter Summary

This chapter presented the evolution of the Internet, along with various ways to connect to the Internet, how data travels the Internet, and how the Internet works with domain names and IP addresses. It discussed the web at length, including topics such as browsing, navigating, web addresses, web apps and mobile apps, searching, and online social networks. It presented various types of websites and media on the web. It also introduced other services available on the Internet, such as email, email lists, Internet messaging, chat rooms, online discussions, VoIP, and FTP. Finally, the chapter listed rules of netiquette.

Discover More: Visit this chapter's free resources for additional content that accompanies this chapter and also includes these features: Technology Innovators: Tim Berners-Lee, Yahoo! and Google, Arianna Huffington, and LinkedIn; Technology Trends: Uses of Bookmarking Sites and Responsive Web Design; and High-Tech Talks: IP Addresses and DNS Servers.

Test your knowledge of chapter material by accessing the Study Guide, Flash Cards, and Practice Test resources from your smartphone, tablet, laptop, or desktop.

TECHNOLOGY @ WORK

Transportation

What is transportation like without computers and mobile devices? Delivery drivers use clipboards to hold their records. Human navigators use paper maps to track routes for pilots. Ship captains rely solely on experience to navigate through shallow waters. Today, the transportation industry relies heavily on computer and mobile device usage.

Many vehicles include onboard navigation systems to help you navigate from one location to another. Some of these systems provide other services, such as dispatching roadside assistance, unlocking the driver's side door if you lock the keys in your vehicle, and tracking the vehicle if it is stolen.

The shipping and travel industries identify items during transport using bar codes, which are identification codes that consist of lines and spaces of different lengths. When you ship a package, the shipping company, such as UPS or FedEx, places a bar code on the package to indicate its destination to a computer. Because a package might travel to its destination by way of several trucks, trains, and airplanes,

computers automatically route the package as efficiently as possible. You are able to visit a website or sign up for text message notifications to track a package's progress during shipment.

When you travel by airplane, baggage handling systems ensure that your luggage reaches its destination on time. When you check in your baggage at the airport, a bar code identifies the airplane on which the bags should be placed. If you change planes, automated baggage handling systems route your bags to connecting flights with very little, if any, human intervention. When the bags reach their destination, they are routed automatically to the baggage carousel in the airport's terminal building.

Pilots of high-technology commercial, military, and space aircraft today work in a glass cockpit, which features computerized instrumentation, navigation, communications, weather reports, and an autopilot. The electronic flight information shown on high-resolution displays is designed to reduce pilot workload, decrease fatigue, and enable pilots to concentrate on flying safely.

Boats and ships also are equipped with computers that include detailed electronic maps, which help the captain navigate, as well as calculate the water depth and provide a layout of the underwater surface so that the captain can avoid obstructions.

As you travel the roadways, airways, and waterways, bear in mind that computers often are responsible for helping you to reach your destination as quickly and safely as possible.

Consider This: In what other ways do computers and technology play a role in the transportation industry?

Digital Vision / Getty Images

Study Guide

The Study Guide exercise reinforces material you should know for the chapter exam.

Discover More: Visit this chapter's premium content to **test your knowledge of digital content** associated with this chapter and **access the Study Guide resource** from your smartphone, tablet, laptop, or desktop.

Instructions: Answer the questions below using the format that helps you remember best or that is required by your instructor. Possible formats may include one or more of these options: write the answers; create a document that contains the answers; record answers as audio or video using a webcam, smartphone, or portable media player; post answers on a blog, wiki, or website; or highlight answers in the book/e-book.

1. Explain how ARPANET contributed to the growth of the Internet.

2. Describe the role of a host on a network.

3. Identify the role of the W3C.

4. Define the terms, dongle and broadband. List popular wired and wireless broadband Internet services.

5. State the purpose of a hot spot, and list tips for using hot spots safely.

6. ISP stands for _____.

7. Briefly describe how data and information travel the Internet.

8. Describe the purpose and composition of an IP address. Differentiate between IPv4 and IPv6.

9. Define the term, domain name. List general steps to register for a domain name.

10. Identify the purpose of several generic TLDs. Identify ICANN's role with TLDs.

11. Describe how and why cybersquatters register domain names.

12. State the purpose of a DNS server.

13. Differentiate between static and dynamic webpages.

14. Distinguish among the web, a webpage, a website, and a web server.

15. Explain the purpose of a browser. Describe the function of tabbed browsing.

16. List ways you can browse safely.

17. Name examples of popular browsers for personal computers and mobile devices.

18. Define the term, web address. Name a synonym.

19. Name and give examples of the components of a web address.

20. Describe the purpose of a web feed.

21. Explain the relationship between web and mobile apps.

22. Describe the purpose of GPS receivers, and why manufacturers embed them in smartphones.

23. Explain the risks and concerns involved in letting apps track your location. List any benefits.

24. Describe how to use a search engine. What are some ways you can refine a search?

25. Besides webpages, identify other items a search engine can find.

26. Differentiate between a search engine and a subject directory.

27. Explain how to use an online social network for personal or business use.

28. List ways to use online social networks securely.

29. Describe the purpose of these types of websites: informational and research; media sharing; bookmarking; news, weather, sports, and other mass media; educational; business, governmental, and organizational; blogs; wikis and collaboration; health and fitness; science; entertainment; banking and finance; travel and tourism; mapping; retail and auctions; careers and employment; e-commerce; portals; content aggregation; and website creation and management.

30. Is it ethical to use a fake name online? Why or why not? List techniques to protect yourself from identity theft.

31. Describe the uses of tags. List steps to tag digital content.

32. Define the term, e-commerce. Differentiate among B2C, C2C, and B2B e-commerce.

33. List uses and benefits of content aggregation websites and apps.

34. Identify and briefly describe the steps in web publishing.

35. The _____ web design approach adapts the layout of the website to fit the screen on which it is displayed.

36. List the seven criteria for evaluating a website's content.

37. _____ refers to any application that combines text with media.

38. Explain how webpages use graphics, animation, audio, video, virtual reality, and plug-ins.

39. Define the terms, thumbnail and infographic.

40. Name the types of graphics formats used on the web and how they use compression.

41. List general steps to download digital media.

42. Describe the purpose of these Internet services and explain how each works: email, email lists, messaging, chat rooms, online discussions, VoIP, and FTP.

43. Describe the components of an email address.

44. _____ refers to Internet communications in which both parties communicate at the same time.

45. List steps to set up a personal VoIP service and make a call.

46. Describe how a home user interacts with digital communications.

47. Define the term, netiquette.

48. Describe cyberbullying, and explain why it is difficult to catch the perpetrators.

49. Describe how the transportation industry uses technology.

You should be able to define the Primary Terms and be familiar with the Secondary Terms listed below.

Key Terms

Discover More: Visit this chapter's premium content to view definitions for each term and to access the Flash Cards resource from your smartphone, tablet, laptop, or desktop.

Primary Terms (shown in **bold-black** characters in the chapter)

blog (78)
blogger (78)
browser (65)
chat (91)
chat room (91)
Chrome (67)
content
   aggregation (83)
domain name (63)
e-commerce (82)
email (88)
email list (90)
email program (88)
emoticons (94)
favorites (67)
Firefox (67)

FTP (92)
GB (61)
GPS (70)
GPS receiver (70)
graphic (85)
home page (66)
hot spot (59)
Internet (56)
Internet Explorer (67)
Internet messaging (90)
Internet service provider
   (ISP) (61)
IP address (62)
MB (61)
mobile service
   provider (61)

netiquette (94)
online auction (82)
online discussion (91)
online social network (72)
Opera (67)
PDF (86)
pop-up blocker (66)
pop-under blocker (66)
portal (82)
responsive web design (84)
Safari (67)
search engine (71)
social media (76)
streaming (79)
tabbed browsing (66)
tag (75)

traffic (62)
user name (88)
virtual reality (87)
VoIP (92)
web (65)
web address (68)
web publishing (84)
web server (65)
webpage (65)
website (65)
wiki (78)
World Wide Web
   (WWW) (65)

Secondary Terms (shown in *italic* characters in the chapter)

analog (60)
animation (86)
anonymous FTP (92)
Anticybersquatting Consumer
   Protection Act (64)
ARPANET (56)
audio (86)
bandwidth (61)
blogosphere (78)
bookmarks (67)
bookmarking site (75)
broadband (58)
business-to-business (B2B)
   e-commerce (82)
business-to-consumer (B2C)
   e-commerce (82)
cable Internet service (59)
cache (66)
catfishing (77)
ccTLD (63)
cloud storage (69)
consumer-to-consumer (C2C)
   e-commerce (82)
contacts folder (89)
content management system (84)
curation website (83)
cyberbullying (94)
discussion forum (91)
DNS server (64)
domain name system (DNS) (64)
dongle (58)

DSL (59)
dynamic webpage (65)
electronic storefront (81)
e-retail (81)
email address (88)
extended contacts (73)
FAQ (94)
Fiber to the Premises (FTTP) (59)
fixed wireless (59)
flames (94)
flame wars (94)
friends (73)
FTP server (92)
gigabyte (61)
hashtag (73)
hits (71)
host (56)
http (69)
ICANN (63)
infographic (86)
Internet backbone (62)
intranet (78)
JPEG (86)
keyloggers (80)
like (73)
LISTSERV (90)
location sharing (66)
m-commerce (82)
media player (87)
media sharing site (75)
megabyte (61)

microblog (78)
mobile app (69)
mobile broadband (59)
mobile browser (65)
MP3 (87)
multimedia (85)
news feed (73)
phishing (66)
phishing filter (66)
plug-in (88)
PNG (86)
pop-up ad (66)
pop-under ad (66)
private browsing (66)
proxy server (66)
real time (90)
registrar (63)
satellite Internet service (59)
search text (71)
shopping cart (81)
social networking site (72)

spoiler (94)
static webpage (65)
status update (73)
subscribe (90)
subject directory (72)
tethering (60)
thread (91)
thumbnail (85)
top-level domain (TLD) (63)
troll (77)
unsubscribe (90)
uploading (93)
URL (68)
video (87)
W3C (58)
Web 2.0 (65)
web app (69)
web feed (69)
web hosting service (64)
Wi-Fi (59)
wireless modem (58)

wiki (78)

Checkpoint

The Checkpoint exercises test your knowledge of the chapter concepts. The page number containing the answer appears in parentheses after each exercise. The Consider This exercises challenge your understanding of chapter concepts.

Discover More: Visit this chapter's premium content to **complete the Checkpoint exercises** interactively; complete the **self-assessment in the Test Prep resource** from your smartphone, tablet, laptop, or desktop; and then **take the Practice Test.**

True/False   Mark T for True and F for False.

_____ 1. No single person or government agency controls or owns the Internet. (58)

_____ 2. The W3C is responsible for maintaining all networks and content on the Internet. (58)

_____ 3. Users typically pay additional fees for mobile hot spot and tethering services. (60)

_____ 4. A gigabyte (GB) is the basic storage unit on a computer or mobile device and represents a single character. (61)

_____ 5. A dynamic webpage's contents generate each time a user displays the page. (65)

_____ 6. Most browsers are available for download at no cost. (67)

_____ 7. Mobile apps sometimes have fewer features than a web app. (69)

_____ 8. A subject directory is software that finds websites, webpages, images, videos, maps, and other information related to a specific topic. (71)

_____ 9. When you post digital content online, it is a good idea to tag it so that it is easy to locate and organize. (76)

_____ 10. The term, blogosphere, refers to the worldwide collection of blogs. (78)

_____ 11. Tethering is the process of transferring data in a continuous and even flow, which allows users to access and use a file while it is transmitting. (79)

_____ 12. One way to protect yourself from identity theft online is to retain all your cookies in your browser. (80)

Multiple Choice   Select the best answer.

1. A(n) _____ is any computer that provides services and connections to other computers on a network. (56)
   a. host
   b. client
   c. FTP site
   d. subject directory

2. A(n) _____ is a sequence of numbers that uniquely identifies the location of each computer or device connected to the Internet. (62)
   a. Internet backbone
   b. domain name
   c. IP address
   d. ccTLD

3. You register a domain name through _____, which is an organization that sells and manages domain names. (63)
   a. a cybersquatter
   b. a registrar
   c. ICANN
   d. an ISP

4. The _____ is the method the Internet uses to store domain names and their corresponding IP addresses. (64)
   a. domain name system (DNS)
   b. top-level domain (TLD)
   c. File Transfer Protocol (FTP)
   d. W3C

5. One way to protect your identity while browsing is to use a(n) _____, which is another computer that screens all your incoming and outgoing messages. (66)
   a. password
   b. anonymous FTP
   c. phishing filter
   d. proxy server

6. _____ is a set of rules that defines how webpages transfer on the Internet. (69)
   a. Top-level domain
   b. Hypertext Transfer Protocol
   c. IPv4
   d. Web 2.0

7. A(n) _____ website contains factual material, such as libraries, encyclopedias, dictionaries, directories, guides, and other types of reference. (74)
   a. wikis and collaboration
   b. media sharing
   c. business
   d. informational and research

8. A _____ is a website that offers a variety of Internet services from a single, convenient location. (82)
   a. LISTSERV
   b. microblog
   c. portal
   d. cache

Checkpoint

Matching   Match the terms with their definitions.

_____ 1. tethering (60)

_____ 2. Internet backbone (62)

_____ 3. domain name (63)

_____ 4. web server (65)

_____ 5. tag (75)

_____ 6. catfishing (77)

_____ 7. wiki (78)

_____ 8. curation website (83)

_____ 9. chat (91)

_____ 10. cyberbullying (94)

a. text-based name that corresponds to the IP address of a server that hosts a website

b. website or web app that allows users to collect and compile content from a variety of websites about a particular topic or theme

c. harassment, often involving teens and preteens, using technology

d. collaborative website that allows users to create, add, modify, or delete website content via a browser

e. technique that transforms a smartphone or Internet-capable tablet into a portable communications device that shares its Internet access with other computers and devices wirelessly

f. real-time typed conversation that takes place on a computer or mobile device with many other online users

g. computer that delivers requested webpages to your computer or mobile device

h. online practice of creating a fake profile to form relationships with unsuspecting users

i. term used to refer to the major carriers of network traffic

j. short descriptive label that you assign to digital content so that it is easier to locate at a later time

✳ Consider This   Answer the following questions in the format specified by your instructor.

1. Answer the critical thinking questions posed at the end of these elements in this chapter: Ethics & Issues (64, 70, 77, 94), How To (63, 76, 87, 92), Mini Features (67, 73, 93), Secure IT (59, 66, 74, 80), and Technology @ Work (95).

2. What were ARPA's original goals? (56)

3. What are the advantages of using a broadband Internet service? (58)

4. What is the relationship between domain names and IP addresses? (62)

5. Is cybersquatting ethical? Why or why not? (64)

6. What is a cybersquatter? (64) What is the goal of the Anticybersquatting Consumer Protection Act (ACPA)? (64)

7. How does a static webpage differ from a dynamic webpage? (65)

8. How does using a proxy server help protect your online identity? (66)

9. What are some safe browsing techniques? (66)

10. What are some popular mobile browsers? (67)

11. How do GPS receivers track their location on earth? (70)

12. What are the advantages and risks associated with allowing an app to track your location? (70)

13. What techniques can you use to improve search results? (72)

14. What precautions can you take to minimize privacy and security risks associated with online social networks? (74)

15. Would you use a public computer to check email or do online banking? Why or why not? What are the risks? (80)

16. How do e-commerce and m-commerce differ? (82)

17. What should you determine during the planning stage of a website? (84)

18. What steps are involved in web publishing? (84)

19. What are some criteria you can use to evaluate a website or webpage before relying on its content? (85)

20. How do JPEG and PNG formats differ? (86)

21. What are some practical applications of virtual reality? (88)

22. Where can you obtain plug-ins? (88)

23. Besides the web, what other Internet services are available? (88)

24. What are some good practices to follow when using email? (89)

25. What elements do you need to place an Internet phone call? (92)

26. What is anonymous FTP? (92)

27. What activities might be considered cyberbullying? (94)

STUDENT ASSIGNMENTS

✸ Problem Solving

The Problem Solving exercises extend your knowledge of chapter concepts by seeking solutions to practical problems with technology that you may encounter at home, school, work, or with nonprofit organizations. The Collaboration exercise should be completed with a team.

Instructions: You often can solve problems with technology in multiple ways. Determine a solution to the problems in these exercises by using one or more resources available to you (such as a computer or mobile device, articles on the web or in print, blogs, podcasts, videos, television, user guides, other individuals, electronics or computer stores, etc.). Describe your solution, along with the resource(s) used, in the format requested by your instructor (brief report, presentation, discussion, blog post, video, or other means).

Personal

1. **Cyberbullying Message** While reviewing the email messages in your email account, you notice one that you interpret as cyberbullying. You do not recognize the sender of the email message, but still take it seriously. What are your next steps?

2. **Unsolicited Friend Requests** You recently signed up for an account on the Facebook online social network. When you log in periodically, you find that people you do not know are requesting to be your friend. How should you respond?

3. **Unexpected Search Engine** A class project requires that you conduct research on the web. After typing the web address for Google's home page and pressing the ENTER key, your browser redirects you to a different search engine. What could be wrong?

4. **Images Do Not Appear** When you navigate to a webpage, you notice that no images are appearing. You successfully have viewed webpages with images in the past and are not sure why images suddenly are not appearing. What steps will you take to show the images?

5. **Social Media Password** Your social media password has been saved on your computer for quite some time and the browser has been signing you in automatically. After deleting your browsing history and saved information from your browser, the online social network began prompting you again for your password, which you have forgotten. What are your next steps?

Source: Twitter

Professional

6. **Suspicious Website Visits** The director of your company's information technology department sent you an email message stating that you have been spending an excessive amount of time viewing websites not related to your job. You periodically visit websites not related to work, but only on breaks, which the company allows. How does he know your web browsing habits? How will you respond to this claim?

7. **Automatic Response** When you return from vacation, a colleague informs you that when she sent email messages to your email address, she would not always receive your automatic response stating that you were out of the office. Why might your email program not respond automatically to every email message received?

8. **Email Message Formatting** A friend sent an email message containing a photo to your email account at work. Upon receiving the email message, the photo does not appear. You also notice that email messages never show any formatting, such as different fonts, font sizes, and font colors. What might be causing this?

9. **Mobile Hot Spot Not Found** Your supervisor gave you a mobile hot spot to use while you are traveling to a conference in another state. When you attempt to connect to the hot spot with your computer, tablet, and phone, none of the devices is able to find any wireless networks. What might be the problem, and what are your next steps?

10. **Sporadic Email Message Delivery** The email program on your computer has been displaying new messages only every hour, on the hour. Historically, new email messages would arrive and be displayed immediately upon being sent by the sender. Furthermore, your coworkers claim that they sometimes do not receive your email messages until hours after you send them. What might be the problem?

Collaboration

11. **Technology in Transportation** Your project team has been assigned to present a business proposal to a group of potential investors. Because the presentation will take place in Kansas City, Missouri, you will need to transport people and ship some materials to that location. Form a team of three people and determine how to use technology to ship materials and how to make travel arrangements. One team member should research the steps required to use a website to make flight reservations, one team member should determine the steps necessary to print a package shipping label from his or her computer and track the package while it is en route, and another team member should find directions from Kansas City International Airport to a nearby hotel.

The How To: Your Turn exercises present general guidelines for fundamental skills when using a computer or mobile device and then require that you determine how to apply these general guidelines to a specific program or situation.

How To: Your Turn

Discover More: Visit this chapter's premium content to **challenge yourself with this additional How To: Your Turn exercises**, which include App Adventure.

Instructions: You often can complete tasks using technology in multiple ways. Figure out how to perform the tasks described in these exercises by using one or more resources available to you (such as a computer or mobile device, articles on the web or in print, online or program help, user guides, blogs, podcasts, videos, other individuals, trial and error, etc.). Summarize your 'how to' steps, along with the resource(s) used, in the format requested by your instructor (brief report, presentation, discussion, blog post, video, or other means).

1 Determine Your IP (Internet Protocol) Address

Knowing a computer or mobile device's IP address can help you identify it on a network and can help you trouble-shoot any problems you may experience connecting to the Internet or other computers and devices on your network. The following steps guide you through the process of determining your IP address.

a. Run a browser and then navigate to a search engine of your choice.

b. Search for a website that can determine your IP address and then navigate to one of these websites.

c. Your IP address should be displayed upon navigating to the website. If it does not, return to the search results and navigate to a different site.

or

a. Run a browser and then navigate to a search engine of your choice.

b. Search for a website that explains how to determine the IP address for your specific operating system and version.

c. View the search results and then navigate to the website that provides you with the best guidance.

d. Follow the instructions on your computer or mobile device to determine the IP address.

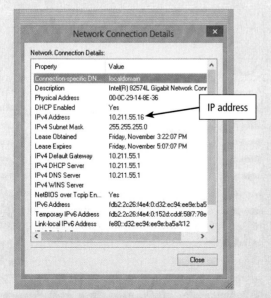

Source: Microsoft Corporation

Exercises

1. Summarize the process you used to determine your IP address.
2. What is your IP address?
3. Is it possible for a computer to have more than one IP address at the same time? Why or why not?

2 Participate in an Online Auction

Online auctions allow consumers to bid on products that other people are selling. If you are the highest bidder at the end of the bidding period, you often can arrange payment through the online auction. The following steps guide you through the process of participating in an online auction. **WARNING: Do not purchase or bid on an item if you do not intend to purchase it. If you win the auction, you legally may be obligated to provide payment for the item.**

a. Run a browser and then navigate to www.ebay.com.

b. Tap or click the link to register for a new account.

c. Enter the requested information to create the account.

d. Search for an item on which you would like to bid. If you want to browse items in a specific category instead, tap or click the link to browse for items by category.

e. When the search results appear, tap or click an item that interests you to see more details about the item.

f. Review the item details to determine whether you would like to bid on this item. If the item does not interest you, return to the search results and select another item.

g. The seller may have a "Buy It Now" option that allows you to purchase the item immediately at a predetermined price. Alternatively, you can bid on the item by making an offer. The highest bidder at the end of the auction will win the item. **Remember: If you bid on and win an item, you are obligated to provide payment.**

h. You will be notified if you are the winning bidder when the auction closes. At that time, follow the instructions to arrange to pay the seller.

i. When you are finished, sign out of eBay.

✳ How To: Your Turn

Exercises

1. What item(s) did you view? If the buyer had the "Buy It Now" option available, do you think the asking price was fair?
2. Would you purchase an item from an online auction? Why or why not?
3. What items might you post for sale on an online auction?

❸ View and Manage Data Usage

Many people have limited data plans, so it is important to know how to view the amount of data you have used on your phone or tablet when you are not connected to the Internet using a Wi-Fi connection. If you are using a phone or tablet where Wi-Fi is available, you should strongly consider using the Wi-Fi connection not only to limit data plan usage, but also to experience faster speed. If you find that your data usage is high each month, you may be able to see which apps are using the most data and adjust usage of those apps accordingly. The following steps guide you through the process of viewing and managing data usage.

a. Display the settings on your mobile device.
b. Select the option to view data usage.
c. If necessary, tap the option to display a list of apps and how much data each app uses. If necessary, select the time period for which you want to see the data usage.
d. If you notice an app using a large amount of data, tap the app to see details for that app. If necessary, disable background data transfer for the app. Background data transfer is data the app downloads and uploads even while you are not actively using the app.
e. If you want your mobile device to notify you when you are approaching your monthly data limit, set the necessary notification option and select a value under your monthly data limit in the appropriate area.

f. If you want your mobile device to turn off data (this does not include Wi-Fi) when you reach a certain limit, set the necessary option and then select a value that is just less than your monthly data limit to ensure you never reach or exceed the limit.
g. Save all changes.

Exercises

1. Do you have a data limit on your mobile data plan? If so, what is it?
2. When you enter an area with Wi-Fi, do you configure your mobile device to connect to the Wi-Fi? Why or why not?
3. Review the mobile data usage on your mobile device. Which app uses the most data? Which app uses the least data?

❹ Search for a Job Online

If you know the company for which you would like to work, you may be able to visit that company's website and search for a webpage with current job postings. If you would like to search for openings in multiple companies, consider using a job search website. The following steps guide you through the process of searching for a job online.

a. Run a browser.
b. Use a search engine to locate a job search website and then navigate to the website.
c. Many job search websites allow you to search for jobs by criteria, such as keyword, category or location. If

How To: Your Turn ✲

you are searching for a job in a specific field, enter relevant keyword(s) (i.e., software developer) or select an appropriate category (i.e., technology). To limit your search results to a specific geographical area, specify a location (i.e., Atlanta).

d. Some websites allow you to search for jobs based on additional criteria, such as company, salary, job type, education, and experience. Specify these additional criteria by performing an advanced search.

e. After entering the job search criteria, start the search.

f. When the search results appear, scroll through the results. To find out more about a particular job, tap or click the job listing.

g. If desired, follow the instructions in the job listing to apply for the job.

Exercises

1. Review three job search websites. Which one did you like the best? Why?

2. Which keywords would you use on a job search website to search for a job in your desired field?

3. Before completing this exercise, have you ever searched for a job online? Do you think it is better to search for a job using a job search website, or by vising company websites directly and viewing their job postings? Justify your answer.

❺ Send Email Messages Using Various Email Programs and Web Apps

The process required to send an email message using a computer or mobile device from various email programs and web apps is very similar. The following steps guide you through the process of sending email messages using various email programs and web apps.

a. Run the email program or navigate to the email web app on your computer or mobile device.

b. Locate and then tap or click the button to compose a new email message.

c. Type the recipient's email address in the To text box. If you are sending the email message to multiple recipients, separate each email address with a semicolon (;).

d. If you would like to send a carbon copy of the email message to one or

more people, type their email address(es) in the Cc text box (which stands for carbon copy).

e. To send a copy of the email message to someone while hiding his or her email address from the other recipients, enter his or her email address in the Bcc text box (which stands for blind carbon copy). The email recipients listed in the To or Cc text boxes will not be able to see the recipients you specified in the Bcc text box.

f. Enter a descriptive subject in the Subject text box. It is not good practice to leave the subject blank when you send an email message because the recipient's email server may place messages without a subject in a spam or junk mail folder.

g. Type the body of the email message in the appropriate area.

h. If your email program supports it, check the spelling of your email message and correct any errors found.

i. Tap or click the Send button, which sends the email message to everyone listed in the To, Cc, and Bcc text boxes.

Exercises

1. Under what circumstances might you want to send a blind carbon copy of an email message to one or more people?

2. Send an email message to your instructor and put your email address in the Cc text box. Use an appropriate subject and tell your instructor you have successfully completed this exercise.

3. Search for and evaluate three web apps that can send and receive email. Which one is your favorite, and why?

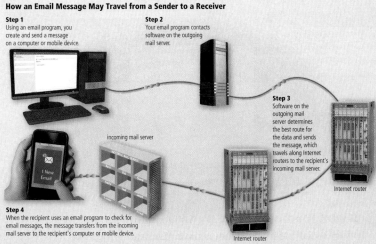

How an Email Message May Travel from a Sender to a Receiver

Step 1
Using an email program, you create and send a message on a computer or mobile device.

Step 2
Your email program contacts software on the outgoing mail server.

Step 3
Software on the outgoing mail server determines the best route for the data and sends the message, which travels along Internet routers to the recipient's incoming mail server.

Step 4
When the recipient uses an email program to check for email messages, the message transfers from the incoming mail server to the recipient's computer or mobile device.

incoming mail server

Internet router

Internet router

1 New Email

✳ Internet Research

The Internet Research exercises broaden your understanding of chapter concepts by requiring that you search for information on the web.

Discover More: Visit this chapter's premium content to **challenge yourself with additional Internet Research exercises**, which include Search Sleuth, Green Computing, Ethics in Action, You Review It, and Exploring Technology Careers.

Instructions: Use a search engine or another search tool to locate the information requested or answers to questions presented in the exercises. Describe your findings, along with the search term(s) you used and your web source(s), in the format requested by your instructor (brief report, presentation, discussion, blog post, video, or other means).

❶ Making Use of the Web
Online Social Networks and Media Sharing

Every second, an average of 5,700 Tweets and 41,000 Facebook posts are created. With these impressive numbers, it is no wonder that online social media have become ubiquitous throughout the world. Twitter, Facebook, and other online social networks, especially those featured in Mini Feature 2-2 in this chapter, are popular among users of all ages. Likewise, media sharing sites, such as YouTube, which is shown in Figure 2-11 in this chapter, are popular means of managing and sharing photos, videos, and music.

Research This: Visit two of the websites discussed in Mini Feature 2-2 or other online social networks and create a profile if you do not currently have one. What personal information is required to join? Does either website ask for personal information that you are uncomfortable sharing? How does the content of these two websites differ? Which features are beneficial for casual users, and which are targeted toward business or professional users? Then, visit two social media sites. What personal information is required to join? Are these websites supported by advertisements? Locate the instructions for posting media. Are these instructions straightforward? Do these websites impose a limit on the number and/or size of media files a user can post?

newspapers, advertisements generally are not used to fund the majority of operating costs, nor are users required to pay monthly or annual fees for basic services that they receive at no cost. One method that social media sites use to generate start-up and ongoing subsidies is through venture capitalists' funding. These investors scrutinize business plans and market trends in an effort to locate Internet start-up companies with the potential to generate substantial returns. Once the businesses are running, additional monies are needed to maintain and improve the websites. At this point, some websites display advertisements. The charge for companies to place an advertisement generally increases as the number of subscribers grows. Another method of generating income is to charge users for accessing premium content. Online dating services use this tactic successfully, for they allow people to browse online profiles free of charge but require them to pay to contact a potential dating match.

Research This: Locate venture capitalists who are seeking Internet start-up companies. Which criteria do they use to make investment decisions? Who are the successful venture capitalists, and which companies have they funded? Which types of advertisements are displayed on specific social media and online social networks? How does the content of these ads pertain to the demographics and interests of users?

Source: Facebook

❷ Social Media

Most social media companies have invested millions of dollars to develop and maintain their websites. Unlike other commercial media, such as television, radio, and

❸ Search Skills
Understand Search Results

Search results display the most relevant results first. Search results may include links to websites, news stories, images, videos, maps, and information from Wikipedia and other online databases. Results also may show links to similar searches, related people, or posts from online social networks or social media sites.

Because many search engines rely on advertising for revenue, some search results are paid advertisements. Companies and organizations may pay search providers to display links to their websites prominently in the

Internet Research ❋

search results when search text contains words relevant to their products and services. Paid ads often appear at the top or along the side of a search results page. A search results page may display an icon or use shading to specify that the search result is an advertisement.

When evaluating the reliability of search results, consider the sources of the information provided. Specialized information such as medical advice or stock performance should come from recognizable sources in those areas, while you might rely on reviews from customers when selecting a restaurant or purchasing a smartphone.

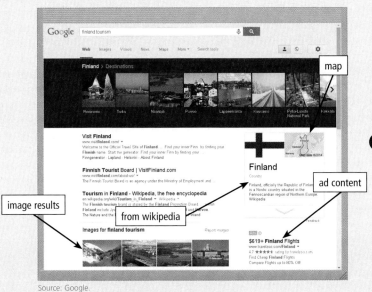

Source: Google.

Research This: Type each search text phrase listed in the paragraph below into the search boxes in Bing, Google, and Yahoo! and then take a screenshot of the first page of search results from each. Compare them, identifying ads, news, images, videos, social media results, information from online databases, search tools, and common links that both search engines returned. Which search engine's results do you find more useful in each case? Why?

Type the following search text: (1) internet service providers, (2) google corporate headquarters, (3) flights from boston to los angeles, and (4) identity theft.

4 Security

Cybercriminals may lurk in public Wi-Fi hot spots, as you learned in Secure IT 2-1 in this chapter. These thieves also may be on the lookout for customers entering their PIN at keypads near cash registers

or at ATMs. Body heat from fingers touching the keys remains for a short time, and a device with infrared-scanning capabilities can detect which keys are warmer than others. This device, which is readily available for purchase at cell phone accessories stores, snaps on the back of cell phones. It captures the thermal heat signatures, with the most recently touched keys glowing red and the cooler keys glowing light green. The thief, therefore, knows which keys comprise the PIN and the sequence of numbers by looking at the intensity of colors on the infrared scan.

Research This: How much does a thermal imaging cell phone case cost? Which brand of phone is more commonly used to capture thermal imaging? What steps can consumers take to thwart thieves using infrared scanning? Which key materials are less apt to retain the thermal signatures: metal, rubber, or plastic? Researchers from which university published a paper discussing thermal camera-based attacks?

5 Cloud Services

Collaboration and Productivity (SaaS)

Microsoft's Office Online and Google Docs are online productivity suites for creating documents, presentations, spreadsheets, and other projects. Microsoft and Google offer these apps as part of their respective cloud storage services. Because documents are stored on the cloud, you can access them from any computer or device connected to the Internet.

These are examples of SaaS (software as a service), a service of cloud computing that allows access to software using a browser, without the need to install software on a computer or device. As providers update their software, users receive the latest version upon signing in. SaaS apps often allow users to collaborate and share their work with other users. Many providers offer SaaS titles at no cost; others require users to purchase a subscription or pay a fee for the features they use.

Research This: (1) Sign up for accounts on Microsoft OneDrive and Google Drive to create and store documents with Office Online and Google Docs. With each app, create a document, share it with another user, and edit it simultaneously. What is an advantage of sharing documents over sending the files by email to collaborators? (2) How do Microsoft Office Online and Google Docs compare with Microsoft Office installed on your computer? What features are available on the cloud that are not possible on a desktop version?

✳ Critical Thinking

The Critical Thinking exercises challenge your assessment and decision-making skills by presenting real-world situations associated with chapter concepts. The Collaboration exercise should be completed with a team.

Instructions: Evaluate the situations below, using personal experiences and one or more resources available to you (such as articles on the web or in print, blogs, podcasts, videos, television, user guides, other individuals, electronics or computer stores, etc.). Perform the tasks requested in each exercise and share your deliverables in the format requested by your instructor (brief report, presentation, discussion, blog post, video, or other means).

1. Mobile Browser Comparison

Although most mobile devices include a mobile browser, users have the option of downloading and installing other browsers.

Source: Google, Inc.

Do This: Evaluate and compare reviews of at least four mobile browsers, such as Android, Firefox, Opera, Safari, or Silk. Discuss the major differences among the browsers you researched, including number and types of features, which devices are compatible, how they display webpages, security features, and the speed at which they perform. Discuss any experiences you or your classmates have had with various browsers. Include in your discussion which mobile browser you would recommend and why.

2. Acceptable Use Policy

Most businesses provide Wi-Fi and Internet access, as well as compatible computers or devices, to employees while they are at work. While the intention is for employees to use the Internet for work-related purposes, employees often find it easy to become distracted with other activities on the Internet, such as social media, checking personal email messages, playing games, or visiting websites for entertainment. These activities can degrade Internet access for others or lead to poor performance, as well as expose the company to malware or other risks. Many businesses create an acceptable use policy (AUP) that outlines how employees should use the Internet. It also may outline consequences for unauthorized Internet use.

Do This: Locate two AUPs published online. Compare the two policies and then create a policy you believe would be fair to employees of a small business. Include guidelines for Internet use during breaks, use of smartphones, and restrictions for using social media.

3. Case Study

Amateur Sports League You are the new manager for a nonprofit amateur soccer league. The league needs a website. You prepare information about the website to present to the board of directors.

Do This: First, you plan the website by determining its purpose and audience. Use a search engine to locate two sports league websites, and print their home pages. Identify what you like and do not like about each. Think about the design of your website, and select the colors you would recommend. Describe the types of media you would include on the webpage and give specific examples, such as a logo, photos or a slide show, or links to videos. Make a sketch of the home page layout, including navigation, media, and text. Research content management systems. Evaluate whether you could use a preformatted template to meet your needs, and find what types of customization options are available. Determine whether you need a separate ISP for hosting the website, and calculate the costs. List ways you will maintain and update the site content. Compile your findings.

Collaboration

4. Website Evaluation

You and three teammates want to open a new chain of fast food sandwich shops. You envision a website that includes a menu, nutritional options, and allergy information, and that has regular promotions and special offers.

Do This: With your teammates, evaluate existing fast food and sandwich websites by comparing the advantages and disadvantages of each. Assign each member the task of evaluating one chain. Team members should print the home page of the assigned website and evaluate each restaurants' website. Pay particular attention to the following areas: (1) design, (2) ease of use, (3) menu, (4) nutritional information, (5) allergy information, (6) special offers, (7) location information and directions, and (8) hours and contact information. Summarize your evaluations and rank the websites in terms of their effectiveness. Be sure to include brief explanations supporting your rankings.

People use or interact with a variety of computers or mobile devices every day.

"I use my laptop at home and school and an all-in-one at work. I send messages and access the Internet on my smartphone, take photos with my digital camera, and read books on my e-book reader. What more do I need to know about computers and mobile devices?"

While you may be familiar with some of the content in this chapter, do you know how to …

- Protect computers and devices from malware infections?
- Determine which mobile computer, desktop, or mobile device to purchase?
- Safely use an ATM?
- Rent a movie using a DVD kiosk?
- Help eliminate e-waste?
- Use a mobile device safely in a public area?
- Identify a DisplayPort or an HDMI port?
- Pair Bluetooth devices?
- Connect your phone to a Wi-Fi network to save data charges?
- Protect your hardware from theft, vandalism, and failure?
- Prevent technology-related tendonitis or CTS?
- Tell if you are addicted to technology?
- Manage power for your computers and mobile devices

In this chapter, you will discover how to perform these tasks along with much more information essential to this course. For additional content available that accompanies this chapter, visit the free resources and premium content. Refer to the Preface and the Intro chapter for information about how to access these and other additional instructor-assigned support materials.

© iStockPhoto / German

✔ Objectives

After completing this chapter, you will be able to:

1 Describe the characteristics and uses of laptops, tablets, desktops, and all-in-ones
2 Describe the characteristics and types of servers
3 Differentiate among POS terminals, ATMs, and self-service kiosks
4 Describe cloud computing and identify its uses
5 Describe the characteristics and uses of smartphones, digital cameras, portable and digital media players, e-book readers, and wearable devices
6 Describe the characteristics of and ways to interact with game devices, including gamepads, joysticks and wheels, dance pads, and motion-sensing controllers
7 Identify uses of embedded computers
8 Differentiate a port from a connector, identify various ports and connectors, and differentiate among Bluetooth, Wi-Fi, and NFC wireless device connections
9 Identify safeguards against hardware theft and vandalism and hardware failure
10 Discuss ways to prevent health-related injuries and disorders caused from technology use, and describe ways to design a workplace ergonomically

Computers and Mobile Devices

BTW
Peripheral Devices
A *peripheral device* is a device you connect to a computer or mobile device to expand its capabilities. Examples include a keyboard, mouse, microphone, monitor, printer, scanner, external hard drive, webcam, and speakers.

As Chapter 1 discussed, a **computer** is an electronic device, operating under the control of instructions stored in its own memory, that can accept data (input), process the data according to specified rules, produce information (output), and store the information for future use. A **mobile device** is a computing device small enough to hold in your hand. Types of computers and mobiles devices include laptops, tablets, and desktops; servers and terminals; smartphones, digital cameras, e-book readers, portable and digital media players, and wearable devices; game devices; and embedded computers. Figure 3-1 shows a variety of computers and mobile devices.

In addition to discussing features, functions, and purchasing guidelines of computers and mobile devices, this chapter also presents ways to connect peripheral devices, protect computers and mobile devices from theft and failure, and minimize your health risks while using computers and mobile devices.

Mobile Computers and Desktops

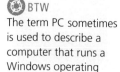
BTW
The term PC sometimes is used to describe a computer that runs a Windows operating system.

A **mobile computer** is a portable personal computer, such as a laptop or tablet, designed so that a user easily can carry it from place to place, whereas a desktop is designed to be in a stationary location. A *personal computer* (PC) is a mobile computer or desktop that can perform all of its input, processing, output, and storage activities by itself and is intended to be used by one person at a time. Personal computers often are differentiated by the type of operating system they use, with Windows and Mac operating systems leading the market share. Companies such as Acer, Dell, Lenovo, HP (Hewlett-Packard), and Samsung sell personal computers that use the Windows operating system, and Apple sells personal computers that use the Mac operating system. Other operating systems for personal computers include Linux and Chrome OS.

Read Secure IT 3-1 for suggestions about how to avoid malware infections on your computers and mobile devices.

Computers and Mobile Devices

Figure 3-1   Computers and mobile devices are available in a variety of shapes and sizes.

SECURE IT 3-1

Avoid Malware Infections

Some websites contain tempting offers to download free games and music, install toolbars that offer convenience, enter contests, and receive coupons on your computers or mobile devices. Danger, however, may lurk in those files, for they secretly could install malware with effects ranging from a mild annoyance to a severe problem such as identity theft. Recall that malware is malicious software that acts without your knowledge and deliberately alters operations of your computer or mobile device. As a general rule, do not install or download unfamiliar software. Follow these guidelines to minimize the chance of your computer or mobile device becoming infected with malware:

- **Social media:** Malware authors often focus on social media, with the goal of stealing personal information, such as passwords, profiles, contact lists, and credit card account details. Their websites urge unsuspecting users to take surveys, tap or click links to obtain free merchandise and games, and download antivirus programs. Ignore these deceitful tactics.

- **Email:** Spam (unsolicited email messages) can be loaded with malware, but even email messages from friends can be a culprit. If the message does not contain a subject line or contains links or an attachment, exercise caution. One option is to save the attachment to your computer so that antivirus software can scan the file for possible malware before you open it. Your best practice is to avoid opening suspicious messages at all costs.

- **Flash memory storage:** Colleagues and friends may hand you a USB flash drive or memory card with software, photos, and other files. Scan these media with security software before opening any files.

- **Pop-up windows:** At times, a window may open suddenly (called a pop-up window), with a warning that your computer is infected with a virus or that a security breach has occurred, and then make an urgent request to download free software to scan your computer or mobile device and correct the alleged problem. Beware. Many of these offers actually are rogue security software that will infect a computer.

- **Websites:** Websites you visit or pop-up windows may present instructions to download new software or update current programs installed on a computer or mobile device. If you are uncertain of their legitimacy, exit and research the software by reading reviews online before you decide to install it.

- **Software:** Occasionally, some seemingly safe software attempts to install malware. Even worse, some software touted as offering malware protection actually installs more malware. Always obtain software from reputable sources and, if possible, update software directly from manufacturers' websites. Consider using the custom installation option to ensure that only the desired software is installed. Read the permissions dialog boxes that are displayed on your screen before tapping or clicking the OK or Agree buttons. If you are uncertain about the messages you are viewing, cancel the installation.

- **Smartphones:** Malware creators are targeting smartphones, particularly those using the Android operating system. While an estimated 80 percent of all smartphones are unprotected now, savvy users are obtaining protection from malware attacks. Read reviews before downloading antimalware apps from trusted sources.

 Consider This: What online activities might cause malware to be installed on your computer? Which specific websites provide reputable antimalware apps for mobile devices? What new techniques will you use to avoid malware?

Figure 3-2   Shown here is a partial motherboard in a laptop.
© rawgroup / Fotolia

motherboard

 CONSIDER THIS

What is inside a personal computer?

The electronic components and circuitry of a personal computer usually are part of or are connected to a motherboard (Figure 3-2). A *motherboard*, sometimes called a system board, is the main circuit board of the personal computer. Many electronic components attach to the motherboard; others are built into it. Two main components on the motherboard are the processor and memory. Many motherboards also integrate sound, video, and networking capabilities. A *processor*, also called a *CPU* (central processing unit), is the electronic component that interprets and carries out the basic instructions that operate a computer. Memory consists of electronic components that store instructions waiting to be executed and data needed by those instructions.

Internet Research

What is a computer chip?

Search for: computer chip

Laptops, Tablets, and Other Mobile Computers

A **laptop**, also called a *notebook computer*, is a thin, lightweight mobile computer with a screen in its lid and a keyboard in its base (Figure 3-3). Designed to fit on your lap and for easy transport, most laptops weigh up to 7 pounds (varying by manufacturer and specifications) and can be as powerful as the average desktop.

Laptops have input devices, such as a keyboard, touchpad, and webcam; output devices, such as a screen and speakers; a storage device(s), such as a hard drive and maybe an optical disc drive; and usually built-in wireless communications capability. Some laptops have touch screens. Most can operate on batteries or a power supply or both. Read Ethics & Issues 3-1 to consider issues related to laptops and other devices with cameras.

BTW
Technology Innovator
Discover More: Visit this chapter's free resources to learn about Samsung (multinational technology company).

traditional laptop

ultrathin laptop

Figure 3-3 Traditional laptops weigh more than ultrathin laptops.
© Sergey Peterman / Shutterstock.com; © iStockphoto / Skip Odonnell; Microsoft; Apple, Inc.

⊛ ETHICS & ISSUES 3-1

What Punishment for Webcam Spying Is Appropriate?

Microphones, digital cameras, and webcams have many practical and harmless uses. These technologies also can leave you open to spying. For example, one school district used software, which was supposed to track the school-distributed laptops in case of theft, to take photos and screen captures of students. In another instance, a person noticed that when she gave a customer service rep access to her computer, he turned on her webcam without asking for her permission.

Cybercriminals can use spy tools that take photos, or record video or audio, without turning on a light or other notification that

indicates your camera or microphone is in use. The Flame virus is one way for spy tools to infect your computer. Security experts recommend using a sticker to cover your webcam, and inserting a dummy plug in the microphone port when you are not using it. These technologies also allow people to take photos or videos in a public setting and share them without your knowledge. A director at the American Civil Liberties Union stated that when you are in a public place, people have the right to photograph you. Privacy advocates criticize *Google Street View*, however, which takes images captured using moving vehicles equipped with GPS and cameras and then creates a

panoramic view of an area, including people entering and exiting buildings or relaxing on a beach.

Many states' laws do not cover these types of acts. Massachusetts, however, recently passed a law that made secretly taking photos or videos that focused on people's private body parts a criminal offense. Lawmakers continue to debate and expand current laws, as well as pass new ones.

Consider This: Should webcam spying punishments be comparable to other types of spying? Why or why not? What kind of privacy should you expect when you are in a public place?

Ultrathin laptops weigh less than traditional laptops, usually have a longer battery life, and generally run the Windows operating system. In order to minimize their thickness, many ultrathin laptops have fewer ports than traditional laptops, do not include an optical disc drive, and often require the use of special dongles to attach cables that connect to external displays or a network. (Recall that a dongle is a small device that connects to a computer and enables additional functions when attached.)

BTW
Ultrabooks
An ultrathin laptop that uses a low-power Intel processor often is called an *ultrabook*.

Tablets Usually smaller than a laptop but larger than a phone, a **tablet** is a thin, lighter-weight mobile computer that has a touch screen.

Two popular form factors (shapes and sizes) of tablets are the slate and convertible (Figure 3-4). Resembling a letter-sized pad, a *slate tablet* is a type of tablet that does not contain a physical keyboard. A *convertible tablet* is a tablet that has a screen it its lid and a keyboard in its base, with the lid and base connected by a swivel-type hinge. You can use a convertible tablet like a traditional laptop, or you can rotate the display and fold it down over the keyboard so that it looks like a slate tablet. As with laptops, tablets run on batteries or a power supply or both; however, batteries in a tablet typically last longer than those in laptops.

Some tablets include a *stylus*, which looks like a small ink pen, that you can use instead of a fingertip to enter data, make selections, or draw on a touch screen. A stylus may include buttons you can press to simulate clicking a mouse. As an alternative to interacting with the touch screen, some users prefer to purchase a separate physical keyboard that attaches to or wirelessly communicates with the tablet (shown with the slate tablet in Figure 3-4).

Tablets are useful especially for taking notes in class, at meetings, at conferences, and in other forums where the standard laptop is not practical. Because slate tablets can have a more durable construction, they often are used in the medical field and other areas where exposure to germs, heat, humidity, dust, and other contaminants is greater.

 BTW

Pens
Some tablet manufacturers refer to a stylus as a pen.

Figure 3-4 Examples of slate and convertible tablets.
Courtesy of Microsoft; © iStockPhoto / rasslava

⚙ **CONSIDER THIS**

What is a phablet?
Some manufacturers use the term, *phablet*, to refer to a device that combines features of a smartphone with a tablet (Figure 3-5). These devices are larger than smartphones but smaller than full-sized tablets. The screen on a phablet usually measures five to seven inches diagonally. Some include a stylus.

Figure 3-5 A phablet combines features of a smartphone and a tablet.
© iStockPhoto / Krystian Nawrocki

Handheld Computers

A *handheld computer* is a computer small enough to fit in one hand. Many handheld computers communicate wirelessly with other devices or computers. Some handheld computers have miniature or specialized keyboards. Others have a touch screen and also include a stylus for input.

Many handheld computers are industry-specific and serve the needs of mobile employees, such as parcel delivery people or warehouse employees (Figure 3-6), whose jobs require them to move from place to place. Handheld computers often send data wirelessly to central office computers.

Figure 3-6 This handheld computer is a lightweight computer that enables warehouse employees to take inventory and check supplies.
© iStockphoto / Ermin Gutenberger

Mini Feature 3-1: Mobile Computer Buyer's Guide

If you need computing capability while traveling and during lectures or meetings, you may find a laptop or tablet to be an appropriate choice. Read Mini Feature 3-1 for tips to consider when purchasing a mobile computer.

 MINI FEATURE 3-1

Mobile Computer Buyer's Guide

© iStockPhoto / vtls

With the abundance of mobile computer manufacturers, research each before making a purchase. The following are purchasing considerations unique to mobile computers.

1. **Determine which mobile computer form factor fits your needs.** Consider a tablet or ultrathin laptop if you require a lightweight device and the most mobility. If you require additional ports or want the computer's capabilities to be more comparable to a desktop, consider purchasing a traditional laptop.

2. **Consider a mobile computer with a sufficiently large screen.** Laptops and tablets are available with various screen sizes. For example, most traditional and ultrathin laptop screens range in size from 11 to 18 inches, while most tablet screens range in size from 7 to 12 inches.

3. **Experiment with different keyboards and pointing devices.** Mobile computers often vary in size, and for that reason have different keyboard layouts. Familiarize yourself with the keyboard layout of the computer you want to purchase, and make sure it is right for you. If you have large fingers, for example, you should not purchase a computer with a small, condensed keyboard. Laptops typically include a touchpad to control the pointer. Tablets have a touch screen and an on-screen keyboard.

4. **Consider processor, memory, and storage upgrades at the time of purchase.** As with a desktop, upgrading a mobile computer's memory and internal storage may be less expensive at the time of initial purchase. Some internal storage is custom designed for mobile computer manufacturers, meaning an upgrade might not be available in the future.

5. **The availability of built-in ports and slots is important.** Determine which ports and slots (discussed later in this chapter) you require on the mobile computer. If you plan to transfer photos from a digital camera using a memory card, consider a mobile computer with a built-in card slot compatible with your digital camera's memory card. If you plan to connect devices such as a printer or USB flash drive to your mobile computer, consider purchasing one with a sufficient number of USB ports. In addition, evaluate mobile computers with ports enabling you to connect an external monitor.

6. **If you plan to use your mobile computer for a long time without access to an electrical outlet, or if the battery life for the mobile computer you want to purchase is not sufficient, consider purchasing a second battery.** Some mobile computers, such as most tablets and ultrathin laptops, have built-in batteries that can be replaced only by a qualified technician. In that case, you might look into options for external battery packs or power sources.

7. **Purchase a well-padded and well-designed carrying case that is comfortable and ergonomic.** An amply padded carrying case will protect your mobile computer from the bumps it may receive while traveling. A well-designed carrying case will have room for accessories such as USB flash drives, pens, and paperwork. Although a mobile computer may be small enough to fit in a handbag, make sure that the bag has sufficient padding to protect the computer. Test the carrying case with the laptop inside to ensure it is comfortable and ergonomic.

8. **If you plan to connect your mobile computer to a video projector, make sure the mobile computer is compatible with the video projector.** You should check, for example, to be sure that your mobile computer will allow you to display an image on the screen and projection device at the same time. Also, ensure that the mobile computer has the ports required or that you have the necessary dongle and cables to connect to the video projector.

Discover More: Visit this chapter's free resources to learn more about mobile computer manufacturers, form factors, screens, keyboards, pointing devices, upgrades, batteries, carrying cases, and video projectors.

☀ **Consider This:** Based on your current computing needs, should you purchase a traditional laptop, ultrathin laptop, or tablet? What are the specifications of the mobile computer you would purchase?

Desktops and All-in-Ones

A **desktop**, or desktop computer, is a personal computer designed to be in a stationary location, where all of its components fit on or under a desk or table (Figure 3-7). Components that typically occupy space outside of a desktop include peripheral devices such as a keyboard, mouse, and webcam (input devices); speakers and printer (output devices); external hard drive (storage device); and possibly a router and/or modem (communications devices). Depending on the form factor of the desktop, it may also require an external monitor.

Some people use the term, *system unit*, to refer to the case that contains and protects the motherboard, internal hard drive, memory, and other electronic components of the computer from damage. A desktop may have a system unit tower that is a separate device from a monitor. A *tower*, which is made of metal or plastic, is a frame that houses the system unit on a desktop. Towers are available in a variety of form factors. Although they can range in height from 12 inches to 30 inches or more, the trend is toward smaller desktop tower form factors. An **all-in-one** (AIO) or *all-in-one desktop*, by contrast, does not have a tower and instead houses the display, system unit, and possibly an optical drive, in the same case.

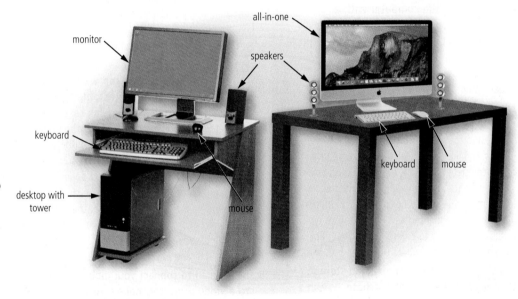

Figure 3-7 The desktop with a tower shown in this figure is a Windows computer, and the all-in-one is a Mac computer.
© George Dolgikh / Shutterstock.com; © iStockphoto / Skip Odonnell; © iStockphoto / Evgeny Kuklev; © Cengage Learning; Microsoft; Apple, Inc.

⊛ CONSIDER THIS

Who uses desktops?
Home and business users who do not require the portability of a mobile computer may work with desktops for their everyday computing needs. Gaming enthusiasts often choose a *gaming desktop*, which offers high-quality audio, video, and graphics with optimal performance for sophisticated single-user and networked or Internet multiplayer games. Power users may work with a high-end desktop, sometimes called a *workstation*, that is designed to handle intense calculations and sophisticated graphics. For example, architects use powerful desktops to design buildings and homes, and graphic artists use them to create computer-animated special effects for full-length motion pictures and video games. Some users configure a desktop to function as a server on a network (servers are discussed later in this chapter).

Mini Feature 3-2: Desktop Buyer's Guide

Desktops are a suitable option if you work mostly in one place and have plenty of space in a work area. Read Mini Feature 3-2 for tips to consider when purchasing a desktop.

 **MINI FEATURE 3-2**

Desktop Buyer's Guide

Today, desktop manufacturers emphasize desktop style by offering bright colors, trendy displays, and theme-based towers so that the computer looks attractive if it is in an area of high visibility. If you have decided that a desktop is most suited to your technology needs, the next step is to determine specific software, hardware, peripheral devices, and services to purchase, as well as where to buy the computer. The following considerations will help you determine the appropriate desktop to purchase.

1. **Determine the specific software to use on the desktop.** Decide which software contains the features necessary for the tasks you want to perform. Your hardware requirements depend on the minimum requirements of the software you plan to use on the desktop.

2. **Know the system requirements of the operating system.** Determine the operating system you want to use because this also dictates hardware requirements. If, however, you purchase a new desktop, chances are it will include the latest version of your preferred operating system (Windows, Mac OS, or Linux).

3. **Look for bundled software.** Purchasing software at the same time you purchase a desktop may be less expensive than purchasing the software at a later date.

4. **Avoid purchasing the least powerful desktop available.** Technology changes rapidly, which means a desktop that seems powerful enough today may not serve your computing needs in the future. Purchasing a desktop with the most memory, largest hard drive capacity, and fastest processor you can afford will help delay obsolescence.

5. **Consider upgrades to the keyboard, mouse, monitor, printer, microphone, and speakers.** You use these peripheral devices to interact with the desktop, so make sure they meet your standards.

6. **Consider a touch screen monitor.** A touch screen monitor will enable you to interact with the latest operating systems and apps using touch input.

7. **Evaluate all-in-ones, which may be less expensive than purchasing a tower and monitor separately.** In addition, all-in-ones take up less space and often look more attractive than desktops with separate towers.

8. **If you are buying a new desktop, you have several purchasing options:** buy directly from a school bookstore, a local computer dealer, or a large retail store, or order from a vendor by mail, phone, or the web. Each purchasing option has its advantages. Explore each option to find the best combination of price and service.

9. **Be aware of additional costs.** Along with the desktop itself, you also may need to make extra purchases. For example, you might purchase computer furniture, an uninterruptable power supply (UPS) or surge protector (discussed later in the chapter), an external hard drive, a printer, a router, or a USB flash drive.

10. **If you use your computer for business or require fast resolution of major computer problems, consider purchasing an extended warranty or a service plan through a local dealer or third-party company.** Most extended warranties cover the repair and replacement of computer components beyond the standard warranty.

Discover More: Visit this chapter's free resources to learn more about desktop manufacturers, software, upgrades, touch screen monitor options, all-in-ones, hidden costs, and warranties.

✳ **Consider This:** Shop around for a desktop that meets your current needs. Which desktop would you purchase? Why?

Table 3-1 Dedicated Servers

Type	Main Service Provided
Application server	Stores and runs apps
Backup server	Backs up and restores files, folders, and media
Database server	Stores and provides access to a database
Domain name server	Stores domain names and their corresponding IP addresses
File server (or storage server)	Stores and manages files
FTP server	Stores files for user upload or download via FTP
Game server	Provides a central location for online gaming
Home server	Provides storage, Internet connections, or other services to computers and devices in a household
List server	Stores and manages email lists
Mail server	Stores and delivers email messages
Network server	Manages network traffic
Print server	Manages printers and documents being printed
Web server	Stores and delivers requested webpages to a computer via a browser

© Cengage Learning

Servers

A **server** is a computer dedicated to providing one or more services to other computers or devices on a network. Services provided by servers include storing content and controlling access to hardware, software, and other resources on a network. In many cases, a server accesses data, information, and programs on another server. In other cases, personal computers, devices, or terminals (discussed in the next section) access data, information, and programs on a server. Servers can support from two to several thousand connected computers or devices at the same time.

Some servers, called dedicated servers, perform a specific service and can be placed with other dedicated servers to perform multiple services (Table 3-1). Each type of dedicated server uses software designed specifically to manage its service. Dedicated servers typically require a faster processor, more memory, and additional storage.

Servers typically include a processor, memory, storage, and network connections. Depending on its function, a server may or may not require a monitor or an input device. Some servers are controlled from remote computers. Form factors for servers include rack server, blade server, and tower server, which are shown in Figure 3-8 and briefly described below.

- A *rack server*, sometimes called a rack-mounted server, is a server that is housed in a slot (bay) on a metal frame (rack). A rack can contain multiple servers, each in a different bay. The rack is fastened in place to a flat surface.
- A *blade server* is a server in the form of a single circuit board, or blade. The individual blades insert in a blade server chassis that can hold many blades. Like a rack server, the chassis is fastened in place to a flat surface.
- A *tower server* is a server built into an upright cabinet (tower) that stands alone. The tower can be similar in size and shape to a desktop tower or larger.

✳ CONSIDER THIS

Which server should you use?

Home or small business users and organizations with ample floor space often choose tower servers. (Some home users even use a desktop tower or powerful laptop to act as a home server.) Data centers and other organizations looking to conserve floor space often choose rack servers or blade servers. Organizations that require a large quantity of servers usually opt for blade servers.

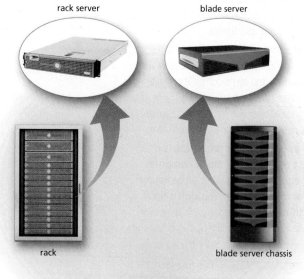

rack server   blade server

rack   blade server chassis

tower server

Figure 3-8 Shown here are a rack server, blade server, and tower server.
© iStockphoto / Godfried Edelman; © iStockphoto / luismmolina; © iStockphoto / evirgen;
© iStockphoto / Alexander Shirokov; © iStockphoto / luismmolina

Some organizations use virtualization to improve utilization of technology. *Virtualization* is the practice of sharing or pooling computing resources, such as servers and storage devices. *Server virtualization* uses software to enable a physical server to emulate the hardware and computing capabilities of one or more servers, known as virtual servers. Users can use software to configure the storage, processing power, memory, operating system, and other characteristics of virtual servers. From the end user's point of view, a virtual server behaves just like a physical server. The advantages are that a virtual server can be created and configured quickly, does not require a new physical server, and is easier to manage. Cloud computing, discussed later in this chapter, uses server virtualization.

Major corporations use server farms, mainframes, or other types of servers for business activities to process everyday transactions (Figure 3-9). A *server farm* is a network of several servers together in a single location. Server farms make it possible to combine the power of multiple servers. A *mainframe* is a large, expensive, powerful server that can handle hundreds or thousands of connected users simultaneously. Enterprises use server farms, mainframes, or other large servers to bill millions of customers, prepare payroll for thousands of employees, and manage millions of items in inventory.

Figure 3-9 Server farms and mainframes can handle thousands of connected computers and process millions of instructions per second.
© Sashkin / Shutterstock.com

Terminals

A *terminal* is a computer, usually with limited processing power, that enables users to send data to and/or receive information from a server, or host computer. The host computer processes the data and then, if necessary, sends information (output) back to the terminal. Terminals may include a monitor and/or touch screen, keyboard, and memory.

A *thin client* is a terminal that looks like a desktop but has limited capabilities and components. Because thin clients typically do not contain a hard drive, they run programs and access data on a network or the Internet. Public locations, such as libraries and schools, and enterprises sometimes use thin clients because they cost less, are easier to maintain, last longer, use less power, and are less susceptible to malware attacks than desktops.

Special-purpose terminals perform specific tasks and contain features uniquely designed for use in a particular industry. Three widely used special-purpose terminals are point-of-sale (POS) terminals, ATMs, and self-service kiosks.

Point-of-Sale Terminals

The location in a retail or grocery store where a consumer pays for goods or services is the point of sale (POS). Most retail stores use a *POS terminal* to record purchases, process credit or debit cards, and update inventory.

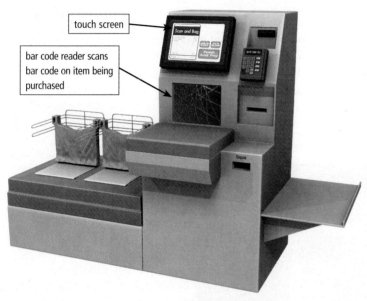

touch screen

bar code reader scans bar code on item being purchased

Figure 3-10 Many grocery stores offer self-service checkouts, where consumers use POS terminals to scan purchases, scan their store or saver card and coupons, and then pay for the goods.
© Valentyna Chukhlyebova / Shutterstock; © iStockPhoto / 00one

In a grocery store, the POS terminal is a combination of an electronic cash register, bar code reader, and printer (Figure 3-10). A *bar code reader* is an input device that uses laser beams to read bar codes on products. When the checkout clerk or customer scans the bar code on the grocery item, the computer uses the manufacturer name and item numbers to look up the price of the item and the complete product name. Then, the price of the item shows on the display device, the name of the item and its price print on a receipt, and the item being sold is recorded so that the inventory can be updated. Thus, the output from a POS terminal serves as input to other computers to maintain sales records, update inventory, verify credit, and perform other activities associated with the sales transactions that are critical to running the business. Some POS terminals are Internet capable, which allows updates to inventory at geographically separate locations.

Many POS terminals handle credit card or debit card payments. After swiping your card through the reader, the POS terminal connects to a system that authenticates the purchase. Once the transaction is approved, the terminal prints a receipt for the customer.

BTW

Technology Trend
Discover More: Visit this chapter's free resources to learn about Bitcoin (digital currency).

ATMs

An *ATM* (automated teller machine) is a self-service banking terminal that connects to a host computer through a network (Figure 3-11). Banks place ATMs in public locations, including grocery stores, convenience stores, retail outlets, shopping malls, sports and concert venues, and gas stations, so that customers can access their bank accounts conveniently.

Figure 3-11 An ATM is a self-service banking terminal that allows customers to access their bank accounts.
© bankerwin / Fotolia

Using an ATM, people withdraw and deposit money, transfer funds, or inquire about an account balance. Some ATMs have a touch screen; others have special buttons or keypads for entering data. To access a bank account, you insert a plastic bank card in the ATM's card reader. The ATM asks you to enter a numeric password, called a *PIN* (personal identification number), which verifies that you are the holder of the bank card. When your transaction is complete, the ATM prints a receipt for your records. Read Secure IT 3-2 for ATM safety tips.

SECURE IT 3-2

ATM Safety

Visiting an ATM to withdraw or deposit money is convenient, but it also is ripe with potential for criminal activity. Avoid being a victim by exercising common sense and following these guidelines.

- **Location:** Choose an ATM in a well-lit public area away from bushes and dividers and near the entrance of a building. If using a drive-up ATM, keep the engine running and doors locked, roll windows up while waiting for the ATM to process your request, and leave adequate room to maneuver between your vehicle and the one in the lane in front of you. Observe your surroundings and be suspicious of people sitting in vehicles or loitering nearby.

- **ATM card and PIN:** Handle the ATM card like cash by keeping it in a safe location and storing it in a protective sleeve. Do not write the PIN on the back of the card or store it in a text file on your smartphone; instead, memorize the numbers. (For information about password manager apps, read Secure IT 5-3 in Chapter 5.) Report a lost or stolen card immediately.

- **Transaction:** Minimize time by having the ATM card ready as you approach the machine. Do not allow people to watch

your activity. Cover the keypad or screen with one hand as you enter the PIN, and use your body to block as much of the area as possible. If the ATM screen appears different, behaves unusually, or offers options with which you are unfamiliar or uncomfortable, cancel the transaction and leave the area.

- **Be suspicious of skimmers:** Thieves can capture a credit card number and PIN by placing a *skimmer* on an ATM (shown in the figure) or on other self-service stations, such as gas pumps, where users swipe their credit cards for payment. Sophisticated skimmers are Bluetooth enabled or are entire panels placed directly on top of the ATM faces and are virtually undetectable. Less-technical devices are false card readers secured to the card slot with double-sided tape and a hidden camera or an overlay on the keypad. Many ATMs have security stickers informing customers to notify attendants if the seal is broken.

- **Valuables:** Expensive clothes and jewelry can be incentives to potential assailants. Dress modestly and leave jewels at home.

- **Exiting:** Do not count cash in public; immediately put it in your pocket or fold it in your hand. If you receive a receipt, take

skimmer

© photobeginner / Shutterstock

it with you and do not discard it in a trash can near the area. As you leave, be certain you are not being followed. If you suspect someone is tracking you, immediately walk to a populated area or business, or drive to a police or fire station.

- **Statements:** Review your balances and bank statements frequently. Be certain all deposits and withdrawals are listed, and look for unusual or unfamiliar activity.

Consider This: Which of these tips do you follow, and how will you change your behavior the next time you visit an ATM or other self-service stations? Which ATMs in your neighborhood appear to be in safe locations?

Self-Service Kiosks

A self-service *kiosk* is a freestanding terminal that usually has a touch screen for user interaction. Table 3-2 identifies several widely used self-service kiosks. Because users interact with self-service kiosks independently, without a salesperson nearby, it is important the kiosk is simple and easy to use. In many cases, a web app or mobile app can extend or enhance the capability of the kiosk. For example, you can reserve an item via the app on a computer or mobile device and then use the kiosk to finalize the transaction.

 **Internet Research**

What is a mobile boarding pass?

Search for: mobile boarding pass

Table 3-2   Self-Service Kiosks

Type	Typical Services Provided
Financial kiosk	Pay bills, add minutes to phone plans, add money to prepaid cards, and perform other financial activities.
Photo kiosk	Print photos from digital images. Some allow editing of digital photos. Users may print directly at the kiosk or may send an order to a photo lab to be printed.
Ticket kiosk	Print tickets. Located in airports, amusement parks, movie theaters, rental companies, and train stations.
Vending kiosk	Dispense item after payment is received. Examples include DVD rentals and license plate renewals.
Visitor kiosk	Manage and track visitors upon check-in. Located in businesses, schools, hospitals, and other areas where access is controlled or registration is required.

© Cengage Learning

touch screen

insert returned DVDs in this slot

Figure 3-12 A DVD kiosk is a self-service DVD rental terminal.
Courtesy of Redbox

A *DVD kiosk*, for example, is a self-service DVD rental machine that connects to a host computer through a network (Figure 3-12). DVD kiosks are associated with a particular vendor. To rent a movie online, for example, a customer establishes an account or connects to an existing account on the vendor's website, selects the desired movie, and then chooses a nearby DVD kiosk where the movie will be picked up. Customers also usually can select movies directly at the DVD kiosk via a touch screen or some other input device on the kiosk. After presenting identifying information and swiping a credit card through the reader, the DVD kiosk dispenses the rented movie to the customer. The customer returns it to any of the vendor's nationwide DVD kiosks, at which time the customer's account is charged a fee based on the time elapsed.

Supercomputers

Internet Research

How is the fastest supercomputer used?

Search for: fastest supercomputer

A *supercomputer* is the fastest, most powerful computer — and the most expensive (Figure 3-13). Supercomputers are capable of processing many trillions of instructions in a single second. With weights that exceed 100 tons, these computers can store more than 20,000 times the data and information of an average desktop.

Applications requiring complex, sophisticated mathematical calculations use supercomputers. For example, large-scale simulations and applications in medicine, aerospace, automotive design, online banking, weather forecasting, nuclear energy research, and petroleum exploration use a supercomputer.

Figure 3-13 Supercomputers can process more than one quadrillion instructions in a single second.
Los Alamos National Laboratory

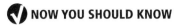 **NOW YOU SHOULD KNOW** ─────────────────────────

Be sure you understand the material presented in the sections titled Computers and Mobile Devices, Mobile Computers and Desktops, Servers, Terminals, and Supercomputers, as it relates to the chapter objectives. *Now you should know . . .*

- What you should consider when purchasing a desktop or mobile computer (Objective 1)

- When you would use specific types of servers (Objective 2)

- How you use a POS terminal, ATM, and self-service kiosk (Objective 3)

Discover More: Visit this chapter's premium content for practice quiz opportunities.

Cloud Computing

Cloud computing refers to an environment that provides resources and services accessed via the Internet (Figure 3-14). Resources include email messages, schedules, music, photos, videos, games, websites, programs, web apps, servers, storage, and more. Services include accessing software, storing files online, and configuring an environment of servers for optimal performance. That is, instead of accessing these resources and services locally, you access them on the cloud. For example, you use cloud computing capabilities when you store or access documents, photos, videos, and other media online; use programs and apps online (i.e., email, productivity, games, etc.); and share ideas, opinions, and content with others online (i.e., online social networks).

BTW
The Cloud
The cloud-shaped symbol, which today universally represents cloud computing, stems from early diagrams that visually portrayed the Internet as a cloud, intangible and widespread.

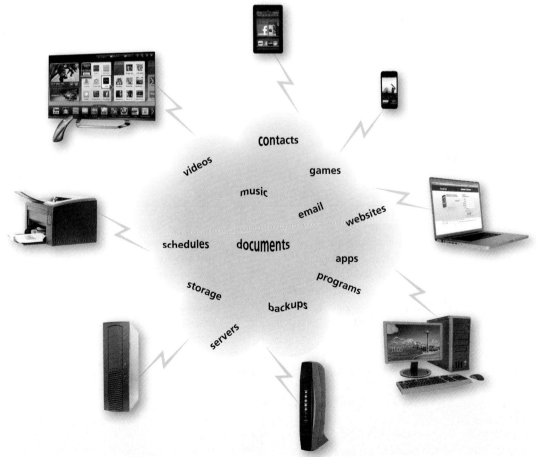

Figure 3-14 Users access resources on the cloud through their Internet connections.

© iStockphoto / Petar Chernaev; © iStockphoto / cotesebastien; © Cengage Learning; © iStockphoto / Jill Fromer; © Cengage Learning; © iStockphoto / 123 render; © Cengage Learning; © Pablo Eder / Shutterstock.com; © Peter Gudella / Shutterstock.com; © Mr.Reborn55 / Shutterstock.com; Courtesy of LG Electronics USA Inc.; © Cengage Learning

Businesses use cloud computing to more efficiently manage resources, such as servers and programs, by shifting usage and consumption of these resources from a local environment to the Internet. For example, an employee working during the day in California could use computing resources located in an office in Paris that is closed for the evening. When the company uses the computing resources, it pays a fee that is based on the amount of computing time and other resources it consumes, much in the way that consumers pay utility companies for the amount of electricity used.

Cloud computing allows a company to diversify its network and server infrastructure. Some cloud computing services automatically add more network and server capacity to a company's website as demand for services of the website increases. The network and server capacity may be duplicated around the world so that, for example, an outage of a single server does not affect the company's operations.

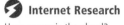 **Internet Research**

How secure is the cloud?

Search for: cloud privacy issues

 CONSIDER THIS

Are all cloud services available to everyone?
Some cloud services are public and others are private. A public cloud is made available free or for a fee to the general public or a large group, usually by a cloud service provider. A private cloud is dedicated to a single organization. Some cloud services are hybrid, combining two or more cloud types.

Discover More: Visit this chapter's free resources to learn more about business uses of cloud computing and cloud service providers.

Mobile Devices

A mobile device is a computing device small enough to hold in your hand. Because of their reduced size, the screens on mobile devices are small — often between 3 and 5 inches. Popular types of mobile devices are smartphones, digital cameras, portable and digital media players, e-book readers, and wearable devices. Read Ethics & Issues 3-2 to consider issues related to recycling computers and mobile devices.

ETHICS & ISSUES 3-2

Should Recycling of Electronics Be Made Easier?

As technology advances and prices fall, many people think of computers and mobile devices as disposable. Worldwide, consumers generate an estimated 20 to 50 million tons of e-waste annually. (Recall that e-waste consists of discarded computers and mobile devices.) E-waste releases lead, mercury, barium, and other elements into soil and water.

Electronics recycling is known as eCycling. Only about 12 percent of e-waste is eCycled. Electronics recycling can take several forms: reusing parts; creating new products from old products; or melting down or reducing parts to basic elements or materials.

Many not-for-profit organizations, retail websites, mobile service providers, and big box retailers offer reselling and eCycling options. Several electronics companies allow you to trade your device for a gift certificate. The Sustainable Materials Management (SMM) Electronics Challenge promotes eCycling by certifying recycling businesses that meet or pass qualification guidelines. Other companies focus exclusively on eCycling. One business has developed automated kiosks that tell you what your device is worth, connect you to a buyer, take your device, and dispense cash back on the spot. The U.S. Environmental Protection Agency (EPA) lists eCycling, reselling, and donation resources on its website.

A large amount of e-waste pollutes developing countries that may accept the materials for profit. A proposed federal bill, supported by many electronics manufacturers and resellers, makes it illegal for companies to export e-waste to developing countries. Currently, several states have laws that mandate eCycling.

Consider This: Should the government, manufacturers, or users be responsible for recycling of obsolete equipment? Why? What impact does exporting toxic waste have on developing nations? Should the state or federal government mandate an eCycling program for electronics? Why or why not?

Smartphones

A **smartphone** is an Internet-capable phone that usually also includes a calendar, an address book, a calculator, a notepad, games, browser, and numerous other apps. In addition to basic phone capabilities, many smartphones include these features:

- Send and receive email messages and access the web — via Wi-Fi or a mobile data plan
- Communicate wirelessly with other devices or computers
- Function as a portable media player
- Include a built-in digital camera
- Talk directly into the smartphone's microphone or into a Bluetooth headset that wirelessly communicates with the phone
- Conduct live video calls, where the parties can see each other as they speak
- Receive GPS signals to determine a user's current location
- Synchronize data and information with a computer or another mobile device
- Support voice control so that you can speak instructions to the phone and it speaks responses back to you
- Connect to external devices wirelessly, such as via BlueTooth
- Serve as a wireless access point

Many smartphones have touch screens. Instead of or in addition to an on-screen keyboard, some have a built-in mini keyboard on the front of the phone or a keyboard that slides in and out from behind the phone. Others have keypads that contain both numbers and letters. Some also include a stylus.

 BTW

High-Tech Talk
Discover More: Visit this chapter's free resources to learn how voice recognition technology works.

✳ CONSIDER THIS

How do you type text messages on a phone that has only a numeric keypad and no touch screen?
Each key on the keypad represents multiple characters, which are identified on the key. For example, the 2 key on the phone's keypad displays the letters a, b, and c on the key's face. On many phones, you cycle through the number, letters, and other symbols associated with a particular key by pressing a key on the keypad multiple times. To type the word, hi, for instance, you would press the 4 key (labeled with the letters g, h, and i) twice to display the letter h, pause momentarily to advance the cursor, and then press the 4 key three times to display the letter i.

A variety of options are available for typing on a smartphone (Figure 3-15). Many can display an *on-screen keyboard*, where you press keys on the screen using your fingertip or a stylus. Some phones support a *swipe keyboard app*, on which users enter words by tracing a path on an on-screen keyboard with their fingertip or stylus from one letter to the next in a continuous motion. With other phones, you press letters on the phone's keyboard or keypad. Some phones use *predictive text*, where you press one key on the keyboard or keypad for each letter in a word, and software on the phone predicts the word you want. Swipe keyboard apps and predictive text save users time when entering text on the phone.

on-screen keyboard   swipe keyboard app   mini keyboard   keypad

slide out keyboard   portable keyboard   virtual keyboard   speech to text

Figure 3-15 A variety of options for typing on a smartphone.
© iStockphoto / TommL; Courtesy of Nuance; © FreezeFrameStudio / Photos.com; © iStockphoto / webphotographeer; Courtesy of Jorno; © Italianestro / dreamstime .com; © iStockPhoto / Giorgio Magini; © Oleksiy Mark / Fotolia; Courtesy of Blackberry

Instead of typing on a phone's keyboard or keypad, users can enter text via a *portable keyboard*, which is a full-sized keyboard that communicates with a smartphone via a dock, cables, or wirelessly. Some portable keyboards physically attach to and remove from the device; others are wireless. Another option is a *virtual keyboard* that projects an image of a keyboard on a flat surface. Finally, some phones work with apps that convert your spoken word to text.

Messaging Services   With messaging services, users can send and receive messages to and from smartphones, mobile phones, handheld game devices, other mobile devices, and computers. The type of messages you send depends primarily on the services offered by the mobile service provider that works with the phone or other mobile device you select. Many users have unlimited wireless messaging plans, while others pay a fee per message sent or received. Messaging services include text and picture/video.

With text messaging service, or *SMS (short message service)*, users can send and receive short text messages, typically fewer than 300 characters, on a phone or other mobile device or computer. Text message services typically provide users with several options for sending and receiving messages, including:

- Mobile to mobile: Send a message from your mobile device to another mobile device.
- Mobile to email: Send a message from your mobile device to any email address.
- Mobile to provider: Send a message by entering a *common short code (CSC)*, which is a four- or five-digit number assigned to a specific content or mobile service provider, sometimes followed by the message, for example, to a vote for a television program contestant or donate to a charity.
- Web to mobile: Send a message from a website to a mobile device or notification from a website to a mobile device with messages of breaking news and other updates, such as sports scores, stock prices, weather forecasts, incoming email messages, game notifications, and more.

 CONSIDER THIS

What is the difference between push and pull notifications?
A *push notification*, sometimes called a server push, is a message that initiates from the sending location (such as a server) without a request from the receiver. With a *pull notification*, by contrast, receiver requests information from the sending location.

With picture messaging service, users can send photos and audio files, as well as short text messages, to a phone or other mobile device or computer. With video messaging services, users can send short video clips, usually about 30 seconds in length, in addition to all picture messaging services. Smartphones and other mobile devices with picture/video messaging services, also called *MMS (multimedia message service)*, typically have a digital camera built into the device. Users who expect to receive numerous picture/video messages should verify the phone has sufficient memory. Picture/video message services typically provide users these options for sending and receiving messages:

- Mobile to mobile: Send the picture/video from your mobile device to another mobile device.
- Mobile to email: Send the picture/video from your mobile device to any email address.

 **Internet Research**

What messaging apps are recommended?

Search for: best messaging apps

If you send a picture message to a phone that does not have picture/video messaging capability, the phone usually displays a text message directing the user to a webpage that contains the picture/video message. Some online social networks allow you to send a picture/video message directly to your online profile.

 CONSIDER THIS

Do you need a messaging service to send a text or picture/video message?
Instead of using a messaging plan from your mobile service provider, you can use a mobile messaging app to send and receive text, picture, and other message from users. Many messaging apps also provide group chat capabilities. Most messaging apps can be downloaded to your mobile device at no cost.

Voice mail, which functions much like an answering machine, allows someone to leave a voice message for one or more people. Unlike answering machines, however, a computer in the voice mail system converts an analog voice message into digital form. Once digitized, the message is stored in a voice mailbox. A voice mailbox is a storage location on a hard drive in the voice mail system. To help users manage voice mail messages, some systems offer visual voice mail. With *visual voice mail*, users can view message details, such as the length of calls and, in some cases, read message contents instead of listening to them. Some voice mail systems can convert a voice mail message to a text message for display on a computer or mobile device, such as a smartphone, which you then can manage like any other text message.

Messaging services and voice mail systems also may be able to send messages to groups of phone numbers or email addresses. Read Secure IT 3-3 for tips about safely using smartphones and other mobile devices in public.

Discover More: Visit this chapter's free resources to learn more about speech to text.

 BTW

Analog vs. Digital
Human speech is analog because it uses continuous (wave form) signals that vary in strength and quality. Most computers and electronic devices are digital, which use only two discrete states: on and off.

 SECURE IT 3-3

Safe Mobile Device Use in Public Areas

Sending a text message, updating a Facebook status, posting a Tweet, selecting a new playlist, and checking email messages are tasks you may perform using a mobile device many times each day. They all require some concentration as you focus on the device, usually while looking downward, and they distract you from events occurring around you. Using technology responsibly and safely can prevent theft and injuries.

One common method of thwarting a smartphone thief is to avoid using the phone to check the time. Potential thieves randomly ask people for the correct time. If a person stops and takes a phone out of a pocket or purse, the thief glances at the make and model and decides if it is worth snatching.

Bus stops and train stations are common places for mobile device theft. People in these locations tend to use their smartphones to check schedules, send text messages, and make phone calls. Headphones and earbuds are giveaways that you are using a mobile device and may not be focused on your surroundings. Recent studies show that more than 100 mobile phones are stolen every minute in the United States. Thieves are likely to snatch the devices while the doors are closing just before the train or bus departs from a station so that the victim is unable to pursue the thief. To decrease the chance of theft or pickpocketing, keep your mobile device(s) in a front pocket or in a zippered backpack. Keep your head up and stay aware of your surroundings. If possible, when in public, avoid using accessories that indicate the type of device to which they are connected.

Cognitive psychologists have studied the effects of inattentional blindness, which occurs when a person's attention is diverted while performing a natural activity, such as walking. The researchers have determined that diverted attention is particularly pronounced when people are talking on a mobile phone and, to a lesser extent, using a portable media player. Emergency room reports indicate that distracted walking accidents are on the rise, especially when people trip over cracks in sidewalks or run into fixed objects, such as parked cars and telephone poles.

Consider This: Do you know anyone who has had a mobile device stolen? If so, how did the theft occur? Have you ever experienced inattentional blindness or distracted walking?

Digital Cameras

A **digital camera** is a mobile device that allows users to take photos and store the photographed images digitally. A *smart digital camera* also can communicate wirelessly with other devices and can include apps similar to those on a smartphone. Mobile computers and devices, such as smartphones and tablets, often include at least one integrated digital camera.

 CONSIDER THIS

Do you need a digital camera if you have a camera built into your mobile phone?
If you use a camera only for posts on social media sites, then you may choose to use your mobile phone's built-in camera. If, however, you want increased zoom capabilities, more powerful flash, image stabilization, manual control of settings, and to reduce the drain on your phone's battery, then you may want to opt for a separate digital camera.

In addition to cameras built into phones and other devices, types of digital cameras include point-and-shoot cameras and SLR cameras (Figure 3-16). A *point-and-shoot camera* is an affordable and lightweight digital camera with lenses built into it and a screen that displays an approximation of the image to be photographed. Point-and-shoot cameras, which range in size and features, provide acceptable quality photographic images for the home or small office user. An *SLR camera* (single-lens reflex camera), by contrast, is a high-end digital camera that has interchangeable lenses and uses a mirror to display on its screen an exact replica of the image to be photographed. SLR cameras are much heavier and larger than point-and-shoot cameras. They also can be quite expensive, with a variety of available lens sizes and other attachments.

point-and-shoot camera

SLR camera

camera in smartphone

smart digital camera

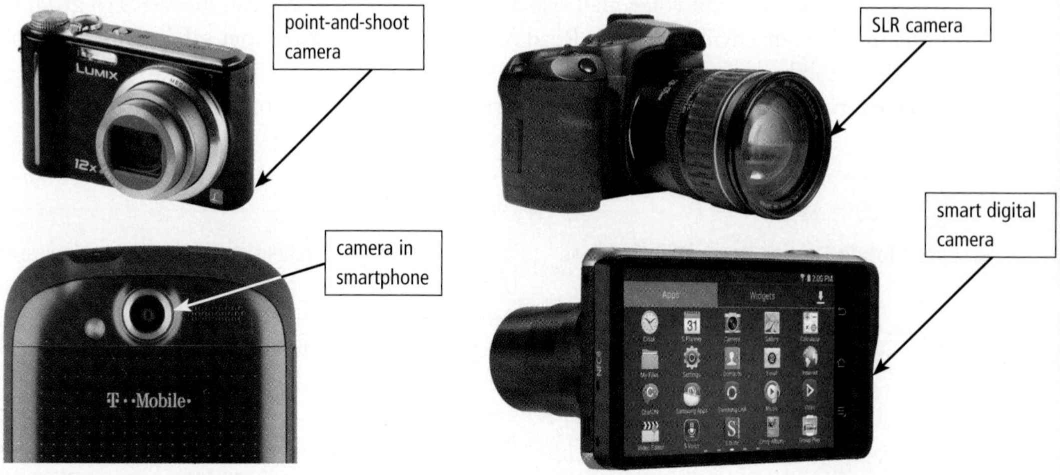

Figure 3-16 SLR digital cameras have lenses and other attachments, whereas the lenses on point-and-shoot cameras are built into the device. Many smartphones also have built-in digital cameras.
© iStockphoto / andrew-thief;
© Pawel Gaul / Photos.com;
© iStockphoto / Stephen Krow;
Courtesy of Samsung

Most point-and-shoot cameras include zoom and autofocus capability, use a built-in flash, store images on memory cards, and enable you to view and sometimes edit images directly on the camera. Many can take video in addition to still photos. Some are equipped with GPS, giving them the capability to record the exact location where a photo was taken and then store these details with the photo. Others are waterproof. Figure 3-17 illustrates how a point-and-shoot digital camera might work.

Internet Research

What is an SD card?

Search for: sd card information

How a Digital Camera Might Work

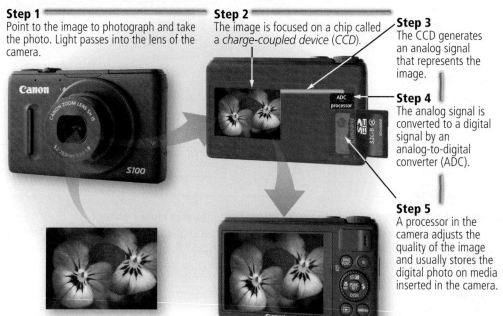

Step 1
Point to the image to photograph and take the photo. Light passes into the lens of the camera.

Step 2
The image is focused on a chip called a *charge-coupled device (CCD)*.

Step 3
The CCD generates an analog signal that represents the image.

Step 4
The analog signal is converted to a digital signal by an analog-to-digital converter (ADC).

Step 5
A processor in the camera adjusts the quality of the image and usually stores the digital photo on media inserted in the camera.

Figure 3-17 This figure shows how a point-and-shoot digital camera might work.
© iStockphoto / David Birkbeck;
© iStockphoto / David Birkbeck;
© Johan Larson / Shutterstock.com;
Courtesy of Kingston Technology Company, Inc

Smart digital cameras include all the features of point-and-shoot cameras and also enable you to connect wirelessly via Wi-Fi. Using the wireless capability, you instantly can save captured photos or videos on a networked computer or the cloud, share them on your online social network, upload them to a video sharing site, send them via email, and more. With a smart digital camera, you typically can download apps (just like on a smartphone) from an app store.

Digital cameras store captured images on storage media in the camera or on some type of memory card. Although most cameras enable you to review, edit, print, and share photos directly from the camera, some users prefer to transfer photos from a digital camera or the memory card to a computer's hard drive to perform these tasks.

Photo Quality   Resolution affects the quality of digital camera photos. **Resolution** is the number of horizontal and vertical pixels in a display. A *pixel* (short for picture element) is the smallest element in an electronic image (Figure 3-18). Digital camera resolution typically is stated in *megapixels* (*MP*), or millions of pixels. For example, a 16 MP resolution means 16 million pixels. The greater the number of pixels the camera uses to capture a picture, the better the quality of the picture but the larger the file size and the more expensive the camera. Most digital cameras provide a means to adjust the resolution. At a lower resolution, you can capture and store more images in the camera.

The actual photographed resolution is known as the *optical resolution*. Some manufacturers state enhanced resolution, instead of, or in addition to, optical resolution. The *enhanced resolution* usually is higher because it uses a special formula to add pixels between those generated by the optical resolution. Be aware that some manufacturers compute a digital camera's megapixels from the enhanced resolution, instead of optical resolution.

Discover More: Visit this chapter's free resources to learn more about resolution.

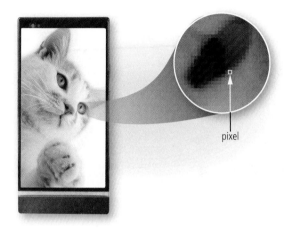

Figure 3-18   A pixel is the smallest element in an electronic image.
© Lingong / Dreamstime.com

pixel

Portable and Digital Media Players

A **portable media player** is a mobile device on which you can store, organize, and play or view digital media (Figure 3-19). Smartphones and other mobile devices often can function as a portable media player. Portable media players enable you to listen to music; view photos; watch videos, movies, and television shows; and even record audio and video. Some include a digital camera and also offer a calendar, address book, games, and other apps. Others communicate wirelessly with other devices or computers and enable you to synchronize your digital media with a computer, another mobile device, or cloud storage.

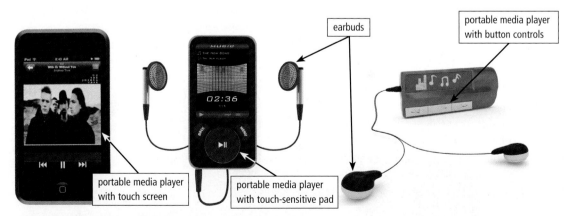

earbuds

portable media player with button controls

portable media player with touch screen

portable media player with touch-sensitive pad

Figure 3-19   Some portable media players have touch screens; others have touch-sensitive pads or buttons that enable you to access your media library.
© iStockphoto / Stephen Krow; © iStockphoto / rzelich; © iStockphoto / AleksVF

Portable media players usually require a set of *earbuds*, which are small speakers that rest inside each ear canal. Available in a variety of sizes and colors, some portable media player models have a touch screen. Others have a *touch-sensitive pad*, which is an input device that contains buttons and/or wheels you operate with a thumb or finger. Using the touch-sensitive pad, you can scroll through and play music; view pictures; watch videos or movies; navigate through song, picture, or movie lists; display a menu; adjust volume; customize settings; and perform other actions. Some portable media players have only button controls.

Portable media players are a mobile type of digital media player. A **digital media player** or *streaming media player* is a device, typically used in a home, that streams digital media from a computer or network to a television, projector, or some other entertainment device (Figure 3-20). Some can stream from the Internet, enabling users to access video on websites. Some users opt for a digital media player instead of subscribing to cable or satellite subscription services to watch television programs.

Your collection of stored digital media is called a *media library*. Portable media players and some digital media players house your media library on a storage device in the player and/or on some type of memory card. With most, you transfer the digital media from a computer or the Internet, if the device is Internet capable, to the player's media library. Read How To 2-3 in Chapter 2 for instructions about how to download digital media from online services.

digital media player

Figure 3-20 A digital media player streams media to a home entertainment device.
Courtesy of Apple, Inc.

Mini Feature 3-3: Mobile Device Buyer's Guide

When purchasing a smartphone, digital camera, or portable or digital media player, you should consider several factors. Read Mini Feature 3-3 for tips to consider when purchasing these mobile devices.

 MINI FEATURE 3-3

Mobile Device Buyer's Guide

Mobile devices such as smartphones, digital cameras, and portable and digital media players are extremely popular. Research the manufacturers and then consider the following guidelines before purchasing a mobile device.

Smartphone Purchase Guidelines

1. Choose a mobile service provider and plan that satisfies your needs and budget. Choose a sufficient voice, text, and data plan that is appropriate.

2. Decide on the size, style, and weight of the smartphone that will work best for you.

3. Determine whether you prefer an on-screen keyboard, keypad, or mini keyboard.

4. Select a smartphone that is compatible with the program you want to use for synchronizing your email messages, contacts, calendar, and other data.

5. Choose a smartphone with sufficient battery life that meets your lifestyle.

6. Make sure your smartphone has enough memory and storage for contacts, email messages, photos, videos, and apps.

7. Consider purchasing accessories such as extra batteries, earbuds, screen protectors, and carrying cases.

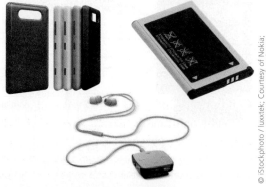

Digital Camera Purchase Guidelines

1. Determine the type of digital camera that meets your needs, such as a point-and-shoot camera or SLR camera.

2. Choose a camera with an appropriate resolution.

3. Evaluate memory cards, because different cameras require different memory cards.

4. Consider a camera with built-in photo editing features.

5. Make sure that you can see the screen easily.

6. If the photos you plan to take will require you to zoom, choose a camera with an appropriate optical zoom.

7. Purchase accessories such as extra batteries and battery chargers, extra memory cards, lenses, and carrying cases.

Portable or Digital Media Player Purchase Guidelines

1. Choose a device with sufficient storage capacity for your media library and apps.

2. Consider how the portable or digital media player will connect to the Internet. Some devices connect using a wired and/or wireless connection. Choose a player that is compatible with the type of connection you can provide.

3. Read reviews about sound quality. If you are purchasing a portable device, consider higher-quality earbuds, headphones, or external speakers.

4. Select a player that is compatible with other devices you already own.

5. Consider additional memory cards to increase the storage capacity of your portable or digital media player.

6. Consider the accessories. If your portable or digital media player connects to a television or other display, consider purchasing a keyboard so that you can type easily. If the device is portable, consider additional batteries or a protective case.

Discover More: Visit this chapter's free resources to learn more about smartphone, digital camera, and portable and digital media player manufacturers and specifications.

✸ **Consider This:** Although most smartphones also can function as digital media players and digital cameras, would you have a separate digital media player and digital camera? Why?

E-Book Readers

An **e-book reader** (short for electronic book reader), or *e-reader*, is a mobile device that is used primarily for reading e-books and other digital publications (Figure 3-21). An *e-book*, or digital book, is an electronic version of a printed book, readable on computers and other mobile devices. Digital publications include books, newspapers, and magazines. Mobile computers and devices that display text also can function as e-book readers.

E-book readers usually are smaller than tablets but larger than smartphones. Most e-book reader models can store thousands of books, have a touch screen, and are Internet capable with built-in wireless technology. You use an on-screen keyboard to navigate, search, make selections, take notes, and highlight. Some have a *text-to-speech feature*, where the device speaks the contents of the printed page. E-book readers are available with an electronic paper black-and-white screen or with a color screen. Most have settings to adjust text size and

Figure 3-21 E-book readers enable you to read e-books and other digital publications such as newspapers and magazines.
© iStockPhoto / Petar Chernaev

for various lighting conditions, such as bright sunlight or dim lighting. Batteries usually have a long life, providing more than 75 hours of use before needing to be recharged.

Similar to how a portable media player stores digital media, e-book readers store digital publications in a library on a storage device in the e-book reader and/or on memory cards. You typically transfer the digital publication from a computer or the Internet, if the device is Internet capable, to the e-book reader. Read How To 2-3 in Chapter 2 for instructions about how to download digital media from online services.

Discover More: Visit this chapter's free resources to learn more about e-book readers.

 CONSIDER THIS ───────────────────────────

Do you need a separate e-book reader if you have a tablet or other device that can function as an e-book reader?
If you want the flexibility of reading on one device while using a tablet or other device for separate tasks, you will want to purchase a separate e-book reader. Also, e-book readers have a design suited for optimal readability of on-screen text and a longer battery life.

Wearable Devices

A **wearable device** or *wearable* is a small, mobile computing device designed to be worn by a consumer (Figure 3-22). These devices often communicate with a mobile device or computer using Bluetooth. Three popular types of wearable devices are activity trackers, smartwatches, and smartglasses.

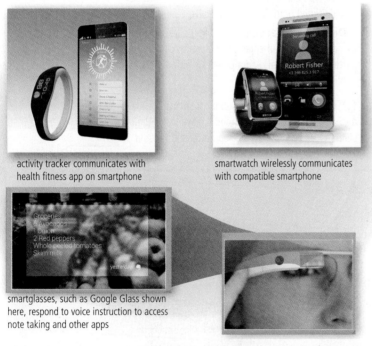

activity tracker communicates with health fitness app on smartphone

smartwatch wirelessly communicates with compatible smartphone

smartglasses, such as Google Glass shown here, respond to voice instruction to access note taking and other apps

Figure 3-22 Three popular wearable devices include activity trackers, smartwatches, and smartglasses.
© iStockPhoto / Petar Chernaev; © iStockPhoto / Chesky_W; © iStockPhoto / scanrail; © iStockPhoto / Wavebreak; Source: Google Inc

An *activity tracker* is a wearable device that monitors fitness-related activities such as distance walked, heart rate, pulse, calories consumed, and sleep patterns. These devices typically sync, usually wirelessly, with a web or mobile app on your computer or mobile device to extend the capability of the wearable device.

A *smartwatch* is a wearable device that, in addition to keeping time, can communicate wirelessly with a smartphone to make and answer phone calls, read and send messages, access the web, play music, work with apps such as fitness trackers and GPS, and more. Most include a touch screen.

Smartglasses, also called *smart eyewear*, are wearable head-mounted eyeglass-type devices that enable the user to view information or take photos and videos that are projected to a miniature screen in the user's field of vision. For example, the device wearer could run an app while wearing smartglasses that display flight status information when he or she walks into an airport. Users control the device

through voice commands or by touching controls on its frame. Some smartglasses also include mobile apps, such as fitness trackers and GPS.

Discover More: Visit this chapter's free resources to learn more about wearable devices.

Game Devices

A **game console** is a mobile computing device designed for single-player or multiplayer video games. Gamers often connect the game console to a television or a monitor so that they can view gameplay on the screen. Some models also allow you to listen to music and watch movies or view photos. Typically weighing between 3 and 11 pounds, many game console models include storage for games and other media. Optical disc drives in the game consoles provide access to games and movies on optical disc. Some use memory cards and accept USB flash drives. Game consoles that are Internet capable enable gamers to download games, stream games or movies, and play with others online. Some gamers connect keyboards or webcams so that they more easily can send text messages or conduct video chats with other gamers.

BTW
Technology Innovator
Discover More: Visit this chapter's free resources to learn about Nintendo (multinational consumer electronics company).

A **handheld game device** is a small mobile device that contains a screen, speakers, controls, and game console all in one unit. Some include a stylus. Some handheld game device models have touch screens and built-in digital cameras. Some are Internet capable for downloading games and apps. Most handheld game devices can communicate wirelessly with other similar devices for multiplayer gaming.

With a game console or computer video game, players direct movements and actions of on-screen objects via a controller, voice, or air gestures. Game controllers include gamepads, joysticks and wheels, dance pads, and a variety of motion-sensing controllers (Figure 3-23). The following list describes each of these types of game controllers. Most communicate via wired or wireless technology.

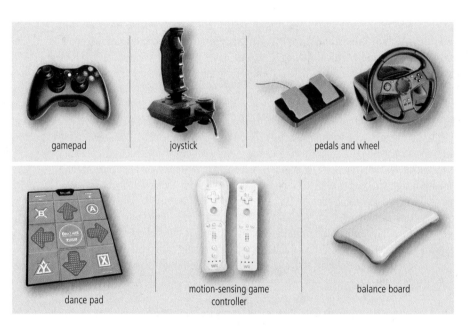

Figure 3-23 Game players have a variety of ways to direct movements and actions of on-screen objects.

© iStockphoto / peng wu; © aquariagirl1970 / Shutterstock.com; © George Dolgikh / Shutterstock.com; Courtesy of DDR Game; © iStockphoto / Florea Marius Catalin; © Stuartkey / Dreamstime.com

- A *gamepad*, which is held with both hands, controls the movement and actions of players or objects in video games or computer games. On the gamepad, users press buttons with their thumbs or move sticks in various directions to trigger events. Several gamepads can communicate with the game console simultaneously for multiplayer gaming.
- Users running flight and driving simulation software often use a joystick or wheel. A *joystick* is a handheld vertical lever, mounted on a base, that you move in different directions to control the actions of the simulated vehicle or player. The lever usually includes buttons, called triggers, that you press to initiate certain events. A *wheel* is a steering-wheel-type input device that users turn to simulate driving a car, truck, or other vehicle. Most wheels also include foot pedals for acceleration and braking actions.
- A *dance pad* is a flat, electronic device divided into panels that users press with their feet in response to instructions from a music video game. These games test the user's ability to step on the correct panel at the correct time, following a pattern that is synchronized with the rhythm or beat of a song.

Internet Research

Which video games are the most widely used?

Search for: popular video games

- *Motion-sensing game controllers* allow users to guide on-screen elements with air gestures, that is, by moving their body or a handheld input device through the air. Some motion-sensing game controllers are sold with a particular type of game; others are general purpose. Sports games, for example, use motion-sensing game controllers, such as baseball bats and golf clubs. With general-purpose motion-sensing game controllers, you simulate batting, golfing, and other actions with a universal handheld device or no device at all.
- Other controllers include those used for music and fitness games. Controllers that resemble musical instruments, such as guitars, drums, keyboards, and microphones work with music video games that enable game players to create sounds and music by playing the instrument. Fitness games often communicate with a *balance board*, which is shaped like a weight scale and contains sensors that measure a game player's balance and weight. Read Ethics & Issues 3-3 to consider whether games and apps are qualified to provide medical advice.

Discover More: Visit this chapter's free resources to learn more about game devices.

 ETHICS & ISSUES 3-3 ────────────────────────────

Are Fitness Video Games and Apps Qualified to Provide Medical Advice?

Most video games and smartphone apps provide a workout only for your fingers. A host of games and apps, however, attempt to track calories, suggest workout routines, and more. Because you can take your smartphone anywhere, one advantage is that apps can provide tips for eating healthfully at a restaurant, act as a pedometer to track your steps, and send reminders to exercise. Wearable fitness devices can track your steps or use GPS to trace your route when running or biking. Another advantage is you can receive instant feedback and support from fitness apps and games that

allow you to post workouts, calorie counts, and even weight loss to online social networks. Some apps even reward you for working out.

Some critics find fault with these apps, claiming that medical personnel have not evaluated either the game or app developers, or the games and apps themselves. Because they do not take into account the amount of lean muscle mass and body fat, health and weight loss goals can be miscalculated. Experts say that games that simulate sports, such as tennis, burn half the calories you would burn if you participated in the actual sport. Some medical professionals also note that apps do not consider a participant's

medical history when recommending activities. Proponents of fitness-related games and apps say that the games encourage people to be more active and can provide positive feedback, especially the elderly and children who might otherwise not get much physical activity.

Consider This: Should game and app developers provide medical advice? Why or why not? Can fitness-related games provide a quality workout? Can an app give accurate calorie recommendations? Why or why not? As long as the games make people more active, should you ignore a games' shortcomings? Why or why not?

Embedded Computers

An **embedded computer** is a special-purpose computer that functions as a component in a larger product. Embedded computers are everywhere — at home, in your car, and at work. The following list identifies a variety of everyday products that contain embedded computers.

- **Consumer electronics:** Mobile phones, digital phones, digital televisions, cameras, video recorders, DVD players and recorders, answering machines
- **Home automation devices:** Thermostats, sprinkling systems, security systems, vacuum systems, appliances, lights
- **Automobiles:** Antilock brakes, engine control modules, electronic stability control, airbag control unit, cruise control, navigation systems and GPS receivers
- **Process controllers and robotics:** Remote monitoring systems, power monitors, machine controllers, medical devices
- **Computer devices and office machines:** Keyboards, printers, fax and copy machines

Because embedded computers are components in larger products, they usually are small and have limited hardware. These computers perform various functions, depending on the requirements of the product in which they reside. Embedded computers in printers, for example, monitor the amount of paper in the tray, check the ink or toner level, signal if a paper jam has occurred, and so on. Figure 3-24 shows some of the many embedded computers in vehicles. Read Ethics & Issues 3-4 to consider whether in-vehicle technology fosters a false sense of security.

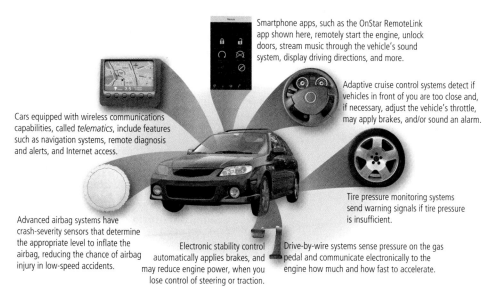

Smartphone apps, such as the OnStar RemoteLink app shown here, remotely start the engine, unlock doors, stream music through the vehicle's sound system, display driving directions, and more.

Adaptive cruise control systems detect if vehicles in front of you are too close and, if necessary, adjust the vehicle's throttle, may apply brakes, and/or sound an alarm.

Cars equipped with wireless communications capabilities, called *telematics*, include features such as navigation systems, remote diagnosis and alerts, and Internet access.

Tire pressure monitoring systems send warning signals if tire pressure is insufficient.

Advanced airbag systems have crash-severity sensors that determine the appropriate level to inflate the airbag, reducing the chance of airbag injury in low-speed accidents.

Electronic stability control automatically applies brakes, and may reduce engine power, when you lose control of steering or traction.

Drive-by-wire systems sense pressure on the gas pedal and communicate electronically to the engine how much and how fast to accelerate.

Figure 3-24 Some of the embedded computers designed to improve your safety, security, and performance in today's vehicles.

© Nir Levy / Shutterstock.com; © Santiago Cornejo / Shutterstock.com; © iStockphoto / narvikk; © iStockphoto / kenneth-cheung; © iStockphoto / Marcin Laska; © iStockPhoto / pagadesign; Source: OnStar, LLC

 ETHICS & ISSUES 3-4

Does In-Vehicle Technology Foster a False Sense of Security?

Embedded computers in vehicles can guide you when backing out of a driveway, warn you if a vehicle or object is in your blind spot, or alert you to unsafe road conditions. Apps can track gas mileage or notify you when your car needs an oil change or other services. Recently, all new cars were required to include electronic stability control, which can assist with steering the car in case of skidding, and backup cameras. Other technologies adjust vehicle speed or headlight usage, and can even activate the brakes.

All of this technology is intended to make driving safer.

Critics of in-vehicle technology claim that it can provide drivers with a false sense of security. If you rely on a sensor for assistance while backing up, parking, or changing lanes, for example, you may miss other obstructions that could cause a crash. Reliance on electronic stability control or other crash-avoidance technologies may cause you to drive faster than conditions allow or to pay less attention to the distance between your vehicle and others.

The effect on new, teen drivers is especially of concern. If teens learn to drive using vehicles

equipped with features such as video rearview mirrors, they may be unable to drive older, less-equipped vehicles safely. Many apps and devices help parents protect their teens while driving. Apps can program mobile devices to block incoming calls or text messages while the vehicle is moving. GPS can track a vehicle's location and speed. Sensors can monitor seatbelt usage and number of passengers in the vehicle.

Consider This: Does in-vehicle technology make driving safer? Why or why not? What basic skills should all drivers have, regardless of their vehicle's technology?

 CONSIDER THIS

Can embedded computers use the Internet to communicate with other computers and devices?
Many already do, on a small scale. For example, a Smart TV enables you to browse the web, stream video from online media services, listen to Internet radio, communicate with others on social media sites, play online games, and more — all while watching a television show.

A trend, called the *Internet of Things*, describes an environment where processors are embedded in every product imaginable (things), and those 'things' communicate with one another via the Internet (i.e., alarm clocks, coffeemakers, apps, vehicles, refrigerators, phones, washing machines, doorbells, streetlights, thermostats, navigation systems, etc.). For example, when your refrigerator detects the milk is low, it sends your phone a text message that you need milk and adds a 'buy milk' task to your scheduling app. On the drive home, your phone determines the closest grocery store that has the lowest milk price and sends the address of that grocery store to your vehicle's navigation system, which, in turn, gives you directions to the store. In the store, your phone directs you to the dairy aisle, where it receives an electronic coupon from the store for the milk. Because this type of environment provides an efficient means to track or monitor status, inventory, behavior, and more — without human intervention — it sometimes is referred to as machine-to-machine (M2M) communications. For additional information about the Internet of Things, read Mini Feature 6-1 in Chapter 6.

Putting It All Together

BTW

Technology Trend
Discover More: Visit this chapter's free resources to learn about volunteer computing, where you can donate your computer's resources to promote scientific research projects.

Industry experts typically classify computers and mobile devices in six categories: personal computers (desktop), mobile computers and mobile devices, game consoles, servers, supercomputers, and embedded computers. A computer's size, speed, processing power, and price determine the category it best fits. Due to rapidly changing technology, however, the distinction among categories is not always clear-cut. Table 3-3 summarizes the categories of computers discussed on the previous pages.

Table 3-3   Categories of Computers and Mobile Devices

Category	Physical Size	Number of Simultaneously Connected Users	General Price Range
Personal computers (desktop)	Fits on a desk	Usually one (can be more if networked)	Several hundred to several thousand dollars
Mobile computers and mobile devices	Fits on your lap or in your hand	Usually one	Less than a hundred dollars to several thousand dollars
Game consoles	Small box or handheld device	One to several	Several hundred dollars or less
Servers	Small cabinet to room full of equipment	Two to thousands	Several hundred to several million dollars
Supercomputers	Full room of equipment	Hundreds to thousands	Half a million to several billion dollars
Embedded computers	Miniature	Usually one	Embedded in the price of the product

© Cengage Learning

✔ NOW YOU SHOULD KNOW

Be sure you understand the material presented in the sections titled Cloud Computing, Mobile Devices, Game Devices, Embedded Computers, and Putting It All Together, as it relates to the chapter objectives.
Now you should know . . .

- When you are using cloud computing (Objective 4)
- What you should consider when purchasing a mobile device (Objective 5)
- What types of controllers you might use with game consoles (Objective 6)
- When you are using an embedded computer (Objective 7)

Discover More: Visit this chapter's premium content for practice quiz opportunities.

BTW

Instead of the term, port, the term, *jack*, sometimes is used to identify audio and video ports (i.e., audio jack or video jack).

Ports and Connections

Computers and mobile devices connect to peripheral devices through ports or by using wireless technologies. A **port** is the point at which a peripheral device (i.e., keyboard, printer, monitor, etc.) attaches to or communicates with a computer or mobile device so that the peripheral device can send data to or receive information from the computer or mobile device. Most computers and mobile devices have ports (Figure 3-25). Some ports have a micro or mini version for mobile devices because of the smaller sizes of these devices.

A **connector** joins a cable to a port. A connector at one end of a cable attaches to a port on the computer or mobile device, and a connector at the other end of the cable attaches to a port on the peripheral device. Table 3-4 shows a variety of ports you may find on a computer or mobile device. USB and Thunderbolt are more general-purpose ports that allow connections to a wide variety of devices; other ports are more specific and connect a single type of device.

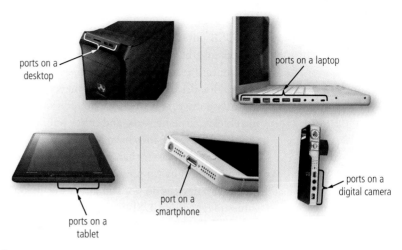

Figure 3-25   Most computers and mobile devices have ports so that you can connect the computer or device to peripherals.

Courtesy of Gateway; © Ultraone / Dreamstime.com; Courtesy of Lenovo; © iStockphoto / Nikada; © eduard ionescu / Shutterstock

Table 3-4   Popular Ports and Connectors

Port Type	Connector Photo	Port Photo	Port Type	Connector Photo	Port Photo
DisplayPort (audio/video)			Mini USB		
DVI (digital video interface)			Mini HDMI (audio/video)		
HDMI (audio/video)			Network (Ethernet)		
Headphones			Speaker		
Lightning			Thunderbolt		
Microphone			USB (Type A)		
Micro USB			USB (Type B)		
Mini DisplayPort			VGA		

Discover More: Visit this chapter's free resources for an expanded list of ports and connectors.

© Cengage Learning; © Steveheap / Dreamstime.com; © iStockphoto / Hans Martens; © iStockphoto / Ksenia Krylova; © iStockphoto / Lusoimages; © Jorge Salcedo / Shutterstock.com; © Aarrows / Dreamstime.com; © iStockphoto / Lusoimages; © Pcheruvi / Dreamstime.com; © iStockphoto / Potapova Vaeriya; © iStockphoto / Jivko Kazakov; © iStockphoto / TimArbaev; © iStockphoto / Ashok Rodrigues; © iStockphoto / Jon Larson; © Aarrows / Dreamstime.com; © iStockphoto / Denis Sokolov; © Germán Ariel Berra / Shutterstock.com; © Aarrows / Dreamstime.com; © iStockphoto / Li Ding; © iStockphoto / TimArbaev; © iStockphoto / Matthew Brown; © Jorge Salcedo /Shutterstock.com; © Pcheruvi / Dreamstime.com; © Anton Malcev / Photos.com; © iStockphoto / alexander kirch; © iStockphoto / Nick Smith; © iStockphoto / Mohamed Badawi; © Jorge Salcedo /Shutterstock © iStockphoto / Brandon Laufenberg; © getIT / Shutterstock.com; © stavklem / Shutterstock.com; © iStockphoto / Lusoimages; © lexan / Shutterstock; © iStockPhoto / NikiLitov; © iStockPhoto / Peter Hermus; © Jarp / Fotolia; Courtesy of Samsung

USB Ports

A **USB port**, short for universal serial bus port, can connect up to 127 different peripheral devices together with a single connector. Devices that connect to a USB port include the following: card reader, digital camera, external hard drive, game console, joystick, modem, mouse, optical disc drive, portable media player, printer, scanner, smartphone, digital camera, speakers, USB flash drive, and webcam. In addition to computers and mobile devices, you find USB ports in vehicles, airplane seats, and other public locations.

Several USB versions have been released, with newer versions (i.e., USB 3.0) transferring data and information faster than earlier ones (i.e., USB 2.0). Newer versions are *backward compatible*, which means they support older USB devices as well as newer ones. Keep in mind, though, that older USB devices do not run any faster in a newer USB port. In addition to transferring data, cables plugged into USB ports also may be able to transfer power to recharge many smartphones and tablets. Newer versions of USB can charge connected mobile devices even when the computer is not in use.

To attach multiple peripheral devices using a single USB port, you can use a USB hub. A *USB hub* is a device that plugs in a USB port on the computer or mobile device and contains multiple USB ports, into which you plug cables from USB devices. Some USB hubs are wireless. That is, a receiver plugs into a USB port on the computer and the USB hub communicates wirelessly with the receiver. Read Secure IT 3-4 for tips when using USB charging stations.

 SECURE IT 3-4

Public USB Charging Stations — Safe or Not?

Although you might be tempted to recharge your smartphone or mobile device at a public charging station, think twice before plugging your USB cable into the charging kiosk's port. The station may be *juice jacking*, which occurs when a hacker steals data from or transfers malware to the device via a USB cable at a charging station. (A hacker is someone who accesses a computer or network illegally.)

This process is possible because the USB cable is used for two purposes: supplying power and syncing data. It can occur within one minute after plugging into the charger.

Anything on the device is susceptible, including photos, contacts, and music, and some malware can create a full backup of your data, leaving you prone to identity theft. Once the phone or mobile device is infected, it can continue to transmit data via Wi-Fi. Security experts claim that the only method of erasing this malware is to restore the device to its factory settings.

Charging stations are common in airports, business centers, and conference rooms. While most are safe, you can reduce the possibility of juice jacking by taking these precautions:

- Use a travel charger, also called a power bank, which can recharge a device several times before needing recharging itself.

- Keep the phone or mobile device locked so that it requires a password to sync data with another device. Turning off the device while charging may not provide sufficient protection against accessing the storage media.

- Use a power-only USB cable that does not allow data transmission.

✸ **Consider This:** Should warning signs be posted by public charging stations? Would you use a public charging kiosk if your smartphone or mobile device was running low on battery power?

Discover More: Visit this chapter's free resources to learn more about USB versions.

Port Replicators and Docking Stations

Instead of connecting peripheral devices directly to ports on a mobile computer, some mobile users prefer the flexibility of port replicators and docking stations. A *port replicator* is an external device that provides connections to peripheral devices through ports built into the device. The mobile user accesses peripheral devices by connecting the port replicator to a USB port or a special port on the mobile computer. Port replicators sometimes disable ports on the mobile computer to prevent conflicts among the devices on the computer and port replicator.

A docking station is similar to a port replicator, but it has more functionality. A *docking station*, which is an external device that attaches to a mobile computer or device, contains a power connection and provides connections to peripheral devices (Figure 3-26). Docking stations also may include slots for memory cards, optical disc drives, and other devices. With the mobile computer or device in the docking station, users can work with a full-sized keyboard, a mouse, and other desktop peripheral devices from their laptop or tablet.

Wireless Device Connections

Instead of connecting computers and mobile devices to peripheral devices with a cable, some peripheral devices use wireless communications technologies, such as Bluetooth, Wi-Fi, and NFC.

Bluetooth **Bluetooth** technology uses short-range radio signals to transmit data between two Bluetooth-enabled computers or devices. In addition to computers, mobile devices and many peripheral devices, such as a mouse, keyboard, printer, or headset, and many vehicles and consumer electronics are Bluetooth enabled. Bluetooth devices have to be within about 33 feet of each other, but the range can be extended with additional equipment. If you have a computer that is not Bluetooth enabled, you can purchase a Bluetooth wireless port adapter that will convert an existing USB port into a Bluetooth port. Read How To 3-1 for instructions about setting up two Bluetooth devices to communicate with each other.

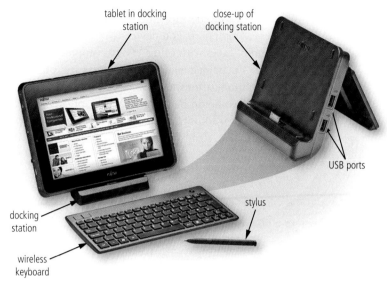

tablet in docking station

close-up of docking station

USB ports

stylus

docking station

wireless keyboard

Figure 3-26 Docking stations often are used with tablets and other mobile computers, providing connections to peripheral devices.
Courtesy of Fujitsu Technology Solutions; © Cengage Learning

 HOW TO 3-1

Pair Bluetooth Devices

Before two Bluetooth devices will communicate with each other, they might need to be paired. *Pairing* is the process of initiating contact between two Bluetooth devices and allowing them to communicate with each other. It is important to have the documentation for the Bluetooth devices you are pairing readily available. The following steps will help you pair two Bluetooth devices.

1. Make sure the devices you intend to pair are charged completely or plugged into an external power source.

2. Turn on the devices to pair, ensuring they are within your immediate reach.

3. If necessary, enable Bluetooth on the devices you are pairing.

4. Place one device in *discoverable mode*, which means it is waiting for another Bluetooth device to locate its signal. If you are connecting a smartphone to a Bluetooth headset, for example,

the smartphone would need to be in discoverable mode.

5. Refer to the other device's documentation and follow the necessary steps to locate the discoverable device from the other device you are pairing.

6. After no more than about 30 seconds, the devices should initiate communications.

7. You may be required to enter a passkey (similar to a PIN) on one device for the other device with which you are pairing. For example, if you are pairing a smartphone with a Bluetooth headset, you may be required to enter the Bluetooth headset's passkey on the smartphone. In this case, you would refer to the Bluetooth headset's documentation to obtain the passkey. Common passkeys are 0000 and 1234.

8. After entering the correct passkey, the two devices should be paired successfully.

⁂ **Consider This:** Why is a passkey required when pairing two Bluetooth devices? Do you need to pair Bluetooth devices before each use?

© Normal Chan / Shutterstock.com

Wi-Fi Short for wireless fidelity, **Wi-Fi** uses radio signals that conform to 802.11 standards, which were developed by the Institute of Electrical and Electronics Engineers (IEEE).

Computers and devices that have the appropriate Wi-Fi capability can communicate via radio waves with other Wi-Fi computers or devices. Most mobile computers and devices are Wi-Fi enabled, along with routers and other communications devices. For successful Wi-Fi communications in open or outdoor areas free from interference, the Wi-Fi computers or devices should be within 300 feet of each other. In closed areas, the wireless range is about 100 feet. To obtain communications at the maximum distances, you may need to install extra hardware. Read How To 3-2 for instructions about connecting a phone to a Wi-Fi network.

 HOW TO 3-2

Connect Your Phone to a Wi-Fi Network to Save Data Charges

Many of today's data plans limit the amount of data you can transfer each month on your mobile service provider's network. Connecting a smartphone to a Wi-Fi network enables you to transfer data without using your phone's data plan and risking costly overages. The following steps describe how to connect your phone to a Wi-Fi network.

1. Make sure you are in a location where a Wi-Fi network is available. Obtain any necessary information you need to connect to the Wi-Fi network.

2. Navigate to the settings on your phone.

3. Locate and enable Wi-Fi in your phone's settings.

4. When your phone displays a list of available wireless networks, choose the network to which you want to connect.

5. If necessary, enter any additional information, such as a password, required to connect to the network.

6. Your phone should indicate when it successfully is connected to the network.

7. When you are finished using the Wi-Fi connection or are not within range of the Wi-Fi network, disable Wi-Fi on your phone to help conserve battery life.

Consider This: If you have a data plan allowing unlimited data and you are within range of a Wi-Fi network, is it better to use your mobile service provider's network or the Wi-Fi network? Why?

NFC NFC (near field communications) uses close-range radio signals to transmit data between two NFC-enabled devices. Examples of NFC-enabled devices include smartphones, digital cameras, computers, televisions, and terminals. Other objects, such as credit cards and tickets, also use NFC technology. For successful communications, the devices either touch or are within an inch or two of each other.

Discover More: Visit this chapter's free resources to learn more about transfer rates of wireless communications technologies and 802.11 standards.

CONSIDER THIS

What are some uses of NFC devices?

- Pay for goods and services (i.e., smartphone to terminal)

- Share contacts, photos, and other files (i.e., smartphone to smartphone or digital camera to television)

- Download apps (i.e., computer to smartphone)

- Gain access or admittance (i.e., smartphone to terminal)

Protecting Hardware

Users rely on computers and mobile devices to create, store, and manage important information. Thus, you should take measures to protect computers and devices from theft, vandalism, and failure.

Hardware Theft and Vandalism

Companies, schools, and other organizations that house many computers are at risk of hardware theft and vandalism, especially those with smaller computers that easily can fit in a backpack or briefcase. Mobile users are susceptible to hardware theft because the size and weight of their computers and devices make them easy to steal. Thieves may target laptops of company executives so that they can use the stolen computer to access confidential company information illegally.

To help reduce the chances of theft, companies and schools use a variety of security measures. Physical access controls, such as locked doors and windows, usually are adequate to protect the equipment. Many businesses, schools, and some homeowners install alarm systems for additional security. School computer labs and other facilities with a large number of semifrequent users often attach additional physical security devices, such as cables that lock the equipment to a desk, cabinet, or floor. Mobile users sometimes lock their mobile computers temporarily to a stationary object, for example, a table in a hotel room. Small locking devices also exist that require a key to access a hard drive or optical disc drive.

Users also can install a security or device-tracking app on their mobile computers and devices. Some security apps shut down the computer and sound an alarm if the computer moves beyond a specified distance. Others can be configured to photograph the thieves when they use the computer. Device-tracking apps use GPS, Wi-Fi, IP addresses, and other means to determine the location of a lost or stolen computer or device.

Users can configure computers and mobile devices to require identification before allowing access. For example, you can require entry of a user name and password to use the computer or device. Some computers and mobile devices have built-in or attached fingerprint readers (Figure 3-27), which can be used to verify a user's identity before allowing access. A *fingerprint reader* captures curves and indentations of a fingerprint. This type of security does not prevent theft, but it renders the computer or device useless if it is stolen.

Discover More: Visit this chapter's free resources to learn more about device-tracking apps.

Internet Research
How prevalent is theft of mobile devices?
Search for: mobile device theft

BTW
Lost Computers or Devices
You usually can instruct the password screen to display your name and phone number, so that a Good Samaritan can return a lost computer or device to you.

Figure 3-27 Some mobile computers and devices include fingerprint readers, which can be used to verify a user's identity.

fingerprint reader

Hardware Failure

Hardware can fail for a variety of reasons: aging hardware; random events, such as electrical power problems; and even errors in programs or apps. Not only could hardware failure require you to replace or repair a computer or mobile device, but it also can cause loss of software, data, and information.

One of the more common causes of system failure is an electrical power variation, which can cause loss of data and loss of equipment. If computers and mobile devices are connected to a network, a single power disturbance can damage multiple devices at once. Electrical disturbances that can cause damage include undervoltages and overvoltages.

- An **undervoltage** occurs when the electrical supply or voltage drops, often defined as more than five percent, below the normal volts. A *brownout* is a prolonged (more than a minute) undervoltage. A *blackout* is a complete power failure. Undervoltages can cause data loss but generally do not cause equipment damage.
- An **overvoltage**, or **power surge**, occurs when the incoming electrical supply or voltage increases, often defined as more than five percent, above the normal volts. A momentary overvoltage, called a *spike*, occurs when the increase in power lasts for less than one millisecond (thousandth of a second). Uncontrollable disturbances such as lightning bolts can cause spikes. Overvoltages can cause immediate and permanent damage to hardware.

To protect against electrical power variations, use a surge protector. A **surge protector**, also called a *surge suppressor*, uses electrical components to provide a stable current flow and minimize the chances of an overvoltage reaching the computer and other electronic equipment (Figure 3-28). Sometimes resembling a power strip, the computer and other devices plug in the surge protector, which plugs in the power source.

Figure 3-28   Circuits inside a surge protector safeguard against electrical power variations.
© iStockPhoto / missisya

The surge protector absorbs small overvoltages — generally without damage to the computer and equipment. To protect the computer and other equipment from large overvoltages, such as those caused by a lightning strike, some surge protectors stop working completely when an overvoltage reaches a certain level. Surge protectors also usually protect the computer from undervoltages. No surge protectors are 100 percent effective. Large power surges can bypass the protector. Repeated small overvoltages can weaken a surge protector permanently. Some experts recommend replacing a surge protector every two to three years.

For additional electrical protection, some users connect an uninterruptible power supply to the computer. An **uninterruptible power supply** (**UPS**) is a device that contains surge protection circuits and one or more batteries that can provide power during a temporary or permanent loss of power (Figure 3-29). A UPS connects your computer and a power source. Read How To 3-3 for purchasing suggestions regarding surge protectors and UPSs.

Figure 3-29 If power fails, a UPS uses batteries to provide electricity for a limited amount of time.
© rendeep kumar r / Shutterstock

✳ HOW TO 3-3

 Evaluate Surge Protectors and UPSs

Electrical power surges are a part of everyday life, and they are especially prevalent during thunderstorms and peak energy consumption periods. These unavoidable occurrences can damage or ruin sensitive electronic equipment. The processor in a computer is particularly sensitive to fluctuations in current. Two devices can help protect electronic components: a surge protector and an uninterruptible power supply (UPS).

Purchase the best surge protector you can afford. Typically, the amount of protection offered by a surge protector is proportional to its cost. That is, the more expensive the

surge protector, the more protection it offers. When evaluating surge protectors and UPSs, they should meet or exceed these specifications:

- Sufficient outlets to accommodate each device needing protection
- Individual on/off switch for each device
- Built in fuse
- UL 1449 rating that ensures quality control and testing
- Joule rating of at least 600
- Indicator light showing the device is functioning properly

- Warranty for damages to any connected equipment
- Low clamping voltage
- High energy-absorption rating
- Low response time, preferably less than ten nanoseconds
- Protection for a modem, communications lines, and cables

✳ **Consider This:** What other factors might you consider while evaluating surge protectors? Why?

✳ CONSIDER THIS

What other measures can organizations implement if their computers must remain operational at all times?

Some companies use duplicate components or duplicate computers to protect against hardware failure. A *fault-tolerant computer* has duplicate components so that it can continue to operate when one of its main components fail. Airline reservation systems, communications networks, ATMs, and other systems that must be operational at all times use duplicate components, duplicate computers, or fault-tolerant computers.

Health Concerns of Using Technology

The widespread use of technology has led to some important user health concerns. You should be proactive and minimize your chance of risk.

Repetitive Strain Injuries

A *repetitive strain injury* (*RSI*) is an injury or disorder of the muscles, nerves, tendons, ligaments, and joints. Technology-related RSIs include tendonitis and carpal tunnel syndrome.

- Tendonitis is inflammation of a tendon due to repeated motion or stress on that tendon.
- Carpal tunnel syndrome (CTS) is inflammation of the nerve that connects the forearm to the palm of the hand.

Repeated or forceful bending of the wrist can cause tendonitis of the wrist or CTS. Symptoms of tendonitis of the wrist include extreme pain that extends from the forearm to the hand, along with tingling in the fingers. Symptoms of CTS include burning pain when the nerve is compressed, along with numbness and tingling in the thumb and first two fingers.

Long-term computer work can lead to tendonitis or CTS. Factors that cause these disorders include prolonged typing, prolonged mouse usage, or continual shifting between the mouse and the keyboard. If untreated, these disorders can lead to permanent physical damage.

 CONSIDER THIS

What can you do to prevent technology-related tendonitis or CTS?
Follow these precautions:

- Take frequent breaks to exercise your hands and arms (Figure 3-30).
- Do not rest your wrists on the edge of a desk. Instead, place a wrist rest between the keyboard and the edge of your desk.
- Place the mouse at least six inches from the edge of the desk. In this position, your wrist is flat on the desk.
- Minimize the number of times you switch between the mouse and the keyboard.
- Keep your forearms and wrists level so that your wrists do not bend.
- Avoid using the heel of your hand as a pivot point while typing or using the mouse.
- Keep your shoulders, arms, hands, and wrists relaxed while you work.
- Maintain good posture.
- Stop working if you experience pain or fatigue.

Hand Exercises
- Spread fingers apart for several seconds while keeping wrists straight.
- Gently push back fingers and then thumb.
- Dangle arms loosely at sides and then shake arms and hands.

Figure 3-30 To reduce the chance of developing tendonitis or carpal tunnel syndrome, take frequent breaks during computer sessions to exercise your hands and arms.
© iStockphoto / Denis Kartavenko; © Oleksiy Mark / Shutterstock.com; © Cengage Learning

Other Physical Risks

With the growing use of earbuds and headphones in computers and mobile devices, some users are experiencing hearing loss. Read How To 3-4 for guidelines for evaluating earbuds and headphones.

Computer vision syndrome (*CVS*) is a technology-related health condition that affects eyesight. You may have CVS if you have sore, tired, burning, itching, or dry eyes; blurred or double vision after prolonged staring at a display device; headache or sore neck; difficulty shifting focus between a display device and documents; difficulty focusing on the screen image; color fringes or after-images when you look away from the display device; and increased sensitivity to light. Eyestrain associated with CVS is not thought to have serious or long-term consequences. Figure 3-31 outlines some techniques you can follow to ease eyestrain.

People who spend their workday using the computer sometimes complain of lower back pain, muscle fatigue, and emotional fatigue. Lower back pain sometimes is caused from poor posture. Always sit properly in the chair while you work. To alleviate back pain, muscle fatigue, and emotional fatigue, take a 15- to 30-minute break every 2 hours — stand up, walk around, stretch, and relax.

Techniques to Ease Eyestrain

- Every 10 to 15 minutes, take an eye break.
  - Look into the distance and focus on an object for 20 to 30 seconds.
  - Roll your eyes in a complete circle.
  - Close your eyes and rest them for at least one minute.
- Blink your eyes every five seconds.
- Place your display about an arm's length away from your eyes with the top of the screen at or below eye level.
- Use large fonts.
- If you wear glasses, ask your doctor about computer glasses.
- Adjust the lighting.

Figure 3-31 Following these tips may help reduce eyestrain while using technology.
© grublee / Shutterstock.com

 HOW TO 3-4

Evaluate Earbuds and Headphones

Earbuds and headphones are used to listen to music and other audio files on computers and mobile devices. Selecting the proper product not only depends on the style you prefer, but also the type of audio you will be playing. Prices for earbuds and headphones can range from only a few dollars to several hundred dollars, so it is important to know what you are purchasing. The following guidelines describe what to look for when evaluating earbuds and headphones.

- Determine which style you prefer. Earbuds rest inside your ear, while headphones rest over your ear. Experiment with both types

and determine which is more comfortable for you.

- Determine the quality you desire. If you listen to music casually and typically do not notice variations in sound quality, a higher-end product might not be necessary. Alternatively, if sound quality is important, you may consider a more expensive set. Note that a higher price does not always indicate better quality; read online product reviews for information about the sound quality of various products.
- Decide whether you would like a noise cancelling feature. *Noise cancelling* helps block external noise while you are

listening to the audio on your device. Noise cancelling headphones sometimes require batteries, and you are able to turn the noise cancelling feature on and off. If you will be listening to audio in locations where you also need to hear what is going on around you, consider purchasing a product without this feature.

Consider This: Based on your preferences and needs, which type of product (earbuds or headphones) is best for you? Locate a product online that meets your specifications. What brand is it? How much does it cost? Where is this product available?

 **Internet Research**

What is a text neck?

Search for: text neck

Another way to help prevent these injuries is to be sure your workplace is designed ergonomically. **Ergonomics** is an applied science devoted to incorporating comfort, efficiency, and safety into the design of items in the workplace. Ergonomic studies have shown that using the correct type and configuration of chair, keyboard, display, and work surface helps users work comfortably and efficiently and helps protect their health (Figure 3-32). You can hire an ergonomic consultant to evaluate your workplace and recommend changes.

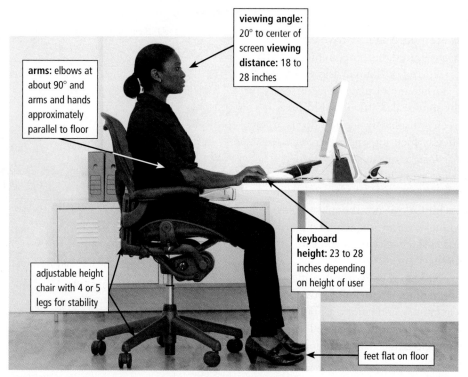

viewing angle: 20° to center of screen **viewing distance:** 18 to 28 inches

arms: elbows at about 90° and arms and hands approximately parallel to floor

keyboard height: 23 to 28 inches depending on height of user

adjustable height chair with 4 or 5 legs for stability

feet flat on floor

Figure 3-32 A well designed work area should be flexible to allow adjustments to the height and build of different individuals.
© Science Photo Library / Alamy

Behavioral Health Risks

Some technology users become obsessed with computers, mobile devices, and the Internet. **Technology addiction** occurs when technology use consumes someone's entire social life. Technology addiction is a growing health problem, but it can be treated through therapy and support groups.

People suffering from *technology overload* feel distressed when deprived of technology, even for a short length of time, or feel overwhelmed with the amount of technology they are required to manage. To cope with the feelings of distraction and to control the impact that technology can have on work and relationships, set aside technology-free time.

 CONSIDER THIS

How can you tell if you are addicted to technology?

Symptoms of a user with technology addiction include the following:

• Craves computer time

• Overjoyed when using a computer or mobile device

• Unable to stop using technology

• Irritable when not using technology

• Neglects family and friends

• Problems at work or school

◆ NOW YOU SHOULD KNOW

Be sure you understand the material presented in the sections titled Ports and Connections, Protecting Hardware, and Health Concerns of Using Technology as it relates to the chapter objectives.
Now you should know...

- How you can connect a peripheral device to a computer or mobile device (Objective 8)

- How you can protect your hardware from theft, vandalism, and failure (Objective 9)

- How you can minimize your risk of health-related injuries and disorders that can result from using technology (Objective 10)

Discover More: Visit this chapter's premium content for practice quiz opportunities.

◆ Chapter Summary

This chapter presented characteristics of and purchasing guidelines for laptops, tablets, desktops, smartphones, digital cameras, and portable and digital media players. It also discussed servers, supercomputers, point-of-sale terminals, ATMs, self-service kiosks, e-book readers, wearable devices, game devices, embedded computers, and cloud computing. It presented a variety of ports and connections, ways to protect hardware, and health concerns of using technology use along with preventive measures.

Discover More: Visit this chapter's free resources for additional content that accompanies this chapter and also includes these features: Technology Innovators: Samsung, Dell/Michael Dell, Sony, and Nintendo; Technology Trends: Bitcoin and Volunteer Computing; and High-Tech Talks: Touch Screen Technology and Voice Recognition Technology.

Test your knowledge of chapter material by accessing the Study Guide, Flash Cards, and Practice Test resources from your smartphone, tablet, laptop, or desktop.

◆ TECHNOLOGY @ WORK

Energy Management

When you walk into your office at the start of a new day, you give little thought to the fact that the lights are on and the temperature is comfortable. For all you know, the air conditioner and lighting were on all night; however, energy management systems are hard at work conserving energy and reducing energy costs. When you return home, you also might take for granted the fact that your dryer automatically stops when it senses that your clothes are dry, or that your dishwasher or washing machine uses only enough water to sufficiently clean its contents. Individuals in the energy management field always are looking for ways to use technology to manage energy use.

Building automation systems are devices that can control various building components, such as complex air conditioning systems and lighting systems. Building automation systems adjust these components to provide a comfortable, safe working environment without wasting energy. For example, in an office building where employees all work weekdays from 8:00 a.m. until 5:00 p.m., the

building automation system might prompt the air conditioner to turn on one or two hours before the first employees arrive. After the employees leave for the day, the air conditioner either may turn off for the evening or maintain a higher temperature to conserve energy. Some systems used in hotel rooms may include motion sensors that turn off the air conditioner if they sense no motion or noise in the room. Cruise ship cabins and hotel rooms with doors to a balcony may automatically shut down the air conditioner if the door is left open. Air conditioning systems often are one of the largest consumers of energy, and money spent toward automating one of these systems often can be recovered in smaller electricity bills. In addition to controlling the air conditioning system, building automation systems also can control and monitor lighting. Many newer buildings include motion and sound sensors in each room and automatically turn off lights when the rooms are unoccupied. Lighting in common areas of these buildings might turn off after hours when the building is unoccupied. Alternatively, if the building

has plenty of natural light coming in, sensors automatically can turn off lights when sufficient sunlight is available, or turn on the lights when the sunlight decreases.

The energy management field has made significant advancements because of computer technologies. Businesses not only are able to reduce their energy costs, but they also are conserving energy at the same time.

☀ **Consider This:** In what other ways do computers and technology play a role in the energy management field?

© Viktor Gladkov / Shutterstock

Study Guide

The Study Guide exercise reinforces material you should know for the chapter exam.

Discover More: Visit this chapter's premium content to **test your knowledge of digital content** associated with this chapter and **access the Study Guide resource** from your smartphone, tablet, laptop, or desktop.

Instructions: Answer the questions below using the format that helps you remember best or that is required by your instructor. Possible formats may include one or more of these options: write the answers; create a document that contains the answers; record answers as audio or video using a webcam, smartphone, or portable media player; post answers on a blog, wiki, or website; or highlight answers in the book/e-book.

1. List types of computers and mobile devices.
2. Describe how personal computers often are differentiated.
3. Explain how to avoid malware infections.
4. Define the term, motherboard.
5. Describe the roles of the processor and memory.
6. Differentiate among traditional and ultrathin laptops, tablets, phablets, and handheld computers.
7. To interact with a tablet, you may use a touch screen or a(n) _____.
8. List steps to protect yourself from webcam spying.
9. List considerations when purchasing a mobile computer. Explain the importance of built-in ports and slots.
10. A(n) _____ desktop may be less expensive and take up less space.
11. Identify types of desktop users and explain how each user's computer needs may differ.
12. Identify how you can purchase the appropriate desktop computer for your needs.
13. Describe the purpose and functions of a server. Differentiate among rack, blade, and tower servers.
14. Define virtualization as it relates to servers. Define the terms, server farm and mainframe.
15. Define the terms, terminal and thin client. List the advantages of a thin client.
16. Identify situations where POS terminals, ATMs, and self-service kiosks might be used. List ATM safety guidelines.
17. A(n) _____ is used to solve complex, sophisticated mathematical calculations, such as those used in petroleum exploration.
18. List cloud computing resources. Describe how businesses use cloud computing to manage resources.
19. List types of mobile devices. Describe features of a smartphone.
20. Explain the issues surrounding the recycling of e-waste.
21. Identify methods for typing on a smartphone.
22. List options provided by text, picture/video message, and voicemail services.
23. Distinguish between push and pull notifications.
24. _____ occurs when a person's attention is diverted, such as by talking on a mobile phone.

25. Describe the types of digital cameras, how they store captured images, and how to transfer photos to a computer.
26. Explain how resolution affects digital picture quality.
27. Identify the features of portable media and digital media players.
28. List considerations when purchasing different types of mobile devices.
29. List features of e-book readers and wearable devices.
30. Identify types of game controllers.
31. Explain whether fitness video games are an effective form of exercise.
32. List products that contain embedded computers. List the disadvantages of in-vehicle technology.
33. Describe the trend, the Internet of Things.
34. Describe categories of computers and mobile devices, and identify general characteristics of size, user type, and price.
35. Explain how a computer uses ports and connectors.
36. List devices that connect to a USB port. Explain risks of using public USB charging stations.
37. Define the term, backward compatible.
38. Distinguish between a port replicator and a docking station.
39. Describe the following technologies: Bluetooth, Wi-Fi, and NFC.
40. _____ is the process of initiating contact between two Bluetooth devices.
41. List steps to connect your phone to a Wi-Fi network.
42. List methods for securing against hardware theft and vandalism.
43. Define the terms, undervoltage and overvoltage, and explain how each can damage a computer or data.
44. Describe the purposes of surge protectors and UPS devices. Explain the purpose a fault-tolerant computer.
45. Identify causes and types of repetitive strain injuries. List symptoms of CVS.
46. List guidelines for evaluating earbuds and headphones.
47. Describe the role of ergonomics in a workplace.
48. List symptoms of technology addiction. Define the term, technology overload.
49. Describe how technology is used in the energy management industry.

You should be able to define the Primary Terms and be familiar with the Secondary Terms listed below.

Key Terms

Discover More: Visit this chapter's premium content to **view definitions** for each term and to **access the Flash Cards resource** from your smartphone, tablet, laptop, or desktop.

Primary Terms (shown in **bold-black** characters in the chapter)

all-in-one (114)
Bluetooth (137)
cloud computing (121)
computer (108)
computer vision
  syndrome (143)
connector (135)
desktop (114)
digital camera (125)
digital media player (128)

e-book reader (129)
embedded computer
  (132)
ergonomics (144)
game console (131)
handheld game device
  (131)
laptop (111)
mobile computer (108)
mobile device (108)

NFC (138)
overvoltage (140)
port (134)
portable media player
  (127)
power surge (140)
resolution (127)
server (116)
smartphone (123)
surge protector (140)

tablet (112)
technology addiction
  (144)
undervoltage (140)
uninterruptible power
  supply (UPS) (140)
USB port (136)
wearable device (130)
Wi-Fi (138)

Secondary Terms (shown in *italic* characters in the chapter)

all-in-one desktop (114)
activity tracker (130)
application server (116)
ATM (118)
backup server (116)
backward compatible (136)
balance board (132)
bar code reader (118)
blackout (140)
blade server (116)
brownout (140)
building automation systems (145)
charge-coupled device (CCD) (126)
common short code (CSC) (124)
convertible tablet (112)
CPU (110)
CVS (143)
dance pad (131)
database server (116)
discoverable mode (137)
docking station (136)
domain name server (116)
DVD kiosk (120)
earbuds (128)
EarPods (128)
e-book (129)
enhanced resolution (127)
e-reader (129)
fault-tolerant computer (141)
file server (116)
fingerprint reader (139)
FTP server (116)
game server (116)
gamepad (131)
gaming desktop (114)
Google Street View (111)

handheld computer (112)
home server (116)
Internet of Things (133)
jack (134)
joystick (131)
juice jacking (136)
kiosk (119)
list server (116)
mail server (116)
mainframe (117)
media library (128)
megapixel (MP) (127)
*MMS (multimedia message
  service) (124)*
motherboard (110)
motion-sensing game controller (132)
network server (116)
noise cancelling (143)
notebook computer (111)
on-screen keyboard (123)
optical resolution (127)
pairing (137)
peripheral device (108)
personal computer (108)
phablet (112)
PIN (118)
pixel (127)
point-and-shoot camera (125)
port replicator (136)
portable keyboard (124)
POS terminal (118)
predictive text (123)
print server (116)
processor (111)
pull notification (124)
push notification (124)

rack server (116)
repetitive strain injury (RSI) (142)
server farm (117)
server virtualization (117)
slate tablet (112)
SLR camera (125)
smart digital camera (125)
smart eyewear (130)
smartglasses (130)
smartwatch (130)
SMS (short message service) (124)
spike (140)
storage server (116)
streaming media player (128)
stylus (112)
supercomputer (120)
surge suppressor (140)
swipe keyboard app (123)
system unit (114)
technology overload (144)

telematics (133)
terminal (117)
text-to-speech feature (129)
thin client (117)
touch-sensitive pad (128)
tower (114)
tower server (116)
ultrabook (111)
USB hub (136)
virtual keyboard (124)
virtualization (117)
visual voice mail (125)
voice mail (125)
wearable (130)
web server (116)
wheel (131)
workstation (114)

phablet (112)

Checkpoint

The Checkpoint exercises test your knowledge of the chapter concepts. The page number containing the answer appears in parentheses after each exercise. The Consider This exercises challenge your understanding of chapter concepts.

Discover More: Visit this chapter's premium content to **complete the Checkpoint exercises** interactively; complete the **self-assessment in the Test Prep resource** from your smartphone, tablet, laptop, or desktop; and then **take the Practice Test**.

True/False   Mark T for True and F for False.

_____ 1. Malware authors often focus on social media, with the goal of stealing personal information. (110)

_____ 2. The disadvantages of a virtual server are that it is difficult to manage and takes a long time to create and configure. (117)

_____ 3. A mainframe is a small terminal that looks like a desktop, but has limited capabilities and components. (117)

_____ 4. Thin clients contain powerful hard drives. (117)

_____ 5. Applications requiring complex, sophisticated mathematical calculations use mainframes. (120)

_____ 6. Most computers and electronic devices are analog, which use only two discrete states: on and off. (125)

_____ 7. SLR cameras are much heavier and larger than point-and-shoot cameras. (125)

_____ 8. Because embedded computers are components in larger products, they usually are small and have limited hardware. (132)

_____ 9. Instead of the term, port, the term, connector, sometimes is used to identify audio and video ports. (134)

_____ 10. Newer versions of USB are backward compatible, which means they support only new USB devices, not older ones. (136)

_____ 11. A port replicator is an external device that provides connections to peripheral devices through ports built into the device. (136)

_____ 12. Because the processor in a computer is particularly sensitive to fluctuations in current, you always should use a surge protector. (141)

Multiple Choice   Select the best answer.

1. Which of the following is *not* true of ultrathin laptops? (111)
   a. They weigh less than traditional laptops.
   b. They have a shorter battery life.
   c. Many have fewer ports than traditional laptops.
   d. They do not include an optical disc drive.

2. Some people use the term _____ to refer to the case that contains and protects the motherboard, internal hard drive, memory, and other electronic components of the computer from damage. (114)
   a. system unit
   b. phablet
   c. thin client
   d. USB hub

3. Power users may work with a high-end desktop, sometimes called a(n) _____, that is designed to handle intense calculations and powerful graphics. (114)
   a. laptop
   b. gaming desktop
   c. server farm
   d. workstation

4. Services provided by _____ include storing content and controlling access to hardware, software, and other resources on a network. (116)
   a. jacks
   b. servers
   c. fault-tolerant computers
   d. mainframes

5. A dedicated server that backs up and restores files, folders, and media is referred to as a _____. (116)
   a. web server
   b. file server
   c. storage server
   d. backup server

6. A four- or five-digit number assigned to a specific content or mobile service provider is referred to as a(n) _____. (124)
   a. CSC
   b. MMS
   c. SMS
   d. SLR

7. A(n) __ is a special-purpose computer that functions as a component in a larger product. (132)
   a. server
   b. embedded computer
   c. thin client
   d. ultrabook

8. A(n) _____ can connect up to 127 different peripheral devices together with a single connector. (136)
   a. SLR device
   b. USB port
   c. port replicator
   d. docking station

Checkpoint

Matching   Match the terms with their definitions.

_____ 1. peripheral device (108)

_____ 2. motherboard (110)

_____ 3. CPU (110)

_____ 4. slate tablet (112)

_____ 5. phablet (112)

_____ 6. server virtualization (117)

_____ 7. thin client (117)

_____ 8. kiosk (119)

_____ 9. push notification (124)

_____ 10. fault-tolerant computer (141)

a. term used to refer to a device that combines the features of a smartphone with a tablet

b. computer with duplicate components so that it can continue to operate when one of its main components fail

c. tablet that does not contain a physical keyboard

d. component you connect to a computer or mobile device to expand its capabilities

e. terminal that looks like a desktop but has limited capabilities and components

f. the use of software to enable a physical server to emulate the hardware and computing capabilities of one or more servers

g. electronic component that interprets and carries out the basic instructions that operate a computer

h. freestanding terminal that usually has a touchscreen for user input

i. message that initiates from a sending location without a request from the receiver

j. the main circuit board of a personal computer

Consider This   Answer the following questions in the format specified by your instructor.

1. Answer the critical thinking questions posed at the end of these elements in this chapter: Ethics & Issues (111, 122, 132, 133), How To (137, 138, 141, 143), Mini Features (113, 115, 128), Secure IT (110, 119, 125, 136), and Technology @ Work (145).

2. How do malware authors use social media to spread infection? (110)

3. What are the two main components of the motherboard? (110)

4. How do ultrathin laptops differ from traditional laptops? (111)

5. What privacy issues have arisen with webcams in mobile devices? (111)

6. What are the two types of tablets? (112)

7. What is a stylus? (112)

8. What is in the system unit? (114)

9. What are the features of a gaming desktop? (114)

10. Who might use a workstation? (114)

11. What additional requirements are associated with a dedicated server? (116)

12. What are the three form factors for servers? (116)

13. What are the advantages of virtual servers? (117)

14. How does a POS terminal serve as input? (118)

15. What are some examples of self-serve kiosks? (119)

16. How does cloud computing allow businesses to more efficiently manage resources? (122)

17. What are three types of cloud computing? (122)

18. What information might you receive from a web to mobile text message? (124)

19. For what purpose is a common short code (CSC) used? (124)

20. How do push notifications differ from pull notifications? (124)

21. How do SLR cameras differ from point-and-shoot cameras? (125)

22. What is the difference between enhanced and optical resolution? (127)

23. What are three popular wearable devices? (130)

24. Why are embedded computers usually small with limited hardware? (132)

25. What are some types of ports you might find on a computer or mobile device? (135)

26. What is the purpose of a docking station? (137)

27. What is necessary before two Bluetooth devices can communicate? (138)

28. Why might you want to connect your phone to a Wi-Fi network? (138)

29. How does a surge protector work? What is the purpose of an uninterruptible power supply? (140)

30. How can you prevent RSIs and CTS? (142)

✳ Problem Solving

The Problem Solving exercises extend your knowledge of chapter concepts by seeking solutions to practical problems with technology that you may encounter at home, school, or work. The Collaboration exercise should be completed with a team.

Instructions: You often can solve problems with technology in multiple ways. Determine a solution to the problems in these exercises by using one or more resources available to you (such as a computer or mobile device, articles on the web or in print, blogs, podcasts, videos, television, user guides, other individuals, electronics or computer stores, etc.). Describe your solution, along with the resource(s) used, in the format requested by your instructor (brief report, presentation, discussion, blog post, video, or other means).

Personal

1. **Slow Computer Performance**   Your computer is running exceptionally slow. Not only does it take the operating system a long time to start, but programs also are not performing as well as they used to perform. How might you resolve this?

2. **Faulty ATM**   When using an ATM to deposit a check, the ATM misreads the amount of the check and credits your account the incorrect amount. What can you do to resolve this?

Source: Google

3. **Wearable Device Not Syncing**   Your wearable device synchronized with your smartphone this morning when you turned it on, but the two devices no longer are synchronized. What might be wrong, and what are your next steps?

4. **Battery Draining Quickly**   Although the battery on your smartphone is fully charged, it drains quickly. In some instances when the phone shows that the battery has 30% remaining, it shuts down immediately. What might be wrong?

5. **Potential Virus Infection**   While using your laptop, a message is displayed stating that your computer is infected with a virus and you should tap or click a link to download a program designed to remove the virus. How will you respond?

Professional

6. **Excessive Phone Heat**   While using your smartphone, you notice that throughout the day it gets extremely hot, making it difficult to hold up to your ear. What steps can you take to correct this problem?

7. **Server Not Connecting**   While traveling on a business trip, your phone suddenly stops synchronizing your email messages, calendar information, and contacts. Upon further investigation, you notice an error message stating that your phone is unable to connect to the server. What are your next steps?

8. **Mobile Device Synchronization**   When you plug your smartphone into your computer to synchronize the data, the computer does not recognize that the smartphone is connected. What might be the problem?

9. **Cloud Service Provider**   Your company uses a cloud service provider to back up the data on each employee's computer. Your computer recently crashed, and you need to obtain the backup data to restore to your computer; however, you are unable to connect to the cloud service provider's website. What are your next steps?

10. **Connecting to a Projector**   Your boss asked you to give a presentation to your company's board of directors. When you enter the boardroom and attempt to connect your laptop to the projector, you realize that the cable to connect your laptop to the projector does not fit in any of the ports on your laptop. What are your next steps?

Collaboration

11. **Technology in Energy Management**   Your science instructor is teaching a lesson about how technology has advanced the energy management field. Form a team of three people to prepare a brief report about how technology and energy management are connected. One team member should research how computers play a role in conserving energy. Another team member should research other types of technology present in today's homes and buildings that can conserve energy, and the third team member should research other benefits (such as cost savings) resulting from proper energy management.

The How To: Your Turn exercises present general guidelines for fundamental skills when using a computer or mobile device and then require that you determine how to apply these general guidelines to a specific program or situation.

How To: Your Turn

Discover More: Visit this chapter's premium content to **challenge yourself with additional How To: Your Turn exercises**, which include App Adventure.

Instructions: You often can complete tasks using technology in multiple ways. Figure out how to perform the tasks described in these exercises by using one or more resources available to you (such as a computer or mobile device, articles on the web or in print, online or program help, user guides, blogs, podcasts, videos, other individuals, trial and error, etc.). Summarize your 'how to' steps, along with the resource(s) used, in the format requested by your instructor (brief report, presentation, discussion, blog post, video, or other means).

1 Synchronize a Device

Synchronizing a mobile device with the cloud or a computer provides a backup location for your data should your device fail, or become lost or stolen. While companies such as Google and Apple typically will allow you to download your purchased apps again free of charge, you also should synchronize your data so that it is available in the event a problem with your device arises. The following steps guide you through the process of synchronizing a device.

© iStockPhoto / Krystian Nawrocki

Synchronize with the Cloud

a. Search for an app compatible with your device that allows you to synchronize the data on your device with the cloud. Some device manufacturers, such as Apple, provide a service to synchronize your device with the cloud.

b. If necessary, download and install the app.

c. The first time you run the app, you may need to enter some personal information so that you are able to sign in and access your data in the future.

d. Configure the app to synchronize at your desired interval. If you are synchronizing a smartphone, keep in mind that synchronizing with the cloud will require a data plan. Be sure your data plan supports the amount of data that will be synchronized.

e. Once you have configured the synchronization settings successfully, select the option to manually synchronize your device at this time.

Synchronize with a Computer

a. Install and run the app designed to synchronize your device with your computer. For instance, iTunes is used to synchronize Apple devices with a computer.

b. Connect the device to the computer using the synchronization cable provided.

c. When the synchronization is complete, a message will inform you that it is safe to disconnect the device. Do not disconnect the device before the synchronization is complete, as that may damage the data on the device.

Retrieve Synchronized Data

If you lose your device or the data on your device, you can retrieve the data previously synchronized. To retrieve data synchronized previously, follow the instructions in the program or app used to synchronize your data.

Exercises

1. What type of device are you attempting to synchronize? What programs and apps are available to synchronize your device with the cloud? What programs and apps are available to synchronize your device with a computer?

2. Which program or app did you use to synchronize your device? Why did you choose that program or app instead of the others?

3. How long did it take to synchronize your device? What data on your device did the program or app synchronize?

2 Find, Download, and Read an E-Book on an E-Book Reader

Most e-book readers enable you to find and download new e-books without having to connect to a computer first. To search for and download an e-book, you need to establish an Internet connection through either Wi-Fi or a mobile data plan. The following steps guide you through the process of finding, downloading, and reading an e-book on an e-book reader.

a. Turn on your e-book reader and establish an Internet connection.

b. Navigate to the store on your e-book reader where you can search for and download e-books.

c. Locate the option to search available e-books and then enter the desired search text. You usually can search by the book's title, author, or genre.

✳ How To: Your Turn

d. Perform the search and then browse the search results for the book you want to download and install.

e. Select the option to download the book. Please note that many books cost money to download. If your payment information was entered previously, you may be charged for downloading this e-book. If you do not want to be charged, locate and download an e-book that is free.

f. When the download is complete, return to your list of installed e-books.

g. Select the e-book you have just downloaded to read the e-book.

Exercises

1. What type of e-book reader do you have? Are you happy with the selection of e-books on your e-book reader?

2. In addition to e-book readers, what other types of devices allow you to read e-books?

3. Do e-books cost more or less than traditional print books? What are the advantages and disadvantages of using e-books?

© iStockPhoto / Petar Chernaev

❸ Manage Power for Mobile Computers and Devices

Configuring power management settings on mobile computers and devices will help ensure your battery life is maximized. The following steps guide you

through the process of configuring power management features on mobile computers and devices.

a. Display the Control Panel or Settings on your mobile computer or device.

b. Tap or click the option to display power management or battery settings.

c. If necessary, select a power plan setting to view or modify.

d. Make the necessary adjustments to the settings that affect power consumption. For example, configure the display to dim or turn off after 30 seconds of inactivity. This will allow you enough time to read what is on the screen without having to touch the screen or move the mouse.

e. Save all changes.

Exercises

1. What power management settings have you configured on your mobile computer or device?

2. Compare battery life on your device before and after configuring power management settings. Have you noticed an improvement in battery life? If so, how vmuch?

3. What other power management settings are you able to configure on your mobile computer or device?

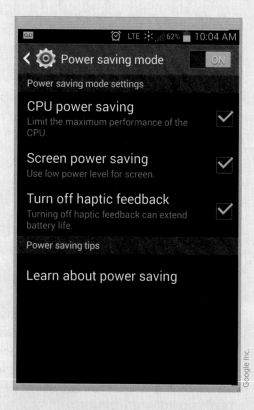

Google Inc.

How To: Your Turn

4 **Use your Mobile Device Ergonomically**

Individuals are using various mobile devices, such as phones and tablets, more frequently, and using these devices ergonomically can help prevent unnecessary injury. The following guidelines will help you use your mobile device ergonomically:

- Use shortcuts and abbreviations whenever possible to avoid excessive hand movement.
- Make sure your hands, wrists, and arms are at a natural angle, and avoid holding the device in a position that causes discomfort.
- Use hands-free devices and voice recognition features whenever possible to avoid hand movement.
- Do not use the device for extended periods of time without taking frequent breaks.
- Avoid resting the device on your lap during use.
- Sit in an upright position or stand when using the device.
- Consider using a separate keyboard and mouse if you will be interacting with the device extensively.
- Use the device in a setting with natural light.

Exercises

1. Have you been following the above guidelines while using mobile computers and devices? If not, what have you been doing differently?
2. What types of health risks might nonergonomic use of a mobile device pose?
3. What are some additional guidelines you can follow to help minimize health risks while using your mobile device?

© Marcin Balcerzak / Shutterstock

5 **Transfer Media from a Mobile Device to a Computer**

Many individuals take photos and record videos using mobile devices such as digital cameras, smartphones, and tablets. After taking the photos and recording the videos, transferring them to a computer allows you easily to create backup copies, edit the media, and create digital albums. The following steps describe multiple ways to transfer media from a mobile device to a computer.

To transfer photos from a mobile device to a computer using a memory card:

a. Safely remove the memory card from the mobile device.
b. Properly insert the memory card into the appropriate memory card slot on the computer.
c. When the computer detects the memory card, navigate to the location of the media to transfer.
d. Select the files to transfer and then drag them to the destination folder on the computer.
e. Use the operating system's "Eject" or "Safely Remove" feature to remove the memory card from the computer safely and insert it back in the mobile device.

To transfer photos from a mobile device to a computer using a USB cable:

a. Connect the cable to the mobile device and to the computer.
b. When the computer detects the mobile device, navigate to the location on the mobile device containing the media to transfer.
c. Select the files to transfer and then drag them to the destination folder on the computer.
d. Disconnect the USB cable from the computer and from the mobile device.

    Some mobile devices also allow you to transfer media using wireless technologies, such as Bluetooth and Wi-Fi. The steps required to transfer photos wirelessly vary greatly for each device. Thus, read your mobile device's documentation to see if and how you can transfer media to your computer wirelessly. Be aware that transferring photos using your mobile data plan could increase your data charges. Consider using Wi-Fi or Bluetooth to transfer the media.

Exercises

1. Of the above techniques, which way do you find is easiest to transfer media from your mobile device to a computer? Why?
2. What other technologies might you be able to use to transfer media from a mobile device to a computer?
3. Would you rather transfer media from your mobile device to a computer, or transfer it to the cloud? Why?

✳ Internet Research

The Internet Research exercises broaden your understanding of chapter concepts by requiring that you search for information on the web.

Discover More: Visit this chapter's premium content to **challenge yourself with additional Internet Research exercises**, which include Search Sleuth, Green Computing, Ethics in Action, You Review It, and Exploring Technology Careers.

Instructions: Use a search engine or another search tool to locate the information requested or answers to questions presented in the exercises. Describe your findings, along with the search term(s) you used and your web source(s), in the format requested by your instructor (brief report, presentation, discussion, blog post, video, or other means).

① Making Use of the Web
Retail and Auctions

E-retailers are changing the ways consumers shop for goods. One market research firm reports that nearly three-fourths of shoppers complete one-half of all their transactions online. As shoppers grow increasingly loyal to e-commerce, retail websites have become more sophisticated, and brick-and-mortar stores have adapted to the online presence. Nearly 90 percent of smartphone owners use their devices to compare prices, locate promotional offers, and determine directions and store hours.

Online auctions offer another convenient method of shopping for and selling practically anything imaginable. Most auction sites organize products in categories and provide photos and descriptions. eBay is one of thousands of Internet auction websites and is the world's largest personal online trading community. In addition, craigslist is a free online equivalent of classified advertisements.

Research This: (a) Visit two retail websites and search for the latest e-book readers. Which features do these websites offer compared with the same offerings in brick-and-mortar stores? What are the advantages and disadvantages of shopping online? What policies do these websites offer for returning items? Which items have you purchased online?

(b) Visit an auction website and search for two objects pertaining to your favorite musical artist, sports team, or celebrity. For example, search for an autographed photo or ticket stubs. Describe these two items. How many people have bid on these items? Who are the sellers? What are the opening and current bids?

Source: eBay

② Social Media

Businesses know that using social media is an efficient and effective method of building brand loyalty and promoting the exchange of ideas. The informal communication between consumers and company representatives can help maintain credibility and promote trust. According to a recent study, more than 70 percent of American Internet users visit online social networks, and 65 percent of these people discover particular brands, products, and services by reading material posted on these websites. Twitter, Facebook, and other social media often are used to befriend customers, give a positive feeling about services and goods, engage readers, and market new ideas. Subscribers share their opinions, thoughts, and experiences, either positive or negative, through product and service reviews.

Research This: Visit at least three Twitter, Facebook, or other online social network sites and review the content. How many Twitter followers or Facebook 'likes' does the website have? Identify three organizations, businesses, products, or causes that have a presence on Facebook, Twitter, or other online social networks. How many followers or fans do they have? Which posts are engaging and promote positive attitudes about the company and the products or services offered? How many user-generated reviews and product ratings are shown? How do the online social networks encourage sharing opinions? In which ways do the companies respond to and interact with followers and fans? If negative posts are written, does the company respond professionally and positively?

③ Search Skills
Search Operators

Search engines provide operators, or special symbols, that will help narrow down search results. Use quotation marks around search text to search for an exact word or phrase. For example, type the following as your search text: "wireless communications technologies" (be sure to include the quotation marks) to search for those three words in that exact order. Search results will display matching pages with the quoted search phrase highlighted or in bold.

Internet Research

To match one or more words in a phrase, you can use an asterisk (*), also called a wildcard operator, as part of your search text. Each asterisk represents one or more words. For example, type the following as your search text: "wireless * technologies" (with the quotation marks) to find search results that match wireless communications technologies, wireless Internet technologies, wireless and related technologies, and others. If you are searching for a phrase or quotation with many words, consider using the asterisk wildcard operator in place of some of the words in the search text. This technique is useful if you have a quotation, and you want to find out who said it or where it may have appeared.

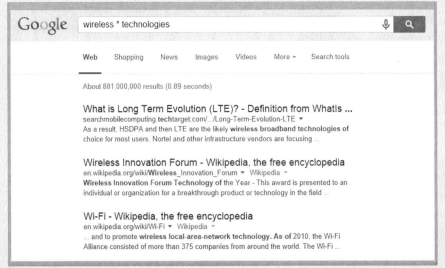

Source: Google

Research This: Create search queries using quotation marks and/or the wildcard operator to answer the following questions and use a search engine to find the answers. (1) Someone once said, "Life is not fair, get used to it." Who was it? (2) What are three websites containing digital camera reviews? (3) How do businesses use near field communications? (4) Find five different words that complete the phrase, handheld ___ devices, by typing appropriate search text into a search engine.

❹ Security

Surge protectors and uninterruptible power supplies offer protection from electrical power surges, as you learned in the Protecting Hardware section of this chapter. While these surges are part of everyday life, they are more likely to occur during thunderstorms and peak energy consumption periods. These unavoidable occurrences can damage or ruin sensitive electronic equipment. The processor in a computer is particularly sensitive to the fluctuations in current. When shopping for a surge protector, purchase the best product you can afford. Typically, the amount of protection offered by a surge protector is proportional to its cost. That is, the more expensive the surge protector, the more protection it offers.

Research This: Visit an electronics store or view websites with a variety of surge protectors from several manufacturers. Read the packaging or specifications to determine many of the features. Compare at least three surge protectors by creating a table using these headings: manufacturer, model, price, Joule rating (a Joule is the unit of energy the device can absorb before it can be damaged; the higher the Joule rating, the better the protection), warranty, energy-absorption rating, response time, and other features. Which surge protector do you recommend? Why?

❺ Cloud Services
Data Providers and Mashups (DaaS)

The web has made it possible for many information providers to make business, housing, weather, demographic, and other data available on demand to third parties. Accessing online data on demand is an example of DaaS (data as a service), a service of cloud computing that provides current data over the Internet for download, analysis, or use in new applications.

Mashups are apps that combine data from one or more online data providers. Mapping mashups are popular because users can visualize locations associated with data originating from a variety of online sources, including real estate listings, crime statistics, current Tweets, live traffic conditions, or digital photos.

Research This: (1) Use a search engine to find two different online data markets. Write a report sharing the sources or focus of information each provides, the availability of visualization tools to preview data, and how developers can access or incorporate the data into their own apps and websites. (2) Use a search engine to find a popular mapping mashup based on data from one of the sources listed above, or another topic. Identify the provider of the data and the provider of the maps on which the data is displayed. (3) Use a search engine to find an app or website that will help you create your own map mashup showing locations of your online data: Facebook friends, Flickr or Instagram photos, or Tweets. Take a screenshot of the mashup you made.

Critical Thinking

The Critical Thinking exercises challenge your assessment and decision-making skills by presenting real-world situations associated with chapter concepts. The Collaboration exercise should be completed with a team.

Instructions: Evaluate the situations below, using personal experiences and one or more resources available to you (such as articles on the web or in print, blogs, podcasts, videos, television, user guides, other individuals, electronics or computer stores, etc.). Perform the tasks requested in each exercise and share your deliverables in the format requested by your instructor (brief report, presentation, discussion, blog post, video, or other means).

1. Technology Purchases

You are the director of information technology at a company that specializes in designing and selling customizable sportswear for local high school and college sports teams. Most of the technology equipment is out of date and must be replaced. You need to evaluate the requirements of individual employees so that you can order replacements.

Do This: Determine the type of computer or mobile device that might be most appropriate for the following employees: a graphic designer who exclusively works in the office, a cashier who is responsible for assisting customers with purchases, and a sales representative who travels to various locations and needs wireless communications capabilities. Consider the varying requirements of each, including mobility, security, and processing capabilities. Discuss various options that might work for each user, and considerations when purchasing each type of device.

2. Game Devices

You manage a youth recreation center and have been given a grant to purchase a game console and accessories, along with fitness games, for use at the center.

Do This: Use the web to research three popular recent game consoles. Choose five characteristics to compare the game consoles, such as Internet capabilities, multiplayer game support, storage capacity, television connection, and game controllers. Research fitness games for each console and what accessories are needed to run the games. Determine the goals of each game, such as skill-building, weight loss, or entertainment. Read user reviews of each game, as well as professional reviews by gaming industry experts. If possible, survey your friends and classmates to learn about their experiences with each game, such as heart rate while playing the games, any fitness goals reached, and their enjoyment of the game.

3. Case Study

Amateur Sports League   You are the new manager for a nonprofit amateur soccer league. The league would like to purchase a digital camera to upload pictures of players, games, and fundraising events to its Facebook page and its website.

Do This: You need to prepare information about digital camera options to present to the board of directors. First, research the cost and quality differences between point-and-shoot cameras and SLR cameras. Use the web to find a recent model of both camera types and compare the reviews, as well as the costs, for each. Make a list of additional features, such as video capabilities, editing capabilities, lens, megapixels, GPS, flash, and zoom. Determine how each camera stores the images, the amount of storage available, and how to transfer images to a computer or mobile device. Explore whether software is included with the camera that can be used to edit, store, or organize the images after they are transferred to a computer. Compare your findings with the camera capabilities of a recent model smartphone. Determine what type of camera would be best for the league's needs and the capabilities that are most important.

Courtesy of Samsung

Collaboration

4. National Security Uses for Technology

Technology is an integral part of military operations. Many military research projects use simulators that resemble civilian computer games. Your company has been contacted by the Department of Defense for a research project.

Do This: Form a four-member team, and then form two two-member groups. Assign each group one of the following topics to research: (1) How have mobile computers and cloud computing affected issues of national security? (2) How can the utilization of microchips worn by soldiers, or wearable computers, be integrated into civilian use? Meet with your team and discuss your findings. Determine any advantages or disadvantages, as well as any legal ramifications that may arise.

PROGRAMS AND APPS: Productivity, Graphics, Security, and Other Tools

People use a variety of programs and apps on their computers and mobile devices.

"I use my computer and mobile devices to complete homework assignments, pay bills, edit digital photos, post social media updates, and play games. I also use an antivirus program. What other programs and apps could I need?"

While you may be familiar with some of the content in this chapter, do you know how to …

- Determine safe websites for downloading software?
- Ensure you are not plagiarizing Internet content?
- Safely use a personal finance app?
- Use project management software?
- Avoid risks when using payment apps?
- Edit and share photos?
- Use voice command personal assistant apps?
- Identify different types of viruses and malware?
- Recognize a virus hoax?
- Protect your smartphone against malware threats?
- Recognize a phishing message?
- Uninstall a program or remove an app?
- Compress and uncompress files and folders?

In this chapter, you will discover how to perform these tasks along with much more information essential to this course. For additional content available that accompanies this chapter, visit the free resources and premium content. Refer to the Preface and the Intro chapter for information about how to access these and other additional instructor-assigned support materials.

✔ Objectives

After completing this chapter, you will be able to:

1 Identify the general categories of programs and apps

2 Describe how an operating system interacts with applications and hardware

3 Differentiate among the ways you can acquire programs and apps: retail, custom, web app, mobile app, mobile web app, shareware, freeware, open source, and public-domain

4 Identify the key features of productivity applications: word processing, presentation, spreadsheet, database, note taking, calendar and contact management, project management, accounting, personal finance, legal, tax preparation, document management, support services, and enterprise computing

5 Identify the key features of graphics and media applications: computer-aided design, desktop publishing, paint/image editing, photo editing and photo management, video and audio editing, multimedia and website authoring, media player, and disc burning

6 Identify the uses of personal interest applications: lifestyle, medical, entertainment, convenience, and education

7 Identify the purpose of software used in communications

8 Identify the key features of security tools: personal firewall, antivirus programs, malware removers, and Internet filters

9 Identify the key features of file, disk, and system management tools: file manager, search, image viewer, uninstaller, disk cleanup, disk defragmenter, screen saver, file compression, PC maintenance, and backup and restore

Programs and Apps

Using programs and apps, you can accomplish a variety of tasks on computers and mobile devices (Figure 4-1). Recall from Chapter 1 that a **program**, or **software**, consists of a series of related instructions, organized for a common purpose, that tells the computer what tasks to perform and how to perform them. An **application**, or **app**, sometimes called *application software*, consists of programs designed to make users more productive and/or assist them with personal tasks.

An *operating system* is a set of programs that coordinates all the activities among computer or mobile device hardware. Other programs, often called *tools* or *utilities*, enable you to perform maintenance-type tasks usually related to managing devices, media, and programs used by computers and mobile devices. The operating system and other tools are collectively known as *system software* because they consist of the programs that control or maintain the operations of the computer and its devices.

Role of the Operating System

To use applications, such as a browser or word processing program on a desktop or laptop, your computer must be running an operating system. Similarly, a mobile device must be running an operating system to run a mobile app, such as a navigation or payment app. Desktop operating systems include Mac OS, Windows, Linux, and Chrome OS. Mobile operating systems include Android, iOS, and Windows Phone. The operating system, therefore, serves as the interface between the user, the applications and other programs, and the computer's or mobile device's hardware (Figure 4-2).

Internet Research

Which mobile operating system is the most widely used?

Search for: mobile operating system market share

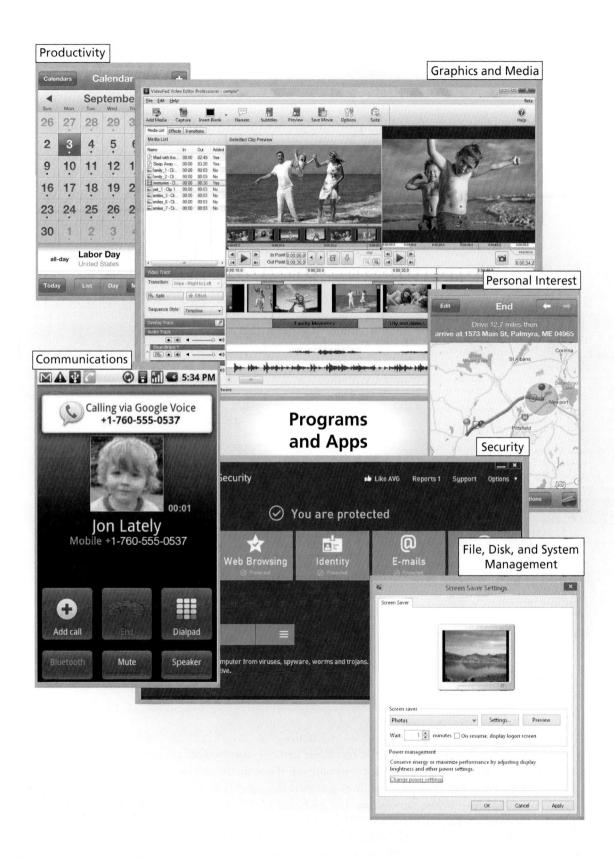

Figure 4-1 Users work with a variety of programs and apps, some of which are shown in this figure.

© Cengage Learning; Courtesy of NCH Software; Source: Apple Inc.; Source: Google Inc.; Courtesy of AVG Technologies; Source: Microsoft

An Example of How an Operating System Interacts with a User, an Application, and Hardware

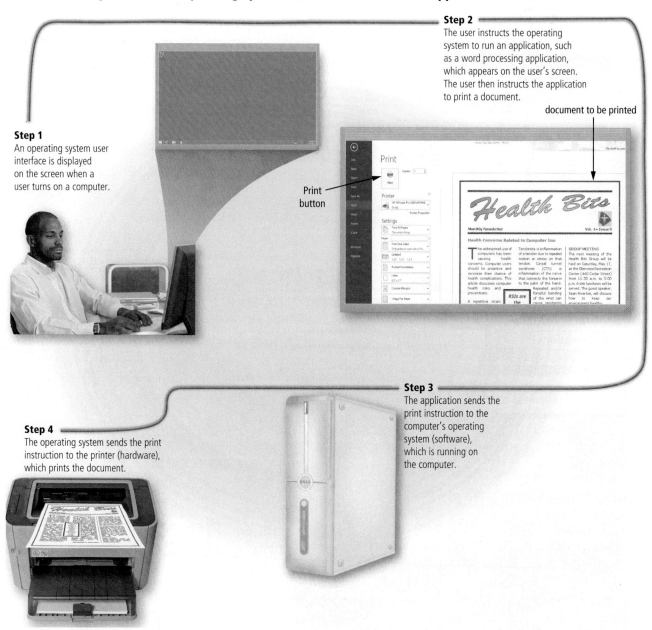

Step 1
An operating system user interface is displayed on the screen when a user turns on a computer.

Step 2
The user instructs the operating system to run an application, such as a word processing application, which appears on the user's screen. The user then instructs the application to print a document.

document to be printed

Print button

Step 3
The application sends the print instruction to the computer's operating system (software), which is running on the computer.

Step 4
The operating system sends the print instruction to the printer (hardware), which prints the document.

Figure 4-2   This figure shows how the operating system is the interface between the user, the application, and the hardware.
© photoguy_76 / Fotolia; © Cengage Learning; © restyler / Shutterstock.com; © StockLite / Shutterstock; Source: Microsoft

Each time you start a computer or mobile device, the operating system is loaded (copied) from the computer's hard drive or mobile device's storage media into memory. Once the operating system is loaded, it coordinates all the activities of the computer or mobile device. This includes running applications and transferring data among input and output devices and memory. While the computer or mobile device is running, the operating system remains in memory.

Discover More: Visit this chapter's free resources to learn more about desktop and mobile operating systems.

Obtaining Software

Software is available in a variety of forms: retail, custom, web app, mobile app, mobile web app, shareware, freeware, open source, and public domain.

- *Retail software* is mass-produced, copyrighted software that meets the needs of a wide variety of users, not just a single user or company. Some retail software, such as an operating system, is preinstalled on new computers and mobile devices. You also can purchase retail software from local stores and on the web. With online purchases, you may be able to download purchased programs immediately instead of waiting for the software to arrive by mail.
- *Custom software* performs functions specific to a business or industry. Sometimes a company cannot locate retail software that meets its unique requirements. In this case, the company may use software developers to create tailor-made custom software. Custom software usually costs more than retail software.
- A *web app* is an application stored on a web server that you access through a browser. Users typically interact with web apps directly by visiting a website, but some web apps also can be accessed locally offline. Many websites provide free access to their apps. Some charge a one-time fee, while others charge recurring monthly or annual subscription fees. You may be able to use part of a web app free and pay for access to a more comprehensive program or pay a fee when a certain action occurs.
- A *mobile app* is an application you download from a mobile device's app store, sometimes called a *marketplace*, or other location on the Internet to a smartphone or other mobile device. Some mobile apps are preinstalled on a new mobile computer or device. Many mobile apps are free; others have a minimal cost — often less than a few dollars.
- A *mobile web app* is a web app that is optimized for display in a browser on a mobile device, regardless of screen size or orientation. Many app developers opt for web delivery because they do not have to create a different version for each mobile device's app store. Many web apps use a responsive design, which means the app displays properly on any computer or device.
- *Shareware* is copyrighted software that is distributed at no cost for a trial period. To use a shareware program beyond that period, you send payment to the software developer or you might be billed automatically unless you cancel within a specified period of time. Some developers trust users to send payment if software use extends beyond the stated trial period. Others render the software useless if no payment is received after the trial period expires. In some cases, a scaled-down version of the software is distributed free, and payment entitles the user to the fully functional product.
- *Freeware* is copyrighted software provided at no cost by an individual or a company that retains all rights to the software. Thus, software developers typically cannot incorporate freeware in applications they intend to sell. The word, free, in freeware indicates the software has no charge.
- *Open source software* is software provided for use, modification, and redistribution. This software has no restrictions from the copyright holder regarding modification of the software's internal instructions and its redistribution. Open source software usually can be downloaded from a web server on the Internet, often at no cost. Promoters of open source software state two main advantages: users who modify the software share their improvements with others, and customers can personalize the software to meet their needs.
- *Public-domain software* has been donated for public use and has no copyright restrictions. Anyone can copy or distribute public-domain software to others at no cost.

 BTW

Trial Versions
Some retail and other programs have a *trial version*, which is an application you can use at no charge for a limited time, to see if it meets your needs. Some trial versions have limited functionality.

BTW

Copyright
A copyright gives authors, artists, and other creators of original work exclusive rights to duplicate, publish, and sell their materials.

Thousands of shareware, freeware, and public-domain programs are available on the Internet for users to download. Examples include communications, graphics, and game programs. Read Secure IT 4-1 for tips about safely downloading shareware, freeware, or public-domain software.

Discover More: Visit this chapter's free resources to learn more about software availability.

✦ SECURE IT 4-1

📄 Safe Downloading Websites

Websites tempt potential customers with catchy offers for software promising to speed up the computer or to obtain the latest versions of games and music. The temptation to download shareware, freeware, and public-domain software is high, especially when the cost of such useful or fun programs is free or extremely reasonable. This action could be dangerous, however, because some of these websites are filled with virus-infected software just waiting to be installed on an unsuspecting user's computer or mobile device.

Before downloading any software, consider these factors when locating and evaluating shareware, freeware, or public-domain websites:

- Search for popular shareware, freeware, and public-domain download websites.

The software generally is organized into evaluation categories, such as outstanding and recommended, or grouped into purpose, such as tools and gaming.

- Look for websites with programs for your particular type of computer or mobile device. Some websites exclusively offer Windows- or Apple-based products.

- Obtain the latest versions of shareware, freeware, and public-domain software. Many developers update their programs frequently in an effort to include new features and to thwart viruses. The newest versions, therefore, often are safer and easier to use than previous versions.

- Locate websites with a variety of programs in a specific category. For example, if you need antivirus software, you can search

to find which shareware, freeware, and public-domain software is available.

- Read ratings for and reviews of products. Often, comments from users provide guidance in selecting the most desirable software for your needs.

If you follow these tips, you may find shareware, freeware, and public-domain software to be one of the best software bargains in the marketplace.

☀ Consider This: Have you ever used or downloaded programs or apps from a shareware, freeware, or public-domain software website? If so, what software did you acquire? If not, would you consider locating shareware, freeware, or public-domain software for your particular needs? Why or why not?

☀ CONSIDER THIS

What is software as a service?

Software as a service (SaaS) describes a computing environment where an Internet server hosts and deploys applications. Editing projects or photos, sending email messages, and managing finances are common consumer tasks of SaaS applications. For an exercise related to SaaS, see the Internet Research: Cloud Services exercise at the end of this chapter.

Installing Software

Recall from Chapter 1 that you typically need to install desktop apps on a computer. Installing is the process of setting up the software to work with a computer, printer, and other hardware. Mobile apps typically install automatically after you download the app from the device's app store. You usually do not need to install web apps before you can use them, but you may need to install plug-ins, such as Java or Flash, so that the web apps work.

During installation of software or before the first use, a program or app may ask you to register and/or activate the software. *Software registration* typically is optional and usually involves submitting your name and other personal information to the software manufacturer or developer. Registering the software often entitles you to product support. *Product activation* is a technique that some software manufacturers use to ensure that you do not install the software on more computers than legally licensed. Usually, the software can be run a preset number of times, has limited

BTW

Syncing Apps
When you install an app on one computer or device, it also will install automatically on any other computers and devices on the same subscription plan.

functionality, or does not function until you activate it via the Internet or by phone. Thus, activation is a required process for programs that request it. Some software allows multiple activations; for example, you can install it and run it on a laptop and a desktop. Registering and/ or activating software also usually entitles you to free program updates for a specified time period, such as a year.

Many desktop and mobile apps use an *automatic update* feature, where the updates can be configured to download and install automatically. With web apps, by contrast, you always access the latest version of the software.

✳ **CONSIDER THIS** ———————————————————————

What is a license agreement?

A *license agreement*, sometimes called an end-user license agreement (*EULA*), is the right to use a program or app. The license agreement provides specific conditions for use of the software, which a user typically must accept before using the software (Figure 4-3). Unless otherwise specified by a license agreement, you do not have the right to copy, loan, borrow, rent, or in any way distribute programs or apps. Doing so is a violation of copyright law; it also is a federal crime.

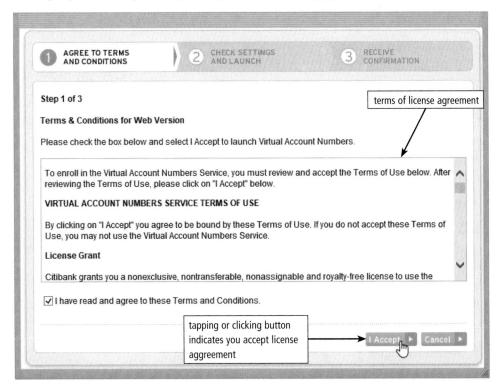

Figure 4-3   A user must accept the terms in a license agreement before using the software.
Source: Citigroup Inc

Categories of Programs and Apps

With programs and apps, you can work on a variety of projects — such as creating letters, memos, reports, and other documents; developing presentations; preparing and filing taxes; drawing and altering images; recording and enhancing audio and video clips; obtaining directions or maps; playing games individually or with others; composing email and other messages; protecting computers and mobile devices from malware; organizing media; locating files; and much more. Table 4-1 categorizes popular categories of programs and apps by their general use.

Table 4-1 Programs and Apps by Category

Category	Types of Programs and Apps	
Productivity (Business and Personal)	• Word Processing • Presentation • Spreadsheet • Database • Note Iaking • Calendar and Contact Management • Project Management	• Accounting • Personal Finance • Legal • Tax Preparation • Document Management • Support Services • Enterprise Computing
Graphics and Media	• Computer-Aided Design (CAD) • Desktop Publishing • Paint/Image Editing • Photo Editing and Photo Management • Clip Art/Image Gallery	• Video and Audio Editing • Multimedia and Website Authoring • Media Player • Disc Burning
Personal Interest	• Lifestyle • Medical • Entertainment • Convenience • Education	
Communications	• Blog • Browser • Chat Room • Online Discussion • Email • File Transfer	• Internet Phone • Internet Messaging • Mobile Messaging • Videoconference • Web Feeds
Security	• Personal Firewall • Antivirus • Malware Removers • Internet Filters	
File, Disk, and System Management	• File Manager • Search • Image Viewer • Uninstaller • Disk Cleanup	• Disk Defragmenter • Screen Saver • File Compression • PC Maintenance • Backup and Restore

CONSIDER THIS

Are the categories of programs and apps shown in Table 4-1 mutually exclusive?

Programs and apps listed in one category may be used in other categories. For example, photo editing applications, which appear in the graphics and media category, often also are used for business or personal productivity. Additionally, the programs and apps in the last three categories (communications; security; and file, disk, and system management) often are used in conjunction with or to support programs and apps in the first three categories (productivity, graphics and media, and personal interest). For example, email appears in the communications category but also is a productivity application.

Productivity Applications

Productivity applications can assist you in becoming more effective and efficient while performing daily activities at work, school, and home. Productivity applications include word processing, presentation, spreadsheet, database, note taking, calendar and contact management, project management, accounting, personal finance, legal, tax preparation, document management, and enterprise computing.

A variety of manufacturers offer productivity apps in each of these areas, ranging from desktop to mobile to web apps. Many have a desktop version and a corresponding mobile version adapted for smaller screen sizes and/or touch screens.

Developing Projects

With productivity applications, users often create, edit, format, save, and distribute projects. Projects include documents, presentations, spreadsheets, notes, calendars, contact lists, budgets, and more.

During the process of developing a project, you likely will switch back and forth among the following activities.

1. When you *create* a project, you enter text or numbers, insert images, add contacts, schedule appointments, and perform other tasks using a variety of input methods, such as a keyboard, a mouse, touch, or voice.
2. To *edit* a project means to make changes to its existing content. Common editing tasks include inserting, deleting, cutting, copying, and pasting.
   a. Inserting involves adding text, images, or other content.
   b. Deleting involves removing text, images, or other content.
   c. Cutting is the process of removing content and storing it in a temporary storage location, called a *clipboard*.
   d. Copying is the process of placing content on a clipboard, with the content remaining in the project. Read Ethics & Issues 4-1 for a discussion about unethical copying.
   e. Pasting is the process of transferring content from a clipboard to a specific location in a project.

✸ ETHICS & ISSUES 4-1

What Can Schools and Employers Do to Prevent Internet Plagiarism?
The Internet has made it easier for students and employees to plagiarize; in contrast, it also provides tools that schools and employers can use to detect illegal copying. Schools often have specific rules about what constitutes plagiarism. Employees, such as journalists, are expected to follow ethical guidelines when copying or citing content.

The Internet offers many ways for students to cheat intentionally, including websites that allow you to purchase a research paper. Students may not realize that copying information without properly citing it also is plagiarism. Students who intentionally plagiarize blame competition. Teachers have several tools to catch plagiarists,

including services that compare papers to others on the Internet and produce a report highlighting content resembling previously published writing.

A journalist might be expected not only to produce multiple articles daily but also to use social media to keep readers engaged. This pressure tempts some journalists to copy content, sometimes without giving credit or linking to the original source. The laws against plagiarism are the same whether copying content from a respected news source, a personal blog, or social media. The pressures of time and expectations of content can create high-profile cases of plagiarism that affect not only the journalist but the news source for which he or she writes.

Some argue that the best way to prevent cheating is to educate. First, teach the values and discuss the consequences of cheating. Next, teach how to cite sources properly and summarize information. Before copying or paraphrasing another person's work, contact him or her to request permission. When in doubt, check with a librarian, editor, or instructor.

Consider This: How should educators and employers deal with plagiarism? Should schools use a paper-comparison service in an attempt to stop cheating? Why or why not? Does linking to the original source excuse a journalist who copies content? Why or why not?

3. When users *format* a project, they change its appearance. Formatting is important because the overall look of a project significantly can affect its capability to communicate information clearly. Examples of formatting tasks are changing the font, font size, and font style (Figure 4-4).

   a. A *font* is a name assigned to a specific design of characters. Cambria and Calibri are examples of fonts.

   b. *Font size* indicates the size of the characters in a particular font. Font size is gauged by a measurement system called points. A single point is about 1/72 of an inch in height.

   c. A *font style* adds emphasis to a font. Bold, italic, underline, and color are examples of font styles.

4. During the process of creating, editing, and formatting a project, the computer or mobile device holds it in memory. To keep the project for future use requires that you save it. When you *save* a project, the computer transfers the project from memory to a local storage medium, such as a USB flash drive or hard drive, or cloud storage, so that you can retrieve it later.

5. You can distribute a project as a hard copy or electronically. A *hard copy* is information that exists on a physical medium, such as paper. To generate a hard copy, you *print* a project. Sending electronic files via email or posting them for others to view, on websites for example, saves paper and printer supplies. Many users opt for electronic distribution because it contributes to green computing.

Figure 4-4 The Cambria and Calibri fonts are shown in two font sizes and a variety of font styles.
© Cengage Learning

 CONSIDER THIS

How often should you save a project, and why do some apps not require you save?
Saving at regular intervals, such as every 5 or 10 minutes, ensures that the majority of your work will not be lost in the event of a power loss or system failure. Many programs have an AutoSave feature that automatically saves open projects at specified time intervals, such as every 10 minutes.

Some web and mobile apps, such as online productivity apps, save your work instantly as you type. These apps and the document both are stored on the cloud. Thus, the app automatically saves your changes to a cloud server with every keystroke.

CONSIDER THIS

What is a clip art/image gallery?
Applications often include a **clip art/image gallery**, which is a collection of clip art and photos. Some applications contain links to additional clips available on the web or are available as web apps. You also can purchase clip art/image gallery software that contains thousands of images.

In addition to clip art and photos, many clip art/image galleries provide fonts, animations, sounds, video clips, and audio clips. You can use the images, fonts, and other items from the clip art/image gallery in all types of projects, including documents, brochures, worksheets, and slide shows.

Word Processing

Word processing software, sometimes called a word processor, is an application that allows users to create and manipulate documents containing mostly text and sometimes graphics (Figure 4-5). Millions of people use word processing software on their computers and mobile devices every day to develop documents such as letters, memos, reports, mailing labels, newsletters, and webpages.

A major advantage of using word processing software is that it enables users to change their written words easily. Word processing software also has many features to make documents look professional and visually appealing. For example, you can change the font, size, and color of characters; apply special effects, such as three-dimensional shadows; use built-in styles to format documents; and organize text in newspaper-style columns.

Most word processing software allows users to incorporate graphics, such as digital photos and clip art, in documents. In Figure 4-5, a user inserted an image of a tractor in the document. With word processing software, you easily can modify the appearance of an image after inserting it in the document.

You can use word processing software to define the size of the paper on which to print and to specify the margins. A feature, called wordwrap, allows users to type words in a paragraph continually without pressing the ENTER key at the end of each line. While you edit a paragraph or change the paragraph margins, the words in the paragraph automatically wrap, or reflow within the paragraph. As you type more lines of text than can be displayed on the screen, the top portion of the document moves upward, or scrolls, off the screen.

Internet Research

What are the guidelines for writing business letters?

Search for: business letter writing

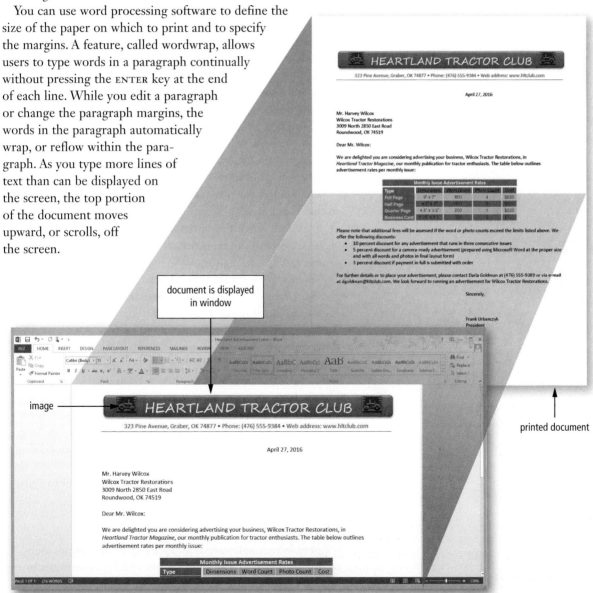

document is displayed in window

image

printed document

Figure 4-5 Word processing software enables users to create professional and visually appealing documents.
Microsoft; © Cengage Learning

Figure 4-6 This presentation created with presentation software consists of five slides.
Source: Microsoft; © Cengage Learning

Word processing software typically includes tools to assist you with the writing process. For example, a spelling checker reviews the spelling of individual words, sections of a document, or the entire document. A grammar checker detects passive voice, run-on sentences, and grammatical errors. A format checker identifies extraneous spaces, capitalization errors, and more.

Discover More: Visit this chapter's free resources to learn more about word processing software and features.

Presentation

Presentation software is an application that allows users to create visual aids for presentations to communicate ideas, messages, and other information to a group. The presentations can be viewed as slides, sometimes called a *slide show*, that are displayed on a large monitor or on a projection screen from a computer or mobile device (Figure 4-6).

Presentation software typically provides a variety of predefined presentation formats that define complementary colors for backgrounds, text, and graphical accents on the slides. This software also provides a variety of layouts for each individual slide such as a title slide, a two-column slide, and a slide with clip art, a chart, a table, or a diagram. In addition, you can enhance any text, charts, and graphics on a slide with 3-D effects, animation, and other special effects, such as shading, shadows, and textures.

When building a presentation, users can set the slide timing so that the presentation automatically displays the next slide after a preset delay. Presentation software allows you to apply special effects to the transition between slides. One slide, for example, might fade away as the next slide appears.

Presentation software typically includes a clip gallery that provides images, photos, video clips, and audio clips to enhance presentations. Some audio and video editing applications work with presentation software, providing users with an easy means to record and insert video, music, and audio commentary in a presentation.

You can view or print a finished presentation in a variety of formats, including a hard copy outline of text from each slide and handouts that show completed slides. Presentation software also incorporates features such as checking spelling, formatting, researching, and creating webpages from existing slide shows.

Discover More: Visit this chapter's free resources to learn more about presentation software.

Spreadsheet

Spreadsheet software is an application that allows users to organize data in columns and rows and perform calculations on the data. These columns and rows collectively are called a **worksheet**. Most spreadsheet software has basic features to help users create, edit, and format worksheets. A spreadsheet file also is known as a workbook because it can contain thousands of related individual worksheets. Data is organized vertically in columns and horizontally in rows on each worksheet (Figure 4-7).

Each worksheet usually can have thousands of columns and rows. One or more letters identify each column, and a number identifies each row. Only a small fraction of these columns and rows are visible on the screen at one time. Scrolling through the worksheet displays different parts of it on the screen.

A cell is the intersection of a column and row. The spreadsheet software identifies cells by the column and row in which they are located. For example, the intersection of column B and row 4 is referred to as cell B4. As shown in Figure 4-7, cell B4 contains the number, $1,000.29, which represents the wages for January.

Many of the worksheet cells shown in Figure 4-7 contain a number, called a value, that can be used in a calculation. Other cells, however, contain formulas that generate values. A formula performs calculations on the data in the worksheet and displays the resulting value in a cell, usually the cell containing the formula. When creating a worksheet, you can enter your own formulas. In Figure 4-7, for example, cell B17 could contain the formula =B9+B10+B11+B12+ B13+B14+B15+B16, which would add (sum) the contents of cells B9, B10, B11, B12, B13, B14, B15, and B16. That is, this formula calculates the total expenses for January.

A *function* is a predefined formula that performs common calculations, such as adding the values in a group of cells or generating a value such as the time or date. For example, the function =SUM(B9:B16) instructs the spreadsheet application to add all of the numbers in the range of cells B9 through B16. Spreadsheet applications contain many built-in functions.

One of the more powerful features of spreadsheet software is its capability to recalculate the rest of the worksheet when data in a cell changes. Spreadsheet software's capability of recalculating data also makes it a valuable budgeting, forecasting, and decision-making tool. Another standard feature of spreadsheet software is charting, which depicts the data in graphical form, such as bar charts or pie charts. A visual representation of data through charts often makes it easier for users to see at a glance the relationship among the numbers.

Discover More: Visit this chapter's free resources to learn more about spreadsheet software and built-in functions.

BTW

Formulas
In many spreadsheet apps, a formula begins with an equal sign (=).

BTW

Technology Innovator
Discover More: Visit this chapter's free resources to learn about Dan Bricklin (cocreator of the first spreadsheet program).

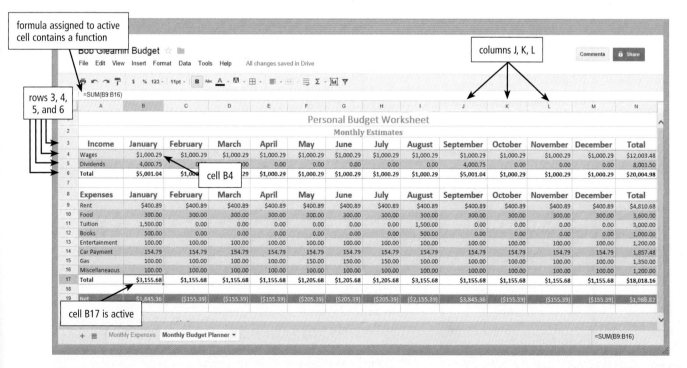

Figure 4-7 With spreadsheet software, you create worksheets that contain data arranged in columns and rows, and you can perform calculations on the data in the worksheets.
Source: Google Inc.

Database

A **database** is a collection of data organized in a manner that allows access, retrieval, and use of that data. In a manual database, you might record data on paper and store it in a filing cabinet. With a database stored electronically, such as the one shown in Figure 4-8, the computer stores the data on a storage medium, such as a hard drive or optical disc, or on cloud storage.

Database software is an application that allows users to create, access, and manage a database. Using database software, you can add, change, and delete data in a database; sort and retrieve data from the database; and create forms and reports using the data in the database.

With most personal computer database programs, a database consists of a collection of tables, organized in rows and columns. Each row, called a record, contains data about a given item in the database, which is often a person, product, object, or event. Each column, called a field, contains a specific category of data within a record. The Publishing database shown in Figure 4-8 consists of two tables: a Customer table and a Book Rep table. The Customer table contains 15 records (rows), each storing data about one customer. The customer data is grouped into 10 fields (columns): CU # (customer number), Customer Name, Street, City, State, Postal Code, Amount Paid, Current Due, Returns, and BR # (book rep number). The Current Due field, for instance, contains the amount of money the customer owes the publisher. The Customer and Book Rep tables relate to each other through a common field, BR # (book rep number).

Users run queries to retrieve data. A query is a request for specific data from the database. For example, a query might request a list of customers whose balance is greater than $20,000. After obtaining the results of a query, database applications can present them on the screen, send them to a printer, or save them in a file.

✴ CONSIDER THIS

When should you use a database instead of a spreadsheet program?
Although databases and spreadsheets both store data, these programs have different purposes and capabilities. Spreadsheet programs are ideal for calculating results or creating charts from value in the worksheet. You should use a database program, however, if want to collect, reorganize and filter data, and/or create reports from the data.

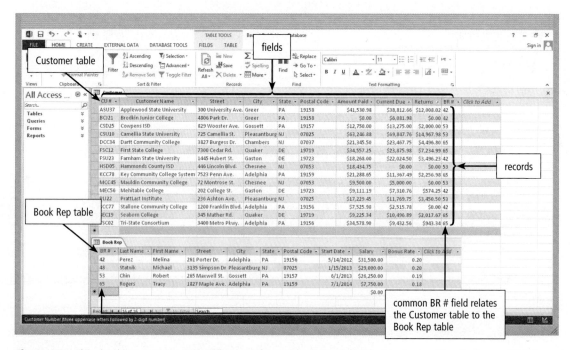

Figure 4-8   This database contains two tables: one for customers and one for book reps. The Customer table has 15 records and 10 fields; the Book Rep table has 4 records and 10 fields.
Source: Microsoft

Discover More: Visit this chapter's free resources to learn more about personal computer database programs.

Note Taking

Note taking software is an application that enables users to enter typed text, handwritten comments, drawings, sketches, photos, and links anywhere on a page and then save the page as part of a notebook (Figure 4-9). Users also can include audio recordings as part of their notes. Some enable users to sync their notes to the cloud so that they can access the notes on any computer or mobile device. Many note taking applications also include a calendar feature.

Users find note taking software convenient during meetings, class lectures and conferences, and in libraries and other settings that previously required pencil and paper for recording thoughts and discussions.

Discover More: Visit this chapter's free resources to learn more about note taking applications.

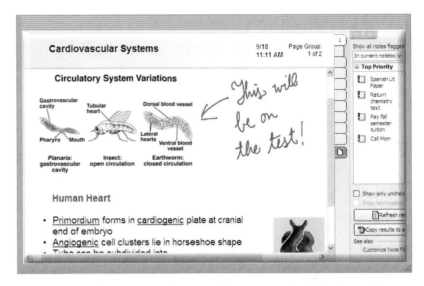

Figure 4-9 With note taking software, mobile users can handwrite notes, draw sketches, insert photos and links, and type text.
Source: Microsoft

Calendar and Contact Management

Calendar and contact management software is an application that helps you organize your calendar, keep track of contacts, and share this information with other users, who can view it on their computers and mobile devices (Figure 4-10). This software provides a way for individuals and workgroups to organize, find, view, and share appointment and contact information easily. Although sometimes available separately, calendar and contact management software often exists as a unit in a single program. Many email applications include calendar and contact management features.

 BTW
Technology Trend

Discover More: Visit this chapter's free resources to learn about the note taking app, Evernote.

Figure 4-10 Users can share schedules with other users via calendar and contact management applications.
Google Inc.

Calendar and contact management applications enable you to synchronize information. This means that all of your computers and mobile devices, along with your organization's server or cloud storage, have the latest version of any updated information.

Discover More: Visit this chapter's free resources to learn more about calendar and contact management applications.

Software Suite

A **software suite** is a collection of individual related applications available together as a unit. Productivity software suites typically include, at a minimum, word processing, presentation, spreadsheet, and email applications. While several productivity suites are designed to be installed on a local computer, some are web apps and/or mobile web apps that enabling you to share and collaborate with projects stored on the cloud.

 CONSIDER THIS

Why would you use a software suite instead of a stand-alone application?
Software suites offer three major advantages: lower cost, ease of use, and integration.

- When you purchase a software suite, the suite usually costs significantly less than purchasing each application individually, or as stand-alone applications.

- Software suites provide ease of use because the applications in the suite normally use a consistent interface and share features, such as clip art and spelling checker.

- Applications in a software suite often are integrated, which makes it easy to share information among them. For example, you can copy a chart created from a worksheet in a spreadsheet program and paste it into a slideshow in the presentation software.

Discover More: Visit this chapter's free resources to learn more about software suites.

Project Management

Project management software is an application that allows a user to plan, schedule, track, and analyze the events, resources, and costs of a project. Project management software helps users manage project variables, allowing them to complete a project on time and within budget. A marketing manager, for example, might use project management software to schedule the processes required in a product launch (Figure 4-11). Read How To 4-1 to learn how you can manage a project using project management software.

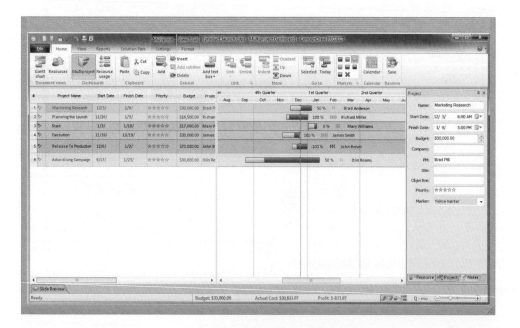

Figure 4-11 With project management software, you can plan and schedule the tasks and processes required in a project.
Courtesy of CS Odessa

HOW TO 4-1

Manage a Project Using Project Management Software

Several project management programs and apps exist that are both free and fee based. Project management programs and apps are designed for projects of specific sizes, so be sure to research the various programs and apps on the market and choose one that best suits your needs. To manage a project using project management software, follow these steps:

1. Make sure you understand the project in its entirety, as well as the steps you must take to bring the project to completion.

2. Determine the date by which the project must be completed.

3. Verify you have the appropriate resources (people and materials) to complete the project. If you do not have the necessary resources, you should obtain them.

4. Determine the order of the steps that must be taken to bring the project to completion. Identify steps that must be taken before other steps, as well as steps that can be completed at the same time as other steps.

5. Verify the feasibility of the plan.

6. During the project, it will be necessary to update the progress and possibly adjust dates. Changes to the project and its dates should be communicated to the entire project team.

Consider This: Do you think project management software can help individuals complete a project more quickly? Why or why not?

CONSIDER THIS

Does the term, project, have two meanings in the technology field?

Yes. As discussed earlier in this chapter, a project can be a deliverable you create using application software, such as a document, presentation, spreadsheet, notes, calendar, contact list, budget, and more. A project also describe the collection of tasks and processes required to develop a solution to a problem.

Accounting

Accounting software is an application that helps businesses of all sizes record and report their financial transactions. With accounting software, business users perform accounting activities related to the general ledger, accounts receivable, accounts payable, purchasing, invoicing (Figure 4-12), and payroll functions. Accounting software also enables business users to write and print checks, track checking account activity, and update and reconcile balances on demand.

Most accounting software supports online credit checks, bill payment, direct deposit, and payroll services. Some offer more complex features, such as job costing and estimating, time tracking, multiple company reporting, foreign currency reporting, and forecasting the amount of raw materials needed for products. The cost of accounting software for small businesses ranges from less than one hundred to several thousand dollars. Accounting software for large businesses can cost several hundred thousand dollars.

Discover More: Visit this chapter's free resources to learn more about accounting software.

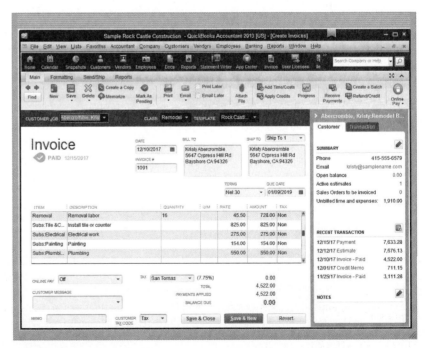

Figure 4-12   Accounting software helps businesses record and report their financial transactions.
Courtesy of Intuit

Personal Finance

Personal finance software is a simplified accounting application that helps home users and small/home office users balance their checkbooks, pay bills, track personal income and expenses, verify account balances, transfer funds, track investments, and evaluate financial plans (Figure 4-13). Personal finance software helps determine where, and for what purpose, you are spending money so that you can manage your finances.

Most personal finance software includes financial planning features, such as analyzing home and personal loans, preparing income taxes, and managing retirement savings. Other features include managing home inventory and setting up budgets. Most of these applications also offer a variety of online services, such as online banking and online investing. Read Secure IT 4-2 for safety tips when using personal finance apps on your smartphone or other mobile device.

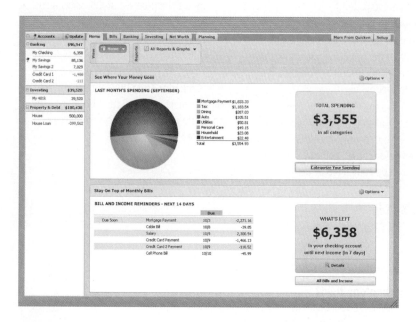

Figure 4-13   Personal finance software assists home users with tracking personal accounts.
Courtesy of Intuit

⊛ SECURE IT 4-2

📄 Using Personal Finance Apps Safely

Personal finance apps offer convenient and easy methods to pay bills, deposit checks, examine account balances, verify payments, and transfer funds. They also are a magnet for cybercriminals to snatch an unsuspecting user's personal information and send it to someone else anywhere in the world, who then can use the information for monetary transactions. Nearly one-third of malware banking apps target customers in the United States with malicious instructions that invade their smartphones and gain access to information stored on their devices. Users in Brazil, Australia, and France also are becoming extremely popular targets for banking thieves. By using caution and common sense, however, users can take steps to safeguard their funds and their identities by following these practices:

- **Evaluate the apps.** Fraudulent apps may resemble legitimate apps from financial institutions. They often, however, are riddled with misspellings and awkward sentences. In addition, legitimate companies rarely promote downloading an app from a pop-up or pop-under advertisement. If you desire an app from a bank or other financial institution, visit that company's website for instructions about downloading and installing its authentic apps.

- **Use strong passwords to access the apps.** Many of the more secure personal finance apps have dual passwords that involve typing a string of characters and also validating a picture. In addition, be certain to password protect your mobile device.

- **Guard your smartphone.** At least 100 smartphones are lost or stolen every minute in the United States according to MicroTrax, an asset protection company. With that figure in mind, store as little personal information as possible on your phone so that if the mobile device is lost, the chance of having your identity stolen and your accounts compromised is lessened. Also install software to locate your lost or stolen device and to erase its content remotely.

- **Verify the transactions.** Always verify your transactions by scrutinizing monthly statements. In addition, periodically check balances and alert your financial institution if any activity seems abnormal.

⊛ **Consider This:** Have you used finance apps? If so, which ones? When making transactions, do you follow some of the tips described in this box? If not, would you consider downloading an app to complete some common banking transactions? Why or why not?

Legal

Legal software is an application that assists in the preparation of legal documents and provides legal information to individuals, families, and small businesses (Figure 4-14). Legal software provides standard contracts and documents associated with buying, selling, and renting property; estate planning; marriage and divorce; and preparing a will or living trust. By answering a series of questions or completing a form, the legal software tailors the legal document to specific needs. Read Ethics & Issues 4-2 to consider whether an attorney should review documents created with legal software.

Discover More: Visit this chapter's free resources to learn more about legal software.

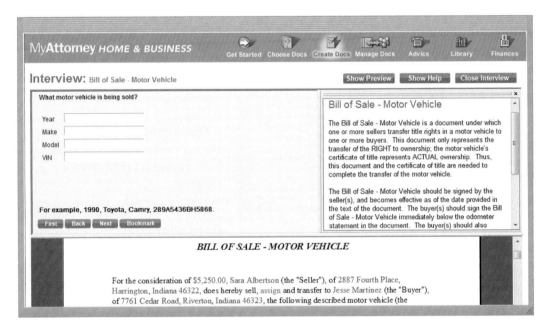

Figure 4-14   Legal software assists individuals, families, and small businesses in the preparation of legal documents.
Source: Avanquest Software

✷ ETHICS & ISSUES 4-2

Should an Attorney Review Documents Created with Legal Software?

If you want to sublet your apartment or buy or sell a used car, should you seek legal help? Hiring an attorney to create a lease or sale agreement can cost hundreds of dollars. Legal software or website services, on the other hand, typically cost less than $100 and sometimes are free. While it is tempting to opt for the route that will save money, you should evaluate the program to make sure it is up to date, addresses the latest laws and provisions that are specific to your state, and includes a legal dictionary. If you use a program that is out of date or creates an incomplete or invalid legal document, the cost for an attorney to correct the document

could exceed the amount you originally spent on the program.

A lease that you create or sign regarding subletting or renting an apartment should have provisions for payment of any damages, breaking or extending the agreement, and who is responsible for routine maintenance and repair. In some states, the property owner must disclose any mold, lead paint, or water quality issues. Sales agreements, such as for used cars, should include language that protects the buyer from undisclosed damage to the car, as well as clearly specify any further responsibility of the car seller.

Attorneys caution against using legal software unless you intend to have an attorney review the document. Not only can

they validate the accuracy of the document, attorneys claim they can provide for gaps in the software; further, they are versed in laws specific to your state or circumstance. Others argue that any legal document is better than a verbal agreement and can protect both parties.

Consider This: Would you use legal software to create a legal document? Why or why not? Would you sign a legal document created with software without consulting an attorney? Why or why not? How do mistakes made as a result of using legal software differ from mistakes that result from human error?

Tax Preparation

Tax preparation software is an application that can guide individuals, families, or small businesses through the process of filing federal and state taxes (Figure 4-15). These programs forecast tax liability and offer money-saving tax tips, designed to lower your tax bill. After you answer a series of questions and complete basic forms, the software creates and analyzes your tax forms to search for missed potential errors and deduction opportunities.

Once the forms are complete, you can print any necessary paperwork; then, they are ready for filing. Some tax preparation programs also allow you to file your tax forms electronically, a process called *e-filing*.

Discover More: Visit this chapter's free resources to learn more about tax preparation programs.

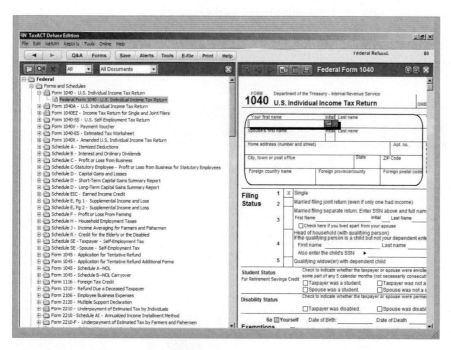

Figure 4-15 Tax preparation software guides individuals, families, or small businesses through the process of filing federal taxes.
Source: 2nd Story Software

Document Management

Document management software is an application that provides a means for sharing, distributing, and searching through documents by converting them into a format that can be viewed by any user. The converted document, which mirrors the original document's appearance, can be viewed and printed without the software that created the original document. Some document management software allows users to edit content and add comments to the converted document (Figure 4-16).

Many businesses use document management software to share and distribute company brochures, literature, and other documents electronically. Home users distribute flyers, announcements, and graphics electronically. A popular electronic image file format that document management software uses to save converted documents is **PDF** (Portable Document Format), developed by Adobe Systems.

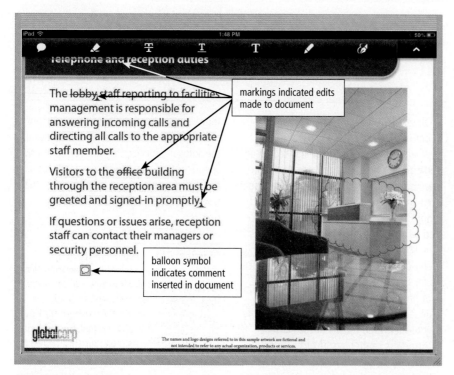

Figure 4-16 Users can edit content and add comments to a converted document.
Source: Adobe Systems Incorporated

To view and print a PDF file, you need Adobe Reader software, which can be downloaded free from Adobe's website.

Discover More: Visit this chapter's free resources to learn more about document management software.

 **CONSIDER THIS** ————————————————————

Can you create a PDF file only in document management applications?
No. Many productivity applications, such as word processing and spreadsheet programs, provide a method of saving a project as a PDF. This enables other users to view your document without requiring the application that created the project.

Enterprise Computing

A large organization, commonly referred to as an enterprise, requires special computing solutions because of its size and geographic distribution. A typical enterprise consists of a wide variety of departments, centers, and divisions — collectively known as functional units. Nearly every enterprise has the following functional units: human resources, accounting and finance, engineering or product development, manufacturing, marketing, sales, distribution, customer service, and information technology.

Software used in functional units is not mutually exclusive; however, each functional unit in an enterprise uses specific software, as outlined below.

- Human resources software manages employee information, such as pay rate, benefits, personal information, performance evaluations, training, and vacation time.
- Accounting software manages everyday transactions, such as sales and payments to suppliers. Finance software helps managers budget, forecast, and analyze.
- Engineering or product development software allows engineers to develop plans for new products and test their product designs.
- Manufacturing software assists in the assembly process, as well as in scheduling and managing the inventory of parts and products.
- Marketing software allows marketing personnel to create marketing campaigns, target demographics, and track their effectiveness.
- Sales software enables the salesforce to manage contacts, schedule meetings, log customer interactions, manage product information, and take customer orders.
- Distribution software analyzes and tracks inventory and manages product shipping status.
- Customer service software manages the day-to-day interactions with customers, such as phone calls, email messages, web interactions, and messaging sessions.
- Information technology staff use a variety of programs and apps to maintain and secure the hardware and software in an enterprise.

Discover More: Visit this chapter's free resources to learn more about software used in an enterprise.

Mini Feature 4-1: Web and Mobile Apps for Personal and Business Productivity

A variety of applications provide a service intended to make business or personal tasks easier to accomplish. Some applications focus on a single service, while others provide several services in a single application. Read Mini Feature 4-1 to learn about some popular web and mobile apps for personal and business productivity.

 Internet Research
Are alternatives to Adobe Reader available?
Search for: adobe reader alternatives

 BTW
Technology Innovator
Discover More: Visit this chapter's free resources to learn about Adobe Systems.

 BTW
Technology Innovator
Discover More: Visit this chapter's free resources to learn about eBay and PayPal, each with apps that can be used for personal and business productivity.

MINI FEATURE 4-1

Web and Mobile Apps for Personal and Business Productivity

Whether you are checking appointments, sending or reading email messages, arranging travel, banking or looking up information online, making a purchase, scanning QR (quick response) codes or bar codes, or checking in with friends on online social networks, web and mobile apps can assist your personal and business productivity.

Calendar and Email

Maintaining a calendar and checking email messages are common tasks of calendar and email web and mobile apps. Calendar apps keep track of your appointments and synchronize information entered on a mobile device with your online or desktop calendar software. Email mobile apps integrate with your device's address book to display names from your device's contact list that match a recipient's name as you type it, and with your device's photo gallery for sending photos.

Source: Kayak

Travel

Purchasing flights, hotels, rental cars, or travel services is a common online task for personal and business travelers. Travel apps display available options and allow you to filter results. Many allow you to share travel plans with your online social networks.

Financial

You can access bank accounts or investments using a financial app. Financial mobile apps track expenses as you spend money and notify you when a bill is due. To help secure information, financial mobile apps can disable access if your device is stolen or lost. Some banking mobile apps allow you to upload a photo of a check taken with the device's camera to process the deposit.

Reference

Dictionaries, encyclopedias, books, and directories are available online as reference apps. Many have associated mobile apps that format information for mobile devices, or take advantage of their features. For example, rather than typing a search term in a dictionary web app to look up its definition, a mobile app also might offer voice input. On the mobile version of an encyclopedia app, you might shake the device to display random topics or redisplay the app's home

screen. Some reference mobile apps also can download information directly to your phone for offline access.

Retail

Online marketplaces and payment services support buying and selling items and transferring funds from one party to another. Marketplace apps enable customers to research products, enter or examine product reviews, and make purchases. A retail store mobile app might use a device's GPS to offer special deals closest to the customer's location. You also might use a device's camera to scan a product's bar code and then place the item in a shopping cart. Payment services allow customers to send money or pay for items using mobile devices. Read Secure IT 4-3 for safety tips when using payment apps.

Scanning

Scanning apps use a mobile device's camera to scan a QR code or bar code. A **QR code** is a square-shaped graphic that represents a web address or other information. A QR code reader app scans a QR code, and then displays its corresponding information. A bar code scanner reads a bar code and may provide product information, price, or reviews. Some supermarkets provide shopping apps for customers to scan bar codes of items they purchase.

© iStockPhoto / franckreporter

These apps create a customized shopping list, ordering items by their aisle location in the store, to provide a more efficient shopping experience.

Online Social Networks

Many users connect with family, friends, and coworkers using online social network mobile apps. Online social network web apps often integrate instant messaging and video chat communications. Online social network mobile apps allow users to include photos and videos from their device in their updates easily.

☀ **Consider This:** Compare the web and mobile versions of the same app for personal and business productivity. Which features are common to both? Which features in the mobile version are not found in the web version? Which features in the web version are not found in the mobile version? Why do you think the developers made these decisions? Which features would you like to see that are missing from either version of the app?

Discover More: Visit this chapter's free resources to learn more about web and mobile apps for personal and business productivity.

SECURE IT 4-3

Avoiding Risks Using Payment Apps

Paying for coffee at the local coffee shop or buying tools at the hardware store has become streamlined with the advent of mobile payment apps. More than 15 percent of Starbucks transactions are accomplished using a smartphone app instead of using cash or credit card, and many merchants are accepting this form of payment as mobile wallet apps become more secure. The users enjoy the convenience of maintaining control when they scan their phone at the checkout counter instead of handing a credit card to a clerk. This security factor becomes even more pronounced at restaurants, where unscrupulous employees can take credit cards away from the table and then have full access to the personal information on the cards.

Mobile payment providers state that using their apps is more secure than using plastic credit cards. The apps use a payment system on phones equipped with an *NFC chip*, which stores data that is transmitted to a contactless terminal and verified as a legitimate sale. A smartphone user never enters an account number at the cash register because all financial information is stored on the mobile payment system. If, however, an unauthorized charge is made, the Electronic Fund Transfer Act protects users as long as the claim is made promptly, generally within two days.

If you use your smartphone to make purchases, follow this advice from the security experts:

• Use a password on your phone.

• Select a payment app that requires you to enter a password to start the transaction.

• Choose a payment app that issues a receipt so that you can verify every purchase.

• Be vigilant about checking mobile transactions against monthly statements from the credit card company.

Consider This: Should additional merchants allow payments using mobile apps? Should merchants be required to pay when customers use payment apps, like they do when customers use credit cards? Why or why not? Where would you like to pay for transactions using your smartphone?

Google Inc.

NOW YOU SHOULD KNOW

Be sure you understand the material presented in the sections titled Programs and Apps and Productivity Applications as it relates to the chapter objectives.
Now you should know ...

• What categories of programs and apps you might find on a computer or mobile device (Objective 1)

• Why you need an operating system on computers and mobile devices (Objective 2)

• How you can obtain software (Objective 3)

• Which productivity applications might be suited to your needs (Objective 4)

Discover More: Visit this chapter's premium content for practice quiz opportunities.

Graphics and Media Applications

In addition to productivity applications, many people work with software designed specifically for their field of work. Power users, such as engineers, architects, desktop publishers, and graphic artists, often use sophisticated software that allows them to work with graphics and media. Many of these applications incorporate user-friendly interfaces or scaled-down versions, making it possible for the home and small business users also to create projects using these types of programs.

Graphics and media applications include computer-aided design, desktop publishing, paint/image editing, photo editing and photo management, video and audio editing, multimedia and website authoring, media players, and disc burning.

Figure 4-17 Architects use CAD software to design building structures.
© iStockPhoto / GordanD

Computer-Aided Design

Computer-aided design (CAD) software is a type of application that assists professionals and designers in creating engineering, architectural, and scientific designs and models. For example, engineers create design plans for vehicles and security systems. Architects design building structures and floor plans (Figure 4-17). Scientists design drawings of molecular structures.

Three-dimensional CAD programs allow designers to rotate designs of 3-D objects to view them from any angle. Some CAD software even can generate material lists for building designs.

Home and small business users work with less sophisticated design and modeling software. These applications usually contain thousands of predrawn plans that users can customize to meet their needs. For example, *home design/landscaping software* is an application that assists users with the design, remodeling, or improvement of a home, deck, or landscape.

Discover More: Visit this chapter's free resources to learn more about CAD software.

Desktop Publishing

Desktop publishing software (DTP software) is an application that enables designers to create sophisticated publications that contain text, graphics, and many colors. Professional DTP software is ideal for the production of high-quality color projects such as textbooks, corporate newsletters, marketing literature, product catalogs, and annual reports. Designers and graphic artists can print finished publications on a color printer, take them to a professional printer, or post them on the web in a format that can be viewed by those without DTP software.

Home and small business users create newsletters, brochures, flyers, advertisements, postcards, greeting cards, letterhead, business cards, banners, calendars, logos, and webpages using personal DTP software (Figure 4-18). Although many word processing programs include DTP features, home and small business users often prefer to create DTP projects using DTP software because of its enhanced features. These programs typically guide you through the development of a project by asking a series of questions. Then, you can print a finished publication on a color printer or post it on the web.

Many personal DTP programs also include paint/image editing software and photo editing and photo management software (discussed next), enabling users to embellish their publications with images.

Discover More: Visit this chapter's free resources to learn more about professional and personal DTP software.

Figure 4-18 With personal DTP software, such as Microsoft Publisher shown here, home users can create newsletters.
Courtesy of Joy Starks; Source: Microsoft

Paint/Image Editing

Graphic artists, multimedia professionals, technical illustrators, and desktop publishers use paint software and image editing software to create and modify graphics, such as those used in DTP projects and webpages. **Paint software**, also called *illustration software*, is an application that allows users to draw pictures, shapes, and other graphics with various on-screen tools, such as a pen, brush, eyedropper, and paint bucket. **Image editing software** is an application that provides the capabilities of paint software and also includes the capability to enhance and modify existing photos and images.

Modifications can include adjusting or enhancing image colors, adding special effects such as shadows and glows, creating animations, and image stitching (combining multiple images into a larger image).

Paint/image editing software for the home or small business user provides an easy-to-use interface; includes various simplified tools that allow you to draw pictures, shapes, and other images (Figure 4-19); and provides the capability of modifying existing graphics and photos. These products also include many templates to assist you in adding images to projects, such as greeting cards, banners, calendars, signs, labels, business cards, and letterhead.

Discover More: Visit this chapter's free resources to learn more about paint and image editing software.

BTW
Built-In Image Editing
Word processing, presentation, and other productivity applications usually include basic image editing capabilities.

Figure 4-19 Home users can purchase affordable paint/image editing programs that enable them to draw images.
DrawPlus X5 © Serif (Europe) Ltd, | www.serif.com

Photo Editing and Photo Management

Photo editing software is a type of image editing software that allows users to edit and customize digital photos. With photo editing software, users can retouch photos, crop images, remove red-eye, erase blemishes, restore aged photos, add special effects, enhance image quality, change image shapes, color-correct images, straighten images, remove or rearrange objects in a photo, add layers, and more (Figure 4–20). Many applications also provide a means for creating digital photo albums.

Figure 4-20 With photo editing software, users can edit digital photos, such as by adjusting the appearance of images as shown here.
PhotoPlus X6 © Serif (Europe) Ltd | www.serif.com

When you purchase a digital camera, it usually includes photo editing software. Many digital cameras also include basic photo editing software so that you can edit the image directly on the camera. Read How To 4-2 for instructions about editing and sharing photos. Read Ethics & Issues 4-3 to consider issues related to altering digital photos.

With **photo management software**, you can view, organize, sort, catalog, print, and share digital photos. Some photo editing software includes photo management functionality. Many online photo storage services enable you to create scrapbooks — selecting photos, adding captions, selecting backgrounds, and more.

⊗ BTW

Technology Trend
Discover More: Visit this chapter's free resources to learn about the photo sharing app, Instagram.

⊗ HOW TO 4-2

Edit and Share Photos
When you take a photo using a digital camera or smartphone, you sometimes may want to edit the photo to remove unwanted areas, correct imperfections, or change its file size. Many apps allow you to edit photos easily. Several are simple to use and do not require advanced photo editing experience. Before editing a photo, you first should make a backup of the original photo. The table below describes common ways to edit photos using a photo editing app.

After you have edited a photo to your satisfaction, you may want to share the photo with others. Many mobile devices, such as smartphones and tablets, as well as most photo editing apps, have built-in options that allow you to share photos. To share a photo on a mobile device or from within a photo editing app, follow these steps:

1. Open the photo to share.
2. Select the sharing option in the photo editing app or on the mobile device.
3. Choose the method by which to share the photo. Common ways to share

photos include sending the photo as an email attachment, posting the photo to an online social network or photo sharing site, and sending the photo as a picture message to another mobile device.

⊗ Consider This: Examine your digital camera or other mobile device with a camera feature. Which of the photo editing features discussed here does it have? Did you notice any photo editing features in addition to those listed here?

ACTION	PURPOSE	STEPS
Crop	Removes unwanted areas of a photo	1. Select cropping tool. 2. Adjust photo border to define area(s) of the photo to keep and discard.
Remove *red-eye*	Removes the appearance of red eyes caused by the camera flash	1. Select red-eye removal tool. 2. Tap or click areas of the photo with the red-eye effect *or* drag a border around the affected areas.
Resize	Changes the physical dimensions of the photo	1. Select resizing tool. 2. Drag sizing handles to increase or decrease the photo's dimensions *or* type the desired height and width in the appropriate text boxes.
Compress	Decreases the photo's file size	1. Select option to compress photo. 2. Choose desired level of compression.
Adjust *sharpness*	Increases or decreases crispness of objects in the photo	1. Select option to adjust sharpness. 2. Drag sharpness slider to desired value *or* type the desired sharpness level into appropriate text box.
Adjust *brightness*	Adjusts lightness or darkness in the photo	1. Select option to adjust brightness. 2. Drag brightness slider to desired value *or* type the desired brightness level into appropriate text box.
Adjust *contrast*	Adjusts the difference in appearance between light and dark areas of the photo	1. Select option to adjust contrast. 2. Drag contrast slider to desired value *or* type the desired contrast level into appropriate text box.

⚜ ETHICS & ISSUES 4-3

Is It Ethical to Alter Digital Photos?

Many commercial artists, photojournalists, and creators of magazine covers and billboards use photo editing software to alter digital photos. Artists use photo editing software to enhance digital photos by changing colors, adding or removing objects, and more. When does photo manipulation become unethical?

In several high-profile cases, news sources published intentionally altered photos that misrepresented the facts, in one case publishing photos of an aging world leader edited to remove his hearing aid. One school received criticism when it altered necklines on yearbook photos to be more modest.

Real estate agents on occasion have altered photos of homes for online listings or print brochures. Also making news are celebrity or model photos that artists retouch to change their physical appearance.

The National Press Photographers Association expresses reservations about digital altering and subscribes to the following belief: "As [photo]journalists we believe the guiding principle of our profession is accuracy; therefore, we believe it is wrong to alter the content of a photo in any way ... that deceives the public." Yet, some insist that the extent to which a photo "deceives the public" is in the eye of the beholder. Many differentiate between

technical manipulation to improve photo quality and an intent to deceive. Some governments are attempting to legislate photo manipulation. One country banned a magazine in which a celebrity's appearance appeared visibly altered. Some celebrities refuse to allow airbrushing or other manipulation of photos of them.

Consider This: Is it ethical to alter digital photos? Why or why not? Does the answer depend on the reason for the alteration, the extent of the alteration, or some other factor? Should magazines stop altering pictures of people to change their appearance? Why or why not?

Video and Audio Editing

Video editing software is an application that allows professionals to modify a segment of a video, called a clip. For example, users can reduce the length of a video clip, reorder a series of clips, or add special effects such as words that move across the screen. Video editing software typically includes audio editing capabilities. **Audio editing software** is an application that enables users to modify audio clips, produce studio-quality soundtracks, and add audio to video clips (Figure 4-21). Most television shows and movies are created or enhanced using video and audio editing software.

Many home users work with easy-to-use video and audio editing software, which is much simpler to use than its professional counterpart, for small-scale movie making projects. With these programs, home users can edit home movies, add music or other sounds to the video, and share their movies on the web. Some operating systems include video editing and audio editing applications.

Discover More: Visit this chapter's free resources to learn more about video and audio editing software.

Figure 4-21 With audio editing software, users modify audio clips.

Source: Adobe Systems Incorporated

Multimedia and Website Authoring

Multimedia authoring software allows users to combine text, graphics, audio, video, and animation in an interactive application (Figure 4-22). With this software, users control the placement of text and images and the duration of sounds, video, and animation. Once created, multimedia presentations often take the form of interactive computer-based presentations or web-based presentations designed to facilitate learning, demonstrate product functionality, and elicit direct user participation. Training centers, educational institutions, and online magazine publishers use multimedia authoring software to develop interactive applications. These applications may be distributed on an optical disc, over a local area network, or via the Internet as web apps.

Website authoring software helps users of all skill levels create related webpages that include graphics, video, audio, animation, special effects with interactive content, and blog posts. In addition, many website authoring programs allow users to organize, manage, and maintain websites. Website authoring software often has capabilities of multimedia authoring software.

 CONSIDER THIS

What is computer-based or web-based training?

Computer-based training (*CBT*) is a type of education in which students learn by using and completing exercises with instructional software. *Web-based training* (*WBT*) is a type of CBT that uses Internet technology to deliver the training. CBT and WBT typically consist of self-directed, self-paced instruction about a topic so that the user becomes actively involved in the learning process instead of being a passive recipient of information. Beginning athletes use CBT programs to learn the intricacies of participating in a sport. The military and airlines use CBT simulations to train pilots to fly in various conditions and environments. WBT is popular in business, industry, and schools for teaching new skills or enhancing existing skills of employees, teachers, and students.

Discover More: Visit this chapter's free resources to learn more about multimedia and website authoring software.

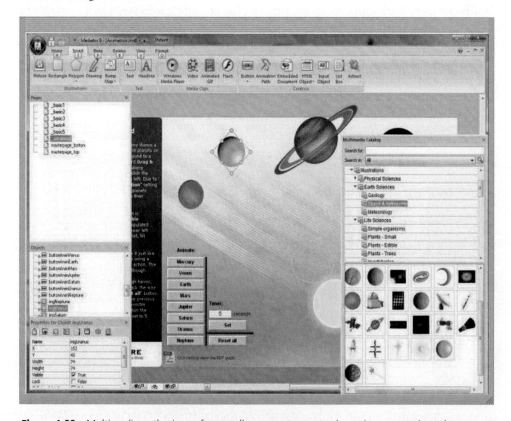

Figure 4-22 Multimedia authoring software allows you to create dynamic presentations that include text, graphics, audio, video, and animation.
Courtesy of Matchware Inc.

Media Player

A **media player** is a program that allows you to view images and animations, listen to audio, and watch video files on your computer or mobile device (Figure 4-23). Media players also may enable you to organize media files by genre, artist, or other category; create playlists; convert files to different formats; connect to and purchase media from an online media store or market-place; stream radio stations' broadcasting over the Internet; download podcasts; burn audio CDs; and transfer media to portable media players.

Discover More: Visit this chapter's free resources to learn more about media players.

Figure 4-23   A media player.
Source: Rhapsody

Disc Burning

Disc burning software writes text, graphics, audio, and video files on a recordable or rewritable disc. This software enables home users easily to back up contents of their hard drive on an optical disc (CD/DVD) and make duplicates of uncopyrighted music or movies. Disc burning software usually also includes photo editing, audio editing, and video editing capabilities.

Personal Interest Applications

Countless desktop, mobile, and web apps are designed specifically for lifestyle, medical, entertainment, convenience, or education activities. Most of the programs in this category are relatively inexpensive; many are free. Some applications focus on a single service, while others provide several services in a single application.

- Lifestyle applications: Access the latest news or sports scores, check the weather forecast, compose music, research genealogy, find recipes, or locate nearby restaurants, gas stations, or points of interest.
- Medical applications: Research symptoms, establish a fitness or health program, track exercise activity, refill prescriptions, count calories, or monitor sleep patterns.

Internet Research

What is geocaching?

Search for: geocaching basics

BTW

Technology Trend

Discover More: Visit this chapter's free resources to learn about the education app, iTunes U.

- Entertainment applications: Listen to music or the radio, view photos, watch videos or shows, read a book or other publication, organize and track fantasy sports teams, and play games individually or with others.
- Convenience applications: Obtain driving directions or your current location, remotely start your vehicle or unlock/lock the doors, set an alarm or timer, check the time, calculate a tip, use your phone as a flashlight, or use a personal assistant that acts on your voice commands (read How To 4-3 for instructions about using personal assistant apps).
- Education applications: Access how-to guides, learn or fine-tune a particular skill, follow a tutorial, run a simulation, assist children with reading and other elementary skills, or support academics.

HOW TO 4-3

Use Features in Voice Command Personal Assistant and Mobile Search Apps

Many mobile operating systems include a virtual personal assistant that processes voice commands and performs certain tasks. Some mobile search apps also act on spoken commands.. For example, you can issue voice commands to set an alarm, add an appointment to your calendar, send a text message, or run an app. The following table describes ways to use features in voice command personal assistant apps:

Task	Sample Voice Command(s)
Change phone settings	"Turn on Wi-Fi." "Turn off Bluetooth."
Dial a number	"Call Madelyn's Cell." "Call Mom Home." "Dial 407-555-8275."
Obtain information	"When was George Washington born?" "How many ounces are in a pound?" "What is the closest Chinese restaurant?"
Obtain driving instructions	"Navigate to 123 Main Street, Orlando, Florida." "Navigate to The Home Depot." "Navigate to Manchester, New Hampshire."
Perform a search	"What is the gas mileage for a Ford Explorer?" "Search butterfly lifespan."
Run an app	"Run calendar." "Run email."
Schedule a meeting	"Schedule a meeting with Traci at the library at 3:00 p.m. tomorrow."
Send a text message	"Text Samuel meet me at the pool."
Set a reminder	"Remind me to go grocery shopping tomorrow."
Set a timer	"Set timer for five minutes."
Set an alarm	"Set an alarm for 6:00 a.m. tomorrow." "Set an alarm for 6:30 a.m. every weekday."

Consider This: What other voice commands are available on your phone? Do you use voice commands? Why or why not?

Mini Feature 4-2: Web and Mobile Apps for Media and Personal Interest

A variety of applications provide a service intended to make media and personal interest tasks easier to accomplish. Some applications focus on a single service, while others provide several services in a single application. Read Mini Feature 4-2 to learn about some popular web and mobile apps for media and personal interests.

Web and Mobile Apps for Media and Personal Interests

Whether sharing, viewing, and purchasing media, such as photos; streaming audio and video; or playing games by yourself or with others, countless web and mobile apps are available to meet your needs. You also can use web and mobile apps to look up news, sports, and weather; obtain maps and directions; help you reach your health and fitness goals; and assist you with academic objectives.

Media Sharing

With media sharing mobile apps, you use the digital camera on your mobile device to take quality photos and/or videos and then instantly can share the photos or videos on online social networks. Using the corresponding media sharing web app, you can categorize, tag, organize, and rank the media posted by you, your friends, and your contacts.

Instagram

Streaming Audio and Video

Podcasts, video blogs, clips or episodes from a television show, or even entire movies are available through a variety of streaming media web and mobile apps. Some services are available only with membership, and may charge a monthly fee. Others are free, but include ads. Streaming media enables you to view and listen to content without downloading it to your computer or device, saving valuable disc or media storage space.

Gaming

Game web and mobile apps often offer a social component, enabling you to chat within the game environment, find friends who play the same game apps, and post your scores on social media. Word, puzzle, and board games are just some examples of apps you can play by yourself or with friends or others using the same apps.

News, Sports, and Weather

Many apps provide access to the latest news, stories, current events, sports scores, sporting events, and weather forecasts. Some of these mobile apps use GPS technology to provide current or customized information based on the location of your mobile device. You also can configure these apps to deliver text messages and other types of alerts to your device when certain events occur, such as when a football team scores a touchdown or when severe weather is near.

Mapping

Using your mobile device's GPS capability, you can use mapping mobile apps to obtain directions, maps, and recommendations for restaurants or other points of interest based on your current location. Some mapping apps even help you to locate friends based on their GPS signals (if they enable you to do so). Others allow you to share your current location on social media using a check-in feature. Web apps help you decide on a route, print directions or a map, and even find amenities along your route, such as public rest stops or restaurants.

Health and Fitness

Losing weight, training for a race, or following a low-calorie diet are some uses of health and fitness apps. Using a mobile device as a pedometer or GPS receiver can help you count your steps or create a map of a route you run and then update your profile with the data it tracked. You can use corresponding web apps to chart and analyze your progress, schedule your next workout, or determine the next steps to reach your goals. These apps also can help plan your meals and track the nutritional value of food you consume.

MyFitnessPal LLC

Academic

If you need to study terms or topics, flash card apps can provide reinforcement. This book's premium content for example, has an accompanying Flash Cards app designed to improve your retention of chapter key terms. Schools often subscribe to educational apps that provide students with games, quizzes, and lessons about course topics. Using these apps, teachers can keep track of students' progress and pinpoint areas where they may need extra help. You also can access complete college or high school courses and take advantage of free or fee-based digital content provided by publishers and teachers.

Discover More: Visit this chapter's free resources to learn more about web and mobile apps for media and personal interests.

⚜ **Consider This:** Which web and mobile apps have you used for media sharing; streaming audio and video; gaming; news, sports, and weather; mapping; health and fitness; and education? Will you try others after reading this mini feature? Why or why not?

BTW

Mobile Communications Apps

Most of the communications apps in Table 4-2 are available as mobile apps, as well.

Communications Applications

One of the main reasons people use computers is to communicate and share information with others. Earlier chapters presented a variety of communications applications, which are summarized in Table 4-2. Read Ethics & Issues 4-4 to consider whether your email provider should be allowed to read or scan your email messages.

Table 4-2 Communications Applications

Blog

- Time-stamped articles, or posts, in diary or journal format, usually listed in reverse chronological order
- Bloggers (author) use blogging software to create/maintain blog
  - Some blog services provide blogging software so users do not have to install it on their own servers

Browsing

- Allows users to access and view webpages on the Internet
- Requires browser
  - Integrated in most operating systems
  - Alternative browsers are available on the web for download, usually for free

Chat

- Real-time, online typed conversation with one or more users
- Requires chat client software
  - Integrated in some operating systems and most browsers
  - Available for download on the web, usually for free
  - Included with some paid ISPs
  - Built into some websites

Online Discussion

- Online areas where users have written discussions
- May require a reader program
- Integrated in some operating systems, email programs, and browsers

Email

- Messages and files sent via a network, such as the Internet
- Requires an email program
  - Integrated in many software suites and operating systems
  - Available free at portals on the web
  - Included with a paid ISP
  - Can be purchased separately

File Transfer

- Method of uploading files to and downloading files from servers on the Internet
- May require an FTP client program
  - Integrated in some operating systems
  - Available for download on the web; many free or open source alternatives are available
  - Many applications (such as web editing software) that require frequent transfer of files to the Internet have built-in FTP capabilities

Internet Phone

- Allows users to speak to other users via an Internet connection
- Requires a microphone, a speaker, a high-speed Internet connection, and VoIP software
  - Some subscription services also require a separate phone and VoIP router
  - With a webcam, some services also support video chat or videoconferences

Internet Messaging

- Real-time exchange of messages, files, images, audio, and/or video with another online user
- Requires messaging software
  - Integrated in some operating systems
  - Available for download on the web, usually for free, or available as a browser plug-in
  - Included with some paid ISPs

Mobile Messaging

- Short text, picture, or video messages sent and received, mainly on mobile devices
- May require messaging plan from mobile service provider
  - Requires messaging software
  - Integrated in most mobile devices
  - Available for download on the web, usually for free

Videoconference

- Meeting between geographically separated people who use a network to transmit video/audio
- Requires videoconferencing software, a microphone, a speaker, and a webcam

Web Feeds

- Keeps track of changes made to blogs by checking feeds
- Requires a feed reader
  - Integrated in some email programs and browsers
  - Available for download on the web, usually for free

ETHICS & ISSUES 4-4

Should Your Email Provider Be Allowed to Read or Scan Your Email?
When using any email program or service, you expect the app to scan incoming and outgoing mail to prevent the spread of malware. One web-based email service recently released a service update that includes automatic scanning of all email messages in order to provide targeted advertisements. Privacy experts point out that the scan includes all email messages sent or received, whether or not both the sender and recipient subscribe to the service.

Ad-supported web services, including email, often collect information in your profile, as well as your search results and other Internet activity. When you agree to

use these services, you give consent to this type of monitoring. In this case, the extent of the monitoring exceeds the policies of other web-based services. In a court filing, one email provider stated that users of web-based services have no "reasonable expectation" of privacy with respect to the content of email messages.

A further complication to this instance is that many educational institutions use this service for email, collaboration software, and more. The service admits to collecting data from students, even when the school has opted out of ad displays. Laws are unclear whether collecting student data is legal. Several schools have joined to create a class-action lawsuit against the provider. Many

argue that collection of student data, which could include grades received and more, is a violation of the Family Educational Rights and Privacy Act (FERPA). Although FERPA predates cloud-based Internet services, it states that "schools must have written permission from the parent or eligible student in order to release any information from a student's education record."

Consider This: Should an email service provider disclose data collection practices? Why or why not? Is it ethical for an email provider to scan email sent by a nonsubscriber? Why or why not? Is collecting student data a violation of FERPA? Why or why not?

NOW YOU SHOULD KNOW

Be sure you understand the material presented in the sections titled Graphics and Media Applications, Personal Interest Applications, and Communications Applications, as it relates to the chapter objectives.
Now you should know ...

- When you might use a graphics or media application (Objective 5)
- Which personal interest applications you would find useful (Objective 6)
- When you are interacting with communications applications (Objective 7)

Discover More: Visit this chapter's premium content for practice quiz opportunities.

Security Tools

To protect your computers and mobile devices, you can use one or more security tools. Security tools include personal firewalls, antivirus programs, malware removers, and Internet filters. Although some of these tools are included with the operating system, you also can purchase stand-alone programs that offer improvements or added functionality.

Personal Firewall

A **personal firewall** is a security tool that detects and protects a personal computer and its data from unauthorized intrusions (Figure 4-24). Personal firewalls constantly monitor all transmissions to and from a computer or mobile device and may inform a user of attempted intrusions. When connected to the Internet, your computer or mobile device is vulnerable to attacks from

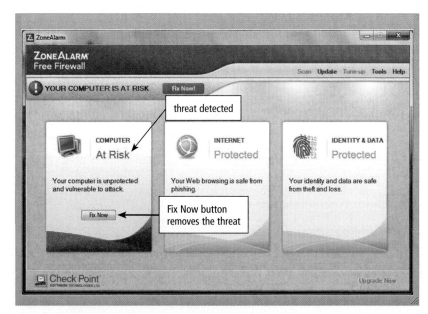

Figure 4-24   This personal firewall detected a threat to the computer and provided a means to remove the threat.
Courtesy of Checkpoint Software Technologies Ltd.

hackers who try to access a computer or network illegally. These attacks may destroy your data, steal information, damage your computer, or carry out some other malicious action.

 CONSIDER THIS

What is a hardware firewall?
A *hardware firewall* is a device intended to stop network intrusions before they attempt to affect your computer or network maliciously. Many routers also can function as a hardware firewall.

Discover More: Visit this chapter's free resources to learn more about personal firewalls.

Mini Feature 4-3: Viruses and Malware

A computer **virus** is a potentially damaging program that affects a computer or device negatively by altering the way it works. This occurs without the user's knowledge or permission. Once the virus is in a computer or device, it can spread and may damage your files, programs and apps, and operating system. Read Mini Feature 4-3 to learn more about viruses and other malware.

 MINI FEATURE 4-3

Viruses and Malware

Viruses do not generate by chance. The programmer of a virus, known as a virus author, intentionally writes a virus program. Writing a virus program usually requires significant programming skills. The virus author ensures the virus can replicate itself, conceal itself, monitor for certain events, and then deliver its payload. A *payload* is the destructive event or prank the virus delivers. Viruses can infect all types of computers and devices. Most variations of viruses have two phases involved in their execution: infection and delivery.

The first step in the infection phase is activation of the virus. The most common way viruses spread is by users running infected programs or apps. During the infection phase, viruses typically perform one or more of the following actions:

1. First, a virus replicates by attaching itself to program files. A macro virus hides in a macro, which is a standard feature of many productivity applications, such as word processing and spreadsheet apps. A boot sector virus targets the computer's start-up files. A file virus attaches itself to program files. The next time an infected program or app is run, the virus executes and infects the computer or device.

2. Viruses conceal themselves to avoid detection. A stealth virus disguises itself by hiding in fake code sections, which it inserts within working code in a file. A polymorphic virus actually changes its code as it delivers the infection.

3. Finally, viruses watch for a certain condition or event and activate when that condition or event occurs. The event might be starting the computer or device, or reaching a date on the system clock. A logic bomb activates when it detects a specific condition

(say, a name deleted from the employee list). A time bomb is a logic bomb that activates on a particular date or time. If the triggering condition does not exist, the virus simply replicates.

During the delivery phase, the virus unleashes its payload, which might be a harmless prank that displays a meaningless message — or it might be destructive, corrupting or deleting data and files. The most dangerous viruses do not have an obvious payload. Instead, they quietly modify files. One way antivirus software detects computer viruses is by monitoring files for unknown changes.

In addition to viruses, other malware includes worms, trojan horse programs, and rootkits.

- A *worm* resides in active memory and replicates itself over a network to infect computers and devices, using up system resources and possibly shutting down the system.

- A *trojan horse* is a destructive program disguised as a real program, such as a screen saver. When a user runs a seemingly innocent program, a trojan horse hiding inside can capture information, such as user names and passwords, from your computer or enable someone to control your computer remotely. Unlike viruses, trojan horses do not replicate themselves.

- A *rootkit* is a program that easily can hide and allow someone to take full control of your computer from a remote location, often for nefarious purposes. For example, a rootkit can hide in a folder on your computer. The folder appears empty because the rootkit has instructed your computer not to display the contents of the folder. Rootkits can be very dangerous and often require special software to detect and remove.

Studies show that malware can infect an unprotected computer within minutes after connecting to the Internet. Due to the increasing threat of viruses attacking your computer, it is more important than ever to protect your computer from viruses and other malware. Secure IT 1-2 in Chapter 1 lists steps you can follow to protect your computer from a virus infection.

Discover More: Visit this chapter's free resources to learn more about file viruses, polymorphic viruses, rootkits, and antivirus software.

✳ **Consider This:** If your computer or mobile device is infected with a virus or malware, how will you know? How will you find instructions for removing a virus?

Signs of Virus Infection

- An unusual message or image is displayed on the computer screen.
- An unusual sound or music plays randomly.
- The available memory is less than what should be available.
- A program or file suddenly is missing.
- An unknown program or file mysteriously appears.

- The size of a file changes without explanation.
- A file becomes corrupted.
- A program or file does not work properly.
- System properties change.
- The computer operates much slower than usual.

© Cengage Learning

Antivirus Programs

To protect a computer from virus attacks, users should install an antivirus program and keep it updated by purchasing revisions or upgrades to the software. An **antivirus program** protects a computer against viruses by identifying and removing any computer viruses found in memory, on storage media, or on incoming files (Figure 4-25). Antivirus programs scan for programs that attempt to modify a computer's start-up files, the operating system, and other programs that normally are read from but not modified. In addition, many antivirus programs automatically scan files downloaded from the web, email attachments, opened files, and all types of removable media inserted in the computer or mobile device.

If an antivirus program identifies an infected file, it attempts to remove the malware. If the antivirus program cannot remove the infection, it often quarantines the infected file. A *quarantine* is a separate area of a hard drive that holds the infected file until the infection can be removed. This step ensures other files will not become infected. Quarantined files remain on your computer or mobile device until you delete them or restore them.

Most antivirus programs also include protection against other malware, such as worms, trojan horses, and spyware. When you purchase a new computer, it may include a trial version of antivirus software. Many email servers also have antivirus programs installed to check incoming and outgoing email messages for viruses and other malware. Read Secure IT 4-4 for tips about recognizing virus hoaxes.

⚙ BTW

Antivirus and Malware Detection Programs You should run only one antivirus program on your computer but can run more than one malware detection program.

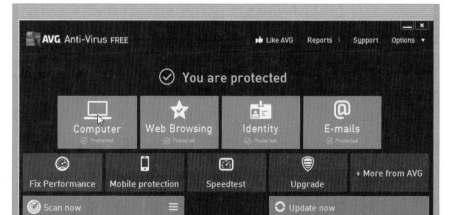

Figure 4-25 An antivirus program scans memory, media, and incoming email messages and attachments for viruses and attempts to remove any viruses it finds.
Courtesy of Checkpoint Software Technologies Ltd.

Recognizing Virus Hoaxes

Computer hoaxes spread across the Internet in record time and often are the source of urban legends. These hoaxes take several forms and often disappear for months or years at a time, only to resurface some time later.

Most alarming to some users are the computer virus hoaxes that warn the computer is infected and needs immediate attention. Some warnings state the problem is so severe that the computer or device will explode or that the entire hard drive will be erased in a matter of seconds. The warnings cite prominent companies, such as Microsoft and Intel Security. These messages claim to offer a solution to the problem, generally requesting a fee for a program to download. Snopes.com compiles these hoaxes and describes their sources and histories.

In reality, these fake messages are generated by unscrupulous scammers preying upon gullible people who panic and follow the directions in the message. These users divulge credit card information and then often download files riddled with viruses.

If you receive one of these virus hoaxes, never respond to the message. Instead, delete it. Most importantly, never forward it to an unsuspecting friend or coworker. If you receive the virus hoax from someone you know, send him or her a separate email message with information about the hoax.

Consider This: Have you ever received a virus hoax? If so, what action did you take?

CONSIDER THIS

How do antivirus programs detect viruses?

Many antivirus programs identify viruses by looking for virus signatures. A *virus signature,* also called a virus definition, is a known specific pattern of virus code. Computer users should update their antivirus program's signature files regularly. This extremely important activity allows the antivirus program to protect against viruses written since the antivirus program was released and/or its last update. Most antivirus programs contain an automatic update feature or regularly prompts users to download the updated virus signatures, usually at least once a week. The vendor usually provides this service to registered users at no cost for a specified time.

Discover More: Visit this chapter's free resources to learn more about antivirus programs.

Spyware, Adware, and Other Malware Removers

Spyware is a type of program placed on a computer or mobile device without the user's knowledge that secretly collects information about the user and then communicates the information it collects to some outside source while the user is online. Some vendors or employers use spyware to collect information about program usage or employees. Internet advertising firms often collect information about users' web browsing habits. Spyware can enter your computer when you install a new program, through a graphic on a webpage or in an email message, or through malware.

Adware is a type of program that displays an online advertisement in a banner or pop-up or pop-under window on webpages, email messages, or other Internet services. Sometimes, Internet advertising firms hide spyware in adware.

A **spyware remover** is a type of program that detects and deletes spyware and similar programs. An **adware remover** is a program that detects and deletes adware. Malware removers detect and delete spyware, adware, and other malware. Read Secure IT 4-5 for measures you can take to protect your mobile device from malware.

CONSIDER THIS

Are cookies spyware?

A *cookie* is a small text file that a web server stores on your computer. Cookie files typically contain data about you, such as your user name, viewing preferences, or shopping cart contents. Cookies are not considered spyware because website programmers do not attempt to conceal the cookies.

Discover More: Visit this chapter's free resources to learn more about malware removers.

⊛ SECURE IT 4-5

📱 Malware Risks to Mobile Devices

Practically every smartphone is vulnerable to hacking attacks. Threats to smartphones and mobile devices are growing in record numbers due to the rising popularity of these products and the variety of marketplace sources for downloading apps.

Often the malware is disguised as a popular app and steals personal and sensitive information and phone numbers. It also can allow hackers to control the mobile device from remote locations. Once the hacker takes over the device, all the information on it is available, including passwords and account numbers. One of the fastest growing threats within mobile apps is *toll fraud malware*,

which is a malicious mobile app that uses a variety of fraudulent schemes to charge unsuspecting users for premium messaging services.

Smartphone users can take several precautions to guard against malware threats. They include:

- Read reviews of apps and the companies that create them before downloading the apps to your mobile device.
- Use mobile malware and antivirus protection.
- Turn off location-based apps that track your movements.
- Do not connect to unknown wireless networks.

- Keep the operating system up to date.
- Enable the screen lock feature, and use a strong password to unlock the device.
- Reset the mobile device before selling or trading it in.
- Practice the same safe computing measures you take on your home computer.

⊛ **Consider This:** Which of these guidelines do you follow now when using your smartphone or mobile device? How will you modify your usage after reading these tips?

Internet Filters

Filters are programs that remove or block certain items from being displayed. Four widely used Internet filters are anti-spam programs, web filters, phishing filters, and pop-up and pop-under blockers.

Anti-Spam Programs **Spam** is an unsolicited email message or posting sent to many recipients or forums at once. Spam is considered Internet junk mail. The content of spam ranges from selling a product or service, to promoting a business opportunity, to advertising offensive material. Spam also may contain links or attachments that contain malware.

An **anti-spam program** is a filtering program that attempts to remove spam before it reaches your inbox or forum. If your email program does not filter spam, many anti-spam programs are available at no cost on the web. ISPs often filter spam as a service for their subscribers.

Web Filters **Web filtering software** is a program that restricts access to certain material on the web. Some restrict access to specific websites; others filter websites that use certain words or phrases. Many businesses use web filtering software to limit employee's web access. Some schools, libraries, and parents use this software to restrict access to websites that are not educational.

Phishing Filters **Phishing** is a scam in which a perpetrator sends an official looking email message that attempts to obtain your personal and/or financial information (Figure 4-26). Some phishing messages ask you to reply with your information; others direct you to a phony website or a pop-up or pop-under window that looks like a legitimate website, which then collects your information.

A **phishing filter** is a program that warns or blocks you from potentially fraudulent or suspicious websites. Some browsers include phishing filters.

Internet Research

What are current phishing scams?

Search for: recent phishing scams

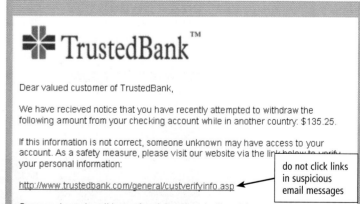

Figure 4-26 An example of a phishing email message.
Source: Andrew Levine

Pop-Up and Pop-Under Blockers A *pop-up ad* is an Internet advertisement that suddenly appears in a new window on top of a webpage. Similarly, a *pop-under ad* is an Internet advertisement that is hidden behind the browser window so that it will be viewed when users close their browser windows. A **pop-up blocker** or **pop-under blocker** is a filtering program that stops pop-up or pop-under ads from displaying on webpages. Many browsers include these blockers. You also can download pop-up and pop-under blockers from the web at no cost.

Discover More: Visit this chapter's free resources to learn more about Internet filters.

File, Disk, and System Management Tools

To perform maintenance-type tasks related to managing a computer, its devices, or its programs, you can use one or more file, disk, and system management tools. Functions provided by these tools include the following: managing files, searching, viewing images, uninstalling software, cleaning up disks, defragmenting disks, setting up screen savers, compressing files, maintaining a personal computer, and backing up files and disks. Although some of these tools are included with the operating system, you also can purchase stand-alone programs that offer improvements or added functionality.

File Manager

A **file manager** is a tool that performs functions related to file management. Some of the file management functions that a file manager performs are displaying a list of files on a storage medium (Figure 4-27); organizing files in folders; and copying, renaming, deleting, moving, and sorting files. A **folder** is a specific named location on a storage medium that contains related files. Operating systems typically include a file manager.

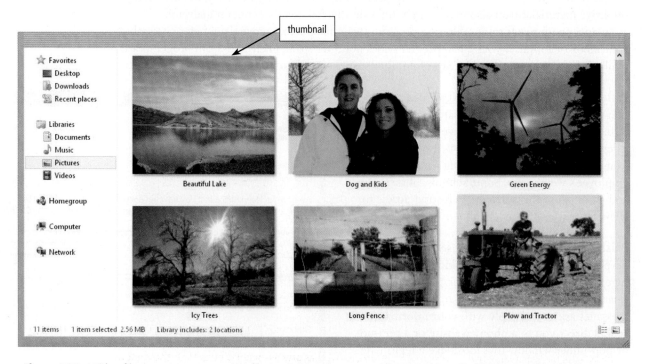

Figure 4-27 With a file manager, you can view files containing documents, photos, and music. In this case, thumbnails of photos are displayed.

Source: Microsoft

Search

A **search tool** is a program, usually included with an operating system, that attempts to locate a file, contact, calendar event, app or any other item stored on your computer or mobile device based on criteria you specify (Figure 4-28). The criteria could be a word(s), date, location, and other similar properties. Search tools can look through documents, photos, music, calendars, contacts, and other items on your computer or mobile device and/or on the Internet, combining search results in a single location.

Search tools typically use an index to assist with locating items quickly. An *index* stores a variety of information about a file, including its name, date created, date modified, author name, and so on. When you enter search criteria, instead of looking through every file and folder on the storage medium, the search tool looks through the index first to find a match. Each entry in the index contains a link to the actual file on the storage media for easy retrieval.

Figure 4-28 This search displays all files on the mobile device that match the search criticia, Map. Notice the search results show map apps, email with a map, and a calendar event.
Source: Apple Inc

Image Viewer

An **image viewer** is a tool that allows users to display, copy, and print the contents of a graphics file, such as a photo (Figure 4-29). With an image viewer, users can see images without having to open them in a paint or image editing program. Many image viewers include some photo editing capabilities. Most operating systems include an image viewer.

Figure 4-29 An image viewer allows users to see the contents of a photo file.
Source: Microsoft

Uninstaller

An **uninstaller** is a tool that removes a program, as well as any associated entries in the system files. When you install a program, the operating system records the information it uses to run the software in the system files. The uninstaller deletes files and folders from the hard drive, as well as removes program entries from the system files. Read How To 4-4 for instructions about uninstalling programs and removing apps from your computers and mobile devices.

HOW TO 4-4

Uninstall a Program or Remove an App
You may choose to uninstall a program or remove an app from your computer or mobile device for a variety of reasons. For example, you may uninstall a program if you need more space on your hard drive, or if you no longer have a use for that program. Uninstalling unwanted programs and apps will keep your hard drive free from clutter and maximize your computer or mobile device's performance. The following steps describe how to uninstall a program or remove an app.

Windows
1. Open the Control Panel.
2. Tap or click the option to uninstall a program.

3. Tap or click to select the program to uninstall.
4. Tap or click the Uninstall button and then follow the prompts on the screen.

Mac
1. Open the Finder.
2. Tap or click Applications in the left pane.
3. Scroll to display the app you wish to uninstall.
4. Drag the app's icon to the Trash.

iPhone, iPad, or iPod Touch
1. Press and hold the icon for the app you wish to delete until the app icons begin to animate.

2. Tap the X on the icon for the app you wish to delete to remove the app from your device.

Android
1. Display the Settings menu.
2. Tap the command to display a list of installed applications.
3. Tap the application to uninstall.
4. Tap the Uninstall button.
5. Tap the OK button.

 Consider This: In addition to the reasons stated here, what other reasons might you choose to uninstall an app from your computer or mobile device?

CONSIDER THIS

Can you use a file manager to delete a program?
If an uninstaller exists and you remove software from a computer by deleting the files and folders associated with the program without running the uninstaller, the system file entries might not be updated. This may cause the operating system to display error messages when you start the computer.

Disk Cleanup

A **disk cleanup** tool searches for and removes unnecessary files (Figure 4-30). Unnecessary files may include downloaded program files, temporary Internet files, deleted files, and unused program files. Operating systems usually include a disk cleanup tool.

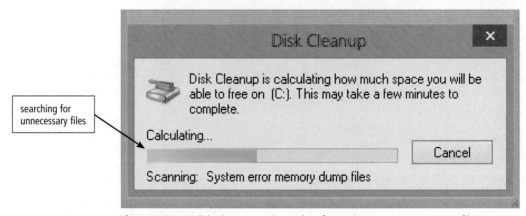

searching for unnecessary files

Figure 4-30 A disk cleanup tool searches for and removes unnecessary files.
Source: Microsoft

Disk Defragmenter

A **disk defragmenter** is a tool that reorganizes the files and unused space on a computer's hard disk so that the operating system accesses data more quickly and programs run faster. When an operating system stores data on a disk, it places the data in the first available sector (a storage location on a disk in the shape of an arc). The operating system attempts to place data in sectors that are contiguous (next to each other), but this is not always possible. When the contents of a file are scattered across two or more noncontiguous sectors, the file is fragmented.

Fragmentation slows down file access and, thus, the performance of the entire computer. Defragmenting the disk, or reorganizing it so that the files are stored in contiguous sectors, solves this problem (Figure 4-31). Operating systems usually include a disk defragmenter.

BTW

SSDs
Defragmenting is necessary only on hard disks. You do not need to defragment an SSD (solid-state drive).

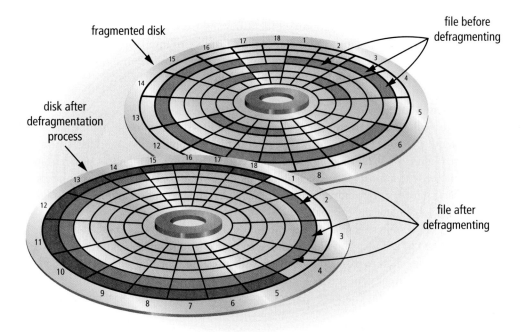

Figure 4-31   A fragmented disk has many files stored in noncontiguous sectors. Defragmenting reorganizes the files so that they are located in contiguous sectors, which speeds access time.
© Cengage Learning

Screen Saver

A **screen saver** is a tool that causes a display device's screen to show a moving image or blank screen if no keyboard or mouse activity occurs for a specified time. When you press a key on the keyboard, tap the screen, or move the mouse, the screen saver disappears and the screen returns to the previous state.

CONSIDER THIS ———————————————————————————

What is the purpose of a screen saver?

Screen savers originally were developed to prevent a problem called ghosting, in which images could be etched permanently on a monitor's screen. Although ghosting is not as severe of a problem with today's displays, manufacturers continue to recommend that users install screen savers for this reason. Screen savers also are popular for security, business, and entertainment purposes. To secure a computer, users configure their screen saver to require a password to deactivate.

⚙ BTW
High-Tech Talk
Discover More: Visit
this chapter's free
resources to learn about
compression algorithms

File Compression

A **file compression tool** shrinks the size of a file(s). A compressed file takes up less storage space than the original file. Compressing files frees up room on the storage media. You may need to compress a file so that it will fit on a smaller storage medium, such as a USB flash drive. Attaching a compressed file to an email message, for example, reduces the time needed for file transmission. Uploading and downloading compressed files to and from the Internet reduces the file transmission time.

Compressed files sometimes are called **zipped files**. When you receive or download a compressed file, you must uncompress it. To **uncompress** (or unzip or expand) a file, you restore it to its original form. Some operating systems include file compression and uncompression capabilities.

Discover More: Visit this chapter's free resources to learn more about file compression tools.

PC Maintenance

A **PC maintenance tool** is a program that identifies and fixes operating system problems, detects and repairs drive problems, and includes the capability of improving a computer's performance. Additionally, some personal computer maintenance utilities continuously monitor a computer while you use it to identify and repair problems before they occur.

Backup and Restore

A **backup tool** allows users to copy, or back up, selected files or the contents of an entire storage medium to another storage location, such as another hard drive, optical disc, USB flash drive, or cloud storage (Figure 4-32). During the backup process, the backup tool monitors progress and alerts you if it needs additional media, such as another disc. Many backup programs compress files during the backup process. By compressing the files, the backup program requires less storage space for the backup files than for the original files.

Because they are compressed, you usually cannot use backup files in their backed up form. In the event you need to use a backup file, a **restore tool** reverses the process and returns backed up files to their original form. Backup tools work with a restore tool. You should back up files and disks regularly in the event your originals are lost, damaged, or destroyed.

Discover More: Visit this chapter's free resources to learn more about backup tools.

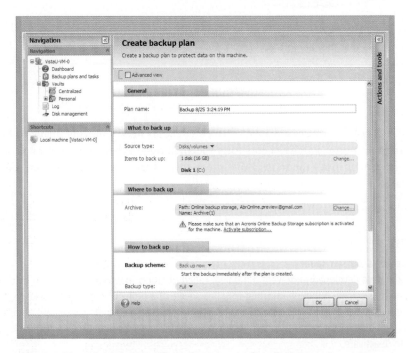

Figure 4-32   A backup tool allows users to copy files, folders, or the entire contents from one storage medium to another location.
Source: Acronis

NOW YOU SHOULD KNOW ─────────────────────────────

Be sure you understand the material presented in the sections titled Security Tools and File, Disk, and System Management Tools as it relates to the chapter objectives.
Now you should know ...

- Why you should use personal firewalls, antivirus programs, malware removers, and Internet filters (Objective 8)
- Which file, disk, and system management tools you would find useful (Objective 9)

Discover More: Visit this chapter's premium content for practice quiz opportunities.

Chapter Summary

This chapter presented a variety of programs and apps available for computers and mobile devices. You learned about the role of the operating system and the various ways software is distributed. The chapter presented the features of a variety of productivity applications, graphics and media applications, and personal interest applications. It reviewed several communications applications and then presented features of a variety of security tools and file, disk, and system management tools.

Discover More: Visit this chapter's free resources for additional content that accompanies this chapter and also includes these features: Technology Innovators: Dan Bricklin, Google/Sergey Brin/Larry Page, Adobe Systems, and eBay/PayPal; Technology Trends: Evernote, Instagram, and iTunes U; and High-Tech Talks: Filtering Data and Compression Algorithms.

Test your knowledge of chapter material by accessing the Study Guide, Flash Cards, and Practice Test resources from your smartphone, tablet, laptop, or desktop.

TECHNOLOGY @ WORK ──────────────────────────────

Entertainment

Do you wonder how music on the radio sounds so perfectly in tune, how animated motion pictures are created, or how one controls and technology lighting during a concert? Not only does the entertainment industry rely on computers and technology to advertise and sell their services, computers also assist in other aspects, including audio and video composition, lighting control, computerized animation, and computer gaming.

Entertainment websites provide music and movies you can purchase and download to your computer or mobile device; live news broadcasts, performances, and sporting events; games you can play with other online users; and much more.

As early as 1951, computers were used to record and play music. Today, computers play a much larger role in the music industry. For example, if you are listening to a song on the radio and notice that not one note is out of tune, it is possible that a program or app was used to change individual notes without altering the rest of the song.

Many years ago, creating cartoons or animated motion pictures was an extremely time-consuming task because artists were responsible for sketching thousands of drawings by hand. Currently, artists use computers to create these drawings in a fraction of the time, which significantly reduces the time and cost of development. Technology also is used in other areas of movie production to add visual effects.

Technology also is used in the gaming industry. While some game developers create games from scratch, others might use game engines that simplify the development process. For example, LucasArts created the GrimE game engine, which is designed to create adventure games.

During a concert, lighting technicians use computer programs to control lights by turning them off and on, changing their color, or changing their placement at specified intervals. In fact, once a performance begins, the technicians often merely are standing by, monitoring the computer as it performs most of the

work. A significant amount of time and effort, however, is required to program the computer to execute its required tasks during a live show.

The next time you listen to a song, watch a movie, play a game, or attend a concert, think about the role technology plays in contributing to your entertainment.

Consider This: How else might computers and technology be used in the entertainment industry?

© Horizons WWP / Alamy

Study Guide

The Study Guide exercise reinforces material you should know for the chapter exam.

Discover More: Visit this chapter's premium content to **test your knowledge of digital content** associated with this chapter and **access the Study Guide resource** from your smartphone, tablet, laptop, or desktop.

Instructions: Answer the questions below using the format that helps you remember best or that is required by your instructor. Possible formats may include one or more of these options: write the answers; create a document that contains the answers; record answers as audio or video using a webcam, smartphone, or portable media player; post answers on a blog, wiki, or website; or highlight answers in the book/e-book.

1. List categories of programs and apps. _____ is another word for program.

2. Define these terms: operating system, tools, and system software.

3. List examples of desktop and mobile operating systems.

4. Describe how an operating system interacts with the computer.

5. _____ software performs functions specific to a business or industry.

6. Differentiate among web apps, mobile apps, and mobile web apps.

7. List any restrictions for shareware, freeware, open source, and public-domain software.

8. Explain considerations for safely downloading software and apps.

9. Describe steps to register and activate software.

10. Explain the purpose of a license agreement.

11. List types of productivity applications.

12. Describe the activities that occur during project development.

13. Differentiate among font, font size, and font style.

14. Explain the impact of the Internet on plagiarism.

15. Applications often include a(n) _____ gallery, which is a collection of clip art and photos.

16. Identify functions of the following software: word processing, presentation, spreadsheet, database, note taking, calendar and contact management, software suite, project management, accounting, personal finance, legal, tax preparation, and document management.

17. Identify tools word processing programs provide that can assist you when writing.

18. Define the following terms: worksheet and function.

19. Describe when you should use a database and when to use a spreadsheet.

20. List advantages of using a software suite.

21. Identify ways you can manage a project using project management software.

22. List safety considerations when using personal finance apps.

23. Describe issues that might arise when using legal software.

24. Name the types of software used by various functional units in an enterprise.

25. Identify functions of the following apps: calendar and email, scanning, financial, reference, retail, travel, and online social networks.

26. Identify risks when using payment apps.

27. Identify functions of the following software: computer-aided design, desktop publishing, paint/image editing, photo editing and photo management, video and audio editing, multimedia and website authoring, media player, and disc burning.

28. List ways to edit digital photos. Identify issues surrounding altered digital photos.

29. _____ authoring software allows users to combine text, graphics, audio, video, and animation in an interactive application.

30. Define the terms, CBT and WBT.

31. List types of personal interest applications.

32. Describe ways to use voice command personal assistant apps.

33. Identify functions of the following apps: media sharing; streaming audio and video; game; news, sports, and weather; mapping; health and fitness; and academic.

34. Identify types of communications applications.

35. List issues surrounding an email provider scanning users' emails.

36. Identify functions of the following tools: personal firewalls, hardware firewalls, antivirus programs, malware removers, and Internet filters.

37. Describe ways a virus infects programs or apps.

38. List types of malware. Identify signs of a virus infection.

39. Explain the risks of and how to avoid computer virus hoaxes.

40. A virus _____ is a known specific pattern of virus code. Differentiate between spyware and adware.

41. Identify ways to avoid malware when using a mobile device.

42. List and describe four types of Internet filters.

43. Identify functions of the following tools: file manager, search, image viewer, uninstaller, disk cleanup, disk defragmenter, screen saver, file compression, PC maintenance, and backup and restore.

44. Define the terms, folder and index.

45. List steps to uninstall a program or remove an app.

46. Describe the disk defragmentation process.

47. Compressed files are sometimes called _____ files.

48. List storage media for backups.

49. Describe uses of technology in the entertainment industry.

You should be able to define the Primary Terms and be familiar with the Secondary Terms listed below.

Key Terms

STUDENT ASSIGNMENTS

Discover More: Visit this chapter's premium content to **view definitions** for each term and to **access the Flash Cards resource** from your smartphone, tablet, laptop, or desktop

Primary Terms   (shown in **bold-black** characters in the chapter)

accounting software (173)
adware remover (192)
anti-spam program (193)
antivirus program (191)
app (158)
application (158)
audio editing software (183)
backup tool (198)
calendar and contact management software (171)
clip art/image gallery (166)
computer-aided design (180)
database (170)
database software (170)
desktop publishing software (180)

disc burning software (185)
disk cleanup (196)
disk defragmenter (197)
document management software (176)
file compression tool (198)
file manager (194)
folder (194)
image editing software (181)
image viewer (195)
legal software (175)
media player (185)
multimedia authoring software (184)
note taking software (171)
paint software (181)
PC maintenance tool (198)

PDF (176)
personal finance software (174)
personal firewall (189)
phishing (193)
phishing filter (193)
photo editing software (181)
photo management software (182)
pop-under blocker (194)
pop-up blocker (194)
presentation software (168)
program (158)
project management software (172)
QR code (178)
restore tool (198)
screen saver (197)
search tool (195)
software (158)

software suite (172)
spam (193)
spreadsheet software (168)
spyware remover (192)
tax preparation software (176)
uncompress (198)
uninstaller (195)
video editing software (183)
virus (190)
web filtering software (193)
website authoring software (184)
word processing software (167)
worksheet (168)
zipped files (198)

Secondary Terms   (shown in *italic* characters in the chapter)

adware (192)
application software (158)
automatic update (163)
brightness (182)
clipboard (165)
compress (182)
computer-based training (CBT) (184)
contrast (182)
cookie (192)
create (165)
crop (182)
custom software (161)
edit (165)
e-filing (176)
EULA (163)
font (166)
font size (166)
font style (166)
format (166)
freeware (161)
function (169)

hard copy (166)
hardware firewall (190)
home design/landscaping software (180)
illustration software (181)
index (195)
license agreement (163)
marketplace (161)
mobile app (161)
mobile web app (161)
NFC chip (179)
open source software (161)
operating system (158)
payload (190)
pop-under ad (194)
pop-up ad (194)
print (166)
product activation (162)
productivity applications (165)
public-domain software (161)
quarantine (191)
red-eye (182)

resize (182)
retail software (161)
rootkit (190)
save (165)
security suite (189)
shareware (161)
sharpness (182)
slide show (168)
software as a service (SaaS) (162)
software registration (162)
spyware (192)

system software (158)
toll fraud malware (193)
tools (158)
trial version (161)
trojan horse (190)
utilities (158)
virus signature (192)
web app (161)
web-based training (WBT) (184)
worm (190)

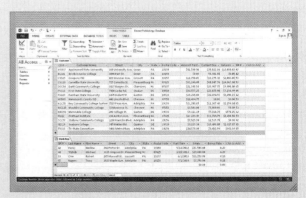

database software (170)

Checkpoint

The Checkpoint exercises test your knowledge of the chapter concepts. The page number containing the answer appears in parentheses after each exercise. The Consider This exercises challenge your understanding of chapter concepts.

Discover More: Visit this chapter's premium content to **complete the Checkpoint exercises** interactively; complete the **self-assessment in the Test Prep resource** from your smartphone, tablet, laptop, or desktop; and then **take the Practice Test.**

True/False   Mark T for True and F for False.

_____ 1. Application software serves as the interface between the user, the apps, and the computer's or mobile device's hardware. (158)

_____ 2. While a computer or mobile device is running, the operating system remains in memory. (160)

_____ 3. Open source software is mass-produced, copyrighted software that meets the needs of a wide variety of users. (161)

_____ 4. When downloading shareware, freeware, or public-domain software, it is good practice to seek websites with ratings for and reviews of products. (162)

_____ 5. With web apps, you always access the latest version of the software. (163)

_____ 6. With database software, users run functions to retrieve data. (170)

_____ 7. Software suites offer three major advantages: lower cost, ease of use, and integration. (172)

_____ 8. A PDF file can be viewed and printed without the software that created the original document. (176)

_____ 9. The military and airlines use CBT simulations to train pilots to fly in various conditions and environments. (184)

_____ 10. A router also can function as a hardware firewall. (190)

_____ 11. A worm is a destructive program designed as a real program. (190)

_____ 12. Cookies typically are considered a type of spyware. (192)

Multiple Choice   Select the best answer.

1. _____ software performs functions specific to a business or industry. (161)
   a. Retail
   b. Open source
   c. Shareware
   d. Custom

2. A(n) _____ is the right to use a program or app. (163)
   a. license agreement
   b. product activation
   c. software registration
   d. automatic update

3. _____ software is an application that allows users to organize data in columns and rows and perform calculations on the data. (168)
   a. Spreadsheet
   b. Database
   c. Presentation
   d. Document management

4. Mobile payment apps use a payment system on phones equipped with a(n) _____, which stores data that is transmitted to a contactless terminal and verified as a legitimate sale. (179)
   a. QR chip
   b. EULA
   c. NFC chip
   d. trojan horse

5. _____ is a type of application that assists professionals and designers in creating engineering, architectural, and scientific designs and models. (180)
   a. Enterprise software
   b. CAD software
   c. Public-domain software
   d. A software suite

6. The term _____ refers to removing unwanted areas of a photo. (182)
   a. crop
   b. snip
   c. compress
   d. shrink

7. A(n) _____ is a device intended to stop network intrusions before they attempt to affect your computer or network maliciously. (190)
   a. anti-spam program
   b. pop-under blocker
   c. hardware firewall
   d. quarantine drive

8. _____ is a small text file that a web server stores on your computer. (192)
   a. A pop-under blocker
   b. A cookie
   c. Adware
   d. Spyware

Checkpoint

Matching Match the terms with their definitions.

_____ 1. tools (158)

_____ 2. shareware (161)

_____ 3. software as a service (162)

_____ 4. QR code (178)

_____ 5. CBT (184)

_____ 6. personal firewall (189)

_____ 7. payload (190)

_____ 8. worm (190)

_____ 9. quarantine (191)

_____ 10. phishing (193)

a. destructive event or prank a virus was created to deliver

b. copyrighted software that is distributed at no cost for a trial period

c. malware that resides in active memory and replicates itself over a network to infect computers and devices, using up the system resources and possibly shutting down the system

d. program that enables you to perform maintenance-type tasks usually related to managing devices, media, and programs used by computers and mobile devices

e. computing environment where an Internet server hosts and deploys applications

f. security tool that detects and protects a personal computer and its data from unauthorized intrusions

g. type of education in which students learn by using and completing exercises with instructional software

h. scam in which a perpetrator sends an official looking email message that attempts to obtain personal and/or financial information

i. square-shaped graphic that represents a web address or other information

j. separate area of a hard drive that holds an infected file until the infection can be removed

✳ **Consider This** Answer the following questions in the format specified by your instructor.

1. Answer the critical thinking questions posed at the end of these elements in this chapter: Ethics & Issues (165, 175, 183, 189), How To (173, 182, 186, 196), Mini Features (178, 187, 190), Secure IT (162, 174, 179, 192, 193), and Technology @ Work (199).

2. What is the role of the operating system? (158)

3. What is system software? (158)

4. What are the advantages of open source software? (161)

5. Why do app developers opt for web delivery? (161)

6. What is the difference between software registration and product activation? (162)

7. What activities does a license agreement restrict? (163)

8. What does it mean to edit a project? (165)

9. What is the clipboard? (165)

10. What is meant by font style? (166)

11. How often should you save a project? (166)

12. How does a spreadsheet organize data? (169)

13. How are cells identified in a spreadsheet? (169)

14. When might you choose to use a database instead of a spreadsheet? (170)

15. What features are included in personal finance software? (174)

16. What steps can you take to safeguard your funds and identity when using personal finance apps? (174)

17. Who might use CAD? (180)

18. Should journalists edit or enhance digital photos? Why or why not? (183)

19. What tasks can you accomplish using mapping apps? (187)

20. How does a personal firewall protect your computer? (189)

21. What happens during the delivery phase of a virus? (190)

22. How do a virus, worm, trojan horse, and rootkit differ? (190)

23. In reference to malware, what is a quarantine? (191)

24. What is a phishing scam? (193)

25. Why is spam potentially dangerous? (193)

26. What are the different types of file, disk, and system management tools? (194)

27. How does a search tool locate a file on your computer or mobile device? (195)

28. What is a fragmented disk? (197)

29. How does fragmentation affect a computer's performance? (197)

30. What tasks does a PC maintenance tool perform? (198)

✳ Problem Solving

The Problem Solving exercises extend your knowledge of chapter concepts by seeking solutions to practical problems with technology that you may encounter at home, school, work, or with nonprofit organizations. The Collaboration exercise should be completed with a team.

Instructions: You often can solve problems with technology in multiple ways. Determine a solution to the problems in these exercises by using one or more resources available to you (such as a computer or mobile device, articles on the web or in print, blogs, podcasts, videos, television, user guides, other individuals, electronics or computer stores, etc.). Describe your solution, along with the resource(s) used, in the format requested by your instructor (brief report, presentation, discussion, blog post, video, or other means).

Personal

1. **Antivirus Program Not Updating** You are attempting to update your antivirus program with the latest virus definitions, but you receive an error message. What steps will you take to resolve this issue?

2. **Operating System Does Not Load** Each time you turn on your computer, the operating system attempts to load for approximately 30 seconds and then the computer restarts. You have tried multiple times to turn your computer off and on, but it keeps restarting when the operating system is trying to load. What are your next steps?

3. **Unwanted Programs** When you displayed a list of programs installed on your computer so that you

   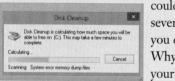

   Source: Microsoft

   could uninstall one, you noticed several installed programs that you do not remember installing. Why might these programs be on your computer?

4. **News Not Updating** Each morning, you run an app on your smartphone to view the news for the current day. For the past week, however, you notice that the news displayed in the app is out of date. In fact, the app now is displaying news that is nearly one week old. Why might the app not be updating? What are your next steps?

5. **Incompatible App** You are using your Android tablet to browse for apps in the Google Play store. You found an app you want to download, but you are unable to download it because a message states it is incompatible with your device. Why might the app be incompatible with your device?

Professional

6. **Videoconference Freezes** While conducting a videoconference with colleagues around the country, the audio sporadically cuts out and the video freezes. You have attempted several times to terminate and then reestablish the connection, but the same problem continues to occur. What might be the problem?

7. **License Agreement** You are planning to work from home for several days, but you are unsure of whether you are allowed to install a program you use at work on your home computer. What steps will you take to determine whether you are allowed to install the software on your home computer?

8. **Low on Space** The computer in your office is running low on free space. You have attempted to remove as many files as possible, but the remaining programs and files are necessary to perform your daily job functions. What steps might you take to free enough space on the computer?

9. **Unacceptable File Size** Your boss has asked you to design a new company logo using a graphics application installed on your computer. When you save the logo and send it to your boss, she responds that the file size is too large and tells you to find a way to decrease the file size. What might you do to make the image file size smaller?

10. **Disc Burning Not Working** While attempting to back up some files on your computer on an optical disc, the disc burning software on your computer reports a problem and ejects the disc. When you check the contents of the disc, the files you are trying to back up are not there. What might be wrong?

Collaboration

11. **Technology in Entertainment** The film department at a local high school is considering developing a movie and has asked for your help. The film teacher would like to incorporate technology wherever possible, in hopes that it would decrease the cost of the movie's production. Form a team of three people to determine what technology can be used to assist in the movie's production. One team member should research the type of technology that can be used during the filming process. Another team member should research the types of hardware and software available for editing footage, and the third team member should research the hardware and software requirements for producing and distributing the media.

The How To: Your Turn exercises present general guidelines for fundamental skills when using a computer or mobile device and then require that you determine how to apply these general guidelines to a specific program or situation.

How To: Your Turn

Discover More: Visit this chapter's premium content to challenge yourself with **additional How To: Your Turn exercises**, which include App Adventure.

Instructions: You often can complete tasks using technology in multiple ways. Figure out how to perform the tasks described in these exercises by using one or more resources available to you (such as a computer or mobile device, articles on the web or in print, online or program help, user guides, blogs, podcasts, videos, other individuals, trial and error, etc.). Summarize your 'how to' steps, along with the resource(s) used, in the format requested by your instructor (brief report, presentation, discussion, blog post, video, or other means).

1 Obtain Help about Programs and Apps

Multiple ways are provided to obtain help while using the programs and apps on a computer or mobile device. The program or app developer usually includes a Help feature in the program and/or online. In addition, third parties often post resources online that can provide further assistance. The following steps describe how to obtain help about various programs and apps using various methods.

Help System

You typically can access help in a program or app using one of the following methods:

- Tap or click the Help or Information icon in the program or app. The appearance of Help or Information icons may vary, but typically they are identified by a question mark or the letter 'i' formatted in italic.
- Navigate the program or app's menu to locate the Help command.
- If you are using a program or app on a Windows laptop or desktop, press the F1 key on the keyboard to display Help content.

Online Help

Online help usually is available from the program or app developer. The following steps describe how to obtain online help.

a. Navigate to the program or app developer's website.
b. Locate, and then tap or click a Help or Support link.
c. Select the program or app for which you wish to obtain help to display the help information.

Searching for Help

In addition to obtaining help from within a program or app or on the developer's website, you also can search the web for help as described in the following steps.

a. Navigate to a search engine, such as google.com or yahoo.com.
b. Type the program or app name, as well as the type of help for which you are searching, as the search text, and then press the ENTER key or tap or click the Search (or a similar) button.
c. Scroll through the search results and then tap or click the search result to display more information. Be aware that not all help originates from reputable or accurate sources.

Exercises

1. Under what circumstances would you use each of these methods to obtain help with a program or app you are using?
2. Compare and contrast the different methods of obtaining help. Which method do you think is the best? Why?
3. What are some reputable websites that can provide you with help for the operating system installed on your computer? Why do you consider them reputable?

2 Compress/Uncompress Files and Folders

You may want to compress files if your hard drive is running out of available space. While the operating system may be able to compress some files by 50 percent or more, other files' sizes may not decrease significantly when they are compressed. Compressed files typically are stored by default in a file with a .zip file extension. The following steps describe how to compress a file or folder and then uncompress (expand or extract) the compressed file.

a. Press and hold or right-click the file(s) or folders you wish to compress to display a shortcut menu.
b. Tap or click the option to compress the file(s) or folder(s). (You may need to select a Send to or other command to display the compression options.)
c. If necessary, type the desired file name for the compressed file.

Uncompressing (or expanding) compressed files or folders returns them to their original form. The following steps uncompress a compressed file.

a. Double-tap or double-click the compressed file.
b. If necessary, tap or click the option to uncompress (expand or extract) the file.

or

a. Press and hold or right-click the compressed file to display a shortcut menu.
b. Tap or click the option to uncompress (expand or extract) the file.

✸ How To: Your Turn

Exercises

1. In addition to the operating system's built-in functionality to compress files and folders, what other programs and apps exist that can compress files and folders?

2. In addition to trying to free space on your storage device, for what other reasons might you want to compress files and folders?

3. Try compressing various types of files on your hard drive, such as a Word document and an image. Compare the file sizes before and after compression. What did you notice with each type of file?

❸ View Current Virus Threats

One important way to protect your computer or mobile device from viruses is to be aware of current threats. Several websites exist that not only provide a list of current virus threats but also describe how best to protect your computer or mobile device from these threats. As new virus threats are introduced, it is important to make sure your antivirus program is updated and running properly. The following steps describe how to view a list of current virus threats.

a. Run a browser and then navigate to a search engine of your choice.

b. Perform a search for websites that display current virus threats.

c. Review the search results and visit at least two websites that display current virus threats.

d. View the list of virus threats on each of these websites.

or

a. Run a browser and then navigate to a search engine of your choice.

b. Perform a search for websites created by companies that make antivirus software. Some companies that make antivirus software include Symantec, McAfee, and Microsoft.

c. Navigate to one of these company's websites and then search for a link to a webpage displaying current virus threats.

d. Tap or click the link to display current virus threats.

Courtesy of Checkpoint Software Technologies Ltd.

Exercises

1. Which websites did you access? Compare these websites and determine which you think provided the most helpful information. Why, in your opinion, does the website you chose provide the best information?

2. Has your computer or mobile device ever been infected with a virus? If so, what steps have you taken to remove the virus?

3. Is your computer or mobile device adequately protected from viruses? What steps do you take to keep your computer safe?

❹ Back Up Your Computer

Backing up your computer is an important way to protect your programs, apps, and data from loss. The frequency at which people back up their computers can vary. For instance, if you create and modify a lot of files on your computer, you may choose to back up your computer frequently. If you rarely use your computer or primarily use your computer for answering email messages and browsing the web, you might not back up your computer as often. The following steps guide you through the process of backing up a computer.

a. Decide which backup program you wish to use. Some operating systems have built-in tools you can use to back up a computer, or you can install a third-party program.

b. Run the program you will use to back up the computer.

c. If necessary, connect the storage device, such as an external hard drive, you will use to store the backup. If you plan to store the backup on an optical disc or another hard drive that already is installed, you will not need to connect an additional storage device.

d. Make sure the storage medium has enough available space for the backed up files. If you are storing the backup on optical discs, make sure you have enough optical discs for the backup.

e. Select the type of backup (full, incremental, differential, or selective) you wish to perform.

f. If you are performing a selective backup, choose the files, programs, and apps you wish to include in the backup.

g. Run the backup. The backup process may take up to several hours, depending on the number of files you are including in the backup.

h. If you are storing the backup on optical discs, the backup program may prompt you to insert new, blank optical discs throughout the backup process.

How To: Your Turn

i. When the backup is complete, store the backup in a safe location. In the event you lose data or information on the computer, you will need to retrieve the backup.

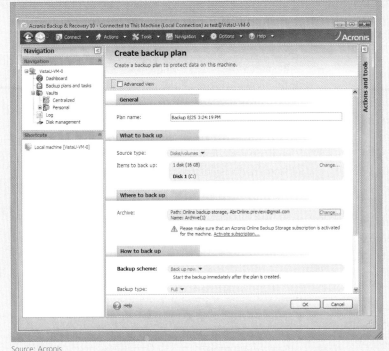

Source: Acronis

Exercises

1. How often do you feel you should back up your computer? Justify your answer.
2. Which storage medium do you feel is most appropriate for your backup? Justify your answer.
3. Research at least three programs that you can use to back up your computer. Which programs did you research? Which program or app do you feel is the best? Why?

5 **Share Your Online Calendar**

If you keep track of your meetings, appointments, and other obligations using an online calendar, you might want to share your calendar with others so that they know when you are available. For instance, you might want to share your calendar with fellow employees so that they can verify your availability before scheduling meetings. Your family members may share their calendars with one another so that it is easier to plan family events when everyone is available. The

following steps describe how to share your online calendar.

a. If necessary, run a browser and navigate to an online calendar.
b. Display the calendar's settings.
c. Select the option to display the calendar's sharing settings.
d. Specify with whom you want to share the calendar.
e. Determine your sharing settings for each person. For example, you may select whether a person only can view your calendar or view and edit your calendar. You also can select the level of detail you want to share with others. For example, you can share the times you are free or busy, or you can share the specific details for each appointment.
f. If necessary, repeat the two previous steps for each additional person with whom you wish to share the calendar.
g. Save the settings.
h. Verify the people with whom you shared the calendar are able to access the calendar.

Exercises

1. For what other reasons might you share your calendar?
2. In addition to the steps outlined previously, in what other ways can you share your calendar online?
3. In addition to sharing online calendars, is it possible to share calendars you create in programs such as Microsoft Outlook? If so, how?

Google Inc.

✳ Internet Research

The Internet Research exercises broaden your understanding of chapter concepts by requiring that you search for information on the web.

Discover More: Visit this chapter's premium content to **challenge yourself with additional Internet Research exercises**, which include Search Sleuth, Green Computing, Ethics in Action, You Review It, and Exploring Technology Careers.

Instructions: Use a search engine or another search tool to locate the information requested or answers to questions presented in the exercises. Describe your findings, along with the search term(s) you used and your web source(s), in the format requested by your instructor (brief report, presentation, discussion, blog post, video, or other means).

❶ Making Use of the Web
Website Creation and Management

Retailers and organizations realize the importance of having a website to promote their goods and services. An online presence helps a business connect with an audience and ultimately builds trust and respect. Innovative and dynamic websites deliver information to current and potential customers and clients. Creating these websites requires a methodology of planning, designing, creating, hosting, and maintaining. A business must identify the website's purpose, demographics of the target audience, appropriate content and functionality, page layout, and usability. Once the website is implemented, it must be monitored to determine usage. Logs list the number of visitors, the browsers they used, and usage patterns. In addition, the website should be maintained to update content and features.

Products are available to help build and manage a website. Most offer well-designed templates that can be customized to accommodate specific personal and business needs. They can include calendars, photos, videos, maps, and blogs. Some of these design and management tools, such as those offered on Google Sites, are available at no cost, while others require fees for specific features, such as technical support or exclusive designs.

Research This: Visit Google Sites and two other online content management systems for building websites. Compare these web apps by creating a table using these headings: Name, Number of Templates, Price, Maximum Storage, Customer Support, and Features. The Features column could include the availability of items such as customizable color schemes, e-commerce, drag and drop, website logs and analytics, and mobile editing. Which website builder would you choose if you were creating a website? Why?

❷ Social Media

Gaming via social media has seen explosive growth in recent years, especially among adult males. Exponential gaming growth has spawned companion businesses that facilitate and manage the gaming experience. Some mobile and desktop apps provide gamers a portal for tracking all their online gaming results in a central location that can be shared with friends and others with similar game interests. These apps integrate with the major Internet messaging services, have personalized news feeds, and incorporate a "suggestion" engine for new game discoveries. Many gaming blogs offer game tricks, work-arounds, and hidden features. Beginning gamers can engage their minds during downtime and expand their circle of online friends.

Research This: Visit at least two online social networks for gamers. How many games are shown? Which topics are featured in community discussions and live chats? Are rewards available? If so, what are they? Which online leagues and tournaments are offered? What are some of the latest news articles about specific games and the gaming industry? Have you participated in gaming online social networks? If so, which ones?

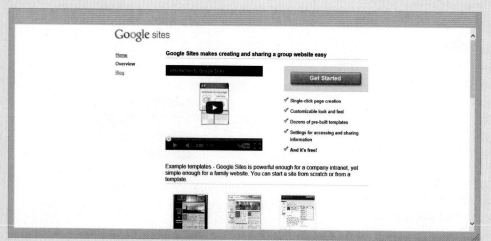

Google Inc.

Internet Research

3 **Search Skills**

Narrowing Your Search Results

One strategy for narrowing search results is to specify what you are or are not looking for as part of your search text. Precede words with a plus sign (+) if you want to ensure that they appear in your search results, and precede a word with a minus sign (-) if you want to exclude that word from search results. For example, typing the phrase, windows +microsoft, will search for information about the operating system; typing the phrase, windows –microsoft, also will find information about windows that are made of glass.

Include the keyword, and, between words or phrases in search text if you want search results to include both words or phrases, or the keyword, or, if search results containing either word or phrase are acceptable. Group terms with parentheses to clarify search text. For example, type the phrase, iPhone and "Steve Jobs" (including the quotation marks), to search for articles about the inventor of the iPhone. Type the phrase, (iPhone or iPad) and "Steve Jobs" (including the parentheses and quotation marks), to search for information about iPhone or iPad devices that also mentions Steve Jobs.

Google, Inc.

Research This: Create search text using the techniques described above or in previous Search Skills exercises, and type it in a search engine to answer these questions. (1) What is an open source FTP application that has versions for both Windows and Mac? (2) Other than TurboTax, what are two examples of online tax preparation software? (3) Find reviews comparing Internet Explorer, Chrome, and Firefox browsers. (4) What are the more popular calendar management and task management apps on Google Play?

4 **Security**

Virus hoaxes are widespread and sometimes cause panic among Internet users. Secure IT 4-4 in this chapter gives advice on recognizing and avoiding virus hoaxes. Snopes.com provides further insight on the sources and variations of a wide variety of rumors, deceptions, and folklore.

Research This: Visit snopes.com and type the search text phrase, virus hoaxes & realities, in the Search box at the top of the page. Review the list of the more recent real (indicated by a green dot) and false (indicated by a red dot) rumors circulating on the Internet. Which are the three newest actual warnings, and which are the three latest virus hoaxes? What harm is predicted to occur if a user downloads each of these real or false viruses or views a website laden with malware? What is the origin of the website's name, Snopes?

5 **Cloud Services**

Photo Editing (SaaS)

Online photo editing apps provide browser-based capabilities to modify digital images, and often contain many similar features as their desktop counterparts. They are an example of SaaS (software as a service), a service of cloud computing that provides access to software solutions accessed through a browser. In addition to drawing shapes, touching up colors, and adding filters to images, online photo editing apps allow users to access, store, and share their photos on the cloud. Online photo editing apps often include the ability to share photos with friends easily by sending a link, or posting the photo to online social networks.

Research This: (1) Use a search engine to research various online photo editing apps. Compare the features of two of them as you explore their capabilities. Summarize your findings in a table, regarding image formats you can import or save, sharing capabilities, special editing features, and ways to organize photos online. Which features take advantage of the fact that the app is cloud based? (2) If you have access to computers running two different operating systems, such as Windows and Mac, try running the photo editing app in a browser on both computers. What similarities and differences do you notice between the two versions?

Critical Thinking

The Critical Thinking exercises challenge your assessment and decision-making skills by presenting real-world situations associated with chapter concepts. The Collaboration exercise should be completed with a team.

Instructions: Evaluate the situations below, using personal experiences and one or more resources available to you (such as articles on the web or in print, blogs, podcasts, videos, television, user guides, other individuals, electronics or computer stores, etc.). Perform the tasks requested in each exercise and share your deliverables in the format requested by your instructor (brief report, presentation, discussion, blog post, video, or other means).

1. File, Disk, and System Management Tools

You are the director of information technology at a company that frequently hires student interns. The interns tend to have limited experience with using file, disk, and system management tools. As part of your job, you lead workshops that teach the interns the many tasks and functions they can perform using these tools.

Do This: Choose three categories of tools, such as disk cleanup, PC maintenance, and file compression. Determine whether your computer's operating system includes these tools. Use the web to research popular tools for each category, whether they can be purchased separately or if they are available only as part of an operating system, and the costs for each tool. Choose one program from each category, and read user reviews and articles by industry experts. Describe situations where you would use each type of tool. Share any experiences you have with using the tools.

2. Web and Mobile App Comparison

You recently purchased a new smartphone and want to research mobile apps that also have accompanying web apps.

Do This: Choose three categories of apps, and find an example for each that has both a free web and mobile version. Read user reviews of each app, and search for articles by industry experts. Research any known safety risks for the apps. If you determine the app is safe, have access to the appropriate device, and would like to test the mobile app, you can download it

to a smartphone or other mobile device. Try accessing the web app on a computer. Using your experience or research, note the differences in functionality between the web and mobile app. Is one or the other easier to use? Why or why not?

3. Case Study

Amateur Sports League You are the new manager for a nonprofit amateur soccer league. The league needs productivity software in order to keep track of participant and budget information and to prepare flyers. You prepare information about productivity software options to present to the board of directors.

Do This: Use the web to research popular word processing, spreadsheet, and accounting software. Choose three programs from each category. List common features of each, find pricing information, and note any feedback or ratings by users. Which programs would you recommend? Why? Describe the steps involved in developing a project, creating a flyer for the league as an example. Identify possible uses the league may have for the spreadsheet and accounting software. Compile your findings.

Source: © Cengage Learning

Collaboration

4. Educational Program and App Effectiveness

The principal of the local elementary school has recommended that educational apps should play a major role in the learning process, believing that these apps enable students to learn at their own pace. Some enable teachers to track an individual student's progress and understanding.

Do This: Form a three-member team and research the use of educational apps. Each member of your team should choose a different type of app, such as flash cards, testing, or CBT. List the advantages and disadvantages of using that type of app. If possible, download or access a free version of an educational app from each category and spend some time using it. Read user reviews of popular apps, and search for articles by industry experts. Would you recommend using an app for educational purposes? Why or why not? Meet with your team, and discuss and compile your findings.

DIGITAL SECURITY, ETHICS, AND PRIVACY:
Threats, Issues, and Defenses

Users should take precautions to protect their digital content.

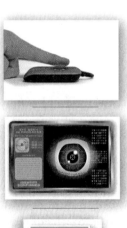

"I am careful when browsing the web, use antivirus software, and never open email messages from unknown senders. I use a cloud storage provider to back up my computer and mobile devices. What more do I need to know about digital safety and security?"

While you may be familiar with some of the content in this chapter, do you know how to . . .

- Avoid risks when playing online games?
- Determine if an email message has been spoofed?
- Tell if your computer or device is functioning as a zombie?
- Set up a personal firewall?
- Protect computers and devices from viruses and other malware?
- Protect your passwords?
- Use two-step verification?
- Prevent your data from being lost on the cloud?
- Follow a disaster recovery plan?
- Secure your wireless network?
- Safeguard your hardware and data from a disaster?
- Protect against a phishing scam?
- Protect yourself from social engineering scams?
- Evaluate your electronic profile?

In this chapter, you will discover how to perform these tasks along with much more information essential to this course. For additional content available that accompanies this chapter, visit the free resources and premium content. Refer to the Preface and the Intro chapter for information about how to access these and other additional instructor-assigned support materials.

✔ Objectives

After completing this chapter, you will be able to:

1   Define the term, digital security risks, and briefly describe the types of cybercriminals

2   Describe various types of Internet and network attacks (malware, botnets, denial of service attacks, back doors, and spoofing) and explain ways to safeguard against these attacks, including firewalls

3   Discuss techniques to prevent unauthorized computer access and use, including access controls, user names, passwords, possessed objects, and biometric devices

4   Explain ways that software manufacturers protect against software piracy

5   Discuss how encryption, digital signatures, and digital certificates work

6   Identify safeguards against hardware theft, vandalism, and failure

7   Explain options available for backing up

8   Identify risks and safeguards associated with wireless communications

9   Recognize issues related to information accuracy, intellectual property rights, codes of conduct, and green computing

10   Discuss issues surrounding information privacy, including electronic profiles, cookies, phishing, spyware and adware, social engineering, privacy laws, employee monitoring, and content filtering

Digital Security Risks

Today, people rely on technology to create, store, and manage their critical information. Thus, it is important that computers and mobile devices, along with the data and programs they store, are accessible and available when needed. It also is crucial that users take measures to protect or safeguard their computers, mobile devices, data, and programs from loss, damage, and misuse. For example, organizations must ensure that sensitive data and information, such as credit records, employee and customer data, and purchase information, is secure. Home users must ensure that their credit card numbers are secure when they make online purchases.

A **digital security risk** is any event or action that could cause a loss of or damage to computer or mobile device hardware, software, data, information, or processing capability. The more common digital security risks include Internet and network attacks, unauthorized access and use, hardware theft, software theft, information theft, and system failure (Figure 5-1).

While some breaches to digital security are accidental, many are intentional. Some intruders do not disrupt a computer or device's functionality; they merely access data, information, or programs on the computer or mobile device before signing out. Other intruders indicate some evidence of their presence either by leaving a message or by deliberately altering or damaging data.

Cybercrime

An intentional breach to digital security often involves a deliberate act that is against the law. Any illegal act involving the use of a computer or related devices generally is referred to as a **computer crime**. The term **cybercrime** refers to online or Internet-based illegal acts such as distributing malicious software or committing identity theft. Software used by cybercriminals sometimes is called *crimeware*. Today, combating cybercrime is one of the FBI's top priorities.

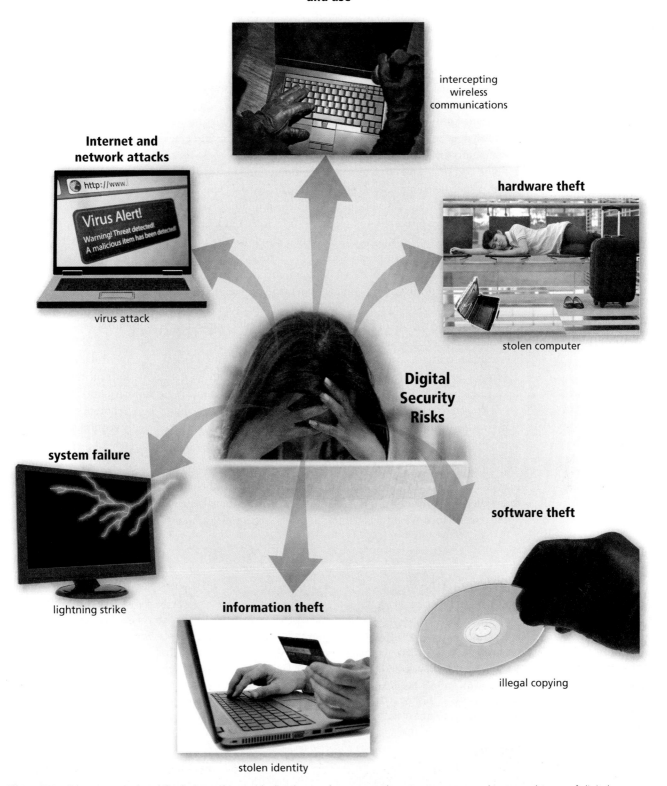

Figure 5-1 Computers and mobile devices, along with the data and programs they store, are exposed to several types of digital security risks.

Perpetrators of cybercrime typically fall into one of these basic categories: hacker, cracker, script kiddie, corporate spy, unethical employee, cyberextortionist, and cyberterrorist.

- The term **hacker**, although originally a complimentary word for a computer enthusiast, now has a derogatory meaning and refers to someone who accesses a computer or network illegally. Some hackers claim the intent of their security breaches is to improve security.

- A **cracker** also is someone who accesses a computer or network illegally but has the intent of destroying data, stealing information, or other malicious action. Both hackers and crackers have advanced computer and network skills.

Internet Research

How do script kiddies use malware?

Search for: script kiddie malware

- A **script kiddie** has the same intent as a cracker but does not have the technical skills and knowledge. Script kiddies often use prewritten hacking and cracking programs to break into computers and networks.

- Some corporate spies have excellent computer and networking skills and are hired to break into a specific computer and steal its proprietary data and information, or to help identify security risks in their own organization. Unscrupulous companies hire corporate spies, a practice known as corporate espionage, to gain a competitive advantage.

- Unethical employees may break into their employers' computers for a variety of reasons. Some simply want to exploit a security weakness. Others seek financial gains from selling confidential information. Disgruntled employees may want revenge.

- A **cyberextortionist** is someone who demands payment to stop an attack on an organization's technology infrastructure. These perpetrators threaten to expose confidential information, exploit a security flaw, or launch an attack that will compromise the organization's network — if they are not paid a sum of money.

- A **cyberterrorist** is someone who uses the Internet or network to destroy or damage computers for political reasons. The cyberterrorist might target the nation's air traffic control system, electricity-generating companies, or a telecommunications infrastructure. The term, *cyberwarfare*, describes an attack whose goal ranges from disabling a government's computer network to crippling a country. Cyberterrorism and cyberwarfare usually require a team of highly skilled individuals, millions of dollars, and several years of planning.

Read Ethics & Issues 5-1 to consider how cybercriminals should be punished. Some organizations hire individuals previously convicted of computer crimes to help identify security risks and implement safeguards because these individuals know how criminals attempt to breach security.

Discover More: Visit this chapter's free resources to learn more about cybercriminals.

⊛ ETHICS & ISSUES 5-1

How Should Cybercriminals Be Punished?
A hacker received a 10-year jail sentence for selling credit card information from several large corporations, costing one company approximately $200 million. In another case, a hacker accessed the personal online accounts of celebrities, as well as people he knew, and distributed revealing photos and information. He also received 10 years in jail, in part for the emotional distress his actions caused his victims. Do these sentences seem too harsh? Some legal experts point out that the punishment given to some hackers is not in line with crimes of a violent nature.

In addition to the extent of the punishment, other issues surrounding

cybercrime laws include whether an action is defamation or free speech and who should be punished, the hacker or those who were hacked. If a hacker's actions damage the reputation of another via libel or slander, should the hacker be prosecuted under the defamation law or be protected under the First Amendment? A *hacktivist*, which is a type of hacker whose actions are politically or socially motivated, believes his or her actions should be protected under the First Amendment. Should companies whose systems have been breached be punished for their lax security? The Federal Trade Commission (FTC) has fined companies whose security flaws enabled hackers to access their systems.

Legislators have made efforts to define and prevent cybercrime, both with new laws and the expansion of existing laws. Cybercrime laws vary between states and countries, making it difficult to establish what is illegal. Determining who has jurisdiction over a case can create more legal hassles. For example, which area is responsible for determining punishment: where the victim(s) resides or where the criminal lives?

Consider This: Should hacktivism be punishable? Why or why not? Should corporations be liable for damages caused by hackers? Why or why not? Should hackers receive comparable punishment to violent criminals? Why or why not?

Internet and Network Attacks

Information transmitted over networks has a higher degree of security risk than information kept on an organization's premises. In an organization, network administrators usually take measures to protect a network from security risks. On the Internet, where no central administrator is present, the security risk is greater. Internet and network attacks that jeopardize security include malware, botnets, denial of service attacks, back doors, and spoofing.

Malware

Recall that **malware**, short for *malicious software*, consists of programs that act without a user's knowledge and deliberately alter the operations of computers and mobile devices. Table 5-1 summarizes common types of malware, all of which have been discussed in previous chapters. Some malware contains characteristics in two or more classes. For example, a single threat could contain elements of a virus, worm, and trojan horse.

Malware can deliver its *payload*, or destructive event or prank, on a computer or mobile device in a variety of ways, such as when a user opens an infected file, runs an infected program, connects an unprotected computer or mobile device to a network, or when a certain condition or event occurs, such as the computer's clock changing to a specific date. A common way that computers and mobile devices become infected with viruses and other malware is through users opening infected email attachments (Figure 5-2). Read Secure IT 5-1 to learn about how malware can affect online gaming.

Table 5-1	Common Types of Malware
Type	**Description**
Virus	A potentially damaging program that affects, or infects, a computer or mobile device negatively by altering the way the computer or device works without the user's knowledge or permission.
Worm	A program that copies itself repeatedly, for example in memory or on a network, using up resources and possibly shutting down the computer, device, or network.
Trojan horse	A program that hides within or looks like a legitimate program. Unlike a virus or worm, a trojan horse does not replicate itself to other computers or devices.
Rootkit	A program that hides in a computer or mobile device and allows someone from a remote location to take full control of the computer or device.
Spyware	A program placed on a computer or mobile device without the user's knowledge that secretly collects information about the user and then communicates the information it collects to some outside source while the user is online.
Adware	A program that displays an online advertisement in a banner, pop-up window, or pop-under window on webpages, email messages, or other Internet services.

Discover More: Visit this chapter's free resources to learn more about malware.

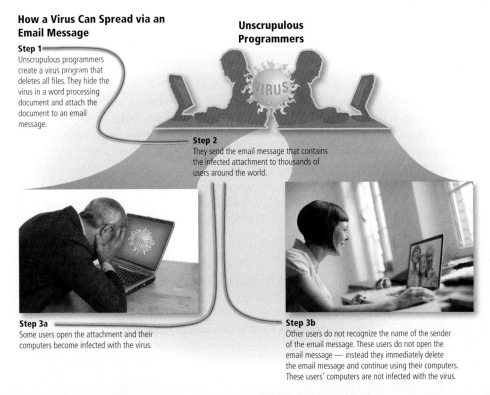

How a Virus Can Spread via an Email Message

Unscrupulous Programmers

Step 1
Unscrupulous programmers create a virus program that deletes all files. They hide the virus in a word processing document and attach the document to an email message.

Step 2
They send the email message that contains the infected attachment to thousands of users around the world.

Step 3a
Some users open the attachment and their computers become infected with the virus.

Step 3b
Other users do not recognize the name of the sender of the email message. These users do not open the email message — instead they immediately delete the email message and continue using their computers. These users' computers are not infected with the virus.

Figure 5-2 This figure shows how a virus can spread via an email message.
© Cengage Learning;
© iStockphoto / Steve Cukrov;
© iStockphoto / Casarsa

What if you cannot remove malware?
In extreme cases, in order to remove malware from a computer or mobile device, you may need to erase, or reformat, an infected computer's hard drive, or reset a mobile device to its factory settings. For this reason, it is critical you have uninfected (clean) backups of all files. Consider creating recovery media when you purchase a new computer, and be sure to keep all installation media in the event you need to reinstall the computer's operating system and your apps. Seek advice from a technology specialist before performing a format or reformat instruction on your media.

 Internet Research

What are the latest malware threats?

Search for: malware news

 SECURE IT 5-1 ———

Play It Safe to Avoid Online Gaming Risks

Gamers often understand general security issues regarding online behavior, but they may not be aware of a different set of technology and social risks they may encounter as they interact in the online world. Anyone experiencing the joys of playing games online or playing games with others through online services should realize that thieves and hackers lurking behind the scenes may take advantage of security holes and vulnerabilities that can turn a gaming session into a nightmare.

Viruses, worms, and malware can be hidden in downloaded game files, mobile apps, email message attachments, and messaging software. In addition, messages on online social networks may encourage gamers to visit fraudulent websites filled with malware. If the game requires a connection to the Internet, then any computer connected to the game's server is subject to security cyberthreats. Thieves can take control of a remote computer that does not have a high level of security protection and use it to control other computers, or they could break into the computer and install malware to discover personal information.

Malicious users know that the gaming community uses social media intensely, so they also create accounts and attempt to mislead uninformed users into revealing personal information. The thieves may claim to have software updates and free games, when they really are luring users to bogus websites that ask users to set up profiles and accounts.

Gamers should follow these practices to increase their security:

• Before downloading any software or apps, including patches to games, or disclosing any private details, check the developer to be certain the website or the person making the request is legitimate.

• Read the permissions notices to learn what information is being requested or being collected. Avoid games requiring passwords to be saved to an online account on a smartphone.

• Exercise extreme caution if the game requires ActiveX or JavaScript to be enabled or if it must be played in administrator mode.

• Use a firewall and make exceptions to allow only trusted individuals to access your computer or mobile device when playing multiplayer online games.

• Do not share personal information with other gamers whom you meet online.

☀ **Consider This:** Have you played online games or downloaded gaming apps and followed the advice listed here? How will you change your gaming behavior now that you are aware of specific security threats?

Botnets

A **botnet**, or *zombie army*, is a group of compromised computers or mobile devices connected to a network, such as the Internet, that are used to attack other networks, usually for nefarious purposes. A compromised computer or device, known as a **zombie**, is one whose owner is unaware the computer or device is being controlled remotely by an outsider.

A *bot* is a program that performs a repetitive task on a network. Cybercriminals install malicious bots on unprotected computers and devices to create a botnet. The perpetrator then uses the botnet to send spam via email, spread viruses and other malware, or commit a distributed denial of service attack (discussed in the next section).

 CONSIDER THIS ———

How can you tell if your computer or mobile device is functioning as a zombie?
Your computer or mobile device may be a zombie if you notice an unusually high drive activity, a slower than normal Internet connection, or connected devices becoming increasingly unresponsive. The chances of your computer or devices becoming part of a botnet greatly increase if your devices are not protected by an effective firewall.

Denial of Service Attacks

A **denial of service attack** (**DoS attack**) is an assault whose purpose is to disrupt computer access to an Internet service, such as the web or email. Perpetrators carry out a DoS attack in a variety of ways. For example, they may use an unsuspecting computer to send an influx of confusing data messages or useless traffic to a computer network. The victim computer network slows down considerably and eventually becomes unresponsive or unavailable, blocking legitimate visitors from accessing the network.

A more devastating type of DoS attack is the *distributed DoS attack* (*DDoS attack*) in which a zombie army is used to attack computers or computer networks. DDoS attacks have been able to stop operations temporarily at numerous websites, including powerhouses such as Yahoo!, eBay, Amazon.com, and CNN.com.

The damage caused by a DoS or DDoS attack usually is extensive. During the outage, retailers lose sales from customers, news websites and search engines lose revenue from advertisers, and time-sensitive information may be delayed. Repeated attacks could tarnish reputations, causing even greater losses.

Internet Research

Are DoS attacks still prevalent?

Search for: news of dos attacks

 CONSIDER THIS

Why would someone execute a Dos or DDoS attack?
Perpetrators have a variety of motives for executing a DoS or DDoS attack. Hactivists, or those who disagree with the beliefs or actions of a particular organization, claim political anger motivates their attacks. Some perpetrators use the attack as a vehicle for extortion. Others simply want the recognition, even though it is negative.

Back Doors

A **back door** is a program or set of instructions in a program that allows users to bypass security controls when accessing a program, computer, or network. Once perpetrators gain access to unsecure computers, they often install a back door or modify an existing program to include a back door, which allows them to continue to access the computer remotely without the user's knowledge. A rootkit can be a back door. Some worms leave back doors, which have been used to spread other worms or to distribute spam from the unsuspecting victim computers.

Programmers often build back doors into programs during system development. These back doors save development time because the programmer can bypass security controls while writing and testing programs. Similarly, a computer repair technician may install a back door while troubleshooting problems on a computer. If a programmer or computer repair technician fails to remove a back door, a perpetrator could use the back door to gain entry to a computer or network.

Spoofing

Spoofing is a technique intruders use to make their network or Internet transmission appear legitimate to a victim computer or network. Two common types of spoofing schemes are IP and email spoofing.

- *IP spoofing* occurs when an intruder computer fools a network into believing its IP address is associated with a trusted source. Perpetrators of IP spoofing trick their victims into interacting with the phony website. For example, the victim may provide confidential information or download files containing viruses, worms, or other malware.
- *Email spoofing* occurs when the sender's address or other components of an email header are altered so that it appears that the email message originated from a different sender. Email spoofing commonly is used in virus hoaxes, spam, and phishing scams (Figure 5-3). Read How To 5-1 to learn about how to determine if an email message has been spoofed.

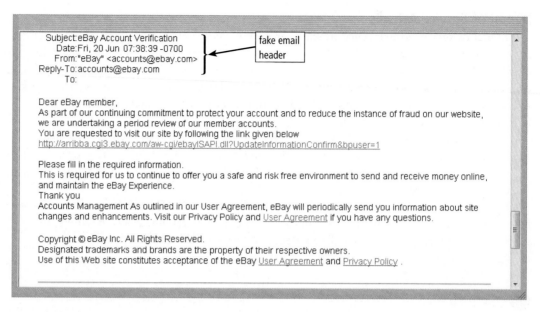

Figure 5-3 With email spoofing, the components of an email header are altered so that it appears the email message originated from a different sender.
Source: Privacy Rights Clearinghouse

 HOW TO 5-1

Determine If an Email Message Has Been Spoofed

Spoofed email messages appear to originate from one source, but in reality originate from another source. Spoofed email messages often are sent by nefarious people attempting to obtain personal information. For example, an email message appearing to be sent from a reputable source, such as your financial institution, may ask you to reply with personal information, such as a password, Social Security number, or account number. If you reply, you will be sending personal information to an unknown third party that could use the information to steal your identity, make unauthorized purchases, and more. The following steps describe some ways to determine if an email message has been spoofed.

- The email message requests personal information, such as account numbers, passwords, Social Security numbers, and credit card numbers.

- The email message contains spelling and/or grammatical errors.

- The email message encourages you to tap or click a link that takes you to another website.

- The header in the email message contains a different domain in the MessageID than the domain of the supposed sender.

- The "From" and "Reply-To" email addresses do not match.

If you ever are unsure of whether an email message was spoofed, contact the supposed sender either via phone or a new email message (do not reply to the original email message) to verify the authenticity of the message.

❋ **Consider This:** Have you ever received a spoofed email message? Did you know it was spoofed? What steps did you take?

Safeguards against Internet and Network Attacks

Methods that protect computers, mobile devices, and networks from attacks include the following:

- Use antivirus software.
- Be suspicious of unsolicited email attachments.
- Scan removable media for malware before using it.
- Implement firewall solutions.
- Back up regularly.

Secure IT 1-2 in Chapter 1 provided some measures you can take to protect your computers and mobile devices from malware. Read Secure IT 5-2 for additional tips to protect home users against Internet and network attacks. The next section discusses firewalls in more depth.

 BTW

Antivirus Programs
In addition to protecting against viruses and other malware, many antivirus programs also include protection from DoS and DDoS attacks.

SECURE IT 5-2

Protection from Viruses and Other Malware

It is impossible to ensure a virus or malware never will attack a computer, but you can take steps to protect your computer by following these practices:

- **Use virus protection software.** Install a reputable antivirus program and then scan the entire computer to be certain it is free of viruses and other malware. Update the antivirus program and the virus signatures (known specific patterns of viruses) regularly.

- **Use a firewall.** Set up a hardware firewall or install a software firewall that protects your network's resources from outside intrusions.

- **Be suspicious of all unsolicited email and text messages.** Never open an email message unless you are expecting it, *and* it is from a trusted source. When in doubt, ask the sender to confirm the message is legitimate before you open it. Be especially

cautious when deciding whether to tap or click links in email and text messages or to open attachments.

- **Disconnect your computer from the Internet.** If you do not need Internet access, disconnect the computer from the Internet. Some security experts recommend disconnecting from the computer network before opening email attachments.

- **Download software with caution.** Download programs or apps only from websites you trust, especially those with music and video sharing software.

- **Close spyware windows.** If you suspect a pop-up or pop-under window may be spyware, close the window. Never tap or click an Agree or OK button in a suspicious window.

- **Before using any removable media, scan it for malware.** Follow this procedure even for shrink-wrapped software

from major developers. Some commercial software has been infected and distributed to unsuspecting users. Never start a computer with removable media inserted in the computer unless you are certain the media are uninfected.

- **Keep current.** Install the latest updates for your computer software. Stay informed about new virus alerts and virus hoaxes.

- **Back up regularly.** In the event your computer becomes unusable due to a virus attack or other malware, you will be able to restore operations if you have a clean (uninfected) backup.

Consider This: What precautions do you take to prevent viruses and other malware from infecting your computer? What new steps will you take to attempt to protect your computer?

CONSIDER THIS

How can you determine if your computer or mobile device is vulnerable to an Internet or network attack? You could use an **online security service,** which is a web app that evaluates your computer or mobile device to check for Internet and email vulnerabilities. The online security service then provides recommendations of how to address the vulnerabilities.

Organizations requiring assistance or information about Internet security breaches can contact or visit the website for the *Computer Emergency Response Team Coordination Center*, or *CERT/CC*, which is a federally funded Internet security research and development center.

Discover More: Visit this chapter's free resources to learn more about online security services.

Firewalls

A **firewall** is hardware and/or software that protects a network's resources from intrusion by users on another network, such as the Internet. All networked and online users should implement a firewall solution.

Organizations use firewalls to protect network resources from outsiders and to restrict employees' access to sensitive data, such as payroll or personnel records. They can implement a firewall solution themselves or outsource their needs to a company specializing in providing firewall protection.

Large organizations often route all their communications through a proxy server, which typically is a component of the firewall. A *proxy server* is a server outside the organization's network that controls which communications pass in and out of the organization's network. That is, a proxy server carefully screens all incoming and outgoing messages. Proxy servers use a variety of screening techniques. Some check the domain name or IP address of the message for legitimacy. Others require that the messages have digital signatures (discussed later in this chapter).

BTW

Technology Innovators
Discover More: Visit
this chapter's free
resources to learn about
AVG, Intel Security,
and Symantec (security
product developers).

Home and small/home office users often protect their computers with a personal firewall. As discussed in Chapter 4, a **personal firewall** is a software firewall that detects and protects a personal computer and its data from unauthorized intrusions. Personal firewalls constantly monitor all transmissions to and from the computer and may inform a user of any attempted intrusions. Both Windows and Mac operating systems include firewall capabilities, including monitoring Internet traffic to and from installed applications. Read How To 5-2 for instructions about setting up a personal firewall.

Some small/home office users purchase a hardware firewall, such as a router or other device that has a built-in firewall, in addition to or instead of a personal firewall. Hardware firewalls stop malicious intrusions before they attempt to affect your computer or network. Figure 5-4 illustrates the purpose of hardware and software firewalls.

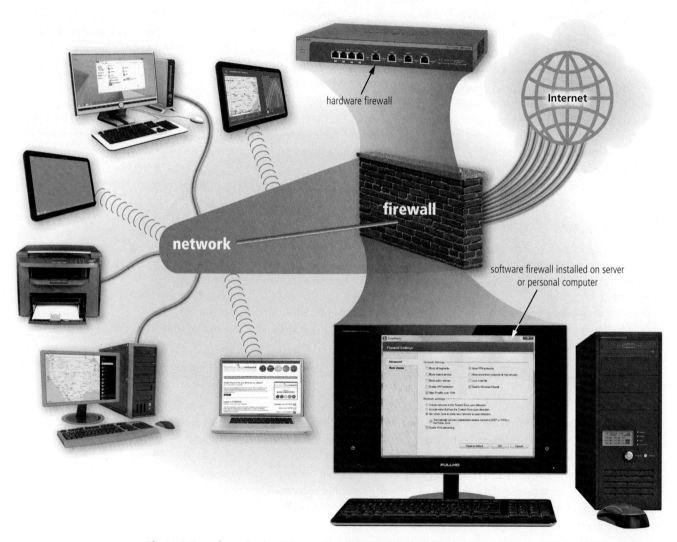

Figure 5-4 A firewall is hardware and/or software that protects a home or business's network resources from intrusion by users on another network, such as the Internet.

Courtesy of NETGEAR; © Cengage Learning; Courtesy of CheckPoint Software Technologies; © iStockphoto / Skip Odonnell; Source: Nutrition Blog Network; © iStockphoto / 123render; Source: Microsoft; © Iakov Filimonov / Shutterstock.com; © iStockphoto / Oleksiy Mark; Source: Microsoft; © iStockphoto / Ayaaz Rattansi; Source: Microsoft; © iStockphoto / Oleksiy Mark; Source: Microsoft; © Cengage Learning; Microsoft

HOW TO 5-2

Set Up a Personal Firewall
A personal firewall is a program that helps protect your computer from unauthorized access by blocking certain types of communications. For example, if somebody knows the IP address of your computer and attempts to access it using a browser or other program, the personal firewall can be configured to deny the incoming connection. The following steps describe how to set up a personal firewall.

1. Locate and purchase a personal firewall. You can purchase personal firewalls online and in stores that sell software. Many operating systems include a personal firewall. Computers typically can have only one active personal firewall running at a time. If you purchase a personal firewall, you may need to disable the one that is included with the operating system.

2. If you purchase a personal firewall, follow the instructions to install the program on your computer.

3. Run the personal firewall.

4. If necessary, ensure the personal firewall is enabled.

5. Review the settings for the incoming and outgoing rules. Incoming rules display programs and services that are allowed to access your computer. Outgoing rules display programs and services on your computer that are allowed to communicate with other computers and mobile devices on your network or the Internet.

6. Back up or export your current list of incoming and outgoing rules. If your computer does not function properly after you adjust the rules (in Steps 7 and 8), you will be able to restore the current rules.

7. Adjust your incoming rules to disallow devices, programs, and services you do

not want accessing your computer. Be careful adjusting these settings, as adding or removing rules may hinder a legitimate program's capability to work properly.

8. Adjust your outgoing rules to allow only appropriate programs on your computer to communicate with other computers and mobile devices on your network or the Internet. Examples include a browser, email program, or other communications programs.

9. Save your settings.

10. Test programs on your computer that require Internet access. If any do not function properly, restore the list of rules you backed up or exported in Step 6.

11. Exit the personal firewall.

Consider This: Which programs on your computer should have access to the Internet? Which programs should not?

Unauthorized Access and Use

Unauthorized access is the use of a computer or network without permission. *Unauthorized use* is the use of a computer or its data for unapproved or possibly illegal activities.

Home and business users can be a target of unauthorized access and use. Unauthorized use includes a variety of activities: an employee using an organization's computer to send personal email messages, an employee using the organization's word processing software to track his or her child's soccer league scores, or a perpetrator gaining access to a bank computer and performing an unauthorized transfer.

Safeguards against Unauthorized Access and Use

Organizations take several measures to help prevent unauthorized access and use. At a minimum, they should have a written *acceptable use policy (AUP)* that outlines the activities for which the computer and network may and may not be used. An organization's AUP should specify the acceptable use of technology by employees for personal reasons. Some organizations prohibit such use entirely. Others allow personal use on the employee's own time, such as a lunch hour. Whatever the policy, an organization should document and explain it to employees. The AUP also should specify the personal activities, if any, that are allowed on company time. For example, can employees check personal email messages or respond to personal text messages during work hours?

To protect your personal computer from unauthorized intrusions, you should disable file and printer sharing in your operating system (Figure 5-5). This security measure attempts to ensure that others cannot access your files or your printer. You also should be sure to use a firewall. The following sections address other techniques for protecting against unauthorized access and use. The technique(s) used should correspond to the degree of risk that is associated with the unauthorized access.

Figure 5-5 To protect files on your device's hard drive from hackers and other intruders, turn off file and printer sharing on your device.
Source: Microsoft

Access Controls

Many organizations use access controls to minimize the chance that a perpetrator intentionally may access or an employee accidentally may access confidential information on a computer, mobile device, or network. An *access control* is a security measure that defines who can access a computer, device, or network; when they can access it; and what actions they can take while accessing it. In addition, the computer, device, or network should maintain an *audit trail* that records in a file both successful and unsuccessful access attempts. An unsuccessful access attempt could result from a user mistyping his or her password, or it could result from a perpetrator trying thousands of passwords.

Organizations should investigate unsuccessful access attempts immediately to ensure they are not intentional breaches of security. They also should review successful access for irregularities, such as use of the computer after normal working hours or from remote computers. The security program can be configured to alert a security administrator whenever suspicious or irregular activities are suspected. In addition, an organization regularly should review users' access privilege levels to determine whether they still are appropriate.

User Names and Passwords

A **user name** — also called a *user ID* (identification), log on name, or sign in name — is a unique combination of characters, such as letters of the alphabet or numbers, that identifies one specific user. A **password** is a private combination of characters associated with the user name that allows access to certain computer resources.

Most operating systems that enable multiple users to share computers and devices or that access a home or business network require users to enter a user name and a password correctly before they can access the data, information, and programs stored on a computer, mobile device, or network. Many systems that maintain financial, personal, and other confidential information also require a user name and password as part of their sign-in procedure (Figure 5-6).

Some systems assign a user name and/or password to each user. For example, a school may use a combination of letters from a student's first and last names as a user name. For example, Brittany Stearn's user name might be stearns_brit. Some websites use your email address as the user name. Information technology (IT) departments may assign passwords so that they have a record in case the employee leaves or forgets the password.

With other systems, users select their own user names and/or passwords. Many users select a combination of their first and last names for their user

Figure 5-6 Many websites that maintain personal and confidential data, such as Citibank's credit card system, require a user to enter a user name (user ID) and password.
Source: Citigroup Inc

⚙ BTW

Single Sign On
When you enter your user name into a *single sign on* account, such as for Microsoft, Google, Twitter, and Facebook, you automatically are signed in to other accounts and services. Many also recognize your information to provide additional customized content.

names. Many online social networks, media sharing sites, and retail and other websites allow you to choose your own user name. You might select a name that is formed from parts of your real name or nickname and possibly some numbers, if the name you want is taken (such as britstearns04). If you wish to remain more anonymous, choose a user name that combines common words, or reflects your interests (such as guitarboston27).

Once you select a password, change it frequently. Read Secure IT 1-3 in Chapter 1 for tips about creating strong passwords. Do not disclose your password to anyone or write it on a slip of paper kept near the computer, especially taped to the monitor or under the keyboard. Email and telemarketing scams often ask unsuspecting users to disclose their credit card numbers, so be wary if you did not initiate the inquiry or phone call. Read Secure IT 5-3 for tips about using a password manager.

SECURE IT 5-3

Safely Use a Password Manager

If you use the same password to access your banking, shopping, online social networks, and school accounts, you are not alone. Many people think one password is sufficient protection for all their vital online accounts, but cyberthieves are aware of this flawed thinking and take advantage of this practice. Security experts recommend using different user names and passwords for every account and changing the passwords frequently.

Keeping track of all these accounts can be an overwhelming task. A *password manager*, also called a *password organizer*, is a convenient service that stores all your account information securely. Once you select a service, you download and install the software and create one master password. The first time you view a password-protected website and enter your user name and password, the password manager saves this information. The next time you visit one of these websites or apps, the software supplies the account information automatically. Password managers use two-step verification and advanced encryption techniques (discussed later in this chapter) to ensure information is stored securely.

Some managers offer the option to generate random passwords, which have a unique combination of jumbled numbers and letters that are difficult for criminals to steal, for each account. Other features include the ability to auto-fill information, such as your name, address, and phone number, on forms and to provide a hint if you have forgotten your master password.

Password manager services can be free to use or may require a small annual fee. Some security experts recommend using a service that charges a fee, stating that these companies may provide more features. Before using any manager, call the company and ask about security measures, the ability to sync with multiple mobile devices, 24-hour customer service via live chat or phone, and limits on the number of passwords that can be saved.

Consider This: Do you use a password manager? If so, do you feel secure storing all your sign in and password information in this service? If not, how do you keep track of your passwords?

CONSIDER THIS

Why do some websites allow you to use your email address as a user name?

No two users can have the same email address; that is, your email address is unique to you. This means you can use your email address and password from one website to validate your identity on another website. Facebook, Google, and Twitter, for example, are three popular websites that provide authentication services to other applications. By using your email address from one of these websites to access other websites, you do not have to create or remember separate user names and passwords for the various websites you visit.

In addition to a user name and password, some systems ask users to enter one of several pieces of personal information. Such items can include a grandparent's first name, your favorite food, your first pet's name, or the name of the elementary school you attended. These items should be facts that you easily remember but are not easy for others to discover about you when using a search engine or examining your profiles on online social networks. As with a password, if the user's response does not match information on file, the system denies access.

Passphrase Instead of passwords, some organizations use passphrases to authenticate users. A *passphrase* is a private combination of words, often containing mixed capitalization and punctuation, associated with a user name that allows access to certain computer resources. Passphrases, which often can be up to 100 characters in length, are more secure than passwords, yet can be easy to remember because they contain words.

PIN A **PIN** (personal identification number), sometimes called a *passcode*, is a numeric password, either assigned by a company or selected by a user. PINs provide an additional level of security. Select PINs carefully and protect them as you do any other password. For example, do not use the same four digits, sequential digits, or dates others could easily determine, such as birth dates.

 BTW

Default Passwords
If a program or device has a default or preset password, such as admin, be sure to change it to prevent unauthorized access.

CONSIDER THIS

Why do some websites display distorted characters you must reenter along with your password?

These websites use a CAPTCHA, which stands for Completely Automated Public Turing test to tell Computers and Humans Apart. A *CAPTCHA* is a program developed at Carnegie Mellon University that displays an image containing a series of distorted characters for a user to identify and enter in order to verify that user input is from humans and not computer programs (Figure 5-7).

A CAPTCHA is effective in blocking computer-generated attempts to access a website, because it is difficult to write programs for computers to detect distorted characters, while humans generally can recognize them. For visually impaired users or if words are too difficult to read, the CAPTCHA text can be read aloud; you also have the option of generating a new CAPTCHA.

Figure 5-7 To continue with the ticket order process at the Ticketmaster website, the user must enter the characters in the CAPTCHA, which consists of the letters, themssr neillso, in this case.
Source: Carnegie Mellon University

Possessed Objects

A possessed object is any item that you must possess, or carry with you, in order to gain access to a computer or computer facility. Examples of possessed objects are badges, cards, smart cards, and keys. The card you use in an ATM (automated teller machine), for example, is a possessed object that allows access to your bank account.

Biometric Devices

A **biometric device** authenticates a person's identity by translating a personal characteristic, such as a fingerprint, into a digital code that is compared with a digital code stored in a computer or mobile device verifying a physical or behavioral characteristic. If the digital code in the computer or mobile device does not match the personal characteristic code, the computer or mobile device denies access to the individual.

Biometric devices grant access to programs, computers, or rooms using computer analysis of some biometric identifier. Examples of biometric devices and systems include fingerprint readers, face recognition systems, hand geometry systems, voice verification systems, signature verification systems, iris recognition systems, and retinal scanners.

Fingerprint Reader A **fingerprint reader**, or fingerprint scanner, captures curves and indentations of a fingerprint (Figure 5-8). Organizations use fingerprint readers to secure doors, computers, and software. With the cost of fingerprint readers often less than $100, some home and small business users install fingerprint readers to authenticate users before they can access a personal computer.

Figure 5-8 A fingerprint reader.
© Flynavyjp / Dreamstime.com

The reader also can be set up to perform different functions for different fingers; for example, one finger starts a program and another finger shuts down the computer. External fingerprint readers usually plug into a USB port.

Some laptops, smartphones, and smartwatches have a built fingerprint reader. Using their fingerprint, users can unlock the computer or device, sign in to programs and websites via their fingerprint instead of entering a user name and password, and on some devices, even test their blood pressure and heart rate.

Discover More: Visit this chapter's free resources to learn more about fingerprint readers.

 CONSIDER THIS

What is a lock screen?

A *lock screen* is a screen that restricts access to a computer or mobile device until a user performs a certain action. Some simply require a user swipe the screen to unlock the screen. Others verify a user's identity by requiring entry of a password, PIN, or passcode; a fingerprint scan; or a gesture swipe (Figure 5-9). Gestures are motions users make on a touch screen with the tip of one or more fingers or their hand. For example, to unlock the screen on a phone, a user could connect the dots on the screen using a pattern previously defined by the user.

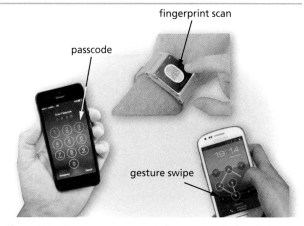

Figure 5-9 Some ways users unlock screens include entering a passcode, scanning a fingerprint, and swiping a gesture.
© iStockPhoto / franckreporter; © Alexey Boldin / Shutterstock; © iStockPhoto / Carpe89

Figure 5-10 A hand geometry system verifies identity based on the shape and size of a person's hand.
Courtesy of Ingersoll Rand Security Technologies

BTW
Technology Trend
Discover More: Visit this chapter's free resources to learn more about uses of face recognition technology.

Face Recognition System A *face recognition system* captures a live face image and compares it with a stored image to determine if the person is a legitimate user. Some buildings use face recognition systems to secure access to rooms. Law enforcement, surveillance systems, and airports use face recognition to protect the public. Some mobile devices use face recognition systems to unlock the device. Face recognition programs are becoming more sophisticated and can recognize people with or without glasses, makeup, or jewelry, and with new hairstyles.

Hand Geometry System A *hand geometry system* measures the shape and size of a person's hand (Figure 5-10). Because hand geometry systems can be expensive, they often are used in larger companies to track workers' time and attendance or as security devices. Colleges use hand geometry systems to verify students' identities. Daycare centers and hospital nurseries use them to identify parents who pick up their children.

Voice Verification System A *voice verification system* compares a person's live speech with their stored voice pattern. Larger organizations sometimes use voice verification systems as time and attendance devices. Many companies also use this technology for access to sensitive files and networks. Some financial services use voice verification systems to secure phone banking transactions.

Signature Verification System A *signature verification system* recognizes the shape of your handwritten signature, as well as measures the pressure exerted and the motion used to write the signature. Signature verification systems use a specialized pen and tablet. Signature verification systems often are used to reduce fraud in financial institutions.

 CONSIDER THIS

Do retailers use a signature verification system for credit card purchases?

No. With a credit card purchase, users sign their name on a signature capture pad using a stylus attached to the device. Software then transmits the signature to a central computer, where it is stored. Thus, the retailers use these systems simply to record your signature.

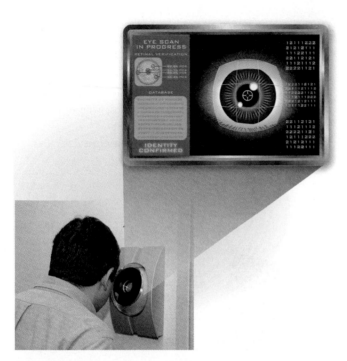

Iris Recognition System

High security areas use iris recognition systems. The camera in an iris recognition system uses iris recognition technology to read patterns in the iris of the eye (Figure 5-11). These patterns are as unique as a fingerprint. Iris recognition systems are quite expensive and are used by government security organizations, the military, and financial institutions that deal with highly sensitive data. Some organizations use retinal scanners, which work similarly but instead scan patterns of blood vessels in the back of the retina.

Figure 5-11 An iris recognition system.
© iStockPhoto / NKND200; © Robert F. Balazik / Shutterstock.com; © Cengage Learning

✳ CONSIDER THIS

How popular are biometric devices?

Biometric devices are gaining popularity as a security precaution because they are a virtually foolproof method of identification and authentication. For example, some grocery stores, retail stores, and gas stations use *biometric payment*, where the customer's fingerprint is read by a fingerprint reader that is linked to a payment method, such as a checking account or credit card. Users can forget their user names and passwords. Possessed objects can be lost, copied, duplicated, or stolen. Personal characteristics, by contrast, are unique and cannot be forgotten or misplaced.

Biometric devices do have disadvantages. If you cut your finger, a fingerprint reader might reject you as a legitimate user. Hand geometry readers can transmit germs. If you are nervous, a signature might not match the one on file. If you have a sore throat, a voice recognition system might reject you. Many people are uncomfortable with the thought of using an iris scanner.

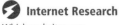 **BTW**

Two-Step Verification
Users should register a landline phone number, alternate email address, or other form of contact beyond a mobile phone number so that they still can access their accounts even if they lose their mobile phone.

🌀 **Internet Research**

Which websites use two-step verification?

Search for: two-step verification websites

Two-Step Verification

In an attempt to further protect personal data and information from online thieves, many organizations such as financial institutions or universities that store sensitive or confidential items use a two-step verification process. With **two-step verification**, also known as *two-factor verification*, a computer or mobile device uses two separate methods, one after the next, to verify the identity of a user.

ATMs (automated teller machines) usually requires a two-step verification. Users first insert their ATM card into the ATM (Step 1) and then enter a PIN (Step 2) to access their bank account. Most debit cards and some credit cards use PINs. If someone steals these cards, the thief must enter the user's PIN to access the account.

Another use of two-step verification requires a mobile phone and a computer. When users sign in to an account on a computer, they enter a user name and a password (Step 1). Next, they are prompted to enter another authentication code (Step 2), which is sent as a text or voice message or via an app on a smartphone (Figure 5-12). This second code generally is valid for a set time, sometimes only for a few hours. If users do not sign in during this time limit, they must repeat the process and request another verification code. Microsoft and Google commonly use two-step verification when you sign in to their websites. If you sign in from a device you use frequently, you can elect to bypass this step.

Step 1
User signs in to an account on a computer.

Step 2
User is prompted to enter an authentication code, received via text message or email message, before being granted access to the account.

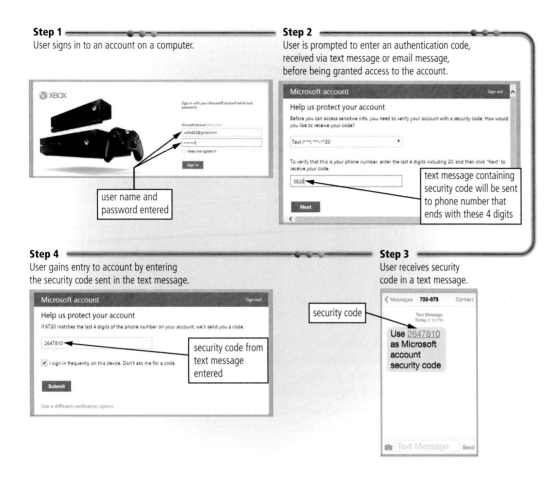

Step 4
User gains entry to account by entering the security code sent in the text message.

Step 3
User receives security code in a text message.

Figure 5-12 This figure shows an example of two-step authentication.
Source: Microsoft

 CONSIDER THIS

Can users circumvent the two-step verification process?
Users may be able to specify a computer as a trusted device during a two-step verification so that future sign-in attempts on that same computer will bypass the two-step verification. Only limited-use computers in safe areas should be identified as a trusted device.

Digital Forensics

Digital forensics, also called *cyberforensics*, is the discovery, collection, and analysis of evidence found on computers and networks. Digital forensics involves the examination of media, programs, data and log files on computers, mobile devices, servers, and networks. Many areas use digital forensics, including law enforcement, criminal prosecutors, military intelligence, insurance agencies, and information security departments in the private sector.

A digital forensics examiner must have knowledge of the law, technical experience with many types of hardware and software products, superior communication skills, familiarity with corporate structures and policies, a willingness to learn and update skills, and a knack for problem solving.

BTW
High-Tech Talk
Discover More: Visit this chapter's free resources to learn more about digital forensics.

NOW YOU SHOULD KNOW ───────────────────────────

Be sure you understand the material presented in the sections titled Digital Security Risks, Internet and Network Attacks, and Unauthorized Access and Use, as it relates to the chapter objectives.
Now you should know ...

- How cybercriminals' backgrounds and intent vary (Objective 1)
- How you can protect your computers and devices from malware, botnets, DoS attacks, back doors, and spoofing (Objective 2)
- Why you should use a firewall (Objective 2)
- How you can prevent unauthorized users from accessing your home or office computers and devices (Objective 3)

Discover More: Visit this chapter's premium content for practice quiz opportunities.

Software Theft

Software theft occurs when someone steals software media, intentionally erases programs, illegally registers and/or activates a program, or illegally copies a program.

 BTW
BSA
To promote understanding of software piracy, a number of major worldwide software companies formed the *Business Software Alliance (BSA)*. The BSA operates a website and antipiracy hotlines around the world.

- Physically stealing software: A perpetrator physically steals the media that contains the software, or steals the hardware that contains the media that contains the software. For example, an unscrupulous library patron might steal a game CD/DVD.
- Intentionally erasing software: A perpetrator erases the media that contains the software. For example, a software developer who is terminated from a company may retaliate by removing or disabling the programs he or she has written from company computers.
- Illegal registration/activation: A perpetrator illegally obtains registration numbers and/or activation codes. A program called a *keygen*, short for key generator, creates software registration numbers and sometimes activation codes. Some unscrupulous individuals create and post keygens so that users can install software without legally purchasing it.
- Illegal copying: A perpetrator copies software from manufacturers. **Software piracy**, often referred to simply as **piracy**, is the unauthorized and illegal duplication of copyrighted software. Piracy is the most common form of software theft.

Safeguards against Software Theft

To protect software media from being stolen, owners should keep original software boxes and media or the online confirmation of purchased software in a secure location, out of sight of prying eyes. All computer users should back up their files and drives regularly, in the event of theft. When some companies terminate a software developer or if the software developer quits, they escort the employee off the premises immediately. These companies believe that allowing terminated employees to remain on the premises gives them time to sabotage files and other network procedures.

Many manufacturers incorporate an activation process into their programs to ensure the software is not installed on more computers than legally licensed. During the **product activation**, which is conducted either online or by phone, users provide the software product's identification number to associate the software with the computer or mobile device on which the software is installed. Usually, the software can be run a preset number of times, has limited functionality, or does not function until you activate it.

To further protect themselves from software piracy, software manufacturers issue users license agreements. As discussed in Chapter 4, a **license agreement** is the right to use software. That is, you do not own the software. The most common type of license included with software purchased by individual users is a *single-user license agreement*, also called an *end-user license agreement (EULA)*. The license agreement provides specific conditions for use of the software, which a user must accept before using the software. These terms usually are displayed when you install

Internet Research
What are the penalties for piracy?
Search for: piracy penalties

the software. Use of the software constitutes acceptance of the terms on the user's part. Figure 5-13 identifies the conditions of a typical single-user license agreement.

To support multiple users' access of software, most manufacturers sell network versions or site licenses of their software, which usually costs less than buying individual stand-alone copies of the software for each computer. A *network license* is a legal agreement that allows multiple users to access the software on the server simultaneously. The network license fee usually is based on the number of users or the number of computers attached to the network. A *site license* is a legal agreement that permits users to install the software on multiple computers — usually at a volume discount.

Discover More: Visit this chapter's free resources to learn more about license agreements.

Typical Conditions of a Single-User License Agreement

You can…
- Install the software on only one computer or device. (Some license agreements allow users to install the software on a specified number of computers and/or mobile devices.)
- Make one copy of the software as a backup.
- Give or sell the software to another individual, but only if the software is removed from the user's computer first.

You cannot…
- Install the software on a network, such as a school computer lab.
- Give copies to friends and colleagues, while continuing to use the software.
- Export the software.
- Rent or lease the software.

Figure 5-13 A user must accept the terms of a license agreement before using the software.
© Cengage Learning

 CONSIDER THIS

Can you install software on work computers or work-issued smartphones?
Many organizations and businesses have strict written policies governing the installation and use of software and enforce their rules by checking networked or online computers or mobile devices periodically to ensure that all software is licensed properly. If you are not completely familiar with your school's or employer's policies governing installation of software, check with the information technology department or your school's technology coordinator.

Information Theft

Information theft occurs when someone steals personal or confidential information. Both business and home users can fall victim to information theft. An unethical company executive may steal or buy stolen information to learn about a competitor. A corrupt individual may steal credit card numbers to make fraudulent purchases. Information theft often is linked to other types of cybercrime. For example, an individual first might gain unauthorized access to a computer and then steal credit card numbers stored in a firm's accounting department.

Safeguards against Information Theft

Most organizations will attempt to prevent information theft by implementing the user identification and authentication controls discussed earlier in this chapter. These controls are best suited for protecting information on computers located on an organization's premises. To further protect information on the Internet and networks, organizations and individuals use a variety of encryption techniques.

Encryption

Encryption is the process of converting data that is readable by humans into encoded characters to prevent unauthorized access. You treat encrypted data just like any other data. That is, you can store it or send it in an email message. To read the data, the recipient must **decrypt**, or decode it. For example, users may specify that an email application encrypt a message before sending it securely. The recipient's email application would need to decrypt the message in order for the recipient to be able to read it.

In the encryption process, the unencrypted, readable data is called *plaintext*. The encrypted (scrambled) data is called *ciphertext*. An *encryption algorithm*, or *cypher*, is a set of steps that can convert readable plaintext into unreadable ciphertext. A simple encryption algorithm might switch the order of characters or replace characters with other characters. Encryption programs typically use more than one encryption algorithm, along with an encryption key. An *encryption key* is a set of characters that the originator of the data uses to encrypt the plaintext and the recipient of the data uses to decrypt the ciphertext.

Two basic types of encryption are private key and public key. With *private key encryption*, also called *symmetric key encryption*, both the originator and the recipient use the same secret key to encrypt and decrypt the data. *Public key encryption*, also called *asymmetric key encryption*, uses two encryption keys: a public key and a private key (Figure 5-14). Public key encryption software generates both the private key and the public key. A message encrypted with a public key can be decrypted only with the corresponding private key, and vice versa. The public key is made known to message originators and recipients. For example, public keys may be posted on a secure webpage or a public-key server, or they may be emailed. The private key, by contrast, should be kept confidential.

Some operating systems and email programs allow you to encrypt the contents of files and messages that are stored on your computer. You also can purchase an encryption program to encrypt files. Many browsers use encryption when sending private information, such as credit card numbers, over the Internet.

Mobile users today often access their company networks through a virtual private network. When a mobile user connects to a main office using a standard Internet connection, a *virtual private network* (*VPN*) provides the mobile user with a secure connection to the company network server, as if the user has a private line. VPNs help ensure that data is safe from being intercepted by unauthorized people by encrypting data as it transmits from a laptop, smartphone, or other mobile device.

Discover More: Visit this chapter's free resources to learn more about encryption algorithms and programs.

An Example of Public Key Encryption

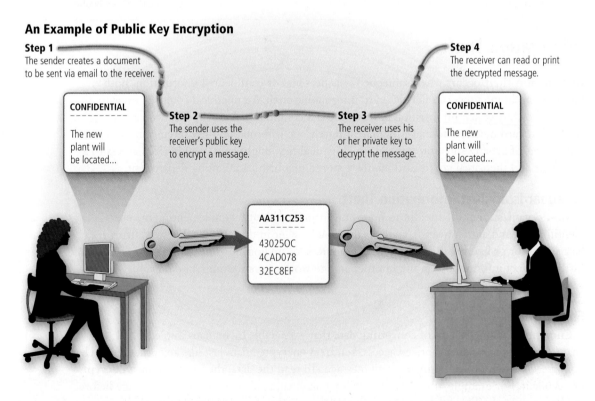

Step 1
The sender creates a document to be sent via email to the receiver.

Step 2
The sender uses the receiver's public key to encrypt a message.

Step 3
The receiver uses his or her private key to decrypt the message.

Step 4
The receiver can read or print the decrypted message.

CONFIDENTIAL
The new plant will be located...

AA311C253
43025OC
4CAD078
32EC8EF

CONFIDENTIAL
The new plant will be located...

Figure 5-14 This figure shows an example of public key encryption.
© Cengage Learning

Digital Signatures and Certificates

A **digital signature** is an encrypted code that a person, website, or organization attaches to an electronic message to verify the identity of the message sender. Digital signatures often are used to ensure that an impostor is not participating in an Internet transaction. That is, digital signatures can help to prevent email forgery. A digital signature also can verify that the content of a message has not changed.

A **digital certificate** is a notice that guarantees a user or a website is legitimate. E-commerce applications commonly use digital certificates. Browsers often display a warning message if a website does not have a valid digital certificate.

A website that uses encryption techniques to secure its data is known as a **secure site** (Figure 5-15). Web addresses of secure sites often begin with https instead of http. Secure sites typically use digital certificates along with security protocols.

 CONSIDER THIS ———————————————————————————————

Who issues digital certificates?
A *certificate authority* (*CA*) is an organization that issues digital certificates. Each CA is a trusted third party that takes responsibility for verifying the sender's identity before issuing a certificate. Individuals and companies can purchase digital certificates from one of more than 35 online CA providers. The cost varies depending on the desired level of data encryption, with the strongest levels recommended for financial and e-commerce transactions.

Discover More: Visit this chapter's free resources to learn more about security protocols, digital certificates and signatures, and CA providers.

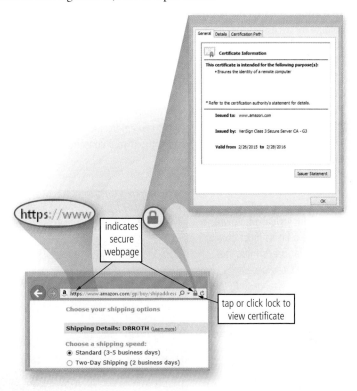

Figure 5-15   Web addresses of secure sites, such as the Amazon.com checkout, often begin with https instead of http. Browsers also often display a lock symbol in the window, which you usually can tap or click to see the associated digital certificate.
Source: Amazon.com and Microsoft

Mini Feature 5-1: Cloud Data Privacy

Privacy and security concerns arise when consumers and businesses consider moving their data to an online storage service. Read Mini Feature 5-1 to learn about privacy issues surrounding cloud data storage. Read Ethics & Issues 5-2 to consider who is responsible for data left on the cloud.

MINI FEATURE 5-1

Cloud Data Privacy

Privacy and security concerns arise when consumers and businesses consider moving their data to an online storage service. While the cloud offers a tremendous amount of storage space at a relatively low cost, the security of data and the reliability of cloud companies trigger concerns.

When people register for a cloud computing service, they sign a written contract or tap or click an online OK or Agree button to affirm they read and understand the terms of the agreement. Any data saved on the cloud is entrusted to the third-party provider, which has a legal obligation to protect the data from security breaches. The company also must guard against data loss due to physical disasters, such as power outages, cooling failures, and fire. When data has been compromised, many states require the company to disclose the issue to the data owner promptly.

The Cloud Security Alliance (CSA) warns of hackers who register for the service with a credit card or for a free trial period and then unleash malware in an attempt to gain access to passwords. Because the registration and validation procedure for accessing the cloud is relatively anonymous, authorities can have difficulty locating the abusers.

Another concern arises when transferring data over a network to the cloud. When the data is traveling to or from a computer and the cloud service, it is subject to interception. To minimize risk, security experts emphasize that the web address of the website you are visiting must begin with https, and the data should be encrypted and authenticated.

Law enforcement's access to the data raises another security issue. Email messages stored on a private server belong to the company or individual who owns the computer, so law enforcement officials must obtain a search warrant to read a particular user's messages. In contrast, law enforcement officials can access email messages stored on the cloud by requesting the information from the company that owns the cloud service. The user might not be notified of the search until up to 90 days after the search occurred; moreover, the search may occur without limitations and may include continuous monitoring of an individual's email communications.

International laws and industry regulations protect sensitive and personal data. Germany has some of the strictest cloud data privacy laws, and, in general, the European Union's privacy regulations are more

protective that those in the United States. In much of Europe, for example, consumers must agree to have their personal information collected, and they can review the data for accuracy. The education, health care, and financial services industries in the United States have strict data privacy regulations that affect cloud storage. For example, the Family Educational Rights and Privacy Act (FERPA) regulates the confidentiality of students' educational records, so colleges must obtain students' consent to share data with cloud storage providers and other third parties.

Cloud storage companies have increased their privacy and security features in recent years. Many allow consumers and businesses to protect files with passwords or require two-step authentication to access files, to delete data if a mobile device has been stolen or lost, and to delete data that has been stored past an expiration date.

Discover More: Visit this chapter's free resources to learn more about cloud security breaches, international laws and industry regulations, and protecting online data.

✳ **Consider This:** How much of your personal data is stored on the cloud? Do you have concerns about the security of this data? Have you ever received a notice that any of your online data has been compromised? Should online social networks or email providers give more explicit notice that data is stored on the cloud? Should law enforcement officials be able to access your data without your consent? Why or why not?

© iStockPhoto / maxkabakov

BTW
Technology Trend
Discover More: Visit this chapter's free resources to learn more about cloud security.

Who Is Responsible for Data Left on the Cloud?

Businesses often contract with cloud storage providers for data storage. Many businesses also use cloud storage providers to store customer data. This data could include contact information, credit card numbers, and ordering history.

Ownership of cloud data becomes an issue when a cloud storage provider or the business using the cloud services closes. Other issues include what happens if the business fails to pay the cloud storage provider, or when a contract ends. Many feel that it is the responsibility of the business owner to remove and destroy company data before a contract ends. Supporters of this argument believe that cloud storage providers should not be accessing data they host. Others contend that if a business fails to remove and destroy its data before its cloud storage contract ends, cloud storage providers should return the data, or remove the data permanently.

An ongoing debate exists related to who is responsible for cloud data security. Many experts put the responsibility of securing data in the hands of the data owner. Others advocate for a shared security model, in which the cloud storage provider includes security tools, but the company provides additional security as needed.

Ownership and security of data should be included in any contract between a business and cloud storage provider. Contracts also should specify what happens in a variety of scenarios, including if either party stops its operations, or if hackers access the data.

Consider This: If a business stops its operations, who should remove its data from cloud storage? Why? If a customer does not remove its data before a contract ends, should a cloud storage provider return the data, or can it remove or sell the data? Why or why not? Who is responsible for data security? Why?

Hardware Theft, Vandalism, and Failure

Users rely on computers and mobile devices to create, store, and manage important information. As discussed in Chapter 3, you should take measures to protect computers and devices from theft, vandalism, and failure.

Hardware theft is the act of stealing digital equipment. Hardware vandalism involves defacing or destroying digital equipment. Hardware can fail for a variety of reasons: aging hardware, natural or man-made disasters, or random events such as electrical power problems, and even errors in programs or apps. Figure 5-16 summarizes the techniques you can use to safeguard hardware from theft, vandalism, and failure.

Hardware Theft and Vandalism Safeguards
- Physical access controls (i.e., locked doors and windows)
- Alarm system
- Physical security devices (i.e., cables and locks)
- Device-tracking app

Hardware Failure Safeguards
- Surge protector
- Uninterruptible power supply (UPS)
- Duplicate components or duplicate computers
- Fault-tolerant computer

Figure 5-16 Summary of safeguards against hardware theft, vandalism, and failure.
© Cengage Learning; © iStockphoto / Norebbo

Backing Up — The Ultimate Safeguard

To protect against data loss caused by hardware/software/information theft or system failure, users should back up computer and mobile device files regularly. As previously described, a **backup** is a duplicate of a file, program, or media that can be used if the original is lost, damaged, or destroyed; and to **back up** a file means to make a copy of it. In the case of system failure or the discovery of corrupted files, you **restore** the files by copying the backed up files to their original location on the computer or mobile device.

If you choose to back up locally, be sure to use high-quality media. A good choice for a home user might be optical discs or an external hard drive. Keep your backup media in a fireproof and heat-proof safe or vault, or offsite. *Off-site* means in a location separate from where you typically store or use your computer or mobile device. Keeping backup copies off-site minimizes the chance that a single disaster, such as a fire, would destroy both the original and the backup media. An off-site location can be a safe deposit box at a bank, a briefcase, or cloud storage or cloud backup.

Cloud storage provides storage to customers, usually along with synchronization services but often on smaller amounts of data. By contrast, cloud backup provides only backup and retrieval services, but generally provides continuous data protection (discussed next) to the cloud. More customers are opting for cloud backup because it saves them the cost of maintaining hardware (Figure 5-17).

 BTW

Technology Innovator
Discover More: Visit this chapter's free resources to learn about the device-tracking app, LoJack.

Backup programs are available from many sources. Most operating systems include a backup program. Backup devices, such as external disk drives, also include backup programs. Numerous stand-alone backup tools exist. Cloud storage providers may offer backup services. Users of a cloud backup service install software on their computers that backs up files to the cloud as they are modified.

Figure 5-17 Cloud storage, such as Carbonite shown here, is a popular method for off-site backups.
Source: Carbonite, Inc.

Business and home users can perform four types of backup: full, differential, incremental, or selective. A fifth type, continuous data protection, often is used only by large enterprises to back up data to an in-house network storage device purchased and maintained by the enterprise. Cloud backup services, a sixth option, are providing continuous data protection capabilities at a lower cost. Table 5-2 summarizes the purpose, advantages, and disadvantages of each of these backup methods.

Some users implement a three-generation backup policy to preserve three copies of important files. The *grandparent* is the oldest copy of the file. The *parent* is the second oldest copy of the file. The *child* is the most recent copy of the file. When a new backup is performed, the child becomes the parent, the parent becomes the grandparent, and the media on which the grandparent copy was stored may be erased and reused for a future backup.

Table 5-2 Various Backup Methods

Type of Backup	Description	Advantages	Disadvantages
Full backup	Copies all of the files on media in the computer.	Fastest recovery method. All files are saved.	Longest backup time.
Differential backup	Copies only the files that have changed since the last full backup.	Fast backup method. Requires minimal storage space to back up.	Recovery is time-consuming because the last full backup plus the differential backup are needed.
Incremental backup	Copies only the files that have changed since the last full or incremental backup.	Fastest backup method. Requires minimal storage space to back up. Only most recent changes saved.	Recovery is most time-consuming because the last full backup and all incremental backups since the last full backup are needed.
Selective backup	Users choose which folders and files to include in a backup.	Fast backup method. Provides great flexibility.	Difficult to manage individual file backups. Least manageable of all the backup methods.
Continuous data protection (CDP)	All data is backed up whenever a change is made.	The only real-time backup. Very fast recovery of data.	Very expensive and requires a great amount of storage.
Cloud backup	Files are backed up to the cloud as they change.	Cloud backup provider maintains backup hardware. Files may be retrieved from anywhere with an Internet connection on any device.	Requires an Internet connection, otherwise files are marked for backup when the computer goes back online.

Mini Feature 5-2: Disaster Recovery

A **disaster recovery plan** is a written plan that describes the steps an organization would take to restore its computer operations in the event of a disaster. Read Mini Feature 5-2 to learn about steps an organization takes in the event of a disaster.

⚙ MINI FEATURE 5-2

Disaster Recovery

A disaster can be natural or man-made (hackers, viruses, etc.). Each company and each department or division within an organization usually has its own disaster recovery plan. The following scenario illustrates how an organization might implement a disaster recovery plan.

Rosewood Associates is a consulting firm that helps clients use social media for marketing and customer outreach. Last week, a fire broke out in the office suite above Rosewood. The heat and smoke, along with water from the sprinkler system, caused extensive damage. As a result, Rosewood must replace all computers, servers, and storage devices. Also, the company lost all of the data it had not backed up.

Rosewood currently backs up its systems daily to an internal server and weekly to a remote cloud server. Because of damage to the internal server, the company lost several days of data. Rosewood does not have a plan for replacing hardware. Thus, they will lose several additional days of productivity while purchasing, installing, and configuring new hardware.

To minimize the chance of this type of loss in the future, the company hired you as a consultant to help create a disaster recovery plan. You first discuss the types of disasters that can strike, as shown in the table. You then explain that the goal of a disaster recovery plan is to prevent, detect, and correct system threats, and to restore the most critical systems first.

A disaster recovery plan typically contains these four components: emergency plan, backup plan, recovery plan, and test plan.

Emergency Plan: An emergency plan specifies the steps Rosewood will take as soon as a disaster strikes. The emergency plan is organized by type of disaster, such as fire, flood, or earthquake, and includes:

1. Names and phone numbers of people and organizations to notify (company management, fire and police department, clients, etc.)
2. Computer equipment procedures, such as equipment or power shutoff, and file removal; employees should follow these procedures only if it is safe to do so
3. Employee evacuation procedures
4. Return procedures (who can enter the facility and what actions they are to perform)

Backup Plan: The backup plan specifies how Rosewood will use backup files and equipment to resume computer operations, and includes:

1. The location of backup data, supplies, and equipment
2. Who is responsible for gathering backup resources and transporting them to an alternate computer facility
3. The methods by which data will be restored from cloud storage

Considerations for Disaster Recovery

Disaster Type	What to Do First	What Might Occur	What to Include in the Plan
Natural (earthquake, hurricane, tornado, etc.)	Shut off power Evacuate, if necessary Pay attention to advisories Do not use phone lines if lightning occurs	Power outage Phone lines down Structural damage to building Road closings, transportation interruptions Flooding Equipment damage	Generator Satellite phone, list of employee phone numbers Alternate worksite Action to be taken if employees are not able to come to work/leave the office Wet/dry vacuums Make and model numbers and vendor information to get replacements
Man-made (hazardous material spill, terrorist attacks, fire, hackers, malware, etc.)	Notify authorities (fire departments, etc.) of immediate threat Attempt to suppress fire or contain spill, if safe to do so Evacuate, if necessary	Data loss Dangerous conditions for employees Criminal activity, such as data hacking and identity theft Equipment damage	Backup data at protected site Protective equipment and an evacuation plan Contact law enforcement Make and model numbers and vendor information to obtain replacements

© Cengage Learning

4. A schedule indicating the order and approximate time each application should be up and running

Recovery Plan: The recovery plan specifies the actions Rosewood will take to restore full computer operations. As with the emergency plan, the recovery plan differs for each type of disaster. You recommend that Rosewood set up planning committees. Each committee would be responsible for different forms of recovery, such as replacing hardware or software.

Test Plan: The test plan includes simulating various levels of disasters and recording Rosewood's ability to recover. You run a test in which the employees follow the steps in the disaster recovery plan. The test uncovers a few needed recovery actions not specified in the plan, so you modify the plan. A few days later, you run another test without giving the employees any advance notice to test the plan again.

Discover More: Visit this chapter's free resources to learn more about lost productivity, backup plans, and alternate computer facilities.

✳ **Consider This:** For what kinds of natural and man-made disasters should a company plan? What roles can cloud storage providers play in helping to recover from a disaster? How involved should employees be in developing and testing disaster recovery plans?

© iStockphoto / Hans Laubel;
© iStockphoto / William Sen;
© Gewoldi / Photos.com

Figure 5-18 Wireless access points or routers around campus allow students to access the school network wirelessly from their classrooms, the library, dorms, and other campus locations.
© Robert Kneschke / Shutterstock.com; © iStockphoto / CEFutcher; © Natalia Siverina / Shutterstock.com; © Downunderphoto / Fotolia; © Natalia Siverina / Shutterstock.com; © Cengage Learning

Wireless Security

Billions of home and business users have laptops, smartphones, and other mobile devices to access the Internet, send email and Internet messages, chat online, or share network connections — all wirelessly. Home users set up wireless home networks. Mobile users access wireless networks in hot spots at airports, hotels, shopping malls, bookstores, restaurants, and coffee shops. Schools have wireless networks so that students can access the school network using their mobile computers and devices as they move from building to building (Figure 5-18).

Although wireless access provides many conveniences to users, it also poses additional security risks. Some perpetrators connect to other's wireless networks to gain free Internet access; others may try to access an organization's confidential data.

To access a wireless network, the individual must be in range of the wireless network. Some intruders intercept and monitor communications as they transmit through the air. Others connect to a network through an unsecured wireless access point (WAP) or combination router/WAP. Read How To 5-3 for instructions about ways to secure a wireless network, in addition to using firewalls.

⊛ HOW TO 5-3

Secure Your Wireless Network

When you set up a wireless network, it is important to secure the network so that only your computers and mobile devices can connect to it. Unsecured wireless networks can be seen and accessed by neighbors and others nearby, which may make it easier for them to connect to and access the data on the computers and mobile devices on your network. The following list provides suggestions for securing your wireless network.

- Immediately upon connecting your wireless access point and/or router, change the password required to access administrative features. If the password remains at its default setting, others may possibly be able to connect to and configure your wireless network settings.

- Change the *SSID* (service set identifier), which is a network name, from the default to something that uniquely identifies your network, especially if you live in close proximity to other wireless networks.

- Do not broadcast the SSID. This will make it more difficult for others to detect your

wireless network. When you want to connect a computer or mobile device to your wireless network, it will be necessary to enter the SSID manually.

- Enable an encryption method such as WPA2 (Wi-Fi Protected Access 2), and specify a password or passphrase that is difficult for others to guess. The most secure passwords and passphrases contain more than eight characters, uppercase and lowercase letters, numbers, and special characters.

- Enable and configure the MAC (Media Access Control) address control feature. A *MAC address* is a unique hardware identifier for your computer or device. The *MAC address control* feature specifies the computers and mobile devices that can connect to your network. If a computer or device is not specified, it will not be able to connect.

- Choose a secure location for your wireless router so

that unauthorized people cannot access it. Someone who has physical access to a wireless router can restore factory defaults and erase your settings.

⊛ **Consider This:** In addition to safeguarding the data and information on your computers from others, why else might it be a good idea to secure your wireless network?

| Home | Wi-Fi | LAN | WWAN | Security | Advanced | ıll Verizon EvDO Rev.Ae | Dormant | ıllll |

Wi-Fi

Wi-Fi Profiles	
Current Profile	Secure
Selected Profile	Secure
Network Name (SSID)	smith
802.11 Mode	802.11g + 802.11b
WMM (Wi-Fi Multimedia)	Off
	With older Droids and devices that aren't working, use "Backward compatibility".
Channel	Auto
Security	WPA2
Authentication	Open Access
Network Key	68c2c067
	8 - 63 ASCII characters
For greater security, use a mixture of digits, upper case, lower case, and other symbols

Update Profile   Apply   Revert

Source: Verizon Wireless

 **CONSIDER THIS**

Can you detect if someone is accessing your wireless home network?
If you notice the speed of your wireless connection is slower than normal, it may be a sign that someone else is accessing your network. You also may notice indicator lights on your wireless router flashing rapidly when you are not connected to your wireless network. Most wireless routers have a built-in utility that allows you to view the computers currently connected to your network. If you notice a computer that does not belong to you, consult your wireless router's documentation to determine how to remove it from the network.

Mini Feature 5-3: Mobile Security

As the number of smartphones and mobile devices in use increases, the possibility of security breaches and lost devices increases proportionally. Read Mini Feature 5-3 to learn about ways you can protect sensitive and personal data on your mobile devices.

 MINI FEATURE 5-3

Mobile Security

The consequences of losing a smartphone or mobile device are significant given the amount of storage and the variety of personal and business data stored. Symantec, one of the world's leading online security companies, projects that only one-half of lost or stolen phones eventually will be returned to their owners. Chances are that the people who find the missing phones likely will have viewed much of the content on the devices in a quest to find the owners and possibly to gain access to private information.

The goal, therefore, for mobile device users is to make their data as secure as possible. Follow these steps to protect sensitive and personal data and to fight mobile cybercrime.

- **Be extra cautious locating and downloading apps.** Any device that connects to the Internet is susceptible to mobile malware. Cyberthieves target apps on widely used phones and tablets. Popular games are likely candidates to house malware, and it often is difficult to distinguish the legitimate apps from the fake apps. Obtain mobile device apps from well-known stores, and before downloading anything, read the descriptions and reviews. Look for

misspellings and awkward sentence structure, which could be clues that the app is fake. If something looks awry, do not download. Scrutinize the number and types of permissions the app is requesting. If the list seems unreasonable in length or in the personal information needed, deny permission and uninstall the app.

- **Use a PIN.** Enable the passcode feature on a mobile device as the first step in stopping prying eyes from viewing contents. This four-to-eight-digit code adds a layer of protection. Only emergency functions can be accessed without entering the correct sequence of numbers. This strong code should not be information easily guessed, such as a birthdate.

- **Turn off GPS tracking.** GPS technology can track the mobile device's location as long as it is transmitting and receiving signals to and from satellites. This feature is helpful to obtain directions from your current location, view local news and weather reports, find a lost device, summon emergency personnel, and locate missing children. Serious privacy concerns can arise, however, when the technology is used in malicious ways, such as to stalk individuals or trace their whereabouts. Unless you want to allow others to follow your locations throughout the day, disable the GPS tracking feature until needed.

- **Use mobile security software.** Protection is necessary to stop viruses and spyware and to safeguard personal and business data. Mobile security apps can allow you to lock your mobile device and SIM card remotely, erase the

turn off location services until needed

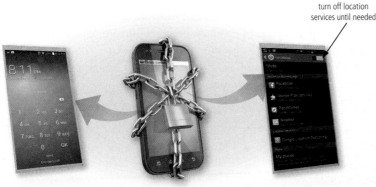

© iStockphoto / Henk Badenhorst; © iStockphoto / Marcello Bortolino;
© Cengage Learning

(Continued)

memory, and activate the GPS function. Other apps prevent cyberthieves from hijacking your phone and taking pictures, making recordings, placing calls to fee-imposed businesses, and sending infected messages to all individuals in your contact list. Look for security software that can back up data to a cloud account, set off a screeching alarm on the lost or stolen mobile device, offer live customer service, and provide theft, spam, virus, and malware protection.

- **Avoid tapping or clicking unsafe links.** Tapping or clicking an unknown link can lead to malicious websites. If you receive a text message from someone you do not know or an invitation to tap or click a link, resist the urge to fulfill the request. Your financial institution never will send you a message requesting you to enter your account user name and password. Malicious links can inject malware on the mobile

device to steal personal information or to create toll fraud, which secretly contacts wireless messaging services that impose steep fees on a monthly bill.

Discover More: Visit this chapter's free resources to learn more about methods to protect your mobile device and personal information.

 Consider This: As the number of smartphones and mobile devices in use increases, the possibility of security breaches and lost devices increases proportionally. How can manufacturers and wireless carriers emphasize the importance of mobile security and convince users to take the precautions suggested in this mini feature? What mobile security safeguards have you taken to protect your smartphone or mobile device? What steps will you take after reading this mini feature?

✅ NOW YOU SHOULD KNOW

Be sure you understand the material presented in the sections titled Software Theft; Information Theft; Hardware Theft, Vandalism, and Failure; Backing Up – The Ultimate Safeguard; and Wireless Security as it relates to the chapter objectives.

Now you should know ...

- What actions you are allowed according to a software license agreement (Objective 4)
- Why you would want to use encryption, digital signatures, or digital certificates (Objective 5)
- How you can protect your hardware from theft, vandalism, and failure (Objective 6)
- Which backup method is most suited to your needs (Objective 7)
- How you can protect your wireless communications (Objective 8)

Discover More: Visit this chapter's premium content for practice quiz opportunities.

Ethics and Society

As with any powerful technology, computers and mobile devices can be used for both good and bad intentions. The standards that determine whether an action is good or bad are known as ethics.

Technology ethics are the moral guidelines that govern the use of computers, mobile devices, information systems, and related technologies. Frequently discussed areas of computer ethics are unauthorized use of computers, mobile devices, and networks; software theft (piracy); information accuracy; intellectual property rights; codes of conduct; green computing; and information privacy. The questionnaire in Figure 5-19 raises issues in each of these areas.

Previous sections in this chapter discussed unauthorized use of computers, mobile devices and networks, and software theft (piracy). The following sections discuss issues related to information accuracy, intellectual property rights, codes of conduct, green computing, and information privacy.

Your Thoughts?

		Ethical	Unethical
1.	An organization requires employees to wear badges that track their whereabouts while at work.	☐	☐
2.	A supervisor reads an employee's email message.	☐	☐
3.	An employee uses his computer at work to send email messages to a friend.	☐	☐
4.	An employee sends an email message to several coworkers and blind copies his supervisor.	☐	☐
5.	An employee forwards an email message to a third party without permission from the sender.	☐	☐
6.	An employee uses her computer at work to complete a homework assignment for school.	☐	☐
7.	The vice president of your Student Government Association (SGA) downloads a photo from the web and uses it in a flyer recruiting SGA members.	☐	☐
8.	A student copies text from the web and uses it in a research paper for his English Composition class.	☐	☐
9.	An employee sends political campaign material to individuals on her employer's mailing list.	☐	☐
10.	As an employee in the registration office, you have access to student grades. You look up grades for your friends, so that they do not have to wait for grades to be posted online.	☐	☐
11.	An employee makes a copy of software and installs it on her home computer. No one uses her home computer while she is at work, and she uses her home computer only to finish projects from work.	☐	☐
12.	An employee who has been laid off installs a computer virus on his employer's computer.	☐	☐
13.	A person designing a webpage finds one on the web similar to his requirements, copies it, modifies it, and publishes it as his own webpage.	☐	☐
14.	A student researches using only the web to write a report.	☐	☐
15.	In a society in which all transactions occur online (a cashless society), the government tracks every transaction you make and automatically deducts taxes from your bank account.	☐	☐
16.	Someone copies a well-known novel to the web and encourages others to read it.	☐	☐
17.	A person accesses an organization's network and reports to the organization any vulnerabilities discovered.	☐	☐
18.	Your friend uses a neighbor's wireless network to connect to the Internet and check email.	☐	☐
19.	A company uses recycled paper to print a 50-page employee benefits manual that is distributed to 425 employees.	☐	☐
20.	An employee is fired based on the content of posts on his or her online social network.	☐	☐

Figure 5-19 Indicate whether you think the situation described is ethical or unethical. Be prepared to discuss your answers.
© Cengage Learning

Information Accuracy

Information accuracy is a concern today because many users access information maintained by other people or companies, such as on the Internet. Do not assume that because the information is on the web that it is correct. As discussed in Chapter 2, users should evaluate the value of a webpage before relying on its content. Be aware that the organization providing access to the information may not be the creator of the information. Read Secure IT 5-4 to consider the risks associated with inaccurate data.

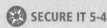

SECURE IT 5-4

Risks Associated with Inaccurate Data

Mapping and navigation software is invaluable for locating unfamiliar destinations. Problems arise, however, when satellite images are outdated or when the desired address cannot be found on a map. Inaccurate data can result in lost revenues for businesses when potential customers cannot find the storefront. It also has caused accidents when drivers followed turn-by-turn GPS directions and drove the wrong way on one-way streets, made illegal turns, or ended at ponds where a road stopped.

Business owners can report incorrect address data to some mapping services. They can, for example, state that the satellite image needs updating, their address has changed, the directions are incorrect, or the street names are inaccurate. In some cases,

the maps and addresses are updated quickly, often within a day.

Data entry errors also can lead to lost business, lawsuits, and expenses. In an extreme example, a $125 million Mars Climate Orbiter spacecraft was lost in space because Lockheed Martin engineers performed calculations using English units (pounds) to fire the thrusters guiding the spacecraft, but NASA engineers assumed the data was in metric units (Newtons) and sent the spacecraft 60 miles off course. In another unit conversion error, an axle broke on a Space Mountain roller coaster car at Tokyo Disneyland because it was the wrong size; the error occurred when engineers performed calculations to convert the original Space Mountain master plan from English units to metric units.

In the business world, mistakes can occur when software has not been updated or when employees are overworked, distracted, or faced with repetitive tasks. Software should have safeguards to verify valid data has been entered, such as checking that phone numbers have 10 numeric characters. Data cleaning software can eliminate duplicate database records, locate missing data, and correct discrepancies.

✳ **Consider This:** Have you ever used a mapping app or website and encountered incorrect information? Would you consider notifying mapping companies of errors in their satellite images or directions? What steps can companies take to help employees enter data accurately?

Figure 5-20 This digitally edited photo shows a fruit that looks like an apple on the outside and an orange on the inside.
© Cengage Learning.

In addition to concerns about the accuracy of computer input, some individuals and organizations raise questions about the ethics of using computers to alter output, primarily graphic output, such as a retouched photo. With graphics equipment and software, users easily can digitize photos and then add, change (Figure 5-20), or remove images.

Intellectual Property Rights

Intellectual property (*IP*) refers to unique and original works, such as ideas, inventions, art, writings, processes, company and product names, and logos. *Intellectual property rights* are the rights to which creators are entitled for their work. Certain issues arise surrounding IP today because many of these works are available digitally and easily can be redistributed or altered without the creator's permission.

A *copyright* gives authors, artists, and other creators of original work exclusive rights to duplicate, publish, and sell their materials. A copyright protects any tangible form of expression.

A common infringement of copyright is piracy, where people illegally copy software, movies, and music. Many areas are not clear-cut with respect to the law, because copyright law gives the public fair use to copyrighted material. The issues surround the phrase, fair use, which allows use for educational and critical purposes. This vague definition is subject to widespread interpretation and raises many questions:

- Should individuals be able to download contents of your website, modify it, and then put it on the web again as their own?
- Should a faculty member have the right to print material from the web and distribute it to all members of the class for teaching purposes only?
- Should someone be able to scan photos or pages from a book, publish them on the web, and allow others to download them?
- Should someone be able to put the lyrics of a song on the web?
- Should students be able to take term papers they have written and post them on the web, making it tempting for other students to download and submit them as their own work?

These issues with copyright law led to the development of *digital rights management* (DRM), a strategy designed to prevent illegal distribution of movies, music, and other digital content.

Codes of Conduct

A **code of conduct** is a written guideline that helps determine whether a specification is ethical/unethical or allowed/not allowed. An IT code of conduct focuses on acceptable use of technology. Employers and schools often specify standards for the ethical use of technology in an IT code of conduct and then distribute these standards to employees and students (Figure 5-21). You also may find codes of conduct online that define acceptable forms of communications for websites where users post commentary or other communications, such as blogs, wikis, online discussions, and so on.

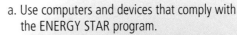

Sample IT Code of Conduct

1. Technology may not be used to harm other people.
2. Employees may not meddle in others' files.
3. Employees may use technology only for purposes in which they have been authorized.
4. Technology may not be used to steal.
5. Technology may not be used to bear false witness.
6. Employees may not copy or use software illegally.
7. Employees may not use others' technology resources without authorization.
8. Employees may not use others' intellectual property as their own.
9. Employees shall consider the social impact of programs and systems they design.
10. Employees always should use technology in a way that demonstrates consideration and respect for fellow humans.

Figure 5-21 Sample IT code of conduct employers may distribute to employees.
© Cengage Learning; © iStockphoto / Oleksiy Mark

Green Computing

People use, and often waste, resources such as electricity and paper while using technology. Recall from Chapter 1 that **green computing** involves reducing the electricity and environmental waste while using computers, mobile devices, and related technologies. Figure 5-22 summarizes measures users can take to contribute to green computing.

Personal computers, displays, printers, and other devices should comply with guidelines of the ENERGY STAR program. The United States Department of Energy (DOE) and the United States Environmental Protection Agency (EPA) developed the *ENERGY STAR program* to help reduce the amount of electricity used by computers and related devices. This program encourages manufacturers to create energy-efficient devices. For example, many devices switch to sleep or power save mode after a specified number of inactive minutes or hours. Computers and devices that meet the ENERGY STAR guidelines display an ENERGY STAR label (shown in Figure 5-22).

Enterprise data centers and computer facilities consume large amounts of electricity from computer hardware and associated devices and utilities, such as air conditioning, coolers, lighting, etc. Organizations can implement a variety of measures to reduce electrical waste:

Green Computing Tips

1. Conserve Energy
    a. Use computers and devices that comply with the ENERGY STAR program.
    b. Do not leave a computer or device running overnight.
    c. Turn off the monitor, printer, and other devices when not in use.

2. Reduce Environmental Waste
    a. Use paperless methods to communicate.
    b. Recycle paper and buy recycled paper.
    c. Recycle toner and ink cartridges, computers, mobile devices, printers, and other devices.
    d. Telecommute.
    e. Use videoconferencing and VoIP for meetings.

Figure 5-22 A list of suggestions to make computing healthy for the environment.
US Environmental Protection Agency, ENERGY STAR program; © Roman Sotola / Shutterstock.com; © Cengage Learning

- Consolidate servers by using virtualization.
- Purchase high-efficiency equipment.
- Use sleep modes and other power management features for computers and devices.
- Buy computers and devices with low power consumption processors and power supplies.
- When possible, use outside air to cool the data center or computer facility.

Some organizations continually review their *power usage effectiveness* (*PUE*), which is a ratio that measures how much power enters the computer facility or data center against the amount of power required to run the computers and devices.

 **Internet Research**

Where can I recycle outdated electronics?

Search for: recycle old electronics

CONSIDER THIS

Should you save out-of-date computers and devices?
Users should not store obsolete computers and devices in their basement, storage room, attic, warehouse, or any other location. Computers, monitors, and other equipment contain toxic materials and potentially dangerous elements including lead, mercury, and flame retardants. In a landfill, these materials release into the environment. Recycling and refurbishing old equipment are much safer alternatives for the environment. Manufacturers can use the millions of pounds of recycled raw materials to make products such as outdoor furniture and automotive parts. Before recycling, refurbishing, or discarding your old computer, be sure to erase, remove, or destroy its hard drive so that the information it stored remains private.

Discover More: Visit this chapter's free resources to learn more about the ENERGY STAR program.

How to Safeguard Personal Information

1. Fill in only necessary information on rebate, warranty, and registration forms.
2. Do not preprint your phone number or Social Security number on personal checks.
3. Have an unlisted or unpublished phone number.
4. If you have Caller ID, find out how to block your number from displaying on the receiver's system.
5. Do not write your phone number on charge or credit receipts.
6. Ask merchants not to write credit card numbers, phone numbers, Social Security numbers, and driver's license numbers on the back of your personal checks.
7. Purchase goods with cash, rather than credit or checks.
8. Avoid shopping club and buyer cards.
9. If merchants ask personal questions, find out why they want to know before releasing the information.
10. Inform merchants that you do not want them to distribute your personal information.
11. Request, in writing, to be removed from mailing lists.
12. Obtain your credit report once a year from each of the three major credit reporting agencies (Equifax, Experian, and TransUnion) and correct any errors.
13. Request a free copy of your medical records once a year from the Medical Information Bureau.
14. Limit the amount of information you provide to websites. Fill in only required information.
15. Install a cookie manager to filter cookies.
16. Clear your history file when you are finished browsing.
17. Set up a free email account. Use this email address for merchant forms.
18. Turn off file and printer sharing on your Internet connection.
19. Install a personal firewall.
20. Sign up for email filtering through your ISP or use an anti-spam program.
21. Do not reply to spam for any reason.
22. Surf the web anonymously or through an anonymous website.

Figure 5-23 Techniques to keep personal data private.
© iStockphoto / Norebbo; © Cengage Learning

Information Privacy

Information privacy refers to the right of individuals and companies to deny or restrict the collection, use, and dissemination of information about them. Organizations often use huge databases to store records, such as employee records, medical records, financial records, and more. Much of the data is personal and confidential and should be accessible only to authorized users. Many individuals and organizations, however, question whether this data really is private. That is, some companies and individuals collect and use this information without your authorization. Websites often collect data about you, so that they can customize advertisements and send you personalized email messages. Some employers monitor your computer usage and email messages.

Figure 5-23 lists measures you can take to make your personal data more private. The following sections address techniques companies and employers use to collect your personal data.

Discover More: Visit this chapter's free resources to learn more about your credit report.

Electronic Profiles

When you fill out a printed form, such as a magazine subscription or contest entry, or an online form to sign up for a service, create a profile on an online social network, or register a product warranty, the merchant that receives the form usually stores the information you provide in a database. Likewise, every time you tap or click an advertisement on the web or perform a search online, your information and preferences enter a database. Some merchants may sell or share the contents of their databases with national marketing firms and Internet advertising firms. By combining this data with information from public records, such as driver's licenses and vehicle registrations, these firms can create an electronic profile of individuals. Electronic profiles may include personal details, such as your age, address, phone number, marital status, number and ages of dependents, interests, and spending habits.

Direct marketing supporters claim that using information in this way lowers overall selling costs, which lowers product prices. Critics contend that the information in an electronic profile reveals more about an individual than anyone has a right to know. They argue that companies should inform people if they plan to provide personal information to others, and people should have the right to deny such use. Many websites allow people to specify whether they want their personal information shared or preferences retained (Figure 5-24).

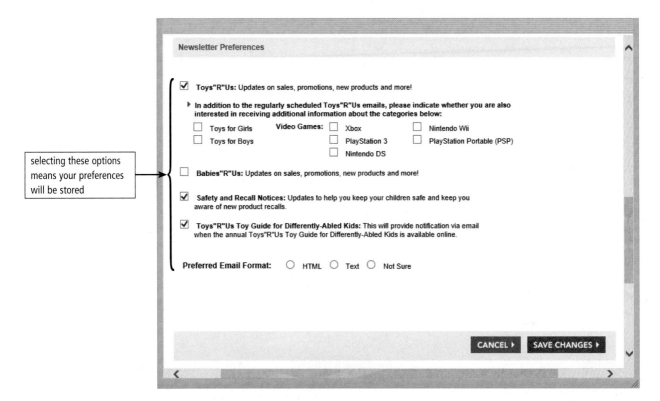

Figure 5-24 Many companies, such as Toys"R"Us shown here, allow users to specify whether they want the company to retain their preferences.
Source: Geoffrey, LLC

Cookies

A **cookie** is a small text file that a web server stores on your computer. Cookie files typically contain data about you, such as your user name, postal code, or viewing preferences. Websites use cookies for a variety of purposes:

- Most websites that allow for personalization use cookies to track user preferences. These cookies may obtain their values when a user fills in an online form requesting personal information. Some websites, for example, store user names in cookies in order to display a personalized greeting that welcomes the user, by name, back to the website. Other websites allow users to customize their viewing experience with preferences, such as local news headlines, the local weather forecast, or stock quotes.
- Some websites use cookies to store user names and/or passwords, so that users do not need to enter this information every time they sign in to the website.
- Online shopping sites generally use a *session cookie* to keep track of items in a user's shopping cart. This way, users can start an order during one web session and finish it on another day in another session. Session cookies usually expire after a certain time, such as a week or a month.

- Some websites use cookies to track how often users visit a site and the webpages they visit while at the website.
- Websites may use cookies to target advertisements. These websites store a user's interests and browsing habits in the cookie.

 **CONSIDER THIS**

Do websites ever sell information stored in cookies?
Some websites sell or trade information stored in your cookies to advertisers — a practice many believe to be unethical. If you do not want personal information distributed, you should limit the amount of information you provide to a website or adjust how your browser handles cookies. You can regularly clear cookies or set your browser to accept cookies automatically, prompt if you want to accept a cookie, or disable all cookie use. Keep in mind if you disable cookie use, you may not be able to use some e-commerce websites. As an alternative, you can purchase software that selectively blocks cookies.

Many commercial websites send a cookie to your browser; your computer's hard drive then stores the cookie. The next time you visit the website, your browser retrieves the cookie from your hard drive and sends the data in the cookie to the website. Figure 5-25 illustrates how websites work with cookies. A website can read data only from its own cookie file stored on your hard drive. That is, it cannot access or view any other data on your hard drive — including another cookie file.

How Cookies Work

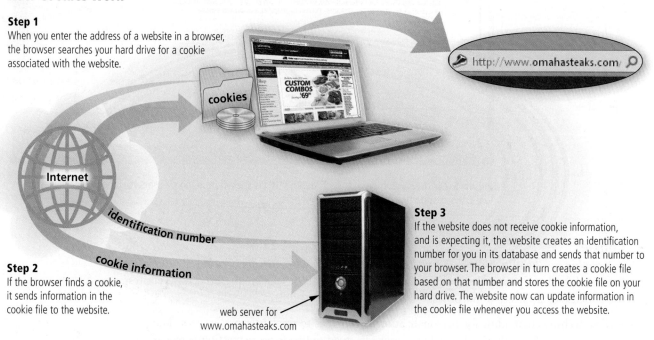

Step 1
When you enter the address of a website in a browser, the browser searches your hard drive for a cookie associated with the website.

cookies

http://www.omahasteaks.com

Internet

identification number

cookie information

Step 2
If the browser finds a cookie, it sends information in the cookie file to the website.

web server for www.omahasteaks.com

Step 3
If the website does not receive cookie information, and is expecting it, the website creates an identification number for you in its database and sends that number to your browser. The browser in turn creates a cookie file based on that number and stores the cookie file on your hard drive. The website now can update information in the cookie file whenever you access the website.

Figure 5-25 This figure shows how cookies work.
© Alex Staroseltsev / Shutterstock.com; Source: Omaha Steaks International, Inc; © iStockphoto / Norman Chan; © Cengage Learning

Phishing

Recall from Chapter 4 that **phishing** is a scam in which a perpetrator sends an official looking email message that attempts to obtain your personal and/or financial information. These messages look legitimate and request that you update credit card numbers, Social Security numbers, bank account numbers, passwords, or other private information. Read How To 5-4 for instructions about protecting yourself from phishing scams.

HOW TO 5-4

Protect against a Phishing Scam
Phishing scams can be perpetrated via email messages, websites, and even on the phone. The following guidelines will help protect you against a phishing scam.

Phone Scams
- If you receive a phone call from someone claiming to be from a company with which you do business, record his or her name and the time of the call. Do not disclose personal or financial information to the caller. If the caller is offering a product or service and is requesting a payment, call the company back at the number you have on file, and ask to be transferred to the person who called you initially.

- Whenever possible, enter your payment information on secure websites instead of reading credit card numbers or bank account information on the phone. You never know whether the caller is recording your payment information to use later for malicious purposes.

Email Scams
- If you receive an email message from someone requesting you to verify online account or financial information, do not reply with this information.

- Never tap or click links in email messages, even if the message appears to be from someone you know. Nor should you copy and paste the link from the email message to a browser. Instead, type the link's web address into a browser's address bar manually, and make sure you type it correctly. If you are visiting your financial institution's website, make sure the web address you enter matches the web address you have on file for them.

- Do not reply to email messages asking you for financial assistance — even if the email message appears to originate from someone you know. If you receive this type of email message from someone you know, call the person to verify the message's authenticity.

Website Scams
- When visiting a website, such as your financial institution's website, that will require you to enter confidential information, be sure to type the web address correctly. Typing it incorrectly may take you to a phishing website where the information you enter can be collected by an unknown party.

- Make sure websites requiring your confidential information use the https://protocol.

- Websites with misspellings, poor grammar, or formatting problems may indicate a phishing website. Do not enter personal or financial information on a website that looks suspicious.

- Enable the *phishing filter* in your browser that can warn or block you from potentially fraudulent or suspicious websites.

Consider This: Have you experienced a phishing scam? If so, how did it attempt to trick you into providing personal or financial information? How did you respond?

Clickjacking is yet another similar scam. With *clickjacking*, an object that can be tapped or clicked — such as a button, image, or link — on a website, pop-up ad, pop-under ad, or in an email message or text message contains a malicious program. When a user taps or clicks the disguised object, a variety of nefarious events may occur. For example, the user may be redirected to a phony website that requests personal information, or a virus may download to the computer or mobile device. Browsers typically include clickjacking protection.

Internet Research

Which phishing scams are prevalent?

Search for: recent phishing scams

Spyware and Adware

Recall from Chapter 4 that **spyware** is a program placed on a computer or mobile device without the user's knowledge that secretly collects information about the user and then communicates the information it collects to some outside source while the user is online. Some vendors or employers use spyware to collect information about program usage or employees. Internet advertising firms often collect information about users' web browsing habits. Spyware can enter your computer when you install a new program, through malware, or through a graphic on a webpage or in an email message.

Adware is a program that displays an online advertisement in a banner, a pop-up window, or pop-under window on webpages, email messages, or other Internet services. Adware on mobile phones is known as *madware*, for mobile adware. Sometimes, spyware is hidden in adware.

To remove spyware and adware, you can obtain spyware removers, adware removers, or malware removers that can detect and delete spyware and adware. Some operating systems and browsers include spyware and adware removers.

Social Engineering

As related to the use of technology, **social engineering** is defined as gaining unauthorized access to or obtaining confidential information by taking advantage of the trusting human nature of some victims and the naivety of others. Some social engineers trick their victims into revealing confidential information, such as user names and passwords, on the phone, in person, or on the Internet. Techniques they use include pretending to be an administrator or other authoritative figure, feigning an emergency situation, or impersonating an acquaintance. Social engineers also obtain information from users who do not destroy or conceal information properly. These perpetrators sift through company dumpsters, watch or film people dialing phone numbers or using ATMs, and snoop around computers or mobile devices looking for openly displayed confidential information.

To protect yourself from social engineering scams, follow these tips:

• Verify the identity of any person or organization requesting personal or confidential information.
• When relaying personal or confidential information, ensure that only authorized people can hear your conversation.
• When personal or confidential information appears on a computer or mobile device, ensure that only authorized people can see your screen.
• Shred all sensitive or confidential documents.
• After using a public computer, clear the cache in its browser.
• Avoid using public computers to conduct banking or other sensitive transactions.

Privacy Laws

The concern about privacy has led to the enactment of federal and state laws regarding the storage and disclosure of personal data, some of which are shown in Table 5-3. Common points in some of these laws are as follows:

1. Information collected and stored about individuals should be limited to what is necessary to carry out the function of the business or government agency collecting the data.
2. Once collected, provisions should be made to protect the data so that only those employees within the organization who need access to it to perform their job duties have access to it.
3. Personal information should be released outside the organization collecting the data only when the person has agreed to its disclosure.
4. When information is collected about an individual, the individual should know that the data is being collected and have the opportunity to determine the accuracy of the data.

Read Ethics & Issues 5-3 to consider the legal issues surrounding your digital footprint.

Table 5-3   Major U.S. Government Laws Concerning Privacy

Law	Purpose
Children's Internet Protection Act	Protects minors from inappropriate content when accessing the Internet in schools and libraries
Children's Online Privacy Protection Act (COPPA)	Requires websites to protect personal information of children under 13 years of age
Computer Abuse Amendments Act	Outlaws transmission of harmful computer code such as viruses
Digital Millennium Copyright Act (DMCA)	Makes it illegal to circumvent antipiracy schemes in commercial software; outlaws sale of devices that copy software illegally
Electronic Communications Privacy Act (ECPA)	Provides the same right of privacy protection of the postal delivery service and phone companies to various forms of electronic communications, such as voice mail, email, and mobile phones
Financial Modernization Act	Protects consumers from disclosure of their personal financial information and requires institutions to alert customers of information disclosure policies
Freedom of Information Act (FOIA)	Enables public access to most government records
HIPAA (Health Insurance Portability and Accountability Act)	Protects individuals against the wrongful disclosure of their health information
PATRIOT (Provide Appropriate Tools Required to Intercept and Obstruct Terrorism)	Gives law enforcement the right to monitor people's activities, including web and email habits
Privacy Act	Forbids federal agencies from allowing information to be used for a reason other than that for which it was collected

Discover More: Visit this chapter's free resources to learn about more privacy laws.

ETHICS & ISSUES 5-3

Do You Have the Right to Be Digitally Forgotten?

Privacy experts, such as The Institute for Responsible Online and Cell-Phone Communication (IROC2), warn that "Your digital activity is public and permanent" and is available permanently to anyone using a search engine. Does it have to be? Do you have a "right to be forgotten" as was ruled by a court in the European Union recently?

In this case, the court ordered a popular search engine to remove links to information that was "inadequate, irrelevant, or no longer relevant." The content in question included many factual articles published by a major news source. Examples included stories about a university student arrested for driving while intoxicated and a referee who

lied about a mistake. Free speech advocates criticize the law. They state that a government should not be able to deny access to accurate information. Others argue that a person should be able to request removal of information that is damaging to his or her reputation. Some are concerned that negative incidents may be necessary information for an employer to know about a job seeker, or for those considering a relationship with another person. You can never truly delete your digital footprint because everything you do online has the potential to be forwarded, captured as a screenshot, or archived in databases.

Among the debated issues is whether the rights of a private citizen should differ from those of a public figure. Many argue that different rules apply for celebrities, politicians,

and others who choose such professions. Some feel that the responsibility rests on search engines to provide methods that enable individuals to comment on, explain, or select what information is displayed when they are the subject of an Internet search. For example, Google developed the Google Inactive Account Manager, where you can specify what happens to your data after a period of inactivity.

Consider This: Does a government have a right to legislate search engine links? Why or why not? In what, if any, situations should individuals be able to request removal of digital content? Should search engines provide users with tools to control what information about them appears? Why or why not?

Employee Monitoring

Employee monitoring involves the use of computers, mobile devices, or cameras to observe, record, and review an employee's use of a technology, including communications such as email messages, keyboard activity (used to measure productivity), and websites visited. Many programs exist that easily allow employers to monitor employees. Further, it is legal for employers to use these programs.

CONSIDER THIS

Do employers have the right to read employee email messages?

Actual policies vary widely. Some organizations declare that they will review email messages regularly, and others state that email messages are private. In some states, if a company does not have a formal email policy, it can read email messages without employee notification.

Content Filtering

One of the more controversial issues that surround the Internet is its widespread availability of objectionable material, such as prejudiced literature, violence, and obscene photos. Some believe that such materials should be banned. Others believe that the materials should be filtered, that is, restricted.

Content filtering is the process of restricting access to certain material. Many businesses use content filtering to limit employees' web access. These businesses argue that employees are unproductive when visiting inappropriate or objectionable websites. Some schools, libraries, and parents use content filtering to restrict access to minors. Content filtering opponents argue that banning any materials violates constitutional guarantees of free speech and personal rights. Read Ethics & Issues 5-4 to consider whether content filtering violates first amendment rights.

Does Content Filtering in a Public Library Violate First Amendment Rights?

Among the resources libraries offer are Internet-enabled computers. The use of content filtering software on library computers controls the type of information a patron can access. Free speech advocates argue that this violates the First Amendment because it restricts library patrons from viewing certain websites and content.

The Children's Internet Protection Act (CIPA) requires that schools and libraries use content filtering software in order to receive certain federal funds. The purpose of CIPA is to restrict access to objectionable material, protect children when communicating online,

prohibit children from sharing personal information, and restrict children's identities or accounts being hacked. Proponents of CIPA claim it is necessary to protect children. CIPA does allow libraries to turn off the filters, if an adult patrons requests it. Some libraries use content filtering software on computers used only by children.

Critics of content filtering software argue that the programs do not always work as intended. They can overfilter content, blocking information or education websites based on a single word. Some websites and services that filtering software may block include online social networks, or software platforms, such as Google Drive, which students may need to access to submit assignments.

Conversely, they can underfilter content, which could result in access to webpages with inappropriate media. Others argue that it gives unequal access to students doing research who rely on library computers to do schoolwork and those who have unfiltered Internet access at home.

Libraries typically have a policy stating acceptable use of the Internet. Libraries' policies also should state whether they use content filtering software, so that the patrons are aware.

Consider This: Is it fair for a government to require that libraries use content filtering software? Why or why not? Do free speech laws cover content on the Internet? Why or why not?

Web filtering software is a program that restricts access to specified websites. Some also filter sites that use specific words (Figure 5-26). Others allow you to filter email messages, chat rooms, and programs. Many Internet security programs include a firewall, antivirus program, and filtering capabilities combined. Browsers also often include content filtering capabilities.

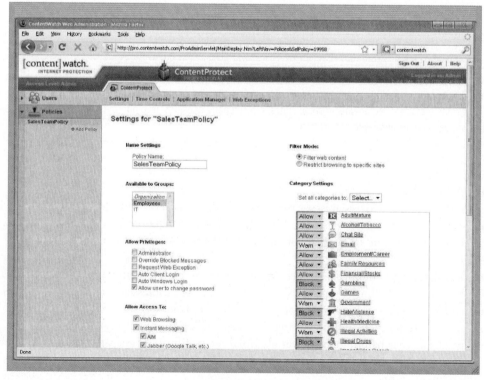

Figure 5-26 Web filtering software restricts access to specified websites.
Courtesy of ContentWatch, Inc.

NOW YOU SHOULD KNOW

Be sure you understand the material presented in the sections titled Ethics and Society and Information Privacy as it relates to the chapter objectives.
Now you should know ...

- What issues you might encounter with respect to information accuracy, intellectual property, codes of conduct, and green computing (Objective 9)
- How you can make your personal data more private (Objective 10)
- Why your computer might have a cookie (Objective 10)

Discover More: Visit this chapter's premium content for practice quiz opportunities.

 Chapter Summary

This chapter presented a variety of digital security risks. You learned about cybercrime and cybercriminals. The chapter discussed risks and safeguards associated with Internet and network attacks, unauthorized access and use, software theft, information theft, and hardware theft, vandalism, and failure. It presented various backup strategies and methods of securing wireless communications. You learned about ethical issues in society and various ways to protect the privacy of personal information.

Discover More: Visit this chapter's free resources for additional content that accompanies this chapter and also includes these features: Technology Innovators: AVG, Intel Security, Symantec, and LoJack; Technology Trends: Uses of Face Recognition Technology and Cloud Security; and High-Tech Talks: Digital Forensics and Encryption Algorithms.

Test your knowledge of chapter material by accessing the Study Guide, Flash Cards, and Practice Test resources from your smartphone, tablet, laptop, or desktop.

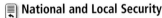 **TECHNOLOGY @ WORK**

National and Local Security
Since 2001, the federal government, local governments, businesses, and individuals have been implementing aggressive new security measures because of the increase in terrorist activity. A security threat can exist anywhere, and it is nearly impossible for humans alone to protect the country. As a result, technology now assists governments, law enforcement officials, business owners, and other individuals with monitoring and maintaining security.

Advancements in computer vision enable computers to monitor indoor and outdoor areas that might be subject to a high volume of criminal activity. For example, some cities are installing cameras in problematic areas. A program analyzes the output from the camera and can determine whether two or more people in close proximity to one another might be engaged in a physical confrontation. If the computer detects suspicious behavior, it automatically notifies local law enforcement.

Computers also use facial recognition to identify individuals who do not belong in a particular area. For example, one theme park takes a picture of individuals they escort out of and ban from the park. As visitors walk from their cars to the park, surveillance cameras positioned in strategic locations scan visitors' faces and compare them with the database containing images of those who are banned from the park. If the computer finds a match, it alerts a security officer who then can investigate the situation. Thousands of people visit theme parks each day, and computers make it easier to perform the otherwise impossible task of identifying those who might be trespassing.

The federal government, particularly the Department of Homeland Security, uses a computerized No Fly List to track individuals who are not authorized to travel on commercial flights within the United States. When an individual makes a reservation, a computer compares his or her name to the names on the No Fly List. If the computer finds a match, the individual must prove that he or she is not the person on the list before being allowed to board an aircraft.

Whether you are walking outside, visiting an attraction, or traveling, the chances are good that computers are, in some way, ensuring your safety.

Consider This: In what other ways do computers and technology play a role in national and local security?

Study Guide

The Study Guide exercise reinforces material you should know for the chapter exam.

Discover More: Visit this chapter's premium content to **test your knowledge of digital content** associated with this chapter and **access the Study Guide resource** from your smartphone, tablet, laptop, or desktop.

Instructions: Answer the questions below using the format that helps you remember best or that is required by your instructor. Possible formats may include one or more of these options: write the answers; create a document that contains the answers; record answers as audio or video using a webcam, smartphone, or portable media player; post answers on a blog, wiki, or website; or highlight answers in the book/e-book.

1. Define the terms, digital security risk, computer crime, cybercrime, and crimeware.

2. Differentiate among hackers, crackers, script kiddies, cyberextortionists, and cyberterrorists. Identify issues with punishing cybercriminals.

3. List common types of malware. A(n) ___ is the destructive event or prank malware delivers.

4. Identify risks and safety measures when gaming.

5. Define these terms: botnet, zombie, and bot.

6. Describe the damages caused by and possible motivations behind DoS and DDoS attacks.

7. A(n) ___ allows users to bypass security controls when accessing a program, computer, or network.

8. Define the term, spoofing. How can you tell if an email is spoofed?

9. List ways to protect against Internet and network attacks.

10. Describe the purpose of an online security service.

11. Define the terms, firewall and proxy server. List steps to set up a personal firewall.

12. Give examples of unauthorized access and use of a computer or network.

13. Identify what an AUP should specify. Why might you disable file and printer sharing?

14. Explain how an organization uses access controls and audit trails.

15. Differentiate among user names, passwords, passphrases, and pass codes.

16. List tips for using a password manager safely.

17. What is a single sign on account? PIN stands for ___.

18. Describe the purpose of a CAPTCHA.

19. Define the terms, possessed objects and biometric devices.

20. What is the purpose of a lock screen?

21. Describe how companies use the following recognition, verification, or payment systems: fingerprint, face, hand, voice, signature, and iris. List disadvantages of biometric devices.

22. Explain the two-step verification process.

23. Define the term, digital forensics. Name areas in which digital forensics are used.

24. Define the terms, software theft, keygen, and software piracy. Identify methods to prevent software theft.

25. Explain the process of product activation.

26. Describe the following license agreement types: single- or end-user, network, and site. List conditions provided in a license agreement.

27. Give examples of information theft. How can you protect yourself from information theft?

28. Describe the functions of an encryption algorithm and an encryption key. Differentiate between private and public key encryption.

29. Unencrypted data is called ___; encrypted data is called ___.

30. Describe the purpose of a VPN.

31. Define these terms: digital signature, digital certificate, and secure site.

32. List concerns and responsibilities regarding cloud data storage and privacy.

33. Describe what occurs during hardware theft or vandalism.

34. Define the terms, backup and restore.

35. List six types of backups. Describe the three-generation backup policy.

36. Identify the components of a disaster recovery plan.

37. Describe security risks associated with wireless access. Identify ways to secure your wireless network.

38. List guidelines to protect your mobile device data.

39. Describe technology ethics, information accuracy, intellectual property rights, copyrights, and codes of conduct.

40. Describe issues surrounding inaccurate data.

41. List measures users can take to contribute to green computing.

42. Explain how companies, websites, and employers might infringe on your right to information privacy.

43. Describe how the following techniques are used to collect personal data: electronic profiles, cookies, phishing, clickjacking, spyware, adware, and madware.

44. How can you protect against phishing scams?

45. Identify methods to protect yourself from social engineering scams.

46. List examples of privacy laws. Should you be able to remove personal information from the Internet? Why or why not?

47. Describe what a company might track when monitoring employees.

48. Define and identify issues surrounding content and web filtering.

49. Describe uses of technology in the national and local security industry.

You should be able to define the Primary Terms and be familiar with the Secondary Terms listed below.

Key Terms

Discover More: Visit this chapter's premium content to **view definitions** for each term and to access the Flash Cards **resource** from your smartphone, tablet, laptop, or desktop.

Primary Terms (shown in **bold-black** characters in the chapter)

adware (244)
back door (217)
back up (233)
backup (233)
biometric device (224)
botnet (216)
code of conduct (241)
computer crime (212)
content filtering (247)
cookie (243)
cracker (214)
cybercrime (212)
cyberextortionist (214)
cyberterrorist (214)

decrypt (229)
denial of service attack
   (DoS attack) (217)
digital certificate (231)
digital forensics (227)
digital security risk (212)
digital signature (231)
disaster recovery plan
   (234)
employee monitoring
   (247)
encryption (229)
fingerprint reader (224)
firewall (219)

green computing (241)
hacker (214)
information privacy (242)
information theft (229)
license agreement (228)
malware (215)
online security service
   (219)
password (222)
personal firewall (220)
phishing (244)
PIN (223)
piracy (228)
product activation (228)

restore (233)
script kiddie (214)
secure site (231)
social engineering (245)
software piracy (228)
software theft (228)
spoofing (217)
spyware (215)
technology ethics (238)
two-step verification (226)
user name (242)
web filtering software
   (248)
zombie (216)

Secondary Terms (shown in *italic* characters in the chapter)

acceptable use policy (AUP) (231)
access control (222)
adware (215)
asymmetric key encryption (230)
audit trail (222)
biometric payment (226)
bot (216)
Business Software Alliance
   (BSA) (228)
CAPTCHA (224)
CERT/CC (219)
certificate authority (CA) (231)
child (234)
ciphertext (230)
clickjacking (245)
cloud backup (234)
Computer Emergency Response Team
   Coordination Center (219)
continuous data protection
   (CDP) (234)
copyright (240)
crimeware (212)
cyberforensics (227)
cyberwarfare (214)
cypher (230)

differential backup (234)
digital rights management (240)
distributed DoS attack (DDoS
   attack) (217)
email spoofing (217)
encryption algorithm (230)
encryption key (230)
end-user license agreement
   (EULA) (228)
ENERGY STAR program (241)
face recognition system (225)
full backup (234)
grandparent (234)
hacktivist (214)
hand geometry system (225)
incremental backup (234)
intellectual property (IP) (240)
intellectual property rights (240)
IP spoofing (217)
keygen (228)
lock screen (225)
MAC address (236)
MAC address control (236)
madware (245)
malicious software (215)

network license (229)
off-site (233)
parent (234)
passcode (223)
passphrase (223)
password manager (223)
password organizer (223)
payload (215)
phishing filter (244)
plaintext (230)
power usage effectiveness
   (PUE) (241)
private key encryption (230)
proxy server (219)
public key encryption (230)
rootkit (215)
selective backup (234)
session cookie (243)
signature verification
   system (225)
single sign on (222)
single-user license
   agreement (228)
site license (229)
spyware (215)

SSID (236)
symmetric key encryption (230)
trojan horse (215)
two-factor verification (226)
unauthorized access (221)
unauthorized use (221)
user ID (222)
virtual private network
   (VPN) (230)
virus (215)
voice verification system (225)
worm (215)
zombie army (216)

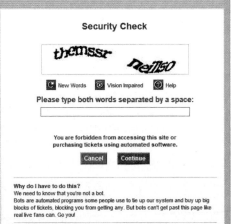

CAPTCHA (224)

Checkpoint

The Checkpoint exercises test your knowledge of the chapter concepts. The page number containing the answer appears in parentheses after each exercise. The Consider This exercises challenge your understanding of chapter concepts.

Discover More: Visit this chapter's premium content to **complete the Checkpoint exercises interactively;** complete the **self-assessment in the Test Prep resource** from on your smartphone, tablet, laptop, or desktop; and then **take the Practice Test.**

True/False   Mark T for True and F for False.

_____ 1. Any illegal act involving the use of a computer or related devices generally is referred to as a crimeware. (212)

_____ 2. A rootkit displays an online advertisement in a banner or pop-up window on webpages, email, or other Internet services. (215)

_____ 3. Viruses, worms, and other malware can be hidden in downloaded game files and mobile apps. (216)

_____ 4. An audit trail records in a file both successful and unsuccessful access attempts. (222)

_____ 5. It is good practice to change your password frequently. (222)

_____ 6. Intentionally erasing software would be considered software theft. (228)

_____ 7. A typical license agreement allows you to rent or lease the software. (229)

_____ 8. Unencrypted, readable data is called ciphertext. (230)

_____ 9. Private key encryption also is called asymmetric key encryption. (230)

_____ 10. VPNs encrypt data to help ensure that the data is safe from being intercepted by unauthorized people. (230)

_____ 11. When data is traveling to or from a computer to a cloud service, it is subject to interception. (232)

_____ 12. A good practice to secure your wireless network is to immediately broadcast the SSID. (236)

Multiple Choice   Select the best answer.

1. A _____ is someone who demands payment to stop an attack on an organization's technology infrastructure. (214)
   a. cyberterrorist
   b. script kiddie
   c. cracker
   d. cyberextortionist

2. _____ is a program that hides in a computer or mobile device and allows someone from a remote location to take full control of the computer or device. (215)
   a. A rootkit
   b. Spyware
   c. A trojan horse
   d. Adware

3. A _____ is a program or set of instructions in a program that allows users to bypass security controls when accessing a program, computer, or network. (217)
   a. zombie
   b. botnet
   c. back door
   d. session cookie

4. An employee using an organization's computer to send personal email messages might be an example of _____. (221)
   a. cybercrime
   b. hardware vandalism
   c. intellectual property rights violation
   d. unauthorized access and use

5. A _____ is a private combination of words, often up to 100 characters in length and containing mixed capitalization and punctuation, associated with a user name that allows access to certain computer resources. (223)
   a. passphrase
   b. private key
   c. passcode
   d. encryption algorithm

6. A(n) _____ is a set of characters that the originator of the data uses to encrypt the text and the recipient of the data uses to decrypt the text. (230)
   a. cipher
   b. plaintext
   c. public key
   d. encryption key

7. A(n) _____ backup method is the only real-time back up, providing very fast recovery of data. (234)
   a. selective
   b. full
   c. incremental
   d. continuous data protection

8. Online shopping websites generally use a _____ to keep track of items in a user's shopping cart. (243)
   a. phishing filter
   b. session cookie
   c. location sharing algorithm
   d. keygen

Checkpoint

Matching   Match the terms with their definitions.

_____ 1. script kiddie (214)

_____ 2. zombie (216)

_____ 3. bot (216)

_____ 4. spoofing (217)

_____ 5. access control (222)

_____ 6. keygen (228)

_____ 7. digital certificate (231)

_____ 8. technology ethics (238)

_____ 9. digital rights management (240)

_____ 10. cookie (243)

a. compromised computer or device whose owner is unaware the computer or device is being controlled remotely by an outsider

b. technique intruders use to make their network or Internet transmission appear legitimate to a victim computer or network

c. program that performs a repetitive task on a network

d. small text file that a web server stores on your computer

e. notice that guarantees a user or website is legitimate

f. strategy designed to prevent illegal distribution of movies, music, and other digital content

g. program that creates software registration numbers and sometimes activation codes

h. hacker who does not have the technical skills and knowledge of a cracker

i. security measure that defines who can access a computer, device, or network; when they can access it; and what actions they can take while accessing it

j. moral guidelines that govern the use of computers, mobile devices, information systems, and related technologies

✳ Consider This   Answer the following questions in the format specified by your instructor.

1. Answer the critical thinking questions posed at the end of these elements in this chapter: Ethics & Issues (214, 233, 246, 247), How To (218, 221, 236, 244), Mini Features (232, 235, 237), Secure IT (216, 219, 223, 240), and Technology @ Work (249).

2. What are some common digital security risks? (212)

3. How does a hacker differ from a cracker? (214)

4. What is cyberwarfare? (214)

5. What is a hacktivist? (214)

6. How does malware deliver its payload? (215)

7. What is a botnet? (216)

8. What practices should gamers follow to increase their security? (216)

9. What is the purpose of a DoS attack? (217)

10. Why would a programmer or computer repair technician build a back door? (217)

11. How is email spoofing commonly used? (217)

12. What are methods to protect computers, mobile devices, and networks from attacks? (218)

13. Who would an organization requiring assistance or information about Internet security breach contact? (219)

14. What screening techniques do proxy servers use? (219)

15. How does unauthorized access differ from unauthorized use? (221)

16. What is a single sign-on account? (222)

17. What is a password manager? (223)

18. Are passphrases more secure than passwords? Why or why not? (223)

19. How are fingerprint readers used with personal computers and mobile devices? (225)

20. What conditions are found in a typical single-user license agreement? (229)

21. Who issues digital certificates? (231)

22. What is meant by a three-generation backup policy? (234)

23. What should you include in a disaster recovery plan for natural disasters? What should you include for man-made disasters? (235)

24. What steps can you take to secure your wireless network? (236)

25. How can mobile security apps protect your mobile device data? (237)

26. What are some questions that arise surrounding fair use with respect to copyrighted material? (240)

27. What role does the ENERGY STAR program play in green computing? (241)

28. For what purposes do websites use cookies? (243)

29. What is clickjacking? (245)

✳ Problem Solving

The Problem Solving exercises extend your knowledge of chapter concepts by seeking solutions to practical problems with technology that you may encounter at home, school, work, or with nonprofit organizations. The Collaboration exercise should be completed with a team.

Instructions: You often can solve problems with technology in multiple ways. Determine a solution to the problems in these exercises by using one or more resources available to you (such as a computer or mobile device, articles on the web or in print, blogs, podcasts, videos, television, user guides, other individuals, electronics or computer stores, etc.). Describe your solution, along with the resource(s) used, in the format requested by your instructor (brief report, presentation, discussion, blog post, video, or other means).

Personal

1. **No Browsing History**   While using the browser on your tablet, you realize that it is not keeping a history of websites you have visited. Why might this be happening, and what is the first step you will take to correct this problem?

2. **Phishing Scam**   You just received an email message from someone requesting personal identification information. Believing the message was legitimate, you provided the requested information to the original sender. You now realize, however, that you might have fallen victim to a phishing scam. What are your next steps?

Source: Privacy Rights Clearinghouse

3. **Suspicious File Attachment**   You receive an email message that appears to be from someone you know. When you try to open the attachment, nothing happens. You attempt to open the attachment two more times without any success. Several minutes later, your computer is running slower and you are having trouble running apps. What might be wrong?

4. **Antivirus Software Outdated**   After starting your computer and signing in to the operating system, a message is displayed stating that your virus definitions are out of date and need to be updated. What are your next steps?

5. **Laptop's Physical Security**   You plan to start taking your laptop to school so that you can record notes in class. You want to make sure, however, that your computer is safe if you ever step away from it for a brief period of time. What steps can you take to ensure the physical security of your laptop?

Professional

6. **Corporate Firewall Interference**   You installed a new browser on your work computer because you no longer wish to use the default browser provided with the operating system. When you run the new browser, an error message appears stating that a user name and password are required to configure the firewall and allow this program to access the Internet. Why has this happened?

7. **Problems with CAPTCHA**   You are signing up for an account on a website and encounter a CAPTCHA. You attempt to type the characters you see on the screen, but an error message appears stating that you have entered the incorrect characters. You try two more times and get the same result. You are typing the characters to the best of your ability but think you still might be misreading at least one of the characters. What are your next steps?

8. **Unclear Acceptable Use Policy**   You read your company's acceptable use policy, but it is not clear about whether you are able to use the computer in your office to visit news websites on your lunch break. How can you determine whether this type of activity is allowed?

9. **Two-Step Verification Problem**   A website you are attempting to access requires two-step verification. In addition to entering your password, you also have to enter a code that it sends to you as a text message. You no longer have the same phone number, so you are unable to receive the text message. What are your next steps?

10. **Issue with Virus Protection**   You receive a notification that the antivirus program on your computer is not enabled. While attempting to enable the antivirus program, an error message is displayed stating that a problem has prevented the antivirus program from being enabled. What are your next steps?

Collaboration

11. **Technology in National and Local Security**   National and local security agencies often use technology to protect citizens. For example, computers are used to maintain a No Fly List, which contains a list of individuals not cleared to board a commercial aircraft. Form a team of three people to create a list of the various ways technology helps to keep the public safe. One team member should research how local agencies, such as police departments, use technology to ensure security. Another team member should research ways national security agencies use technology to protect the public from threats, and the last team member should research ways that private businesses use technology to enhance security. Compile these findings into a report and submit it to your instructor.

The How To: Your Turn exercises present general guidelines for fundamental skills when using a computer or mobile device and then require that you determine how to apply these general guidelines to a specific program or situation.

How To: Your Turn

Discover More: Visit this chapter's premium content to **challenge yourself with additional How To: Your Turn exercises,** which include App Adventure.

Instructions: You often can complete tasks using technology in multiple ways. Figure out how to perform the tasks described in these exercises by using one or more resources available to you (such as a computer or mobile device, articles on the web or in print, online or program help, user guides, blogs, podcasts, videos, other individuals, trial and error, etc.). Summarize your 'how to' steps, along with the resource(s) used, in the format requested by your instructor (brief report, presentation, discussion, blog post, video, or other means).

❶ Evaluating Your Electronic Profile

When you make purchases online, tap or click advertisements, follow links, and complete online forms requesting information about yourself, you are adding to your electronic profile. While an electronic profile may help businesses guide you toward products and services that are of interest to you, some people view them as an invasion of privacy. The following steps guide you through the process of locating online information about yourself and taking steps to remove the information, if possible.

a. Run a browser.

b. Navigate to a search engine of your choice.

c. Perform a search for your full name.

d. In the search results, follow a link that you feel will display a webpage containing information about you. If the link's destination does not contain information about you, navigate back to the search results and follow another link.

e. Evaluate the webpage that contains information about you. If you wish to try removing the information, locate a link that allows you to contact the site owner(s) or automatically request removal of the information.

f. Request that your information be removed from the website. Some websites may not honor your request for removal. If you feel that the information must be removed, you may need to solicit legal advice.

g. If the search results display information from an account you have on an online social network, such as Facebook or LinkedIn, you may need to adjust your privacy settings so that the information is not public. If the privacy settings do not allow you to hide your information, you may need to consider deleting the account.

h. Repeat Steps d – g for the remaining search results. When you no longer see relevant search results for the search engine you used, search for other variations of your name (use your middle initial instead of your middle name, exclude your middle name, or consider using commonly used nicknames instead of your first name).

i. Use other search engines to search for different variations of your name. Some search engines uncover results that others do not.

j. If you have an account on an online social network, navigate to the website's home page and, without signing in, search for your name. If information appears that you do not want to be public, you may need to adjust your privacy settings or remove your account.

k. Follow up with requests you have made to remove your online information.

Exercises

1. What personal information have you uncovered online? Did you have any idea that the information was there?

2. What additional steps can you take to prevent people and businesses from storing information about you?

3. What steps might you be able to take if you are unsuccessful with your attempts to remove online information that identifies you?

✳ How To: Your Turn

❷ Update Virus Definitions

In addition to installing or activating an antivirus program on your computer or mobile device to keep it safe from viruses, it also is necessary to keep the virus definitions updated so that the antivirus program can search for and detect new viruses on your computer or mobile device. New virus definitions can be released as often as once per day, depending on the number of new viruses that are created. Antivirus programs either can search for and install new virus definitions automatically at specified intervals, or you can update the virus signatures manually. The following steps describe how to update the virus definitions for an antivirus program.

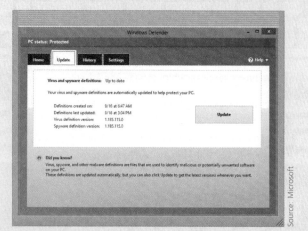

Source: Microsoft

Update Virus Definitions Manually

a. If necessary, establish an Internet connection so that you will be able to update the virus definitions.
b. Run an antivirus program.
c. Tap or click the button to check for updated virus definitions.
d. If new virus definitions are available for the antivirus program, tap or click the link to download the definitions to the computer or mobile device.
e. When the update is complete, tap or click the button to scan the computer or mobile device for viruses.

Configure Automatic Updates for Virus Definitions

a. If necessary, establish an Internet connection so that you will be able to update the virus definitions.
b. Run an antivirus program.
c. Tap or click the option to update virus definitions automatically.
d. Tap or click the option to display the virus definition update schedule.
e. To provide the maximum protection from viruses, configure the antivirus program to update definitions as frequently as possible.
f. After configuring the update schedule, tap or click the button to update virus definitions manually.
g. When the update is complete, tap or click the button to scan the computer or mobile device for viruses.

Exercises

1. What antivirus program, if any, currently is installed on your computer? Is it scheduled to update virus definitions automatically?
2. In addition to downloading and installing virus definitions from within the antivirus program, are other ways available to obtain the latest virus definitions?
3. In addition to keeping the antivirus program's virus definitions current, what other ways can you protect a computer or mobile device from viruses?

❸ Determine Whether a Computer or Mobile Device Is Secured Properly

Several steps are required to secure a computer or mobile device properly. In addition to installing antivirus software and updating the virus definitions regularly, you also should install and configure a firewall, keep the operating system up to date, and be careful not to open suspicious email messages, visit unsecure webpages, or download untrusted files while using the Internet. The following steps guide you through the process of making sure your computer or mobile device is secured properly by verifying antivirus software is installed and running, a firewall is enabled and configured, and the operating system is up to date.

Verify Antivirus Software

a. Use the search tool in the operating system or scan the programs on the computer or mobile device for antivirus software. Some operating systems include antivirus software.
b. If you are unable to locate antivirus software on the computer or mobile device, obtain an antivirus program and install it.
c. Run the antivirus program.
d. Verify the virus definitions in the antivirus program are up to date.

Verify the Firewall

a. Use the search tool in the operating system or scan the programs, apps, and settings on the computer or mobile device to access and configure the firewall.
b. If you are unable to locate a firewall on the computer or mobile device, obtain a firewall program and install it.
c. Run the firewall program.
d. View the firewall settings and verify the firewall is turned on.
e. View the list of programs, apps, and features allowed through the firewall. If you do not recognize or use one or more of the programs, apps, or features, remove them from the list of allowed programs, apps, and features.

How To: Your Turn

Verify Operating System Updates

a. If necessary, establish an Internet connection.

b. Navigate to the area of the operating system where you can access the button, link, or command to search for operating system updates. For example, in Microsoft Windows, you would display the settings for Windows Update.

c. Tap or click the button, link, or command to check for updates.

d. If no updates are available, your operating system is up to date. If the operating system locates additional updates, download and install the updates. **NOTE: If the computer or mobile device you are using does not belong to you, check with its owner before downloading and installing updates for the operating system.**

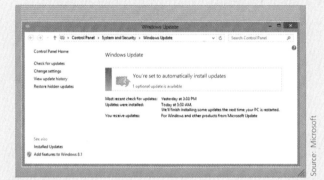

Source: Microsoft

Exercises

1. Before you began this exercise, was your computer or mobile device secured properly? How did you know your computer or mobile device was secured properly? If it was not, what actions did you need to perform to secure it?

2. Which programs, apps, and features do you think are safe to allow through your firewall? Which programs, apps, and features do you feel are not safe to allow through your firewall?

3. What additional ways can you properly secure your computer?

④ Clear Your Browsing History

A browser keeps track of the webpages that you have visited previously unless you have changed your settings. Although you can clear the browsing history on your computer or mobile device, your Internet service provider still may have logs that show a history of websites you have visited. The following steps guide you through the process of clearing your browsing history.

a. Run the browser.

b. Display the browser's settings.

c. If necessary, navigate to the settings that configure the browser's security settings. These settings often are found in the Security, Safety, or Privacy category.

d. Select the option to delete the browsing history. In addition to deleting the list of websites you have visited, you also may be able to clear passwords the browser has remembered, clear cookies and temporary internet files, clear data you entered in forms, and clear a history of downloads.

e. When the browsing history has been deleted, run the browser again.

f. Follow the above steps for each additional browser you have installed on your computer or mobile device.

Exercises

1. What are some reasons why you might want to delete your browsing history?

2. Can you configure your browser to automatically delete your browsing history? If so, how?

3. What are the advantages of keeping your browsing history? If you do keep your browsing history, how long do you keep it?

⑤ Configure a Browser's Cookie Settings

As discussed in this chapter, cookies can be used for a variety of reasons. Websites can install cookies on your computer or mobile device that can store information on your computer or mobile device, or track your browsing habits. You can configure a browser's settings to disallow websites from storing and accessing cookies on your computer or mobile device. The following steps guide you through the process of configuring a browser's cookie settings.

a. Run the browser.

b. Display the browser's settings.

c. Navigate to the settings that configure the browser's cookie settings. These settings often are found in the Security, Safety, or Privacy category.

d. Configure how the browser handles first-party cookies and third-party cookies. Some users choose to reject all cookies. To function properly, however, some websites require that you accept their cookies.

e. Save the changes to the settings.

f. Run the browser again.

Exercises

1. What is the difference between first-party cookies and third-party cookies?

2. Configure the browser to deny all first-party and third-party cookies and then navigate to five websites you visit most frequently. Do the websites display any differently now that you are denying all cookies? Describe your browsing experience while the browser is configured to deny all cookies.

3. What security risks are associated with cookies?

✳ Internet Research

The Internet Research exercises broaden your understanding of chapter concepts by requiring that you search for information on the web.

Discover More: Visit this chapter's premium content to **challenge yourself with additional Internet Research exercises,** which include Search Sleuth, Green Computing, Ethics in Action, You Review It, and Exploring Technology Careers.

Instructions: Use a search engine or another search tool to locate the information requested or answers to questions presented in the exercises. Describe your findings, along with the search term(s) you used and your web source(s), in the format requested by your instructor (brief report, presentation, discussion, blog post, video, or other means).

❶ Making Use of the Web
News, Weather, and Sports

Apps on tablets, smartphones, and other mobile devices are changing the delivery of the day's major news, weather, and sports stories. In one study, approximately one-half of American adults reported that they get some of their news on a tablet or mobile device. They view video and photos from eyewitnesses and fans, read analyses from investigators and coaches, and comment on stories. Men and college-educated people are the heaviest users of mobile news websites, and they are likely to read in-depth investigations and analyses. Online social networks also are a major source of information for many people.

Research This: (a) Visit two news websites or apps and locate one national event covered in both sources. Compare the coverage of the two stories. What information is provided in addition to the text, such as video, graphics, or links to related articles? Which story offers a better analysis? Which source is easier to navigate and read? Then, using another website or app, locate and read today's top international news story. What did you learn by reading the story? Were you aware of this event prior to reading the online story? Does the coverage include videos and photos to increase your comprehension?

(b) Visit a weather website or app and obtain the five-day forecast for your hometown. Include details about information that supplements the current and forecast conditions, such as a pollen or air quality index, storm tracking, travel advisories, or season summaries.

Source: National Weather Service

(c) Visit a sports website or app and read the first story reported. Describe the coverage of this event. Which sources are quoted in the story? Which links are included to other stories? Describe the features provided on this website, such as the ability to chat, customize the page for your favorite teams, or share the content with media sharing sites.

❷ Social Media

Sharing photos on your social media sites of yesterday's visit to the ballpark might be at the top of today's to-do list, but these images might be just the clues cyberthieves need to access your account. Facebook, in particular, is one website that scammers and advertisers use to gather information regarding your whereabouts and your personal life. Their malicious attacks begin with a visit to your timeline or other record of your activities. Searching for keywords on your page, they send targeted messages appearing to originate from trusted friends. If you open their attachments or tap or click their links, you have given these unscrupulous individuals access to your account. In addition, you may think you have crafted a password no one could guess. With your page open for others to view, however, the thieves scour the contents in hopes of locating starting clues, such as children's names, anniversary dates, and pet breeds, which could be hints to cracking your password.

Research This: In the Help section of an online social network you use, search for information about changing your profile's security and privacy settings. What steps can you take to mitigate the chance of becoming the victim of a hack? For example, can you adjust the connection settings to restrict who can see stories, send friend requests and messages, or search for you by name or contact information? Can you hide certain posts or block people from posting on your page? Can you report posts if they violate the website's terms? What are other potential threats to someone accessing your account?

❸ Search Skills
Social Media Search

Search engines provide access to millions of search results by finding webpages, documents, images, or

Internet Research ☀

other information that match the search text you provide. Recommendations from people who use social media to share what they have read can be a possible alternative to using a search engine. People who take the time to Tweet pin an article or image on Twitter or Pinterest often do so because they found it useful, and hope others will as well.

To search Twitter, type the search text, search twitter, in a search engine to find the web address for the Twitter Search website, or sign in to Twitter with your credentials. In the Search Twitter text box, type the search text. For example, type the text, best mapping app, to find recommendations of links to articles or websites about mapping apps. You also can search Twitter for hashtags (a keyword preceded by a # symbol) to find Tweets about current events or popular discussion topics.

To search Pinterest, sign in to your Pinterest account and then type the search text into the search box. For example, type the search text, information security, into the search box to view related pins from Pinterest users. Pinterest users often pin links to infographics, images, and websites.

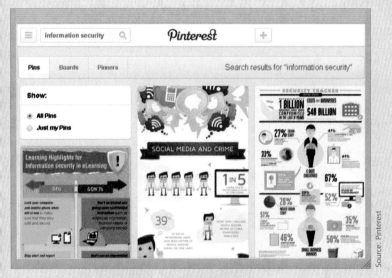

Source: Pinterest

Research This: Use Twitter and Pinterest to search for information about the following topics and then compare your results with those you would find using a search engine such as Bing, Google, or Yahoo!. (1) green computing, (2) computer virus, (3) cyber-crime, and (4) malware. How are the results different? What type of information are you more likely to find on Twitter, on Pinterest, and using a search engine?

❹ Security

Digital certificates and signatures detect a sender's identity and verify a document's authenticity. In this chapter you learned that many e-commerce companies use them in an attempt to prevent digital eavesdroppers from intercepting confidential information. The online certificate authority (CA) vendors generate these certificates using a standard, called X.509, which is coordinated by the International Telecommunication Union and uses algorithms and encryption technology to identify the documents.

Research This: Visit websites of at least two companies that issue digital certificates. Compare products offered, prices, and certificate features. What length of time is needed to issue a certificate? What is a green address bar, and when is one issued? What business or organization validation is required? Then, visit websites of at least two companies that provide digital signatures. Compare signing and sending requirements, types of supported signatures, and available security features. Which documents are required to obtain a digital signature? When would a business need a Class 2 rather than a Class 3 digital signature?

❺ Cloud Services
Cloud Security (SecaaS)

Antivirus software offers regular, automatic updates in order to protect a server, computer, or device from viruses, malware, or other attacks. Antivirus software is an example of cloud security, or security as a service (SecaaS), a service of cloud computing that delivers virus definitions and security software to users over the Internet as updates become available, with no intervention from users. Security as a service is a special case of software as a service, but is limited to security software solutions.

Individuals and enterprise users take advantage of antivirus software and security updates. Enterprise cloud users interact with cloud security solutions via a web interface to configure apps that provide protection to email servers, preventing spam before it arrives, keeping data secure, and watching for online threats and viruses. As the use of cloud-based resources continues, the market for security as a service solutions is expected to increase significantly in coming years.

Research This: (1) Use a search engine to find two different providers of security as a service solutions. Research the different solutions they provide, and report your findings. (2) How are enterprise security requirements different from those of individual users?

Critical Thinking

The Critical Thinking exercises challenge your assessment and decision-making skills by presenting real-world situations associated with chapter concepts. The Collaboration exercise should be completed with a team.

Instructions: Evaluate the situations below, using personal experiences and one or more resources available to you (such as articles on the web or in print, blogs, podcasts, videos, television, user guides, other individuals, electronics or computer stores, etc.). Perform the tasks requested in each exercise and share your deliverables in the format requested by your instructor (brief report, presentation, discussion, blog post, video, or other means).

1. Online Gaming Safety

You and your friend frequently play a popular online role-playing game. Your friend's computer had a virus recently, which was traced back to a malware-infected website. Your friend tells you that she visited the website after following a link while playing the game. What risks are involved when playing online games?

Do This: Use the web to find articles about incidents of malware infections associated with online gaming. Research tips for increasing security when playing online games. Did you find other threats and security tips in addition to the ones mentioned in this chapter? Have you ever downloaded updates to a game? If so, how did you ensure the updates were safe? Locate a list of games that are known to cause malware infections. Share your findings and any online gaming security problems you have experienced with the class.

2. Ensuring Safety and Security Online

You work in the information technology department for a large enterprise. An increasing number of users are contacting the help desk complaining about slow computer performance. Help desk representatives frequently attribute the decreased performance to malware. Although the help desk has installed security software on each computer, users also must practice safe computing. Your manager asked you to prepare information that teaches employees how to guard against malware and other security threats.

Do This: Include information such as how to determine if a website is safe, how to identify email and other spoofing schemes, guidelines for downloading programs and apps, email attachment safety, and how to avoid phishing scams. Create a list of how organizations use common safeguards to protect other users on the network, such as firewalls, proxy servers, user names and passwords, access controls, and audit trails.

3. Case Study

Amateur Sports League You are the new manager for a nonprofit amateur soccer league. The league's board of directors asked you to develop a disaster recovery plan for its main office. The main office consists of a small storefront with two back rooms: one room is the office, with all of the electronic equipment and paper files; the other is for storage of nonelectronic equipment. The staff members — you, an administrative assistant, and an information technology (IT) specialist — work in the office. The electronic equipment in the office includes two desktops, a laptop, an external hard drive for backups, a wireless router, and two printers. In addition, each staff member has a smartphone.

Do This: Choose either a natural or man-made disaster. Create a disaster recovery plan that outlines emergency strategies, backup procedures, recovery steps, and a test plan. Assign staff members roles for each phase of the disaster recovery plan.

Collaboration

4. **Implementing Biometric Security** You are the chief technology officer of a large company. You have been reading an article about computer security that discussed several examples of security breaches, including thieves breaking into an office and stealing expensive equipment, and a recently terminated employee gaining access to the office after hours and corrupting data. Because of these incidents, your company would like to start using biometric devices to increase its security.

Do This: Form a three-member team and research the use of biometric devices to protect equipment and data. Each member of your team should choose a different type of biometric device, such as fingerprint readers, face recognition systems, and hand geometry systems. Find products for each device type, and research costs and user reviews. Search for articles by industry experts. Would you recommend using the biometric device for security purposes? Why or why not? Meet with your team, discuss and compile your findings, and then share with the class.

Technology Timeline

1937 Dr. John V. Atanasoff and Clifford Berry design and build the first electronic digital computer. Their machine, the Atanasoff-Berry-Computer, or ABC, provides the foundation for advances in electronic digital computers.

1945 John von Neumann poses in front of the electronic computer built at the Institute for Advanced Study. This computer and its von Neumann architecture served as the prototype for subsequent stored program computers worldwide.

1947 William Shockley, John Bardeen, and Walter Brattain invent the transfer resistance device, eventually called the transistor. The transistor would revolutionize computers, proving much more reliable than vacuum tubes.

1952 Dr. Grace Hopper considers the concept of reusable software in her paper, "The Education of a Computer." The paper describes how to program a computer with symbolic notation instead of detailed machine language.

AP Images/Frederick News-Post (2); J. R. Eyerman/The LIFE Picture Collection/Getty Images

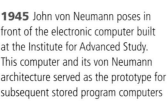

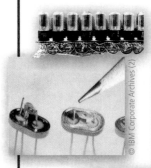

Photo: Alan Richards, from the Shelby White and Leon Levy Archives Center, Institute for Advanced Study, Princeton, NJ, USA (2)

© IBM Corporate Archives (2)

Courtesy of Hagley Museum and Library

| 1937 | 1943 | 1945 | 1946 | 1947 | 1951 | 1952 | 1953 |

Bletchley Park Trust/SSPL/The Image Works

From the Collections of the University of Pennsylvania Archives

© IBM Corporate Archives

S. M./Sueddeutsche Zeitung Photo/The Image Works

1943 During World War II, British scientist Alan Turing designs the Colossus, an electronic computer created for the military to break German codes. The computer's existence is kept secret until the 1970s.

1946 Dr. John W. Mauchly and J. Presper Eckert, Jr. complete work on the first large-scale electronic, general-purpose digital computer. The ENIAC (Electronic Numerical Integrator And Computer) weighs 30 tons, contains 18,000 vacuum tubes, occupies a 30 × 50 foot space, and consumes 160 kilowatts of power.

Courtesy Unisys Corporation

1951 The first commercially available electronic digital computer, the UNIVAC I (UNIVersal Automatic Computer), is introduced by Remington Rand. Public awareness of computers increases when the UNIVAC I correctly predicts that Dwight D. Eisenhower will win the presidential election.

1953 Core memory, developed in the early 1950s, provides much larger storage capacity than vacuum tube memory.

1953 The IBM model 650 is one of the first widely used computers. The computer is so successful that IBM manufactures more than 1,000. IBM will dominate the mainframe market for the next decade.

1957 The IBM 305 RAMAC computer is the first to use magnetic disk for external storage. The computer provides storage capacity similar to magnetic tape that previously was used but offers the advantage of semi-random access capability.

1959 More than 200 programming languages have been created.

1959 IBM introduces two smaller, desk-sized computers: the IBM 1401 for business and the IBM 1620 for scientists.

1965 Dr. John Kemeny of Dartmouth leads the development of the BASIC programming language.

1968 In a letter to the editor titled, "GO TO Statements Considered Harmful," Dr. Edsger Dijkstra introduces the concept of structured programming, developing standards for constructing computer programs.

© IBM Corporate Archives

Courtesy of Dartmouth College

© IBM Corporate Archives

1965 Digital Equipment Corporation (DEC) introduces the first microcomputer, the PDP-8. The machine is used extensively as an interface for time-sharing systems.

1968 Computer Science Corporation (CSC) becomes the first software company listed on the New York Stock Exchange.

© Cengage Learning

1957 FORTRAN (FORmula TRANslation), an efficient, easy-to-use programming language, is introduced by John Backus.

© IBM Corporate Archives

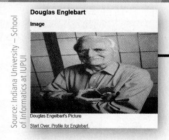

Courtesy of Hewlett-Packard Company

1957 · 1958 · 1959 · 1960 · 1964 · 1965 · 1967 · 1968

Courtesy of Texas Instruments (2)

Courtesy of Hagley Museum and Library

Source: Indiana University – School of Informatics at IUPUI

Douglas Englebart
Image

Douglas Engelbart's Picture
Start Over, Profile for Englebart

1967 Douglas Engelbart applies for a patent for his wooden mouse.

© IBM Corporate Archives

1958 Jack Kilby of Texas Instruments invents the integrated circuit, which lays the foundation for high-speed computers and large-capacity memory. Computers built with transistors mark the beginning of the second generation of computer hardware.

1960 COBOL, a high-level business application language, is developed by a committee headed by Dr. Grace Hopper.

1964 The number of computers has grown to 18,000. Third-generation computers, with their controlling circuitry stored on chips, are introduced. The IBM System/360 computer is the first family of compatible machines, merging science and business lines.

1968 Alan Shugart at IBM demonstrates the first regular use of an 8-inch floppy disk.

© IBM Corporate Archives (3)

1964 IBM introduces the term, word processing, for the first time with its Magnetic Tape/Selectric Typewriter (MT/ST). The MT/ST was the first reusable storage medium that allowed typed material to be edited without requiring that the document be retyped.

1969 Under pressure from the industry, IBM announces that some of its software will be priced separately from the computer hardware, allowing software firms to emerge in the industry.

1969 The ARPANET network is established, which eventually grows to become the Internet.

1975 MITS, Inc. advertises one of the first microcomputers, the Altair. The Altair is sold in kits for less than $400, and within the first three months 4,000 orders are taken.

1975 Ethernet, the first local area network (LAN), is developed at Xerox PARC (Palo Alto Research Center) by Robert Metcalfe.

1976 Steve Jobs and Steve Wozniak build the first Apple computer. A subsequent version, the Apple II, is an immediate success. Adopted by elementary schools, high schools, and colleges, for many students, the Apple II is their first contact with the world of computers.

1980 IBM offers Microsoft Corporation cofounder, Bill Gates, the opportunity to develop the operating system for the soon-to-be announced IBM personal computer. With the development of MS-DOS, Microsoft achieves tremendous growth and success.

1980 Alan Shugart presents the Winchester hard disk, revolutionizing storage for personal computers.

| 1969 | 1970 | 1971 | 1975 | 1976 | 1979 | 1980 | 1981 |

1970 Fourth-generation computers, built with chips that use LSI (large-scale integration) arrive. While the chips used in 1965 contained up to 1,000 circuits, the LSI chip contains as many as 15,000.

1971 Dr. Ted Hoff of Intel Corporation develops a microprocessor, or microprogrammable computer chip, the Intel 4004.

1979 VisiCalc, a spreadsheet program written by Bob Frankston and Dan Bricklin, is introduced.

1979 The first public online information services, CompuServe and the Source, are founded.

1981 The IBM PC is introduced, signaling IBM's entrance into the personal computer marketplace. The IBM PC quickly garners the largest share of the personal computer market and becomes the personal computer of choice in business.

1981 The first computer virus, Elk Cloner, is spread via Apple II floppy disks, which contained the operating system. A short rhyme would appear on the screen when the user pressed the Reset button after the 50th boot of an infected disk.

Microsoft

© Lane V. Erickson/Shutterstock
Courtesy of Microsoft® Corporation

1986 Microsoft has public stock offering and raises approximately $61 million.

3.275 Million

1982 3,275,000 personal computers are sold, almost 3,000,000 more than in 1981.

1982 Hayes introduces the 300 bps smart modem. The modem is an immediate success.

1982 Compaq, Inc. is founded to develop and market IBM-compatible PCs.

COMPAQ

Courtesy of Hewlett-Packard Company

1988 Microsoft surpasses Lotus Development Corporation to become the world's top software vendor.

© Cengage Learning

1991 Kodak announces the first digital SLR (single-lens reflex) camera. The Kodak DCS 100 is developed mostly for photojournalism purposes and stores the photos and batteries in a separate unit.

©NMPFT/SSPL / The Image Works

1991 World Wide Web Consortium releases standards that describe a framework for linking documents on different computers.

© Cengage Learning

1982 | **1983** | **1984** | **1986** | **1988** | **1989** | **1991**

1983 Instead of choosing a person for its annual award, TIME magazine names the computer Machine of the Year for 1982, acknowledging the impact of computers on society.

© IBM Corporate Archives

1983 Lotus Development Corporation is founded. Its spreadsheet software, Lotus 1-2-3, which combines spreadsheet, graphics, and database programs in one package, becomes the best-selling program for IBM personal computers.

© iStockphoto /audioundwerbung

Apple

1984 Apple introduces the Macintosh computer, which incorporates a unique, easy-to-learn, graphical user interface.

Courtesy of Hewlett-Packard Company

1984 Hewlett-Packard announces the first LaserJet printer for personal computers.

1989 Nintendo introduces the Game Boy, its first handheld game console.

SSPL / The Image Works

Hank Morgan / Science Source

1989 While working at CERN, Switzerland, Tim Berners-Lee invents the World Wide Web.

Courtesy of Intel Corporation

1989 The Intel 486 becomes the world's first 1,000,000 transistor microprocessor. It executes 15,000,000 instructions per second — four times as fast as its predecessor, the 80386 chip.

Courtesy of Microsoft Corporation

1993 Microsoft releases Microsoft Office 3 Professional, the first version of Microsoft Office for the Windows operating system.

1993 Several companies introduce computers using the Pentium processor from Intel. The Pentium chip contains 3.1 million transistors and is capable of performing 112,000,000 instructions per second.

Courtesy of Intel Corporation

Source: amazon.com

1994 Amazon is founded and later begins business as an online bookstore. Amazon eventually expands to sell products of all types and facilitates the buying and selling of new and used goods. Today, Amazon employs more than 88,400 people.

1994 Linus Torvalds creates the Linux kernel, a UNIX-like operating system that he releases free across the Internet for further enhancement by other programmers.

Courtesy of Larry Ewing and The Gimp

1995 eBay, an online auction website, is founded. Providing an online venue for people to buy and sell goods, it quickly becomes the world's largest online marketplace as it approaches 100 million active users worldwide.

AP Images/Nigel Treblin/dapd

Oracle and Java are registered trademarks of Oracle and/or its affiliates. Other names may be trademarks of their respective owners.

1995 Sun Microsystems launches Java, an object-oriented programming language that allows users to write one program for a variety of computer platforms.

1995 Microsoft releases Windows 95, a major upgrade to its Windows operating system. Windows 95 consists of more than 10,000,000 lines of computer instructions developed by 300 person-years of effort.

/Reuters/Landov

1992   1993   1994   1995

Courtesy of Microsoft® Corporation

1992 Microsoft releases Windows 3.1, the latest version of its Windows operating system. Windows 3.1 offers improvements such as TrueType fonts, multimedia capability, and object linking and embedding (OLE). In two months, 3,000,000 copies of Windows 3.1 are sold.

1993 The U.S. Air Force completes the Global Positioning System by launching its 24th Navstar satellite into orbit. Today, GPS receivers can be found in cars, laptops, and smartphones.

Courtesy of Garmin International

1993 The White House launches its website, which includes an interactive citizens' handbook and White House history and tours.

© Orhan Cam/Shutterstock.com

1994 Jim Clark and Marc Andreessen found Netscape and launch Netscape Navigator 1.0, a browser.

Courtesy of Netscape Communications Corporation

1994 Apple introduces the first digital camera intended for consumers. The Apple QuickTake 100 is connected to home computers using a serial cable.

Courtesy of Mark D. Martin

1994 Yahoo!, a popular search engine and portal, is founded by two Stanford Ph.D. students as a way to keep track of their personal interests on the Internet. Currently, Yahoo! has approximately 11,500 employees in 25 countries, provinces, and territories.

AP Photo/Paul Sakuma

1997 Intel introduces the Pentium II processor with 7.5 million transistors. The new processor, which incorporates MMX technology, processes video, audio, and graphics data more efficiently and supports programs such as movie editing, gaming, and more.

Courtesy of Intel Corporation

1999 Intel introduces the Pentium III processor. This processor succeeds the Pentium II and can process 3-D graphics more quickly. The Pentium III processor contains between 9.5 and 44 million transistors.

Courtesy of Intel Corporation

1999 Governments and businesses frantically work to make their computers Y2K (Year 2000) compliant, spending more than $500 billion worldwide.

© Cengage Learning

1997 Microsoft releases Internet Explorer 4.0 and seizes a key place in the Internet arena.

AP Photo

1999 Open source software, such as the Linux operating system and the Apache web server created by unpaid volunteers, begins to gain wide acceptance among computer users.

© Tan Kian Khoon/Shutterstock

1996   **1997**   **1998**   **1999**

Courtesy of Palm, Inc.

1996 U.S. Robotics introduces the PalmPilot, an inexpensive user-friendly personal digital assistant (PDA).

1996 Microsoft releases Windows NT 4.0, an operating system for client-server networks.

Box shot reprinted with permission from Microsoft Corporation.

Courtesy of Google, Inc.

Google

1998 Google files for incorporation and is now the most used search engine, capturing more than 60 percent of the market over other search engines.

Brad Cherson / Alamy

1998 E-commerce booms. Companies such as Amazon.com, Dell, and E*TRADE spur online shopping, allowing buyers to obtain a variety of goods and services.

© iStockphoto/juniorbeep

1998 Apple introduces the iMac, the next version of its popular Macintosh computer. The iMac wins customers with its futuristic design, see-through case, and easy setup.

Source: Napster

2000 Shawn Fanning, 19, and his company, Napster, turn the music industry upside down by developing software that allows computer users to swap music files with one another without going through a centralized file server.

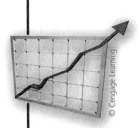

© Cengage Learning

2000 E-commerce achieves mainstream acceptance. Annual e-commerce sales exceed $100 billion, and Internet advertising expenditures reach more than $5 billion.

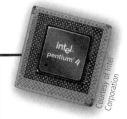

Courtesy of Intel Corporation

2001 Intel unveils its Pentium 4 chip with clock speeds starting at 1.4 GHz. The Pentium 4 includes 42 million transistors.

Wikimedia Foundation

2001 Wikipedia, a free online encyclopedia, is introduced. Additional wikis begin to appear on the Internet, enabling people to share information in their areas of expertise. Although some might rely on wikis for research purposes, the content is not always verified for accuracy.

2002 Digital video cameras, DVD burners, easy-to-use video editing software, and improvements in storage capabilities allow the average computer user to create Hollywood-like videos with introductions, conclusions, rearranged scenes, music, and voice-over.

Courtesy of Intel Corporation

2002 After several years of negligible sales, the Tablet PC is reintroduced to meet the needs of a more targeted audience.

Courtesy of ViewSonic Corporation

2000 2001 2002

© Cengage Learning

2000 Dot-com (Internet based) companies go out of business at a record pace — nearly one per day — as financial investors withhold funding due to the companies' unprofitability.

Microsoft .net

Source: Microsoft

2002 Microsoft launches its .NET strategy, which is a new environment for developing and running software applications featuring ease of development of web-based services.

© Tatiana Popova / Shutterstock.com

2002 DVD burners begin to replace CD burners (CD-RW). DVDs can store up to eight times as much data as CDs. Uses include storing home movies, music, photos, and backups.

Kenneth Murray / Science Source

2000 Telemedicine uses satellite technology and videoconferencing to broadcast consultations and to perform distant surgeries. Robots are used for complex and precise tasks.

2002 Intel ships its revamped Pentium 4 chip with the 0.13 micron processor and Hyper-Threading (HT) Technology, operating at speeds of 3.06 GHz. This new development eventually will enable processors with a billion transistors to operate at 20 GHz.

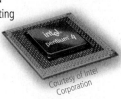

Courtesy of Intel Corporation

2004 Mozilla releases its first version of the Firefox browser. Firefox provides innovative features that enhance the browsing experience for users, including tabbed browsing and a Search box. Firefox quickly gains popularity and takes market share away from Microsoft's Internet Explorer.

AP Photo/screenshot

2004 Facebook, an online social network originally available only to college students, is founded. Facebook eventually opens registration to all people and immediately grows to more than 110 million users.

Courtesy of Facebook

2004 Sony unveils the PlayStation Portable (PSP). This handheld game console is the first to use optical discs.

ISSEI KATO/Reuters/Landov

2004 Companies such as RealNetworks, Microsoft, Sony, and Walmart stake out turf in the online music store business started by Apple.

© Cengage Learning

2004 Flat-panel LCD monitors overtake bulky CRT monitors as the popular choice of computer users.

2004 Linux, an open source operating system, makes major inroads into the server market as a viable alternative to Microsoft Windows Server 2003, Sun's Solaris, and UNIX.

2004 106 million, or 53 percent, of the 200 million online population in America accesses the Internet via broadband.

Courtesy of Larry Ewing and The Gimp

2003

2004

2003 In an attempt to maintain their current business model of selling songs, the Recording Industry Association of America (RIAA) files more than 250 lawsuits against individual computer users who offer copyrighted music over peer-to-peer networks.

© Getty Images

REUTERS/Mannie Garcia / Landov

2003 Wireless computers and devices, such as keyboards, mouse devices, home networks, and wireless Internet access points become commonplace.

© wavebreakmedia/Shutterstock.com; ©Tom Grill/ CORBIS; © iStockphoto /hocus-pocus; © StockLite / Shutterstock.com; ©iStockphoto / LifesizeImages

Courtesy of Palm Inc.

2004 USB flash drives become a cost-effective way to transport data and information from one computer to another.

Courtesy of SanDisk Corporation

2004 Major retailers begin requiring suppliers to include radio frequency identification (RFID) tags or microchips with antennas, which can be as small as one-third of a millimeter across, in the goods they sell.

Courtesy of Intermec Technologies

2004 The smartphone overtakes the PDA as the mobile device of choice.

Courtesy of Palm Inc.

2004 Apple introduces the sleek all-in-one iMac G5. The new computer's display device contains the system unit.

/Reuters /Landov

Source: YouTube

2005 YouTube, an online community for video sharing, is founded. YouTube includes content such as home videos, movie previews, and clips from television shows. In November 2006, Google acquires YouTube.

© Cengage Learning

LPETTET / iStockphoto.com

2006 Sony launches its PlayStation 3. New features include a Blu-ray Disc player, high-definition capabilities, and always-on online connectivity.

2006 Apple begins selling Macintosh computers with Intel microprocessors.

2006 Web 2.0, a term coined in 2004, becomes a household term with the increase in popularity of online social networks, wikis, and web applications.

Video iPod

HANDOUT/KRT/Newscom

2005 Apple releases the latest version of its popular pocket-sized iPod portable media player. First it played songs, then photos, then podcasts, and now, in addition, up to 150 hours of music videos and television shows on a 2.5″ color display.

Courtesy of Intel Corporation

© iStockphoto / robiyannucci

2006 Nintendo releases the Nintendo DS Lite, a handheld game console with new features such as dual screens and improved graphics and sound.

Toru Hanai/Reuters/Corbis

2005

2006

2005 Spam, spyware, phishing, and pharming take center stage, along with viruses and other malware, as major nuisances to the 801 million computer users worldwide.

2005 Blogging and podcasting become mainstream methods for distributing information via the web.

Source: Microsoft

2005 Microsoft releases the Xbox 360, its latest game console. Features include the capability to play music, display photos, and communicate with computers and other Xbox gamers.

Courtesy of Intel Corporation

© Cengage Learning (2)

2006
Intel introduces its Core 2 Duo processor family. Boasting record-breaking performance while using less power, the family consists of five desktop computer processors and five mobile computer processors. The desktop processor includes 291 million transistors, yet uses 40 percent less power than the Pentium processor.

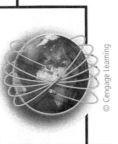
© Cengage Learning

2006 IBM produces the fastest supercomputer, Blue Gene/L. It can perform approximately 28 trillion calculations in the time it takes you to blink your eye, or about one-tenth of a second.

ISSEI KATO/Reuters/Corbis

2006 Nintendo Wii is introduced and immediately becomes a leader in game consoles. The Wii is being used in revolutionary ways, such as training surgeons.

2007 Intel introduces Core 2 Quad, a four-core processor made for dual-processor servers and desktop computers. The larger number of cores allows for more energy-efficient performance and optimizes battery performance in laptops.

Courtesy of Intel Corporation

2007 VoIP (Voice over Internet Protocol) providers expand usage to include Wi-Fi phones. The phones enable high-quality service through a Wireless-G network and high-speed Internet connection.

Courtesy of Belkin International

2007 Apple introduces the iPhone and sells 270,000 phones in the first 2 days. iPhone uses iTouch technology that allows you to make a call simply by tapping a name or number in your address book. In addition, it stores and plays music like an iPod. Also, Apple sells its one billionth song on iTunes.

© Neville Elder/Corbis

2007 Apple releases its Mac OS X version 10.5 "Leopard" operating system, available in a desktop version and server version. The system includes a significantly revised desktop, with a semitransparent menu bar and an updated search tool that incorporates the same visual navigation interface as iTunes.

© oliver leedham /Alamy

2008 Smartphones become smarter. Smartphones introduced this year include enhanced features such as touch screens with multi-touch technology, mobile TV, tactile feedback, improved graphics, GPS receivers, and better cameras.

AP Photo/Mark Lennihan

Courtesy of Microsoft Corporation

2008 Bill Gates retires from Microsoft. He continues as chairman and advisor on key development projects.

2008 Google releases its new browser. Google Chrome uses an entirely unique interface and offers other features such as dynamic tabs, crash control, and application shortcuts.

Source: Google

2007

2008

2007 Half of the world's population uses mobile phones. More and more people are using a mobile phone in lieu of a landline in their home.

© Sean Locke/iStockphoto

2007 Blu-ray Discs increase in popularity, overcoming and replacing HD DVD in less than one year. A Blu-ray Disc can store approximately 9 hours of high-definition (HD) video on a 50 GB disc or approximately 23 hours of standard-definition (SD) video.

Helene Rogers/Art Directors & Trips Photo/ AGE Fotostock

© Rtimages /Shutterstock.com

2007 Wi-Fi hot spots are popular in a variety of locations. People bring their computers to coffeehouses, fast food restaurants, or bookstores to access the Internet wirelessly, either free or for a small fee.

2008 Netflix, an online movie rental company, and TiVo, a company manufacturing digital video recorders (DVRs), make Netflix movies and television episodes available on TiVo DVRs.

Source: Netflix

©1998–2013 TiVo Inc. All rights reserved.

2008 Computer manufacturers begin to offer solid-state drives (SSDs) instead of hard disks, mostly in laptops. Although SSDs have a lower storage capacity, are more expensive, and slightly more susceptible to failure, they are significantly faster.

© Bedo / Dreamstime.com

iStockphoto

2008 WiMAX goes live! The advantage of this technology is the capability to access video, music, voice, and video calls wherever and whenever desired. Average download speeds are between 2 Mbps and 4 Mbps. By year's end, Sprint has approximately 100 million users on its network.

2009 Intel releases the Core i5 and Core i7 line of processors. These processors offer increased performance for some of the more demanding tasks. Intel also enhances its Core processor family by releasing multi-core processors, designed to increase the number of instructions that can be processed at a given time.

2009 Online social networks revolutionize communications. Schools, radio stations, and other organizations develop pages on popular online social networks, such as Facebook, creating closer connections with their stakeholders.

2009 In June 2009, federal law requires that all full-power television stations broadcast only in digital format. Analog television owners are required to purchase a converter box to view over-the-air digital programming.

Courtesy of Intel Corporation

2009 Computers and mobile devices promote fitness by offering games and programs to help users exercise and track their progress. These games and programs also are used to assist with physical rehabilitation.

© Stuartkey/ Dreamstime.com

Google docs
Source: Google

2009 Web apps continue to increase in popularity. Web apps make it easier to perform tasks such as word processing, photo editing, and tax preparation without installing software on your computer.

Courtesy of Coby Electronics Corporation

2011 Netbooks offer a smaller, lighter alternative to laptops. Netbooks have screens between seven and ten inches, and are used mostly for browsing the web and communicating online.

PRNewsFoto/ Verizon Wireless)

2011 More than 200 types of mobile devices are using Google Android, an operating system originally designed for mobile devices.

© iStockphoto/Brightrock

2011 A new generation of browsers is released to support HTML5, enabling webpages to contain more vivid, dynamic content.

HTML 5
HTML5 Logo by World Wide Web Consortium

2011 E-books and e-book readers explode in popularity. Many novels, textbooks, and other publications now are available digitally and can be read on an e-book reader, computer, or mobile device.

© iStockphoto /MichaelJay

© iStockphoto /EdStock

2011 Steve Jobs, a cofounder of Apple, passes away after a long battle with cancer. Jobs is remembered for revolutionizing the computer and music industries.

2009   2010   2011

2010 Hard disk capacity continues to increase at an exponential rate, with the largest hard disks storing more than 2.5 TB of data and information.

Source: Seagate Technology LLC

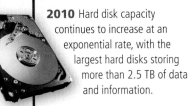

2011 Google introduces its Google+ online social network and integrates it across many of its products and services.

Source: Google

Source: AMD

2010 AMD develops a 12-core processor, which contains two 6-core processors, each on an individual chip. Power consumption is similar to that of a 6-core processor but offers reduced clock speed.

2010 Kinect for Xbox 360 changes the way people play video games. Game players now can interact with the game with a series of sensors, as well as a camera, tracking their movements in 3-D.

Source: Microsoft

2010 Apple releases the iPad, a revolutionary mobile device with a 9.7-inch multi-touch screen. The iPad boasts up to 10 hours of battery life, connects wirelessly to the Internet, and is capable of running thousands of apps.

© iStockphoto / hanibaram

Source: Lenovo

2011 Intel introduces Ultrabooks, which are powerful, lightweight alternatives to laptops. Ultrabooks normally weigh three pounds or less, have great performance and battery life, and are usually less than one inch thick.

2012 Microsoft announces the Surface, a tablet designed to compete with Apple's iPad. The Surface has a built-in stand, runs the Windows 8 operating system and its apps, and supports a cover that also can serve as a keyboard.

Source: Microsoft

2013 Twitter users generate more than 500 million Tweets per day.

2012 Microsoft releases Windows 8, its newest version of the Windows operating system. Windows 8 boasts a completely redesigned interface and supports touch input.

2012 Apple releases the iPhone 5. This newest iPhone has a four-inch screen, contains a new, smaller connector, and uses Apple's A6 processor.

Source: Apple

2013 Amazon announces it will use drones to deliver packages to its customers.

2013 Sony releases the PlayStation 4 (PS4) game console and Microsoft releases the Xbox One game console.

2013 Tablet sales grow at a faster rate than personal computer sales ever grew.

Courtesy of Amazon

2012

2013

2012 Google's Android surpasses Apple's iOS as the most popular operating system used on smartphones. Although the iPhone still is the bestselling smartphone, competing products are gaining market share quickly.

Source: Google

2013 Samsung releases the Galaxy Gear, a smartwatch that synchronizes with a Samsung Galaxy smartphone using Bluetooth technology.

© Ivan Garcia / Shutterstock

2013 QR codes rapidly gain in popularity, giving mobile device users an easy way to access web content.

© Cengage Learning

2013 Windows 8.1, a significant update to Microsoft's Windows 8 operating system, is released.

Source: Microsoft

Source: qr-code-generator.com

2012 Microsoft releases Office 2013. Office 365, which uses the familiar Office 2013 interface, also is released, allowing users to use their Microsoft accounts to access Office apps from computers that do not have Office installed.

2012 Nintendo releases the Wii U game console.

© iStockPhoto / Mlenny

2013 Apple releases the iPhone 5S, the first iPhone with TouchID. TouchID verifies a user's identity using an integrated fingerprint reader.

2013 Many consumers prefer tablets for their mobile computing needs. Tablets provide ultimate portability while still allowing users to access a vast array of apps, as well as access to the Internet and their email messages.

© iStockphoto/mozcann

Green Computing

© Cengage Learning

2014 Individuals and enterprises increase their focus on green computing. Computer manufacturers not only sell more energy-efficient hardware, they also provide easy ways in which customers can recycle their old computers and devices.

2014 Solid-state storage is becoming more popular, with storage capacities increasing and prices decreasing.

©Oleksiy Mark /Shutterstock.com

2014 Apple releases the Apple Watch, a wearable device that runs apps and can monitor various aspects of your health and fitness.

Courtesy of Apple, Inc.

2014 Decreases in storage costs and increases in Internet connection speeds persuade more users to use cloud storage for their data. Cloud storage also provides users with the convenience of accessing their files from almost anywhere.

© Cengage Learning

2015 3-D printing decreases in price and increases in popularity.

© dreamikon / Fotolia

2015 Microsoft releases Windows 10, the latest version of its operating system. Windows 10 expands on many of the new features introduced in Windows 8, and also brings back popular features, such as the Start menu, from previous versions of Windows.

© iStockPhoto / xefstock

2015 Individuals and families are increasingly turning to streaming video on the Internet and abandoning their cable companies.

2014 | 2015

2014 Bitcoin continues to grow as a digital currency and online payment system.

Courtesy of Mark Frydenberg

2014 Apple releases the iPhone 6 and iPhone 6 Plus. Both devices have significantly larger screens than its predecessors.

Courtesy of Apple, Inc.

2014 Televisions with features such as curved screens and Ultra HD displays begin to increase in popularity.

© iStockPhoto / JazzIRT

2014 Google Glass goes on sale to the public in the United States.

© iStockPhoto / ferrantraite

2014 Amazon drops the price of its Fire Phone to $0.99, possibly indicating that apps and services are valued more than the device.

© iStockPhoto / Ilya_Starikov

2015 Emerging protocols, such as ITF-A and Wi-Fi 802.11 ac, ad, aq, and ah, increase performance on mobile and wireless networks.

2015 Approximately 91% of all Internet traffic is video, including HD and 3-D video.

Notes

Computers and mobile devices contain a variety of electronic components.

"I bought my laptop a couple of years ago, and it appears to be working well. Although at times it runs a little slow and generates a lot of heat, I really have not had problems with it. Why would I need to learn about hardware inside my laptop and other devices?"

While you may be familiar with some of the content in this chapter, do you know how to . . .

- Protect computers and mobile devices from theft?
- Select the right processor?
- Recognize the Internet of Things?
- Make use of cloud computing services?
- Prevent a computer from overheating?
- Determine memory requirements?
- Install memory?
- Erase your mobile phone's memory?
- Familiarize yourself with efforts related to technology products made with fair trade practices?
- Identify which ports you might need on a computer or mobile device?
- Clean a computer or mobile device?
- Conserve battery life on mobile computers and devices?

In this chapter, you will discover how to perform these tasks along with much more information essential to this course. For additional content available that accompanies this chapter, visit the free resources and premium content. Refer to the Preface and the Intro chapter for information about how to access these and other additional instructor-assigned support materials.

© iStockPhoto / arosoft

✔ Objectives

After completing this chapter, you will be able to:

1   Describe the various computer and mobile device cases and the contents they protect
2   Describe multi-core processors, the components of a processor, and the four steps in a machine cycle
3   Identify characteristics of various personal computer processors on the market today, and describe the ways processors are cooled
4   Describe what is meant by the Internet of Things
5   Explain the advantages and services of cloud computing
6   Define a bit, and describe how a series of bits represents data
7   Explain how program and application instructions transfer in and out of memory
8   Differentiate among the various types of memory: RAM, cache, ROM, flash memory, and CMOS
9   Describe the purpose of adapter cards and USB adapters
10 Explain the function of a bus
11 Explain the purpose of a power supply and batteries
12 Describe how to care for computers and mobile devices

Inside the Case

Whether you are a home user or a business user, you most likely will purchase a new computer or mobile device, or upgrade an existing computer at some time in the future. Thus, you should understand the purpose of each component in a computer or mobile device. As Chapter 1 discussed, computers and mobile devices include components that are used for input, processing, output, storage, and communications. Many of these components are inside the case that contains and protects the electronics of the computer or mobile device from damage. These cases, which are made of metal or plastic, are available in a variety of shapes and sizes (Figure 6-1).

- Recall that the term, *system unit* (or *chassis*), refers to the case on a desktop that contains and protects the motherboard, hard drive, memory, and other electronic components. Some desktops have a tower system unit that is a device separate from the monitor. Others that house the display and the system unit in the same case are called an all-in-one. Peripheral devices normally occupy space outside the system unit and communicate with the system unit using wired or wireless technology.
- On most laptops, including ultrathin laptops, the keyboard and pointing device often occupy the area on top of the case, and the display attaches to the case by hinges.
- With a slate tablet, which typically does not include a physical keyboard, the case is behind the display. Keyboard options for slate tablets include an on-screen keyboard, a wireless keyboard, or a keyboard that attaches to the slate via a clip, magnets, or other mechanism. On a convertible tablet, by contrast, the case is positioned below a keyboard, providing functionality similar to a laptop. The difference is that the display attaches to the case with a swivel-type hinge, enabling the user to rotate the display and fold it down over the keyboard to look like a slate tablet.
- With game consoles, the input and output devices, such as controllers and a television, reside outside the case.
- Like a slate tablet, the case on a smartphone often is behind the display.
- The case on wearable devices, portable media players, digital cameras, and handheld game devices typically consumes the entire device and houses the display and input devices.

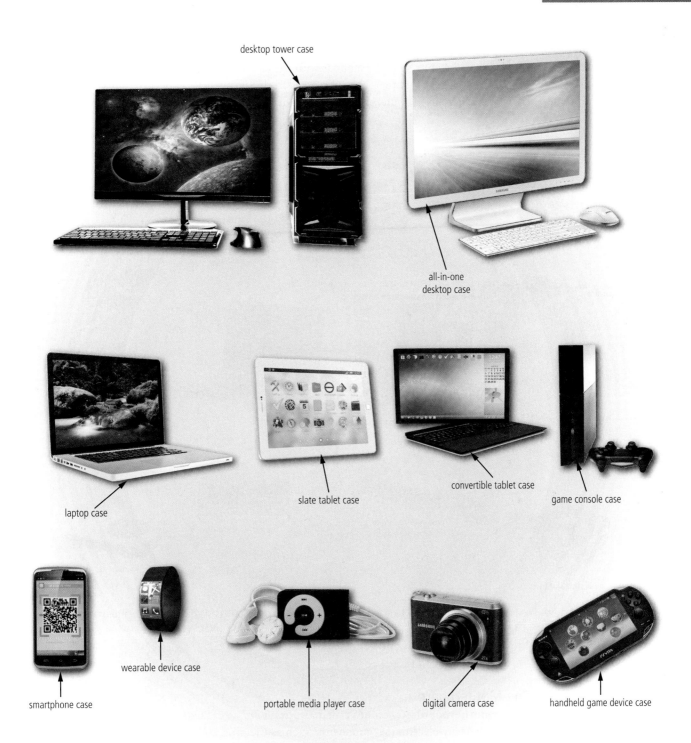

Figure 6-1 Cases for computers and mobile devices are available in a variety of shapes and sizes.

 **Internet Research**

Which laptops are the most popular?

Search for: laptop market share

At some point, you might have to open the case on a desktop or access panels on a laptop to replace or install a new electronic component, or hire a professional to assist with this task. For this reason, you should be familiar with the electronic components inside the case, some of which are shown in Figure 6-2 and discussed in this chapter. Read Secure IT 6-1 for tips related to protecting your computers and mobile devices from theft.

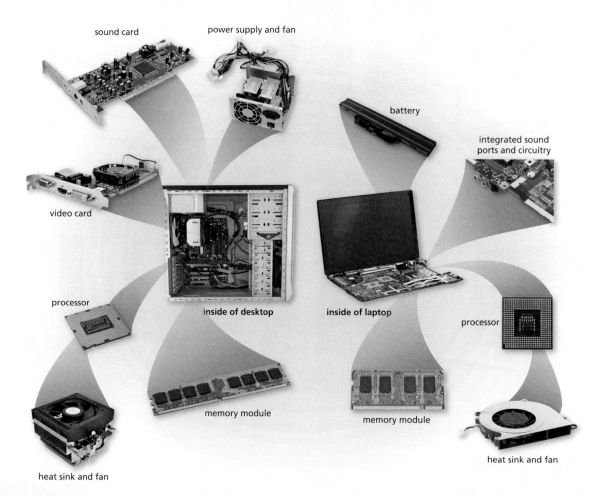

Figure 6-2 This figure shows typical components in a higher-end desktop and laptop. Many basic desktops have integrated video and sound capability, similar to the laptop image shown here.

The Motherboard

The **motherboard**, sometimes called a *system board*, is the main circuit board of the computer. Many electronic components, such as the processor and memory, attach to the motherboard; others are built into it. Figure 6-3 shows photos of current desktop and laptop motherboards.

On personal computers, the circuitry for the processor, memory, and other components reside on a computer chip(s). A computer **chip** is a small piece of semiconducting material, usually silicon, on which integrated circuits are etched. An *integrated circuit* contains many microscopic pathways capable of carrying electrical current. Each integrated circuit can contain millions of elements such as resistors, capacitors, and transistors. A *transistor*, for example, can act as an electronic switch that opens or closes the circuit for electrical charges. Today's computer chips contain millions or billions of transistors.

Most chips are no bigger than one-half-inch square. Manufacturers package chips so that the chips can be attached to a circuit board, such as a motherboard.

✪ SECURE IT 6-1

Securing Computers and Mobile Devices

Millions of smartphones, mobile devices, and computers are stolen in the United States every year, but only a small percent of these devices are recovered. Many devices can help deter potential thieves and also help trace and recover stolen goods. The following products may be useful in securing and tracking hardware.

- **Clamps, cables, and locks:** Lock kits include mounting plates, glue, cables, and padlocks to protect desktops, monitors, laptops, and peripheral devices.

- **Ultrasonic sensors:** Thieves do not need to remove a computer from an office building or school to commit their crimes; instead, they can open the case on a desktop or server on site and then remove a hard drive or other expensive component. To prevent such tampering, hardware manufacturers have developed an alarm system to install in the case. If the computer is moved or the case is opened,

an ear-piercing alarm sounds and a security company is alerted.

- **Tracking software:** Many smartphones and mobile devices have software that shows the approximate location of devices and computers. The owner can issue commands remotely to have the device play a sound, lock the screen, display a message, or erase all personal information.

- **Asset tags:** Metal security plates affixed to hardware contain unique bar codes that are registered to the owner and are stored in a security company's database. If a lost or stolen device is recovered, the finder can call the phone number on the tag, and the company will notify the owner.

- **Personal safes:** Protective cases that are approximately the size of a cereal box can store a smartphone, keys, tablet, and other valuables. The attached security cable

can be secured to a stationary object, such as a chair or table. Some personal safes have built-in electronic locks; others can be secured with a combination lock. The safe can be useful in a hotel room, at the gym, or on campus.

❇ **Consider This:** Have you seen any of these security devices at school or at businesses? If so, where? Do you know someone whose computer or mobile device was lost or stolen? If so, was the hardware recovered? What other measures can organizations take to prevent security breaches?

Courtesy of SentrySafe

Figure 6-3 A desktop motherboard and a laptop motherboard.
Courtesy of GIGABYTE; © iStockphoto / RAW group

BTW

Technology Trend

Discover More: Visit this chapter's free resources to learn about medical robotics.

Processors

The **processor**, also called the **central processing unit** (**CPU**), interprets and carries out the basic instructions that operate a computer. The processor significantly impacts overall computing power and manages most of a computer's operations. On larger computers, such as mainframes and supercomputers, the various functions performed by the processor extend over many separate chips and often multiple circuit boards. On a personal computer, all functions of the processor usually are on a single chip. Some computer and chip manufacturers use the term *microprocessor* to refer to a personal computer processor chip.

Most processor chip manufacturers now offer multi-core processors. A processor core, or simply core, contains the circuitry necessary to execute instructions. The operating system views each processor core as a separate processor. A **multi-core processor** is a single chip with two or more separate processor cores. Multi-core processors are used in all sizes of computers. Read Secure IT 6-2 to learn how chips can help to identify and secure animals.

 CONSIDER THIS

Are multi-core processors better than single-core processors?

Each processor core on a multi-core processor generally runs at a slower speed than a single-core processor, but multi-core processors typically increase overall performance. For example, although a dual-core processor does not double the processing speed of a single-core processor, it can approach those speeds. The performance increase is especially noticeable when users are running multiple programs simultaneously, such as antivirus software, spyware remover, email program, Internet messaging, media player, and photo editing software. Multi-core processors also are more energy efficient than separate multiple processors, requiring lower levels of power consumption and emitting less heat inside the case.

 SECURE IT 6-2

Chip Implants Secure Animals' Identity

The search for lost dogs or cats can be traumatic for their owners. The animals' safe return home may be based on data stored on a chip that veterinarians have implanted under the skin, usually at the neck or shoulder blades.

The chip — sometimes called a microchip because it is so small (about the size of a grain of rice) — has a unique number that is registered to the owner's name and address. It contains an antenna and transponder encased in a glass tube. The antenna receives low-frequency radio waves when a scanning device passes over the chip, and the transponder sends a signal with the chip's number back to the scanner.

Shelters and animal control centers routinely scan runaway pets for chips in an attempt to reunite animals with their owners.

Most shelters require pets to have the implant before the animals are adopted or before a once-lost pet is returned to its owner. Some veterinarians also scan new pets for chips to ensure the animal does not belong to someone else.

Some pet owners are concerned that microchipping can cause health problems, particularly if the chip moves from its original injection site. Most humane societies and veterinarians, however, state that no long-term adverse health effects or discomfort occurs.

Microchips also are implanted or attached externally in other animals, including horses, elephants, cows, birds, fish, lizards, and snakes. Breeders, farmers, and animal associations implant the chips to deter thieves. Chips also can monitor an animal's temperature, so that a farmer can prevent the spread of disease by identifying and removing an ill animal from a herd.

Researchers, including those at the U.S. Fish and Wildlife Service, also use this technology to track migration of wild animals, reptiles, and fish. They study how these species interact with their environment, and conservation authorities can identify endangered species, such as sea turtles, that have been confiscated from smugglers.

Consider This: Do you have or know anyone who has a pet that has been implanted with a chip? If so, why do you think they did it? Besides possible health problems, why might some people oppose mandatory animal chipping? Do you think people someday might choose to have a chip implanted to eliminate the need to carry identification? Why or why not?

Processors contain a control unit and an arithmetic logic unit (ALU). These two components work together to perform processing operations. Figure 6-4 illustrates how other devices connected to the computer communicate with the processor to carry out a task. When a user runs an application, for example, its instructions transfer from a storage device to memory. Data needed by programs and applications enters memory from either an input device or a storage device. The control unit interprets and executes instructions in memory, and the arithmetic logic unit performs calculations on the data in memory. Resulting information is stored in memory, from which it can be sent to an output device or a storage device for future access, as needed.

Discover More: Visit this chapter's free resources to learn more about processor chip manufacturers and multi-core processors.

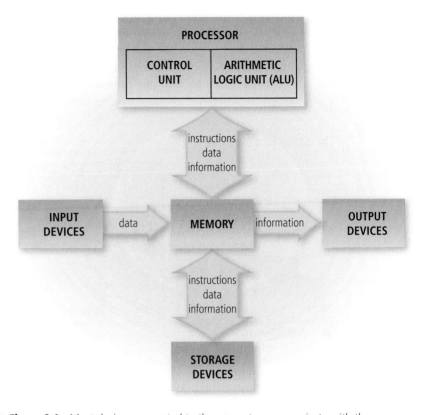

Figure 6-4 Most devices connected to the computer communicate with the processor to carry out a task.
© Cengage Learning

The Control Unit

The **control unit** is the component of the processor that directs and coordinates most of the operations in the computer. That is, it interprets each instruction issued by a program or an application and then initiates the appropriate action to carry out the instruction. Types of internal components that the control unit directs include the arithmetic logic unit, registers, and buses, each discussed in this chapter.

The Arithmetic Logic Unit

The **arithmetic logic unit** (*ALU*), another component of the processor, performs arithmetic, comparison, and other operations.

Arithmetic operations include basic calculations, such as addition, subtraction, multiplication, and division. *Comparison operations* involve comparing one data item with another to determine whether the first item is greater than, equal to, or less than the other item. Depending on the result of the comparison, different actions may occur. For example, to determine if an employee should receive overtime pay, software instructs the ALU to compare the number of hours an employee worked during the week with the regular time hours allowed (e.g., 40 hours). If the hours worked exceed 40, for example, software instructs the ALU to perform calculations that compute the overtime wage.

Machine Cycle

For every instruction, a processor repeats a set of four basic operations, which comprise a *machine cycle:* (1) fetching, (2) decoding, (3) executing, and, if necessary, (4) storing.

* *Fetching* is the process of obtaining a program or an application instruction or data item from memory.
* *Decoding* refers to the process of translating the instruction into signals the computer can execute.
* *Executing* is the process of carrying out the commands.
* *Storing*, in this context, means writing the result to memory (not to a storage medium).

Internet Research
What is Moore's Law?
Search for: moores law

Internet Research
What is Wolfram|Alpha?
Search for: wolfram alpha

Figure 6-5 illustrates the steps in a machine cycle. In some computers, the processor fetches, decodes, executes, and stores only one instruction at a time. With others, the processor fetches a second instruction before the first instruction completes its machine cycle, resulting in faster processing. Some use multiple processors simultaneously to increase processing times.

Discover More: Visit this chapter's free resources to learn about two additional ways to increase processing times, pipelining and parallel processing.

The Steps in a Machine Cycle

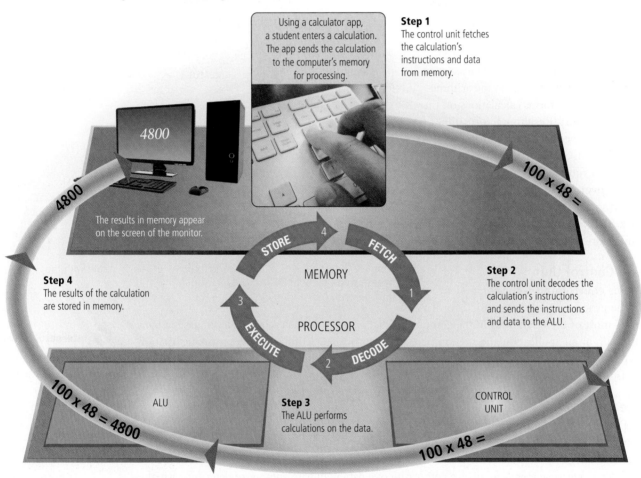

Step 1
The control unit fetches the calculation's instructions and data from memory.

Step 2
The control unit decodes the calculation's instructions and sends the instructions and data to the ALU.

Step 3
The ALU performs calculations on the data.

Step 4
The results of the calculation are stored in memory.

Using a calculator app, a student enters a calculation. The app sends the calculation to the computer's memory for processing.

The results in memory appear on the screen of the monitor.

Figure 6-5   This figure shows the steps in a machine cycle.
© iStockphoto / sweetym; © slavchovr / Shutterstock.com; © Cengage Learning

Registers

A processor contains small, high-speed storage locations, called *registers*, that temporarily hold data and instructions. Registers are part of the processor, not part of memory or a permanent storage device. Processors have many different types of registers, each with a specific storage function. Register functions include storing the location from where an instruction was fetched, storing an instruction while the control unit decodes it, storing data while the ALU calculates it, and storing the results of a calculation.

The System Clock

The processor relies on a small quartz crystal circuit called the **system clock** to control the timing of all computer operations. Just as your heart beats at a regular rate to keep your body functioning, the system clock generates regular electronic pulses, or ticks, that set the operating pace of components of the system unit.

BTW

System Clock and Peripheral Devices
The speed of the system clock has no effect on peripheral devices such as a printer or hard drive.

Each tick equates to a *clock cycle*. Processors today typically are *superscalar*, which means they can execute more than one instruction per clock cycle.

The pace of the system clock, called the **clock speed**, is measured by the number of ticks per second. Current personal computer processors have clock speeds in the gigahertz range. Giga is a prefix that stands for billion, and a *hertz* is one cycle per second. Thus, one **gigahertz (GHz)** equals one billion ticks of the system clock per second. A computer that operates at 3 GHz has 3 billion (giga) clock cycles in one second (hertz).

The faster the clock speed, the more instructions the processor can execute per second. The speed of the system clock is just one factor that influences a computer's performance. Other factors, such as the type of processor chip, amount of cache, memory access time, bus width, and bus clock speed, are discussed later in this chapter.

Internet Research

What are the fastest processor clock speeds?

Search for: fastest processor

 CONSIDER THIS

Does the system clock also keep track of the current date and time?
No, a separate battery-backed chip, called the *real-time clock*, keeps track of the date and time in a computer. The battery continues to run the real-time clock even when the computer is off.

Personal Computer and Mobile Device Processors

The leading manufacturers of personal computer processor chips are Intel and AMD. AMD manufactures *Intel-compatible processors*, which have an internal design similar to Intel processors, perform the same functions, and can be as powerful, but often are less expensive. These manufacturers often identify their processor chips by a model name or model number. Read How To 6-1 for items to consider when selecting a processor for a computer.

In the past, chip manufacturers listed a processor's clock speed in marketing literature and advertisements. As previously mentioned, though, clock speed is only one factor that impacts processing speed in today's computers. To help consumers evaluate various processors, manufacturers such as Intel and AMD now use a numbering scheme that more accurately reflects the processing speed of their chips.

 BTW

Technology Innovators
Discover More: Visit this chapter's free resources to learn about Intel, Gordon Moore, and AMD.

 HOW TO 6-1

Select the Right Processor
When you are shopping for a new computer, it is important to select one with a processor that will meet your needs. For example, some processors are designed for home users, some are designed for power users, and others are designed for mobile users. Performing basic research before you shop for a new computer can help you select the most appropriate processor. The following steps describe how to select the right processor.

1. **Determine your needs.** Think about how you will use your computer and the programs and applications you plan to run. If you will be using your computer for basic tasks, such as web browsing or checking email, you may require a less expensive processor than a user who will be running many programs and applications simultaneously.

2. **Determine your current processor.** If you are replacing your existing computer with a new computer, determine the processor in your existing computer so that you can make sure the new processor is better and faster than the one in use currently.

3. **Research processor models.** While shopping for computers in your price range, pay attention to the types of processors they include. Visit the processor manufacturer's website and verify that the processor will meet your computing needs adequately. Reviewing the minimum system requirements on the programs and apps you wish to run may help you determine the processor you need. Choose a processor that exceeds the minimum system requirements of the programs and apps you wish to run, but remember that it is not

always necessary to purchase the most expensive computer with the fastest processor.

Courtesy of Intel

 Consider This: What type of processor is in your current computer? If you were to upgrade your processor, which one would you choose? Why?

BTW
Technology Innovator
Discover More: Visit this chapter's free resources to learn about Nvidia, maker of high-performance graphics processors.

Processor chips include technologies to improve processing performance (for example, to improve performance of media and 3-D graphics). Some also include technology to track computer hardware and software, diagnose and resolve computer problems, and secure computers from outside threats. Processors for mobile computers also include technology to optimize and extend battery life and integrate wireless capabilities. Smaller mobile devices often use more compact processors that consume less power, yet offer high performance.

Discover More: Visit this chapter's free resources to learn more about processor chips.

CONSIDER THIS

Can you upgrade an existing computer's processor?

You might be able to upgrade a processor to increase the computer's performance. Be certain the processor you buy is compatible with your computer's motherboard; otherwise, you will have to replace the motherboard, too.

BTW
Mobile Device Cooling
Mobile devices often use low-voltage processors, which have such low power demands that they do not require additional cooling.

Processor Cooling

Processor chips for laptops, desktops, and servers can generate quite a bit of heat, which could cause the chip to malfunction or fail. Although the power supply on some computers contains a main fan to generate airflow, today's personal computer processors often require additional cooling. Some computer cases locate additional fans near certain components, such as a processor, to provide additional cooling. Heat sinks, liquid cooling technologies, and cooling mats often are used to help further dissipate processor heat.

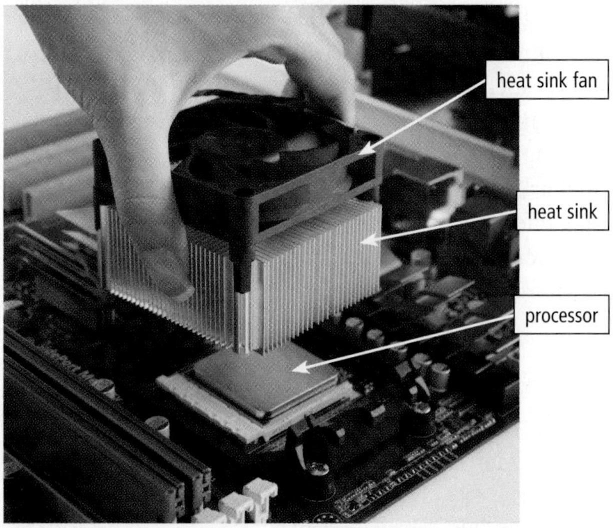

Figure 6-6 This photo shows a heat sink being attached to the top of a processor to prevent the chip from overheating.
© Claudio Bravo / Shutterstock.com

A *heat sink* is a small ceramic or metal component with fins on its surface that absorbs and disperses heat produced by electrical components, such as a processor. Many heat sinks have fans to help distribute air dissipated by the heat sink. Some heat sinks are packaged as part of a processor chip. Others are installed on the top or the side of the chip (Figure 6-6).

Some computers use liquid cooling technology to reduce the temperature of a processor. *Liquid cooling technology* uses a continuous flow of fluid(s), such as water and glycol, in a process that transfers the heated fluid away from the processor to a radiator-type grill, which cools the liquid, and then returns the cooled fluid to the processor.

Laptop users often use a cooling pad to help further reduce the heat generated by their computer. A *cooling pad* rests below a laptop and protects the computer from overheating and also the user's lap from excessive heat (Figure 6-7). Some cooling pads contain a small fan to transfer heat away from the laptop. These types of cooling pads often draw power from a USB port. Instead of using power, other pads absorb heat through a conductive material inside the pad.

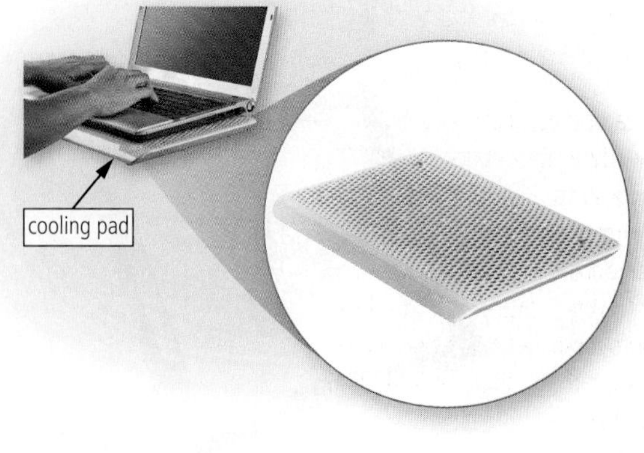

Figure 6-7 A laptop cooling pad helps reduce heat generated by a laptop.
Courtesy of Targus Group International, Inc; Courtesy of Targus Group International, Inc.

Mini Feature 6-1: The Internet of Things

The *Internet of Things* (*IoT*) describes a computing environment where everyday objects, or things, are connected to the Internet. Sensors connected to these objects may gather, share, transmit, and receive data about the objects with other devices or servers online. Users can access the data or control individual objects using web or mobile apps. Read Mini Feature 6-1 to learn about types of devices used as things and technologies used to enable the IoT. Read Ethics & Issues 6-1 to consider whether the IoT discriminates, and read Secure IT 6-3 for privacy issues related to the IoT.

BTW
Technology Trend
Discover More: Visit this chapter's free resources to learn about self-driving cars.

 MINI FEATURE 6-1

The Internet of Things

Analysts predict that the IoT will be a multitrillion-dollar business as the number of "smart" devices and things connected to the Internet continues to increase. As watches, thermostats, fitness trackers, appliances, clothing, and other "things" become equipped with sensors that can transmit data to and from the Internet, keeping every "thing" connected could become one of the world's largest industries.

From Devices to Things

Computers and mobile devices are not the only things that connect to the Internet. You can buy a thermostat, such as the one from Nest Labs shown in the figure, that

Source: Nest Labs

allows you to adjust the temperature of your home from anywhere using an app on your smartphone. The thermostat contains a temperature sensor that can send and receive data. A wireless chip attached to your medicine bottle can send text messages to remind you to take your medication and then contact your pharmacy to refill the prescription when it is due for a refill. Smart trash cans in public places have sensors that monitor the amount of trash deposited and then send a message notifying owners when the containers need to be emptied. This saves garbage collectors from checking the containers every day; instead, they can empty the containers only when receiving a message that they are full.

Wearable technology, such as smartwatches and wristbands, can track your pulse and heart rate, as well as accept calls and display notifications from a smartphone. Many public buses and subways have GPS sensors that report their locations so that travelers can track them with mobile apps. Retailers can use beacons, which are devices that send low-energy Bluetooth signals to nearby smartphones, to notify customers who use a payment app such as Paypal, of personalized offers in their stores.

Washers and dryers in many college dormitory laundry rooms are connected to sensors that report the availability of an individual machine. Students can visit a website, use a mobile app, or request text message alerts to locate available machines before carrying their laundry to the laundry room.

Technologies Enable the IoT

The IoT brings together several recent technology developments. Communications technologies, such as Bluetooth, RFID tags, near-field communications (NFC) tags, and sensors tracking heat (temperature), light, weight, or location have become readily available. Sensors and tags can transmit messages to a server on the Internet over a wireless network at frequent intervals for analysis and storage. Developments in Big Data have made it possible to access, store, and process all of this data reported by sensors efficiently. (To learn more about Big Data, read Mini Feature 11-1 in Chapter 11.) Mobile service providers offer connectivity to a variety of devices at broadband speeds, so transmitting and retrieving data can take place quickly. The size and cost of wireless radios has decreased, enabling more things to have embedded sensors, tags, and transmitters.

The capability of computers, devices, and everyday objects to communicate with one another over the Internet has opened new possibilities for both consumers and the enterprise to be more productive, efficient, and informed.

Discover More: Visit this chapter's free resources to learn more about the Internet of Things.

Consider This: Research one of the smart products described in the "From Devices to Things" section of this mini feature. Who manufactures or uses it? How does it work? What are the benefits to such a smart product? What object or thing do you wish was connected to the Internet? What data would you like it to send or capture? How might an app help you to control this object or access information about it? How would this improve your life?

Source: Mac-Gray Corporation

ETHICS & ISSUES 6-1

Does the Internet of Things Discriminate?

Technology experts expect that the advantages brought by the expansion of the Internet of Things (IoT) will enhance the comfort, safety, and efficiency of a large population across the globe. Where does that leave people who are struggling to make ends meet? What about those who live in developing countries?

Among the IoT technologies that exist or are in development include the following examples. Students can find accurate information quickly and use cloud-based apps to store data so that it is accessible. The coordination of traffic lights based on GPS data will lead to a lessening of commute times. Wearable and implanted devices can collect and communicate health-related

data. Sensors that monitor temperature, air and water quality and usage, and more, will reduce home ownership costs and security risks. Agricultural devices can monitor, track, and provide assessment of livestock and crops to lower costs and improve access to food.

Individuals or countries that cannot afford these and other IoT-related technologies may feel a negative impact as others take advantage of the effects brought by these technologies. Students without access to these technologies could be at a disadvantage. Workers with shorter travel times may enjoy a better quality of life. Those who cannot afford health-related devices may be at higher risk for illnesses or medical complications. Homeowners without

IoT-enabled homes may be more prone to dangers, such as fires. Countries involved in agricultural exporting may lose business as others are able to reduce costs.

As costs of these technologies decrease, it is likely that the divide between the more and less fortunate will decrease. Awareness of the impact of the inequalities also may give rise to nonprofits or organizations that focus on providing IoT technologies to a larger population.

Consider This: In what other ways will IoT affect individuals and countries who cannot afford these technologies? What responsibility exists to make IoT technologies available to all?

SECURE IT 6-3

Does the Internet of Things Encroach on Privacy?

Being digitally observed in the connected world is inescapable. Every day, smart electric meters, wearable technology, and vehicles' black boxes submit data about us as part of the Internet of Things (IoT). Researchers predict billions of devices will be part of the IoT by the end of this decade. With all these devices in nearly every facet of our daily lives, data is being accumulated and sold to health care providers, home security businesses, utility companies, and researchers.

Savvy consumers can take some steps to attempt to limit exposure to data collection.

They can enable privacy settings, for example, but that does not guarantee that data is not being gathered, transmitted, and compiled. The report of Smart TVs secretly collecting data about audiences' viewing habits sparked privacy and security concerns. Consumers need to urge companies to design products with built-in privacy protections. These devices could have default settings that prevent the sharing of data until obtaining the consumer's consent. Companies should explain what data is being collected and whether it will be used to help people live more productive lives or to create personal profiles that predict behavior. In addition, companies bear the responsibility

of ensuring sensitive data being collected is kept secure and confidential.

Privacy and security concerns abound with the Internet of Things, but most consumers and technology experts believe that the security, health, and productivity benefits of this technology outweigh the potential risks.

Consider This: Should companies inform consumers about the data being collected in homes, vehicles, schools, and workplaces? What role should governmental agencies, such as the Federal Trade Commission, play in overseeing companies' secure products and commercial data collection techniques?

 NOW YOU SHOULD KNOW

Be sure you understand the material presented in the sections titled Inside the Case and Processors as it relates to the chapter objectives.

Now you should know . . .

- Why you should protect the contents of computers and mobile devices (Objective 1)

- How processors in computers and mobile devices operate (Objective 2)

- Which processors might be best suited to your needs, and how to keep processors and other components from overheating (Objective 3)

- How you might interact with the Internet of Things (Objective 4)

Discover More: Visit this chapter's premium content for practice quiz opportunities.

Cloud Computing

Recall that cloud computing refers to an environment of servers that house and provide access to resources users access via the Internet. Home and business users choose cloud computing for a variety of reasons:

- **Accessibility:** Data and/or applications are available worldwide from any computer or device with an Internet connection.
- **Cost savings:** The expense of software and high-end hardware, such as fast processors and high-capacity memory and storage devices, shifts away from the user.
- **Space savings:** Floor space required for servers, storages devices, and other hardware shifts away from the user.
- **Scalability:** Provides the flexibility to increase or decrease computing requirements as needed.

Cloud computing consists of a front end and a back end, connected to each other through a network. The front end includes the hardware and software with which a user interacts to access the cloud. For example, a user might access a resource on the cloud through a browser on a laptop. The back end consists of the servers and storage devices that manage and store the resources accessed by users.

Mini Feature 6-2: Cloud Computing Services

Cloud computing allows companies to outsource, or contract to third-party providers, elements of their information technology infrastructure. They pay only for the computing power, storage, bandwidth, and access to applications that they actually use. As a result, companies need not make large investments in equipment, or the staff to support it. Read Mini Feature 6-2 to learn about available types of cloud computing services.

 BTW
Technology Innovator
Discover More: Visit this chapter's free resources to learn about VMware, a provider of virtualization software and cloud computing services.

 Internet Research
Which companies offer cloud computing services?
Search for: cloud computing providers

 MINI FEATURE 6-2 ————————————————————————————————

Cloud Computing Services

Consumers and organizations rely on cloud computing services to manage IT infrastructure (infrastructure as a service), provide applications (software as a service), access online data (data as a service), and create, test, and deploy applications using web-based development tools (platform as a service).

Infrastructure as a Service

IaaS (infrastructure as a service) uses software to emulate hardware capabilities, enabling companies to scale, or adjust up or down, storage, processing power, or bandwidth as needed. For example, retailers may need to increase these capabilities to accommodate additional traffic to their websites during busy holiday shopping seasons. When the season ends, retailers easily can reduce these settings.

Two specific instances of IaaS are storage as a service and desktop as a service:

- **Storage as a Service:** Cloud storage providers offer file management services such as storing files online, system backup, and archiving earlier versions

of files. Cloud storage is especially useful to tablet and smartphone users, because it enables them to access their files from all of their devices.

- **Desktop as a Service:** Some companies specify the applications, security settings, and computing resources available to employees on their desktop computers. These images, or configurations, provide a common desktop work environment available to employees across an entire organization. Because the desktop and its applications appear to be installed on the user's own computer, desktop as a service also is known as a *virtual desktop*.

Software as a Service

SaaS (software as a service) describes a computing environment where an Internet server hosts and deploys applications. Editing documents or photos, sending email messages, and managing finances are common consumer tasks of SaaS applications. A pioneering provider of SaaS applications for companies is Salesforce (shown in the figure in this mini feature), which offers customer relationship management (CRM) software. Salesforce users subscribe to modules to handle tasks such as sales and marketing campaigns and customer services.

(*continued*)

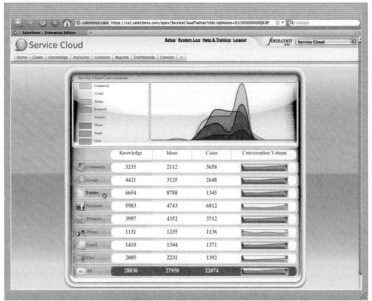

Source: Courtesy Salesforce.com

are applications that incorporate data from multiple providers into a new application. Displaying homes or crime statistics on a map are examples of mashups that require data from real estate, police records, and mapping providers.

Platform as a Service

Application developers need to maintain computers running specific hardware, operating systems, development tools, databases, and other software. *PaaS (platform as a service)* allows developers to create, test, and run their solutions on a cloud platform without having to purchase or configure the underlying hardware and software.

Discover More: Visit this chapter's free resources to learn more about the various cloud services described in this mini feature.

Consider This: Cloud computing services are based on a "pay as you go" model. How are cloud services different from desktop or mobile applications? What services are customers paying for from an SaaS provider? Under what circumstances might it be advantageous to purchase an external hard drive to store your files, rather than storing them on a third-party server on the cloud?

Data as a Service

Government agencies, companies, and social media sites make data available for developers to incorporate in applications or to use when making business decisions and plans. *DaaS (data as a service)* allows users and applications to access a company's data. *Mashups*

Data Representation

To understand how a computer processes data, you should know how a computer represents data. People communicate through speech by combining words into sentences. Human speech is **analog** because it uses continuous (wave form) signals that vary in strength and quality. Most computers are **digital**. They recognize only two discrete states: on and off. This is because computers are electronic devices powered by electricity, which also has only two states: on and off.

Bits and Bytes

The two digits, 0 and 1, easily can represent these two states (Figure 6-8). The digit 0 represents the electronic state of off (absence of an electronic charge). The digit 1 represents the electronic state of on (presence of an electronic charge).

When people count, they use the 10 digits in the decimal system (0 through 9). The computer, by contrast, uses a binary system because it recognizes only two states. The **binary system** is a number system that has just two unique digits, 0 and 1, called bits. A **bit** (short for *binary digit*) is the smallest unit of data the computer can process. By itself, a bit is not very informative.

When 8 bits are grouped together as a unit, they form a **byte**. A byte provides enough different combinations of 0s and 1s to represent 256 different characters. These characters include numbers, uppercase and lowercase letters of the alphabet, punctuation marks, and other keyboard symbols, such as an asterisk (*), ampersand (&), and dollar sign ($).

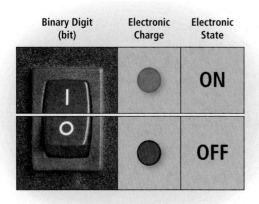

Figure 6-8 The circuitry in a computer or mobile device represents the on or the off states electronically by the presence or absence of an electronic charge.

© iStockphoto / rjmiz; © Cengage Learning

Coding Schemes

The combinations of 0s and 1s that represent uppercase and lowercase letters, numbers, and special symbols are defined by patterns called a coding scheme. Coding schemes map a set of *alphanumeric characters* (letters and numbers) and special symbols to a sequence of numeric values that a computer can process. *ASCII* (pronounced ASK-ee), which stands for American Standard Code for Information Interchange, is the most widely used coding scheme to represent a set of characters. In the ASCII coding scheme, for example, the alphabetic character E is represented as 01000101; the symbolic character * is represented as 00101010; the numeric character 6 is represented as 00110110 (Figure 6-9).

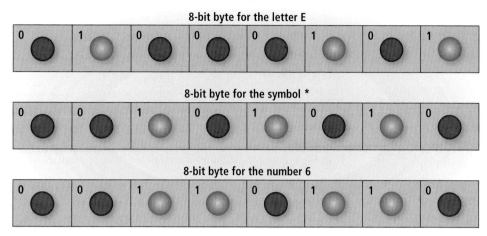

Figure 6-9 Eight bits grouped together as a unit are called a byte. A byte represents a single character in the computer or mobile device.
© Cengage Learning

When you press a key on a keyboard, a chip in the keyboard converts the key's electronic signal into a special code, called a scan code, that is sent to the electronic circuitry in the computer. Then, the electronic circuitry in the computer converts the scan code into its ASCII binary form and stores it as a byte value in its memory for processing. When processing is finished, the computer converts the byte into a human-recognizable number, letter of the alphabet, or special character that is displayed on a screen or is printed (Figure 6-10). All of these conversions take place so quickly that you do not realize they are occurring.

How a Letter Is Converted to Binary Form and Back

Step 1
A user presses the capital letter **T** (SHIFT+T keys) on the keyboard, which in turn creates a special code, called a scan code, for the capital letter **T**.

Step 2
The scan code for the capital letter **T** is sent to the electronic circuitry in the computer.

Step 4
After processing, the binary code for the capital letter **T** is converted to an image and displayed on the output device.

Step 3
The electronic circuitry in the computer converts the scan code for the capital letter **T** to its ASCII binary code (01010100) and stores it in memory for processing.

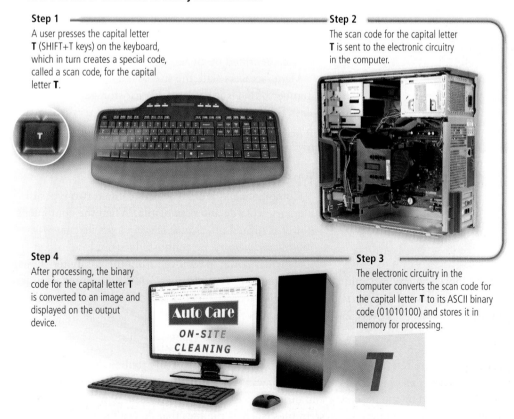

Figure 6-10 This figure shows how a letter is converted to binary form and back.
© Chiyacat / Shutterstock.com; © Kitch Bain / Shutterstock.com; © Cengage Learning; Source: Microsoft; © iStockphoto / sweetym

---

✳️ **CONSIDER THIS** ——————————————————————

Why are coding schemes necessary?
Computers rely on logic circuits, which are controlled by electronic switches whose state can be either on or off. Each switch's on/off state is represented by one bit, whose value is either 0 or 1. Coding schemes translate real-world data into a form that computers can process easily.

Memory

Memory consists of electronic components that store instructions waiting to be executed by the processor, data needed by those instructions, and the results of processing the data (information). Memory usually consists of one or more chips on the motherboard or some other circuit board in the computer. Memory stores three basic categories of items:

1. The operating system and other programs that control or maintain the computer and its devices
2. Applications that carry out a specific task, such as word processing
3. The data being processed by the applications and the resulting information

This role of memory to store both data and programs is known as the *stored program concept*.

Bytes and Addressable Memory

A byte (character) is the basic storage unit in memory. When an application's instructions and data are transferred to memory from storage devices, the instructions and data exist as bytes. Each byte resides temporarily in a location in memory that has an address. Simply put, an *address* is a unique number that identifies the location of a byte in memory. To access data or instructions in memory, the computer references the addresses that contain bytes of data. The photo in Figure 6-11 shows how seats in a stadium are similar to addresses in memory: (1) a seat, which is identified by a unique seat number, holds one person at a time, and a location in memory, which is identified by a unique address, holds a single byte; and (2) both a seat, identified by a seat number, and a byte, identified by an address, can be empty.

Manufacturers state the size of memory in terms of the number of bytes it has available for storage. Common sizes for memory are in the gigabyte and terabyte range. A *gigabyte (GB)* equals approximately 1 billion bytes. A *terabyte (TB)* is equal to approximately 1 trillion bytes.

seat J20 is empty

seat J21 is occupied

Figure 6-11 Seats in a stadium are similar to addresses in memory: a seat holds one person at a time, and a location in memory holds a single byte; and both a seat and a byte can be empty.
© iStockPhoto / GeorgePeters

Types of Memory

Computers and mobile devices contain two types of memory: volatile and nonvolatile. When the computer's power is turned off, *volatile memory* loses its contents. *Nonvolatile memory*, by contrast, does not lose its contents when power is removed from the computer. Thus, volatile memory is temporary and nonvolatile memory is permanent. RAM is the most common type of volatile memory. Examples of nonvolatile memory include ROM, flash memory, and CMOS. The following sections discuss these types of memory.

RAM

Users typically are referring to RAM when discussing computer and mobile device memory. **RAM** *(random access memory)*, also called *main memory*, consists of memory chips that can be read from and written to by the processor and other devices. When you turn on power to a computer or mobile device, certain operating system files (such as the files that determine how the desktop or home screen appears) load into RAM from a storage device such as a hard drive. These files remain in RAM as long as the computer or mobile device has continuous power. As additional applications and data are requested, they also load into RAM from storage.

The processor interprets and executes a program or application's instructions while the program or application is in RAM. During this time, the contents of RAM may change (Figure 6-12). RAM can accommodate multiple programs and applications simultaneously.

Most RAM is volatile, which means it loses its contents when the power is removed from the computer. For this reason, you must save any data, instructions, and information you may need in the future. Saving is the process of copying data, instructions, and information from RAM to a storage device such as a hard drive.

How Program Instructions Transfer in and out of RAM

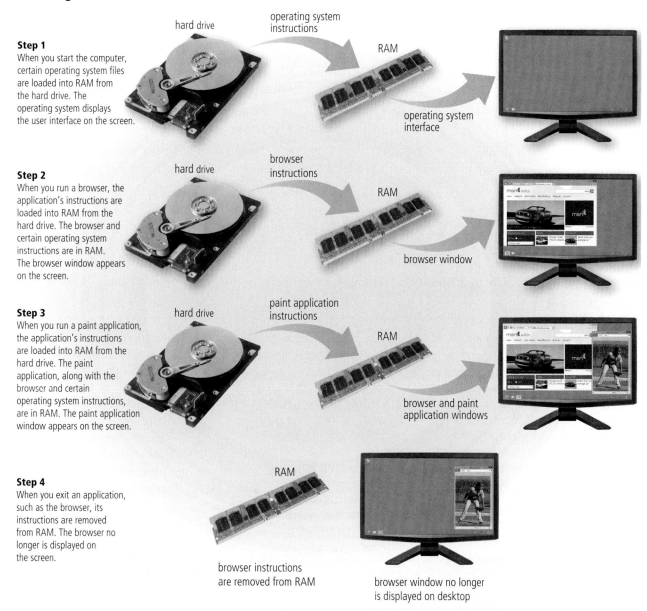

Step 1
When you start the computer, certain operating system files are loaded into RAM from the hard drive. The operating system displays the user interface on the screen.

hard drive

operating system instructions

RAM

operating system interface

Step 2
When you run a browser, the application's instructions are loaded into RAM from the hard drive. The browser and certain operating system instructions are in RAM. The browser window appears on the screen.

hard drive

browser instructions

RAM

browser window

Step 3
When you run a paint application, the application's instructions are loaded into RAM from the hard drive. The paint application, along with the browser and certain operating system instructions, are in RAM. The paint application window appears on the screen.

hard drive

paint application instructions

RAM

browser and paint application windows

Step 4
When you exit an application, such as the browser, its instructions are removed from RAM. The browser no longer is displayed on the screen.

RAM

browser instructions are removed from RAM

browser window no longer is displayed on desktop

Figure 6-12 This figure shows how program and application instructions transfer in and out of RAM.

Types of RAM   Two common types of RAM are dynamic RAM and static RAM:

- *Dynamic RAM* (*DRAM* pronounced DEE-ram) chips must be reenergized constantly or they lose their contents. Many variations of DRAM chips exist, most of which are faster than the basic DRAM (Table 6-1).
- *Static RAM* (*SRAM* pronounced ESS-ram) chips are faster and more reliable than any variation of DRAM chips. These chips do not have to be reenergized as often as DRAM chips; hence, the term, static. SRAM chips, however, are much more expensive than DRAM chips. Special applications, such as cache, use SRAM chips. A later section in this chapter discusses cache.

Read How To 6-2 for instructions about determining memory requirements.

Table 6-1   Common DRAM Variations

Name	Comments
SDRAM (Synchronous DRAM)	• Synchronized to the system clock • Much faster than DRAM
DDR SDRAM (Double Data Rate SDRAM)	• Transfers data twice, instead of once, for each clock cycle • Faster than SDRAM
DDR2	• Second generation of DDR • Faster than DDR
DDR3	• Third generation of DDR • Designed for computers with multi-core processors • Faster than DDR2
DDR4	• Fourth generation of DDR • Faster than DDR3
RDRAM (Rambus DRAM)	• Much faster than SDRAM

Discover More: Visit this chapter's free resources to learn about additional DRAM variations.

   HOW TO 6-2

Determine Memory Requirements

If you are shopping for a new computer or looking to upgrade your existing computer, be sure that it will have sufficient memory. When a computer has insufficient memory, its performance can slow significantly. On the other hand, it would be an unnecessary expense to purchase a computer with more memory than you will ever use. The following steps describe how to determine memory requirements.

1. If you are upgrading the memory in your existing computer, determine the following:
   a. Amount of memory currently installed
   b. Amount of memory the computer can support
   c. Type of memory modules currently installed
   d. Whether memory modules must be installed in pairs
   e. Number of available slots for memory modules

2. Determine the amount of memory your computer requires by checking the memory requirements for the operating system and programs and applications you plan to run. You can find the system requirements, which will specify the memory requirements, on product packaging or on a software manufacturer's website. If you are planning to upgrade your computer and the amount of memory you require exceeds the amount of memory your computer currently can support, you may need to purchase a new computer. If you are purchasing a new computer, view the computer's specifications to make sure it has sufficient memory. Some online vendors offer a web app that will check the configuration on your computer to determine the memory modules that are compatible and offer options to you for purchase.

3. Once you have determined your memory requirements, you are ready to purchase the memory modules. Memory modules are

available for purchase in many computer and electronic stores, directly from computer manufacturers, and on various websites. When you are purchasing memory modules, keep the following in mind:

   a. Many types of memory modules are available. Purchase a type, size, and speed that is compatible with your computer.
   b. If your computer requires that you install memory in pairs, be sure to purchase two memory modules that are the same type, size, and speed.
   c. Do not purchase more memory modules than you have slots available. You may need to remove existing memory modules to make room for new memory modules.

   ✷ **Consider This:** How much memory would be appropriate for your computer based on your current computing needs?

Memory Modules RAM chips usually reside on a memory module, which is a small circuit board. Memory slots on the motherboard hold memory modules.

Two types of memory modules are SIMMs and DIMMs (Figure 6-13). A *SIMM* (single inline memory module) has pins on opposite sides of the circuit board that connect together to form a single set of contacts. With a *DIMM* (dual inline memory module), by contrast, the pins on opposite sides of the circuit board do not connect and, thus, form two sets of contacts. Read How To 6-3 for instructions about installing memory modules.

🔘 **BTW**
High-Tech Talk
Discover More: Visit this chapter's free resources to learn how data is written to RAM.

Figure 6-13 Memory modules contain memory chips.
© mycola / Shutterstock.com; © TerryM / Shutterstock.com

🌟 HOW TO 6-3

Install Memory Modules
Installing additional memory modules in a desktop or laptop can be a relatively easy process. The following steps describe how to install new memory modules.

1. Turn off and unplug your computer from the power source. If you are using a laptop, remove its battery.

2. Wear an antistatic wristband to protect the computer from static electricity.

3. Remove or open the computer case. If you are upgrading a laptop, you may be able to locate the slots for the memory modules through an access panel.

4. If necessary, remove any existing memory modules you no longer need. If clips are holding the memory module in place, you may need to pull the clips away from the memory module before removing it. Remove the memory modules by lifting them out by the side edges.

5. Remove the new memory modules from the packaging.

6. Slowly and carefully insert the memory modules into the slots on your computer's motherboard. Be sure they are facing the correct way as you insert them. The memory modules should "click" in place once they are inserted completely.

7. Close the computer case or any access panel you have opened.

8. Plug in the computer and turn it on.

9. Check the system information in the operating system to make sure it is recognizing the new amount of memory installed.

🌟 **Consider This:** Why might it not be possible to install memory modules in some types of computers?

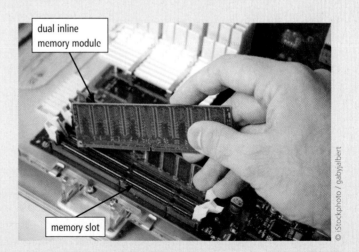

Cache

Most of today's computers improve their processing times with **cache** (pronounced cash), which is a temporary storage area. Two common types of cache are memory cache and disk cache. This chapter discusses memory cache. Chapter 8 discusses disk cache.

Memory cache helps speed the processes of the computer because it stores frequently used instructions and data. Most personal computers today have two types of memory cache: Level 1 (L1) cache and Level 2 (L2) cache. Some also have Level 3 (L3) cache.

- *L1 cache* is built directly on the processor chip. L1 cache usually has a very small capacity.
- *L2 cache* is slightly slower than L1 cache but has a much larger capacity. Current processors include *advanced transfer cache* (*ATC*), a type of L2 cache built directly on the processor chip. Processors that use ATC perform at much faster rates than those that do not use it.
- *L3 cache* is a cache on the motherboard that is separate from the processor chip. L3 cache exists only on computers that use L2 advanced transfer cache.

When the processor needs an instruction or data, it searches memory in this order: L1 cache, then L2 cache, then L3 cache (if it exists), then RAM — with a greater delay in processing for each level of memory it must search (Figure 6-14). If the instruction or data is not found in memory, then it must search a slower speed storage medium, such as a hard drive or optical disc.

Discover More: Visit this chapter's free resources to learn more about memory cache.

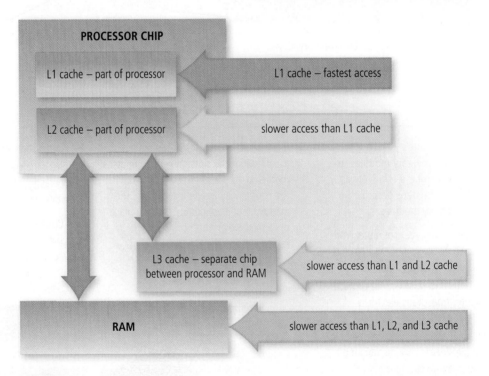

Figure 6-14 Memory cache helps speed processing times when the processor requests data, instructions, or information.
© Cengage Learning

ROM

Read-only memory (**ROM** pronounced rahm) refers to memory chips storing permanent data and instructions. The data on most ROM chips cannot be modified — hence, the name read-only. ROM is nonvolatile, which means its contents are not lost when power is removed from the computer. In addition to computers and mobile devices, many peripheral devices contain ROM chips. For example, ROM chips in printers contain data for fonts.

Manufacturers of ROM chips often record data, instructions, or information on the chips when they manufacture the chips. These ROM chips, called **firmware**, contain permanently written data, instructions, or information, such as a computer or mobile device's start-up instructions. Read Ethics & Issues 6-2 to consider issues related to the manufacture of computer and mobile device components.

Should Companies Reveal Which Products They Manufacture Using Fair Trade Practices?

Despite the increased cost, many coffee and tea drinkers gladly purchase fair trade products. Fair trade labels indicate that the workers who pick the coffee beans or tea leaves work in humane conditions and receive fair pay for their labor.

With respect to technology, several cases of unfair labor practices exist. Some technology manufacturers use products or components made in areas of extreme poverty. In these cases, factory owners coerce workers, including children, to work long hours in unsafe or unsanitary conditions for little pay and without breaks. In another example, mining for the raw materials needed to manufacture technology components may occur in areas where military conflict exists. Those involved in the military conflict may use the revenue from mining this material, sometimes called conflict minerals, to fund the soldiers and continue the discord.

Under a rule recently adopted by the U.S. Securities and Exchange Committee (SEC), manufacturers must review their supply sources and file a form disclosing any materials mined in areas of conflict. Failure to disclose may have legal consequences, as well as attract the attention of human rights and environmental activists. Critics of this rule state that it does not address methods to ease situations of conflict, and may take jobs away from the workers. In addition, the rule applies only to manufacturers, not to retailers or distributors.

The Fair Labor Association (FLA) provides workplace standards for the environment and treatment of workers at all stages of product development. Many technology companies are making efforts to comply with the SEC ruling, as well as FLA guidelines. Providing a living wage, ensuring worker safety, and mandating that workers receive breaks are some of the guidelines.

Consider This: Would you pay more for a fair trade smartphone or laptop? Why or why not? Are retailers responsible for the source of the materials used in products they sell? Why or why not? Should the government require companies to comply with fair trade policies? Why or why not?

Flash Memory

Flash memory is a type of nonvolatile memory that can be erased electronically and rewritten. Most computers use flash memory to hold their start-up instructions because it allows the computer to update its contents easily. For example, when the computer changes from standard time to daylight savings time, the contents of a flash memory chip (and the real-time clock chip) change to reflect the new time.

Flash memory chips also store data and programs on many mobile devices and peripheral devices, such as smartphones, portable media players, printers, digital cameras, automotive devices, and digital voice recorders. When you enter names and addresses in a smartphone, for example, a flash memory chip stores the data. Some portable media players store music on flash memory chips; others store music on tiny hard drives or memory cards. Memory cards contain flash memory on a removable device instead of a chip. Read Secure IT 6-4 for tips about deleting data on a smartphone.

Wiping Mobile Phone Memory

If you ever have lent your smartphone to someone, left it sitting on your desk at school or work, or placed it in your car's center console at valet parking, you might have provided someone access without your consent to all your personal data stored on that device. A thief can plug a small device, called a *Cellular Seizure Investigation (CSI) stick*, into the phone and then download sensitive data in seconds.

While this unscrupulous activity seems alarming, a similar action occurs every day when smartphone users recycle or sell their devices without wiping all their personal records from memory. A person buying or acquiring the phone then can access the sensitive data left in memory. Some recyclers claim that 95 percent of the mobile phones they receive are not completely cleaned.

A kill switch allows smartphone owners to delete all data or to disable their devices remotely in the event of theft or loss. Since 2015, all smartphones sold in California must include this device, and federal and other state lawmakers have proposed requiring all manufacturers to include this switch in their products.

Deleting all data from a mobile phone's memory is a relatively simple process, but it is not a universal procedure. Each device has its own set of steps described in the owner's manual or online. In general, users must locate their device's settings area on a menu and then look for a reset command. Most electronics manufacturers post instructions for this process on their websites. Mobile phone retailers often can offer help in clearing personal data; if you resort to this measure, be certain to watch the sales associate perform this action. If your mobile phone has a SIM or memory card, remove and destroy it if you are not going to transfer it to another phone. Employees who use their phone to access email messages on corporate servers sometimes are required to enter a passcode on the phone so that if it is lost or stolen, the data can be wiped remotely.

Consider This: Have you ever wiped the memory of your mobile phone? What action would you take if you received or bought a used mobile phone and then discovered the previous owner's personal information stored in memory? Should lawmakers require smartphone manufacturers to include a kill switch in their products? Why or why not?

CMOS

Some RAM chips, flash memory chips, and other memory chips use complementary metal-oxide semiconductor (*CMOS* pronounced SEE-moss) technology because it provides high speeds and consumes little power. CMOS technology uses battery power to retain information even when the power to the computer is off. Battery-backed CMOS memory chips, for example, can keep the calendar, date, and time current even when the computer is off. The flash memory chips that store a computer's start-up information often use CMOS technology.

Memory Access Times

Access time is the amount of time it takes the processor to read data, instructions, and information from memory. A computer's access time directly affects how fast the computer processes data. For example, accessing data in memory can be more than 200,000 times faster than accessing data on a hard disk because of the mechanical motion of the hard disk.

Today's manufacturers use a variety of terminology to state access times (Table 6-2). Some use fractions of a second, which for memory occurs in nanoseconds. A *nanosecond* (abbreviated *ns*) is one billionth of a second. A nanosecond is extremely fast (Figure 6-15). In fact, electricity travels about one foot in a nanosecond.

10 million operations = 1 blink

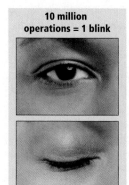

Figure 6-15 It takes about one-tenth of a second to blink your eye, in which time a computer can perform some operations 10 million times.
© iStockphoto / drbimages;
© iStockphoto / drbimages

Table 6-2	Access Time Terminology	
Term	**Abbreviation**	**Speed**
Millisecond	ms	One-thousandth of a second
Microsecond	μs	One-millionth of a second
Nanosecond	ns	One-billionth of a second
Picosecond	ps	One-trillionth of a second

 CONSIDER THIS

What if a manufacturer states access times in megahertz instead of fractions of a second?
Some manufacturers state access times in MHz; for example, 800 MHz DDR2 SDRAM. If a manufacturer states access time in megahertz, you can convert it to nanoseconds by dividing 1 billion ns by the megahertz number. For example, 800 MHz equals approximately 1.25 ns (1,000,000,000/800,000,000). The higher the megahertz, the faster the access time; conversely, the lower the nanoseconds, the faster the access time.

While access times of memory greatly affect overall computer performance, manufacturers and retailers often list a computer's memory in terms of its size, not its access time. For example, an advertisement might describe a computer as having 8 GB of RAM.

 NOW YOU SHOULD KNOW

Be sure you understand the material presented in the sections titled Cloud Computing, Data Representation, and Memory, as it relates to the chapter objectives.
Now you should know . . .

- Which cloud computing service is best suited to your needs (Objective 5)
- How your computers and mobile devices represent data (Objective 6)
- How memory on your computer or mobile device works with your programs and applications (Objective 7)
- When you are using RAM, cache, ROM, flash memory, and CMOS (Objective 8)

Discover More: Visit this chapter's premium content for practice quiz opportunities.

Adapters

Although the circuitry in many of today's computers integrates all the necessary functionality, some require additional capabilities in the form of adapters. Desktops and servers use adapter cards; mobile computers use USB adapters. Read How To 6-4 to learn about ports you might consider including in a computer or mobile device that can eliminate the need for adapters.

 HOW TO 6-4

Determine Which Ports You Need on a Computer or Mobile Device
When purchasing a computer or mobile device, it is important to make sure it has the correct ports so that you can connect your peripheral devices. The following list will help identify the ports you need on a computer or mobile device.

- **Displays:** If you plan to connect your computer or mobile device to a display such as a monitor or projector, make sure your computer or mobile device has a port that is compatible with the display. For example, if you plan to connect a laptop to a monitor that has an HDMI port, your computer or mobile device should have a port capable of HDMI output.

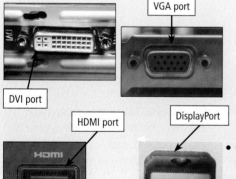

DVI port

VGA port

HDMI port

DisplayPort

- **Networking:** If you plan to connect your computer or mobile device to a wired computer network, it should have an Ethernet port to which you can connect network cables.

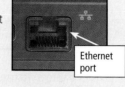
Ethernet port

- **Audio:** If you plan to connect your computer or mobile device to an audio output device, such as speakers, head-phones, or earbuds, your computer or mobile device should have a port for audio output. If you are connecting an external microphone or other device that provides audio, your computer or mobile device should have a port for audio input.

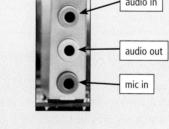
audio in

audio out

mic in

- **Other Input, Output, and Storage Devices:** If you plan to connect other devices, such as a keyboard, mouse, external hard drive, or printer, look at the

cable that connects this device to the computer, and make sure your computer has a port that will accept the connector on the cable. In many cases, these devices will connect to your computer using a USB connection. Make sure your computer has a sufficient number of USB ports to support the devices you want to connect. If you are unable to connect a computer with enough USB ports, you can purchase a USB hub.

USB ports

If your computer or mobile device does not have the ports you need, you may be able to purchase an adapter that converts an existing port to one that can connect to the desired device.

Consider This: In addition to the devices discussed in this box, what other devices might you connect to your computer or mobile device?

© paulrommer / Shutterstock.com; © iStockphoto / Günay Mutlu; © WitthayaP / Shutterstock.com; © ludinko / Shutterstock.com; © WitthayaP / Shutterstock.com; © ludinko / Shutterstock.com

Adapter Cards
An **adapter card**, sometimes called an *expansion card* or *adapter board*, is a circuit board that enhances the functions of a component of a desktop or server system unit and/or provides connections to peripheral devices. An **expansion slot** is a socket on a desktop or server motherboard that can hold an adapter card. Figure 6-16 shows some adapter cards in expansion slots on a desktop motherboard.

Two popular adapter cards are sound cards and video cards. A *sound card* enhances the sound-generating capabilities of a personal computer by allowing sound to be input through a

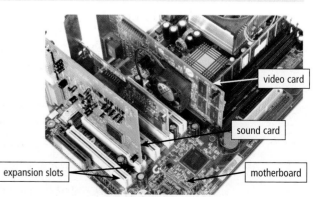
video card

sound card

expansion slots

motherboard

Figure 6-16 Cards inserted in expansion slots on a desktop motherboard.
© Olga Lipatova / Shutterstock.com

microphone and output through external speakers or headphones. A *video card*, also called a *graphics card*, converts computer output into a video signal that travels through a cable to the monitor, which displays an image on the screen. Table 6-3 identifies the purpose of some adapter cards. Sometimes, all functionality is built in the adapter card. With others, a cable connects the adapter card to a device, such as a digital video camera, outside the computer.

Today's computers support **Plug and Play** technology, which means the computer automatically can recognize peripheral devices as you install them. Plug and Play support means you can plug in a device and then immediately begin using it. Read Secure IT 6-5 for issues related to Plug and Play technology.

Table 6-3 Adapter Cards

Type	Purpose
Bluetooth	Enables Bluetooth connectivity
MIDI	Connects to musical instruments
Modem	Connects to transmission media, such as cable television lines or phone lines
Network	Provides network connections, such as to an Ethernet port
Sound	Connects to speakers or a microphone
TV tuner	Allows viewing of digital television broadcasts on a monitor
USB	Connects to high-speed USB ports
Video	Provides enhanced graphics capabilities, such as accelerated processing or the ability to connect a second monitor
Video capture	Connects to a video camera

SECURE IT 6-5

Plug and Play Security Flaws

Plug and Play technology allows your computer to recognize peripheral devices and begin using them immediately after they are installed. This support permits computers to connect and communicate with devices easily, but it also creates security flaws that allow hackers to take control of security systems, routers, Smart TVs, printers, webcams, and other devices connected to the Internet.

According to Rapid7, a security firm that uncovered these defects, between 40 and 50 million devices are susceptible to remote attacks. Rapid7 has developed a scanner tool to check vulnerabilities and identify affected hardware. Security experts recommend turning off or disabling any Plug and Play device not being used on a network that accesses the Internet.

Consider This: Would you consider checking your home network to discover Plug and Play security weaknesses or disabling devices? What steps can manufacturers take to minimize these vulnerabilities?

USB Adapters

Because of their smaller size, mobile computers typically do not have expansion slots. Instead, users can purchase a **USB adapter**, which is a dongle that plugs into a USB port, enhances functions of a mobile computer, and/or provides connections to peripheral devices (Figure 6-17). USB adapters can be used to add memory, communications, multimedia, security, and storage capabilities to mobile computers. A USB flash drive is a common USB adapter that provides computers and mobile devices with additional storage capability as long as it is plugged in. Read Ethics & Issues 6-3 to consider whether manufacturers should eliminate proprietary connectors.

Unlike adapter cards that require you to open the system unit and install the card on the motherboard, you can change a removable flash memory device without having to open the system unit or restart the computer. This feature, called *hot plugging*, allows you to insert and remove a device while the computer is running (be sure, though, to stop or eject the device before removing it).

Should Manufacturers Eliminate Proprietary Connectors?

If you need to replace the cable that connects your mobile device to a USB port, you might have a choice of many makes, models, and prices. Some devices, however, require the use of proprietary connectors, limiting your options to those manufacturers who make connectors that match the port on your mobile device.

When Apple released the iPhone 5 in 2012, for example, it required the use of a proprietary connector that was incompatible with connectors used with prior iPhone models and other Apple devices. Apple developed the connector, called Lightning,

in part to eliminate problems caused by attempts to attach the cord the wrong way. With Lightning, users can attach the cord in either direction without causing damage to the port or device. Critics argue that requiring customers to purchase proprietary connectors increases the cost of purchasing or upgrading a mobile device.

The International Electronics Commission (IEC) is working with major technology providers to make micro USB the universal connector standard used to charge mobile devices. This type of universal standard has several advantages. It will save customers money because they will not have to purchase a new connector with their new

device, even if it is a different brand. A universal standard connector also will enable users with different device models to share connectors. The environment will benefit because fewer outdated or incompatible cords will find their way into landfills. Further, the manufacturing process will generate less waste because fewer cords will be required.

Consider This: Should customers pressure manufacturers to use a universal connector standard? Why or why not? Would you consider the connector type when purchasing a new phone? Why or why not?

Figure 6-17 A USB adapter inserts into a USB port on a computer or mobile device.
© vetkit / Shutterstock.com; © vetkit / Shutterstock.com

Buses

As explained earlier in this chapter, a computer processes and stores data as a series of electronic bits. These bits transfer internally within the circuitry of the computer along electrical channels. Each channel, called a **bus**, allows the various devices both inside and attached to the system unit to communicate with one another. Just as vehicles travel on a highway to move from one destination to another, bits travel on a bus (Figure 6-18).

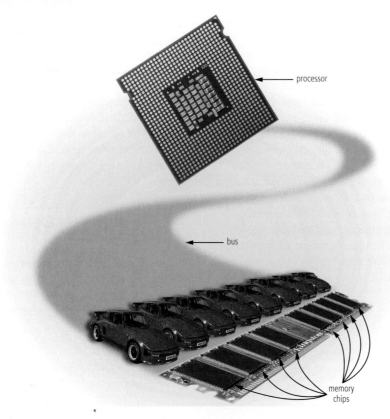

Buses are used to transfer bits from input devices to memory, from memory to the processor, from the processor to memory, and from memory to output or storage devices. Buses consist of a data bus and an address bus. The *data bus* is used to transfer actual data, and the *address bus* is used to transfer information about where the data should reside in memory.

Bus Width

The size of a bus, called the *bus width*, determines the number of bits that the computer can transmit at one time. For example, a 32-bit bus can transmit 32 bits (4 bytes) at a time. On a 64-bit bus, bits transmit from one location to another 64 bits (8 bytes) at a time. The larger the number of bits handled by the bus, the faster the computer transfers data. Using the highway analogy again, assume that one lane on a highway can carry one bit. A 32-bit bus is like a 32-lane highway. A 64-bit bus is like a 64-lane highway.

If a number in memory occupies 8 bytes, or 64 bits, the computer must transmit it in two separate steps when using a 32-bit bus: once for the first 32 bits and once for the second 32 bits.

Figure 6-18 Just as vehicles travel on a highway, bits travel on a bus. Buses are used to transfer bits from input devices to memory, from memory to the processor, from the processor to memory, and from memory to output or storage devices.
© divgradcurl / Shutterstock.com; © Cengage Learning

Using a 64-bit bus, the computer can transmit the number in a single step, transferring all 64 bits at once. The wider the bus, the fewer number of transfer steps required and the faster the transfer of data. Most personal computers today use a 64-bit bus.

In conjunction with the bus width, many computer professionals refer to a computer's word size. **Word size** is the number of bits the processor can interpret and execute at a given time. That is, a 64-bit processor can manipulate 64 bits at a time. Computers with a larger word size can process more data in the same amount of time than computers with a smaller word size. In most computers, the word size is the same as the bus width.

 CONSIDER THIS

How is bus speed measured?
Every bus also has a clock speed. Just like the processor, manufacturers state the clock speed for a bus in hertz. The higher the bus clock speed, the faster the transmission of data, which results in programs running faster.

Types of Buses

A computer has a system bus, possibly a backside bus, and an expansion bus.

- A *system bus*, also called the *front side bus* (*FSB*), is part of the motherboard and connects the processor to main memory.
- A *backside bus* (*BSB*) connects the processor to cache.
- An *expansion bus* allows the processor to communicate with peripheral devices.

When computer professionals use the term, bus, by itself, they usually are referring to the system bus.

Power Supply and Batteries

Many personal computers plug in standard wall outlets, which supply an alternating current (AC) of 115 to 120 volts. This type of power is unsuitable for use with a computer or mobile device, which requires a direct current (DC) ranging from 5 to more than 15 volts. The **power supply** or laptop AC adapter converts the wall outlet AC power into DC power (Figure 6-19). Different motherboards and computers require different wattages on the power supply. If a power supply is not providing the necessary power, the computer will not function properly.

desktop power supply

laptop AC adapter

Figure 6-19 Examples of desktop power supply and laptop AC adapter.
© robootb / Shutterstock.com; © iStockphoto / Freer Law

Built into the power supply is a fan that keeps the power supply cool. Some have variable speed fans that change speed or stop running, depending on temperature in the case. Many newer computers have additional fans near certain components in the system unit, such as the processor, hard drive, and ports. Some users install more fans to help dissipate heat generated by the components of the computer.

✹ CONSIDER THIS

How many fans are in a desktop case?
Most have at least three fans: one in the power supply, one in the case, and one on the processor heat sink. In addition, you also might find a fan on a video card or other adapter card. While some computers contain fans that are designed to be quiet or operate in quiet mode, others allow you to turn off noisy fans until they are needed. You also can purchase programs that slow or stop the fan until the temperature reaches a certain level.

Some external peripheral devices, such as a cable modem, speakers, or a printer, have an AC adapter, which is an external power supply. One end of the AC adapter plugs in the wall outlet and the other end attaches to the peripheral. The AC adapter converts the AC power into the DC power that the peripheral requires, and also often charges the battery in a mobile computer or device.

Mobile computers and devices can run using either a power supply or batteries. The batteries typically are rechargeable lithium-ion batteries (Figure 6-20). Some mobile devices and computers, such as some ultrathin laptops, do not have removable batteries.

 Internet Research

How effective are solar chargers?

Search for: portable solar charger reviews

Figure 6-20 Rechargeable batteries for mobile computers and devices.
© Thejipen / Dreamstime.com; © Anaken2012 / Dreamstime.com

CONSIDER THIS

How often do batteries for mobile computers and devices need to be replaced?
Battery life depends on usage. While some may last several years, you may need to replace a battery much sooner than that. When the battery no longer can hold a charge, you should replace it with a battery made by, or recommended by, the manufacturer of the computer or device. Read Ethics & Issues 6-4 to consider issues surrounding mobile phone policies.

ETHICS & ISSUES 6-4

Should Businesses Be Allowed to Make Policies Regarding Customer Mobile Phone Use?
Diners who use mobile devices while at a restaurant or moviegoers whose devices make noise or light up an otherwise dark theater can cause distractions and frustrations for employees and other patrons. One deli counter posted a sign that said it would not serve customers until they put away their phone. Another similar business said it would levy an additional charge to anyone using a phone while ordering, stating that "It's rude."

Restaurant owners who want to ban mobile phones insist that "distracted dining" adds considerably to the time a customer spends occupying a table, which results in more time elapsing before the restaurant can seat new customers. Food service may be slower because customers are not promptly reading the menu and deciding on their order. This has prompted many owners to adopt a zero tolerance policy for mobile phone use. One movie theater escorted a patron from the theater for refusing to turn off her phone. The theater argued that the purchase of a ticket, which states that it can refuse service without a refund for anyone causing disturbances, is a contract.

You can expect to see more and more restaurants, movie theaters, and other businesses posting or stating guidelines for use of mobile devices beyond asking customers to silence their devices. Some businesses institute rules that state acceptable use for mobile phones, rather than an outright ban. Many businesses designate mobile phone areas. Others give a discount for patrons who leave devices with the host or front desk. Still others allow use of photography, as long as no flash is involved. One etiquette blogger suggested that patrons dining in a group stack their phones in the middle of the table. Whoever first reaches for his or her phone must pay the entire bill.

Consider This: Do businesses have a right to refuse service or otherwise restrict phone usage by customers? Why or why not? Is it ever acceptable to use a mobile phone in a restaurant or theater? Under what circumstances? Have you ever been negatively affected by another person's inappropriate use of a mobile phone? How did you resolve the problem?

Mini Feature 6-3: Proper Care for Computers and Mobile Devices

Taking proper care of computers and mobile devices not only will help prolong their life, but also will keep them running optimally. Read Mini Feature 6-3 to learn about properly caring for computers and mobile devices.

 **MINI FEATURE 6-3**

Proper Care for Computers and Mobile Devices

Caring for a computer or mobile device requires keeping hardware in good condition and maintaining programs and apps.

Hardware Maintenance

Before performing any of the following steps to care for your computer or mobile device, turn off and unplug the device from its power source. If the computer or mobile device has a removable battery, you also should remove the battery. All hardware maintenance should be performed in an area that is clean and free from clutter.

- Use a damp cloth to clean the screen gently. Do not use any special cleaners to clean the display, as they may damage the display. Water is sufficient to remove dust and most dirt. Read How To 6-5 for additional ways to protect screens and replace them if necessary.

- If the computer or mobile device has a keyboard, use a can of compressed air to free the keyboard from any dirt and debris that might interfere with the operation of the keys or pose a risk of getting inside the computer or mobile device. When using compressed air, hold the can upright, and not at an angle, when dispensing the air. Holding the can at an angle can cause the can to dispense a very cold liquid instead of air, which can damage components in your computer or mobile device.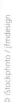

- If you are transporting a laptop, be sure to store it in a case with plenty of padding. If you are using a mobile device, protect it with a case. A case will protect the device better in the event you drop it and may make it easier for you to grip the device while using it.

- If the computer or mobile device has an air vent where a fan removes heat, make sure the vent is free of dust and debris. A blocked vent can prohibit heat from escaping, which ultimately can cause the computer or mobile device to overheat. If the air vent is dirty, contact a trained professional to have it cleaned properly. Improperly cleaning an air vent can result in more debris entering the computer or mobile device.

© Raw Group / Shutterstock.com

- When you insert media such as an optical disc, be sure the media is clean. Inserting dirty media can damage a computer or mobile device's internal components.

Software Maintenance

Maintaining the software on your computers and mobile devices can help them run optimally. While no specific recommendation exists for the frequency with which you should perform the following actions, you should do so if you begin to notice a decline in your computer or mobile device's performance.

- Uninstall programs and remove apps you no longer need on your computer or mobile device. These programs and apps may consume a significant amount of space on your storage medium and decrease the performance of your computer or mobile device. More information about uninstalling programs and removing apps can be found in How To 4-4 in Chapter 4.

- If you are using a desktop or laptop, defragment the computer's hard disk if you notice a decline in the computer's performance. More information about defragmenting can be found in the Disk Defragmenter section in Chapter 4.

- Install programs and apps only from reputable software manufacturers. In addition, make sure you are installing the program or app from the original installation media, the software manufacturer's website, or from your mobile device's app store or marketplace. You also should read reviews for programs and apps before you download and/or install them to make sure the program or app will meet your needs.

Discover More: Visit this chapter's free resources to learn about additional ways to care for your hardware.

✳ **Consider This:** In addition to the methods mentioned in this mini feature, what other ways can you care for your computer or mobile device?

CONSIDER THIS

How does an antistatic wristband work?
When working with electronic components, such as a motherboard, you should wear an antistatic wristband. An *antistatic wristband* is a bracelet designed to protect electronics from an electrostatic discharge by preventing a buildup of static electricity on a user. The wristband has an attached clip that you connect to any bare metal surface, which acts as a ground.

 HOW TO 6-5

Protect and Replace Screens
One way to protect the screen on your mobile device is to use a screen protector. A *screen protector* is a thin plastic film that adheres to the screen of your device. While screen protectors may not protect the screen if you drop your device or an object impacts it with excessive force, it will protect the screen from minor scratches obtained through normal use. Screen protectors often can be purchased from the same place you bought your mobile device and also are available online. If you cannot find a screen protector that is the exact same size as the screen on your mobile device, you can purchase a larger one and then trim it to fit your screen.

In the event the screen on your mobile device breaks, the following steps will guide you through the process of replacing it. Even if your device continues to work with a broken screen, you still should replace it as soon as possible to avoid injury. **NOTE: Screen replacement should be attempted only by advanced users. If you are**
uncomfortable following these steps, seek help from a trained professional. In addition, the exact steps to replace a broken screen can vary with each device. If the steps for your device vary from the steps listed below, follow the instructions from your device's manufacturer.

1. Back up the data on your mobile device before starting a screen replacement. While a successful screen replacement should not threaten the data, it is a good idea to keep a backup in case a problem arises unexpectedly.

2. Turn off the mobile device and disconnect it from all power sources. If the device uses a removable battery, remove it.

3. Protect your hands and eyes before beginning glass replacement.

4. If possible, carefully remove all pieces of broken glass. Consider using compressed air to remove any dust.

5. Remove the display assembly. Refer to your device's documentation for information about removing the display. You may
need a small, nonmagnetic screwdriver and/or metal or plastic tool to remove the assembly. If the display assembly is connected to the mobile device with a cable, carefully disconnect the cable.

6. Unpack the new screen and connect it to the mobile device, connecting any necessary cables.

7. Reassemble the mobile device, reconnect the power source and/or the battery, and turn on the device.

 Consider This: Why might you replace a cracked screen instead of replacing the entire mobile device?

iStockPhoto / deepblue4you

 NOW YOU SHOULD KNOW

Be sure you understand the material presented in the sections titled Adapters, Buses, and Power Supply and Batteries, as it relates to the chapter objectives.
Now you should know . . .

- When you would use an adapter card and a USB adapter (Objective 9)

- How your computer uses buses (Objective 10)

- Why your computers and mobile devices need power supplies or batteries (Objective 11)

- How to care for your computers and mobile devices (Objective 12)

Discover More: Visit this chapter's premium content for practice quiz opportunities.

Chapter Summary

This chapter presented the various components inside computers and mobile devices. It discussed types of processors, steps in a machine cycle, and processor cooling methods. You learned about advantages and services of cloud computing. The chapter discussed how memory stores data and described various types of memory. You learned about adapters, buses, power supplies and batteries, and ways to care for computers and mobile devices.

Discover More: Visit this chapter's free resources for additional content that accompanies this chapter and also includes these features: Technology Innovators: Intel and Gordon Moore, AMD, Nvidia, and VMware; Technology Trends: Medical Robotics and Self-Driving Cars; and High-Tech Talks: How Data is Written to RAM and Coding Schemes and Number Systems.

Test your knowledge of chapter material by accessing the Study Guide, Flash Cards, and Practice Test resources from your smartphone, tablet, laptop, or desktop.

⚡ TECHNOLOGY @ WORK

📃 Publishing

Today, virtually any printed material that you read exists additionally in electronic form. In publishing's early years, and before computers existed, authors and writers recorded content using a typewriter, which then would be duplicated and bound into a publication. When word processors were introduced, writers not only could type their work, but also were able to apply basic formatting and check their spelling. While typewriters and word processors performed their tasks adequately, they pale in comparison to the extent to which today's computers and mobile devices have improved the publishing process.

Before computers and other related technological advances, publishing a book would be a very long process. After the authors wrote a manuscript, it was converted into a form that was ready to print; the printing process then could take several weeks to complete. Today, authors can use programs and apps to write material in a format that will require minimal, if any, conversion before it is ready to print.

Many book, magazine, and newspaper publishers are turning away from the print medium and encouraging consumers to read content electronically. In fact, some publishers are turning exclusively to publishing in electronic form and abandoning the print medium altogether. As mentioned previously in this book, you can read book content or magazine and newspaper articles either on the web or using an e-book reader. Content on the web usually is available free or for a fee. For example, some newspapers allow people to read articles for free, while others may charge a digital subscription fee. If you are using an e-book reader, you often have to pay to download and read content, although some items are available for free.

Programs and apps, including web apps, also are enabling individuals to publish content themselves. Individuals easily can publish content to a blog on the web, or they can use an app to create and publish an e-book for others to purchase and download.

Many libraries also are taking advantage of advances in technology by enabling users to check out books electronically. Similar to a print book, library patrons can reserve an e-book on their computer or mobile device. When the e-book is available, it will download to the user's computer or mobile device automatically. When the e-book is due or when the user decides to return the book, it will remove itself from the user's computer or mobile device. While many people believe that libraries can check out unlimited copies of the same e-book simultaneously, this is not true. Libraries are able to check out simultaneously only the number of copies, or licenses, of the e-book they purchase. For example, if a library purchases two licenses of an e-book, only two copies of that e-book can be checked out simultaneously. If a third user wants to check out this e-book, he or she must wait for one copy to be returned.

Technology has greatly improved the publishing industry. Not only is content published more quickly and in an easily accessible form, but it also now is less prone to errors because the development process is much more streamlined.

✴ **Consider This:** In what other ways do computers and technology play a role in the publishing industry?

Study Guide

The Study Guide exercise reinforces material you should know for the chapter exam.

Discover More: Visit this chapter's premium content to **test your knowledge of digital content** associated with this chapter and **access the Study Guide resource** from your smartphone, tablet, laptop, or desktop.

Instructions: Answer the questions below using the format that helps you remember best or that is required by your instructor. Possible formats may include one or more of these options: write the answers; create a document that contains the answers; record answers as audio or video using a webcam, smartphone, or portable media player; post answers on a blog, wiki, or website; or highlight answers in the book/e-book.

1. Describe the hardware referred to by the terms, system unit and chassis.

2. Name the typical location of the case for a laptop, slate tablet, convertible tablet, smartphone, game console, wearable device, portable media player, digital camera, and handheld game device.

3. List products for securing and tracking hardware and how each is used.

4. Define the terms, motherboard, chip, integrated circuit, and transistor.

5. Describe the purpose of the processor and how multi- and single-core processors differ.

6. Describe how a chip can be used to locate a lost animal.

7. Explain the role of the control unit and ALU in performing computer operations.

8. Describe what happens during each step in the machine cycle.

9. Define these terms: registers, system clock, and superscalar. Describe how clock speed is measured.

10. List two leading manufacturers of personal computer processor chips. List considerations when choosing a processor.

11. List technologies that processor chips often include.

12. List options for cooling a processor, and describe how each works.

13. Define the term, Internet of Things (IoT). List IoT-enabled devices and technologies.

14. Describe issues related to access and privacy regarding IoT.

15. Explain why a home or business user might choose cloud computing. Describe services offered with cloud computing.

16. Human speech is ___ because it uses continuous (wave form) signals that vary in strength and quality. Most computers are ____, meaning that they recognize only two discrete states: on and off.

17. Define the terms, bit and byte. Describe the binary system and the ASCII coding scheme.

18. List categories of items stored in memory. Explain how manufacturers state memory size.

19. Differentiate between volatile and nonvolatile memory. List an example of each.

20. Describe how RAM works. List two types of RAM.

21. Explain how to determine memory requirements.

22. Describe the function of a memory module. List two types of memory modules.

23. List the steps to install memory modules.

24. Describe how a computer uses cache. Differentiate among L1, L2, and L3 cache.

25. Describe what is stored in ROM. ____ are ROM chips that contain permanently written data, instructions, or information.

26. Explain if a company is responsible for using components manufactured using fair trade practices.

27. Identify uses for flash memory.

28. List methods to wipe the memory of a mobile device when recycling or selling.

29. Describe CMOS technology and its possible uses.

30. Define the term, access time. List different methods used to state access time.

31. Identify the port options for computers and mobile devices. Explain the function of each type.

32. Describe the purpose of an adapter card and the role of an expansion slot. List types of adapter cards.

33. Explain Plug and Play technology.

34. List security concerns regarding Plug and Play technology.

35. Describe the functions of USB adapters.

36. Explain the advantages of using a universal standard connector.

37. Define the term, hot plugging.

38. Identify the role of a bus. Differentiate between a data bus and an address bus.

39. Describe how bus width and word size affect and are used to measure computer speed.

40. List types of buses and describe the purpose of each.

41. Explain how a power supply converts AC current into DC current.

42. Explain the purpose of and roles of fans in power supplies.

43. Describe issues surrounding use of mobile devices in restaurants or movie theatres.

44. Explain how to maintain hardware and software on your computer or mobile device.

45. A(n) ____ wristband is a bracelet designed to protect electronics from an electrostatic discharge by preventing a buildup of static electricity on a user.

46. List steps and precautions to take when replacing the screen on a mobile device.

47. Identify how technology is used in the publishing industry.

You should be able to define the Primary Terms and be familiar with the Secondary Terms listed below.

Key Terms

Discover More: Visit this chapter's premium content to **view definitions for each term** and to **access the Flash Cards resource** from your smartphone, tablet, laptop, or desktop.

Primary Terms   (shown in **bold-black** characters in the chapter)

access time (296)
adapter card (297)
analog (288)
arithmetic logic unit
   (281)
binary system (288)
bit (288)
bus (299)
byte (288)

cache (293)
central processing unit
   (CPU) (280)
chip (278)
clock speed (283)
control unit (281)
digital (283)
eCycling (297)
expansion slot (297)

firmware (294)
flash memory (295)
gigahertz (GHz) (283)
memory (290)
memory cache (294)
motherboard (278)
multi-core processor
   (280)
Plug and Play (298)

power supply (301)
processor (280)
RAM (290)
read-only memory
   (ROM) (294)
system clock (282)
USB adapter (298)
word size (300)

Secondary Terms   (shown in *italic* characters in the chapter)

adapter board (297)
address (290)
address bus (300)
advanced transfer cache (ATC) (294)
alphanumeric characters (289)
ALU (281)
antistatic wristband (304)
arithmetic operations (281)
ASCII (289)
backside bus (BSB) (300)
binary digit (288)
bus width (300)
*Cellular Seizure Investigation (CSI)
   stick (295)*
chassis (276)
clock cycle (283)
CMOS (296)
comparison operations (281)
cooling pad (284)
DaaS (data as a service) (288)

data bus (300)
DDR SDRAM (292)
DDR2 (292)
DDR3 (292)
DDR4 (292)
decoding (281)
*DIMM (dual inline memory
   module) (293)*
*dynamic RAM
   (DRAM) (292)*
executing (281)
expansion bus (300)
expansion card (297)
fetching (281)
front side bus (FSB) (300)
gigabyte (GB) (290)
graphics card (298)
heat sink (284)
hertz (283)
hot plugging (298)

*IaaS (infrastructure as a
   service) (287)*
integrated circuit (278)
Intel-compatible processors (283)
Internet of Things (IoT) (284)
L1 cache (294)
L2 cache (294)
L3 cache (294)
liquid cooling technology (284)
machine cycle (281)
main memory (290)
mashups (288)
microprocessor (280)
nanosecond (ns) (296)
nonvolatile memory (290)
PaaS (platform as a service) (288)
random access memory (290)
RDRAM (292)
real-time clock (283)
registers (282)

screen protector (304)
SDRAM (292)
*SIMM (single inline memory
   module) (293)*
software as a service (SaaS) (287)
sound card (297)
static RAM (SRAM) (292)
stored program concept (290)
storing (281)
superscalar (283)
system board (278)
system bus (300)
system unit (276)
terabyte (TB) (290)
transistor (278)
video card (298)
virtual desktop (287)
volatile memory (290)

power supply (301)

Checkpoint

The Checkpoint exercises test your knowledge of the chapter concepts. The page number containing the answer appears in parentheses after each exercise. The Consider This exercises challenge your understanding of chapter concepts.

Discover More: Visit this chapter's premium content to **complete the Checkpoint exercises** interactively; complete the **self-assessment in the Test Prep resource** from your smartphone, tablet, laptop, or desktop; and then **take the Practice Test**.

True/False   True/False Mark T for True and F for False.

_____ 1. The motherboard also is called a system board. (278)

_____ 2. On a personal computer, all functions of the processor usually are on a single chip. (280)

_____ 3. A dual-core processor doubles the processing speed of a single-core processor. (280)

_____ 4. In general, multi-core processors are less energy efficient than separate multiple processors. (280)

_____ 5. The system clock keeps track of the date and time in a computer. (283)

_____ 6. In cloud computing, the back end consists of the servers and storage devices that manage and store the resources accessed by users. (287)

_____ 7. In the binary system, the digit 1 represents the absence of an electronic charge. (288)

_____ 8. Most RAM is nonvolatile. (291)

_____ 9. The processor interprets and executes a program or application's instructions while the program or application is in nonvolatile memory. (291)

_____ 10. ROM chips also are called firmware. (294)

_____ 11. As with processors, manufacturers state the clock speed for a bus in hertz. (300)

_____ 12. The power supply converts the wall outlet AC power into DC power. (301)

Multiple Choice   Select the best answer.

1. The _____ is the main circuit board of the computer. (278)
   a. ALU
   b. CPU
   c. motherboard
   d. system chassis

2. A _____ is a single chip with two or more separate processor cores. (280)
   a. transistor
   b. multi-core processor
   c. resistor
   d. capacitor

3. _____ include basic calculations such as addition, subtraction, multiplication, and division. (281)
   a. Arithmetic operations
   b. Comparison operations
   c. Machine cycles
   d. Transistors

4. In the machine cycle, the _____ operation obtains a program or application instruction or data item from memory. (281)
   a. fetching
   b. decoding
   c. executing
   d. storing

5. The term, _____, describes a computing environment where everyday objects are connected to the Internet. (284)
   a. IoT
   b. DaaS
   c. IaaS
   d. ASCII

6. An aspect of cloud computing that allows developers to create, test, and run their solutions on a cloud platform without having to purchase or configure the underlying hardware and software is known as _____. (288)
   a. DaaS
   b. IaaS
   c. SaaS
   d. PaaS

7. _____ are applications that incorporate data from multiple providers into a new application. (288)
   a. Plug and Play apps
   b. Firmware
   c. Mashups
   d. DDR2s

8. A(n) _____ is a circuit board that enhances the functions of a component of a desktop or server system unit and/or provides connections to peripheral devices. (297)
   a. expansion slot
   b. USB adapter
   c. front side bus
   d. adapter card

Checkpoint

Matching   Match the terms with their definitions.

_____ 1. motherboard (278)

_____ 2. chip (278)

_____ 3. transistor (278)

_____ 4. control unit (281)

_____ 5. registers (282)

_____ 6. IaaS (287)

_____ 7. ASCII (289)

_____ 8. firmware (294)

_____ 9. bus width (300)

_____ 10. word size (300)

a. small, high-speed storage locations contained in a processor

b. component of the computer that directs and coordinates most of the operations in the computer

c. widely used coding scheme to represent a set of characters

d. the main circuit board of the computer

e. integrated circuit component that acts as an electronic switch that opens or closes the circuit for electrical charges

f. ROM chips that contain permanently written data, instructions, or information

g. determines the number of bits that the computer can transmit at one time

h. the use of software to emulate hardware capabilities, enabling computers to scale, or adjust up or down, storage, processing power, or bandwidth as needed

i. small piece of semiconducting materials, usually silicon, on which integrated circuits are etched

j. number of bits the processor can interpret and execute at a given time

✳ Consider This   Answer the following questions in the format specified by your instructor.

1. Answer the critical thinking questions posed at the end of these elements in this chapter: Ethics & Issues (286, 295, 299, 302), How To (283, 292, 293, 297, 304), Mini Features (285, 287, 303), Secure IT (279, 280, 286, 295, 298), and Technology @ Work (305).

2. Where is the typical location of the case on a laptop, tablet, smartphone, game console, wearable device, portable media player, digital camera, and handheld game device? (276)

3. How does tracking software help secure hardware? (279)

4. What is meant by the term, microprocessor? (280)

5. What are the two components contained in the processor? (281)

6. How do arithmetic operations and comparison operations differ? (281)

7. What are the four operations performed during the machine cycle? (281)

8. What are registers? (282)

9. In addition to the clock speed, what other factors influence the computer's performance? (283)

10. What does the term superscalar mean, with regard to the clock cycle? (283)

11. What is clock speed? (283)

12. What is a heat sink? (284)

13. How does a cooling pad reduce the heat generated by a computer? (284)

14. How might the Internet of Things (IoT) invade privacy? (286)

15. In reference to cloud computing, what do the front end and back end include, respectively? (287)

16. What is the binary system? (289)

17. How do volatile and nonvolatile memory differ? (290)

18. Which type of memory is RAM? (291)

19. How do DRAM and SRAM chips differ? (292)

20. What are the two types of memory modules? (293)

21. How do L1, L2, and L3 cache differ? (294)

22. What is the function of an adapter card? (297)

23. What does Plug and Play allow you to do? (298)

24. Should a universal connector standard be adopted? Why or why not? (299)

25. How does bus width measure a computer's processing speed? (300)

26. How does the data bus differ from the address bus? (300)

27. What are three types of buses? (300)

✳ Problem Solving

The Problem Solving exercises extend your knowledge of chapter concepts by seeking solutions to practical problems with technology that you may encounter at home, school, work, or with nonprofit organizations. The Collaboration exercise should be completed with a team.

Instructions: You often can solve problems with technology in multiple ways. Determine a solution to the problems in these exercises by using one or more resources available to you (such as a computer or mobile device, articles on the web or in print, blogs, podcasts, videos, television, user guides, other individuals, electronics or computer stores, etc.). Describe your solution, along with the resource(s) used, in the format requested by your instructor (brief report, presentation, discussion, blog post, video, or other means).

Personal

1. **No Matching Port** Your uncle has given you a new monitor for your computer. When you attempt to connect it, you notice that none of the ports on the back of your computer is able to accept the connector at the end of the monitor's cable. What are your next steps?

2. **Incompatible Power Adapter** While using your laptop, you notice the battery life is running low. When you plug in the AC adapter that was included with the laptop, an error message is displayed stating that the AC adapter is incompatible. You unplug the AC adapter and plug it back in, but the same message keeps appearing. Why might this be happening?

© iStockphoto / Freer Law

3. **Nonworking Fan** Each time you turn on your computer, you hear the noise generated by the fans in the system unit. Recently, however, you turned on the computer and noticed that the noise was not as loud and that the fan in the back of the system unit was not spinning. What are your next steps?

4. **Missing Smartphone** You have just returned from the mall and seem to have forgotten your smartphone. You checked all over your house and your car, and it is nowhere to be found. What are your next steps?

5. **Low Battery Life** You have had your laptop for more than one year and notice that your battery is losing its charge more quickly than normal. What are some ways you can conserve battery life so that your smartphone does not lose its charge as quickly?

Professional

6. **Determining Memory Requirements** Your computer has been running slowly and you suspect it is because it is low on memory. You review the computer's hardware configuration and find that the computer has only 4 GB of RAM. How can you determine how much memory your computer should have to run properly?

7. **Selecting the Right Processor** Your boss has given you permission to purchase a new processor for your aging desktop computer, but many models are available. What steps will you take to make sure you purchase the processor that is best for you?

8. **Plug and Play Error** You have connected an external hard drive to your computer so that you can back up your important files, but the computer is not recognizing the external hard drive when it is connected. What might be wrong?

9. **Internet Access Unavailable** You are using a cloud storage provider to save files you want to use both at work and at home, so that you do not have to carry a USB flash drive back and forth with your files. When you arrive at work, you notice that your Internet connection is unavailable and you are unable to access the files stored on the cloud. What steps can you take to prevent this in the future?

10. **System Password** You started working at a company to replace someone who has just been terminated. When you turn on your computer, which previously was used by the terminated employee, the computer immediately asks for a system password. You do not know the password but need to access the computer so that you can start working. What are your next steps?

Collaboration

11. **Technology in Publishing** You have been hired to select employees for the IT (information technology) department in a start-up publishing company. Before you can begin hiring employees, you must familiarize yourself with the technology requirements in the publishing industry. Form a team of three people to compose a plan for creating the IT department. One team member should research the hardware requirements for people working in the publishing industry. Another team member should research the types of software used in this industry, and the third team member should compile a list of interview questions to ask each candidate.

The How To: Your Turn exercises present general guidelines for fundamental skills when using a computer or mobile device and then require that you determine how to apply these general guidelines to a specific program or situation.

How To: Your Turn

Discover More: Visit this chapter's premium content to **challenge yourself with additional How To: Your Turn exercises**, such as App Adventure.

Instructions: You often can complete tasks using technology in multiple ways. Figure out how to perform the tasks described in these exercises by using one or more resources available to you (such as a computer or mobile device, articles on the web or in print, online or program help, user guides, blogs, podcasts, videos, other individuals, trial and error, etc.). Summarize your 'how to' steps, along with the resource(s) used, in the format requested by your instructor (brief report, presentation, discussion, blog post, video, or other means).

❶ Conserve Battery Life of Mobile Computers and Devices

As consumers rely on mobile computers and devices more and more every day, it is increasingly important for the battery life on these devices to support high usage demands. Unfortunately, battery life on these devices often is not sufficient for many users to make it throughout the day with moderate activity on their devices. For this reason, it is important to conserve battery life so that a mobile computer or device can remain functional until it is possible to connect it to a battery charger. The following steps guide you through the process of conserving battery life on mobile computers and devices:

a. When you first obtain a new mobile computer or device or purchase a new battery for your computer or mobile device, charge the battery completely. Most new mobile computers and devices will indicate how long to charge the battery before its first use. Refrain from using the device before the battery is fully charged.

b. Charge the battery only when it is drained completely. Many batteries on computers and mobile devices can be charged only a certain number of times before they fail completely. For this reason, you should charge batteries only when absolutely necessary.

c. When you charge your mobile computer or device, try not to unplug the battery charger until the battery is charged completely.

d. Use the battery charger supplied with the mobile computer or device. Connecting inexpensive battery chargers from other vendors may damage the battery.

e. If you want to use the mobile computer or device while it is plugged in to an external power source, remove the battery, if possible, if it is fully charged. Leaving the mobile computer or device connected to an external power source while the battery has a full charge can shorten the life of the battery.

f. If you are using a laptop or tablet, disable Wi-Fi and Bluetooth unless you are using them.

g. Adjust the display's brightness. Brighter displays consume more battery life, so keep the display as dim as you can without having to strain your eyes.

h. Download and install an app that will inform you which other apps are running and consuming battery life. If an app does not need to run, you should exit it so that the app does not consume your battery.

i. Avoid turning your mobile computer or device on and off multiple times per day. The power-saving features on mobile computers and devices often require less power than turning on your computer or mobile device from a powered-off state.

j. Turn off automatic app update capabilities on your phone or mobile device, so that your device is not constantly checking for new apps and downloading them to your device.

Exercises

1. What other ways can you think of to conserve the battery life on your mobile computer or device?
2. Approximately how long do batteries on your mobile computers and devices last before they no longer are able to hold a charge?
3. What else can shorten the battery life on a mobile computer or device?

© Thejipen / Dreamstime.com; © Anaken2012 / Dreamstime.com

❷ Locate a Lost Mobile Computer or Device

Mobile computers and devices sometimes contain a feature that can help you locate it in the event you lose it. If the device does not contain this feature, you may be able to download and install an app that can help you track its location. The following steps guide you through the process of locating a lost mobile computer or device.

✷ How To: Your Turn

a. Before you lose or misplace a mobile computer or device, enable the feature that allows you to track its location remotely.

b. Make sure the GPS feature on your device is enabled. If GPS is not enabled, the device might be more difficult to locate.

c. If you lose your smartphone, try calling it to see if someone answers. He or she may have located your misplaced phone. If nobody answers, send it a text message inquiring about the phone's location.

d. If you lose a device, you can run an app or navigate to a website that will enable you to track the device's location. The device's location typically will be displayed on a map and include the approximate address.

e. If the device is in an unfamiliar location, use a service such as Google Maps to obtain driving directions to the location.

f. If the device is in a location other than where you originally lost it, exercise extreme caution while trying to retrieve your device. You might consider contacting a local law enforcement agency to accompany you while trying to retrieve your device.

g. If you are unable to track your device using the above suggestions, consider contacting your mobile service provider to see if they have a way to locate the device.

© iStockPhoto / Krystian Nawrocki

Exercises

1. What privacy concerns might arise as a result of keeping the GPS feature on a device enabled?

2. What are names of some apps that can help you track your device's location in the event it is lost or stolen?

3. In addition to GPS, what other ways might you be able to determine your device's location?

❸ Run Diagnostic Tools and Check for Computer Hardware Errors

If your computer is not functioning properly and you believe the problem is related to the computer's hardware, you can run diagnostic tools to check for hardware errors. If the diagnostic tool identifies a hardware error, you then can communicate information about the error to technical support personnel so that they either can correct the problem or suggest replacing the problematic hardware. The following

steps guide you through the process of running diagnostic tools and checking for hardware errors.

Obtain Diagnostic Tools

Your computer may have included diagnostic tools you can use to check for hardware errors. If it did not include diagnostic tools, follow these steps to download diagnostic tools from the computer manufacturer's website:

a. Navigate to the computer manufacturer's website.

b. Tap or click the necessary links to display information about the computer.

c. Tap or click the link to display a page containing drivers and/or downloads for the computer's model.

d. Browse for a diagnostic tool that you can download to your computer.

e. Some diagnostic tools can run within the operating system, and some require that you copy them to an optical disc or USB flash drive so that you can start the computer from this media and run the diagnostic tools. If necessary, copy the diagnostic tools to an optical disc or USB flash drive.

Run Diagnostic Tools

a. Run the program containing the diagnostic tools. If you copied the diagnostic tools to an optical disc or USB flash drive, restart the computer with the optical disc or USB flash drive inserted, and be sure to select the option to boot (start) from that device.

b. Select the option to scan all computer hardware for errors.

c. Begin the scan. Please note that because the program is scanning all hardware, it may take some time to complete. Some specific tests during the scan will require input from you, so watch the computer closely while the scan is in progress.

d. When the scan is complete, note any errors and, if desired, report them to the computer manufacturer's technical support team.

e. When the scan is complete, if necessary, restart the computer.

Exercises

1. What might cause you to use diagnostic tools to scan a computer for hardware errors?

2. After scanning your computer for hardware errors, were any found?

3. In addition to downloading drivers from the computer manufacturer's website, are there any other websites offering tools to help you diagnose your computer hardware problems? If so, what are some?

How To: Your Turn

4 Determine How Much Memory Is Being Used on Your Computer or Mobile Device

If your computer or mobile device is running slowly, it could be running low on memory. A number of factors can contribute to the slow performance, but checking the memory usage is fast and easy. If the computer or mobile device's memory is almost all used, you may be able to determine which programs and apps are using the most memory. Exiting these programs and apps may make more memory available and increase a computer or mobile device's performance. The following steps guide you through the process of determining how much memory is being used on a computer or mobile device.

a. Restart the computer or mobile device.

b. If necessary, sign in to the operating system.

c. Navigate to the window or screen showing a list of running tasks. On a computer, you may be able to search for the Task Manager or Activity Monitor. On a mobile device, a list of running processes may be found in the system settings.

d. Tap or click the option to show the list of running processes. This list will show you how much memory each process is using. This list also includes the programs and apps currently running. If you notice that a program or app is consuming a high amount of memory, consider exiting the program or app to make the memory available.

e. When you are finished, return to the desktop or home screen.

Source: Microsoft

Exercises

1. How much memory is installed on your computer or mobile device? How much currently is being used?

2. Which three processes are using the largest amount of memory on your computer or mobile device?

3. If the programs and apps you run consume nearly all available memory on your computer or mobile device, what additional steps might you be able to take?

5 Check Your Computer's Hardware Configuration

If you are experiencing a problem with a hardware component on your computer, you can check the computer's hardware configuration to determine the manufacturer's name and model number for the hardware in question. With this information, you then can search for ways to correct the problem. Alternatively, if you reinstall the operating system on the computer, you may check the computer's hardware configuration to make sure the operating system is recognizing correctly all hardware connected to the computer. The following steps guide you through the process of checking a computer's hardware configuration.

a. If you are using a Mac, display the Apple menu and then select the option to display information about the computer. If you are running Windows, display the Control Panel.

b. Navigate to the area that displays information about the hardware and devices currently connected to the computer. (*Hint:* In Windows, display the Device Manager. On a Mac, display the System Report.)

c. Tap or click the categories of hardware devices to see details related to those types of devices.

d. If you are familiar with the hardware devices on the computer, verify that the operating system is recognizing these devices correctly.

e. If you notice a problem with the operating system detecting any of these devices, you might need to run the installation software and/or install the drivers for the hardware device so that the operating system can communicate with the device. If necessary, contact the computer manufacturer's technical support for assistance.

Exercises

1. List at least three hardware devices listed in the System Report or in the Device Manager.

2. In addition to the reasons mentioned above, what are some other reasons why you might want to check the hardware configuration on a computer?

3. What steps can you take if one or more hardware devices are not identified by your computer?

Source: Microsoft

✳ Internet Research

The Internet Research exercises broaden your understanding of chapter concepts by requiring that you search for information on the web.

Discover More: Visit this chapter's premium content to **challenge yourself with additional Internet Research exercises**, which include Search Sleuth, Green Computing, Ethics in Action, You Review It, and Exploring Technology Careers.

Instructions: Use a search engine or another search tool to locate the information requested or answers to questions presented in the exercises. Describe your findings, along with the search term(s) you used and your web source(s), in the format requested by your instructor (brief report, presentation, discussion, blog post, video, or other means).

1 Making Use of the Web
Content Aggregation and Curation

Locating valuable information to read on particular topics or to share with your online social network may take some effort. To help find material, you may want to use content aggregation, an automated process that uses keywords to gather and filter materials someone else has written or produced on the Internet. Another option is content curation, which is a manual process of acquiring this information and then expanding the content into original and useful material to post. A good content curator can edit the content to share, add annotations and notes, give attributions to the original source, and provide additional viewpoints. As a starting point, Twitter and blog feeds, bookmarking tools such as StumbleUpon, and services that provide email notifications, such as Google Alerts, provide the opportunity to view webpages, photos, videos, and additional material about celebrities, sports, politics, businesses, and other people and subjects.

Research This: (a) Visit StumbleUpon and two other bookmarking services. If necessary, sign in to these services and compare the features. How do users select the categories to view? What information is required to create a profile? What opportunities for feedback are provided? What procedure would users follow to delete their profiles and terminate their accounts?

(b) Visit Google Alerts and two other email alerting services. If necessary, create an alert for at least two words for which you would want to receive email notifications. What options are available to customize these alerts? For example, can you specify the frequency of the alerts, the types of websites to search, the geographical region, or the number of messages sent?

2 Social Media

Companies review the conversations, comments, complaints, and feedback written on online social networks to obtain valuable information that ultimately enhances developing or improving products and services. In some cases, companies have asked consumers to view videos of product demonstrations, Tweet their immediate impressions, and suggest improvements. Small companies with limited marketing and advertising budgets, in particular, increasingly view social media as an inexpensive means of building relationships with and among customers. Social media users interact with others who have similar interests and exchange information about their experiences. In general, companies have found that customers are eager to provide feedback and recommend improvements.

Research This: View at least two automotive websites and describe the social media that are featured. Choose one of the websites and review the content. What topics are being discussed? In which ways is the company encouraging participation, such as by sponsoring contests or providing opportunities for consumers to upload photos and videos? Can consumers create an account to share advice, rate and review vehicles, and discuss mechanical issues?

3 Search Skills
Limiting Search Results by Website, Date, and Location

You can instruct a search engine to look for results on a specific website that match your search text. To do so, in your search text include the operator site: followed by a domain name you would like to search, with no spaces between the colon and the domain name. For example, to read articles from the Cnet website about solid state drives, type the search text, site:cnet.com "solid state drives".

Some search engines provide additional search tools to specify a date range such as the past day, week, or month, to limit your results. Limiting search results by date can help you to find current information because the search engine will return results published during

Source: StumbleUpon

Internet Research ✸

a specified period. Providing a location or ZIP code as search options (beneath the search box) will limit search results to the geographic area you specify. Location search can help you find results for a specific area, such as computer stores in Boise, Idaho.

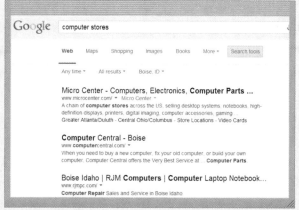

Source: Google

Research This: Create search text using the techniques described above or in previous Search Skills exercises, and type it in a search engine to answer these questions. (1) Find information on Intel's website about core I7 processors that was posted within the past month. (2) Where in your local area can you recycle used computer equipment and electronics? (3) Find reviews of digital cameras posted within the past week. (4) Which laptops reviewed during the past six months have the longest battery life?

4 Security

More than 3 million smartphones are stolen each year, according to a *Consumer Reports* survey. In addition, 1.4 million smartphone users never have recovered a lost phone. Secure IT 6-1 in this chapter describes categories of products that can help secure and track hardware that has been stolen or lost.

Research This: Which apps are available for your smartphone to erase data remotely? Which location-tracking apps allow you to take a photo of the thief and then send an email message that contains the image to you automatically? If your device is lost and you file a police report, you will need the device's serial number. Locate that number now and write it on a piece of paper. Also, locate the phone's 15-digit International Mobile Equipment Identity

(IMEI) number and record that number. Store the document with these two numbers in a secure location. In addition, research the efforts by the U.S. Federal Communications Commission (FCC) and the Cellular Telecommunications Industry Association (CTIA) to create a centralized database of lost and stolen mobile phones. What is the status of this database? What legislation has been proposed or passed that requires wireless carriers and phone manufacturers to develop technological solutions that can curb the growing problem of violent smartphone theft?

5 Cloud Services

Public, Private, Hybrid, and Personal Clouds (IaaS)

When deciding how to host data and apps on the cloud, companies often choose between sharing a server on the cloud with other organizations, configuring a dedicated server on the cloud, or using both options. Companies must consider the type of data involved and the level of security required to keep it safe. Public, private, and hybrid clouds are examples of IaaS (infrastructure as a service), a service of cloud computing that uses a provider's hardware to manage, store and access files and apps over the Internet. On a public cloud, several companies store data or apps on the same physical server on the cloud. On a private cloud, a company has its own servers in the cloud to host its apps and data. On a hybrid cloud, organizations may host confidential data on a private cloud and rely on a public cloud for information that does not require such a high degree of security.

Individual users may set up a personal cloud by purchasing a networked hard drive. A networked hard drive connects directly to a router, providing access to its files over the Internet. This is a useful solution for having access to files from several devices.

Research This: (1) Use a search engine to find IaaS providers that offer public, private, and hybrid cloud solutions. Summarize the different solutions they provide. (2) Under what circumstances might an individual or enterprise set up a public, private, or hybrid cloud? (3) Research networked hard drive models from different manufacturers. Compare their costs, storage sizes, and additional features to consider when creating a personal cloud. (4) When might you create a personal cloud instead of using a cloud storage provider?

Critical Thinking

The Critical Thinking exercises challenge your assessment and decision-making skills by presenting real-world situations associated with chapter concepts. The Collaboration exercise should be completed with a team.

Instructions: Evaluate the situations below, using personal experiences and one or more resources available to you (such as articles on the web or in print, blogs, podcasts, videos, television, user guides, other individuals, electronics or computer stores, etc.). Perform the tasks requested in each exercise and share your deliverables in the format requested by your instructor (brief report, presentation, discussion, blog post, video, or other means).

1. Cloud Storage

The owner of the motorcycle repair shop where you work as a part-time office manager is seeking alternatives to using a network server to store and back up files. She asks you to investigate the feasibility of using cloud storage, rather than purchasing additional storage media for the company's computers, mobile devices, and network servers.

Do This: Analyze the advantages and disadvantages of using cloud storage. Include in your discussion security concerns, costs, and a comparison between two different cloud storage offerings. Which company offers the better arrangement? Why? Explore one other area of cloud computing, such as SaaS (software as a service), and determine how the service might benefit the shop. Find three providers of the cloud service and compare prices, user reviews, and features. List the risks and benefits of using the cloud for storage and other services.

2. Upgrading Memory

You are an IT consultant at a bank. An analyst at the bank is complaining that her laptop is performing slowly. You determine that the laptop's memory is insufficient for the complex calculations and reports the analyst is running.

Do This: Search the web to learn more about current memory modules available to increase memory capacity. Evaluate the differences among various options, including type, size, speed, and price. Find articles from industry experts that list methods and recommendations for upgrading a laptop's memory. Also determine how to add memory to a laptop, obtaining answers to the following questions: How can you determine the type and correct amount of memory to add? Why should you not purchase more memory than your computer can support? How do you determine the available slots for memory modules? What safety measures should you take when upgrading memory? Is it better to upgrade the memory or purchase a new laptop?

3. Case Study

Amateur Sports League You are the new manager for a nonprofit amateur soccer league. You recently purchased replacement smartphones for yourself and another employee, along with an upgraded tablet that the staff can use. Because you are discarding the outdated devices, the league's board of directors is concerned about how to secure and protect data when selling, donating, or recycling the devices. The board asked you to prepare information it can use in a press release to educate the league's customers about keeping data secure when discarding a device.

Do This: Determine the possible steps needed to wipe the memory and storage media in the devices. What kind of data is important to delete? Why? What are the risks of not wiping the memory and storage media in a device before you discard it? What responsibility does the league have to protect members' personal data? Why? Does choosing whether to sell, donate, or recycle the devices change your approach and need to wipe the devices' memory? Why or why not?

© mycola / Shutterstock.com

Collaboration

4. **Mobile Device Batteries** You work in the IT department for a large publishing company that just purchased new tablets for all employees. The department manager asked you to prepare information about how to conserve the battery life of the tablets.

Do This: Form a three-member team. Each member of your team should choose a different type of tablet. Find information about the battery life for each device type, including recommendations for use by the manufacturer and user reviews of the device and its chargers. Research apps that track battery life. Search for articles by industry experts that give tips on conserving the battery life of a tablet. Meet with your team, and discuss and compile your findings. Which tablet would you recommend? Why? How does the charger affect the battery life? What did you learn about battery conservation? Which apps would you recommend? Why?

INPUT AND OUTPUT: Extending Capabilities of Computers and Mobile Devices

Users interact with a variety of input and output devices every day.

"After work or school, I video chat with my friends and discuss our gaming strategies. I print photos from my digital camera on my ink-jet printer. I have a wireless speaker system that works with my laptop and phone. What more should I know about input and output?"

While you may be familiar with some of the content in this chapter, do you know how to . . .

- Decide if you should take notes electronically or by hand?
- Use motion and gestures for input?
- Use touch input on various devices?
- Use DV technology?
- Set up and use a webcam or integrated DV camera?
- Prevent unauthorized use of a webcam?
- Improve the quality of scanned documents?
- Scan QR codes safely?
- Prevent electronic pickpockets from obtaining information stored on your credit cards and other personal documents?
- Protect yourself from hardware radiation?
- Show media on a Smart TV from a computer or tablet?
- Print from a smartphone or tablet?
- Acquire assistive technologies for input and output?

In this chapter, you will discover how to perform these tasks along with much more information essential to this course. For additional content available that accompanies this chapter, visit the free resources and premium content. Refer to the Preface and the Intro chapter for information about how to access these and other additional instructor-assigned support materials.

✔ Objectives

After completing this chapter, you will be able to:

1 Differentiate among various types of keyboards: standard, compact, on-screen, virtual, ergonomic, gaming, and wireless

2 Describe characteristics of various pointing devices: mouse, touchpad, and trackball

3 Describe various uses of touch screens

4 Describe various types of pen input: stylus, digital pen, and graphics tablet

5 Describe various uses of motion input, voice input, and video input

6 Differentiate among various scanners and reading devices: optical scanners, optical readers, bar code readers, RFID readers, magstripe readers, MICR readers, and data collection devices

7 Identify the types of output

8 Explain the characteristics of various displays

9 Summarize the various types of printers: ink-jet printers, photo printers, laser printers, all-in-one printers, thermal printers, mobile printers, label printers, plotters and large-format printers, and impact printers

10 Identify the purpose and features of speakers, headphones and earbuds, data projectors, interactive whiteboards, and force-feedback game controllers and tactile output

11 Identify various assistive technology input and output methods

What Is Input?

Input is any data and instructions entered into the memory of a computer. As shown in Figure 7-1, people have a variety of options for entering data and instructions into a computer.

As discussed in Chapter 1, *data* is a collection of unprocessed items, including text, numbers, images, audio, and video. Once data is in memory, a computer or mobile device interprets and executes instructions to process the data into information. Instructions that a computer or mobile device processes can be in the form of software (programs and apps), commands, and user responses.

- *Software* is a series of related instructions, organized for a common purpose, that tells a computer or mobile device what tasks to perform and how to perform them. When software developers write programs or apps, they usually enter the instructions into the computer or mobile device by using a keyboard, mouse, or other input method. The software developer then stores the program in a file that a user can execute (run). When a user runs a program or app, the computer or mobile device loads the program or app from a storage medium into memory. Thus, a program or app is entered into a computer's or mobile device's memory.

- A *command* is an instruction that causes a program or app to perform a specific action. Programs and apps respond to commands that a user issues. Users issue commands by touching an area on a screen, pressing keys on the keyboard, clicking a mouse button to control a pointer on the screen, or speaking into a microphone.

- A *user response* is an instruction a user issues by responding to a message displayed by a program or app. A response to the message instructs the program or app to perform certain actions. For example, when a program or app asks the question, 'Do you want to save the changes made to this file?', and you respond with the instruction of 'Yes', the program will save the file with the changes you made. If you respond with the instruction of 'No', the program will not save your changes before exiting.

Commonly used input methods include the keyboard, pointing devices, touch screens, pen input, motion input, voice input, video input, and scanners and reading devices. This chapter discusses each of these input methods.

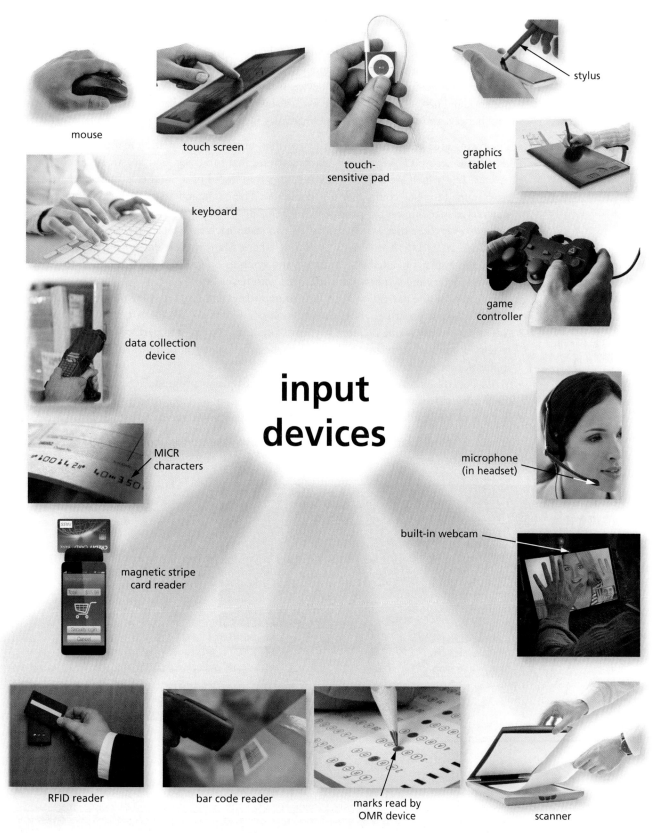

mouse

touch screen

touch-sensitive pad

stylus

graphics tablet

keyboard

game controller

data collection device

input devices

microphone (in headset)

MICR characters

built-in webcam

magnetic stripe card reader

RFID reader

bar code reader

marks read by OMR device

scanner

Figure 7-1 Users can enter data and instructions into computers and mobile devices in a variety of ways.

Keyboards

Most computers and mobile devices include a keyboard or keyboarding capabilities. As discussed in previous chapters, a **keyboard** is an input device that contains keys you press to enter data and instructions into a computer or mobile device. Nearly all keyboards have a typing area, function keys, toggle keys, and navigation keys (Figure 7-2). Many also include media control buttons, Internet control buttons, and other special keys. Others may include a fingerprint reader or a pointing device.

- The typing area includes letters of the alphabet, numbers, punctuation marks, and other basic keys. Read Secure IT 7-1 to learn about software that can track your keystrokes.
- *Function keys*, which are labeled with the letter F followed by a number, are special keys programmed to issue commands to a computer. The command associated with a function key may vary, depending on the program you are using.
- A *toggle key* is a key that switches between two states each time a user presses the key. CAPS LOCK and NUM LOCK are examples of toggle keys. Many mobile devices have keys that toggle the display of alphabetic, numeric, and symbols on touch keyboards in order to display more characters and symbols on a keyboard with fewer keys.
- Users can press the navigation keys, such as arrow keys and PAGE UP/PG UP and PAGE DOWN/ PG DN on the keyboard, to move the insertion point in an application left, right, up, or down.
- A *keyboard shortcut* is one or more keyboard keys that you press to perform an operating system or application-related task. Some keyboard shortcuts are unique to a particular application or operating system.
- Media control buttons allow you to control a media player program, access the computer's optical disc drive, and adjust speaker volume.
- Internet control buttons allow you to run an email application, run a browser, and search the web.

Discover More: Visit this chapter's free resources to learn more about function key commands, toggle keys, and keyboard shortcuts.

⚙ BTW

Insertion Point
The *insertion point*, also known as a *cursor* in some applications, is a symbol on the screen, usually a blinking vertical bar, that indicates where the next character you type will appear.

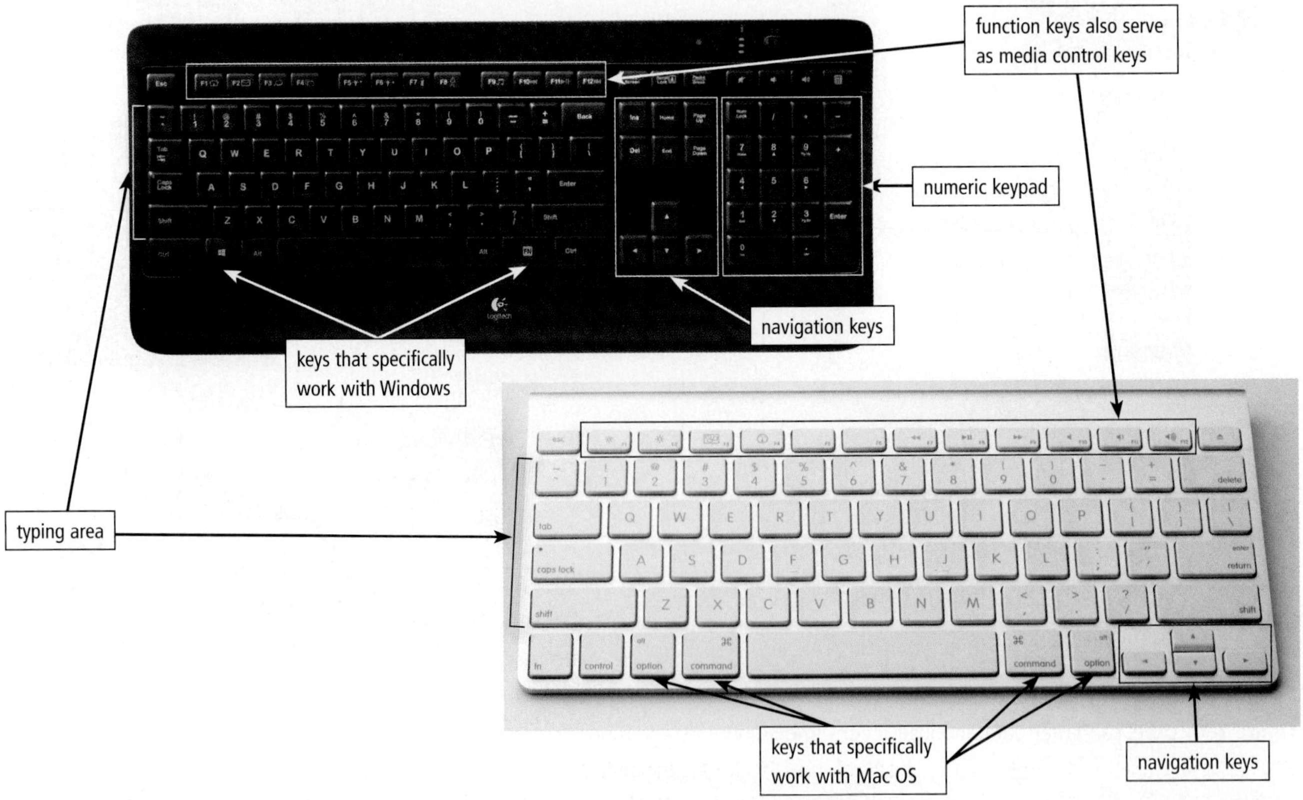

Figure 7-2 On a standard keyboard, you type using keys in the typing area and on the numeric keypad. Some of the keys on standard keyboards differ, depending on the operating system with which they are designed to work.
Courtesy of Logitech; © iStockphoto / Jill Fromer

SECURE IT 7-1

Keyboard Monitoring

Some employers and parents want to monitor everything that has been entered into a computer to ensure that employees and children are using the computer for appropriate purposes. They may use *keyboard monitoring software*, also called *keylogging software*, to accomplish this task. This software runs undetected and stores every keystroke in a file for later retrieval.

These programs have both criminal and beneficial purposes. When used in a positive fashion, employers can measure the efficiency of data entry personnel. This software also can verify that employees are not releasing company secrets, are not viewing personal or inappropriate content on work computers, and are not engaging in activities that could subject the company to harassment, hacking, or other similar charges. Employers sometimes use the software to troubleshoot technical problems and to back up their networks. Parents, likewise, can verify their children are using the home computer safely and are not visiting inappropriate websites. Educators and

researchers can capture students' input to analyze how well they are learning a second language or improving their typing skills. This software also can monitor activity in chat rooms and other similar locations.

When used for malicious purposes, criminals use the programs on both public and private computers to capture user names, passwords, credit card numbers, and other sensitive data and then use this data to access financial accounts and private networks.

Many keylogging programs are available, and they perform a variety of functions. Some simply record keystrokes in a hidden file stored on the hard drive that can be accessed by supplying the correct password. More sophisticated programs record software used, websites visited, and periodic screenshots and then transmit this data to a remote computer.

It can be difficult to locate keylogging software on a computer, but taking these steps may help detect the programs:

- **Run detection software regularly.** Several antivirus and spyware detection programs check for known keylogging programs.

- **Review hard drive files.** Regularly look at the most recent files and note any that are updated continually. These files might be the keylogging software's logs.

- **Check running programs.** Periodically examine which software is loaded from the computer's hard drive into memory when you start the computer and which are running while you are using the computer. If you are uncertain of any program names, perform a search to learn the software's function and if it is a known keylogging program.

💥 **Consider This:** Do you know anyone who has installed keylogging software or who has found keylogging software installed on his or her computer? Is keylogging software an invasion of privacy? Should employers inform employees if the software is installed? Why or why not?

Types of Keyboards

Desktops include a standard keyboard. Standard keyboards typically have from 101 to 105 keys, which include function keys along the top and a numeric keypad on the right (shown in the top keyboard in Figure 7-2).

As discussed in previous chapters, you have a variety of keyboard options for mobile computers and devices (Figure 7-3). These devices often use a *compact keyboard*, which is smaller than a standard keyboard and usually does not include the numeric keypad or navigation keys. Typically, the keys on a compact keyboard serve two or three purposes in order to provide the same functionality as standard keyboards. Some compact keyboards are built into the computer or mobile device and/or are permanently attached with hinges, a sliding mechanism, or some other technique. Other compact keyboards are separate devices that communicate wirelessly or attach to the computer or device with a magnet, clip, or other mechanism. Some users prefer to work with on-screen or virtual keyboards instead of a physical keyboard. Others, however, prefer to use a standard keyboard with their mobile devices because these keyboards provide added functionality and tactile comfort.

built-in laptop keyboard

clip-on tablet keyboard

on-screen keyboards

Figure 7-3   Users have a variety of keyboard options for mobile computers and devices.
© iStockphoto / EricVega; © iStockphoto / pictafolio; Courtesy of Logitech

💥 **CONSIDER THIS**

What is the rationale for the arrangement of keys in the typing area?

The keys originally were arranged on old mechanical typewriters to separate frequently used keys, which caused typists to slow down. This arrangement, called a QWERTY keyboard because the six first letters on the top row of letter keys spell QWERTY, reduced the frequency with which the mechanical levers jammed.

Figure 7-4 An ergonomic keyboard.
© Dmitry Melnikov / Shutterstock.com

An *ergonomic keyboard* has a design that reduces the chance of repetitive strain injuries (RSIs) of wrist and hand (Figure 7-4). Recall that the goal of ergonomics is to incorporate comfort, efficiency, and safety in the design of the workplace. Even keyboards that are not ergonomically designed attempt to offer a user more comfort by including a wrist rest.

A *gaming keyboard* is a keyboard designed specifically for users who enjoy playing games on the computer. Gaming keyboards typically include programmable keys so that gamers can customize the keyboard to the game being played. The keys on gaming keyboards light up so that the keys are visible in all lighting conditions. Some have small displays that show important game statistics, such as time or targets remaining.

 Internet Research

How prevalent are RSIs?

Search for: rsi statistics

 CONSIDER THIS

Why use a wireless keyboard?
Although some keyboards connect via a cable to a USB port on the computer, some users choose a wireless keyboard to eliminate the clutter of a cord and/or to free USB ports for other uses. A *wireless keyboard* is a battery-powered device that transmits data to the computer or mobile device using wireless technology. For example, Bluetooth keyboards are especially popular with tablets because they do not require a USB port and are easy to pair with computers and devices. Many vendors offer tablet cases with a built-in Bluetooth keyboard so that you easily can transport a keyboard with the tablet.

BTW

Technology Innovator

Discover More: Visit this chapter's free resources to learn about Logitech, a global company that makes a variety of input and output devices.

Pointing Devices

In a graphical user interface, a **pointer** is a small symbol on the screen whose location and shape change as a user moves a pointing device. A pointing device can enable you to select text, graphics, and other objects, such as buttons, icons, links, and menu commands. The following pages discuss a variety of pointing devices.

Mouse

A **mouse** is a pointing device that fits under the palm of your hand comfortably. As you move a mouse, the pointer on the screen also moves. The bottom of a mouse is flat and contains a mechanism that detects movement of the mouse. Desktop users have an optical mouse or a touch mouse, both of which can be placed on nearly all types of flat surfaces (Figure 7-5).

An *optical mouse* uses optical sensors that emit and sense light to detect the mouse's movement. Similarly, a *laser mouse* uses laser sensors that emit and sense light to detect the mouse's movement. Some mouse devices use a combination of both technologies. The top and sides of an optical or laser mouse may have one to four buttons; some may also have a small wheel. Some are more sensitive than others for users requiring more precision, such as graphic artists, engineers, or game players.

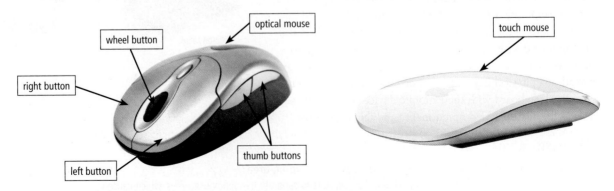

Figure 7-5 An optical mouse has buttons. A touch mouse often has no buttons.
© Anton Derevschuk / Shutterstock.com; Courtesy of Apple, Inc.

A *touch mouse* is a touch-sensitive mouse that recognizes touch gestures, in addition to detecting movement of the mouse and traditional click and scroll operations. For example, you press a location on a touch mouse to simulate a click, sweep your thumb on the mouse to scroll pages, or slide multiple fingers across the mouse to zoom.

As with keyboards, you can purchase an ergonomic mouse to help reduce the chance of RSIs or to reduce pain and discomfort associated with RSIs.

 **Internet Research**
What are mouse gestures?
Search for: mouse gestures

 CONSIDER THIS ————————————————————————

Why use a wireless mouse?
As with keyboards, some users choose a wireless mouse to eliminate the clutter of a cord. A *wireless mouse* is a battery-powered device that transmits data using wireless technology. A wireless mouse typically transmits data to a receiver that plugs in a USB port or uses Bluetooth technology to pair with the device.

Touchpad

A **touchpad** is a small, flat, rectangular pointing device that is sensitive to pressure and motion (Figure 7-6). Touchpads are found most often on laptops and convertible tablets. Desktop users who prefer the convenience of a touchpad can purchase a separate touchpad, which usually communicates wirelessly with the computer.

To move the pointer using a touchpad, slide your fingertip across the surface of the pad. Some touchpads have one or more buttons around the edge of the pad that work like mouse buttons; others have no buttons. On most touchpads, you also can tap the pad's surface to imitate mouse operations, such as clicking. Some touchpads also recognize touch gestures, such as swipe, pinch, and stretch motions.

 BTW
Trackpad
Apple uses the term, *trackpad*, to refer to the touchpad on its laptops.

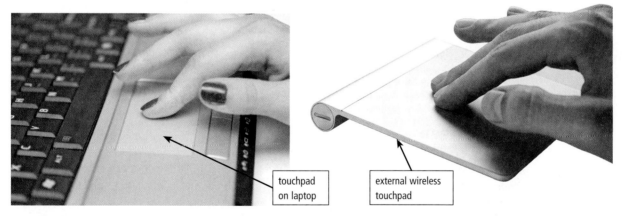

touchpad on laptop

external wireless touchpad

Figure 7-6 Laptop users often use the touchpad to control movement of the pointer. You also can purchase an external wireless touchpad for use with desktops and tablets.
© Andrew Donehue / Shutterstock.com; © iStockPhoto / Goldmund

---

 CONSIDER THIS ————————————————————————

What is a pointing stick?
Some mobile computer keyboards contain a pointing stick, which is a pressure-sensitive pointing device shaped like a pencil eraser positioned between its keys. To move the pointer using a pointing stick, you push the pointing stick with a finger.

Trackball

A **trackball** is a stationary pointing device with a ball on its top or side. The ball in most trackballs is about the size of a Ping-Pong ball. Some devices, called a trackball mouse, combine the functionality of both a trackball and a mouse (Figure 7-7).

To move the pointer using a trackball, you rotate the ball with your thumb, fingers, or the palm of your hand. In addition to the ball, a trackball usually has one or more buttons that work like mouse buttons.

 CONSIDER THIS —————————————————————

Why use a trackball instead of a mouse?
For users who have limited desk space, a trackball is a good alternative to a mouse because the device is stationary. Keep in mind, however, that a trackball requires frequent cleaning because it picks up oils from fingers and dust from the environment.

Figure 7-7 Shown here is a trackball mouse, which is a single device that provides the functionality of both a trackball and a mouse.
© iStockphtoo / peng wu

Touch Screens

A **touch screen** is a touch-sensitive display. Touch screens are convenient because they do not require a separate device for input. Smartphones and tablets, and many laptops and all-in-ones offer touch screens.

You can interact with a touch screen by touching areas of the screen with your finger or a stylus to make selections or to begin typing. Many touch screens also respond to gestures. A *gesture* is a motion you make on a touch screen with the tip of one or more fingers or your hand. For example, you can slide your finger to drag an object or pinch your fingers to zoom out. (Read How To 1-1 in Chapter 1 for a description of widely used touch screen gestures.)

Touch screens that recognize multiple points of contact at the same time are known as *multi-touch*. Because gestures often require the use of multiple fingers (points of contact), touch screens that support gestures are multi-touch.

Mini Feature 7-1: Touch Input

Many new computers and devices are using touch as a primary method of input. In fact, newer operating systems are optimizing their user interfaces for touch input. Read Mini Feature 7-1 to learn about various devices that use touch input.

MINI FEATURE 7-1

Touch Input

Devices that utilize touch input include monitors for desktops and screens on laptops and tablets, smartphones, wearable devices, portable media players, digital cameras, tablets, kiosks, and navigation systems.

Desktop Monitors and Screens on Laptops and Tablets

An increasing number of desktop monitors and screens on laptops and tablets support touch input. These touch-enabled monitors and screens allow users to interact with the operating system without a keyboard or pointing device. Instead of using a mouse to click an object on the screen, users simply can tap or double-tap the item they otherwise would have

clicked. For example, users can tap or double-tap an icon to run a program or an application, slide their finger to scroll, or use their finger to drag items across the screen.

Smartphones

Smartphones are becoming more functional, lighter weight, and now often do not include a physical keyboard. Touch input can help smartphone manufacturers achieve all these goals. The gestures you might perform on a smartphone that supports touch input include tapping to run an app, sliding or swiping to scroll, and pinching and stretching to zoom. The absence of a physical keyboard makes it more difficult to type without looking at the screen, so it is not advisable to use a smartphone when performing actions that require undivided attention, such as driving a car or walking.

Wearable Devices

Wearable devices, such as smartwatches, do not have room for a physical keyboard, so they mainly rely on touch input. The gestures you might perform on a wearable device include tapping to make a selection, and sliding or swiping to scroll through the various screens.

Portable Media Players

Portable media players widely use touch as the primary method of input so that the size of the screen on the device is maximized. That is, space on the device does not have to be dedicated to other controls, such as buttons or click wheels. Users slide and swipe to browse their music libraries on their portable media players and then tap to select the song they want to play. While songs are playing, users can tap the screen to display controls so that they can pause or stop the song, navigate to another song, or adjust the volume.

Digital Cameras

As digital cameras start to include built-in features to browse through and edit photos without requiring a computer, touch input helps digital camera users perform these functions with greater accuracy. For example, you can perform gestures such as swiping left and right on the screen to browse your photos, tapping the screen to identify the area on which you wish to focus when taking a picture, pinching and stretching to zoom while viewing photos, tapping areas of photos to remove red-eye, and dragging borders of photos to crop them.

Kiosks

Touch input also is used on devices where a keyboard and pointing device might not endure its high volume of use. Kiosks, such as those at an airport allowing you to check in for a flight, can be used by hundreds of people per day. Because kiosks are designed to help you perform a specific function as quickly as possible, touch input is ideal for their user-friendly interfaces. Users typically interact with kiosks by tapping various areas of the screen to select options (as discussed in Chapter 3). If typing is required, an on-screen keyboard is displayed so that users can enter information, such as their name or a confirmation number. Kiosks requiring sensitive or a significant amount of input also might include a separate keyboard and pointing device. For example, ATMs with touch screens often have a separate keypad to enter your PIN so that others are not able to see what you are typing.

Navigation Systems

Navigation systems in cars and other vehicles use touch input because typing on a separate keyboard is not wise while in a vehicle. Navigation system users can perform actions such as tapping to enter a destination address, dragging to display different areas of the map, or pinching and stretching to zoom. Operating a navigation system with touch input requires you to take your eyes off the road to interact with the device, so you should operate a navigation system only while your vehicle is parked or stopped. To reduce the chances of driver distraction, some built-in navigation systems reduce functionality while the vehicle is in motion. Read Ethics & Issues 7-1 to consider issues associated with using navigation and other mobile devices while driving.

Discover More: Visit this chapter's free resources to learn more about operating systems, monitors, smartphones, portable media players, and navigation systems that use touch input.

✴ **Consider This:** Do you find it is easier to use touch input instead of using a keyboard or mouse? Does your answer depend on the type of device you are using or the task you are trying to accomplish? Why?

ETHICS & ISSUES 7-1

Should a Vehicle Be Able to Prevent User Input on a Mobile Device while the Vehicle is in Motion?

As you are driving, you receive a text message from a friend. Is it safe to read the text message? Is it legal? Should you respond to it? Millions of Americans acknowledge that they use mobile phones while driving. Today's newer vehicles include sophisticated hands-free systems that use Bluetooth and other technologies to connect mobile devices to the vehicle's sound system.

Other technologies restrict or block usage while a vehicle is moving. Motion sensors can detect if the car is in motion. A phone's camera can tell whether the user is the driver or a passenger by the angle of the scenery in the background. Some cars will not start unless the mobile device is plugged into a socket that blocks all signals and can send a message to a parent if the device is removed. Parents can install apps on their children's smartphones that use GPS, cameras, and motion sensors to track or restrict teens' usage.

The debate about mobile phone safety while driving elicits different points of view from vehicle insurance companies, consumer safety groups, and the telecommunications industry. The U.S. Department of Transportation says that users who text while driving have a crash risk 23 times higher than those who refrain. In some states, it is illegal to send, read, or respond to text messages while driving. Other states have outlawed the use of mobile phones or they require drivers to use hands-free devices while driving. Many states have different laws for teens or new drivers.

A recent study stated that talking on a phone while driving affects drivers' response times as much as if they had consumed alcohol. Critics of hands-free and signal blocking technology claim that drivers can be just as easily distracted if they are discussing business or emotional matters.

Consider This: Would you use technology that limited your device usage while driving? Why or why not? Do you think laws that target teens or new drivers are fair? Why or why not? Do you believe hands-free devices are safe? Why or why not?

CONSIDER THIS

What is the purpose of a touch-sensitive pad?
Portable media players that do not have touch screens typically have a touch-sensitive pad. A *touch-sensitive pad* is an input device that contains buttons and/or wheels you operate with a thumb or other finger. Using the touch-sensitive pad, you can scroll through and play music; view photos; watch videos or movies; navigate through song, photo, or movie lists; display a menu; adjust volume; customize settings; and perform other actions. For example, users can rotate a portable media player's touch-sensitive pad to browse through the device's playlists and press the pad's buttons to play or pause media (Figure 7-8).

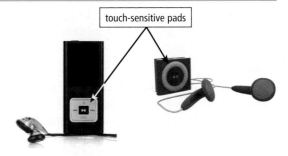
touch-sensitive pads

Figure 7-8 You use your thumb or finger to rotate or press buttons on a touch-sensitive pad, which commonly is found on portable media players.
© iStockphoto / Jorge Juan Pérez Suárez; © iStockphoto / Lusoimages

Pen Input

Some displays and mobile devices support pen input. With **pen input**, you touch a stylus or digital pen on a flat surface to write, draw, or make selections.

Stylus

BTW

Stylus
Some manufacturers refer to a stylus as a pen.

A **stylus** is a small metal or plastic device that looks like a tiny ink pen but uses pressure instead of ink (Figure 7-9). Nearly all tablets and mobile devices, some laptop screens, and a few desktop monitors have touch screens that support pen input, in addition to touch input. These computers and devices may include a stylus. Some stylus designs include buttons you can press to simulate clicking a mouse.

To capture a handwritten signature, a user writes his or her name on a **signature capture pad** with a stylus that is attached to the device. Software then transmits the signature to a central computer, where the signature is stored. Retailers use signature capture pads to record purchasers' signatures. Signature capture pads often work with POS terminals and include a magnetic stripe card reader, discussed later in the chapter.

Figure 7-9   You use a stylus to write, draw, or make selections on a touch screen that supports pen input.
© iStockphoto / Petar Chernaev; © iStockphoto / pictafolio; © iStockphoto / tirc83

Digital Pen

A **digital pen**, which is slightly larger than a stylus, is an input device that captures and converts a user's handwriting or drawings into a digital format, which users can upload (transfer) to a computer or mobile device. Some require the user to write or draw on special paper or a tablet; others can write or draw on any surface (Figure 7-10).

Once uploaded, *handwriting recognition software* on the computer or mobile device translates the handwritten letters and symbols created on the screen into typed text or objects that the computer or device can process. For this reason, digital pens most often are used for taking notes. Some are battery operated or USB powered; others use wireless technology, such as Bluetooth. Read Ethics & Issues 7-2 to consider whether you should take notes electronically or by hand.

Discover More: Visit this chapter's free resources to learn more about digital pens.

Figure 7-10   Users take notes with a digital pen and then upload the notes to a computer or mobile device, where software translates the notes to typed text.
Courtesy of LiveScribe

 Internet Research
Which digital pens are the most accurate?
Search for: digital pen reviews

Is It More Efficient to Take Notes by Hand or with a Digital Device?
When an instructor starts a lecture, he or she looks out at the classroom to see some students bent over a tablet, others frantically typing on a laptop, and still others using pen and paper to take notes. Which method is most effective for retaining knowledge?

A recent study concluded that students who used traditional pen and paper to take notes in class and while studying had better understanding and recall of information. The study concluded that when taking notes on a laptop, students tended to write down the speaker's exact words. Taking notes longhand required students to process the information, use their own words, and select what information is important enough to write down. Tablet users tended to have a mix of both transcribed and selected content. Regardless of the note-taking method, students performed equally when asked to recall factual information. Laptop users, however, were less able to answer conceptual or interpretive questions than those who took notes longhand.

Another concern when using laptops and mobile devices in a classroom is distractibility. Students may receive notifications about activity on an online social network, or use Internet messaging or text messaging to communicate with others about unrelated topics. Research shows that laptop users have unrelated programs or apps on their screen up to 40 percent of class time. Many instructors encourage students to use their computers and mobile devices for class related purposes. For example, some encourage students to Tweet answers to questions or research articles to support a fact or opinion. Others provide access to online forums in order for students to communicate with one another during or after class.

Consider This: Should instructors inform students about the benefits of longhand note taking? Why or why not? Should students be required to take notes longhand? Why or why not? How else might you use your computer or mobile device during class time to further your own learning?

Graphics Tablet

To use pen input on a computer that does not have a touch screen, you can attach a graphics tablet to the computer. A **graphics tablet,** also called a *digitizer*, is an electronic plastic board that detects and converts movements of a stylus or digital pen into digital signals that are sent to the computer (Figure 7-11). Each location on the graphics tablet corresponds to a specific location on the screen. Architects, mapmakers, designers, and artists, for example, use graphics tablets to create images, sketches, or designs.

pen

graphics tablet

Figure 7-11 Architects use a graphics tablet to create blueprints.
© iStockphoto / small_frog

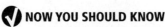

NOW YOU SHOULD KNOW

Be sure you understand the material presented in the sections titled What is Input?, Keyboards, Pointing Devices, Touch Screens, and Pen Input, as it relates to the chapter objectives.
Now you should know . . .

- What types of keyboards are available for computer and mobile devices, and which are best suited your needs (Objective 1)
- When you would use a mouse, touchpad, and trackball (Objective 2)
- What devices use touch screens (Objective 3)
- When you might use a stylus, digital pen, and graphics tablet (Objective 4)

Discover More: Visit this chapter's premium content for practice quiz opportunities.

Motion, Voice, and Video Input

Many of today's computers, mobile devices, and game devices support motion, voice, and video input. The following sections discuss each of these input methods.

Mini Feature 7-2: Motion Input

Internet Research

What are other uses of gesture recognition?

Search for: gesture recognition uses

With *motion input*, sometimes called *gesture recognition*, users can guide on-screen elements using air gestures. *Air gestures* involve moving your body or a handheld input device through the air. With motion input, a device containing a camera detects your gesture and then converts it to a digital signal that is sent to a computer, mobile, or game device. For example, gamers can swing their arm or a controller to simulate rolling a bowling ball down a lane toward the pins. Read Mini Feature 7-2 to learn how a variety of fields use motion input.

Motion Input

Until a few years ago, the idea of controlling a computer by waving your hands was seen only in Hollywood science fiction movies. Today, the entertainment industry (such as for gaming and animating movies), the military, athletics, and the medical field have found uses for motion input.

Motion-sensing devices communicate with a game console or a personal computer using wired or wireless technology. The console or computer translates a player's natural gestures, facial movements, and full-body motion into input. Although these devices originally were intended for gaming, developers are working on adapting them or using similar technology outside of the gaming and entertainment industries.

Entertainment

Motion-sensing game controllers enable a user to guide on-screen elements by moving a handheld input device through the air. Examples include handheld devices that enable gamers to use sweeping arm movements to simulate sports activities, such as a golf swing (shown in the figure below), balance boards that judge stability and motion when holding yoga poses, and remote control attachments, such as a steering wheel used to guide a car along a race course.

Some controllers track peripheral motion within a specific area. With these devices, users can move their finger to draw or move their whole body to dance or exercise. Some use a device that can track small finger gestures, enabling users to be more precise in their movements.

Facial motion capture converts people's facial movements into a digital format while they talk, smile,

and more. Animators, for example, use the digital data to simulate facial movements to create realistic gaming avatars, or computer-generated characters in movies. Facial movements, however, are more subtle and difficult to detect. Thus, the technology used for capturing facial motions requires more precision and a higher resolution than that required by gaming devices.

Military

Military uses of motion input include training, such as flight simulation or weapon usage. To ensure safety, trainees maneuver a helicopter or other device using motion input from a remote location. Motion input also aids in physical rehabilitation for wounded soldiers by providing a method for conducting physical therapy exercises outside of a military hospital. Another use of motion input is to assist in recovery from post-traumatic stress disorder. Sufferers of this ailment can use avatars and simulators to work through scenarios in a comfortable environment.

Athletics

Coaches and sports trainers use motion input to improve athletes' performance and to correct inefficient or injury-causing motions. Analyzing the arc of a pitcher's arm, and factoring the speed of the motion and the trajectory of the ball, can help improve a pitcher's accuracy and speed. Combining the athlete's motion input with complex algorithms can pinpoint areas in which the athlete can improve.

Medical Field

The medical field also uses motion input for training. For example, surgeons can practice new technologies in a simulated environment. Using motion input that enhances movements, surgeons also can operate less invasively. Surgeons even operate remotely, enabling experts to manipulate surgical devices and share their expertise to save lives around the world. Sports medicine specialists use motion input to assess injuries, determine treatment, and assist in physical therapy.

Discover More: Visit this chapter's free resources to learn more about motion-sensing devices and controllers, controllers that track peripheral motion, and other uses of motion input.

✳ **Consider This:** Have you used a motion-sensing device or game controller? What were your impressions? What security issues surround military use of motion input? What issues might the medical field encounter when using motion input?

controller translates motion of golf swing to move the golf ball on the screen

screen shows the position and movements of the avatar

player moves controller to simulate a golf swing

© iStockphoto / Chris Schmidt, © iStockphoto / Anthony Rosenberg, © Dani McDaniel / Shutterstock.com; © iStockPhoto / Cobalt88

Figure 7-12 With Siri, you can speak instructions and commands to the smartphone and its apps. As shown here, the user asks Siri about the weather, to which Siri replies by speaking a message and displaying the forecast.
© iStockphoto / alexander kirch

Internet Research

How accurate is voice recognition?

Search for: voice recognition accuracy

BTW

Technology Trend
Discover More: Visit this chapter's free resources to learn about the use of drones with technology.

Voice and Audio Input

Voice input is the process of entering input by speaking into a microphone. The microphone may be built in the computer or device, in a headset, or an external peripheral device that sits on top of a desk or other surface. Some external microphones have a cable that attaches to a port on a computer; others communicate using wireless technology, such as Bluetooth.

Uses of voice input include Internet messaging that supports voice conversations, chat rooms that support voice chats, video calls, videoconferencing, VoIP, and voice recognition. Recall that VoIP enables users to speak to other users via their Internet connection. **Voice recognition**, also called *speech recognition*, is the computer or mobile device's capability of distinguishing spoken words. Some computers and mobile devices make use of built-in and third-party voice recognition applications, which have a natural language interface (Figure 7-12). A *voice recognition application* allows users to dictate text and enter instructions by speaking into a microphone.

On mobile devices, these applications allow users to speak simple, task-based instructions to the device, such as setting an alarm, entering a calendar appointment, or making a call. Some mobile devices have a *speech-to-text* feature, which recognizes a user's spoken words and enters them into email messages, text messages, or other applications that support typed text entry.

Discover More: To learn how voice recognition works, visit the free resources in Chapter 3 and read the High-Tech Talk article on this topic.

Audio Input Voice input is part of a larger category of input called audio input. *Audio input* is the process of entering any sound into the computer, such as speech, music, and sound effects. To enter high-quality sound into computer, the computer uses a sound card or integrated sound capability. Users enter sound into computers and mobile devices via devices such as microphones, CD/DVD/Blu-ray Disc players, or radios, each of which plugs in a port on the computer or device.

Some users also record live music and other sound effects into a computer by connecting external music devices, such as an electronic keyboard (Figure 7-13), guitar, drums, harmonica, and microphones, to a computer. Music production software allows users to record, compose, mix, and edit music and sounds. For example, music production software enables you to change the speed, add notes, or rearrange the score to produce an entirely new arrangement.

Figure 7-13 This sound engineer uses a computer to mix music.
© iStockphoto / Chris Schmidt

Discover More: Visit this chapter's free resources to learn more about voice recognition applications and music production software.

⚙ CONSIDER THIS

How do external music devices connect to a computer?
External music devices typically connect to USB and MIDI ports. When purchasing a music device, check its specifications for the type(s) of ports to which it connects.

Mini Feature 7-3: Digital Video Technology

Video input is the process of capturing full-motion images and storing them on a computer or mobile device's storage medium, such as a hard disk or optical disc. A **digital video (DV) camera** records video as digital signals, which you can transfer directly to a computer or mobile device with the appropriate connection. Read Mini Feature 7-3 to learn the steps involved in using DV technology.

Digital Video Technology

Everywhere you look, people are capturing videos using DV (digital video) cameras and mobile devices with built-in digital cameras. Using **DV technology**, you can input, edit, manage, publish, and share your videos. You can enhance digital videos by adding scrolling titles and transitions, cutting out or adding scenes, and adding background music and voice-over narration. The following sections outline the steps involved in the process of using DV technology.

Step 1: Select a DV Camera

DV cameras range from inexpensive consumer versions to high-end DV camera models that support Blu-ray or HDV standards. Many mobile devices allow you to record digital video that you later can transmit to your computer or email from the device. When selecting a DV camera, consider features such as zoom, sound quality, editing capabilities, and resolution.

Step 2: Record a Video

With most DV cameras, you have a choice of recording programs that include different combinations of camera settings. These programs enable you to adjust the exposure and other functions to match the recording environment. You also have the ability to select special digital effects, such as fade, wipe, and black and white.

Step 3: Transfer and Manage Videos

You can connect most video cameras and mobile devices to a computer using a USB port. With many devices, you can transfer the videos to a media sharing or an online social network. Before doing this, however, consider the frame rate and video file format. The *frame rate* of a video refers to the number of frames per second (fps). A smaller frame rate results in a smaller file size for the video, but playback of the video will not be as smooth as one recorded with a higher frame rate. A video file format holds the video information in a manner specified by a vendor.

Step 4: Edit a Video

When editing, you first split the video into smaller pieces, or scenes, that you can manipulate easily. Most video editing software automatically splits the video into scenes at locations that you specify. After splitting, you should delete, or prune, unwanted scenes or portions of scenes. You can crop (or resize) scenes, and add logos, special effects, or titles. Special effects include warping, changing from color to black and white, morphing, or zoom motion. *Morphing* transforms one video image into another image over the course of several frames of video.

The next step is to add audio effects, including voice-over narration and background music. Using many video editing programs, you can add more tracks, or layers, of sound to a video in addition to the sound that the video camera or mobile device recorded. Adding audio tracks enables you to set a mood by providing background music or sounds. In the final step, you use video editing software to combine the scenes into a complete video by ordering scenes and adding transition effects. Transition effect options include fades, wipes, blurs, bursts, ruptures, and erosions.

Step 5: Distribute a Video

Some mobile devices allow you to upload video directly to video sharing and online social networks, as well as to send a video message. You can save digital video to media such as a DVD or Blu-ray Disc and package it for individual distribution or sale.

Discover More: Visit this chapter's free resources to learn more about DV cameras, Blu-ray and HDV standards, special digital effects, transferring videos to a computer or online site, video file formats, video editing software, and adding logos.

Consider This: If your computer or mobile device is capable of recording video, how often and for what purposes do you generally record videos? What settings can you adjust to improve the quality of the video? Which file format does your mobile device use to save video files?

DV camera captures video

edited video posted online

video available to view on mobile device using video sharing site

Figure 7-14 During a video call, users see one another as they communicate.
© iStockphoto / Anatoliy Babiy

Webcams and Integrated DV Cameras

A **webcam** is a type of DV camera that enables you to capture video and still images, and usually audio input, for viewing or manipulation on a computer or mobile device. Some webcams are separate peripheral devices, which usually attach to the top of a desktop monitor. Many laptops, tablets, and smartphones have built-in webcams. Smartphones and other mobile devices have built-in integrated DV cameras. Read How To 7-1 for instructions about setting up and using a webcam or integrated DV camera.

Using a webcam or integrated DV camera, you can send email messages with video attachments, broadcast live images or video over the Internet, conduct videoconferences, and make video calls. During a **video call**, all parties see one another as they communicate over the Internet (Figure 7-14).

⚙ HOW TO 7-1

Set Up and Use Webcams and Integrated DV Cameras

As mentioned, webcams and DV cameras are used to record and/or send live video to others. Before you can record and send video to others, you must have a webcam or integrated DV camera on your computer or mobile device. Some computers and mobile devices have integrated DV cameras; others require you to set up a separate webcam. The following steps describe how to set up a webcam, and use a webcam or integrated DV camera:

Setting Up a Webcam

1. If the webcam included software, install the software on your computer before connecting the webcam.

2. Connect the webcam to your computer or mobile device either when the software prompts you or after you have installed the necessary software. If no software accompanied your webcam, connect the webcam to the computer or mobile device.

3. When the computer or mobile device acknowledges that a webcam has been connected, you are ready to begin using it.

Yuganov Konstantin / Shutterstock.com

Using a Webcam or Integrated DV Camera

1. Run the app that will use the webcam or integrated DV camera.

2. Display the app's settings and make sure the app recognizes the webcam or integrated DV camera.

3. If you are using the camera to record a video, record a short clip and then replay it to make sure the camera properly captured audio and video. If you are using the camera for a videoconference, place a call to somebody using the videoconferencing app and make sure he or she is able to see and hear you.

4. If you experience problems with the camera capturing audio or video, try the following:

    a. Run the program that came with the camera and see if a troubleshooter can identify and correct the problem you are experiencing.

    b. If you are using a webcam, disconnect the webcam from the computer, restart the computer or mobile device, and then reconnect the webcam.

    c. If you are using a webcam, disconnect the webcam, uninstall the program(s) included with the webcam, restart the computer or mobile device, and then follow the previous steps to set up and use the webcam.

    d. If you continue experiencing problems after attempting these steps, contact the technical support team for the camera's manufacturer.

⚙ **Consider This:** What are some reasons why you might use a webcam or integrated DV camera on your computer or mobile device?

What is the purpose of a videoconference versus a video call?

Where video calls usually are for personal use, videoconferences typically are for business use. A **videoconference** is a meeting between two or more geographically separated people who use a network or the Internet to transmit audio and video data (Figure 7-15). To participate in a videoconference using a computer, you need videoconferencing software or access to a videoconferencing web app, along with a microphone, speakers, and a video camera attached to or built into a computer. As you speak, members of the meeting hear your voice on their speakers. Any image in front of the video camera, such as a person's face, appears in a window on each participant's screen.

Figure 7-15   To save on travel expenses, many large businesses use videoconferencing.
Idprod / Fotolia

Discover More: Visit this chapter's free resources to learn more about videoconference software.

You can configure some webcams to display the images they capture remotely on a webpage, or via an app on a mobile device. This use of a webcam attracts website visitors by showing images that change regularly. Home or small business users might use webcams to show a work in progress, weather and traffic information, or employees at work; they also might use it as a security system. Some websites have live webcams that display still pictures and update the displayed image at a specified time or time intervals, such as every 15 seconds. A *streaming cam* has the illusion of moving images because it sends a continual stream of still images. Read Secure IT 7-2 to learn about security issues related to using webcams.

✹ SECURE IT 7-2

Digital Video Security

Sales of home security systems are on the rise due to their low costs and easy setup. These systems use cameras and sensors to monitor activity, and most send a message via mobile phone to alert a user of movement and entrance or exit into the dwelling and send the webcam's live feed of the scene.

This use of webcams serves a practical use in a private setting. Similarly, webcams in public areas, such as shopping malls, parking lots, and school cafeterias, help with surveillance measures and record everyday activity.

Webcam use, however, is criticized when the live feeds are used in a manner without the recorded parties' consent. Ethics and Issues 3-1 in Chapter 3 discusses the appropriate punishment for webcam spying, citing examples of criminals who hacked into home computers and streamed live video feeds, school administrators who took 66,000

pictures and screen captures of students using school-distributed laptops at home, and rent-to-own stores that rented laptops with spyware that captured photos of customers in their homes. Digital video recorders also are hidden in products resembling remote car keys, wall and desk clocks, sunglasses, smoke detectors, and electrical boxes.

If you have a webcam, follow these measures to prevent its unauthorized use:

- **Unplug the webcam.** This obvious suggestion offers the most secure solution. If the webcam is not connected to the computer, it cannot reveal what is occurring in front of the lens.

- **Cover the lens and plug the microphone.** Place a piece of black electrical tape over the lens, and insert a dummy plug in the microphone port. This solution is ideal for tablets and laptops equipped with cameras.

- **Register the hardware.** Hardware manufacturers continually update their firmware to fix issues. If you register your product, the companies can notify you of known security holes and offer updates to download.

- **Use a strong password.** When connecting a webcam to a network, you may need to configure the device for features such as sending an email or text message when motion is detected. If you are prompted to create a password, be certain it can resist hackers and malicious software. Read Secure IT 1-3 in Chapter 1 for tips about creating strong passwords.

✹ **Consider This:** If you have a webcam, what actions will you take to protect your privacy? Should you be warned of webcam use when you are in a public area? If so, how can these warnings be given? Would you consider buying a digital video recorder for surveillance purposes?

Scanners and Reading Devices

Some input devices save users time by capturing data directly from a *source document*, which is the original form of the data. Examples of source documents include time cards, order forms, invoices, paychecks, advertisements, brochures, photos, inventory tags, or any other document that contains data to be processed.

Devices that can capture data directly from a source document include optical scanners, optical readers, bar code readers, RFID (radio frequency identification) readers, magnetic stripe card readers, and MICR (magnetic-ink character recognition) readers.

Optical Scanners

An optical scanner, usually called a **scanner**, is a light-sensing input device that reads printed text and graphics and then translates the results into a form the computer can process. A flatbed scanner works in a manner similar to a copy machine except it creates a file of the document in memory instead of a paper copy (Figure 7-16). Once you scan a picture or document, you can display the scanned object on the screen, modify its appearance, store it on a storage medium, print it, attach it to an email message, include it in another document, or post it on a website or photo community for everyone to see.

The quality of a scanner is measured by its resolution, that is, the number of bits it stores in a pixel and the number of pixels per inch. The higher each number, the better the quality, but the more expensive the scanner.

Many scanners include *OCR* (optical character recognition) *software*, which can read and convert text documents into electronic files. OCR software converts a scanned image into a text file that can be edited, for example, with a word processing application.

 CONSIDER THIS ———————————————————————————————————————

How can you improve the quality of scanned documents?
Place a blank sheet of paper behind translucent papers, newspapers, and other transparent types of paper. If the original is crooked, draw a line on the back at the bottom of the image. Use that mark to align the original on the scanner. Use photo editing software to fix imperfections in images.

How a Flatbed Scanner Works

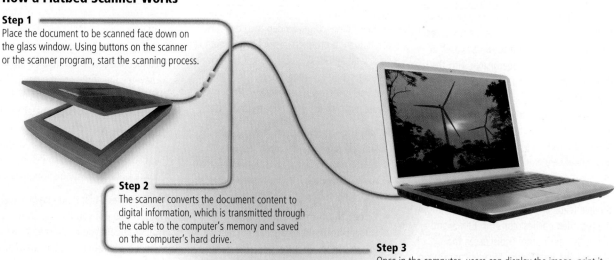

Step 1
Place the document to be scanned face down on the glass window. Using buttons on the scanner or the scanner program, start the scanning process.

Step 2
The scanner converts the document content to digital information, which is transmitted through the cable to the computer's memory and saved on the computer's hard drive.

Step 3
Once in the computer, users can display the image, print it, send it in an email message, include it in a document, or place it on a webpage.

Figure 7-16 This figure shows how a flatbed scanner works.
© Cengage Learning; © Mile Atanasov / Shutterstock.com; © Alex Staroseltsev / Shutterstock.com

Optical Readers

An optical reader is a device that uses a light source to read characters, marks, and codes and then converts them into digital data that a computer can process. Two technologies used by optical readers are optical character recognition (OCR) and optical mark recognition (OMR).

- Most **OCR devices** include a small optical scanner for reading characters and sophisticated software to analyze what is read. OCR devices range from large machines that can read thousands of documents per minute to handheld wands that read one document at a time. OCR devices read printed characters in a special font.
- **OMR devices** read hand-drawn marks, such as small circles or rectangles. A person places these marks on a form, such as a test, survey, or questionnaire answer sheet (shown in Figure 7-1 at the beginning of this chapter).

BTW
Technology Innovators
Discover More: Visit this chapter's free resources to learn about Masahiro Hara and Denso Wave, QR code inventors.

Internet Research
What are current uses of QR codes?
Search for: qr code uses

Bar Code Readers

A **bar code reader**, also called a *bar code scanner*, is an optical reader that uses laser beams to read bar codes (Figure 7-17). A **bar code** is an identification code that consists of either a set of vertical lines and spaces of different widths or a two-dimensional pattern of dots, squares, and other images. The bar code represents data that identifies the manufacturer and the item.

Manufacturers print a bar code either on a product's package or on a label that is affixed to a product, such as groceries, books, clothing, vehicles, mail, and packages. Each industry uses its own type of bar code. The United States Postal Service (USPS) uses a POSTNET bar code. Retail and grocery stores use the *UPC* (*Universal Product Code*) bar code.

Figure 7-17   A bar code reader uses laser beams to read bar codes on products such as clothing, shown here.
© iStockPhoto / klaptoman

A **QR code** (quick response code) is known as a 2-D bar code because it stores information in both a vertical and horizontal direction (Figure 7-18). The information it stores can correspond to a web address or other content, such as contacts or phone numbers. QR codes can be read with a QR bar code reader or a QR code reader app on a smartphone or other mobile device. All types of material, from posters to textbooks to merchandise, include QR codes that consumers scan to obtain additional information, which may be in the form of a website or may display text for the user to read. For information about safely scanning QR codes, read Secure IT 7-3.

Discover More: Visit this chapter's free resources to learn more about QR code reader apps.

Figure 7-18   This customer pays her bills by scanning an on-screen QR code.
© iStockPhoto / gpointstudio

RFID Readers

RFID (radio frequency identification) is a technology that uses radio signals to communicate with a tag placed in or attached to an object, an animal, or a person. RFID tags, which contain a memory chip and an antenna, are available in many shapes and sizes. An **RFID reader** reads information on the tag via radio waves. RFID readers can be handheld devices or mounted in a stationary object, such as a doorway.

Many retailers see RFID as an alternative to bar code identification because it does not require direct contact or line-of-site transmission. Each product in a store would contain a tag that identifies the product. As consumers remove products from the store shelves and walk through a checkout area, an RFID reader reads the tag(s) and communicates with a computer that calculates the amount due and updates inventory.

Other uses of RFID include tracking times of runners in a marathon; tracking location of people, airline baggage, and misplaced or stolen goods; checking lift tickets of skiers; managing inventory; gauging temperature and pressure of tires on a vehicle; checking out library books; providing access to rooms or buildings (Figure 7-19); managing purchases; and tracking payment as vehicles pass through booths on tollway systems.

Figure 7-19 This electronic key system locks and unlocks doors using RFID technology.
© iStockPhoto / iggy1965

Magstripe Readers

A **magstripe reader**, short for *magnetic stripe card reader*, reads the magnetic stripe on the back of credit cards, entertainment cards, bank cards, identification cards, and other similar cards (Figure 7-20). The stripe contains information identifying you and the card issuer. Some information stored in the stripe may include your name, account number, the card's expiration date, and a country code.

magstripe reader

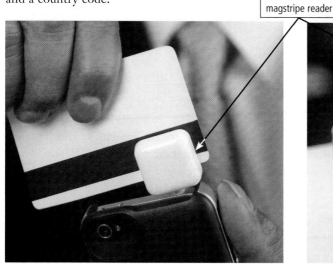

Figure 7-20 A magstripe reader reads information encoded on the stripe on the back of a credit card.
© EdBockStock / Shutterstock.com; © iStockPhoto / hocus-focus

Most magstripe readers are separate devices that communicate with a POS (point-of-sale) terminal, such as those in retail stores. Home or small business users, however, may attach a small plastic magstripe reader to a smartphone or tablet so that they can accept payments using a mobile app. When a credit card is swiped through a magstripe reader, it reads the information stored on the magnetic stripe on the card. Read Secure IT 7-4 for tips about how to protect credit cards from scanning devices.

⚡ Internet Research

What types of mobile magstripe readers are available?

Search for: mobile magstripe readers

✴ SECURE IT 7-4

📄 Protecting Credit Cards from Scanning Devices

One-third of the 775 million credit and debit cards issued in the United States are likely targets for high-tech thieves who can steal the account information quickly and silently. RFID technology embedded in these cards transmits signals with the coded account information to scanners, which thieves place in their coat pockets, purses, and other nonmetallic containers. Some signals have a range as far as 30 feet, so that the electronic pickpockets simply walk among crowds in search of obtaining these radio waves.

The RFID technology embedded in the credit cards is approximately the size of a postage stamp. It consists of a coil of wire connected to an electronic circuit that generates a pattern of electrical pulses with coded account information

unique to a specific card. An antenna transmits these radio waves to a scanner.

The radio waves do not penetrate metal or water easily. You, consequently, can protect these cards and documents by wrapping them in aluminum foil or placing them near water bottles. Security experts also recommend stacking several credit cards in an attempt to scramble the signals. Place the cards in your wallet with the magnetic strip facing inside. RFID-blocking wallets also are manufactured to prevent scanners from obtaining the emitted signals.

To determine if your credit or debit card has this RFID technology, look for the words, PayPass, PayWave, Blink, or a radio wave symbol, as shown in the figure. If you do not see this information, call customer service or search the company's website. This technology

also is found in passports, driver's licenses, hotel room keys, and university and employee identification cards, so you may need to protect these documents and cards from electronic pickpockets, too.

☀ **Consider This:** Are any of your credit or debit cards or personal documents embedded with RFID technology? If so, what precautions will you take to block the signals from scanners?

CONSIDER THIS ───────────────────────────

Why are some magnetic stripes not readable by a magstripe reader?
If the magstripe reader rejects the card, it is possible that the magnetic stripe is scratched, dirty, or erased. Exposure to a magnet or magnetic field can erase the contents of a card's magnetic stripe.

 CONSIDER THIS ───────────────────────────

What is a smart card?
A smart card stores data on an integrated circuit embedded in a card, such as a credit card. Chapter 8 discusses smart cards in more depth.

Figure 7-21 The MICR characters preprinted on the check represent the bank routing number, customer account number, and check number. The amount of the check in the lower-right corner is added after the check is cashed.
© Cengage Learning

MICR Readers

MICR (magnetic-ink character recognition) *devices* read text printed with magnetized ink. An MICR reader converts MICR characters into a form the computer can process. The banking industry almost exclusively uses MICR for check processing. Each check in your checkbook has precoded MICR characters beginning at the lower-left edge (Figure 7-21).

When a bank receives a check for payment, it uses an MICR inscriber to print the amount of the check in MICR characters in the lower-right corner. Each check is inserted in an MICR reader, which sends the check information — including the amount of the check — to a computer for processing.

Data Collection Devices

Instead of reading or scanning data from a source document, a *data collection device* obtains data directly at the location where the transaction or event takes place. For example, employees use bar code readers, handheld computers, or other mobile devices to collect data wirelessly (Figure 7-22). These types of data collection devices are used in restaurants, grocery stores, factories, warehouses, the outdoors, or other locations where heat, humidity, and cleanliness are not easy to control. For example, factories and retail stores use data collection devices to take inventory and order products.

Data collection devices and many mobile computers and devices have the capability of wirelessly transmitting data over a network or the Internet. Increasingly more users today send data wirelessly to central office computers using these devices.

Figure 7-22 An employee in a warehouse uses this data collection device to scan items, which wirelessly transmits information about the scanned item to the store's inventory system.
© endostock / Fotolia

NOW YOU SHOULD KNOW ─────────────────────────

Be sure you understand the material presented in the sections titled Motion, Voice, and Video Input, and Scanners and Reading Devices, as it relates to the chapter objectives.
Now you should know…

• Which type of motion, voice, and video input are best suited to your needs (Objective 5)

• Why you would use optical scanners and readers, bar code readers, RFID readers, magstripe readers, MICR readers, and data collection devices (Objective 6)

Discover More: Visit this chapter's premium content for practice quiz opportunities.

What Is Output?

Output is data that has been processed into a useful form. Recall that computers process data (input) into information (output). The form of output varies, depending on the hardware and software being used and the requirements of the user. Users view or watch output on a screen, print it, or hear it through speakers, headphones, or earbuds. While working with a computer or mobile device, a user encounters four basic types of output: text, graphics, audio, and video (Figure 7-23). Very often, a single form of output, such as a webpage, includes more than one of these types of output.

Text

Graphics

Audio

Video

Figure 7-23   Four types of output are text, graphics, audio, and video.

- **Text:** Examples of output that primarily contain text are text messages, Internet messages, memos, letters, press releases, reports, classified advertisements, envelopes, and mailing labels. On the web, users read blogs, news and magazine articles, books, television show transcripts, stock quotes, speeches, and lectures.
- **Graphics:** Many forms of output include graphics to enhance visual appeal and convey information. Business letters have logos. Reports include charts. Newsletters use drawings, clip art, and photos. Users print high-quality photos taken with a digital camera. Many websites use animation.
- **Audio:** Users download their favorite songs and listen to the music. Software, such as games, encyclopedias, and simulations, often include musical accompaniments and audio clips, such as narrations and speeches. On the web, users listen to radio broadcasts, audio clips, podcasts, sporting events, news, music, and concerts. They also use VoIP.
- **Video:** As with audio, software and websites often include video clips and video blogs. Users watch news reports, movies, sporting events, weather conditions, and live performances on a computer or mobile device. They attach a video camera to a computer or mobile device to watch video or programs.

 CONSIDER THIS

Are storage devices categorized as input or output devices?

When storage devices write on storage media, they are creating output. Similarly, when storage devices read from storage media, they function as a source of input. Nevertheless, they are categorized as storage devices, not as input or output devices.

Common methods of output include displays, printers, speakers, headphones and earbuds, data projectors, interactive whiteboards, and force-feedback game controllers and tactile output. The following sections discuss each of these output devices.

Displays

A *display device*, or simply **display**, is an output device that visually conveys text, graphics, and video information. Sometimes called *soft copy*, information on a display exists electronically and appears for a temporary period. Displays consist of a screen and the components that produce the information on the screen. Most current displays are a type of *flat-panel display*, which means they have a shallow depth and a flat screen. Figure 7-24 shows displays for a variety of computers and mobile devices.

Desktops often use a monitor as their display. A **monitor** is a display that is packaged as a separate peripheral device. Some monitors have a tilt-and-swivel base, which allows you to adjust the angle of the screen to minimize neck strain and reduce glare from overhead lighting. With some, you also can rotate the screen. Adjustable monitor stands allow you to

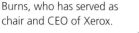

Figure 7-24 A variety of displays.

adjust the height of the monitor. Monitor controls enable you to adjust the brightness, contrast, positioning, height, and width of images. Some have touch screens, integrated speakers, and/or a built-in webcam. Today's monitors have a small footprint; that is, they do not take up much desk space. For additional space savings, some monitors are wall mountable.

Most mobile computers and devices integrate the display and other components into the case. Size of these displays varies depending on the mobile computer or device. Some mobile computers and many mobile devices have touch screens. Traditional laptops have a display that attaches with a hinge to the case. (Read How To 7-2 to learn how to connect a laptop to an external display.) Tablets are available with two types of displays: one that attaches with a hinge and one built into the top of the case. Some smartphone and digital camera displays also attach with a hinge to the device. On other smartphones and most portable media players, digital cameras, and handheld game consoles, the display is built into the case. Newer vehicles integrate a display in the dashboard, enabling drivers to control audio, video, navigation, temperature, and other settings.

Discover More: Visit this chapter's free resources to learn more about monitor and display sizes and manufacturers.

 BTW

Measuring Displays
You measure the screen on a monitor, laptop, tablet, smartphone, or other mobile device the same way you measure a television; that is, you measure diagonally from one corner to the other.

HOW TO 7-2

Connect a Laptop to an External Display

When you are using a laptop, you may need to connect it to an external display for a variety of reasons. If you are giving a presentation, connecting a laptop to a projector or television will allow attendees to view presentation slides or other media content. If you use your laptop at a desk, you might want to connect it to a larger display so that you can more easily see the content without straining your eyes, or you may want to work with two open programs simultaneously with one displaying on the laptop screen and the other on the external display. The following steps describe how to connect a laptop to an external display.

1. Verify that your laptop is compatible with the external display.

2. Make sure that you have a cable that can connect from a port on your laptop to a port or cable connected to the external display. If not, you may need to purchase an adapter.

3. Verify that your laptop supports a screen resolution that the external display also supports.

4. Use the cable to connect your laptop's video port to the video input port for the external display.

5. External displays often have multiple video input ports; make sure the external display is configured to display the content from the port to which your laptop is connected.

6. If necessary, configure the laptop to display content on the external display. This often can be done by pressing a

key on the keyboard or accessing the operating system's display settings.

7. If necessary, change the screen resolution on the laptop so that the contents display properly on the external display.

Consider This: What are some other reasons why you might want to connect your laptop to an external display?

© Goygel-Sokol Dmitry / Shutterstock.com

Display Technologies

Many desktop monitors, along with the screens on mobile computers and devices, use some type of LCD technology. A *liquid crystal display* (**LCD**) sandwiches a liquid compound between two sheets of material that presents sharp, flicker-free images on a screen when illuminated. The light source, called the *backlight*, often uses either CCFL (cold cathode fluorescent lamp) or *LED* (light-emitting diode) technology.

 Internet Research

What is in-plane switching (IPS)?

Search for: ips display

A display that uses LED for the backlight often is called an *LED display* or an LED LCD display. LED displays consume less power, last longer, and are thinner, lighter, and brighter than a display that uses CCFL technology, but they also may be more expensive. Screens in laptops and mobile devices often use LED backlight technology.

LCD displays typically produce color using *active-matrix*, or *TFT* (thin-film transistor), technology, which uses a separate transistor to apply charges to each liquid crystal cell and, thus, displays high-quality color that is viewable from all angles. Several types of active matrix displays, or panels, are available, with some providing higher quality than others.

Instead of LCD or traditional LED, some displays use OLED technology. *OLED* (organic LED) uses organic molecules that are self-illuminating and, thus, do not require a backlight. OLED displays consume less power and produce an even brighter, easier-to-read display than LCD or LED displays, but they can have a shorter life span. OLEDs also can be fabricated on thin, flexible surfaces.

Many mobile computers and devices use either AMOLED or Retina Display technology. An *AMOLED* (active-matrix OLED) screen uses both active-matrix and OLED technologies, combining the benefits of high-quality viewing from all angles with lower power consumption. Variations of AMOLED provide different levels of viewing quality. *Retina Display*, developed by Apple, produces vibrant colors and supports viewing from all angles because the LCD technology is built into the screen instead of behind it and contains more pixels per inch of display. Recall that a *pixel* (short for picture element) is a single point in an electronic image.

Discover More: Visit this chapter's free resources to learn more about active-matrix displays.

Display Quality

The quality of a display depends primarily on its resolution, response time, brightness, dot pitch, and contrast ratio.

- **Resolution** is the number of horizontal and vertical pixels in a display. For example, a monitor or screen that has a 1600 × 900 resolution displays up to 1600 pixels per horizontal row and 900 pixels per vertical row, for a total of 1,440,000 pixels to create a screen image. A higher resolution uses a greater number of pixels and, thus, provides a smoother, sharper, and clearer image. As the resolution increases, however, some items on the screen appear smaller.

  Displays are optimized for a specific resolution, called the *native resolution*. Although you can change the resolution to any setting, for best results, use the monitor or screen's native resolution setting.

- *Response time* of a display refers to the time in milliseconds (ms) that it takes to turn a pixel on or off. Response times of displays range from 2 to 16 ms. The lower the number, the faster the response time.

- Brightness of a display is measured in nits. A *nit* is a unit of visible light intensity equal to one candela (formerly called candlepower) per square meter. The *candela* is the standard unit of luminous intensity. Displays today range from 250 to 550 nits. The higher the nits, the brighter the images.

- *Dot pitch*, sometimes called *pixel pitch*, is the distance in millimeters between pixels on a display. Text created with a smaller dot pitch is easier to read. Advertisements normally specify a display's dot pitch or pixel pitch. Average dot pitch on a display should be .30 mm or lower. The lower the number, the sharper the image.

- *Contrast ratio* describes the difference in light intensity between the brightest white and darkest black that can be produced on a display. Contrast ratios today range from 500:1 to 2000:1. Higher contrast ratios represent colors better.

Graphics Chips, Ports, and Flat-Panel Monitors A cable on a monitor plugs in a port on the computer, which enables communications from a graphics chip. This chip, called the *graphics processing unit* (GPU), controls the manipulation and display of graphics on a display device. The GPU either is integrated on the motherboard or resides on a video card in a slot on the motherboard.

Today's monitors use a digital signal to produce a picture. To display the highest quality images, the monitor should plug in a DVI port, an HDMI port, or a DisplayPort.

- A *DVI (Digital Video Interface) port* enables digital signals to transmit directly to a monitor.
- An *HDMI (High-Definition Media Interface) port* combines DVI with high-definition (HD) television, audio, and video. Some ultrathin laptops have mini-HDMI ports that require the use of an adapter (or dongle) when connecting to a standard-size HDMI display.
- A *DisplayPort* is an alternative to DVI that also supports high-definition audio and video.

Over the years, several video standards have been developed to define the resolution, aspect ratio, number of colors, and other display properties. The *aspect ratio* defines a display's width relative to its height. A 2:1 aspect ratio, for example, means the display is twice as wide as it is tall. The aspect ratio for a *widescreen monitor* is 16:9 or 16:10. Some displays support multiple video standards. For a display to show images as defined by a video standard, both the display and GPU must support the same video standard.

Discover More: Visit this chapter's free resources to learn more about video standards.

DTVs and Smart TVs

Home users sometimes use a digital television (DTV) as a display. Gamers also use a television as their output device. They plug one end of a cable in the game console and the other end in the video port on the television.

HDTV (*high-definition television*) is the most advanced form of digital television, working with digital broadcast signals, transmitting digital sound, supporting wide screens, and providing high resolutions. A *Smart TV* is an Internet-enabled HDTV from which you can browse the web, stream video from online media services, listen to Internet radio, communicate with others on online social media, play online games, and more — all while watching a television show (Figure 7-25). Using a SmartTV, you can stream content from the TV to other Internet-enabled devices, such as a tablet or smartphone, and use cloud storage services to share content. Read How To 7-3 to learn how to show media on a Smart TV from your computer or device.

Figure 7-25 Smart TVs enable you to connect to the Internet and/or watch television shows.
Courtesy of LG Electronics USA Inc.

✹ HOW TO 7-3

Show Media on a Smart TV from Your Computer or Device

Smart TVs can connect to the network in your home using a wired or wireless connection. Compatible computers and devices connected to the same network can display content on the Smart TV. For example if you connect your smartphone to the same network as the Smart TV, you can display pictures from the phone on the Smart TV. The following steps describe how to show media on a Smart TV from a computer or device.

1. Verify that your computer or device is capable of displaying content on the Smart TV.

2. Make sure that the computer or device is connected to the same network as the Smart TV.

3. Navigate to the settings on the computer or device and specify that you want to mirror the display on the Smart TV.

4. Navigate to the settings on the Smart TV, if necessary, and enable the setting that allows content from computers and devices to be displayed.

5. Continue to use the computer or device when the video from your computer or device is displayed on the Smart TV.

6. When you no longer wish to display the content from your computer or device on the Smart TV, change the setting on your computer or mobile device to disable this feature.

✹ **Consider This:** What type of media might you display on your Smart TV? Why?

© iStockPhoto / chargerv8

DTVs often use LCD, LED, or plasma technology. A *plasma display* uses gas plasma technology, which sandwiches a layer of gas between two glass plates. When voltage is applied, the gas releases ultraviolet (UV) light. This UV light causes the pixels on the screen to glow and form an image. Read Ethics & Issues 7-3 to consider the effects of radiation from monitors and other devices.

 ETHICS& ISSUES 7-3

Should We Be Concerned with Hardware Radiation?

When you work on a computer or talk on a mobile phone, could you be at risk from harmful radiation? Every electronic device emits some level of radiation. While the amounts for computers and mobile devices may not be harmful in low doses, some critics argue that constant exposure, such as sitting in an office all day or wearing a Bluetooth headset for several hours at a time, can cause levels of radiation that, over time, may cause cancer or other health concerns. In addition to the computer itself, peripheral devices, such as printers, along with the wireless or cordless methods to connect the devices, emit radiation.

Research is inconclusive about safe levels and long-term risks. Most agree that it is not the level from any one device, but rather the cumulative effect from long-term exposure (several hours a day over many years) to multiple devices simultaneously that causes harm.

You can protect yourself and minimize your risks. Replace older equipment, such as CRT (cathode-ray tube) monitors, with devices such as LCD monitors, which meet current emission standards. Sit back from your monitor as far as possible, and place a barrier between your computer and your lap. Move other electronic sources, such as hard drives and printers, as far away as possible. Minimize your wireless connections, such

as a wireless keyboard or a wireless mouse. Remove your Bluetooth headset when not in use, and frequently switch the headset from one ear to the other. Turn off devices when not in use. Recycle or donate older, unused devices to eliminate any radiation exposure from older devices, even when they are not in use.

Consider This: Do you consider computers and mobile devices to be harmful to your health? Why or why not? Would you change your electronic device usage, change your habits, or rearrange your computer work area to minimize your risk? Why or why not? What modifications can you make?

 **Internet Research**

What are popular television streaming media services?

Search for: television streaming media

 CONSIDER THIS

Can you view the output from your display remotely?

With a television streaming media device, you can view and control a home DVR or TV from a remote computer or mobile device.

 NOW YOU SHOULD KNOW

Be sure you understand the material presented in the sections titled What is Output? and Displays, as it relates to the chapter objectives.

Now you should know…

• What types of output you may encounter (Objective 7)

• What to consider when purchasing computers and devices with various displays (Objective 8)

Discover More: Visit this chapter's premium content for practice quiz opportunities.

Printers

A **printer** is an output device that produces text and graphics on a physical medium, such as paper. Printed information (hard copy) exists physically and is a more permanent form of output than that presented on a display (soft copy).

A hard copy, also called a *printout*, is either in portrait or landscape orientation. A printout in *portrait orientation* is taller than it is wide, with information printed across the shorter width of the paper. A printout in *landscape orientation* is wider than it is tall, with information printed across the widest part of the paper. Letters, reports, and books typically use portrait orientation. Spreadsheets, slide shows, and graphics often use landscape orientation.

Can you print documents and photos from a mobile computer and device without physically connecting to the printer with a cable?

Yes. Many printers contain memory card slots, so that you can remove the memory card from a camera, insert it in the printer, and print photos directly from the card. You also can connect a printer to a wireless network so that devices with a Wi-Fi connection can print wirelessly. With *Bluetooth printing*, a computer or other device transmits output to a printer via radio waves. The computer or other device and the printer do not have to be aligned with each other; rather, they need to be within an approximate 30-foot range.

To meet the range of printing needs from home users to enterprise users, many different types and styles of printers exist with varying speeds, capabilities, and printing methods. Figure 7-26 presents a list of questions to help you determine the printer best suited to your needs.

Nonimpact Printers

A **nonimpact printer** forms characters and graphics on a piece of paper without actually contacting the paper. Some spray ink, while others use heat or pressure to create images.

Commonly used nonimpact printers are ink-jet printers, photo printers, laser printers, all-in-one printers, thermal printers, mobile printers, label printers, plotters, and large-format printers.

Ink-Jet Printers

An **ink-jet printer** is a type of nonimpact printer that forms characters and graphics by spraying tiny drops of liquid ink onto a piece of paper. Ink-jet printers have become a popular type of color printer for use in the home.

Ink-jet printers produce text and graphics in both black-and-white and color on a variety of paper types and sizes (Figure 7-27). These printers normally use individual sheets of paper stored in one or two removable or stationary trays. Most ink-jet printers can print lab-quality photos. Ink-jet printers also print on other materials, such as envelopes, labels, index cards, greeting card paper (card stock), transparencies, and iron-on T-shirt transfers. Many ink-jet printers include software for creating greeting cards, banners, business cards, and letterhead.

The speed of an ink-jet printer is measured by the number of pages per minute (ppm) it can print. Graphics and colors print at a slower rate than text.

Discover More: Visit this chapter's free resources to learn more about ink-jet printers.

1. What is my budget?
2. How fast must my printer print?
3. Do I need a color printer?
4. What is the cost per page for printing?
5. Do I need multiple copies of documents?
6. Will I print graphics?
7. Do I want to print photos?
8. Do I want to print directly from a memory card?
9. What types of paper does the printer use?
10. What sizes of paper does the printer accept?
11. Do I want to print on both sides of the paper?
12. How much paper can the printer tray hold?
13. Will the printer work with my computer and software?
14. How much do supplies such as ink, toner, and paper cost?
15. Can the printer print on envelopes?
16. How many envelopes can the printer print at a time?
17. How much do I print now, and how much will I be printing in a year or two?
18. Will the printer be connected to a network?
19. Do I want wireless printing capability?

Figure 7-26   Questions to consider before purchasing a printer.
© Cengage Learning

Figure 7-27   Ink-jet printers are a popular type of color printer used at home and in the office.
© iStockphoto / Greg Nicholas; JurgaR / iStockphoto; Courtesy of Xerox Corporation; JurgaR / iStockphoto; Courtesy of Xerox Corporation

⊛ **CONSIDER THIS**

How does resolution affect print quality?
As with many other input and output devices, one factor that determines the quality of an ink-jet printer is its resolution. Printer resolution is measured by the number of *dots per inch* (*dpi*) a printer can print. With an ink-jet printer, a dot is a drop of ink. A higher dpi means the print quality is higher because the drops of ink are smaller and more drops fit in an area.

The difference in quality becomes noticeable when the size of the printed image increases. That is, a wallet-sized image printed at 1200 dpi may look similar in quality to one printed at 2400 dpi. When you increase the size of the image, to 8 × 10 for example, the printout of the 1200 dpi resolution may look grainier than the one printed using a 2400 dpi resolution.

Ink Cartridges   The printhead mechanism in an ink-jet printer contains ink-filled cartridges. Each cartridge has fifty to several hundred small ink holes, or nozzles. The steps in Figure 7-28 illustrate how a drop of ink appears on a page. The ink propels through any combination of the nozzles to form a character or image on the paper.

When the cartridge runs out of ink, you simply replace the cartridge. Most ink-jet printers use two or more ink cartridges, one containing black ink and the other(s) containing colors. Some color cartridges contain a variety of ink colors; others contain only a single color. Consider the number of ink cartridges a printer requires, along with the cost of the cartridges, when purchasing a printer. To reduce the expense of purchasing cartridges, some users opt to purchase refilled cartridges or have empty cartridges refilled by a third-party vendor.

⚡ **Internet Research**

How much do ink cartridges cost?

Search for: ink cartridge cost comparison

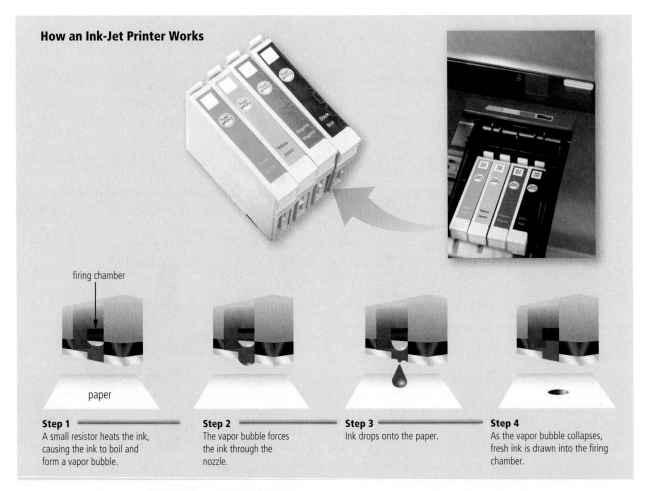

How an Ink-Jet Printer Works

firing chamber

paper

Step 1
A small resistor heats the ink, causing the ink to boil and form a vapor bubble.

Step 2
The vapor bubble forces the ink through the nozzle.

Step 3
Ink drops onto the paper.

Step 4
As the vapor bubble collapses, fresh ink is drawn into the firing chamber.

Figure 7-28   This figure shows how an ink-jet printer works.
© BoyanDimitrov / Shutterstock.com; © Almaamor / Dreamstime.com; © Cengage Learning

Photo Printers

A **photo printer** is a color printer that produces lab-quality photos (Figure 7-29). Some photo printers print just one or two sizes of photos, for example, 3 × 5 inches and 4 × 6 inches. Others print up to 8 × 10 or even larger. Some even print panoramic photos. Generally, the more sizes the printer prints, the more expensive the printer.

Many photo printers use ink-jet technology. With models that can print letter-sized documents, users connect the photo printer to their computer and use it for all their printing needs. For a few hundred dollars, this type of photo printer is ideal for the home or small business user.

Most photo printers are PictBridge enabled, so that you can print photos without a computer. *PictBridge* is a standard technology that allows you to print photos directly from a digital camera by connecting a cable from the digital camera to a USB port on the printer. Photo printers also usually have a built-in card slot(s) so that the printer can print digital photos directly from a memory card. Read How To 7-4 for instructions about printing from a smartphone or tablet.

Discover More: Visit this chapter's free resources to learn more about photo printers.

Figure 7-29   A photo printer.
© iStockphoto / Tamás Ambrits

⚙ **HOW TO 7-4**

Print from a Smartphone or Tablet

As smartphones and tablets become more widely used and packed with features, you may need to print items stored on these devices. For example, you may capture a great photo while spending time with your family and want to print the photo to place on your desk, or you may take notes on your tablet and want to print a hard copy. You have several options available to print from a smartphone or tablet. The method you use will depend primarily on the type of mobile device and printer you are using, and the printer must support printing from a mobile device. The following steps describe how to print from a smartphone or tablet:

1. Verify your mobile device or tablet is connected to the same network as the printer.
2. If necessary, download and install an app on your device or tablet to enable you to print. The printer's documentation will inform you if you need an app and, if so, where to obtain it.

3. When you are viewing the item that you want to print on your smartphone or tablet, select the option to print on your printer and then retrieve the printout.

In addition to using an app or built-in features on your mobile device or computer to print, you may be able to configure your printer so that you can attach files and send them to a specified email address. The following steps describe how to use this feature on supported printers:

1. Access your printer's settings and make sure the printer is connected to your network.
2. Configure the option to set up an email address for receiving print jobs and write down that email address.
3. On your computer or mobile device, send the file you want to print as an attachment to an email message addressed to the email address determined in Step 2.
4. When the printer receives the email message with the file attachment, it will print the file.

If your mobile device or printer does not support wireless printing, you also can print

by transferring the file from your smartphone or tablet to your laptop, desktop, or printer. The following steps describe how to print from a smartphone or tablet when wireless printing is not supported:

1. Remove the memory card from your smartphone or tablet and insert it into your laptop, desktop, or printer. *Note:* If your smartphone or tablet does not have a removable memory card, you can connect the smartphone or tablet to a desktop, laptop, or printer using the USB cable included with your device.
2. On the laptop, desktop, or printer, navigate to and select the file you want to print, and then select the option to print the file.
3. When the printer stops, safely remove the memory card from the laptop, desktop, or printer and insert it in your smartphone or tablet.

✷ **Consider This:** What are some other reasons why you might want to print from a smartphone or tablet?

Figure 7-30 A laser printer.
Courtesy of Xerox Corporation

Laser Printers

A **laser printer** is a high-speed, high-quality nonimpact printer (Figure 7-30). Laser printers are available in both black-and-white and color models. A laser printer for personal computers ordinarily uses individual 8 1/2 × 11-inch sheets of paper stored in one or more removable trays that slide in the printer case.

Laser printers print text and graphics in high-quality resolutions. While laser printers usually cost more than ink-jet printers, many models are available at affordable prices for the home user. Laser printers usually print at faster speeds than ink-jet printers.

Depending on the quality, speed, and type of laser printer, the cost ranges from a few hundred to a few thousand dollars for the home and small office user, and several hundred thousand dollars for the enterprise user.

When printing a document, laser printers process and store the entire page before they actually print it. For this reason, laser printers sometimes are called page printers. Storing a page before printing requires that the laser printer has a certain amount of memory in the device. The more memory in the printer, the faster it usually can print.

Operating in a manner similar to a copy machine, a laser printer creates images using a laser beam and powdered ink, called *toner*. The laser beam produces an image on a drum inside the printer. The light of the laser alters the electrical charge on the drum wherever it hits. When this occurs, the toner sticks to the drum and then transfers to the paper through a combination of pressure and heat (Figure 7-31). When the toner runs out, you replace the toner cartridge.

Internet Research

How much does toner for a laser printer cost?

Search for: laser printer toner cost comparison

How a Black-and-White Laser Printer Works

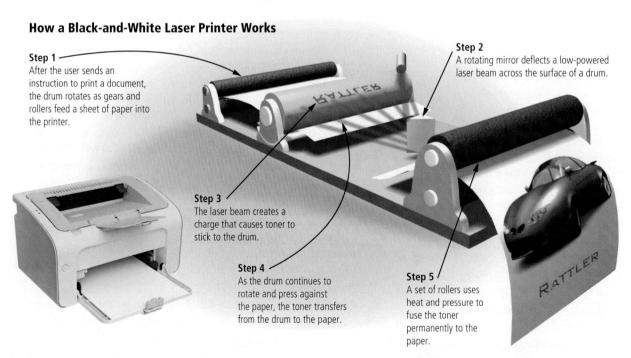

Step 1
After the user sends an instruction to print a document, the drum rotates as gears and rollers feed a sheet of paper into the printer.

Step 2
A rotating mirror deflects a low-powered laser beam across the surface of a drum.

Step 3
The laser beam creates a charge that causes toner to stick to the drum.

Step 4
As the drum continues to rotate and press against the paper, the toner transfers from the drum to the paper.

Step 5
A set of rollers uses heat and pressure to fuse the toner permanently to the paper.

Figure 7-31 This figure shows how a black-and-white laser printer works.
© Cengage Learning; © Serg64 / Shutterstock.com

All-in-One Printers

An **all-in-one printer**, also called a *multifunction printer* (MFP), is a single device that looks like a printer or a copy machine but provides the functionality of a printer, scanner, copy machine, and perhaps a fax machine (Figure 7-32). Some use color ink-jet printer technology, while others use laser technology.

Figure 7-32   An all-in-one printer.
Courtesy of Epson America, Inc.

 CONSIDER THIS

Who uses all-in-one printers?
Small/home office users have all-in-one printers because these devices require less space than having a separate printer, scanner, copy machine, and fax machine. Another advantage of these devices is they are significantly less expensive than if you purchase each device separately. If the device breaks down, however, you lose all four functions, which is the primary disadvantage.

 **BTW**
High-Tech Talk
Discover More: Visit this chapter's free resources to learn how 3-D printers work.

3-D Printers

A **3-D printer** uses a process called additive manufacturing to create an object by adding material to a three-dimensional object, one horizontal layer at a time. 3-D printers can print solid objects, such as clothing, prosthetics, eyewear, implants, toys, parts, prototypes, and more (Figure 7-33).

Using a digital model created with CAD (computer-aided design) software, 3-D printers begin creating an object at the bottom and add layers of material to the object until it is complete. Depending on the type of printer, the layers are built with liquid polymer, gel, or resin.

In the past, 3-D printers were quite expensive and used only by large corporations. Today, home and small business users work with more affordable desktop 3-D printers.

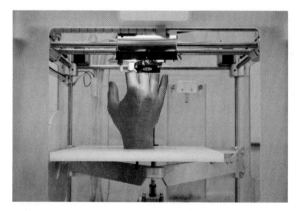

Figure 7-33   A 3-D printer.
© dreamnikon / Fotolia

Thermal Printers

A **thermal printer** generates images by pushing electrically heated pins against heat-sensitive paper. Basic thermal printers are inexpensive, but the print quality is low, the images tend to fade over time, and thermal paper can be expensive. Self-service gas pumps often print gas receipts using a built-in, lower-quality thermal printer. Many point-of-sale terminals in retail and grocery stores also print purchase receipts on thermal paper.

Some thermal printers have high print quality and can print at much faster rates than ink-jet and laser printers. A *dye-sublimation printer*, sometimes called a *digital photo printer*, uses heat to transfer colored dye to specially coated paper. Photography studios, medical labs, security identification systems, and other professional applications requiring high image quality use dye-sublimation printers that can cost thousands of dollars (Figure 7-34). Dye-sublimation printers for the home or small business user, by contrast, typically are much slower and less expensive than their professional counterparts. Some are small enough for the mobile user to carry in a briefcase.

Figure 7-34   A dye-sublimation printer.
Courtesy of Mitsubishi Electric Visual Solutions America, Inc.

Mobile Printers

A **mobile printer** is a small, lightweight, battery-powered printer that allows a mobile user to print from a laptop, smartphone, or other mobile device while traveling (Figure 7-35). Barely wider than the paper on which they print, mobile printers fit easily in a briefcase alongside a laptop.

Mobile printers mainly use ink-jet or thermal technology. Many connect to a USB port. Others have a built-in wireless port through which they communicate with the computer.

Figure 7-35   A mobile printer is small enough to fit in a backpack.
Courtesy of Brother International Corporation

Label Printers

A **label printer** is a small printer that prints on an adhesive-type material that can be placed on a variety of items, such as envelopes, packages, optical discs, photos, and file folders (Figure 7-36). Most label printers also print bar codes. Label printers typically use thermal technology.

Plotters and Large-Format Printers

Plotters are sophisticated printers used to produce high-quality drawings, such as blueprints, maps, and circuit diagrams. These printers are used in specialized fields such as engineering and drafting and usually are very costly. Current plotters use a row of charged wires (called styli) to draw an electrostatic pattern on specially coated paper and then fuse toner to the pattern. The printed image consists of a series of very small dots, which provides high-quality output.

Using ink-jet printer technology, but on a much larger scale, a **large-format printer** creates photo-realistic-quality color prints. Graphic artists use these high-cost, high-performance printers for signs, posters, and other professional quality displays (Figure 7-37).

Figure 7-36   A label printer.
© iStockphoto.com /ZavgSG

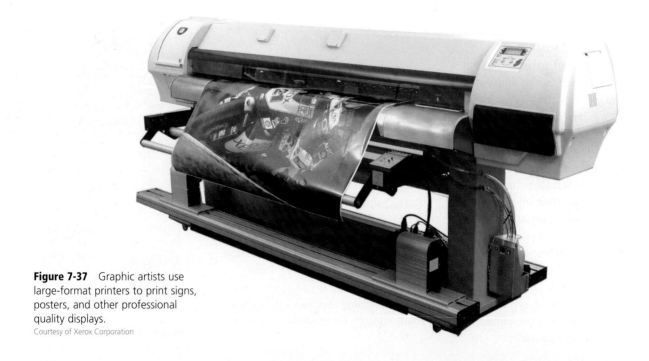

Figure 7-37   Graphic artists use large-format printers to print signs, posters, and other professional quality displays.
Courtesy of Xerox Corporation

Impact Printers

An **impact printer** forms characters and graphics on a piece of paper by striking a mechanism against an inked ribbon that physically contacts the paper. Impact printers characteristically are noisy because of this striking activity (Figure 7-38). Impact printers are ideal for printing multipart forms because they print through many layers of paper easily. Factories, warehouses, and retail counters may use impact printers because these printers withstand dusty environments, vibrations, and extreme temperatures.

Discover More: Visit this chapter's free resources to learn more about impact printers.

Other Output Devices

In addition to displays and printers, other output devices are available for specific uses and applications. These include speakers, headphones and earbuds, data projectors, interactive whiteboards, and force-feedback game controllers and tactile output.

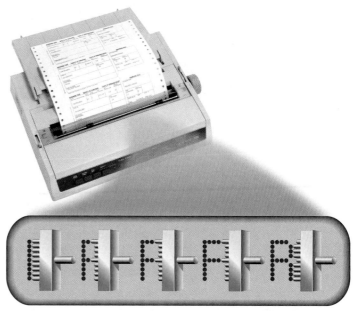

Figure 7-38   An impact printer produces printed images when tiny pins strike an inked ribbon.
Courtesy of Oki Data Americas, Inc.; © Cengage Learning

Speakers

Most personal computers and mobile devices have a small internal speaker that usually emits only low-quality sound. Thus, many users attach surround sound **speakers** or speaker systems to their computers, game consoles, and mobile devices to generate higher-quality sounds for playing games, interacting with multimedia presentations, listening to music, and viewing movies (Figure 7-39).

Most surround sound computer speaker systems include one or two center speakers and two or more *satellite speakers* that are positioned so that sound emits from all directions. Speakers typically have tone and volume controls, allowing users to adjust settings. To boost the low bass sounds, surround sound speaker systems also include a *subwoofer*.

In some configurations, a cable connects the speakers or the subwoofer to a port on the computer or device. With wireless speakers, however, a transmitter connects to a port on the computer, which wirelessly communicates with the speakers.

center speaker

subwoofer

satellite speakers

satellite speakers

Figure 7-39   Users often attach high-quality surround sound speaker systems to their computers, game consoles, and mobile devices.
Courtesy of Logitech

 CONSIDER THIS

What do the numbers mean in surround sound configurations?
The first number refers to the number of speakers, and the second number refers to the number of subwoofers. For example, a 2.1 speaker system contains two speakers and one subwoofer. A 5.1 speaker system has five speakers (i.e., four satellite speakers, one center speaker) and one subwoofer. A 7.2 speaker system has seven speakers (i.e., four satellite speakers, two side speakers, one center speaker) and two subwoofers.

 **Internet Research**

Which wireless speakers are the best?

Search for: wireless speaker reviews

Figure 7-40 In a crowded environment where speakers are not practical, users can wear headphones to hear audio output.
© Terrie L. Zeller / Shutterstock.com

headphones

Internet Research

Which Bluetooth headset is best?

Search for: bluetooth headset reviews

Headphones and Earbuds

When using speakers, anyone in listening distance can hear the output. In a computer laboratory or other crowded environment, speakers might not be practical. Instead, users can listen through headphones or earbuds so that only the individual wearing the headphones or earbuds hears the sound from the computer. The difference is that **headphones** cover or are placed outside of the ear (Figure 7-40), whereas **earbuds** (shown with the audio output devices in Figure 7-23 earlier in the chapter) rest inside the ear canal. Both headphones and earbuds usually include noise-cancelling technology to reduce the interference of sounds from the surrounding environment.

A *headset* is a device that functions as both headphones and a microphone (shown in Figure 7-1 at the beginning of the chapter). Computer and smartphone users wear a headset to free their hands for typing and other activities while talking or listening to audio output. Many headsets communicate wirelessly with the computer or mobile device.

As an alternative to headphones, earbuds, or headsets, you can listen to audio from mobile devices, such as a portable media player or smartphone, through speakers in a vehicle or on a stereo system at home or work. Or, you can purchase speakers specifically designed to play audio from the device.

Data Projectors

A **data projector** is a device that projects the text and images displaying on a computer or mobile device screen on a larger screen so that an audience can see the image clearly (Figure 7-41). For example, many classrooms use data projectors so that all students easily can see an instructor's presentation on the screen.

data projector

Figure 7-41 A data projector projects an image from a computer or mobile device screen on a larger screen so that an audience easily can see the image.
©iStockphoto / poba; © iStockphoto / Michal Szwedo

Some data projectors are large devices that attach to a ceiling or wall in an auditorium. Others, designed for the mobile user, are small portable devices that can be transported easily. Two types of smaller, lower-cost units are LCD projectors and DLP projectors.

- An *LCD projector*, which uses liquid crystal display technology, attaches directly to a computer or mobile device and uses its own light source to display the information shown on the computer screen. Because LCD projectors tend to produce lower-quality images, users often prefer DLP projectors for their sharper, brighter images.
- A *digital light processing (DLP) projector* uses tiny mirrors to reflect light, which produces crisp, bright, colorful images that remain in focus and can be seen clearly, even in a well-lit room. Some newer televisions use DLP instead of LCD or plasma technology.

Interactive Whiteboards

An **interactive whiteboard** is a touch-sensitive device, resembling a dry-erase board, that displays the image on a connected computer screen, usually via a projector. A presenter controls the program by clicking a remote control, touching the whiteboard, drawing on or erasing the whiteboard with a special digital pen and eraser, or writing on a special tablet. Notes written on the interactive whiteboard can be saved directly on the computer and/or printed. Interactive whiteboards are used frequently in classrooms as a teaching tool (Figure 7-42), during meetings as a collaboration tool, and to enhance delivery of presentations.

Force-Feedback Game Controllers and Tactile Output

Joysticks, wheels, gamepads, and motion-sensing game controllers are input devices used to control movements and actions of a player or object in computer games, simulations, and video games. These devices also function as output devices when they include *force feedback*, which is a technology that sends resistance to the device in response to actions of the user (Figure 7-43). For example, as you use the simulation software to drive from a smooth road onto a gravel alley, the steering

Figure 7-42   Teachers and students can write directly on an interactive whiteboard, or they can write on a slate that communicates wirelessly with the whiteboard.
Courtesy of SMART Technologies

wheel trembles or vibrates, making the driving experience as realistic as possible. These devices also are used in practical training applications, such as in the military and aviation.

Some input devices, such as a mouse, and mobile devices, such as a smartphone, include *tactile output* that provides the user with a physical response from the device. For example, users may sense a bumping feeling on their hand while scrolling through a smartphone's contact list.

Figure 7-43   Gaming devices often use force feedback, giving the user a realistic experience.
© Vetkit / Dreamstime.com; © shutswis / Shutterstock.com; © Robseguin / Dreamstime.com

Assistive Technology Input and Output

The ever-increasing presence of computers in everyone's lives has generated an awareness of the need to address computing requirements for those who have or may develop physical limitations. **The Americans with Disabilities Act (ADA)** requires any company with 15 or more employees to make reasonable attempts to accommodate the needs of physically challenged workers. Read Ethics & Issues 7-4 to consider who should pay for assistive technologies.

BTW
Technology Trend
Discover More: Visit this chapter's free resources to learn more about assistive technologies.

Who Should Pay for Assistive Technologies?

Public institutions, such as schools and libraries, are required to accommodate visitors or students who require wheelchairs or other devices to enter and move about the building. These institutions install wide doors and ramps and modify restroom facilities to ensure accessibility. Should the same accommodations be available for those who need assistive technologies?

Assistive technologies include devices you can operate with your foot; one example is a mouse. Braille keyboards, printers, and display devices exist for visually impaired users. Several sources are available to fund assistive technologies. Health insurance covers many assistive technologies. Government programs, such as Medicare, Medicaid, or Social Security, offer some funding. In addition, private or nonprofit groups may provide grants or donations.

Many libraries offer digital versions of books, including digital Braille and audio, for those with visual impairments or dyslexia. Patrons must submit a request that includes recommendations from a doctor. The Individuals with Disabilities Education Act (IDEA) requires that public schools provide free and appropriate education for all students. Technology increasingly is an important part of a student's education. Thus, schools are required to purchase or acquire funding for adaptive technologies for students who need them. If a student's parents provide an assistive technology that a student uses at school, the school must pay to repair and service the device.

Consider This: Should parents of children who need assistive technology devices be required to provide funding or partial funding? Why or why not? What resources should public libraries provide to patrons with disabilities?

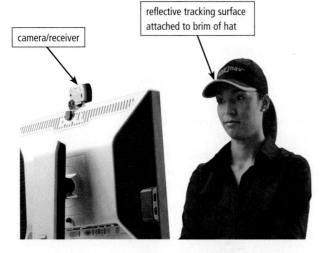

Figure 7-44 A camera/receiver mounted on the monitor tracks the position of the head-mounted pointer, which is the reflective material on the brim of the hat. As the user moves her head, the pointer on the screen also moves.
Courtesy of NaturalPoint, Inc.

Besides voice recognition, which is ideal for blind or visually impaired users, several other input options are available. Users with limited hand mobility who want to use a keyboard can use an on-screen keyboard or a keyboard with larger keys. Users with limited hand movement can use a head-mounted pointer to control the pointer or insertion point (Figure 7-44). To simulate the functions of a mouse button, a user works with switches that control the pointer. The switch might be a hand pad, a foot pedal, a receptor that detects facial motions, or a pneumatic instrument controlled by puffs of air.

For users with mobility, hearing, or vision disabilities, many different types of output options are available. Hearing-impaired users, for example, can instruct programs to display words instead of sounds. Visually impaired users can change screen settings, such as increasing the size or changing the color of the text to make the words easier to read. Instead of using a monitor, blind users can work with voice output. That is, the computer speaks out loud the information that appears on the screen. Another alternative is a Braille printer, which prints information on paper in Braille (Figure 7-45).

Internet Research

What are new developments related to assistive technologies?

Search for: assistive technology devices

Figure 7-45 A Braille printer.
Courtesy of Enabling Technologies; © Don Farrall / Getty Images

✔ NOW YOU SHOULD KNOW

Be sure you understand the material presented in the sections Printers, Other Output Devices, and Assistive Technology Input and Output, as it relates to the chapter objectives.
Now you should know...

- Which type of printer might be suited to your needs (Objective 9)

- When you would use speakers, headphones, earbuds, data projectors, interactive whiteboards, and game controllers (Objective 10)

- Which types of assistive technology options are available (Objective 11)

Discover More: Visit this chapter's premium content for practice quiz opportunities.

✔ Chapter Summary

This chapter presented a variety of options for input and output. Input options included the keyboard, mouse and other pointing devices, touch screens, pen input, motion input, voice input, video input, and scanners and reading devices. Output options included displays, printers, speakers, headphones and earbuds, data projectors, interactive whiteboards, and force-feedback game controllers and tactile output. The chapter also presented several assistive technology options for input and output.

Discover More: Visit this chapter's free resources for additional content that accompanies this chapter and also includes these features: Technology Innovators: HP, Logitech, Masahiro Hara and Denso Wave, and Ursula Burns; Technology Trends: Drones and Assistive Technology; and High-Tech Talks: Biometric Input and How 3-D Printers Work.

Test your knowledge of chapter material by accessing the Study Guide, Flash Cards, and Practice Test resources from your smartphone, tablet, laptop, or desktop.

⚡ TECHNOLOGY @ WORK

📰 Finance

Watching the television, you notice a ticker at the bottom of the screen showing how various stocks currently are performing. You realize that the price of a stock you own has risen significantly, most likely the result of a recent press release about a new product they plan to release. A notification on your smartphone also alerts you of the sharp rise, and you decide to keep a closer eye on the price for the rest of the day in case you wish to sell some shares. You then use the app on your smartphone to check the balances in your accounts.

Because timely decisions often are important in the financial industry, technology helps provide important information to all who participate in various financial transactions. In the stock market, large displays on the trading floors of various exchanges help provide timely information to those buying and selling shares of stock. With the advancements in technology, stock traders now can see up-to-the-minute stock information on their computers and mobile

devices using various finance programs and apps. Users can configure these programs and apps to display notifications when a certain stock's price reaches a certain value so that they can decide whether they want to buy or sell shares. The program or app then can facilitate the sale or purchase of stock shares, all within seconds. Technology also enables users to buy or sell stock shares automatically when they reach a certain price, all without additional user intervention.

In addition to technology playing a role in the stock market, it also helps with banking for individuals and businesses. In fact, technology makes it possible to perform the majority of banking transactions, all without having to visit a bank teller. ATMs allow people the flexibility to deposit and withdraw funds from many locations around the globe. Web and mobile apps also are available and provide users with the ability to access account information, transfer funds between accounts, pay bills electronically, apply for loans, and complete the necessary

information to open new accounts. Some financial institutions allow their users to use a mobile app on their smartphone to deposit checks by taking a picture of the front and back of an endorsed check. The next time you are able to perform a financial transaction easily with little or no human intervention, think about all the ways technology has made this possible.

✳ **Consider This:** How else might computers and technology be used in the finance industry?

© Andrey_Popov / Shutterstock.com

Study Guide

The Study Guide exercise reinforces material you should know for the chapter exam.

Discover More: Visit this chapter's premium content to **test your knowledge of digital content** associated with this chapter and **access the Study Guide resource** from your smartphone, tablet, laptop, or desktop.

Instructions: Answer the questions below using the format that helps you remember best or that is required by your instructor. Possible formats may include one or more of these options: write the answers; create a document that contains the answers; record answers as audio or video using a webcam, smartphone, or portable media player; post answers on a blog, wiki, or website; or highlight answers in the book/e-book.

1. ___ is any data and instructions entered into the memory of a computer.

2. Define these terms: data, software, and command. Give an example of a user response.

3. List features that are common to most keyboards. Describe how to use a keyboard shortcut.

4. Explain the criminal and beneficial purposes of keyboard monitoring software.

5. Differentiate among compact, ergonomic, gaming, and wireless keyboards.

6. Define the term, pointer. Name objects a pointing device can select.

7. List different mouse types.

8. Describe the following input devices: touchpad, pointing stick, and trackball.

9. Explain how to interact with a touch screen.

10. Describe how desktop monitors, laptop and mobile device screens, smartphones, wearable devices, portable media players, digital cameras, kiosks, and navigation systems use touch input.

11. Explain technologies and laws aimed to prevent use of mobile devices while driving.

12. List methods and devices for using pen input. Define the term, digitizer.

13. Explain how hand-writing notes during class could impact your knowledge retention.

14. Define the term, motion input. Describe how the entertainment industry, the military, athletes, and the medical field use motion input.

15. Name hardware and devices used for voice and audio input.

16. Outline steps involved in using DV technology.

17. List steps for setting up and using a webcam.

18. Explain what occurs during a videoconference and the technology needed.

19. Outline steps to secure your privacy when using a device with a webcam.

20. Describe types of scanners and reading devices.

21. A(n) ___ code stores information that can correspond to a web address or other content.

22. List guidelines for safely scanning QR codes.

23. Explain why a retailer would use RFID technology, and list uses for magstripe readers.

24. List guidelines to protect your credit card from scanning devices.

25. Describe how a bank uses MICR technology.

26. Give examples of data collection devices and describe how they are used.

27. Define the term, output. List types and methods of output.

28. Define the terms, display and monitor. Describe different types of monitors.

29. List steps to connect a laptop to an external display.

30. Differentiate among LCD, CCF, LED, TFT, OLED, and AMOLED technologies.

31. Describe how display quality is determined. Define these terms: resolution, response time, nit, candela, dot pitch, and contrast ratio.

32. Explain the purpose of the GPU. List and describe port types for monitors.

33. Describe the technologies used by HDTV. Explain the capabilities of a Smart TV.

34. List steps to show media on a Smart TV from a computer or mobile device.

35. Explain safety issues surrounding hardware radiation.

36. Describe orientation options for printouts. Explain what is needed to print using Bluetooth.

37. Explain how an ink-jet printer works, and describe the mechanics of the ink cartridge.

38. Explain how resolution affects printer quality.

39. Explain how a photo printer uses PictBridge.

40. Outline steps for printing from a smartphone or tablet.

41. Compare the price and quality of laser printers to ink-jet printers.

42. Describe the following printer types: all-in-one, 3-D, thermal, mobile, label, plotter, and impact.

43. Explain how computers and mobile devices use speakers, such as satellite speakers, to emit sound.

44. Differentiate among headphones, earbuds, and headsets.

45. Define the term, data projector. Differentiate between LCD and DLP projector technology.

46. Describe uses of interactive whiteboards and force-feedback game controllers. Define the term, tactile output.

47. List types of assistive technologies for input and output.

48. Explain issues surrounding payment for assistive technologies.

49. Explain how the finance field uses technology.

You should be able to define the Primary Terms and be familiar with the Secondary Terms listed below.

Key Terms

Discover More: Visit this chapter's premium content to **view definitions** for each term and to **access the Flash Cards resource** from your smartphone, tablet, laptop, or desktop.

Primary Terms (shown in **bold-black** characters in the chapter)

3-D printer (349)
all-in-one printer (349)
Americans with Disabilities Act (ADA) (353)
bar code (335)
bar code reader (335)
data projector (352)
digital pen (327)
digital video (DV) camera (330)
display (340)
DV technology (331)
earbuds (352)
graphics tablet (328)

HDTV (343)
headphones (352)
impact printer (351)
ink-jet printer (345)
input (318)
interactive whiteboard (353)
keyboard (320)
label printer (350)
large-format printer (350)
laser printer (348)
LCD (341)
magstripe reader (339)
mobile printer (350)

monitor (340)
mouse (322)
nonimpact printer (345)
OCR devices (335)
OMR devices (335)
output (339)
pen input (326)
photo printer (347)
plotters (350)
pointer (322)
printer (344)
QR code (335)
resolution (342)
RFID (336)

RFID reader (336)
scanner (334)
signature capture pad (326)
speakers (351)
stylus (326)
thermal printer (349)
touch screen (324)
touchpad (323)
trackball (324)
video call (332)
videoconference (333)
voice recognition (330)
webcam (332)

Secondary Terms (shown in *italic* characters in the chapter)

active-matrix (342)
air gestures (328)
AMOLED (342)
aspect ratio (343)
audio input (330)
backlight (341)
bar code scanner (335)
Bluetooth printing (345)
candela (342)
command (318)
compact keyboard (321)
contrast ratio (342)
cursor (320)
data (318)
data collection device (338)
digital light processing (DLP) projector (352)
digital photo printer (349)
digitizer (328)
display device (340)
DisplayPort (343)
dot pitch (342)
dots per inch (dpi) (346)
DVI (Digital Video Interface) port (343)
dye-sublimation printer (349)
ergonomic keyboard (322)
flat-panel display (340)
force feedback (353)
frame rate (331)

function keys (320)
gaming keyboard (322)
gesture (324)
gesture recognition (328)
graphics processing unit (342)
handwriting recognition software (327)
HDMI (High-Definition Media Interface) port (343)
headset (352)
high-definition television (343)
insertion point (320)
keyboard monitoring software (321)
keyboard shortcut (320)
keylogging software (321)
landscape orientation (344)
laser mouse (322)
LCD projector (352)
LED (341)
LED display (342)
liquid crystal display (341)
magnetic stripe card reader (337)
MICR devices (338)
morphing (331)
motion input (328)
multifunction printer (348)
multi-touch (324)
native resolution (342)
nit (342)
OCR software (334)

OLED (342)
optical mouse (322)
PictBridge (347)
pixel (342)
pixel pitch (342)
plasma display (344)
portrait orientation (344)
printout (344)
response time (342)
Retina Display (342)
satellite speakers (351)
Smart TV (343)
soft copy (340)
software (318)
source document (334)
speech recognition (330)
speech-to-text (330)

streaming cam (333)
subwoofer (351)
tactile output (353)
TFT (342)
toggle key (320)
toner (348)
touch mouse (323)
touch-sensitive pad (326)
trackpad (323)
UPC (Universal Product Code) (335)
user response (318)
voice input (330)
voice recognition application (330)
widescreen monitor (343)
wireless keyboard (322)
wireless mouse (323)

QR code (335)

Checkpoint

The Checkpoint exercises test your knowledge of the chapter concepts. The page number containing the answer appears in parentheses after each exercise. The Consider This exercises challenge your understanding of chapter concepts.

Discover More: Visit this chapter's premium content to **complete the Checkpoint exercises** interactively; complete the **self-assessment in the Test Prep resource** from your smartphone, tablet, laptop, or desktop; and then **take the Practice Test**.

True/False   Mark T for True and F for False.

_____ 1. CAPS LOCK and NUM LOCK are two examples of toggle keys. (320)

_____ 2. Keylogging software runs undetected and stores every keystroke in a file for later retrieval. (321)

_____ 3. Wearable devices mainly rely upon touch input. (325)

_____ 4. A smaller frame rate results in a smaller file size for a video, as well as a smoother playback. (331)

_____ 5. Optical character recognition (OCR) and optical mark recognition (OMR) are two technologies used by QR code readers. (335)

_____ 6. Many retailers do not believe RFID is an alternative to bar code identification because it requires line-of-sight transmission. (336)

_____ 7. A data collection device reads and scans data from a source document. (338)

_____ 8. In terms of response time, the lower the number, the faster the response time. (342)

_____ 9. Contrast ratio defines a display's width relative to its height. (342)

_____ 10. Every electronic device emits some level of radiation. (344)

_____ 11. Printer resolution is measured by the number of pixels per inch a printer can print. (346)

_____ 12. A dye-sublimation printer uses heat to transfer colored dye to specially coated paper. (349)

Multiple Choice   Select the best answer.

1. A _____ is an instruction a user issues by responding to a message displayed by a program or app. (318)
   a. command
   b. user response
   c. keyboard shortcut
   d. function

2. Which of the following is not an example of a pointing device? (324)
   a. touchpad
   b. trackball
   c. touch screen
   d. pointing stick

3. A(n) _____ is an input device that contains buttons and/ or wheels you operate with a thumb or finger. (326)
   a. digitizer
   b. interactive whiteboard
   c. touch-sensitive pad
   d. OCR device

4. _____ read hand-drawn marks, such as small circles or rectangles. (335)
   a. MICR readers
   b. Digitizers
   c. OMR devices
   d. OCR devices

5. LCD displays typically produce color using _____ technology, which uses a separate transistor to supply charges to each liquid crystal cell. (342)
   a. passive-matrix
   b. OLED
   c. Retina Display
   d. active-matrix

6. _____ displays use organic molecules that are self-illuminating and, thus, do not require a backlight. (342)
   a. OLED
   b. TFT
   c. LED
   d. CCFL

7. _____ orientation refers to a printout that is wider than it is tall. (344)
   a. Cinematic
   b. Portrait
   c. Landscape
   d. Widescreen

8. How many subwoofers would a 7.2 speaker system contain? (351)
   a. 1   c. 7
   b. 2   d. 9

Checkpoint

Matching   Match the terms with their definitions.

_____ 1. command (318)

_____ 2. keyboard shortcut (320)

_____ 3. touchpad (323)

_____ 4. multi-touch (324)

_____ 5. voice recognition (330)

_____ 6. scanner (334)

_____ 7. QR code (335)

_____ 8. graphics processing unit (342)

_____ 9. headset (352)

_____ 10. interactive whiteboard (353)

a. a type of 2-D bar code that stores information in both horizontal and vertical directions

b. small, flat, rectangular pointing device that is sensitive to pressure and motion

c. touch screen capability of recognizing more than one point of contact at the same time

d. device that functions as both headphones and a microphone

e. touch-sensitive device that displays the image on a connected computer screen, usually via projector

f. chip that controls the manipulation and display of graphics on a display device

g. instruction that causes a program or app to perform a specific action

h. computer or mobile device's capability of distinguishing spoken words

i. light-sensing input device that reads printed text and graphics and then translates the result into a form the computer can process

j. one or more keyboard keys that you press to perform an operating system or application-related task

✳ Consider This   Answer the following questions in the format specified by your instructor.

1. Answer the critical thinking questions posed at the end of these elements in this chapter: Ethics & Issues (326, 327, 344, 354), How To (332, 341, 343, 347), Mini Features (325, 329, 331), Secure IT (321, 333, 336, 337), and Technology @ Work (355).

2. What are some examples of data? (318)

3. What are some commonly used input methods? (319)

4. What happens when you press a toggle key? (320)

5. What steps can you take to detect keyboard monitoring software? (321)

6. What are some types of keyboards? (321)

7. How does an optical mouse differ from a touch mouse? (322)

8. How does a stylus differ from a digital pen? (326)

9. Who might use a graphics tablet? (328)

10. What are some disciplines in which motion input is being used? (329)

11. What is meant by the term, morphing? (331)

12. How does a video call differ from a videoconference? (333)

13. What steps should you take to secure a webcam? (333)

14. How do OCR and OMR devices differ? (335)

15. What do bar codes represent? (335)

16. What guidelines should you follow to use a QR code safely? (336)

17. What are some uses of RFID? (336)

18. What is contained in an RFID tag? (336)

19. Why might some magstripes become unreadable? (338)

20. What are the four basic types of output? (340)

21. What are some advantages and a disadvantage of OLED technology? (342)

22. On today's displays, what is the range for nits? (342)

23. What are commonly used nonimpact printers? (345)

24. If your mobile device does not support wireless printing, how can you print photos from it? (347)

25. What types of businesses use a dye-sublimation printer? (349)

26. Why might a user prefer a DLP projector over an LCD projector? (352)

27. What does the Americans with Disabilities Act (ADA) require? (353)

28. Should schools and companies be required to pay for assistive technologies? Why or why not? (354)

✷ Problem Solving

The Problem Solving exercises extend your knowledge of chapter concepts by seeking solutions to practical problems with technology that you may encounter at home, school, or work. The Collaboration exercise should be completed with a team.

Instructions: You often can solve problems with technology in multiple ways. Determine a solution to the problems in these exercises by using one or more resources available to you (such as a computer or mobile device, articles on the web or in print, blogs, podcasts, videos, television, user guides, other individuals, electronics or computer stores, etc.). Describe your solution, along with the resource(s) used, in the format requested by your instructor (brief report, presentation, discussion, blog post, video, or other means).

Personal

1. **Assistive Technologies**   You have just purchased a new computer and, because of a visual impairment, you are having trouble reading the information on the screen. What are your next steps?

2. **Smart TV Issues**   You are watching a movie on your Smart TV using a streaming media service.

© Courtesy of LG Electronics USA Inc.

Every few minutes, a message is displayed on the TV stating that the movie is buffering. Why might this be happening, and what can you do to resolve this issue?

3. **Touch Gestures Not Working**   You are using the stretch touch gesture to zoom on your mobile device. Each time you perform the gesture, however, instead of zooming, one of your fingers appears to be dragging an item around the screen. What might be the problem?

4. **Dim Screen**   While using your laptop, the screen suddenly becomes dim. You set the brightness to its highest setting before it dimmed and wonder why it suddenly changed. After resetting the brightness to its highest setting, you continue working. What might have caused the screen to dim?

5. **Malfunctioning Earbud**   While listening to music on your portable media player, one side of the earbuds suddenly stops working. What might have caused this?

Professional

6. **Printer Problem**   You are attempting to print on a wireless printer from your laptop, but each time you tap or click the Print button, you receive an error message that the printer is not connected. What are your next steps?

7. **Projector Resolution Issue**   You are preparing for a meeting in your company's conference room and have connected your laptop to the projector. When the projector displays the information from your laptop screen, the resolution drops significantly and not everything fits on the screen. What steps can you take to correct this problem?

8. **Fingerprints Not Recognized**   To increase security, your company now requires employees to sign in to their computer accounts using a fingerprint reader instead of entering a user name and password. This past weekend, you cut the finger you use to sign in, and your computer now does not recognize your fingerprint. As a result, you are unable to access your computer. What are your next steps?

9. **Access Denied**   Your company uses security badges with embedded RFID tags to authenticate the rooms to which employees have access. This badge also grants employees access to the company's parking lot. When arriving at work one morning, you wave your badge in front of the RFID reader, but the gate that allows access to the parking lot does not open. In addition, a red light blinks on the RFID reader. What are your next steps?

10. **Monitors Reversed**   You have two monitors on your desk at work: the monitor on the left is your primary monitor and displays the taskbar and the applications you are currently using, and you typically use the monitor on the right to display an email program. When you arrive at work and sign in to your Windows account, you realize that the monitor on the right is now the primary monitor. What might have happened?

Collaboration

11. **Technology in Finance**   Technology enables individuals and businesses to conduct transactions in the finance industry with great convenience and speed; however, many individuals do not realize the extent to which technology impacts the industry. Form a team of three people to learn more about the important role that technology plays in today's finance industry. One team member should research the different ways that technology impacts and improves personal financial transactions, such as home banking. Another team member should research how large businesses use technology to manage their finances, and the other team member should research the different ways technology has helped improve the stock market. Write a brief report summarizing your findings.

The How To: Your Turn exercises present general guidelines for fundamental skills when using a computer or mobile device and then require that you determine how to apply these general guidelines to a specific program or situation.

How To: Your Turn

Discover More: Visit this chapter's premium content to **challenge yourself with additional How To: Your Turn exercises,** which include App Adventure.

Instructions: You often can complete tasks using technology in multiple ways. Figure out how to perform the tasks described in these exercises by using one or more resources available to you (such as a computer or mobile device, articles on the web or in print, online or program help, user guides, blogs, podcasts, videos, other individuals, trial and error, etc.). Summarize your 'how to' steps, along with the resource(s) used, in the format requested by your instructor (brief report, presentation, discussion, blog post, video, or other means).

1 Work with QR Codes

QR codes initially were used in the automotive industry to track vehicles during the production process. Today, QR codes often are used in publications and advertisements to convey information, direct users to a website, suggest users download a file, or direct users to an app store or marketplace to download an app. Exercise caution when scanning QR codes, because they may direct your mobile computer or device to a malicious website or file. For example, it probably is wise to avoid scanning QR codes appearing on homemade flyers and other similar sources.

Scanning QR Codes

When you encounter a QR code that you want to scan, you should use an app capable of reading QR codes. The following steps guide you through the process of scanning QR codes.
a. Download and install an app that can read QR codes.
b. When you see a QR code you want to scan, run the app on your mobile computer or device. If necessary, select the option to scan a QR code.
c. Hold the device still and point its camera toward the QR code to scan it.
d. Once your device scans the QR code, it will display the associated information. If the QR code represents a web address, the app will run a browser and navigate to that address.

Generating QR Codes

If you want to generate a QR code to make it easier for others to navigate to a particular location or perform an action, you should use a QR code generator. The following steps describe how to generate QR codes:
a. Use a search engine to locate a website that contains a QR code generator and then navigate to it.
b. Enter the information, such as a web address, phone number, word, or short phrase, that you want the QR code to contain, and then tap or click the button to generate the QR code.
c. Copy the generated QR code image and then paste it in the desired location.
d. Scan the QR code to make sure it displays the results you expect.

Exercises

1. Compare and contrast at least three apps that can scan QR codes. Which one is your favorite? Why?
2. Compare and contrast at least three websites or apps that can generate QR codes. Which app would you use to generate QR codes? Why?
3. List at least three places you remember seeing QR codes. Did you scan them? Why or why not?

Source: Cengage Learning

2 Record and Edit a Video

Once you have finished recording a video, you may want to edit it before sharing it with others. For example, you might want to remove portions of the video, add special effects, or play an audio track instead of the audio recorded with the video. The following steps guide you through the process of recording and editing a video.

Record a Video

a. Verify your camera's battery is charged and that the device has sufficient space available to store the video you are about to record.
b. If you plan to record the video from one location, consider placing the camera on a stable surface so that it does not move.
c. If you intend to record outside where it is windy, shield the camera from the wind.
d. Start the recording.

❋ How To: Your Turn

e. If you plan to move the camera during recording, do so with slow, smooth movements.

f. Stop the recording.

Edit a Video

a. If you are using video editing software on your computer, transfer the video to the computer. If you are using video editing capabilities on your mobile device, run the video editing app.

b. Make a copy of the video so that you can revert to the original if you make a mistake.

c. Run a video editing program on your computer and open the video.

d. To trim a video — that is, remove portions from the beginning and/or end of the video — tap or click the command to trim the video. Select the new starting and ending position for the video.

e. To add a special effect to the video, select the location in the video where you want to add the special effect, and then tap or click the command corresponding to the special effect you want to add.

f. To add music that will play while the video is playing, tap or click the command to add a separate audio track to the video. Next, navigate to and select the music file you want to add. Finally, select the starting and ending locations in the video for the music.

g. Preview the video.

h. Save your changes.

i. Exit the video editing program.

Exercises

1. What reasons might you have for wanting to trim a video?

2. What type of device do you use to record videos? Why?

3. Compare and contrast at least three programs or apps that can be used to edit videos. Which one do you prefer? Why?

❸ Save as or Print to a PDF File

In an effort to conserve paper, people today think twice before printing a hard copy of a document. Instead of printing a hard copy of a document, many applications have a built-in feature enabling you to print soft copies in various formats, such as PDF. You can print to a PDF file from many apps, including Microsoft Office. When you save as or print to a PDF file (both saving as or printing to PDF produce the same results), anyone with an app capable of reading PDF files will be able the view the file without necessarily having to open it in the same program from which it was created. Several free apps you can use to view PDF files are available. The following steps guide you through the process of printing to a PDF file.

a. Verify the app from which you want to print has a built-in feature to save files in or print files to PDF format. If this feature is not available, search for and install an app that enables you to save files to or print files in PDF format.

b. Open the file you want to save in or print to PDF format.

c. If you want to save the file as a PDF format, display the app's Save As dialog box and check if PDF is one of the available file types.

d. If you want to print the file to a PDF, display the screen to print the file and select the appropriate printer to print the file to PDF.

Source: Microsoft

e. Tap or click the button to save or print the file.

f. Specify a file name and save location for the PDF file.

Exercises

1. What are some applications you can use to view PDF files?

2. In addition to saving paper, what are some other reasons why you might save or print to a PDF?

❹ Take Screenshots

Many computer and mobile device operating systems allow you to take screenshots, which are snapshots of the screen that are saved as an image. In addition, third-party programs and apps also allow you to take screenshots. The following steps guide you through the process of taking a screenshot on your computer or mobile device.

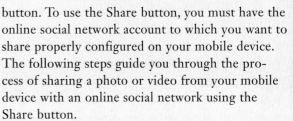

a. If you wish to use a third-party app to take a screenshot, search for, download, and install the desired app. Next, run the app and review the required steps to take the screenshot.

b. Display the desired programs, apps, or windows on the screen of which you want to take a screenshot.

c. Issue the desired command to take the screenshot. On computers, you may need to press a specific key combinations (such as CTRL+PRINT SCREEN). On mobile devices, you may need to press specific buttons at the same time (such as the Home button and the Power button) or perform a specific hand gesture (such as swiping your hand across the screen).

d. Locate the screenshot. If you used a third-party app, it may be displayed immediately upon taking the screenshot. If you used an operating system such as Windows or Mac OS, you may need to run another app (such as Microsoft Word) and paste the image into the document. If you took the screenshot on a mobile device, you may be able to locate the screenshot in the image gallery.

Exercises

1. What are at least three reasons why you may need to take a screenshot?

2. Why might you want to use a third-party program or app to take a screenshot instead of using the built-in function in your computer or device's operating system?

3. If you take a screenshot of an entire screen but require information in only one window on the screen, what steps can you take to manipulate the screenshot so that it shows only the portions of the screen you desire?

⑤ Share a Photo or Video from Your Mobile Device with an Online Social Network

If you take a photo or record a video on your mobile device and want to share it with your friends, you might consider uploading it to an online social network. You can share a photo or video from your mobile device with an online social network in several ways, depending upon the online social network and how your mobile device is configured. This exercise describes two common ways to share a photo or video from your mobile device to an online social network.

Share Button

You may be able to share photos or videos with an online social network easily by using the Share

button. To use the Share button, you must have the online social network account to which you want to share properly configured on your mobile device. The following steps guide you through the process of sharing a photo or video from your mobile device with an online social network using the Share button.

a. Locate and display the photo or video on your mobile device that you want to share with the online social network.

b. Tap the Share button.

c. Tap the desired online social network with which you want to share the photo or video.

d. If desired, type a caption or message to share with the photo or video.

e. Tap the necessary button to share the photo or video.

Uploading Photos or Videos Manually

If you are unable to share your photo or video using the Share button, you can sign in to the online social network and upload it manually. The following steps guide you through the process of sharing a photo or video on an online social network by uploading it manually to your online social network account.

a. If necessary, take a photo or record a video you want to share.

b. Using an app installed on your mobile device or the online social network's website, sign in to your account on the online social network on which you want to share the photo or video.

c. Tap the appropriate button to post or share a photo or video.

d. Navigate to and select the photo or video you want to share.

e. If desired, type a caption or message to share with the photo or video.

f. Tap the necessary button to share the photo or video.

Exercises

1. What types of photos or videos do you share with online social networks?

2. Research the potential privacy risks associated with uploading photos or videos of yourself or your family. Are you comfortable sharing photos or videos on online social networks? Why or why not?

3. Why might individuals want to share photos and videos on online social networks instead of using other methods such as sending them as attachments to email messages?

☀ Internet Research

The Internet Research exercises broaden your understanding of chapter concepts by requiring that you search for information on the web.

Discover More: Visit this chapter's premium content to **challenge yourself with additional Internet Research exercises**, which include Search Sleuth, Green Computing, Ethics in Action, You Review It, and Exploring Technology Careers.

Instructions: Use a search engine or another search tool to locate the information requested or answers to questions presented in the exercises. Describe your findings, along with the search term(s) you used and your web source(s), in the format requested by your instructor (brief report, presentation, discussion, blog post, video, or other means).

1 Making Use of the Web
Health and Fitness

More than 70 percent of Internet users search online for health information, and their most commonly researched topics are specific diseases or conditions, treatments and procedures, and doctors or other health professionals. One-half of these online diagnosticians say that the information they found for themselves or someone else led them to seek medical attention.

Fitness websites and apps can provide guidance and motivation for all fitness levels and lifestyles. Expert advice is offered for designing customized workout routines, maintaining a nutritious diet, and buying equipment. Other features include downloadable MP3 workouts, videos demonstrating correct exercise techniques, and the ability to locate a virtual supportive workout buddy. Users often can set goals and then track their performance and overall progress with logs and detailed graphs.

Research This: (a) Visit WebMD and two other health websites and describe the features of each. Which of the three is the most user-friendly? Why? Search for the difference between the flu and a cold. Describe the symptoms of each and the recommended foods to eat when you are suffering from either ailment.

(b) Visit WebMD and two fitness websites. What similar features do these websites have, such as fitness tools, effective exercises, and food planners? Which website is the easiest to navigate? Why? Which articles, planners, and tools would you use to start or continue your fitness routines?

2 Social Media

Aspiring musicians have turned to online social networks to break into the music business and to promote their material. Musical artists are urged to develop accounts on YouTube, Facebook, OurStage, MP3.com, Ourwave, Twitter, Myspace, Last.fm, PureVolume, and other online social networks to interact and stay connected with their fans. They can post information about concerts and album releases and sell concert tickets. They also can add music that fans can listen to, download at no charge, or purchase. Some online social networks sponsor contests for bands to showcase their talents and vie for fans' votes to play live at a local venue. Others are crowd-funding websites where bands can ask fans to pledge a specific amount of money to support the artists' creative efforts.

Research This: View at least two websites that allow listeners to recommend music and share playlists. What similarities and differences do these websites have? Locate one of your favorite artists on an online social network and describe the content displayed. For example, are concerts and new releases being promoted? Then, search for and then view at least two musician websites. What types of music are available? Which new artists and songs did you hear?

Source: WebMD

Internet Research

❸ Search Skills
News Search

Performing a news search using a search engine will limit search results to news stories that appeared recently or in the past in newspapers and magazines, news websites, and other electronic media news sources. To search for news articles about assistive technology devices, for example, type the search text, assistive technology devices, in the search engine's search box and then tap or click the News link on the search page. You may narrow the results by specifying a date range or location. Tap or click the search button to see the results.

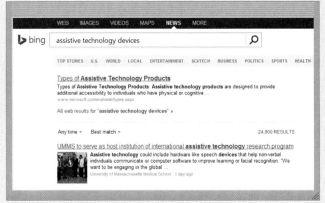

Source: Microsoft

Research This: Create search text using the techniques described above or in previous Search Skills exercises, and type it into a search engine to answer these questions. Present a summary of your findings. (1) Find news articles about the enterprise uses of 3-D printing. (2) Find news articles suggesting capabilities to be included in the next iPhone. (3) Find a news story published within the past week describing how any company uses QR codes. (4) Select a technology company and then find news stories about its financial earnings during the past three months.

❹ Security

The Office of Cyber and Infrastructure Analysis (OCIA), a division of the U.S. Department of Homeland Security, strives to thwart and respond to physical or cyberthreats and hazards. Part of the office's role is to implement two policies: (1) Presidential Policy Directive 21 - Critical Infrastructure Security and Resilience, and (2) Executive Order 13636 - Improving Critical Infrastructure Cybersecurity. These two policies are designed to strengthen and secure the country's critical physical assets and services, such as air traffic control, natural gas supplies, water treatment, power plants, and finance, which are likely targets of cyberattacks. Federal agencies must comply with and routinely assess privacy standards and civil liberties protections. The government must share information regarding the cyberthreats, such as malicious code found on networks, but not contents of personal email messages. The private companies are urged to adopt the security incentives and increase their security systems, but participation is voluntary.

Research This: Locate Presidential Policy Directive 21 - Critical Infrastructure Security and Resilience and Executive Order 13636 - Improving Critical Infrastructure Cybersecurity and read their contents. Then, research news articles describing lawmakers' and businesses' support and criticism of these orders. What components are proposed to increase the nation's cybersecurity? What positions do the Internet Security Alliance and The Internet Association take on this matter? What efforts has Congress made to pass legislation addressing computer security?

❺ Cloud Services
Virtualization (IaaS)

An online business's website receives higher traffic during peak holiday shopping times. Purchasing and configuring additional servers to meet this demand for the short term can be an expensive task for companies managing complex computing environments. To minimize cost and maximize performance, companies often use virtualization software rather than purchasing and installing additional memory, storage, or processing power. Virtualization software allows one physical machine to emulate the capabilities of one or more servers. Virtualization is an example of infrastructure as a service (IaaS), a service of cloud computing that allows users to configure a computing environment's hardware, devices, storage, and operating systems using software. Amazon Web Services and Microsoft Azure are two cloud providers of virtualization services. (To learn more about virtualization, visit Chapter 9's free resources and read the High-Tech Talk article on this topic.)

Research This: (1) Use a search engine to find current articles, websites, or reviews of the virtualization offerings of Microsoft Azure and Amazon Web Services. (2) Find a case study about a company using Microsoft Azure or Amazon's virtualization services, summarize the problem the company was trying to solve, and describe how virtualization played a part in solving it. (3) Refer to the Chapter 6 Internet Research activity on private, public, and hybrid clouds. Why is running a private cloud in a virtualized environment a popular cloud computing solution?

Critical Thinking

The Critical Thinking exercises challenge your assessment and decision-making skills by presenting real-world situations associated with chapter concepts. The Collaboration exercise should be completed with a team.

Instructions: Evaluate the situations below, using personal experiences and one or more resources available to you (such as articles on the web or in print, blogs, podcasts, videos, television, user guides, other individuals, electronics or computer stores, etc.). Perform the tasks requested in each exercise and share your deliverables in the format requested by your instructor (brief report, presentation, discussion, blog post, video, or other means).

1. Bar Codes versus RFID

You work as an efficiency analyst at one of the largest retail companies in the world, with multiple stores in every state, as well as in many other countries. For the past 25 years, the company has used bar code readers at checkout counters that scan the bar code on products to determine from a database the price to charge customers and to keep a record of inventory. The company is considering replacing the bar codes and bar code readers with RFID.

Do This: Analyze and discuss the impact such a change would have on the company, its suppliers, and its customers. Include in your discussion any security risks. Find two examples of RFID readers and compare prices, user reviews, and features. Are handheld options for RFID readers available for store clerks to use on the store floor or for customer checkout? Compile your findings. List advantages and disadvantages of implementing RFID. Include information about reliability and costs.

2. Carpal Tunnel Syndrome

While attending college for the past two years, you have worked part-time as a data entry clerk. Recently, you began to feel a pain in your right wrist. Your doctor diagnosed the problem as carpal tunnel syndrome, which is the most well-known of a series of musculoskeletal disorders that fall under the umbrella of repetitive strain injuries (RSIs). Your doctor made several recommendations to relieve the pain. You want to learn more about this debilitating injury.

Do This: Use the web to investigate carpal tunnel syndrome. Research the carpal tunnel syndrome warning signs and risk factors. Find suggestions about proper workstation ergonomics to avoid carpal tunnel syndrome. Evaluate the differences among various treatment options. Does insurance typically cover treatment? Include in your discussion the average length of time of recovery. How should you change your workspace to help heal and prevent further damage? Should the company's insurance pay for changes to your workspace? Why or why not?

3. Case Study

Amateur Sports League You are the new manager for a nonprofit amateur soccer league. You recently hired a part-time employee who is visually impaired. The league's board of directors has asked you to assess your current input and output devices and make recommendations for assistive technologies. The new employee will need to enter data and review on-screen and printed information to ensure accuracy and identify trends.

Do This: Use the web to find information about assistive input devices, such as voice recognition and larger keyboards. Research output devices, such as large-screen monitors and Braille printers. In addition to devices, research assistive software that you can install on existing computers and devices shared by others. Find reviews from users of these assistive devices. Research costs for implementation, and find information about any grants your company can apply for as a nonprofit to ease the costs. Compile your findings.

© Don Farrall / Getty Images

Collaboration

4. Printer Comparison
You work for a local real estate agency as an IT consultant. The agency needs a new, networked printer it can use to print high-quality, custom color brochures for the homes it is showing. Each brochure is printed double-sided on glossy paper, and the agency prints an average of 200 per week.

Do This: Form a three-member team. Refer to Figure 7-26 in this chapter, which lists several questions to consider when choosing a printer, and divide the questions among your team. Each team member should answer each question according to what the employer needs. Then, each team member should use the web to research at least two printers that meet the requirements. Meet with your team, and discuss and compile your findings. Share information about the printers you researched, describe their features, and evaluate their advantages and disadvantages. Identify any additional questions you might have for the employer, such as needs for wireless printing and printing from mobile devices. Which printer you would recommend? Why?

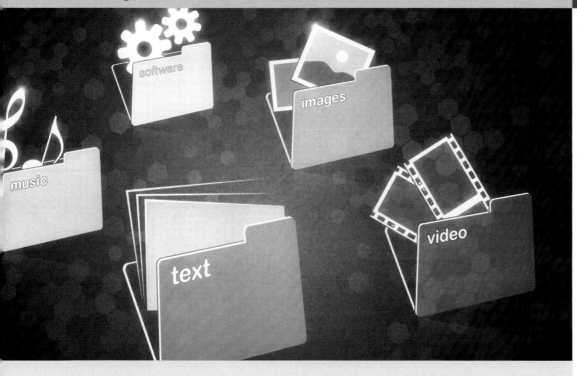

Users have a variety of storage options available.

"I use cloud storage for all my homework files. I transfer my digital photos from an SD card to my laptop's hard drive, which has plenty of extra space for my music. Weekly, I back up files from my computer to an external hard drive. What more do I need to know about storage?"

While you may be familiar with some of the content in this chapter, do you know how to . . .

- Share media?
- Defragment a hard disk?
- Decide between a hard disk and an SSD?
- Transfer files from one internal hard drive to another?
- Encrypt data and files?
- Safely remove a portable flash memory storage device?
- Evaluate cloud storage providers?
- Fix a scratch on a CD or DVD?
- Use your own device to access company data responsibly?
- Protect your credit card?
- Limit data breaches when using NFC technology?
- Create a backup plan?
- Determine how much data a company should keep?

In this chapter, you will discover how to perform these tasks along with much more information essential to this course. For additional content available that accompanies this chapter, visit the free resources and premium content. Refer to the Preface and the Intro chapter for information about how to access these and other additional instructor-assigned support materials.

✔ Objectives

After completing this chapter, you will be able to:

1 Differentiate between storage and memory
2 Describe the characteristics of internal hard disks
3 Describe the benefits of solid-state drives
4 Identify uses of external hard drives and RAID
5 Differentiate among various types of memory cards and USB flash drives
6 Discuss the benefits and uses of cloud storage
7 Describe characteristics of and differentiate among types of optical discs
8 Explain types of enterprise storage: RAID, NAS, SAN, and tape
9 Identify uses of magnetic stripe cards, smart cards, RFID tags, and NFC tags

Storage

A storage medium, also called *secondary storage*, is the physical material on which a computer keeps data, information, programs, and applications. Examples of storage media include hard disks, solid-state drives (both of which can be internal or external), memory cards, USB flash drives, optical discs, network attached storage devices, magnetic stripe cards, smart cards, RFID tags, and NFC tags. Another storage option is cloud storage, which keeps information on servers on the Internet. Because the user accesses files on cloud storage through a browser using an app from the storage provider, the actual media on which the files are stored are transparent to the user. Figure 8-1 shows a variety of storage options.

In addition to programs and apps, users store a variety of data and information on storage media in their computers and mobile devices or on cloud storage. For example, many users store digital photos, appointments, schedules, contacts, email messages, and tax records. A home user also might store budgets, bank statements, a household inventory, stock purchase records, homework assignments, recipes, music, and videos. In addition or instead, a business user stores reports, financial records, travel records, customer orders and invoices, vendor payments, payroll records, inventory records, presentations, quotations, and contracts. Business and power users store diagrams, drawings, blueprints, designs, marketing literature, corporate newsletters, and product catalogs.

A **storage device** is the hardware that records and/or retrieves items to and from storage media. **Writing** is the process of transferring data, instructions, and information from memory to a storage medium. **Reading** is the process of transferring these items from a storage medium into memory. When storage devices write on storage media, they are creating output. Similarly, when storage devices read from storage media, they function as a source of input. Nevertheless, they are categorized as storage devices, not as input or output devices.

 CONSIDER THIS

Does the amount of storage on a computer or mobile device affect the speed at which it operates?
Although the amount of storage does not directly affect the speed of a processor in a computer or mobile device, storage capacity (discussed next) could indirectly affect the overall performance. For example, a computer or mobile device with extra available storage may perform faster because the unused space can be used to hold temporary files while you browse the web and for virtual memory, discussed later in this chapter. Storage access times are discussed in more depth later in this chapter.

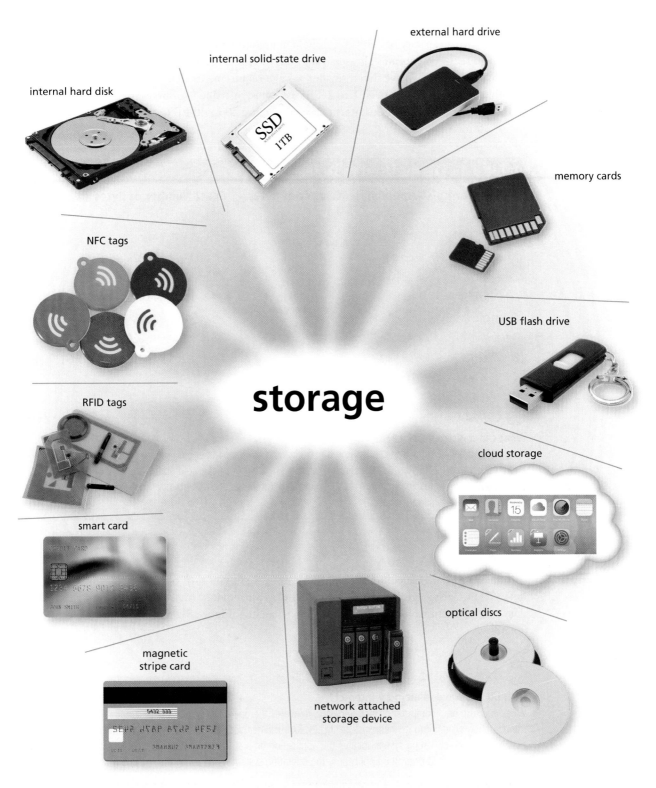

Figure 8-1 A variety of storage options.

Storage Capacity

Capacity is the number of bytes (characters) a storage medium can hold. Table 8-1 identifies the terms manufacturers may use to define the capacity of storage media. For example, a storage medium with a capacity of 750 GB can hold approximately 750 billion bytes.

Storage requirements among users vary greatly. Home users, small/home office users, and mobile users typically have much smaller storage requirements than enterprise users. For example, home users may need 1 to 2 TB (terabytes, or trillions of bytes) of storage for all of their digital content, while enterprises may require 20 to 40 PB (petabytes, or quadrillions of bytes) of storage.

 Table 8-1   Terms Used to Define Storage

Storage Term	Approximate Number of Bytes	Exact Number of Bytes
Kilobyte (KB)	1 thousand	2^{10} or 1,024
Megabyte (MB)	1 million	2^{20} or 1,048,576
Gigabyte (GB)	1 billion	2^{30} or 1,073,741,824
Terabyte (TB)	1 trillion	2^{40} or 1,099,511,627,776
Petabyte (PB)	1 quadrillion	2^{50} or 1,125,899,906,842,624
Exabyte (EB)	1 quintillion	2^{60} or 1,152,921,504,606,846,976
Zettabyte (ZB)	1 sextillion	2^{70} or 1,180,591,620,717,411,303,424
Yottabyte (YB)	1 septillion	2^{80} or 1,208,925,819,614,629,174,706,176

✸ CONSIDER THIS

What can a gigabyte store?
The total number of items that can be stored in a gigabyte will vary, depending on file size, quality of media, and a variety of other factors. As a general guide, though, a gigabyte can hold approximately 500,000 pages of text, 600 medium-resolution photos, 250 songs (2 to 3 minutes each), 4 hours of low-resolution video, or 15 minutes of high-definition video.

Storage versus Memory

Items on a storage medium remain intact even when you turn off a computer or mobile device. Thus, a storage medium is nonvolatile. Most memory (i.e., RAM), by contrast, holds data and instructions temporarily and, thus, is volatile. Figure 8-2 illustrates this concept of volatility.

✸ CONSIDER THIS

How do storage and memory interact?
When you turn on a computer or mobile device, it locates the operating system on its storage medium and loads the operating system into its memory (specifically, RAM). When you issue a command to run an application, such as a browser, the operating system locates the application on a storage medium and loads it into memory (RAM). When you are finished using the application, the operating system removes it from RAM, but the application remains on the storage medium.

A storage medium is similar to a filing cabinet that holds file folders, and memory is similar to the top of your desk. When you want to work with a file, you remove it from the filing cabinet (storage medium) and place it on your desk (memory). When you are finished with the file, you remove it from your desk (memory) and return it to the filing cabinet (storage medium).

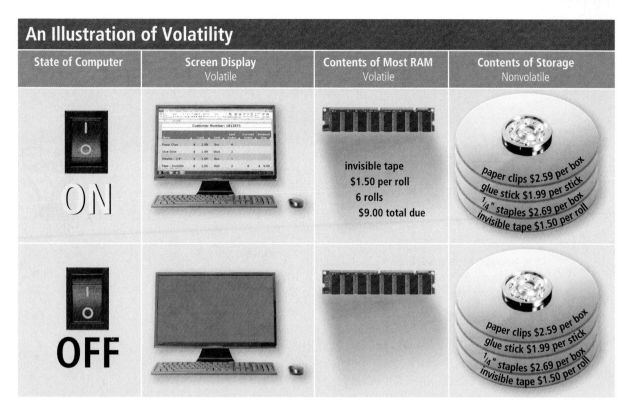

Figure 8-2 A screen display is considered volatile because its contents disappear when power is removed. Likewise, most RAM is volatile. That is, its contents are erased when power is removed from a computer or mobile device. Storage, by contrast, is nonvolatile. Its contents remain when power is off.

ImageState Royalty Free / Alamy; © Anson0618/Shutterstock.com; © Hellen Sergeyeva/Shutterstock.com; ImageState Royalty Free/Alamy; © Anson0618/Shutterstock.com; © Hellen Sergeyeva/Shutterstock.com; Source: Microsoft; © Cengage Learning

Storage Access Times

The speed of storage devices and memory is defined by access time. **Access time** measures (1) the amount of time it takes a storage device to locate an item on a storage medium or (2) the time required to deliver an item from memory to the processor. The access time of storage devices is slow, compared with the access time of memory. Memory (chips) accesses items in billionths of a second (nanoseconds). Storage devices, by contrast, access items in thousandths of a second (milliseconds) or millionths of a second (microseconds).

Instead of, or in addition to, access time, some manufacturers state a storage device's transfer rate because it affects access time. *Transfer rate* is the speed with which data, instructions, and information transfer to and from a device. Transfer rates for storage are stated in *KBps* (kilobytes per second), *MBps* (megabytes per second), and *GBps* (gigabytes per second).

Numerous types of storage media and storage devices exist to meet a variety of users' needs. Figure 8-3 shows how different types of storage media and memory compare in terms of transfer rates and uses. This chapter discusses these and other storage media.

Mini Feature 8-1: Media Sharing

Users often want to share photos, videos, and music they have stored on computers and mobile devices with others using social media. Read Mini Feature 8-1 to learn about sharing media.

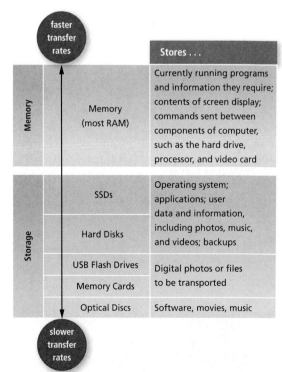

Figure 8-3 A comparison of different types of storage media and memory in terms of relative speed and uses. Memory is faster than storage but is expensive and not practical for all storage requirements. Storage is less expensive but is slower than memory.

© Cengage Learning

⚙ **MINI FEATURE 8-1**

Media Sharing

Online services offer a host of tools for sharing photos, video, and music with friends and family. When researching locations to share media files, ask yourself the following questions:

- **Where do my original files need to reside?** Can I upload from my computer, mobile device, or camera? Can I send via text message or email?

- **What is the cost?** Is the service free, or must I pay a monthly or annual fee? What happens to my files if I miss a payment or cancel my account?

- **How do I access and share the files safely?** Is the service password protected? Can I use Facebook, Twitter, blogs, and email to share the files?

- **What privacy rights are available?** Can I determine who can access the files and see my profile? Can I use a *geotag*, which is geographical data that can pinpoint where a photo was taken?

- **Can I annotate my media?** Does the service allow me to add notes, tags, and locations?

- **Are online reviews of the services available?** What experiences have other people had using the websites? Are they generally pleased or displeased with the service's reliability and ease of use?

- **What help and website support are available?** Does the service have an extensive Help section? Are FAQs, tutorials, and user forums posted?

Photos

Some photo sharing sites have millions of images to view and possibly download. When deciding which websites to use, consider the following factors:

- **Services:** Many services allow users to print the images. They also offer photo-customizing products.

- **Tools:** Owners can create webpages and keep photos organized by using albums, titles, and tags. They also can join forums to share experiences.

- **Features:** It is efficient if you can upload many files simultaneously in one batch. Many websites allow visitors to write comments on uploaded photos.

- **Storage space:** Some services offer unlimited storage, while others may limit members to a maximum number of stored photos or limit the total storage space.

Video

With video recording available on most smartphones and cameras, virtually anyone who owns these devices can produce videos to distribute. The following features are found on popular video sharing sites:

- **Video creation:** Editing tools allow special effects, editing, titles, and descriptions.

- **Audience interaction:** On-screen and keyboard controls allow viewers to play, pause, fast-forward, and stop the videos. Audience members can rate the videos and browse specific categories.

- **Features:** Most services accept files saved in a variety of file formats, but the maximum file size may be restricted or limited.

- **Genre:** Some websites accept a wide variety of content, while others require original work.

© Maximus256/Shutterstock.com

Music

Online social networks and personal radio stations are popular sources of music. Some of these services are for listening only, while others sell songs to download. The following features are found on music sharing sites:

- **Playlists:** Musicians and listeners can organize the songs and albums into specific categories, such as by artist or genre. In a playlist, each song can be played sequentially or shuffled to play in random order.

© Dmitrydesign / Shutterstock.com

- **Compatibility:** Some file types will not play on specific mobile devices, so check permissible formats before attempting to upload or download songs.

- **Features:** Services show the album cover, list artist information, and provide song previews.

- **Titles:** Musicians use music hosting websites as a convenient method of distributing their works.

Protecting Your Rights to Files You Share

When you post your files on many media sharing sites, you can give permission to people who want to use or republish your photos, documents, or other digital content for a variety of purposes. *Creative Commons* is a nonprofit organization that provides standard licensing options that owners of creative works may specify when granting permission for others to use their digital content. When posting and downloading media files, ensure you are not infringing on copyright protection. Creative Commons simplifies the process of asking for permission to reuse online content.

Discover More: Visit this chapter's free resources to learn more about photo, video, and music sharing sites, Creative Commons, and copyright protection.

⚙ **Consider This:** Have you used photo, video, or music sharing sites? If so, which ones? How did you decide the services to use? If not, would you like to try uploading or viewing one of these websites?

⚙ **BTW**
Technology Innovators
Discover More: Visit this chapter's free resources to learn about the bookmarking site Pinterest and its founder, Ben Silbermann.

© iStockphoto/Baris Simsek

Hard Drives

The term, **hard drive**, refers collectively to hard disks and SSDs. Hard drives can be internal or external. That is, they can reside inside a computer or mobile device, or they can be an external device that connects to a computer or some mobile devices. The following sections discuss the characteristics of internal and external hard disks and SSDs.

Hard Disk

A **hard disk**, also called a **hard disk drive (HDD)**, is a storage device that contains one or more inflexible, circular platters that use magnetic particles to store data, instructions, and information. Depending on how the magnetic particles are aligned, they represent either a 0 bit or a 1 bit. Recall from Chapter 7 that a bit (binary digit) is the smallest unit of data a computer can process. Thus, the alignment of the magnetic particles represents the data.

Desktops and laptops often contain at least one hard disk. The entire hard disk is enclosed in an airtight, sealed case to protect it from contamination (Figure 8-4). Read Ethics & Issues 8-1 to consider whether governments should be able to confiscate computers and mobile devices to search the content of hard drives and other media.

 BTW
Technology Innovators
Discover More: Visit this chapter's free resources to learn about the storage solutions company, Seagate, and storage pioneer, Al Shugart.

hard disk mounted inside a laptop

close-up of laptop hard disk

hard disk mounted inside a desktop

close-up of desktop hard disk

Figure 8-4 The hard disk in a personal computer is enclosed inside an airtight, sealed case. In these photos of the desktop and laptop hard disks, the top plate is removed for illustration purposes. The laptop hard disk is much smaller than the desktop hard disk.

Is Government Search and Seizure of Computers Ethical?

In the interest of national security, the Department of Homeland Security may search and seize any computer or mobile device belonging to anyone arriving in the United States. Authorities can conduct the sometimes random searches without a warrant or even a reason. Additionally, the government has taken computers from schools and libraries in a similar manner. Authorities who confiscate computers and mobile devices for an off-site inspection may hold them for any amount of time.

The Fourth Amendment protects against unreasonable search and seizure. Yet sometimes, authorities do not return the devices and provide little or no reason for the seizure. At airports and other points

of entry to the country, the government considers computers and mobile devices to be containers, just as a piece of luggage is a container. Authorities, therefore, can search and seize computers and mobile devices without reasonable suspicion, just as they can with luggage.

Opponents claim that users may be unaware of some of the contents of a hard drive, such as with a shared or repurposed computer or device. Users also may not realize that the media on the computer or mobile device contains Internet search history, access to cloud storage, online social network activity, deleted email messages and documents, and drafts of email messages or documents that they never sent or saved. Opponents also claim that the government should be able to inspect the hardware but

not the contents of memory or a hard drive. Librarians and school administrators have stated that the government is invading the privacy of patrons and students. Privacy experts warn that, even without physically inspecting a computer or device, the government may still be able to access digital content you save, search for, or post.

Consider This: Is government search and seizure of computers without a warrant ethical? Why or why not? Do you believe a government employee should have the power to inspect the data on your mobile computer or device? Why or why not? If memories or thoughts someday are decipherable by a computer at a security checkpoint, should it be legal for the government to scan them? Why or why not?

Internet Research

What is the largest storage capacity available today for hard disks?

Search for: largest hard disk

The storage capacity of hard disks varies and is determined by the number of platters the hard disk contains, the composition of the magnetic coating on the platters, whether it uses longitudinal or perpendicular recording, and its density.

- A *platter* is made of aluminum, glass, or ceramic and has a thin coating of alloy material that allows items to be recorded magnetically on its surface.
- *Longitudinal recording* aligns the magnetic particles horizontally around the surface of the disk. With *perpendicular recording*, by contrast, hard disks align the magnetic particles vertically, or perpendicular to the disk's surface, making much greater storage capacities possible.
- *Density* is the number of bits in an area on a storage medium. A higher density means more storage capacity.

Hard disks are read/write storage media. That is, you can read from and write on a hard disk any number of times. Before any data can be read from or written on a hard disk, however, the disk must be formatted. *Formatting* is the process of dividing the disk into tracks and sectors (Figure 8-5) so that the operating system can store and locate data and information on the disk. A *track* is a narrow recording band that forms a full circle on the surface of the disk. The disk's storage locations consist of wedge-shaped sections, which break the tracks into small arcs called *sectors*. On a hard disk, a sector typically stores up to 512 bytes of data. Sometimes, a sector has a flaw and cannot store data. When you format a disk, the operating system marks these bad sectors as unusable.

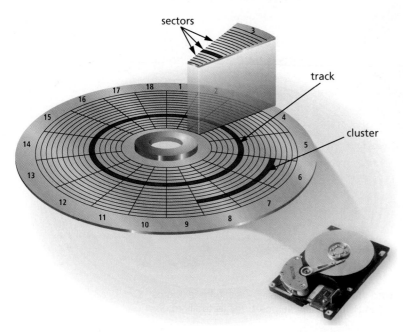

Figure 8-5 Tracks form circles on the surface of a hard disk. The disk's storage locations are divided into wedge-shaped sections, which break the tracks into small arcs called sectors. Several sectors form a cluster.

© Cengage Learning; © Gilmanshin / Shutterstock.com

On desktops, the platters most often have a form factor (size) of approximately 3.5 inches in diameter. On laptops, mobile devices, and some servers, the form factor is 2.5 inches or less. A typical hard disk has multiple platters stacked on top of one another. Each platter has two read/write heads, one for each side. A **read/write head** is the mechanism that reads items and writes items in the drive as it barely touches the disk's recording surface. A head actuator on the hard disk attaches to arms that move the read/write heads to the proper location on the platter (Figure 8-6).

While the computer is running, the platters in the hard disk rotate at a high rate of speed. This spinning, which usually is 5,400 to 15,000 *revolutions per minute (rpm)*, allows nearly instant access to all tracks and sectors on the platters. The platters may continue to spin until power is removed from the computer, or more commonly today, the platters stop spinning or slow down after a specified time to save power. The spinning motion creates a cushion of air between the platter and its read/write head. This cushion ensures that the read/write head floats above the platter instead of making direct contact with the platter surface. The distance between the read/write head and the platter is about two-millionths of one inch.

How a Hard Disk Works

Step 1
The circuit board controls the movement of the head actuator and a small motor.

Step 2
A small motor spins the platters while the computer is running.

Step 3
When software requests disk access, the read/write heads determine the current or new location of the data.

Step 4
The head actuator positions the read/write head arms over the correct location on the platters to read or write data.

Figure 8-6 This figure shows how a hard disk works.
© Alias Studiot Oy / Shutterstock.com; © Cengage Learning

✷ **CONSIDER THIS**

What happens if dust touches the surface of a platter on a hard disk?
Because of the close clearance between the read/write head and the platter on a hard disk, dust, dirt, hair, smoke, or any other contaminant could cause a disk to crash (Figure 8-7). A *head crash* occurs when a read/write head touches the surface of a platter, usually resulting in a loss of data or sometimes loss of the entire disk.

Although current internal hard disks are built to withstand shocks and are sealed tightly to keep out contaminants, head crashes occasionally still do occur. Thus, it is crucial that you back up a hard disk regularly.

🕥 **Internet Research**

Can you recover data after a disk crash?

Search for: disk crash recovery

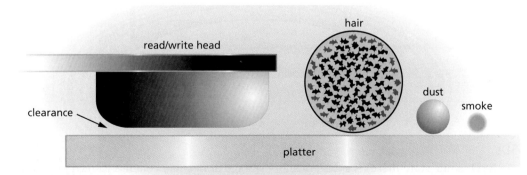

Figure 8-7 The clearance between a hard disk read/write head and the platter is about two-millionths of an inch. Any contaminant could render the disk unusable.
© Cengage Learning

 **BTW**

High-Tech Talk
Discover More: Visit this chapter's free resources to learn how data is recovered.

Most manufacturers guarantee their hard disks to last approximately three to five years. Many last much longer with proper care. To prevent the loss of items stored on a hard disk, you regularly should perform preventive maintenance such as defragmenting or scanning the disk for errors. Read How To 8-1 for instructions about defragmenting a hard disk.

Discover More: Visit this chapter's free resources to learn more about adding a second hard drive to a computer, hard disk storage capacity, sectors, read/write heads, and disk cache.

HOW TO 8-1

Defragment a Hard Disk

As discussed in Chapter 4, defragmenting a hard disk can improve your computer's performance by storing all related files for a particular program together. This can reduce the amount of time it takes the hard disk to locate and access the files necessary for programs to run. Windows has a built-in tool to defragment a computer's hard disk. Because the Mac OS defragments files automatically and writes smaller files closer together, Mac users generally do not have to defragment their hard

disks. The following steps describe how to defragment a hard disk using the Windows operating system.

1. Open the Control Panel window.
2. Tap or click the Control Panel link on the Settings menu to display the Control Panel.
3. Tap or click the 'System and Security' link.
4. If necessary, scroll to display the 'Defragment and optimize your drives' link.
5. Tap or click the 'Defragment and optimize your drives' link.

6. Tap or click the hard disk you wish to defragment.
7. Tap or click the Optimize button to begin defragmenting the selected hard disk. This process may take from several minutes to more than one hour.

Consider This: What other tools can help optimize the performance of your computer?

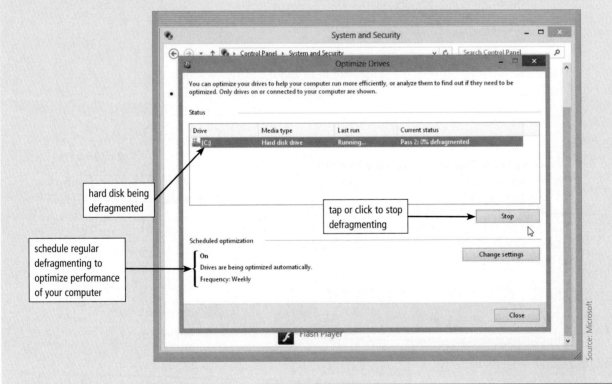

hard disk being defragmented

schedule regular defragmenting to optimize performance of your computer

tap or click to stop defragmenting

Source: Microsoft

SSDs

Internet Research

What is the largest storage capacity available today for SSDs?

Search for: largest ssd

An **SSD** (**solid-state drive**) is a flash memory storage device that contains its own processor to manage its storage (Figure 8-8). As discussed in Chapter 6, flash memory is a type of non-volatile memory that can be erased electronically and rewritten. Flash memory chips are a type of *solid-state media*, which means they consist entirely of electronic components, such as integrated circuits, and contain no moving parts. The lack of moving parts makes flash memory storage more durable and shock resistant than other types of media, such as magnetic hard disks or optical discs.

SSDs may be in the form of flash memory chips installed directly on a motherboard or an adapter card. They also may be housed in a separate casing that attaches to the motherboard, as shown in Figure 8-8, which are available in a variety of form factors including 3.5 inches, 2.5 inches, and 1.8 inches. SSDs are used in all types of computers, including servers, desktops, laptops, tablets, and a variety of mobile devices, such as portable media players and DV cameras. Some computers have both a hard disk and an SSD. Read How To 8-2 for instructions about transferring files from one internal hard drive to another.

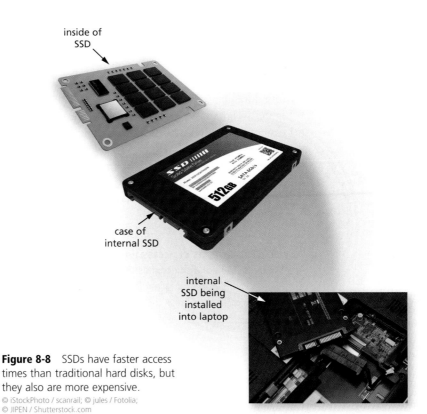

inside of SSD

case of internal SSD

internal SSD being installed into laptop

Figure 8-8   SSDs have faster access times than traditional hard disks, but they also are more expensive.
© iStockPhoto / scanrail; © jules / Fotolia;
© JIPEN / Shutterstock.com

✳ HOW TO 8-2

Transfer Files from One Internal Hard Drive to Another

If you are replacing an existing internal hard drive (hard disk or SSD), you may want to transfer the files from one internal hard drive to another one. The following list describes ways to transfer files from one internal hard drive to another.

- Connect the new internal hard drive as a second internal hard drive in your computer (refer to your computer's documentation to learn more about how to purchase and install a hard drive). When the operating system finishes loading, use the file manager in the operating system to drag the files you want to transfer from the original internal hard drive to the second one.

- Use a docking station or an external enclosure to connect the second internal hard drive to the computer that contains the original internal hard drive. (An enclosure is a case

that contains the same adapters found on a motherboard with which to connect the internal hard drive. The enclosure usually connects to a computer through a USB port. Be sure to select an enclosure that matches the dimensions and connections of your hard drive.) Use the file manager in the operating system to move or copy files from the original internal hard drive to the new one.

Xigmatek

- Move or copy the files you want to transfer from the original internal hard drive to a separate storage device, such as a USB flash drive, or to a cloud storage provider. Next, connect the second internal hard drive and then move or copy the files from the storage device or cloud storage provider to the second internal hard drive.

- Install and run a program designed to transfer files from an old internal hard drive to a new one. Some programs not only will transfer files but also may transfer programs and settings.

✳ **Consider This:** If you are purchasing a new internal hard drive, what types of files might you want to transfer from your existing internal hard drive? What types of files would you not transfer? Why?

SSDs have several advantages over traditional (magnetic) hard disks, including the following:

Internet Research
Where might you buy a hard drive enclosure?
Search for: purchase hard drive enclosure

- Faster access times (can be more than 100 times faster)
- Faster transfer rates
- Quieter operation
- More durable
- Lighter weight
- Less power consumption (leads to longer battery life)
- Less heat generation
- Longer life (more than 10 times longer)
- Defragmentation is not required

BTW
SSD Access Times
You do not need to defragment an SSD because the location of the stored data has no impact on its access times.

 CONSIDER THIS

Why do SSDs have faster access times than hard disks?
Access time on a hard disk depends on the location of the data. That is, the data on the platter near the read/write head is accessed faster. The data on an SSD, by contrast, can be accessed almost instantly wherever it is located because the drive contains no moving parts.

The disadvantages of SSDs are that they typically have lower storage capacities than hard disks, data recovery in the event of failure can be more difficult than for traditional hard disks, and their cost is higher per gigabyte. In order to keep the price of a laptop affordable, laptops with SSDs usually have a lower storage capacity than laptops with a traditional hard disk.

CONSIDER THIS

Which should you use, a hard disk or SSD?
You may want to opt for a hard disk if you are looking for a looking for the lowest-cost option, use the computer or mobile device only for basic tasks at one location, or if you require a large amount of storage space on a hard drive, such as for high-end media. If you transport the computer or mobile device frequently, want faster access to stored items, need a quieter drive (such as for audio recording), you may want to choose an SSD. Another option is a dual-drive computer, that is, one that includes both a hard disk and SSD, so that you can take advantage of the benefits of both drives.

Discover More: Visit this chapter's free resources to learn more about SSDs.

External Hard Drives

An **external hard drive** is a separate freestanding storage device that connects with a cable to a USB port or other port on a computer or mobile device (Figure 8-9). Both hard disks and SSDs are available as external hard drives.

Sizes and storage capacities of external hard drives vary, with some having greater capacities than internal hard drives. Smaller external hard drives are portable and enable mobile users to transport photos and other files from one computer to another easily. As with an internal hard drive, an entire external hard drive is enclosed in an airtight, sealed case. External hard drives units can include multiple hard drives that you can use for different purposes, if desired.

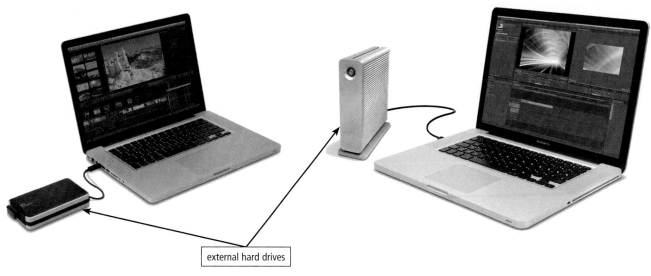

external hard drives

Figure 8-9   Examples of external hard drives.
Courtesy of Western Digital; Courtesy of LaCie

✸ CONSIDER THIS

Why would you use an external hard drive instead of a second internal hard drive?
Although the transfer rate of external hard drives usually is slower than that of internal hard drives, external hard drives do offer many advantages over internal hard drives:

- Transport a large number of files.
- Back up important files or an entire internal hard drive (most external hard drive models include backup software).
- Easily store large audio and video files.
- Secure your data; for example, at the end of a work session, you can relocate or lock up an external hard drive, leaving no data in a computer. Read Secure IT 8-1 for instructions about encrypting files or drives to protect data.
- Add storage space to a mobile computer, such as a laptop or tablet.
- Add storage space to a desktop without having to open the case or connect to a network.

✸ SECURE IT 8-1

 Encrypting Data and Files on Storage Devices

Hard drives and other storage devices are necessary tools for keeping, backing up, and transporting data and files. If they fall into the wrong hands, however, the data may be unprotected and subject to unrestricted access. Encryption encodes the data so that only authorized people can access the data.

Some operating systems provide a feature allowing users to encrypt individual files, folders, or the entire contents of a hard drive or external storage device. In addition, third-party programs are designed to encrypt data.

While each program may use a different method of encrypting files, they all use the process of cryptography. Mathematical functions, called algorithms, scramble the data. A password generally is needed to decrypt, or reassemble, this data. If this password is lost, the program or operating system's documentation may identify a procedure that allows users to access the encrypted files. In some cases, however, the software will not decrypt the files without the password, so people might reconsider encryption if they anticipate great risk when losing access to these files.

Encrypted files offer security, but users might notice that the operating system may require more time to open and access encrypted files. While no encryption program is infallible, security experts recommend using this process to protect individual files, folders, or entire storage media with personal or sensitive information.

✸ **Consider This:** What types of files would you encrypt on media in or attached to your computer or mobile device? Would you consider not using encryption in the chance that you might lose the password?

Figure 8-10 An example of RAID for the home or small business user.
Courtesy of LaCie

RAID

Some personal computer manufacturers provide a hard drive configuration that connects multiple smaller hard disks or SSDs into a single unit that acts like a single large hard drive. A group of two or more integrated hard drives is called a **RAID** (redundant array of independent disks). RAID is an ideal storage solution in situations where uninterrupted access to the data is critical (Figure 8-10). Because enterprises often use RAID, the characteristics of these devices are discussed in more depth in the enterprise storage section of this chapter.

 Internet Research

How much does RAID cost for the home user?

Search for: raid home storage

 BTW

Serial versus Parallel
With serial transfers, data is sent one bit at a time. Parallel transfers, by contrast, send several bits at once.

★ **CONSIDER THIS**

How do drives connect to a computer?
A *controller*, formerly called a disk controller, consists of a special-purpose chip and electronic circuits that control the transfer of data, instructions, and information from a drive to and from the system bus and other components in the computer. The controller may be part of a drive, may be on the motherboard, or may be a separate adapter card inside the computer.

In personal computer advertisements, vendors usually state the type of interface supported by the controller. In addition to USB, which can function as an interface for an external hard drive, four other types of interfaces for use in personal computers are EIDE, SCSI, SAS, and SATA.

- *EIDE* (Enhanced Integrated Drive Electronics) is an interface that uses parallel signals to transfer data, instructions, and information. EIDE interfaces provide connections for hard disks, SSDs, RAID, optical disc drives, and tape drives.
- Like EIDE, *SCSI* (Small Computer System Interface) also uses parallel signals, but can support up to 8 or 15 peripheral devices. Supported devices include hard disks, SSDs, RAID, optical disc drives, tape drives, printers, scanners, network cards, and more.
- *SAS (serial-attached SCSI)* is a type of SCSI that uses serial signals to transfer data, instructions, and information. Advantages of SAS over parallel SCSI include thinner, longer cables; reduced interference; lower cost; support for many more connected devices at once; and faster speeds. SAS interfaces support connections to hard disks, SSDs, RAID, optical disc drives, printers, scanners, digital cameras, and other devices.
- *SATA* (Serial Advanced Technology Attachment) uses serial signals to transfer data, instructions, and information. The primary advantage of SATA interfaces is that their cables are thinner, longer, more flexible, and less susceptible to interference than cables that use parallel signals. SATA interfaces support connections to hard disks, SSDs, RAID, and optical disc drives. External drives can use the *eSATA* (external SATA) interface, which is much faster than USB.

Discover More: Visit this chapter's free resources to learn more about drive interfaces.

✔ **NOW YOU SHOULD KNOW**

Be sure you understand the material presented in the sections titled Storage and Hard Drives, as it relates to the chapter objectives.
Now you should know ...

- When you would use storage and when you use memory (Objective 1)
- What type of internal hard drive you would find in a desktop or laptop (Objective 2)
- Why you would use an SSD (Objective 3)
- Why you would use an external hard drive or RAID (Objective 4)

Discover More: Visit this chapter's premium content for practice quiz opportunities.

Portable Flash Memory Storage

In addition to SSDs discussed in the previous section, two other widely used types of flash memory storage include memory cards and USB flash drives. Users opt for memory cards and USB flash drives because they are portable.

Memory Cards

Memory cards enable mobile users easily to transport digital photos, music, videos, or other files to and from mobile devices and computers or other devices. As mentioned in Chapter 1, a **memory card** is a removable flash memory storage device, usually no bigger than 1.5 inches in height or width, that you insert in and remove from a slot in a computer, mobile device, or card reader/writer (Figure 8-11).

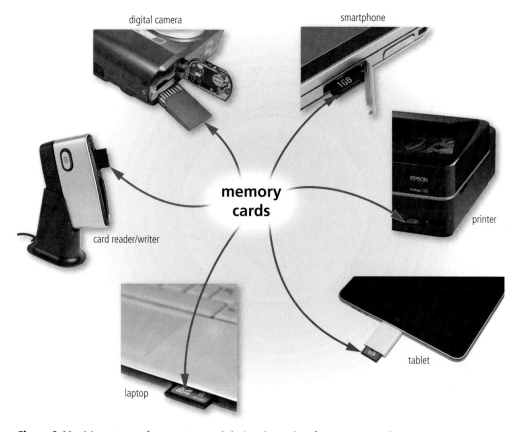

Figure 8-11   Many types of computers and devices have slots for memory cards.
© iStockphoto / Tomasz Zajaczkowski; Courtesy of Epson America Inc; © Verisakeet / Fotolia; © Thejipen / Dreamstime.com; © iStockphoto/Brian Balster; © Cengage Learning; © iStockPhoto/hanibaram

Common types of memory cards include **SDHC (Secure Digital High Capacity)**, **SDXC (Secure Digital Expanded Capacity)**, **miniSD, microSDHC, microSDXC, CF (CompactFlash), xD Picture Card, Memory Stick PRO Duo**, and **M2 (Memory Stick Micro)**. Capacities of memory cards vary. A slot on a computer or device often accepts multiple types of cards. For example, an SD slot will accept an SDHC and SDXC card. To read a mini or micro card in a computer, you insert it in an adapter that fits in a standard-sized slot on the computer or device (shown in Figure 8-1 at the beginning of this chapter).

If your computer or printer does not have a built-in card slot, you can purchase a *card reader/ writer*, which is a device that reads from and writes on memory cards. Card reader/writers usually connect to the USB port on a computer. The type of card determines the type of card reader/ writer needed. Some accept multiple types of cards; others accept one type. Figure 8-12 shows how one type of memory card works with a card reader/writer.

How SD Cards Work

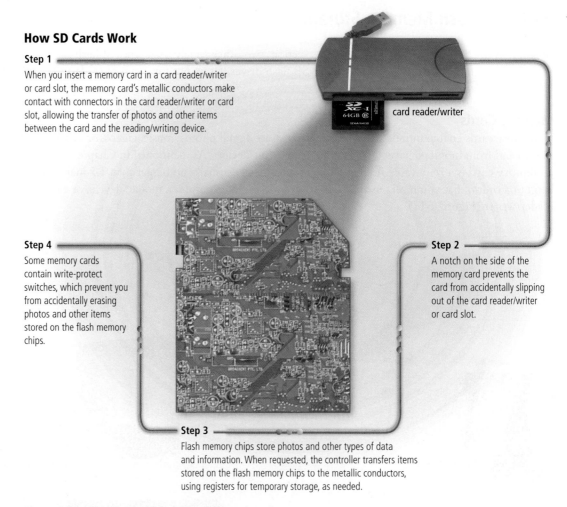

Step 1

When you insert a memory card in a card reader/writer or card slot, the memory card's metallic conductors make contact with connectors in the card reader/writer or card slot, allowing the transfer of photos and other items between the card and the reading/writing device.

card reader/writer

Step 4

Some memory cards contain write-protect switches, which prevent you from accidentally erasing photos and other items stored on the flash memory chips.

Step 2

A notch on the side of the memory card prevents the card from accidentally slipping out of the card reader/writer or card slot.

Step 3

Flash memory chips store photos and other types of data and information. When requested, the controller transfers items stored on the flash memory chips to the metallic conductors, using registers for temporary storage, as needed.

Figure 8-12   This figure shows how an SD card works.

© iStockphoto/Hugo Oswaldo Lara Gámez; Courtesy of Kingston Technology Company Inc.; © Cengage Learning

---

✸ **CONSIDER THIS**

What is the life span of a memory card?

Depending on the card, manufacturers claim their media can last from 10 to 100 years with proper care, including the following:

- Do not bend the card.
- Avoid dropping the card.
- Keep cards away from direct sunlight.
- Do not expose cards to extreme temperatures.
- Do not remove the card while data is transferring to or from it.

 Internet Research

Which memory cards are best?

Search for: memory card reviews

Discover More: Visit this chapter's free resources to learn more about memory cards.

USB Flash Drives

 Internet Research

What is the largest USB flash drive storage capacity available today?

Search for: largest usb flash drive

As mentioned in Chapter 1, a **USB flash drive**, sometimes called a *thumb drive*, is a flash memory storage device that plugs in a USB port on a computer or mobile device (Figure 8-13). USB flash drives are convenient for mobile users because they are small and lightweight enough to be transported on a keychain or in a pocket. With a USB flash drive, users easily transfer documents, photos, music, and videos from one computer to another. Storage capacities of USB flash drives vary. Read Secure IT 8-2 for pointers about safely removing a USB flash drive and other media.

Discover More: Visit this chapter's free resources to learn more about USB flash drives.

Figure 8-13 A close-up of the flash memory and circuitry inside a USB flash drive.
© cheyennezj / Shutterstock.com; © iStockPhoto / werny; © Cengage Learning

---

 **SECURE IT 8-2**

Safely Remove Media

If you are using portable flash memory storage with your computer or mobile device, you should not remove the device or media while it is in use. Likewise, you should not remove a smartphone, digital camera, or portable media player that actively is connected to your computer. Although you might not be accessing files, the operating system still might be accessing the device, and disconnecting it may damage the files.

Operating systems typically provide an option to remove or eject the device or media safely and then will notify you when the device or media no longer is in use and can be removed. To remove or eject removable storage media, follow these steps:

1. Close any files or exit any programs that are open or running on the media.

2. Open the window displaying all the drives and media connected to your computer or mobile device and then select the drive or media you want to remove safely.

3. Tap or click the command to safely remove or eject the removable storage media. (If you are unable to locate this command, you may need to press and hold or right-click the icon representing the device or media to display a shortcut menu and then tap or click the command to remove or eject the device or media safely.)

4. When the notification appears stating that the device or media is safe to remove or eject, disconnect or remove it from your computer. If a notification does not appear, you can disconnect or remove the device or media once it no longer appears

in your operating system as connected to your computer.

These guidelines generally apply to all types of portable flash memory storage, including USB flash drives, memory cards, and solid-state drives. When handling these storage devices, do not subject them to extreme temperatures, moisture, dust, or static electricity. Store them in cases, and try to avoid dropping them.

Consider This: Do you follow the guidelines described here before disconnecting portable flash memory storage, smartphones, digital cameras, and portable media players from your computer? If not, have you encountered damaged files on your storage devices? Should storage companies provide instructions on their packaging materials about how to remove media safely?

Cloud Storage

Some users choose cloud storage in addition to storing data locally on a hard disk, SSD, or other media. As discussed in previous chapters, **cloud storage** is an Internet service that provides storage to computer or mobile device users.

Cloud storage is available for home and business users, with various levels of storage services available. Cloud storage fee arrangements vary, depending on the user's storage requirements.

CONSIDER THIS

What are some advantages of cloud storage?
Users subscribe to cloud storage for a variety of reasons:

- To access files on the Internet from any computer or device that has Internet access
- To store large audio, video, and graphics files on the Internet instantaneously, instead of spending time downloading to a local hard drive or other media
- To allow others to access their files on the Internet so that others can listen to an audio file, watch a video clip, or view a photo — instead of sending the file to them via an email message
- To view time-critical data and images immediately while away from the main office or location; for example, doctors can view X-ray images from another hospital, home, or office, or while on vacation
- To store off-site backups of data
- To provide data center functions, relieving enterprises of this task

 CONSIDER THIS

What is a personal cloud?
Some hard drive manufacturers sell networked hard drives that make your data available on a cloud that exists within your home or office. That is, the networked hard drive connects directly to your router, creating a *personal cloud* that allows you to access its files over the Internet. With a personal cloud, you maintain the storage device on which the files are located versus a cloud storage provider where your files are stored on servers on the Internet that a cloud storage provider configures, maintains, and backs up.

Mini Feature 8-2: Services Offered by Cloud Storage Providers

Cloud storage provides access to your files across many devices. Read Mini Feature 8-2 to learn about services provided by cloud storage providers.

 **MINI FEATURE 8-2**

Services Offered by Cloud Storage Providers

Microsoft OneDrive, Google Drive, Apple's iCloud, Amazon Cloud Drive, Dropbox, and Box are among the many options that consumers consider for cloud storage. These and other cloud storage providers enable you to synchronize files, write documents, back up files on your computer or mobile device, share project work, stream music, post photos, and play games online. Many offer a limited amount of free storage and make additional storage available for a fee.

© iStockPhoto/Aaltazar

Synchronize Files

Many cloud storage providers place a folder on your computer with contents you can synchronize across multiple devices. Other providers allow you to upload files for storage online, and download them via a web app or mobile app. Cloud storage providers often retain previous versions of your files, in case you need to revert to an earlier one.

Write Documents

Google Drive and OneDrive provide integrated web apps to edit documents in a browser and store them on the cloud. Some third-party tools such as Evernote, an online note taking application, synchronize your notes with popular cloud storage providers.

Back Up Files

Storing files on the cloud is an easy way to back them up in case the hard drive on your computer fails or your mobile device is lost, stolen, or damaged. Some cloud backup services, such as Carbonite, automatically copy a computer or mobile device's new or changed files to the cloud, freeing users of performing backups themselves. Backup providers generally do not synchronize files across a user's multiple devices, but only provide capabilities to store and retrieve files on the cloud.

Stream Music

You can play music and videos stored offline (i.e., on your computer or mobile devices) in places without Internet access. Many people also store their media files on the cloud, so as not to use up the limited internal storage available on mobile devices. Some services, such as Google Play, support streaming music stored on the cloud to Android, iOS, and other devices.

Courtesy of Farrel Buchinsky; Source: Google, Inc.

Post Photos

Photo sharing sites and online social networks provide apps that support uploading photos taken with a smartphone or tablet to the cloud.

Play Games

Internet-connected game consoles enable you to save games in progress. Because game information is stored on the cloud, you can continue playing where you left off, regardless of whether you are using your own or another's game console.

Evaluating Providers

With so many providers offering free and paid cloud storage services, it is important to compare features to take advantage of the capabilities that each offers. Criteria to consider include the amount of free storage offered,

the cost to purchase more if needed, and the maximum file size that each service allows you to upload. Keep the files you use most on the service on which you have the most storage space; use services that support streaming to store and play media files. Photos, songs, and videos take longer to upload than smaller text or webpage files, so it is important to select a provider whose servers have sufficient bandwidth to support large file transfers.

It also is important to read a cloud storage provider's privacy policy and terms of agreement to which you must consent before using its services. Some cloud storage providers may not guarantee the protection of the files you upload, so you still should keep a backup of the files you stored on the cloud. Read How To 8-3 to learn about selecting a cloud storage provider and deciding what to upload.

Discover More: Visit this chapter's free resources to learn more about cloud storage providers and their offerings.

☀ **Consider This:** What are advantages of storing your files on the cloud? When does it make sense to use physical storage media, such as a USB flash drive, to store your files? Storing files on the cloud encourages collaboration and sharing. How can you share files stored on the cloud with your team members? Are you concerned about the security of your files when stored on the cloud? What information, if any, would you not store on the cloud?

 HOW TO 8-3

Select a Cloud Storage Provider and Decide What to Upload to the Cloud
Many people are choosing to back up data to the cloud in addition to, or instead of, backing up to storage media such as external hard drives and optical discs. Cloud storage providers enable you to synchronize data on your computers and mobile devices effortlessly to one or more servers in remote locations. Various cloud storage providers exist, and it is important to select one that adequately meets your needs. In addition to selecting a cloud storage provider, you also should decide what to upload to the cloud.

Selecting a Cloud Storage Provider
Consider the following guidelines when selecting a cloud storage provider:

- Verify the company is reputable and has been in business for an extended period of time.
- Choose a provider that encrypts your files.
- Make sure the company has not fallen victim to major security breaches.

- Determine whether the provider's service is compatible with your computer(s) and mobile device(s).
- Compare the price of various storage plans and choose a provider that offers competitive pricing.
- Verify the cloud storage provider will support the types of files you want to back up. For example, some cloud storage providers might allow you only to back up photos, so they would not be a good choice to back up your personal files, such as documents and spreadsheets.
- If desired, choose a cloud storage provider that allows you to share selected files with others.
- Consider whether the provider offers a mobile app that you can use to access your files using a mobile device.

Deciding What to Upload to the Cloud
Consider the following guidelines when determining what to upload to the cloud. Before ultimately deciding what to upload, make sure the cloud storage provider you choose will adequately protect your files.

- Consider uploading files that you cannot afford to lose, such as financial documents or scanned copies of insurance paperwork.
- Upload files that might have sentimental value, such as photos and video. In the unlikely event of a disaster that ruins your computer, mobile device, and backups you possess, the cloud storage provider will retain these files.
- Do not back up programs and apps if you have access to the installation media or files.
- If your cloud storage provider offers only a limited amount of storage space, back up only the files you are sure you will need again in the future.
- Routinely review the files you have stored on the cloud storage provider and remove files you no longer need.

☀ **Consider This:** Which of your files would you back up to the cloud? Why? After reviewing at least three cloud storage providers, which one would you choose? Why?

Optical Discs

An **optical disc** is a type of storage medium that consists of a flat, round, portable disc made of metal, plastic, and lacquer that is written and read by a laser. Optical discs used in computers typically are 4.75 inches in diameter and less than 1/20 of an inch thick. Game consoles and mobile devices, however, may use a *mini disc* that has a diameter of 3 inches or less; mini discs also work in standard-sized optical disc drives. Three widely used types of optical discs are CDs (compact discs), DVDs (digital versatile discs or sometimes digital video discs), and Blu-ray Discs.

On some computers, you push a button to slide out a tray, insert the disc, and then push the same button to close the tray; others are slot loaded, which means you insert the disc in a narrow opening on the drive (Figure 8-14). When you insert the disc, the operating system automatically may run a program, play music, or start a video on the disc. Desktops and traditional laptops usually have an optical disc drive. Ultrathin laptops, tablets, and mobile devices typically do not have an optical disc drive.

Many different formats of optical discs are available today. Some are read only, meaning users cannot write (save) on the media. Others are read/write, which allows users to save on the disc just as they save on a hard drive. With most discs, you can read and/or write on one side only. Manufacturers usually place a silk-screened label on the top layer of these single-sided discs. You insert a single-sided disc in the drive with the label side up.

optical disc

Figure 8-14 An optical disc in a disc drive.
© ra2studio/Shutterstock.com

Characteristics of Optical Discs

Optical discs store items by using microscopic pits (indentations) and lands (flat areas) that are in the middle layer of the disc (Figure 8-15). A high-powered laser light creates the pits. A lower-powered laser light reads items from the disc by reflecting light through the bottom of

How a Laser Reads Data on an Optical Disc

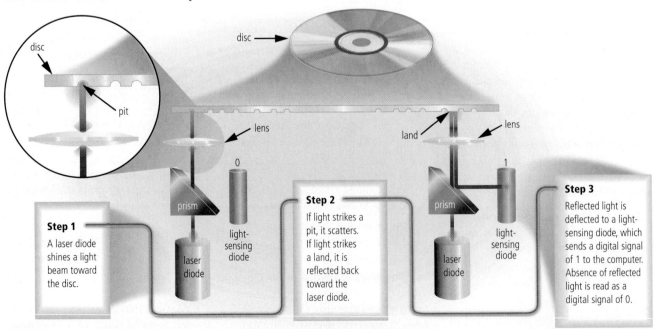

disc

disc

pit

lens

land

lens

0

1

prism

prism

Step 1

A laser diode shines a light beam toward the disc.

laser diode

light-sensing diode

Step 2

If light strikes a pit, it scatters. If light strikes a land, it is reflected back toward the laser diode.

laser diode

light-sensing diode

Step 3

Reflected light is deflected to a light-sensing diode, which sends a digital signal of 1 to the computer. Absence of reflected light is read as a digital signal of 0.

Figure 8-15 This figure shows how a laser reads data on an optical disc.
© Cengage Learning

the disc. The reflected light is converted into a series of bits the computer can process. A land causes light to reflect, which is read as binary digit 1. Pits absorb the light; this absence of light is read as binary digit 0.

Optical discs commonly store items in a single track that spirals from the center of the disc to the edge of the disc. As with a hard disk, this single track is divided into evenly sized sectors on which items are stored (Figure 8-16).

Discover More: Visit this chapter's free resources to learn more about optical disc formats.

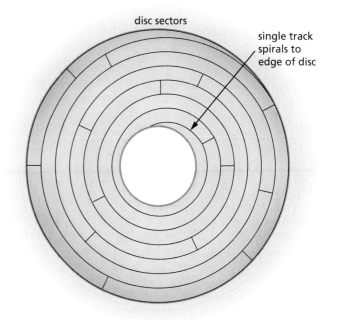

disc sectors

single track spirals to edge of disc

Figure 8-16 An optical disc typically stores data, instructions, and information in a single track that spirals from the center of the disc to the edge of the disc.
© Cengage Learning

 CONSIDER THIS

What is the life span of an optical disc?
Manufacturers claim that a properly cared for, high-quality optical disc will last 5 years but could last up to 100 years. Tips for proper care of optical discs include the following:

- Never bend a disc; it may break.
- Do not expose discs to extreme temperatures or humidity. The ideal temperature range for disc storage is 50 to 70 degrees Fahrenheit.
- Stacking discs, touching the underside of discs, or exposing them to any type of contaminant may scratch a disc. Read How To 8-4 for instructions about cleaning and fixing scratches on a disc.
- Place an optical disc in its protective case, called a *jewel case*, when you are finished using it, and store it in an upright (vertical) position.

 HOW TO 8-4

Clean an Optical Disc and Fix Scratches
If you are having trouble accessing programs and files on an optical disc, such as a CD or DVD, you may need to clean the disc or fix scratches on its surface. To avoid the risk of not being able to access a disc because it is dirty, you should clean a disc when you first notice dirt on its surface. The following steps describe how to clean or fix scratches on an optical disc:

Cleaning an Optical Disc
1. While holding the disc by its edges, use compressed air to blow excess dust off of its surface. Hold the can of compressed air upright while using it.
2. Use a soft, nonabrasive cloth to gently wipe debris off of the disc's surface. Wipe the disc from the center out to its edges.

3. If any dirt remains on the disc, dip a soft cloth or cotton ball in isopropyl alcohol (or a cleaner designed for optical discs) and then gently wipe the soiled areas.
4. Use a soft cloth to dry the disc's surface or allow it to air dry. You never should insert a wet disc in a computer.

Fixing Scratches on an Optical Disc
1. Complete the previous Steps 1 – 4 to clean the disc. If it still contains scratches, follow the remaining steps.
2. As with any maintenance you perform, risks are associated with attempting to fix scratches on an optical disc. For this reason, if possible, you should back up the data on the disc before attempting to fix a scratch.

3. Place a very small amount of rubbing compound (available at a hardware store) on a soft, nonabrasive cloth and rub the compound on the disc from its center outward at the location of the scratch. If rubbing compound is not available, place a small amount of toothpaste (not a gel) on the scratched area and rub from the inside of the disc outward.
4. Test the disc. If you still are experiencing problems because of the scratch(es), consider having a professional remove the scratch.

 Consider This: What other household products can be used to clean or fix scratches on an optical disc?

CDs

CDs are available in three basic formats: read-only, recordable, and rewritable.

- A **CD-ROM** (CD-read-only memory) is a type of optical disc that users can read but not write on (record) or erase — hence, the name read-only. Manufacturers write the contents of standard CD-ROMs and distribute them to consumers. A standard CD-ROM is called a *single-session disc* because manufacturers write all items on the disc at one time. Software manufacturers sometimes distribute their programs using CD-ROMs. The term, *photo CD*, sometimes is used to refer to CDs that contain only photos.

- A **CD-R** (CD-recordable) is an optical disc on which users can write once, but not erase, their own items, such as text, graphics, and audio. Because a CD-R can be written on only one time, the format of these discs sometimes is called *WORM* (write once, read many). Some CD-Rs are *multisession*, which means you can write on part of the disc at one time and another part at a later time — if the disc has free space.

- A **CD-RW** (CD-rewritable) is an erasable multisession disc users can write on multiple times. CD-RW overcomes the major disadvantage of CD-R because it allows users to write and rewrite data, instructions, and information on the CD-RW disc multiple times — instead of just once. Reliability of the disc tends to drop, however, with each successive rewrite.

A popular use of CD-RW and CD-R discs is to create audio CDs. For example, you can record your own music and save it on a CD, purchase and download songs from the web, or rearrange tracks on a purchased music CD.

 BTW

Burning and Ripping
The process of writing on an optical disc is called *burning*. The process of copying audio and/or video data from a purchased disc and saving it on your own media is called *ripping*.

✷ CONSIDER THIS

Can all CD drives read all CD formats?
A CD-ROM drive or a CD player may be able to read only CD-ROMs and sometimes CD-Rs. Because audio CDs and CD-ROMs use the same laser technology, you may be able to use a CD-ROM drive to listen to an audio CD while using the computer.

Most CD-R drives can read audio CDs, CD-ROMs, CD-Rs, and sometimes CD-RWs. Most CD-RW drives can read audio CDs, CD-ROMs, CD-Rs, and CD-RWs. To write on a CD-R disc, you must have a CD-R drive. Similarly, to write on a CD-RW disc, you must have a CD-RW drive.

DVDs

DVD quality for storing videos far surpasses that of CDs because items are stored in a slightly different manner, which enables DVDs to have greater storage capacities and higher resolutions than CDs. The first storage technique involves making the disc denser by packing the pits closer together. The second involves using two layers of pits. This technique doubles the capacity of the disc because the lower layer of pits is semitransparent, which allows the laser to read through it to the upper layer. Finally, some DVDs are double-sided. A more expensive DVD format is **Blu-ray**, which has a higher capacity and better quality than standard DVDs, especially for high-definition audio and video.

As with CDs, DVDs are available in three basic formats: read-only, recordable, and rewritable.

BTW

DVD/CD-RW
Some drives, called DVD/CD-RW drives, are combination drives that read and write on DVD and CD media. Current computers that include optical drives often use these combination drives.

- A **DVD-ROM** (DVD-read-only memory) is a high-capacity optical disc that users can read but not write on or erase. Manufacturers write the contents of DVD-ROMs and distribute them to consumers. DVD-ROMs store movies, music, music videos, huge databases, and applications you install on a computer.

- **DVD-R** and **DVD+R** are competing DVD-recordable WORM formats, on which users can write once but not erase their own items, including video, audio, photos, graphics, and text.

- **DVD-RW**, **DVD+RW**, and **DVD+RAM** are competing DVD-rewritable formats that users can write on multiple times.

CONSIDER THIS

Can all DVD drives read all DVD formats?

No. In addition to DVD-ROMs, most DVD-ROM drives also can read audio CDs, CD-ROMs, CD-Rs, and CD-RWs. Recordable and rewritable DVD drives usually can read a variety of DVD and CD media. Blu-ray Disc (BD) drives and players are backward compatible with DVD and CD formats. Before investing in equipment, check to be sure it is compatible with the media on which you intend to record.

 NOW YOU SHOULD KNOW

Be sure you understand the material presented in the sections titled Portable Flash Memory Storage, Cloud Storage, and Optical Discs, as it relates to the chapter objectives.
Now you should know …

- Whether you should use a memory card or a USB flash drive (Objective 5)
- Why you would use cloud storage (Objective 6)
- Which optical disc format is best suited to your needs (Objective 7)

Discover More: Visit this chapter's premium content for practice quiz opportunities.

Enterprise Storage

Enterprise hardware allows large organizations to manage and store data and information using devices intended for heavy use, maximum efficiency, and maximum availability. The availability of hardware to users is a measure of how often it is online. Highly available hardware is accessible 24 hours a day, 365 days a year. To meet these needs, enterprise hardware often includes levels of *redundancy*, which means that if one component fails or malfunctions, another can assume its tasks.

Some organizations manage an enterprise storage system in-house. Others elect to offload all (or at least the backup) storage management to an outside organization or a cloud storage provider, a practice known as *outsourcing*. Enterprises use a combination of storage techniques to meet their large-scale needs, including cloud storage and some of the other previously discussed methods, along with RAID, network attached storage, storage area networks, and tape. Read Ethics & Issues 8-2 to consider issues with employees bringing their own devices into an enterprise.

 BTW
Technology Trend
Discover More: Visit this chapter's free resources to learn about how organizatons are digitizing nondigital media, such as microfilm and microfiche.

 ETHICS & ISSUES 8-2

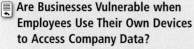 **Are Businesses Vulnerable when Employees Use Their Own Devices to Access Company Data?**
BYOD (bring your own device) strategies enable employees to access company data from a personal smartphone, tablet, or laptop. Companies might adopt or allow a BYOD policy to save money on the cost of buying and maintaining devices. Employers might increase productivity by allowing employees to work in the environment in which they are most comfortable.

BYOD raises many privacy and security concerns. IT managers, security experts, and human resource directors work together to create and enforce a BYOD policy. BYOD guidelines should balance securing company

data and preventing unauthorized network access with ensuring personal autonomy and privacy over employees' personal data. IT managers express concern over the potential need to service many different types of devices, if the company policy requires it to troubleshoot or secure employee devices. A company's security team must protect company data. In some cases, employees must install a tool to remotely wipe data, including personal data, if the device is lost, damaged, or stolen. Human resource directors help devise guidelines regarding cost-sharing and how to protect employees' private data and activities. Some industries may not be able to allow BYOD, as it may violate data privacy laws.

Many companies ban certain apps, such as gaming or file sharing, because of concerns over malware risks. In many cases, employees must agree to back up data. Employees should protect the device with a password or biometric security feature. Some companies employ a *geofence*, which is a virtual perimeter or boundary, to disable certain apps or cameras in secure areas, such as labs or meeting rooms.

Consider This: If you use your own device for work, would you be willing to give some control over the device to your company? Why or why not? Should companies be able to punish employees who violate BYOD policies? Why or why not?

Enterprise storage often uses *Fibre Channel* (*FC*) technology as the interface that connects the devices to the network because FC technology has much faster transmission rates than SCSI and other previously discussed interfaces.

Discover More: Visit this chapter's free resources to learn more about FC technology.

Figure 8-17 Shown here is a rack-mounted RAID chassis, including many integrated hard disks.
© stavklem/Shutterstock.com

RAID

For applications that depend on reliable data access, users must have the data available when they attempt to access it. Some manufacturers provide a type of hard drive system that connects several smaller drives into a single unit that acts like a single large hard drive. As mentioned earlier in this chapter, a group of two or more integrated hard drives is called a RAID (Figure 8-17). Although RAID can be more expensive than traditional hard drives, it is more reliable. Computers and enterprise storage devices often use RAID.

RAID duplicates data, instructions, and information to improve data reliability. RAID implements this duplication in different ways, depending on the storage design, or level, being used. The simplest RAID storage design is *level 1*, called *mirroring*, which writes data on two drives at the same time to duplicate the data (Figure 8-18a). A level 1 configuration enhances storage reliability because, if a drive should fail, a duplicate of the requested item is available elsewhere within the array of drives.

Other RAID levels use a technique called *striping*, which splits data, instructions, and information across multiple drives in the array (Figure 8-18b). Striping improves drive access times, but does not offer data duplication. For this reason, some RAID levels combine both mirroring and striping.

(a)

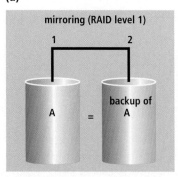

(b)

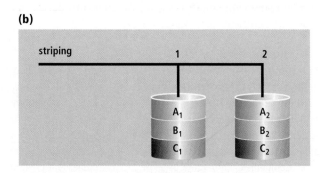

Figure 8-18 In RAID level 1, called mirroring, a backup disk exists for each drive. Other RAID levels use striping; that is, portions of each drive are placed on multiple drives.
© Cengage Learning

NAS and SAN

Network attached storage (NAS) is a server that is placed on a network with the sole purpose of providing storage to users, computers, and devices attached to the network (Figure 8-19). A network attached storage server, often called a *storage appliance*, has its own IP address, usually does not have a keyboard or display, and contains at least one hard drive, often configured in a RAID. Administrators can add storage to an existing network quickly by connecting a network attached storage server to a network.

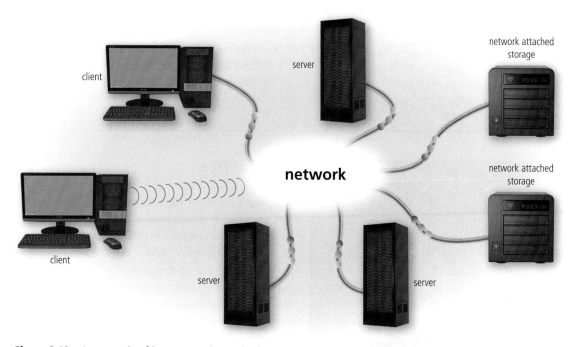

Figure 8-19   An example of how network attached storage connects on a network.
© iStockphoto/luismmolina; © lucadp/Shutterstock.com; © Cengage Learning; © Oleksiy Mark/Shutterstock.com; Source: Microsoft

A **storage area network (SAN)** is a high-speed network with the sole purpose of providing storage to other attached servers (Figure 8-20). In fact, a storage area network includes only storage devices. High-speed fiber-optic cable usually connects other networks and servers to the storage area network, so that the networks and servers have fast access to large storage capacities. A storage area network can connect to networks and other servers that are miles away using high-speed network connections.

Both network attached storage and storage area network solutions offer easy management of storage, fast access to storage, sharing of storage, and isolation of storage from other servers. Isolating the storage enables the other servers to concentrate on performing a specific task, rather than consuming resources involved in the tasks related to storage. Both storage solutions include disk, optical disc, and magnetic tape types of storage.

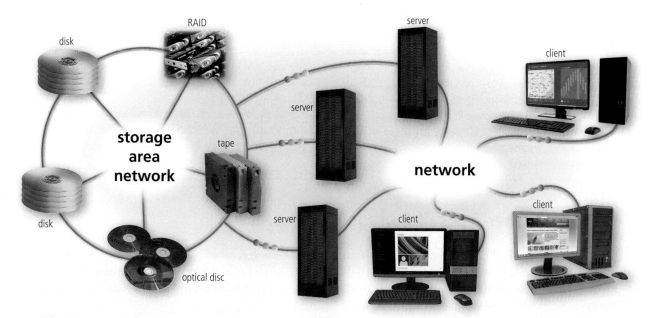

Figure 8-20   A storage area network provides centralized storage for servers and networks.
© Cengage Learning; © stavklem/Shutterstock.com; © iStockphoto/luismmolina; © Cengage Learning; © bigmagic/Shutterstock.com; © Oleksiy Mark/Shutterstock.com;
© iStockphoto/sweetym; © iStockphoto/123render; Source: Microsoft

CONSIDER THIS

Which do enterprises typically use, network attached storage or storage area networks?
Enterprises sometimes choose to implement both network attached storage and storage area network solutions.
A network attached storage server is better suited for adding storage to an existing network, such as a department's
file server. A company typically implements a storage area network solution as central storage for an entire
enterprise.

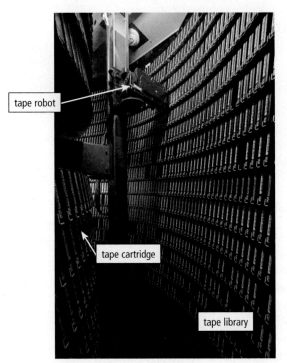

tape robot

tape cartridge

tape library

Figure 8-21　A tape robot retrieves tape cartridges.
Courtesy of Oak Ridge National Laboratory

Magnetic Tape

One of the first storage media used with enterprise computers was tape. **Tape** is a magnetically coated ribbon of plastic that is capable of storing large amounts of data and information at a low cost. Before the use of digital music players became widespread, cassette tapes were a popular medium to store music. Tape no longer is used as a primary method of storage. Instead, businesses use tape most often for long-term storage and backup.

Comparable to a cassette recorder, a *tape drive* reads from and writes on a magnetic tape. Although older computers used reel-to-reel tape drives, today's tape drives use tape cartridges. A *tape cartridge* is a small, rectangular, plastic housing for tape. Enterprises typically use a *tape library*, where individual tape cartridges are mounted in a separate cabinet. Often, a tape robot automatically retrieves tape cartridges (Figure 8-21), which are identified by location or bar code.

 CONSIDER THIS

Is tape as fast as other storage techniques?
No. Tape storage requires *sequential access*, which refers to reading or writing data consecutively. In much the
same way you would find a specific song on a cassette tape or videotape, you must forward or rewind to a specific
position to access a specific piece of data. On a tape, for example, to access items ordered A, B, C, and D, you must
pass through items A, B, and C sequentially before you can access item D.

Hard drives, flash memory storage, and optical discs all use direct access. *Direct access*, also called *random
access*, means that the device can locate a particular data item or file immediately, without having to move
consecutively through items stored in front of the desired data item or file. When writing or reading specific data,
direct access is much faster than sequential access.

 BTW
Technology Trend
Discover More: Visit this
chapter's free resources
to learn about how
RECAPTCHAs are used
to digitize media.

Other Types of Storage

In addition to the previously discussed types of storage, other options are available for specific uses and applications. These include magnetic stripe cards, smart cards, RFID tags, and NFC chips and tags. Read Ethics & Issues 8-3 to consider the ramifications of devices not secured after product development.

Should Manufacturers Be Required to Close Back Doors after Product Development?

As discussed in Chapter 5, a back door is a program or set of instructions that allows users to bypass security controls when accessing a program, computer, or network. Software developers often include a back door during product development to modify program code when troubleshooting. In these instances, a back door is necessary. What happens, though, when a hacker finds or creates a back door?

Hackers look for known security issues in software to access a computer or mobile device through a back door. If a hacker is unable to find and use a back door, they use trojan horses (previously discussed in Chapter 5) to deliver a payload that creates a back door. Hackers use back doors to gain control over a computer or mobile device so that they can use its resources to mount further malware attacks or to send spam. Using an unsuspecting user's resources to distribute spam or malware enables the hacker to avoid detection from and identification by authorities.

Back doors pose a serious security risk because they allow unauthorized access to your computer or mobile device's resources, files, and network whenever you are on the Internet.

Not only can hackers control your computer or mobile device, but they can look through your files to find and steal your personal information. Users often are unaware of a back door's existence and do not know when it is breached. If your computer acts strangely or performance decreases, you may have been the victim of a hacker. Do not connect to the Internet until you run an antivirus program.

Consider This: Should software developers close back doors created during product development? Why or why not? Has your computer or device ever been hacked using a back door? If so, how did you detect and resolve the issue?

Magnetic Stripe Cards

A **magnetic stripe card** is a credit card, entertainment card, bank card, or other similar card with a stripe that contains information identifying you and the card (Figure 8-22). The card issuer, such as a financial organization, encodes information in the stripe. The information in the stripe often includes your name, account number, and the card's expiration date. When you swipe the card through a magstripe reader, discussed in the previous chapter, it reads information stored on the stripe.

Smart Cards

A **smart card**, which is an alternative to a magnetic stripe card, stores data on an integrated circuit embedded in the card (Figure 8-23). Two types of smart cards, also called *chip cards*, are contact and contactless. When you insert a contact smart card in a specialized card reader, the information on the smart card is read and, if necessary, updated. Contactless smart cards communicate with a reader using a radio frequency, which means the user simply places the card near the reader.

magnetic stripe

Figure 8-22 The magnetic stripe on the back of credit cards and other ID cards contain information that identifies you and the card.
© iStockphoto/Ryan Warnick

🔎 **Internet Research**
Which credit cards are smart cards?
Search for: credit card chips

contact smart card

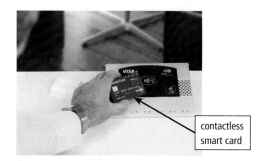
contactless smart card

Figure 8-23 Examples of contact and contactless smart cards and their readers.
© iStockphoto/oytun karadayi; © iStockphoto/alexander kirch

✳ CONSIDER THIS

What are some uses of smart cards?
Uses of smart cards include storing medical records, vaccination data, and other health care and identification information; tracking information, such as employee attendance or customer purchases; storing a prepaid amount of money, such as for student purchases on campus or fares for public transportation; and authenticating users, such as for Internet purchases or building access. In addition, a smart card can double as an ID card or credit card. Read Secure IT 8-3 for tips about protecting your credit cards.

SECURE IT 8-3

Using Credit Cards Safely

Consumers in the United States own more than 775 million credit and debit cards, and the average cardholder has multiple cards available to use. With this widespread use, the potential for theft is high.

The newest smart cards have embedded RFID tags that allow vendors to obtain the account number without physically touching the card. While this technology is convenient for both the merchant and consumer, it also enables thieves with remote scanners to capture the card's information without the owner's knowledge.

Thieves also use a handheld device to swipe the card and then obtain and store account details. This action, called *skimming*, is prevalent at gas stations, restaurants, and lounges, where unscrupulous employees sell the information to criminals who then spend your money or steal your identity.

Follow these tips to help keep your credit card account safe:

Do

- Use a card with added security features, such as a photo.
- Draw a line through blank areas on restaurant charge slips. If you have left a cash tip on the table, write the words, On Table, in the slip's tip amount section.
- Cover the keypad when entering a PIN.
- Save charge receipts and check them against monthly statements or online postings.
- Keep a record in a safe place of all your credit card numbers, expiration dates, and toll-free numbers to call if you need to report a lost or stolen card.
- Purchase an RFID-proof wallet to shield smart cards from remote readers.
- Shred new credit account mail solicitations.
- Look for skimmers, which can capture a credit card number. (Read Secure IT 3-2 in Chapter 3 for information about skimmers at ATMs and other self-service stations.)

Do Not

- Reveal your account number during a phone call unless you have initiated the call.
- Write your PIN on the card or on the protective envelope.
- Sign a blank charge slip.
- Carry extra cards, especially when traveling to unfamiliar locations.
- Let your card out of sight. While you may not be able to follow this advice at a restaurant when you hand the card to a server, you can be observant of employees' behaviors.

☀ **Consider This:** Do you know anyone who has been a victim of credit card theft? What steps will you take to use credit cards more safely after reading this information?

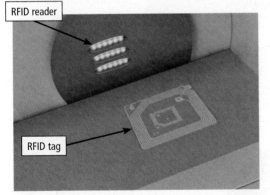

RFID reader

RFID tag

Figure 8-24 An RFID reader reads radio signals from an RFID tag that is affixed to this box.
© iStockPhoto/luismmolina

RFID Tags

Recall that RFID is a technology that uses radio signals to communicate with a tag placed in or attached to an object, an animal, or a person. The **RFID tag** consists of an antenna and a memory chip that contains the information to be transmitted via radio waves (Figure 8-24). An RFID reader reads the radio signals and transfers the information to a computer or computing device.

RFID tags are either passive or active. An active RFID tag contains a battery that runs the chip's circuitry and broadcasts a signal to the RFID reader. A passive RFID tag does not contain a battery and, thus, cannot send a signal until the reader activates the tag's antenna by sending out electromagnetic waves. Because passive RFID tags contain no battery, these can be small enough to be embedded in skin.

 **CONSIDER THIS**

How do RFID tags differ from contactless smart cards?

The physical size of the chip and storage capacities in an RFID tag typically are much smaller than the chips in contactless smart cards. The chips in RFID tags usually are read only, whereas the chips in contactless smart cards can function as a processor. Also, RFID tags often are not as secure as contactless smart cards. Thus, credit cards that contain RFID tags, called RFID-enabled credit cards, may not be as secure as those that use contactless technology.

NFC Chips and Tags

Recall that NFC is a technology (based on RFID) that uses close-range radio signals to transmit data between two NFC-enabled devices or an NFC-enabled device and an NFC tag. NFC-enabled devices include smartphones, digital cameras, computers, televisions, and terminals. An NFC-enabled device, such as a smartphone, contains an NFC chip (Figure 8-25). Other objects, such as credit cards and tickets, can contain an NFC chip. An *NFC tag*, similar to RFID tag, contains a chip and an antenna that contains information to be transmitted (shown in Figure 8-1 at the beginning of the chapter). Most NFC tags are self-adhesive, so that they can be attached to any location.

When a user places the NFC-enabled device close to another NFC-enabled device or an NFC tag, radio waves enable communications between the chips in the NFC-enabled devices or the chip in the NFC-enabled device and the NFC tag. Uses of NFC communications includes using a mobile device to pay for goods or services, displaying a webpage, making a phone call, sending a text message, or exchange contact information. Read Secure IT 8-4 for how to secure NFC transactions.

Discover More: Visit this chapter's free resources about uses of NFC technology.

Figure 8-25 This NFC-enabled phone communicates with the NFC reader to send a mobile payment.
© iStockPhoto/scyther5

 SECURE IT 8-4

Keeping NFC Transactions Safe

NFC-enabled phones offer convenience when making contactless payments at the point of sale. A user simply waves his or her smartphone above a reader attached to a register, and money is deducted from a credit card or account that is registered when the NFC application is installed. The security of this technology, however, raises major issues.

Eavesdropping is one concern. The phones and the merchant's receivers need to be less than 8 inches apart to communicate with each other and complete the wireless data transfer, but even this short distance leads to vulnerabilities that allow cyberthieves to steal financial and other personal data. Attackers can stand near the sales counter to intercept the smartphone's signals or use antennas to

extend the signal's range. Another issue is data corruption and modification, when the high-tech criminals change or delete communications between the devices. Customers also are uneasy when the technology allows merchants to load coupons, advertisements, and other adware on the phone during the NFC transaction without the shopper's permission.

Hardware manufacturers and software engineers are working to improve security between the smartphones and the readers that receive the signals, but consumers need to exercise common sense and be proactive in protecting their sensitive information. They should follow these procedures in an attempt to avoid security breaches:

• Use a strong passcode on the phone and a PIN for the NFC transaction.

• Lock the phone when it has not been used for several minutes.

• Install antivirus software.

• Install an app that takes a photograph of a person trying to access a phone without permission and then sends a message to another mobile device when the phone has been stolen, or uses the phone's GPS to track its locations.

• Turn off Bluetooth discoverable status when not using this feature.

Consider This: Have you used NFC transactions? If so, did you take any precautions to keep your data safe? If not, would you consider using NFC technology to pay for goods and services? Why or why not?

Mini Feature 8-3: Backup Plans

To protect against data loss, users should back up the contents of their storage devices regularly. Read Mini Feature 8-3 to learn about backup plans.

 MINI FEATURE 8-3

Backup Plans

Data loss or corruption can cause many issues. A user who accidentally misplaces a mobile device may lose contact information. A small business owner whose hard drive is infected with a virus may lose financial data, making billing and tax preparation difficult. A power user whose office floods and ruins a desktop not only may lose work completed on complex projects but also may need to replace expensive software. The best method for protecting against data loss from these types of unforeseen circumstances is to back up data.

A backup plan specifies a regular schedule for copying and storing important data, information, apps, and

programs. Organizations should state their backup plans clearly, document them in writing, and follow them consistently. Home and small business users can use a calendar app or other reminder to keep a backup schedule for their computers or mobile devices, or use a program or app that performs automatic backups. Backup plans should weigh the time and expense of performing a backup against the value of the data, information, apps, and programs. For example, a small business may perform one type of backup daily, while a home user may find that monthly backups are sufficient. Read Ethics & Issues 8-4 to consider storage requirements for public companies.

As briefly discussed in Chapter 5, business and home users can use four methods for backup: full, differential, incremental, or selective. Typically, only large enterprises uses a fifth type, continuous data protection. Cloud backup services, a sixth option, provide continuous data protection capabilities at a lower cost. Users can choose to backup to external media, or, as increasingly more are choosing to do, to the cloud.

- A *full backup*, sometimes called an *archival backup*, provides the best protection against data loss because it copies all program and data files. Generally, users should perform a full backup at regular intervals, such as at the end of each week and at the end of the month.

- Between full backups, you can perform differential or incremental backups. A *differential backup* copies only the files that have changed since the last full backup. An *incremental backup* copies only the files that have changed since the last full or last incremental backup.

- A *selective backup*, sometimes called a *partial backup*, allows the user to choose specific files to back up, regardless of whether or not the files have changed since the last incremental backup.

Backup software enables you to schedule backups, select the appropriate backup type, and choose the storage media for the backup. Traditional storage media includes CDs or DVDs, external hard drives, or removable SSDs, including USB flash drives or memory cards. Whichever storage media you choose, it should be stored separately from the device you are backing up to ensure it is available in case of theft or disaster. When choosing storage media, consider price and reliability. A USB flash drive may be inexpensive, but it also could be corrupted or lost easily. Cloud storage may be more expensive, but your data will be in a remote location and accessible from anywhere at any time.

Many smartphones and other mobile devices include services that sync data to a computer or to a cloud service. To sync data to a computer, the mobile device either requires cables to connect via a USB port or uses wireless methods, such as Wi-Fi or Bluetooth. Many mobile apps sync data to web apps automatically, which means you may not need to schedule a procedure to back up items on a mobile device, such as contacts, calendars, email messages, notes, and apps. For additional protection, however, some users still back up certain mobile data for easy retrieval if the device is lost or corrupted.

December					
MONDAY	**TUESDAY**	**WEDNESDAY**	**THURSDAY**	**FRIDAY**	**SAT/SUN**
28 DAILY INCREMENTAL BACKUP	**29** DAILY INCREMENTAL BACKUP	**30** END OF MONTH FULL BACKUP	**1** DAILY INCREMENTAL BACKUP	**2** WEEKLY FULL BACKUP	3/4
5 DAILY INCREMENTAL BACKUP	**6** DAILY INCREMENTAL BACKUP	**7** DAILY INCREMENTAL BACKUP	**8** DAILY INCREMENTAL BACKUP	**9** WEEKLY FULL BACKUP	10/11
12 DAILY INCREMENTAL BACKUP	**13** DAILY INCREMENTAL BACKUP	**14** DAILY INCREMENTAL BACKUP	**15** DAILY INCREMENTAL BACKUP	**16** WEEKLY FULL BACKUP	17/18
19 DAILY INCREMENTAL BACKUP	**20** DAILY INCREMENTAL BACKUP	**21** DAILY INCREMENTAL BACKUP	**22** DAILY INCREMENTAL BACKUP	**23** WEEKLY FULL BACKUP	24/25
26 DAILY INCREMENTAL BACKUP	**27** DAILY INCREMENTAL BACKUP	**28** DAILY INCREMENTAL BACKUP	**29** DAILY INCREMENTAL BACKUP	**30** END OF MONTH FULL BACKUP	31/1

© Cengage Learning

Discover More: Visit this chapter's free resources to learn more about continuous data protection, incremental backups, backup software, and syncing data.

Consider This: Do you have a backup plan for your mobile device and/or computer? Why or why not? How often do you think you need to back up your devices? Why? What storage media is best suited for your backup needs? Why?

ETHICS & ISSUES 8-4

How Much Data Should Companies Be Required to Keep?
More than a decade ago, after a string of corporate scandals, lawmakers enacted the *Sarbanes-Oxley (SOX) Act*. SOX provides a myriad of financial reporting requirements and guidelines for publicly traded companies. A main focus of SOX is the retention of business records. Because of SOX, companies have been confronted with massive new data storage requirements. For example, a company must retain all of its email messages just as it would other business records. Deleting stored email messages can result in a destruction of evidence infraction. Employees face penalties of up to 20 years in prison for altering or destroying records or documents. IT departments must not only understand

this complex law, but they also must ensure accuracy of financial data, determine policies for record retention, and provide storage capacity to hold all of the data.

Supporters of SOX state that it is essential to avoid corporate scandals caused by lack of accuracy in financial reporting. They also say that consumer confidence has increased because the financial statements are more transparent. Further, the financial costs for complying with SOX have decreased since companies have implemented plans. Opponents claim that the law is overreaching and costs too much for the added benefits. In addition, opponents blame the law for a decline in the number of IPOs (initial public offerings), as well as the transfer of several large companies

to foreign countries. Recently, the U.S. government passed the Jumpstart Our Business Startup (JOBS) Act. Supported by technology companies, startup businesses, and venture capitalists, the JOBS Act aims to support smaller and emerging companies. By redefining the size of companies, as well as tiers of responsibilities related to SOX, supporters of the JOBS Act hope to help new businesses grow.

Consider This: Is the Sarbanes-Oxley Act an unfair burden on companies? Why or why not? Should the government distinguish between large and smaller companies? Why or why not? Are such laws necessary in order to protect the public? Why or why not?

 NOW YOU SHOULD KNOW

Be sure you understand the material presented in the sections titled Enterprise Storage and Other Types of Storage, as it relates to the chapter objectives.
Now you should know ...

- When you might use RAID, network attached storage, storage area network, and tape (Objective 8)
- Where you would use a magnetic stripe card, smart card, RFID tag, and NFC tag (Objective 9)

Discover More: Visit this chapter's premium content for practice quiz opportunities.

🔖 Chapter Summary

This chapter presented a variety of storage options. You learned about storage capacity and storage access times. The chapter discussed characteristics of hard disks, SSDs, external hard drives, and RAID. It discussed portable flash memory storage, including memory cards and USB flash drives. It presented advantages and various uses of cloud storage. Next, the chapter discussed characteristics of optical discs. Enterprise storage options were presented. You also learned about magnetic stripe cards, smart cards, RFID tags, and NFC chips and tags.

    Discover More: Visit this chapter's free resources for additional content that accompanies this chapter and also includes these features: Technology Innovators: Pinterest/Ben Silbermann, Seagate/Al Shugart, SanDisk, and Amazon/Jeff Bezos; Technology Trends: Digitizing Nondigital Media and Digitizing Media with RECAPTCHAs; and High-Tech Talks: How Data Is Recovered and RAID Levels.

Test your knowledge of chapter material by accessing the Study Guide, Flash Cards, and Practice Test resources from your smartphone, tablet, laptop, or desktop.

🔗 TECHNOLOGY @ WORK

📑 Automotive

The automotive industry plays a crucial role in today's society. To keep up with our growing population's increasing demand for transportation, organizations explore ways to streamline manufacturing processes in the automotive industry while simultaneously minimizing costs. These organizations often find that using technology in the manufacturing process requires fewer people-hours, and automobiles are manufactured with greater accuracy and less waste.

Automakers manufacture cars on an assembly line. In the early years of car manufacturing, people were involved at all stages of the manufacturing process. It was not uncommon to find hundreds or thousands of individuals working along the line. Although the assembly line allowed individuals to manufacture cars as quickly as they could, companies soon realized that computer-aided manufacturing (CAM) would increase output and decrease labor costs. In fact, CAM proved to be most

effective when used in conjunction with computer-aided design (CAD). CAD designs an item, such as a car, to manufacture; CAM then manufactures the car according to the original design. Computers also determine the exact amount of material necessary to build the car, as well as the expected output.

Communications during the assembly process is critical. Computers automatically communicate with each other along the assembly line and provide alerts when factors arise that can interrupt the process. For example, running out of hinges that attach the door to the car's body will halt the line until someone replenishes the hinges. Computers, however, often alert individuals to low supplies before they run out and the assembly halts. Failure to detect the missing hinges might result in the machinery attempting to manufacture the car without hinges. This could result in damage to the door and/or the car's body further along the assembly line.

Today, technology helps create quality automobiles efficiently. Although some might argue that computers perform jobs that people once held, their introduction has helped to meet society's increased demand for products and desire for low prices.

✳ **Consider This:** How else might computers and technology be used in the automotive industry?

Study Guide

The Study Guide exercise reinforces material you should know for the chapter exam.

Discover More: Visit this chapter's premium content to **test your knowledge of digital content** associated with this chapter and **access the Study Guide resource** from your smartphone, tablet, laptop, or desktop.

Instructions: Answer the questions below using the format that helps you remember best or that is required by your instructor. Possible formats may include one or more of these options: write the answers; create a document that contains the answers; record answers as audio or video using a webcam, smartphone, or portable media player; post answers on a blog, wiki, or website; or highlight answers in the book/e-book.

1. Define the term, secondary storage. List types of storage media.

2. Differentiate between writing and reading data to storage media.

3. ___ refers to the number of bytes a storage medium can hold. Identify terms manufacturers use to determine this.

4. Differentiate between storage and memory and describe how they interact.

5. Explain what access time measures and how transfer rates are stated.

6. Identify questions to ask before deciding how to share media files.

7. Define the term, hard drive.

8. Explain the ethical issues surrounding government search and seizure of computers.

9. List characteristics and functions of a hard disk.

10. ___ is the process of dividing the disk into tracks and sectors.

11. Define the term, read/write head.

12. List steps to defragment a hard drive.

13. Define the term, SSD. List devices that use SSDs.

14. Describe how to transfer files from one internal hard drive to another.

15. List advantages and disadvantages of SSDs versus magnetic hard disks.

16. Define the term, external hard drive. Explain why you would use an external hard drive instead of a second internal hard drive.

17. Explain how to encrypt files.

18. RAID is an acronym for ___.

19. Explain the role of a controller for transferring data from a drive to the computer components.

20. In addition to USB, list four other types of interfaces for use in personal computers.

21. Describe memory cards and their uses. List types of memory cards.

22. Explain who might use a USB flash drive, and for what purpose.

23. Explain how to eject removable storage media safely.

24. Define the term, cloud storage. List advantages of cloud storage.

25. List uses of a personal cloud.

26. Name uses of cloud storage. Explain criteria for evaluating cloud storage providers.

27. Define the term, optical disc. List types of optical discs.

28. List characteristics of optical discs.

29. List steps for cleaning and fixing scratches on optical discs.

30. Differentiate among CD-ROM, CD-R, and CD-RW discs.

31. The process of writing on an optical disc is called ___. The process of copying audio and/or video data from a purchased disc and saving it on your own media is called ___.

32. Describe the storage techniques that make DVD storage higher capacity than CD storage.

33. Define the terms, redundancy and outsourcing, as they relate to enterprise computing.

34. Explain issues surrounding BYOD policies in the workplace.

35. List and describe the levels of RAID used in enterprises.

36. Differentiate between a network attached storage (NAS) and a storage area network (SAN).

37. Explain how enterprise computers use tape for storage.

38. Differentiate between sequential and direct access.

39. Explain issues surrounding the use of back doors in software development.

40. Define the terms, magnetic stripe card and smart card. Describe the uses of each.

41. List tips for using credit cards safely. ___ occurs when thieves use a handheld device to swipe the card and then obtain and store account details.

42. Differentiate between active and passive RFID tags.

43. Describe NFC technology and its uses.

44. List guidelines for conducting NFC transactions safely.

45. Describe types of backup used by business and home users. Explain considerations when creating a backup plan.

46. Explain the ethical issues surrounding the Sarbanes-Oxley Act.

47. Describe how technology is used in the automotive industry.

You should be able to define the Primary Terms and be familiar with the Secondary Terms listed below.

Key Terms

Discover More: Visit this chapter's premium content to **view definitions** for each term and to **access the Flash Cards resource** from your smartphone, tablet, laptop, or desktop.

Primary Terms (shown in **bold-black** characters in the chapter)

access time (371)
Blu-ray (388)
capacity (370)
CD-R (388)
CD-ROM (388)
CD-RW (388)
CF (CompactFlash) (383)
cloud storage (383)
DVD-R (388)
DVD-ROM (388)
DVD-RW (388)
DVD+R (388)
DVD+RAM (388)

DVD+RW (388)
external hard drive (378)
hard disk (373)
hard disk drive (HDD) (373)
hard drive (373)
M2 (Memory Stick Micro) (381)
magnetic stripe card (393)
memory card (381)
Memory Stick PRO Duo (381)

microSDHC (381)
microSDXC (381)
miniSD (381)
network attached storage (NAS) (390)
optical disc (386)
RAID (380)
read/write head (375)
reading (368)
RFID tag (394)
SDHC (Secure Digital High Capacity) (381)

SDXC (Secure Digital Expanded Capacity) (381)
smart card (393)
SSD (solid-state drive) (376)
storage area network (SAN) (391)
storage device (368)
tape (392)
USB flash drive (382)
writing (368)
xD Picture Card (381)

Secondary Terms (shown in *italic* characters in the chapter)

archival backup (396)
burning (388)
card reader/writer (381)
chip cards (393)
controller (380)
Creative Commons (372)
density (374)
differential backup (396)
direct access (392)
EIDE (380)
eSATA (380)
exabyte (EB) (370)
Fibre Channel (FC) (390)
formatting (374)
full backup (396)
GBps (371)
geofence (389)

geotag (372)
gigabyte (GB) (370)
head crash (375)
incremental backup (396)
jewel case (387)
KBps (371)
kilobyte (KB) (370)
level 1 (390)
longitudinal recording (374)
MBps (371)
megabyte (MB) (370)
mini disc (386)
mirroring (390)
multisession (388)
NFC tag (396)
outsourcing (390)
partial backup (396)

perpendicular recording (374)
personal cloud (384)
petabyte (PB) (370)
photo CD (388)
platter (374)
random access (392)
redundancy (389)
revolutions per minute (rpm) (375)
ripping (388)
Sarbanes-Oxley Act (SOX) (390)
SAS (serial-attached SCSI) (380)
SATA (380)
SCSI (380)
secondary storage (368)
sectors (374)
selective backup (396)
sequential access (392)

single-session disc (388)
skimming (394)
solid-state media (376)
storage appliance (390)
striping (390)
tape cartridge (392)
tape drive (392)
tape library (392)
terabyte (TB) (370)
thumb drive (382)
track (374)
transfer rate (371)
WORM (388)
yottabyte (YB) (370)
zettabyte (ZB) (370)

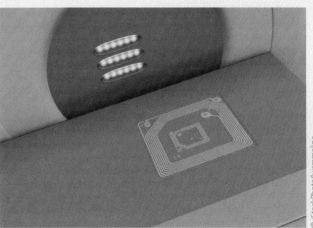

RFID tag (394)

Checkpoint

The Checkpoint exercises test your knowledge of the chapter concepts. The page number containing the answer appears in parentheses after each exercise. The Consider This exercises challenge your understanding of chapter concepts.

Discover More: Visit this chapter's premium content to **complete the Checkpoint exercises** interactively; complete the **self-assessment in the Test Prep resource** from your smartphone, tablet, laptop, or desktop; and then **take the Practice Test.**

True/False   Mark T for True and F for False.

_____ 1. Storage devices can be categorized as input or output devices. (368)

_____ 2. A storage medium is volatile; that is, items stored on it remain intact even when you turn off a computer or mobile device. (370)

_____ 3. Compared with the access time of memory, the access time of storage devices is slow. (371)

_____ 4. On storage media, a higher density means less storage capacity. (374)

_____ 5. Because of current standards, head crashes no longer occur. (375)

_____ 6. The access time of a hard disk can be more than 100 times faster than an SSD. (378)

_____ 7. While encrypted files offer greater security than unencrypted files, an operating system may require more time to open and access encrypted files. (379)

_____ 8. While each program may use a different method of encrypting files, they all use the process of cryptography. (379)

_____ 9. With serial transfers, data is sent one bit at a time. (380)

_____ 10. When you are finished using a USB flash drive, simply remove it from the USB port. (383)

_____ 11. Mini discs require a separate mini disc drive; that is, they do not work in standard-sized optical disc drives. (386)

_____ 12. An active RFID tag contains a battery than runs the chip's circuitry and broadcasts a signal to the RFID reader; because they are so small, they can be embedded in skin. (394)

Multiple Choice   Select the best answer.

1. _____ measures the amount of time it takes a storage device to locate an item on a storage medium and/or the time required to deliver an item from memory to the processor. (371)
   a. Rpm(s)
   b. Transfer time
   c. Access time
   d. Clock speed

2. A(n) _____ is a storage device that contains one or more inflexible, circular platters that use magnetic particles to store data, instructions, and information. (373)
   a. hard disk
   b. SSD
   c. USB flash drive
   d. optical disc

3. Which of the following is *not* an advantage of SSDs over hard disks? (378)
   a. faster transfer time
   b. lighter weight
   c. more durable
   d. higher storage capacity

4. A group of two or more integrated hard drives is called a(n)_____. (380)
   a. RAID
   b. SSD
   c. HDD
   d. EIDE

5. A disc you can read but not write on or erase is a _____. (388)
   a. CD-RW
   b. CD-ROM
   c. multisession
   d. WORM

6. The process of copying audio and/or video data from a purchased disc and saving it on your own media is called _____. (388)
   a. ripping
   b. burning
   c. tearing
   d. formatting

7. Enterprise storage often uses _____ technology as the interface that connects the devices to the network because it has much faster transmission rates than SCSI. (390)
   a. SAS
   b. serial transfer
   c. Fibre Channel (FC)
   d. SATA

8. A selective backup sometimes is called a(n) _____ backup. (396)
   a. differential
   b. incremental
   c. partial
   d. archival

Checkpoint

Matching   Match the terms with their definitions.

_____ 1. writing (368)

_____ 2. reading (368)

_____ 3. capacity (370)

_____ 4. perpendicular recording (374)

_____ 5. longitudinal recording (374)

_____ 6. solid-state media (376)

_____ 7. controller (380)

_____ 8. thumb drive (382)

_____ 9. network attached storage (390)

_____ 10. sequential access (392)

a. storage method in which the magnetic particles are aligned horizontally around a disk's surface

b. server whose sole purpose is providing storage to users, computers, and devices attached to the network

c. the number of bytes a storage medium can hold

d. special-purpose chip and electronic circuits that control the transfer of data, instructions, and information from a drive to and from the system bus and other components in the computer

e. flash memory chip type that consists entirely of electronic components, such as integrated circuits, and contains no moving parts

f. flash memory storage device that plugs in a USB port on a computer or mobile device

g. process of transferring data, instructions, and information from memory to a storage medium

h. storage method in which the magnetic particles are aligned vertically to a disk's surface, making much greater storage capacities possible

i. storage technique that reads or writes data consecutively

j. process of transferring data, instructions, and information from a storage medium into memory

✳ Consider This   Answer the following questions in the format specified by your instructor.

1. Answer the critical thinking questions posed at the end of these elements in this chapter: Ethics & Issues (373, 389, 393, 396), How To (376, 377, 385, 387), Mini Features (372, 384, 395), Secure IT (379, 383, 394, 395), and Technology @ Work (397).

2. In terms of storage devices, what is reading and writing? (368)

3. Is a screen display volatile or nonvolatile? (371)

4. What does access time measure? (371)

5. How does the access time of storage compare with the access time of memory? (371)

6. What does Creative Commons provide? (372)

7. How does longitudinal recording differ from perpendicular recording? (374)

8. What is a head crash? (375)

9. What are some disadvantages of SSDs? (378)

10. Why might you opt for a hard disk rather than an SSD? (378)

11. Why is it not necessary to defrag an SSD? (378)

12. What advantages does SAS have over SCSI? (380)

13. What is the life span of a memory card? (382)

14. How do optical discs store items? (386)

15. What is the life span of an optical disc? (387)

16. What are the differences among a CD-ROM, a CD-R, and a CD-RW? (388)

17. What does redundancy mean with respect to enterprise storage? (389)

18. What does the term, geofence, mean? (389)

19. How does mirroring differ from striping? (389)

20. How do businesses most often use tape? (392)

21. Which is faster: sequential or direct access? Why? (392)

22. Why would a developer include a backdoor in a program? (393)

23. What are the two types of smart cards? (393)

24. How do contactless smart cards communicate with a reader? (393)

25. What is skimming? (394)

26. What is contained in an NFC card? (395)

27. What are three types of backup plans? (396)

✳ Problem Solving

The Problem Solving exercises extend your knowledge of chapter concepts by seeking solutions to practical problems with technology that you may encounter at home, school, or work. The Collaboration exercise should be completed with a team.

Instructions: You often can solve problems with technology in multiple ways. Determine a solution to the problems in these exercises by using one or more resources available to you (such as a computer or mobile device, articles on the web or in print, blogs, podcasts, videos, television, user guides, other individuals, electronics or computer stores, etc.). Describe your solution, along with the resource(s) used, in the format requested by your instructor (brief report, presentation, discussion, blog post, video, or other means).

Personal

1. **Unrecognized Storage Device**   You have connected an external storage device to your new MacBook Pro, but the operating system is not recognizing the device's contents. Instead, it asks whether you want to format the device. Why might this be happening?

2. **Second Hard Drive Connection**   While installing a second hard drive in your computer, you realize that your computer does not include a cable to connect the hard drive to the motherboard. How can you determine what type of cable to purchase?

3. **Incompatible Memory Card**   While attempting to copy files from your digital camera to your laptop, you realize that the memory card from your camera does not fit in the memory card slot on your laptop. What other steps can you take to copy the photos from the camera to the laptop?

4. **Missing Files**   You stored some files on a USB flash drive, but when you attempted to access them you noticed that they no longer were there. What might have happened, and what next steps will you take to attempt to recover these files?

5. **Media Not Supported**   You purchased a program that came on a DVD, but your laptop does not have an optical disc drive. What next steps can you take to install this program?

© ra2studio/Shutterstock.com

Professional

6. **Inaccessible Files**   Your company requires you to store your files on a remote server so that you can access the files from any location within the company. When you sign in to another computer using your account, you cannot see your files. What might be causing this?

7. **Encrypted Storage Device**   You have purchased an external storage device so that you can back up files on your office computer. The IT department in your company informs you that you must make sure the data on the device is encrypted. What are your next steps?

8. **Alternative to Tape Storage**   Your company still uses tape storage to back up important files, but your manager has asked you to begin researching alternatives to the aging technology. What steps will you take to research current storage technologies that are suitable to store company backups?

9. **Faulty RFID Card**   You use an RFID card to obtain access to your office. When you attempt to scan your card, the RFID reader acts like it does not recognize your card is nearby. What are your next steps?

10. **Files Not Synchronizing**   You have saved files on the cloud from your home computer, but the files are not appearing on the computer in your office. What might have happened, and what steps can you take to retrieve the files?

Collaboration

11. **Technology in the Automotive Industry**   Technology is used in the automotive industry to increase speed and efficiency. Your instructor would like everyone to realize the importance of technology in this industry and the different ways it is used. Form a team of three people. One team member should investigate how technology is used to build automobiles. Another team member should investigate how technology is used to help ensure the safety of individuals working in the automobile manufacturing process, and the last team member should research how technology is used to market and sell cars. Write a brief report summarizing your findings.

The How To: Your Turn exercises present general guidelines for fundamental skills when using a computer or mobile device and then require that you determine how to apply these general guidelines to a specific program or situation.

How To: Your Turn

Discover More: Visit this chapter's premium content to **challenge yourself with additional How To: Your Turn exercises**, which include App Adventure.

Instructions: You often can complete tasks using technology in multiple ways. Figure out how to perform the tasks described in these exercises by using one or more resources available to you (such as a computer or mobile device, articles on the web or in print, online or program help, user guides, blogs, podcasts, videos, other individuals, trial and error, etc.). Summarize your 'how to' steps, along with the resource(s) used, in the format requested by your instructor (brief report, presentation, discussion, blog post, video, or other means).

1 Determine Your Device's Storage Capacity

It may be necessary to determine your device's storage capacity before you decide to install a new operating system, program, or app, or if you want to transfer a large number of files to your computer or mobile device. For example, a new program you want to install may state that it requires a certain amount of storage capacity, so you should verify the storage capacity available on your device before deciding to purchase and install the program. One way to determine a device's total storage capacity is to review the documentation or specifications that were included with your computer or mobile device. The following steps guide you through the process of determining your device's storage capacity using other methods.

Computers

a. Open the window that shows the available storage devices on the computer.
b. Press and hold or right-click the drive for which you want to display the total storage capacity and then select the option to display the drive properties.
c. Navigate to the location showing the total storage capacity and available storage space.

or

a. Some operating systems allow you to hover your pointer over the icon representing the drive for which you want to determine the storage capacity, and the storage information will appear.

Mobile Devices

a. Display the device settings.
b. Navigate to the storage settings.
c. If necessary, navigate to the screen showing the total storage capacity and available storage space.

Exercises

1. What are other reasons why you might need to determine the total storage capacity or available storage space on your computer or mobile device?

2. Does the total storage capacity displayed on your computer or mobile device match the exact amount advertised when you purchased your computer or mobile device? If not, what might cause the discrepancy?

3. How much storage space is available on your computer or mobile device? What steps can you take if the storage on your device is almost completely used?

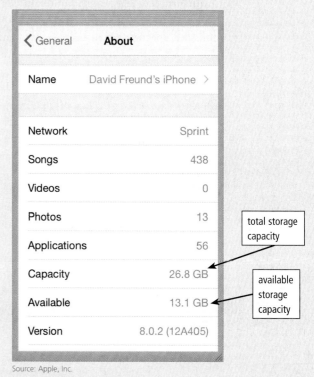

Source: Apple, Inc.

2 Organize Files on a Storage Device Using Folders

Organizing the files on a storage device not only can improve your computer's performance, but it also can make your files easy to locate. If you are accustomed to saving files to your desktop or to a folder on your storage device, you should consider organizing the files by storing them in appropriate folders. The following steps guide you through the process of using folders to organize files on a storage device.

a. Review the types of files you currently store on your device.

✷ How To: Your Turn

b. Current operating systems, such as Windows and Mac OS, include locations for storing different types of files, such as documents, music, video, and photos. Within these locations, however, you should create additional folders to further organize these file types. The method you use to organize each file type might vary.

1. Create folders to store your documents by the type of content they contain. For example, you might create separate folders to store files related to academics, finances, and entertainment. Then, consider whether you should create folders within these folders. For instance, you might create additional folders within the Academics folder to organize your files by subject.

2. Create folders to store your music by genre. Within each genre, create additional folders to sort your music by artist. If you have many songs for a particular artist, consider creating folders within the artist's folder to store the songs by album.

3. Create folders to store your photos and videos either by date, event, or a combination of the two. For example, you could have a folder for a particular year, and then within that folder, create additional folders for all events that occurred within that year.

c. Although the desktop seems to be a convenient location to store files, it quickly can become cluttered. The only files you should store on the desktop are the ones you will need in the immediate future. If will not need a file again for at least several days, consider storing it in one of the folders mentioned previously.

d. Review the files on your storage device periodically and delete the ones you no longer need. Delete only the files you have placed on your storage device; be careful not to delete files that any programs or the operating system may need to run.

Exercises

1. Review the files and folders on your storage device. In your opinion, do you feel they are organized effectively? Why or why not?

2. How are the files and folders on your storage device organized?

3. When you take photos on a digital camera, the camera often generates a file name consisting of a generic prefix and sequential number. What are some ways to identify the photos easily on your digital camera's memory card?

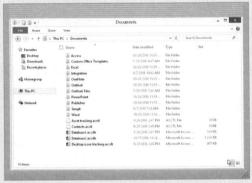

Source: Microsoft

③ Copy Individual Files to Another Storage Device, and Copy Files to Cloud Storage

If you save a file on your computer or mobile device and later will need to access it on another device, you likely will have to copy the file to another storage device or to the cloud so that you can access the file on the other device. The following steps guide you through the process of copying files to another storage device or to the cloud.

Copying Files to Another Storage Device

a. Navigate to the location containing the file you want to copy. If the file is on an external storage device or memory card, connect the storage device to your computer or insert the memory card into your computer's card reader. Next, navigate to the location containing the file you want to copy.

b. Navigate to the location to which you want to copy the file. If the location to which you want to copy the file is on an external storage device or on a memory card, connect the external storage device to your computer or insert the memory card into your computer's card reader. Next, navigate to the location to which you want to copy the file.

c. Drag the file you want to copy to the destination location. After you drag the file, make sure the file exists both in the source and destination location.

How To: Your Turn

Copying Files to the Cloud

a. If necessary, sign up for an account with an online service that can store your files. Some online services store only photos and videos, while other services store all types of files, such as documents and other media files.

b. Sign in to the online service and navigate to the page where you can upload files.

c. Tap or click the button or link to upload a file.

d. Navigate to and then tap or click the file you want to upload.

e. Tap or click the button or link to upload the file.

Exercises

1. What types of files might you want to copy to the cloud? Why would you copy files to the cloud instead of copying them to an external storage device?

2. What are at least three online services that allow you to store files? Are they free, or do they charge a fee? How much space do they provide? How do you obtain more storage space?

3. What steps would you take to copy a file from the cloud to your computer or mobile device?

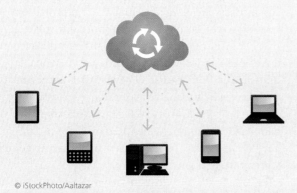

© iStockPhoto/Aaltazar

4 **Manage Space on a Storage Device**

As you use your computer or mobile device, chances are that you are storing more files and installing additional programs and apps. At some point, you might require additional space or need to improve performance on your storage device. While purchasing an additional storage device might seem like the best option, ways may be available to help you manage the space on your existing storage device so that an additional purchase is not necessary. The following steps guide you through the process of managing space on a storage device.

a. Review the files on your storage device and identify unused files you might be able to delete. Be careful not to remove files that the operating system, programs, or apps require to run properly.

b. View the list of programs and apps you have installed on your computer or mobile device. If you no longer need a program or app, uninstall it.

c. If you have files you may need in the future but not immediately, consider compressing them or copying them to an external storage device or to cloud storage. Verify the files have copied properly and then remove the files from your primary storage device.

d. If possible, defragment the storage device. If the storage device has not been defragmented recently, this process might improve performance significantly.

e. Search for and use any other tools that might be available in your operating system to maximize available space or improve performance. Note that some programs that claim to increase free space by compressing the files on your hard drive may slow your computer's performance.

f. If the above options do not increase performance enough or create sufficient free space, you might need to purchase an additional storage device.

Exercises

1. What files on your storage device might you consider deleting to save space? Why?

2. Does your computer or mobile device contain any programs or apps that you no longer need? How can you uninstall programs and apps from your computer or mobile device?

3. How does defragmentation help increase performance on your computer?

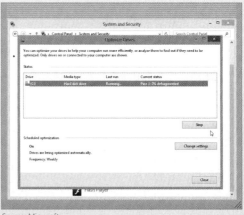

Source: Microsoft

✳ Internet Research

The Internet Research exercises broaden your understanding of chapter concepts by requiring that you search for information on the web.

Discover More: Visit this chapter's premium content to **challenge yourself with additional Internet Research exercises**, which include Search Sleuth, Green Computing, Ethics in Action, You Review It, and Exploring Technology Careers.

Instructions: Use a search engine or another search tool to locate the information requested or answers to questions presented in the exercises. Describe your findings, along with the search term(s) you used and your web source(s), in the format requested by your instructor (brief report, presentation, discussion, blog post, video, or other means).

❶ Making Use of the Web
Educational and Science

General reference websites, which include online encyclopedias, almanacs, and reference collections, are excellent sources of comprehensive, accurate, and organized facts on specific topics. For example, history and literary buffs can appreciate the websites that translate text, contain thousands of free books to download, and provide literary analyses. Among the more comprehensive websites are those sponsored by the American Library Association and the Library of Congress.

Answers to perplexing science questions and math problems are available on several educational websites that include practice tests, conversion tables, and current news articles. Environmental websites seek to educate and often persuade citizens to become aware of issues. The information helps consumers to make environmentally responsible purchasing decisions and urges people to become involved in solving global environmental problems. Scientists' research efforts extend beyond investigating this planet to exploring the great frontier of space. Their science websites contain information about current studies, conferences, and breakthroughs in such areas as biology, earth and ocean sciences, physics, and chemistry.

Research This: (a) Visit a general reference website and locate any free resources that you can download to your computer or mobile device. What materials are available to download? Which general topics are available? For which classes would you find the contents useful? Are you able to browse and search the collections? What types of current news articles are displayed? Are links to news stories or research articles shown? How often are they updated? Are previous stories archived so that you can research these events?

(b) Visit two environmental or science websites or apps, such as NASA, and browse their contents or download related apps. Which general topics are available for students? What types of current news articles are displayed? Are additional resources, such as videos and photos, available? Are online social network accounts listed to interact with scientists and researchers?

Source: NASA

❷ Social Media

Digital footprints tracking your Internet activity are relatively easy to find. Maintaining online anonymity is difficult to achieve once you have established online social network accounts with your actual name. While deleting an online social network account is a fairly easy process, deleting all remnants of information relating to the account can be a more difficult task. Just because you no longer can sign in to the account does not mean your posts, photos, and personal information do not exist somewhere on a website.

If you desire to remove an Internet presence for security or personal reasons, begin by searching for your name or account user names. Remove your profiles from any online social network account that is displayed in the search results. Each of the online social network websites has a process to close an account, generally through the account's settings page. Next, contact the websites listed in the search results and ask that your name be removed. Many companies have a form to complete and submit. A third place to hunt for your information is on websites listing public records and people searches. Again, attempt to contact these companies and request that your personal information be removed. As a last resort, some services will perform these tasks for a fee.

Research This: Use a search engine to locate instances of your name or user names. Did the search results list these names? If so, which online social networks or companies have records of your name? Then, search for your name on at least two websites that have public records or people databases. Did you see your name on these websites? If so, do you want the details, such as a phone number or address, available for anyone to see? If not, attempt to remove this data and write a report of the steps you took and your success in deleting the personal information.

Internet Research ✳

3 **Search Skills**
Image Search
An image search locates photos and images related to your search text or similar to other images. Tap or click the Images link on a search engine's home page and then type the search text describing images you would like to find. For example, type the search text, solid state drive, to find photos of solid state drives. Search engines allow you to narrow your results by specifying additional conditions on the images found. These may include size (icon, wallpaper, or dimensions in pixels), color, time taken (past day, week, or month), type (photo, clip art, face, animation, or drawing), shape (wide, tall, square), usage rights (whether a photo may be reused, and under what conditions), and safe search. Safe search filters content inappropriate for minors.

Some search engines allow you to upload or specify the web address for an image, so that the search engine can locate images with similar features. Searching for similar images can be effective if the image is of a well-known person, place, or object.

Image search results usually display an arrangement of thumbnail images; tap or click each thumbnail to see it in full size, download it, or obtain its web address from the browser's address bar.

Source: Yahoo!

Research This: Create search text using the techniques described above or in previous Search Skills exercises and then type it in a search engine to find these images: (1) an RFID tag, exactly 400 x 400; (2) an external DVD drive, with a transparent background; (3) an internal hard drive, labeled for noncommercial reuse; (4) a person holding an SD card; and (5) images similar to a photo of a laptop computer (take a photo of a laptop and upload it). How successful was your image search?

Create a document containing each image, its web address, and the name or web address of the website on which it appears.

4 **Security**
Permanently destroying files on storage media is recommended when donating or selling a computer. Federal laws have imposed strict requirements and penalties for data security, particularly regarding health and insurance records and credit transactions. While procedures exist to restore deleted files or erased media, often companies and individuals truly desire that the data never can be recovered. Sensitive medical and financial information, in particular, should be erased so that savvy criminals and digital forensics examiners cannot recover deleted files. The U.S. Department of Defense and the National Security Agency set standards for sanitizing magnetic media and specify that degaussing, or demagnetizing, is the preferred method in lieu of permanently destroying the storage medium.

Research This: What types of degaussers are available? How do they wipe a drive's contents? How are Gauss and Oersted ratings applied? What length of time is required to degauss a drive? Some companies offer degaussing services. What procedures do they use to ensure secure practices?

5 **Cloud Services**
Cloud Backups (IaaS)
Backing up files to the cloud provides a systematic way for organizations and individuals to create off-site copies of their files. Backing up files to the cloud is an example of infrastructure as a service (IaaS), a service of cloud computing which allows users to access and store files online.

Cloud backup providers offer continuous backup of new and changed files, transmitting them over a secure Internet connection. Like many cloud services, they offer a "pay as you go" pricing model, where customers subscribe to a service for a period, and pay for the features or storage they use. Many cloud backup providers offer web and mobile apps to access and restore files.

Cloud backup services differ from cloud storage services. Cloud backup services offer the software and infrastructure to back up and restore files only. They generally do not support synchronizing files across devices or sharing files with many users, which are common features of cloud storage services.

Research This: (1) Use a search engine to find two different cloud backup providers. Compare their pricing plans, storage offered, file types backed up, security features, and other services offered. (2) Why are cloud backup services attractive options for small to medium-sized businesses? (3) When is it practical to use cloud backup services, and when is it practical to use cloud storage?

Critical Thinking

The Critical Thinking exercises challenge your assessment and decision-making skills by presenting real-world situations associated with chapter concepts. The Collaboration exercise should be completed with a team.

Instructions: Evaluate the situations below, using personal experiences and one or more resources available to you (such as articles on the web or in print, blogs, podcasts, videos, television, user guides, other individuals, electronics or computer stores, etc.). Perform the tasks requested in each exercise and share your deliverables in the format requested by your instructor (brief report, presentation, discussion, blog post, video, or other means).

1. Increasing Storage Capacity

You are the office manager at a local boutique. The store needs to increase its storage capacity, and so decides to buy an external hard drive. Your boss asks you to research access times and storage capacities of various external hard drives.

Do This: Use the web to learn more about available hard drive options. What other factors should you evaluate when determining the appropriate hard drive to purchase? Analyze the advantages and disadvantages of using external hard drives for storage. Include in your discussion backup plans, costs, and alternate options. Recommend two hard drives to your boss. Include user reviews and any information by industry experts in your comparison between the two different hard drives. Which is the best option? Why? Compile your findings.

2. NFC

Your new smartphone includes NFC capabilities. You are curious about its uses but are concerned about potential risks. Before you enable NFC and install apps that can use this technology, you want to do some research.

Do This: Use the web to find and then list current and developing uses of NFC. If possible, find reviews or blog posts about these technologies. Describe any safety issues you found in your research. List ways you can protect yourself when using NFC technology. Locate apps that can use NFC. For what purposes can you use this new technology? What disadvantages and risks exist? How can you avoid any negative experiences and protect your data? Do any current laws govern or restrict the use of NFC for data collection? What are they? Can you provide additional potential uses for NFC at home, school, or work?

3. Case Study

Amateur Sports League   You are the new manager for a nonprofit amateur soccer league. The board of directors has asked you to create a backup plan for the league's computers and devices. The employees in the league office have access to multiple shared laptops, a desktop, and a tablet. Several employees use their own smartphones and tablets for work, according to the league office's BYOD policy.

Do This: Use the web to find industry experts' recommendations for backing up data. Write a sample backup plan and schedule for the board, and include types of backups you will use. Describe each backup type you propose and why you recommend it. Is any special software required to back up the different devices? The board asked you to present reasons for using cloud storage as part of your backup plan. Research the benefits of using cloud storage over other backup methods. Why would you choose cloud storage? What are the cost differences? Compare three cloud storage providers, ranking them by cost and storage capacity.

Collaboration

4. Computers in Telemarketing

Your team is performing IT research for a magazine-subscription telemarketing company. The company's 150 telemarketers must make a minimum of 100 calls a day. If telemarketers do not meet the minimum number, they must finish the calls from home. The company must decide on the type of storage device to provide the telemarketers so that they can take the necessary data home. Management has narrowed the choice to three storage options: rewritable optical discs, cloud storage, or USB flash drives.

Do This: Form a three-member team and assign an option to each member. Each team member should evaluate the advantages and disadvantages. Include features such as capacity, access time, durability of media, ease of transporting between home and office, and cost. Meet with your team, and discuss and compile your findings. Which method would you recommend? Why? What are the advantages of each? Share your findings with the class.

© science photo/Fotolia

OPERATING SYSTEMS: Managing, Coordinating, and Monitoring Resources

9

Operating systems provide a variety of functions to users.

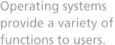

"My laptop is running slower than when I bought it, but it seems to be working properly. I install operating system updates regularly on my computer and smartphone. I added a printer using my operating system's configuration options. Aside from knowing where my files are stored, what more could I learn about operating systems?"

While you may be familiar with some of the content in this chapter, do you know how to . . .

- Remove a program or app?
- Prevent a computer from thrashing?
- Resolve a low memory issue with a mobile device?
- Locate and install a driver for a device connected to your computer?
- Identify bloatware?
- Evaluate an operating system's built-in security tools?
- Use the Windows interface?
- Use the Mac OS interface?
- Determine whether to use an open or closed source operating system?
- Set up a virtual machine?
- Use the Windows operating system on a Mac computer?
- Recognize BYOD security issues?

In this chapter, you will discover how to perform these tasks along with much more information essential to this course. For additional content available that accompanies this chapter, visit the free resources and premium content. Refer to the Preface and the Intro chapter for information about how to access these and other additional instructor-assigned support materials.

✔ Objectives

After completing this chapter, you will be able to:

1 Explain the purpose of an operating system

2 Describe the start-up process and shutdown options on computers and mobile devices

3 Explain how an operating system provides a user interface, manages programs, manages memory, and coordinates tasks

4 Describe how an operating system enables users to configure devices, establish an Internet connection, and monitor performance

5 Identify file management and other tools included with an operating system, along with ways to update operating system software

6 Explain how an operating system enables users to control a network or administer security

7 Summarize the features of several desktop operating systems: Windows, OS X, UNIX, Linux, and Chrome OS

8 Briefly describe various server operating systems: Windows Server, OS X Server, UNIX, and Linux

9 Summarize the features and uses of several mobile operating systems: Google Android, Apple iOS, and Windows Phone

Operating Systems

When you purchase a computer or mobile device, it usually has an operating system and other tools installed. As previously discussed, the operating system and related tools collectively are known as system software because they consist of the programs that control or maintain the operations of the computer and its devices. An **operating system (OS)** is a set of programs that coordinate all the activities among computer or mobile device hardware. Other tools, which were discussed in Chapter 4, enable you to perform maintenance-type tasks usually related to managing devices, media, and programs used by computers and mobile devices.

Most operating systems perform similar functions that include starting and shutting down a computer or mobile device, providing a user interface, managing programs, managing memory, coordinating tasks, configuring devices, monitoring performance, establishing an Internet connection, providing file management and other device or media-related tasks, and updating operating system software. Some operating systems also allow users to control a network and administer security (Figure 9-1).

Although an operating system often can run from a USB flash drive, media in an optical drive, or an external drive, in most cases, an operating system resides inside a computer or mobile device. For example, it is installed on a hard drive in a laptop or desktop. On mobile devices, the operating system may reside on firmware in the device. *Firmware* consists of ROM chips or flash memory chips that store permanent instructions.

Operating systems often are written to run on specific types of computers, based on their computing needs and capabilities. That is, servers do not run the same operating system as tablets or laptops because these computers perform different computing tasks. For example, a tablet or laptop operating system might have a feature to turn the device off after a few minutes of inactivity in order to conserve battery power. A server, by contrast, always is plugged in and generally remains on all of the time, which means its operating system would not need this power-saving feature. The same types of computers, such as laptops, may run different operating systems. It also is possible to run more than one operating system on the same computer.

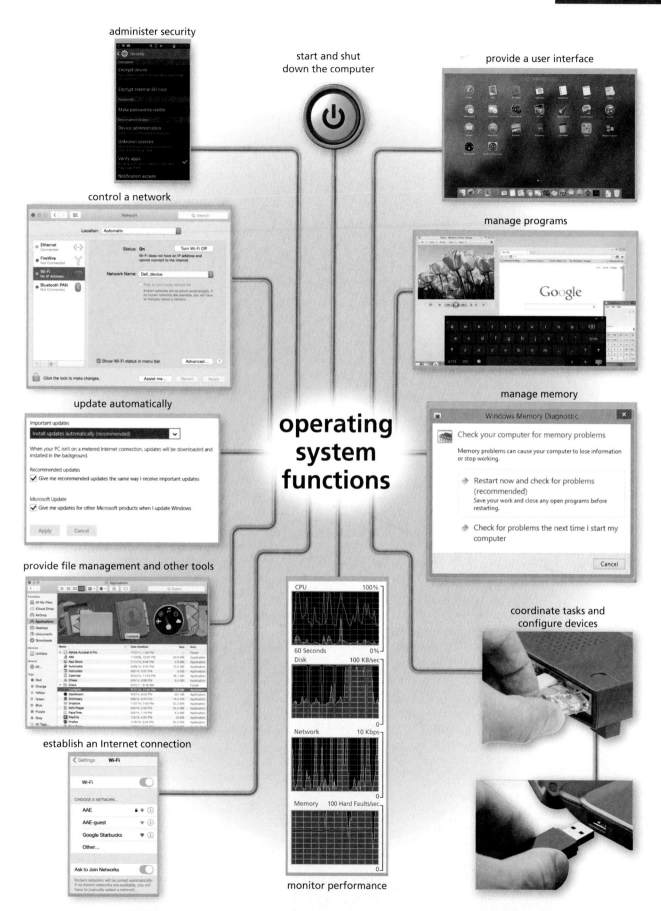

administer security

start and shut down the computer

provide a user interface

control a network

manage programs

update automatically

manage memory

operating system functions

Windows Memory Diagnostic

Check your computer for memory problems

Memory problems can cause your computer to lose information or stop working.

Restart now and check for problems (recommended)
Save your work and close any open programs before restarting.

Check for problems the next time I start my computer

Cancel

provide file management and other tools

coordinate tasks and configure devices

establish an Internet connection

monitor performance

Figure 9-1 Most operating systems perform similar functions, a variety of which are illustrated above.

When purchasing a program or an application, you must ensure that it works with the operating system installed on your computer or mobile device. The operating system that a computer uses sometimes is called the *platform* because applications are said to run "on top of" it, or because the platform supports the applications. With purchased applications, their specifications will identify the required platform(s), or the operating system(s), on which they will run. A *cross-platform application* is an application that runs the same way on multiple operating systems.

Operating System Functions

Every computer and mobile device has an operating system. Regardless of the type of the computer or device, however, their operating systems provide many similar functions. The following sections discuss functions common to most operating systems. These functions include starting and shutting down computers and mobile devices, providing a user interface, managing programs, managing memory, coordinating tasks, configuring devices, monitoring performance, establishing an Internet connection, updating operating system software, providing file and disk management tools, controlling a network, and administering security.

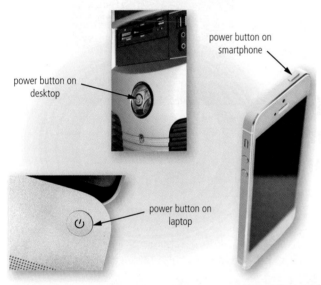

power button on desktop

power button on smartphone

power button on laptop

Figure 9-2 Examples of power buttons on computers and mobile devices.
© Olinchuk / Shutterstock.com; © iStockphoto / kizilkayaphotos; © iStockphoto / Nikada

Starting Computers and Mobile Devices

If a computer or mobile device is off, you press a power button to turn it on (Figure 9-2). If it is on, you may need to restart (also called reboot) the computer or mobile device for a variety of reasons. For example, you might install a new program or app, update existing software, or experience network or Internet connectivity problems. Alternatively, you might notice that the performance of the computer or device is sluggish, or it may stop responding altogether. The method you use to restart a computer or device differs, depending on the situation and also the hardware. You may be able to use operating system instructions or press keys on the keyboard to restart the computer or device. Or, you might be required to respond to on-screen prompts. Sometimes, the computer or device restarts automatically.

When you start or restart a computer or mobile device, a series of messages may appear on the screen. The actual information displayed varies depending on the make and type of the computer or mobile device and the equipment installed. The start-up process, however, is similar for large and small computers and mobile devices, as described in the following steps.

Step 1: When you turn on the computer or mobile device, the power supply or battery sends an electrical current to circuitry in the computer or mobile device.

Step 2: The charge of electricity causes the processor chip to reset itself and finds the firmware that contains start-up instructions.

Step 3: The start-up process executes a series of tests to check the various components. These tests vary depending on the type of computer or devices and can include checking the buses, system clock, adapter cards, RAM chips, mouse, keyboard, and drives. It also includes making sure that any peripheral devices are connected properly and operating correctly. If any problems are identified, the computer or device may beep, display error messages, or cease operating — depending on the severity of the problem.

Step 4: If the tests are successful, the kernel of the operating system and other frequently used instructions load from the computer or mobile device's internal storage media to its memory (RAM). The *kernel* is the core of an operating system that manages memory and devices, maintains the internal clock, runs programs, and assigns the resources, such as devices, programs, apps, data, and information. The kernel is *memory resident*, which means it remains in memory while the computer or mobile device is running. Other parts of the operating system are *nonresident*; that is, nonresident instructions remain on a storage medium until they are needed, at which time they transfer into memory (RAM).

Step 5: The operating system in memory takes control of the computer or mobile device and loads system configuration information. The operating system may verify that the person attempting to use the computer or mobile device is a legitimate user. Finally, the user interface appears on the screen, and any start-up applications, such as antivirus software, run.

 **CONSIDER THIS** ——————————————————————————————

What is meant by the phrase, booting a computer?

The process of starting or restarting a computer or mobile device is called *booting*. Some people use the term *cold boot* to refer to the process of starting a computer or mobile device from a state when it is powered off completely. Similarly, *warm boot* refers to the process of restarting a computer or mobile device while it remains powered on.

A warm boot generally is faster than a cold boot because it skips some of the operating system start-up instructions that are included as part of a cold boot. If you suspect a hardware problem, it is recommended that you use a cold boot to start a computer or device because this process detects and checks connected hardware devices. If a program or app stops working, a warm boot often is sufficient to restart the device because this process clears memory.

A **boot drive** is the drive from which your personal computer starts, which typically is an internal hard drive, such as a hard disk or SSD. Sometimes, an internal hard drive becomes damaged and the computer cannot boot from it, or you may want to preview another operating system without installing it. In these cases, you can start the computer from a *boot disk*, which is removable media, such as a CD or USB flash drive, that contains only the necessary operating system files required to start the computer.

When you purchase a computer, it may include recovery media in the form of a CD. If it does not, the operating system usually provides a means to create one. When the word, live, is used with a type of media, such as *Live USB* or *Live CD*, this usually means the media can be used to start the computer.

 BTW

Recovery Media
In situations when a boot disk is required to restart a computer or device that will not start from its boot drive, the boot disk often is referred to as *recovery media*.

Discover More: Visit this chapter's free resources to learn more about restarting computers and mobile devices.

Shutting Down Computers and Mobile Devices

Some users choose to leave their computers or mobile devices running continually and rarely turn them off. Computers and devices that are left on always are available, and users often run back up or other similar programs while the computer or device is not being used. These users also do not need to wait for the boot process, which can be time consuming on older computers. Other users choose to shut down their computers and mobile devices regularly. These users might be concerned with security, want to reduce energy costs, or prefer to clear memory often. To turn off a computer or mobile device, you may be required to use operating system commands, press keyboard key(s), push a power button, or a combination of these methods. Read Secure IT 8-2 in Chapter 8 for tips on safely removing media before shutting down a computer or mobile device.

Power options include shutting down (powering off) the computer or mobile device, placing it in sleep mode, or placing it in hibernate mode. Both sleep mode and hibernate mode are designed to save time when you resume work on the computer or device. *Sleep mode* saves any open documents and running programs or apps to RAM, turns off all unneeded functions, and then places the computer in a low-power state. If, for some reason, power is removed from a computer or device that is in sleep mode, any unsaved work could be lost. *Hibernate mode*, by contrast, saves any open documents and running programs or apps to an internal hard drive before removing power from the computer or device.

The function of the power button on a computer or mobile device varies, and users typically are able to configure its default behavior. For example, you typically can place a computer or mobile device in sleep mode by quickly pressing its power button or closing its lid or cover (for example, on a laptop or tablet). Pressing and holding down the power button may remove all power from the computer or mobile device.

 **Internet Research**

When should I turn off a computer, and when should I use sleep mode?

Search for: shut down or sleep computer

Providing a User Interface

You interact with an operating system through its user interface. That is, a **user interface** (**UI**) controls how you enter data and instructions and how information is displayed on the screen. Two types of operating system user interfaces are graphical and command line. Operating system user interfaces often use a combination of these techniques to define how a user interacts with a computer or mobile device.

Graphical User Interface   Most users today work with a graphical user interface. With a *graphical user interface* (*GUI*), you interact with menus and visual images by touching, pointing, tapping, or clicking buttons and other objects to issue commands (Figure 9-3). Many current GUI operating systems incorporate features similar to those of a browser, such as links and navigation buttons (i.e., Back button and Forward button) when navigating the computer or mobile device's storage media to locate files.

A graphical user interface designed for touch input sometimes is called a *touch user interface*. Some operating systems for desktops and laptops and many operating systems for mobile devices have a touch user interface.

Internet Research

Which operating systems have a touch user interface?

Search for: touch operating systems

🌣 CONSIDER THIS

What is a natural user interface?
With a **natural user interface** (**NUI**), users interact with the software through ordinary, intuitive behavior. NUIs are implemented in a variety of ways: touch screens (touch input), gesture recognition (motion input), speech recognition (voice input), and virtual reality (simulations).

Figure 9-3   Examples of operating system graphical user interfaces on a variety of computers and mobile devices.
Courtesy of Apple Inc.; Courtesy of SAMSUNG; Courtesy of Microsoft; Courtesy of SAMSUNG; Courtesy of Apple Inc.

Command-Line Interface   To configure devices, manage system resources, automate system management tasks, and troubleshoot network connections, network administrators and other technical users work with a command-line interface. In a *command-line interface*, a user types commands represented by short keywords or abbreviations (such as dir to view a directory, or list of files) or presses special keys on the keyboard (such as function keys or key combinations) to enter data and instructions (Figure 9-4).

Some people consider command-line interfaces difficult to use because they require exact spelling, form, and punctuation. Minor errors, such as a missing period, generate an error message. Command-line interfaces, however, give a user more control to manage detailed settings. When working with a command-line interface, the set of commands used to control actions is called the *command language*.

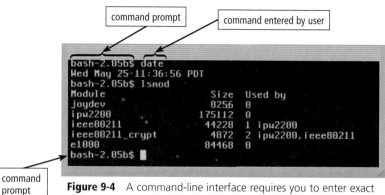

Figure 9-4 A command-line interface requires you to enter exact spelling, form, and punctuation.
© Cengage Learning

Managing Programs

How an operating system handles programs directly affects your productivity. An operating system can be single tasking or multitasking:

- A single tasking operating system allows only one program or app to run at a time. For example, if you are using a browser and want to check email messages, you must exit the browser before you can run the email program. Operating systems on embedded computers and some mobile devices use a single tasking operating system.
- Most operating systems today are multitasking. A *multitasking* operating system allows two or more programs or apps to reside in memory at the same time. Using the example just cited, if you are working with a multitasking operating system, you do not have to exit the browser to run the email program. Both programs can run concurrently.

When a computer is running multiple programs concurrently, one program is in the foreground and the others are in the background (Figure 9-5). The one in the *foreground* is the active program, that is, the one you currently are using. The other programs running but not in use are in the *background*. The foreground program typically is displayed on the screen, and the background programs are hidden partially or completely behind the foreground program. A multitasking operating system's user interface easily allows you to switch between foreground and background programs.

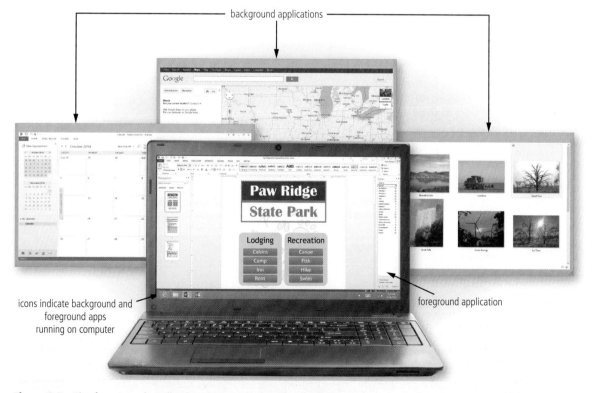

Figure 9-5 The foreground application, Microsoft Word, is displayed on the screen. The other applications (Microsoft Outlook, Google Maps in Internet Explorer, and File Explorer) are in the background.
© donatas1205 / Shutterstock.com; © Cengage Learning; Source: Google Inc.; Source: Microsoft

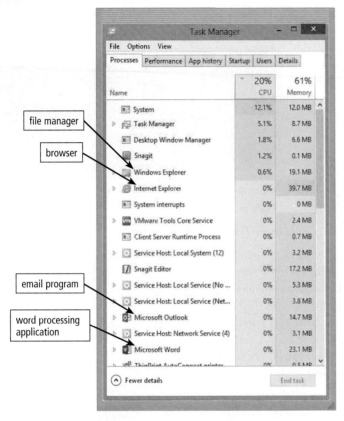

file manager

browser

email program

word processing application

Figure 9-6 An operating system manages multiple programs and processes while you use a computer or mobile device.
Source: Microsoft

In addition to managing applications, an operating system manages other processes. These processes include programs or routines that provide support to other programs or hardware. Some are memory resident. Others run as they are required. Figure 9-6 shows a list of some processes running on a Windows computer; notice the list contains the applications running in Figure 9-5, as well as other programs and processes.

Some operating systems support a single user; others support thousands of users running multiple programs. A *multiuser* operating system enables two or more users to run programs simultaneously. Networks, servers, and supercomputers allow hundreds to thousands of users to connect at the same time and, thus, use multiuser operating systems.

Through the operating system, you also can install programs and apps, as well as remove them. For instructions on installing programs and apps, refer to How To 1-4 in Chapter 1. Read How To 9-1 for instructions on removing a program or app.

Discover More: Visit this chapter's free resources to learn more about single tasking, multitasking, and multiuser operating systems.

⚙ **HOW TO 9-1**

Remove a Program or App
If you are running low on space on your computer or mobile device, you may want to remove programs and apps you no longer use. The following steps describe how to remove a program or app from your computer or mobile device:

1. Sign in to a user account that has administrative privileges; that is, the user account should have the capability

to perform functions such as removing programs or apps.

2. Make sure the program or app you want to remove is not running.

3. Display the list of programs or apps installed on your computer or mobile device.

4. Select the program or app you wish to remove.

5. Tap or click the button to remove the program or app.

6. If necessary, when the installation is complete, restart your computer or device.

7. Verify the program or app you removed no longer is on your computer or mobile device.

☀ **Consider This:** What are some other reasons why you might want to remove a program or app from your computer or mobile device?

Managing Memory

The purpose of memory management is to optimize the use of a computer or device's internal memory, i.e., RAM. As Chapter 6 discussed, RAM (random access memory) consists of one or more chips on the motherboard that hold items such as data and instructions while the processor interprets and executes them. The operating system allocates, or assigns, data and instructions to an area of memory while they are being processed. Then, it carefully monitors the contents of memory. Finally, the operating system releases these items from being monitored in memory when the processor no longer requires them.

If several programs or apps are running simultaneously, your computer or mobile device may use up its available RAM. For example, assume an operating system requires 2 GB of RAM to run, an antivirus program — 256 MB, a browser — 512 MB, a productivity software suite — 1 GB, and a photo editing program — 512 MB. With all these programs running simultaneously, the total RAM required would be 4.352 GB (2048 MB + 256 MB + 512 MB + 1024 MB + 512 MB) (Figure 9-7). If the computer has only 4 GB of RAM, the operating system may have to use virtual memory in order to run all of the applications at the same time. When a computer or mobile device runs low on available RAM, this often results in the computer or mobile device running sluggishly.

Applications Using RAM

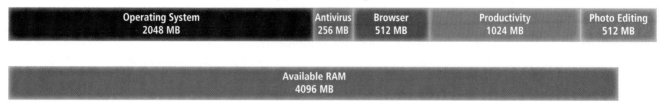

Operating System 2048 MB	Antivirus 256 MB	Browser 512 MB	Productivity 1024 MB	Photo Editing 512 MB

Available RAM 4096 MB

Figure 9-7   Many applications running at the same time may deplete a computer's or device's available RAM.
© Cengage Learning

With **virtual memory**, the operating system allocates a portion of a storage medium, such as a hard drive or a USB flash drive, to function as additional RAM (Figure 9-8). As you interact with a program, part of it may be in physical RAM, while the rest of the program is on the hard drive as virtual memory. Because virtual memory is slower than RAM, users may notice the computer slowing down while it uses virtual memory.

How a Computer Might Use Virtual Memory

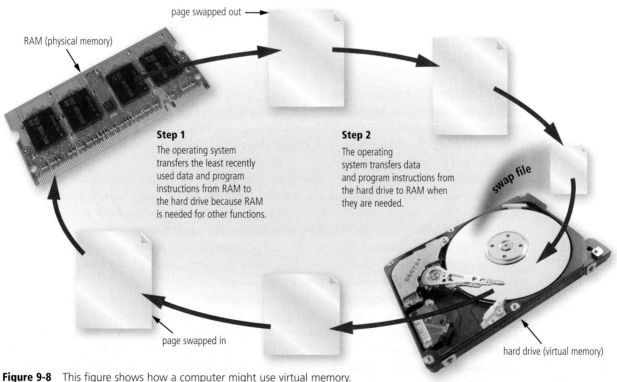

page swapped out

RAM (physical memory)

Step 1
The operating system transfers the least recently used data and program instructions from RAM to the hard drive because RAM is needed for other functions.

Step 2
The operating system transfers data and program instructions from the hard drive to RAM when they are needed.

swap file

page swapped in

hard drive (virtual memory)

Figure 9-8   This figure shows how a computer might use virtual memory.
© TungCheung / Shutterstock.com; © kastianz / Shutterstock.com; © Cengage Learning

The area of the hard drive used for virtual memory is called a *swap file* because it swaps (exchanges) data, information, and instructions between memory and storage. A *page* is the amount of data and program instructions that can swap at a given time. The technique of swapping items between memory and storage, called *paging*, is a time-consuming process for the computer. When an operating system spends much of its time paging, instead of executing application software, it is said to be *thrashing*.

 CONSIDER THIS —————————————————————

What happens if an application stops responding or the computer appears to run sluggishly?
If an application, such as a browser, has stopped responding, the operating system may be thrashing. When this occurs, try to exit the program. If that does not work, try a warm boot and then a cold boot. To help prevent future occurrences of thrashing, you might consider the following:

1. Remove unnecessary files and uninstall seldom used programs and apps. (Read How To 9-1 earlier in this chapter for instructions about removing programs and apps.)

2. If your computer has a hard disk (instead of an SSD), try defragmenting the hard disk. (Read How To 8-1 in Chapter 8 for instructions about defragmenting a hard disk.)

3. Purchase and install additional RAM. (Read How To 6-3 in Chapter 6 for instructions about installing memory modules.)

 CONSIDER THIS —————————————————————

What if my smartphone runs out of memory?
If your smartphone or other mobile device displays a message that it is running low on memory, try the following:

1. Exit unnecessary applications that are running.

2. Restart the smartphone or mobile device.

3. Uninstall seldom used applications. (Read How To 9-1 earlier in this chapter for instructions about removing programs and apps.)

4. Remove unnecessary files, including photos and videos (you may want to copy them to cloud storage, a computer, or a memory card first).

5. If your smartphone supports the use of a memory card, specify that applications, photos, videos, or downloaded files should be saved on a memory card instead of the smartphone's internal memory.

Coordinating Tasks

The operating system determines the order in which tasks are processed. A task, or job, is an operation the processor manages. Tasks include receiving data from an input device, processing instructions, sending information to an output device, and transferring items from storage to memory and from memory to storage.

Sometimes, a device already may be busy processing one task when it receives a request to perform a second task. For example, if a printer is printing a document when the operating system sends it a request to print another document, the printer must store the second document in memory until the first document has completed printing.

While waiting for devices to become idle, the operating system places items in buffers. A *buffer* is a segment of memory or storage in which items are placed while waiting to be transferred from an input device or to an output device.

An operating system commonly uses buffers with printed documents. This process, called *spooling*, sends documents to be printed to a buffer instead of sending them immediately to the printer. If a printer does not have its own internal memory or if its memory is full, the operating system's buffer holds the documents waiting to print while the printer prints from the buffer at its own rate of speed. By spooling documents to a buffer, the computer or mobile device's processor can continue interpreting and executing instructions while the printer prints. This allows users to perform other activities on the computer while a printer is printing. Multiple documents line up in a **queue** (pronounced Q) in the buffer. A program, called a *print spooler*, intercepts documents to be printed from the operating system and places them in the queue (Figure 9-9).

 BTW

Higher-Priority Tasks
A multiuser operating system does not always process tasks on a first-come, first-served basis. If a user or task has been assigned a higher priority than others by the network administrator, the operating system performs higher-priority tasks first. For example, an operating system on a corporate server may process tasks to check for incoming email more frequently than it processes tasks to access archived documents.

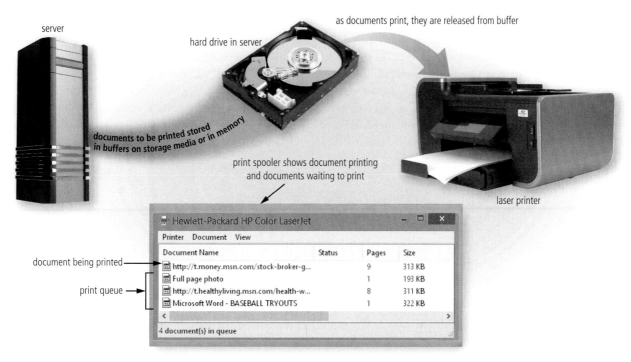

Figure 9-9 Spooling increases both processor and printer efficiency by placing documents to be printed in a buffer or on storage media before they are printed. This figure shows three documents in the queue with one document printing.
© iStockphoto / luismmolina; © iStockphoto / Lee Rogers; © Kitch Bain / Shutterstock.com; © Cengage Learning

Configuring Devices

A **driver**, short for *device driver*, is a small program that tells the operating system how to communicate with a specific device. Each device connected to a computer, such as a mouse, keyboard, monitor, printer, card reader/writer, digital camera, webcam, portable media player, or smartphone, has its own specialized set of commands and, thus, requires its own specific driver. When you start a computer or connect a device via a USB port, the operating system loads the device's driver. Drivers must be installed for each connected device in order for the device to function properly. Read How To 9-2 for instructions about finding the latest drivers for devices.

If you attach a new device, such as a portable media player or smartphone, to a computer, its driver must be installed before you can use the device. Today, most devices and operating systems support Plug and Play. As discussed in Chapter 6, *Plug and Play* means the operating system automatically configures new devices as you install or connect them. Specifically, it assists you in the device's installation by loading the necessary drivers automatically from the device and checking for conflicts with other devices. With Plug and Play, a user plugs in a device and then immediately can begin using the device without having to configure it manually.

🛠 HOW TO 9-2

Find the Latest Drivers for Devices
Device manufacturers sometimes release updated driver versions either to correct problems with previous drivers, enhance a device's functionality, or increase compatibility with new operating system versions. The following steps describe how to find the latest drivers for devices:

1. Search for and navigate to the device manufacturer's website.

2. Tap or click the link on the website to display the webpage containing technical support information.

3. Select or enter the device's model number to display support information for the device.

4. Browse the device's support information and then tap or click the link or button to download the most current driver. Manufacturers often create different versions of drivers for different operating systems, so make sure you download the driver that is compatible with the operating system you currently are using.

5. When the download is complete, follow the instructions that accompanied the driver to install it.

☀ **Consider This:** What might you do if you are unable to locate your device's driver on the manufacturer's website?

Monitoring Performance

Operating systems typically include a performance monitor. A **performance monitor** is a program that assesses and reports information about various computer resources and devices (Figure 9-10). For example, users can monitor the processor, drives, network, and memory usage.

The information in performance reports helps users and administrators identify a problem with resources so that they can try to resolve any issues. If a computer is running extremely slow, for example, the performance monitor may determine that the computer's memory is being used to its maximum. Thus, you might consider installing additional memory in the computer.

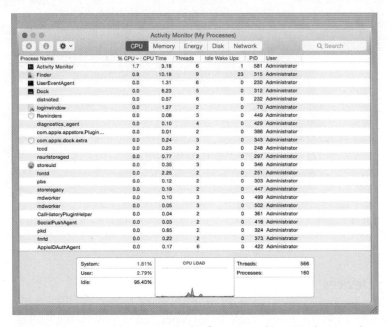

Figure 9-10 The Activity Monitor in this figure is tracking CPU (processor) usage.
Source: Apple Inc.

Establishing an Internet Connection

Operating systems typically provide a means to establish Internet connections. You can establish wired connections, such as cable and DSL, or wireless connections, such as Wi-Fi, mobile broadband, and satellite. Some connections are configured automatically as soon as you connect to the Internet. With others, you may need to set up a connection manually (Figure 9-11).

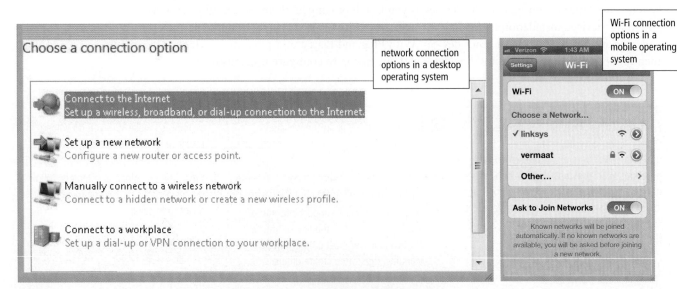

Figure 9-11 Shown here are Internet connection options for desktop and mobile operating systems.
Source: Microsoft; Source: Apple Inc.

Some operating systems also include a browser and an email program, enabling you to begin using the web and communicating with others as soon as you set up an Internet connection. Operating systems also sometimes include firewalls and other tools to protect computers and mobile devices from unauthorized intrusions and unwanted software. Read Ethics & Issues 9-1 to consider whether operating systems should include antivirus and other programs.

 ETHICS & ISSUES 9-1

Should Manufacturers Include Extra Programs in Operating Systems for Computers and Mobile Devices?
OEMs (original equipment manufacturers) often include and profit from including extra programs installed with a computer or device's operating system. These additional programs and apps, often called *bloatware*, mostly are harmless. Users object to their inclusion, however, because these programs and apps take up space, may slow start-up time, and can decrease the computer or device's overall efficiency.

Bloatware can come in many forms: antivirus programs, games, productivity apps, and more. Some programs or apps cause nuisances for the user, such as those that display alarming messages about a computer's virus protection and then

offer more protection for additional costs. Programs that run when the operating system starts or run in the background cause unnecessary slowdowns. Websites exist that you can use to check your installed programs or apps against a list of those other users commonly have uninstalled, as well as the reasons for uninstalling. Independent computer programmers post fixes to remove bloatware. These fixes may or may not be legal, depending on your license agreement, and could violate any warranties for which you may be eligible.

Critics of this practice state that OEMs and operating system manufacturers should offer users the option to purchase a computer or device with a clean installation (without bloatware) of the operating system. A clean install may lead to an increased

cost to make up for the lost revenue the manufacturer receives by including the extra programs or apps. Many say that charging more for a clean installation is unethical. Some recommend giving users the option to install the programs or apps that provide additional functionality as plug-ins or add-ons. Open source software advocates state that these versions offer more options to avoid bloatware.

Consider This: Should OEMs be able to install programs and apps to run alongside capabilities built into a computer or mobile device's operating system? Why or why not? Would you pay more for a clean installation of your operating system? Why or why not?

NOW YOU SHOULD KNOW

Be sure you understand the material presented in the section titled Operating Systems and the first nine sections in Operating System Functions, as it relates to the chapter objectives.
Now you should know...

- The purpose of an operating system (Objective 1)

- What processes are occurring when you start up or shut down your computers or mobile devices (Objective 2)

- How an operating system enables you to interact with the user interface, manage programs, manage memory, coordinate tasks, configure devices, monitor performance, and establish an Internet connection (Objectives 3 and 4)

Discover More: Visit this chapter's premium content for practice quiz opportunities.

Updating Operating System Software

Many programs, including operating systems, include an **automatic update** feature that regularly provides new features or corrections to the program. That is, the operating system automatically checks to see if new updates are available, and if so, downloads them from the Internet and installs them on your computer. With an operating system, these updates can include fixing program errors, improving program functionality, expanding program features, enhancing security, and modifying device drivers (Figure 9-12).

Figure 9-12 An operating system usually includes a means to download and install important updates.
Source: Google Inc.

BTW
Bugs
An error in a program sometimes is called a *bug*.

Many software makers provide free downloadable updates, sometimes called a *service pack*, to users who have registered and/or activated their software. With operating systems, the automatic update feature can be configured to alert users when an update is available or to download and install the update automatically. Users without an Internet connection usually can order the updates on an optical disc for a minimal shipping fee. Read Secure IT 9-1 for issues related to automatic updates.

SECURE IT 9-1

Automatic Updates — Safe or Not?

Software updates often improve security and reliability, and they also may add significant features that optimize the computer's performance. In most cases, you have the choice either to allow the software to update automatically or to assess and then decide whether to install each update individually. Software manufacturers often recommend you download and install all available updates when they become available.

The automatic update option occasionally has caused problems. In one case, people

preparing their income tax returns were unable to print forms when a leading software company issued an automatic update one week before the filing deadline. In another situation, an automatic update was installed on all computers — even those with this feature disabled. The company claimed that the update was harmless and was for the benefit of its customers. Only later did some users realize that this secret update caused serious problems. One problem, ironically, was that updates no longer could be installed on the affected

computers. Customers were furious about the issues, especially because the company made the changes without informing the computer owners. One consequence of the ensuing outrage was that many people turned off the automatic update feature, fearing that future updates might cause even more damage.

Consider This: Is the automatic update feature enabled or disabled on your computer? Why? Should software companies be able to send automatic updates to your computer without your knowledge? Why or why not?

Providing File, Disk, and System Management Tools

Operating systems often provide users with a variety of tools related to managing a computer, its devices, or its programs. These file, disk, and system management tools were discussed in Chapter 4 and are summarized in Table 9-1. Read Secure IT 9-2 to learn more about an operating system's built-in security tools.

Table 9-1 File, Disk, and System Management Tools

Tool	Function
File Manager	Performs functions related to displaying files; organizing files in folders; and copying, renaming, deleting, moving, and sorting files
Search	Attempts to locate files on your computer or mobile device based on specified criteria
Image Viewer	Displays, copies, and prints the contents of graphics files
Uninstaller	Removes a program or app, as well as any associated entries in the system files
Disk Cleanup	Searches for and removes unnecessary files
Disk Defragmenter	Reorganizes the files and unused space on a computer's hard disk so that the operating system accesses data more quickly and programs and apps run faster
Screen Saver	Causes a display's screen to show a moving image or blank screen if no keyboard or mouse activity occurs for a specified time
File Compression	Shrinks the size of a file(s)
PC Maintenance	Identifies and fixes operating system problems, detects and repairs drive problems, and includes the capability of improving a computer's performance
Backup and Restore	Copies selected files or the contents of an entire storage medium to another storage location

Using and Evaluating an Operating System's Built-In Security Tools

Security software must run constantly to protect against new viruses and malware and spyware attacks. Operating systems can include the following security tools:

- **Firewall:** Security experts recommend using a firewall and configuring it to turn on or off automatically.

- **Automatic updating:** Security updates are issued at least once daily, and other updates are generated on an as-needed basis. Many people enjoy the convenience offered by allowing these fixes to install automatically instead of continually checking for new files to download. Users can view the update history to see

when specific updates were installed. If an update caused a problem to occur, a user can uninstall these new files.

- **Antivirus software:** Many operating systems include antivirus programs that are updated regularly. Some users mistakenly think they should install and run another antivirus program simultaneously for more protection. They should not run more than one antivirus program on a computer because multiple programs might conflict with one another and slow overall performance.

- **Spyware and malware detection software:** Sophisticated malware and spyware threats are emerging at an unparalleled rate, so comprehensive

spyware and malware detection software is mandatory to fend off attacks on the computer or device.

The operating system generally is scheduled to scan and update when the computer is idle, such as in the middle of the night. Overall, the security tools should run constantly and quietly in the background to ensure a safe computing experience.

⊛ **Consider This:** Does your operating system have a firewall and protection against spyware and malware? Do updates occur automatically or manually? Which operating systems are more susceptible to malware attacks? Why?

Controlling a Network

Some operating systems are designed to work with a server on a network. These multiuser operating systems allow multiple users to share a printer, Internet access, files, and programs.

Some operating systems have network features built into them. In other cases, the operating system for the network is a set of programs that are separate from the operating system on the client computers or mobile devices that access the network. When not connected to the network, the client computers use their own operating system. When connected to the network, the operating system on the network may assume some of the operating system functions on the client computers or mobile devices.

The *network administrator*, the person overseeing network operations, uses the server operating system to add and remove users, computers, and other devices to and from the network. The network administrator also uses the operating system on the network to configure the network, install software, and administer network security.

⊛ BTW

Guest Account
If you want to provide someone temporary access to your computer, you can create a secure guest account that provides access to basic functions.

Administering Security

Network administrators, as well as owners of computers, typically have an *administrator account* that enables them to access all files and programs, install programs, and specify settings that affect all users on a computer, mobile device, or network. Settings include creating user accounts and establishing permissions. These *permissions* define who can access certain resources and when they can access those resources.

For each user, the network administrator or computer owner establishes a user account. A user account enables a user to **sign in** to, or access resources on, a network or computer (Figure 9-13). Each user account typically consists of a user name and password. Recall that a **user name**, or user ID, is a unique combination of characters, such as letters of the alphabet and/or numbers, that identifies a specific user.

Figure 9-13 Most multiuser operating systems allow each user to sign in, which is the process of entering a user name and a password into the computer. Single-user operating systems often use a password to lock an entire device or computer.
Source: Microsoft

BTW

Passwords
While users type a password, most computers and mobile devices hide the actual password characters by displaying some other characters, such as asterisks (*) or dots.

A **password** is a private combination of characters associated with the user name that allows access to certain computer, mobile device, or network resources. Some operating systems allow the network administrator to assign passwords to files and commands, restricting access to only authorized users. Mobile device owners often assign a password to the entire device, restricting all access until the correct password is entered. Read Secure IT 1-3 in Chapter 1 for tips on creating strong passwords.

To prevent unauthorized users from accessing computer resources, keep your password confidential. After entering a user name and/or password, the operating system compares the user's entry with the authorized user name(s) and password(s). If the entry matches the user name and/or password stored in a file, the operating system grants the user access. If the entry does not match, the operating system denies access to the user.

The operating system on a network records successful and unsuccessful sign-in attempts in a file. This allows the network administrator to review who is using or attempting to use the computer. The administrators also use these files to monitor computer usage. Read Ethics & Issues 9-2 to consider who is responsible for operating system security flaws.

ETHICS & ISSUES 9-2 ─────────────────────

Should Operating System Manufacturers Be Liable for Breaches Due to Security Flaws?
If you purchase a household device with a warranty, you can hold the manufacturer responsible for replacing and fixing it. Some argue that the same product liability laws that protect consumers in other industries should apply to software. Users' devices and data are vulnerable when security flaws exist in operating systems for computers and mobile devices. A flaw in an operating system can affect the performance of the computer or mobile device and subject data to corruption or unauthorized use. A user may not even be aware when a computer or mobile device is corrupted.

Hackers look for ways to break into a computer or mobile device using flaws in the operating system. An operating system is complex software that includes millions of lines of code. Developers write code as securely as possible, but with the volume of code, mistakes are bound to occur. Users sometimes are unaware of their own role in infecting their own computer or mobile device. Perhaps a hacker took advantage of a user with an unsecured Wi-Fi connection, or the user did not install or enable the latest updates to the operating system.

Some argue that making software manufacturers responsible for flaws will inhibit innovation. If a company spends

more time looking for potential security flaws, it has less time to spend enhancing the software. In addition, some of the same features that enhance an operating system, such as web integration, increase the software's vulnerability.

─────────────────────

Consider This: Has your computer or mobile device become infected with malware due to a flaw in the operating system? How did you know? What responsibility does a software manufacturer have for preventing and fixing operating system flaws? Should users expect their software to be perfect? Why or why not?

 CONSIDER THIS ─────────────────────

What are some alternatives to passwords?
Many computers and mobile devices offer alternatives to setting and entering a password in order to gain access. Alternatives to passwords include specifying passcodes containing only numeric characters, swiping or touching areas of the screen in a specified order or pattern, or fingerprint or facial recognition.

 CONSIDER THIS ─────────────────────

Do operating systems encrypt data and files?
To protect sensitive data and information further as it travels over a network, the operating system may encrypt it. Recall that *encryption* is the process of encoding data and information into an unreadable form. Administrators can specify that data be encrypted as it travels over a network to prevent unauthorized users from reading the data. When an authorized user attempts to read the data, it is automatically decrypted, or converted back into a readable form.

Types of Operating Systems

Many of the first operating systems were device dependent and proprietary. A *device-dependent* program is one that runs only on a specific type or make of computer or mobile device. *Proprietary software* is privately owned and limited to a specific vendor or computer or device model. Some operating systems still are device dependent. The trend today, however, is toward *device-independent* operating systems that run on computers and mobile devices provided by a variety of manufacturers. The advantage of device-independent operating systems is you can retain existing applications and data files even if you change computer or mobile device models or vendors.

When you purchase a new computer or mobile device, it typically has an operating system preinstalled. As new versions of the operating system are released, users often upgrade their existing computers and mobile devices to incorporate features of the new versions. Some upgrades are free; some offer an upgrade price that is less than the cost of purchasing the entire operating system. Read Ethics & Issues 9-3 to consider when you should upgrade.

Discover More: Visit this chapter's free resources to learn more about device-independent operating systems.

 ETHICS & ISSUES 9-3

Should You Be an Early Adopter of a New Technology?
Consumers' reactions to the release of a new device, program or app, or operating system fall into two camps: those who cannot wait, and those who exercise caution. Early adopters is the term given to users who sleep in line on the street outside a store in order to be one of the first to own a new device, or those who stay up until midnight to start the download of a program or app the moment it is released.

Some early adopters of new technology do so for the same reasons one might purchase a new item of clothing — to make a statement. Others do so out of curiosity, or for a desire to Tweet, blog, or post on social media his or her experiences. Manufacturers and developers rely on early adopters to provide valuable feedback and insight into the user experience, as well as to help generate excitement. In some cases, early adopters receive additional customer assistance in exchange for feedback. As one manufacturer said, the more people who initially use the product, the better the resulting product will be.

Critics of early adoption cite security risks and usability issues that may be uncovered. Many feel that waiting until the initial reviews, and subsequent patches or updated releases, are available is prudent. Others are concerned with compatibility issues between syncing the new technology with the user's current devices, data, or apps. Another factor in waiting is that the price of the new technology often drops within a few months of its release. Early adopters may have paid more for a less satisfying experience than those who wait.

Consider This: Have you ever been an early adopter of a new technology? What was your experience? Will you be an early adopter in the future? Why or why not? Should manufacturers give benefits to early adopters? Why or why not?

New versions of an operating system usually are *backward compatible*, which means they recognize and work with applications written for an earlier version of the operating system (or platform). The application, by contrast, may or may not be *upward compatible*, meaning it may or may not run on new versions of the operating system.

The three basic categories of operating systems on computers and mobile devices are desktop, server, and mobile. Table 9-2 lists examples in each of these categories, which are discussed on the following pages.

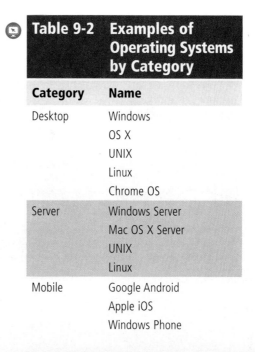

Table 9-2	Examples of Operating Systems by Category
Category	**Name**
Desktop	Windows
	OS X
	UNIX
	Linux
	Chrome OS
Server	Windows Server
	Mac OS X Server
	UNIX
	Linux
Mobile	Google Android
	Apple iOS
	Windows Phone

Desktop Operating Systems

Internet Research

What is the most widely used desktop operating system?

Search for: desktop os market share

A **desktop operating system**, sometimes called a *stand-alone operating system*, is a complete operating system that works on desktops, laptops, and some tablets. Desktop operating systems sometimes are called *client operating systems* because they also work in conjunction with a server operating system. Client operating systems can operate with or without a network.

Examples of the more widely used desktop operating systems are Windows, Mac OS, UNIX, Linux, and Chrome OS.

Windows/Mini Feature 9-1

In the mid-1980s, Microsoft developed its first version of Windows, which provided a graphical user interface. Since then, Microsoft continually has updated its Windows operating system, incorporating innovative features and functions with each subsequent version. In addition to basic capabilities, the latest versions of Windows offer these features:

BTW

Networking

Some desktop operating systems include networking capabilities, allowing the home and small business user to set up a small network.

- Uses tiles to access apps
- Includes the desktop interface
- Support for input via touch, mouse, and keyboard
- Email app, calendar app, and browser (*Internet Explorer*) included
- Photos, files, and settings can sync with *OneDrive*, Microsoft's cloud server
- Enhanced security through an antivirus program, firewall, and automatic updates
- Windows Store offers additional applications for purchase

Discover More: Visit this chapter's free resources to learn more about the Windows Store. Read Mini Feature 9-1 to learn more about the interface of the Windows operating system.

BTW

PC

The term, PC, sometimes is used to describe a computer that runs a Windows operating system.

MINI FEATURE 9-1

Windows User Interface

The following screens show the components of the Windows interface. The Windows operating system simplifies the process of working with documents and apps by organizing the manner in which you interact with the computer.

The Windows interface includes tiles and icons, as shown in the figure below. You tap or click tiles to run apps, and double-tap or double-click icons to run apps.

When you run an app in Windows, it may appear in an on-screen work area app, called the desktop, shown in the second figure in this mini feature. Many Office and Windows programs, such as Paint, contain common elements.

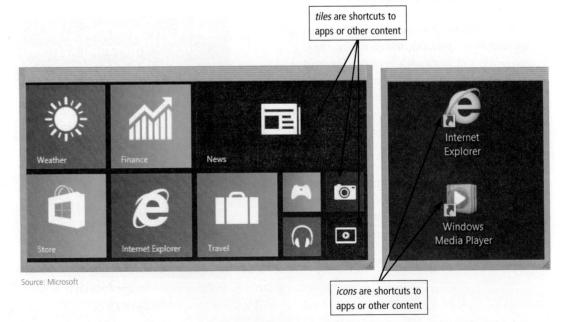

tiles are shortcuts to apps or other content

icons are shortcuts to apps or other content

Source: Microsoft

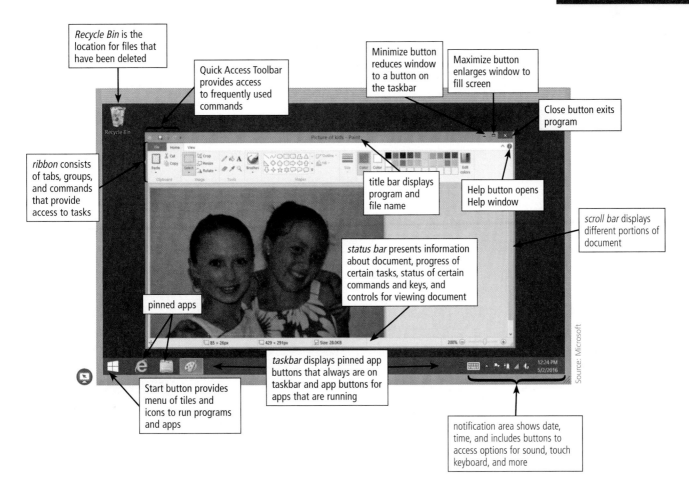

Recycle Bin is the location for files that have been deleted

Quick Access Toolbar provides access to frequently used commands

Minimize button reduces window to a button on the taskbar

Maximize button enlarges window to fill screen

Close button exits program

ribbon consists of tabs, groups, and commands that provide access to tasks

title bar displays program and file name

Help button opens Help window

scroll bar displays different portions of document

status bar presents information about document, progress of certain tasks, status of certain commands and keys, and controls for viewing document

pinned apps

Start button provides menu of tiles and icons to run programs and apps

taskbar displays pinned app buttons that always are on taskbar and app buttons for apps that are running

notification area shows date, time, and includes buttons to access options for sound, touch keyboard, and more

Source: Microsoft

Discover More: Visit this chapter's free resources to learn about the current Windows version.

✸ **Consider This:** Have you used Windows? If so, which version? What was your experience? What features of the Windows interface make it easy to run apps and open documents? Why? How does the ribbon help make learning a new program easier?

Mac OS/Mini Feature 9-2

Since it was released in 1984 with Macintosh computers, Apple's *Macintosh operating system* (*Mac OS*) has earned a reputation for its ease of use and has been the model for most of the new GUIs developed for non-Macintosh systems. The latest version, **OS X**, is a multitasking operating system available for computers manufactured by Apple. Features of the latest version of OS X include the following:

- Mail, calendars, contacts, and other items sync with *iCloud*, Apple's cloud server
- Communicate and play games with users of mobile devices running Apple's mobile operating system (iOS)
- Built-in Facebook and Twitter support allows you to post a status, comments, or files from any app
- Browser (*Safari*)
- Open multiple desktops at once
- Dictated words convert to text
- Support for Braille displays
- Mac App Store provides access to additional apps and software updates

Discover More: Visit this chapter's free resources to learn more about the Mac App Store. Read Mini Feature 9-2 to learn more about the interface of the Mac operating system.

MINI FEATURE 9-2

Mac OS User Interface

The following screens show the components of the OS X user interface. Mac OS is installed on Apple computers, such as iMacs, MacBook Pros, MacBook Airs, Mac Pros, and Mac minis. The user interface contains components such as the Dock, icons, and windows.

The OS X user interface begins with the desktop. Many OS X programs and apps contain common elements, as shown in the desktop figure below.

You can use the Launchpad to view, organize, and run apps, as shown in the second figure below.

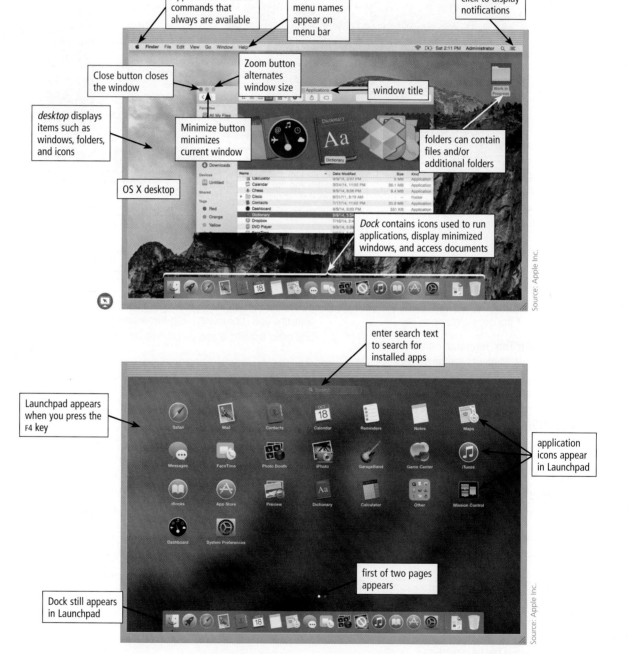

Discover More: Visit this chapter's free resources to learn more about the latest version of Mac OS.

☀ **Consider This:** How is the user interface in OS X similar to the Windows user interface? How is it different?

UNIX

UNIX (pronounced YOU-nix) is a multitasking operating system developed in the early 1970s by scientists at Bell Laboratories. Bell Labs (a subsidiary of AT&T) was prohibited from actively promoting UNIX in the commercial marketplace because of federal regulations. Bell Labs instead licensed UNIX for a low fee to numerous colleges and universities, where UNIX obtained a wide following. UNIX was implemented on many different types of computers. In the 1980s, the source code for UNIX was licensed to many hardware and software companies to customize for their devices and applications. As a result, several versions of this operating system exist, each with slightly different features or capabilities.

Today, a version of UNIX is available for most computers of all sizes. Although some versions of UNIX have a command-line interface, most versions of UNIX offer a graphical user interface (Figure 9-14). Power users often work with UNIX because of its flexibility and capabilities. An industry standards organization, *The Open Group*, now owns UNIX as a trademark.

BTW
OS X
OS X is a UNIX-based operating system.

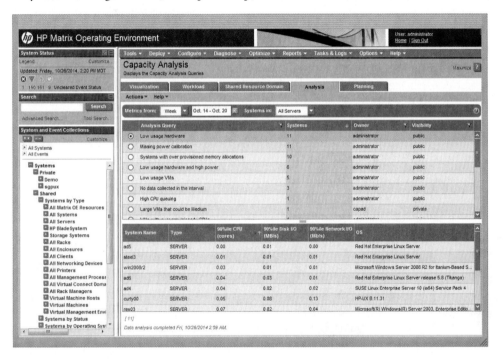

Figure 9-14 One version of the UNIX operating system.
Courtesy of Hewlett-Packard Company

Linux

Linux (pronounced LINN-uks), introduced in 1991, is a popular, multitasking UNIX-based operating system that runs on a variety of personal computers, servers, and devices. In addition to the basic operating system, Linux also includes many free tools and programming languages.

Linux is not proprietary software like the operating systems discussed thus far. Instead, Linux is *open source software*, which means its code is provided for use, modification, and redistribution. Many programmers have donated time to modify and redistribute Linux to make it the most popular UNIX-based operating system.

BTW
Technology Innovator
Discover More: Visit this chapter's free resources to learn about Linus Torvalds, the creator of Linux.

BTW
Technology Trend
Discover More: Visit this chapter's free resources to learn more about innovations of Linux powering the Internet of Things.

 **CONSIDER THIS**

Why use open source software?
Open source software has no restrictions from the copyright holder regarding modification of the software's internal instructions and redistribution of the software. Promoters of open source software state two main advantages: users who modify the software share their improvements with others, and customers can personalize the software to meet their needs. Read Secure IT 9-3 to consider security issues associated with open and closed source programs.

Open Source or Closed Source — Which Is More Secure?

Supporters of open source software maintain that this operating system enables developers to create high-quality programs. Source code, along with any changes, remains public, so communities of open source programmers can examine, correct, and enhance programs. They also can make changes immediately when security issues arise.

Many proponents of open source software use Linux, which is known for its speed and stability. Of the 500 fastest supercomputers, more than 90 percent use variants of Linux. Many of these computers perform high-performance tasks, including detecting and preventing fraud. Companies and nonprofit

organizations can distribute and sell their versions of Linux, which enables those without the expertise to modify open source software and to benefit from the creative efforts of the Linux community.

Developers of closed source operating systems, on the other hand, refuse to share some or all of the code. They believe that companies and developers should be able to control, and profit from, the operating systems they create. Their philosophy may hinder third-party software developers who create programs and apps for the operating system.

Fear of viruses and other security concerns can lead some to question about whether open source software is worthwhile. While

dishonest and anonymous developers can use open source software to create programs that may be or may include malware, cryptography experts emphasize that Linux systems have fewer reported security exposures than Windows-based systems. In general, Linux systems do not run antivirus software, but they do use detection programs that check for signs of attacks and probes.

Consider This: Are the security concerns about open source software legitimate? Why or why not? Why is antivirus software not needed on Linux-based systems? Does the open source model lead to higher-quality software? Why or why not?

Figure 9-15 A GUI distribution of Linux.
Courtesy of KDE

 BTW

Technology Innovator
Discover More: Visit this chapter's free resources to learn about Red Hat, a distributor of Linux.

Linux is available in a variety of forms, known as distributions. Some distributions of Linux are command line. Others are GUI (Figure 9-15). Some companies market software that runs on their own distribution of Linux. Many application programs, tools, and plug-ins have Linux distributions.

Users obtain versions of Linux in a variety of ways. Some download it free from a provider's website and create media to install it on a computer, or they create a Live CD or Live USB from which to preview it. Others purchase optical discs from vendors who may bundle their own software with the operating system or download it from their websites. Some retailers will preinstall Linux on a new computer on request.

Discover More: Visit this chapter's free resources to learn more about Linux distributions and Live CDs/Live USBs.

Chrome OS

Chrome OS, introduced by Google, is a Linux-based operating system designed to work primarily with web apps (Figure 9-16). Apps are available through the Chrome Web Store, and data is stored on Google Drive. The only apps typically installed on the computer are the Chrome browser, a media player, and a file manager. A specialized laptop that runs Chrome OS is called a *Chromebook*, and a specialized desktop that runs Chrome OS is called a *Chromebox*. Chromebooks and Chromeboxes typically use SSDs for internal storage. Users also can run Chrome OS as a virtual machine (which is discussed in the next section).

Because computers running Chrome OS work mostly with web apps, they do not require as much internal storage capacity as other desktop operating systems discussed in this section. Their start-up and shutdown time also is considerably less than other desktop operating systems because Chrome OS uses a streamlined start-up procedure.

Discover More: Visit this chapter's free resources to learn more about Chromebooks and Chromeboxes.

Figure 9-16   Chrome OS is a Linux-based operating system by Google.
Courtesy of Volha Kryvets; Source: Google Inc.

Running Multiple Desktop Operating Systems

If you want to run multiple operating systems on the same computer, you could partition the hard drive or you could create a virtual machine. *Partitioning* divides a hard drive in separate logical storage areas (partitions) that appear as distinct drives. When you partition a drive, you can install a separate operating system in each partition, sometimes called a dual boot. Because partitioning requires advanced skills, users often opt to create a virtual machine instead. A *virtual machine* (*VM*) is an environment on a computer in which you can install and run an operating system and programs. VMs enable you to install a second operating system on a computer. Read How To 9-3 for instructions about creating a virtual machine. Another option for Mac users who want to run Windows programs is a program called Boot Camp. Read How To 9-4 for instructions about installing the Windows operating system on a Mac computer.

HOW TO 9-3

Set Up and Use a Virtual Machine

A virtual machine enables a computer to run another operating system in addition to the one installed. Various reasons exist for using a virtual machine. For example, if you are running the latest version of Windows on a computer but require an app that runs only in a previous version of Windows, you might set up a virtual machine running the previous version of Windows so that you can run the desired app. The computer still will have the latest version of Windows installed, but you easily will be able to switch to the previous version when necessary.

To set up a virtual machine, you will need the required software, as well as installation media for the operating system you want to install in the virtual machine. The following steps describe how to set up a virtual machine:

1. Obtain and install an app that creates and runs virtual machines.

2. Run the app and select the option to create a new virtual machine.

3. Specify the settings for the new virtual machine.

4. If necessary, insert the installation media for the operating system you want to run in the virtual machine.

5. Run the virtual machine. Follow the steps to install the operating system in the virtual machine.

6. When the operating system has finished installing, remove the installation media.

7. While the virtual machine is running, if desired, install any apps you want to run.

8. When you are finished using the virtual machine, shut down the operating system in the same manner you would shut down your computer.

9. Exit the virtual machine software.

After you set up the virtual machine, you can use the virtual machine any time by performing the following steps:

1. Run the virtual machine software.

2. Select the virtual machine you want to run.

3. Tap or click the button to run the virtual machine.

4. When you are finished using the virtual machine, shut down the operating system similar to how you would shut down your computer.

5. Exit the virtual machine software.

Consider This: What are some other reasons that might require you to set up and use a virtual machine on a computer?

HOW TO 9-4

Use Boot Camp to Install the Windows Operating System on a Mac

If you are using an Apple computer, such as an iMac or MacBook Pro, you may encounter instances where you need to run apps in the Windows operating system. Newer versions of Mac OS enable you to install Windows on a computer using a program called *Boot Camp*. The following steps describe how to use Boot Camp to install the Windows operating system on a Mac:

1. Obtain the installation media for the version of Windows you want to install.

2. Use the operating system's search feature to locate the Boot Camp Assistant application. (*Hint:* Use the search text, boot camp.)

3. Click the search result for the Boot Camp Assistant application.

4. When the Boot Camp Assistant runs, read the introduction and then click the Continue button.

5. Next, you create a partition, which is a section of storage or memory reserved for a specific program or application. Partitions enable a single drive to be treated as multiple drives. Follow the remaining steps to create a Windows partition and install Windows:

   a. Specify the amount of disk space to use for the Windows partition. The partition should be large enough to store all operating system files, apps you want to run in Windows, and any files you want to store using Windows.

   b. Complete the steps described in the Windows installation process.

6. When the installation is complete and Windows starts, if necessary, enter your user name and password to sign in to Windows.

   If you want to switch between Mac OS and Windows, press and hold the option key on the keyboard while turning on or restarting the computer. When the list of operating systems is displayed, select the operating system you want to run.

 Consider This: What apps might someone want to run in Windows that are unavailable in Mac OS? How does Boot Camp differ from a virtual machine?

✔ NOW YOU SHOULD KNOW

Be sure you understand the material presented in the last four sections in Operating System Functions and the sections titled Types of Operating Systems and Desktop Operating Systems, as it relates to the chapter objectives. *Now you should know ...*

- How to update your operating system and tools (Objective 5)
- How you can use an operating system to control a network or administer security (Objective 6)
- Which desktop operating system is best suited to your needs (Objective 7)

Discover More: Visit this chapter's premium content for practice quiz opportunities.

Server Operating Systems

A **server operating system** is a multiuser operating system that organizes and coordinates how multiple users access and share resources on a network. Client computers on a network rely on server(s) for access to resources.

Many of the desktop operating systems discussed in the previous section function as clients and work in conjunction with a server operating system. Although desktop operating systems may include networking capability, server operating systems are designed specifically to support all sizes of networks, including medium- to large-sized businesses and web servers. Server operating systems can handle high numbers of transactions, support large-scale messaging and communications, and have enhanced security and backup capabilities.

Many also support virtualization. Recall that *virtualization* is the practice of sharing or pooling computing resources, such as servers or storage devices. Through virtualization, for example, server operating systems can separate a physical server into several virtual servers. Each virtual server then can perform independent, separate functions.

Examples of server operating systems include the following:

- **Windows Server:** Developed by Microsoft, Windows Server enables organizations to manage applications and websites on-site and/or on the cloud.
- **OS X Server:** Developed by Apple, OS X Server enables organizations to collaborate, share files, host websites and mail servers, and more on Mac computers and iOS devices.

- **UNIX:** Capable of handling a high volume of transactions in a multiuser environment and working with multiple processors, UNIX often is used on web servers.
- **Linux:** Because it provides a secure, stable multiuser environment, Linux often is used on web servers and on supercomputers.

Discover More: Visit this chapter's free resources to learn more about the latest versions of Windows Server and OS X Server.

Mobile Operating Systems

The operating system on mobile devices and many consumer electronics is called a **mobile operating system** and resides on firmware. Mobile operating systems typically include or support the following: calendar and contact management, text messaging, email, touch screens, accelerometer (so that you can rotate the display), digital cameras, media players, speech recognition, GPS navigation, a variety of third-party apps, a browser, and wireless connectivity, such as cellular, Wi-Fi, and Bluetooth. Read Ethics & Issues 9-4 to consider the privacy of text messages.

 Internet Research

What is the most widely used server operating system?

Search for: server os market share

BTW

Technology Innovators
Discover More: Visit this chapter's free resources to learn about the products and services of Sun and IBM.

 ETHICS & ISSUES 9-4

Should Text Messages Sent by Employees Be Private?

When an employer asks a worker to disclose work-related text messages, is the employee legally required to reveal all messages, even personal ones? Is the employer liable for damages caused by inappropriate messages sent by an employee?

Many companies provide employees with mobile devices, such as smartphones, for work communications. Employers typically create acceptable use policies. These policies address ownership of electronic communications, including email messages, voice mail messages, and text messages. Regardless of the policy,

employees may believe they have the rights of privacy and self-expression when they use a company-issued mobile device for personal use. The issue is complicated further when companies employ BYOD (bring your own device) policies. When an employee uses a personal device for business-related communications, it is unclear who owns the communications, and who takes responsibility for any misuse. Read Secure IT 9-4 for security issues associated with BYOD.

The U.S. Supreme Court ruled that an employer can read workers' text messages on company-owned devices if the employer has reason to believe the text messages violate workplace rules. The Court held that employees

can purchase their own mobile devices for personal use. Critics state that employees have a reasonable expectation of privacy. Supporters of the decision argue that employers own the devices because they provide the devices and pay for the service for the employee. They claim, therefore, that employers have a right to view the content of all text messages.

Consider This: Should text messages sent by employees be private? Why or why not? How can employers impose policies regarding text messages sent on company-issued mobile devices? Should employers be able to access work-related communications on an employee-owned device? Why or why not?

 SECURE IT 9-4

BYOD Security Issues

Effective BYOD (bring your own device) policies can lead to many benefits for businesses, but they also give rise to many issues that affect information security and data protection. When employees bring their smartphones, tablets, and laptops into the workplaces, the companies surrender much control over this hardware compared to devices they own.

One of the biggest problems is that employees can carry their devices everywhere outside of work. If these devices are lost or stolen, the company's sensitive information can land in the hands of criminals. Many of these allegedly lost devices are sold on online auctions and other services websites, even if the original owners have wiped their devices remotely.

Companies need to educate employees on *mobile device management (MDM)*. One point they need employees to know is that phishing scams abound in email messages, text messages, Facebook posts, and Tweets. Other security measures to emphasize are the need to use strong passwords, to not reveal these passwords to other employees, and to avoid apps that collect information about the user, especially those that monitor the employee's location and shopping habits.

BYOD policies should be developed that address technical, legal, and human resources issues. The language in these policies should cover these topics:

- Ensuring that work data will not be merged with the employee's personal data

- Requiring that nonemployees, such as family members who use the device, will not access work data

- Following procedures when an employee resigns or is terminated

- Alerting management immediately when the device is lost or stolen

Consider This: Do you or people you know work at a business that allow employees to bring their own devices to work? If so, do these businesses have a BYOD policy? If so, how were the policy's terms communicated? For example, were they explained verbally and available in written form?

Popular mobile operating systems include Android, iOS, and Windows Phone. The following sections discuss each of these operating systems.

✴ **CONSIDER THIS**

Do other mobile operating systems exist?

Yes. Several other mobile operating systems exist, although they are not as widely used as Android, iOS, and Windows Phone. For example, the *Blackberry operating system* is a proprietary mobile operating system that runs on Blackberry smartphones and Blackberry tablets. *Firefox OS* is a Linux-based open source operating system that runs on smartphones and tablets developed by Mozilla. *Fire OS* is a Linux-based operating system for Amazon Kindle tablets and Amazon Fire Phones. Several phones also run a version of Linux.

Android tablet

Android phone

Figure 9-17 An Android phone and tablet.
© iStockPhoto / deepblue4you; Courtesy of Sony Corporation

Android

Android is an open source, Linux-based mobile operating system designed by Google for smartphones and tablets (Figure 9-17). A variety of manufacturers produce devices that run the Android operating system, adding their own interface elements and bundled software. As a result, an Android smartphone manufactured by Samsung may have different user interface features from one manufactured by Google.

Features unique to recent versions of the Android operating system include the following:

- *Google Play* app store provides access to apps, songs, books, and movies.
- *Google Drive* provides access to email, contacts, calendar, photos, files, and more.
- Face recognition or fingerprint scanner can unlock the device.
- Share contacts and other information by touching two devices together (using NFC technology).
- Speech output assists users with vision impairments.
- Voice recognition capability enables users to speak instructions.
- Built-in heart rate monitor works with phone apps.

Discover More: Visit this chapter's free resources to learn more about the Android operating system.

iOS

iOS (originally called iPhone OS), developed by Apple, is a proprietary mobile operating system specifically made for Apple's mobile devices (Figure 9-18). Supported devices include the iPhone, iPod Touch, and iPad. Features unique to recent versions of the iOS operating system include the following:

- *Siri*, a voice recognition app, enables you to speak instructions or questions to which it takes actions or responds with speech output.
- Apple Pay provides a centralized, secure location for credit and debit cards, coupons, boarding passes, loyalty cards, and mobile payment accounts.
- iCloud enables you to sync mail, calendars, contacts, and other items.
- *iTunes Store* provides access to music, books, podcasts, ringtones, and movies.
- Integrates with iPod to play music, video, and other media.
- Improves connectivity with other devices running the Mac operating system.
- Mac App Store provides access to additional apps and software updates.

Discover More: Visit this chapter's free resources to learn more about the iOS operating system.

iOS tablet

iOS phone

Figure 9-18 An iOS phone and tablet.
© iStockPhoto / cotesebastien

Windows Phone

Windows Phone, developed by Microsoft, is a proprietary mobile operating system that runs on some smartphones (Figure 9-19). Features unique to recent versions of the Windows Phone operating system include the following:

- Sync photos, files, and settings with OneDrive.
- Use your phone as a remote control for your television.
- Access a global catalog of music, videos, or podcasts, or listen to iTunes music.
- Geofencing enables your phone to send or receive notification when you enter or exit a geographic location. (Read Ethics & Issues 8-2 in Chapter 8 for other uses of geofencing.)
- *Windows Phone Store* provides access to additional apps and software updates.
- *Wallet* app provides a centralized location for coupons, credit cards, loyalty cards, and memberships in a single, easily accessible location.

Discover More: Visit this chapter's free resources to learn more about the Windows Phone operating system.

Figure 9-19   A Windows Phone.
Courtesy of Microsoft

Mini Feature 9-3: Mobile versus Desktop Operating Systems

While mobile and desktop operating systems share many similarities, they also have differences designed for their operating environment. Read Mini Feature 9-3 for a comparison of mobile and desktop operating systems.

 MINI FEATURE 9-3

Mobile versus Desktop Operating Systems

An operating system has the same role, whether for a desktop or mobile device. It manages operations and provides a user interface. Because of this shared role, many similarities exist between the functions of desktop and mobile operating systems. From a user's perspective, operating systems enable you to work with apps and to monitor and maintain the functions of the computer or device. Typical functions included in mobile operating systems include the following:

- Main areas, such as a desktop or home screen, enable you to access and organize apps

- Methods to return to the main area quickly

- The ability to organize the app icons or tiles in the main areas easily by moving them to pages or folders or by adding them to menus

- System tools, such as to manage battery power and Internet connections

- Options for security settings

Whether you are purchasing a computer or mobile device, the choice of an operating system plays an important role.

Historically, the two types of operating systems have had different uses and capabilities. The differences are due in part to the disparity in screen size, keyboards, and processing power. Because of convergence, as well as the increased reliance on mobile devices for communications and productivity, the use and function of mobile and desktop operating systems are becoming more similar. The prevalence of web apps and cloud storage services enables users to access the same programs and files they work with on their desktop from a mobile device. Some developers now create operating systems that share code and have common features, regardless of whether they are installed on a computer or mobile device. Features, such as tiles and icons (typically used in mobile devices), make the transition between using a mobile device and computer easier. For example, mobile device operating systems include capabilities that allow users to take advantage of the touch screen displays. As more computer desktop monitors today are touch enabled, computer users can take advantage of this feature.

Many differences exist in the way a user interacts with a mobile operating system.

 BTW

Technology Trend
Discover More: Visit this chapter's free resources to learn more about mobile versus desktop operating system usage.

Source: SAMSUNG

Source: Google Inc.

Source: SAMSUNG

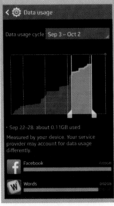

Source: Google Inc.

- A desktop operating system may use menus, windows, and bars to run apps and to access features within apps. On a desktop, you can run multiple programs simultaneously and seamlessly due to the large screen and the use of pointing devices. This feature makes desktops more relevant than mobile operating systems to productivity and multitasking.

- A mobile operating system typically has one program running at a time, although others may be running in the background. Quick movements and gestures are often all that you need to perform tasks on a mobile device. Mobile operating systems use technologies such as cellular, Bluetooth, Wi-Fi, GPS, and NFC to communicate with other devices and to connect to the Internet. Mobile devices also typically include cameras, video cameras, voice recorders, and sometimes speech recognition.

Discover More: Visit this chapter's free resources to learn more about mobile and desktop operating systems.

Consider This: What similarities have you noticed between mobile and desktop operating systems? What differences have you noticed between mobile and desktop operating systems? What features work better with a mobile versus a desktop operating system? Why? Is the convergence trend beneficial or should each device type take advantage of its strengths? Why?

✳ CONSIDER THIS

Do embedded computers use mobile operating systems?

Typically, an embedded computer uses an embedded operating system, sometimes called a *real-time operating system* (*RTOS*). Examples of products that use embedded operating systems include digital cameras, ATMs, digital photo frames, HDTV receivers, fuel pumps, ticket machines, process controllers, robotics, and automobile components. Embedded operating systems often perform a single task, usually without requiring input from a user. Several embedded operating systems are available, each intended for various uses.

✅ NOW YOU SHOULD KNOW

Be sure you understand the material presented in the sections titled Server Operating Systems and Mobile Operating Systems, as it relates to the chapter objectives.

Now you should know ...

- When you might use a server operating system (Objective 8)
- Which mobile operating system you would prefer to use (Objective 9)

Discover More: Visit this chapter's premium content for practice quiz opportunities.

Chapter Summary

This chapter discussed the functions common to most operating systems: starting and shutting down computers and mobile devices, providing a user interface, managing programs, managing memory, coordinating tasks, configuring devices, monitoring performance, establishing an Internet connection, updating operating system software, providing file, system, and disk management tools, controlling a network, and administering security. It also presented a variety of desktop operating systems, server operating systems, and mobile operating systems.

Discover More: Visit this chapter's free resources for additional content that accompanies this chapter and also includes these features: Technology Innovators: Linus Torvalds, Red Hat, Sun, and IBM; Technology Trends: Linux Powering the Internet of Things and Mobile versus Desktop Operating System Usage; and High-Tech Talks: Benchmarking and Virtualization.

Test your knowledge of chapter material by accessing the Study Guide, Flash Cards, and Practice Test apps that run on your smartphone, tablet, laptop, or desktop.

TECHNOLOGY @ WORK

Meteorology

With the television tuned to the local weather station, you anxiously are awaiting to see the projected path of a hurricane in the tropics. Having experienced hurricanes in the past, you rely heavily on the accuracy of weather forecasts so that you can prepare adequately if a storm travels through the area. Technology allows meteorologists to better estimate the severity and path of storms, enabling people to make potentially life-saving preparations.

The National Hurricane Center uses powerful computers to generate multiple computer models to determine a storm's path. These models consider factors such as the storm's current strength, the effects of nearby weather systems, the storm's central pressure, and whether the storm may travel over land. These models also may consider previous storms that traveled a similar path. While these models are not 100 percent accurate, they do ensure that everyone who may be affected by the storm has enough time to prepare.

Violent, rotating thunderstorms potentially can spawn tornadoes, which sometimes cause catastrophic damage. For this reason, it is important for everyone to watch or listen closely to the weather during the storm. Meteorologists can monitor weather systems on multiple radars and send additional severe weather warnings automatically to weather radios and apps. Technology enables these messages to be broadcast automatically to weather radios and apps only in areas that may be affected.

In addition to computers helping us stay safe during severe storms, they also assist with day-to-day weather forecasting. Several years ago, meteorologists could predict the weather for only a few days into the future. Beyond that point, the forecast was very uncertain. Meteorologists presently are able to predict the weather, including temperature and chance of precipitation, one week or more into the future with much greater accuracy because computers create models using historical weather data and behavior to predict the future path of various weather systems.

News and weather stations have weather apps and also post their weather forecasts online. In fact, several websites have interactive radars that allow visitors to zoom in and view how weather is affecting their immediate neighborhood.

The meteorology field has made significant advancements because of computer technologies. Weather forecasts are more accurate, which not only helps us prepare on land, but also helps to protect those traveling by air or by sea.

Consider This: In what other ways do computers and technology play a role in the meteorology field?

National Oceanographic and Atmospheric Administration

Study Guide

The Study Guide exercise reinforces material you should know for the chapter exam.

Discover More: Visit this chapter's premium content to **test your knowledge of digital content** associated with this chapter and **access the Study Guide resource** from your smartphone, tablet, laptop, or desktop.

Instructions: Answer the questions below using the format that helps you remember best or that is required by your instructor. Possible formats may include one or more of these options: write the answers; create a document that contains the answers; record answers as audio or video using a webcam, smartphone, or portable media player; post answers on a blog, wiki, or website; or highlight answers in the book/e-book.

1. Define the term, operating system. List the functions of an operating system.

2. Define the term, firmware. Name another term for an operating system.

3. List methods to start a computer or device.

4. Identify the five steps in the start-up process.

5. The _____ is the core of an operating system. Differentiate between resident and nonresident, with respect to memory.

6. Explain the role of a boot drive.

7. List reasons why users might shut down computers or mobile devices regularly. Differentiate between sleep mode and hibernate mode.

8. Define the term, user interface. Distinguish between GUI, natural-user, and command-line interfaces.

9. Define the terms, foreground and background, in a multitasking operating system.

10. List steps for removing a program or app.

11. Describe how a computer manages memory. Define the term, virtual memory.

12. The technique of swapping items between memory and storage is called _____.

13. Explain what occurs during thrashing, and list steps to prevent it.

14. List actions you should take if a mobile device displays a message that it is running low on memory.

15. Explain how a computer coordinates tasks. Define these terms: buffer, spooling, and queue.

16. Describe the role of a driver. Explain how to find the latest drivers for a device.

17. Describe the role of a performance monitor.

18. Explain how an operating system establishes an Internet connection.

19. Explain the issues surrounding an operating system's inclusion of additional software.

20. Identify changes that may be made to an operating system during an automatic update. List security concerns regarding automatic updates.

21. List file and disk management tools, and describe the function of each.

22. List and describe security tools used by operating systems.

23. Describe the role of a network administrator.

24. Explain the capabilities of administrator and user accounts on a network.

25. Explain the use of permissions on a network.

26. Explain issues surrounding responsibility for operating system security flaws.

27. List alternatives to using passwords.

28. Explain how an operating system uses encryption.

29. Differentiate between device-dependent and device-independent programs.

30. Define these terms: proprietary software, backward compatible, and upward compatible.

31. Explain issues surrounding being an early adopter of a new technology.

32. List two other names for a desktop operating system.

33. Identify features of Windows. Define the term, desktop, with respect to Windows and Mac OS.

34. The term, _____, sometimes is used to describe a computer that runs a Windows operating system.

35. Identify features of OS. You can use the _____ to view, organize, and run apps.

36. Describe uses and features of the UNIX operating system.

37. Define the term, open source software. _____ is an example of an open source operating system.

38. Explain the issues surrounding open source versus closed source operating systems.

39. Identify features of Chrome OS.

40. Identify reasons to use a virtual machine. List steps for setting up a virtual machine.

41. List steps for using Boot Camp to install the Windows operating system on a Mac computer.

42. Describe a server operating system. List examples of server operating systems.

43. Identify common features of mobile operating systems.

44. Explain issues surrounding ownership of text messages sent using company-issued devices.

45. Explain security concerns regarding BYOD policies.

46. Differentiate among the features of the Android, iOS, and Windows Phone mobile operating systems.

47. List differences and similarities between how a user interacts with mobile versus desktop operating systems.

48. Describe how embedded computers use operating systems.

49. Explain how the meteorology industry uses technology.

You should be able to define the Primary Terms and be familiar with the Secondary Terms listed below.

Key Terms

Discover More: Visit this chapter's premium content to **view definitions** for each term and to **access the Flash Cards resource** from your smartphone, tablet, laptop, or desktop.

Primary Terms (shown in **bold-black** characters in the chapter)

Android (434)
automatic
 update (421)
boot drive (413)
Chrome OS (430)
desktop operating
 system (426)
driver (419)

iOS (434)
Linux (429)
mobile operating
 system (433)
natural user interface
 (NUI) (414)
operating system
 (OS) (410)

OS X (427)
password (424)
performance
 monitor (420)
queue (418)
server operating
 system (432)
sign in (423)

UNIX (429)
user interface
 (UI) (414)
user name (423)
virtual memory (417)
Windows Phone (435)

Secondary Terms (shown in *italic* characters in the chapter)

administrator account (423)
background (415)
backup and restore (422)
backward compatible (425)
Blackberry operating system (434)
bloatware (421)
Boot Camp (432)
boot disk (413)
booting (413)
buffer (418)
bug (422)
Chromebook (430)
Chromebox (430)
client operating systems (426)
cold boot (413)
command language (415)
command-line interface (414)
cross-platform application (412)
desktop (428)
device driver (419)
device-dependent (425)
device-independent (425)
disk cleanup (422)
disk defragmenter (422)
Dock (428)
encryption (424)
file compression (422)
file manager (422)
Fire OS (434)
Firefox OS (434)
firmware (410)
foreground (415)

Google Drive (434)
Google Play (434)
*graphical user interface
 (GUI) (414)*
hibernate mode (413)
iCloud (427)
icons (426)
image viewer (422)
Internet Explorer (426)
iTunes Store (434)
kernel (412)
Live CD (413)
Live USB (413)
*Macintosh operating system
 (MAC OS) (427)*
memory resident (413)
*mobile device management
 (MDM) (433)*
*multipurpose operating
 systems (432)*
multitasking (415)
multiuser (416)
*network administrator
 (423)*
nonresident (413)
OneDrive (426)
*open source software
 (429)*
page (418)
paging (418)
partitioning (431)
PC maintenance (422)

permissions (423)
platform (412)
Plug and Play (419)
print spooler (418)
proprietary software (425)
*real-time operating system (RTOS)
 (436)*
recovery media (413)
Recycle Bin (427)
ribbon (427)
Safari (427)
screen saver (422)
scroll bars (427)
search (422)
service pack (422)
Siri (434)
sleep mode (413)

spooling (418)
stand-alone operating system (426)
status bar (427)
swap file (418)
taskbar (427)
The Open Group (429)
thrashing (418)
tiles (426)
touch user interface (414)
uninstaller (422)
upward compatible (425)
virtual machine (VM) (431)
virtualization (432)
Wallet (435)
warm boot (413)
Windows Phone Store (435)

sign in (423)

STUDENT ASSIGNMENTS

Checkpoint

The Checkpoint exercises test your knowledge of the chapter concepts. The page number containing the answer appears in parentheses after each exercise. The Consider This exercises challenge your understanding of chapter concepts.

Discover More: Visit this chapter's premium content to **complete the Checkpoint exercises** interactively; complete the **self-assessment in the Test Prep resource** from your smartphone, tablet, laptop, or desktop; and then **take the Practice Test**.

True/False   Mark T for True and F for False.

_____ 1. An operating system must reside inside a computer or mobile device; that is, it cannot run from a USB flash drive or other external drives. (410)

_____ 2. The kernel is nonresident, which means it remains in memory while the computer or mobile device is running. (413)

_____ 3. A user interface controls how you enter data and instructions and how information is displayed on the screen. (414)

_____ 4. Most users today work with a command-line interface. (414)

_____ 5. Most operating systems today are multitasking. (415)

_____ 6. The area of the hard drive used for virtual memory is called a swap file. (418)

_____ 7. Each device connected to a computer requires its own specific driver. (419)

_____ 8. Hackers often look for ways to break into a computer or device using flaws in the operating system. (424)

_____ 9. Many of the first operating systems were device dependent and proprietary. (425)

_____ 10. An upward compatible application means it can recognize and work with applications written for an earlier version of the operating system. (425)

_____ 11. Linux is proprietary software. (429)

_____ 12. Operating systems that function as both desktop and server operating systems sometimes are called multipurpose operating systems. (432)

Multiple Choice   Select the best answer.

1. A _____ application is an application that runs the same on multiple operating systems. (412)
   a. cross-platform
   b. stand-alone
   c. device driver
   d. multitasking

2. Placing a computer in _____ mode saves any open documents and running programs or apps to an internal hard drive before power is removed from the computer or device. (413)
   a. sleep
   b. hibernate
   c. kernel
   d. NUI

3. With a _____ interface, users interact with the software through ordinary, intuitive behavior. (414)
   a. command-line interface
   b. proprietary software
   c. natural user interface
   d. graphical user interface

4. A _____ operating system allows two or more programs or apps to reside in memory at the same time. (415)
   a. foreground
   b. background
   c. multiuser
   d. multitasking

5. With _____, the operating system allocates a portion of a storage medium to function as additional RAM. (417)
   a. Live USB
   b. a natural user interface
   c. virtual memory
   d. spooling

6. The technique of swapping items between memory and storage is called _____. (418)
   a. thrashing
   b. paging
   c. spooling
   d. buffering

7. In Windows, a _____ is a shortcut to apps or other content. (426)
   a. tile
   b. Launchpad
   c. ribbon
   d. Recycle Bin

8. A _____ is a multiuser operating system that organizes and coordinates how multiple users access and share resources on a network. (432)
   a. stand-alone operating system
   b. server operating system
   c. virtual machine
   d. multipurpose operating system

Checkpoint

Matching   Match the terms with their definitions.

_____ 1. firmware (410)

_____ 2. command language (415)

_____ 3. thrashing (418)

_____ 4. buffer (418)

_____ 5. driver (419)

_____ 6. bloatware (421)

_____ 7. proprietary software (425)

_____ 8. device-independent (425)

_____ 9. icons (426)

_____ 10. open source software (429)

a. operating system problem that occurs when it spends much of its time paging, instead of executing application software

b. small program that tells the operating system how to communicate with a specific device

c. Windows term for a shortcut to an app or other content

d. software that is privately owned and limited to a specific vendor or computer or device model

e. ROM chips or flash memory chips that store permanent instructions

f. operating system that runs on computers and mobile devices provided by a variety of manufacturers

g. software whose code is provided for use, modification, and redistribution

h. additional programs and apps included with operating systems, usually for profit

i. segment of memory or storage in which items are placed while waiting to be transferred from an input device or to an output device

j. set of commands used to control actions performed in a command-line interface

✱ Consider This   Answer the following questions in the format specified by your instructor.

1. Answer the critical thinking questions posed at the end of these elements in this chapter: Ethics & Issues (421, 424, 425, 433), How To (416, 419, 431, 432), Mini Features (426, 428, 435), Secure IT (422, 423, 430, 433), and Technology @ Work (437).

2. What is the role of the operating system? (410)

3. What does firmware do? (410)

4. What is a platform? (412)

5. What is a cross-platform application? (412)

6. What does the kernel do? (412)

7. How do resident and nonresident memory differ? (413)

8. What does the word, live, signify when used to describe a type of media (i.e., Live USB or Live CD)? (413)

9. What is the difference between a cold and warm boot? (413)

10. How does sleep mode differ from hibernate mode? (413)

11. Why do some users find command-line interfaces difficult to use? (415)

12. What is the role of virtual memory? (417)

13. In terms of speed, how does virtual memory compare with RAM? (417)

14. What does it mean when an operating system is thrashing? (418)

15. What is meant by the term, swap file? (418)

16. What remedies can you try if your computer or application runs sluggishly? (418)

17. What is a buffer? (418)

18. In a multiuser operating system, are tasks processed on a first-come, first-served basis? Why or why not? (418)

19. Why do some users object to bloatware? (421)

20. What is a service pack? (422)

21. How do users without an Internet connection obtain updates? (422)

22. What built-in security tools are included in most operating systems? (422)

23. What duties does a network administrator perform? (423)

24. What is the advantage of device-independent operating systems? (425)

25. What are some widely used desktop operating systems? (426)

26. How are tiles used in the Windows user interface? (426)

27. What elements are contained in the OS Dock? (428)

28. Why do computers running Chrome OS require less internal storage capacity than those running other desktop operating systems? (430)

29. What are some popular mobile operating systems? (434)

✳ Problem Solving

The Problem Solving exercises extend your knowledge of chapter concepts by seeking solutions to practical problems with technology that you may encounter at home, school, or work. The Collaboration exercise should be completed with a team.

Instructions: You often can solve problems with technology in multiple ways. Determine a solution to the problems in these exercises by using one or more resources available to you (such as a computer or mobile device, articles on the web or in print, blogs, podcasts, videos, television, user guides, other individuals, electronics or computer stores, etc.). Describe your solution, along with the resource(s) used, in the format requested by your instructor (brief report, presentation, discussion, blog post, video, or other means).

Personal

1. **Difficulty Signing In to Operating System** You are attempting to sign in to your operating system, but you receive an error message stating that you have entered an invalid password. What are your next steps?

2. **Missing Customization Settings** When you sign in to your operating system, your customized desktop background does not appear. Instead, the operating system displays the default desktop background. What might have happened?

3. **Incompatible Program** You have upgraded to the latest version of an operating system on your computer. After the upgrade, you realize that programs that used to run without issue now do not run. What are your next steps?

4. **Insufficient Access** You are attempting to install a program on your computer and a dialog box appears informing you that you have insufficient privileges to install the program. What might be wrong?

Source: Google Inc.

5. **Software Update Issues** You have heard that new software updates are available for your operating system, but when the operating system checks for updates, it shows that no updates are available. Why might this be the case?

Professional

6. **Virtual Machine Error** You use virtual machines on your office computer so that you can run and test software in multiple operating system versions. When you attempt to run one of the virtual machines, you receive an error message that the virtual machine already is running. You are certain that the virtual machine is not running. What steps can you take to correct the problem?

7. **Missing Files and Settings** When you sign in to various computers at work with the credentials assigned by your IT department, you typically see all your files. When you recently signed in to the computer in your office, however, you were unable to view your files. What are your next steps?

8. **Faulty Update** Your computer is set to install updates for the operating system, programs, and apps automatically. You have learned through your company's IT department that a recent operating system update causes a problem to occur with a program you use regularly. What are your next steps?

9. **Mobile Device Operating System Upgrade** A notification appears on your mobile phone stating that an operating system upgrade has been downloaded and is ready to install. Your company has provided the mobile phone to you for work-related business, and you are hesitant to install the upgrade. What are your next steps?

10. **Slow System Performance** Your office computer has been running slow lately, and you are attempting to determine the cause. What steps can you take to determine what might be slowing your computer's performance?

Collaboration

11. **Technology in Meteorology** Your environmental sciences instructor is teaching a lesson about how technology has advanced the meteorology field. Form a team of three people to prepare a brief report about how technology and meteorology are connected. One team member should research how meteorologists predicted weather patterns before computer use became mainstream. Another team member should create a timeline illustrating when and how technology was introduced to the meteorology field, and the third team member should research the technology required for a typical news station to forecast and present the weather.

The How To: Your Turn exercises present general guidelines for fundamental skills when using a computer or mobile device and then require that you determine how to apply these general guidelines to a specific program or situation.

How To: Your Turn

Discover More: Visit this chapter's premium content to **challenge yourself with additional How To: Your Turn exercises,** which include App Adventure.

Instructions: You often can complete tasks using technology in multiple ways. Figure out how to perform the tasks described in these exercises by using one or more resources available to you (such as a computer or mobile device, articles on the web or in print, online or program help, user guides, blogs, podcasts, videos, other individuals, trial and error, etc.). Summarize your 'how to' steps, along with the resource(s) used, in the format requested by your instructor (brief report, presentation, discussion, blog post, video, or other means).

1 Determine Your Operating System Version

Companies such as Microsoft, Apple, and Google release new versions of operating systems periodically. Software and drivers sometimes are designed for specific operating system versions, which means you may need to determine your operating system version so that you can obtain the proper software. The following steps describe how to determine your operating system version.

a. If necessary, turn on your computer or mobile device and, if necessary, sign in to the operating system. Some operating systems will display the version when they run. If the operating system version is not displayed, continue following these steps.

b. If you are using a Mac computer, click the command on the Apple menu to display information about the computer to determine the operating system version. If you are running an operating system other than Mac OS, continue following these steps.

c. Display the control panel or settings for your computer or mobile device.

d. Navigate to and then tap or click the command to display system information about the computer or device, and then locate the operating system version.

Source: Google, Inc.

Exercises

1. What operating system are you running?
2. What are some other reasons why you might need to know the operating system version on your computer or mobile device?
3. What might happen if you attempt to install a program or app that is not designed for your operating system version?

2 Search for Files on a Computer

Advances in technology enable users to store a large number of files, such as documents, photos, videos, and music, on their computers. Users store contacts, appointments, email messages, and other information on mobile devices to retrieve at a later time. With all the information you can store on computers and mobile devices, it sometimes can be difficult to locate an item you need to access. Today's operating systems contain a search tool that provides an easy way to locate files stored on a computer or mobile device. To search for an item on a computer or mobile device, you should know information about the item for which you are searching. The following steps guide you through the process of searching a computer or mobile device.

a. If necessary, run the search tool on your computer or mobile device. If you are using a mobile device, such as a smartphone or tablet, you may be able to access the search tool by pressing a search button on the phone or tablet.

Courtesy of Volha Kryvets; Source: Google Inc.

✷ How To: Your Turn

b. If you remember all or part of the name of the file for which you are searching, enter all or part of the file name in the search box.

c. Tap or click the search button to display the search results. Depending upon the number of files and folders on your computer or mobile device, it may take several minutes for search results to appear.

d. If no search results are displayed, consider searching again and entering less information in the search box.

e. When you locate the file for which you are searching, you can open it either by tapping, double-tapping, or double-clicking the file. The method you should use to open the file will depend on the operating system you are using.

Exercises

1. Have you used the search tool on your computer? If so, what files were you attempting to locate? If not, do you think the search tool will be helpful to you?

2. Have you used the search tool on a mobile device? What were you attempting to locate?

3. In addition to searching for files, what other items might the search tool locate?

❸ Personalize Your Operating Environment

When you purchase a new computer or mobile device, the first task you might want to complete is to personalize the operating environment to suit your tastes. For example, you might want to have your favorite sports team's logo as your desktop background, a screen saver consisting of a slide show containing photos of your recent vacation, or specific sounds that play when certain events occur. The following steps guide you through the process of personalizing your operating environment.

a. If necessary, sign in to your operating system.

b. Display your operating system's control panel, settings, or system preferences.

c. Tap or click the option to modify the display settings and then navigate to the specific setting to change the desktop background (the desktop background also may be referred to as wallpaper).

d. Tap or click the option to locate the image to use as your desktop background. If you are planning to download an image from the web, you should do

so before completing this step. Download only an image that is not protected by copyright.

e. Navigate to the location of the image to use as the desktop background and then select the image to set it as your desktop background.

f. Navigate to the screen saver settings and then select the desired screen saver. If necessary, set the desired preferences for the screen saver.

g. Navigate to the sound settings.

h. Select the event for which you want to assign or change the sound.

i. Select the sound you want to play. If you are not using one of the operating system's prerecorded sounds, navigate to the location of the sound you want to use and then select the sound.

j. If necessary, save the changes and close the control panel, settings, or system preferences.

Exercises

1. What image are you currently using as your desktop background or wallpaper?

2. Do you have a screen saver configured on your computer or mobile device? If so, what does it look like?

3. What other personalization settings do you customize?

Courtesy of KDE

❹ Configure Accessibility Settings

Many modern operating systems allow users to configure accessibility settings to make it easier for some individuals to interact with them. Accessibility features can perform functions such as enhancing the contrast between colors on the display device, narrating text that is displayed on the screen, and allowing the user to control the pointer using keys on

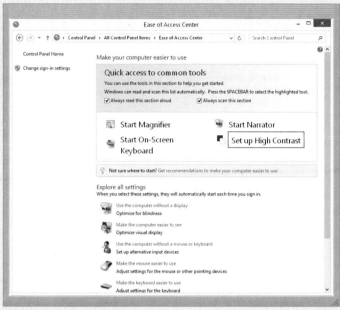

Source: Microsoft

the keyboard. The following steps guide you through the process of configuring accessibility settings.

a. If necessary, sign in to the operating system.

b. Display your operating system's control panel, settings, or system preferences.

c. Tap or click the command to display accessibility settings.

d. Select the accessibility setting you want to configure, and specify your desired settings.

e. Repeat the previous step for all remaining accessibility settings you want to configure.

f. When you have finished configuring the accessibility settings, save your changes and then close the window containing the control panel, settings, or system preferences.

g. If you no longer require the accessibility settings, display your operating system's control panel, settings, or system preferences, display the setting you want to disable, and then disable the setting.

Exercises

1. Accessibility settings are not only for people with impairments; these settings can make it easier for anyone to use a computer. Can you think of any accessibility settings that you might consider using to make it easier to interact with the computer?

2. Which third-party programs can provide additional features for accessibility?

3. Do you feel that the accessibility features in your computer or mobile device's operating system are sufficient? Why or why not?

How To: Your Turn

STUDENT ASSIGNMENTS

❺ Add Users to an Operating System

If you share your computer with others, you can add more user accounts to the operating system. When users sign in to their accounts, they can customize their settings and store files in locations that may not be accessible to other users on the computer. The following steps guide you through the process of adding users to an operating system.

a. Sign in to a user account that has administrative privileges; that is the user account should have the capability to perform functions such as adding users.

b. Display the operating system settings.

c. Tap or click the option to display user accounts.

d. Tap or click the option to add a new user account.

e. Specify the options for the new user account:

- Enter a name to identify the user account.
- Specify a default password for the user account.
- Select the type of user account (administrative, standard, etc.). You should create user accounts with administrative access only if you want the user to be able to perform tasks such as change computer settings; add or remove programs and apps; and add, modify, or remove a user account.
- If necessary, set parental controls for the user account.

f. Save the settings for the new user account.

g. Sign out of the existing user account.

h. Sign in to the newly created user account and make sure everything works as intended.

Exercises

1. Do you have multiple user accounts on your computer? Why or why not?

2. Do you think it is a good idea for students in a school computer lab to have administrative access to the computers? Why or why not?

3. What types of parental controls can you enable using your operating system? Do you think these controls are relevant only to parents, or can you determine other people who might benefit from using parental controls? What parental controls might those other people use, and why?

Source: Microsoft

✳ Internet Research

The Internet Research exercises broaden your understanding of chapter concepts by requiring that you search for information on the web.

Discover More: Visit this chapter's premium content to **challenge yourself with additional Internet Research exercises**, which include Search Sleuth, Green Computing, Ethics in Action, You Review It, and Exploring Technology Careers.

Instructions: Use a search engine or another search tool to locate the information requested or answers to questions presented in the exercises. Describe your findings, along with the search term(s) you used and your web source(s), in the format requested by your instructor (brief report, presentation, discussion, blog post, video, or other means).

❶ Making Use of the Web
Banking and Finance

Managing money and making wise investments and are among the most important skills consumers need to master. Abundant advice is available on a variety of banking and financial websites. More than 80 percent of Americans who manage household finances have enrolled in online banking programs, and 20 percent have used a banking app on their smartphones or mobile devices. Whether their financial institutions are a retail bank, a virtual bank, or a credit union, they enjoy the convenience of monitoring account balances, depositing checks, transferring funds, receiving text message alerts, and paying bills.

Personal finance websites provide information on portfolio management, tax preparation, real estate investing, mortgage rates, retirement planning, credit card and student loan advice, and a host of other lifestyle and educational topics. Also available are calculators to help make saving, spending, and real estate decisions. Business finance websites include market data, company earnings, interest rates, and corporate news.

Research This: (a) Visit two online banking websites: one for a financial institution that has a physical presence in your community and another that is virtual. Compare the services and featured products. For example, do they offer bill payment, retirement accounts, and mobile banking apps? What fees are charged for these services? Which bank has the highest money market and certificate of deposit rates?

(b) Visit two financial websites, such as Yahoo! Finance, that feature information about managing personal credit and debt. Read two stories discussing student loans, credit card debt, overspending, or retirement planning. According to these articles, what mistakes do people make managing their money? Who are the economic professionals writing or being quoted in the articles? What advice is given that can help you handle your expenses?

❷ Social Media

Operating systems constantly evolve as developers add new features, fix security issues, and modify functions. Computer and mobile device users need to stay abreast of these changes, especially when the updates affect performance and safety. Many blogs feature content about operating systems. Their posts cover industry news, photos, product reviews, previews of forthcoming software and hardware, and management changes. Most of these blogs are unofficial, meaning that the writers are not necessarily employees of the companies that develop the operating systems. The bloggers generally have extensive experience in the technology field and desire to share their expertise with others.

Research This: Search online for a blog that tracks features or updates to a mobile, desktop, or other operating system that you use or about which you would like more information. Report the web address of the blog, along with a summary of the most recent blog post.

Source: Yahoo

Internet Research

❸ Search Skills

Video, Audio, and Voice Search

A video search allows you to locate video files posted or shared online. Tap or click the Videos link on a search engine's home page and then type the search text. For example, type the search text, linux tutorial, in the search box to find videos for learning about Linux. You can narrow your results by specifying additional conditions. These may include length (in minutes), time taken (such as past day, week, or month), quality, popularity (based on number of views), and source (YouTube or other websites).

To search for audio files, type the search text, audio search, in a search engine's search box and look for a search engine that specializes in finding audio clips, streaming audio, and other audio files. Alternatively, visit a website for sharing audio and music files, and search that site directly. For example, type the search text, ios podcast, in an audio sharing site's search box to find podcasts about Apple's mobile operating system.

Some search apps allow you to speak your search text. For example, using Google, tap or click the microphone button in the search box or say the phrase, "ok google" to activate voice search and then speak your question. The app will convert your speech to text and provide the search results.

Source: SoundCloud

Research This: Using a search app that accepts voice input, either speak the search text or find an audio sharing site in which to type search text to find podcasts, audio files, or videos about these topics: (1) a video about how to manage security settings on your computer posted within the past month; (2) a video tutorial about how to use the Mac Finder, shorter than four minutes in length; (3) a video that was not posted on YouTube, describing how to partition a hard

drive; and (4) audio files of Windows operating system start-up sounds.

Create a document containing the web address of each audio or video clip and the name or web address of the website on which it appears. Watch or listen to comments on how accurately they reflect your search text.

❹ Security

An operating system should include antivirus and spyware and malware detection software to fend off intrusions. The use of this security software is discussed in Secure IT 9-2 in this chapter. Major companies that provide this software often include information on their websites about recently discovered virus threats and hoaxes. They also track scheduled virus payload strikes and map global and regional virus attacks.

Research This: Visit at least two virus protection websites to obtain virus information. When were the latest active threats discovered and updated? What are their names and risk levels? When is the next virus payload strike scheduled? What type of malware is spreading via mobile device use? Which virus removal tools and resources are available?

❺ Cloud Services

Cloud Development Platforms (PaaS)

Developers have many choices for the programming languages, operating systems, databases, and tools they use to create apps hosted on the cloud. Microsoft Azure, Amazon Web Services, and Google App Engine are providers of platform as a service (PaaS), a service of cloud computing that delivers tools for developing, testing, and deploying apps on the cloud.

A PaaS provider manages the computing resources required to run apps on the cloud so that developers can concentrate on writing the code, logic, interfaces, and operations of the software.

Research This: (1) Read a customer case study about Microsoft Azure, Amazon Web Services, or Google App Engine. In what industry is the customer involved? What was the challenge for which the customer was seeking a PaaS solution? How did this solution meet their needs? (2) Research one of these PaaS providers. Which operating systems and development tools does it support? How does it support scalability when additional computing resources are required? What pricing model is in place?

Critical Thinking

The Critical Thinking exercises challenge your assessment and decision-making skills by presenting real-world situations associated with chapter concepts. The Collaboration exercise should be completed with a team.

Instructions: Evaluate the situations below, using personal experiences and one or more resources available to you (such as articles on the web or in print, blogs, podcasts, videos, television, user guides, other individuals, electronics or computer stores, etc.). Perform the tasks requested in each exercise and share your deliverables in the format requested by your instructor (brief report, presentation, discussion, blog post, video, or other means).

1. Using Operating System Tools

You are the office manager at a social media consulting business. The office recently upgraded and replaced several computers. You now are running the latest version of Windows on all of your computers. Your boss asks you to explore the various tools that are included with the operating system and to evaluate any additional needs you might have.

Do This: Use the web to learn more about the following Windows operating system tools: firewalls, automatic updates, and software that scans for viruses, spyware, and other malware. Read reviews by industry experts and users. Analyze the advantages and disadvantages of using built-in operating system tools. Do any built-in operating system tools present

Source: Microsoft

security concerns? If so, what would you recommend? Explore alternatives for each of the tools, and determine whether you should disable the Windows tool and if any risks exist. Compile your findings.

2. Complete Security Solutions

Your neighbor started a new construction business. He would like to hire you to set up his new computers. His business will use the Internet to communicate with clients via email, store backups of data, and access cloud-based accounting software. The office will include two networked computers, which will share a printer and an Internet connection. In addition, he will use a tablet so that he can access the cloud-based accounting software using Wi-Fi. Because of security concerns with

using the Internet, he first would like you to install a program(s) designed to protect his computers from various security threats.

Do This: Use the web to find answers to the following questions. What types of security threats exist on the Internet that could impact his business? What types of security measures should he use? Evaluate two programs that provide a comprehensive security solution. What are the programs' functions? What are their costs? Do the services charge subscription fees in order to receive automatic updates? Which would you recommend? Why?

3. Case Study

Amateur Sports League You are the new manager for a nonprofit amateur soccer league. The board of directors has asked you to recommend options for mobile operating systems for the new smartphones they would like to purchase.

Do This: Select two mobile operating systems to explore (such as Android, iOS, and Windows Phone). Use the web to find industry experts' recommendations and user reviews for each operating system. Include the different device types for which each is available. Examine differences in security, features, speed, and reliability. What security concerns exist? What security features enable you to protect the smartphone and its data? Which mobile operating system offers the best features? Which is considered faster and/or more reliable? Your office computers run the Mac OS operating system. Do compatibility issues exist with any of the mobile operating systems? If so, what are the issues? Can you find solutions that would enable you to sync data? Compile your findings.

Collaboration

4. Desktop Operating Systems

You are an analyst for a large manufacturer of laundry soaps. The company currently uses an early version of the Windows operating system on its 5,000 desktops. This year, the company plans to upgrade the operating system and, if necessary, its desktops. The company asks your team to compare the latest versions of the Windows, Mac OS, and Linux operating systems.

Do This: Form a three-member team and assign each member an operating system. Each member should use the web to develop a feature/benefit analysis and answer the following questions. What is the initial cost of the operating system per computer? What are the memory and storage requirements? Will the operating system require the company to purchase new computers? Which is best at protecting against viruses, spam, and spyware? Which support touch input? As a team, compile your findings and share your recommendation with the class.

COMMUNICATING DIGITAL CONTENT:
Wired and Wireless Networks and Devices

A variety of media are used for worldwide communications.

"I use my smartphone to make phone calls, send text messages, video chat with family and friends, listen to voice mail messages, and navigate using a GPS app. At home, I have a broadband Internet connection, and I access the Internet wirelessly at local hot spots and on campus. What more could I learn about communications and networks?"

While you may be familiar with some of the content in this chapter, do you know how to . . .

- Add a computer or mobile device to a network?
- Determine if you should use a BAN to monitor medical data?
- Use mobile communications?
- Evaluate the risks and benefits of telemedicine?
- Use Bluetooth technology?
- Prevent Bluebugging?
- Use an NFC tag?
- Use your smartphone as a mobile hot spot?
- Strengthen a wireless signal?
- Detect an intruder accessing your wireless signal?
- Plan and design a home network?
- Add a wireless printer to a network?
- Describe how fake cell towers are intercepting calls?

In this chapter, you will discover how to perform these tasks along with much more information essential to this course. For additional content available that accompanies this chapter, visit the free resources and premium content. Refer to the Preface and the Intro chapter for information about how to access these and other additional instructor-assigned support materials.

✓ Objectives

After completing this chapter, you will be able to:

1 Discuss the purpose of components required for successful communications (sending device, communications device, transmission media, and receiving device) and identify various sending and receiving devices

2 Differentiate among LANs, MANs, WANs, and PANs

3 Differentiate between client/server and peer-to-peer networks

4 Explain the purpose of communications software

5 Describe various network communications standards and protocols: Ethernet, token ring, TCP/IP, Wi-Fi, Bluetooth, UWB, IrDA, RFID, NFC, and LTE

6 Describe various types of communications lines: cable, DSL, ISDN, FTTP, T-carrier, and ATM

7 Describe commonly used communications devices: broadband modems, wireless modems, wireless access points, routers, network cards, and hubs and switches

8 Discuss ways to set up and configure a home network

9 Differentiate among physical transmission media: twisted-pair cable, coaxial cable, and fiber-optic cable

10 Differentiate among wireless transmission media: infrared, broadcast radio, cellular radio, microwaves, and communications satellite

Communications

The process in which two or more computers or devices transfer data, instructions, and information is known as digital communications. Today, even the smallest computers and devices can communicate directly with one another, with hundreds of computers on a corporate network, or with millions of other computers around the globe — often via the Internet.

Figure 10-1 shows a sample communications system. Some communications involve cables and wires; others are sent wirelessly through the air. For successful communications, you need the following:

• A **sending device** that initiates an instruction to transmit data, instructions, or information
• A communications device that connects the sending device to transmission media
• **Transmission media**, or a *communications channel*, on which the data, instructions, or information travel
• A communications device that connects the transmission media to a receiving device
• A **receiving device** that accepts the transmission of data, instructions, or information

As shown in Figure 10-1, all types of computers and mobile devices serve as sending and receiving devices in a communications system. This includes servers, desktops, laptops, tablets, smartphones, portable media players, handheld game devices, and GPS receivers. Communications devices, such as modems, wireless access points, and routers, connect transmission media to a sending or receiving device. Transmission media can be wired or wireless.

This chapter presents types of networks, along with various types of communications lines and devices, and transmission media.

Communications System

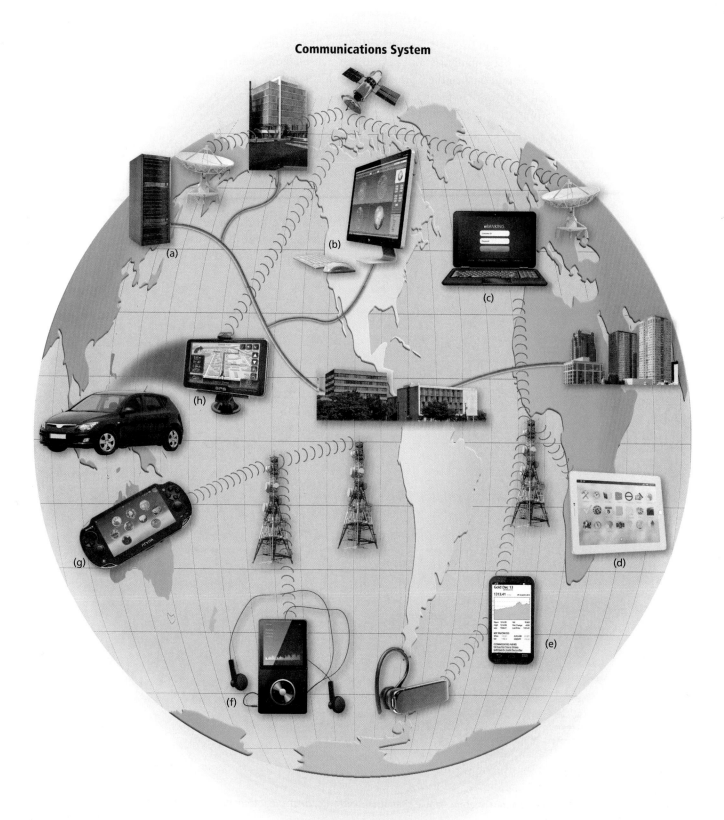

Figure 10-1 A simplified example of a communications system. Some devices that serve as sending and receiving devices are (a) servers, (b) desktops, (c) laptops, (d) tablets, (e) smartphones and headsets, (f) portable media players, (g) handheld game devices, and (h) GPS receivers in vehicles. Transmission media consist of phone and power lines, cable television and other underground lines, microwave stations, and satellites.

Networks

As discussed in Chapter 1, a **network** is a collection of computers and devices connected together via communications devices and transmission media. A network can be internal to an organization or span the world by connecting to the Internet. Many home and business users create a network to facilitate communications, share hardware, share data and information, share software, and transfer funds (Figure 10-2):

- **Facilitate communications.** Using a network, people communicate efficiently and easily via email, Internet messaging, chat rooms, blogs, wikis, online social networks, video calls, online meetings, videoconferences, VoIP, text messaging, and more. Some of these communications occur within an internal network. Other times, they occur globally over the Internet.
- **Share hardware.** Each computer or device on a network can be provided access to hardware on the network. For example, each computer and mobile device user can access a printer on the network, as they need it. Thus, home and business users create networks to save money on hardware expenses.

Figure 10-2 Networks facilitate communications; enable sharing of hardware, data and information, and software; and provide a means for transferring funds.

- **Share data and information**. Any authorized user can access data and information stored on a network. A large company, for example, might have a database of customer information. Any authorized employee can access the database using a computer or mobile device connected to the network.

  Most businesses use a standard, such as *EDI* (*electronic data interchange*), that defines how business documents travel across transmission media. For example, businesses use EDI to send bids and proposals, place and track orders, and send invoices.

- **Share software.** Users connected to a network can access software on the network. To support multiple users' software access, vendors often sell versions of their software designed to run on a network or as a web app on the Internet. These network and Internet subscription versions usually cost less than buying individual copies of the software for each computer. The license fees for these programs typically are based on the number of users or the number of computers or mobile devices attached to the network.

- **Transfer funds.** *Electronic funds transfer* (*EFT*) allows users connected to a network to exchange money from one account to another via transmission media. Both businesses and consumers use EFT. Examples include wire transfers, use of credit cards and debit cards, direct deposit of funds into bank accounts, online banking, and online bill payment.

Instead of using the Internet or investing in and administering an internal network, some companies hire a value-added network provider for network functions. A *value-added network* (*VAN*) provider is a third-party business that provides networking services such as EDI services, secure data and information transfer, storage, or email. Some VANs, such as PayPal, charge an annual or monthly fee; others charge by the service used.

Discover More: Visit this chapter's free resources to learn more about sharing hardware, data, and information.

 BTW
Sharing Network Software
When you use a network to share software, you sometimes have to install the software on your computer, and a server on the network manages the licenses.

 Internet Research
How do you physically transfer files without a network connection?
Search for: sneakernet

 CONSIDER THIS

What is an intranet?

Recognizing the efficiency and power of the Internet, many organizations apply Internet and web technologies to their internal networks. An *intranet* (intra means within) is an internal network that uses Internet technologies. Intranets generally make company information accessible to employees and facilitate collaboration within an organization. Files on an intranet generally are not accessible from the Internet.

One or more servers on an intranet host an organization's internal webpages, applications, email messages, files, and more. Users locate information, access resources, and update content on an intranet using methods similar to those used on the Internet. A company hosts its intranet on servers different from those used to host its public webpages, apps, and files.

Sometimes a company uses an *extranet* (extra means outside or beyond), which allows customers or suppliers to access part of its intranet. Package shipping companies, for example, allow customers to access their intranet via an extranet to print air bills, schedule pickups, and track shipped packages as the packages travel to their destinations.

LANs, MANs, WANs, and PANs

Networks usually are classified as a local area network, metropolitan area network, wide area network, or personal area network. The main difference among these classifications is their area of coverage.

LAN A **local area network** (**LAN**) is a network that connects computers and devices in a limited geographical area, such as a home, school, office building (Figure 10-3), or closely positioned group of buildings. Each computer or device on the network, called a *node*, often shares resources, such as printers, large hard drives, and programs. Often, the nodes are connected via cables.

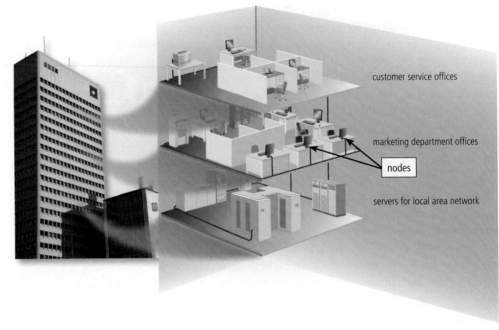

Figure 10-3 Computers and devices on different floors access the same LAN in an office building. Computers and devices on the network often are identified as nodes.
© Xtuv Photography / Shutterstock.com; © Cengage Learning

A **wireless LAN (WLAN)** is a LAN that uses no physical wires. Computers and devices that access a wireless LAN must have built-in wireless capability or the appropriate wireless network card, USB adapter, or other wireless device. A WLAN may communicate with a wired LAN for access to its resources, such as software, hardware, and the Internet (Figure 10-4). Read How To 10-1 for instructions about adding mobile computers or devices to wireless networks.

Figure 10-4 Computers and mobile devices on a WLAN may communicate via a wireless access point with a wired LAN to access its hardware, software, Internet connection, and other resources.
© iStockphoto / Stephen Krow; © Oleksiy Mark / Shutterstock.com; © iStockphoto / 123render; © iStockphoto / pictafolio; © iStockphoto / Moncherie; © Natalia Siverina / Shutterstock.com; © Ruslan Kudrin / Shutterstock.com; © Cengage Learning

🏵 HOW TO 10-1

Add a Computer or Mobile Device to a Wi-Fi Network

If you are using a mobile computer or device, such as a tablet or smartphone, in a location that has a Wi-Fi network, you might want to add the device to the network. When a mobile device is connected to a Wi-Fi network, you not only can transfer data and information more quickly, but you also might save charges imposed by a mobile service provider if you subscribe to a mobile data plan. The following steps describe how to add a mobile computer or device to a Wi-Fi network:

1. Obtain the necessary network information required to connect. This might include the network's SSID and password. Read How To 5-3 in Chapter 5 for additional information about SSIDs.
2. If necessary, enable the device's capability of connecting to Wi-Fi networks.

3. If necessary, display the list of available Wi-Fi networks that are in range of the mobile computer or device.
4. Select the Wi-Fi network to which you want to connect.
5. If necessary, enter the required password for the network.
6. If desired, disconnect from the mobile network so that your device communicates using only the Wi-Fi network.
7. Run a browser and navigate to a webpage to verify that the device is connected to the network properly.

🏵 **Consider This:** What other reasons might you have for wanting to connect a mobile computer or device to a Wi-Fi network?

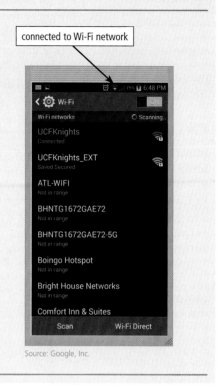

connected to Wi-Fi network

Source: Google, Inc.

MAN   A *metropolitan area network* (*MAN*) is a high-speed network that connects local area networks in a metropolitan area, such as a city or town, and handles the bulk of communications activity across that region. A MAN typically includes one or more LANs, but covers a smaller geographic area than a WAN.

A MAN usually is managed by a consortium of users or by a single network provider that sells the service to the users. Local and state governments, for example, regulate some MANs. Phone companies, cable television providers, and other organizations provide users with connections to the MAN.

WAN   A **wide area network** (**WAN**) is a network that covers a large geographic area (such as a city, country, or the world) using a variety of wired and wireless transmission media (Figure 10-5). A WAN can be one large network or can consist of multiple LANs connected together. The Internet is the world's largest WAN.

PAN   A **personal area network** (**PAN**) is a network that connects computers and devices in an individual's workspace using wired and wireless technology. Devices

Figure 10-5   A simplified example of a WAN.

BTW
High-Tech Talk
Discover More: Visit this chapter's free resources to learn about the star, bus, and ring network topologies.

include smartphones, digital cameras, printers, and more. A PAN may connect devices through a router using network cables or directly using special USB cables. PANs also may use Bluetooth or Wi-Fi technology. A *body area network* (*BAN*), sometimes called a body sensor network (BSN), is a type of PAN that wirelessly connects sensors worn by, carried by, implanted in, or attached to a human body. Read Ethics & Issues 10-1 to consider how BANs are used to monitor medical data.

ETHICS & ISSUES 10-1

Would You Use a BAN to Monitor Medical Data?

By wearing, carrying, implanting, or attaching small devices to a person's body, medical professionals can track vital signs and monitor heart rhythms, breathing rates, and much more via a BAN, which uses low-powered sensors to collect data. The BAN sends the collected data wirelessly to an Internet-connected device, which relays the data to a medical data server. In some cases, the data transmits directly to emergency services. Some devices also automatically can dispense medications based on the data collected.

Because of these devices, a patient may not have to visit a medical facility to receive treatment. Heart patients, diabetics, or those

with asthma or other similar conditions can perform regular daily activities while wearing the device. If it collects any unusual data, the patient can receive medical resources immediately. First responders also use these devices. A fire chief, for example, can monitor firefighters' body temperature and oxygen levels as they battle a fire.

The disadvantages of BANs include data validity and security. What happens if a device stops working or its data becomes corrupt? Serious health complications could result if the patient is not monitoring conditions via another technique. For example, devices that administer medication could cause an overdose or underdose if not working properly. Medical data is highly sensitive. An unscrupulous individual could

intercept vital signs and other personal data during transfer, violating a patient's confidentiality. Privacy advocates also have concerns about nonmedical uses of BANs. The FCC (Federal Communications Commission) controls the registration of MBANs (medical BANs). The FCC regulates the radio frequency in which an MBAN can transmit data. Some types of MBANs are restricted to be used only within a licensed medical facility.

Consider This: Should insurance companies be required to pay for BANs? Why or why not? Would you use a BAN for a medical condition? Why or why not?

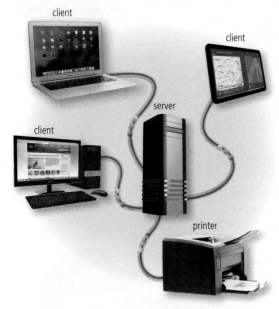

Figure 10-6 As illustrated by the communications in this simplified diagram, on a client/server network, one or more computers act as a server, and the client computers and mobile devices access the server(s). Connections can be wired or wireless and may occur through a communications device.
© iStockphoto / Oleksiy Mark; © iStockphoto / Stephen Krow; © Oleksiy Mark / Shutterstock.com; © Mr.Reborn55 / Shutterstock.com; © iStockphoto / luismmolina; © Cengage Learning

Network Architectures

The configuration of computers, devices, and media on a network is sometimes called the *network architecture*. Two examples of network architectures are client/server or peer-to-peer.

Client/Server On a **client/server network**, one or more computers act as a server, and the other computers on the network request services from the server (Figure 10-6). A **server**, sometimes called a *host computer*, controls access to the hardware, software, and other resources on the network and provides a centralized storage area for programs, data, and information. The **clients** are other computers and mobile devices on the network that rely on the server for its resources. For example, a server might store an organization's email messages. Clients on the network, which include any users' connected computers or mobile devices, access email messages on the server. Both wired and wireless networks can be configured as a client/server network.

Although it can connect a smaller number of computers, a client/server network architecture typically provides an efficient means to connect 10 or more computers. Most client/server networks require a person to serve as a network administrator because of the large size of the network.

As discussed in Chapter 3, some servers are dedicated servers that perform a specific task. For example, a network server manages network traffic (activity), and a web server delivers requested webpages to computers or mobile devices.

Peer-to-Peer   A *peer-to-peer (P2P) network* is a simple, inexpensive network architecture that typically connects fewer than 10 computers. Each computer or mobile device, called a *peer*, has equal responsibilities and capabilities, sharing hardware (such as a printer), data, or information with other computers and mobile devices on the peer-to-peer network (Figure 10-7). Peer-to-peer networks allow users to share resources and files located on their computers and to access shared resources found on other computers on the network. Peer-to-peer networks do not have a common file server. Instead, all computers can use any of the resources available on other computers on the network. For example, you might set up a P2P network between an Android tablet and a Windows laptop so that they can share files using Bluetooth or so that you can print from the tablet to a printer accessible to all devices on the network. Both wired and wireless networks can be configured as a peer-to-peer network.

P2P networks are ideal for very small businesses and home users. Some operating systems include a P2P networking tool that allows users to set up a peer-to-peer network. Many businesses also see an advantage to using P2P. That is, companies and employees can exchange files using P2P, freeing the company from maintaining a network server for this purpose. Business-to-business e-commerce websites find that P2P easily allows buyers and sellers to share company information such as product databases.

Figure 10-7   As illustrated by the communications in this simplified diagram, each computer or mobile device on a P2P network shares its hardware and software with other computers and mobile devices on the network. Connections can be wired or wireless and may occur through a communications device.
© Alex Staroseltsev / Shutterstock.com; © iStockphoto / 123render; © Sergey Peterman / Shutterstock.com; © Oleksiy Mark / Shutterstock.com; Source: Microsoft; © Cengage Learning

---

 CONSIDER THIS

What is P2P file sharing?
P2P file sharing, sometimes called a *file sharing network*, describes a network configuration on which users access one another's hard drives and exchange files directly via a file sharing program. As more users connect to the network, each user has access to shared files on other users' hard drives. When users sign out of the network, others no longer have access to their hard drives.
   Discover More: Visit this chapter's free resources to learn more about file sharing programs.

Internet Research
Why have some file sharing networks been shut down?
Search for: file sharing network shutdown

Communications Software

Communications software consists of programs and apps that (1) help users establish a connection to another computer, mobile device, or network; (2) manage the transmission of data, instructions, and information; and (3) provide an interface for users to communicate with one another. The first two often are provided by or included as tools with an operating system or bundled with a communications device. The third is provided by applications such as email, FTP, browser, discussion boards, chat rooms, Internet messaging, videoconferencing, and VoIP.

Sometimes, communications devices are preprogrammed to accomplish communications tasks. Some routers, for example, contain firmware for various protocols. Other communications devices require separate communications software to ensure proper transmission of data. Communications software works with the network standards and protocols (presented in a later section) to ensure data moves through the network or the Internet correctly.

Internet Research
What are examples of apps that provide free text messaging services?
Search for: free text messages

Mini Feature 10-1: Mobile Communications

Users often communicate with one another via mobile computers and devices. Read Mini Feature 10-1 to learn about communications options for mobile devices and associated data plans.

MINI FEATURE 10-1

Mobile Communications

After visiting your parents for the weekend, you receive an email message from your mom asking about your trip home. You respond that it was fine and that you were able to send text messages over the Internet to your sister because the bus had a Wi-Fi connection. Meanwhile, your roommate sends you a text message with directions to the restaurant where you are meeting for dinner. That night, you chat on Facebook with a classmate about your homework and catch up on your friends' updates. You see your brother is online, so you invite him to a video call where you talk about the ball game streaming on your phone. From email and text messages to voice and video calls, computers and mobile devices offer many ways to communicate.

Email is best for sharing longer, detailed messages. For shorter or time-sensitive messages, consider using the following forms of immediate communications.

Text/Picture/Video Messaging

Text, picture, and video messages often take the place of phone conversations among many people, who find exchanging these messages to be less intrusive and more efficient than voice conversations. SMS (short message service) text messages are messages of 300 or fewer characters sent from one user to another through a mobile service provider's cell phone tower. With MMS (multimedia message service), users also can send and receive photos, videos, and audio files. Occasional users might subscribe to a text-messaging plan, where providers charge a small fee for each message sent or received. In contrast, avid users, who send frequent text, picture, or video messages, might subscribe to an unlimited plan. To avoid paying fees to mobile service providers for sending text messages, some people opt for free messaging apps and services available via third-party providers. These services send messages over the Internet rather than a provider's network. Some of these services are free when both parties subscribe. Free messaging apps often include advertising content alongside the messages.

Internet Messaging

With Internet messaging services, you can send text or media messages in real time to other online users. To access an Internet messaging service, you need the service's desktop, web, or mobile app, and an Internet connection on your computer or mobile device. Users with accounts on multiple Internet messaging services often use an Internet messaging aggregator app to manage contact lists and chat on different Internet messaging networks simultaneously.

Some providers allow you to merge your text/picture/video (SMS and MMS) and Internet messages so that you can see messages of both types from the same contact in a single conversation.

Voice and Video Calling

VoIP services, such as Skype and FaceTime, also provide voice and video calling services over the Internet. These often are much less expensive than making phone calls over a mobile service provider's network. It also is possible to make calls from a VoIP program to a mobile or landline phone. Voice and video calling require large amounts of bandwidth. As a result, some carriers prohibit the use of calling services over their networks, requiring users to connect via Wi-Fi to make these calls. Read Ethics & Issues 10-2 to consider video calling and other issues associated with communications technologies and medical care.

© radub85 / Fotolia

Data Plans

Your mobile device's data plan enables you to access the Internet through your mobile service provider's network when Wi-Fi is not available. Without a data plan, you must use Wi-Fi or a wired connection to access the Internet on your computer or mobile device. Some mobile service providers offer an unlimited data plan for your device, while many offer limited data plans. If you exceed your data limit in a given month, additional fees apply. By monitoring your data usage to see how much you use on average over a few months, you can decide on the best plan for you. Some carriers offer a shared data plan that provides an allotted amount of data to be shared across several smartphones, tablets, laptops, gaming devices, and mobile hot spots. Using Wi-Fi when available to access the Internet will save on data usage charges if you have a limited data plan.

Discover More: Visit this chapter's free resources to learn more about mobile communications, messaging, and voice and video calling.

✴ **Consider This:** Think about how you use different forms of mobile communications to share information or communicate with your family, friends, or coworkers as part of your daily routine. For what purposes do you generally send email messages or text messages? After exchanging text messages, when might you make a phone call or use VoIP service to talk in real time? Under what circumstances is each form of communication most efficient?

ETHICS & ISSUES 10-2

Do the Benefits of Telemedicine Outweigh the Risks?

After your doctor asks you several questions, she gives you a diagnosis and sends a prescription to your local pharmacy electronically. Instead of walking out of the exam room, you turn off your tablet's webcam, receiving medical care without leaving your home. *Telemedicine* is the use of communications and information technology to provide and assist with medical care. Patients use telemedicine to communicate with a doctor, nurse, or pharmacist from their home or workplace. Healthcare professionals benefit from collaborating and consulting with specialized physicians in other locations.

Proponents of telemedicine state that its use can provide healthcare access to patients in remote areas, or those who are unable to leave their home safely. The Mayo Clinic is testing in-office kiosks which enable employees to videoconference with a medical professional to diagnose minor health conditions without the employee having to leave work. Another benefit of telemedicine is in cases where spread of infectious disease is a concern.

Some healthcare experts state that the cost of the equipment and time spent training healthcare professionals outweighs the benefits. The inability of healthcare professionals to perform hands-on tasks, such as take a temperature or examine the patient's ears or throat, can lead to misdiagnosis or an incomplete exam. If a patient requires immediate care, such as for an allergic reaction, a medical professional is not on hand to give treatment, causing delays. Insurance companies may require physicians to have medical licenses in the state where the patient resides in order to cover the expenses. Privacy advocates warn that hackers can access shared data or spy on videoconferences between doctors and patients.

Consider This: Have you ever used telemedicine to communicate with your healthcare provider? Why or why not? Would you use a kiosk at your workplace to communicate with a healthcare provider? Why or why not? Is it practical to relay on telemedicine to provide care to people in remote areas? Why or why not?

NOW YOU SHOULD KNOW

Be sure you understand the material presented in the sections titled Communications, Networks, and Communications Software, as it relates to the chapter objectives.
Now you should know . . .

- When you are using a sending device, a communications device, transmission media, and a receiving device (Objective 1)
- When you might use a LAN, MAN, WAN, and PAN (Objective 2)
- Why you would use a client/server or a P2P network (Objective 3)
- Why you would use communications software and what types of mobile communications you might use (Objective 4)

Discover More: Visit this chapter's premium content for practice quiz opportunities.

Network Communications Standards and Protocols

Today's networks connect terminals, devices, and computers from many different manufacturers across many types of networks. For the different devices on various types of networks to be able to communicate, the network must use similar techniques of moving data through the network from one application to another.

To alleviate the problems of incompatibility and ensure that hardware and software components can be integrated into any network, various organizations such as ANSI (American National Standards Institute) and IEEE (Institute of Electrical and Electronics Engineers) propose, develop, and approve network standards. A *network standard* defines guidelines that specify the way computers access the medium to which they are connected, the type(s) of medium used, the speeds used on different types of networks, and the type(s)

BTW
High-Tech Talk
Discover More: Visit this chapter's free resources to learn about the OSI reference model.

Table 10-1 Network Communications Standards and Protocols

Name	Type	Sample Usage
Ethernet	Standard	LAN
Token ring	Standard	LAN
TCP/IP	Protocol	Internet
Wi-Fi	Standard	Hot spots
Bluetooth	Protocol	Wireless headset
UWB	Standard	Inventory tracking
IrDA	Standard	Remote control
RFID	Protocol	Tollbooth
NFC	Protocol	Mobile phone payment
LTE	Standard	Mobile phones

of physical cable and/or the wireless technology used. Hardware and software manufacturers design their products to meet the guidelines specified in a particular standard, so that their devices can communicate with the network. A standard that outlines characteristics of how two devices communicate on a network is called a *protocol*. Specifically, a protocol may define data format, coding schemes, error handling, and the sequence in which data transfers over a network.

Table 10-1 identifies some of the more widely used network communications standards and protocols for both wired and wireless networks. The following sections discuss each of these standards and protocols.

 CONSIDER THIS

Do network standards and protocols work together?
Network standards and protocols often work together to move data through a network. Some of these standards define how a network is arranged physically, while others specify how messages travel along a network. Thus, as data moves through a network from one program to another, it may use one or more of these standards.

 BTW

Technology Innovator
Discover More: Visit this chapter's free resources to learn about Robert Metcalfe, Ethernet inventor.

 BTW

Data Transfer Rates
Mbps (megabits per second) is one million bits per second, and *Gbps* (gigabits per second) is one billion bits per second.

Ethernet

Ethernet is a network standard that specifies no central computer or device on the network (nodes) should control when data can be transmitted. That is, each node attempts to transmit data when it determines the network is available to receive communications. If two computers or devices on an Ethernet network attempt to send data at the same time, a collision will occur. When this happens, the computers or devices resend their messages until data transfer is successful.

The Ethernet standard defines guidelines for the physical configuration of a network (e.g., cabling, network devices, and nodes). Ethernet currently is the most popular network standard for LANs because it is relatively inexpensive and easy to install and maintain. Depending on the transmission media used, Ethernet networks have data transfer rates that range from 10 Mbps for home/small office users to 100 Gbps for enterprise users.

Token Ring

The **token ring** standard specifies that computers and devices on the network share or pass a special signal, called a token, in a unidirectional manner and in a preset order. A *token* is a special series of bits that functions like a ticket. The device with the token can transmit data over the network. Only one token exists per network. This ensures that only one computer transmits data at a time. Although token ring is not as widely used today, many networks use the concept of a token.

The token ring standard defines guidelines for the physical configuration of a network (e.g., cabling, network cards, and devices). Some token ring networks connect up to 72 devices. Others use a special type of wiring that allows up to 260 connections. The data transfer rate on a token ring network ranges from 4 Mbps to 1 Gbps.

TCP/IP

Short for Transmission Control Protocol/Internet Protocol, **TCP/IP** is a network protocol that defines how messages (data) are routed from one end of a network to the other, ensuring the data arrives correctly. TCP/IP describes rules for dividing messages into small pieces, called *packets*; providing addresses for each packet; checking for and detecting errors; sequencing packets; and regulating the flow of messages along the network.

TCP/IP has been adopted as the network standard for Internet communications. Thus, all hosts on the Internet follow the rules defined in this standard. As shown in Figure 10-8, Internet communications also use other standards, such as the Ethernet standard, as data is routed to its destination.

When a computer sends data over the Internet, the data is divided into packets. Each packet contains the data, as well as the recipient (destination), the origin (sender), and the sequence information used to reassemble the data at the destination. Each packet travels along the fastest individual available path to the recipient's computer or mobile device via routers. This technique of breaking a message into individual packets, sending the packets along the best route available, and then reassembling the data is called *packet switching*. Read Secure IT 10-1 for another use of packets.

How Communications Standards Might Work Together

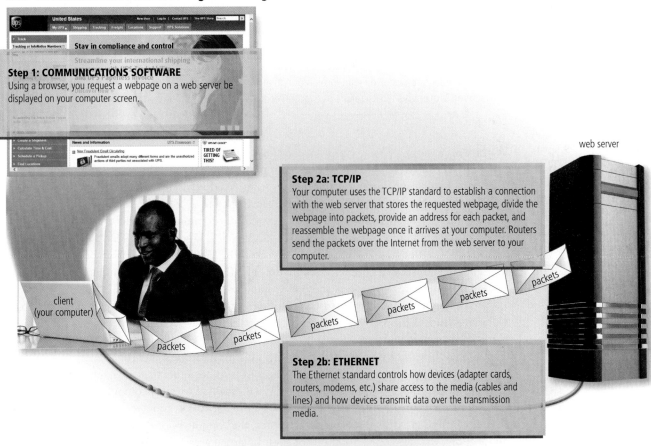

Step 1: COMMUNICATIONS SOFTWARE
Using a browser, you request a webpage on a web server be displayed on your computer screen.

Step 2a: TCP/IP
Your computer uses the TCP/IP standard to establish a connection with the web server that stores the requested webpage, divide the webpage into packets, provide an address for each packet, and reassemble the webpage once it arrives at your computer. Routers send the packets over the Internet from the web server to your computer.

Step 2b: ETHERNET
The Ethernet standard controls how devices (adapter cards, routers, modems, etc.) share access to the media (cables and lines) and how devices transmit data over the transmission media.

web server

client
(your computer)

packets

Figure 10-8 This figure illustrates how Internet communications use TCP/IP and Ethernet to ensure that data travels correctly to its destination.

© lenetstan / Shutterstock.com; © iStockphoto / luismmolina; © Cengage Learning

SECURE IT 10-1

Monitoring Network Traffic

Network monitoring software constantly assesses the status of a network and sends an email or text message, usually to the network administrator, when it detects a problem. These messages may state that an outage has occurred, the server's available memory space is near capacity, a new user account has been added, or some other critical event has developed.

Monitoring software can measure the amount of network traffic, graph network usage, determine when a specific program uses the network, and show the bandwidth used by each computer or mobile device. On networks that use the TCP/IP protocol, for example, *packet sniffer software* monitors and logs packet traffic for later analysis. Packet sniffing can detect problems, such as why traffic is flowing slowly.

The software also can play a security role, including identifying unusual or excessive network activity. For example, it can flag a remote computer always connected to the network or someone making repeated attempts to sign in to an account. Hackers use packet sniffer software to hijack a computer, which means they capture a user's packets and then reconstruct the contents of webpages that were visited, obtain user names and passwords, and trace photos and videos viewed.

Consider This: How would you determine if your employer or school has network monitoring software? Would you change your computer activities, including browsing certain websites, if you knew the software could track your computer or mobile device usage?

CONSIDER THIS

Can IP addresses be used to determine a computer or device's location?

In many cases, you can determine a computer or a device's location from its IP address. For example, if an IP address begins with 132.170, a small amount of research will uncover that the University of Central Florida assigns IP addresses beginning with these numbers; however, additional research would be necessary to determine where the computer or mobile device is located on the network. Certain websites allow visitors to find a location by entering an IP address. Some web apps infer your approximate location from your IP address when GPS is not available in order to provide you with local information or nearby search results.

Discover More: Visit this chapter's free resources to learn more about finding locations based on IP addresses.

Internet Research

What does it mean to be Wi-Fi CERTIFIED?

Search for: wifi certified

Wi-Fi

Computers and devices that have the appropriate wireless capability can communicate via radio waves with other computers or devices using **Wi-Fi** (wireless fidelity), which identifies any network based on the 802.11 standards. Developed by IEEE, **802.11** is a series of network standards that specifies how two wireless devices communicate over the air with each other. Common standards include 802.11a, 802.11b, 802.11g, 802.11n, 802.11ac, 802.11ad, and 802.11af, with data transfer rates ranging from 11 Mbps to 7 Gbps. Many devices support multiple standards. For example, a designation of 802.11 ac/b/g/n on a computer, router, or other device indicates it supports those four standards (ac, b, g, and n).

Wi-Fi sometimes is referred to as *wireless Ethernet* because it uses techniques similar to the Ethernet standard to specify how physically to configure a wireless network. Thus, Wi-Fi networks easily can be integrated with wired Ethernet networks. When a Wi-Fi network accesses the Internet, it works in conjunction with the TCP/IP network standard.

One popular use of the Wi-Fi network standard is in hot spots that offer mobile users the ability to connect to the Internet with their Wi-Fi-enabled wireless computers and devices. Many homes and small businesses also use Wi-Fi to network computers and devices wirelessly. In open or outdoor areas free from interference, the computers or devices should be within 300 feet of a wireless access point or hot spot. In closed areas, the wireless network range is about 100 feet. To obtain communications at the maximum distances, you may need to install extra hardware to extend or strengthen a wireless signal.

Discover More: Visit this chapter's free resources to learn more about 802.11 standards.

LTE

LTE (Long Term Evolution) is a network standard that defines how high-speed cellular transmissions use broadcast radio to transmit data for mobile communications. Developed by the Third Generation Partnership Project (3GPP), LTE has the potential of 100 Mbps *downstream rate* (receiving data) and 30 Mbps *upstream rate* (sending data). Based on the TCP/IP network standard, LTE supports data, messaging, voice, and video transmissions. Many mobile service providers, including AT&T and Verizon Wireless, offer LTE service.

Two competing standards for LTE are WiMax (Worldwide Interoperability for Microwave Access) and UMB (Ultra Mobile Broadband).

Discover More: Visit this chapter's free resources to learn more about LTE.

 BTW

Technology Innovators
Discover More: Visit this chapter's free resources to learn about AT&T and Verizon.

Bluetooth/Mini Feature 10-2

Bluetooth is a network protocol that defines how two Bluetooth devices use short-range radio waves to transmit data. The data transfers between devices at a rate of up to 3 Mbps. To communicate with each other, Bluetooth devices often must be within about 33 feet but can be extended to about 325 feet with additional equipment.

A Bluetooth device contains a small chip that allows it to communicate with other Bluetooth devices. For computers and devices not Bluetooth-enabled, you can purchase a Bluetooth wireless port adapter that will convert an existing USB port into a Bluetooth port. Most current operating systems have built-in Bluetooth support. When connecting two devices using Bluetooth, the originating device sends a code to the connecting device. The codes must match to establish the connection. Devices that share a Bluetooth connection are said to be paired. Read Mini Feature 10-2 to learn about Bluetooth uses, advantages, and disadvantages.

 MINI FEATURE 10-2 ────────────────────

Bluetooth Technology

Most mobile devices and computers manufactured today are equipped with Bluetooth capability. One of the earliest and most popular uses of Bluetooth is to connect hands-free headsets to a mobile phone. Bluetooth has many additional uses, and device manufacturers are increasingly including Bluetooth technology.

Uses

You can use Bluetooth-enabled or Bluetooth-enhanced devices in many ways, including the following:

- Connect devices, such as mobile phones, portable media players, or GPS devices, with vehicle stereos, which use the vehicle's speakers to project sound (shown in the figure).

- Use GPS receivers to send directions to a mobile phone or GPS-enabled device.

- Transfer photos wirelessly from a digital camera to a laptop or server.

- Play music on a smartphone through the speakers on a computer or other Bluetooth-enabled device.

- Send signals between video game accessories, video game devices, and a television.

- Establish a PAN (personal area network).

- Allow communications between a computer and devices, such as a keyboard, printer, Smart TV, or mobile phone. Connecting these devices enables you to print documents, share calendar appointments, and more.

- Replace wired communications devices, such as bar code readers, with wireless devices to enhance portability.

- Transmit data from a medical device, such as a blood glucose monitor, to a mobile phone or other device.

- Change the channel, pause a program, or schedule a recording using a Bluetooth-compatible or Bluetooth-enabled television and remote control.

- Track objects that include tags or nodes used to send wireless signals read by a real-time location system.

 Internet Research

What are future uses of Bluetooth?

Search for: future bluetooth uses

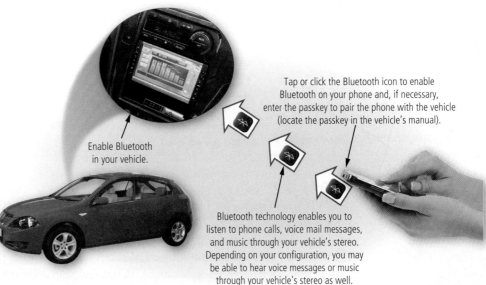

Enable Bluetooth in your vehicle.

Tap or click the Bluetooth icon to enable Bluetooth on your phone and, if necessary, enter the passkey to pair the phone with the vehicle (locate the passkey in the vehicle's manual).

Bluetooth technology enables you to listen to phone calls, voice mail messages, and music through your vehicle's stereo. Depending on your configuration, you may be able to hear voice messages or music through your vehicle's stereo as well.

©Fotolia; © Adisa / Shutterstock.com; © Vartanov Anatoly / Shutterstock.com; © Pakhnyushcha / Shutterstock.com

(continued)

Advantages and Disadvantages

Advantages of using Bluetooth technology include the following:

- If a device has Bluetooth capability, using Bluetooth technology is free.
- Although Bluetooth devices need to be near each other, they do not have to be in the same room, within the same line of sight, or facing each other.
- Bluetooth devices typically require low processing power and use little energy, so using Bluetooth technology will not drain a device's batteries.
- Establishing a wireless Bluetooth connection is easy. With most Bluetooth-enabled devices, you simply tap or click a Bluetooth shortcut or icon to enable Bluetooth. Once enabled, the devices usually immediately recognize a connection. (Before initial use, you may need to pair two Bluetooth devices so that they can communicate with each other. Read How To 3-1 in Chapter 3 for instructions about pairing Bluetooth devices.)
- Bluetooth connections have low security risks. If you want to secure a Bluetooth channel, you would define an identification number for the connection and create a PIN that you can distribute as needed. If the secured computer or device detects an unknown Bluetooth connection, you can choose to accept or reject it. Read Secure IT 10-2 to learn about security risks associated with using Bluetooth technology.
- Bluetooth technology is standardized globally, meaning it can be used to connect devices that are not the same make or model.
- Bluetooth connections have little risk of interference with other wireless networks because the strength of the wireless signals is weak and because of frequency hopping, which changes frequency channels periodically.

One disadvantage of Bluetooth technology is its low bandwidth. Because of its slow data transfer speeds, Bluetooth technology is not an ideal solution for replacing a LAN. Because Bluetooth-enabled mobile payment services are new, security risks may exist. Most agree that the advantages of Bluetooth technology far outweigh the disadvantages.

Discover More: Visit this chapter's free resources to learn more about Bluetooth technology.

✸ **Consider This:** Have you used Bluetooth technology to connect two devices? What devices did you connect, and what was your experience? In your opinion, what is the best reason to use Bluetooth? Why? What devices do you think will include Bluetooth technology in the future?

 SECURE IT 10-2

Preventing Bluebugging

One reason why Bluetooth technology is so popular is because connections generally have low security risks, as described in Mini Feature 10-2. Despite this advantage, security experts have seen an increase in *Bluebugging*, which occurs when cyberthieves exploit Bluetooth devices that have been paired. Smartphones and other mobile devices are discoverable to other Bluetooth devices only for a short period when they first are turned on, but during this time the hackers can intercept the signals or use hardware that has the same identifying characteristics as the smartphone or other mobile device. Once hackers have intercepted a device, they take control and read or download personal data, place calls, monitor conversations, review text and email messages, and modify contacts.

Security experts recommend following these practices to prevent Bluebugging:

- Turn off Bluetooth capability if it is not required. Use a Bluetooth earpiece only when you need to be hands free.
- Use your device in a remote area. Bluebuggers often work in crowded and public places, such as shopping centers, parks, and public transportation, and they can intercept signals up to 30 feet away from the device.
- Prevent hackers from intercepting your device by pairing it for the first time in a secure location, such as your home.
- If Bluetooth is required, be certain the device's visibility setting is hidden and all paired devices are set to unauthorized so that the user must authorize each connection request.
- Upgrade your phone. Older devices are more vulnerable to these intrusions.

✸ **Consider This:** Have you paired your phone with any Bluetooth devices? If so, did you pair them in a private location? Which of these guidelines will you follow to attempt to prevent Bluebugging?

UWB

UWB, which stands for **ultra-wideband**, is a network standard that specifies how two UWB devices use short-range radio waves to communicate at high speeds with each other. At distances of about 33 feet, the data transfer rate is 110 Mbps. At closer distances, such as about 6.5 feet, the transfer rate is at least 480 Mbps. UWB can transmit signals through doors and other obstacles. Because of its high transfer rates, UWB is best suited for transmission of large files, such as video, graphics, and audio. Examples of UWB uses include locating and tracking inventory, equipment, or personnel (especially in remote or dangerous areas).

IrDA

Some devices, such as television remote controls, use the **IrDA** (Infrared Data Association) standard to transmit data wirelessly to each other via infrared (IR) light waves. The devices transfer data at rates from 115 Kbps (thousand bits per second) to 4 Mbps between their IrDA ports. Infrared requires *line-of-sight transmission*; that is, the sending device and the receiving device must be in line with each other so that nothing obstructs the path of the infrared light wave. Because Bluetooth and UWB do not require line-of-sight transmission, these technologies are more widespread than IrDA.

RFID

RFID (*radio frequency identification*) is a protocol that defines how a network uses radio signals to communicate with a tag placed in or attached to an object, an animal, or a person. The tag, called a transponder, consists of an antenna and a memory chip that contains the information to be transmitted via radio waves. Through an antenna, an RFID reader, also called a transceiver, reads the radio signals and transfers the information to a computer or computing device. Read Secure IT 6-2 in Chapter 6 for uses of animal implants.

Depending on the type of RFID reader, the distance between the tag and the reader ranges from 5 inches to 300 feet or more. Readers can be handheld or embedded in an object, such as a doorway or a tollbooth (Figure 10-9).

Discover More: Visit this chapter's free resources to learn more about RFID tags.

⊘ Internet Research

Are RFID chips safe?

Search for: rfid implant side effects

How Electronic RFID Toll Collection Works

Step 1
Motorist purchases an RFID transponder or RFID tag and attaches it to the vehicle's windshield.

Step 2
As the vehicle approaches the tollbooth, the RFID reader in the tollbooth sends a radio wave that activates the windshield-mounted RFID tag. The activated tag sends vehicle information to the RFID reader.

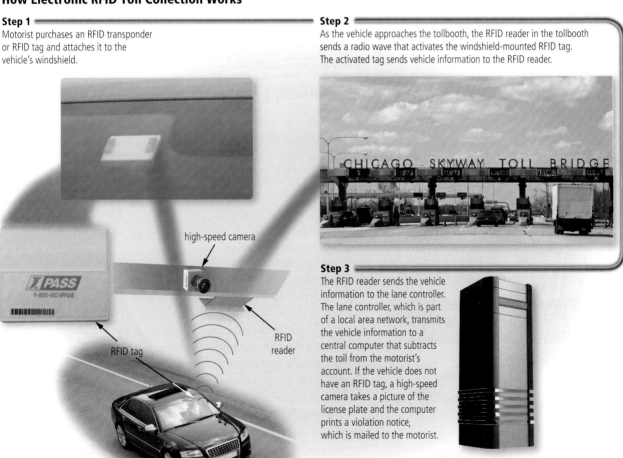

high-speed camera

Step 3
The RFID reader sends the vehicle information to the lane controller. The lane controller, which is part of a local area network, transmits the vehicle information to a central computer that subtracts the toll from the motorist's account. If the vehicle does not have an RFID tag, a high-speed camera takes a picture of the license plate and the computer prints a violation notice, which is mailed to the motorist.

RFID reader

RFID tag

Figure 10-9 This figure shows how electronic RFID toll collection works.

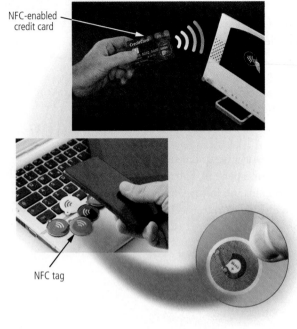

NFC-enabled credit card

NFC tag

Figure 10-10 Some objects, such as credit cards, are NFC enabled. You also can program NFC tags yourself.
© Alexander Kirch / Shutterstock.com; © iStockphoto / Gianni Furlan; © iStockphoto / pierrephoto

NFC

NFC (*near field communications*) is a protocol, based on RFID, that defines how a network uses close-range radio signals to communicate between two devices or objects equipped with NFC technology (Figure 10-10). Examples of NFC-enabled devices include smartphones, digital cameras, televisions, and terminals. Credit cards, tickets, and NFC tags are examples of objects that also use NFC technology. An NFC tag is a chip that can store small amounts of data. NFC tags are in a variety of objects, such as posters, ski lift tickets, business cards, stickers, and wristbands.

For successful communications, the devices or objects touch or are placed within an inch or two of each other. For example, you can touch two NFC-enabled phones together to transfer contacts, touch an NFC-enabled phone to an NFC tag to display a map, or hold an NFC-enabled phone near a parking meter to pay for parking. Contactless payment, such as the parking meter example, is a popular use of NFC technology. Other uses of NFC technology include sharing contacts or photos, downloading apps, and gaining access or admittance.

 Internet Research

How secure is contactless payment?

Search for: contactless payment security

CONSIDER THIS

Can you buy a blank NFC tag?
Yes. Consumers can purchase blank NFC tags (shown in the bottom photo in Figure 10-10) at a reasonable cost and easily program them to perform certain actions. For example, you can program an NFC tag to contain your home network user name and password. Visitors to your home can touch their phones to the NFC tag to access your home network without entering the user name and password.

Discover More: Visit this chapter's free resources to learn more about NFC-enabled devices.

Communications Lines

A **dedicated line** is a type of always-on physical connection that is established between two communications devices. Businesses often use dedicated lines to connect geographically distant offices. Dedicated lines can be either analog or digital. Digital lines increasingly are connecting home and business users to networks around the globe because they transmit data and information at faster rates than analog lines.

Digital dedicated lines include cable television lines, DSL, ISDN lines, FTTP, T-carrier lines, and ATM. Table 10-2 shows speeds of various dedicated digital lines.

Table 10-2	Speeds of Various Dedicated Digital Lines
Type of Line	**Transfer Rates**
Cable	256 Kbps to 52 Mbps
DSL	256 Kbps to 8.45 Mbps
ISDN	Up to 1.54 Mbps
FTTP	5 Mbps to 300 Mbps
Fractional T1	128 Kbps to 768 Kbps
T1	1.544 Mbps
T3	44.736 Mbps
ATM	155 Mbps to 622 Mbps, can reach 10 Gbps

Cable

The cable television (CATV) network provides high-speed Internet connections, called *cable Internet service*. The CATV signal enters a building through a single line, usually a coaxial cable. This cable connects to a modem (discussed in the next section), which typically attaches to your computer via an Ethernet cable. Home and small business users often subscribe to cable Internet service.

DSL

DSL (*Digital Subscriber Line*) transmits on existing standard copper phone wiring. Some DSL installations include a dial tone, providing users with both voice and data communications. These DSL installations often require that filters be installed to reduce noise interference when voice communications share the same line. DSL is a popular digital line alternative for the small business or home user.

ADSL is a popular type of DSL. As shown in Figure 10-11, *ADSL* (*asymmetric digital subscriber line*) is a type of DSL that supports faster downstream rates than upstream rates. ADSL is ideal for Internet access because most users download more information from the Internet than they upload.

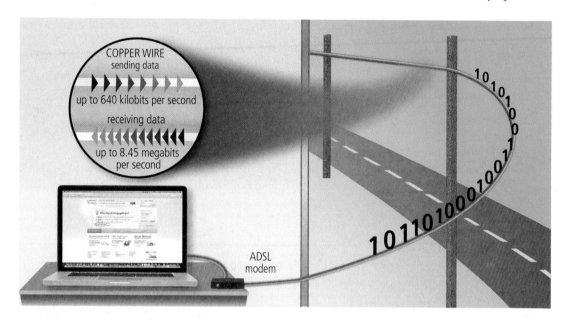

Figure 10-11   ADSL connections transmit data downstream (receiving) at a much faster rate than upstream (sending).
© artjazz / Shutterstock.com; © Cengage Learning

 CONSIDER THIS

Which is a better choice, DSL or cable Internet service?

Each has its own advantages. DSL uses a line that is not shared with other users in the neighborhood. With cable Internet service, by contrast, users might share the node with up to hundreds of other cable Internet users. Simultaneous access by many users can cause the cable Internet service to slow down. Cable Internet service, however, has widespread availability and usually has faster transmission rates.

ISDN

Not as widely used today as in the past, *ISDN* (Integrated Services Digital Network) is a set of standards for digital transmission of data over standard copper phone lines. With ISDN, the same phone line that could carry only one computer signal now can carry three or more signals at once through the same line, using a technique called *multiplexing*.

FTTP

FTTP, which stands for **Fiber to the Premises**, uses fiber-optic cable to provide extremely high-speed Internet access to a user's physical permanent location.

- *FTTH* (*Fiber to the Home*) provides home users with Internet access via fiber-optic cable.
- *FTTB* (*Fiber to the Building*) refers to small businesses that use fiber-optic cables to access the Internet.

With FTTP service, an optical terminal at your location receives the signals and transfers them to a router connected to a computer. As the cost of installing fiber decreases, more homes and businesses are expected to choose FTTP.

T-Carrier

A **T-carrier line** is any of several types of long-distance digital phone lines that carry multiple signals over a single communications line. Whereas a standard phone line carries only one signal, digital T-carrier lines use multiplexing so that multiple signals share the line. T-carrier lines provide very fast data transfer rates. Only medium to large companies usually can afford the investment in T-carrier lines because these lines are so expensive.

The most popular T-carrier line is the *T1 line*. Businesses often use T1 lines to connect to the Internet. Home and small business users purchase *fractional T1*, in which they share a connection to the T1 line with other users. Fractional T1 is slower than a dedicated T1 line, but it also is less expensive. Users who do not have other high-speed Internet access in their areas can opt for fractional T1. With fractional T1 lines, the data transfer rates become slower as additional users are added.

A *T3 line* is equal in speed to 28 T1 lines. T3 lines are quite expensive. Main users of T3 lines include large corporations, phone companies, and ISPs connecting to the Internet backbone. The Internet backbone itself also uses T3 lines.

ATM

ATM (Asynchronous Transfer Mode) is a service that carries voice, data, video, and media at very high speeds. Phone networks, the Internet, and other networks with large amounts of traffic use ATM. Some experts predict that ATM eventually will become the Internet standard for data transmission, replacing T3 lines.

✔ NOW YOU SHOULD KNOW

Be sure you understand the material presented in the sections titled Network Communications Standards and Protocols and Communications Lines, as it relates to the chapter objectives.
Now you should know . . .

- Which network communications standards and protocols you have used (Objective 5)
- Which communications line is best suited to your needs (Objective 6)

Discover More: Visit this chapter's premium content for practice quiz opportunities.

Communications Devices

⚙ BTW
Transmission Media
Computers process data as digital signals. Data, instructions, and information travel along transmission media in either analog or digital form, depending on the transmission media.

A **communications device** is any type of hardware capable of transmitting data, instructions, and information between a sending device and a receiving device. At the sending end, a communications device sends the data, instructions, or information from the sending device to transmission media. At the receiving end, a communications device receives the signals from the transmission media.

The following pages describe a variety of communications devices: modems, wireless access points, routers, network cards, and hubs and switches.

Digital Modems: Cable, DSL, and ISDN

A *broadband modem*, also called a *digital modem*, is a communications device that sends and receives data and information to and from a digital line. Three types of broadband modems are cable modems, DSL modems, and ISDN modems. These modems typically include built-in Wi-Fi connectivity.

A **cable modem** is a broadband modem that sends and receives digital data over the CATV network. To access the Internet using the CATV service, as shown in Figure 10-12, the CATV provider installs a splitter inside your house. From the splitter, one part of the cable runs to your televisions and the other part connects to the cable modem. Many CATV providers include a cable modem as part of the installation; some offer a rental plan, and others require that you purchase one separately. A cable modem usually is an external device, in which one end of a cable connects to a CATV wall outlet and the other end plugs in a port on a computer.

A **DSL modem** is a broadband modem that sends digital data and information from a computer to a DSL line and receives digital data and information from a DSL line. Similarly, an *ISDN modem* is a broadband modem that sends digital data and information from a computer to an ISDN line and receives digital data and information from an ISDN line. DSL and ISDN modems usually are external devices, in which one end connects to the phone line and the other end connects to a port on the computer.

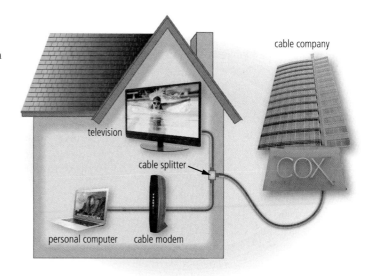

Figure 10-12 A typical cable modem installation.
© tiridifilm / iStockphoto; © image100 / Alamy; © Erik S. Lesser / Landov; © iStockphoto / Stephen Krow; © Pablo Eder / Shutterstock.com; © Cengage Learning

 **BTW**
Cable and DSL
Cable and DSL are more widely used than ISDN.

 CONSIDER THIS

What are dial-up modems?
A *dial-up modem* is a communications device that converts digital signals to analog signals and analog signals to digital signals, so that data can travel along an analog phone line. For example, a dial-up modem connected to a sending computer converts the computer's digital signals into analog signals. The analog signals then can travel over a standard phone line. A dial-up modem connected to a receiving computer converts the analog signals from a standard phone line into digital signals that the computer can process.

A dial-up connection must be reestablished each time the modem is used. With transfer rates of only up to 56 Kbps, dial-up connections also are much slower than broadband connections. For these reasons, dial-up connections are used only in remote areas or where high-speed or wireless options are not available.

Wireless Modems

Some mobile users have a *wireless modem* that uses a mobile service provider's network to connect to the Internet wirelessly from a computer or mobile device (Figure 10-13). Wireless modems, which have an external or built-in antenna, are available as USB adapters and other devices.

Some smartphones also can function as a wireless modem, called a *mobile hot spot*, when tethered to a personal computer or mobile device. Read How To 10-2 for instructions about using your phone as a mobile hot spot.

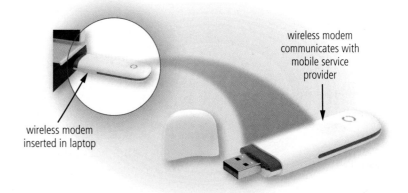

Figure 10-13 Wireless modems allow users to access the Internet wirelessly using a mobile service provider's network. Some manufacturers refer to the type of wireless modem shown in this figure as a USB modem.
© iStockphoto / nolimitpictures; © Cengage Learning

HOW TO 10-2

Use Your Phone as a Mobile Hot Spot

If you are in a location without a wireless Internet connection, you may be able to access the Internet from your desktop or mobile computer if you enable your smartphone as a mobile hot spot. When you enable a phone as a mobile hot spot, the phone acts as a wireless access point. You then can connect your desktop or mobile computer to the phone and utilize the data plan on your phone to access the Internet. If you have a limited data plan with your mobile service provider, you should be careful not to use your phone as a hot spot too often. While the speed from a mobile hot spot might not be as fast as your home or office network, it should be more than sufficient for performing tasks such as browsing the web or sending and receiving email messages that contain mostly text. The next steps describe how to use your phone as a mobile hot spot:

1. Contact your mobile service provider and determine whether your plan allows for your phone to be used as a mobile hot spot. Using your phone as a mobile hot spot may carry an additional monthly charge.

2. Determine whether your phone has built-in functionality to be used as a

mobile hot spot. If not and if supported by your service plan, you may be able to download a separate app that allows your phone to function as a mobile hot spot.

3. Access your phone's settings and enable the mobile hot spot. Your phone should display the SSID and password to access the hot spot. Read How To 5-3 in Chapter 5 for additional information about SSIDs.

4. Connect to the mobile hot spot on a computer or mobile device using

the SSID and password displayed in the previous step.

5. When you are finished using the hot spot, disconnect from the wireless network on your computer and disable the hot spot feature on your phone.

Consider This: How can you determine how much data you are using on your smartphone's data plan?

© Peter Bernik/Shutterstock.com; © Cengage Learning

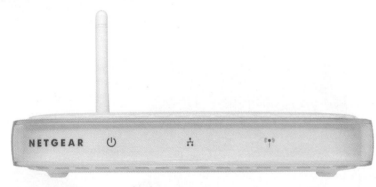

Figure 10-14 Wireless access point.
Copyright 2013 NETGEAR

Wireless Access Points

A *wireless access point* (WAP) is a central communications device that allows computers and devices to transfer data wirelessly among themselves or to a wired network using wireless technologies, such as Wi-Fi (Figure 10-14). Wireless access points have high-quality internal or external antennas for optimal signals. For the best signal, some manufacturers suggest positioning the wireless access point at the highest possible location and using a device to strengthen your wireless signal. Read How To 10-3 for tips to strengthen your wireless signal. A wireless access point either connects to a router via an Ethernet or other cable or is part of a router.

HOW TO 10-3

Strengthen Your Wireless Signal

If you reside in a large apartment or house and use a wireless network, you may find that you either experience poor network performance or you are unable to access the network in certain locations. These problems may be related to a weak wireless signal in your home. Various options are available to strengthen a wireless signal to increase network performance and ensure you have a wireless connection throughout your home. The following points describe how to strengthen a wireless signal:

- If your wireless router or wireless access point has an antenna(s), make sure the antenna(s) is extended completely.

- If you are able to remove the antenna(s) from your wireless router or wireless access point, consider replacing it with a wireless signal booster. Check your device's and the wireless signal booster's documentation to determine whether it will work with your device.

- If possible, position the wireless router or wireless access point in a central location of your home and away from appliances or other electronic devices that may degrade the signal.

- Purchase a range extender for your wireless router or wireless access point. Some range extenders are compatible only with specific wireless routers or wireless access points, and others are universal. Make sure the range extender you purchase is compatible with your device. Once installed, follow the range extender's instructions to enable it on your network.

- If you still experience problems with the strength of your wireless signal after following the suggestions above, consider replacing your wireless router or wireless access point with a newer model.

Consider This: What problems may arise if your wireless network's range extends beyond the confines of your home? How can you determine the range of your wireless network?

Copyright 2013 NETGEAR

Routers

A *router* is a communications device that connects multiple computers or other routers together and transmits data to its correct destination on a network. A router can be used on a network of any size. On the largest scale, routers along the Internet backbone forward data packets to their destination using the fastest available path. For smaller business and home networks, a router allows multiple computers and mobile devices to share a single broadband Internet connection, such as through a cable modem or DSL modem (Figure 10-15).

If the network has a separate router, it connects to the router via a cable. Similarly, if the network has a separate wireless access point, it connects to the router via a cable. Many users, however, opt for routers that provide additional functionality:

- A *wireless router* is a device that performs the functions of a router and also a wireless access point.

- A *broadband router* is a device that performs the functions of a router and also a broadband modem.

Internet Research

What is a core router?

Search for: core router definition

Figure 10-15 Through a router, home and small business networks can share access to a broadband Internet connection, such as through a cable or DSL modem.

Copyright 2013 NETGEAR; © iStockphoto / Stephen Krow; © iStockphoto / Dane Wirtzfeld; © Kitch Bain / Shutterstock.com; © Oleksiy Mark / Shutterstock.com; © Pablo Eder / Shutterstock.com; © Cengage Learning; 1125089601 / Shutterstock.com

BTW

Hardware Firewall
To prevent unauthorized users from accessing files and computers, many routers are protected by a built-in firewall, called a *hardware firewall*. Some also have built-in antivirus protection.

- A *broadband wireless router* is a device that performs the functions of a router, a wireless access point, and a cable or DSL modem.
- A *mobile broadband wireless router* is a device that performs the functions of a router, a wireless access point, and a wireless modem (Figure 10-16). Consumers use mobile broadband wireless routers to create a mobile hot spot.

These combination devices eliminate the need for a separate wireless access point and/or modem on a network. These routers also enable you easily to configure and secure the device against unauthorized access.

✳ CONSIDER THIS

How many connections can a router support?
Although a router may be able to connect more than 200 wired and/or wireless computers and mobile devices, the performance of the router may decline as you add connections. Some mobile service providers limit the number of connections to their mobile broadband wireless routers.

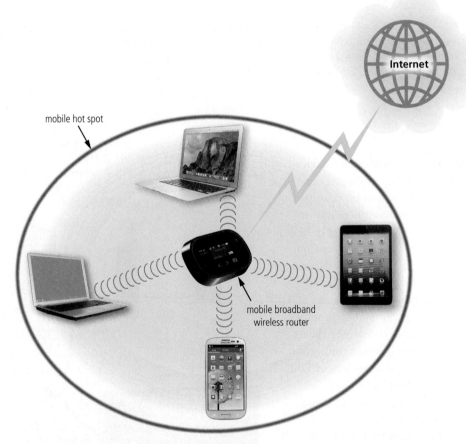

Figure 10-16 Through a mobile broadband wireless router, users can create a mobile hot spot via 3G or 4G mobile broadband Internet service.
Courtesy of Verizon Wireless; © iStockphoto / Stephen Krow; © iStockphoto / Dane Wirtzfeld; © iStockphoto / Moncherie; © Alex Staroseltsev / Shutterstock.com; © Cengage Learning

 **BTW**

Motherboards
Many computers and mobile devices have motherboards that integrate networking capability, eliminating the need for a separate network card.

Network Cards

A *network card*, sometimes called a *network interface card* (*NIC* pronounced nick), is a communications device that enables a computer or device that does not have built-in networking capability to access a network. The network card coordinates the transmission and receipt of data, instructions, and information to and from the computer or device containing the network card.

Network cards are available in a variety of styles. A network card for a desktop is an adapter card that has a port to which a cable connects (Figure 10-17). A network card for mobile computers and devices is in the form of a USB adapter or other device. A network card follows the guidelines of a particular network communications standard, such as Ethernet or token ring.

Figure 10-17 Network card for a desktop computer.
Courtesy of D-Link Corporation

Hubs and Switches

Today, thousands of computer networks exist, ranging from small networks operated by home users to global networks operated by widespread telecommunications firms. Interconnecting these many types of networks requires various types of communications devices. A *hub* or *switch* is a device that provides a central point for cables in a network (Figure 10-18). Larger networks typically use a hub, while smaller networks use a switch. Some hubs and/or switches include routers. That is, the hub or switch receives data from many directions and then forwards it to one or more destinations.

BTW
Technology Innovator
Discover More: Visit this chapter's free resources to learn about Cisco, a leading networking products corporation.

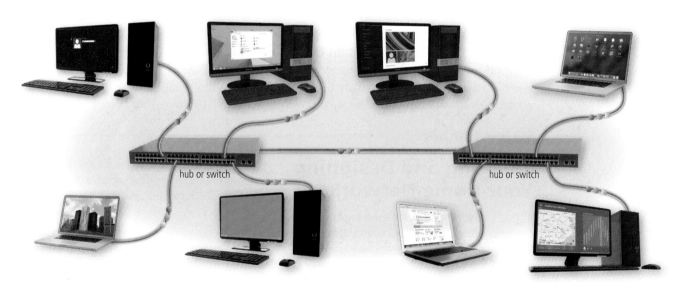
hub or switch   hub or switch

Figure 10-18 A hub or switch is a central point that connects several devices in a network together, as well as connects to other networks, as shown in this simplified diagram.
Courtesy of D-Link Corporation; © iStockphoto / sweetym; © Oleksiy Mark / Shutterstock.com; © Oleksiy Mark / Shutterstock.com; © iStockphoto / Skip ODonnell; © Natalia Siverina / Shutterstock.com; © iStockphoto / Skip ODonnell; © iStockphoto / sweetym; © Alex Staroseltsev / Shutterstock.com; © iStockphoto / sweetym; © Cengage Learning

Home Networks

Many home users connect multiple computers and devices together in a **home network**. Vendors typically offer home networking packages that include all the necessary hardware and software to network your home using wired or wireless techniques. You no longer need extensive knowledge of networks to set up a home network. For example, desktop operating systems often enable you to connect all computers in your house to a home network easily. Read Secure IT 10-3 to learn how to detect if an intruder is accessing your network.

Internet Research
What is an intelligent home network?

Search for: intelligent home network

SECURE IT 10-3

 Detecting an Intruder Accessing Your Wireless Home Network

One of the largest Internet security threats is *IP hijacking*, which occurs when cyberthieves tap into home routers or cable modems or other Internet access point to intercept a paid Internet service. Some cyberthieves use the connection to commit illegal acts; others just steal the Internet connection. The incidences of IP hijacking are growing, and catching thieves is a difficult task for law enforcement officials.

Unscrupulous people hijack Internet service in one of two ways. Either the network has no security, or the thieves determine the network name and password and then reprogram their modem's settings to duplicate the network's settings. The Electronic Communications Privacy Act (ECPA) and a lack of funding prevent fraud examiners from investigating and prosecuting many IP hijackers.

Experts recommend using the following steps to determine if someone is accessing a wireless network without permission:

- **Sign in to the administrative interface.** The modem's user's guide will provide instructions to view wireless clients actively using a wireless access point.

- **Count the number of connected devices.** Each device connected wirelessly to the network should be displayed in a table that shows, at a minimum, the device's name, MAC address, and IP address. (Read How To 5-3 in Chapter 5 for additional information about MAC address controls.) Wireless devices that might be connected to the network include smartphones, game consoles, DVD players, and other hardware. If the number of devices seems extraordinarily high, use a MAC lookup website, which can help you

to determine the manufacturer of wireless devices in the list.

- **Secure the network.** The router's manufacturer's website should provide instructions about upgrading the security strength. Change the default network name and password, and be certain to use the latest wireless encryption technology. Enable the router's firewall and, if possible, use "stealth mode" to make the network less visible to outsiders. Disable the feature that allows users to administer the router wirelessly, so that changes can be made only when using a physical connection with an Ethernet cable.

✸ **Consider This:** If you use a wireless router, have you taken any of these steps to prevent IP hijacking? Which steps will you now take? Do you know anyone who has had a cyberthief access his or her network?

Mini Feature 10-3: Planning and Designing Your Home Network

As with any network, a home network's basic purpose is to share resources and connect devices. You can use a home network to share files and folders or to allow multiple devices to share a printer. Read Mini Feature 10-3 to learn about planning and designing your home network.

 MINI FEATURE 10-3

Planning and Designing Your Home Network

A home network enables you to use a common Internet connection among many computers and mobile devices. Other uses include connecting entertainment devices, such as digital video recorders (DVRs) and televisions, to the Internet and establishing a connection between devices in order to play multiplayer games.

Before purchasing hardware, or contracting a network expert to set up your network, consider how your network will be used, and by whom. Ask yourself the following questions:

- What devices will connect to the network? The number of devices, as well as the operating system or platform on which the devices operate will determine the speed and strength needed to run your wireless network.

- How large of a range do you need, and where will most of the use take place? If you have a small apartment, your needs will differ from those with a large home.

- How many users typically will be using the network, how will they use it, and for what purposes? The number of users affects the capabilities of the network and determines whether you need to define permissions for certain users or devices.

- How secure do you need your network? Hiding the network name, requiring passwords, or having a user with network administration capabilities can help ensure your network is safe from unauthorized use.

A home network can be as simple as using a cable to connect two devices. More complex home networks include wireless technologies that connect several devices to one another and to the Internet. Hardware needed for a wireless, Internet-connected home network includes the following:

- A modem, such as a cable or DSL modem, that connects to an ISP and establishes the Internet connection for the network

- A router, which establishes the connection between the Internet and all computers and devices on the home network and also enables the devices to communicate with one another

- A wireless access point, often included as part of the router, in order to connect wireless devices

- Computers and devices, such as desktops, laptops, tablets, smartphones, televisions, cable set-top boxes, or a VoIP phone, that you connect to the home network

Read How To 10-4 for instructions about creating a home network. Once you configure your wireless network, you can create user names and user groups. Names and groups establish network users, who can share files (such as documents, music, and photos), as well as devices (such as printers), with others connected to the network.

Maintaining the network involves monitoring the security settings and network activity, establishing connections to new devices as needed, and enhancing the wireless signal if necessary. Wireless home network speeds and ranges vary. The strength of the wireless signal affects the range of the network. Read How To 10-3 earlier in this chapter for instructions about strengthening a wireless signal.

Discover More: Visit this chapter's free resources to learn more about planning and designing a home network.

✳ **Consider This:** Do you have a home network? What devices are connected to it? Is your network password protected? Why or why not? Is the signal weaker in certain areas in your home? If so, where? What can you do to increase the effectiveness and security of your network?

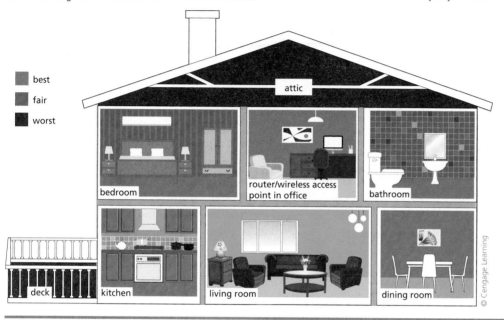

✳ **HOW TO 10-4**

📄 Create a Home Network

If you have multiple computers and mobile devices in your home and want to share resources, you can create a home network. The following steps describe how to create a home network:

1. Establish a connection to the Internet. In many cases, your ISP will provide a modem that serves as the connection between the computers and mobile devices in your home and the Internet connection.

2. Most modems allow you to connect only one computer or mobile device and may not have the capability to serve also as a wireless access point. If you intend to use more than one computer or mobile device with your Internet connection, purchase and connect a router with a sufficient number of ports and then connect it to the modem. If you want wireless access in your home, purchase and connect a wireless router or mobile hot spot.

3. For computers that will use a wired network connection, connect a network cable from the computer to an available port on the router.

4. Follow the router's instructions to configure it. If you are configuring wireless access, you may need to perform the following steps:

   a. Set an SSID to uniquely identify your wireless network.

   b. Select an encryption method and choose an encryption key that will be easy for you to remember but very difficult for others to guess.

   c. Connect the wireless devices to the network by enabling the wireless card if necessary, selecting the SSID of your wireless network, and specifying the proper encryption key. Read How To 5-3 in Chapter 5 for additional information about SSIDs and encryption methods.

5. Test the connection on all devices, whether wired or wireless, that are connected to the network. You can verify that your network is working properly by running a browser and navigating to a webpage.

6. If desired, enable file sharing so that you can share files among the computers and mobile devices on your home network. Operating systems today typically include a feature that allows you to enable sharing with other computers on the same network. For another computer or mobile device to access shared files on your computer, the user will need to know the IP address or name of your computer, as well as the location of the files.

7. For maximum security, disable Internet and network connections when you are not using them.

✳ **Consider This:** What are some other benefits of creating a home network? What disadvantages might be associated with creating a home network?

An Example of Sending a Request over the Internet Using a Variety of Transmission Media

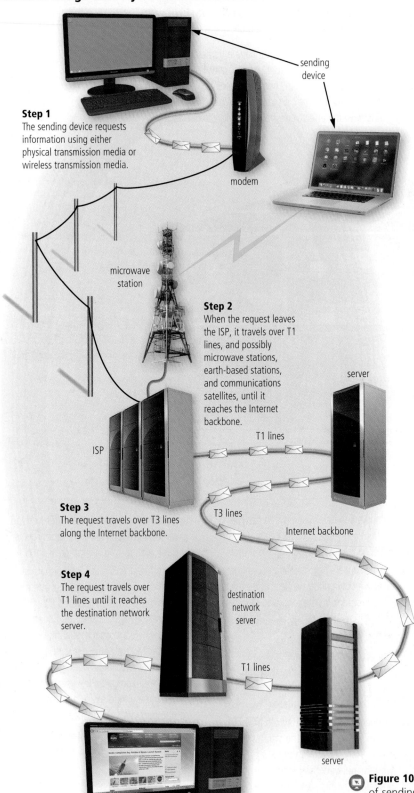

sending device

Step 1
The sending device requests information using either physical transmission media or wireless transmission media.

modem

microwave station

Step 2
When the request leaves the ISP, it travels over T1 lines, and possibly microwave stations, earth-based stations, and communications satellites, until it reaches the Internet backbone.

server

ISP

T1 lines

Step 3
The request travels over T3 lines along the Internet backbone.

T3 lines

Internet backbone

Step 4
The request travels over T1 lines until it reaches the destination network server.

destination network server

T1 lines

server

Transmission Media

Transmission media consist of materials or substances capable of carrying one or more communications signals. When you send data from a computer or mobile device, the signal that carries the data may travel over various transmission media. This is especially true when the transmission spans a long distance. Figure 10-19 illustrates the variety of transmission media, including both physical and wireless, used to complete a data request over the Internet. Although many media and devices are involved, the entire communications process could take less than one second.

Broadband media transmit multiple signals simultaneously. The amount of data, instructions, and information that can travel over transmission media sometimes is called the **bandwidth**. The higher the bandwidth, the more data transmitted. For transmission of text only, a lower bandwidth is acceptable. For transmission of music, graphics, photos, virtual reality images, or 3-D games, however, you need a higher bandwidth. When the bandwidth is too low for the application, you will notice a considerable slowdown in system performance.

Latency, with respect to communications, is the time it takes a signal to travel from one location to another on a network. Several factors that negatively can affect latency include the distance between the two points, the type of transmission media, and the number of nodes through which the data must travel over the network. For best performance, bandwidth should be high and latency low. Read Ethics & Issues 10-3 to consider whether ISPs should be able to control Internet usage.

Figure 10-19 This figure shows a simplified example of sending a request over the Internet using a variety of transmission media.

Should ISPs Be Allowed to Control Your Internet Usage?

People often compare the early days of the Internet and web to a wild frontier. ISPs simply offered customers an Internet connection and exerted no control over how the customer used the connection. This is similar to a phone company, which does not control who a customer calls, the length of a call, or the reason for the call. Online gaming, VoIP, video and audio streaming, and the use of web apps and cloud services led to an increased reliance on the Internet. Because of these increases, ISPs are attempting to regulate and limit their customers' usage.

Capping is a practice ISPs use that provides a certain amount of data usage at the optimal speed. Once a customer has used his or her allotted amount, the customer's Internet access is restricted, is slowed, or incurs additional costs. *Throttling* occurs when a network reduces upload and download speeds of certain high-data users at peak times in order not to tie up network resources for a small pool of users.

Controversy surrounds capping and throttling practices. Providers argue that caps are necessary to regulate traffic and ensure equal access to the Internet for all of its users. Critics argue that ISPs use limits to unfairly increase customer fees. Legislators are attempting to resolve the issues surrounding *net neutrality*, which is the concept of an open Internet, accessible to all users, without interference from ISPs or other third-parties. Proposals include standardizing how data transfer rates are measured and involving the Federal Communications Commission (FCC). The FCC would evaluate the regulations to ensure that ISPs intend merely to regulate traffic, rather than make a profit. It would examine whether caps or throttling are appropriate for low-usage times, such as in the middle of the night, and other related issues.

Consider This: Should ISPs control your Internet usage? Why or why not? Are data caps at peak usage times reasonable? Why or why not? Should the government enforce net neutrality? Why or why not?

Physical Transmission Media

Physical transmission media use wire, cable, and other tangible materials to send communications signals. These wires and cables typically are used underground or within or between buildings. Ethernet and token ring LANs often use physical transmission media.

Table 10-3 lists the transfer rates of LANs using various physical transmission media. The following sections discuss each of these types.

Twisted-Pair Cable

One of the more widely used transmission media for network cabling and landline phone systems is twisted-pair cable. **Twisted-pair cable** consists of one or more twisted-pair wires bundled together (Figure 10-20). Each *twisted-pair wire* consists of two separate insulated copper wires that are twisted together. The wires are twisted together to reduce **noise**, which is an electrical disturbance that can degrade communications.

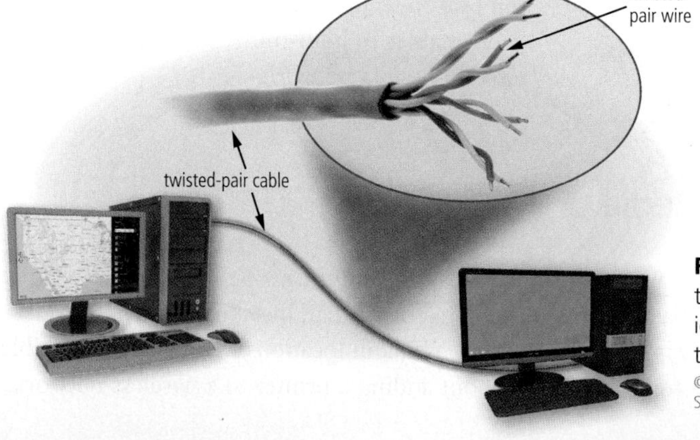

Table 10-3 Transfer Rates for Physical Transmission Media Used in LANs	
Type of Cable and LAN	**Maximum Transfer Rate**
Twisted-Pair Cable	
• 10Base-T (Ethernet)	10 Mbps
• 100Base-T (Fast Ethernet)	100 Mbps
• 1000Base-T (Gigabit Ethernet)	1 Gbps
• Token ring	4 Mbps to 16 Mbps
Coaxial Cable	
• 10Base2 (ThinWire Ethernet)	10 Mbps
• 10Base5 (ThickWire Ethernet)	10 Mbps
Fiber-Optic Cable	
• 10Base-F (Ethernet)	10 Mbps
• 100Base-FX (Fast Ethernet)	100 Mbps
• FDDI (Fiber Distributed Data Interface) token ring	100 Mbps
• Gigabit Ethernet	1 Gbps
• 10-Gigabit Ethernet	10 Gbps
• 40-Gigabit Ethernet	40 Gbps
• 100-Gigabit Ethernet	100 Gbps

twisted-pair wire

twisted-pair cable

Figure 10-20 A twisted-pair cable consists of one or more twisted-pair wires. Each twisted-pair wire usually is color coded for identification. Landline phone networks and LANs often use twisted-pair cable.

© Galushko Sergey / Shutterstock.com; © iStockphoto / 123render; © Oleksiy Mark / Shutterstock.com; © Cengage Learning

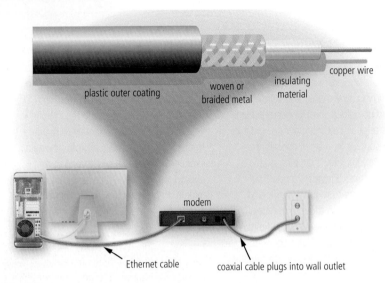

Figure 10-21 On coaxial cables, data travels through a copper wire. This simplified illustration shows a computer connected to a modem, which also is connected to the CATV network through a coaxial cable.
© iStockphoto / THEPALMER; © iStockphoto / Evgeny Karandaev; Courtesy of Zoom Telephonics, Inc.; © Cengage Learning

Coaxial Cable

Coaxial cable, often referred to as *coax* (pronounced KO-ax), consists of a single copper wire surrounded by at least three layers: (1) an insulating material, (2) a woven or braided metal, and (3) a plastic outer coating (Figure 10-21).

CATV network wiring often uses coaxial cable because it can be cabled over longer distances than twisted-pair cable. Most of today's computer networks, however, do not use coaxial cable because other transmission media, such as fiber-optic cable, transmit signals at faster rates.

Fiber-Optic Cable

The core of a **fiber-optic cable** consists of dozens or hundreds of thin strands of glass or plastic that use light to transmit signals. Each strand, called an *optical fiber*, is as thin as a human hair. Inside the fiber-optic cable, an insulating glass cladding and a protective coating surround each optical fiber (Figure 10-22).

Fiber-optic cables have the following advantages over cables that use wire, such as twisted-pair and coaxial cables:

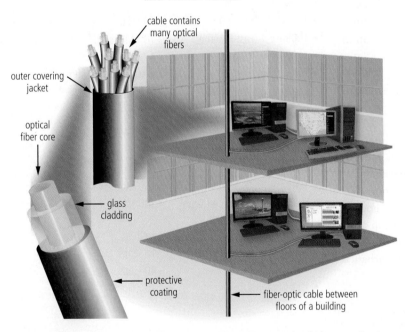

Figure 10-22 A fiber-optic cable consists of hair-thin strands of glass or plastic that carry data as pulses of light, as shown in this simplified example.
© Cengage Learning; © Oleksiy Mark / Shutterstock.com; © iStockphoto /123render; © Oleksiy Mark / Shutterstock.com; © Oleksiy Mark / Shutterstock.com

- Capability of carrying significantly more signals than wire cables
- Faster data transmission
- Less susceptible to noise (interference) from other devices, such as a copy machine
- Better security for signals during transmission because they are less susceptible to noise
- Smaller size (much thinner and lighter weight)

Disadvantages of fiber-optic cable are it costs more than twisted-pair or coaxial cable and can be difficult to install and modify. Despite these limitations, many phone companies replaced original analog phone lines with fiber-optic cables, enabling them to offer fiber-optic Internet access to home and business users. Businesses also use fiber-optic cables in high-traffic networks or as the backbone in a network.

Wireless Transmission Media

Wireless transmission media send communications signals through the air or space. Many users opt for wireless transmission media because it is more convenient than installing cables. In addition to convenience, businesses use wireless transmission media in locations where it is impossible to install cables. Read How To 10-5 for instructions about adding a printer to a wireless network.

HOW TO 10-5

Add a Wireless Printer to a Home/Small Office Network

Adding a wireless printer to a home or small office network has several advantages. For example, multiple computers and mobile devices on the network can use the printer. You also can place the printer anywhere in the home or office, as long as it is within range of the wireless signal. For example, a wireless router can be on the first floor of your house, and a wireless printer can be on the second floor. The following steps describe how to add a wireless printer to a home/small office network:

1. Determine the location to install the wireless printer. This location must have an electrical outlet for the printer and also be within range of the wireless network. You can check the strength of wireless signals in your home or office by walking

around with a mobile computer or device while connected to the network and monitoring the signal strength.
2. Be sure to place the printer on a stable surface.
3. Access the printer's settings and navigate to the network settings.
4. Connect to the wireless network in your home or small office. If necessary, specify the encryption key for your network.
5. Enter any remaining required information.
6. Install the printer software on the computer(s) from which you want to print to the wireless printer. During the installation process, you will select the wireless printer that you have connected and configured. If the printer does not appear, return to Step 4 and try connecting the printer to the wireless network again. If

the problem persists, consider contacting the printer's manufacturer.
7. Verify the computers are able to print successfully to the wireless printer.

Consider This: What are some ways to prevent some computers or mobile devices on your network from printing on your wireless printer?

© iStockphoto / btrenkel; © Cengage Learning

Types of wireless transmission media used in communications include infrared, broadcast radio, cellular radio, microwaves, and communications satellites. Table 10-4 lists transfer rates of various wireless transmission media, which are discussed in the following sections.

Infrared

As discussed earlier in the chapter, infrared (IR) is a wireless transmission medium that sends signals using infrared light waves. Mobile computers and devices, such as a mouse, printer, and smartphone, may have an IrDA port that enables the transfer of data from one device to another using infrared light waves.

Broadcast Radio

Broadcast radio is a wireless transmission medium that distributes radio signals through the air over long distances, such as between cities, regions, and countries, and short distances, such as within an office or home.

For radio transmissions, you need a transmitter to send the broadcast radio signal and a receiver to accept it. To receive the broadcast radio signal, the receiver has an antenna that is located in the range of the signal. Some networks use a transceiver, which both sends and receives signals from wireless devices. Broadcast radio is slower and more susceptible to noise than physical transmission media, but it provides flexibility and portability.

Bluetooth, UWB, and Wi-Fi communications technologies discussed earlier in this chapter use broadcast radio signals. Bluetooth and UWB are alternatives to infrared communications, with the latter designed for high-bandwidth transmissions. Hot spots use Wi-Fi.

Table 10-4 Wireless Transmission Media Transfer Rates

Medium		Maximum Transfer Transmission Rate
Infrared		115 Kbps to 4 Mbps
Broadcast radio	• Bluetooth	1 Mbps to 24 Mbps
	• 802.11b	11 Mbps
	• 802.11a	54 Mbps
	• 802.11g	54 Mbps
	• 802.11n	300 Mbps
	• 802.11ac	500 Mbps to 1 Gbps
	• 802.11ad	up to 7 Gbps
	• UWB	110 Mbps to 480 Mbps
Cellular radio	• 2G	9.6 Kbps to 144 Kbps
	• 3G	144 Kbps to 3.84 Mbps
	• 4G	Up to 100 Mbps
Microwave radio		Up to 10 Gbps
Communications satellite		Up to 2.56 Tbps

 BTW

Data Transfer Rates
Tbps (terabits per second) is one trillion bits per second.

Cellular Radio

Cellular radio is a form of broadcast radio that is in wide use for mobile communications, specifically wireless modems and mobile phones (Figure 10-23). A mobile phone uses high-frequency radio waves to transmit voice and digital data messages. Because only a limited number of radio frequencies exist, mobile service providers reuse frequencies so that they can accommodate the large number of users. Some users install an amplifier or booster to improve the signal strength. Read Secure IT 10-4 to consider issues related to fake cell towers.

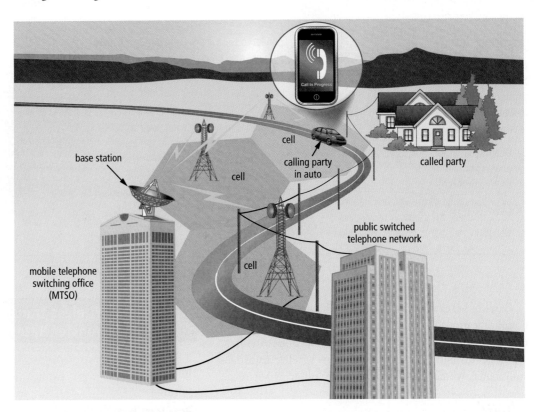

Figure 10-23 As a person with a mobile phone drives from one cell to another, the radio signals transfer from the base station (microwave station) in one cell to a base station in another cell.
© Stuartmile / Dreamstime.com; © Cengage Learning

🛡️ SECURE IT 10-4

📱 Fake Cell Towers Are Tracking Devices

At least 17 cell towers located throughout the United States are intercepting mobile phone calls, according to technical security company ESD America. The company has identified these towers but does not know who owns them. It does know, however, that they do not belong to a mobile service provider or to the National Security Agency (NSA).

Every mobile device has a unique *International Mobile Subscriber Identity* (*IMSI*) that allows it to communicate with a cell tower. The interceptor technology on fake towers grasps, or catches, this IMSI

signal; hence, it is known as an IMSI catcher. According to some reports, cyberthieves can purchase IMSI catchers for $1,800 or can build the devices themselves. The interceptors, also called stingrays, slow the protocol, so consumers may notice that the display on their smartphone shows that the 4G connection has dropped to 2G and that the performance has degraded. Higher-quality interceptors, however, will not change the phone's display when the phone has been attacked.

The Federal Communications Commission (FCC) is investigating these fake towers to determine who or what entity is intercepting the calls. It has established a task force to

protect cellular networks and to address the threat of illicit IMSI catcher technology. It also is working with several industry organizations to develop new, secure cybersecurity standards. In addition, the FCC urges consumers to update their mobile devices' operating systems and apps because the latest software often addresses security vulnerabilities.

☀️ **Consider This:** Have you read any articles or publications disclosing the illicit and unauthorized use of IMSI catchers? Who or what organization do you think is using these interceptors?

Several categories of cellular radio transmissions exist, defining the development of cellular networks. Although the definitions of these categories may vary by mobile service providers, below are some general guidelines:

- *1G* (first generation of cellular transmissions)
    - o Analog data transfer at speeds up to 14.4 Kbps
- *2G* (second generation of cellular transmissions)
    - o Digital data transfer at speeds from 9.6 Kbps to 144 Kbps
    - o Improved voice transmissions, added data communications, and added SMS (short message service) or text messaging services
    - o Standards include *GSM* (Global System for Mobile Communications) and *GPRS* (General Packet Radio Service)
- *3G* (third generation of cellular transmissions)
    - o Digital data transfer at speeds from 144 Kbps to 3.84 Mbps
    - o Improved data transmissions, added MMS (multimedia message services)
    - o Standards include *UMTS* (Universal Mobile Telecommunications System), CDMA (Code Division Multiple Access), EDGE (Enhanced Data GSM Environment), and EVDO (Evolution Data Optimized)
- *4G* (fourth generation of cellular transmissions)
    - o Digital data transfer at speeds up to 100 Mbps
    - o Improved video transmissions
    - o Standards include Long Term Evolution (LTE), Ultra Mobile Broadband (*UMB*), and IEEE 802.16 (WiMAX)
- *5G* (fifth generation of cellular transmissions)
    - o Future generation of cellular transmissions
    - o Expected to improve bandwidth
    - o Expected to provide artificial intelligence capabilities on wearable devices

Read Ethics & Issues 10-4 to consider whether mobile service providers should be able to force customers to switch from landlines to mobile phones.

✳ ETHICS & ISSUES 10-4

Should Phone Companies Be Allowed to Force Customers to Switch from Landlines to Mobile Phones?
Many people today rely solely on a mobile phone and have no need for a traditional landline installed in their home. A mobile phone enables users to keep their same phone number if they move and ensures that they can receive communications when not at home. Around 100 million Americans still rely on a landline for phone access, especially in rural areas. As the copper lines that connect these phones deteriorate from age and rust, phone companies are pushing customers to purchase VoIP or mobile services instead of a landline.

Critics of these measures cite that mobile phones are less reliable in certain areas and during extended power failures, and may or may not properly connect to emergency services. The elderly and people with certain illnesses rely on medical devices that use a landline to send medical information or alerts. The FCC (Federal Communications Commission) would need to approve the phone companies' plans to eliminate landline service. Because of rules known as 'common carrier' guidelines, phone companies must provide phone access to all users, at a fair price. Different pricing rules exist for Internet usage and mobile phones, which some fear may lead phone companies to raise prices unfairly.

Phone companies argue that the current landlines are expensive to maintain. Many feel that they have a right to refuse to repair, install, or continue service to areas for which they do not see a profit. They argue that uses of satellites and Internet technologies can provide service to even the most rural areas. Two major phone providers have proposed eliminating landline service by 2020.

Consider This: Do you have a landline? Why or why not? Should phone companies require users to switch to mobile phones? Why or why not? Should the government force phone companies to provide service without a profit? Why or why not?

Microwaves

Microwaves are radio waves that provide a high-speed signal transmission. Microwave transmission, often called *fixed wireless*, involves sending signals from one microwave station to another (Figure 10-24). A *microwave station* is an earth-based reflective dish that contains the antenna, transceivers, and other equipment necessary for microwave communications. As with infrared, microwaves use line-of-sight transmission. To avoid possible obstructions, such as buildings or mountains, microwave stations often sit on the tops of buildings, towers, or mountains.

Microwave transmission typically is used in environments where installing physical transmission media is difficult or impossible and where line-of-sight transmission is available. For example, microwave transmission is used in wide-open areas, such as deserts or lakes, between buildings in a close geographic area, or to communicate with a satellite. Current users of microwave transmission include universities, hospitals, city governments, CATV providers, and phone companies. Homes and small businesses that do not have other high-speed Internet connections available in their area also opt for lower-cost fixed wireless plans.

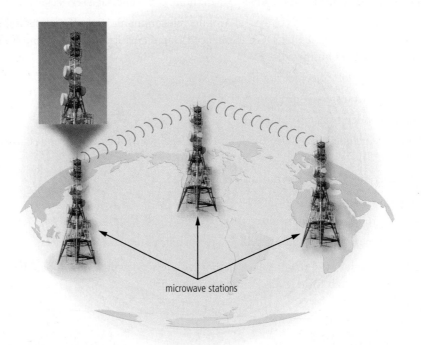

microwave stations

Figure 10-24 A microwave station is a ground-based reflective dish that contains the antenna, transceivers, and other equipment necessary for microwave communications.
© Cengage Learning; © Alfonso de Tomas / Shutterstock.com

Communications Satellite

A **communications satellite** is a space station that receives microwave signals from an earth-based station, amplifies (strengthens) the signals, and broadcasts the signals back over a wide area to any number of earth-based stations (Figure 10-25). These earth-based stations often are microwave stations. Other devices, such as smartphones and GPS receivers, also can function as earth-based stations. Transmission from an earth-based station to a satellite is an *uplink*. Transmission from a satellite to an earth-based station is a *downlink*.

Applications such as air navigation, television and radio broadcasts, weather forecasting, videoconferencing, paging, GPS, and Internet connections use communications satellites. With the proper satellite dish and a satellite modem, consumers can access the Internet using satellite technology. With satellite Internet connections, however, uplink transmissions usually are slower than downlink transmissions. This difference in speeds usually is acceptable to most Internet satellite users because they download much more data than they upload. Although a satellite Internet connection is more expensive than cable Internet or DSL connections, sometimes it is the only high-speed Internet option in remote areas.

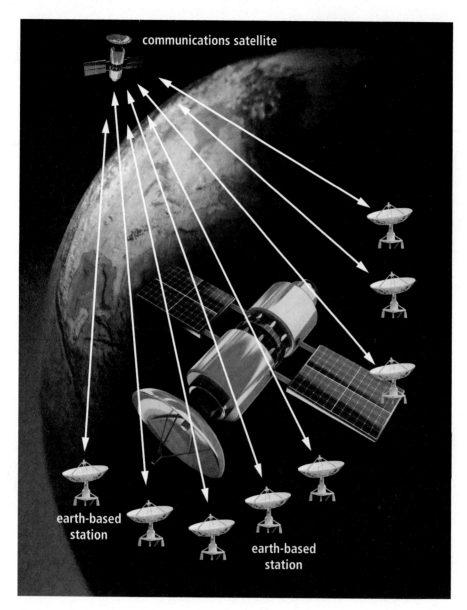

Figure 10-25   Communications satellites are placed about 22,300 miles above the Earth's equator.

GPS   As described previously, a **GPS** (*global positioning system*) is a navigation system that consists of one or more earth-based receivers that accept and analyze signals sent by satellites in order to determine the receiver's geographic location.

Many mobile devices, such as smartphones, have GPS capability built into the device or as an add-on feature. Some users carry a handheld GPS receiver; others mount a receiver to an object such as an automobile, a boat, an airplane, farm and construction equipment, or a computer or mobile device. A GPS receiver is a handheld, mountable, or embedded device that contains an antenna, a radio receiver, and a processor. Many include a screen display that shows an individual's location on a map. Figure 10-26 shows how a GPS works.

BTW
Technology Trend
Discover More: Visit this chapter's free resources to learn about geocaching.

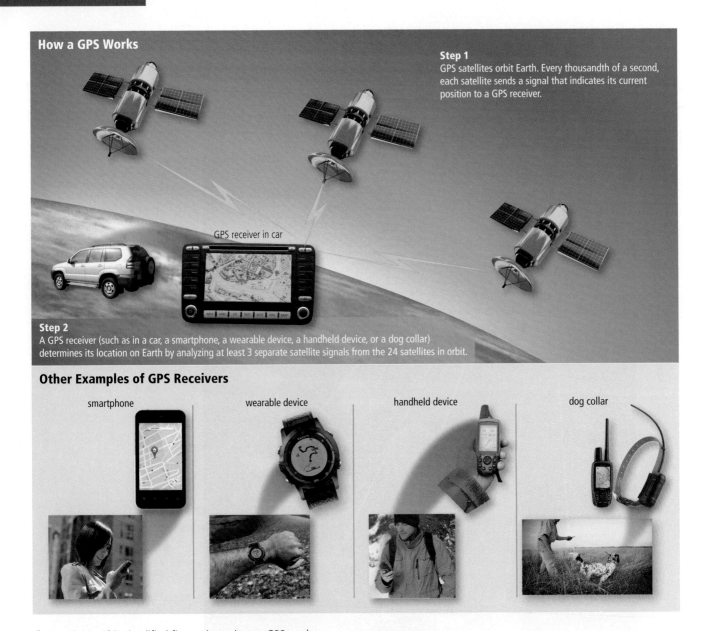

Figure 10-26 This simplified figure shows how a GPS works.

© Mmaxer / Shutterstock.com; © Tupungato / Shutterstock.com; © kaczor58 / Shutterstock.com; © 3Dstock / Shutterstock.com; © iStockphoto / PhotoTalk; Courtesy of Garmin International;
© iStockphoto / cotesebastien; © Evgeny Vasenev / Shutterstock.com; © Lithiumphoto / Shutterstock.com; Courtesy of Garmin International; Courtesy of Garmin International; © Cengage Learning

✳ CONSIDER THIS

What are uses of GPS?

The first and most used application of GPS technology is to assist people with determining where they are located. The data obtained from a GPS, however, can be applied to a variety of other uses: creating a map, ascertaining the best route between two points, locating a lost person or stolen object, monitoring the movement of a person or object, determining altitude, and calculating speed.

Many vehicles use GPSs to provide drivers with directions or other information, such as alternate traffic routes, automatically call for help if the airbag is deployed, dispatch roadside assistance, unlock the driver's side door if keys are locked in the car, and track the vehicle if it is stolen. Newer GPS receivers also give drivers information about nearby points of interest, such as gas stations, restaurants, and hotels. Hikers and remote campers may carry GPS receivers in case they need emergency help or directions.

Some GPS receivers work in conjunction with a cellular radio network. Parents, for example, can locate the whereabouts of a child who carries a mobile phone with GPS capability or other GPS-enabled device.

 **NOW YOU SHOULD KNOW** ——————————————

Be sure you understand the material presented in the sections titled Communications Devices, Home Networks, Transmission Media, Physical Transmission Media, and Wireless Transmission Media, as it relates to the chapter objectives. *Now you should know ...*

- When you would use various communications devices (Objective 7)
- How you can set up and configure a home network (Objective 8)
- Which types of transmission media are best suited to your needs (Objectives 9 and 10)

Discover More: Visit this chapter's premium content for practice quiz opportunities.

✔ Chapter Summary

This chapter presented a variety of networks and communications technologies. It discussed various types of network architectures and standards and protocols. It explained communications software. Several types of communications lines and communications devices were presented. The chapter discussed how to create a home network. It also presented a variety of physical transmission media and wireless transmission media.

Discover More: Visit this chapter's free resources for additional content that accompanies this chapter and also includes these features: Technology Innovators: Robert Metcalfe, AT&T and Verizon, and Cisco; Technology Trends: Wireless Charging and Geocaching; and High-Tech Talks: Network Topologies: Star, Bus, Ring, and the OSI Reference Model.

Test your knowledge of chapter material by accessing the Study Guide, Flash Cards, and Practice Test apps that run on your smartphone, tablet, laptop, or desktop.

⚡ TECHNOLOGY @ WORK ——————————————————————————

Agriculture

The world's dependence on the agriculture industry is enormous. The demand to keep food prices affordable encourages those working in this industry to operate as efficiently as possible. Although people have worked in agriculture for more than 10,000 years, advances in technology assist with maintaining and protecting land and crops.

Almost all individuals and organizations in this industry have many acres of land that they must maintain. It is not always feasible for farmers to take frequent trips around the property to perform basic tasks, such as watering soil in the absence of rain. The number of people-hours required to water soil manually on several thousand acres of land might result in businesses spending thousands of dollars in labor and utility costs. If an irrigation system is installed instead, one or more individuals still are responsible for deciding when to water and how long to water. If the irrigation process is automated, sensors detect how much rain has fallen recently, as well as whether the soil is in need of watering. The sensors then send

this data to a computer that processes it and decides when and how much to water. Many automated home irrigation systems also are programmable and use rain sensors, which regulate operation of the irrigation system.

In addition to keeping the soil moist and reducing maintenance costs, computers also can use sensors to analyze the condition of crops in the field and determine whether pests or diseases are affecting the crops. If sensors detect pests and/or diseases, computers send a notification to the appropriate individual to take corrective action. In some cases, the discovery of pests might trigger a pesticide to discharge in the affected area automatically.

Until recently, the lack of adequate cellular and wireless network signals in the fields made communications difficult for farmers. Mobile cellular antennas and amplifiers stretch mobile broadband coverage across entire farms, enabling farmers to receive wireless signals up to eight times farther from the cellular tower than they would without the antennas and amplifiers. Wireless access

throughout the farm also allows farmers to monitor their farms and communicate with colleagues from remote locations.

The next time you take a bite of a delicious carrot or juicy cucumber, you can appreciate how technology has helped to maintain an ideal environment for these vegetables to grow and protected them from unwanted pests, all for a reasonable price when you purchase them from your local supermarket.

✳ **Consider This:** How else might computers and technology be used in the agriculture industry?

eliandric / iStockphoto

Study Guide

The Study Guide exercise reinforces material you should know for the chapter exam.

Discover More: Visit this chapter's premium content to **test your knowledge of digital content** associated with this chapter and **access the Study Guide resource** from your smartphone, tablet, laptop, or desktop.

Instructions: Answer the questions below using the format that helps you remember best or that is required by your instructor. Possible formats may include one or more of these options: write the answers; create a document that contains the answers; record answers as audio or video using a webcam, smartphone, or portable media player; post answers on a blog, wiki, or website; or highlight answers in the book/e-book.

1. List the device types and media you need for successful communications.

2. A(n) _____ is a collection of computers and devices connected together via communications devices and transmission media.

3. List reasons home and business users create a network. Identify how networks facilitate communications.

4. A(n) _____ is a third-party business that provides networking services, such as EDI.

5. Define the terms, intranet and extranet.

6. Differentiate among LANs, WLANs, MANs, WANs, and PANs.

7. List steps to add a computer or mobile device to a wireless network.

8. Explain issues surrounding the use of BANs.

9. Name and describe two types of network architectures. Define the terms, client and server.

10. Explain how P2P networks function, and describe the uses of P2P file sharing.

11. List functions of communications software. List and describe forms of immediate mobile communications.

12. Explain issues surrounding the use of telemedicine.

13. Define the terms, network standard and protocol. Explain whether they work together.

14. Define the term, Ethernet. Explain what happens when two devices on an Ethernet attempt to send data at the same time.

15. Describe how a network transmits data using a token.

16. TCP/IP is the network standard for _____ communications. Describe how packet switching works.

17. Explain how network monitoring software and packet sniffers identify network security risks.

18. Explain whether you can use an IP address to determine a computer or device's location.

19. Describe how Wi-Fi enables users to connect to the Internet.

20. _____ is a network standard that defines how high-speed cellular transmissions use broadcast radio to transmit data for mobile communications.

21. List uses for Bluetooth devices. Name advantages and disadvantages of using Bluetooth.

22. Describe how to prevent Bluebugging.

23. Differentiate among UWB, IrDA, RFID, and NFC technologies.

24. Identify the role of a dedicated line. List types of digital dedicated lines.

25. Explain the advantages of cable Internet services and DSL.

26. List and differentiate among different T-carrier lines.

27. Define the term, communications device.

28. List and describe three widely used types of broadband modems. Define the term, dial-up modem.

29. Define the terms, wireless modem and mobile hot spot.

30. List the steps to use your phone as a mobile hot spot.

31. Define the term, wireless access point. Explain how to strengthen your wireless signal.

32. Identify the role of a router. List types of routers that offer additional functionality.

33. To prevent unauthorized users from accessing files and computers, many routers are protected by a built-in _____ firewall.

34. Describe the function of a network card.

35. Identify the roles of hubs and switches on a network.

36. List questions to ask when planning a home network. Identify hardware needed to set up a home network.

37. List steps to create a home network.

38. Explain how to determine if someone is accessing a wireless network without permission.

39. Define the terms, broadband, bandwidth, and latency.

40. Explain issues surrounding ISPs setting limits on Internet usage.

41. Name types of physical transmission media. Define the term, noise.

42. Identify advantages and disadvantages of fiber-optic cables.

43. List steps to add a wireless printer to a home/small office network.

44. Name types of wireless transmission media.

45. Explain how cyberthieves use fake cell towers to intercept communications.

46. Differentiate among 1G, 2G, 3G, 4G, and 5G cellular transmissions.

47. Explain issues surrounding phone companies forcing customers to switch to mobile phones.

48. List uses of GPS.

49. Explain how the agriculture industry uses technology.

You should be able to define the Primary Terms and be familiar with the Secondary Terms listed below.

Key Terms

Discover More: Visit this chapter's premium content to **view definitions** for each term and to **access the Flash Cards resource** from your smartphone, tablet, laptop, or desktop.

Primary Terms   (shown in **bold-black** characters in the chapter)

802.11 (462)
ATM (468)
bandwidth (476)
Bluetooth (463)
broadband (476)
broadcast radio (479)
cable modem (469)
cellular radio (480)
client/server
   network (456)
clients (456)
coaxial cable (478)
communications
   device (468)

communications
   satellite (482)
communications software
   (457)
dedicated line (466)
DSL (467)
DSL modem (469)
Ethernet (460)
fiber-optic cable (478)
FTTP (Fiber to the
   Premises) (467)
GPS (483)
home network (473)
IrDA (465)

latency (476)
local area network
   (LAN) (453)
LTE (462)
microwaves (482)
network (452)
NFC (466)
noise (477)
personal area network
   (PAN) (455)
receiving device (450)
RFID (465)
sending device (450)
server (456)

T-carrier line (468)
TCP/IP (461)
token ring (460)
transmission media (450)
twisted-pair cable (477)
UWB (ultra-wideband)
   (464)
wide area network
   (WAN) (455)
Wi-Fi (462)
wireless LAN
   (WLAN) (454)

Secondary Terms   (shown in *italic* characters in the chapter)

1G (481)
2G (481)
3G (481)
4G (481)
5G (481)
*ADSL (asymmetric digital subscriber
   line) (467)*
Bluebugging (464)
body area network (BAN) (456)
broadband modem (468)
broadband router (471)
broadband wireless router (472)
cable Internet service (466)
capping (477)
coax (478)
communications channel (450)
dial-up modem (469)
digital modem (468)
Digital Subscriber Line (467)
downlink (482)
downstream rate (462)
*EDI (electronic data interchange)
   (453)*
*electronic funds transfer
   (EFT) (453)*
extranet (453)
file sharing network (457)

fixed wireless (482)
fractional T1 (468)
FTTB (Fiber to the Building) (467)
FTTH (Fiber to the Home) (467)
Gbps (460)
global positioning system (483)
GPRS (481)
GSM (481)
hardware firewall (472)
host computer (456)
hub (473)
*International Mobile Subscriber
   Identity (IMSI) (480)*
intranet (453)
IP hijacking (474)
ISDN (467)
ISDN modem (469)
line-of-sight transmission (465)
Mbps (460)
*metropolitan area network
   (MAN) (455)*
microwave station (482)
*mobile broadband wireless
   router (472)*
mobile hot spot (469)
multiplexing (467)
near field communications (466)

net neutrality (477)
network architecture (456)
network card (472)
network interface card (NIC) (472)
network monitoring software (462)
network standard (459)
node (453)
optical fiber (478)
packet sniffer software (462)
packet switching (461)
packets (461)
peer (457)
peer-to-peer (P2P) network (457)
protocol (460)
radio frequency identification (465)
router (471)
switch (473)
T1 line (468)

T3 line (468)
Tbps (479)
telemedicine (459)
throttling (477)
token (460)
twisted-pair wire (477)
UMB (481)
UMTS (481)
uplink (482)
upstream rate (463)
value-added network (VAN) (453)
wireless access point (470)
wireless Ethernet (462)
wireless modem (469)
wireless router (471)

wireless modem (469)

Checkpoint

The Checkpoint exercises test your knowledge of the chapter concepts. The page number containing the answer appears in parentheses after each exercise. The Consider This exercises challenge your understanding of chapter concepts.

Discover More: Visit this chapter's premium content to **complete the Checkpoint exercises interactively;** complete the **self-assessment in the Test Prep resource** from your smartphone, tablet, laptop, or desktop; and then **take the Practice Test.**

True/False   Mark T for True and F for False.

_____ 1. All types of computers and mobile devices serve as sending and receiving devices in a communications system. (450)

_____ 2. Files on an intranet also are accessible from the Internet. (453)

_____ 3. Disadvantages of BANs include data validity and security. (456)

_____ 4. A client computer sometimes is called a host computer. (456)

_____ 5. Voice and video calling require large amounts of bandwidth. (458)

_____ 6. UWB requires line-of-sight transmission, so its technology is not as widespread as IrDA. (465)

_____ 7. For successful communications with NFC devices, the devices or objects must touch or be placed within an inch or two of each other. (466)

_____ 8. DSL transmits on existing standard copper phone wiring. (467)

_____ 9. Large corporations, phone networks, the Internet, and other networks with large amounts of traffic use DSL. (468)

_____ 10. A broadband modem is a communications device that converts digital signals to analog signals and analog signals to digital signals, so that data can travel along an analog phone line. (469)

_____ 11. Although some routers may be able to connect more than 200 wired and/or wireless computers and mobile devices, the performance of the router may decline as you add connections. (472)

_____ 12. With satellite Internet connections, uplink transmissions usually are slower than downlink transmissions. (483)

Multiple Choice   Select the best answer.

1. For successful communications, you need all of the following *except* a _____. (450)
   a. sending device
   b. transponder
   c. communications channel
   d. receiving device

2. A(n) _____ is an internal network that uses Internet technologies. (453)
   a. router
   b. extranet
   c. intranet
   d. communications channel

3. A _____ is a network that connects computers and devices in an individual's workspace using wired and wireless technology. (455)
   a. LAN
   b. PAN
   c. BAN
   d. WAN

4. A(n) _____ network is a simple, inexpensive network architecture that typically connects fewer than 10 computers. (457)
   a. protocol
   b. WAN
   c. extranet
   d. P2P

5. A _____ is a special series of bits that functions like a ticket. (460)
   a. packet
   b. Bluebug
   c. token
   d. host

6. _____ occurs when cyberthieves exploit Bluetooth devices that have been paired. (464)
   a. Bluebugging
   b. IP hijacking
   c. Capping
   d. Throttling

7. Which of the following is *not* a digital dedicated line? (466)
   a. NFC
   b. ISDN
   c. FTTP
   d. T-carrier lines

8. The practice used by some ISPs that provides a certain amount of data usage at the optimal speed is known as _____. (477)
   a. Bluebugging
   b. IP hijacking
   c. capping
   d. throttling

Checkpoint

Matching   Match the terms with their definitions.

_____ 1. value-added network (VAN) (453)

_____ 2. client (456)

_____ 3. network standard (459)

_____ 4. Ethernet (460)

_____ 5. protocol (460)

_____ 6. TCP/IP (461)

_____ 7. packet sniffer software (462)

_____ 8. LTE (462)

_____ 9. bandwidth (476)

_____ 10. latency (476)

a. standard that outlines characteristics of how two devices communicate on a network

b. guidelines that specify the way computers access the medium to which they are connected, the type(s) of medium used, the speeds used on different types of networks, and the type(s) of physical cable and/or the wireless technology used

c. third-party business that provides networking services, such as EDI services, secure data and information transfer, storage, or email

d. program that monitors and logs packet traffic for later analysis

e. network protocol that defines how messages are routed from one end of a network to the other, ensuring the data arrives correctly

f. the amount of data, instructions, and information that can travel over transmission media

g. network standard that specifies no computer or device on the network should control when data can be transmitted

h. computers or mobile devices on the network that rely on the server for its resources

i. the time it takes a signal to travel from one location to another on a network

j. network standard that defines how high-speed cellular transmissions use broadcast radio to transmit data for mobile communications

✳ Consider This   Answer the following questions in the format specified by your instructor.

1. Answer the critical thinking questions posed at the end of these elements in this chapter: Ethics & Issues (456, 459, 477, 481), How To (455, 470, 471, 475, 479), Mini Features (458, 463, 474), Secure IT (462, 464, 474, 480), and Technology @ Work (485).

2. What elements are necessary for successful communications? (450)

3. For what purposes do home and business users create networks? (452)

4. What are EDI and EFT? (453)

5. Why might a company use an intranet or extranet? (453)

6. What are disadvantages of BANs? (456)

7. How might small business and home users benefit from a P2P network? (457)

8. What does communications software do? (457)

9. What are some benefits and drawbacks of telemedicine? (459)

10. What are some network communications standards and protocols? (460)

11. What happens when a collision occurs on an Ethernet network? (460)

12. What is a disadvantage of using Bluetooth? (464)

13. What practices can you follow to prevent Bluebugging? (464)

14. Which wireless technology requires line-of-sight transmission? (465)

15. What are some examples of NFC-enabled devices? (466)

16. How might you use an NFC tag for personal purposes? (466)

17. What types of objects might contain an NFC tag? (466)

18. How does DSL differ from cable Internet service? (466)

19. Why is ADSL ideal for Internet access? (467)

20. What are three types of broadband modems? (468)

21. What steps can you take to strengthen a wireless signal? (471)

22. What steps are involved in maintaining a network? (475)

23. What factors negatively affect latency? (476)

24. What is throttling? (477)

25. What advantages do fiber-optic cables have over cables that use wires? (478)

26. What are some examples of wireless transmission media? (479)

27. How does an uplink differ from a downlink? (482)

✸ Problem Solving

The Problem Solving exercises extend your knowledge of chapter concepts by seeking solutions to practical problems with technology that you may encounter at home, school, or work. The Collaboration exercise should be completed with a team.

Instructions: You often can solve problems with technology in multiple ways. Determine a solution to the problems in these exercises by using one or more resources available to you (such as a computer or mobile device, articles on the web or in print, blogs, podcasts, videos, television, user guides, other individuals, electronics or computer stores, etc.). Describe your solution, along with the resource(s) used, in the format requested by your instructor (brief report, presentation, discussion, blog post, video, or other means).

Personal

1. **Problems Exchanging Files** You are attempting to use Bluetooth to send files from your phone to your computer. When you try sending the files from your phone, it does not display your computer as a device to which it can send the file. What might be the problem?

2. **Cannot Connect to Hot Spot** You are sitting in a fast food restaurant that offers free Wi-Fi. When you search for available hot spots using your computer, the restaurant's hot spot does not appear in the computer's list of wireless networks. What are your next steps?

3. **Paired Bluetooth Devices** You and your brother each have your Bluetooth-enabled smartphones paired with your car so that you can talk through the car's microphone and listen through its speakers. When you and your brother are both in the car at the same time, his phone rings but it is not connected to the car's audio. Why might this be the case?

4. **Slow Internet Connection** Your Internet speed has suffered a sharp decline in performance recently. You have not added any computers or mobile devices to your house that might be accessing the network, and you are puzzled by the sudden performance problems. What might be the problem?

5. **Wireless Network Coverage** You installed a new wireless network in your house. You notice that you  sometimes have trouble connecting to the network from certain locations in the house, but other times you can connect from the same location without issue. What might be causing the problem?

Professional

6. **Cannot Access Network** You brought your personal laptop to your place of employment so that you can take care of some personal obligations while you are on lunch break. You successfully connect to your company's wireless network but are unable to access the Internet. What might be the problem?

7. **Cannot Sign In** Your corporate network requires you to sign in with a user name and password as soon as your computer or mobile device connects. After entering your user name and password, the computer still does not connect to the network. What might be the problem?

8. **Too Many Networks** While attempting to connect to the wireless network at your job, you notice that five different wireless networks are available. How can you determine the network to which you should connect?

9. **No Network Connection** You have unpacked, installed, and turned on a new computer at your desk. When the operating system starts and you run the browser to display a webpage, you receive an error message stating that you are not connected to the Internet. You check the network card on the back of the computer and although the cable is plugged in, the lights next to the port are not flashing. What are your next steps?

10. **Connecting Corporate Email** You are visiting your company's remote office for the day and realize that you do not have the necessary information to connect to their wireless network. Your boss has asked you to check your email throughout the day, so it is important that you connect to the Internet. What are your next steps?

Collaboration

11. **Technology in Agriculture** Your employer owns hundreds of acres of orange groves and realizes labor and utility costs can be decreased by installing automated systems to manage the property. As a digitally literate employee of the organization, your supervisor asks you to research automated systems that can help decrease expenses. Form a team of three people to research automated agricultural solutions. One team member should research automated irrigation systems that water the trees only as needed. Another team member should research solutions that can keep the trees healthy and free from pests, and the third team member should create a list of reasons why these automated systems can decrease costs, bolster efficiency, and increase profit. Compile your findings and submit them to your instructor.

The How To: Your Turn exercises present general guidelines for fundamental skills when using a computer or mobile device and then require that you determine how to apply these general guidelines to a specific program or situation.

How To: Your Turn

Discover More: Visit this chapter's premium content to **challenge yourself with additional How To: Your Turn exercises**, which include App Adventure.

Instructions: You often can complete tasks using technology in multiple ways. Figure out how to perform the tasks described in these exercises by using one or more resources available to you (such as a computer or mobile device, articles on the web or in print, online or program help, user guides, blogs, podcasts, videos, other individuals, trial and error, etc.). Summarize your 'how to' steps, along with the resource(s) used, in the format requested by your instructor (brief report, presentation, discussion, blog post, video, or other means).

1 Evaluate Internet Access Plans

If you are planning to connect to the Internet from your computer or mobile device, you will need to subscribe to an Internet access plan. Cable companies, phone companies, and mobile service providers all offer Internet access plans, so it is important to evaluate the plans in your area to determine which one is best for you. The following steps guide you through the process of evaluating Internet access plans.

a. Create a budget. Internet access plans are available for a monthly fee, so determine how much money you are able to spend for Internet access on a monthly basis.

b. Locate and list the Internet access plans available in your area. To determine Internet access plans that are available, check the local cable or phone company's website and search for available plans. You may have to enter your ZIP code to determine whether certain plans are available in your area. Alternatively, visit a local electronics store and inquire about wireless Internet access plans available in your area.

c. Compare Internet access speeds. Each Internet access plan may offer a different speed, so determine which speed is sufficient for you. If you mainly browse webpages and send or receive email messages, you may not need a plan that offers the fastest transfer rates. If you plan to download files, play online games, and watch movies on the Internet, you should consider a plan with faster transfer rates. You also should consider a plan with faster transfer rates if you will have multiple devices accessing the Internet simultaneously in your household. If an ISP offers multiple plans with a variety of transfer rates, it often will let you switch back and forth between plans without penalty so that you can find the one with the transfer rate that is best for you.

d. Check for package deals. If you already have service with an existing CATV or phone provider, they may be able to add Internet access to your current services at a reduced rate. Bundling multiple services can make each service (such as Internet access) less expensive, but you should be careful not to sign up for services you do not need.

e. Think about how much data you intend to transfer each month. Some Internet access plans limit the amount of data you can upload or download each month. While it can be difficult to determine how much data you will upload or download, you first should purchase a plan that might allow you to transfer more than you think you will need. Monitor your data usage each month and consider downgrading to a plan that provides the amount of data transfer that better represents your use.

f. Determine where you require Internet access. Some ISPs will allow you to use their hot spots for free in locations such as shopping malls, coffeehouses, and airports. Consider the additional locations from where you can access the Internet for free, and determine whether it makes the Internet access plan more desirable.

g. Consider whether a wireless Internet access plan is appropriate. While these plans can cost more and transfer rates often are not as fast, they do provide the flexibility of allowing you to connect to the Internet from almost anywhere. If you often travel and regularly need to access the Internet while away from home, a wireless Internet access plan might be right for you.

Exercises

1. What Internet access plans are available in your area?
2. Prepare a table comparing the Internet access plans in your area. Based on your current Internet usage, which plan appears to be the best? Why?
3. How can you determine approximately how much data you will transfer each month?

2 Locate Hot Spots

If you are using a mobile computer or device and need to access the Internet, you will need to locate a hot spot. Hot spots are available in a variety of locations, such as coffeehouses, shopping malls, public libraries, airports, and educational institutions. Once you locate a hot spot, be sure to use it safely. Read Secure IT 2-1 in Chapter 2 for more information about using public Wi-Fi hot spots safely. If you plan to connect

✸ How To: Your Turn

to a wireless hot spot, make sure you are authorized to connect. For example, you should not connect to people's or businesses' hot spots without their knowledge or consent. If you are unsure of whether you are authorized to connect to a hot spot, contact someone representing the residence or business providing the hot spot. The following are guidelines that can assist you in locating a hot spot:

- Enable (turn on) your mobile computer or device's Wi-Fi and see whether it automatically detects any wireless networks. If one or more wireless networks are detected, connect to the one with the SSID that accurately describes your location. For example, if you are at a coffeehouse, the SSID of the wireless network might be the coffeehouse's name. If you unsure of the wireless network to which you should connect, contact an employee at the location and inquire. If the wireless network is protected with a password, the employee may be able to provide the password.
- You can check the location's website or app in advance to determine whether it has free Wi-Fi. For example, if you are flying out of your local airport, the airport's website might indicate whether Wi-Fi is available.
- Businesses offering free Wi-Fi sometimes have a decal on a front door or window indicating the location has Wi-Fi. If necessary, contact an employee to determine how to connect to the wireless network.
- Search for and navigate to a website that lists Wi-Fi hot spots in a particular area. These websites sometimes do not provide the most up-to-date information, so do not rely completely on the information you locate.

© DeiMosz / Shutterstock.com

Exercises

1. What public hot spots are available near where you live?
2. Have you connected to a public hot spot before? If so, when?
3. What security risks may be associated with connecting to a public hot spot?

❸ Test Your Internet Speed

Internet connection speeds will vary depending on the type of Internet connection you currently are using. If you believe your Internet speed is not what was promised by your Internet access provider, you can

test your Internet speed to see how it is performing. The following steps guide you through the process of testing your Internet speed:

a. Turn off any computers or mobile devices that might be accessing the Internet, except for the computer on which you want to test your broadband speed.

b. If your broadband Internet service is provided through your phone company, do not talk on the phone during the test. If your CATV company provides your broadband Internet service, turn off all devices accessing the cable television. If you have cable boxes or converters, disconnect them from their power source so that they cannot communicate using the Internet connection while you are testing your broadband speed.

c. Run the browser.

d. Search for and navigate to a website that can test your Internet speed.

e. Tap or click the button to start the test. The test may take up to one minute to complete before displaying results.

f. Internet speeds sometimes can vary with the time of day or day of the week. Repeat the previous steps to test your Internet speed at various times throughout the day, as well as on weekdays and weekends.

g. If you have any concerns regarding your Internet speed, contact your Internet access provider.

Exercises

1. What is the speed of the Internet connection on the computer or mobile device you currently are using?
2. Test your Internet speed while other computers and mobile devices also are using the Internet connection. How do the results vary from when your other devices are turned off?
3. Do you see differences in the Internet speed when you test it during the day versus at night? If so, what might explain these differences in speed?

speedtest.net

How To: Your Turn ✴

4 Connect Your Computer and Mobile Device via Bluetooth and Exchange Files

Bluetooth enables you to exchange files wirelessly between computers and mobile devices via Bluetooth. Before you are able to transfer files between devices, you first must enable Bluetooth and pair the devices so that they can communicate.

Connecting Your Computer and Mobile Device

The following steps guide you through the process of connecting your computer and mobile device via Bluetooth:

a. If necessary, display the settings on your computer and enable (turn on) Bluetooth.

b. If necessary, display the settings on your mobile device and enable (turn on) Bluetooth. Configure the mobile device so that it is discoverable to other Bluetooth devices. The mobile device must be discoverable so that your computer will be able to locate it.

c. In the Bluetooth settings on the computer, select the option to add a device.

d. When the computer has finished locating nearby discoverable Bluetooth devices, select your mobile device.

e. When the devices communicate with each other, the computer will display a passcode. Enter the passcode into your mobile device to complete the pairing, or verify the passcode on the computer and the mobile device match. The steps required to connect Bluetooth devices will vary, depending on the types of devices and operating system in use. Be sure to follow all instructions on the screen while connecting the computer to the mobile device.

Exchanging Files between Devices

When the computer and mobile device have been paired successfully, you are able to transfer files between the devices. The following steps guide you through the process of exchanging files between devices.

Transferring Files from a Mobile Device to a Computer

a. Display the file on the mobile device that you want to transfer to the computer.

b. Tap the button to share the file.

c. Select the option to share the file via Bluetooth.

d. Select the device to which you want to send the file.

e. Tap the button to begin the transfer.

f. On the computer, verify that you want to receive the incoming file. If necessary, specify a name and location for the file.

g. When the file has finished transferring, locate the file and open it so that you can verify it has transferred properly.

Transferring Files from a Computer to a Mobile Device

a. Display the location containing the file you want to transfer to the mobile device.

b. Select the file you want to transfer to the mobile device.

c. Select the command to send the file via Bluetooth (this command may be on a shortcut menu, so you may need to press and hold or right-click the file).

d. Select the device to which you want to send the file.

e. On the mobile device, verify that you want to receive the incoming file and, if necessary, specify a name and location for the file.

f. When the file has finished transferring, locate the file and open it so that you can verify it has transferred properly.

When you have finished transferring files between your computer and mobile device, disable Bluetooth if you do not intend to use it.

Exercises

1. In addition to using Bluetooth to connect a computer to a mobile device, what other types of devices can you connect to your mobile device?

2. Are any risks associated with leaving Bluetooth enabled (turned on) even when you are not using it?

3. What types of files might you want to transfer between your computer and mobile device using Bluetooth?

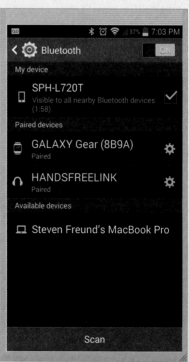

Source: Google, Inc.

✹ Internet Research

The Internet Research exercises broaden your understanding of chapter concepts by requiring that you search for information on the web.

Discover More: Visit this chapter's premium content to **challenge yourself with additional Internet Research exercises**, which include Search Sleuth, Green Computing, Ethics in Action, You Review It, and Exploring Technology Careers.

Instructions: Use a search engine or another search tool to locate the information requested or answers to questions presented in the exercises. Describe your findings, along with the search term(s) you used and your web source(s), in the format requested by your instructor (brief report, presentation, discussion, blog post, video, or other means).

❶ Making Use of the Web
Blogs, Wikis, and Collaboration

Writers can publish their views and share their interests using blogs, as you learned in Chapter 2. The blogosphere began as an easy way for individuals to express their opinions on the web. Today, this communications vehicle has become a powerful tool for individuals, groups, and corporations to promote their ideas and to advertise their products. Individuals easily may set up a blog free or for a fee, and they do not need to have knowledge of web design or programming.

Wikis are collaborative websites. As discussed in Chapter 2, users can develop, modify, and delete content on these public or private websites. This information can include articles, documents, photos, and videos. Other collaboration websites, such as Google Docs, allow users to share documents and to work together in real time. All files are stored online, so participants can access these documents everywhere at any time.

Research This: (a) Visit two blogging services, such as Tumblr, WordPress, or Blogger. What steps are required to start a blog? Do these services have monthly or annual fees? Do storage limitations exist? What options are available to customize the design? Can products or services be sold or advertised? If you were to set up a blog, which topics would you cover? Could you assign your own domain name to your blog?

(b) Visit two reference wikis. Which subjects are featured? Which organizations host the websites? How are the wikis funded? Are they public or private? Who may edit the content? What procedure is used to add, modify, or delete information?

(c) Visit two collaboration websites. What features are available for sharing content, such as managing projects, scheduling, blogging, discussing forum topics,

Source: Tumblr, Inc.

publishing information, delivering announcements, or uploading photos and videos? Are chat windows and whiteboards offered? What is the charge for using these services? Do they offer a mobile app? Do members receive notifications when content is updated?

❷ Social Media

Using social media can be an excellent opportunity to unite with people who share similar interests. In some cases, local groups form for members to improve themselves and their communities. Dog owners, runners, photographers, entrepreneurs, parents, and travelers are among the thousands of groups with members who met online. In addition, more than 41 million people in the United States have subscribed to at least one of the 2,500 online dating services. Online dating can offer a safe opportunity to meet a variety of people if some practical advice is followed. Reputable dating services keep information confidential and have many members. Some have niche dating demographics, such as age, professions, religion, cultural interests, or geographical regions, and members can search for matches with desired criteria.

Research This: Search at least two online dating websites for information about these services. How many members do they have? What is the cost to join? What are the monthly membership fees? What claims do their privacy statements make about not disclosing personal information? What policies are in place to report members who have acted inappropriately?

❸ Search Skills
Map Search

Search engines provide capabilities to search for maps, directions, and local attractions. Type search text in a search engine and then tap or click the Maps link on a search engine's home page to see a map of locations for your search text. For example, type the search text, verizon wireless chicago, in the search box to find locations of Verizon Wireless stores in Chicago. Type the search text, cisco boston, to view the location of the Boston Cisco office on a map. To obtain directions, type the address to or from which to obtain directions, and specify walking, driving, or by public transportation. On mobile devices with GPS capability, you can

Internet Research

specify to use your current location as a starting or ending location. You also can search near a location. For example, type the search text, pizza near 125 high street boston, to display the names of pizza restaurants near that location. Some mapping search tools allow you to zoom, pan, and navigate a map in aerial view or street view, showing the location when looking from above or on the street.

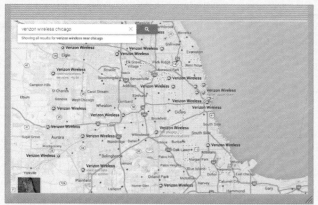

Source: Google, Inc.

Research This: Create search text using the techniques described above or in previous Search Skills exercises, and type it in a search engine to create maps that provide this information: (1) aerial and street view of your home, (2) directions to a local store that sells wireless networking equipment, (3) locations of your mobile service provider's retail stores in your current city, and (4) distance between Microsoft's headquarters in Redmond, Washington and Apple's headquarters in Cupertino, California. Take screenshots to capture and document your results.

4 Security

The Social Media exercise in this section discusses online dating websites. According to some of these dating services, 20 percent of people currently in committed relationships met online. While using these dating websites may result in a positive experience, the Better Business Bureau and other consumer-oriented organizations receive thousands of complaints each year about these services. Online dating fraud is rising, so security experts caution online dating members to follow safe practices, including the following:

- Compose a profile carefully, and be certain it reflects the image you want to portray. Do not post your full name, phone number, or home or work location.
- Use the service's messaging system before sending email or text messages or having a phone conversation.
- When arranging a first date, meet in a safe location, such as a restaurant during a busy time of the day.

Share your plans with a friend, and keep a mobile phone handy.
- Trust your instincts. If you feel uncomfortable or threatened, leave the location and call a friend.

Research This: Visit at least two websites providing advice for online dating members. What guidance is provided in addition to the four safe practices listed above? What behaviors may signal potentially dangerous situations? Where can members verify other members' reputations? How can members report fraud and inappropriate behavior?

5 Cloud Services

Streaming Media from the Cloud (SaaS)

Streaming media allows users to play music or videos from the cloud without having to wait for the entire file to download. Streaming media is an example of software as a service (SaaS), a service of cloud computing that allows access to software apps using a browser, without the need to install software on a computer or device. Streaming media has become popular because of the decreasing cost of cloud storage; the increasing download speeds for business, home, and mobile users; and the growing number of devices available to play downloaded content.

When streaming, a provider sends the media to the user's device over the Internet in a compressed format. The user runs a media player app to uncompress the data as it arrives and then play the resulting audio data as sound; or, the user can display the resulting video data on mobile devices, computers, Smart TVs, and other devices that have an appropriate player.

Content providers, such as Netflix, Hulu, and Amazon, allow users to subscribe to their services for a monthly fee and watch videos on demand, or instantly, by streaming them to Internet-connected devices.

Individuals and businesses use streaming services to broadcast video of their events live, on the Internet in high definition. Many will use this service to broadcast presentations, product demonstrations, performances, and other events online.

Research This: (1) What file formats are used to compress audio and video files for streaming? (2) Compare the offerings of Netflix, Hulu, and Amazon for providing video on demand. Do you use any of these services? Which would you choose? Why? (3) Find a television or radio broadcast that is streamed live on the Internet and simultaneously broadcast "on air." Watch or listen to part of the live stream and then do the same for the broadcast on television or radio. How do the experiences and quality compare? What other events often are streamed live online?

Critical Thinking

The Critical Thinking exercises challenge your assessment and decision-making skills by presenting real-world situations associated with chapter concepts. The Collaboration exercise should be completed with a team.

Instructions: Evaluate the situations below, using personal experiences and one or more resources available to you (such as articles on the web or in print, blogs, podcasts, videos, television, user guides, other individuals, electronics or computer stores, etc.). Perform the tasks requested in each exercise and share your deliverables in the format requested by your instructor (brief report, presentation, discussion, blog post, video, or other means).

1. Transmission Media

You work as an intern in the IT department for a local newspaper. The newspaper's management team recently approved a budget for redesigning the interior of its century-old building as part of an urban rehabilitation project. Because the employees at the newspaper more often use mobile devices and laptops than desktops, the newspaper plans to set up a wireless LAN.

Do This: Prepare information that summarizes the issues surrounding wireless network setup. Include the following information: What hardware is required for a wireless network? Could the thick walls in the building present a problem? If so, how can the issue be resolved? Does a wireless network present any health hazards? What security concerns exist for a wireless network? What advantages does a wireless network have over a wired network for the newspaper's needs?

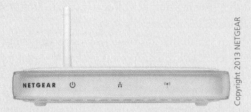

Copyright 2013 NETGEAR

2. Wireless Networking Standards

Several networking standards exist for wireless networks, including 802.11a, 802.11b, 802.11g, 802.11n, 802.11ac, 802.11ad, and 802.11af. You want to install a wireless network in your house and want to ensure that you choose the standard that best meets your needs.

Do This: Use the web to research the various wireless networking standards and answer the following questions: Which was the first developed standard? Are any of the standards more susceptible to interference from other wireless devices in your home, such as alarm systems and mobile phones? Which standard is the fastest? Is the fastest standard always the best, or do other factors on your wireless network or on the Internet affect performance? Is equipment to support one standard more expensive than the equipment that supports the other standards? Which would you recommend? Why? Address the answers to those questions, as well as any other information you find pertinent. Compile your findings.

3. Case Study

Amateur Sports League You are the new manager for a nonprofit amateur soccer league. The league's office equipment consists of a few laptops and tablets, a printer, and several smartphones. The board of directors has asked you to investigate how the league might use Bluetooth technology in its offices.

Do This: Review the uses of Bluetooth technology listed in Mini Feature 10-2 in this chapter. Which uses might apply to the league? Can you think of other ways the league might use Bluetooth technology? What are the advantages of using Bluetooth technology? Use the web to find industry experts' recommendations for Bluetooth use in a small office. What other wireless technologies might the league's office use? Examine issues related to bandwidth, speed, and reliability. What security concerns exist? What measures should the league take to prevent Bluebugging? Would you recommend the league use Bluetooth in its offices? Why or why not? Should the league replace its LAN with Bluetooth? Why or why not? Compile your findings.

Collaboration

4. **Network Security** You are a network administrator for a small security firm. The company's main office includes 20 workers, most of whom use laptops. This year, the company plans to upgrade the network. The company asks your team to create a list of common network security issues, to make recommendations for hardware and software, and to create guidelines to secure the network.

Do This: Form a three-member team. As a team, list different networking security risks discussed in this chapter. Each member should choose a different risk to research. Members should determine the following: Describe the risk. Find an example of an industry article or blog post describing an experience with the risk. What damage was done? What steps did the network administrator take to recover from the damage, and/or prevent future attacks? What hardware or software can be used to safeguard against the risk? What guidelines for network users should be in place to help avoid the risk? As a team, compile your findings and share your recommendation with the class.

BUILDING SOLUTIONS: Database, System, and Application Development Tools

Users share data and information using solutions created by analysts and developers.

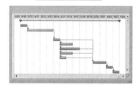

"I check my grades on the school's portal and recently learned the school finished upgrading its database and related systems. The conversion process has been lengthy, but seems worth it because the new features are quite useful. Although I am just a user of these and other systems, what more should I know about databases, system development, and application development?"

While you may be familiar with some of the content in this chapter, do you know how to . . .

- Recover from identity theft?
- Tell how your personal data is being used?
- Identify uses of databases on the web?
- Recognize Big Data?
- Import data from a spreadsheet into a database?
- Secure and maintain a database?
- Participate in system development?
- Identify security issues that can arise from outsourcing business tasks?
- Justify whether schools should teach hacking?
- Determine which object-oriented programming language or application development tool to use?
- Record a macro?
- Protect your computer from macro viruses?
- Publish a webpage?
- Develop a web application?

In this chapter, you will discover how these tasks are performed along with much more information essential to this course. For additional content available that accompanies this chapter, visit the free resources and premium content. Refer to the Preface and the Intro chapter for information about how to access these and other additional instructor-assigned support materials.

✓ Objectives

After completing this chapter, you will be able to:

1 Differentiate among a character, field, record, and data file and describe validation techniques
2 Differentiate between file processing systems and the database approach
3 Describe uses of web databases, types of databases, and Big Data
4 Discuss functions common to most database management systems: data dictionary, file retrieval and maintenance, data security, and backup and recovery
5 Define system development, list the system development phases, and identify the guidelines for system development
6 Discuss the importance of project management, feasibility assessment, documentation, and data and information gathering techniques
7 Discuss the purpose of and tasks conducted in each system development phase
8 Differentiate between low-level languages and procedural languages
9 Identify the benefits of object-oriented programming languages and application development tools
10 Describe various ways to develop webpages and web applications

Databases, Data, and Information

As presented in Chapter 4, a **database** is a collection of data organized in a manner that allows access, retrieval, and use of that data. As discussed in previous chapters, data is a collection of unprocessed items, which can include text, numbers, images, audio, and video. Information is processed data; that is, it is organized, meaningful, and useful.

Computers process data in a database to generate information for users. A database at a school, for example, contains data about its students and classes. When students are accepted to a school, they typically complete an online admission form that is displayed as a form in a browser. Students type their personal information into an online form and, at a later date, stop by the school to have their photo taken. Upon submitting the form, the page uploads the student's personal information in a database on a server at the school. When the school takes the student's photo, it also is stored in the school's database. The school's admission system assigns an ID number to the student and stores it in the database. The system then sends the student an email message with advising information. When the student's photo is taken on campus, relevant information is sent to an ID card printer, where the student's photo, name, and address is printed on the front of the card and the ID number is encoded on a magnetic stripe on the back of the card. Figure 11-1 illustrates this process.

With **database software**, often called a **database management system** (**DBMS**), users create a computerized database; add, modify, and delete data in the database; sort and retrieve data from the database; and create forms and reports from the data in the database.

How a School's Admissions Department Might Process New Student Data into Information

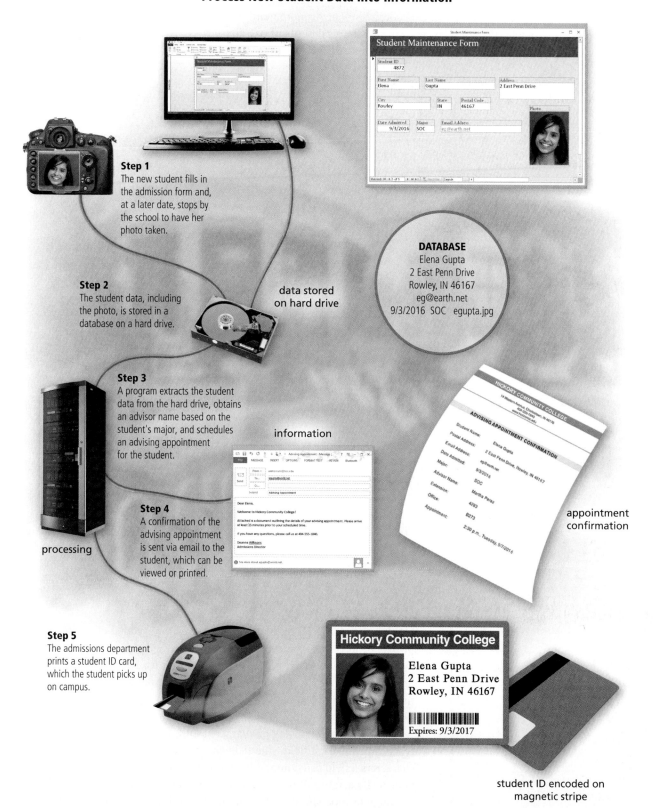

Step 1
The new student fills in the admission form and, at a later date, stops by the school to have her photo taken.

Step 2
The student data, including the photo, is stored in a database on a hard drive.

data stored on hard drive

DATABASE
Elena Gupta
2 East Penn Drive
Rowley, IN 46167
eg@earth.net
9/3/2016 SOC egupta.jpg

Step 3
A program extracts the student data from the hard drive, obtains an advisor name based on the student's major, and schedules an advising appointment for the student.

information

Step 4
A confirmation of the advising appointment is sent via email to the student, which can be viewed or printed.

appointment confirmation

processing

Step 5
The admissions department prints a student ID card, which the student picks up on campus.

student ID encoded on magnetic stripe

Figure 11-1   This figure shows how a school's admissions department might process new student data into information.

The Hierarchy of Data

Data is organized in levels. Information technology (IT) professionals classify data in a hierarchy. Each higher level of data consists of one or more items from the lower level. Depending on the application and the user, different terms describe the various levels of the hierarchy.

As shown in Figure 11-2, a database contains a group of related data files. A data file contains records, a record contains fields, and a field is composed of one or more characters. This sample School database contains four data files: Student, Instructor, Schedule of Classes, and Student Schedule.

- The Student file contains records about enrolled students.
- The Instructor file contains records about current instructors.
- The Schedule of Classes file contains records about class offerings in a particular semester.
- The Student Schedule file contains records about the classes in which a student is enrolled for a given semester.

BTW

Tables
In some database programs, a data file is referred to as a table (i.e., Student table, Instructor table, etc.).

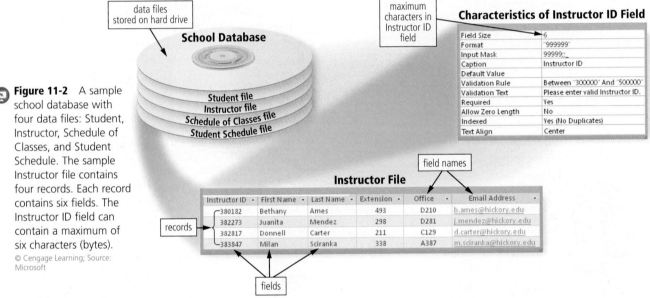

Figure 11-2 A sample school database with four data files: Student, Instructor, Schedule of Classes, and Student Schedule. The sample Instructor file contains four records. Each record contains six fields. The Instructor ID field can contain a maximum of six characters (bytes).
© Cengage Learning; Source: Microsoft

Characters of Instructor ID Field

Field Size	6
Format	"999999"
Input Mask	99999;;
Caption	Instructor ID
Default Value	
Validation Rule	Between "300000" And "500000"
Validation Text	Please enter valid Instructor ID.
Required	Yes
Allow Zero Length	No
Indexed	Yes (No Duplicates)
Text Align	Center

Instructor File

Instructor ID	First Name	Last Name	Extension	Office	Email Address
380182	Bethany	Ames	493	D210	b.ames@hickory.edu
382273	Juanita	Mendez	298	D281	j.mendez@hickory.edu
382817	Donnell	Carter	211	C129	d.carter@hickory.edu
383847	Milan	Sciranka	338	A387	m.sciranka@hickory.edu

Instructor File

Instructor ID	Text
First Name	Text
Last Name	Text
Extension	Number
Office	Text
Email Address	Hyperlink

Student File

Student ID	AutoNumber
First Name	Text
Last Name	Text
Address	Text
City	Text
State	Text
Postal Code	Text
Email Address	Hyperlink
Date Admitted	Date/Time
Major	Text
Photo	Attachment

Characters As discussed in Chapter 6, a bit is the smallest unit of data the computer can process. Eight bits grouped together in a unit constitute a byte. In the ASCII coding scheme, each byte represents a single **character**, which can be a number (4), letter (R), blank space (SPACEBAR), punctuation mark (?), or other symbol (&).

Fields A **field** is a combination of one or more related characters or bytes and is the smallest unit of data a user accesses. A **field name** uniquely identifies each field. When searching for data in a database, you often specify the field name. For example, field names for the data in the Instructor file are Instructor ID, First Name, Last Name, Extension, Office, and Email Address.

A database uses a variety of characteristics, such as field size and data type, to define each field. The field size defines the maximum number of characters a field can contain. For example, the Instructor ID field contains 6 characters and thus has a field size of 6 (shown in Figure 11-2).

The **data type** specifies the kind of data a field can contain and how the field is used. Figure 11-3 identifies the data types for fields in the Instructor and Student files.

Figure 11-3 Data types of fields in the Instructor and Student files.
© Cengage Learning

⚙ CONSIDER THIS ───

What are common data types?
Common data types include the following:

- Text: Letters, numeric characters, or special characters

- Number (also called numeric values): Positive or negative numbers, and the number zero, with or without decimal points

- AutoNumber: Unique number automatically assigned by the DBMS to each added record, which provides a value that identifies the record (such as a student ID)

- Currency: Dollar and cent amounts or numbers containing decimal values

- Date (also called date/time): Month, day, year, and sometimes time

- Memo (also called long text): Lengthy text entries, which may or may not include separate paragraphs

- Yes/No (also called *Boolean*): Only the values Yes or No (or True or False)

- Hyperlink: Email address or web address that links to a webpage on the Internet or document on a network

- Object (also called *BLOB*, for binary large object): Photo, audio, video, or a document created in other programs or apps, such as word processing or spreadsheet, stored as a sequence of bytes in the database

- Attachment: Document or image that is attached to the field, which can be opened in the program that created the document or image (functions similarly to email attachments)

⚙ BTW
Field Names
Some database programs do not allow the use of the space character in field names. For example, you may see the Last Name field name written as LastName or last_name.

Records   A **record** is a group of related fields. For example, a student record includes a set of fields about one student. A **primary key** is a field that uniquely identifies each record in a file. The data in a primary key is unique to a specific record. For example, the Student ID field uniquely identifies each student because no two students can have the same student ID. In some files, the primary key consists of multiple fields, called a *composite key*. For example, the primary key for the Schedule of Classes file could consist of the fields Semester Code, Class Code, and Class Section, which together would uniquely identify each class listed in a schedule.

Data Files   A **data file**, often simply called a file, is a collection of related records stored on a storage medium, such as a hard drive, or on cloud storage. A Student file at a school might consist of thousands of individual student records. Each student record in the file contains the same fields. Each field, however, contains different data. Figure 11-4 shows a small sample Student file that contains four student records, each with eleven fields. A database includes a group of related data files.

Sample Student File

Student ID	First Name	Last Name	Address	City	State	Postal Code	Email Address	Date Admitted	Major	Photo
2295	Milton	Brewer	54 Lucy Court	Charlestown	IN	46176		6/10/2016	EE	mbrewer.jpg
3876	Louella	Drake	33 Timmons Place	Bonner	IN	45208	lou@world.com	8/9/2016	BIO	ldrake.jpg
3928	Adelbert	Ruiz	99 Tenth Street	Sheldon	IN	46033		10/8/2016	CT	aruiz.jpg
2872	Benjamin	Tu	2204 Elm Court	Rowley	IN	46167	tu@indi.net	9/14/2016	GEN	btu.jpg

records   key field   fields

Figure 11-4   This sample data file, stored on a hard drive, contains four records, each with eleven fields.
© Cengage Learning

⚙ CONSIDER THIS ───

Why do some fields that store only numbers have a text data type?
Fields that contain numeric characters whose values will not be used in calculations, such as postal codes or phone numbers, usually are assigned a text data type.

File Maintenance

File maintenance refers to the procedures that keep data current. File maintenance includes adding records to, modifying records in, and deleting records from a file. Users add new records to a file when they obtain additional data that should be stored, such as data about a new student admitted to a school. Generally, users modify a record in a file for two reasons: (1) to correct inaccurate data or (2) to update old data with new data, such as replacing a student's address when she moves to a new address. When a record no longer is needed, a user deletes it from a file. For example, if a student was accepted for admission but later notifies the school that he chose to attend another college, the school might delete the student's records from its database. Read Ethics & Issues 11-1 to consider how organizations use data they collect.

 ETHICS & ISSUES 11-1

 Should Companies Inform Consumers about How Collected Data Is Used?

A department store came under scrutiny recently for using customers' shopping habits and purchases to determine whether a customer was pregnant. The store used the data to send ads for baby products before some customers even announced that they were expecting. If you willingly purchase products at a store, can the business analyze your purchases to create a profile to use for marketing purposes? Can it sell that data to a third party?

Function creep occurs when a company uses the technology intended for one purpose for an entirely different purpose. One example of function creep is when companies use or sell customer data collected through sales transactions using customer loyalty cards or other customer tracking methods. While some companies use data for their own purposes, such as to plan inventory or identify sales trends, others sell to data brokers or businesses that perform marketing surveys or generate credit reports. Privacy advocates are concerned about any use of personal data for purposes other than what the customer intended.

Online social networks and search engines often use activities, such as posts, pages viewed, and search terms, to suggest sponsored ads. Online vendors state that the data enables them to provide custom product suggestions and streamline ordering processes. Some customers acknowledge that a company has the right to use data to enhance the customers' experience or to make business decisions.

Many consumers would like more control over their data. The FTC Fair Information Practices (FIP) attempt to address data privacy concerns. FIP states that companies must inform customers of their data use and must allow customers to provide or deny consent. Privacy advocates argue further that limits should be imposed regarding the amount and type of data a company can collect and that the customer has a right to access the information.

Consider This: Have you experienced examples of a company using your personal data? For what purpose? Do you read a company's data privacy policy before using its website or service? Why or why not? How should the government enforce data privacy laws?

DBMSs use a variety of techniques to manage deleted or obsolete records. Sometimes, the DBMS removes the record from the file immediately, which means the deleted record cannot be restored. Other times, the record is flagged, or marked, so that the DBMS will not process it again. In this case, the DBMS places an asterisk (*) or some other character at the beginning of the record to indicate that it was deleted. DBMSs that maintain inactive data for an extended period commonly flag records. For example, a school might flag courses no longer offered or former employees no longer employed. When a DBMS flags a deleted record, the record remains physically on the drive. The record, however, is deleted logically because the DBMS will not process it. DBMSs will ignore flagged records unless an instruction is issued to process them.

 CONSIDER THIS

Can you permanently delete flagged records?

From time to time, users should run a program that removes flagged records and reorganizes current records. For example, the school may remove from the drive the names of applicants who chose to attend other schools instead. Deleting unneeded records reduces the size of files, thereby freeing up storage space.

Validating Data

Validation is the process of comparing data with a set of rules or values to determine if the data meets certain criteria. Many programs perform a validity check that analyzes data, either as you enter the data or after you enter it, to help ensure that it is valid. For instance, when an admissions department specialist adds or modifies data in a student record, the DBMS tests the entered data to verify it meets certain criteria.

If the data fails a validity check, the computer either should not allow the invalid data to be stored, or it should display an error message that instructs the user to enter the data again. Validity checks, sometimes called validation rules, reduce data entry errors and thus enhance the data's integrity.

Alphabetic/Numeric Check   An *alphabetic check* ensures that users enter only alphabetic data into a field. A *numeric check* ensures that users enter only numeric data into a field. For example, data in a First Name field should contain only characters from the alphabet. Data in a Current Enrollment field should contain integers.

Range Check   A *range check* determines whether a number is within a specified range. Assume the lowest per credit hour fee at the school is $75.00 and the highest is $370.75. A range check for the Credit Hour Fee field ensures it is a value between $75.00 and $370.75.

Consistency Check   A *consistency check* tests the data in two or more associated fields to ensure that the relationship is logical and their data is in the correct format. For example, the value in a Date Admitted field cannot occur earlier in time than a value in a Birth Date field.

Completeness Check   A *completeness check* verifies that a required field contains data. For example, some fields cannot be left blank; others require a minimum number of characters. One completeness check can ensure that data exists in a Last Name field. Another can ensure that a day, month, and year are included in a Birth Date field.

Check Digit   A *check digit* is a number(s) or character(s) that is appended to or inserted in a primary key value. A check digit often confirms the accuracy of a primary key value. Bank account, credit card, and other identification numbers often include one or more check digits.
   Discover More: Visit this chapter's free resources to learn more about check digits.

Internet Research
How do you know if a credit card number is valid?
Search for: luhn algorithm

Other Checks   DBMSs that include the hyperlink and attachment data types can perform validity checks on data entered in those fields. Hyperlink entries (web addresses and email addresses) can be tested to ensure that the address follows the correct format. Similarly, an attachment entry can be validated by confirming that the file exists.

Table 11-1 illustrates some of the validity checks just discussed and shows valid data that passes the check and invalid data that fails the check.

Table 11-1   Sample Valid and Invalid Data

Validity Check	Field(s) Being Checked	Valid Data	Invalid Data
Alphabetic Check	First Name	Karen	Ka24n
Numeric Check	Current Enrollment	24	s8q
Range Check	Per Credit Hour Fee	$220.25	$2,120.00
Consistency Check	Date Admitted, Birth Date	9/19/2016 8/27/1998	9/19/2016 8/27/2017
Completeness Check	Last Name	Gupta	
Other Check	Email Address	eg@earth.net	egearth.net

File Processing Systems and Databases

Almost all applications use the file processing approach, the database approach, or a combination of both approaches to store and manage data. The next sections discuss these two approaches.

File Processing Systems

In the past, many organizations exclusively used file processing systems to store and manage data. In a typical **file processing system**, each department or area within an organization has its own set of files. The records in one file may not relate to the records in any other file. Many of these systems have two major weaknesses: redundant data and isolated data.

- **Redundant data:** Because each department or area in an organization has its own files in a file processing system, the same fields are stored in multiple files. If a file processing system is used at a school, for example, the Student file and the Student Schedule file both might store the same students' names and addresses.

  Duplicating data in this manner can increase the chance of errors. If a student changes his or her address, for example, the school must update the address in each file in which it appears. If the Address field is not changed in all the files where it is stored or is changed incorrectly in one location, then discrepancies among the files exist. This duplication also wastes resources, such as storage space and time. When new students are added or student data is modified, file maintenance tasks consume additional time because employees must update multiple files that contain the same data.

- **Isolated data:** It often is difficult to access data that is stored in separate files in different departments. Assume, for example, that the student email addresses exist in the Student files and class room numbers (locations) are in the Schedule of Classes file. To send an email message informing students about a room change, data is needed from both the Student file and the Schedule of Classes file. Sharing data from multiple, separate files to generate such a list in a file processing system often is a complicated procedure and usually requires an experienced programmer.

The Database Approach

When an organization uses a database approach, many programs and users share the data in the database. A school's database most likely, at a minimum, contains data about students, instructors, schedule of classes, and student schedules. As shown in Figure 11-5, various areas within the school share and interact with the data in this database. The database does secure its data, however, so that only authorized users can access certain data items. Read Ethics & Issues 11-2 to consider whether criminal databases are useful for law enforcement.

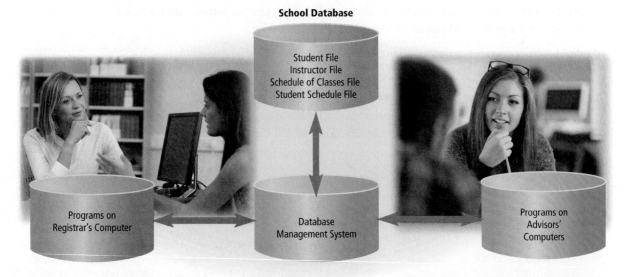

School Database

Student File
Instructor File
Schedule of Classes File
Student Schedule File

Programs on Registrar's Computer

Database Management System

Programs on Advisors' Computers

Figure 11-5 In a school's database, the computer used by the registrar and the computers used by advisors access data in the same database through the DBMS.

Does the Use of Criminal Databases Help or Hinder Investigations?

On television, detectives use databases to quickly compile a list of suspects for a crime. In these depictions, the list is complete, accurate, and leads to a speedy conviction. In reality, criminal databases are a helpful tool in solving crimes, but they are not without limitations. As with any database, the value depends on the quality of its information. If a criminal database contains data that is incomplete, inaccurate, or outdated, is it useful for law enforcement?

Many criminal databases exist at the county, state, and federal levels. Some information is mandatory, but other contributions to databases are voluntary or require only periodic updates. States' departments of correction record and share arrest records and jail time, but county or local jail records may not be included. Some courts and law enforcement use these databases for background checks to narrow a list of suspects or when determining sentencing. Others allow the use during an investigation, but findings are not admissible in court.

Megan's Law refers to a group of U.S. laws that require law enforcement agencies to share information in a national database about criminals who commit unlawful acts on children. States decide which information to make public and how to distribute the information. Often, states release criminals' names, photos, addresses, and information about the crime on a searchable, public website. Some states share information with one another regarding almost all criminals, and a few allow citizens to search for convicted criminals by name. Privacy experts feel that publishing this information makes it impossible for an offender who has served time to lead a normal life. Proponents state that the public's right to know outweighs the rights of privacy of those convicted.

Consider This: Are criminal databases useful in law enforcement? Why or why not? Should information from criminal databases be admissible in court? Why or why not? What information should states provide to the public regarding people convicted of crimes? Why?

While a user is working with the database, the DBMS resides in the computer's memory. Instead of working directly with the DBMS, some users interact with a front end. A *front end* is a program that generally has a more user-friendly interface than the DBMS. For example, a registration department specialist interacts with the Class Registration program by filling out a form. This front-end program interacts with the DBMS, which, in turn, interacts with the database. Many programs today use forms on a webpage as their front end. An application that supports a front-end program by interacting directly with the database sometimes is called the *back end*. In this case, the DBMS is the back end.

⚛ BTW

Technology Trend
Discover More: Visit this chapter's free resources to learn about uses of forensic databases.

Advantages of a Database Approach
The database approach addresses many of the weaknesses associated with file processing systems. Advantages of the database approach include the following:

- **Reduced data redundancy:** Most data items are stored in only one file, which greatly reduces duplicate data. For example, a school's database would record a student's name and address only once. When student data is entered or changed, one employee makes the change once. Figure 11-6 demonstrates the differences between how a file processing application and a database application might store data.

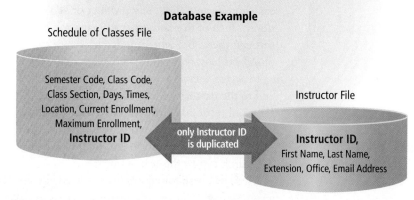

File Processing Example

Schedule of Classes File

Semester Code, Class Code, Class Section, Days, Times, Location, Current Enrollment, Maximum Enrollment, **Instructor ID, First Name, Last Name, Extension, Office, Email Address**

↔ duplicated data

Instructor File

Instructor ID, First Name, Last Name, Extension, Office, Email Address

Database Example

Schedule of Classes File

Semester Code, Class Code, Class Section, Days, Times, Location, Current Enrollment, Maximum Enrollment, **Instructor ID**

← only Instructor ID is duplicated

Instructor File

Instructor ID, First Name, Last Name, Extension, Office, Email Address

Figure 11-6 With file processing, both files contain all six instructor data fields. With a database, only the Instructor file contains the First Name, Last Name, Extension, Office, and Email Address fields. Other files, such as the Schedule of Classes file, contain only the Instructor ID — which links to the Instructor file when instructor data is needed.
© Cengage Learning

- **Improved data integrity:** When users modify data in the database, they make changes to one file instead of multiple files. Thus, the database approach increases the data's integrity by reducing the possibility of introducing inconsistencies.
- **Shared data:** The data in a database environment belongs to and is shared, usually over a network, by the entire organization. This data is independent of, or separate from, the programs that access the data. Organizations that use databases typically have security settings to define who can access, add, modify, and delete the data in a database.
- **Easier access:** The database approach allows nontechnical users to access and maintain data, provided they have the necessary privileges. Many computer users also can develop smaller databases themselves, without professional assistance.
- **Reduced development time:** It often is easier and faster to develop programs that use the database approach. Many DBMSs include several tools to assist in developing programs, which further reduces the development time.

 CONSIDER THIS

Can a database eliminate redundant data completely?

No. A database reduces redundant data; it does not eliminate it. Key fields link data together in a database. For example, a Student ID field will exist in any database file that requires access to student data. Thus, a student ID is duplicated (exists in more than one file) in the database.

Disadvantages of a Database Approach   A database can be more complex than a file processing system. People with special training usually develop larger databases and their associated applications. Databases also require more memory and processing power than file processing systems.

Data in a database can be more vulnerable than data in file processing systems because it can store a lot of data in a single physical file. Many users and programs share and depend on this data. If the database is not operating properly or is damaged or destroyed, users may not be able to perform their jobs. Further, unauthorized users potentially could gain access to a single database file that contains several data files of personal and confidential data. To protect their database resource, individuals and companies should establish and follow security procedures.

Despite these limitations, business and home users often work with databases because of their numerous advantages.

Mini Feature 11-1: Web Databases

The web offers information about jobs, travel destinations, television programming, photos, movies, videos, local and national weather, sporting events, and legislative information. You can shop for just about any product or service, buy or sell stocks, and make airline reservations. Much of this and other information exists in databases that are stored on or are accessible through the web. Some web databases are *collaborative databases*, where users store and share photos, videos, recordings, and other personal media with other registered users.

To access data in a web database, you fill in a form on a webpage. The webpage is the front end to the database. Many search engines use databases to store and index content from websites for rapid retrieval. Thus, the search engine's home page, containing a form in which to type search text, is the front end to the database. To access the search engine's database, you enter search text in a search form and then tap or click a search button that instructs the form to send the search text to the search engine.

A web database for an organization usually resides on a database server. A *database server* is a computer that stores and provides access to a database. For smaller databases, many desktop database programs provide a variety of web publishing tools that enable users without computer programming experience to create a home or small office database. Read Mini Feature 11-1 to learn about types of web databases.

Web Databases

A database service, or a website that acts as a portal for a database, enables government agencies, schools, and companies to share information with a wide audience. Some web databases are accessible to the public. Examples of public databases include shopping and travel databases. Other databases contain information accessible only to authorized users. Examples of protected databases include certain government databases or entertainment and research databases that are subscription based.

Government

Government web database services can provide access to information about the government, as well as information created and used by government agencies. Some information that government agencies publish in databases is available to the public. Through these database services, for example, users can locate information about current laws. Other database services, such as those for criminal databases, allow access only to those individuals with necessary clearance. Government database services also enable officials around the world to share data.

Entertainment

You can search an entertainment web database service to find out who guest-starred on your favorite television program or locate video or audio clips. Using a subscription-based entertainment web database service allows you to access media content, such as music. These database services often enable you to create and share playlists. Entertainment professionals use subscription-based web databases to view and post casting notices or update artist profiles.

Travel

Booking online travel through a travel web database service enables you to view multiple vendors and options. You can limit a search to desired locations and dates. These database services help you find deals on air travel, car rentals, hotel rooms, and vacation packages. Travel web database services can save your personal data and travel history. These services will send notifications about upcoming travel deals and communicate changes or updates to your travel plans.

Shopping

Shopping web database services enable you to locate the right size and color, sort by price or featured products, and more. Vendors can use a web database service to show photos of items they sell and track inventory. Some shopping database services search for bargains, presenting a variety of purchasing options so that you can find the lowest price. These database services also use your search and order history to suggest products in their databases that you may be interested in buying.

Research

You can interact with web databases to research product information when shopping for a new appliance or car. Information accessible through these web database services includes costs, safety concerns, and industry and user reviews. Some research web database services provide financial information for potential investors, including company histories and stock analysis. Research web database services are available to help you find a college or university and then provide information about admission requirements, financial information, and application advice.

Education

Teachers can search education web database services to locate and share curricula, worksheets, and lesson plans. Schools use web database services to store and distribute student contact information and grades. Students interact with web database services when signing up for their courses online. Using these services during enrollment helps a school determine when a class has reached its maximum size.

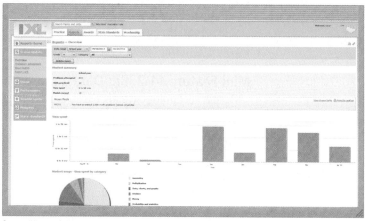

Source: IXL Learning

Discover More: Visit this chapter's free resources to find examples of web databases.

Consider This: Which web database services have you used? How do web databases help you in your daily life? Would you use a web database for research? Why or why not?

Types of Databases

Every database and DBMS is based on a specific data model. A data model consists of rules and standards that define how the database organizes data. A **data model** defines how users view the organization of the data. It does not define how the operating system actually arranges the data on the storage media. A database typically is based on one data model. Three popular data models in use today are relational, object-oriented, and multidimensional.

Relational Database   A *relational database* is a database that stores data in tables that consist of rows and columns. In addition to storing data, a relational database also stores data relationships. A relationship is a link within the data. Applications best suited for relational databases are those whose data can be organized into a two-dimensional table, that is, tables with rows and columns. Many organizations use relational databases for payroll, accounts receivable, accounts payable, general ledger, inventory, order entry, invoicing, and other business-related functions.

Object-Oriented Database   An *object-oriented database* (*OODB*) stores data in objects. An *object* is an item that contains data, as well as the actions that read or process the data. Examples of applications appropriate for an object-oriented database include media databases that store images, audio clips, and/or video clips; groupware databases that store documents, such as schedules, calendars, manuals, memos, and reports; and CAD (computer-aided design) databases that store data about engineering, architectural, and scientific designs.

Multidimensional and Other Database Types   A *multidimensional database* stores data in dimensions. Whereas a relational database is a two-dimensional table, a multidimensional database can store more than two dimensions of data. These multiple dimensions allow users to access and analyze any view of the database data. One application that uses multi-dimensional databases is a data warehouse. A *data warehouse* is a huge database that stores and manages the data required to analyze historical and current transactions. The database in a data warehouse often is distributed. The data in a *distributed database* exists in many separate locations throughout a network or the Internet. Although the data is accessible through a single server, the physical location of the server on which it is stored is transparent and often unknown, to the user.

Mini Feature 11-2: Big Data

Recent technology trends have resulted in activities that generate large quantities of data. These trends include the following:

- Growth of online commerce, social, and government applications
- Increased use of mobile devices
- Emergence of the Internet of Things
- Development of cloud computing
- Availability of Internet connectivity through wired and wireless networks

Online business transactions, posts on social networks, government agencies, media and text messages from tablets and smartphones, and automated sensors produce data that is stored in databases located stored on servers distributed across the Internet. **Big Data** refers to large-scale data sets that require advanced technologies beyond the capabilities of typical database software to gather, store, process, retrieve, or analyze. Read Mini Feature 11-2 to learn more about characteristics and sources of Big Data, and technologies that facilitate working with large-scale distributed databases.

BTW
Technology Innovator
Discover More: Visit this chapter's free resources to learn about E. F. Codd, the inventor of the relational database model.

BTW
Technology Innovator
Discover More: Visit this chapter's free resources to learn about Oracle and its cofounder Larry Ellison.

BTW
High-Tech Talk
Discover More: Visit this chapter's free resources to learn more about types of databases, relational database design, and the normalization process.

Internet Research
What is data mining?
Search for: data mining

Big Data

Through their daily activities, consumers, businesses, and machines produce large quantities of data to be stored on the Internet. Making sense of Big Data can provide valuable information to organizations trying to improve their business processes and make intelligent business decisions.

Characteristics of Big Data

Analysts often refer to the three V's when describing characteristics of Big Data: volume, velocity, and variety. Large-scale data sets grow in volume (how much data is generated), velocity (the rate at which data is generated), and variety (the different formats in which data can appear).

Volume refers to the amount of data that individuals and organizations generate. As data formats expand from text to images, files, audio, and video, it is common to need storage for multiple terabytes (1,000 gigabytes) of data. In the future, some organizations may require storage for petabytes (1,000 terabytes) and exabytes (1,000 petabytes) of data.

Velocity refers to the rate at which data is processed. In one day, for example, Google performs more than 6 billion searches, Facebook records more than 4.5 billion "likes," Twitter receives more than 500 million Tweets, and temperature and barometric sensors located across the world gather and transmit more than 200 million observations. In one minute, YouTube processes 100 hours of uploaded video. In one second, Amazon processes more than 400 transactions from customers during the holiday shopping period.

Variety refers to the different formats to represent or store data for use by humans and computer applications. Some data, such as census records, stock values, and corporate sales, is structured, meaning it can be organized neatly in tables. Unstructured data generally is more complex and may include items such as Tweets, media files, Wikipedia articles, and fingerprints.

Some analysts have expanded the three V's to include veracity (how accurate the data is), value (how organizations use their data), and viability (whether organizations can make predictions based on this data).

Sources and Uses of Big Data

One way businesses generate Big Data is by capturing customer behaviors. For example, in addition to storing information about a customer's purchase, some shopping websites also gather data about how much time customers spend on a webpage, how many items they view before making a purchase, and which pages on the company's website that customers visited, in order to create a more customized experience. Amazon and other retailers compile data from customer purchases in process

called collaborative filtering to recommend related products. For example, Amazon recommends that customers who purchase a digital camera might also want to purchase a storage card or a camera case.

Government agencies generate large amounts of data in real time from satellite images, social media posts, and media. By analyzing this data, they can monitor transportation systems, dispatch first responders in emergencies, and provide consumers with information to make informed choices about health care, schools, and community services.

Temperature and barometric sensors, wearable devices, and buses and trains equipped with GPS capability all transmit data over the Internet to be used in a variety of web and mobile applications.

Source: Amazon.com, Inc.

Data Visualization

Data visualization is the process of presenting data graphically as charts, maps, or other pictorial formats in order to understand the resulting information easily. As the size of databases grows, data visualizations make it possible to interpret complex data sets, find relationships among data items, and discover patterns that can provide useful information. The "Racial Dot Map" shown in the figure is a visualization that displays one dot per person in the United States. Each dot is colored by ethnicity. The figure shows the map zoomed in on the Boston area.

Source: Weldon Cooper Center for Public Service, Rector and Visitors of the University of Virginia (Dustin A. Cable, creator)

Discover More: Visit this chapter's free resources to learn more about Big Data and the technologies that make it possible to capture, store, and retrieve data from distributed databases.

✳ **Consider This:** What websites or apps do you use that generate or take advantage of Big Data? How have cloud computing, online social networks, and the Internet of Things contributed to and enabled the growth of Big Data? What visualizations have you seen that help make sense of complex data sets?

NOW YOU SHOULD KNOW

Be sure you understand the material presented in the section titled Databases, Data, and Information; and File Processing Systems and Databases as it relates to the chapter objectives.

Now you should know . . .

- How you organize and maintain data (Objective 1)
- Why you would choose a database approach over a file processing approach (Objective 2)
- When you use a web database, relational database, and Big Data (Objective 3)

Discover More: Visit this chapter's premium content for practice quiz opportunities.

Database Management Systems

Internet Research
Which is the most widely used DBMS?
Search for: dbms share

BTW
Metadata
Because the data dictionary contains details about data, some call it *metadata* (meta means more comprehensive).

As previously discussed, a database management system (DBMS), or database program, is software that allows you to create, access, and manage a database. Managing a company's databases requires a great deal of coordination. The *database administrator* (*DBA*) is the person in the organization who is responsible for managing and coordinating all database activities, including development, maintenance, and permissions.

DBMSs are available for many sizes and types of computers. Whether designed for a small or large computer, most DBMSs perform common functions. The following pages discuss these functions.

Discover More: Visit this chapter's free resources to learn more about specific database management systems.

Data Dictionary

A **data dictionary**, sometimes called a *repository*, contains data about each file in the database and each field in those files. For each file, it stores details such as the file name, a description, the file's relationship to other files, and the number of records in the file. For each field, it stores details such as the field name, description, field type, field size, default value, validation rules, and the field's relationship to other fields. Figure 11-7 shows how a data dictionary might list data for a Student file.

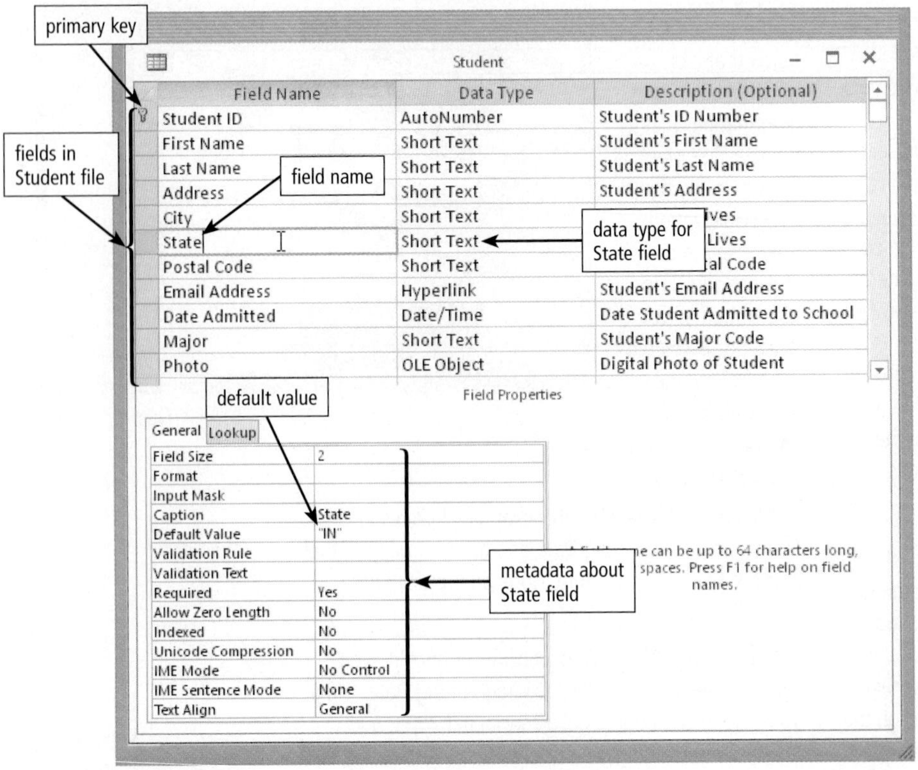

Figure 11-7 A sample data dictionary entry shows the fields in the Student file and the properties of the State field.
Source: Microsoft

A DBMS uses the data dictionary to perform validation checks to maintain the integrity of the data. When users enter data, the data dictionary verifies that the entered data matches the field's data type. For example, the data dictionary allows only dates to be entered in a Date Admitted field. The data dictionary also can limit the type of data that can be entered, often allowing a user to select from a list. For example, the data dictionary ensures that the State field contains a valid two-letter state code, such as IN, by presenting a list of valid state codes to the user.

File Retrieval and Maintenance

A DBMS provides several tools that allow users and programs to retrieve and maintain data in the database. To retrieve or select data in a database, you query it. A **query** is a request for specific data from the database. Users can instruct the DBMS to return or store the results of a query. The capability of querying a database is one of the more powerful database features.

A DBMS offers several methods to retrieve and maintain its data. The four more commonly used are query languages, query by example, forms, and report writers. Another method is by importing data. Read How To 11-1 for instructions about importing spreadsheet data into a database and vice versa.

HOW TO 11-1

Import Spreadsheet Data into a Database and Export Database Data to a Spreadsheet

If you periodically use spreadsheets and databases, you may find it beneficial to import data from a spreadsheet into a database or export data from a database to a spreadsheet. As mentioned in this book, spreadsheet applications and database applications each have unique advantages; therefore, you may need to convert the data from one application's format to use in the other. For example, if you have a spreadsheet with many rows of customer data, you might want to import the data from the spreadsheet into a database so that you can perform simple or complex queries on the data. If you have a database with many records and you want to perform calculations or a statistical analysis of the data, you might export data from the database to a spreadsheet. If you are exporting data from a relational database to a spreadsheet, the relationships will not be reflected in the spreadsheet. The following steps describe how to accomplish these tasks.

Import Data from a Spreadsheet into a Database

1. Run the spreadsheet application. Open the spreadsheet you want to import to the database and make sure your data is organized properly. For example, each column should represent a field, and each row should represent a record. The first row in the spreadsheet should contain the field names for each respective column. Make the necessary changes to the spreadsheet.

2. Save and close the spreadsheet.

3. Run the database application.

4. Create a new database or open the database to which you want to import the spreadsheet.

5. Navigate to and then tap or click the command to import data from an external file.

6. Select the type of file you want to import (spreadsheet, in this case). Some database applications may identify types of files by the name of the program that created them. For example, if you are importing an Excel spreadsheet into an Access database, you would select the option in Access to import an Excel file.

7. Navigate through the remaining steps to verify that the data in the spreadsheet will import properly. This includes:

   - Choosing the table into which you want to import the data in the spreadsheet
   - Verifying field names
   - Setting a field to act as a primary key
   - Choosing data types for each field

8. Tap or click the button or command to finish the import.

9. Open the table in the database with the data you just imported, and verify it all was imported properly.

Export Data from a Database to a Spreadsheet

1. Run the database application. Open the database containing the data you want to export.

2. Open the table containing the data you want to export.

3. Navigate to and then tap or click the option to export the data.

4. Select the option to export the database to a spreadsheet. Some database applications might require you to select the name of the spreadsheet application to which you want to export the database. For example, in Microsoft Access, you should specify that you want to export to a Microsoft Excel file.

5. Specify a file name for the spreadsheet.

6. Tap or click the button or command to complete the export.

7. Run the spreadsheet application and open the file you have just created. Verify the data has been exported properly from the database.

Consider This: What are some other reasons why you might want to import data from a spreadsheet into a database or export data from a database to a spreadsheet?

	A	B	C	D	E	F	G	H	I	J	K
1	Student ID	First Name	Last Name	Address	City	State	Postal Code	Email Address	Date Admitted	Major	Photo
2	2295	Milton	Brewer	54 Lucy Court	Charlestown	IN	46176		6/10/2016	EE	mbrewer.jpg
3	3876	Louella	Drake	33 Timmons Place	Bonner	IN	45208	lou@world.com	8/9/2016	BIO	ldrake.jpg
4	3928	Adelbert	Ruiz	99 Tenth Street	Sheldon	IN	46033		10/8/2016	CT	aruiz.jpg
5	2872	Benjamin	Tu	2204 Elm Court	Rowley	IN	46167	tu@indi.net	9/14/2016	GEN	btu.jpg
6											
7											

Source: Microsoft

Figure 11-8a (SQL statement)

```
SELECT CLASS_TITLE, CLASS_SECTION,
 MAXIMUM_ENROLLMENT - CURRENT_ENROLLMENT AS SEATS_REMAINING
FROM SCHEDULE_OF_CLASSES, CLASS_CATALOG
WHERE SCHEDULE_OF_CLASSES.CLASS_CODE = CLASS_CATALOG.CLASS_CODE
ORDER BY CLASS_TITLE
```

Figure 11-8b (SQL statement results)

Class Title	Class Section	Seats Remaining
Algebra 1	51	14
Art Appreciation	52	19
English Composition 1	02	5
Introduction to Sociology	01	14

Figure 11-8 A sample SQL statement and its results. Notice that the query results show meaningful column headings instead of the actual SQL field names.
Source: Microsoft; © Cengage Learning

Query Language A **query language** consists of simple, English-like statements that allow users to specify the data they want to display, print, store, update, or delete. Each query language has its own formats and vocabulary.

Structured Query Language (SQL pronounced S-Q-L or sequel) is a popular query language that allows users to manage, update, and retrieve data. SQL has special keywords and rules that users include in SQL statements. Figure 11-8a shows an SQL statement that creates the results shown in Figure 11-8b.

Discover More: Visit this chapter's free resources to learn about query wizards.

Internet Research
What is a NoSQL database?
Search for: nosql database

Query by Example Most DBMSs include *query by example* (QBE), a feature that has a graphical user interface to assist users with retrieving data. Figure 11-9 shows a sample QBE screen for a query that searches for and lists students majoring in sociology; that is, their Major field value is equal to SOC.

Figure 11-9a (all records in Student table)

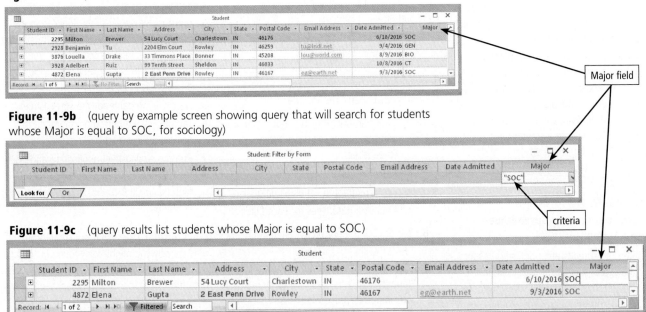

Figure 11-9b (query by example screen showing query that will search for students whose Major is equal to SOC, for sociology)

Figure 11-9c (query results list students whose Major is equal to SOC)

Figure 11-9 Shown here is a Microsoft Access QBE, which searches for students whose major is sociology.
Source: Microsoft

Form A **form**, sometimes called a *data entry form*, is a window on the screen that provides areas for entering or modifying data in a database. You use forms (such as the Student Maintenance Form in Figure 11-1 at the beginning of this chapter) to retrieve and maintain the data in a database. To reduce data entry errors, well-designed forms should validate data as it is entered.

Report Writer A **report writer**, also called a *report generator*, allows users to design a report on the screen, retrieve data into the report design, and then display or print the report (Figure 11-10). Unlike a form, you use a report writer only to retrieve data. Report writers usually allow you to format page numbers and dates; titles and column headings; subtotals and totals; and fonts, font sizes, color, and shading; and to include images. Some report writers allow you to create a report as a webpage.

Data Security

Most organizations and people realize that data is one of their more valuable assets. To ensure that data is accessible on demand, an organization must manage and protect its data just as it would any other resource. Thus, it is vital that the data is kept secure. For example, data in a database often is encrypted to prevent unauthorized users from reading its contents, and its access is restricted to only those who need to process the data.

A DBMS provides means to ensure that only authorized users can access data. In addition, most DBMSs allow different levels of access privileges to be identified for each field in the database. Access privileges define the actions that a specific user or group of users can perform on the data. For example, in the Schedule of Classes file, the student would have read-only privileges. That is, the student could view the list of classes offered in a semester but could not change them. A department head, by contrast, would have full-update privileges to classes offered during a particular semester, meaning he or she can view and modify the data. Finally, some users have no access privileges to the data; that is, they cannot view or modify any data in the database. Read How To 11-2 for ways to secure and maintain a database. Read Ethics and Issues 11-3 to consider issues surrounding users who accidentally access confidential data. Read Secure IT 11-1 for steps to take if you become a victim of identity theft due to your personal data being compromised.

Student List by Major

Major	Last Name	Student ID	First Name	Address	City	Date Admitted
BIO						
	Drake	3876	Louella	33 Timmons Place	Bonner	8/9/2016
CT						
	Ruiz	3928	Adelbert	99 Tenth Street	Sheldon	10/8/2016
GEN						
	Tu	2928	Benjamin	2204 Elm Court	Rowley	9/4/2017
SOC						
	Brewer	2295	Milton	54 Lucy Court	Charlestown	6/10/2016
	Gupta	4872	Elena	2 East Penn Drive	Rowley	9/3/2016

Figure 11-10 This report, created in Microsoft Access, displays student information by major.
Source: Microsoft

 Internet Research
What are recent data security breaches?
Search for: security breaches news

 BTW
Principle of Least Privilege
Many organizations adopt a *principle of least privilege policy*, where users' access privileges are limited to the lowest level necessary to perform required tasks to prevent accidental or intentional misuse of the data.

🏵 HOW TO 11-2

Secure and Maintain a Database
As you add and delete tables and records from your database, you should secure and maintain the database so that it can continue operating securely and efficiently. If you neglect to secure and maintain a database, chances increase that the data can become compromised or inaccessible. The following guidelines describe how to secure and maintain a database.

Secure the Database
- Each person accessing the database should have a profile that includes a user name, a strong password that must be changed frequently, and limits on database system-level access.
- Only administrators should have access to create and delete tables.

- Consider allowing typical users only to view or modify records.
- Restrict users to accessing only database tables and records that are necessary to perform their job function(s).
- Limit the number of unsuccessful sign-in attempts in a specified period, and record when users access the database.

Maintain the Database
- If the database contains a table that you do not need (and you do not foresee a future need for the data in that table), remove the table from the database.
- Evaluate the fields in all remaining tables and make sure they are assigned the proper data type. Make any necessary adjustments.

- Remove fields you no longer need from the tables in your database.
- If the database contains a large number of records, consider deleting records you no longer need.
- Navigate to and then tap or click the command to compact and repair the database (if available).
- If you want to protect the data in the database, consider selecting the option to encrypt the database.

🏵 **Consider This:** What problems may arise from individuals or companies failing to properly secure and maintain their databases?

ETHICS & ISSUES 11-3

What Should the Consequences Be If a User Accidentally Accesses Confidential Data?

A student discovered private student data on a publicly accessible area of a university computer. Instead of notifying authorities, he took the information to the student newspaper. The newspaper advisor authorized the publication of an article about the situation. Although the article did not include any student names or personal information, the administration fired the newspaper's adviser for violating the university's computer policies and nearly expelled the student. Was the student obligated to report the vulnerability to the administration? Was the school right to fire the advisor for not reporting the breach?

In another case, a student accessed personal data for school employees from the school's network. In this instance, the student allegedly attempted to profit from the data. Administrators charged the high school student with criminal trespassing. Other examples include students attempting to alter grades, access test questions, or disrupt or trace a school's network activity.

Institutions often attempt to resolve security breaches quietly. Some fear that publicity may cause financial loss and may encourage hackers to target the institution. In some cases, an institution may file lawsuits against those who make security breaches public, including reporters. Some

feel that protecting data privacy partially is the responsibility of the person who uncovers the breach. Others feel that it is the responsibility of the institution or organization to secure its servers and educate employees about protection of confidential data.

Consider This: Is an institution responsible for unauthorized access of its personal data, or is the person who accessed it responsible? Why? Even if a person is not trying to profit from a data breach, is he or she still responsible for the discovery? Why or why not? Are journalists wrong to expose breaches, even if they do not publish the accessed data? Why or why not?

SECURE IT 11-1

Recovering from Identity Theft

In the past 10 years, more than 640 million Americans fell victim to identity theft, according to the Identity Theft Resource Center. Data breaches in businesses, banks, medical centers, and schools have affected nearly 39 percent of Americans. This crime is the complaint most often reported to the Federal Trade Commission (FTC).

On average, victims of identity theft spend 25 hours settling the resulting issues. Experts recommend that people who have experienced identity theft should follow this advice as part of their resolution efforts:

• **Request a fraud alert**. Contact the fraud department at the three national credit reporting companies: Experian, Equifax, and TransUnion. (Refer to the How To: Your Turn student assignment in this chapter for details about contacting these agencies.) One agency should report the theft to the other two companies, but you might want to contact all three to be certain the fraud has been noted. Request that a fraud alert be placed on your accounts to help prevent credit accounts from being opened in your name. This free service requires lenders to contact the

account owners if a new request for credit is submitted. This fraud alert must be renewed every 90 days.

• **Order credit reports.** Once you file a fraud alert, you are entitled to receive a free credit report. Wait at least 30 days from the theft to obtain the report, however, because creditors may report activity on a monthly basis, and your most current report may not include current information. Request that only the last four digits of your Social Security number are shown on the report.

• **Obtain an FTC affidavit and file it with law enforcement agencies.** The FTC's Identity Theft Victim's Complaint and Affidavit is accepted as proof of your identity. Download the form from the FTC's website and then file it with the police. The form also can be used to dispute claims with creditors.

• **Report Internet crime to the Internet Crime Complaint Center.** Report stolen finances or identities and other cybercrime to the Internet Crime Complaint Center. This organization is a partnership between the Federal Bureau of Investigation and the National White Collar Crime Center.

• **Keep records of your actions.** Create a journal that records the names of people you called, phone numbers, dates, and correspondence sent.

• **Review financial accounts.** Look for unusual activity, and check to see if any accounts were opened recently. Continue reviewing the accounts even if you do not see any questionable transactions.

• **Enroll in a credit monitoring service.** Each of the three national credit reporting agencies and many credit card companies provide this service. The companies send messages to subscribers when unusual activity is detected on a credit card account to alert consumers to possible identity theft. This service can be useful for people who have large balances in savings and checking accounts, travel frequently, or fail to check their bank statements and credit reports regularly.

Consider This: Do you know someone who has been a victim of identity theft? If so, which type of fraud occurred? What activity did this person take to report this crime and to restore personal records and accounts?

Backup and Recovery

Occasionally, a database is damaged or destroyed because of hardware failure, a problem with the software, human error, or a catastrophe, such as fire or flood. A DBMS provides a variety of techniques to restore the database to a usable form in case it is damaged or destroyed.

- A backup, or copy, of the entire database should be made on a regular basis. Some DBMSs have their own built-in backup tools. Others require users to purchase a separate backup program, or use one included with the operating system.
- More complex DBMSs maintain a **log**, which is a listing of activities that modify the contents of the database. If a registration department specialist modifies a student's address, for example, the change appears in the log.
- A DBMS **recovery utility** uses logs and/or backups, and either a rollforward or a rollback technique, to restore a database when it becomes damaged or destroyed. In a *rollforward*, also called *forward recovery*, the DBMS uses the log to reenter changes made to the database since the last save or backup. In a *rollback*, also called *backward recovery*, the DBMS uses the log to undo any changes made to the database during a certain period. The rollback restores the database to its condition prior to the failure. Depending on the type of failure, the DBMS determines which type of recovery technique to use.
- **Continuous backup** is a backup plan in which changes are backed up as they are made. This backup technique can cost more than other backup strategies but is growing in popularity for businesses whose data must be available at all times, because it provides recovery of damaged data in a matter of seconds. Organizations such as hospitals, communications companies, and financial institutions often use continuous backup.

Discover More: Visit this chapter's free resources to learn more about database recovery utilities.

System Development

An *information system* is a collection of hardware, software, data, people, and procedures that work together to produce information. As a user of technology in a business, you someday may participate in the modification of an existing information system or the development of a new one. Thus, it is important that you understand system development.

System development is a set of activities used to build an information system. System development activities often are grouped into larger categories called *phases*. This collection of phases sometimes is called the **system development life cycle** (**SDLC**). Many traditional SDLCs contain five phases (Figure 11-11):

1. Planning
2. Analysis
3. Design
4. Implementation
5. Support and Security

Each system development phase consists of a series of activities, and the phases form a loop. In theory, the five system development phases often appear sequentially, as shown in Figure 11-11. In reality, activities within adjacent phases often interact with one another, making system development a dynamic, iterative process.

Discover More: Visit this chapter's free resources to learn more about system development life cycles.

Internet Research

What is agile development?

Search for: agile development

System Development

1. Planning
- Review project requests
- Prioritize project requests
- Allocate resources
- Form project development team

Ongoing Activities
- Project management
- Feasibility assessment
- Documentation
- Data/information gathering

5. Support and Security
- Perform maintenance activities
- Monitor system performance
- Assess system security

2. Analysis
- Conduct preliminary investigation
- Perform detailed analysis activities:
  - Study current system
  - Determine user requirements
  - Recommend solution

4. Implementation
- Develop programs and apps, if necessary
- Install and test new system
- Train users
- Convert to new system

3. Design
- Acquire hardware and software, if necessary
- Develop details of system

Figure 11-11 System development often consists of five phases that form a loop. Several ongoing activities also take place throughout system development.

System Development Guidelines

System development should follow three general guidelines: group activities into phases, involve users, and define standards.

1. **Group activities into phases.** Many SDLCs contain the same phases shown in Figure 11-11. Others have more or fewer phases. Regardless, all system development cycles have similar activities and tasks.
2. **Involve users.** Users include anyone for whom the system is being built. Customers, employees, students, data entry specialists, accountants, sales managers, and owners all are examples of users. Users are more apt to accept a new system if they contribute to its design.
3. **Define standards.** *Standards* are sets of rules and procedures an organization expects employees to accept and follow. Standards help people working on the same project produce consistent results.

Who Participates in System Development?

System development should involve representatives from each department in which the proposed system will be used. This includes both nontechnical users and IT professionals. Although the roles and responsibilities of members of the system development team may change from organization to organization, this chapter presents general descriptions of tasks for various team members.

During system development, the systems analyst meets and works with a variety of people. A **systems analyst** is responsible for designing and developing an information system. The systems analyst is the users' primary contact person. Depending on the size of the organization, the tasks performed by the systems analyst may vary. Smaller organizations may have one systems analyst or even one person who assumes the roles of both systems analyst and software developer. Larger organizations often have multiple systems analysts who discuss various aspects of the development project with users, management, other analysts, database analysts, database administrators, network administrators, web developers, software developers, vendors, and the steering committee.

For each system development project, an organization usually forms a *project team* to work on the project from beginning to end. The project team consists of users, the systems analyst, and other IT professionals.

Discover More: Visit this chapter's free resources to learn more about skills required for a systems analyst.

 BTW
Steering Committee
A *steering committee* is a decision-making body in an organization.

Project Management

Project management is the process of planning, scheduling, and then controlling the activities during system development. The goal of project management is to deliver an acceptable system to the user in an agreed-upon time frame, while maintaining costs.

In smaller organizations or projects, one person manages the entire project. For larger projects, the project management activities often are separated between a project manager and a project leader. In this situation, the *project leader* manages and controls the budget and schedule of the project, and the *project manager* controls the activities during system development. Project leaders and/or project managers are part of the project team. If the systems analyst is not the project manager, he or she works closely with the project manager.

To plan and schedule a project effectively, the project leader identifies the following elements:

- Goals, objectives, and expectations of the project, collectively called the *scope*
- Required activities
- Time estimates for each activity
- Cost estimates for each activity
- Order of activities
- Activities that can take place at the same time

After these items are identified, the project leader usually records them in a project plan. Project leaders can use **project management software** to assist them in planning, scheduling, and controlling development projects. One aspect of managing projects is to ensure that everyone submits deliverables on time and according to plan. A *deliverable* is any tangible item, such as a chart, diagram, report, or program file.

Gantt and PERT Charts Popular tools used to plan and schedule the time relationships among project activities are Gantt and PERT charts (Figure 11-12).

- A *Gantt chart*, developed by Henry L. Gantt, is a bar chart that uses horizontal bars to show project phases or activities. The left side, or vertical axis, displays the list of required activities. A horizontal axis across the top or bottom of the chart represents time.
- Developed by the U.S. Department of Defense, a *PERT chart*, short for Program Evaluation and Review Technique chart, analyzes the time required to complete a task and identifies the minimum time required for an entire project.

PERT charts, sometimes called network diagrams, can be more complicated to create than Gantt charts, but are better suited than Gantt charts for planning and scheduling large, complex projects.

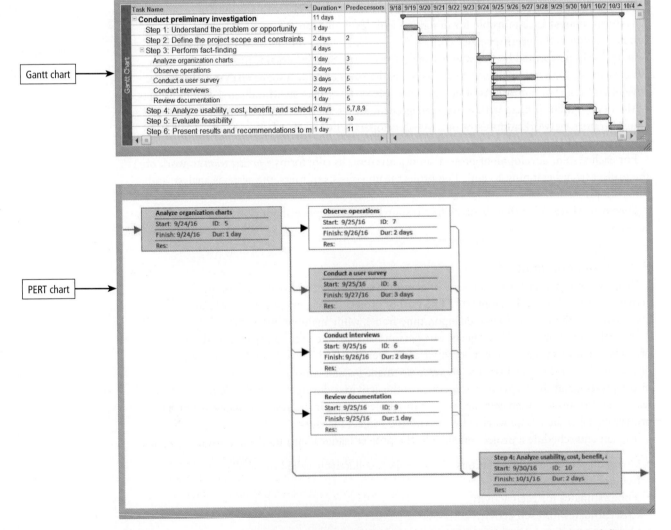

Figure 11-12 Project managers use software to create Gantt charts, PERT charts, and other charts and diagrams.
© Cengage Learning

 CONSIDER THIS ─────────────────────────────────

How do project leaders adjust when a project changes?

After the project features and deadlines have been set, the project leader monitors and controls the project. Some activities take less time than originally planned. Others take longer. The project leader may realize that an activity is taking excessive time or that scope creep has begun. *Scope creep*, also called *feature creep*, occurs when one activity has led to another that was not planned originally; thus, the scope of the project now has grown.

Project leaders should use *change management*, which is the process of recognizing when a change in the project has occurred, taking actions to react to the change, and planning for opportunities because of the change. For example, the project leader may recognize the team will not be able to meet the original deadline of the project due to scope creep. Thus, the project leader may extend the deadline or may reduce the scope of the system development. If the latter occurs, the users will receive a less comprehensive system at the original deadline. In either case, the project leader revises the first project plan and presents the new plan to users for approval. It is crucial that everyone is aware of and agrees on any changes made to the project plan.

Feasibility Assessment

Feasibility is a measure of how suitable the development of a system will be to the organization. A project that is feasible at one point during system development might become infeasible at a later point. Systems analysts, therefore, frequently reevaluate feasibility during the system development project.

A systems analyst typically uses at least four tests to evaluate feasibility of a project: operational feasibility, schedule feasibility, technical feasibility, and economic feasibility.

- *Operational feasibility* measures how well the proposed information system will work. Will the users like the new system? Will they use it? Will it meet their requirements? Will it cause any changes in their work environment? Is it secure?
- *Schedule feasibility* measures whether the established deadlines for the project are reasonable. If a deadline is not reasonable, the project leader might make a new schedule. If a deadline cannot be extended, then the scope of the project might be reduced to meet a mandatory deadline.
- *Technical feasibility* measures whether the organization has or can obtain the computing resources, software services, and qualified people needed to develop, deliver, and then support the proposed information system. For most information system projects, hardware, software, and people typically are available to support an information system. An organization's choice for using computing resources and software services in-house or on the cloud may impact a system's technical feasibility.
- *Economic feasibility*, also called *cost/benefit feasibility*, measures whether the lifetime benefits of the proposed information system will be greater than its lifetime costs. A systems analyst often consults the advice of a business analyst, who uses many financial techniques, such as return on investment (ROI) and payback analysis, to perform a cost/benefit analysis.

Documentation

During system development, project members produce a large amount of documentation. *Documentation* is the collection and summarization of data, information, and deliverables. It is important that all documentation be well written, thorough, consistent, and understandable. The final information system should be reflected accurately and completely in documentation developed throughout the development project. Maintaining up-to-date documentation should be an ongoing part of system development. Too often, project team members put off documentation until the end of the project because it is time consuming, but these practices typically result in lower-quality documentation.

CONSIDER THIS

How do team members collaborate?

Conferencing software includes tools that enable users to share documents via online meetings and communicate with other connected users. When a meeting takes place on the web, it is called a *web conference*. In an online meeting, the facilitator may share a document for all participants to see at the same time. This allows the participants to edit a document and see the changes being made. Many conferencing software apps allow the facilitator to share his or her computer's desktop screen to demonstrate software apps or show webpages in real time to meeting participants. During the online meeting, participants have the ability to open a chat window and type messages to one another. Conferencing software also usually includes audio and video capabilities.

Discover More: Visit this chapter's free resources to learn more about conferencing software.

Data and Information Gathering Techniques

During system development, members of the project team gather data and information. They need accurate and timely data and information for many reasons. They must keep a project on schedule, evaluate feasibility, and be sure the system meets requirements. Systems analysts and other IT professionals use several techniques to gather data and information. They review documentation, observe, survey, interview, conduct joint-application design sessions, and research.

- **Review documentation:** By reviewing documentation such as organization charts, memos, and meeting minutes, systems analysts learn about the history of a project. Documentation also provides information about the organization, such as its operations, weaknesses, and strengths.

Internet Research

Does the Hawthorne Effect apply to development projects?

Search for: hawthorne effect

- **Observe:** Observing people helps systems analysts understand exactly how they perform a task. Likewise, observing a machine allows you to see how it works.
- **Survey:** To obtain data and information from a large number of people, systems analysts distribute surveys.
- **Interview:** The interview is the most important data and information gathering technique for the systems analyst. It allows the systems analyst to clarify responses and probe during face-to-face feedback.

- **JAD sessions:** Instead of a single one-on-one interview, analysts often use joint-application design sessions to gather data and information. A *joint-application design (JAD) session*, or *focus group*, consists of a series of lengthy, structured group meetings in which users and IT professionals work together to design or develop an application (Figure 11-13).
- **Research:** Newspapers, technology magazines and journals, reference books, trade shows, the web, vendors, and consultants are excellent sources of information. These sources can provide the systems analyst with information, such as the latest hardware and software products and explanations of new processes and procedures. In addition, systems analysts often collect website statistics, such as the number of visitors and most-visited webpages, etc., and then evaluate these statistics as part of their research.

Figure 11-13 During a JAD session, the systems analyst is the moderator, or leader of the discussion. Another member, called the *scribe*, records facts and action items assigned during the session.

© Nyul / Dreamstime.com

 CONSIDER THIS

What circumstances initiate system development?
A user may request a new or modified information system for a variety of reasons. The most obvious reason is to correct a problem, such as an incorrect calculation or a security breach. Another reason is to improve the information system. Organizations may want to improve hardware, software, or other technology to enhance an information system.

Sometimes, situations outside the control of an organization require a modification to an information system. Corporate management or some other governing body may mandate a change. Mergers, reorganizations, and competition also can lead to change.

A user may request a new or modified information system verbally in a phone conversation or written as an email message. In larger organizations, users write a formal request for a new or modified information system, which is called a *project request* or *request for system services*. The project request becomes the first item of documentation for the project. It also triggers the first phase of system development: planning.

Discover More: Visit this chapter's free resources for the introduction to a system development case study, along with an example of a project request.

Planning Phase

The planning phase for a project begins when the steering committee receives a project request. This committee usually consists of five to nine people and typically includes a mix of vice presidents, managers, nonmanagement users, and IT personnel.

During the **planning phase**, four major activities are performed: (1) review and approve the project requests, (2) prioritize the project requests, (3) allocate resources, such as money, people, and equipment to approved projects, and (4) form a project development team for each approved project.

 CONSIDER THIS

How are projects prioritized?
The projects that receive the highest priority are those mandated by management or some other governing body. These requests are given immediate attention. The steering committee evaluates the remaining project requests based on their value to the organization. The steering committee approves some projects and rejects others. Of the approved projects, it is likely that only a few will begin system development immediately. Others will have to wait for additional funds or resources to become available.

Discover More: Visit this chapter's free resources for a discussion of the planning phase in a system development case study.

Analysis Phase

The **analysis phase** consists of two major activities: (1) conduct a preliminary investigation and (2) perform detailed analysis.

The Preliminary Investigation   The main purpose of the **preliminary investigation**, sometimes called the *feasibility study*, is to determine the exact nature of the problem or improvement and decide whether it is worth pursuing. Should the organization continue to assign resources to this project? To answer this question, the systems analyst conducts a general study of the project.

The first task in the preliminary investigation is to interview the user who submitted the project request. Depending on the nature of the request, project team members may interview other users, too. In addition to interviewing, members of the project team may use other data gathering techniques, such as reviewing existing documentation. Often, the preliminary investigation is completed in just a few days.

Upon completion of the preliminary investigation, the systems analyst writes the feasibility report. This report presents the team's findings to the steering committee.

Discover More: Visit this chapter's free resources for a discussion of the preliminary investigation process in the analysis phase in a system development case study, along with an example of a feasibility report.

Does the feasibility report always recommend that the project be continued?
In some cases, the project team may recommend to cancel the project. If the steering committee agrees, the project ends at this point. If the project team recommends continuing and the steering committee approves this recommendation, then detailed analysis begins.

Detailed Analysis   *Detailed analysis* involves three major activities: (1) study how the current system works, (2) determine the users' wants, needs, and requirements, and (3) recommend a solution. Detailed analysis sometimes is called *logical design* because the systems analysts develop the proposed solution without regard to any specific hardware or software. That is, they make no attempt to identify the procedures that should be automated and those that should be manual.

While studying the current system and identifying user requirements, the systems analyst collects a great deal of data and information. A major task for the systems analyst is to document these findings in a way that can be understood by everyone. Systems analysts use diagrams to describe the processes that transform inputs into outputs and diagrams that graphically show the flow of data in the system. Both users and IT professionals refer to this documentation.

The System Proposal   After the systems analyst has studied the current system and determined all user requirements, the next step is to communicate possible solutions for the project in a system proposal. The purpose of the system proposal is to assess the feasibility of each alternative solution and then recommend the most feasible solution for the project, which often involves modifying or expanding the current system. The systems analyst presents the system proposal to the steering committee. If the steering committee approves a solution, the project enters the design phase.

When the steering committee discusses the system proposal and decides which alternative to pursue, it considers whether to modify the existing system, buy retail software from an outside source, use web apps, build its own custom software, and/or outsource some or all of its IT needs to an outside firm. The final decision often is a mix of these options. Read Secure IT 11-2 for issues related to outsourcing.

Discover More: Visit this chapter's free resources for a discussion of the detailed analysis process in a system development case study, along with an example of a feasibility report.

 BTW

High-Tech Talk
Discover More: Visit this chapter's free resources to learn about process and object modeling.

 **Internet Research**

What is the difference between horizontal and vertical market software?

Search for: horizontal and vertical market software

 BTW

Technology Trend
Discover More: Visit this chapter's free resources to learn about custom crime fighting software.

Security Issues Arising from Outsourcing

Businesses outsource noncore functions because third-party vendors may be more efficient and more cost effective than the businesses trying to perform the functions on their own. Noncore functions often include general business tasks, such as maintaining and supporting an organization's information systems and processing customer payments on websites.

Sometimes, however, when a business outsources, the external vendors are not as careful with security and customer information as the business itself might be. The business that outsources this task has spent time and effort to cultivate and then forge a relationship with its customers, and it is in the company's best interest to treat its customers well. The outside vendor, however, has no such bond with the customers.

Security breaches might occur when work is contracted to third parties. For example, personal and confidential information about customers and employees, payroll, credit card numbers, and health records can be transferred to external hard drives or other storage media and taken outside the building. Companies should develop a computer security plan that requires safeguards on the part of the outside vendors. These procedures might include running background checks on personnel, closely monitoring the level of database access and email messages, replacing Social Security numbers with another unique identifier, and conducting security audits. The plan also should include penalties if a security breach occurs.

 Consider This: Does outsourcing lead to a lower level of security and privacy for customers? Why or why not? What can an organization do to ensure that vendors practice the same level of care with customer information as the organization practices? Should customers hold organizations or their vendors responsible for leaks of private customer information? Why?

Design Phase

The **design phase** consists of two major activities: (1) if necessary, acquire hardware and software and (2) develop all of the details of the new or modified information system. The systems analyst often performs these two activities at the same time instead of sequentially.

When the steering committee approves a solution, the systems analyst begins the activity of obtaining additional hardware or software or evaluating cloud providers that offer the computing services to meet the organization's needs. The systems analyst may skip this activity if the approved solution does not require new hardware or software. If this activity is required, it consists of four major tasks: (1) identify technical specifications, (2) solicit vendor proposals, (3) test and evaluate vendor proposals, and (4) make a decision.

Discover More: Visit this chapter's free resources to learn more about cloud providers.

Identify Technical Specifications The first step in acquiring necessary hardware and software is to identify all the hardware and software requirements of the new or modified system. To do this, systems analysts use a variety of research techniques. They talk with other systems analysts, visit vendors' stores, and search the web. Many trade journals, newspapers, and magazines provide some or all of their printed content online.

After the systems analyst defines the technical requirements, the next step is to summarize these requirements for potential vendors. The systems analyst can use three basic types of documents for this purpose: an RFQ, an RFP, or an RFI.

- A *request for quotation* (*RFQ*) identifies the required product(s). With an RFQ, the vendor quotes a price for the listed product(s).
- With a *request for proposal* (*RFP*), the vendor selects the product(s) that meets specified requirements and then quotes the price(s).
- A *request for information* (*RFI*) is a less formal method that uses a standard form to request information about a product or service.

Solicit Vendor Proposals Systems analysts send the RFQ, RFP, or RFI to potential hardware and software vendors. Another source for hardware and software products is a value-added reseller. A *value-added reseller* (*VAR*) is an organization that purchases products from manufacturers and then resells these products to the public — offering additional services with the product (Figure 11-14).

Instead of using vendors, some organizations hire an IT consultant or a group of IT consultants. An *IT consultant* is a professional who is hired based on technical expertise, including service and advice.

Test and Evaluate Vendor Proposals After sending RFQs, RFPs, or RFIs to potential vendors, the systems analyst will receive completed quotations and proposals. Evaluating the proposals and then selecting the best one often is a difficult task.

Systems analysts use many techniques to test the various software products from ven-

Internet Research
What are popular online technology magazines?
Search for: online technology magazines

BTW
Technology Innovator
Discover More: Visit this chapter's free resources to learn about Lenovo (personal computer vendor).

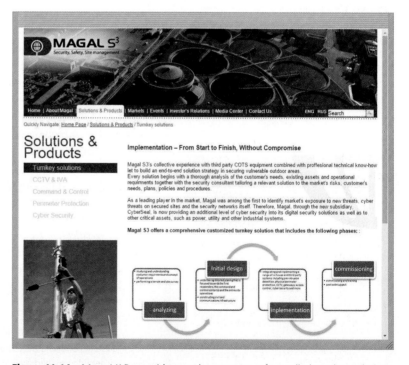

Figure 11-14 Many VARs provide complete systems, often called turnkey solutions.
Source: Magal Security Systems Ltd.

dors. They obtain a list of user references from the software vendors. They also talk to current users of the software to solicit their opinions. Some vendors will provide a demonstration of the product(s) specified. Others supply demonstration copies or trial versions, allowing the organizations to test the software themselves.

 **Internet Research**

What are the best benchmark tests for evaluating personal computers?

Search for: best pc benchmark tests

Sometimes it is important to know whether the software can process a certain volume of transactions efficiently. In this case, the systems analyst conducts a benchmark test. A *benchmark test* measures the performance of hardware or software. For example, a benchmark test could measure the time it takes a payroll program to print 50 paychecks. Comparing the time it takes various accounting programs to print the same 50 paychecks is one way of measuring each program's performance.

Make a Decision Having rated the proposals, the systems analyst presents a recommendation to the steering committee. The recommendation could be to award a contract to a vendor or to not make any purchases at this time.

Discover More: Visit this chapter's free resources for a discussion of the hardware acquisition process in the design phase in a system development case study.

Detailed Design The next step is to develop detailed design specifications for the components in the proposed solution. The activities to be performed include developing designs for the databases, inputs, outputs, and programs.

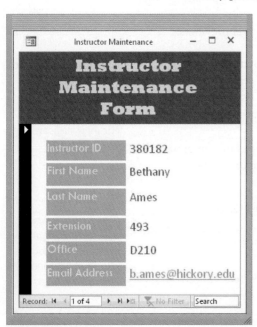

Figure 11-15 Users provide their approval on inputs and outputs. This input screen is a mock-up (containing actual sample data) for users to review.
Source: Microsoft

- During database design, the systems analyst works closely with the database administrators to identify those data elements that currently exist within the organization and those that are new. The systems analyst also addresses user access privileges.
- During detailed design of inputs and outputs, the systems analyst carefully designs every menu, screen, and report specified in the requirements. The outputs often are designed first because they help define the requirements for the inputs.

The systems analyst may develop a mock-up and/or a layout chart for each input and output. A *mock-up* is a sample of the input or output that contains actual data (Figure 11-15). The systems analyst shows mock-ups to users for their approval. After users approve the mock-up, the systems analyst develops a layout chart for the software developer. A layout chart is more technical and contains programming-like notations. Many database programs provide tools for technical design (Figure 11-16).

Other issues that must be addressed during input and output design include the types of media to use (paper, video, or audio); formats (graphical or narrative); and data entry validation techniques, which include making sure the entered data is correct (for example, a state code has to be one of the fifty valid two-letter state abbreviations).

- During program design, the systems analyst prepares the *program specification package*, which identifies required programs and the relationship among each program, as well as the input, output, and database specifications.

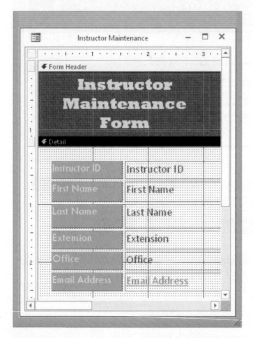

Figure 11-16 Shown here is a technical view in Access of the mock-up in Figure 11-15.
Source: Microsoft

✳ **CONSIDER THIS**

How can systems analysts build relationships with users?
Systems analysts have much more credibility with users if the analysts understand user concerns and have empathy for how the workers are feeling. If users are involved, they are more likely to accept and use the new system — called *user buy-in.* One reason systems fail is because some systems analysts create or modify systems with little or no user participation.

Prototyping Many systems analysts today use prototypes during detailed design. A **prototype**, sometimes called a *proof of concept*, is a working model of the proposed system's essential functionality. The systems analyst actually builds a functional form of the solution during design. The main advantage of a prototype is users can work with the system before it is completed to make sure it meets their needs. As soon as users approve a prototype, systems analysts can implement a solution more quickly than without a prototype.

 CONSIDER THIS

Who reviews the detailed design?

Many people should review the detailed design specifications before they are given to the programming team. The purpose of their review is to ensure the design represents a finished product that will work for the user and the development is feasible. Reviewers should include users, systems analysts, managers, IT staff, and members of the system development team. If the steering committee decides the project still is feasible, which usually is the case, the project enters the implementation phase.

Discover More: Visit this chapter's free resources for a discussion of the detailed design process in a system development case study.

Implementation Phase

The purpose of the **implementation phase** is to construct, or build, the new or modified system and then deliver it to the users. Members of the system development team perform four major activities in this phase: (1) develop programs and apps, (2) install and test the new system, (3) train users, and (4) convert to the new system.

Develop Programs and Apps If the organization purchases retail software or no modifications to existing custom software are required, the development team may skip this activity. For custom software that is new or requires modification, however, programs and apps are developed or modified either by an outside firm or in-house.

Software developers write or modify programs and apps from the program specification package created during the analysis phase. Just as system development follows an organized set of activities, so does program development. These program development activities are known as the *program development life cycle*.

 BTW

High-Tech Talk
Discover More: Visit this chapter's free resources to learn about programming logic.

 CONSIDER THIS

What is a sandbox?

A *sandbox* is an environment that allows software developers to test their programs with fictitious data without adversely affecting other programs, information systems, or data. Sandboxes are used for testing purposes both by developers and users. Users often work with a sandbox to familiarize themselves with a new program or information system before they use it.

Install and Test the New System If the organization acquires new hardware or software, someone must install and test it. The systems analysts should test individual programs. They also should be sure that all the programs work together in the system.

Systems analysts and users develop test data so that they can perform various tests.

- A *unit test* verifies that each individual program or object works by itself.
- A *systems test* verifies that all programs in an application work together properly.
- An *integration test* verifies that an application works with other applications.
- An *acceptance test* is performed by end users and checks the new system to ensure that it works with actual data.

Figure 11-17 Organizations must ensure that users are trained properly on the new system. One training method uses hands-on classes to learn the new system.
© Goodluz / Shutterstock.com

Train Users Training involves showing users exactly how they will use the new hardware and software in the system. Some training takes place as one-on-one sessions or classroom-style lectures (Figure 11-17). Other organizations use web-based training, which is a self-directed, self-paced online instruction method. Whichever technique is used, it should include hands-on sessions with realistic sample data. Users should practice on the actual system during training. Users also should be provided access to printed or online user manuals for reference. It is the systems analyst's responsibility to create user manuals.

Convert to the New System The final implementation activity is to change from the old system to the new system. This change can take place using one or more of the following conversion strategies: direct, parallel, phased, or pilot.

- With *direct conversion*, the user stops using the old system and begins using the new system on a certain date. The advantage of this strategy is that it requires no transition costs and is a quick implementation technique. The disadvantage is that it is extremely risky and can disrupt operations seriously if the new system does not work correctly the first time.
- *Parallel conversion* consists of running the old system alongside the new system for a specified time. Results from both systems are compared. The advantage of this strategy is that you can fix any problems in the new system before you terminate the old system. The disadvantage is that it is costly to operate two systems at the same time.
- In a *phased conversion*, each location converts at a separate time. For example, an accounting system might convert its accounts receivable, accounts payable, general ledger, and payroll sites in separate phases. Each site can use a direct or parallel conversion. Larger systems with multiple sites may use a phased conversion.
- With a *pilot conversion*, only one location in the organization uses the new system — so that it can be tested. After the pilot site approves the new system, other sites convert using one of the other conversion strategies.

Discover More: Visit this chapter's free resources for a discussion of the implementation phase in a system development case study.

Support and Security Phase

The purpose of the **support and security phase** is to provide ongoing assistance for an information system and its users after the system is implemented. The support and security phase consists of three major activities: (1) perform maintenance activities, (2) monitor system performance, and (3) assess system security.

Information system maintenance activities include fixing errors in, as well as improving, a system's operations. To determine initial maintenance needs, the systems analyst should meet with users. The purpose of this meeting, often called the *post-implementation system review*, is to discover whether the information system is performing according to the users' expectations. In some cases, users would like the system to do more. Maybe they have enhancements or additional requirements that involve modifying or expanding an existing information system.

During this phase, the systems analyst monitors performance of the new or modified information system. The purpose of performance monitoring is to determine whether the system is inefficient or unstable at any point. If it is, the systems analyst must investigate solutions to make the information system more efficient and reliable — back to the planning phase.

Most organizations must deal with complex technology security issues. All elements of an information system — hardware, software, data, people, and procedures — must be secure from threats both inside and outside the enterprise. Read Secure IT 11-3 for information about an organization's technology security plan.

 SECURE IT 11-3

Technology Security Plan Components

If an organization experiences a major information system disaster, a computer security plan will guide the recovery process. The document should identify all the security risks that may cause an information system asset loss and include all possible safeguards to detect, prevent, and recover from losses. It should identify all of the organization's information assets, which include hardware, software, documentation, procedures, people, data, facilities, and supplies. Key components should include securing equipment, especially laptops and mobile devices, creating a strong disaster recovery

strategy, developing a security breach detection and response plan, and providing for ongoing training.

One of the responsibilities of a chief security officer (CSO) is to protect the organization's information assets. The goal of the computer security plan is to match an appropriate level of safeguards against the identified risks. The CSO must realize that some degree of risk is unavoidable and that the more secure a system is, the more difficult it is for everyone to use. The security plan should be evaluated annually, or more frequently if information assets have changed dramatically. Microsoft has

developed a Security Development Lifecycle to guide the development, implementation, and review process. Its seven security practices phases — training, requirements, design, implementation, verification, release, and response — help increase security while reducing costs.

Consider This: What method should be used to communicate the plan to all employees and provide adequate training to ensure continued compliance? How can a CSO be assured that employees will comply with the computer security plan?

 NOW YOU SHOULD KNOW

Be sure you understand the material presented in the sections titled Database Management Systems and System Development, as it relates to the chapter objectives.
Now you should know . . .

- How you use a data dictionary, retrieve data in a database, keep data secure in a database, and back up a database (Objective 4)

- Which three guidelines typically are part of system development life cycles? (Objective 5)

- How users are involved with project management, feasibility assessment, documentation, and data and information gathering tasks in a system development project (Objective 6)

- What tasks are performed during the planning, analysis, design, implementation, and support and security phases of system development (Objective 7)

Discover More: Visit this chapter's premium content for practice quiz opportunities.

Application Development Languages and Tools

The previous sections discussed the system development phases. One activity during the implementation phase is to develop programs and apps. Although you may never write a program or app, information you request may require a software developer to create or modify a program or app. Thus, you should understand how software developers, sometimes called programmers, create programs and apps to meet information requirements.

To create a program, software developers sometimes write a program's instructions using a programming language. A **programming language** is a set of words, abbreviations, and symbols that enables a software developer to communicate instructions to a computer or mobile device. Other times, software developers use a program development tool to create a program or app. Software that provides a user-friendly environment for building programs and apps often is called an *application development tool*. An application development tool provides a means for creating, designing, editing, testing, and distributing programs and apps. Software developers use a variety of programming languages and application development tools to create programs and apps.

Several hundred programming languages exist today. Each language has its own rules, or *syntax*, for writing the instructions. Languages often are designed for specific purposes, such as scientific applications, business solutions, or webpage development. When solving a problem or building a solution, software developers often use more than one language; that is, they integrate the languages. Read Ethics & Issues 11-4 to consider whether programming courses should teach students how hackers write programs.

⚜ ETHICS & ISSUES 11-4

Should Colleges Teach Hacking?

Investigators often try to understand criminal minds in an attempt to identify what motivates criminals to commit crimes. Similarly, to allow students to experience the mind-set of a hacker, some colleges teach students how to write computer viruses and other malware. Hacking sometimes is taught as part of an advanced programming course or as a stand-alone course. One instructor teaches students how to thwart antivirus software and how to generate anonymous email spam. He claims that if college students easily bypass antivirus software, then the products clearly are deficient. Does any benefit exist from teaching students to hack?

Proponents of such courses claim that these hacking skills enable the next generation of security experts to think like malicious hackers, thereby helping to stop the spread of malware. They liken the gained skills to physics students who learn about atomic weapons or biology students who learn how poisons work. One software company supports teaching hacking to help software developers evaluate code for security risks.

Critics claim that this practice only encourages more virus authoring and hacking. Some developers of malware detection software have said they would not hire a student who had taken a hacking course. Others claim that knowing how to write malware does not make someone more capable of stopping malware. Questions remain about who is responsible legally, financially, and morally if a student uses the knowledge acquired in the course to release malicious code to the Internet or purposely infect other computers.

Consider This: Should colleges teach hacking? Why or why not? Should companies hire people who are trained in creating malware and computer hacking? Why or why not? What precautions should schools take if they plan to offer such courses? Who is responsible if a student in such a course releases malware? Why?

Procedural Languages

With a **procedural language**, a software developer writes instructions using English-like words that tell the computer what to accomplish and how to do it. For example, ADD stands for addition, or PRINT means to print. Many procedural languages also use arithmetic operators, such as * (asterisk) for multiplication and + (plus sign) for addition. Hundreds of procedural languages exist. Only a few, however, are used widely enough for the industry to recognize them as standards.

One example of a widely used procedural language is C. The **C** programming language, developed in the early 1970s by Dennis Ritchie at Bell Laboratories, originally was designed for writing system software. Today, many programs are written in C (Figure 11-18). C runs on almost any type of computer with any operating system, but it is used most often with the UNIX and Linux operating systems.

Discover More: Visit this chapter's free resources to learn more about the generations of programming languages, including machine languages, assembly languages, and procedural languages.

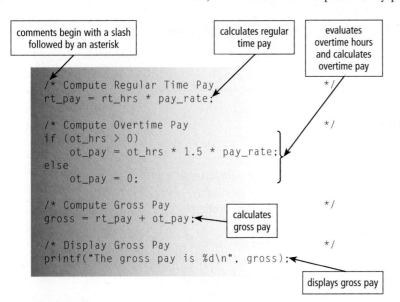

comments begin with a slash followed by an asterisk

calculates regular time pay

evaluates overtime hours and calculates overtime pay

calculates gross pay

displays gross pay

```
/* Compute Regular Time Pay          */
rt_pay = rt_hrs * pay_rate;

/* Compute Overtime Pay              */
if (ot_hrs > 0)
    ot_pay = ot_hrs * 1.5 * pay_rate;
else
    ot_pay = 0;

/* Compute Gross Pay                 */
gross = rt_pay + ot_pay;

/* Display Gross Pay                 */
printf("The gross pay is %d\n", gross);
```

Figure 11-18 An excerpt from a C payroll program. The code shows the computations for regular time pay, overtime pay, and gross pay; the decision to evaluate the overtime hours; and the output of the gross pay.
© Cengage Learning

Compilers and Interpreters Before a computer or mobile device can run (execute) a program or app created with a procedural language, system developers must convert the program into *machine language*, which is the only language the computer directly recognizes. That is, the computer cannot execute the procedural language source program. A *source program* contains the language instructions, or *code*, to be converted to machine language. For procedural languages, software developers typically use either a compiler or an interpreter to perform the conversion.

- A *compiler* is a separate program that converts the entire source program into machine language before executing it. The machine language version that results from compiling the procedural language is called the *object program* or *object code*. The compiler stores the object program on storage media for execution later.

  While it is compiling the source program into the object program, the compiler checks the source program for errors. The compiler then produces a program listing that contains the source code and a list of any errors. This listing helps the software developer make necessary changes to the source code and correct errors in the program. Figure 11-19 shows the process of compiling a source program.

- An *interpreter*, by contrast, translates and executes one instruction at a time. An interpreter reads an instruction, converts it to one or more machine language instructions, and then executes those machine language instructions. It does this all before moving to the next instruction in the program. Each time the source program runs, the interpreter translates and executes it, instruction by instruction. An interpreter does not produce an object program. Figure 11-20 shows the process of interpreting a program.

  One advantage of an interpreter is that when it finds errors, it displays feedback immediately. The software developer can correct any errors before the interpreter translates the next instruction. The disadvantage is that interpreted programs do not run as fast as compiled programs.

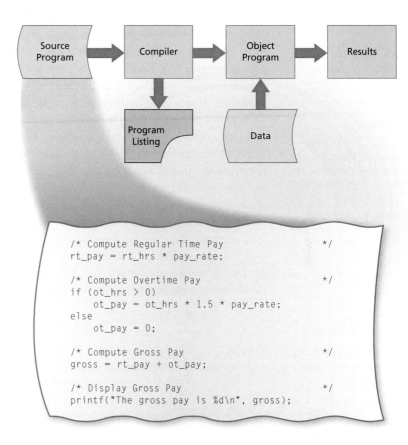

Figure 11-19 A compiler converts the source program (C, in this example) into a machine language object program.
© Cengage Learning

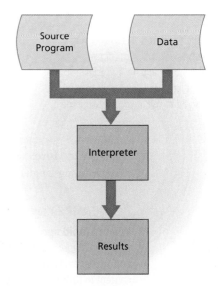

Figure 11-20 With an interpreter, one instruction of the source program at a time is converted into machine language and then immediately executed by the computer or mobile device.
© Cengage Learning

Object-Oriented Programming Languages and Application Development Tools

System developers use an **object-oriented programming (OOP) language** or object-oriented application development tool to implement objects in a program. Recall that an object is an item that can contain both data and the procedures that read or manipulate that data. An object represents a real person, place, event, or transaction.

A major benefit of OOP is the ability to reuse and modify existing objects. For example, once a system developer creates an Employee object, it is available for use by any other existing or future program. Thus, system developers repeatedly reuse existing objects. For example, a payroll program and health benefits program both would use an Employee object. That is, the payroll program would use it to process employee paychecks, and the health benefits program would use it to process health insurance payments.

Programs developed using the object-oriented programming languages and application development tools have several advantages. The objects can be reused in many systems, are designed for repeated use, and become stable over time. In addition, developers create applications faster because they design programs using existing objects. Programming languages, such as Java and C++, and the latest versions of Visual Basic are complete OOP languages. Most object-oriented application development tools, such as Visual Studio, are referred to as an *integrated development environment* (IDE) because they include tools for building graphical interfaces, an editor for entering program code, a compiler and/or interpreter, and a debugger (to remove errors). Some work with a single programming language, and others support multiple languages. Read How To 11-3 for instructions about selecting the object-oriented programming language and application development tools best suited to your needs.

BTW

Technology Innovator
Discover More: Visit this chapter's free resources to learn about Electronic Arts (entertainment software developer).

 HOW TO 11-3

Determine Which Object-Oriented Programming Language or Application Development Tool to Use

Software developers can choose from a variety of object-oriented programming languages and application development tools to write a program or app for a computer or mobile device. The following guidelines describe how to determine which language or tool to use:

• Determine the types of devices on which your program or app will run. For example, if you are writing an app for a mobile device, limited languages and tools may be available for you to use. If you are writing a

program or app that will run on a computer, more options will be available. Perform research and determine which types of programming languages can be used for various devices and operating systems.

• Determine the capabilities of the programming languages you are considering using. Some programming languages have greater capabilities than others.

• Consider the speed at which programs and apps run that are written in a particular programming language. For example, a program or app might run faster if it is written in one language as opposed to another.

• Consider whether you want to write a program using a text editor or an IDE. If you want to use an IDE, your choices of programming languages may be limited.

• Solicit recommendations from other developers. Explain the type of program or app you plan to write, and consider suggestions they might offer.

Consider This: If you are forced to write a program or app using a programming language with which you are not very familiar, what resources can you utilize to obtain assistance?

Discover More: Visit this chapter's free resources to learn more about object-oriented programming languages and application development tools.

CONSIDER THIS

What is rapid application development?
RAD (rapid application development) is a method of developing software in which the software developer writes and implements a program in segments instead of waiting until the entire program is completed. An important concept in RAD is the use of prebuilt components. For example, software developers do not have to write code for buttons and text boxes on Windows forms because they already exist in the programming language or application development tools provided with the language. Object-oriented programming languages and application development tools work well in a RAD environment.

Java **Java** is an object-oriented programming language developed by Sun Microsystems. Figure 11-21 shows a portion of a Java program and the window that the program displays. When software developers compile a Java program, the resulting object program is machine independent. Software developers use various Java Platform implementations, which provide application development tools for creating programs for all sizes of computers and mobile devices.

```
public class BodyMassApplet extends Applet implements ActionListener
{
        //declare variables
        Image logo; //declare an Image object
        int inches, pounds;
        double meters, kilograms, index;

        //construct components
        Label companyLabel = new Label("THE SUN FITNESS CENTER BODY MASS INDEX CALCULATOR");
        Label heightLabel = new Label("Enter your height to the nearest inch   ");
            TextField heightField = new TextField(10);
        Label weightLabel = new Label ("Enter your weight to the nearest pound  ");
            TextField weightField = new TextField(10);
        Button calcButton = new Button("Calculate");
        Label outputLabel = new Label(
        "Click the Calculate button to see your Body Mass Index.");

            inches = Integer.parseInt(heightField.getText());
            pounds = Integer.parseInt(weightField.getText());
            meters = inches / 39.36;
            kilograms = pounds / 2.2;
            index = kilograms / Math.pow(meters,2);
            outputLabel.setText("YOUR BODY MASS INDEX IS " + Math.round(index) + ".");
        }

        public void paint(Graphics g)
        {
            g.drawImage(logo,125,160,this);
        }
}
```

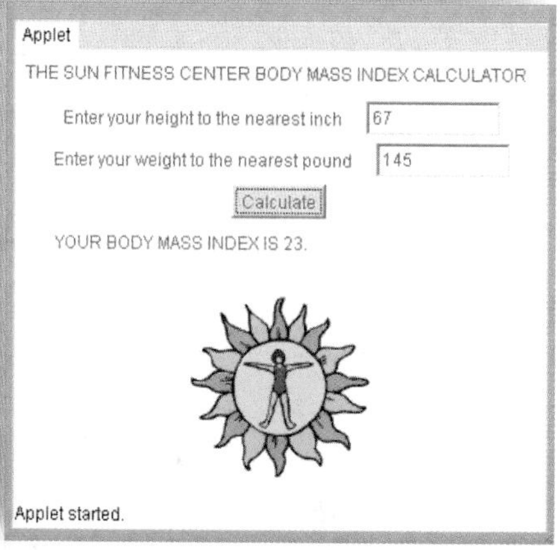

Applet

THE SUN FITNESS CENTER BODY MASS INDEX CALCULATOR

Enter your height to the nearest inch   `67`

Enter your weight to the nearest pound `145`

[Calculate]

YOUR BODY MASS INDEX IS 23.

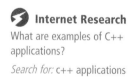

Applet started.

Figure 11-21 A portion of a Java program and the window the program displays.
© Cengage Learning

C++ Developed in the 1980s by Bjarne Sroustrup at Bell Laboratories, **C++** (pronounced SEE-plus-plus) is an object-oriented programming language that is an extension of the C programming language. C++ includes all the elements of the C language, plus it has additional features for working with objects. Software developers commonly use C++ to develop database and web applications.

Visual Studio Developed by Microsoft, **Visual Studio** contains a suite of object-oriented application development tools that assists software developers in building programs and apps for Windows or any operating system that supports the Microsoft .NET Framework. Visual Studio also includes a set of tools for developing programs and apps that work with Microsoft's Office suite. OOPs included in the Visual Studio suite are Visual Basic, Visual C++, and Visual C#.

Internet Research
What are examples of C++ applications?
Search for: c++ applications

Internet Research
What is Visual Studio Express?
Search for: visual studio express

CONSIDER THIS

What is .NET?
The Microsoft .NET Framework, or *.NET* (pronounced dot net), is a set of technologies that allows almost any type of program to run on the Internet or an internal business network, as well as stand-alone computers and mobile devices. Similarly, *ASP.NET* is a web application framework that provides the tools necessary for the creation of dynamic websites.

 BTW
Visual Basic
Visual Basic is based on the BASIC programming language, which was developed by Microsoft Corporation in the early 1960s. Because this language is easy to learn and use, beginning programmers often use it.

 CONSIDER THIS

What is a visual programming language?
A *visual programming language* is a language that uses a visual or graphical interface for creating all source code. The graphical interface, called a *visual programming environment* (*VPE*), allows system developers to drag and drop objects to build programs and apps.
Discover More: Visit this chapter's free resources to learn more about visual programming languages.

Other Languages and Application Development Tools

The following sections discuss a variety of other programming languages and application development tools.

4GLs A **4GL** (*fourth-generation language*) is a nonprocedural language that enables users and software developers to access data in a database. With a *nonprocedural language*, the software developer writes English-like instructions or interacts with a graphical environment to retrieve data from files or a database. Many object-oriented application development tools use 4GLs. One popular 4GL is SQL. As discussed earlier in this chapter, SQL is a query language that allows users to manage, update, and retrieve data in a relational DBMS.

BTW
Technology Trend
Discover More: Visit this chapter's free resources to learn about programs behind Mars Rover.

Classic Programming Languages In addition to the programming languages discussed on the previous pages, software developers sometimes use the languages to maintain legacy systems. These languages, which include BASIC, COBOL, FORTRAN, and RPG, were more widely used in the past than they are today.
Discover More: Visit this chapter's free resources to learn more about classic programming languages.

Application Generators An application generator is a program that creates source code or machine code from a specification of the required functionality. When using an application generator, a software developer or user works with menu-driven tools and graphical user interfaces to define the desired specifications. Application generators most often are bundled with or are included as part of a DBMS. An application generator typically consists of a report writer and forms (discussed earlier in this chapter), and a menu generator. A menu generator enables you to create a menu for the application options.

Macros A **macro** is a series of statements that instructs a program or app how to complete a task. Macros allow users to automate routine, repetitive, or difficult tasks in application software, such as word processing, spreadsheet (Figure 11-22), or database programs. That is, users can create simple programs within the application by writing macros. You usually create a macro in one of two ways: (1) record the macro or (2) write the macro.

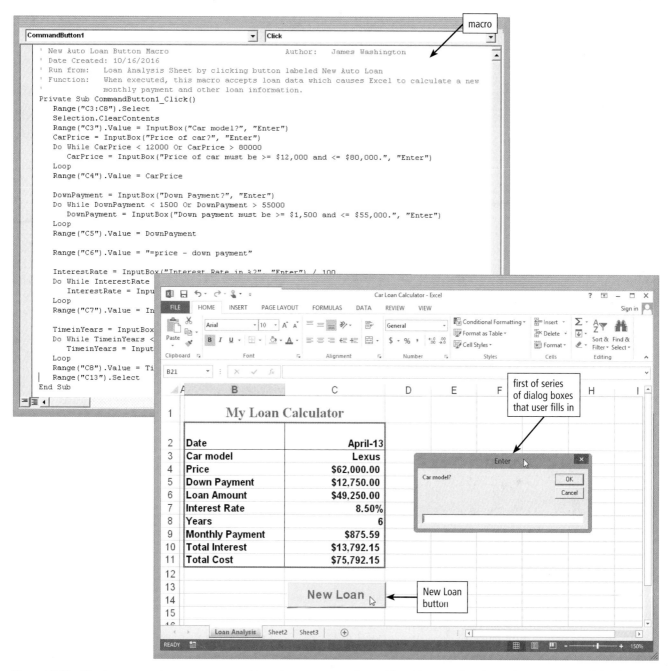

Figure 11-22   The top screen shows a macro used to automate an auto loan. After this macro is written, the user taps or clicks the New Loan button to run the macro. The bottom screen shows the macro guiding the user through part of the data entry process.
Source: Microsoft

CONSIDER THIS

Why and how would you record a macro?

If you want to automate a routine or repetitive task such as formatting or editing, you would record a macro. A *macro recorder* is similar to a movie camera because both record all actions until turned off. To record a macro, start the macro recorder in the software. Then, perform the steps to be part of the macro, such as taps, clicks, or keystrokes. Once the macro is recorded, you can run it any time you want to perform that same sequence of actions. For example, if you always print three copies of certain documents, you could record the actions required to print three copies. To print three copies, you would run the macro called PrintThreeCopies. When you become familiar with programming techniques, you can write your own macros instead of recording them. Read Secure IT 11-4 for security issues related to macros.

SECURE IT 11-4

Protection from Macro Viruses

More than 20 years ago, the first macro viruses wreaked havoc with personal computers. Now, the same macro coding techniques are being used to create malware infecting smartphones. For example, the Selfmite worm sends text messages with malicious links to the owner's contacts.

As the name implies, a macro virus hides in a program's macro language. Malware authors find that one of the easiest methods of spreading viruses and worms is by distributing apps and files containing macro viruses. This type of virus is easy to write, and the damage that results from infecting smartphones and computers can exceed millions of dollars.

Because many computers and smartphones have acquired damaging macro viruses, antivirus and productivity software companies have strengthened their efforts to prevent this malware from infecting their products. One method, for example, disables the macros, which prohibits users from running once-automated tasks on their computers. The users, however, are frustrated when they now must perform routines manually. Other prevention measures include setting the software's macro security level to high, not installing apps from unknown sources, not opening unexpected file attachments, and holding down the SHIFT key when opening a file that may be infected by a macro virus so that any automatic macros are prevented from running.

Many smartphone and computer users claim the software companies should make it impossible for malware authors to take advantage of security problems in the software. The software companies, however, place the blame on users who install apps and open files from unknown sources.

✹ **Consider This:** Should users or software companies be held accountable for macro security threats? Why? How can smartphone and computer users best be educated about opening text messages and documents from unknown sources?

Web Development

The designers of webpages, known as *web developers*, use a variety of techniques to create and publish webpages. The following sections discuss these techniques. Read How To 11-4 for instructions about publishing webpages.

 HOW TO 11-4

Publish a Webpage

After creating a webpage, you will need to publish it on a web server so that it is accessible online. The method you use to publish a webpage can vary, depending upon a number of factors. For example, if you created a webpage using a content management system or web app, the webpage may be available online automatically, or you may be able to use a feature in the content management system or web app to publish the webpage. If you created the webpage using a program or app on your computer, the following sections describe various ways to publish the webpage.

1. Identify the web hosting company you want to use.

2. Navigate to and review the documentation explaining how to publish your webpage. Some web hosting companies require you to publish the webpage using a specific set of steps, while others are more flexible.

3. Publish the webpage using one of the web hosting company's recommended methods:

- Some web hosting companies will allow you to publish your webpage using a web app or file transfer program that is part of their website. Select the files you want to transfer from your computer, select the destination (if necessary), and then tap or click the appropriate button or link that will initiate the transfer.

- Some web hosting companies, businesses, or universities allow you to publish webpages using FTP or SFTP (secure FTP). Download and install a program or app that supports the required protocol (FTP or SFTP). Run the program and enter the required information to connect to the web hosting company's server. (The required information, such as the server address, user name, and password, is available from the web hosting company.) Next, connect to the server, select the file(s) you want to transfer from your computer

and the location on the web hosting company's server where you want to transfer the files, and then initiate the transfer.

4. Once the transfer has completed, run a browser.

5. Navigate to your webpage. Your web hosting company should have provided the web address for accessing the webpage.

6. If your webpage does not display properly, verify that you entered the correct web address and ensure the web server is functional. Lastly, consider contacting your web hosting company's technical support staff for additional assistance.

✹ **Consider This:** Does one method of publishing webpages have any advantages over another? Which method described previously in Step 3 appears to be the easiest?

HTML **HTML** (*Hypertext Markup Language*) is a special formatting language that software developers use to format documents for display on the web. You view a webpage written with HTML in a browser, such as Internet Explorer, Safari, Firefox, Opera, or Chrome. Figure 11-23a shows part of the HTML code used to create the webpage shown in Figure 11-23b.

Figure 11-23a (portion of HTML code)

Figure 11-23b
(portion of resulting
webpage)

Figure 11-23 The portion of the HTML code in Figure 11-23a generates a portion of the Cengage Learning CengageBrain webpage shown in Figure 11-23b.
Source: Cengage Learning

CONSIDER THIS

Is HTML a programming language?

HTML is not actually a programming language. It is, however, a language that has specific rules for defining the placement and format of text, graphics, video, and audio on a webpage. HTML uses tags or elements, which are words, abbreviations, and symbols that specify links to other documents and indicate how a webpage is displayed when viewed on the web.

XML XML (*Extensible Markup Language*) is an increasingly popular format for sharing data that allows web developers to create tags that describe the structure of information. XML separates the webpage content from its format, allowing the browser to display the contents of a webpage in a form appropriate for the display device. For example, RSS feeds (web feeds) are represented as XML. A webpage can read the feed's content as described by XML and then apply styles and consistent formatting to each element (title, link, description) to display it within a browser.

Wireless devices use a subset of XML called WML. *WML (wireless markup language)* allows web developers to design pages specifically for microbrowsers. Many smartphones and other mobile devices use WML as their markup language.

 CONSIDER THIS

What are some applications of XML?

Two applications of XML are the RSS 2.0 and ATOM specifications. *RSS 2.0*, which stands for Really Simple Syndication, and *ATOM* are specifications that content aggregators use to distribute content to subscribers. The online publisher creates an RSS or ATOM document, called a web feed, that is made available to websites for publication. News websites, blogs, and podcasts often use web feeds to publish headlines and stories. Most browsers can read web feeds, meaning they can display titles, links, descriptions, and other information about pages identified in the feed.

Internet Research

What is Ruby on Rails?

Search for: ruby on rails

Scripting and Other Web Development Languages To add interactivity on webpages and to add special media effects, such as animated graphics, scrolling messages, calendars, and advertisements, web developers write small programs called scripts using a variety of scripting languages. Although some use languages previously discussed, such as Java and C++, many developers instead use scripting languages. A *scripting language* is an interpreted language that typically is easy to learn and use. Popular scripting and other web development languages include JavaScript (Figure 11-24), Perl, PHP, Python, and Ruby.

Discover More: Visit this chapter's free resources to learn more about scripting and other web development languages.

Mini Feature 11-3: Web Application Development

Three technologies form the foundation for many web applications: HTML5 specifies the structure of content displayed on a webpage; CSS (cascading style sheets) describes the design and appearance of information on a webpage; and JavaScript is a scripting language that allows users to interact with a webpage's content. Many web applications also access applications running on a server, connect to a database, or access third-party content from online sources. Together, these technologies enable developers to create browser-independent web applications that run on a variety of devices.

As discussed in an earlier chapter, the W3C (World Wide Web Consortium) is an international organization that sets the standards for the technologies and operation of the web. In addition, it defines the standards for HTML5 and CSS. Read Mini Feature 11-3 to learn about technologies that enable developers to create browser-independent web applications.

Figure 11-24a (JavaScript code)

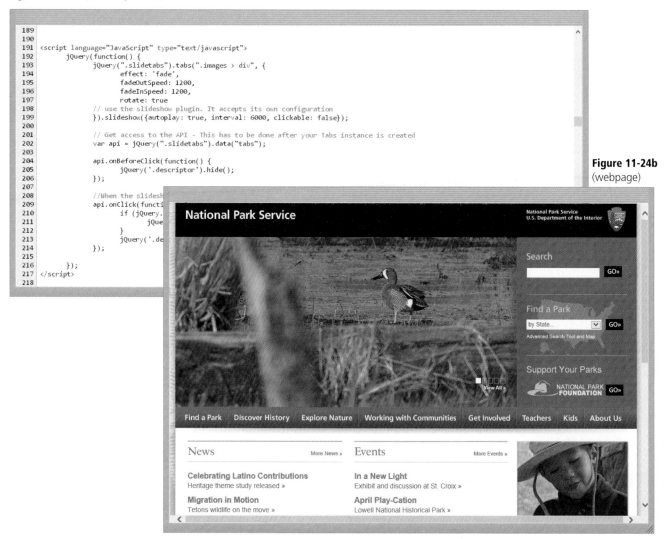

```
189
190
191  <script language="JavaScript" type="text/javascript">
192      jQuery(function() {
193          jQuery(".slidetabs").tabs(".images > div", {
194              effect: 'fade',
195              fadeOutSpeed: 1200,
196              fadeInSpeed: 1200,
197              rotate: true
198          // use the slideshow plugin. It accepts its own configuration
199          }).slideshow({autoplay: true, interval: 6000, clickable: false});
200
201          // Get access to the API - This has to be done after your Tabs instance is created
202          var api = jQuery(".slidetabs").data("tabs");
203
204          api.onBeforeClick(function() {
205              jQuery('.descriptor').hide();
206          });
207
208          //When the slidesh
209          api.onClick(functi
210              if (jQuery.
211                  jQue
212              }
213              jQuery('.de
214          });
215
216      });
217  </script>
218
```

Figure 11-24b
(webpage)

Figure 11-24 Shown here is a portion of the JavaScript code and its associated National Park Service webpage.
Source: National Park Service U.S. Department of the Interior

 **MINI FEATURE 11-3**

Web Application Development

To develop a web application, web developers use HTML5, CSS, and JavaScript.

HTML5

HTML5 is the current HTML standard for creating websites and applications. HTML uses a set of codes called tags to instruct a browser how to structure a webpage's content. HTML tags specify the structure of content on a webpage, such as headings, paragraphs, links, or images. HTML5 includes tags for playing audio and video files without relying on the use of third-party plug-ins or modules, such as Adobe Flash, to perform these tasks. Some mobile devices and computers, such as Apple's iPhone and iPad, do not support displaying media content that requires Flash. Instead, they rely on HTML5-compliant browsers, which are capable of interpreting HTML5 tags, to handle these tasks.

Additional HTML5 features include recognizing gestures, such as swipe or drag-and-drop, on mobile devices; dynamically creating graphics, such as progress bars, charts, and animations; *geolocation* (determining a user's location based on a device's GPS or connection to a cell tower); and offline storage. For example, Google Drive uses HTML5's drag-and-drop feature so that you can organize documents and uses its offline storage feature to allow you to work with your documents when you do not have an Internet connection. Twitter makes use of HTML5's geolocation feature when users search for Tweets that originate near a specific location.

Source: HTML5 Logo by World Wide
WebConsortium

(continued)

These HTML5 features enable web developers to build applications that address the needs of how people use the web today and provide richer user experiences. Each browser implements the HTML5 specification differently and may not support all of its features.

CSS

While HTML describes the structure of a webpage's content as a collection of elements (such as headings, paragraphs, images, and links), CSS allows web designers to separate the code that specifies a webpage's content from the code that specifies the webpage's appearance. For example, a webpage may contain two paragraphs of text that are presented using a variety of fonts and sizes, styles, colors, borders, thicknesses, columns, or backgrounds. CSS provides web designers with precise control over a webpage's layout and allows the designers to apply different layouts to the same information for printing or for viewing in browsers on smartphones, tablets, or computers with varying screen sizes. The current version of CSS is known as CSS3 (cascading style sheets, version 3).

JavaScript

JavaScript is a programming language that adds interactivity to webpages. It often is used to check for appropriate values on web forms, display alert messages, display menus on webpages, control the appearance of a browser window, read and write cookies, display alert boxes, and detect the browser version in order to display a webpage especially designed for that browser. JavaScript code is loaded with a webpage and runs in the browser.

Developing Websites and Applications with HTML5, CSS, and JavaScript

Web developers often use tools, such as the one shown in the figure, to create their code and visualize what it will look like in a browser. In this example, HTML5 specifies a heading, a paragraph, and a link; CSS specifies the page background color and fonts, while JavaScript instructs the page to display an alert box when it loads.

Discover More: Visit this chapter's free resources to learn more about web development using HTML5, CSS3, and JavaScript.

⚙ **Consider This:** What are two advantages and two disadvantages of writing mobile apps using HTML5, CSS, and JavaScript? Before HTML5's geolocation features, how might a web app have determined a user's approximate location? Some web-based email services, such as Gmail, use HTML5, CSS, and JavaScript. Name a feature of Gmail that might demonstrate a characteristic of each of these technologies.

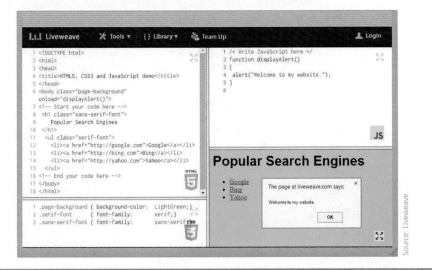

Source: Liveweave

✅ NOW YOU SHOULD KNOW

Be sure you understand the material presented in the section titled Application Development Languages and Tools, as it relates to the chapter objectives.
Now you should know . . .

- How your computer works with low-level and procedural languages (Objective 8)
- Why you would use an OOP language or application development tool (Objective 9)
- How you can develop webpages and web apps (Objective 10)

Discover More: Visit this chapter's premium content for practice quiz opportunities.

🕹 Chapter Summary

This chapter discussed the hierarchy of data, ways to validate data, the advantages of the database versus the file processing approach, and characteristics of database management systems. It also discussed the system development phases and the guidelines for system development, along with activities that occur during system development, including project management, feasibility assessment, documentation, and data and information gathering. This chapter also reviewed various programming languages and application development tools used to create and modify computer programs. Finally, it described a variety of web development tools.

Discover More: Visit this chapter's free resources for additional content that accompanies this chapter and also includes these features: Technology Innovators: E. F. Codd, Oracle/Larry Ellison, Lenovo, and Electronic Arts; Technology Trends: Forensic Databases, Custom Crime Fighting Software, and Programs behind Mars Rover; and High-Tech Talks: Types of Databases, Database Design, and the Normalization Process; Process and Object Modeling; and Programming Logic.

Test your knowledge of chapter material by accessing the Study Guide, Flash Cards, and Practice Test resources from your smartphone, tablet, laptop, or desktop.

⚡ TECHNOLOGY @ WORK

Sports

While watching your local football team play an out-of-state game on television, you notice various player and game statistics appear on the screen, alerting you to how many yards the offense must travel before making a first down. The camera then focuses on the large, colorful, high-resolution scoreboard at the stadium. While sports, such as football, have been around for many decades, the integration of technology has added significantly to the viewing experience.

While watching a baseball game, you notice that the scoreboard shows the number of balls and strikes for the player at bat, as well as other statistics. Behind home plate, an electronic radar gun calculates and records the speed of each pitch. This recorded data, along with the umpire's call (ball or strike) and the player's performance at bat (hit, home run, strike out, etc.) are entered in a computer, which updates the player's batting average automatically. A database stores information about the individual players and other aspects of the baseball game. During this entire time, the video display on the stadium's scoreboard plays audio and video to entertain the fans. The computer storing the player and game statistics, audio, and video communicates with the scoreboard and video display using either a wired or wireless connection. At the

same time, these computers send updated scores and statistics to webpages and mobile devices.

Technology not only is used to keep track of athlete statistics and communicate with scoreboards, but also in racing to help measure a vehicle's performance before a race. Sensors installed on a vehicle can measure throttle inputs, airflow over the body, the distance between the vehicle's frame and the track, and more. The racing teams then can modify the vehicle so that

it achieves maximum performance during a race.

Overall, technology adds enjoyment to various sporting events for many individuals. While waiting for a pitcher to throw the next ball or for a football team to start its next play, keep in mind that the integration of technology entertains you with interesting statistics and replays between the action.

✴ **Consider This:** How else might computers and technology be used in sports?

© Przemek Tokar / Shutterstock.com

Study Guide

The Study Guide exercise reinforces material you should know for the chapter exam.

Discover More: Visit this chapter's premium content to **test your knowledge of digital content** associated with this chapter and **access the Study Guide resource** from your smartphone, tablet, laptop, or desktop.

Instructions: Answer the questions below using the format that helps you remember best or that is required by your instructor. Possible formats may include one or more of these options: write the answers; create a document that contains the answers; record answers as audio or video using a webcam, smartphone, or portable media player; post answers on a blog, wiki, or website; or highlight answers in the book/e-book.

1. Define the terms, database and database software. Identify the role of a file, record, and field in database hierarchy.

2. Define these terms: field, field name, and data type. List common data types.

3. Identify what is stored in a record. Explain the importance of a primary key.

4. Define the term, data file. Identify what is involved in file maintenance.

5. Explain the issues surrounding companies using customer data.

6. Explain how a DBMS might manage deleted or obsolete records.

7. Define the term, validation. List types of validity checks and explain what occurs in each.

8. Explain the disadvantages of typical file processing systems. Describe the database approach to storing data.

9. Explain the issues surrounding use of criminal databases.

10. Differentiate between a front-end and back-end program. Explain the advantages and disadvantages of the database approach.

11. Explain how you access data in a web database. Describe the role of a database server.

12. Identify uses of web databases for government, entertainment, travel, shopping, research, and education.

13. A(n) _____ defines how users view the organization of the data. List four popular data models.

14. List possible uses of an object-oriented database.

15. Explain the characteristics, sources, and uses of Big Data. Describe what occurs during data visualization.

16. Describe the role of the database administrator.

17. Define the term, data dictionary. Explain how a data dictionary helps ensure data integrity.

18. A(n) _____ is a request for specific information from a database.

19. List steps to import and export data between a spreadsheet and a database.

20. Define the terms query language, SQL, and QBE.

21. Define the terms, form and report writer.

22. Explain how access privileges contribute to data security. List steps to secure and maintain a database.

23. Explain issues surrounding accidental access of confidential data. List methods to recover from identity theft.

24. List methods to restore or backup a database. Differentiate between rollforward and rollback recovery.

25. Identify the five phases in the SDLC. Name three guidelines for system development.

26. Identify who participates in system development. Describe the responsibilities of a systems analyst.

27. Define the term, project management. List elements the project leader must identify.

28. Define the function of project management software. A(n) _____ is any tangible item, such as a chart, diagram, report, or program file.

29. Describe how Gantt and PERT charts are used.

30. Define the terms, scope creep and change management.

31. Identify tests used to evaluate feasibility of a project. Explain the importance of documentation.

32. Describe ways that team members collaborate.

33. Identify data and information gathering techniques. A(n) _____ session also is called a focus group.

34. Describe circumstances that can initiate system development.

35. List the four activities of the planning phase. Explain how projects are prioritized.

36. Describe the activities of the analysis phase. List the three activities of the detailed analysis phase.

37. Explain security issues surrounding outsourcing.

38. List the two activities of the design phase. Describe how a systems analyst obtains hardware or software.

39. Differentiate among an RFQ, RFP, and RFI. Describe the roles of VARs and IT consultants when soliciting vendor proposals.

40. Explain what occurs when vendor proposals are tested and evaluated. A(n) _____ test measures the performance of hardware or software.

41. Explain the activities and users involved in the detailed design phase. Define the term, prototype.

42. List the four activities of the implementation phase.

43. List the three activities of the support and security phase. Describe components of a technology security plan.

44. Define the following terms: programming language, application development tool, and syntax.

45. Explain issues surrounding colleges teaching students how to hack.

46. Define the terms, procedural language, compiler, machine language, and interpreter. List benefits of OOP languages.

47. Describe the following: 4GLs, classic programming languages, application generators, and macros. Explain how to protect yourself from macro viruses.

48. List steps to publish a webpage. Explain how web developers use HTML5, XML, WML, CSS, and JavaScript.

49. Explain how the sports industry uses technology.

You should be able to define the Primary Terms and be familiar with the Secondary Terms listed below.

Key Terms

Discover More: Visit this chapter's premium content to **view definitions** for each term and to **access the Flash Cards** resource from your smartphone, tablet, laptop, or desktop.

Primary Terms (shown in **bold-black** characters in the chapter)

4GL (532)
analysis phase (521)
Big Data (508)
C (528)
C++ (531)
character (500)
continuous backup (515)
data dictionary (510)
data file (501)
data model (508)
data type (500)
database (498)
database management system (DBMS) (498)
database software (498)
design phase (523)

feasibility (519)
field (500)
field name (500)
file maintenance (502)
file processing system (504)
form (512)
HTML (535)
implementation phase (525)
Java (531)
log (515)
macro (532)
object-oriented programming (OOP) language (530)

planning phase (521)
preliminary investigation (521)
primary key (501)
procedural language (528)
programming language (527)
project management (517)
project management software (518)
prototype (525)
query (511)
query language (512)
record (501)

recovery utility (515)
report writer (513)
Structured Query Language (SQL) (512)
support and security phase (526)
system development (515)
system development life cycle (SDLC) (515)
systems analyst (517)
training (526)
validation (503)
Visual Studio (531)
XML (536)

Secondary Terms (shown in *italic* characters in the chapter)

.NET (532)
acceptance test (525)
alphabetic check (503)
application development tool (527)
ASP.NET (532)
ATOM (536)
back end (505)
backward recovery (515)
benchmark test (524)
BLOB (501)
Boolean (501)
change management (519)
check digit (503)
code (529)
collaborative databases (506)
compiler (529)
completeness check (503)
composite key (501)
conferencing software (520)
consistency check (503)
cost/benefit feasibility (519)
CSS (cascading style sheets) (537)
data entry form (512)
data warehouse (508)
database administrator (DBA) (510)
database server (506)
deliverable (518)
detailed analysis (522)
direct conversion (526)
distributed database (508)
documentation (519)
economic feasibility (519)

e-form (512)
Extensible Markup Language (536)
feasibility study (521)
feature creep (519)
focus group (520)
forward recovery (515)
fourth-generation language (532)
front end (505)
function creep (502)
Gantt chart (518)
geolocation (537)
HTML5 (537)
Hypertext Markup Language (535)
information system (515)
integrated development environment (IDE) (530)
integration test (525)
interpreter (529)
IT consultant (523)
JavaScript (537)
joint-application design (JAD) session (520)
logical design (522)
machine language (529)
macro recorder (533)
metadata (508)
mock-up (524)
multidimensional database (508)
nonprocedural language (532)
numeric check (503)
object (508)
object code (529)

object program (529)
object-oriented database (OODB) (528)
operational feasibility (519)
parallel conversion (526)
PERT chart (518)
phased conversion (526)
phases (515)
pilot conversion (526)
post-implementation system review (526)
principle of least privilege policy (513)
program development life cycle (525)
program specification package (524)
project leader (517)
project manager (517)
project request (521)
project team (517)
proof of concept (525)
query by example (QBE) (512)
RAD (rapid application development) (530)
range check (503)
relational database (508)
report generator (513)
repository (510)
request for information (RFI) (523)
request for proposal (RFP) (523)
request for quotation (RFQ) (523)
request for system services (521)

rollback (515)
rollforward (515)
RSS 2.0 (536)
sandbox (525)
schedule feasibility (519)
scope (517)
scope creep (519)
scribe (520)
scripting language (536)
source program (529)
standards (517)
steering committee (517)
syntax (528)
systems test (525)
technical feasibility (519)
unit test (525)
user buy-in (524)
value-added reseller (VAR) (523)
visual programming environment (VPE) (532)
visual programming language (532)
web conference (520)
web developers (534)
WML (wireless markup language) (536)

Gantt chart (518)

Checkpoint

The Checkpoint exercises test your knowledge of the chapter concepts. The page number containing the answer appears in parentheses after each exercise. The Consider This exercises challenge your understanding of chapter concepts.

Discover More: Visit this chapter's premium content to **complete the Checkpoint exercises** interactively; complete the **self-assessment in the Test Prep resource** from your smartphone, tablet, laptop, or desktop; and then **take the Practice Test.**

True/False   Mark T for True and F for False.

_____ 1. In a data hierarchy, each higher level of data contains one or more items from the lower level. (500)

_____ 2. A check digit often confirms the accuracy of a primary key value. (503)

_____ 3. In a typical database system, each department or area within an organization has its own set of files. (504)

_____ 4. In a file processing system, duplicated data can increase the chance of errors. (504)

_____ 5. Many programs today use forms on a webpage as their front end. (505)

_____ 6. File processing systems require more memory, storage, and processing power than a database. (506)

_____ 7. To retrieve or select data in a database, you query it. (511)

_____ 8. Unlike a form, you use a report writer only to retrieve data. (513)

_____ 9. One way to secure a database is to allow only administrators to have access to create and delete tables. (513)

_____ 10. In a rollforward, the DBMS uses the log to undo any changes made to the database during a certain period. (515)

_____ 11. Gantt charts are better suited than PERT charts for planning and scheduling large, complex projects. (518)

_____ 12. The planning phase begins when the steering committee receives a project request. (521)

Multiple Choice   Select the best answer.

1. A(n) _____ check tests data in two or more associated fields to ensure that the relationship is logical and their data is in the correct format. (503)
   a. completeness
   b. consistency
   c. range
   d. alphabetic

2. Which of the following is *not* an advantage of a database approach? (506)
   a. data integrity
   b. reduced data redundancy
   c. shared data
   d. requires less memory, storage, and processing power than file processing systems

3. A _____ defines how users view the organization of data in a database. (508)
   a. data dictionary
   b. data mart
   c. data model
   d. report writer

4. A(n) _____ database stores data in tables that consist of rows and columns. (508)
   a. object-oriented   c. relational
   b. multidimensional   d. distributed

5. A _____ contains data about each file in the database and each field in those files. (510)
   a. query
   b. form
   c. data dictionary
   d. data mart

6. Which of the following is *not* a phase in the SDLC? (515)
   a. planning
   b. analysis
   c. implementation
   d. converting

7. _____ feasibility measures whether an organization has or can obtain the computing resources, software services, and qualified people needed to develop, deliver, and then support the proposed information system. (519)
   a. Operational   c. Economic
   b. Technical   d. Schedule

8. Systems analysts use a(n) _____ test to verify that all programs in an application work together properly. (525)
   a. unit   c. integration
   b. systems   d. acceptance

Checkpoint

Matching Match the terms with their definitions.

_____ 1. data type (500)

_____ 2. primary key (501)

_____ 3. file maintenance (502)

_____ 4. validation (503)

_____ 5. check digit (503)

_____ 6. object (508)

_____ 7. standards (517)

_____ 8. feature creep (519)

_____ 9. object program (529)

_____ 10. source program (529)

a. procedures that keep data current

b. item that contains data, as well as the actions that read or process the data

c. field that uniquely identifies each record in a file

d. process of comparing data with a set of rules or values to determine if the data meets certain criteria

e. language instructions, or code, to be converted to machine language

f. machine language version of a program that results from compiling the procedural language

g. number(s) or character(s) that is appended to or inserted in a primary key value

h. specifies the kind of data a field can contain and how the field is used

i. problem that occurs when one activity has led to another that was not planned originally, causing the project to grow in scope

j. sets of rules and procedures an organization expects employees to accept and follow

✳ Consider This Answer the following questions in the format specified by your instructor.

1. Answer the critical thinking questions posed at the end of these elements in this chapter: Ethics & Issues (502, 505, 514, 528), How To (511, 513, 530, 534), Mini Features (507, 509, 537), Secure IT (514, 522, 527, 534), and Technology @ Work (539).

2. What are common data types? (501)

3. What is included in file maintenance? (502)

4. What is function creep? (502)

5. How does a DBMS typically flag deleted records or records that contain inactive data? (502)

6. What should a computer do if data fails a validity check? (503)

7. What are the different types of validity checks? (503)

8. What are two major weaknesses of file processing systems? (504)

9. What are the advantages of a database approach to data storage? (505)

10. What are three popular data models used today? (508)

11. What trends have contributed to Big Data? (508)

12. What is stored in the data dictionary? (510)

13. What steps can you take to recover from identity theft? (514)

14. What are the steps in the SDLC? (515)

15. Who should be included on a project team? (517)

16. How do the responsibilities of a project manager differ from those of a project leader? (517)

17. What four tests does a systems analyst use to evaluate a project's feasibility? (519)

18. What techniques do systems analysts use to gather data and information? (520)

19. What four major activities take place during the planning phase in the SDLC? (521)

20. Why is detailed analysis sometimes called logical design? (522)

21. How do RFQs, RFPs, and RFIs differ? (523)

22. What does a program specification package identify? (524)

23. What are the four major steps in the implementation phase? (525)

24. Why might users work with a sandbox? (525)

25. What tests might a systems analyst perform on test data? (525)

26. How do direct, parallel, phased, and pilot conversion strategies differ? (526)

27. How does a compiler differ from an interpreter? (529)

28. What are some popular object-oriented programming (OOP) languages? (530)

✳ Problem Solving

The Problem Solving exercises extend your knowledge of chapter concepts by seeking solutions to practical problems with technology that you may encounter at home, school, or work. The Collaboration exercise should be completed with a team.

Instructions: You often can solve problems with technology in multiple ways. Determine a solution to the problems in these exercises by using one or more resources available to you (such as a computer or mobile device, articles on the web or in print, blogs, podcasts, videos, television, user guides, other individuals, electronics or computer stores, etc.). Describe your solution, along with the resource(s) used, in the format requested by your instructor (brief report, presentation, discussion, blog post, video, or other means).

Personal

1. **No Search Results** While searching a web database for a hotel room for an upcoming trip, a message is displayed stating that no search results match your criteria. What can you do to correct this problem?

2. **Incorrect Price** You are shopping for groceries and, after loading all items in your cart, it is time to check out. The cashier scans your items, but you realize that the register is not reflecting an advertised discount on one of the items. Why might this be happening?

3. **Webpage Not Readable** You are attempting to view a webpage on your smartphone, but the text is very small and you are having difficulty reading anything. It is extremely time consuming for you to zoom in and constantly scroll around the webpage to view the contents. What might be causing this?

4. **Inaccurate Credit Report** You have obtained a free copy of your credit report and notice that multiple companies are accessing your credit report without your knowledge or permission. Your financial records are very important, and it is troubling that other companies are accessing this information. Why might this be occurring?

5. **Webpage Script** You are viewing a webpage and have just submitted an online form. The browser does not appear to do anything for about one minute, and an error message finally appears stating that a script on the page is taking longer than expected to run. What might be wrong?

Professional

6. **Data Entry Issues** You are in charge of adding student information to your school's database using a front end. When you attempt to enter the street address for one of the students, the entire street name does not fit in the text box. What are your next steps?

Source: Microsoft

7. **Incorrect Postal Codes** Your company's database stores information about its customers, including their names, addresses, phone numbers, email addresses, and order history. While reviewing the database to ensure data integrity, you notice that some of the postal codes, which should be five digits, are only four digits. What might be wrong?

8. **Database Connection Error** While interacting with a web app, an error is displayed informing you that the web app is not able to connect to the database. What might be causing this?

9. **Database Recovery** Your boss has informed you that the main customer database for your company has become corrupt. Fortunately, you can attempt to use the recovery utility to salvage the data in the database. When you attempt to recover the database, you receive an error message that the recovery has failed. What are your next steps?

10. **Content Management System Updates** You are attempting to update your company's website using a content management system. When you make the requested changes in the content management system, they are not reflected on the company website. What might be the problem?

Collaboration

11. **Technology in Sports** You serve as an assistant coach for your former high school's baseball team. The head coach, whose computer is more than five years old, informs you that he would like to create an application that will allow him to keep track of his players' statistics. For instance, he would like to track each player's number of strikeouts, walks, hits, and home runs. Form a team of three people to determine the requirements for implementing his request. One team member will research the types of apps that can track this data, another team member will determine the specifications for a computer or mobile device capable of running the software and storing the data, and the other team member will determine the best way to collect the data during the game.

The How To: Your Turn exercises present general guidelines for fundamental skills when using a computer or mobile device and then require that you determine how to apply these general guidelines to a specific program or situation.

How To: Your Turn

Discover More: Visit this chapter's premium content to **challenge yourself with additional How To: Your Turn exercises**, which include App Adventure.

Instructions: You often can complete tasks using technology in multiple ways. Figure out how to perform the tasks described in these exercises by using one or more resources available to you (such as a computer or mobile device, articles on the web or in print, online or program help, user guides, blogs, podcasts, videos, other individuals, trial and error, etc.). Summarize your 'how to' steps, along with the resource(s) used, in the format requested by your instructor (brief report, presentation, discussion, blog post, video, or other means).

❶ Obtain and Verify the Accuracy of a Credit Report

As discussed in this chapter, you might need to obtain or verify the accuracy of your credit report for a variety of reasons. It is important to obtain your credit report at least one time per year to verify its accuracy, as imperfections on a credit report can lead to problems such as financing being declined or higher interest rates on loans. The following steps guide you through the process of obtaining and verifying the accuracy of a credit report.

a. Run a browser and then navigate to annualcreditreport.com.

b. When you arrive at the website, verify that the browser is using the "https" protocol, indicating a secure connection.

c. Tap or click the button to request the report.

d. Provide the necessary personal information.

e. Select the agency or agencies from which you want a copy of your credit report.

f. Tap or click the button to continue to the credit reporting agency's website.

g. If necessary, enter the additional requested information to validate your request.

h. Follow the remaining instructions on the website to finish obtaining a copy of your credit report.

i. Save and/or print a copy of the credit report.

After you have obtained a copy of your credit report, you should verify it for accuracy. The following points describe what to look for when reviewing the report:

- Verify the list of accounts is accurate.
- Verify your payment history.
- Verify current balances are accurate.
- Review your personal information, and report any inconsistencies to the credit reporting agency.
- Review your rights under the Fair Credit Reporting Act.

Exercises

1. In addition to the reasons mentioned in this exercise, why else might you want to obtain a copy of your credit report?

2. What is a credit score? How can you obtain your credit score? What are the highest and lowest possible credit scores?

3. If you find erroneous information on your credit report, what steps can you take to make the necessary corrections?

Source: Central Source, LLC

❷ Use a Research Database

Students often use one or more research databases to locate information about a particular topic. Research databases often can be accessed in a public or school library, through a library's website, or through the research database's website. The following steps guide you through the process of using a research database:

a. Locate and then navigate to the research database that contains the information you are seeking. Consult a librarian if you need assistance in determining the exact database you should use.

b. Determine the location from which you can access the research database. For instance, you may need to access some research databases from a library computer. Other databases are accessible from anywhere if you can verify your identity as a library patron or a student. Some databases are available to the public at no charge or with no other restrictions.

✳ How To: Your Turn

c. Navigate to the research database you plan to use.

d. If the research database contains an option to perform an advanced search, tap or click the option to perform the advanced search.

e. Specify the search criteria. Note that not all research databases will request the same search criteria. The following list contains some common criteria:
   1. Keywords
   2. Author
   3. Publication date
   4. Publication type
   5. Education level

f. Run the search.

g. Browse the search results and then tap or click the search result that interests you.

Exercises

1. What are some reasons why you might want or need to use a research database?

2. What research databases are available through your school's library?

3. Evaluate three research databases that you may need to use throughout your academic career. Which one do you like the most? Why? Which one do you like the least? Why?

Source: EBSCO Industries, Inc.

❸ Protect Your Data If Your Device Is Lost or Stolen

If you misplace your device or it is stolen, you can use another device to help find yours. Certain apps will help you locate your device, cause your phone to ring, display an alert message, take a photo using the front or back camera, or remotely lock the device so that your data will be safe. Some apps require purchasing the full version to access advanced features, such as remotely locking or wiping your device. The following steps guide you through the process of protecting your data if your device is lost or stolen.

a. Determine whether your device has a built-in feature or app you can use to locate it in the event it is lost or stolen. If not, locate, install, and run an app that can perform this service. The app you locate and install should meet the following criteria:
   1. The app should be reputable and have good reviews.
   2. Reviews should contain no indication that the app is malicious.
   3. The app should be able to locate, lock, and erase data from your device in the event it is lost or stolen.
   4. You should be able to access or control your phone from a variety of devices (such as smartphones, tablets, laptops, and desktops) and operating systems (such as iOS, Android, Mac OS, and Windows).
   5. The app should be secure so that others cannot inadvertently or maliciously control your device.

b. From the app's home screen, configure the necessary settings so that you will be able to locate and control your device in the event that it is lost or stolen. Consider configuring the following settings:
   1. Determine which ringer or sound you want to use if you are attempting to locate a lost device.
   2. Specify how to instruct the device to take an appropriate action. For example, you may be able to instruct a device to play a sound (such as a siren) by sending a text message to it with certain wording, or by tapping or clicking a button on a specific website.
   3. Enable the GPS feature on the device so that you will be able to see its location.

c. Make sure the data on your device is backed up regularly. You can back up your data either to a computer or to the cloud. Some devices have a feature (or apps available) to automatically back up your data in the event it is erased from your device.

d. Test the features of the app to make sure it works as intended.

e. In the event the device is lost or stolen, perform the following steps as soon as possible for the best chance at retrieving the device and its data:
   1. Issue a command to the device to lock it.
   2. If you are attempting to locate a phone, call it to see if someone answers. If so, try to retrieve the phone.
   3. If possible, send a text message to the device with your contact information to see if someone contacts you.

How To: Your Turn

4. Activate the ringer or sound on the device so that you can hear it if it is nearby.

5. If possible, sign in to a web app or access an app on another device to track the device's location using GPS.

6. If possible, take a photo with the device's front and back cameras to see if you can determine where it is located.

7. If you are unsuccessful and you think the data on the device is at risk, issue a command to the device to erase all data. You also might consider contacting law enforcement if you think the device was stolen.

Exercises

1. Have you ever lost or misplaced a device? If so, did you locate it? How?

2. Evaluate at least three apps that can locate and remove data from a lost or stolen device. Which ones did you evaluate? Which is your favorite? Why?

3. Some devices offer a feature that allows you to encrypt the data. Would you encrypt the data on your device? Why or why not? What are the benefits of doing so? What drawbacks exist, if any?

❹ Create and View a Text File

Word processing programs and apps allow you to enter small or large amounts of text into documents; however, these apps apply additional formatting to the document that may not be necessary. For example, if you are writing a program or creating a webpage with HTML, you would not be able to enter the code in a word processing program or app because it would apply additional formatting (such as the font and size used, information about margins, colors, and line spacing) to the file that would interfere with the code you write. A text file stores only the text you write without any additional formatting. For this reason, you are not able to format the text that you enter in a text file. The following steps guide you through the process of creating and viewing a text file.

Creating a Text File

a. Locate and run a text editor, for example, the Notepad app in Windows or the TextEdit app on a Mac. Some word processing programs and apps can save documents as plain text files.

b. If necessary, create a new text file.

c. Enter the desired text, such as HTML or program code, in the file.

d. When you have finished entering the text, save the file with the appropriate file extension for the type of file you are creating, and verify that you are saving it as a text file. If you used a word processing program or app to create the text file and find that it will not save your file as a plain text file, you can copy the text from the word processing program or app and paste it into a text editor and then save the file from the text editor.

e. If necessary, exit the text editor.

Viewing a Text File

a. Run a text editor.

b. Select the option to open a file.

c. Navigate to the text file you want to view.

d. Select the text file you want to view and then tap or click the button to open the file.

e. When you are done viewing the file, close the file and then exit the text editor.

or

a. Navigate to the text file you want to view.

b. Press and hold or right-click the text file's icon to display a shortcut menu.

c. Select the option on the shortcut menu to open the file in the desired text editor.

Note: You should not attempt to view a text file by double-clicking its icon because it may not open in a text editor by default. For example if you create a text file and save it with an .html file extension, double-clicking the file may open it in a browser.

Exercises

1. Have you ever created a file in a text editor? Why? If not, what types of files might you need to create in a text editor?

2. How do file sizes of text files compare with similar files created in a word processing program or app? Why do you think this is the case?

3. Evaluate one third-party text editor that is compatible with your operating system. How does it compare to the one that is included with your operating system? What is the same? What is different?

Source: Cengage Learning

✳ Internet Research

The Internet Research exercises broaden your understanding of chapter concepts by requiring that you search for information on the web.

Discover More: Visit this chapter's premium content to **challenge yourself with additional Internet Research exercises**, which include Search Sleuth, Green Computing, Ethics in Action, You Review It, and Exploring Technology Careers.

Instructions: Use a search engine or another search tool to locate the information requested or answers to questions presented in the exercises. Describe your findings, along with the search term(s) you used and your web source(s), in the format requested by your instructor (brief report, presentation, discussion, blog post, video, or other means).

❶ Making Use of the Web
Entertainment

Americans, on average, spend nearly six percent of their income on entertainment, which includes tickets for concerts and movies, electronic equipment, hobbies, and services. They have scaled back their away-from-home activities in favor of in-home entertainment as they have invested in home theaters, high-speed Internet, and game consoles.

Many websites satisfy our cravings for amusement. For example, the Rock and Roll Hall of Fame and Museum has videos, stories, and a comprehensive "The Story of Rock" to enjoy. The Internet Movie Database (IMDb) has facts about more than 2.7 million movies, television shows, and entertainment programs. It also has video highlights, quotes, quizzes, and movie showtimes. Other entertainment websites have a variety of content aimed at amusing visitors and relieving boredom.

Research This: (a) Locate the Rock and Roll Hall of Fame and Museum website and view the information about the latest inductees. What is the total number of inductees? Which artists have been inducted more than once? Describe two upcoming events. Which classes are being offered in the Rock and Roll Night School?

(b) Locate the Internet Movie Database website. Take the IMDb Internet Icon Quiz. What score did you earn? What are three movies opening this week? What is the top news story of the day?

(c) Visit an entertainment website. What content is featured, such as humorous and sports video clips, photos, animations, and audio clips? What categories are available? Are advertisements included in the content? Which content is available at no cost, and which requires a fee to access?

Source: The Rock and Roll Hall of Fame and Museum, Inc.

❷ Social Media

Companies collect data as people browse websites. Just seconds after individuals visit a specific webpage, advertisements are displayed matching their shopping patterns and favorite products. This tracking is prevalent in online social networks, too, as marketers match users' profiles and other posted information, such as status updates, with specific businesses. Facebook, for example, allows retailers to upload their databases containing email addresses, phone numbers, and other personal facts. This data then is compared with the Facebook users' data. When a match is found, specific advertisements are displayed. Social media may charge the advertisers each time a user clicks an ad, called CPC (cost per click) or PPC (pay per click), which could range from a few cents to several dollars. Another option is to charge for a specific number of times an ad is displayed, called CPI (cost per impression).

Research This: Locate at least two articles discussing targeting ads on online social networks. How do the businesses place their ads based on the users' online identities and profiles? What steps are taken to ensure the users' privacy? Should users expect companies to collect data about some of their online behaviors in return for using the websites at no charge?

❸ Search Skills
Verifying Your Search Results

Even though a link to a website or other online resource may appear first in your list of search results, the information it presents may not be accurate. Several strategies exist to help you determine the credibility of search results. Verify the information you read by finding supporting information on other websites or by comparing search results from different search engines. Often authors will provide links to sources within or at the end of an article. Search for information about the author to help determine his or her credibility, authenticity, or objectivity. Some articles may present opinions, not facts.

If you do not recognize or have doubts about the domain name of a website you are reading, type the search text, whois, in a search engine to locate the

WhoIs database. Then type the domain name of the website in question (such as cengagebrain.com) in the WhoIs search box to find its owner. You then can search for more information about the website's owner. If you are looking for time-sensitive information, check the date when the links or pages were updated. If a webpage is filled with ads or pop-ups, it may be a scam.

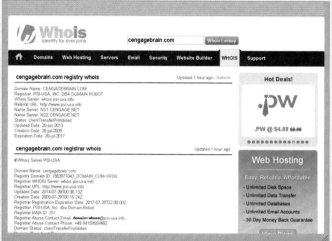

Source: WhoIs

Research This: Use a search engine to answer these questions and report your findings. (1) Find an article on Wikipedia about relational databases. What references reinforce the statements in the article? (2) Find a popular blog about CRM systems and use WhoIs to determine the blog's owner. (3) Search for a news article about web databases and then find two additional articles by the same author on a similar topic. (4) Search for information about the five most popular content management systems in use today. Do different websites give you different results? How was popularity determined?

④ Security

When you use supermarket loyalty cards, enter contests, complete warranty registrations, apply for credit cards, and subscribe to newsletters, businesses automatically store personal data about you, your transactions, and your preferences in their marketing databases. They often use this data to analyze sales, develop advertising campaigns, and solicit more business from you. Unbeknownst to many consumers, some companies also sell or rent this data to other businesses for the purpose

of developing interest-based or online behavioral advertising. Consumers can refuse to receive targeted email messages and marketing materials, but they often must search the websites or paper forms for check boxes to indicate these opt-out preferences. Some consumer advocates view this practice as an invasion of privacy and urge businesses to default to not adding consumers' information to databases unless the consumer opts in to receive additional materials.

Research This: Visit at least two websites that include opt-in or opt-out provisions and read the disclosure notices. What steps can you take to remove yourself from databases? Which organizations help protect consumers and offer information on maintaining online privacy? Then, search for at least two marketing companies that provide online direct advertising campaigns. How do these companies use databases to match consumers' buying preferences with targeted offers?

⑤ Cloud Services
Online Databases (DaaS)

Accessing information from online databases is an example of data as a service (DaaS), a service of cloud computing that provides data on demand for use in applications or visualizations. Federal, state, and local governments provide data online to promote transparency and enable users to perform research online. Independent data markets are websites that aggregate and offer data from leading providers, along with web-based tools for exploring, analyzing, and visualizing online data. Data providers make the data available to developers through an API (application programming interface), who incorporate the data in new products, such as web or mobile apps. Users often can explore the data through a web interface.

Research This: (1) Use a search engine to find and visit the open data site for your city, state, or country's government. Select a topic for which data is available, and use the online tools provided to explore a data set and create a visualization in the form of a map or graph. (2) Use a search engine to find and visit an independent data market website, and browse the data sets listed. Select one of the data sets and read about the data it contains. How might an app make use of this data? What pricing models are available for developers who wish to incorporate this data into their apps?

Critical Thinking

The Critical Thinking exercises challenge your assessment and decision-making skills by presenting real-world situations associated with chapter concepts. The Collaboration exercise should be completed with a team.

Instructions: Evaluate the situations below, using personal experiences and one or more resources available to you (such as articles on the web or in print, blogs, podcasts, videos, television, user guides, other individuals, electronics or computer stores, etc.). Perform the tasks requested in each exercise and share your deliverables in the format requested by your instructor (brief report, presentation, discussion, blog post, video, or other means).

1. Online Movie Reviews

Information about movie titles and television shows is available from the web database IMDb (Internet Movie Database). Visitors can search IMDb using by title, cast member, year produced, characters, genre, awards, or other criteria. Each movie or show's listing offers a brief description and rating and includes links to such items as summary, trivia, reviews, quotes, and even streaming video options.

Do This: Visit imdb.com and search for both recently released and classic movies. Explain the steps you used to query the movie database. Assess how complete the information provided was. Who would benefit most from using the movie database? Why? Answer the following questions about your experiences. Did the information provided differ when viewing recently released titles versus classic movies? What did you learn from your queries? Can you identify a few fields that are included in the records for each movie? What interactive features can you identify? Can you find any HTML5 features that have been incorporated?

2. Spreadsheets versus Databases

Some individuals and small organizations prefer using spreadsheets instead of databases. People who use spreadsheets might argue that similar to databases, spreadsheets have columns and rows, and you can keep track of different sets of data in individual worksheets. This is similar to how you would use tables in a database to store different data sets. In addition, some find it easier to install, use, and maintain spreadsheet software than database software. After reading this chapter, you are convinced that databases have additional advantages, such as the capability of storing more data and more quickly searching for data, as well as generating reports.

Do This: Prepare information aimed toward individuals who prefer spreadsheets to databases. Include reasons why it is not advisable to store large amounts of data in spreadsheets, as well as the reporting and query-ing capabilities of data-bases. Explain benefits for using a database for collaborating and shar-ing information among departments in a business.

Source: Microsoft

3. Case Study

Amateur Sports League   You are the new manager for a nonprofit amateur soccer league. The league uses a database to store information about its players, teams, schedules, and statistics. The league's website uses information stored in the database to display team rosters, league standings, and events. The board of directors has asked you to investigate how the league should secure its database.

Do This: Using information learned in the chapter as well as performing additional research, prepare information about securing a database. What risks exist for databases? Who should determine the security measures to take? What should you include in the database security policy? Include recommendations for backing up data, validation, maintenance, and assigning different access levels to employees, coaches, and players. Is the league responsible for security breaches that put players' personal data at risk? Why or why not? Compile your findings.

Collaboration

4. System Development Life Cycle   A major retail company has hired your team to create and implement the steps in the system development life cycle (SDLC) to create custom inventory software.

Do This: Assign SDLC steps to different teammates and compile a plan for each step. Share your findings. Does the plan contain gaps? Do any steps or tasks overlap? What guidelines should you follow during system development? What roles are needed? How might you use project management software? As a team, answer the following questions to share with the retail company: Would you use a compiler or an interpreter? Why? Would you use an object-orient-ed programming language? Why or why not? What types of information gathering techniques would be most effec-tive? Why? Would you recommend outsourcing parts of the process? Why or why not? What is necessary to create a prototype of the project? Search for popular programming languages. Find industry experts' reviews of each language. Can you find an example of a program that uses each language? Which language might be best suited to this project? Why? As a team, compile your findings and share your recommendation with the class.

WORKING IN THE ENTERPRISE:
Systems, Certifications, and Careers

12

Various careers are available in the technology field.

"I have enjoyed discovering many facets of the technology field through this course. I would like to continue learning about technology, but I am uncertain of my specific career path. What more do I need to know about the technology field and its careers?"

While you may be familiar with some of the content in this chapter, do you know how to . . .

- Manage information using the five components of information literacy?
- Effectively research and compose a project?
- Set up your home office for telecommuting?
- Explain why those who use unlicensed software may be committing a crime?
- Explain issues surrounding outsourcing of jobs?
- Describe issues that may arise when someone jailbreaks a smartphone or mobile device?
- Start your job search online?
- Create a professional online presence?
- Explain how social media can help your job search?
- Use LinkedIn?
- Create a video resume?
- Create a online survey?

In this chapter, you will discover how to perform these tasks along with much more information essential to this course. For additional content available that accompanies this chapter, visit the free resources and premium content. Refer to the Preface and the Intro chapter for information about how to access these and other additional instructor-assigned support materials.

✔ Objectives

After completing this chapter, you will be able to:

1 Identify the qualities of valuable information

2 Describe various information systems used in an enterprise

3 Identify the components of and steps in information literacy

4 Describe career opportunities available in these segments of the computer industry: general business and government organizations and their IT departments; technology equipment field; software and apps field; technology service and repair field; technology sales; technology education, training, and support field; and IT consulting

5 Identify job titles and responsibilities for various technology jobs

6 Identify mobile app development strategies

7 Identify ways to prepare for certification

8 Describe the general areas of IT certification

9 Identify ways to begin a job search

10 Explain how to create a professional online presence

The Technology Industry

Nearly every job requires you to interact with technology to complete projects, exchange information with coworkers, and meet customers' needs. The technology field provides many opportunities for people of all skill levels and interests, and a demand for computer professionals continues to grow. Figure 12-1 identifies some technology-related careers available to today's college graduates. You can use both social media and job search websites to learn about technology careers and to promote yourself to potential employers. By creating a professional online presence, hiring managers can learn more about you beyond what you can convey in a traditional one-page paper resume.

As new technologies emerge, organizations look for potential employees who possess skills and a desire to learn and who are comfortable using all types of technology. This chapter discusses the various types of information systems you may encounter in an organization, as well as technology professionals with whom you might interact. It also explores current technology careers and how you can prepare for them.

Figure 12-1 The technology industry offers many rewarding careers.
© iStockPhoto / jayfish

Information Systems in the Enterprise

BTW
Technology Trend
Discover More: Visit this chapter's free resources to learn about crowd sourcing.

Businesses, and their employees, use many types of systems. A system is a set of components that interact to achieve a common goal. A billing system, for example, allows a company to send invoices and receive payments from customers. Through a payroll system, employees receive paychecks — often deposited directly into their bank accounts. A manufacturing system produces the goods that customers order. Very often, these systems also are information systems. Recall from Chapter 11 that an **information system** is a set of hardware, software, data, people, and procedures that work together to produce information. Information systems support daily, short-term, and long-range information requirements of users in a company.

To assist with sound decision making, information must have value. For it to be valuable, information should be accurate, verifiable, timely, organized, accessible, useful, and cost effective.

- Accurate information is error free. Inaccurate information can lead to incorrect decisions. For example, consumers assume their credit reports are accurate. If your credit report incorrectly shows past-due payments, a bank may not lend you money for a vehicle or a house.
- Verifiable information can be proven as correct or incorrect. For example, security personnel at an airport usually request some type of photo identification to verify that you are the person named on the ticket.
- Timely information is useful only within a specific time period. A decision to build additional schools in a particular district should be based on the most recent census report — not on one that is 10 years old. Most information loses value with time. Some information, however, such as information about trends, gains value as time passes and more information is obtained. For example, your transcript gains value as you take more classes.
- Organized information is arranged to suit the needs and requirements of the decision maker. Two different people may need the same information presented in a different manner. For example, an inventory manager may want an inventory report to list out-of-stock items first. The purchasing agent, instead, wants the report alphabetized by vendor.
- Accessible information is available when the decision maker needs it. Having to wait for information may delay an important decision. For example, a sales manager cannot decide which sales representative deserves the award for highest annual sales if the December sales have not been entered in the database yet.
- Useful information has meaning to the person who receives it. Most information is important only to certain people or groups of people. Always consider the audience when collecting and reporting information. Avoid distributing useless information. For example, an announcement of an alumni association meeting is not useful to students who have not graduated yet.
- Cost-effective information should provide more value than it costs to produce. An organization occasionally should review the information it produces to determine if it still is cost effective to produce. Some organizations create information only on demand, that is, as people request it, instead of on a regular basis. Many make information available online so that users can access it as they need it.

BTW
Technology Innovator
Discover More: Visit this chapter's free resources to learn about Wikimedia Foundation and its founder, Jimmy Wales.

Discover More: Visit this chapter's free resources to learn more about daily, short-term, and long-range information requirements of users.

Functional Units

A large organization, commonly referred to as an enterprise, requires special computing solutions because of its size and geographic distribution. A typical enterprise consists of a wide variety of departments, centers, and divisions — collectively known as functional units. Examples of functional units include human resources, manufacturing, and customer service.

Some information systems are used exclusively by only one type of functional unit within the enterprise. Table 12-1 lists some of the more common information systems that are used by functional units in a typical enterprise. Other information systems that support activities of several functional units include enterprise resource planning, document management systems, and content management systems.

⚙ BTW
Technology Trend
Discover More: Visit this chapter's free resources to learn about how employees and others can monitor their health status.

🖥 **Table 12-1 Information Systems Used Exclusively by Functional Units in an Enterprise**

Functional Unit	Information System
Human Resources (HR)	• *A human resources information system* (*HRIS*) manages one or more administrative human resources functions, such as maintaining and managing employee benefits, schedules, and payroll.
Engineering or Product Development	• *Computer-aided engineering* (*CAE*) aids in the development and testing of product designs, and often includes CAD (computer-aided design).
Manufacturing	• *Computer-aided manufacturing* (*CAM*) controls production equipment, such as drills, lathes, and milling machines. • *Material Requirements Planning* (*MRP*) monitors and controls inventory, material purchases, and other processes related to manufacturing operations. • *Manufacturing Resource Planning II* (*MRP II*) is an extension of MRP that also includes product packaging and shipping, machine scheduling, financial planning, demand forecasting, tracking labor productivity, and monitoring product quality.
Marketing	• Market research systems analyze data gathered from demographics and surveys.
Sales	• *Salesforce automation* (*SFA*) helps salespeople manage customer contacts, schedule customer meetings, log customer interactions, manage product information, and place customer orders.
Customer Service	• *Customer relationship management* (*CRM*) manages information about customers, past purchases, interests, and the day-to-day interactions, such as phone calls, email messages, web communications, and Internet messaging sessions.

© Cengage Learning

Enterprise Resource Planning

Enterprise Resource Planning (**ERP**) integrates MRP II with the information flow across an organization to manage and coordinate the ongoing activities of the enterprise, including product planning, manufacturing and distribution, accounting and finance, sales, human resources, and customer support.

Advantages of ERP include complete integration of information systems across departments, better project management, and improved customer service. Complete integration means information is shared rapidly, and management receives a more complete and timely view of the organization through the information. Project management software often is standardized across an enterprise so that different parts of the enterprise easily can integrate and collaborate on their planning and logistics. Figure 12-2 illustrates how ERP encompasses all major activities of an enterprise.

Figure 12-2 ERP encompasses all of the major activities throughout an enterprise.
© Hurst Photo / Shutterstock.com; © Monkey Business Images / Shutterstock.com; © PKM1 / iStockphoto.com; © Bartlomiej
Magierowski / Shutterstock.com; © Inti St Clair / Getty Images; © iStockphoto / choicegraphx; © John Penezic / Shutterstock.com;
© lucadp / Shutterstock.com; © Andresr / Shutterstock.com; © baki / Shutterstock.com; © StockLite / Shutterstock.com;
© wavebreakmedia / Shutterstock.com; © Tumar / Shutterstock.com; © Cengage Learning

Document Management Systems

Some organizations use document management systems to make collaboration possible among employees. A **document management system (DMS)** allows for storage and management of a company's documents, such as word processing documents, presentations, and spreadsheets. A central library stores all documents within a company or department. The system supports access control, security, version tracking of documents, and search capabilities; it also gives users the ability to check out documents to review or edit them and then check them back in when finished. This information can be used for searches within the document repository. Web-based application document management systems allow individuals and any organization to enjoy the benefits of document management systems as applications running in a browser. Users are granted access to certain parts of the repository, depending on their needs.

Discover More: Visit this chapter's free resources to learn more about web-based application document management systems.

Content Management Systems

A **content management system** (CMS) enables and manages the publishing, modification, organization, and access of various forms of documents and other files, including media and webpages, on a network or the web. CMSs include information about the files and data (metadata). For example, the metadata for a company's employee manual may include the author's name, revision number, a brief summary, and last revision date. A CMS also provides security controls for the content, such as who is allowed to add, view, and modify content and on which content the user is allowed to perform those operations.

Users add content to a CMS through a graphical user interface or webpage. Based on the user's actions, the CMS processes content, categorizes the content, indexes the content so that it later can be searched, and stores the content. Users then access the content stored in the system through a website, company portal, or other application. Read Secure IT 12-1 for security issues related to CMSs.

 BTW
DMS and CMS
A CMS (content management system) typically includes a DMS (document management system).

 Internet Research
What are popular content management systems?
Search for: popular content management systems

 SECURE IT 12-1

How Secure Are Content Management Systems?

Content management systems (CMSs) control many websites and online applications. Much of their popularity is due to their ease of use, especially because CMS operators need minimal technical skills to organize and update documents and files. This simplicity, however, is one reason cyberthieves can accomplish malicious attacks. The operators' lack of networking and security knowledge exposes the CMSs to security risks, especially distributed denial of service attacks (discussed in Chapter 5).

The United States Computer Emergency Readiness Team (US-CERT) and other organizations assess CMS vulnerabilities and offer specific actions for operators to follow. These practices include limiting the amount of website content that is displayed automatically, installing updates regularly, changing passwords, removing unused files, and using antivirus programs.

Because of the CMS's vulnerabilities, some security experts recommend the alternative of using HTML and uploading webpages to a web server. HTML allows the programmer to specify precisely how the custom page will

be displayed instead of relying on the CMS's templates. It also alleviates the need to install software upgrades and security updates. A person skilled in HTML programming may be able to develop and maintain a small, static website more quickly than having to conquer the steep learning curve that is associated with some CMSs.

Consider This: Under which circumstances would a company consider coding HTML directly, rather than maintaining a CMS to develop its website? How would a company evaluate and select a particular CMS?

CONSIDER THIS

What are uses of a CMS?

Publishing entities, such as news services, use CMSs to keep websites and web feeds up to date. As news or information is published, it is categorized and updated on the appropriate sections of the website. For example, a sportswriter may submit a story to the CMS and add metadata that indicates the story is a headline story. The CMS categorizes the story so that it is displayed as the first item with a large headline on the sports section of the website and included in the sports section's web feed. The CMS indexes the information in the story so that users who search the website based on keywords in the story will find a link to the story. Bloggers use CMSs to post to their blogs without having to format each entry manually in HTML. Blog posts can be categorized so that readers can search by category for posts on the same topic. Blogs also are searchable. Readers can use the CMS to comment on blog posts, and the blog owner may need to approve the comments before they are published.

Other Enterprise-Wide Information Systems

Some enterprise-wide information systems focus on the collection, organization, and sharing of information so that users can make decisions based on an up-to-date and accurate view of the information. The following sections discuss these information systems.

Transaction Processing Systems A *transaction processing system* (TPS) is an information system that captures and processes data from day-to-day business activities. Examples of transactions are deposits, payments, orders, and reservations. When you use a credit card to purchase an item, you are interacting with a transaction processing system.

BTW
TPS
Transaction processing systems were among the first computerized systems that processed business data. Many people initially used the term, data processing, to refer to the functions of these systems.

Information systems use batch or online transaction processing systems (Figure 12-3). With *batch processing*, the computer collects data over time and processes all transactions later, as a group. With *online transaction processing (OLTP)*, the computer processes each transaction as it is entered. For example, when you book a flight on the web, the airline probably uses OLTP to schedule the flight, book the flight, and send you a confirmation message.

Most transaction processing systems today use OLTP because users need information immediately. For some routine processing tasks, such as printing monthly invoices or weekly paychecks, they use batch processing.

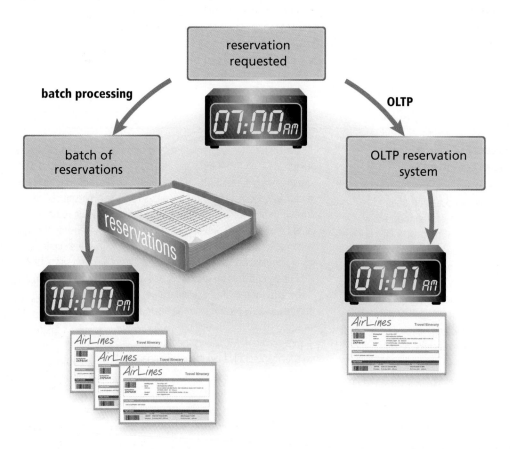

Figure 12-3 With batch processing, all reservations would be processed together at the end of the day. With OLTP, by contrast, reservations are processed immediately.
© Cengage Learning

Management Information Systems A **management information system (MIS)** is an information system that generates accurate, timely, and organized information, so that managers and other users can make decisions, solve problems, supervise activities, and track progress. Management information systems often are integrated with transaction processing systems and focus on creating information that managers and other users need to perform their jobs.

A management information system creates three basic types of reports: detailed, summary, and exception (Figure 12-4). A *detailed report* usually lists just transactions. For example, a Detailed Flight Report lists the number of passengers booked for a given flight. A *summary report* consolidates data usually with totals, tables, or graphs, so that managers can review it quickly and easily. An *exception report* identifies data outside of a normal condition. These out-of-the-ordinary conditions, called the *exception criteria*, define the normal activity or status range. For example, a Premier Club Booking Exception Report notifies the airline's marketing department that some flights have not met minimum goals for booking Premier Club members.

Discover More: Visit this chapter's free resources to learn more about how managers coordinate resources to make decisions.

Detailed Flight Report for Flight #328

Passenger Name	Gender	Birthdate	Seat	Premier Club
Adams, Latisha	F	4/25/92	3C	Y
Brewer, Milton	M	10/14/45	22F	N
Cam, Lin	F	12/16/91	2A	Y
Canaan, Lana	F	4/12/90	21A	N
Cole, Kristina	F	5/10/79	16C	N
Drake, Louella	F	3/4/81	4A	Y
Galens, Lynette	F	11/2/75	2C	N
Gilbert, Laura	F	2/20/78	4F	N
Henreich, Max	M	3/10/85	17C	Y
Hidalgo, Ronald	M	10/15/44	3F	Y
Marsh, Constance	F	11/5/82	2C	N
McGill, Teresa	F	2/27/73	16F	Y
Moretti, Leo	M	9/22/90	17A	Y
Nitz, Dawn	F	7/12/65	3F	N
Ruiz, Albert	M	2/13/93	10D	Y
Stein, Michelle	F	8/16/50	3A	N
Tu, Benjamin	M	1/16/77	22C	N
Van Wijk, Fred	M	6/9/89	10A	Y
Warner, Betty	F	7/1/58	16A	N

Summary Flight Report for March 30

Flight #	Origin/ Destination	Passengers	Premier Club Members
1048	ORD – RSW	108	33
543	ORD – BMI	24	12
715	ORD – LAX	160	62
701	ORD – JFK	26	10

Exception Flight Report for March 30

Flight #	Class	Origin/ Destination	Premier Club Members	Premier Club Member Goal
1048	A	ORD – RSW	1	4
701	C	ORD – JFK	3	5

Figure 12-4 Three basic types of reports generated in an MIS are detailed, summary, and exception.
© Cengage Learning

Decision Support Systems A **decision support system** (DSS) helps users analyze information and make decisions (Figure 12-5). Some decision support systems are company specific and designed solely for managers. Others are available to everyone on the web. Programs that analyze data, such as those in a decision support system, sometimes are called *online analytical processing* (*OLAP*) programs.

A decision support system uses data from internal and external sources. Internal sources of data might include databases, sales orders, MRP and MRP II results, inventory records, or financial data from accounting and financial analyses. Data from external sources could include interest rates, population trends, or raw material pricing.

Some decision support systems include their own query languages, statistical analyses, spreadsheets, and graphics that help users retrieve data and analyze the results. Some also allow managers to create a model of the factors affecting a decision.

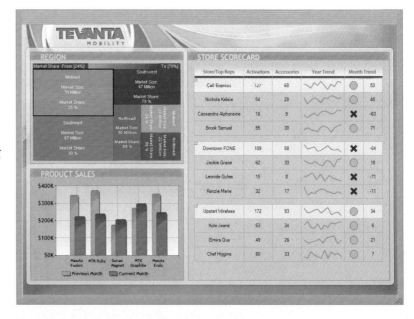

Figure 12-5 This decision support system helps managers analyze sales by product and by sales rep.
Courtesy of Dundas Data Visualation, Inc.

Expert Systems An **expert system** is an information system that captures and stores the knowledge of human experts and then imitates human reasoning and decision making (Figure 12-6). Expert systems consist of two main components: a knowledge base and inference rules. A *knowledge base* is the combined subject knowledge and experiences of the human experts. The *inference rules* are a set of logical judgments that are applied to the knowledge base each time a user describes a situation to the expert system.

Expert systems help all levels of users make decisions. Enterprises employ expert systems in a variety of roles, such as answering customer questions, training new employees, and analyzing data. Expert systems also successfully have resolved such diverse problems as diagnosing illnesses, searching for oil, and making soup.

 BTW

Technology Innovator
Discover More: Visit this chapter's free resources to learn about Ray Kurzweil (technology inventor and futurist).

Internet Research

What are recent developments in artificial intelligence?

Search for: artificial intelligence applications

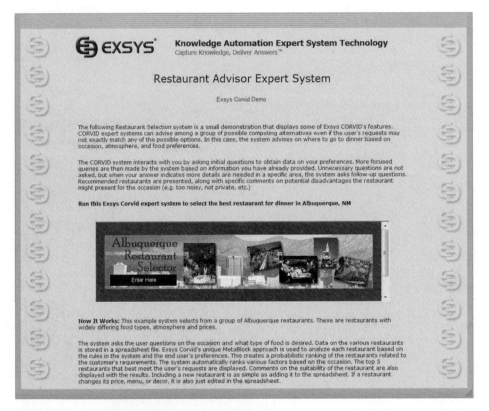

Figure 12-6 This company's restaurant advisor expert system recommends a restaurant based on a user's answers to specific questions.
Courtesy of Exsys

CONSIDER THIS

How do expert systems relate to artificial intelligence?
Expert systems are a component of artificial intelligence. **Artificial intelligence (AI)** is the application of human intelligence to computers. Artificial intelligence technology senses a person's actions and, based on logical assumptions and prior experience, takes the appropriate action to complete the task. Artificial intelligence has a variety of capabilities, including speech recognition, logical reasoning, and creative responses.

Mini Feature 12-1: Information Literacy

To adequately manage information, you should know how to use the five components of information literacy and also know the steps in effective research and composition. Read Mini Feature 12-1 to learn about information literacy.

Information Literacy

Managing the vast amount of information inundating us daily can be an overwhelming task, not only for those involved in technology careers, but also for any digital citizen. This twenty-first century skill set, called *information literacy*, prepares students, employees, and citizens to manage information so that they can be knowledgeable decision makers.

Defining Information Literacy

More than 25 years ago, the American Library Association was the first organization to recognize the importance of information literate citizens. As the web and the Internet became a mainstay in education, business, and home environments, experts realized that the traditional basic literacy skills of reading, writing, and arithmetic were insufficient for living a productive life. According to the Association of College & Research Libraries, also needed are lifelong skills "to locate, evaluate, and use effectively the needed information."

Information Literacy Components

An individual's quality of existence depends upon obtaining quality information. Information literate people know how to locate meaningful sources that can be used to solve problems, make decisions, and set goals. The following five categories are recognized as integral literacy components:

- **Digital literacy:** Using computers, mobile devices, the Internet, and related technologies effectively is a necessity in business and society. Also important is an understanding of the general concerns of having computers in the world, including their integration in employment and education and their effects on national and personal security.

- **Library instruction:** Undergraduates rarely seek the help of librarians when performing academic research. This lack of help may be due, in part, to the fact that the students misunderstand the role of the reference librarian. Information literate individuals use the librarians' expertise in locating relevant sources. They also understand the necessity of using citations, how information is cataloged and organized, search strategies, and the process of locating and evaluating resources.

- **Media literacy:** Skills needed to understand how mass communication and popular culture affect learning and entertainment include the ability to evaluate and analyze how music, film, video, television, and other nonprint media are used effectively to persuade and inform.

- **Numerical literacy:** The ability to use basic math skills and interpret data is essential to solving problems and communicating information. Also important are

understanding how data is gathered and presented in graphs, charts, and other visuals and how to interpret and verify information presented in media.

- **Traditional literacy:** Individuals who can read and understand a variety of documents are likely to complete their educations, obtain employment, and participate in community groups. They also need to think critically about the material they have read and to express their thoughts by writing and speaking coherently.

Steps in Effective Research and Composition

Locating appropriate material, organizing these sources, and producing the final document require effort and careful thought. The following paragraphs discuss steps you should take when crafting research, thinking critically, and drafting strategies:

- **Establish an appropriate topic.** Identify the purpose and audience. Determine an effective method of communicating the information, such as a written paper, oral presentation, or blog. Explore and narrow the topic so that it is manageable within time and logistical constraints. Determine the audience's familiarity with the topic and the need to find reference materials.

- **Identify sources.** Determine where to locate electronic and print resources, including websites, media, databases, and printed materials. Differentiate between primary and secondary sources, popular and scholarly articles, and current and historical materials.

- **Evaluate materials.** Analyze the sources to determine reliability, accuracy, timeliness, and bias. Compare the materials to determine if the authors agree or disagree with topics.

- **Create the final work.** Organize and integrate the source material using direct quotations, paraphrases, and summaries. Document the work to credit sources and avoid plagiarism. Integrate photos, charts, and graphs when necessary to clarify the message. Use the writing process to create, review, revise, and proofread.

Discover More: Visit this chapter's free resources to learn more about information literacy components and the steps in effective research and composition.

✸ **Consider This:** Test your skills at effective research by examining a website for a vehicle you would consider purchasing. Describe the photos, colors, placement of objects, and description. Who is the intended audience? Is any information missing from the website? What message is the company attempting to send? Do you think the message achieves its purpose?

✔ NOW YOU SHOULD KNOW ————————————————————————

Be sure you understand the material presented in the section titled Information Systems in the Enterprise as it relates to the chapter objectives.
Now you should know...

- Whether information is valuable (Objective 1)
- Which enterprise information systems you have used (Objective 2)
- How you can be information literate (Objective 3)

Discover More: Visit this chapter's premium content for practice quiz opportunities.

Technology Careers

With billions of dollars in annual revenue, the technology industry is a major source of career opportunities worldwide. This industry has created thousands of high-tech career opportunities, even in organizations whose primary business is not technology-related. As technology changes, so do the available careers and requirements. New careers are available in social media and mobile technologies that did not exist a few years ago. For this reason, you should stay up to date with technology developments.

General Business and Government Organizations and Their IT Departments

Business and government organizations of all sizes use a variety of computers, mobile devices, and other technology. Most use networks to ensure seamless communications among employees, vendors, and customers. They also use webpages, email, mobile apps, online social networks, and more to communicate with the public.

Larger organizations use computers and other technology to answer and route phone calls, process orders, update inventory, and manage accounts receivable, accounts payable, billing, and payroll activities. Many use mobile devices, web conferencing, and VPNs (virtual private networks) to stay connected with employees who work in other locations or who telecommute (Figure 12-7). Read How To 12-1 for tips related to setting up a home office for telecommuting. Read Ethics & Issues 12-1 to consider whether telecommuting is good or bad for business.

Figure 12-7 Some organizations allow employees to telecommute.
© Goodluz / Shutterstock.com

⚙ HOW TO 12-1

Set Up Your Home Office for Telecommuting

Telecommuting mutually benefits employers and employees. Employers do not have to pay for the physical infrastructure (including office space and parking) for the employee, and telecommuters often work more hours than those who physically commute to an office. Employees benefit from not having to commute and from having a comfortable work environment. The following guidelines describe how to set up your home office for telecommuting:

- Choose a location in your home that is free from noise and distractions. If your home is occupied by others during the hours you plan to telecommute, your office should be located away from potentially noisy areas. For example, an office next to a room where someone else is watching television may not be an ideal choice.

- Make sure your office has a comfortable desk and chair. Although it may be tempting to sit on your couch with your laptop while you work, having a professional workspace will increase productivity.

- Consider acquiring additional furniture, such as a file cabinet and bookshelf, especially if you plan to store files and books for reference.

- If required, verify your office has a sufficient Internet connection. If you are using a wired connection, one should be available near your desk. If you are using a wireless network, make sure the signal strength is sufficient in your office.

- Make sure the office has a phone to place and receive calls. If you will be relying on a mobile phone, verify your phone can receive a strong signal and has a conveniently located charger and power outlet.

- Use a headset with your phone to minimize background noise.

- Obtain supplies that typically are found in an office setting, such as writing utensils, paper, tape, a stapler, paper clips, and sticky notes.

- If your employer does not provide a computer for your use, make sure your computer is sufficiently equipped to complete your job tasks. Make sure you also have accessories, such as USB flash drives and other external storage media, if necessary.

- Consider obtaining an all-in-one printer that can print scan, copy, and fax (if necessary), as well as extra printer cartridges.

⚙ **Consider This:** What other equipment, supplies, and furniture would you prefer to have in an office from where you telecommute?

⚙ ETHICS & ISSUES 12-1

Is Telecommuting Good or Bad for Business?

Studies show that nearly 80 percent of workers dream of leaving the confines of an office to work from the comfort of home, at least part of the time. Although employees may view working from home as an ideal situation, some bosses do not agree. An Internet CEO, for example, made news when she reviewed data such as employees' sign-ins to the company's VPN (virtual private network) and discovered that many employees were not working during company hours. As a result, the CEO made the decision to end telecommuting at her company.

Supporters cite reduced pollution and commuting time. Other benefits include increased productivity due to lack of office gossip and politics. Many feel that they could not be as dedicated to their jobs without telecommuting because of the flexible hours and closeness to home. Others feel that trusted employees should have the privilege if they earn it. Companies benefit by saving on resources, such as office space.

Opponents claim that some lack the self-discipline to work remotely. Employees may be distracted more easily without direct management supervision. Some workers have difficulty setting appropriate boundaries regarding childcare or other family obligations. Additionally, productivity actually may decrease if employees stagger work hours to fit their schedule, limiting times when employees can schedule meetings.

Many experienced workers agree that telecommuting cannot replace valuable face-to-face time with coworkers, vendors, and customers. Some workers fear telecommuting because they feel that the lack of a personal relationship with managers puts them at the top of the list for downsizing.

Consider This: Is telecommuting good or bad for business? Why? Are some businesses or positions better suited for telecommuting? If so, which ones? Do some people lack the self-discipline to be productive while telecommuting? If so, how should managers determine whether to allow this practice and who may participate?

Most medium and large businesses and government organizations have an IT (information technology) department. IT staff are responsible for ensuring that all the computer operations, mobile devices, and networks run smoothly. They also determine when and if the organization requires new hardware, mobile devices, or software. Usually, these jobs are divided into the following areas:

- Management — directs the planning, research, development, evaluation, and integration of technology.
- Research and software development — analyzes, designs, develops, and implements new information technology and maintains and improves existing systems.
- Technical support services — evaluates and integrates new technologies, administers the organization's data resources, and supports the centralized computer operating system and servers.
- Operations — operates the centralized computer equipment and administers the network, including both data and voice communications.
- Training/Support — teaches employees how to use components of the information system or answers specific user questions.
- Information security services — develops and enforces policies that are designed to safeguard an organization's data and information from unauthorized users.
- Marketing/Strategy — directs and implements Internet and social media marketing, and manages customer relationships.

BTW

Technology Innovator
Discover More: Visit this chapter's free resources to learn about Meg Whitman (technology business executive).

Technology Equipment

The *technology equipment field* consists of manufacturers and distributors of computers, mobile devices, and other hardware, such as magnetic and optical drives, monitors, printers, and communications and networking devices. In addition to the companies that make end-user equipment, thousands of companies manufacture components used inside a computer or mobile device, such as chips, motherboards, cables and connectors, and power supplies.

Available careers in this field include positions with companies that design, manufacture, and produce computers and input, output, communications, mobile, and networking devices. Careers include designing and fabricating chips, testing internal components (Figure 12-8), assembling computers and devices, and packing finished products.

Discover More: Visit this chapter's free resources to learn about technology equipment manufacturers.

Software and Apps

The *software and apps field* consists of companies that develop, manufacture, and support a wide range of software and apps for computers, the web, and mobile devices. Some companies specialize in a particular type, such as productivity software or tools, or focus on a device type. Other companies — especially larger firms, such as Microsoft — produce and sell many types of software that work with both computers and mobile devices and may use Internet services to sync data among devices or provide collaborative features.

Some employees develop desktop, web, and mobile apps, such as productivity software, games, simulations, and more; others develop operating systems and related tools. Read Secure IT 12-2 to consider how unlicensed software affects software publishers.

Discover More: Visit this chapter's free resources to learn about leading software companies.

Figure 12-8 This lab technician tests internal computer components.
© iStockPhoto / anyaivanova

SECURE IT 12-2

Using Unlicensed Software Is a Crime

Software publishers own the copyright to their products. These companies are on the lookout for copies of their software that have been duplicated, distributed, or used without their permission. The pirated software denies these publishers revenue they would have earned from sales, which they could have used to produce new products and improve current products. A recent Business Software Alliance (BSA) Global Software Survey revealed that 43 percent of all software has been installed without proper licensing, including one in five pieces in the United States. This software is valued at more than $62 billion.

Software may be considered unlicensed in a number of circumstances: it could have been downloaded illegally from file-sharing websites, it could have an expired license, or it could be installed on multiple computers when the license specifies use on only one computer. Using unlicensed software violates copyright laws and is subject to serious

criminal and civil penalties up to $150,000 for each illegal copy. It is important, therefore, to understand when software can be copied legally. In most circumstances, the software owner can make one copy of the software for backup purposes. Many people make multiple copies, however, either to share or to sell. Often the sharing is done online. In one survey, more than 50 percent of students and 25 percent of instructors admitted that they have copied or would copy software illegally.

People and companies copy software illegally for a variety of reasons, insisting that software prices are too high, that software often is copied for educational or other altruistic purposes, that copied software makes people more productive, that no restrictions should be placed on the use of software after it is purchased, and that software copying is a widespread practice. They also may not be aware that their actions are illegal, but ignorance is not an excuse for illegal actions.

Along with the risk of facing litigation, people and businesses using unlicensed software risk data theft and unauthorized access to their information because they are not receiving program updates and patches that could prevent hacking attempts. If people discover unlicensed software being used on a computer at work or at school, the best practice is to report this situation to managers or IT authorities. The Business Software Alliance encourages people to call its hotline and promises to keep the information confidential.

Consider This: What penalties should be imposed for using unlicensed software? Why? Can you counter the reasons people give for copying software illegally? How? Would you copy software illegally, even if your boss told you to copy it? Why or why not? Should software vendors be allowed to probe your computer secretly for illegally installed software? Why or why not?

Technology Service and Repair

The *technology service and repair field* provides preventive maintenance, component installation, and repair services to customers (Figure 12-9). Some technology service technicians possess general knowledge that enables them to work with a variety of devices from different manufacturers. Other technicians receive training and certifications directly from manufacturers to specialize in devices from that manufacturer. This work is best suited for those individuals who like to troubleshoot and solve problems and who have a strong background in electronics.

Many technology equipment manufacturers include diagnostic software with their computers and devices that assists technicians in identifying problems. Today's technology also allows technicians to diagnose and repair software problems from a remote location; that is, the technician accesses the user's hard drive or smartphone from a different location. Read Ethics & Issues 12-2 to consider the trustworthiness of computer repair services.

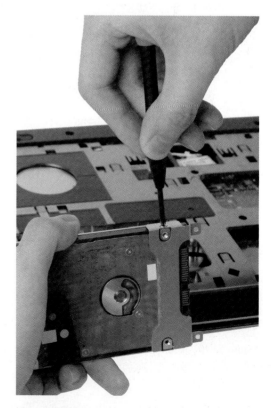

Figure 12-9 This repair technician is replacing a laptop hard drive.
© iStockPhoto / theJIPEN

📖 ❋ ETHICS & ISSUES 12-2

Can You Trust Data Recovery or Computer Repair Services?

While doing legitimate data recovery and device support tasks, IT workers and computer repair technicians often have access to confidential information. Most often you need to provide your password and access to your network, computer, or device during service. In doing so, you also give access to financial information, confidential records, email and other communications, and passwords. The result could be leaked information or identity theft.

IT workers often sign agreements with organizations stating that they will not access any information that is not critical to their jobs. Information systems at many government agencies and some organizations log all access to sensitive information. In some high-profile cases, organizations fired or suspended workers after log information proved they violated policies.

In one state, the law requires computer repair technicians who review or analyze data to have a private investigator license. The law implies that the technician is performing an investigation, in a sense, when business managers and parents hire them to analyze the computer usage habits of employees or children.

Privacy experts recommend backing up and wiping all data before turning over your computer or device to an IT or computer repair technician. You may assume that these professionals likely will follow ethical guidelines. It can be difficult, however, to repair the effects of unauthorized access, use, or distribution of your data.

Consider This: What should the consequences be for IT or computer repair technicians who access unauthorized data? Why? Would licensing and requiring training lessen the impact of unauthorized access? Why or why not? How can you protect your data when repairing or servicing your computer or device?

Technology Sales

Technology salespeople must possess a general understanding of technology and a specific knowledge of the product they are selling. Strong people skills are important, including a keen listening ability and superior verbal communications. Technology salespeople generally determine buyers' needs and direct buyers toward devices, computers, and apps that meet their needs.

Some salespeople work directly for technology equipment manufacturers, mobile device manufacturers, or software manufacturers. Others work for resellers, including retailers that sell personal computer products. The technology salesperson in a retail store often is a suitable entry-level job for students working toward a certificate or degree in computer-related fields (Figure 12-10). Before consulting the opinion of a salesperson, be sure to independently research the product so that you can better determine whether answers to your questions are unbiased. Read How To 12-2 to learn how to evaluate extended warranty options.

Figure 12-10 A salesperson in an electronics store shows a digital camera to customers.
© dotshock / Shutterstock.com

HOW TO 12-2

Evaluate Extended Warranty Options

When you purchase electronic devices, such as computers and mobile devices, retailers and third-party vendors typically offer an extended warranty on the computer or device. These warranties, which are available for a fee, offer services that extend beyond what the device's manufacturer's warranty covers. For example, extended warranties may include replacing parts that break after the manufacturer's warranty expires, accidental damage, or replacing parts that become worn as a result of normal wear and tear. The following guidelines describe how to evaluate extended warranty options:

• Extended warranties can be offered by the manufacturer, retailer, or a third party. Extended warranties offered by a third party sometimes can be less expensive, but it may be more difficult to obtain service for your device. With an extended warranty that is offered by the manufacturer or retailer, it may be easier and faster to obtain service.

• Evaluate the manufacturer's warranty and what it covers. You may find that the additional coverage an extended warranty provides may not be worth the cost, so do your research first on the manufacturer's warranty. Do not rely on a salesperson to inform you of what a manufacturer's warranty does and does not cover.

• Determine an appropriate length for the extended warranty. For example, if you believe the device will be used for only three years before you will consider replacing it, do not purchase an warranty that extends longer than three years.

• Compare the cost of the warranty with costs associated with repairing or replacing the device. It may be less expensive to pay for one or two repairs instead of purchasing an extended warranty.

• Carefully research devices before you purchase them. Read reviews from people who have purchased the same device, and stay away from devices that are prone to problems. By purchasing a reliable device, you reduce the need for an extended warranty.

• Consider purchasing accidental damage protection. This protection offers either a repair or replacement of devices that are damaged accidentally. For example, if you drop your phone and the screen cracks, accidental damage protection may cover the repair. The number of repairs or replacements offered through an accidental damage protection plan may be limited, so do your research before purchasing it.

• Do not fall for sales tactics. Salespeople often earn commission or receive incentives for selling extended warranties. For this reason, they will make every effort to convince you of the possibility that something could go wrong. Educating yourself and determining the risk you want to take before purchasing your device will help you make a more informed decision about purchasing an extended warranty.

Consider This: Have you ever purchased an extended warranty? What other factors do you consider when determining whether to purchase an extended warranty?

Technology Education, Training, and Support

Schools, colleges, universities, and private companies all need qualified educators to provide technology-related education and training. The high demand in this field has led to a shortage of qualified instructors at the college level as instructors increasingly move to careers in private industry, which offers the promise of higher pay.

Corporate trainers teach employees how to use software and apps, design and develop systems, write programs, integrate and sync data from apps used on multiple devices, and perform other technology-related activities (Figure 12-11). Many large companies use their own training departments. Corporations usually require less educational background for trainers than educational institutions require for instructors.

In a more informal setting, a help desk specialist answers hardware, software, and networking questions in person, over the phone, or electronically via email or a chat room. Educational requirements for help desk specialists are less stringent than they are for other careers in the technology field. The help desk specialist position is an ideal entryway into the IT field.

Figure 12-11 A corporate trainer shows employees how to use new software.
© Jenner / Fotolia

IT Consulting

Technology professionals sometimes become IT consultants after gaining experience in one or more technology-related areas, such as software development, systems analysis and design, network configuration, developing mobile devices, using social media, or web development. An **IT consultant**, typically hired based on expertise, provides technology services to his or her clients. Large enterprises often hire teams of consultants to offer advice about technology-related concerns. IT consultants must possess strong technical skills in their specialized area and must be able to communicate effectively to clients. Read Ethics & Issues 12-3 to consider the effects of outsourcing IT jobs.

⚙ ETHICS & ISSUES 12-3

Is Outsourcing Jobs Wrong?
Companies have a long history of outsourcing, or relying on outside companies to perform certain tasks. Outsourcing enables companies to find workers with specialized experience and to control costs. When a company sends jobs overseas, outsourcing becomes offshoring. A skilled computer professional in the United States typically commands a higher salary than an IT worker in other countries. To remain competitive, many companies have chosen to send computer jobs abroad.

Proponents say that the United States has a long history of outsourcing all types of work when the economics of the situation demands it. Companies feel that they have a right to choose to send business tasks abroad if it saves costs. Foreign economies benefit when companies hire and pay

workers a fair wage and provide benefits. American consumers benefit from the reduced cost of goods.

Opponents say that offshoring results in unemployment and harms the economy. Others are concerned that sensitive work, such as health record maintenance or weapons manufacturing, could place U.S. citizens at risk. Some experts state that the work done abroad should be easy to manage and quantifiable in order to ensure it meets company standards. Some companies have received negative press due to inefficiencies in call centers and customer support located abroad.

Government officials and lawmakers struggle with policies regarding offshoring, especially with regard to taxing workers. Politicians debate whether or not companies who keep business in the United States

should receive tax breaks. Many argue that the Unites States should require companies who hire foreign workers to pay a fair salary and provide benefits comparable to those for American workers.

Consider This: Should the government limit a company's ability to outsource computer jobs to other countries? Why or why not? Should companies receive criticism for outsourcing jobs? Why or why not? What are some possible alternatives to outsourcing that would help to keep a company competitive? What steps can people take in their careers to avoid becoming a victim of outsourcing? Would you pay more money for goods manufactured in the United States? Why or why not?

Putting It All Together — Job Titles and Descriptions

The following sections briefly describe some of the more popular technology-related job titles for several categories of IT careers.

System Development   Careers in system development require you to analyze or create software, apps, databases, websites and web-based development platforms, and networks. Some careers are listed in Table 12-2.

Table 12-2   System Development Jobs

Job Title	Job Description
Cloud Architect	Identifies business requirements, strategies, and solutions for cloud storage and services that meet a company's goals or needs
Database Designer	Specifies the structure, interface, and requirements of a large-scale database; determines security and permissions for users
Program and App Developer	Specifies, designs, implements, tests, and documents programs and apps in a variety of fields, including robotics, operating systems, animation, and applications
Systems Analyst	Works closely with users to analyze their requirements, designs and develops new information systems, and incorporates new technologies
Systems Programmer	Installs and maintains operating system software and provides technical support to the programming staff
Web Designer	Designs the layout, navigation, and overall appearance of a website with a focus on user experience; specifies a website's appearance using HTML5, JavaScript, CSS, media, and other web design technologies
Web Developer	Analyzes, develops, and supports the functionality of a website, including applications that often interact with databases or other online resources

Technology Operations   Careers in technology operations require you to have knowledge about how hardware, software, and networks function. Some careers are listed in Table 12-3.

Table 12-3   Technology Operations Jobs

Job Title	Job Description
Computer Technician	Installs, maintains, and repairs hardware and servers; installs, upgrades, and configures software; troubleshoots hardware problems
Help Desk Specialist/ Help Desk Technician	Answers technology-related questions in person, on the phone, or via email or an online chat room
Network Administrator/ Engineer	Installs, configures, and maintains LANs, WANs, wireless networks, intranets, Internet systems, and network software; identifies and resolves connectivity issues
Technical Project Manager	Guides design, development, and maintenance tasks; serves as interface between programmers/developers and management

Web Marketing and Social Media   Careers in web marketing and social media require you to be knowledgeable about web-based development platforms, social media apps, and marketing strategies. Some careers are listed in Table 12-4.

Table 12-4   Web Marketing and Social Media Jobs

Job Title	Job Description
Customer Relationship Management (CRM) Specialist	Integrates apps and data related to customer inquiries, purchases, support requests, and behaviors in order to provide a complete application that manages a company's relationships with its customers
Internet/Social Media Marketing Specialist	Directs and implements an organization's use of Internet and social media marketing, including Facebook pages, Twitter feeds, blogs, and online advertisements
Search Engine Optimization (SEO) Expert	Writes and develops web content and website layouts so that they will appear at the beginning of search results when users search for content
User Experience (UX) Designer	Plans and designs software and apps that consider a user's reaction to a program and its interface, including its efficiency, its effectiveness, and its ease of use

Data Storage, Retrieval, and Analysis   Careers in data storage and analysis require you to be knowledgeable about collecting, analyzing, and reporting data from databases or the web. Some careers are listed in Table 12-5.

Table 12-5   Data Storage, Retrieval, and Analysis Jobs

Job Title	Job Description
Data Scientist	Uses analytics and other Big Data tools to compile statistics on data that an organization can use to plan product development or create strategies for marketing
Database Analyst	Uses data modeling techniques and tools to analyze and specify data usage
Database Administrator	Creates and maintains the data dictionary; monitors database performance
Digital Forensics Examiner	Collects and analyzes evidence found on computers, networks, mobile devices, and databases
Web Analytics Expert	Collects and measures Internet data, such as website traffic patterns and advertising, and develops reports that recommend strategies to maximize an organization's web presence

BTW
Technology Innovator
Discover More: Visit this chapter's free resources to learn about Salesforce (cloud computing company known for its CRM software).

Information and Systems Security   Careers in information and systems security require you to be knowledgeable about potential threats to a device or network, including viruses and hacking. Security specialists need to know the tools and techniques to protect against threats. Some careers are listed in Table 12-6.

Table 12-6 Information and Systems Security Jobs	
Job Title	**Job Description**
Computer Security Specialist/ Mobile Security Specialist	Responsible for the security of data and information stored on computers and mobile devices within an organization
Network Security Administrator	Configures routers and firewalls; specifies web protocols and enterprise technologies
Security Analyst	Implements security procedures and methods, looks for flaws in security of a company's devices and networks, works with and trains employees at all levels, and assigns permissions and network settings
Security System Project Manager	Develops and maintains programs and tools designed to provide security to a network
Digital Forensics Analyst	Inspects electronic data to recover documents and files from data storage devices that may have been damaged or deleted, in order to use them as evidence in a crime investigation

App Development and Mobile Technologies   Careers in app development and mobile technologies require you to have knowledge about trends in the desktop and mobile app market, as well as the ability to develop secure apps for a variety of computers and mobile devices. Some careers are listed in Table 12-7.

Table 12-7 App Development and Mobile Technologies Jobs	
Job Title	**Job Description**
Desktop or Mobile Application Programmer/ Developer	Converts the system design into the appropriate application development language, such as Visual Basic, Java, C#, and Objective C, and toolkits for various platforms
Games Designer/Programmer	Designs games and translates designs into a program or app using an appropriate application development language
Mobile Strategist	Integrates and expands the company's initiatives for mobile users
Mobile Technology Expert	Develops and directs an organization's mobile strategy, including marketing and app development

Mini Feature 12-2: Mobile App Development

When creating mobile apps, selecting a strategy to develop an app is as important as describing its capabilities. Read Mini Feature 12-2 to learn about three approaches to developing mobile apps.

 MINI FEATURE 12-2

Mobile App Development

Developers and technology managers should evaluate several possible approaches for creating mobile apps, and make a decision based on both technical and business considerations. Should they invest the time and money it takes to develop high-performing native apps for many different mobile operating systems? Would they be better off creating mobile web apps, written using standard web technologies, to run in a mobile browser? Or should they use a hybrid, or mixed, approach that can simplify the development process and lower development costs at the expense of a possible inconsistent user experience across platforms?

Native Apps

A *native app* is written for mobile devices running a particular mobile phone operating system, such as Google's Android, Apple's iOS, or Microsoft's Windows Phone. They offer fast performance and can store data for offline use. Native apps can access all of a device's content, including its contacts, calendar, and photos, and can interact with its hardware, including the microphone, camera, or accelerometer to measure movement and motion. For example, the native Instagram app shown in the figure below can access the device's camera to take photos.

Apps developed for a specific mobile platform or device generally will not work on another without significant modification. Creating native apps requires programming languages, presentation technologies, and development tools particular to each platform.

Source: © Instagram Courtesy of Neil Litt

After testing to be sure it works properly, developers deploy, or submit, a native app to an app store for approval and distribution. When deploying native apps to Google Play, Apple's App Store, or the Windows Store, developers must ensure that their apps follow rules and conditions that their publishers issue. For example, apps must run properly, may not contain offensive content, and should notify the user when requesting the current location or access to information stored on the device. Developers pay an annual fee to publish apps in an app store. The store retains a percentage of the sales price of any apps sold as a commission.

Mobile Web Apps

Mobile web apps are actually websites that provide a user experience similar to native apps. Developers write them using standard web technologies including HTML5, CSS, and JavaScript. Mobile web apps are not deployed to an app store; rather, they are deployed to a web server and users access them in a mobile browser. Users, therefore, always have access to the most recent version of an app. Creating a shortcut to the app's website and saving it as an icon or tile on a device's home screen provides easy access to the mobile web app. Many mobile web apps have a responsive web design, so that they will be displayed properly on devices with screens of different sizes.

Some companies choose to develop mobile web apps so that they can write one app that works on all devices that is not subject to the rules of an app store. Mobile web apps can access a limited set of device features, such as basic gestures, working offline, tap-to-call, and GPS, but do not have access to native features, such as the camera, microphone, accelerometer, and device notifications. For example, the Instagram mobile web app shown in the figure to the right runs in a browser and only displays photos, but does not allow you to take photos using your device's camera.

Source: Instagram Courtesy of Neil Litt

Hybrid Apps

A *hybrid app* combines features of native and mobile web apps. Like native apps, hybrid apps are developed for specific platforms and deployed to an app store. They can access many of a device's hardware features, such as its camera. Like mobile web apps, they are built with HTML5, CSS, and JavaScript. Developers use development tools to package this code with a browser and prepare it as a native app to deploy to popular app stores. In this way, hybrid apps are cross-platform, meaning the same code can run on many mobile platforms. This approach often saves development time and costs, but may not provide a consistent user experience or fast performance on all devices.

Discover More: Visit this chapter's free resources to learn more about development technologies for creating mobile apps.

Consider This: If an app is available as both a mobile web app and in an app store for you to download, which would you be more likely to use? Why? Suppose you have a great idea for an app, and you raise enough money to hire an experienced developer to build it for you. Would you ask the developer to code it as a web, hybrid, or native app? Why? Does your choice depend on the capabilities and requirements of the app?

NOW YOU SHOULD KNOW

Be sure you understand the material presented in the section titled Technology Careers as it relates to the chapter objectives.
Now you should know…

- Which technology fields you find interesting (Objective 4)
- Which technology jobs you might like to pursue (Objective 5)
- How mobile apps are developed (Objective 6)

Discover More: Visit this chapter's premium content for practice quiz opportunities.

Technology Certifications

A certification demonstrates your knowledge in a specific area to employers or potential employers. Organizations often require technology certification to ensure quality standards and to confirm their workforce remains up to date with respect to technology.

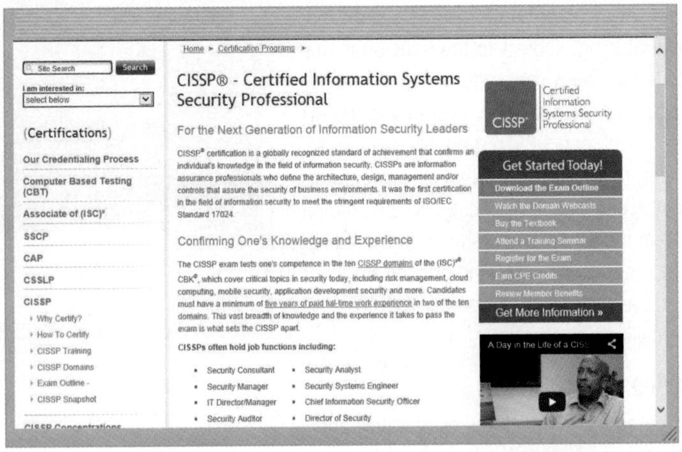

Figure 12-12 Certification exam sponsors, such as (ISC)² shown here, provide ways for you to prepare for exams, register and pay for exams, and more.
Source: (ISC)²

Most certification programs do not require academic coursework. Test results alone determine certification. Few professionals, however, have the experience and skill set to take a certification exam without preparation.

To assist in preparing for a certification exam, several training options are available: self-study, online training, instructor-led training, and web resources. Authorized testing centers provide most certification exams for a fee. The exam sponsor's website typically lists testing centers near you. On the website, you can schedule and pay for your exam (Figure 12-12). At a testing center, you may use a computer to take the examination, or you may mark your answers on a form that will be read by a scanner for grading. You likely will know before you leave the testing center whether you passed the examination. Some tests are in a multiple-choice format. Others are skill based. If you do not pass an exam, you may have to pay the fee again to retake it.

Obtaining a certification requires time and money. Certifications demonstrate your commitment to your chosen area. When deciding whether to obtain a certification, consider your long-term career goals, as well as your current experience. Read evaluations of the certification to determine its value in the industry you have chosen. Examine employment projections and available job opportunities to determine if it is worth obtaining the certification.

Technology certifications are available in many areas, some of which are discussed next.

BTW
Exam Day
Before taking a certification exam, read the instructions provided by the testing center to ensure you bring all necessary supplies, equipment, or technology. Print a copy of the directions in case your GPS device or app fails. Arrive early and silence or turn off your mobile devices. Know approximately how long the exam will take so that you can use your time wisely.

Application Software Certifications

Although numerous types of application software exist, several programs have achieved national recognition for use as business and graphics tools. Most sponsors of application software certifications have a partner training program and encourage computer-training centers to be authorized training representatives. A popular application software certification includes *Microsoft Office Specialist*, which tests a user's skills of Microsoft Office programs.

As with most other certifications, vendor-authorized testing facilities take registrations and administer the certification test. People with the following jobs may be interested in application software certification:

- Corporate trainers
- Help desk specialists
- Office managers/workers
- Technology sales representatives
- Technology teachers

Discover More: Visit this chapter's free resources to learn more about available application software certifications.

Data Analysis and Database Certifications

Data analysis certifications focus on the discovery, collection, and analysis of evidence on computers and networks. These certifications often contain the word, forensics, in their title. Database certifications cover the tasks required to support a database management system. If you are interested in working with data analysis or database certifications, you also may benefit from certifications in hardware, networking, programming, and security.

People with the following jobs may be interested in data analysis and database certification:

- Data scientist
- Database administrators
- Database analysts
- Digital forensics examiners

Discover More: Visit this chapter's free resources to learn more about available data analysis and database certifications.

Hardware Certifications

Hardware certifications vary in scope from a narrow focus with an emphasis on the repair of a specific device to an integrated hardware solution that addresses a company's current and future computing needs. Obtaining an advanced certification in hardware implies that you have achieved a standard of competence in assessing a company's hardware needs, and you can implement solutions to help the company achieve its computing goals. A popular hardware certification includes *A+*, which tests knowledge of computer setup, configuration, maintenance, troubleshooting, basic networking skills, and system software.

People interested in hardware certifications also may benefit from networking and operating system software certifications, which are closely tied to advanced hardware knowledge. People with the following jobs may be interested in hardware certification:

- Cable installation technicians
- Computer repair technicians
- Corporate trainers
- Help desk specialists
- IT consultants
- System engineers and administrators

Discover More: Visit this chapter's free resources to learn more about available hardware certifications.

Networking Certifications

Network expertise is acquired through years of experience and training because so many variables exist for a total network solution. Obtaining an advanced certification in networking implies that you have achieved a standard of competence, enabling you to address the complex issues that arise when planning, installing, managing, and troubleshooting a network. Cisco, Novell, Sun, and others offer certifications that test knowledge of installing, configuring, operating, and administering networks.

People in the following careers may be interested in network certification:

- Hardware service technicians
- IT consultants
- Network managers
- Network engineers
- System administrators

Discover More: Visit this chapter's free resources to learn more about available networking certifications.

 BTW
High-Tech Talk
Discover More: Visit this chapter's free resources to learn about bioinformatics (where biologists use technology to analyze, store, and retrieve biological information).

Operating System Certifications

Several options for various knowledge levels are available to those seeking operating system certifications. These certifications focus on particular skills of the user, the operator, the system administrator, and the software engineer. IBM, Microsoft, Novell, RedHat, Sun, and others offer certifications that test knowledge of their operating systems.

If you are interested in an occupation as an operating system administrator or software engineer, you also may benefit from certifications in networking, hardware, and the Internet. These additional certifications are closely linked to the operating system and serve to broaden expertise in that area. (Read Secure IT 12-3 to learn about risks associated with users who make unauthorized modifications to operating systems.) People with the following jobs may be interested in a certification in operating systems:

- Hardware technicians
- Help desk specialists
- Network administrators
- IT consultants
- System administrators

Discover More: Visit this chapter's free resources to learn more about available operating system certifications.

 SECURE IT 12-3

Risks of Jailbreaking and Rooting

Copyrights protect creators of original works, and digital rights management (DRM) strategies were developed to prevent people from pirating the owners' digital content. (Refer to Chapter 5 for details about copyrights and piracy.) Hardware manufacturers include DRM software on their products to control the apps and other programs that can be installed. When users want to run unapproved apps and customize their smartphones or mobile devices, they can make unauthorized modifications to the operating system and bypass the DRM

restrictions. This process, called *jailbreaking*, generally refers to hacking into Apple's iPhones and iPads, whereas a similar term, *rooting*, refers to products running Android and other operating systems.

When software developers create apps for Apple's iOS, Apple scrutinizes the software to ensure it adheres to strict guidelines. This review process helps maintain integrity and security. When the phone or mobile device is jailbroken, however, this reliability no longer exists. Apple states that jailbreaking causes these issues: security vulnerabilities,

instability, shortened battery life, unreliable voice and data, disruptions of services, and the inability to apply future software updates. The unauthorized modification violates the end-user license agreement (EULA), so the device may no longer be covered by the manufacturer's warranty.

☀ **Consider This:** Do you know anyone with a jailbroken smartphone or mobile device? Should Apple ease the limitations that are placed on changing iOS default settings or installing apps and other software from websites other than the App Store?

 BTW

High-Tech Talk
Discover More: Visit this chapter's free resources to learn how game developers create 3-D graphics, which appear to have height, width, and depth, giving realistic qualities to objects.

Programmer/Developer Certifications

Various certifications are available in the programmer/developer area. These certifications usually are supported with training programs that prepare applicants for the certification test. A popular specific programmer/developer certification includes *Google Apps Certified Specialist*, which tests a user's skills of administering, selling, and deploying Google Apps. A more broad development certification includes *Project Management Professional* (PMP), which tests knowledge of tasks required during system development.

If you are interested in developing applications, you also may benefit from certifications in networking and web design. These certifications are closely tied to programming and may broaden employment opportunities. People with the following jobs may be interested in a programmer/developer certification:

- Game developers
- IT consultants
- Mobile application developers
- Project leaders/managers
- Systems analyst
- Web developers

Discover More: Visit this chapter's free resources to learn more about available programmer/ developer certifications.

Security Certifications

Security certifications measure a candidate's ability to identify and control security risks associated with any event or action that could cause a loss of or damage to computer hardware, software, data, information, or processing capability. (Read Secure IT 12-4 to consider the effects of inadequately protected customer data.) While some security certifications focus solely on network and Internet security, others include measures to secure operating systems, application programs, and information systems, as well as the physical facility and its people. A popular specific security certification includes *Certified Information Systems Security Professional (CISSP)*, which tests in-depth knowledge of access control methods, information systems development, cryptography, operations security, physical security, and network and Internet security. Some security certifications relate specifically to the area of digital forensics.

People in the following careers may be interested in security certification:

- Information security officers and managers
- Law enforcement officials
- Military intelligence officers
- Network administrators
- Wireless network administrators
- Network security specialists
- Security administrators

Discover More: Visit this chapter's free resources to learn more about available security certifications.

 SECURE IT 12-4

Protecting Customer Data

Many for-profit and nonprofit companies and organizations have been affected by malware intrusions into their point-of-sale systems. Hackers have broken into retail servers and accessed data for millions of credit and debit card accounts. In one situation, they broke into a large entertainment company's server, disrupting service to its customers and publishing personal data for millions of customers, including passwords and possibly credit card information. The breached company allegedly waited one week to inform customers about the attack. The hackers who exposed this company's data were part of a well-known activist group that routinely targets large corporations and government agencies to expose data vulnerabilities and to protest policies. The group claimed that the company had not encrypted the exposed data

properly. The group's members are unknown, so officials are unable to hold them responsible for their actions.

Customers, however, sued the company for the breach. One lawsuit stated that the company's lack of encryption and adequate firewalls makes it responsible for the hackers' actions. Officials agreed, with one stating, "If you are responsible for so many payment card details and log-in details, then keeping that personal data secure has to be your priority." Customers held the company responsible for the delay in notification. The attack ultimately cost the company an estimated $170 million. Since the breach, the company changed its user agreement policies. The new policy states that by agreeing to use its products, users give up the right to sue for security breaches.

Thousands of other corporate security breaches have ranged from email phishing

schemes to stolen equipment. Cybersecurity risks affect all businesses because criminals know how to manipulate technology to compromise the networks and install malware. The U.S. Department of Homeland Security, U.S. Secret Service, and the National Cybersecurity and Communications Integration Center work to locate organized criminal groups, warn organizations about potential unauthorized access, and detect intrusions. They provide information about performing risk assessments, installing backup systems, and establishing security policies.

Consider This: Should hackers be punished for exposing customer data? Why or why not? What expectations of security should customers have when they enter personal data on a website or form? Should companies be able to prevent customers from suing them? Why or why not?

BTW

Counselors and Alumni
If your school has a career center or alumni network, take advantage of these valuable resources. Career counselors and experienced alumni can help you prepare for and secure an interview in your chosen field. They also might provide references to potential employers.

Job Searching and Career Planning

Many job opportunities may exist in your industry, so it is important to narrow down the available jobs to ones for which you are qualified and in which you are interested. Tools at your disposal include the career service department at your school (Figure 12-13), career planning websites, and online social networks. Read How To 12-3 to learn how to start your job search online.

Whether you are seeking a new job or currently are employed, you may find a career planning website useful. Career planning websites often allow you to post your resume online or enter your resume information in a form at the website for potential employers to review. Many also offer mobile apps. Examples of popular career planning websites include CareerBuilder, Dice, and Monster. Use a search engine to locate these career planning websites and their mobile apps.

Discover More: Visit this chapter's free resources to learn more about career planning websites.

Figure 12-13 A college or university career services website, such as the Illinois State University one shown here, provides helpful career planning information.
Source: Illinois State University

 HOW TO 12-3

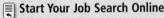 **Start Your Job Search Online**
Starting your job search online will help you locate available jobs and determine whether you are qualified to apply. Performing your research online will save time applying and interviewing for jobs for which you are not qualified. The following steps describe how to start your job search online.

1. Begin your job search by reviewing the information on online social networks, job search websites, and organizations' websites. On these websites, you can learn about career opportunities and prepare for an interview.

2. Follow an organization's activity on Facebook, Twitter, LinkedIn, and other social media channels.

3. Research a company's online activity to become familiar with some of the products, services, and opportunities that they provide.

4. Visit career services websites hosted by your college or university. These websites often contain information about career fairs, resume planning workshops, and campus recruitment activities.

5. Consider visiting a career planning website. These websites offer information about available jobs and local salaries. You

also can use them to research corporate work environments, technology news, and opportunities for professional networking.

6. Upload your resume to career planning websites and job search websites. Create the resume in a word processing program and then save it in the PDF format so that it has a consistent appearance when viewed on a variety of computers or mobile devices.

 Consider This: Have you ever searched for a job online? Why or why not? If so, were you successful in finding a job for which you were qualified?

Mini Feature 12-3: Creating a Professional Online Presence

In addition to the information provided in a job application and resume, many employers will search the web to learn more about job candidates. For this reason, both beginning and established technology professionals promote themselves online. Read Mini Feature 12-3 to learn about creating a professional online presence.

 BTW

Online Social Networks
Online social networks revise their privacy settings often. Periodically revisit your privacy settings on all personal social media accounts to ensure you have chosen the most current options that will secure your privacy.

 MINI FEATURE 12-3

Creating a Professional Online Presence

An understanding of the web, digital media, and online social networks, such as LinkedIn, is beneficial in creating your online presence.

Recommended Online Strategies

A professional online presence that positively conveys your accomplishments, skills, interests, and personality offers potential employers a more complete picture of you beyond what can be conveyed in a resume.

- Register a form of your name as a domain name and host a blog or website at that web address. If your name is not available or you do not have access to a web server, include your name as part of the web address for your website on a free service, such as Blogger or WordPress.

- Avoid informal or humorous names for your account profiles, blog title, or domain name.

- Include a photo of yourself that presents your best self.

- Use a webcam to create a 30-second video in which you introduce yourself. In the video, summarize your skills and professional interests. Post the video on YouTube or another video sharing site and include a link to it on your blog or website.

- Upload a PDF file of your resume, and include a link to it on your blog or website.

- Include links to your LinkedIn and Twitter profiles on your blog or website.

- Include links to any other publications, articles, videos, or digital content you have created.

- Create consistent accounts on online social networks. Read Ethics & Issues 12-4 to consider ways that social media can help in your job search.

- Post appropriate content to your blog, website, or online social networks regularly.

- Before uploading your resume or publishing your blog or website, ask at least two people to proofread content for any spelling and grammar mistakes. Keep the language professional.

Using LinkedIn

LinkedIn is an online social network where professionals, such as Reid Hoffman, founder of LinkedIn, can create profiles and connect with coworkers and industry colleagues. LinkedIn uses the term, contacts, to describe the individuals in your professional network and also stores your relationship with each contact in your network. Read How To 12-4 for steps to create a LinkedIn profile.

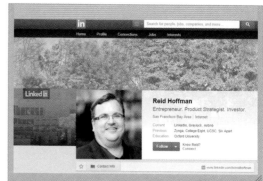

Source: LinkedIn

Use LinkedIn to:

- Connect with or stay in touch with current and former coworkers and classmates.

- Follow companies on LinkedIn to stay informed of job openings.

- Use LinkedIn's employment database to learn about career opportunities. View the job listing to find the name of the person who posted the job and to determine the connections between you and those members you might want to contact in order to learn about a company or open jobs.

- Join groups of people with similar interests or experiences. For example, your school's alumni group, people who work at the same company, people looking to share experiences they had when starting their own businesses, and people who use specific apps might be willing to share their expertise.

- Consider expanding your network by connecting with your contacts' connections. If you invite an extended contact to connect, be sure to include a note that introduces yourself and indicates your professional reason for connecting.

Discover More: Visit this chapter's free resources to learn more about maintaining a professional online presence and using LinkedIn.

Consider This: What online resources should you use to create a professional online presence? Why? What groups or companies should you join or follow on LinkedIn? What steps will you take to enhance your professional online presence?

ETHICS & ISSUES 12-4

 How Can Social Media Help Your Job Search?

It is no secret that what you do or say on social media can affect you in the job search. As previously mentioned, many employers check potential employees' social media profiles, including Facebook, Twitter, Google+, and LinkedIn, as part of the screening process. You likely are aware that you should use privacy settings and to be careful what you post, but how can you use social media tools to aid you in your job search?

Employers not only look for red flags (inappropriate or inflammatory posts, typographical errors, poor grammar, or photos that show unsavory or unethical

activities), but also for reasons to offer the candidate a position. A social media profile that presents you as professional and lists your qualifications can lead an employer to put you ahead of others. Employers also use social media to determine if a candidate's personality would fit into the corporate culture.

Instead of hiding all information behind privacy settings, employment experts recommend several social media strategies for job seekers. Create a profile that shows an interest in topics relevant to your profession. Use LinkedIn and other resources to follow companies and industry professionals to be aware of events, news, or job openings. Network with students,

colleagues, and industry contacts. Present consistent information, especially regarding education and experience, across all social media platforms. Consider using Twitter to share industry news, to demonstrate not only your interest, but your enthusiasm for the field.

Consider This: Does your social media presence reflect your interest in your desired field? What changes can you make so that your profile stands out among other job candidates? How does your profile compare to others in your industry? What can you gain by using social media to network or find industry information?

 HOW TO 12-4

Create a Professional Presence on LinkedIn

Building a professional profile and network on LinkedIn can help you locate professionals who can introduce you to employees at companies where you might like to work. In addition, LinkedIn also helps prospective employers locate you. Upon joining LinkedIn, you specify a profile that allows contacts, prospective contacts, and others to learn about you. The following steps describe how to create a professional presence on LinkedIn.

1. Include your full name, and avoid using nicknames.
2. Select and upload a professional photo. Consider using a high-quality photo that

clearly shows your face, and make certain you are dressed professionally in the photo.
3. Include comprehensive information about your work experience, education, and skills.
4. If you have any professional publications, websites, or blogs, be sure to list them and provide web addresses.
5. Build your network on LinkedIn by finding other LinkedIn members to add to your network. To see if any of your current acquaintances are on LinkedIn, you can import email addresses from your email address book or import profiles of friends from other online social networks. LinkedIn also may suggest

people you may know from a school you attended or company for which you work(ed).
6. Ask other members to provide recommendations about your skills.
7. Review your extended contacts (the network of your contacts' contacts) and determine whether you should connect directly with any of them.
8. As your work experience, education, or skills change, be sure to promptly update your LinkedIn profile.

Consider This: What professional information is, or will you put, in your LinkedIn profile?

NOW YOU SHOULD KNOW

Be sure you understand the material presented in the sections titled Technology Certifications, and Job Searching and Career Planning, as it relates to the chapter objectives.
Now you should know . . .

- How you can prepare for a certification (Objective 7)
- Which types of certifications you find interesting (Objective 8)
- How you can begin a job search (Objective 9)
- How you can create a professional online presence (Objective 10)

Discover More: Visit this chapter's premium content for practice quiz opportunities.

 Chapter Summary

This chapter discussed information systems used in an enterprise. It also presented various technology career fields and specific technology jobs. It then discussed technology certifications. Finally, it described how to begin a job search and create a professional online presence.

Discover More: Visit this chapter's free resources for additional content that accompanies this chapter and also includes these features: Technology Innovators: Wikimedia Foundation/Jimmy Wales, Ray Kurzweil, Meg Whitman, and Salesforce; Technology Trends: Crowd Sourcing and Monitoring Health Status; and High-Tech Talks: 3-D Graphics and Bioinformatics.

Test your knowledge of chapter material by accessing the Study Guide, Flash Cards, and Practice Test resources from your smartphone, tablet, laptop, or desktop.

TECHNOLOGY @ WORK

Architecture and Design

While walking down the city street, you stop to admire a new skyscraper with the most striking architectural features you ever have seen. You think to yourself that those responsible for designing the building are nothing less than brilliant. While a great deal of time is spent by people designing the building, computers and technology also play an important role in making the process more efficient. Today's tools allow architects and designers to see exactly what a finished building will look like before construction even begins.

During the preliminary design process, architects and design firms use CAD software to design the appearance and layout of a new building and can provide clients with a 3-D walk-through of a building so that they can determine whether the proposed design will meet their needs. Later, the program can be used to include the placement of support beams, walls, roof shape, and so on, and also conform to building codes.

CAD software also allows engineers in various fields, such as mechanical and electrical, to design separate layers in a structure. The software then can superimpose the designs to check for interactions and conflicts, such as if a structural beam in one layer interferes with a drain in another layer. The CAD software makes it easy to modify and correct the

structure before it is built, which can save time and money during the construction process. This software also eliminates most, if not all, of the manual drafting required.

Engineers use computers to determine the type of foundation required to support the building and its occupants; the heating, ventilating, and air conditioning (HVAC); the electrical requirements; and how the building may withstand external threats, such as hurricanes and tornadoes.

At the conclusion of the architecture and design process, contractors can use the information from computers to estimate the

total cost to build the structure. If, while construction is ongoing, a need arises to modify the building's design in some way, computers can incorporate a change and quickly provide plans for the new design.

The next time you notice a building under construction, stop to think about how computers and technology have increased the efficiency of the architecture and design process.

Consider This: How else might computers and technology be used in architecture and design?

© LDprod / Shutterstock.com

Study Guide

The Study Guide exercise reinforces material you should know for the chapter exam.

Discover More: Visit this chapter's premium content to **test your knowledge of digital content** associated with this chapter and **access the Study Guide resource** from your smartphone, tablet, laptop, or desktop.

Instructions: Answer the questions below using the format that helps you remember best or that is required by your instructor. Possible formats may include one or more of these options: write the answers; create a document that contains the answers; record answers as audio or video using a webcam, smartphone, or portable media player; post answers on a blog, wiki, or website; or highlight answers in the book/e-book.

1. A(n) _____ system is a set of hardware, software, data, people, and procedures that work together to produce information.

2. List and describe seven criteria that make information valuable.

3. Describe how functional units in an enterprise use information systems.

4. Define the term, enterprise resource planning (ERP). What are the advantages of ERP?

5. Explain the uses of and relationship between a document management system (DMS) and a content management system (CMS).

6. Describe security issues surrounding use of a CMS. List uses of a CMS.

7. List transactions that may occur when using a transaction processing system (TPS). Differentiate between batch and online transaction processing.

8. Define the term, management information system (MIS). Differentiate among the three types of reports an MIS generates.

9. Describe how a decision support system (DSS) is used. OLAP stands for _____.

10. List types of internal and external sources used in a DSS.

11. A(n) _____ system is an information system that captures and stores the knowledge of human experts and then imitates human reasoning and decision making. Define the terms, knowledge base, inference rules, and artificial intelligence (AI).

12. Define the components of information literacy. List steps in effective research and composition.

13. List guidelines for setting up your home office for telecommuting. Explain issues surrounding telecommuting.

14. List and describe the areas typically found in an IT department.

15. Describe the technology equipment field, and list possible jobs in this area.

16. Explain different types of companies in the software and apps field.

17. Explain security issues that arise when using unlicensed software.

18. Describe the technology service and repair field. Explain how technicians use diagnostic software.

19. Explain the issues surrounding data recovery and computer repair services.

20. List criteria needed to be a technology salesperson. Describe various careers in this field.

21. Explain how to evaluate extended warranty options for electronic devices.

22. Describe the role of a corporate trainer.

23. Explain the responsibilities and educational requirements of a help desk specialist.

24. Define the roles an IT consultant might fulfill.

25. Explain issues surrounding outsourcing and offshoring of jobs.

26. List requirements and available careers for the following areas: system development; technology operations; web marketing and social media; data storage, retrieval, and analysis; information and systems security; and app development and mobile technologies.

27. Describe three approaches to developing mobile apps.

28. Explain how and why an employee or employer might value or require technology certifications. What options are available to prepare for a certification exam?

29. Describe the benefits of obtaining an application software certification. List jobs that may require, or jobholders who may benefit from, obtaining this certification.

30. Explain the focus of a data analysis certification. List jobs that may require, or jobholders who may benefit from, obtaining this certification.

31. Explain why an employee might obtain an advanced hardware certification. _____ is a popular hardware certification.

32. List jobs that may require, or jobholders who may benefit from, obtaining a hardware certification.

33. Explain the expertise necessary to achieve a networking certification. List jobs that may require, or jobholders who may benefit from, obtaining this certification.

34. List options that are available for operating system certification. Name companies that offer operating system certifications.

35. List jobs that require, or jobholders who may benefit from, obtaining an operating system certification.

36. Explain security issues surrounding jailbreaking and rooting.

37. List examples of programmer/developer certifications. List jobs that may require, or jobholders who may benefit from, obtaining this certification.

38. Explain what is measured by obtaining a security certification. Name one popular specific security certification.

39. Describe how security breaches of customer data might occur. Explain the responsibility of a company to protect its customer data.

40. List jobs that may require, or jobholders who may benefit from, obtaining a security certification.

41. List steps to start your job search online.

42. Explain how a job seeker might use a career planning website. List examples of popular career planning websites.

43. List strategies to create a professional online presence. Explain how professionals use LinkedIn.

44. Explain how social media can help your job search.

45. List steps to create a professional presence on LinkedIn.

You should be able to define the Primary Terms and be familiar with the Secondary Terms listed below.

Key Terms

Discover More: Visit this chapter's premium content to **view definitions** for each term and to **access the Flash Cards resource** from your smartphone, tablet, laptop, or desktop.

Primary Terms (shown in **bold-black** characters in the chapter)

artificial intelligence (AI) (560)
cloud architect (568)
computer security specialist/mobile security specialist (570)
computer technician (569)
content management system (CMS) (577)
customer relationship management (CRM) specialist (569)
data scientist (569)
database administrator (569)
database analyst (569)
database designer (568)

decision support system (559)
desktop or mobile application programmer/developer (570)
digital forensics analyst (570)
digital forensics examiner (569)
document management system (DMS) (556)
Enterprise Resource Planning (ERP) (555)
expert system (560)
games designer/programmer (570)

help desk specialist/help desk technician (569)
information system (554)
Internet/social media marketing specialist (569)
IT consultant (568)
management information system (MIS) (558)
mobile strategist (570)
mobile technology expert (570)
network administrator/engineer (569)
network security administrator (570)
program and app developer (568)

search engine optimization (SEO) expert (569)
security analyst (570)
security system project manager (570)
systems analyst (568)
systems programmer (568)
technical project manager (596)
user experience (UX) designer (569)
web analytics expert (569)
web designer (568)
web developer (568)

Secondary Terms (shown in *italic* characters in the chapter)

A+ (573)
batch processing (558)
Certified Information Systems Security Professional (CISSP) (575)
computer-aided engineering (CAE) (555)
computer-aided manufacturing (CAM) (555)
customer relationship management (CRM) (555)
detailed report (558)
exception criteria (558)
exception report (558)
Google Apps Certified Specialist (574)
human resources information system (HRIS) (555)

hybrid app (571)
inference rules (560)
information literacy (561)
jailbreaking (574)
knowledge base (560)
Manufacturing Resource Planning II (MRP II) (555)
Material Requirements Planning (MRP) (555)
Microsoft Office Specialist (572)
native app (571)
online analytical processing (OLAP) (559)
online transaction processing (OLTP) (558)
Project Management Professional (574)
rooting (574)

salesforce automation (SFA) (555)
software and apps field (564)
summary report (558)
technology equipment field (564)

technology service and repair field (565)
transaction processing system (TPS) (557)

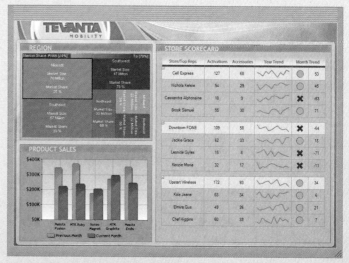

decision support system (559)

Checkpoint

The Checkpoint exercises test your knowledge of the chapter concepts. The page number containing the answer appears in parentheses after each exercise. The Consider This exercises challenge your understanding of chapter concepts.

Discover More: Visit this chapter's premium content to **complete the Checkpoint exercises** interactively; complete the **self-assessment in the Test Prep resource** from your smartphone, tablet, laptop, or desktop; and then **take the Practice Test**.

True/False   Mark T for True and F for False.

_____ 1. Accessible information has meaning to the person who receives it. (554)

_____ 2. A typical enterprise consists of a wide variety of departments, centers, and divisions — collectively known as functional units. (554)

_____ 3. CMSs are popular in large part because of their ease of use; CMS operators need minimal technical skills. (557)

_____ 4. In most circumstances, the licensed software owner can make multiple copies of software, for back up or to share with other users. (565)

_____ 5. It is good practice to back up and wipe all data before turning over your computer or device to an IT or computer repair technician. (566)

_____ 6. With third-party extended warranties, it is easier to obtain quick service for your device than returning it to the retailer. (567)

_____ 7. Educational requirements for help desk specialists are far more stringent than they are for other careers in the technology field. (567)

_____ 8. Apps developed for a specific mobile platform or device generally work on any other device without any modification. (571)

_____ 9. Like native apps, hybrid apps are developed for specific platforms and deployed to an app store. (571)

_____ 10. Most professionals have the experience and skill set to take a certification exam without preparation. (572)

_____ 11. Data analysis certifications focus on the discovery, collection, and analysis of evidence on computers and networks. (573)

_____ 12. Employers often use social media to determine if a candidate's personality would fit into the corporate culture. (578)

Multiple Choice   Select the best answer.

1. _____ information is arranged to suit the needs of the decision maker. (554)
   a. Verifiable
   b. Organized
   c. Timely
   d. Cost-effective

2. A(n) _____ allows for storage and management of a company's documents. (556)
   a. CMS
   b. DMS
   c. MRP II
   d. ERP

3. With _____, the computer processes each transaction as it is entered. (558)
   a. batch processing
   b. inference rules
   c. rooting
   d. online transaction processing

4. A(n) _____ report consolidates data usually with totals, tables, or graphs. (558)
   a. detailed
   b. summary
   c. exception
   d. criteria

5. In an expert system, the _____ is the combined subject knowledge and experiences of the human experts. (560)
   a. inference rules
   b. artificial intelligence (AI)
   c. decision support system
   d. knowledge base

6. Which of the following skills is *not* necessary for technology salespeople? (566)
   a. a general understanding of technology
   b. specific knowledge of the product they are selling
   c. testing internal components
   d. strong people skills

7. A(n) _____ is written for mobile devices running a particular mobile phone operating system. (571)
   a. native app
   b. hybrid app
   c. DSS
   d. expert system

8. If you are interested in developing applications, you also may benefit from certifications in _____. (574)
   a. hardware
   b. operating system
   c. networking and web design
   d. CISSP

Checkpoint

Matching   Match the terms with their definitions.

_____ 1. MRP (555)

_____ 2. CRM (555)

_____ 3. ERP (555)

_____ 4. OLTP (558)

_____ 5. artificial intelligence (560)

_____ 6. inference rules (560)

_____ 7. hybrid app (571)

_____ 8. A+ (573)

_____ 9. jailbreaking (574)

_____ 10. Project Management Professional (574)

a. processing system in which the computer processes each transaction as it is entered

b. application of human intelligence to computers

c. information system that manages information about customers, past purchases, interests, and the day-to-day interactions

d. program that combines features of native and mobile web apps

e. process of hacking into iPhones and iPads in order to make unauthorized modifications to the operating system and bypass DRM restrictions

f. broad development certification that tests knowledge of tasks required during system development

g. information systems that monitors and controls inventory, material purchases, and other processes related to manufacturing operations

h. hardware certification that tests knowledge of computer setup, configuration, maintenance, troubleshooting, basic networking skills, and system software

i. set of logical judgments that are applied to the knowledge base each time a user describes a situation to the expert system

j. integration of MRP II with the information flow across an organization to manage and coordinate the ongoing activities of the enterprise

✳ Consider This   Answer the following questions in the format specified by your instructor.

1. Answer the critical thinking questions posed at the end of these elements in this chapter: Ethics & Issues (563, 566, 568, 578), How To (563, 567, 576, 578), Mini Features (561, 571, 577), Secure IT (557, 565, 574, 575), and Technology @ Work (579).

2. What elements are contained in an information system? (554)

3. What are the qualities of valuable information? (554)

4. What are some common information systems used by functional units in a typical enterprise? (555)

5. What are some advantages of ERP? (555)

6. In addition to documents, what other items can be included in a CMS? (557)

7. What factors make CMSs so popular? (557)

8. Who assesses CMS vulnerabilities? (557)

9. How does batch processing differ from online transaction processing (OLTP)? (558)

10. How do detailed reports, summary reports, and exception reports differ? (558)

11. What are some examples of internal and external sources that a decision support system might use? (559)

12. How do enterprises use expert systems? (560)

13. What are some capabilities of artificial intelligence? (560)

14. What are the five categories recognized as integral literacy components? (561)

15. What are the benefits of telecommuting? (563)

16. What are some responsibilities of IT staff? (564)

17. What careers are available in the technology equipment field? (564)

18. Under what circumstances is software considered unlicensed? (565)

19. What individuals might be best suited for a career in the technology service and repair field? (565)

20. How might your information be compromised if a computer repair technician works on your computer or mobile device? (566)

21. What skills must an IT consultant have? (568)

22. What are some disadvantages of offshoring? (568)

23. What knowledge is required to work in a technology operations job? (569)

24. What are some typical rules and conditions developers must follow in order to deploy an app to an app store? (571)

25. What are the drawbacks of hybrid apps? (571)

26. What options are available to help you prepare for a certification exam? (572)

27. What is meant by the term, rooting? (574)

28. What issues does jailbreaking cause? (574)

29. What tools can help you search for a job? (576)

❁ Problem Solving

The Problem Solving exercises extend your knowledge of chapter concepts by seeking solutions to practical problems with technology that you may encounter at home, school, or work. The Collaboration exercise should be completed with a team.

Instructions: You often can solve problems with technology in multiple ways. Determine a solution to the problems in these exercises by using one or more resources available to you (such as a computer or mobile device, articles on the web or in print, blogs, podcasts, videos, television, user guides, other individuals, electronics or computer stores, etc.). Describe your solution, along with the resource(s) used, in the format requested by your instructor (brief report, presentation, discussion, blog post, video, or other means).

Personal

1. **Keywords for Job Search**   After taking your third computer class, you realize that you would like to train people how to use computers and software. You look for a job online and are asked to enter some keywords for your job search. What keywords will you enter to find a job that allows you to train others how to use computers and software?

2. **Online Job Search**   Having decided to work in the computer equipment field, you begin your job search online. In addition to looking on job search websites for available positions, where else might you find job postings?

3. **Documenting Education and Experience**   You are preparing your resume to submit to a computer service and repair company. You have studied computer service and repair in various classes and want to convince your prospective employer that you are the best candidate for the job. What might convince the employer to offer you a job?

4. **Contemplating a Job Offer**   After graduating from college with a degree in computer science, you send your resume to several companies. Almost immediately, you receive a job offer as a technical support representative in a midsized organization. Will you accept this job offer or wait for additional offers? Why?

5. **Appropriate Certification**   Because you hope to pursue a career as a system administrator, you would like

Source: (ISC)²

to obtain a certification. Many certifications are available, but you want to choose the one(s) that will best prepare you for your future career. Which certification(s) will you consider?

Professional

6. **Staying Current with Technology**   Having accepted a job as a computer salesperson, you now realize the importance of staying up to date with the latest technologies and products. What are three ways that you can stay current in the technology field while working full time?

7. **Outsourcing IT Positions**   As the chief information officer for a large organization, you consider outsourcing various positions within your department to save money. What are some types of positions that can be outsourced easily? What positions might be difficult to outsource? Why?

8. **Conducting an Interview**   You are preparing to conduct several interviews for candidates applying for a job as a senior systems administrator. What types of questions will you ask during the interview to determine whether they have the experience required to fulfill the job responsibilities?

9. **Tough Decision**   Two top candidates who applied for a job within your organization have interviewed well, and you are having difficulty selecting which candidate should be offered the job. One candidate has several certifications and only two years of job-related experience, while the other candidate has six years of experience, but no certifications. What decision will you make, and why?

10. **Training Decision**   Your boss has allocated money to allow everyone in the IT department to attend training related to their job responsibilities. While researching the training available for your job as a system administrator, you learn that you either can take a semester-long course at a local university or attend an accelerated one-week, forty-hour training course. At the end of each training session, you will be ready to become certified. Which type of training will you choose? Why?

Collaboration

11. **Technology in Architecture and Design**   As a student in a drafting class, your instructor has challenged you to design your dream home by using programs and apps wherever possible. Form a team of three people that will determine how to accomplish this objective. One team member should compare and contrast two programs or apps that can be used to create a two-dimensional floor plan, another team member should compare and contrast two computer-aided design programs or apps that can create a more detailed design of the house, and the third team member should compare and contrast two programs or apps that can assist with other aspects of the design process, such as landscaping and interior design.

The How To: Your Turn exercises present general guidelines for fundamental skills when using a computer or mobile device and then require that you determine how to apply these general guidelines to a specific program or situation.

How To: Your Turn

Discover More: Visit this chapter's premium content to **challenge yourself with additional How To: Your Turn exercises**, which include App Adventure.

Instructions: You often can complete tasks using technology in multiple ways. Figure out how to perform the tasks described in these exercises by using one or more resources available to you (such as a computer or mobile device, articles on the web or in print, online or program help, user guides, blogs, podcasts, videos, other individuals, trial and error, etc.). Summarize your 'how to' steps, along with the resource(s) used, in the format requested by your instructor (brief report, presentation, discussion, blog post, video, or other means).

❶ Conduct an Effective Interview

Gathering information is an important task, whether you are trying to assess whether a job candidate would be a good fit for an open position, or if you need to gather feedback about a new system you are developing. An important means of gathering information is the personal interview. Interviews must be thorough and comprehensive. Prior to conducting an interview, you must determine that an interview is the best means for obtaining the information you seek. You have learned a variety of ways to obtain information, and you should use each of them appropriately. Because an interview may interrupt a person's schedule and takes time, you must be sure the information gained in the interview justifies this interruption. Once you have determined you should conduct an interview to gather information, plan to ask questions that will generate useful answers. The following steps guide you through the process of conducting an interview that ultimately will generate useful answers.

a. Your questions should directly address the goals of the interview. Do not expect the person being interviewed to provide a tutorial. Your questions must generate answers that supply you with the information you need to make a decision.

b. Your questions should be thought-provoking. In general, do not ask questions requiring a yes or no answer. Your questions should not lead the interviewee to an answer — rather, the questions should be open-ended and allow the person to develop the answer. As an interviewer, never argue with the person being interviewed, do not suggest answers or give opinions, ask straightforward questions rather than compound questions, never assign blame for any circumstance that might come up in the interview, and never interrupt while the person is talking. Finally, you, as the interviewer, should not talk much. Remember, you are conducting the interview to gain information, and it is the person you are interviewing who has that information. Let him or her talk.

c. Pay attention carefully, with your ears and your eyes. What you hear normally is most important, but body language and other movements often convey information as well. Concentrate on the interviewee — expect that you will make much more eye contact with the person than he or she will with you. Allow silences to linger — the normal impulse in a conversation is to fill the silence quickly; in an interview, however, if you are quiet, the person being interviewed might think of additional information.

d. As you listen, concentrate on the interviewee. When points are being made, do not take notes because that will distract from what the person is saying; stay focused. Once the information has been conveyed, jot down a note so that you will remember.

e. Throughout the interview, offer reinforcing comments, such as, "The way I understand what you just said is …" Make sure when you leave the interview that no misunderstandings exist between you and the person you interviewed.

f. Before you conclude the interview, be sure all your goals have been met. You may not have another opportunity to interview the person, so ensure you have asked sufficient questions to gain the information you need to make a decision.

g. After the interview, it is recommended you send a follow-up email message or letter to the person you interviewed to review the information you learned. This message or letter should invite the interviewee to correct any errors you made in summing up your findings. In addition, for all the people you interview, keep a record of the time and place of the interview. In this way, if any questions arise regarding the interview, you will have a record.

Interviewing Online

If you are not in the same physical location as the people you want to interview, it may be better to conduct the interview online. If you plan to conduct the interview online, consider the following advice:

STUDENT ASSIGNMENTS

❋ How To: Your Turn

- Plug in the computer or device so that you do not have to rely on battery power. If you must rely on battery power, be sure that the battery is fully charged.
- Use a wired Internet connection, rather than connecting to a wireless network, to minimize the risk of losing Internet connectivity during the interview.
- Select a location for the video call that has a neutral background and is free from distractions.
- Know how to initiate or receive a video call.
- Exit your email, chat, and other unnecessary applications during the interview so that you are not distracted or interrupted by alerts and notification messages.
- Test the videoconferencing software in advance to ensure the configuration works.
- Adjust the microphone, webcam, and speakers before the actual interview to ensure optimum call quality.
- Practice switching between the videoconferencing app's chat window and your desktop or a browser window, in case you want to share a link, send a file, or type a message during the interview.
- Keep your eyes focused on the webcam so that you will appear attentive.

Exercises

1. Think about the last time you were involved in an interview (either as an interviewer or an interviewee). What types of questions were you asked? Do you feel the questions solicited useful answers?

2. If you were to interview a candidate for a technology-related position, what types of questions would you ask?

3. What advantages do open-ended questions have? When might a question requiring a brief answer be appropriate?

❷ Create a Video Resume

Resumes are used to inform potential employers about your experience, education, qualifications, and other important information. When using job search services on the web, such as Monster, CareerBuilder, and Dice, you often will submit your resume electronically.

A video resume contains a video of you speaking to your potential employer, explaining your interest in the job and why you think you are the best qualified candidate. The following steps guide you through the process of creating a video resume.

Record the Video

When you record the video resume, you must be aware of several important elements:

a. Make sure you have access to a computer with a webcam. Alternatively, you can record the video with a more sophisticated camera.

b. Prepare your script. Before you start recording, write and memorize the words you will say in the video. The video should be no longer than one minute, so write your script accordingly. Remember — you are trying to impress your potential employer.

c. Set the stage. The lighting and image in the video are critical to making a professional-appearing video. You should use adequate light so that the video is clear. Generally, you should arrange the camera for a head-and-shoulders shot.

d. Practice. You must practice your presentation in front of the camera. You can record and play back your practice recordings until you feel confident about your presentation.

e. Dress for the part. When on camera, the impression you make will be influenced by your attire and your personal grooming. You should dress as if you were doing a live interview.

f. Record the video. Your video should be no longer than one minute, but you might want to divide it into segments. For example, you could separate your statement about why you want to work for a company from your statement about your educational background.

Capture the Video

After you have recorded the video on a video camera, attach the video camera to the computer or insert the memory card from the camera into the computer and then complete the following steps:

a. Run a program or app to capture the video.

b. Select the option to import a video from the location on which it was stored.

c. If necessary, navigate to the location of and select the video to import.

d. Specify a name to identify the imported video.

e. Start the import process. This process may take several minutes to complete.

f. When the import process is complete, display the contents from the camera and verify the video has imported correctly.

Edit the Video

After recording the video, you normally should edit it and save it in a format that can be placed in your resume. To dit the video, complete the following steps:

a. Import the video clip(s) that will comprise your video resume into a new project in the program or app you are using to create your video.

b. If you are working with multiple video clips, arrange them in the correct order.

How To: Your Turn ✳

c. View the video clips in the order you desire to make sure the transition from one video clip to the next is not obvious. If it is obvious, you either can use editing features in the program or app to make the transition less obvious, or you may need to record one or more video clips again.

d. Review the audio quality to make sure it is clear and that the volume is adequate. If necessary, use editing features in the program or app to reduce or eliminate background noise.

e. Avoid using special effects, such as sound effects, transitions, or other visual effects. The purpose of the video resume is to advertise you as a potential employee, so do not include anything that may distract from that.

f. After you have edited the video, play the video from beginning to end to make sure you are pleased with it.

g. Save, but do not close, the project.

h. Export the video to an appropriate format. Because you will be distributing this resume and possibly publishing it on the web, use a format that is of acceptable quality but does not generate an excessively large file.

Share Your Resume

Now that you have edited your resume and exported it, you are ready to share your video resume with potential employers.

Saving in a Document

a. Open the document on your computer.

b. Use the commands in the word processing program to insert the video resume at the desired location.

c. Verify the video plays properly.

d. Save the document.

e. Open the document on another computer and make sure the video plays properly.

Saving on the Web

a. Connect to your web hosting company.

b. Upload the video to the folder that contains your website's files.

c. Modify the webpage that you want to include the video resume. You either can update the webpage so that the video plays on the page itself, or so that the webpage visitor has to tap or click a link to open and play the video in a new window.

d. Save the changes to the webpage.

e. Run a browser, navigate to the webpage containing the video resume, and make sure the video resume plays as intended. You should test your video resume from multiple computers and devices using multiple browsers.

Exercises

1. What type of information would you include in your video resume?

2. Compare and contrast three programs or apps that can edit a video. Which one do you like the most? Why? Which one do you like the least? Why?

❸ Create an Online Survey

If you want to collect information from a group of people, one way is to use an online survey. Online surveys can be sent to many individuals across the globe, allowing you to collect responses in a timely manner. Multiple web apps exist that allow you to create and distribute online surveys either for free or for a fee. Each web app has slightly different features, so evaluate various options before deciding which one to use. The following steps guide you through the process of creating an online survey.

a. Navigate to the website you want to use to create the online survey.

b. If necessary, create an account on the website hosting the web app.

c. Select the option to create a new survey.

d. Enter a descriptive title for the survey.

e. Add the appropriate instructions to the survey.

f. Add the questions to your survey. This includes:
   • Choosing the correct question type
   • Entering a descriptive question
   • If necessary, specifying the answer choices
   • Selecting whether the question is required
   • Specifying whether certain answers should prompt additional questions to appear

g. Save the survey.

h. Test the survey to make sure it functions as intended.

i. Distribute the survey to intended recipients.

j. When the due date for the survey passes, collect the survey results.

Exercises

1. What are at least three reasons you might need to distribute an online survey in your desired field?

2. Compare and contrast at least three online tools that can create and distribute surveys. Which one was your favorite? Why? Which one was your least favorite? Why? What are the differences between their free and fee-based accounts?

✳ Internet Research

The Internet Research exercises broaden your understanding of chapter concepts by requiring that you search for information on the web.

Discover More: Visit this chapter's premium content to **challenge yourself with additional Internet Research exercises**, which include Search Sleuth, Green Computing, Ethics in Action, You Review It, and Exploring Technology Careers.

Instructions: Use a search engine or another search tool to locate the information requested or answers to questions presented in the exercises. Describe your findings, along with the search term(s) you used and your web source(s), in the format requested by your instructor (brief report, presentation, discussion, blog post, video, or other means).

❶ Making Use of the Web
Careers and Employment

It is a good idea to acquire information before graduation about the industry in which you would like to work. While your teachers provide valuable training and knowledge to prepare you for a career, they rarely teach you how to begin a job search. You can broaden your horizon by searching online for career information and job openings.

Career websites provide details about training and education requirements, employment outlook, industry trends, and salary data. They also offer advice on writing a cover letter and resume, applying for jobs online, networking, and preparing for an interview. When you are offered a job, turn to these websites to obtain industry salary comparisons and negotiation techniques.

Job seekers can search employment websites, such as CareerBuilder, Dice, and Monster, for specific position openings worldwide. The jobs can be sorted by category, industry, location, date posted, job title, and keywords. Some websites list job fairs and separate the listings by categories, such as entry level, part time, summer, and temporary.

Source: CareerBuilder

Research This: (a) Visit at least two career websites and review the resources. What type of career advice is given? Are aptitude tests available? What tools are provided to manage a job search, such as tips for writing a cover letter and resume, job search mistakes to avoid, search strategies, and online social network tips?

(b) Use at least two employment websites to search for three job openings in your field. Which positions are available? What are their salaries, locations, required education and experience, and job descriptions? Can job seekers post a resume? Are company profiles and salary comparison available? Do these websites have mobile apps?

❷ Social Media

Companies have created policies that employees must follow when participating in social media and online social networks. Intel, for example, considers participation in social media to be an opportunity, not a right, and requires its employees to disclose their identity, protect the company's confidential and classified information, and use common sense when writing and airing opinions. Apple employees are urged to use good judgment when using online social networks and are barred from discussing the company on their own websites and from commenting on or posting messages regarding the company and its products on any related websites.

Research This: Locate at least two corporate policies for social media participation and summarize the requirements. Do you agree with the companies' guidelines? Are the policies too lenient or too strict? What actions are taken if an employee fails to abide by the policies? In what ways may policies differ among various fields, such as in health care and education?

❸ Search Skills
Using the Web for Research

A search engine may provide targeted results from news websites, blogs, corporate websites, and other sources. In addition, research websites, digital libraries, and specialized search engines can provide valuable information when using the web for research.

Your college or university library's website may list links to online journals, magazines, films, and books that will be helpful resources. It may make available links to online research databases, such as Gartner, Factiva, LexisNexis, and ProQuest, that offer IT

Internet Research

professionals' press releases, analysis, and case studies about companies, technologies, and industries. These sources often present valuable background information, and they offer IT professionals relevant business information to guide their decision-making.

Academic search engines, such as Google Scholar, and digital libraries, such as JSTOR (Journal Storage), provide access to academic journals and conference publications that can be useful when doing academic research. Navigating to these websites from campus may give you additional access to online research databases to which your library has a paid subscription.

Source: Gartner

Research This: Complete these tasks and report your findings. (1) Use your school library's website to find articles in online newspapers about information literacy. (2) Use a research database available from your school library's website to find an article about the fastest-growing IT careers. (3) Use a research database available from your school library's website to find an article about a company or technology discussed in this chapter. (4) Use Google Scholar or JSTOR to find a recent scholarly publication about rapid application development.

4 Security

Microsoft, Apple, Facebook, and Twitter are among the technology companies that have experienced a series of attacks exploiting security flaws in the Java plug-in for browsers. These security intrusions appear to have originated from hackers in China, Russia, or Eastern Europe who were attempting to obtain the companies' intellectual property, sensitive data, and users' personal information. The cyberthieves bypassed Java's built-in protections and installed malware on the compromised computers.

Kaspersky Security estimates that more than one-half of the security threats can originate from Java flaws. Oracle, the company that develops Java, issues patches to address known security vulnerabilities, but the Department of Homeland Security and other experts recommend not using Java until it is needed in browsers because new attacks may occur in the popular programming language.

Research This: Locate at least two articles discussing Java security flaws. How do Oracle and other companies inform users about the need to obtain updates to fix security holes? How many devices worldwide have Java installed? How can users discover if Java is installed on their computer or mobile device and, if it is, learn how to uninstall it?

5 Cloud Services

Enterprise Software Apps

Many companies make use of enterprise software apps to manage customer relationship management (CRM) and Enterprise Resource Planning (ERP). The rise of cloud computing in the enterprise has resulted in these and other enterprise software apps being hosted and managed on the cloud, rather than being purchased and installed in house. Software as a service (SaaS), a service of cloud computing, provides the delivery of software applications that are stored and deployed from servers on the Internet.

Enterprise software applications are popular SaaS offerings because IT departments do not need to install the software or manage the servers on which they run; instead, they can concentrate on configuring and specifying the services that these apps provide. Their "pay as you go" model, where customers are charged only for the capabilities they use, make SaaS apps attractive from a financial perspective. Users always interact with the most up-to-date version, and because the apps are accessed in a browser, it is easy to maintain the app across large organizations.

Research This: (1) Read about Salesforce, a pioneer in cloud-based CRM applications. What services does Salesforce provide? Find a case study about Salesforce, and describe how Salesforce's cloud solutions met one of its customer's needs. (2) Read about enterprise SaaS offerings to manage business operations and customer relations. Select or compare cloud services from companies such as SAP, Microsoft, and Oracle, and prepare a summary of their offerings. What are advantages and disadvantages to companies running these apps on the cloud?

Critical Thinking

The Critical Thinking exercises challenge your assessment and decision-making skills by presenting real-world situations associated with chapter concepts. The Collaboration exercise should be completed with a team.

Instructions: Evaluate the situations below, using personal experiences and one or more resources available to you (such as articles on the web or in print, blogs, podcasts, videos, television, user guides, other individuals, electronics or computer stores, etc.). Perform the tasks requested in each exercise and share your deliverables in the format requested by your instructor (brief report, presentation, discussion, blog post, video, or other means).

1. Offshoring and Outsourcing

The consulting company where you work as a systems analyst has refused to use offshoring, claiming management prefers to employ homeland citizens. The company's competitors have been using offshoring for some time. Your company's management team wants to discuss outsourcing the company's accounting system to an overseas firm.

Do This: Research laws, guidelines, and opinions regarding outsourcing. Address the following questions: Do you think systems should be developed entirely overseas? Why or why not? What are the major advantages and disadvantages of developing systems offshore? What security issues exist when using offshore developments? Does the United States have an obligation to help with employment overseas or in developing nations? Why or why not? What factors should a company consider when determining whether to use offshore developers?

2. Mobile App Development

Your company creates digital quizzes and study guides for nursing students. Currently you deliver these quizzes and other materials through a subscription-based website. Customers have been asking for an app that is optimized for smartphones and tablets. You have been asked to gather necessary information to start the project.

Do This: Determine which type of mobile app might be best suited to this type of product and explain why. Research other quiz and study guide apps. Read user reviews to determine what features customers might find valuable. List common features of the most highly-rated apps. What skills, hardware, and software are necessary to develop this type of app? What resources might your company have to purchase or use to develop the app? Research mobile app development jobs on an employment website to find examples of requirements for this type of job. What certifications might you look for when hiring a mobile app developer?

3. Case Study

Amateur Sports League You are the new manager for a nonprofit amateur soccer league. Several employees of the league have expressed interest in telecommuting a few days per week. You need to present a telecommuting proposal for the next meeting of the board of directors.

Do This: Research benefits and disadvantages of allowing telecommuting. List requirements for employees to be able to work from home, including types of Internet access and hardware. Discuss security issues with allowing employees to telecommute. How can you address security concerns? List guidelines employees should follow when working from home. Should you implement a method for evaluating employee efficiency or productivity when telecommuting? Why or why not? How would you assess individual employee performance? What jobs are better suited to telecommuting? Why? Would you recommend that the league allow telecommuting? Why or why not?

Collaboration

4. Job Search You work in the human resources department of a network security company. You currently have several openings for positions, including a network administrator, a security expert, and a help desk technician.

Do This: Form a three-member team and have each team member choose a different position. As a team, discuss any common requirements or background necessary for all of the positions based on the type of company. Each team member should list the educational background, available certifications, and other requirements for the position. Find listings for available jobs in your area. What responsibilities are listed for the position? What salary information can you locate? Create a list of information potential employees should have as part of their online profile. As a team, meet to discuss and compile your findings.

Technology Acronyms

Acronym	Description	Page
1G	first generation	481
2G	second generation	481
3-D	three-dimensional	15
3G	third generation	481
3GPP	Third Generation Partnership Project	462
4G	fourth generation	481
4GL	fourth-generation language	532
5G	fifth generation	481
AC	alternating current	301
ACPA	Anticybersquatting Consumer Protection Act	64
ADA	Americans with Disabilities Act	353
ADSL	asymmetric digital subscriber line	467
AI	artificial intelligence	560
AIO	all-in-one	114
ALU	arithmetic logic unit	281
AMOLED	active-matrix OLED	342
ANSI	American National Standards Institute	459
API	application programming interface	549
ARPA	Advanced Research Projects Agency	56
ASCII	American Standard Code for Information Interchange	289
ATC	advanced transfer cache	294
ATM	automated teller machine	118
ATM	Asynchronous Transfer Mode	468
AUP	acceptable use policy	106
B2B	business-to-business	82
B2C	business-to-consumer	82
BAN	body area network	456
bcc	blind carbon copy	103
BD	Blu-ray Disc	389
BLOB	binary large object	501
BMP	bitmap	86
BSA	Business Software Alliance	228
BSB	backside bus	300
BSN	body sensor network	456
BTW	by the way	94
BYOD	bring your own device	35

Acronym	Description	Page
C2C	consumer-to-consumer	82
CA	certificate authority	231
CAD	computer-aided design	164
CAE	computer-assisted engineering	555
CAM	computer-aided manufacturing	40
CAPTCHA	Completely Automated Public Turing test to tell Computers and Humans Apart	224
CATV	cable television	466
CBT	computer-based training	184
cc	carbon copy	103
CCFL	cold cathode fluorescent lamp	341
ccTLD	country code top-level domain	63
CD	compact disc	18
CDMA	Code Division Multiple Access	481
CDP	continuous data protection	234
CD-R	CD-recordable	388
CD-ROM	CD-read-only memory	388
CD-RW	CD-rewritable	388
CERT/CC	Computer Emergency Response Team Coordination Center	219
CF	CompactFlash	381
CIPA	Children's Internet Protection Act	247
CISSP	Certified Information Systems Security Professional	575
CMOS	complementary metal-oxide semiconductor	296
CMS	content management system	557
COPPA	Children's Online Privacy Protection Act	246
CPC	cost per click	548
CPI	cost per impression	548
CPU	central processing unit	110
CRM	customer relationship management	287
CRT	cathode-ray tube	344
CSA	Cloud Security Alliance	232
CSC	common short code	124
CSI	Cellular Seizure Investigation	295
CSO	chief security officer	527

Acronym	Description	Page
CSS	cascading style sheets	537
CTIA	Cellular Telecommunications Industry Association	315
CTS	carpal tunnel syndrome	142
CVS	computer vision syndrome	143
DaaS	data as a service	155
DBA	database administrator	510
DBMS	database management system	498
DC	direct current	301
DDoS	distributed DoS	217
DDR SDRAM	Double Data Rate SDRAM	292
DIMM	dual inline memory module	293
DLP	digital light processing	352
DMCA	Digital Millennium Copyright Act	246
DMS	document management system	556
DNS	domain name system	64
DOE	Department of Energy	241
DoS	denial of service	217
dpi	dots per inch	346
DRAM	dynamic RAM	292
DRM	digital rights management	240
DSL	Digital Subscriber Line	59
DSS	decision support system	559
DTP	desktop publishing	180
DTV	digital television	343
DV	digital video	330
DVD	digital versatile disc or digital video disc	18
DVD+R	DVD-recordable	388
DVD+RAM	DVD-random access memory	388
DVD+RW	DVD-rewritable	388
DVD-R	DVD-recordable	388
DVD-ROM	DVD-read-only memory	388
DVD-RW	DVD-rewritable	388
DVI	Digital Video Interface	135
DVR	digital video recorder	474
EB	exabyte	370
ECPA	Electronic Communications Privacy Act	246
EDGE	Enhanced Data GSM Environment	481
EDI	electronic data interchange	453
EFT	electronic funds transfer	453
EIDE	Enhanced Integrated Drive Electronics	380
EPA	Environmental Protection Agency	241
ERP	Enterprise Resource Planning	555

Acronym	Description	Page
eSATA	external SATA	380
EULA	end-user license agreement	163
EVDO	Evolution Data Optimized	481
FAQ	frequently asked questions	94
FC	Fibre Channel	390
FCC	Federal Communications Commission	315
FDDI	Fiber Distributed Data Interface	477
FERPA	Family Educational Rights and Privacy Act	163
FIP	Fair Information Practices	502
FLA	Fair Labor Association	295
FOIA	Freedom of Information Act	246
fps	frames per second	331
FSB	front side bus	300
FTP	File Transfer Protocol	24
FTTB	Fiber to the Building	467
FTTH	Fiber to the Home	467
FTTP	Fiber to the Premises	59
FWIW	for what it's worth	94
FYI	for your information	94
GB	gigabyte	61
GBps	gigabytes per second	371
GHz	gigahertz	283
GIF	Graphics Interchange Format	86
GPRS	General Packet Radio Service	481
GPS	global positioning system	70
GPU	graphics processing unit	342
GSM	Global System for Mobile Communications	481
GUI	graphical user interface	414
HDD	hard disk drive	373
HDMI	High-Definition Media Interface	343
HDTV	high-definition television	15
HIPAA	Health Insurance Portability and Accountability Act	246
HRIS	human resources information system	555
HTML	Hypertext Markup Language	535
http	Hypertext Transfer Protocol	69
HVAC	heating, ventilating, and air conditioning	579
IaaS	infrastructure as a service	53
ICANN	Internet Corporation for Assigned Names and Numbers	63
ID	identification	222

Acronym	Description	Page
IDE	integrated development environment	530
IDEA	Individuals with Disabilities Education Act	354
IEC	International Electronics Commission	299
IEEE	Institute of Electrical and Electronics Engineers	138
IMDb	Internet Movie Database	548
IMEI	International Mobile Equipment Identity	315
IMHO	in my humble opinion	94
IMSI	International Mobile Subscriber Identity	480
IoT	Internet of Things	284
IP	Internet Protocol	62
IP	intellectual property	240
IPO	initial public offering	396
IR	infrared	465
IrDA	Infrared Data Association	465
IROC2	Institute for Responsible Online and Cell-Phone Communication	246
ISDN	Integrated Services Digital Network	467
ISP	Internet service provider	20
IT	information technology	310
JAD	joint-application design	520
JOBS	Jumpstart Our Business Startup	396
JPEG	Joint Photographic Experts Group	86
KB	kilobyte	370
KBps	kilobytes per second	371
L1	Level 1	294
L2	Level 2	294
L3	Level 3	294
LAN	local area network	453
LCD	liquid crystal display	341
LED	light-emitting diode	341
LTE	Long Term Evolution	462
M2	Memory Stick Micro	381
M2M	machine-to-machine	133
MAC	Media Access Control	236
Mac OS	Macintosh operating system	427
MAN	metropolitan area network	455
MB	megabyte	61
MBAN	medical body area network	456
MBps	megabytes per second	371
MDM	mobile device management	433
MFP	multifunction printer	349

Acronym	Description	Page
MICR	magnetic-ink character recognition	338
MIS	management information system	558
MMS	multimedia message service	124
MP	megapixels	127
MRP	Material Requirements Planning	555
MRP II	Manufacturing Resource Planning II	555
ms	millisecond	296
MTSO	mobile telephone switching office	480
NAS	network attached storage	390
NFC	near field communications	138
NIC	network interface card	472
ns	nanosecond	296
NSA	National Security Agency	480
NUI	natural user interface	414
OCIA	Office of Cyber and Infrastructure Analysis	365
OCR	optical character recognition	334
OEM	original equipment manufacturer	421
OLAP	online analytical processing	559
OLED	organic LED	342
OLTP	online transaction processing	558
OMR	optical mark recognition	335
OODB	object-oriented database	508
OOP	object-oriented programming	530
OS	operating system	410
P2P	peer-to-peer	457
PaaS	platform as a service	288
PAN	personal area network	455
PATRIOT	Provide Appropriate Tools Required to Intercept and Obstruct Terrorism	246
PB	petabyte	370
PC	personal computer	4
PDF	Portable Document Format	86
PERT	Program Evaluation and Review Technique	518
PIN	personal identification number	118
PMP	Project Management Professional	574
PNG	Portable Network Graphics	86
POS	point of sale	118
PPC	pay per click	548
ppm	pages per minute	345
ps	picosecond	296
PUE	power usage effectiveness	241
QBE	query by example	512

Acronym	Description	Page
QR	quick response	178
RAD	rapid application development	530
RAID	redundant array of independent disks	380
RAM	random access memory	290
RDRAM	Rambus DRAM	292
RFI	request for information	523
RFID	radio frequency identification	465
RFP	request for proposal	523
RFQ	request for quotation	523
ROI	return on investment	519
ROM	read-only memory	294
rpm	revolutions per minute	375
RSI	repetitive strain injury	142
RSS	Really Simple Syndication	536
RTOS	real-time operating system	436
RWD	responsive web design	84
SaaS	software as a service	105
SAN	storage area network	391
SAS	serial-attached SCSI	380
SATA	Serial Advanced Technology Attachment	380
SCSI	Small Computer System Interface	380
SDHC	Secure Digital High Capacity	381
SDLC	system development life cycle	515
SDRAM	Synchronous DRAM	292
SDXC	Secure Digital Expanded Capacity	381
SEC	Securities and Exchange Committee	295
SecaaS	security as a service	259
SFA	salesforce automation	555
SFTP	secure file transfer protocol	534
SIMM	single inline memory module	293
SLR	single-lens reflex	125
SMM	Sustainable Materials Management	122
SMS	short message service	124
SOX	Sarbanes-Oxley	396
SQL	Structured Query Language	512
SRAM	static RAM	292
SSD	solid-state drive	17
SSID	service set identifier	236
TB	terabyte	290
Tbps	trillion bits per second	479
TCP/IP	Transmission Control Protocol/Internet Protocol	461

Acronym	Description	Page
TFT	thin-film transistor	342
TIFF	Tagged Image File Format	86
TLD	top-level domain	63
TPS	transaction processing system	557
TTFN	ta-ta for now	94
TYVM	thank you very much	94
UI	user interface	414
UMB	Ultra Mobile Broadband	481
UMTS	Universal Mobile Telecommunications System	481
UPC	Universal Product Code	335
UPS	uninterruptible power supply	115
URL	Uniform Resource Locator	68
USB	Universal Serial Bus	17
US-CERT	United States Computer Emergency Readiness Team	557
USPS	United States Postal Service	335
UV	ultraviolet	344
UWB	ultra-wideband	463
VAN	value-added network	453
VAR	value-added reseller	523
VM	virtual machine	431
VoIP	Voice over Internet Protocol	24
VPE	visual programming environment	532
VPN	virtual private network	230
VR	virtual reality	87
W3C	World Wide Web Consortium	58
WAN	wide area network	455
WAP	wireless access point	236
WBT	web-based training	184
Wi-Fi	wireless fidelity	59
WiMAX	Worldwide Interoperability for Microwave Access	463
WLAN	wireless local area network	454
WML	wireless markup language	536
WORM	write once, read many	388
WPA2	Wi-Fi Protected Access 2	236
WWW	World Wide Web	65
XML	Extensible Markup Language	536
YB	yottabyte	370
ZB	zettabyte	370
μs	microsecond	296

Troubleshooting Computer and Mobile Device Problems

While using a computer or mobile device, at some point you probably will experience a technology problem that requires troubleshooting. Technology problems that remain unresolved may impact your ability to use your device. This appendix identifies some common problems you might experience with computers and mobile devices; it also includes some suggestions for correcting these problems. If the recommended solutions in the table below do not solve your problem, or you are uncomfortable performing any of the recommended actions, contact a repair professional (independent computer repair company, technical support department at your job or academic institution, or computer or mobile device manufacturer) for additional options.

This appendix also might assist you with completing some of the Problem Solving exercises found at the end of each chapter in this textbook. Table 1 contains possible solutions for problems that might occur on your computer or mobile device.

Note: The following steps are suggestions; they are not comprehensive solutions. When working with a computer or mobile device, follow all necessary safety precautions before implementing any of these recommended solutions. Contact a professional if you require additional information.

Table 1 Problems and Recommended Solutions					
Problem	**Desktop**	**Laptop**	**Tablet**	**Phone**	**Recommended Solution(s)**
Computer or device does not turn on.	✓	✓	✓		The computer might be in sleep or hibernate mode; to wake up the computer, try pressing a key on the keyboard, pressing the power button, or tapping the touch screen if applicable.
	✓				Make sure power cables are plugged securely into the wall and the back of the computer.
		✓	✓	✓	Make sure the battery is charged if the computer or device is not connected to an external power source. If the battery is charged, connect the external AC adapter and attempt to turn on the computer or device. If the computer or device still does not turn on, the problem may be with the computer or device.
	✓	✓	✓	✓	If none of the above options resolves the issue, the power supply or AC adapter might be experiencing problems; contact a professional for assistance.
Battery does not hold a charge.		✓	✓	✓	Verify the AC adapter used to charge the battery is working properly. If the mobile computer or device can run from the AC adapter without a battery installed, the AC adapter most likely is working properly.
					If the AC adapter works, it may be time to replace the battery.
Computer issues a series of beeps when turned on.	✓	✓			Refer to your computer's documentation to determine what the beeps indicate, as the computer hardware may be experiencing a problem.

Problem	Desktop	Laptop	Tablet	Phone	Recommended Solution(s)
Computer or device turns on, but operating system does not run.	✓	✓	✓	✓	Disconnect all nonessential peripheral devices, remove all storage media, and then restart the computer or device.
					Restart the computer or device; if the problem persists, the operating system might need to be restored. If restoring the operating system does not work, the hard drive might be failing.
Monitor does not display anything.	✓				Verify the monitor is turned on.
					Verify the video cable is connected securely to the computer and monitor.
					Make sure the power cables are plugged securely into the wall and the back of the monitor.
					Make sure the monitor is set to the correct input source.
					Restart the computer.
					If you have access to a spare monitor, see if that monitor will work. If so, your original monitor might be faulty. If not, the problem may be with your computer's hardware or software configuration.
Screen does not display anything.		✓	✓	✓	Restart the device.
					Make sure the device is plugged in or the battery is sufficiently charged.
Keyboard or mouse does not work.	✓	✓	✓		Verify the keyboard and mouse are connected properly to the computer or device.
					If the keyboard and mouse are wireless, make sure they are turned on and contain new batteries.
					If the keyboard and mouse are wireless, attempt to pair them again with the computer or wireless receiver. Read How To 3-1 for more information.
					If you have access to a spare keyboard or mouse, see if it will work. If so, your original keyboard or mouse might be faulty. If not, the problem may be with your computer's hardware or software configuration.
		✓			Make sure the touchpad is not disabled.
Wet keyboard no longer works.	✓	✓			Turn the keyboard upside down to drain the liquid, dab wet areas with a cotton swab, and allow the keyboard to dry.
Speakers do not work.	✓	✓	✓	✓	Verify that headphones or earbuds are not connected.
					Make sure the volume is not muted and is turned up on the computer or mobile device.
	✓	✓			Verify the speakers are turned on.
					Make sure the speakers are connected properly to the computer.
					If necessary, verify the speakers are plugged in to an external power source.
Hard drive makes noise.	✓	✓			If the computer is not positioned on a flat surface, move it to a flat surface.
					If the problem persists, contact a professional.

Problem	Desktop	Laptop	Tablet	Phone	Recommended Solution(s)
Fan contains built-up dust/does not work.	✓	✓			If possible, open the system unit and use a can of compressed air to blow the dust from the fan and away from the system unit.
	✓				Remove obvious obstructions that might be preventing the fan from functioning.
					Verify the fan is connected properly to the motherboard.
					If the fan still does not work, it may need to be replaced.
Computer or device is too hot.	✓	✓			Verify the fan or vents are not obstructed. If the fan or vents are obstructed, use a can of compressed air to blow the dust from the fan or vent and away from the computer or device or remove other obstructions.
		✓			Purchase a cooling pad that rests below the laptop and protects it from overheating.
			✓	✓	Exit apps running in the background.
					Search for and follow instructions how to clear the tablet or phone's cache memory.
					Run an app to monitor the tablet's or phone's battery performance, and exit apps that require a lot of battery power.
					Decrease the brightness of the display.
Cannot read from optical disc.	✓	✓			Clean the optical disc and try reading from it again.
					Try reading from another optical disc. If the second optical disc works, the original disc is faulty.
					If the second disc does not work, the problem may be with the optical disc drive.
External drive (USB flash drive, optical disc drive, or external hard drive) is not recognized.	✓	✓	✓		Remove the drive and insert it into a different USB port, if available.
					Remove the drive, restart the computer, and insert the drive again.
					Try connecting the drive to a different computer. If you still cannot read from the drive, it may be faulty.
Program or app does not run.	✓	✓	✓	✓	Restart the computer or device and try running the program or app again.
					If feasible, uninstall the program or app, reinstall it, and then try running it again. If the problem persists, the problem may be with the operating system's configuration.
Computer or device displays symptoms of a virus or other malware.	✓	✓	✓	✓	Make sure your antivirus software is up to date and then disconnect the computer or device from the network and run antivirus software to attempt to remove the malware. Continue running scans until no threats are detected and then reconnect the computer to the network.
					If you do not have antivirus software installed, obtain and install a reputable antivirus program or app and then scan your computer in an attempt to remove the malware. You should have only one antivirus program or app installed on your computer or mobile device at one time.
					If you are unable to remove the malware, take your computer to a professional who may be able to remove the malicious program or app.

Problem	Desktop	Laptop	Tablet	Phone	Recommended Solution(s)
Computer or device is experiencing slow performance.	✓	✓	✓		Defragment the hard disk.
	✓	✓			Uninstall programs and apps that you do not need.
					Verify your computer or device meets the minimum system requirements for the operating system and software you are running.
					If possible, purchase and install additional memory (RAM).
Screen is damaged physically.	✓	✓	✓	✓	Contact a professional to replace the screen; if the computer or device is covered under a warranty, the repair may be free.
					Replacing a broken screen on a computer or device might be more costly than replacing the computer or device; consider your options before replacing the screen.
Touch screen does not respond.	✓	✓	✓	✓	Clean the touch screen.
					Restart the computer or device.
Computer or device is wet.		✓	✓	✓	Turn off the computer or device, remove the battery, and dry off visible water with a cloth. Fill a plastic bag or box with rice, submerge the computer or device and battery into the rice so that it is surrounded completely, and then do not turn on the computer or device for at least 24 hours.
					If the computer or device does not work after it is dry, contact a professional for your options.
Computer or device does not connect to a wireless network.	✓	✓	✓	✓	Verify you are within range of a wireless access point.
					Make sure the information to connect to the wireless network is configured properly on the computer or device.
					Make sure the wireless capability on the computer or device is turned on.
Computer or device cannot synchronize with Bluetooth accessories.	✓	✓	✓	✓	Verify the Bluetooth device is turned on.
					Verify the Bluetooth functionality on your computer or device is enabled.
					Verify the computer or device has been paired properly with the accessory. Read How To 3-1 for more information.
					Make sure the Bluetooth device is charged.
Device continuously has poor cell phone reception.			✓	✓	Restart the device.
					If you have a protective case, remove the case to see if reception improves.
					If you are using the device inside a building, try moving closer to a window or open doorway.
					Contact your wireless carrier for additional suggestions.

Index

1G (first generation of cellular transmissions): First generation of cellular transmissions., 481

2G (second generation of cellular transmissions): Second generation of cellular transmissions., 481

3-D printer: Printer that uses a process called additive manufacturing to create an object by adding material to a three-dimensional object, one horizontal layer at a time. (Or) Printer that can print solid objects such as clothing, prosthetics, eyewear, implants, toys, parts, prototypes, and more., 15, 349

3G (third generation of cellular transmissions): Third generation of cellular transmissions., 481

4G (fourth generation of cellular transmissions): Fourth generation of cellular transmissions., 481

4GL: A nonprocedural language that enables users and programmers to access data in a database., 532. *See also* **fourth-generation language**

5G (fifth generation of cellular transmissions): Fifth generation of cellular transmissions., 481

802.11: A series of network standards that specifies how two wireless devices communicate over the air with each other., 462

A

acceptable use policy (AUP): Outlines the activities for which a computer and network may and may not be used., 231

acceptance test: Test performed by end users during the program development life cycle that checks the new system to ensure that it works with actual data., 525

access control: A security measure that defines who can access a computer, device, or network, when they can access it, and what actions they can take while accessing it., 222

accessories, gaming, 11

access time: The amount of time it takes a storage device (1) to locate an item on a storage medium or (2) to deliver an item from memory to the processor., 296, 371

accounting software: An application that helps businesses of all sizes record and report their financial transactions., 173

active-matrix: LCD display technology that uses a separate transistor to apply charges to each liquid crystal cell and, thus, displays high-quality color that is viewable from all angles., 342. *See also* **TFT**

activity tracker, 130

ADA: Law that requires any company with 15 or more employees to make reasonable attempts to accommodate the needs of physically challenged workers., 353. *See also* **Americans with Disabilities Act**

adapter board: A circuit board that enhances the functions of a component of a desktop or server system unit and/or provides connections to peripheral devices., 297. *See also* **adapter card; expansion card**

adapter card: A circuit board that enhances the functions of a component of a desktop or server system unit and/or provides connections to peripheral devices., 297–298. *See also* **adapter board; expansion card**

adapters, 297–299

address book, 74

address: Unique number that identifies the location of a byte in memory., 290

administrator account: Type of account typically held by computer owners or network administrators that enables them to access all files and programs, install programs, and specify settings that affect all users on a computer, mobile device, or network., 423

Adobe Reader, 88, 177

ADSL: A type of DSL that supports faster downstream rates than upstream rates., 467. *See also* **asymmetric digital subscriber line**

Advanced Research Projects Agency (ARPA), 56

advanced transfer cache: Type of L2 cache built directly on the processor chip, which increases processor speed., 294. *See also* **ATC**

adware: A program that displays an online advertisement in a banner or pop-up window on webpages, email, or other Internet services., 192, 215, 245

adware remover: A program that detects and deletes adware., 192

agriculture, technology and, 485

A+: Hardware certification that tests knowledge of computer setup, configuration, maintenance, troubleshooting, basic networking skills, and system software., 573

AI, 560

air gestures: Gestures made by moving your body or a handheld input device through the air., 328

all-in-one desktop: Desktop that does not have a tower and instead houses the screen and system unit in the same case., 114

all-in-one printer: A single device that looks like a printer or a copy machine but provides the functionality of a printer, scanner, copy machine, and perhaps a fax machine., 349. *See also* **multifunction printer (MFP)**

alphabetic check: Validity check that ensures that users enter only alphabetic data into a field., 503

alphanumeric characters: Letters and numbers., 289

ALU: Component of the processor that performs arithmetic, comparison, and other operations., 281. *See also* **arithmetic logic unit**

alumni network, 576

Amazon's storefront, 81

Americans with Disabilities Act: Law that requires any company with 15 or more employees to make reasonable attempts to accommodate the needs of physically challenged workers., 353. *See also* **ADA**

AMOLED (active-matrix OLED): Screens that use both active-matrix and OLED technologies, combining the benefits of high-quality viewing from all angles with lower power consumption., 342

analog: Continuous (wave form) signals., 288

analysis phase: Step in the system development life cycle during which two major activities are performed: (1) conduct a preliminary investigation and (2) perform detailed analysis., 521

Android: An open source, Linux-based mobile operating system designed by Google for smartphones and tablets., 434

Animal's identity security, chip implantation, 280

animation: The appearance of motion created by displaying a series of still images in sequence., 86

anonymous FTP: File transfer method whereby anyone can transfer some, if not all, available files., 92

Anticybersquatting Consumer Protection Act (ACPA): Legislation whose goal is to protect trademark owners from being forced to pay a cybersquatter for a domain name that includes their trademark. ACPA for short., 64

anti-spam program: A filtering program that attempts to remove spam before it reaches your inbox or forum., 193

antistatic wristband: Bracelet designed to protect electronics from an electrostatic discharge by preventing a buildup of static electricity on a user., 304

antivirus program: Software that protects a computer against viruses by identifying and removing any computer viruses found in memory, on storage media, or on incoming files., 25, 110, 191, 218

antivirus software, 423

app: Program designed to make users more productive and/or assist them with personal tasks., 27, 158

Apple computers, 27

Apple's iOS, 27

Apple's Mac OS, 27

application: Programs designed to make users more productive and/or assist them with personal tasks., 27, 158

application development languages, 527–538

application development tool, 527

application generators, 532

applications
  categories of (table), 27, 164
  developing, 29
  downloading safely, 162
  graphics and media, 179–185
  help systems, 205
  installing, 29
  vs. software suites, 172
  tracking your location, 70

application server, 116

apps
  fitness videos, apps as medical advice, 132
  fraudulent, 174
  help systems, 205
  payment, 179
  and programs, 26–30
  removing, 195

architecture and design, technology and, 578

archival backup: Backup method that provides the best protection against data loss because it copies all program and data files., 396. *See also* **full backup**

arithmetic logic unit: Component of the processor that performs arithmetic, comparison, and other operations., 281. *See also* **ALU**

arithmetic operations: Operations that involve basic calculations such as addition, subtraction, multiplication, and division., 281

ARPANET: Agency of the U.S. Department of Defense whose goal was to build a network that (1) allowed scientists at different physical locations to share information and work together on military and scientific projects and (2) could function even if part of the network was disabled or destroyed by a disaster such as a nuclear attack. Short for Advanced Research Projects Agency., 56

artificial intelligence: The application of human intelligence to computers., 560. *See also* **AI**

ASCII: American Standard Code for Information Interchange; the most widely used coding scheme to represent a set of characters., 289

aspect ratio: A display's width relative to its height., 343

ASP.NET: A web application framework that provides the tools necessary for the creation of dynamic websites., 532

asset tags, 279

assistive technology, 353–354

asterisk (*), search engine operator, 72

asymmetric digital subscriber line: A type of DSL that supports faster downstream rates than upstream rates., 467. *See also* **ADSL**

asymmetric key encryption: Encryption method that uses two encryption keys: a public key and a **private key.**, 230. *See also* **public key encryption**

Asynchronous Transfer Mode (ATM): Short for Asynchronous Transfer Mode; a service that carries voice, data, video, and media at very high speeds., 468

ATC: Type of L2 cache built directly on the processor chip, which increases processor speed., 294. *See also* **advanced transfer cache**

Athletics, motion input in, 329

ATM: A self-service banking terminal that connects to a host computer through a network. Short for automated teller machine., 118

ATM (Asynchronous Transfer Mode): Short for Asynchronous Transfer Mode; a service that carries voice, data, video, and media at very high speeds, 468

ATOM: Specification that content aggregators use to distribute content to subscribers., 536

at symbol (@), 89

auction websites, 81–82

audio: Music, speech, or any other sound., 86

output, 340

streaming, 187

audio editing software: An application that enables users to modify audio clips, produce studio-quality soundtracks, and add audio to video clips., 183

audio input: The process of entering any sound into the computer such as speech, music, and sound effects., 330

audit trail: Electronic file that records both successful and unsuccessful access attempts., 222

AUP: Outlines the activities for which a computer and network may and may not be used., 231. *See also* **acceptable use policy**

automated teller machine (ATM), 118

automatic update: Feature can be configured to download and install updates automatically.(or) Feature that regularly provides new features or corrections to the program., 163, 421, 423

security and, 422

automobiles, and embedded computers, 132

AutoSave feature, 166

B

back door: A program or set of instructions in a program that allows users to bypass security controls when accessing a program, computer, or network., 217, 393

back end: An application that supports a front-end program., 505

background: Programs that are running, but not in use., 415

backing up

computers, mobile devices, 19

regularly, 25, 233

backlight: Light source in a display that often uses CCFL (cold cathode fluorescent lamp) or LED (light-emitting diode) technology., 341

backside bus: Bus that connects the processor to cache., 300. *See also* **BSB**

backup: A duplicate of content on a storage medium that you can use in case the original is lost, damaged, or destroyed., 233, 422

various methods (table), 234

backup plans, 19, 235, 395–396

backups, 18

backup server, 116

backup tool: A program that allows users to copy, or back up, selected files or the contents of an entire storage medium to another storage location, such as another hard disk, optical disc, USB flash drive, or cloud storage., 198

backward compatible: Term used to refer to a program's or device's capability of supporting older programs or devices, as well as newer programs or devices., 136, 425

backward recovery: Recovery technique where the DBMS uses the log to undo any changes made to the database during a certain period., 515. *See also* **rollback**

balance board: Game controller that is shaped like a weight scale and contains sensors that measure a game player's balance and weight., 132

BAN: A type of PAN that wireless connects sensors worn by, carried by, implanted in, or attached to a human body., 456. *See also* **body area network**

bandwidth: The amount of data, instructions, and information that can travel over transmission media., 61, 476

bar code: An identification code that consists of either a set of vertical lines and spaces of different widths or a two-dimensional pattern of dots, squares, and other images., 335

bar code reader: An input device that uses laser beams to read bar codes on products., 118, 335. *See also* **bar code scanner**

bar code scanner: An optical reader that uses laser beams to read bar codes., 335. *See also* **bar code reader**

batch processing: Processing technique in which the computer collects data over time and processes all transactions later, as a group., 558

Batteries, 301–304

batteries for mobile computers, 113

behavioral health risks with using technology, 144

benchmark test: Test that measures the performance of hardware or software., 524

Berners-Lee, Tim, 63

Big Data: Large-scale data sets that require advanced technologies beyond the capabilities of typical database software, to gather, store, process, retrieve, or analyze., 508

 characteristics of, 509

 data visualization, 509

 sources and uses of, 509

binary digit: The smallest unit of data the computer can process., 288. *See also* **bit**

binary system: Number system that has just two unique digits, 0 and 1, called bits., 288

biometric device: Device that authenticates a person's identity by translating a personal characteristic, such as a fingerprint, into a digital code that is compared with a digital code stored in a computer verifying a physical or behavioral characteristic., 224

biometric payment: Payment method where the customer's fingerprint is read by a fingerprint reader that is linked to a payment method such as a checking account or credit card., 226

bitmaps, 86

bit: The smallest unit of data the computer can process. Short for binary digit., 288. *See also* **binary digit**

Blackberry operating system: A proprietary mobile operating system that runs on Blackberry smartphones and Blackberry tablets., 434

blackout: A complete power failure., 140

blade server: A server in the form of a single circuit board, or blade., 116

bloatware: Additional programs and apps included with an operating system., 421

BLOB: Binary large object., 501

blog: An informal website consisting of time-stamped articles, or posts, in a diary or journal format, usually listed in reverse chronological order. Short for weblog., 24, 39, 78

blogger, 78

blogging, 188

blogosphere: The worldwide collection of blogs., 78

blog software: Software needed to create/maintain a blog., 188

Bluebugging: Security risk that occurs when cyberthieves exploit Bluetooth devices that have been paired., 464

Bluetooth: Wireless communication technology that uses short-range radio signals to transmit data between two Bluetooth-enabled computers or devices to communicate with each other., 32, 137, 463–464

Bluetooth printing: Printing that occurs when a computer or other device transmits output to a printer via radio waves., 345

Bluetooth wireless port adapter: Adapter that will convert an existing USB port into a Bluetooth port., 137

Blu-ray: A more expensive DVD format that has a higher capacity and better quality than standard DVDs, especially for high-definition audio and video., 388

BMP graphics format, 86

body area network: A type of PAN that wirelessly connects sensors worn by, carried by, implanted in, or attached to a human body. Sometimes called a body sensor network (BSN)., 456. *See also* **BAN**

body sensor network (BSN), 456

bookmarking site: A website that enables members to organize, tag, and share links to media and other online content., 75

bookmarks: Links to preferred websites., 67. *See also* **favorites**

Boolean: Data type consisting of Yes or No, or True or False, values., 501

Boot Camp: Apple program that enables you to install Windows on an Apple computer., 432

boot disk: Removable media, such as a CD or USB flash drive, that contains only the necessary operating system files required to start the computer., 413

boot drive: The drive from which your personal computer starts., 413

booting: The process of starting or restarting a computer or mobile device., 413

boot sector viruses, 190

bot: A program that performs a repetitive task on a network., 216

botnet: A group of compromised computers or mobile devices connected to a network such as the Internet that are used to attack other networks, usually for nefarious purposes., 216. *See also* **zombie army**

Braille printer, 354

brightness: Term used to describe how light or dark a photo appears., 182

broadband: Internet connection with fast data-transfer speeds and an always-on connection. (or) Transmission media that transmits multiple signals simultaneously, 58, 476

broadband Internet, 60

broadband modem: A communications device that sends and receives data and information to and from a digital line., 468. *See also* **digital modem**

broadband router: A device that performs the functions of a router and also a broadband modem., 471

broadband wireless router: A device that performs the functions of a router, a wireless access point, and a cable or DSL modem., 472

broadcast radio: A wireless transmission medium that distributes radio signals through the air over long distances such as between cities, regions, and countries and short distances, such as within an office or home., 479

brownout: A prolonged (more than a minute) undervoltage., 140

browser: Software that enables users with an Internet connection to access and view webpages on computers or mobile devices., 21, 65

configuring, 67

displaying webpages using, 64

browsing

communications applications, 188

safe techniques, 66

browsing history: A list of all websites you have visited over a period of time., 257

BSB: Bus that connects the processor to cache., 300. *See also* **backside bus**

buffer: Segment of memory or storage in which items are placed while waiting to be transferred from an input device or to an output device., 418

bug: Error in a program., 421

building automation systems, 145

burning: The process of writing on an optical disc., 388

bus: Electrical channel that transfers electronic bits internally within the circuitry of a computer, allowing the devices both inside and attached to the system unit to communicate with each other., 299–300

bus width, 300

speed measurement, 300

types of, 300

Busey bank, 79

business

uses of online social networks, 73

websites, 77

business networks, 33

Business Software Alliance (BSA): Alliance formed by major worldwide software companies to promote understanding of software piracy., 228

business-to-business (B2B) e-commerce: E-commerce transaction that occurs when businesses provide goods and services to other businesses, such as online advertising, recruiting, credit, sales, market research, technical support, and training., 82

business-to-consumer (B2C) e-commerce: E-commerce action that involves the sale of goods and services to the general public, such as at a shopping website., 82

bus width: The size of a bus, which determines the number of bits that a computer can transmit at one time., 300

buyer's guides

for desktops, 115

for mobile computers, 113

for mobile devices, 128–129

BYOD (bring your own device) strategies, 389, 433

byte (character): Eight bits grouped together as a unit., 61, 288, 290

C

cable Internet service: Broadband Internet access provided through the cable television network via a cable modem., 59, 466, 467

cable modem: A broadband modem that sends and receives digital data over the CATV network., 469

cache: Area of memory that stores the contents of frequently used data or instructions., 66, 293–294

CAD (computer-aided design), 180

calendar and contact management software: An application that helps you organize your calendar, keep track of contacts, and share this information with other devices or users., 171

calls, making VoIP, 92

candela: The standard unit of luminous intensity., 342

C++: An object-oriented programming language developed in the 1980s by Bjarne Sroustrup at Bell Laboratories that is an extension of the C programming language., 531

capacity: The number of bytes (characters) a storage medium can hold., 370

capping: ISP practice of providing a certain amount of data at the optimal speed; once the customer used his or her allotted amount, Internet access is restricted, slowed, or incurs additional costs., 477

CAPTCHA: A program developed at Carnegie Mellon University that displays an image containing a series of distorted characters for a user to identify and enter in order to verify that user input is from humans and not computer programs. Short for Completely Automated Public Turing test to tell Computers and Humans Apart., 224

Carbonite, 234

card reader/writer: A device that reads from and writes on memory cards, 381

career counselors, 576

career planning, 576

career websites, 82

carpal tunnel syndrome (CTS), 142

cascading style sheets: Technology used for web apps that describes the design and appearance of information on a webpage., 536, 538. *See also* **CSS**

cases
of computer, 276–278
of mobile device, 276–278

C : A widely used procedural language developed in the early 1970s by Dennis Ritchie at Bell Laboratories that originally was designed for writing system software., 528

ccTLD: A two-letter country code in a web address., 63

CDP: Backup method in which all data is backed up whenever a change is made., 234. *See also* **continuous data protection**

CD-R: CD-recordable; optical disc on which users can write once, but not erase, their own items, such as text, graphics, and audio., 388

CD-ROM: CD-read-only memory; type of optical disc that users can read but not write on (record) or erase., 388

CD-RW: CD-rewritable; erasable multisession disc users can write on multiple times., 388

CDs as optical discs, 18

cellular radio: A form of broadcast radio that is in wide use for mobile communications, specifically wireless modems and mobile phones., 480

Cellular Seizure Investigation stick: Device used by cyberthieves to download sensitive data from phones and other mobile devices., 295. *See also* **CSI stick**

central processing unit (CPU): The electronic component of a computer that interprets and carries out the basic instructions that operate a computer., 110, 280. *See also* **processor**

CERT/CC, 219

certificate authority: Online providers that issue digital certificates., 231

Certified Information Systems Security Professional: Security certification that tests in-depth knowledge of access control methods, information systems development, cryptography, operations security, physical security, and network and Internet security., 575. *See also* **CISSP**

CF: A type of memory card., 381. *See also* **CompactFlash**

change management: Process of recognizing when a change in a project has occurred, taking actions to react to the change, and planning for opportunities because of the change., 519

character: A number, letter, punctuation mark, or other symbol that is represented by a single byte in the ASCII coding scheme., 500

charge-coupled device (CCD), 126

chassis: The case that contains and protects the motherboard, hard drive, memory, and other electronic components of the computer from damage., 276. *See also* **System unit**

chat: A real-time typed conversation that takes place on a computer or mobile device with many other online users., 91, 188

chat room: A location on an Internet server that permits users to chat with others who are online at the same time., 31, 91

check digit, 503

Children's Internet Protection Act (CIPA), 248

child: Term used in three-generation backups to refer to the most recent copy of the file., 234

chip: A small piece of semiconducting material, usually silicon, on which integrated circuits are etched., 278

chip card: An alternative to a magnetic stripe card, stores data on an integrated circuit embedded in the card., 393. *See also* **smart card**

Chromebook: A specialized laptop that runs Chrome OS., 430

Chromebox: A specialized desktop that runs Chrome OS., 430

Chrome: Google's browser., 67

Chrome OS: Google's Linux-based operating system designed to work primarily with web apps., 430

ciphertext: Encrypted (scrambled) data., 230

CISSP: Security certification that tests in-depth knowledge of access control methods, information systems development, cryptography, operations security, physical security, and network and Internet security., 575. *See also* **Certified Information Systems Security Professional**

classic programming languages, 532

click, 13

clickjacking: Scam in which an object that can be clicked on a website, such as a button, image, or link, contains a malicious program., 245

client operating systems: Desktop operating systems that work in conjunction with a server operating system., 426

client/server network: Network in which one or more computers act as a server, and the other computers on the network request services from the server., 456

clients: The other computers and mobile devices on a network that rely on the server for its resources., 456

clip art: A collection of drawings, photos, and other images., 166

clip art/image gallery: A collection of clip art and photos., 166

clipboard: A temporary storage location., 165

clock cycle: Each tick of the system clock., 283

clock speed: The pace of the system clock., 283, 300

closed source operating systems
security of, 430

cloud architect: Employee who identifies business requirements, strategies, and solutions for cloud storage and services that meet a company's goals or needs., 687

cloud backup: Backup method in which files are backed up to the cloud as they change., 234

cloud computing: An environment of virtual servers that house and provide access to resources users access through the Internet., 121, 287–288

cloud data privacy, 232

cloud storage: An Internet service that provides remote storage to computer users., 18, 34, 69, 234, 383–385
advantages of, 384
selecting provider, 385
services, by providers, 384–385
upload files, 385

CMOS: Complementary metal-oxide semiconductor; technology used by some RAM chips, flash memory chips, and other types of memory chips that provides high speeds and consumes little power by using battery power to retain information even when the power to a computer is off., 296

coaxial cable: Physical transmission media that consists of a single copper wire surrounded by at least three layers: (1) an insulating material, (2) a woven or braided metal, and (3) a plastic outer coating., 478. *See also* **coax**

coax: Physical transmission media that consists of a single copper wire surrounded by at least three layers: (1) an insulating material, (2) a woven or braided metal, and (3) a plastic outer coating., 478. *See also* **coaxial cable**

code of conduct: A written guidelines that helps determine whether a specific action is ethical/unethical or allowed/not allowed., 241

code: The program that contains the language instructions, or code, to be converted to machine language., 529. *See also* **source program**

coding schemes, 289–290

cold boot: The process of starting a computer or mobile device from a state when it is powered off completely., 413

collaborative databases: Web databases where users store and share photos, videos, recordings, and other personal media with other registered users., 506

command: An instruction that causes a program or app to perform a specific action., 318

command language: The set of commands used to control actions in a command-line interface., 415

command-line interface: User interface in which users type commands represented by short keywords or abbreviations or press special keys on the keyboard to enter data and instructions., 414–415

common short code (CSC): A four- or five-digit number assigned to a specific content or mobile service provider, sometimes followed by the message., 124

communications

applications, 28

applications (table), 188

digital, 93, 450–451

netiquette guidelines for online, 94

use of technologies (table), 31

communications channel: Transmission media on which data, instructions, or information travel in a communications system., 450

communications device: Hardware capable of transferring items from computers and devices to transmission media and vice versa., 31, 468

cable modem, 469

digital modems, 468

DSL modem, 469

hubs and switches, 473

ISDN modem, 469

network cards, 472–473

routers, 471–472

wireless access points, 470

wireless modem, 469

communications lines

ATM, 468

cable, 466

DSL, 467

FTTP, 467

ISDN, 467

T-carrier line, 468

communications satellite: A space station that receives microwave signals from an earth-based station, amplifies (strengthens) the signals, and broadcasts the signals back over a wide area to any number of earth-based stations., 482

communications software: Programs and apps that (1) help users establish a connection to another computer, mobile device, or network; (2) manage the transmission of data, instructions, and information; and (3) provide an interface for users to communicate with one another., 457

CompactFlash: A type of memory card., 381. *See also* **CF**

compact keyboard: Keyboard that is smaller than a standard keyboard and usually does not include the numeric keypad., 321

comparison operations: Operations that involve comparing one data item with another to determine whether the first item is greater than, equal to, or less than the other item., 281

compiler: Separate program that converts an entire source program into machine language before executing it., 529

completeness check: Validity check that verifies that a required field contains data., 503

composite key: Primary key that consists of multiple fields., 501

compressed files, 86

compressing files, folders, 198

compress: To decrease a file or photo's file size., 182

computer: An electronic device, operating under the control of instructions stored in its own memory, that can accept data (input), process the data according to specified rules, produce information (output), and store the information for future use., 4, 108

computer-aided design: A type of application that assists professionals and designers in creating engineering, architectural, and scientific designs and models. CAD for short., 180

computer-aided engineering: Information system that aids in the development and testing of product designs, and often includes CAD (computer-aided design)., 555. *See also* **CAE**

computer-aided manufacturing (CAM): The use of computers to assist with manufacturing processes such as fabrication and assembly; CAM for short., 40, 555

computer: An electronic device, operating under the control of instructions stored in its own memory, that can accept data (input), process the data according to specified rules, produce information (output), and store the information for future use.

application, stopped responding, 418

backing up, 19, 233–234

buyer's guide for desktops, 115

buyer's guide for mobile computers, 113

care for, 302–303

cases for, 276–278

categories of (table), 134

connecting peripheral devices, accessories to, 136

easing eyestrain using, 143

entering data and instructions in, 319

external music devices connection, 330

media on smart TV from, 343

memory card slots, 381

mobile, 108–115

and mobile devices, 7, 108

ports for, 297

recycling, refurbishing, 242

removing programs and apps, 416

search and seize, government, 374

securing, 279

synchronizing your, 34

transferring photos from mobile devices to, 153

and transportation, 95

unauthorized access and use, 221–227

computer-based training (CBT): A type of education in which students learn by using and completing exercises with instructional software., 184

computer crime: Any illegal act involving the use of a computer or related devices., 212

Computer Emergency Response Team Coordination Center (CERT/CC): A federally funded Internet security research and development center., 219

computer ethics: The moral guidelines that govern the use of computers, mobile devices, and information systems., 238

computer repair services, 566

computer security specialist: Employee who is responsible for the security of data and information stored on computers and mobile devices within an organization. *See also* **Mobile security specialist,** 570

computer technician: Employee who installs, maintains, and repairs hardware and servers; installs, upgrades, and configures software; troubleshoots hardware problems., 569

computer vision syndrome: Technology-related health condition that affects eyesight., 143. *See also* **CVS**

conferencing software: Software that includes tools that enable users to share documents via online meetings and communicate with other connected users., 520

confidential data, access of, 514

connecting

peripheral devices, accessories to computers, 136

phones to Wi-Fi networks, 138

connections, ports and, 134–138

connector: Device that joins a cable to a port., 135

popular (table)., 135

consistency check: Validity check that tests the data in two or more associated fields to ensure that the relationship is logical and their data is in the correct format., 503

consumer electronics, and embedded computers, 132

consumer-to-consumer (C2C) e-commerce: E-commerce transaction that occurs when one consumer sells directly to another, such as in an online auction., 82

contact management software: Folder used in email programs that contains a list of names, addresses, phone numbers, email addresses, and other details about people with whom you communicate., 171

contacts folder: Folder used in email programs that contains a list of names, addresses, phone numbers, email addresses, and other details about people with whom you communicate., 89

content aggregation, 83

content filtering: The process of restricting access to certain material., 247

content management system (CMS): System that enables and manages the publishing, modification, organization, and access of various forms of documents and other files, including media and webpages, on a network or the web. (or) A program that assists you with creating, editing, and hosting content on a website., 84, 557

continuous backup: A backup plan in which changes are backed up as they are made., 515

continuous data protection (CDP): Backup method in which all data is backed up whenever a change is made., 234. *See also* **CDP**

contrast ratio: The difference in light intensity between the brightest white and darkest black that can be produced on a display., 342

contrast: The difference in appearance between light and dark areas of a photo., 182

controller: A special-purpose chip and electronic circuits that control the transfer of data, instructions, and information from a drive to and from the system bus and other components in the computer. Formerly called a disk controller., 380

control unit: The component of the processor that directs and coordinates most of the operations in the computer., 281

convenience applications, 186

convertible tablet: A tablet that has a screen in its lid and a keyboard in its base, with the lid and base connected by a swivel-type hinge., 112

cookie: A small text file that a web server stores on your computer., 192, 243

cooling pad: Pad that rests below a laptop and protects the computer from overheating and also the user's lap from excessive heat., 284 copying

media from websites, 38

copyright: Exclusive rights given to authors, artists, and other creators of original work to duplicate, publish, and sell their materials., 240

cost/benefit feasibility: Test that measures whether the lifetime benefits of the proposed information system will be greater than its lifetime costs., 519. *See also* **economic feasibility**

CPU: The electronic component of a computer that interprets and carries out the basic instructions that operate a computer. Short for central processing unit., 110. *See also* **processor**

cracker: Someone who accesses a computer or network illegally with the intent of destroying data, stealing information, or other malicious action., 214

create: Process in project development during which you enter text or numbers, insert images, and perform other tasks using a variety of input methods, such as keyboard, a mouse, touch, or voice., 165

Creative Commons: Nonprofit organization that provides several standard licensing options that owners of creative works may specify when granting permission for others to use their digital content., 372

credit cards

protection, 337

safely using, 394

and signature verification system, 225

crimeware: Software used by cybercriminals., 212

criminal databases, 505

CRM: Information system that manages information about customers, past purchases, interests, and the day-to-day interactions, such as phone calls, email messages, web communications, and Internet messaging sessions., 555. *See also* **Customer relationship management**

CRM specialist: Employee who integrates apps and data related to customer inquiries, purchases, support requests, and behaviors in order to provide a complete application that manages a company's relationships with its customers. *See also* **Customer relationship management specialist**, 577

crop: To remove unwanted areas of a photo., 182

cross-platform application: An application that runs the same on multiple operating systems., 412

CSI stick: Device used by cyberthieves to download sensitive data from phones and other mobile devices., 295. *See also* **cellular seizure investigation stick**

CSS: Technology used for web apps that describes the design and appearance of information on a webpage., 536, 538. *See also* **cascading style sheets**

CT scans, 43

curation website, 83

cursor: A symbol on the screen, usually a blinking vertical bar, that indicates where the next character you type will appear., 320. *See also* **insertion point**

customer data protection, 575

customer relationship management: Information system that manages information about customers, past purchases, interests, and the day-to-day interactions, such as phone calls, email messages, web communications, and Internet messaging sessions., 555. *See also* **CRM**

customer relationship management specialist: Employee who integrates apps and data related to customer inquiries, purchases, support requests, and behaviors in order to provide a complete application that manages a company's relationships with its customers. *See also* **CRM specialist**, 569

customer service software, 177

custom software: Software that performs functions specific to a business or industry., 161

CVS: Technology-related health condition that affects eyesight., 143. *See also* **computer vision syndrome**

cyberbullying: Harassment using technology., 94

cybercrime: Online or Internet-based illegal acts such as distributing malicious software or committing identity theft., 212

cyberextortionist: Someone who demands payment to stop an attack on an organization's technology infrastructure., 214

cyberforensics: The discovery, collection, and analysis of evidence found on computers and networks., 227. *See also* **digital forensics**

cybersquatters, 64

cyberterrorist: Someone who uses the Internet or network to destroy or damage computers for political reasons., 214

cyberwarfare: A cybercrime attack whose goal ranges from disabling a government's computer network to crippling a country., 214

cypher: A set of steps that can convert readable plaintext into unreadable ciphertext., 230. *See also* **encryption algorithm**

D

DaaS : Cloud computing service that allows users and applications to access a company's data., 288. *See also* **data as a service**

dance pad: Technology-related health condition that affects eyesight., 131. *See also* **computer vision**

data
  common data types, 501
  file maintenance, 502
  hierarchy of, 500–501
  validating, 503

data: A collection of unprocessed items, which can include text, numbers, images, audio, and video., 12, 318
  how travels on Internet, 62
  usage examples (table), 61

data as a service: Cloud computing service that allows users and applications to access a company's data., 288. *See also* **DaaS**

data scientist: Employee who uses analytics and other Big Data tools to compile statistics on data that an organization can use to plan product development or create strategies for marketing., 569

database: A collection of data organized in a manner that allows access, retrieval, and use of that data., 170, 498
  maintaining, 513
  securing, 513

database administrator: Person in an organization who is responsible for managing and coordinating all database activities, including development, maintenance, and permissions., 510, 569. *See also* **DBA**

database analyst: Employee who uses data modeling techniques and tools to analyze and specify data usage., 569

database approach, 504–505
  advantages of, 505–506
  disadvantages of, 506
  types of, 508

database data, import/export of, 511

database designer: Employee who specifies the structure, interface, and requirements of a large-scale database; determines security and permissions for users., 568

database management system: Software that allows users to create a computerized database; add, modify, and delete data in the database; sort and retrieve data from the database; and create forms and reports from the data in the database., 498. *See also* **DBMS**
  backup and recovery, 515
  data dictionary and, 510
  data security and, 513–514
  file retrieval and maintenance, 511–513

database server: Dedicated server that stores and provides access to a database., 116, 506

database software: An application that allows users to create, access, and manage a database., 170, 498

data collection device: Reading device that obtains data directly at the location where the transaction or event takes place., 338

data dictionary: A DBMS element that contains data about each file in a database and each field in those files., 510. *See also* **repository**

data entry form: A window on the screen that provides areas for entering or modifying data in a database., 512. *See also* **form**

data file: A collection of related records stored on a storage medium such as a hard drive or on cloud storage; often simply called a file., 501

data model: Rules and standards that define how users view the organization of the data in a database., 508

data plans, mobile device, 458

data projector: A device that projects the text and images displaying on a computer or mobile device screen and projects the images on a larger screen so that an audience can see the image clearly., 352

data representation, 288–290
  bits and bytes, 288
  coding schemes, 289–290

data security, 513–514

data transfer rates, 460, 479

data type: Specifies the kind of data a field in a database can contain and how the field is used., 500

data visualization, 509

data warehouse: Huge database that stores and manages the data required to analyze historical and current transactions., 508

DBA: Person in an organization who is responsible for managing and coordinating all database activities, including development, maintenance, and permissions., 510. *See also* **database administrator**

DBMS: Software that allows users to create a computerized database; add, modify, and delete data in the database; sort and retrieve data from the database; and create forms and reports from the data in the database., 498. *See also* **database management system**

DDoS attack: Type of DoS attack in which a zombie army is used to attack computers or computer networks., 217. *See also* **distributed DoS attack**

decision support system (DSS): Information system that helps users analyze information and make decisions; DSS for short., 559

decoding: Processor operation in the machine cycle that translates the instruction into signals the computer can execute., 281

decrypt: The process of decoding encrypted data., 229

dedicated line: A type of always-on physical connection that is established between two communications devices., 466

dedicated servers (table), 116

defragmenting: Reorganizing the contents of a hard disk so that the files are stored in contiguous sectors., 197

hard disks, 197

deliverable: Any tangible item, such as a chart, diagram, report, or program file., 518

denial of service attack (DoS attack): An assault whose purpose is to disrupt computer access to an Internet service such as the web or email., 251

density: The number of bits in an area on a storage medium., 374

design phase: Step in the system development life cycle that consists of two major activities: (1) if necessary, acquire hardware and software and (2) develop all of the details of the new or modified information system., 523

desktop: A personal computer designed to be in a stationary location, where all of its components fit on or under a desk or table. Also called a desktop computer., 6, 114, 428

buyer's guide for, 115

components in, 278

motherboard of, 279

desktop app: Applications stored on a computer., 28

desktop as a service, 287

desktop case, fans, 301

desktop computers, 114–115

desktop monitors, 325

desktop operating system: A complete operating system that works on desktops, laptops, and some tablets., 426–428. *See also* **stand-alone operating system**

Macintosh operating system (Mac OS), 427–428

vs. mobile, 435–436

Windows, 426–427

desktop or mobile application developer: Employee who converts the system design into the appropriate application development language, such as Visual Basic, Java, C#, and Objective C, and toolkits for various platforms. *See also* **Desktop or mobile application programmer**, 570

desktop or mobile application programmer: Employee who converts the system design into the appropriate application development language, such as Visual Basic,

Java, C#, and Objective C, and toolkits for various platforms. *See also* **Desktop or mobile application developer**, 570

desktop publishing software: An application that enables designers to create sophisticated publications that contain text, graphics, and many colors. DTP for short., 180

detailed analysis: Activity during system development that involves three major activities: (1) study how the current system works, (2) determine the users' wants, needs, and requirements, and (3) recommend a solution., 522. *See also* **logical design**

detailed report: Report generated by a management information system that usually lists just transactions., 558

developing programs, applications, 29

device-dependent: A program is one that runs only on a specific type or make of computer or mobile device., 425

device driver: A small program that tells the operating system how to communicate with a specific device., 419. *See also* **driver**

device-independent: Operating systems that run on computers and mobile devices provided by a variety of manufacturers., 425

devices

game, 10, 131–132

recycling, refurbishing, 242

dial-up access: Internet connection that takes place when a modem in a computer connects to the Internet via a standard telephone line that transmits data and informa- tion using an analog (continuous wave pattern) signal., 60

dial-up modem: A communications device that converts digital signals to analog signals and analog signals to digital signals, so that data can travel along an analog phone line., 469

differential backup: Backup method that copies only the files that have changed since the last full backup. (or) Fast backup method that requires minimal storage space to back up., 234, 396

digital camera: A mobile device that allows users to take pictures and store the photographed images digitally., 8, 125–127, 325

vs. smartphones and tablets, 8

digital certificate: A notice that guarantees a user or a website is legitimate., 231

verifying authenticity with, 231

digital communications, 450–451

digital device convergence, 10

digital forensics: The discovery, collection, and analysis of evidence found on computers and networks., 227. *See also* **cyberforensics**

digital forensics analyst: Employee who inspects electronic data to recover documents and files from data storage devices that may have been damaged or deleted, in order to use them as evidence in a crime investigation., 570

digital forensics examiner: Employee who collects and analyzes evidence found on computers, networks, mobile devices, and databases., 569

digital light processing projector: Data projector that uses tiny mirrors to reflect light, which produces crisp, bright, colorful images that remain in focus and can be seen clearly, even in a well-lit room., 352. *See also* **DLP projector**

digital literacy: Having a current knowledge and understanding of computers, mobile devices, the web, and related technologies., 2, 561

digital media: Music, photos, and videos., 8

digital media player, 9

digital modem: A communications device that sends and receives data and information to and from a digital line., 468. *See also* **broadband modem**

digital pen: An input device, slightly larger than a stylus, that captures and converts a user's handwriting or drawings into a digital format, which users can upload (transfer) to a computer or mobile device., 327

digital photo printer: Printer that uses heat to transfer colored dye to specially coated paper., 349. *See also* **dye-sublimation printer**

digital: Representation of data using only two discrete states: on (1) and off (0)., 288

digital rights management (DRM): A strategy designed to prevent illegal distribution of movies, music, and other digital content. DRM for short., 240, 574

digital school, 35–36

digital security and privacy, 24–26

digital security risk: Any event or action that could cause a loss of or damage to computer or mobile device hardware, software, data, information, or processing capability., 212

digital signature: An encrypted code that a person, website, or organization attaches to an electronic message to verify the identity of the message sender., 231

digital subscriber line: Broadband Internet connection provided through the telephone network via a DSL modem., 59, 467. *See also* **DSL**

digital television (DTV), 343–344

digital video (DV) camera: Camera that records video as digital signals, which you can transfer directly to a computer or mobile device with the appropriate connection., 330

Digital Video Interface port: Port that enables digital signals to transmit directly to a monitor., 343. *See also* **DVI port**

digital video security, 333

digitizer: An electronic plastic board that detects and converts movements of a stylus or digital pen into digital signals that are sent to the computer., 328. *See also* **graphics tablet**

direct access: Access method where a device can locate a particular data item or file immediately, without having to move consecutively through items stored in front of the desired data item or file., 392. *See also* **random access**

direct conversion: Conversion strategy where the user stops using the old system and begins using the new system on a certain date., 526

disaster recovery plan: A written plan that describes the steps an organization would take to restore its computer operations in the event of a disaster., 234

disc burning software: Software that writes text, graphics, audio, and video files on a recordable or rewritable disc., 185

discoverable mode: State of a Bluetooth device when it is waiting for another Bluetooth device to locate its signal., 137

Discovering Computers Twitter feed, 78

discussion forum: An online area in which users have written discussions about a particular subject., 91.

disc *vs.* disk, 17

disk cleanup: Tool that searches for and removes unnecessary files., 196, 422

disk defragmenter: A tool that reorganizes the files and unused space on a computer's hard disk so that the operating system accesses data more quickly and programs and apps run faster., 197, 422

disk *vs.* disc, 17

display: An output device that visually conveys text, graphics, and video information., 340–344. *See also* **display device**

measuring, 341

quality of, 342–343

technologies, 341–342

display device: An output device that visually conveys text, graphics, and video information., 340. *See also* **display**

DisplayPort: Port that is an alternative to DVI and also supports high-definition audio and video., 343

displays, 15

distributed database: Database in which the data exists in many separate locations throughout a network or the Internet., 508

distributed DoS attack (DDoS attack): Type of DoS attack in which a zombie army is used to attack computers or computer networks., 217. *See also* **DDoS attack**

distribution software, 177

DLP projector: Data projector that uses tiny mirrors to reflect light, which produces crisp, bright, colorful images that remain in focus and can be seen clearly, even in a well-lit room., 352. *See also* **digital light processing projector**

DMS: System that allows for storage and management of a company's documents, such as word processing documents, presentations, and spreadsheets., 556. *See also* **document management system**

DNS server: A server on the Internet that usually is associated with an ISP. Short for domain name system., 64

Dock, 428

docking station: An external device that attaches to a mobile computer or device and contains a power connection and provides connections to peripheral devices., 136

documentation: The collection and summarization of data, information, and deliverables., 519

document management software: An application that provides a means for sharing, distributing, and searching through documents by converting them into a format that can be viewed by any user., 176

document management system: System that allows for storage and management of a company's documents, such as word processing documents, presentations, and spreadsheets., 556. *See also* **DMS**

domain name: A text-based name that corresponds to the IP address of a server that hosts a website., 63

domain name server, 116

domain name system (DNS): The method that the Internet uses to store domain names and their corresponding IP addresses., 64

dongle: Small device that connects to a computer and acts as a modem., 58

dot pitch: The distance in millimeters between pixels on a display., 342. *See also* **pixel pitch**

dots per inch: One measurement of ink-jet printer resolution., 346. *See also* **dpi**

double-click, 13

double-tap: Touch gesture in which a user quickly touches and releases one finger two times., 5

downlink: Transmission from a satellite to an earth-based station, 482

downloading: The process of transferring content from the Internet to a computer or mobile device., 21

applications, 29

digital media from online services, 87

software safely, 162

downstream rate: The transfer rate that is achieved when data is being sent over a communications channel., 462

dpi: One measurement of ink-jet printer resolution., 346. *See also* **dots per inch**

drag: Touch gesture in which a user presses and holds one finger on an object and then moves the finger to the new location., 5, 13. *See also* **Slide**

DRAM: RAM chips that must be reenergized constantly or they lose their contents., 292. *See also* **dynamic RAM**

driver: A small program that tells the operating system how to communicate with a specific device., 419. *See also* **device driver**

DSL: Broadband Internet connection provided through the telephone network via a DSL modem., 59, 467. *See also* **digital subscriber line**

DSL modem: A broadband modem that sends digital data and information from a computer to a DSL line and receives digital data and information from a DSL line., 469

DTP software, 180

DVD kiosk: A self-service DVD rental machine that connects to a host computer through a network., 120

DVD+RAM: DVD-rewritable formats that users can write on multiple times., 388

DVD+R: DVD-recordable WORM formats, on which users can write once but not erase their own items, including video, audio, photos, graphics, and text., 388

DVD-R: DVD-recordable WORM formats, on which users can write once but not erase their own items, including video, audio, photos, graphics, and text., 388

DVD-ROM: DVD-read-only memory; a high-capacity optical disc that users can read but not write on or erase., 388

DVD+RW: DVD-rewritable formats that users can write on multiple times., 388

DVD-RW: DVD-rewritable formats that users can write on multiple times., 388

DVDs as optical discs, 18

DVI port: Port that enables digital signals to transmit directly to a monitor., 343. *See also* **Digital Video Interface port**

DV technology: Technology used with DV (digital video) cameras that allows you to input, edit, manage, publish, and share your videos., 330, 331

dye-sublimation printer: Printer that uses heat to transfer colored dye to specially coated paper., 349. *See also* **digital photo printer**

Dynamic RAM: RAM chips that must be reenergized constantly or they lose their contents., 292. *See also* **DRAM**

dynamic webpage: A webpage on which visitors can customize some or all of the viewed content., 65

E

earbuds: Small speakers that rest inside each ear canal., 8, 9, 16, 128, 352

EarPods: Term used by Apple to refer to earbuds they designed to match the shape of the human ear., 128

easier access, database approach, 506

eavesdropping, 395

e-book: An electronic version of a printed book, readable on computers and other digital devices. Also called a digital book., 9, 129

e-book reader: A mobile device that is used primarily for reading e-books and other digital publications. Short for electronic book reader., 129. *See also* **e-reader**

vs. smartphones and tablets, 9

e-commerce: A business transaction that occurs over an electronic network such as the Internet. Short for electronic commerce., 82

economic feasibility: Test that measures whether the lifetime benefits of the proposed information system will be greater than its lifetime costs., 519. *See also* **cost/benefit feasibility**

EDI: Standard that defines how business documents transmit across transmission media., 453. *See also* **electronic data interchange**

editing

audio, 183

photos, 181

edit: Process in project development during which you make changes to a project's existing content., 165

education

applications, 186

cyberbullying in schools, 94

Internet plagiarism, 165

technology in, 35

wikis in, 40

educational websites, 77

education web database services, 507

e-filing: The process of filing your tax forms electronically., 176

e-form: Short for electronic form; a form that sends entered data across a network or the Internet., 512

EFT: Service in which users connected to a network can exchange money from one account to another via transmission media., 453. *See also* **electronic funds transfer**

EIDE: Enhanced Integrated Drive Electronics; interface that uses parallel signals to transfer data, instructions, and information., 380

Electronic Communications Privacy Act (ECPA), 474

electronic data interchange: Standard that defines how business documents transmit across transmission media., 453. *See also* **EDI**

electronic funds transfer: Service in which users connected to a network can exchange money from one account to another via transmission media., 453. *See also* **EFT**

electronic profiles, 242–243

electronics recycling, 122

electronic storefront: In e-commerce applications, webpage that contains product descriptions, images, and a shopping cart., 81

email: The transmission of messages and files via a computer network. Short for electronic mail., 24, 31, 88

address book, 74

avoiding malware infections, 110

communications applications, 188

employers monitoring of, 247

scams, 245

suspicious attachments, 25

viruses, how they spread via, 215

email address, 88

email list: A group of email addresses used for mass distribution of a message. Short for electronic mailing list., 90 email messages, sending, 103

email program: Program used to create, send, receive, forward, store, print, and delete email messages., 88

email spoofing: Spoofing that occurs when the sender's address or other components of an email header are altered so that it appears that the email message originated from a different sender., 217

email: The transmission of messages and files via a computer network. Short for electronic mail.

  sending messages, 103

embedded computer: A special-purpose computer that functions as a component in a larger product., 132

emergency plans, 235

emoticons: Symbols used in online communications that express emotion., 94

employee monitoring: The use of computers, mobile devices, or cameras to observe, record, and review an employee's use of a technology, including communications such as email messages, keyboard activity (used to measure productivity), and websites visited., 247

employment websites, 82

encryption: The process of converting data that is readable by humans into encoded characters to prevent unauthorized access., 229

encryption algorithm: A set of steps that can convert readable plaintext into unreadable ciphertext., 230. *See also* **cypher**

encryption key: A set of characters that the originator of the data uses to encrypt the plaintext and the recipient of the data uses to decrypt the ciphertext., 230

encryption: The process of converting data that is readable by humans into encoded characters to prevent unauthorized access., 424

end-user license agreement (EULA): License agreement included with software purchased by individual users., 163, 228. *See also* **single-user license agreement**

ENERGY STAR program: Program developed by the United States Department of Energy (DOE) and the United States Environmental Protection Agency (EPA) to help reduce the amount of electricity used by computers and related devices., 241

enhanced resolution: Digital camera resolution that uses a special formula to add pixels between those generated by the optical resolution., 127

enterprise

  content management systems, 557

  document management systems, 556

  functional units of, 554–555

enterprise computing, 177

Enterprise Resource Planning: Information system that integrates MRP II with the information flow across an organization to manage and coordinate the ongoing activities of the enterprise, including product planning, manufacturing and distribution, accounting and finance, sales, human resources, and customer support., 555

enterprise storage, 389–392

  network attached storage, 390–392

  storage area network, 391–392

enterprise user: Each employee or customer who uses computers, mobile devices, and other technology in an enterprise., 41, 42

entertainment

  applications, 186

  motion input in, 329

  technology in, 38, 199

  web database services, 507

  websites, 79, 199

environmental issues of computer use, 26

e-reader: A mobile device that is used primarily for reading e-books and other digital publications. short for electronic book reader., 9, 129. *See also* **e-book reader**

e-retail: Process of purchasing products or services on the web. Short for electronic retail., 81

ergonomic keyboard: Keyboard design that reduces the chance of repetitive strain injuries (RSIs) of wrist and hand., 322

ergonomics: An applied science devoted to incorporating comfort, efficiency, and safety into the design of items in the workplace., 144

ERP: Information system that integrates MRP II with the information flow across an organization to manage and coordinate the ongoing activities of the enterprise, including product planning, manufacturing and distribution, accounting and finance, sales, human resources, and customer support., 555. *See also* **Enterprise Resource Planning**

eSATA: External SATA; interface used with external drives and that is much faster than USB., 380

Ethernet: A network standard that specifies no central computer or device on the network (nodes) should control when data can be transmitted., 460

ethics

  of altering digital, 182

  punishment for webcam spying, 111

  and society, 238–242

EULA: License agreement included with software purchased by individual users., 163, 228. *See also* **end-user license agreement; single-user license agreement**

e-waste: Discarded computers and mobile devices., 26, 122

exabyte (EB), 370

exception criteria: Out-of-the-ordinary conditions that define the normal activity or status range in an exception report., 558

exception report: Report generated by a management information system that identifies data outside of a normal condition., 558

executing: Processor operation in the machine cycle that carries out the commands., 281

expansion bus: Bus that allows the processor to communicate with peripheral devices., 300

expansion card: A circuit board that enhances the functions of a component of a desktop or server system unit and/or provides connections to peripheral devices., 297. *See also* **adapter board; adapter card**

expansion slot: A socket on a desktop or server motherboard that can hold an adapter card., 297

expert system: An information system that captures and stores the knowledge of human experts and then imitates human reasoning and decision making., 560

extended contacts, 73

extended warranty options, 567

Extensible Markup Language: Popular format for sharing data that allows web developers to create tags that describe the structure of information., 536. *See also* **XML**

external displays, connecting laptop, 341

external hard drive: A separate freestanding storage device that connects with a cable to a USB port or other port on a computer or mobile device., 17, 378–379

extranet: Portion of a company's network that allows customers or suppliers to access part of its intranet., 453

eyestrain, easing while using computers, 16, 143

F

Facebook, 23, 24, 73, 77, 258

face recognition system: Biometric device that captures a live face image and compares it with a stored image to determine if the person is a legitimate user., 225

failure of hardware, 139–140, 233

Fair Information Practices (FIP), 502

Fair Labor Association (FLA), 295

fair trade practices, 295

fake cell towers, device tracking, 480

FAQ, 94

fault-tolerant computer: Computer that has duplicate components so that it can continue to operate when one of its main components fails., 141

favorites: Links to preferred websites., 67. *See also* **bookmark**

fax, 31

FBI's National Crime Information Center (NCIC), 36

FC: Interface often used in enterprise storage because it has much faster transmissions rates than SCSI and other interfaces., 390. *See also* **Fibre Channel**

feasibility: A measure of how suitable the development of a system will be to the organization., 519

feasibility study: Investigation performed in system development that determines the exact nature of the problem or improvement and decide whether it is worth pursuing., 521. *See also* **preliminary investigation**

feature creep: Problem that occurs when one activity has led to another that was not planned originally; thus, the scope of the project now has grown., 519. *See also* **Scope creep**

Federal Communications Commission (FCC), 477, 480

Federal Trade Commission (FTC), 214

fetching: Processor operation in the machine cycle that obtains a program or an application instruction or data item from memory., 281

fiber-optic cable: Physical transmission media that consists of dozens or hundreds of thin strands of glass or plastic that use light to transmit signals., 478

Fiber to the Building: Dedicated line used by small businesses to access the Internet via fiber-optic cables., 467. *See also* **FTTB**

Fiber to the Home: Dedicated line that provides home users with Internet access via fiber-optic cable., 467. *See also* **FTTH**

Fiber to the Premises: Broadband Internet connection that uses fiber-optic cable to provide high-speed Internet access via a modem. FTTP for short., 59

Fiber to the Premises: Dedicated line that uses fiber-optic cable to provide extremely high-speed Internet access to a user's physical permanent location., 467. *See also* **FTTP**

Fibre Channel: Interface often used in enterprise storage because it has much faster transmissions rates than SCSI and other interfaces., 390. *See also* **FC**

field: A combination of one or more related characters or bytes and is the smallest unit of data a user accesses., 500

field name: Name that uniquely identifies each field in a database., 500

file, disk, and system management tools, 194–198

file: A named collection of stored data, instructions, or information that can contain text, images, audio, and video., 18

file compression: Shrink the size of a file(s)., 422

file compression tool: Tool that shrinks the size of a file(s)., 198

file maintenance: Procedures that keep data current., 502

file manager: A tool that performs functions related to displaying files in folders; and copying, renaming, deleting, moving, and sorting files. (or) A tool that performs functions related to file management., 194, 422

  caution about deleting program files, 194

file processing system: System used to store and manage data in which each department or area within an organization has its own set of files., 504

  isolated data, 504

  redundant data, 504

files

  audio, 86–87

  compressed, 86

  compressing, uncompressing, 198

  deleting to uninstall programs, 195

file server, 116

file sharing network: P2P network configuration on which users access each other's hard drives and exchange files directly via a file sharing program., 457

file viruses, 190

filters, Internet, 193

finance websites, 36

financial apps, 178

financial information, entering online, 82

financial websites, 79

fingerprint reader: Biometric device that captures curves and indentations of a fingerprint. Also called a fingerprint scanner., 139, 224

Firefox: Mozilla Corporation's browser., 67

Firefox OS: Linux-based operating system for Amazon Kindle tablets and Amazon Fire phones., 434

Fire OS: Linux-based operating system for Amazon Kindle tablets and Amazon Fire phones., 434

firewall: Hardware and/or software that protects a network's resources from intrusion by users on another network, such as the Internet., 25, 189, 219–220, 423

firmware: ROM chips that contain permanently written data, instructions, or information., 294, 410

First Amendment, and content filtering, 248

fitness and health apps, 187

fixed wireless: Broadband Internet connection that uses a dish-shaped antenna on a building, such as a house or business, to communicate with a tower location via radio signals., 59, 482

flagged records, 502

flames: Abusive or insulting messages., 94

flame wars: Exchanges of flames., 94

flash memory storage, avoiding malware infections, 110

flash memory: Type of nonvolatile memory that can be erased electronically and rewritten., 295

flat-panel display: Display device that has a shallow depth and a flat screen., 340

flat-panel monitors, 332–343

focus group: A series of lengthy, structured group meetings in which users and IT professionals work together to design or develop an application., 520. *See also* **Joint-application design (JAD) session**

folder: A specific named location on a storage medium that contains related documents., 194

  compressing, uncompressing, 198

font: A name assigned to a specific set of characters., 166

font size: The size of the characters in a particular font, measured in points., 166

font style: Formatting task that adds emphasis to a font, such as bold, italic, underline, and color., 166

force feedback: Technology that sends resistance to the device in response to actions of the user., 353

foreground: Program with which the user currently is interacting., 415

format: Process in project development during which change a project's appearance., 166

  graphics, used on the web (table), 86

formatting: The process of dividing the disk into tracks and sectors so that the operating system can store and locate data and information on the disk., 374

form: A window on the screen that provides areas for entering or modifying data in a database., 512. *See also* **data entry form**

formulas in worksheet cells, 169

forward recovery: Recovery technique where the DBMS uses the log to reenter changes made to the database since the last save or backup., 515. *See also* **rollforward**

fourth-generation language: A nonprocedural language that enables users and programmers to access data in a database., 532. *See also* **4G**

FoxNews.com, 90

fractional T1: T-carrier line that home and small business users purchase, in which they share a connection to a T1 line with other users., 468

frame rate: The number of frames per second (fps) in a video, 331

freeware: Copyrighted software provided at no cost by an individual or a company that retains all rights to the software., 161

friends, 73, 74

front end: A program that generally has a more user-friendly interface than a DBMS., 505

front side bus: Bus that is part of the motherboard and connects the processor to main memory., 300. *See also* **FSB**

FSB: Bus that is part of the motherboard and connects the processor to main memory., 300. *See also* **front side bus**

FTP: An Internet standard that permits file uploading and downloading to and from other computers on the Internet. Short for File Transfer Protocol., 24, 31, 92, 188

FTP server: A computer that allows users to upload and/or download files using FTP., 92, 116

FTTB: Dedicated line used by small businesses to access the Internet via fiber-optic cables., 467. *See also* **Fiber to the Building**

FTTH: Dedicated line that provides home users with Internet access via fiber-optic cable., 467. *See also* **Fiber to the Home**

FTTP: Dedicated line that uses fiber-optic cable to provide extremely high-speed Internet access to a user's physical permanent location., 467. *See also* **Fiber to the Premises**

full backup: Backup method that provides the best protection against data loss because it copies all program and data files. (or) Fastest recovery method in which all files are saved., 234, 396. *See also* **archival backup**

function: A predefined formula that performs common calculations such as adding the values in a group of cells or generating a value such as the time or date., 169

function creep: Problem that occurs when a company uses the technology intended for one purpose for an entirely different purpose., 502

function keys: Special keyboard keys, labeled with the letter F followed by a number, programmed to issue commands to a computer., 320

G

game console: A mobile computing device designed for single-player or multiplayer video games., 10, 131, 276

game devices, 131–132

gamepad: Game controller, held with both hands, that controls the movement and actions of players or objects in video games or computer games., 131

game server, 116

game web and mobile apps, 187

games designer: Employee who designs games and translates designs into a program or app using an appropriate application development language. *See also* **Games programmer,** 570

games programmer: Employee who designs games and translates designs into a program or app using an appropriate application development language. *See also* **Games designer,** 570

gaming

accessories and input techniques, 11

in home, 11

online, avoiding risks, 216

gaming desktop: Desktop that offers high-quality audio, video, and graphics with optimal performance for sophisticated single-user and networked or Internet multiplayer games., 114

gaming keyboard: A keyboard designed specifically for users who enjoy playing games on the computer., 322

Gantt chart: Bar chart developed by Henry L. Gantt that uses horizontal bars to show project phases or activities., 518

Gates, Bill, 26

GBps: Gigabytes per second., 371, 460

geofence: Virtual perimeter or boundary to disable certain apps or cameras in secure areas, such as labs or meeting rooms., 389

geolocation: Determining a user's location based on a device's GPS or connection to a cell tower., 537

geotag, 372

gesture: A motion you make on a touch screen with the tip of one or more fingers or your hand., 5, 324

touch screen (table), 5

gesture recognition: Computer capability that allows users to guide on-screen elements using air gestures., 328. *See also* **motion input**

ghosting, 197

GIF graphics format, 86

gigabyte (GB): One billion characters., 61, 290, 370

gigahertz (GHz): One billion ticks of the system clock per second., 283

global positioning system: A navigation system that consists of one or more earth-based receivers that accept and analyze signals sent by satellites in order to determine the receiver's geographic location., 483. *See also* **GPS**

Google, 63

Google Apps Certified Specialist: Programmer/ developer certification that tests a user's skills of administering, selling, and deploying Google Apps., 574

Google Drive: Drive that provides access to email, contacts, calendar, photos, files, and more., 434

Google Maps, 81

Google Play: Google's app store that provides access to apps, songs, books, and movies., 434

Google's Android, 27

Google Street View feature, 111

governmental websites, 77

government web database services, 507

GPRS: General Packet Radio Service; a 2G standard for cellular transmissions., 481

GPS: A navigation system that consists of one or more earth-based receivers that accept and analyze signals sent by satellites in order to determine the receiver's geographic location., 31, 39, 69, 132, 178, 187, 483. *See also* **global positioning system**

GPS receiver: A handheld, mountable, or embedded device that contains an antenna, a radio receiver, and a processor., 69

GPS tracking, disabling, 237

grandparent: Term used in three-generation backups to refer to the oldest copy of the file., 234

graphical user interface (GUI): User interface with which you interact with menus and visual images by touching, pointing, tapping, or clicking buttons and other objects to issue commands., 414. *See also* **video card**

graphics

applications, 27

and media applications, 164

output, 340

graphics card: Adapter card that converts computer output into a video signal that travels through a cable to the monitor, which displays an image on the screen., 298. *See also* **video card**

graphics formats used on the web (table), 86

graphics processing unit (GPU): Chip that controls the manipulation and display of graphics on a display device. Also called GPU., 342

graphics tablet: An electronic plastic board that detects and converts movements of a stylus or digital pen into digital signals that are sent to the computer., 328. *See also* **digitizer**

graphic: Visual representation of nontext information such as a drawing, chart, or photo., 85

green computing: Practices that involve reducing the electricity and environmental waste while using a computers, mobile devices, and related technologies., 26, 241

GSM: Global System for Mobile Communications; a 2G standard for cellular transmissions., 481

GUI (graphical user interface): User interface with which you interact with menus and visual images by touching, pointing, tapping, or clicking buttons and other objects to issue commands., 414

H

hacker: Someone who accesses a computer or network illegally., 193, 214

  punishment for cybercrime, 214

hacking, 528

hand geometry system: Biometric device that measures the shape and size of a person's hand., 225

handheld computer: A computer small enough to fit in one hand., 112

handheld game device: A small mobile device that contains a screen, speakers, controls, and game console all in one unit., 131

hands-free device, 8

handwriting recognition software: Software that translates the handwritten letters and symbols created on the screen into typed text or objects that the computer or mobile device can process., 327

hard copy: Information that exists on a physical medium, such as paper., 14, 166. *See also* **hyperlink**

hard disk drive: Storage device that includes one or more inflexible, circular platters that use magnetic particles to store data, instructions, and information., 373. *See also* **hard disk; HDD**

hard disk: Storage device that includes one or more inflexible, circular platters that use magnetic particles to store data, instructions, and information., 17, 373–376. *See also* **hard disk drive; HDD**

access time on, 376

defragmenting, 197, 376

hard drive: Term used to refer collectively to hard disks and SSDs., 17, 373–380

data and files, encryption, 379

transfer files, internal, 377

hardware: Electric, electronic, and mechanical components contained in a computer., 4

and operating system, 158

protecting, 139–141

hardware firewall: Device intended to stop network intrusions before they attempt to affect your computer or network malicious., 190, 472

hardware radiation, 344

hashtag: A number sign (#) followed by a keyword that describes and categorizes a Tweet., 73

HDD: Storage device that includes one or more inflexible, circular platters that use magnetic particles to store data, instructions, and information., 373. *See also* **hard disk; hard disk drive**

HDMI port: Port that combines DVI with high-definition (HD) television and video., 343. *See also* **High-Definition Media Interface port**

HDTV: The most advanced form of digital television, working with digital broadcast signals, transmitting digital sound, supporting wide screens, and providing high resolutions., 343. *See also* **high-definition television**

head crash: Type of hard disk failure that occurs when a read/write head touches the surface of a platter., 375

headphones: Audio output device that cover or are placed outside the ear., 16, 352

headset: Input device that you can speak into that contains both a microphone and a speaker., 14, 352

health and fitness apps, 187

health care, technology in, 38

health concerns of using technology, 26, 142–144

health websites, 79

heat sink: Small ceramic or metal component with fins on its surface that absorbs and disperses heat produced by electrical components, such as a processor., 284

help desk specialist: Employee who answers technology-related questions in person, on the phone, or via email or an online chat room. *See also* **Help desk technician,** 569

help desk technician: Employee who answers technology-related questions in person, on the phone, or via email or an online chat room. *See also* **Help desk specialist,** 569

help systems, 205

hertz: One clock cycle per second, 283

hibernate mode: Computer power option that saves any open documents and running programs or apps to an internal hard drive before removing power from the computer or device., 413

High-Definition Media Interface port: Port that combines DVI with high-definition (HD) television and video., 343. *See also* **HDMI port**

high-definition television: The most advanced form of digital television, working with digital broadcast signals, transmitting digital sound, supporting wide screens, and providing high resolutions., 343. *See also* **HDTV**

highest priority projects, 521

hits: Webpage names displayed by a search engine that contain the search text specified by a user., 71

home automation, 11

devices, 132

home design/landscaping software, 180

home network: Multiple computers and devices connected together by home users., 33, 473

creating, 475

planning and designing, 474–475

home page: The first page that is displayed on a website., 66

home server, 116

home user: Any person who spends time using technology at home., 41, 42, 236

host: Any computer that provides services and connections to other computers on a network. Also called a server., 56

host computer: Computer that controls access to the hardware, software, and other resources on the network and provides a centralized storage area for programs, data, and information., 456. *See also* **server**

hot plugging: Feature that allows you to insert or remove a removable flash memory device and other devices while the computer is running., 298

hot spot: A wireless network that provides Internet connections to mobile computers and devices., 32, 59

HTML5: Technology used for web apps that specifies the structure of content displayed on a webpage., 537–538

HTML: A special formatting language that software developers use to format documents for display on the web., 535, 536. *See also* **Hypertext Markup Language**

hub: A device that provides a central point for cables in a network., 473. *See also* **switch**

human resources information system (HRIS): Information system that manages one or more administrative human resources functions, such as maintaining and managing employee benefits, schedules, and payroll., 555

human resources software, 177

hybrid app: App that combines features of native and mobile web apps., 571

hyperlink: A built-in connection to other documents, graphics, audio files, videos, other webpages, or websites., 21

Hypertext Markup Language: A special formatting language that software developers use to format documents for display on the web., 535, 536. *See also* **HTML**

Hypertext Transfer Protocol (http), 69

I

IaaS (infrastructure as a service): Cloud computing service that uses software to emulate hardware capabilities, enabling companies to scale, or adjust up or down, storage, processing power, or bandwidth as needed., 287

ICANN: Organization that approves and controls TLDs. Short for Internet Corporation for Assigned Names and Numbers., 63

iCloud: Apple's cloud server., 427

icons, 426

identity theft

  protecting yourself from, 80

  recovering from, 514

illustration software: An application that allows users to draw pictures, shapes, and other graphics with various on-screen tools such as a pen, brush, eyedropper, and paint bucket., 181. *See also* **paint software**

image editing software: An application that provides the capabilities of paint software and also includes the capability to enhance and modify existing photos and image., 181

image viewer: A tool that allows users to display, copy, and print the contents of a graphics file, such as a photo., 195, 422

impact printer, 351

implementation phase, 525

improved data integrity, 506

inattentional blindness: Problem that occurs when a person's attention is diverted while performing a natural activity, such as walking., 125

incremental backup: Fastest backup method that requires minimal storage space to back up because only most recent changes are saved. (or) Backup method that copies only the files that have changed since the last full or incremental backup., 234, 396

index: Feature of a search tool that stores a variety of information about a file, including its name, date created, date modified, author name, and so on., 195

inference rules: A set of logical judgments that are applied to the knowledge base each time a user describes a situation to the expert system., 560

infographic: A visual representation of data or information, designed to communicate quickly, simplify complex concepts, or present patterns or trends. Short for information graphic., 86

informational websites, 74

information literacy: Skill set that prepares people to manage information so that they can be knowledgeable decision makers., 560–561

  components, 561

  defining, 561

  research and composition, steps in, 561

information privacy: The right of individuals and companies to deny or restrict the collection, use, and dissemination of information about them., 242

information: Processed data that conveys meaning to users., 12

  accuracy, 239–240

  described, 12

  how travels on Internet, 62

information system: A set of hardware, software, data, people, and procedures that work together to produce information., 515, 554

information theft: Illegal act that occurs when someone steals person or confidential information., 229

infrared (IR), 479

infrastructure as a service (IaaS): Cloud computing service that uses software to emulate hardware capabilities, enabling companies to scale, or adjust up or down, storage, processing power, or bandwidth as needed., 287

ink cartridges, 346

ink-jet printer: A type of nonimpact printer that forms characters and graphics by spraying tiny drops of liquid ink onto a piece of paper., 345–346

input devices: Any hardware component that allows you to enter data and instructions into a computer or mobile device., 12

input: Term used to refer to data., 4, 318–319

data, 12

with input devices, 12

techniques for gaming, 12

video and voice, 14

insertion point: A symbol on the screen, usually a blinking vertical bar, that indicates where the next character you type will appear., 320. *See also* **cursor**

Instagram, 182

installing applications, mobile apps, 29

instant messaging (IM): A real-time Internet communications service that notifies you when one or more of your established contacts are online and then allows you to exchange messages or files or join a private chat room with them., 31, 178

instructors, 567

integrated circuit: Circuit that contains many microscopic pathways capable of carrying electrical current., 278

integrated development environment (IDE): Object-oriented application development tool that contains tools for building graphical interfaces, an editor for entering program code, a compiler and/or interpreter, and a debugger (to remove errors)., 530

integration test, 525

intel-compatible processors: Processors manufactured by AMD that have an internal design similar to Intel processors, perform the same functions, and can be as powerful, but often are less expensive., 283

intellectual property rights: The rights to which creators are entitled for their work., 240

intellectual property (IP): Unique and original works such as ideas, inventions, art, writings, processes, company and product names, and logos., 240

interactive whiteboard: A touch-sensitive device, resembling a dry-erase board, that displays the image on a connected computer screen, usually via a projector., 353

interactive whiteboards, 35

International Electronics Commission (IEC), 299

International Mobile Subscriber Identity (IMSI): Unique identity of every mobile device that allows it to communicate with a cell tower., 480

Internet: A worldwide collection of computer networks that connects millions of businesses, government agencies, educational institutions, and individuals., 20, 56

addresses, 62–64

communications, 24

connecting to the, 58–64

evolution of the, 56

filters, 193

how data, information travels on, 62

and network attacks, 215–220

plagiarism, schools dealing with, 165

popular broadband service technologies (table), 59

using in daily activities (fig.), 57

World Wide Web Consortium (W3C), 58

Internet backbone: Major carriers of network traffic., 62

internet communications, 24

Internet Explorer: Microsoft's browser., 67, 426

internet marketing specialist: Employee who directs and implements an organization's use of Internet and social media marketing, including Facebook pages, Twitter feeds, blogs, and online advertisements. *See also* **Social media marketing specialist,** 569

internet messaging, 90

internet messaging services, 458

Internet of things (IoT): Term that describes an environment where processors are embedded in every product imaginable (things), and those 'things' communicate with each other via the Internet., 133

Internet of things (IoT): Term that describes an environment where processors are embedded in every product imaginable (things), and those 'things' communicate with each other via the Internet., 284–285

discrimination of, 286

privacy and security concerns, 286

Internet service providers (ISPs): A business that provides individuals and organizations access to the Internet free or for a fee. Sometimes called an Internet access provider., 20, 61

internet usage, ISPs controlling, 477

interpreter: Program used to convert a source program into machine language by translating and then executing the machine language instructions one instruction at a time., 529

interview, 520

intranet: An internal network that uses Internet technologies, 453

iOS: Proprietary mobile operating system specifically made for Apple's mobile devices., 434

IP address: A sequence of numbers that uniquely identifies the location of each computer or device connected to the Internet. Short for Internet Protocol., 62, 462

IP hijacking: Internet security threat that occurs when cyberthieves tap into home routers or cable modems or other Internet access points to intercept a paid Internet service., 474

iPods with earbuds, 9

IP spoofing: Spoofing that occurs when an intruder computer fools a network into believing its IP address is associated with a trusted source., 217

IP: Unique and original works such as ideas, inventions, art, writings, processes, company and product names, and logos., 240

IrDA: Infrared Data Association; standard for devices to transmit data wirelessly to each other via infrared (IR) light waves., 465

iris recognition system: Biometric device that uses iris recognition technology to read patterns in the iris of the eye., 226

IRS website, 77

ISDN modem: A broadband modem that sends digital data and information from a computer to an ISDN line and receives digital data and information from an ISDN line., 469

ISDN (Integrated Services Digital Network): Short for Integrated Services Digital Network; a set of standards for digital transmission of data over standard copper phone lines., 467

IT consultant: A professional, typically hired based on technical expertise, who provides technology services to his or her clients., 523, 568

iTunes, 38, 87

iTunes Store: Store that provides access to music, books, podcasts, ringtones, and movies., 434

iTunes U, 35, 199

J

jack: Term sometimes used to identify audio and video ports., 134

jailbreaking: Process of making unauthorized modifications to operating systems and bypassing the DRM restrictions on Apple iPhones and iPads in order to run unapproved apps., 574

Java: An object-oriented programming language developed by Sun Microsystems., 531

JavaScript: A scripting language that users to interact with a webpage's content., 538

jewel case: Protective case for storing optical discs., 387

Jobs, Steve, 26

job searching, 576

job search websites, 82

joint-application design (JAD) session: A series of lengthy, structured group meetings in which users and IT professionals work together to design or develop an application., 520. *See also* **focus group**

joystick: A handheld vertical lever, mounted on a base, that you move in different directions to control the actions of the simulated vehicle or player., 131

JPEG: Compressed graphics format that attempts to reach a balance between image quality and file size. Short for Joint Photographic Experts Group., 86

juice jacking, 136

Jumpstart Our Business Startup (JOBS) Act, 396

JustCloud.com, 19

K

KBps: Kilobytes per second., 371

kernel: The core of an operating system that manages memory and devices, maintains the internal clock, runs programs, and assigns the resources, such as devices, programs, apps, data, and information., 412–413

keyboard: Input device that contains keys you press to enter data and information into a computer or mobile device., 13, 320–322

types of, 321

keyboard monitoring software: Software that runs undetected and stores every keystroke in a file for later retrieval., 321. *See also* **keylogging software**

keyboard shortcut: One or more keyboard keys that you press to perform an operating system or application-related task., 320

keygen: Program that creates software registration numbers and sometimes activation codes. Short for key generator., 228

keyloggers: Program often found on public computers that records keystrokes in a hidden file., 80

keylogging software: Software that runs undetected and stores every keystroke in a file for later retrieval., 321. *See also* **keyboard monitoring software**

kill switch, smartphone, 295

kilobyte (KB), 370

kiosk: A freestanding terminal that usually has a touch screen for user interaction., 119, 325

knowledge base: The combined subject knowledge and experiences of the human experts used in an expert system., 560

L

L1 cache: Cache built directly on the processor chip., 294

L2 cache: Cache that is slightly slower than L1 cache but has a much larger capacity., 294

L3 cache: Cache on the motherboard that is separate from the processor chip., 294

label printer: A small printer that prints on an adhesive-type material that can be placed on a variety of items such as envelopes, packages, optical discs, photos, and file folders., 350

landscape orientation: A project that is wider than it is tall, with information printed across the widest part of the document., 344

laptop: Thin, lightweight mobile computer with a screen in its lid and a keyboard in its base, designed to fit on your lap., 4, 111, 276. *See also* **notebook computer**

components in, 278

keyboard, 13

motherboard of, 279

vs. tablets, desktops, 6

large-format printer: Printer that uses ink-jet technology, but on a much larger scale, to create photo-realistic-quality color prints., 350

laser mouse: Mouse that uses laser sensors that emit and sense light to detect the mouse's movement., 322

laser printer: Type of high-speed, high-quality nonimpact printer that creates images using a laser beam and powdered ink called toner., 348

latency: The time it takes a signal to travel from one location to another on a network., 476

latest drivers, finding, 419

laws, privacy, 246

LCD: Display technology that sandwiches a liquid compound between two sheets of material that presents sharp, flicker-free images on a screen when illuminated., 341–342. *See also* **liquid crystal display**

LCD projector: Data projector, which uses liquid crystal display technology, that attaches directly to a computer or mobile device and uses its own light source to display the information shown on the computer screen., 352

LED display: A display that uses LED for the backlight. Also called an LED LCD display., 342

LED (light-emitting diode): Light-emitting diode technology used in monitors., 341–342

legal software: An application that assists in the prepa-ration of legal documents and provides legal informa- tion to individuals, families, and small businesses, 175

level 1: RAID storage design that writes data on two disks at the same time to duplicate the data., 390. *See also* **mirroring**

libraries

and content filtering, 247

library instruction, 561

license agreement: The right to use a program or app, which provides specific conditions for use of the soft-ware and that a user typically must accept before using the software., 163, 228

lifestyle applications, 185

like: Terminology used on social networking sites to recommend content., 73

line-of-sight transmission: Requirements that the sending device and the receiving device must be in line with each other so that nothing obstructs the path of the infrared light wave., 465

link: A built-in connection to other documents, graphics, audio files, videos, other webpages, or websites., 21. *See also* **hyperlink**

avoiding clicking unsafe, 238

LinkedIn, 23, 24, 82, 578

Linux: A popular, multitasking UNIX-based operating system that runs on a variety of personal computers, servers, and devices., 429–430

liquid cooling technology: Processor cooling method that uses a continuous flow of fluid(s), such as water and glycol, in a process that transfers the heated fluid away from the processor to a radiator-type grill, which cools the liquid, and then returns the cooled fluid to the processor., 284

liquid crystal display: Display technology that sand-wiches a liquid compound between two sheets of mate-rial that presents sharp, flicker-free images on a screen when illuminated., 341–342. *See also* **LCD**

LISTSERV, 90

list server, 116

literacy, digital, 2

Live CD: CD that can be used to start the computer., 413

Live USB: USB flash drive that can be used to start the computer, 413

loads: The process of copying software from storage to memory., 28

local area network (LAN): A network that connects computers and devices in a limited geographical area such as a home, school, office building., 453

location sharing: Browsing option that gives websites access to your current location., 66

log: A listing of activities that modify the contents of the database, 515

logical design: Activity during system development that involves three major activities: (1) study how the current system works, (2) determine the users' wants, needs, and requirements, and (3) recommend a solution., 522. *See also* **detailed analysis**

logic bombs, 199

longitudinal recording: Storage technique in which magnetic particles are aligned horizontally around the surface of the disk., 374

LTE (Long Term Evolution): Short for Long Term Evolution; a network standard that defines how high-speed cellular transmissions use broadcast radio to transmit data for mobile communications., 462–463

M

M2 (Memory Stick Micro): A type of memory card., 381

MAC address: A unique hardware identifier for a computer or device. Short for Media Access Control address., 236

machine cycle: Set of four basic operations that a processor repeats for every instruction: (1) fetching, (2) decoding, (3) executing, and, if necessary, (4) storing., 281–282

machine language: The only language the computer directly recognizes., 529

machine-to-machine (M2M) communications, 133

Macintosh operating system (Mac OS): Apple's operating system., 427–428

macro: A series of statements that instructs a program or app how to complete a task., 532

macro recorder: A program used with macros that records all actions until turned off., 533

macro viruses, 190

madware: Adware on mobile phones. Short for mobile adware., 245

magnetic stripe card: A credit card, entertainment card, bank card, or other similar card with a stripe that contains information identifying you and the card., 393

magnetic stripe card reader: Reading device that reads the magnetic stripe on the back of credit cards, entertainment cards, bank cards, identification cards, and other similar cards., 337. *See also* **Magstripe reader**

magnetic tape, 392

magstripe reader: Reading device that reads the magnetic stripe on the back of credit cards, entertainment cards, bank cards, identification cards, and other similar cards., 337–338. *See also* **Magnetic stripe card reader**

mail server, 116

mainframe: A large, expensive, powerful server that can handle hundreds or thousands of connected servers simultaneously., 117

main memory: Memory chips that can be read from and written to by the processor and other devices., 290. *See also* **RAM; Random access memory**

malicious software: Programs that act without a user's knowledge and deliberately alter the operations of computers and mobile devices. Short for malicious software., 215. *See also* **malware**

malware: Programs that act without a user's knowledge and deliberately alter the operations of computers and mobile devices. Short for malicious software., 24, 215

avoiding infections, 110

common types of (table), 215

if you can't remove, 216

and viruses, 190–191

management information system (MIS): information system that generates accurate, timely, and organized information, so that managers and other users can make decisions, solve problems, supervise activities, and track progress., 558

manufacturing, technology in, 40–41

Manufacturing Resource Planning II (MRP II): Information system that is an extension of MRP that also includes product packaging and shipping, machine scheduling, financial planning, demand forecasting, tracking labor productivity, and monitoring product quality., 555

manufacturing software, 177

mapping apps, 187

mapping websites, 80–81

mashups: Applications that incorporate data from multiple providers into a new application., 288

mass media websites, 76

Material Requirements Planning (MRP): Information system that monitors and controls inventory, material purchases, and other processes related to manufacturing operations., 555

MBps: Megabytes per second., 371, 460

m-commerce: E-commerce that takes place using mobile devices. Short for mobile commerce., 82

media
applications, 27
downloading digital, from online services, 87
on the web, 76
media and graphics applications, 179–185
media library: A collection of stored digital media., 128
media literacy, 561
media player: Special A program that allows you to view images and animations, listen to audio, and watch video files on your computer or mobile device., 87, 185
buyer's guide for, 129
media sharing, 371–372
media sharing mobile apps, 187
media sharing site: A website that enables members to manage and share media such as photos, videos, and music., 75
medical applications, 185
Medical field, motion input in, 329
megabyte (MB): One million characters., 61, 370
megahertz, 296
Megan's Law, 505
megapixel (MP), 127
memory: Electronic components that store instructions waiting to be executed and the data needed by those instructions., 16, 110
memory cache: Cache that helps speed the processes of a computer by storing frequently used instructions and data., 294
memory card: Removable flash memory, usually no bigger than 1.5 inches in height or width, that you insert and remove from a slot in a computer, mobile device, or card/reader writer., 18, 381–382
life span of, 382
slots, in computer, 381
working of, 382
memory: Electronic components that store instructions waiting to be executed and the data needed by those instructions., 290
access times, 296
bytes and addressable, 290
cache, 294
CMOS, 296
flash memory, 295
modules, 293

RAM (random access memory), 290–292
read-only memory (ROM), 294
requirements, determining, 292
types of, 290
memory modules, 293
memory resident: Instructions that remain in memory while the computer or mobile device is running., 413
Memory Stick PRO Duo: A type of memory card., 381
metadata: Details about data., 510
meteorology, computers and, 437
metropolitan area network (MAN): A high-speed network that connects local area networks in a metropolitan area, such as a city or town, and handles the bulk of communications activity across that region., 455
MICR devices: Magnetic-ink character recognition; reading devices that read text printed with magnetized ink., 338
microblog: Blog that allows users to publish short messages, usually between 100 and 200 characters, for others to read., 78
microchip, 280
microphones: Input device that enables you to speak into a computer or mobile device., 14
microprocessor: Term used by some computer and chip manufacturers to refer to a personal computer processor chip., 280
microSDHC: A type of memory card., 381
microSDXC: A type of memory card., 381
Microsoft, 27
Microsoft Office Specialist: Application software certification that tests a user's skills of Microsoft Office programs., 572
Microsoft's Windows, 27
microwaves: Radio waves that provide a high-speed signal transmission., 482
microwave station: An earth-based reflective dish that contains the antenna, transceivers, and other equipment necessary for microwave communications., 482
Military, motion input in, 329
mini disc: Optical disc used in some game consoles and mobile devices that has a diameter of 3 inches of less., 386
mini keyboards, 13
miniSD, 381
mirroring: RAID storage design that writes data on two disks at the same time to duplicate the data., 390. *See also* **level 1**

MMS (multimedia message service): Smartphone and mobile device service that allows you to send picture/video messages., 124

mobile app: An application you download from a mobile device's application store or other location on the Internet to a smartphone or other mobile device., 28, 69, 161

  locating, installing, running, 29

  for personal, business productivity, 177

mobile app development, 570–571

mobile broadband: Broadband Internet connection that uses the cellular radio network to connect computers and devices with built-in compatible technology (such as 3G, 4G, or 5G) or a wireless modem or other communications device., 59

mobile broadband wireless router, 472

mobile browser: A special type of browser designed for the smaller screens and limited computing power of Internet-capable mobile devices such as smartphones., 65, 67

mobile communications, 457–458

mobile computer: A portable personal computer designed so that a user easily can carry it from place to place., 4, 108

mobile device

  removing programs and apps, 416

mobile device: A computing device small enough to hold in your hand., 108–145

  backing up, 19

  buyer's guide for, 128–129

  categories of (table), 134

  computers and, 7, 108

  connecting peripheral devices, accessories to, 136

  described, 7

  malware risks to, 193

  security in public places, 125

  transferring photos to computers, 153

  transportation and, 95

mobile device cooling, 284

mobile device input, in vehicle, 326

mobile device management (MDM): Company policy that outlines and educates employees about safe mobile device use., 433

mobile devices: A computing device small enough to hold in your hand.

  care for, 302–303

  cases for, 276–278

  entering data and instructions in, 319

  ports for, 297

  securing, 279

mobile hot spot: Smartphones that can function as a wireless modem when tethered to a personal computer or movile device., 469, 470

mobile operating system: The operating system on mobile devices and many consumer electronics., 186, 433–436

  vs. desktop, 435–436

mobile payments, 36

mobile phone memory, wiping of, 295

mobile phone usage, ethics and issues, 302

mobile printer: A small, lightweight, battery-powered printer that allows a mobile user to print from a laptop, smartphone, or other mobile device while traveling., 350

mobile security, 237

mobile security specialist: Employee who is responsible for the security of data and information stored on computers and mobile devices within an organization. *See also* **Computer security specialist**, 570

mobile service provider: An ISP that offers wireless Internet access to computers and mobile devices with the necessary built-in wireless capability, wireless modems, or other communications devices that enable wireless connectivity. Sometimes called a wireless data provider., 61

mobile strategist: Employee who integrates and expands the company's initiatives for mobile users., 570

mobile technology expert: Employee who develops and directs an organization's mobile strategy, including marketing and app development., 570

mobile user: Any person who works with computers or mobile devices while away from a main office, home, or school., 41, 42

mobile web app: A web app that is optimized for display in a browser on a mobile device, regardless of screen size or orientation., 161, 571

mock-up: A sample of the input or output that contains actual data., 524

modems, 31, 58

monitor: A display that is packaged as a separate peripheral device., 340

morphing: Video editing technique that transforms one video image into another image over the course of several frames of video., 331

motherboard: The main circuit board of the personal computer. Also called a system board., 110, 278, 472

motion input: Computer capability that allows users to guide on-screen elements using air gestures., 328–329. *See also* **gesture recognition**

motion-sensing controllers, 131, 132

motion-sensing devices, 329

motion-sensing game controllers: Game controllers that allow the user to guide on-screen elements with air gestures, that is, by moving their body or handheld input device through the air., 132

mouse: A pointing device that fits under the palm of your hand comfortably., 13, 322

  operations (table), 13

MP3: Audio format that reduces an audio file to about one-tenth its original size, while reserving much of the original quality of the sound., 87

MSN portal, 83

multi-core processor: A single chip with two or more separate processor cores., 280

multidimensional database: A database that stores data in dimensions., 508

multifunction printer (MFP): A single device that looks like a printer or a copy machine but provides the functionality of a printer, scanner, copy machine, and perhaps a fax machine., 349. *See also* **all-in-one printer**

multimedia: Any application that combines text with media., 85

multimedia authoring software: Software that allows users to combine text, graphics, audio, video, and animation in an interactive application., 184

multiple desktop operating systems, 431

multiplexing: ISDN line technique of carrying three or more signals at once through the same line., 467

multipurpose operating systems: Operating systems that can function as both desktop and server operating systems., 432

multisession: Optical disc that can be written on more than once, allowing users to save additional data on the disc at a later time., 388

multitasking: An operating system that allows two or more programs or apps to reside in memory at the same time., 415

multi-touch: Capability of touch screens that recognize multiple points of contact at the same time., 324

multiuser: Operating system that enables two or more users to run programs simultaneously., 416

music sharing sites, 75

N

nanosecond (ns): One billionth of a second., 296

National Park Service home page, 68

native apps: Apps written for mobile devices running a particular mobile phone operating system., 571

native resolution: The specific resolution for which displays are optimized., 342

natural user interface (NUI): User interface with which users interact with the software through ordinary, intuitive behavior., 414

navigation systems, 325

near field communications: Type of wireless connection that uses close-range radio signals to transmit data between two NFC-enabled devices., 138, 466. *See also* **NFC**

.NET: A set of technologies that allows almost any type of program to run on the Internet or an internal business network, as well as stand-alone computers and mobile devices., 532

netiquette: The code of acceptable behaviors users should follow while on the Internet. Short for Internet etiquette., 94

net neutrality, 477

network: A collection of computers and mobile devices connected together, often wirelessly, via communications devices and transmission media., 32, 452–453

  architectures, 456–457

  to facilitate communications, 452

  home, business, 33

  local area network, 453

  metropolitan area network, 455

  personal area network, 455–456

  securing wireless, 236

  to share data and information, 453

  to share hardware, 452

  to share software, 453

  to transfer funds, 453

  unauthorized access and use, 221–227

  wide area network, 455

  wireless LAN, 454

network administrator: The person overseeing network operations., 423, 569

network and Internet attacks, 215–220

network architecture: The configuration of computers, devices, and media in a network., 456–457

network attached storage (NAS): A server that is placed on a network with the sole purpose of providing storage to users, computers, and devices attached to the network., 390–392. *See also* **storage appliance**

network card: A communications device that enables a computer or device that does not have built-in networking capability to access a network., 472. *See also* **Network interface card (NIC); NIC (network interface card)**

network engineer: Employee who installs, configures, and maintains LANs, WANs, wireless networks, intranets, Internet systems, and network software; identifies and resolves connectivity issues. *See also* **Network administrator,** 569

networking, defined, 426

network interface card (NIC): A communications device that enables a computer or device that does not have built-in networking capability to access a network., 472. *See also* **network card**

network license: A legal agreement that allows multiple users to access software on the server simultaneously., 229

network monitoring software: Software the constantly assesses the status of a network and sends an email or text message, usually to the network administrator, when it detects a problem., 462

network security administrator: Employee who configures routers and firewalls; specifies web protocols and enterprise technologies., 570

network server, 116

network standard: Guidelines that specify the way computers access the medium to which they are connected, the type(s) of medium used, the speeds used on different types of networks, and the type(s) of physical cable and/or the wireless technology used., 459

neural network: A system that attempts to imitate the behavior of the human brain., 39

news feed: Terminology used on social networking sites to refer to activity updates from your friends that appear on a separate page associated with your account., 73

newsgroups, 31

news mobile apps, 187

news websites, 76

NFC chips: Chip in a smartphone or mobile device that enables communication with other devices simply by being in proximity., 394–395

NFC tags: Tag that contains a chip and an antenna that contains information to be transmitted., 394–395

NFC transactions, security of, 395

NFC: Type of wireless connection that uses close-range radio signals to transmit data between two NFC-enabled devices., 138, 466. *See also* **near field communication**

NIC (network interface card): A communications device that enables a computer or device that does not have built-in networking capability to access a network., 472. *See also* **network card**

Nintendo, 131

nit: A unit of visible light intensity equal to one candela (formerly called candlepower) per square meter., 342

node, 453

No Fly List, 249

noise: An electrical disturbance that can degrade communications., 477

noise cancelling, 143

nonimpact printer: A printer that forms characters and graphics on a piece of paper without actually contacting the paper., 345

nonprocedural language: A programming language in which thesoftware developer writes English-like instructions or interacts with a graphical environment to retrieve data from files or a database., 532

nonresident: Instructions that remain on a storage medium until they are needed, at which time they transfer into memory (RAM)., 413

nonvolatile memory: Memory that does not lose its contents when power is removed from the computer., 290

notebook computer: Thin, lightweight mobile computer with a screen in its lid and a keyboard in its base, designed to fit on your lap., 4, 111. *See also* **laptop computer**

notes taking, hand and digital device, 327

note taking software: An application that enables users to enter typed text, handwritten comments, drawings, sketches, photos, and links anywhere on a page and then save the page as part of a notebook., 171

numerical literacy, 561

numeric check: Validity check that ensures that users enter only numeric data into a field., 503

O

object: An item that can contain both data and the procedures that read or manipulate that data., 508

object code: The machine language version of a program that results from compiling the procedural language., 529. *See also* **Object program**

object-oriented database (OODB): A database that stores data in objects., 508

object-oriented programming (OOP) language: Programming language used to implement objects in a program., 530

object program: The machine language version of a program that results from compiling the procedural language., 529. *See also* **object code**

observing people, system analysts, 520

OCR devices: Devices that usually include a small optical scanner for reading characters and sophisticated software to analyze what is read., 335

OCR software: Optical character recognition; software that can read and convert text documents into electronic files., 334

office network, wireless printer addition, 479

off-site: A location separate from the computer or mobile device site., 233

OLED: Organic LED; display technology that uses organic molecules that are self-illuminating and, thus, do not require a backlight., 342

OMR devices: Devices that read hand-drawn marks, such as small circles or rectangles., 335

onboard navigation systems, 39

OneDrive: Microsoft's cloud server., 426

online analytical processing (OLAP): Programs that analyze data, such as those in a decision support system., 559

online auction: Auction in which users bid on an item being sold by someone else on the web., 82

online gaming, avoiding risks, 216

online help, 205

online photo storage, 182

online security service: A web app that evaluates our computer or mobile device to check for Internet and email vulnerabilities., 219

online services, downloading digital media from, 87

online social network: A website that encourages its members in its online community to share their interests, ideas, stories, photos, music, and videos with other registered users., 23, 72, 73. *See also* **social networking site**

privacy, 74

security, 74

uses of, 73

online: Term used to refer to a the state of a computer or device being connected to a network., 6

online transaction processing (OLTP): Processing technique in which the computer processes each transaction as it is entered., 558

on-screen keyboard: Smartphone feature where you press keys on the screen using a fingertip or a stylus., 5, 12, 13, 123

The Open Group: Industry standards organization that now owns UNIX as a trademark., 429

open source software: Software provided for use, modification, and redistribution and has no restrictions from the copyright holder regarding modification of the software's internal instructions and its redistribution., 161, 429

security of, 430

Opera: Browser used on both computers and mobile devices., 67

operating system (OS): A set of programs that coordinates all the activities among computer or mobile device hardware., 27, 158, 410–412

functions of, 411, 412–424

types of, 425

operating system functions, 411, 412–424

administering security, 423–424

built-in security tools, using and evaluating, 423

configuring devices, 419

coordinating tasks, 418–419

establishing Internet connections, 420–421

managing memory, 416–418

managing programs, 415–416

network, controlling, 423

performance monitor, 420

product liability laws, security flaws, 424

shutting down, computers and mobile devices, 413

starting, computers and mobile devices, 412–413

updating operating system software, 421–422

user interface, providing, 414–415

operational feasibility: Test that measures how well the proposed information system will work., 519

operators, search engine (table), 72

optical disc: Type of storage medium that consists of a flat, round, portable disc made of metal, plastic, and lacquer that is written and read by a laser., 18, 386–389

characteristics of, 386–387

cleaning and fixing scratches on, 387

life span of, 387

optical fiber: Each strand of a fiber-optic cable., 478

optical mouse: Mouse that uses optical sensors that emit and sense light to detect the mouse's movement., 322 optical readers, 335

optical resolution: The actual photographed resolution of a photo taken with a digital camera., 127

OR (search engine operator), 72

organizational websites, 77

OS X: Latest version of Apple's operating system., 427

output: Data that has been processed into a useful form., 4, 339–340

information as, 12

on output devices, 14

output device: Any hardware component that conveys information from a computer or mobile device to one or more people., 14

outsourcing: The practice of off-loading some or all storage management to an outside organization or a cloud storage provider., 390

jobs, 568

security issues and, 522

overvoltage: Electrical disturbance that occurs when the incoming electrical supply or voltage increases above the normal volts., 140. *See also* **power surge**

P

PaaS (platform as a service): Cloud computing service that allows developers to create, test, and run their solutions on a cloud platform without having to purchase or configure the underlying hardware and software., 288

packet sniffer software: Software that monitors and logs packet traffic for later analysis., 462

packets: Small pieces into which messages are divided by TCP/IP., 461

packet switching: Technique of breaking a message into individual packets, sending the packets along the best route available, and then reassembling the data., 461

page: The amount of data and program instructions that can swap at a given time., 418

paging: Technique of swapping items between memory and storage., 418

paint software: An application that allows users to draw pictures, shapes, and other graphics with various on-screen tools such as a pen, brush, eyedropper, and paint bucket., 181. *See also* **illustration software**

pairing: The process of initiating contact between two Bluetooth devices and allowing them to communicate with each other., 137

parallel conversion: Conversion strategy that consists of running the old system alongside the new system for a specified time., 526

parentheses (()), search engine operator, 72

parent: Term used in three-generation backups to refer to the second oldest copy of the file., 234

partial backup: Backup method that allows the user to choose specific files to back up, regardless of whether or not the files have changed since the last incremental backup., 396. *See also* **selective backup**

partitioning: Dividing a hard drive in separate logical storage areas (partitions) that appear as distinct drives., 431

passkeys, 137

passphrase: Similar to a password; several words separated by spaces., 25, 223

password: A private combination of characters associated with the user name that allows access to certain computer, mobile device, or network resources., 222, 424

creating strong, 25

default, 223

payload: The destructive event or prank a virus was created to deliver., 190, 215

payment apps, 179

PC: Computer that can perform all of its input, processing, output, and storage activities by itself and is intended to be used by one person at a time., 426

PC maintenance, 422

PC maintenance tool: A program that identifies and fixes operating system problems, detects and repairs disk problems, and includes the capability of improving a computer's performance., 198

PDF: An electronic image file format by Adobe Systems that mirrors the appearance of an original document. Short for Portable Document Format., 86, 176

peer: Each computer on a peer-to-peer network., 457

peer-to-peer (P2P) network: A simple, inexpensive network architecture that typically connects fewer than 10 computers., 457

pen input: Touching a stylus or digital pen on a flat surface to writem draw, or make selections., 326–328

performance monitor: A program that assesses and reports information about various computer resources and devices., 420

peripheral device: A device you connect to a computer or mobile device to expand its capabilities., 108

connecting to computer, mobile device, 136

permissions: Settings used to define who can access certain resources and when they can access those resources., 423

perpendicular recording: Storage technique in which magnetic particles are aligned vertically, or perpendicular to the disk's surface, making much greater storage capacities possible., 374

personal area network (PAN): A network that connects computers and devices in an individual's workspace using wired and wireless technology., 455–456

personal cloud: Networked hard drive connected directly to a router, allowing access to files over the Internet., 384

personal computer: Computer that can perform all of its input, processing, output, and storage activities by itself and is intended to be used by one person at a time., 4, 108, 426. *See also* **PC**

personal finance software: A simplified accounting application that helps home users and small office/home office users balance their checkbooks, pay bills, track personal income and expenses, verify account balances, transfer funds, track investments, and evaluate financial plans., 174

personal firewall: A security tool that detects and protects a personal computer and its data from unauthorized intrusions., 189, 220

setting up, 220, 221

personal interest applications, 27, 185–187

personal safes, 279

personal VoIP call, making, 92

PERT charts: Short for Program Evaluation and Review Technique chart; chart developed by the U.S. Department of Defense that analyzes the time required to complete a task and identifies the minimum time required for an entire project., 518

petabyte (PB), 370

phablet: A device that combines the features of a smartphone with a tablet., 7, 112

phased conversion: Conversion strategy where each location converts at a separate time., 526

phases: Larger categories of system development activities., 515

phishing: A scam in which a perpetrator sends an official looking email message that attempts to obtain your personal and/or financial information., 66, 193, 244

phishing filter: A program that warns or blocks you from potentially fraudulent or suspicious websites., 66, 193, 244

phishing websites, 245

phones
connecting to Wi-Fi networks, 138

typing text messages without numeric keypad, 123

phone scams, 245

photo CD: CDs that contain only photos., 388

photo editing software: A type of image editing software that allows users to edit and customize digital photos., 181

photographs
editing, 181

transferring from mobile devices to computers, 153

photo management software: Software that allows you to view, organize, sort, catalog, print, and share digital photos., 182

photo printer: A color printer that produces lab-quality photos., 347

photo sharing sites, 75

physical transmission media
coaxial cable, 478

fiber-optic cables, 478

twisted-pair cable, 477

PictBridge: A standard technology that allows you to print photos directly from a digital camera by connecting a cable from the digital camera to a USB port on the printer., 347

picture message: A photo or other image, sometimes along with sound and text, sent to or from a smartphone or other mobile device., 7

picture/video message services, 124

pilot conversion: Conversion strategy where only one location in the organization uses the new system — so that it can be tested., 526

PIN: A numeric password, either assigned by a company or selected by a user., 118, 223. *See also* **personal identification number**

pinch: Touch gesture in which a user moves two fingers together., 5

piracy: The unauthorized and illegal duplication of copyrighted software., 228. *See also* **software piracy**

pixel pitch: The distance in millimeters between pixels on a display., 342. *See also* **dot pitch**

pixel: The smallest element in an electronic image. Short for picture element., 127, 342

plaintext: Unencrypted, readable data., 230

planning phase: Step in the system development life cycle during which four major activities are performed: (1) review and approve the project requests, (2) prioritize the project requests, (3) allocate resources such as money, people, and equipment to approved projects, and (4) form a project development team for each approved project., 521

plasma display: Display that uses gas plasma technology to sandwich a layer of gas between two glass plates., 344

platform as a service (PaaS): Cloud computing service that allows developers to create, test, and run their solutions on a cloud platform without having to purchase or configure the underlying hardware and software., 288

platform: Term used to refer to the operating system that a computer uses, because applications are said to run "on top of" it, or because the it supports the applications., 412

platter: Component of a hard disk that is made of aluminum, glass, or ceramic and is coated with an alloy material that allows items to be recorded magnetically on its surface., 374

plotters: Sophisticated printers used to produce high-quality drawings such as blueprints, maps, and circuit diagrams., 350

plug and play: Technology that gives a computer the capability to recognize peripheral devices as you install them., 298, 419

plug-in: A program that extends the capability of a browser. Also called an add-on., 88

PNG: Patent-free compressed graphics format that restores all image details when the file is viewed. Short for Portable Network Graphics., 86

podcast: Recorded media that users can download or stream to a computer or portable media player., 40, 187

point, 13

point-and-shoot camera: An affordable and lightweight digital camera with lenses built into it and a screen that displays an approximation of the image to be photographed., 125

pointer: A small symbol on the screen whose location and shape change as a user moves a pointing device., 322

pointing devices, 13

  mouse, 322–323

  touchpad, 323

  trackball, 324

pointing stick, 323

point of sale (POS), 118

points (font size), 166

polymorphic viruses, 190

pop-under ad, 66

pop-under blocker, 66

pop-up ad: An Internet advertisement that suddenly appears in a new window on top of a webpage displayed in a browser., 66, 194

pop-up blocker: A filtering program that stops pop-up ads from displaying on webpages., 66, 194

pop-up windows, avoiding malware infections, 110

Portable Document Format (PDF), 86

portable keyboard: A full-sized keyboard that communicates with a smartphone., 124

portable media player: A mobile device on which you can store, organize, and play or view digital media., 8, 10, 127, 325.

portal: A website that offers a variety of Internet services from a single, convenient location., 82

portrait orientation: A project that is taller than it is wide, with information printed across the shorter width of the document., 344

port replicator: An external device that provides connections to peripheral devices through ports built into the device., 136

port: The point at which a peripheral device attaches to or communicates with a computer or mobile device so that the peripheral device can send data to or receive information from the computer., 134

  and connections, 134–138

  popular (table), 135

POS terminal: Terminal used by most retail stores to record purchases, process credit or debit cards, and update inventory. Short for point of sale., 118

post-implementation system review, 526

power supply: Component of the system unit that converts wall outlet AC power to the DC power that is used by a computer., 301–304

power surge: Electrical disturbance that occurs when the incoming electrical supply or voltage increases above the normal volts., 140. *See also* **overvoltage**

power usage effectiveness (PUE): A ratio that measures how much power enters the computer facility or data center against the amount of power required to run the computers and devices., 241

power user: User who requires the capabilities of a powerful computer., 41, 42

predictive text input: Phone technology that allows you to press one key on the keyboard or keypad for each letter in a word, and software on the phone predicts the word you want., 123

preliminary investigation: Investigation performed in system development that determines the exact nature of the problem or improvement and decide whether it is worth pursuing., 521. *See also* **feasibility study**

presentation software: An application that allows users to create visual aids for presentations to communicate ideas, messages, and other information to a group., 168

press and hold: Touch gesture in which a user presses and holds one finger until an action occurs., 5

primary key: A field that uniquely identifies each record in a file., 501

principle of least privilege policy: Policy adopted by some organizations, where users' access privileges are limited to the lowest level necessary to perform required tasks to prevent accidental or intentional misuse of the data., 513

printer: An output device that produces text and graphic on a physical medium such as paper or other material., 14, 344–351

printer resolution, 346

printout: Information that exists on a physical medium, such as paper., 14, 344. *See also* **hard copy**

print server, 116

print spooler, 418

print: To generate a hard copy of a project., 166

privacy, 24–25

  described, 24

  digital security and, 24–26

  information, 242–248

  laws, 246

  and online social networks, 74

private clouds, 122

private key encryption: Encryption method where both the originator and the recipient use the same secret key to encrypt and decrypt the data., 230. *See also* **symmetric key encryption**

procedural language: Programming language in which the software developer writes using English-like words that tell the computer what to accomplish and how to do it., 528

processor cooling, 284

processor: The electronic component of a computer that interprets and carries out the basic instructions that operate a computer., 111, 280–286. *See also* **CPU**

  arithmetic logic unit (ALU) of, 281

  control unit of, 281

  cooling of, 284

  machine cycle, 281–282

  mobile device, 283–284

  personal computer, 283–284

  registers in, 282

  selection, 283

  system clock in, 282–283

product activation: Process in which users, either online or on the phone, provide the software product's identification number to associate the software with the computer or mobile device on which the software is installed., 162, 228

product development software, 177

productivity applications: Software that can assist you in becoming more effective and efficient while performing daily activities at work, school, and home., 27, 165

  types of, 165–179

professional online presence, 577

profiles, electronic, 242–243

program: A series of related instructions, organized for a common purpose, that tells the computer what tasks to perform and how to perform them., 26, 158. *See also* **software**

  antivirus, 191–192

  and apps, 26–30

  categories of (table), 164

  developing, 29

  generally, 163

  specifications, 29

  uninstalling, 196

program and app developer: Employee who specifies, designs, implements, tests, and documents programs and apps in a variety of fields, including robotics, operating systems, animation, and applications., 568

program development life cycle: An organized set of activities performed during program development., 525

programming language: Set of words, abbreviations, and symbols that enables a software developer to communicate instructions to a computer or mobile device., 527

program specification package: Item prepared during program design that identifies the required programs and the relationship among each program, as well as the input, output, and database specifications., 524

project leader: Person who manages and controls the budget and schedule of a system development project., 517

Project Management Professional (PMP): Broad development certification that tests knowledge of tasks required during system development; PMP for short., 574

project management software: An application that allows a user to plan, schedule, track, and analyze the events, resources, and costs of a project., 172, 518

project management: The process of planning, scheduling, and then controlling the activities during system development., 517

project manager: Person who controls the activities during system development., 517

project request: A formal, written request for a new or modified information system., 521. *See also* **request for system service**

projects, saving regularly, 166

project team: Group formed for each system development project, usually consisting of users, the sytstems analyst, and other IT professionals., 517

proof of concept: A working model of the proposed system's essential functionality., 525. *See also* **prototype**

proprietary connector, 299

proprietary software: Software that is privately owned and limited to a specific vendor or computer or device model., 425

protecting
hardware, 139–141

against unauthorized access and use, 221–227

protocol: A standard that outlines characteristics of how two devices communicate on a network., 460

prototype: A working model of the proposed system's essential functionality., 525. *See also* **proof of concept**

proxy server: A server outside the organization's network that controls which communications pass into the organization's network., 66, 219

public clouds, 122

public-domain software: Software that has been donated for public use and has no copyright restrictions., 161

public key encryption: Encryption method that uses two encryption keys: a public key and a private key., 230. *See also* **asymmetric key encryption**

publishing, technology in, 39–40

PUE: A ratio that measures how much power enters the computer facility or data center against the amount of power required to run the computers and devices., 241

pull notification, 124

pull: Request information from a web server., 69

push notification, 124

Q

QR code reader: App that scans a QR code and then displays the corresponding webpage in a browser., 178

QR code (quick response code): Square-shaped graphic that corresponds to a web address or other information. Short for quick response code., 178, 335, 336

quarantine: A separate area of the hard disk that holds infected files until the infection can be removed., 191

query: A request for specific data from a database., 511

query by example (QBE): DBMS feature that has a graphical user interface to assist users with retrieving data., 512

query language: Language used with databases that consists of simple, English-like statements that allows users to specify the data they want to display, print, store, update, or delete., 512

queue: Group of files waiting in the buffer to be printed., 418

quotation marks ("), search engine operator, 72

QWERTY keyboard, 321

R

rack server: A server that is house in a slot (bay) on a metal frame (rack). Also called a rack-mounted server., 116

RAD (rapid application development): A method of developing software in which the software developer writes and implements a program in segments instead of waiting until the entire program is completed., 530

radio frequency identification: Technology that uses radio signals to communicate with a tag placed in or attached to an object, an animal, or a person., 336, 465. *See also* **RFID**

radiology, technology in, 43

RAID: Redundant array of independent disks; a group of two or more integrated hard drives., 380, 390

RAM (random access memory): Memory chips that can be read from and written to by the processor and other devices., 290–293. *See also* **main memory**

types of, 292

random access: Access method where a device can locate a particular data item or file immediately, without having to move consecutively through items stored in front of the desired data item or file., 392. *See also* **direct acces**

random access memory (RAM): Memory chips that can be read from and written to by the processor and other devices., 290-293. *See also* **main memory**

range check: Validity check that determines whether a number is within a specified range., 503

rapid application development (RAD) : A method of developing software in which the software developer writes and implements a program in segments instead of waiting until the entire program is completed., 530

reading: The process of transferring these items from a storage medium into memory., 368

read-only memory (ROM): Memory chips that store permanent data and instructions., 294

read/write head: The mechanism that reads items and writes items in the drive as it barely touches the disk's recording surface., 375

real-time clock: A separate battery-backed chip that keeps track of the date and time in a computer., 283

real-time operating system (RTOS): Operating system used by an embedded computer., 436

real time: Term used with online communications that means you and the people with whom you are conversing are online at the same time., 90

receiving device: Device that accepts the transmission of data, instructions, or information., 450

rechargeable batteries, 302

record: A group of related fields., 501

recovery media: Tool that uses logs and/or backups, and either a rollforward or a rollback technique, to restore a database when it becomes damaged or destroyed., 413

recovery plan, 235

recovery utility, 515

Recycle Bin, 427

recycling
  of electronics, 122
  of old computers, devices, 242

red-eye: The appearance of red eyes caused by a camera's flash., 182

reduced data redundancy, 505, 506

reduced development time, database approach, 506

redundancy: Built-in levels of duplicate components used in enterprise hardware that ensures that if one component fails or malfunctions, another can assume its tasks., 389

reference apps, 178

registers: Small, high-speed storage locations that temporarily hold data and instructions., 282

relational database: A database that stores data in tables that consist of rows and columns., 508

remote controls for home systems, 11

removing apps, 196

repetitive strain injury (RSI): An injury or disorder of the muscles, nerves, tendons, ligaments, and joints., 142

report generator: DBMS feature that allows users to design a report on the screen, retrieve data into the report design, and then display or print the report., 513. *See also* **report writer**

report writer: DBMS feature that allows users to design a report on the screen, retrieve data into the report design, and then display or print the report., 513. *See also* **report generator**

repository: A DBMS element that contains data about each file in a database and each field in those files., 510. *See also* **data dictionary**

request for information (RFI): A less formal document that uses a standard form to request information about a product or service., 523

request for proposal (RFP): Document sent to a vendor during the system development cycle where the vendor selects the product(s) that meets specified requirements and then quotes the price(s)., 523

request for quotation (RFQ): Document sent to a vendor during the system development cycle that identifies required products., 523

request for system services: A formal, written request for a new or modified information system., 521. *See also* **project request**

research, web database services, 507

research websites, 74

resize: To change the physical dimensions of a photo., 182

resolution: The number of horizontal and vertical pixels in a display device., 127, 342

resources: Hardware, software, data, and information., 32
  in the cloud, 121

response time: The time in milliseconds (ms) that it takes to turn a pixel on or off., 342

restore: Copying backed up files to their original location on a computer or mobile device., 233, 422

restore tool: Program that reverses the backup process and returns backed up files to their original form., 198

retail, 36

retail apps, 179

retail software: Mass-produced, copyrighted software that meets the needs of a wide variety of users, not just a single user or company., 161 retail websites, 81–82

Retina Display: LCD technology developed by Apple that produces vibrant colors and supports viewing from all angles because the LCD technology is built into the screen instead of behind it and contains more pixels per inch of display., 342

review documentation, 520

revolutions per minute (rpm): The number of times per minute that a hard disk platter rotates., 375

RFI (request for information) : A less formal document that uses a standard form to request information about a product or service., 523

RFID: Radio frequency identification; technology that uses radio signals to communicate with a tag placed in or attached to an object, an animal, or a person., 336, 465. *See also* **radio frequency identification**

RFID reader: Reading device that reads information on an RFID tag via radio waves., 336

RFID tag: Tag that includes an antenna and a memory chip that contains the information to be transmitted via radio waves., 394

RFP (request for proposal): Document sent to a vendor during the system development cycle where the vendor selects the product(s) that meets specified requirements and then quotes the price(s)., 523

RFQ (request for quotation): Document sent to a vendor during the system development cycle that identifies required products., 523

ribbon, 427

right-click, 13

ripping: The process of copying audio and/or video data from a purchased disc and saving it on your own media., 388

rollback: Recovery technique where the DBMS uses the log to undo any changes made to the database during a certain period., 515. *See also* **backward recovery**

rollforward: Recovery technique where the DBMS uses the log to reenter changes made to the database since the last save or backup., 515. *See also* **forward recovery**

ROM (read-only memory): Memory chips that store permanent data and instructions., 294

rooting: Process of making unauthorized modifications to operating systems and bypassing the DRM restrictions on devices running Android (or other operating systems) in order to run unapproved apps., 574

rootkit: A program that hides in a computer or mobile device and allows someone from a remote location to take full control of the computer or device, often for nefarious purposes., 190, 215

router: A communications device that connects multiple computers or other routers together and transmits data to its correct destination on a network., 471

routers, 31, 190, 220, 236, 237

rpm (revolutions per minute): The number of times per minute that a hard disk platter rotates., 375

RSS 2.0: Short for Really Simple Syndication; specification that content aggregators use to distribute content to subscribers., 536

RSS: A popular specification used to distribute content to subscribers. Short for Really Simple Syndication., 31

running applications, mobile apps, 29

S

SaaS (software as a service): Computing environment where an Internet server hosts and deploys applications., 287–288

Safari: Apple's browser., 67, 427

salesforce automation (SFA): Information system that helps salespeople manage customer contacts, schedule customer meetings, log customer interactions, manage product information, and place customer orders., 555

sales software, 177

Samsung, 111

SAN (storage area network): A high-speed network with the sole purpose of providing storage to other attached servers., 391–392

sandbox: An environment that allows software developers to test their programs with fictitious data without adversely affecting other programs, information systems, or data., 525

San Diego Zoo webpage, 85

Sarbanes-Oxley (SOX) Act: Law that provides financial reporting requirements and guidelines for public companies' retention of business records., 390, 396

SAS (serial-attached SCSI): A type of SCSI that uses serial signals to transfer data, instructions, and information., 380

SATA (Serial Advanced Technology Attachment): Serial Advanced Technology Attachment; interface that uses serial signals to transfer data, instructions, and information., 380

satellite Internet service: Broadband technology that provides Internet connections via satellite to a satellite dish that communicates with a satellite modem., 59

satellite speakers: Speakers in a surround sound system that are positioned so that sound emits from all directions., 351

save: Process of the computer transferring a project from memory to a local storage medium or cloud storage., 165

scams, avoiding, 245

scanner: A light-sensing input device that reads printed text and graphics and then translates the results into a form the computer can process., 14, 178, 334

schedule feasibility: Test that measures whether the established deadlines for the project are reasonable., 519

science, technology in, 38–39

science websites, 79

scope, 517

scope creep: Problem that occurs when one activity has led to another that was not planned originally; thus, the scope of the project now has grown., 519. *See also* **feature creep**

screen protector, 304

screen saver: A tool that causes a display device's screen to show a moving image or blank screen if no keyboard or mouse activity occurs for a specified time., 197, 422

scribe: Member of a joint-application design session who records facts and action items assigned during the session., 520

scripting language: An interpreted language that typically is easy to learn and use., 536

script kiddie: Cybercriminal who has the same intent as a cracker but does not have the technical skills and knowledge., 214

scroll bars, 427

SCSI (Small Computer System Interface): Small Computer System Interface; interface that uses parallel signals and can support up to 8 or 15 peripheral devices., 380

SDHC (Secure Digital High Capacity): A type of memory card., 381

SDLC (system development life cycle): Collection of phases in system development., 515

SDXC (Secure Digital Expanded Capacity): A type of memory card., 381

search: A tool, usually included with an operating system, that attempts to locate a file on your computer or mobile device based on criteria you specify., 422

search engine operators (table), 72

search engine: Software that finds websites, webpages, images, videos, news, maps, and other information related to a specific topic., 22, 71

search engine optimization expert: Employee who writes and develops web content and website layouts so that they will appear at the beginning of search results when users search for content. *See also* **SEO expert,** 569

searching

with search engines, 71–72

web, 22

search text: Word or phrase entered in a search engine to describe the word you want to find., 71

search tool: A program, usually included with an operating system, that attempts to locate a file on your computer or mobile device based on criteria you specify., 195

secondary storage: The physical material on which a computer keeps data, information, programs, and applications., 368

sectors: The small arcs into which tracks on a disk are divided., 374

Secure Digital Expanded Capacity (SDXC): A type of memory card., 381

Secure Digital High Capacity (SDHC): A type of memory card., 381

secure site: A website that uses encryption techniques to secure its data., 231

security

applications, 28

ATM, 118

avoiding malware infections, 110

digital security risks, 212–214

Internet and network attacks, 215–220

in-vehicle technology, 133

mobile, 237

mobile devices in public areas, 125

and online social networks, 74

payment apps, 179

protecting against scams, 245

protecting yourself from identify theft, 80

safe browsing techniques, 66

safeguarding against Internet and network attacks, 218

systems in the home, 11

technology in national and local, 249

tools, 189–194

wireless, 236–237

of wireless networks, 236

security analyst: Employee who implements security procedures and methods, looks for flaws in security of a company's devices and networks, works with and trains employees at all levels, and assigns permissions and network settings., 570

security suite: A collection of individual security tools available together as a unit. These programs often are called Internet security programs., 189

security system project manager: Employee who develops and maintains programs and tools designed to provide security to a network., 570

selective backup: Backup method that allows the user to choose specific files to back up, regardless of whether or not the files have changed since the last incremental backup., 396. *See also* **partial backup**

selective backup: Fast backup method that provides great flexibility., 234

self-service kiosks, 119

sending device: Device that initiates an instruction to transmit data, instructions, or information., 450

sending email messages, 103

SEO expert: Employee who writes and develops web content and website layouts so that they will appear at the beginning of search results when users search for content. *See also* **Search engine optimization expert,** 569

sequential access: Access method where data is read or written consecutively., 392

serial-attached SCSI (SAS): A type of SCSI that uses serial signals to transfer data, instructions, and information., 380

server: A computer dedicated to providing one or more services to other computers or devices on a network. (or) Computer that controls access to the hardware, software, and other resources on the network and provides a centralized storage area for programs, data, and information., 6, 116, 456. *See also* **host computer**

dedicated (table), 116

and networks, 32

server farm: A network of several servers together in single location., 117

server operating system: A multiuser operating system that organizes and coordinates how multiple users access and share resources on a network., 432–433

server virtualization: Technique that uses software to divide a physical server logically into many virtual server., 117

service pack: Free downloadable updates provided by software makers for users who have registered and/or activated their software., 422

session cookie: A file used by online shopping sites to keep track of items in a user's shopping cart., 243

SFA (salesforce automation): Information system that helps salespeople manage customer contacts, schedule customer meetings, log customer interactions, manage product information, and place customer orders., 555

shared data, 506

shareware: Copyrighted software that is distributed at no cost for a trial period., 161

downloading safely, 161

sharpness: Term used to refer to the crispness of objects in photos., 182

shopping cart: Component of an electronic storefront that allows the customer to collect purchases., 81

shopping web database services, 507

shopping websites, 82

signature capture pad: Pen input device that captures handwritten signatures with a stylus that is attached to the device., 326

signature verification system: Biometric device that recognizes the shape of your handwritten signature, as well as measures the pressure exerted and the motion used to write the signature., 225

sign in: To access resources on a network or computer., 423

simulation, gaming category, 35

single-core processors, 280

single-session disc: CD-ROM on which manufacturers write all items at one time., 388

single-user license agreement: License agreement included with software purchased by individual users., 228. *See also* **end-user license agreement**

Siri: iOS voice recognition app that enables you to speak instructions or questions to which it takes actions or responds with speech output., 434

site license: A legal agreement that permits users to install software on multiple computers-usually at a volume discount., 229

skimmer: Virtually undetectable, a device that is placed directly on top of an ATM face and captures credit card numbers and pins., 119

skimming: Crime in which thieves use a handheld device to swipe someone's credit or smart card and then obtain and store account details., 394

slate computers, 5

slate tablet: A type of tablet that does not contain a physical keyboard., 112, 276

sleep mode: Computer power option that saves any open documents and running programs or apps to RAM, turns off all unneeded functions, and then places the computer in a low-power state., 413

slide show: Presentations that are viewed as slides, usually on a large monitor or projection screen., 168

slide: Touch gesture in which a user presses and holds one finger on an object and then moves the finger to the new location., 5. *See also* **Drag**

SLR camera: A high-end digital camera that has interchangeable lenses and uses a mirror to display on its screen an exact replica of the image to be photographed. Short for single-lens reflex camera., 125

small/home office user: Employees of companies with fewer than 50 employees and the self-employed who work from home., 41, 42

smart card: An alternative to a magnetic stripe card, stores data on an integrated circuit embedded in the card., 338, 393. *See also* **chip card**

smart digital camera, 125

smart eyewear, 130

smartglasses, 130

smartphone: An Internet-capable phone that usually also includes a calendar, an appointment book, an address book, a calculator, a notepad, games, browser, and numerous other apps., 7, 123, 325

buyer's guide for, 128

with digital cameras, 125

guarding your, 174

low memory of, 418

mobile security, 237

payment apps, 179

phablets, 112

printing from, 347

typing options on, 123

Smart TV: Television containing an embedded computer that enables you to browse the web, stream video from online media services, listen to Internet radio, communicate with others on social media sites, play online games, and more - all while watching a television show., 15, 133, 343

smartwatch, 130

SMS (short message service): Short text messages, typically fewer than 300 characters., 124

social engineering: Scam in which perpetrators gain unauthorized access to or obtain confidential information by taking advantage of the trusting human nature of some victims and the naivety of others., 245

social media, 76, 110

social media, in job search, 578

social media marketing specialist: Employee who directs and implements an organization's use of Internet and social media marketing, including Facebook pages, Twitter feeds, blogs, and online advertisements. *See also* **Internet marketing specialist,** 569

social networking apps, 178

social networking sites: A website that encourages members in its online community to share their interests, ideas, stories, photos, music, and videos with other registered users., 23, 72. *See also* **online**

soft copy: Information on a display that exists electronically and appears for a temporary period., 340

software and apps field: Specialty area consisting of organizatons and individuals who develop, manufacture, and support a wide range of software and apps for computers, the web, and mobile devices., 564

software as a service (SaaS): Computing environment where an Internet server hosts and deploys applications., 287–288

software: A series of related instructions, organized for a common purpose, that tells the computer what tasks to perform and how to perform them., 26, 158, 318. *See also* **program**

availability, 161

avoiding malware infections, 110

bundled, 115

in enterprise computing, 177

license agreement, 163

theft, 228

software developer: Someone who develops programs and apps or writes the instructions that direct the computer or mobile device to process data into information; sometimes called an application developer or computer programmer., 29

software piracy: The unauthorized and illegal duplication of copyrighted software., 228. *See also* **piracy**

software registration: Optional process that usually involves submitting your name and other personal information to the software manufacturer or developer in order to receive product support., 162

software suite: A collection of individual applications available together as a unit., 172

software theft: Illegal act that occurs when occurs when someone steals software media, intentionally erases programs, illegally registers and/or activates a program or illegally copies a program., 228

solid-state drive (SSD): A storage device that typically uses flash memory to store data, instructions, and information, and that contains no moving parts. (or) Flash memory storage device that contains its own processor to manage its storage., 17, 376–378

solid-state media: Media that consist entirely of electronic components, such as integrated circuits, and contain no moving parts., 376

sound card: Adapter card that enhances the sound-generating capabilities of a personal computer by allowing sound to be input through a microphone and output through external speakers or headphones., 297

sound configurations, numbers in, 351

source document: Document that contains the original form of data to be processed., 334

source: Original location on a storage device., 34

source program: The program that contains the language instructions, or code, to be converted to machine language., 529

space (search engine operator), 72

spam: An unsolicited email message or posting sent to many recipients or forums at once., 193

speakers, 16

speakers: Audio output devices that generate sound., 351

speech recognition: A computer or mobile device's capability of distinguishing spoken words., 330. *See also* **voice recognition**

speech-to-text: Feature that recognizes a user's spoken words and enters them into email messages, text messages, or other applications that support typed text entry., 330

spelling checkers, 168

spike: Electrical disturbance that occurs when the increase in power lasts for less than one millisecond (thousandth of a second)., 140

spoofing: A technique intruders use to make their network or Internet transmission appear legitimate to a victim computer or network., 217

spooling: The process of sending documents to be printed to a buffer instead of sending them immediately to the printer., 418

sports mobile apps, 187

sports websites, 76

spreadsheet data, import/export of, 511

spreadsheet software: An application that allows users to organize data in rows and columns and perform calculations on the data., 168

spyware and malware detection software, 423

spyware: A program placed on a computer or mobile device without the user's knowledge that secretly collects information about the user and then communicates the information it collects to some outside source while the user is online., 192, 215

spyware remover: A program that detects and deletes spyware and similar programs., 192

spyware windows, 25

SQL (Structured Query Language): A popular query language that allows users to manage, update, and retrieve data., 512

SRAM: RAM chips that are faster and more reliable than and do not have to be reenergized as often as DRAM chips., 292. *See also* **Static RAM**

SSD (solid-state drive): A storage device that typically uses flash memory to store data, instructions, and information, and that contains no moving parts. (or) Flash memory storage device that contains its own processor to manage its storage., 376–378

SSID: A network name. Short for service set identifier., 236

stand-alone operating system: A complete operating system that works on desktops, laptops, and some tablets., 426. *See also* **desktop operating system**

standards: Sets of rules and procedures an organization expects employees to accept and follow., 517

Static RAM: RAM chips that are faster and more reliable than and do not have to be reenergized as often as DRAM chips., 292. *See also* **SRAM**

static webpage: A fixed webpage where all visitors see the same content., 65

status bar, 427

status update: Terminology used on social networking sites to inform friends about your activities., 73

steering committee: Decision-making body in an organization., 517

storage

  access time, 371

  capacity, 370

  enterprise, 389–392

  vs. memory, 370

  options of, 369

  processor speed of, computer and, 368

storage and processes of data, 12

storage appliance: A server that is placed on a network with the sole purpose of providing storage to users, computers, and devices attached to the network., 390. *See also* **network attached storage (NAS)**

storage area network (SAN): A high-speed network with the sole purpose of providing storage to other attached servers., 391–392

storage as a service, 287

storage device: Device that records (writes) and/or retrieves (reads) items to and from storage media., 17, 340, 368

storage media: Media, such as hard disks, solid-state drives, USB flash drives, memory cards, and optical discs, on which a computer keeps data, instructions, and information., 17

storage server, 116

stored program concept: Concept of using memory to store both data and programs., 290

storing: Processor operation in the machine cycle that writes the result to memory (not to a storage medium)., 281

streaming: The process of transferring data in a continuous and even flow, which allows users to access and use a file while it is transmitting., 38, 79

audio and video, 187

streaming cam: Camera that has the illusion of moving images because it sends a continual stream of still images., 333

streaming media player: Device, typically used in a home, that streams digital media from a computer or network to a television, projector, or some other entertainment device., 9, 128. *See also* digital media player

stretch: Touch gesture in which a user moves two fingers apart., 5

striping, 390

strong passwords, 25

Structured Query Language (SQL): A popular query language that allows users to manage, update, and retrieve data., 512

stylus: Input device that looks like a small ink pen that you can use instead of a fingertip to enter data, make selections, or draw on a touch screen., 112, 326

subject directory: Search tool that classifies webpages in an organized set of categories and related subcategories., 72

subscribe: Adding your email address to a mailing list., 90

subwoofer: Audio output device that boosts low bass sounds in a surround sound speaker system., 351

summary report: Report generated by a management information system that consolidates data usually with totals, tables, or graphs, so that managers can review it quickly and easily., 558

supercomputer: The fastest, most powerful computer and the most expensive., 120

superscalar: Processors that can execute more than one instruction per clock cycle., 283

support and security phase: Step in the system development life cycle whose purpose is to provide ongoing assistance for an information system and its users after the system is implemented, and consists of three major activities: (1) perform maintenance activities, (2) monitor system performance, and (3) assess system security., 526

surfing the web: Term used to refer to the activity of using links to explore the web., 21

surge protector: Device that uses electrical components to provide a stable current flow and minimize the chances of an overvoltage reaching the computer and other electronic equipment., 140

surge suppressor: Device that uses electrical components to provide a stable current flow and minimize the chances of an overvoltage reaching the computer and other electronic equipment., 140

survey distribution, system analysts, 520

swap file: Area of the hard drive used for virtual memory., 418

swipe keyboard app, 123

swipe: Touch gesture in which a user presses and holds one finger and then moves the finger horizontally or vertically on the screen., 5

switch: A device that provides a central point for cables in a network., 473. *See also* **hub**

symmetric key encryption: Encryption method where both the originator and the recipient use the same secret key to encrypt and decrypt the data., 230. *See also* **private key encryption**

synchronize: Process of matching the files on computers or mobile devices in two or more locations with each other., 34. *See also* **sync**

sync: Process of matching the files on computers or mobile devices in two or more locations with each other ; short for synchronize., 34. *See also* **synchronize**

syntax, 528

system board, 278

system bus, 300

system clock: Small quartz crystal circuit that controls the timing of all computer operations., 282–283

system development: A set of activities used to build an information system., 515

analysis phase, 521–522

circumstances initiating, 521

data and information gathering techniques, 520

design phase, 523–525

documentation, 519

feasibility assessment in, 519

general guidelines of, 517

implementation phase, 525–526

participation in, 517

planning phase, 521

support and security phase, 526–527

system development life cycle (SDLC): Collection of phases in system development., 515

system proposal, 522

systems analyst: Person responsible for designing and developing an information system., 517, 568

systems programmer: Employee who installs and maintains operating system software and provides technical support to the programming staff., 568

system software: Term used to refer to the operating system and other tools that consist of the programs that control or maintain the operations of the computer and its devices., 158

systems test: Test performed during the program development life cycle that verifies all programs in an application work together properly., 525

system unit: The case that contains and protects the motherboard, hard disk drive, memory, and other electronic components of the computer from damage., 114, 276. *See also* **chassis**

T

T1 line: The most popular T-carrier line., 468

T3 line: T-carrier line that is equal in speed to 28 T1 lines., 468

tabbed browsing: Browsing technique where the top of the browser shows a tab (similar to a file folder tab) for each webpage you display., 66

tables, 500

tablet: Thin, lighter weight mobile computer that has a touch screen, usually smaller than a laptop but larger than a phone., 4, 112

vs. laptops, desktops, 6

printing from, 347

tactile output: Feature included with some input devices that provides the user with a physical response from the device., 353

tag: A short descriptive label that you assign to webpages, photos, videos, blog posts, email messages, and other digital content so that it is easier locate at a later time., 75

tape: A magnetically coated ribbon of plastic that is capable of storing large amounts of data and information at a low cost., 392

tape cartridge: A small, rectangular, plastic housing for tape., 392

tape drive: Drive that reads from and writes on a magnetic tape., 392

tape library: Facility where individual tape cartridges are mounted in a separate cabinet., 392

tap: Touch gesture in which a user quickly touches and releases one finger one time., 5

target: Destination location on a storage device., 34

taskbar, 427

tax preparation software: An application that can guide individuals, families, or small businesses through the process of filing federal taxes., 176

TB (terabyte): 1 trillion bytes, 290, 370

Tbps (terabits per second), 479

T-carrier line: Any of several types of long-distance digital phone lines that carry multiple signals over a single communications line., 468

TCP/IP: Network protocol that defines how messages (data) are routed from one end of a network to the other, ensuring the data arrives correctly. Short for Transmission Control Protocol/Internet Protocol., 461

technical feasibility: Test that measures whether the organization has or can obtain the computing resources, software services, and qualified people needed to develop, deliver, and then support the proposed information system., 519

technical specifications, identification, 523

technical project manager: Employee who guides design, development, and maintenance tasks; serves as interface between programmers/developers and management., 569

technology

in entertainments, 199

health concerns of using, 142–144

national and local security, 249

technology addiction: Behavioral health risk that occurs when the technology consumes someone's entire social life., 144 technology careers, 562–571

  app development and mobile technologies, 570

  business and government organizations, 562–564

  information and systems security, 570

  IT consulting, 568

  software and apps field, 564

  system development, 568

  technology education, training, and support, 567

  technology equipment field, 564

  technology operations, 569

  technology sales, 566

  technology service and repair field, 565

technology certificatons

  application software certifications, 572–573

  data analysis and database certifications, 573

  hardware certifications, 573

  networking certifications, 573

  operating system certifications, 574

  programmer/developer certifications, 574–575

  security certifications, 575

technology equipment field: Specialty area consisting of manufacturers and distributors of computers, mobile devices, and other hardware, such as magnetic and optical drives, monitors, printers, and communications and networking devices., 564

technology industry, 552–553

technology overload: Behavioral health risk that occurs when people feel distressed when deprived of technology, even for a short length of time, or feel overwhelmed with the amount of technology they are required to manage., 144

technology-related tendonitis, 142

technology security plan components, 527

technology service and repair field: Specialty area that focuses on providing preventive maintenance, component installation, and repair services to customers., 565

telecommuting, home office for, 563

telematics, 133

telemedicine: The use of communications and information technology to provide and assist with medical care., 459

tendonitis, 142

terabyte (TB): 1 trillion bytes, 290, 370

terminal: A computer, usually with limited processing power, that enables users to send data to and/or receive information from a server, or host computer., 117

test plan, 235

tethering: Technique used to configure a smartphone or Internet-capable tablet to act as a portable communications device that shares its Internet access with other computers and devices wirelessly., 60

text, output, 340

text message: A short note, typically fewer than 300 characters, sent to or from a smartphone or other mobile device., 7

text message services, 124

text/picture/video messaging services, 458

text-to-speech feature, 129

TFT: Thin-film transistor. LCD display technology that uses a separate transistor to apply charges to each liquid crystal cell and, thus, displays high-quality color that is viewable from all angles., 342

theft

  of hardware, 139, 233

  of information, 229–233

  of software, 228–229

thermal printer: Printer that generates images by pushing electrically heated pins against heat-sensitive paper., 349

thermostats, programmable, 11

thin client: A terminal that looks like a desktop but has limited capabilities and components., 117

thrashing: Occurs when an operating system spends much of its time paging, instead of executing application software., 418

thread: In discussion forums, consists of the original article and all subsequent related replies. Also called a threaded discussion., 91

throttling: ISP practice of reducing upload and download speeds of certain high-data users at peak times in order not to tie up network resources for a small pool of users., 477

thumb drive: A portable flash memory storage device that you plug in a USB port., 382. *See also* **USB flash drive**

thumbnail: A small version of a larger object that you usually can tap or click to display a larger image or object., 85

Thunderbolt ports, 135

TIFF graphics format, 86

tiles, 426

time bombs, 190

toggle key: A key that switches between two states each time a user presses the key., 320

token: A special series of bits that functions like a ticket., 460

token ring: Standard that specifies that computers and devices on the network share or pass a special signal, called a token, in a unidirectional manner and in a preset order., 460

toll fraud, 238

toll fraud malware: Malicious mobile app that uses a variety of fraudulent schemes to charge unsuspecting users for premium messaging services., 193

toner: Type of powdered ink that is used by some laser printers and copy machines to produce output., 348

tools: Programs that enable you to perform maintenance-type tasks usually related to managing devices, media, and programs used by computers and mobile devices., 158. *See also* **utilities**

top-level domain: The suffix of the domain name in a web address., 63

 original (table), 63

touch input, 324–325

touch mouse: Touch-sensitive mouse that recognizes touch gestures, in addition to detecting movement of the mouse and traditional click and scroll operations., 323

touchpad: A small, flat, rectangular pointing device that is sensitive to pressure and motion., 13, 323

touch screen: A touch-sensitive display device., 324–326

 gestures (table), 5

 on smartphones, 7

touch-sensitive pad: An input device that contains buttons and/or wheels you operate with a thumb or finger., 128, 326

touch user interface, 414

tourism websites, 80

tower: A frame made of metal or plastic that houses the system unit on a desktop., 114

tower server: A server built into an upright cabinet (tower) that stands alone., 116

Toys "R" Us, 243

trackball: A stationary pointing device with a ball on its top or side., 324

tracking software, 279

track: Narrow recording band that forms a full circle on the surface of the disk., 374

trackpad: Term used by Apple to refer to the touchpad on its laptops., 323

traditional literacy, 561

traffic: Communications activity on the Internet., 62

training: Showing users exactly how they will use the new hardware and software in the system., 526

transaction processing system (TPS): An information system that captures and processes data from day-to-day business activities; TPS for short., 557

transactions, verifying, 174

transfer rate: The speed with which data, instructions, and information transfer to and from a device., 371

transferring media from mobile devices to computers, 153

transistor: Element of an integrated circuit that can act as an electronic switch that opens or closes the circuit for electrical charges., 278

transmission media: Materials or substances capable of carrying one or more communications signals., 450, 476–477

transportation, and computers, mobile devices, 95

travel, technology in, 39

travel apps, 178

travel web database services, 507

travel websites, 80

trial version: An application you can use at no charge for a limited time, to see if it meets your needs., 161

trojan horse: A destructive program that hides within or looks like a legitimate program., 190, 215

twisted-pair cable: Physical transmission media that consists of one or more twisted-pair wires bundled together., 477

twisted-pair wire: Two separate insulated copper wires that are twisted together., 477

Twitter, 23, 24, 78

two-step verification process, 226–227

typing on phone with numeric keypad, 123

U

UI (user interface): Portion of software that controls how you enter data and instructions and how information is displayed on the screen., 414

ultrabook, 111

ultrasonic sensors, 279

ultra-wideband (UWB): A network standard that specifies how two UWB devices use short-range radio waves to communicate at high speeds with each other., 464

UMB (Ultra Mobile Broadband): Ultra Mobile Broadband; a 4G standard for cellular transmissions, 481

UMTS (Universal Mobile Telecommunications System): Universal Mobile Telecommunications System; a 3G standard for cellular transmissions, 481 unauthorized access and use, 221

unauthorized access: The use of a computer or network without permission., 221

unauthorized use: The use of a computer or its data for unapproved or possibly illegal activities., 221

uncompress: To unzip or expand a zipped (compressed) file, which restores it to its original form., 198

undervoltage: Electrical disturbance that occurs when the electrical supply or voltage drops below the normal volts., 140

uninstaller: A tool that removes a program, as well as any associated entries in the system files., 195, 422

uninstalling programs, 195

uninterruptible power supply (UPS): A device that contains surge protection circuits and one or more batteries that can provide power during a temporary or permanent loss of power., 141

United States Computer Emergency Readiness Team (US-CERT), 557

unit test: Test performed during the program development life cycle that verifies each individual program or object works by itself., 525

Universal Product Code (UPC): Bar code used by retail and grocery stores., 335

UNIX: A multitasking operating system developed in the early 1970s by scientists at Bell Laboratories., 429

unlicensed software, 565

unsubscribe: Removing your email address from a mailing list., 90

UPC (Universal Product Code): Bar code used by retail and grocery stores., 335

updates for desktop and mobile apps, 157

uplink: Transmission from an earth-based station to a satellite., 482

uploading: The process of transferring files from your computer or mobile device to a server on the Internet., 92

upstream rate: The transfer rate that is achieved when data is being received on a communications channel., 463

upward compatible: Applications that may not run on new versions of an operating system., 425

URL: Unique address of a webpage. Short for Uniform Resource Locator., 68. *See also* **web address**

USA TODAY website, 76

USB adapters: A dongle that plugs into a USB port, enhances functions of a mobile computer and/or provides connections to peripheral devices., 298–299

USB cable, transferring photos to computers using, 153

USB flash drive: A portable flash memory storage device that you plug in a USB port., 18, 382–383. *See also* **thumb drive**

safely removing, 383

USB hub, 136

USB port: Port that can connect up to 127 different peripheral devices together with a single connector. Short for universal serial bus port., 136

U.S. Department of Homeland Security, 36

user: Anyone who interacts with a computer or mobile device, or utilizes the information it generates., 4

categories of (table), 41, 42

user buy-in: A measure of how likely users are to accept and use a new system., 524

user experience designer: Employee who plans and designs software and apps that consider a user's reaction to a program and its interface, including its efficiency, its effectiveness, and its ease of use. *See also* **UX designer**, 569

user ID: A unique combination of characters, such as letters of the alphabet or numbers, that identifies one specific user. Short for user identification., 222. *See also* **user name**

user interface (UI): Portion of software that controls how you enter data and instructions and how information is displayed on the screen., 29, 414

user name: A unique combination of characters, such as letters of the alphabet or numbers, that identifies one specific user. Also called log on name or sign on name., 88, 242, 423. *See also* **user ID**

user response: An instruction a user issues by responding to a message displayed by a program or app., 318

U.S. Securities and Exchange Committee (SEC), 295

utilities: Programs that enable you to perform maintenance-type tasks usually related to managing devices, media, and programs used by computers and mobile devices., 158. *See also* **tools**

UWB (ultra-wideband): A network standard that specifies how two UWB devices use short-range radio waves to communicate at high speeds with each other., 464

UX designer: Employee who plans and designs software and apps that consider a user's reaction to a program and its interface, including its efficiency, its effectiveness, and its ease of use. *See also* **user experience designer**, 569

V

validation: The process of comparing data with a set of rules or values to determine if the data meets certain criteria., 503

value-added network (VAN): A third-party business that provides networking services, such as EDI services, secure data and information transfer, storage, or email., 453

value-added reseller (VAR): An organization that purchases products from manufacturers and then resells these products to the public — offering additional services with the product., 523

VAN (value-added network): A third-party business that provides networking services, such as EDI services, secure data and information transfer, storage, or email., 453

vandalism of hardware, 139, 233

VAR (value-added reseller): An organization that purchases products from manufacturers and then resells these products to the public — offering additional services with the product., 523

vendor proposals, 523

verification process, two-step, 226–227

video, output, 340

video blog (vlog), 78

video call: Call in which all parties see one another as they communicate over the Internet., 332

video card: Adapter card that converts computer output into a video signal that travels through a cable to the monitor, which displays an image on the screen., 298. *See also* **graphics card**

videoconference: A meeting between two or more geographically separated people who use a network or the Internet to transmit audio and video data., 31, 188, 333

video editing software: An application that allows professionals to modify a segment of a video, called a clip., 183

video games, 132

video: Images displayed in motion and voice input., 14, 87

streaming, 187

video message: A short video clip, usually about 30 seconds, sent to or from a smartphone or other mobile device., 7

video projectors, 113

video sharing sites, 75

virtualization: The practice of sharing or pooling computing resources, such as servers and storage devices., 7, 432

virtual keyboard: Phone technology that projects an image of a keyboard on a flat surface., 124

virtual keyboards, 13

virtual machine (VM): Environment on a computer in which you can install and run an operating system and programs., 431

virtual memory: A portion of a storage medium, such as a hard drive or USB flash drive, that the operating system allocates to function as additional RAM., 417

virtual private network (VPN): Network that provides a mobile user with a secure connection to a company network server, as if the user has a private line., 230

virtual reality (VR): The use of computers to simulate a real or imagined environment that appears as a three-dimensional (3-D) space., 87

virus: A potentially damaging computer program that affects, or infects, a computer negatively by altering the way the computer works without the user's knowledge or permission., 190, 215

detecting, 192

hoaxes, recognizing, 192

how they spread via email, 215

and malware, 190

protection from, 25

signs of infection, 191

virus signature: A known specific pattern of virus code., 192

Visual Basic, 29, 532

visual programming environment (VPE): A graphical interface in a visual programming language that allows system developers to drag and drop objects to build programs and apps., 532

visual programming language: A language that uses a visual or graphical interface for creating all source code., 532

Visual Studio: A suite of object-oriented application development tools that assists software developers in building programs and apps for Windows or any operating system that supports the Microsoft .NET Framework., 531

visual voice mail: A voice mail feature that allows you to view message details such as the length of calls and, in some cases, read message contents instead of listening to them., 125

VM (virtual machine): Environment on a computer in which you can install and run an operating system and programs., 431 voice commands

gaming, 11

and video input, 11

voice input: The process of entering input by speaking into a microphone., 330

voice mail, 31, 125

voice mail message: Short audio recording sent to or from a smartphone or other mobile device., 7

voice recognition: A computer or mobile device's capability of distinguishing spoken words., 330. *See also* **speech recognition**

voice recognition application: Application that allows users to dictate text and enter instructions by speaking into a microphone., 330

voice verification system: Biometric device that compares a person's live speech with their stored voice pattern., 225

VoIP: Technology that uses the Internet (instead of the public switched telephone network) to connect a calling party to one or more local or long-distance called parties and and enables users to speak to other users via their Internet connection. Short for Voice over IP (Internet Protocol)., 24, 31, 92, 188

volatile memory: Memory that loses its contents when the computer's power is turned off., 290

volatility, illustration of, 371

VPE (visual programming environment): A graphical interface in a visual programming language that allows system developers to drag and drop objects to build programs and apps., 532

VPN: Network that provides a mobile user with a secure connection to a company network server, as if the user has a private line., 230

VR world: Three-dimensional (3-D) environment that contains infinite space and depth., 88

W

W3C: Group that oversees research and sets standards and guidelines for many areas of the Internet whose mission is to ensure the continued growth of the web., 58

Wallet: Windows app that provides a centralized location for coupons, credit cards, loyalty cards, and memberships in a single, easily accessible location., 435

WAN (wide area network): A network that covers a large geographic area (such as a city, country, or the world) using a variety of wired and wireless transmission media., 455

warm boot: The process of restarting a computer or mobile device while it remains powered on., 413

wearable device: Small mobile computing consumer device designed to be worn and that often communicate with a mobile device or printer., 9, 130, 325. *See also* **wearable**

wearable: Small mobile computing consumer device designed to be worn and that often communicate with a mobile device or printer, 9. *See also* **wearable device**

wearable technology, 285

weather forecasts, 124

weather websites, 76

Web 2.0: Term to refer to websites that provide a means for users to share personal information, allow users to modify website content, and provide applications through a browser., 65

web address: Unique address of a webpage., 68. *See also* **URL**

web anaytics expert: Employee who collects and measures Internet data, such as website traffic patterns and advertising, and develops reports that recommend strategies to maximize an organization's web presence., 569

web app: An application stored on a web server that you access through a browser., 28, 69, 161

email, 103

for personal, business productivity, 178

web: A worldwide collection of electronic documents; short for World Wide Web., 21, 65

graphics formats used on (table), 86

media on the, 76

searching the, 22

web-based training (WBT): A type of computer-based training that uses Internet technology to deliver the training., 184

webcam: A digital video camera that allows you to capture video and usually audio input for your computer or mobile device., 14, 332

spying, punishment for, 111

web conference: A meeting that takes place on the web., 520

web creation and management, 84

web designer: Employee who designs the layout, navigation, and overall appearance of a website with a focus on user experience; specifies a website's appearance using HTML5, JavaScript, CSS, media, and other web design technologies., 568 web databases, 170, 506–507

web developers: Designers of webpages., 534, 568

web development, 534–538

web feed: Content that has changed on a website that you can display in your browser., 69, 188

web filtering software: A program that restricts access to certain material on the web., 193, 248

web hosting service: Service on the web that provides a program that assists you with creating, editing, and hosting content on a website., 64

web maps, 81

WebMD, 74

webpage: Each electronic document on the web; can contain text, graphics, audio, and video., 21, 65

web publishing: The development and maintenance of websites., 84

web server: A computer that delivers requested webpages to your computer or mobile device., 21, 65, 116

website: A collection of related webpages and associated items stored on a web server., 21, 65

website authoring software: Software that helps users of all skill levels create webpages that include graphics, video, audio, animation, and special effects with interactive content., 184

websites
  avoiding malware infections, 110
  and cookies, 244
  copying media from, 38
  displaying CAPTCHA, 224
  downloading software safely, 162
  finance, 36
  government, 36
  portals, 82
  types of, 71–85
  verifying safety of, 66
  whether correct or accurate, 85

website scams, 245

wheel: A steering-wheel-type input device that users turn to simulate driving a car, truck, or other vehicle., 131

wide area network (WAN): A network that covers a large geographic area (such as a city, country, or the world) using a variety of wired and wireless transmission media., 455

widescreen monitor: Monitor that is wider than it is tall., 343

Wi-Fi (wireless fidelity): Broadband Internet connection that uses radio signals to provide connections to computers and devices with built-in Wi-Fi capability or a communications device that enables Wi-Fi connectivity., 31, 59, 138, 462

Wi-Fi network
  adding computer or mobile device to, 455

wiki: A collaborative website that allows users to create, add to, modify, or delete the content via their browser., 40, 78

Wikipedia, 40, 78

Windows Media Player, 87

Windows Phone: A proprietary mobile operating system that runs on some smartphones., 435

Windows Phone Store: Store that provides access to additional Windows apps and software updates, 435

wireless
  device connections, 137
  Internet access points, 31
  messaging services, 31
  security, 236–237

wireless access point (WAP): A central communications device that allows computers and devices to transfer data wirelessly among themselves or to a wired network using wireless technologies, such as Wi-Fi., 236, 470

wireless Ethernet: Term sometimes used to refer to Wi-Fi because it uses techniques similar to the Ethernet standard to specify how physically to configure a wireless network., 462

wireless keyboard: A battery-powered device that transmits data to the computer or mobile device using wireless technology., 322

wireless LAN (WLAN): A LAN that uses no physical wires., 454

wireless markup language (WML): Subset of XML that allows web developers to design pages specifically for microbrowsers., 536

wireless modem: Modem that uses a wireless communications technology (such as cellular radio, satellite, or Wi-Fi network) to connect to the Internet., 58, 469

wireless mouse: A battery-powered device that transmits data using wireless technology., 323

wireless router: A device that performs the functions of a router and also a wireless access point., 471

wireless signal, strengthening, 471

wireless transmission media, 478–479
  broadcast radio, 479

the complete
aromatherapy
& essential oils
handbook for everyday wellness

the complete
aromatherapy
& essential oils
handbook for everyday
wellness

Nerys Purchon and Lora Cantele

Robert
ROSE

For complete cataloguing information, see page 471.

Disclaimer

This book contains information on a range of essential oils. It is intended as a source of information, not
as a medical reference book. The key to safe and responsible essential oil use is dosage and duration. Some
essential oils, which are beneficial for short-term use, can be harmful if used for a long period. The reader
is advised not to attempt self-treatment for serious or long-term problems without consulting a qualified
health practitioner. Neither the authors nor the publisher can be held responsible for any adverse reactions
to the recipes, recommendations and instructions contained herein, and the use of any essential oil is
entirely at the reader's own risk.

Design and Production: Daniella Zanchetta/PageWave Graphics Inc.
Senior Editor: Judith Finlayson
Editor: Tracy Bordian
Copyeditor and Proofreader: Gillian Watts
Indexer: Gillian Watts

Cover image: Sage leaves in an essential oil bottle © iStockphoto.com/ElenaGaak
Back cover images: Bottle with dropper & purple flowers © iStockphoto.com/Surakit Harntongkul;
Bottle with pink rose & petals © iStockphoto.com/miss_j

Published by Robert Rose Inc.
120 Eglinton Ave East, Suite 800
Toronto, Ontario   M4P 1E2
Tel. (416) 322-6552 Fax: (416) 322-6936
www.robertrose.ca

Printed and bound in Canada

9 10 11 12   MI   23 22 21 20 19 18 17

This book is for my father, a natural-born student, who taught me to love learning for its own sake.

—*Nerys Purchon*

This book is dedicated to Dan, Dominic and Emily—without their patience and support I couldn't have completed this work. Thank you for your love and understanding.

To my grandparents, who were my cheerleaders in their life and continue to support me on this path through their spiritual presence.

To my sister, who never hesitates to say the things I don't want to hear and to push me even further. I love you all *more-er*!

This book is also dedicated to those new to the wonderful world of aromatherapy. I hope you find this book to be a useful and inspiring tool and will incorporate the benefits of this ancient healing art into your everyday lives. May this be a stepping stone on your aromatic journey to wellness.

Namaste.

—*Lora Cantele*

Contents

Preface to the First Edition. 8

Preface to the Second Edition 10

Acknowledgments. 11

Introduction: The Aromatic Apothecary

Using Essential Oils 12

Cautions When Using
  Essential Oils. 16

For Professionals Only. 18

Part 1: The Oils

Properties of Essential Oils 21

Why the Botanical Name
  Is Important 22

Key Essential Oils and
  Their Properties. 24

Essential Oils (A to Y) 28

Hydrolats 118

Fixed (Carrier) Oils and Butters. . . 128

Basic Massage Oil Blends and
  Treatment Bases 139

Infused Oils 141

Part 2: Remedies

Conditions and Remedies
  (Abrasions to Workplace
  Stress). 149

Part 3: Aromatherapy for Daily Living

Aromatherapy
  for Personal Care 353
  Skincare. 353
  Hair Care 387
  Body Care 399

Aromatherapy for the Home 423

Aromatherapy for Massage 440

Part 4: Practicalities

Equipment 449

Measuring and Storing
  Essential Oils. 450

Glossary 454

Resources. 459

Bibliography. 465

Index. 472

Preface to the First Edition

Some of the happiest years of my life were spent on a small farm called Rivendell, where my husband, Prakash, and I, together with family and friends, had a small company making natural herbal and cruelty-free cosmetics. I began to appreciate the heavy perfume in the air as the early morning sun warmed the herbs and released their aromas; I began to notice that on cold, wet days very little perfume was released, even if some of the leaves were crushed; I also began to feel on some days an attraction to a certain plant, only to discover later on that was the very plant I needed at the time. We began to use essential oils extensively in our products. In the late 1970s this was no mean feat, as there were few companies selling quality oils. We also experimented with finding the best ways to make really strong infused oils, thanking our powerful Australian sun, which did such a wonderful job coaxing precious essences to leave the plant material and dissolve gracefully into the oil.

Finally it was time to move on, and from 20 acres (8 hectares) and a house we became gypsies in a motor home, with the whole of Australia as our herb garden and backyard. We now roam slowly all over Australia (creating a mobile traffic jam on hills!) with our two little dogs, avoiding the cold of the south in winter and the heat of the north in summer. Everywhere we travel our needs are met. When we stop for the night, our little oil burner is lit, the kettle goes on the gas ring or the campfire and we are home. On the brilliantly colored autumn slopes of the Snowy Mountains not so very long ago, we picked blackberries for dinner and blackberry shoots to dry for our pharmacy. St. John's wort was in bloom, and we gathered the bright yellow flowers that transform miraculously into a rich ruby-red oil for rubbing into sore muscles. Horehound was gathered in a forest in Victoria, and dried and stored for use if we caught a cold. My oil and herb pharmacy now travels with me in a wooden roll-top box and is used every day in many different ways, and each day I feel a deeper love for and gain a greater understanding of these magical essences. When I rub a leaf or a petal, I feel as excited as Aladdin when he rubbed the magic lamp and released the genie. My genie is the oil that, when released, will perform all sorts of wonderful magic for me. The contents of this book are largely the result of things I have learned during and since this time. I hope that you will find it helpful and, more important, inspirational.

The recipes are not at all difficult. They don't take long to make, and most of them are quite inexpensive—the biggest cost will be buying the oils. If you consider how much you spend in a year on skin- and hair-care items, perfumes, household cleaning and disinfectant products, garden and insect sprays and repellents, and medicinal items, you will realize that your initial outlay is small by comparison. You will feel enriched when you, your family and friends use the gifts of the earth to improve your lives. To see the raw materials transformed into beautiful and richly scented unguents, perfumes, sachets, room fresheners and other lovely things is a very special experience.

Nerys Purchon
Bunbury, Western Australia, January 1999

(Nerys Purchon passed away on January 15, 2011.)

Preface to the Second Edition

My journey in essential oils began like so many others, as a need for an alternative method of care. I was in a car accident (rear-ended) while pregnant with my son. After the accident I was told that I had only 75% use of my back. I was living with pain. Almost one year to the date (and incidentally the last day of my physical therapy), I was again in the same type of car accident. This time I was told I would have only 65% use of my back. My doctor said it would never heal completely but that the pain could be managed with ongoing physical therapy. As a new mom, I knew that multiple visits every week to the therapist would become increasingly difficult, not to mention costly. I shared my concerns with a friend, who gifted me with some beautiful essential oil blends made by a friend of his to treat my back pain. I was struggling to sit for more than 10 minutes at a time, but after applying the essential oils to my back, I found I could sit pain-free for longer periods.

A few weeks later, another friend gave me an essential oil blend to help both my infant son and me to sleep, and it worked! It wasn't until I was packing my things sometime later to move to a new home that I discovered that both essential oil blends had been made by the same person, aromatic alchemist Kris Wrede. My husband and I went to meet her. From the moment we entered her flat, we were enveloped in the most amazing aromas. She shared some of her aromatherapy wisdom as she gave us a tour of her home and production "lab." I left there totally committed to embarking on my own aromatic journey. From the moment I first learned about essential oils, I believed aromatherapy to be the best-kept secret ever—and one to be shared.

Since 1997 essential oils have been a daily part of my life. My children now ask for lavender for their cuts and scrapes, their "roll-on" when they have trouble sleeping and their "throat rub" when they have a sore throat. My husband has used aromas for several years to de-stress at work. Our personal care products are lovingly made in our kitchen with these wonderful gifts from nature.

After several years of study in aromatology and working with clients and seeing their results, I now encourage others to embrace this fragrant way of life. I have found my calling in service to others, as both a health-care provider and an aromatherapy educator.

Reading this book and trying out some of the blends is a good first step to beginning to enjoy the benefits of aromatherapy. The recipes have been developed to be easy to prepare, using products readily available in your local grocery and health-food stores and equipment found in your kitchen.

I encourage you to enhance your health and wellbeing with nature's medicine by incorporating aromatherapy into your everyday life.

Lora Cantele
Boulder, Colorado, April 2014

Acknowledgments

Thank you, Philippa, for being a patient and helpful long-distance friend and agent and for being the most careful, tactful, positive and inspired editor. There have been many days when this book wouldn't have happened if you had not been on the other end of my fax machine giving much needed support.

A special thanks to Jan Purser for the massage section (pages 440 to 447), which has been adapted from the text she provided for *Aromatherapy Secrets*.

—*Nerys Purchon*

I would like to thank Nerys Purchon, who influenced my aromatherapy education long before I knew it; Kris Wrede, for starting me on my journey and for being my constant mentor; Robert Tisserand, Gabriel Mojay, Ann Harmon and Erin Smith, for their wisdom and patience; the many friends and colleagues who help me to learn more every day and to perfect my craft; and to Judith Finlayson and Tracy Bordian, for keeping me on task and working their magic to make this book a reality. Finally, thank you to Jane Colby for my *Under the Tuscan Sun* moment in which she reminded me of my purpose, helping me to realize that a wish I committed to a Post-it note had become a dream come true.

—*Lora Cantele*

Introduction: The Aromatic Apothecary

Using Essential Oils

Essential oils have been variously described as the "life force" or "essence" of plants. Aromatherapy is a method of employing essential oils to protect, heal and beautify. The best-known way to employ the oils is through massage, but as you will see in this book, there are many more ways to use these oils to support your health and enrich your life. The wonderful thing about essential oils is that they are available to everyone and, once you understand the basic concepts and follow the appropriate methods and procedures, they are very easy to use.

> ### What Are Essential Oils?
> Pure essential oils are a product of distillation or expression (or other methods of extraction) of the aromatic substances, or essences, found in plants. The oils are volatile, which means they evaporate on exposure to air and have a powerful aroma. Essential oils differ from cooking or "fixed" oils in that they are not oily to the touch.

Essential oils have been used for centuries. Many books suggest that in their early iterations, before the days of public sanitation, their main use (apart from in religious ceremonies) was to mask and disguise unpleasant smells (of both people and places). This suggestion is a disservice to the intelligence of the people who used these substances. Historical references suggest that their therapeutic actions were well known. Herbs, essential oils and other natural methods of healing were primary tools of medical care until scientists discovered ways of synthesizing drugs.

Our sense of smell is primal and the most evocative sense we possess. It is connected to our limbic system, the part of the brain responsible for memory, breathing, blood circulation and the regulation of hormones. Who hasn't been transported back to other people, places and situations by a sudden waft of a particular aroma? On the other hand, it's all too easy to experience a wave of nausea when confronted by a pungent odor. And who hasn't passed a bakery or coffee shop and been enticed in to buy a little treat?

Our powerful sense of smell is responsible for the pleasure we take in food and wine. Without it, food can scarcely be tasted.

These days, herbs and essential oils are attracting more attention and emerging as scientifically proven and accepted remedies. We now understand how and why certain essential oils heal, but the actions of others still remain a mystery. Skeptics will scoff if you are unable to offer a "scientific" explanation as to how these oils work, yet the medical profession still cannot explain how Aspirin, for instance, performs its painkilling function. This is ironic, because the main ingredient of nonsteroidal anti-inflammatory drugs (NSAIDs) and pain-relieving liniments is a synthetic form of salicylic acid and its derivatives (e.g., methyl salicylate), which occur naturally in sweet birch (*Betula lenta*) and wintergreen (*Gaultheria procumbens*) essential oils, as well as other plant sources.

This book is not intended to take the place of advice from your health-care practitioner. The recipes provided are intended to enhance the healing of diagnosed complaints. Please remember that even simple symptoms can mask serious conditions. If your symptoms are severe or of long duration, the condition needs to be assessed professionally. The purpose of this book is to provide sound information, based on both tradition and contemporary research, on the safe and responsible use of aromatherapy to alleviate everyday health complaints. Essential oils can help the body mitigate everyday ailments; strengthen your immune system, organs and glands; fight bacteria, fungi and viruses; lower your stress levels; and tone, relax and strengthen your muscles. In fact they assist the body in healing itself. They can also enhance your enjoyment of daily living by helping to keep your skin and hair in tiptop condition and your home fragrant and clean, among other uses.

Patch Testing

It is typically recommended to try a skin "patch test" before beginning to use any essential oil. However, this approach has met with some controversy. A patch test may indicate a sensitivity to an essential oil, but it will not clearly specify whether the oil is an irritant or causing an allergic reaction. It may also generate a false positive or false negative result. In addition, patch testing may even initiate sensitivity, through a process of sensitization caused by the test itself.

The decision to perform a skin patch test is an individual one. Should you decide to perform such a test, add 1 drop of the essential oil to be tested to 1 tsp (5 mL) grapeseed or sweet almond oil. Mix well and apply a small amount to the inside crook of your elbow. Cover with a bandage and check in 24 hours to see if there is a reaction. If irritation begins, wash promptly with soap and water and avoid using that oil in your recipes.

Allergies, Sensitization and Essential Oils

Tip: If you are diffusing essential oils (dispersing them into the air), it is neither necessary nor productive to do so for longer than 15 to 20 minutes at a time.

The proteins in plants are removed during the distillation process, so they are not present in an essential oil. Because a protein needs to be present for an allergic reaction to occur, the likelihood that an essential oil will produce an allergic reaction is greatly reduced. However, when an essential oil is applied to the skin, the proteins in the skin may react with the oil, causing an allergic reaction.

One solution to avoiding skin contact is to inhale the scent of essential oils. Although some components may irritate the respiratory tract, there is no documented evidence of an allergic reaction to the inhalation of any essential oil (any allergic reaction that might occur is likely caused by a synthetic fragrance). However, individuals with respiratory disorders should avoid long-term inhalation of lemon-scented and pine-scented essential oils such as citrus, cypress and pine, as they can be irritating to the respiratory system.

It's also important to understand that essential oils are metabolized and excreted from the body in a variety of ways. Constant use of the same essential oils can create "buildup"— they need time to properly metabolize and be excreted. For this reason it is strongly recommended that you allow some "time off" from any essential oil blend. A number of use patterns are taught in aromatherapy; the simplest approach when treating a chronic problem or for ongoing application is to use the oils for 5 days, then take 2 days off. Many people who use essential oils on a steady basis simply take the weekend off. To reduce the possibility that a blend may cause sensitization, add an antioxidant such as vitamin E to it. This slows the process of oxidization and can help to reduce the likelihood that the blend will cause sensitization or other adverse reactions to limonene-rich essential oils. Add 1 drop of vitamin E (with mixed tocopherols) for every teaspoon (5 mL) of your blend (including the carrier oil).

Explore Options

As you begin to embrace your inner aromatherapist, we encourage you to explore the resources presented in the back of this book (pages 459 to 464). You can use alternative versions of the recipes as you become more proficient in understanding and using essential oils. And remember that fixed oils (see pages 128 to 138) also have therapeutic benefit. When combined with essential oils, they create a more effective treatment.

When you venture out to buy your first oils, they may seem expensive. However, when you consider how little is used and how much material is required to yield a tiny amount of oil— thyme, for instance, yields only about 200 mL (6.8 oz) of essential oil from 1,000 kg (2,200 lbs) of plant material!—you will realize that you are getting value for the money. After all, this purchase will be an investment in the future good health and wellbeing of you and your family.

Start by purchasing a few essential oils and add more as you are able (see page 21 for a good starter kit). The remedies provide a list of essential oils that may be beneficial for treating a specific problem. If you do not have an essential oil listed in the recipe, select another from the list. The majority of the recipes call for using grapeseed or sweet almond oil as a carrier (base) oil for massage blends because these oils are readily available and affordable. Other carriers may be specified in recipes where their inclusion greatly benefits the overall effectiveness of the blend.

Ways to Use Essential Oils

- Incorporate with carrier oils to make massage oils.
- Add to water to be used with compresses.
- Add in minute quantities to baths, along with a carrier such as milk.
- Add to alcohol to make toilet waters and perfumes.
- Incorporate with a carrier oil to make insect repellent.
- Incorporate in cosmetics, lotions and healing ointments.
- Use in shampoos, conditioners and hair tonics.
- Use to strengthen the perfume of potpourris.
- Use to add antibacterial and antiviral qualities to room-freshener sprays.
- Add to floor and furniture cleaners.
- Add to basic kitchen ingredients for "green" cleaning of sinks and surfaces.
- Use in a vaporizer to improve the air quality of a sickroom.
- Add to the shower stall for a fragrant morning wakeup.
- Use in a pocket inhaler or aromatic jewelry to revive, restore or relax.

Tip: What proves effective for one individual may not work as well for someone else. For example, while Aspirin may provide headache relief for one person, ibuprofen may work better for someone else. Chemically they are different but they can be used to treat similar conditions. Essential oils work in much the same way. Where one person may find lavender to be quite relaxing and soothing, another person may find Roman chamomile a better choice. If one recipe in this book doesn't work for you, try a different recipe, or tweak the blend by substituting other oils with similar benefits (options are provided at the beginning of each section in Part 2: Remedies).

Cautions When Using Essential Oils

- Do not ingest essential oils. They should be used internally only on the advice of a qualified aromatologist, aromatic medicine practitioner or naturopath.

- Keep essential oils out of the reach of children—they can be lethal if consumed, even in small quantities (see Procedures for Essential Oil Poisoning or Adverse Reaction, page 238).

- Read the cautions that are provided for each oil in Essential Oils (A to Y), pages 28 to 117. Some essential oils must be avoided during pregnancy, are toxic in large quantities, or should not be used when taking certain medications.

- Most essential oils should be combined with a carrier oil, such as sweet almond or grapeseed oil, before using on the skin, as they are too strong to use alone.

- Always use the appropriate proportions of essential oils and carrier oil. The total amount of essential oil in a preparation should rarely exceed 3% or 4% of the total blend, and some oils should be used in far smaller amounts (see Measurement Guide, page 450). The recipes in this book have been adjusted for their intended use and duration of use. Products created for long-term use, such as lotions and massage oils, use a 1.5% dilution. However, some treatments intended to be used as one-offs or in the short term may have higher concentrations of essential oils. When in doubt, use a 1.5% dilution, or 3 drops per 2 tsp (10 mL) carrier oil or lotion.

- Use only the best-quality essential oils. Look for a label that states "100% pure and natural essential oil." There are many synthetic oils of inferior quality on the market. Synthetic oils are usually called "fragrance oil," "compounded oil" or "perfume oil." They have no therapeutic properties.

Caution

Essential oils for home use should never be ingested and should be used only in the dilutions specified. It is important to be particularly cautious when using certain essential oils if you are taking medications such as blood thinners, diabetic medications, heart medicine or antidepressants, because negative interactions have been known to occur. Where essential oil use is contraindicated with certain medications, it is noted it in the "Caution" section of the information on the specific essential oil.

Observe Quantities

Carefully observe the cautions and suggestions about quantities to use that are provided in this book. The difference in action between 1 and 2 drops of any essential oil is considerable!

- Don't be swayed by marketing claims that an oil is "certified therapeutic" or "medicinal" grade. There is no certifying body or grading system for essential oils anywhere in the world. Such claims are merely a marketing ploy.
- Dosage and duration should be your primary concern (see Using Essential Oils, page 12). As noted, it is important to take a break from long-term use of a blend. After 2 or 3 weeks, switch to different oils with similar properties to avoid overtaxing your body.

Using Essential Oils Orally

Although essential oils should never be ingested in home use, they are sometimes used in oral preparations such as gargles and mouthwashes. If using an essential oil in this manner, be sure to prepare a proper dilution (as specified) and spit it all out when treatment is completed.

Label Essentials

When purchasing essential oils, make sure they are properly labeled with the information you need. The label should tell you:

- the common or popular name for the oil (such as "tea tree")
- its botanical name ("*Melaleuca alternifolia*")
- the instructions for use and any warnings or cautions, including
  - "For external use only"
  - "Keep out of reach of children"
  - "Not to be used at more than 3%" (or whatever dilution is applicable; some oils can only be used at 0.5%)
  - "Not to be used during pregnancy or when breastfeeding"

For Professionals Only

The following essential oils should not be used by a home aromatherapist. They all contain high percentages of toxic, narcotic, abortifacient (capable of inducing abortion) or carcinogenic chemicals.

- Almond, bitter (unrectified) (*Prunus amygdalus*)
- Armoise (mugwort) (*Artemisia herba-alba*)
- Arnica (*Arnica montana*)
- Birch, sweet (*Betula lenta*)
- Buchu (*Agothosma betulina*)
- Calamus (*Acorus calamus*)
- Camphor (white, brown and yellow) (*Cinnamomum camphora*; see page 101)
- Cassia (*Cinnamomum cassia*)
- Costus (*Saussurea costus*)
- Elecampane (*Inula helenium*)
- Horseradish (*Armoracia rusticana*)
- Lemon verbena (*Aloysia tryphilla*)
- Mustard (*Brassica nigra*)
- Oakmoss (*Evernia prunastri*)
- Pennyroyal (*Mentha pulegium*)
- Sassafras (*Sassafras albidum*)
- Savin (*Juniperus sabina*)
- Savory (*Satureia hortensis*)
- Tarragon (*Artemisia dracunculus*)
- Thuja and western red cedar (*Thuja occidentalis, T. plicata*)
- Wintergreen (*Gaultheria procumbens*)
- Wormseed (*Chenopodium ambrosioides*)
- Wormwood (*Artemisia absinthium*)

Know Your Purveyor

There are virtually no regulations regarding the quality or type of essential oils available in shops. As a result, it's important that you select well-known high-quality brands from reputable outlets. For example, it is very rare to find essential oils that are not appropriate for home aromatherapy use in reputable health-food stores or aromatherapy specialist outlets. However, you may come across such oils in market stalls.

Troubleshooting

As careful as you may be when using essential oils, problems sometimes crop up. The following are areas of potential concern.

Phototoxicity

When applied to the skin, certain chemicals can cause an excessive reaction to sunlight for up to 12 hours after application (and possibly for much longer). The combination of essential oil plus sunlight can result in burns or darker skin pigmentation, which can range from mild to very severe depending upon the strength of the oil used. Even a mere 0.4% of some oils can cause a phototoxic effect. Take note of the cautions in the profiles of the individual oils regarding potential phototoxicity.

Sensitization

Sensitization is gradual buildup of an allergic reaction or intolerance to a substance even when used in minuscule amounts. This sensitivity may be scarcely apparent on first application, but if the substance is used often, the reaction usually worsens steadily. Take note of warnings on the label. You may want to try a patch test (see page 13) to help you determine if you have become sensitized to an oil.

Skin Irritation

Unlike sensitization, which may develop over a considerable period, some individuals may react immediately to particular oils (this is true for other substances as well). In such a case, irritation and inflammation can occur on the first application. The irritation is localized to where the oil was applied, and once the oil is removed, it begins to dissipate. The severity of the reaction depends on the amount used, whether or not the oil was diluted and how reactive the person is. Some essential oils can produce skin irritation ranging from mild to very severe. If you have sensitive skin or if you frequently develop allergic reactions, you might consider using a patch test (see page 13) before applying any unfamiliar substance.

Part 1
The Oils

Properties of Essential Oils

Most essential oils have healing properties, but some are more efficacious than others. What follows in this section is a description of essential, infused and carrier oils, as well as hydrolats, many of which are included in the remedies and recipes in this book. As you read the entries, it may be useful to keep in mind the previous sections that looked at using essential oils and listed cautions about using these substances (pages 12 to 19).

If you can afford only a couple of essential oils to begin with, make sure that lavender and tea tree are among your first purchases, followed closely by Roman chamomile, lemon and geranium. As you read through the remedies in Part 2 you will notice immediately how often these remarkable essential oils are used. Lavender in particular has a reputation for being gentle and safe enough to use for the whole family.

Five Key Essential Oils

If you can afford only a small number of essential oils to get started, here are our top 5 recommendations, in order of preference:

1. Lavender
2. Tea tree
3. Roman chamomile
4. Lemon
5. Geranium

It is commonly believed that blending essential oils is about synergy, or working together. The theory behind blending is that the whole is greater than the sum of the individual parts. If you blend three or four essential oils that have the same or very similar therapeutic properties, you have created a synergistic blend that is more powerful than the individual oils used on their own. There is research to support this theory; however, other research indicates that antagonism occurs. Synergy and antagonism are opposite actions, and both are difficult to predict. When synergy happens, it is serendipitous, but it cannot be relied upon in every blend. Another factor is *intent*. In the spirit of holism, many aromatherapists visualize their client as well and thriving while they are blending their oils for therapeutic use. It is believed that by blending with intent they are in fact enhancing the efficacy of the blend. Whatever your belief, it's probably best not to use more than three to four essential oils in blends until you are very familiar with all the individual oils and what each of them can do.

Use Oils Carefully

As noted, essential oils should never be taken internally, unless administered or prescribed by a qualified health-care professional trained at an appropriate level in the use and administration of essential oils.

Used externally and in a safe and responsible manner, with attention to dosage and dilution, most essential oils are "generally regarded as safe" (GRAS). Under certain conditions, such as improper storage or in combination with certain medications, essential oils have the potential to produce negative effects. We have highlighted these circumstances in the cautions associated with particular oils.

Why the Botanical Name Is Important

When buying essential oils, it's crucial to know the botanical name of what you are purchasing, because many plants have the same common name. Unless the label includes the botanical name, you could easily end up with the wrong oil. Here are some examples:

Calendula (*Calendula officinalis*) oil is produced only in very small quantities and is difficult to obtain. Tagetes (*Tagetes patula, T. minuta, T. erecta*) oil is often sold as calendula or marigold oil. Tagetes oil is distilled from French, African or Mexican marigolds. The two must not be confused, as tagetes doesn't have the same therapeutic properties as calendula and is very phototoxic.

Atlas cedar (*Cedrus atlantica*) oil is the appropriate oil to use for aromatherapy. However, thuja oil (*Thuja occidentalis*) is sometimes sold as "white cedar oil" or "cedar leaf oil." This oil is severely toxic because of its high alpha- and beta-thujone content, and deaths have been reported from its oral use. White cedar oil should not be confused with Atlas cedar oil.

Lemon verbena (*Aloysia tryphilla*) oil is difficult to obtain, and the oil sold as lemon verbena is often a blend of citrus oils. However, true lemon verbena oil presents many hazards, so in this case it might be safer to use the blend!

Melissa (*Melissa officinalis*) oil is very costly, as huge amounts of plant materials are needed to produce a very small amount of oil. Most of the melissa essential oil offered is adulterated with other lemon-scented oils.

Read These Sections!

- **Label Essentials** (page 17) explains why it is important always to check the botanical name on the essential oil bottle.
- **Cautions When Using Essential Oils** (page 16) discusses some of the properties of essential oils that can cause problems, and how you can avoid them.
- **For Professionals Only** (page 18) discusses toxic compounds found in some essential oils and lists the high-risk essential oils, which should be used only by a trained clinician.

Key Essential Oils and Their Properties

The following properties chart includes the most effective oils suitable for the home aromatherapist to use. It contains only the most important oils in each category, according to the benefit derived.

Term	Property	Essential Oils
Analgesic	Relieves or diminishes pain by exerting a nerve-numbing effect	Cajuput, *Eucalyptus smithii*, silver fir, frankincense, lavandin 'Grosso', spike lavender, lemongrass, Spanish marjoram, sweet marjoram, peppermint, rosemary ct. cineole, tea tree, yarrow
Antibiotic	Combats infection in the body	Bay laurel, bergamot, cajuput, cinnamon, cistus, cypress, eucalyptus (all), frankincense, helichrysum, hyssop, lemon, *Litsea cubeba*, manuka, sweet marjoram, myrtle, neroli, niaouli, peppermint, petitgrain, ravensara, rosewood, sandalwood, tea tree
Antidepressant	Lifts the emotions	Canadian balsam, basil, bergamot, cistus, clary sage, cypress, Douglas fir, frankincense, grapefruit, helichrysum, jasmine, juniper, lavandin 'Super', lavender, lemongrass, mandarin, neroli, peppermint, rose, rosemary, ylang ylang
Antiemetic	Helps to reduce and control vomiting and nausea	Star anise, bergamot, black pepper, cardamom, ginger, lemon, peppermint, spearmint
Anti-inflammatory	Reduces inflammation	Peru balsam, bergamot, cardamom, Roman chamomile, cistus, citronella, eucalyptus (*citriodora*, *radiata*, *staigeriana*), Fragonia, frankincense, geranium, helichrysum, juniper, lavender, lemon, lemongrass, melissa, myrrh, myrtle, naiouli, sweet orange, patchouli, peppermint, petitgrain, pine, plai, rose, spearmint, spikenard, tea tree, thyme ct. linalool, valerian, yarrow

Term	Property	Essential Oils
Antiseptic	Helps to control or destroy some infection-causing bacteria	Most essential oils have some antiseptic qualities, but the following are particularly good: bergamot, cistus, cubeb, eucalyptus, silver fir, juniper, lavender, manuka, niaouli, ravensara
Antispasmodic	Prevents or relieves cramps or spasms in the intestine or uterus	Chamomile, clary sage, ginger, juniper, lavender, Spanish marjoram, sweet marjoram, honey myrtle, orange, peppermint
Antisudorific	Reduces sweating	Clary sage, cypress
Antitoxic	Counteracts the effects of a poison	Bergamot, black pepper
Antiviral	Kills or inhibits the growth of viruses	Bergamot, eucalyptus, Douglas fir, lavender, manuka, palmarosa, ravensara, tea tree
Aphrodisiac	Increases sexual response	Amyris, clary sage, jasmine, neroli, patchouli, rose, rosewood, sandalwood, vetiver, ylang ylang
Astringent	Contracts and tones tissues	Canadian balsam, benzoin, cedarwood, cypress, frankincense, juniper, myrrh, rose, sandalwood
Carminative	Expels gases from the intestines	Angelica, star anise, black pepper, caraway, cardamom, coriander, cubeb, fennel, ginger, lime, anise myrtle, peppermint, spearmint
Cholagogue	Stimulates bile production and flow	Chamomile, lavender, peppermint, rosemary, spearmint
Cicatrizant	Promotes the formation of scar tissue	Bergamot, citronella, cypress, eucalyptus, frankincense, lavender, neroli, patchouli, petitgrain, rosewood
Deodorant	Reduces odors	Cypress, eucalyptus, Douglas fir, lavender, lemongrass, *Litsea cubeba*, patchouli, petitgrain
Depurative	Purifies the blood	Birch bud, carrot seed, clary sage, fennel, juniper, rose
Digestive	Aids digestion and eases indigestion	Star anise, black pepper, cardamom, chamomile, sweet marjoram, rosemary

Term	Property	Essential Oils
Diuretic	Increases the flow of urine	Birch bud, cedarwood, chamomile, cubeb, fennel, geranium, juniper, parsley
Emmenagogue	Encourages and regulates menstrual flow	Basil, chamomile, clary sage, sweet marjoram
Expectorant	Helps remove excess mucus from bronchial passages	Balsam (all), benzoin, cubeb, eucalyptus, frankincense, ginger, lavandin 'Grosso', lavender, marjoram, myrrh, myrtle, sandalwood, saro, tea tree
Febrifuge	Cools and reduces fever	Bergamot, chamomile, eucalyptus, lavender, peppermint, ravensara, spikenard, tea tree, yarrow
Fungicide	Prevents or destroys fungal infection	Fragonia, lavender, myrrh, myrtle, tea tree
Galactagogue	Increases production of milk	Star anise, basil, celery seed, cubeb, fennel
Hemostatic	Helps to stop bleeding	Geranium, lemon, rose, yarrow
Hepatic	Stimulates and strengthens the liver	Angelica, Peru balsam, clary sage, fennel, grapefruit, helichrysum, lemon, peppermint, rose, rosemary, saro, violet
Hypertensive	Raises blood pressure	Black pepper, clary sage, hyssop, peppermint, rosemary
Hypotensive	Lowers blood pressure	Amyris, garlic, lavandin 'Super', lavender, sweet marjoram, melissa, yarrow, ylang ylang
Immunostimulant	Strengthens the body's defenses against infection	Cistus, eucalyptus, Fragonia, helichrysum, lavender, manuka, lemon myrtle, palo santo, ravensara, rosewood, tea tree
Nervine	Strengthens the nervous system	Angelica, basil, chamomile, clary sage, sweet marjoram, melissa, spikenard, valerian
Rubefacient	Produces localized redness and warmth when applied to the skin, by increasing the flow of blood to the area	Birch bud, black pepper, eucalyptus, silver fir, ginger, juniper, sweet marjoram, rosemary, thyme

Term	Property	Essential Oils
Sedative	Reduces stress in the body and calms the nervous system	Benzoin, bergamot, catnip, chamomile, clary sage, frankincense, jasmine, lavandin 'Super', lavender, mandarin, sweet marjoram, melissa, neroli, rose, spikenard, valerian, ylang ylang
Stimulant	Increases energy and quickens the functions of the adrenal and other glands	Basil, bergamot, black pepper, cypress, eucalyptus, geranium, peppermint, rosemary
Stomachic	Aids and tones the digestive system	Angelica, star anise, basil, bergamot, black pepper, carrot seed, chamomile, cinnamon, clary sage, nutmeg, peppermint, rosemary
Styptic	Stops or reduces external bleeding	Benzoin, cypress, lemon, yarrow
Sudorific	Increases sweating	Basil, West Indian bay, cajuput, chamomile, hyssop, juniper, lemon, manuka, peppermint, ravensara, rosemary, spearmint, tea tree
Tonic	Strengthens the whole body or a specific organ	Angelica, basil, bergamot, birch bud, black pepper, clove, Fragonia, geranium, ginger, juniper, lavender, lemon, sweet marjoram, myrrh, neroli, rose, rosemary, saro, tea tree, thyme
Uterine	Tones and strengthens the uterus	Clary sage, frankincense, jasmine, melissa, myrrh, rose
Vasoconstrictor	Causes small blood vessels to contract	Chamomile, cypress, rose
Vasodilator	Causes small blood vessels to dilate	Lemongrass, sweet marjoram, melissa
Vulnerary	Helps wounds to heal	Canadian balsam, benzoin, bergamot, chamomile, geranium, lavender, myrrh, rosemary, tea tree

ESSENTIAL OILS (A TO Y)

Essential oils are widely used in therapeutic massage and in the pharmaceutical, cosmetic and perfume industries. They are volatile non-oily (despite their name) compounds that occur naturally in plants and evaporate when exposed to air. Because these precious essences are composed of molecules small enough to penetrate the skin and enter the bloodstream, essential oils are employed in many ways. These include as massage oils, compresses, diffusions, inhalation sticks, natural perfumes, antiseptics and tonic waters, as well as healing ointments, beauty and skincare products, household cleansers, antibacterial sprays and more.

A plant's essential oil can be found in its leaves (eucalyptus), petals (rose), bark (sandalwood), resin (myrrh), root/rhizome (ginger), rind (citrus fruits) or seeds (carrot). In some cases the oil is excreted, in which case it provides the plant with a characteristic aroma that attracts birds and insects (for example, hyssop, which attracts bees that help to pollinate your garden). In other situations the essential oil isn't apparent until a part of the plant is crushed or dried (for example, root of valerian). With some plants, the essential oil is released from the gum or resin only when an incision is made in the bark (for example, mastic); many of these resins have no aroma until dried.

Essential oils are as individual as fine wines. A Merlot will generally taste like a Merlot, but every Merlot will be different. Each vintage of the same brand of Merlot can taste different too. The wine produced will vary depending on the terroir (the area where the grapes were grown), when the grapes were harvested and how much rain or sunshine they received during the growing season. The same is true of essential oils. Not only do the climate and geography where the plants are grown determine the oil that results, the final product is also affected by whether the plant material was dried or fresh when distilled, the time of day it was picked, how it was produced, and how it was stored. Some of these factors will determine the main chemical component, or chemotype, of the oil and, ultimately, an oil's therapeutic properties.

Using the Properties Table

The table on pages 24 to 27 gives the technical terms for the therapeutic properties of various essential oils, describes those properties, and lists the essential oils that are important in each category. Where a treatment will benefit from a specific type of oil or chemotype, the Latin name and/or the chemotype (see page 29) is indicated.

The essential oil profiles that follow will help you become familiar with the oils and confident about using them. Once you get to know the oils, you will be able to find appropriate substitutes and create your own recipes.

What's in a Name?

The name of an essential oil is very important. Look for essential oils that have the Latin botanical name of the plant used to produce the oil on the label. Latin names are normally shown in italics. The first name is the genus and the second is the species. Becoming familiar with the botanical names will help you to select a good-quality oil that will produce the therapeutic benefits you are seeking.

Often you will come across essential oils that identify specific chemotypes (see below). These are indicated with "ct." after the Latin name—for example, *Hyssopus officinalis* ct. pinocamphone. This identifies the predominant chemical component of the essential oil (in this case, pinocamphone). It is especially important because it can mean the difference between an oil that can be hazardous and one that is gentler and safer.

What Is a Chemotype?

Often the names of essential oils will contain an additional identification: the chemotype. Specific chemotypes are indicated with "ct." after the Latin name—for example, *Hyssopus officinalis* ct. pinocamphone. A chemotype is a chemically distinct component of the plant that, in very general terms, reflects the environment in which it grows. The chemotype identifies the predominant chemical component in the essential oil (in this case, pinocamphone) that distinguishes it from another essential oil from the same plant species.

ALLSPICE See Pimento (page 97)

AMYRIS

Amyris balsamifera

Formerly known as *Schimmerelia oleisera*, the wood of amyris was often called "candle wood" or "torch wood" because it is highly flammable and was used by fishermen and traders as a torch. Amyris is found mainly in Haiti but has been exported to other tropical climates in Central and South America. The pale yellow, sometimes brownish yellow oil possesses a woody, sweet and sometimes faintly peppery aroma. It is used most often in perfumes. The intensely aromatic resin is steam-distilled, which provides an essential oil that is commonly referred to as "West Indian sandalwood oil." It is often used as a less expensive version of East Indian sandalwood, although it is not a true replacement for any sandalwood.

The predominant component of the oil is valerianol (think valerian), which provides its sedative and hypotensive qualities. Its chemical makeup suggests that it may be beneficial as an anti-inflammatory, antiseptic and antifungal and that it is calming to the digestive system. Amyris oil blends well with lavandin and other wood oils such as cedarwood and sandalwood.

Amyris is used as a fixative (see page 38) in soaps and is listed as a flavoring ingredient by the US Food and Drug Administration. A 2010 study, which found that it could repel ticks, suggests that amyris also has insecticidal qualities.

Uses

- Amyris oil is excellent when used in a toner or face wash, helping to maintain clear, healthy skin. It has been recommended as suitable for anti-aging skincare products.

- Amyris has a relaxing effect. It can be used in an inhaler stick or aromatherapy diffuser to ease nervous tension and everyday stresses, hence aiding the immune system.

- When used in an evening bath, the soothing aroma of amyris can help to attain healthy sleep.

ANGELICA

Angelica archangelica

Angelica is a tall, handsome biennial plant long valued for medicinal and culinary purposes. The tender young stems are often candied and are popular for decorating cakes and desserts.

The rich and fragrant essential oil is extracted from the roots and seeds. The whole plant was once used as protection against the plague. A well-known story tells of a monk who dreamed that an angel visited him and told him to use the herb to cure plague-smitten people, hence the name *angelica*.

Angelica essential oil is steam-distilled from the roots and seeds of the plant. It has a sweet, rich, pleasant perfume that blends well with basil, chamomile, geranium, grapefruit, lavender, lemon and mandarin. It is used in the perfume industry as a fragrance for soaps, perfumes and colognes. Another use is in the delicious liqueurs Chartreuse and Benedictine.

Angelica also has medicinal benefits. One 2013 study of college students found that inhaling angelica essential oil not only decreased their level of craving for nicotine, it also extended the period between cravings. A laboratory study of mice concluded that angelica essential oils have an antiseizure effect equal to that of anticonvulsant medications. In 2005 one laboratory study found that angelica essential oils have anticarcinogenic effects.

The herb dong quai (Angelica sinensis), long used in Chinese medicine and now becoming well known for its estrogen-like activity, is a close relation of Angelica archangelica.

Uses

- Angelica oil is excellent in all skincare preparations, both as a tonic and to soften and smooth rough, dry skin. It reduces inflammation and can be useful when applied to irritated skin and for helping with psoriasis.

- Angelica oil is a valuable oil to include in massage blends, as it purifies the blood and acts as a lymphatic stimulator—it drains the body of excess fluid, increases energy and generally quickens the function of glands. It increases perspiration and rids the body of poisons and strengthens bodily systems and the constitution, particularly the heart.

- Angelica oil is an excellent tonic for the entire digestive system. It stimulates the appetite, which means it is useful for treating anemia and anorexia and helping people recover from a severe or long illness. Its toning properties strengthen the liver. It aids digestion and generally boosts the digestive system, helping to dispel intestinal gases and relieve cramps, as well as easing indigestion, stomach ulcers and colic.

- A useful remedy for respiratory infections, angelica helps to decongest the lungs, remove excess mucus and reduce fever during colds, bronchitis, influenza and pleurisy.

- Used in baths, massage oils and compresses, angelica increases the flow of urine and is a useful urinary antiseptic for cystitis and urethritis. It is said to regulate menstrual flow and ease painful periods by relieving cramps in the uterus and encouraging the production of estrogen.

- Angelica quickly relieves exhaustion and stress and strengthens the nerves. It restores and gives strength to a tired mind and can be used to ease the pain of headache, migraine and toothache.

Caution
Avoid using more than 1 drop angelica oil per 2 tsp (10 mL) carrier oil on skin that will be exposed to sunlight or a sunbed within 12 hours of use (see Phototoxicity, page 19).

- Star anise essential oil should not be used over the whole body.

- Not to be used in large percentages or for extended periods.

- Not to be used in pregnancy or during breastfeeding or to treat endometriosis and estrogen-dependent cancers.

- Not to be used with children under 5 years old.

- Make sure this oil is not accidentally ingested. Negative interactions have been known to occur when taking certain medications.

ANISE, STAR

Illicium verum

Star anise essential oil is extracted by steam distillation from the fresh green star-shaped fruits of this East Asian tree. The oil has a licorice-like aroma, similar to aniseed (*Pimpinella anisum*); it blends well with other spice oils such as lavender, pine, orange and rosewood. The oil is used in pharmaceuticals to mask the taste of other, less pleasant-tasting ingredients and by the food industry for flavoring food and drink. It has been widely used in Europe since the 16th century as a flavoring agent for liqueurs.

Although not in the same plant family, star anise and aniseed essential oil share very similar properties. For instance, their perfumes are almost the same. Aniseed is distilled from the seeds of the *Pimpinella anisum* plant. Although the two oils aren't related, both are potentially carcinogenic, so the oil needs to be used with great care. According to experts, star anise oil can affect reproductive hormones and inhibit blood clotting (see Cautions).

Uses

- Star anise oil is useful for adding to inhalations and massage blends at 0.5% to treat respiratory complaints where there is a mucus problem (conditions such as bronchitis, sinusitis and colds).

- Star anise oil is very helpful for easing problems of the digestive system. A hot compress using 3 drops of star anise oil will quickly dispel flatulence and ease the pains of indigestion and colic. It eases constipation by encouraging a stronger action in the bowel.

- Star anise oil has a warming action that could help with pain such as that of rheumatism and lumbago, complaints that are aggravated by the cold.

BALSAM, CANADIAN
(Canadian Fir Needle)

Abies balsamea

Canada balsam is an oleoresin (a mixture of essential oil and resin) exuded by the trunk and branches of the Canadian balsam fir, a tall, cone-shaped evergreen tree. The oleoresin is distilled to make an essential oil; an essential oil can also be distilled from the needles. This sweet, pine-smelling oil was traditionally used by Native Americans to treat burns and wounds and to relieve chest pain. Today it is still used for cuts and burns, as well as for a range of respiratory conditions such as asthma, bronchitis and cough. It is also used as an anti-inflammatory agent for treating sore throat. As an antiseptic it is often used in the treatment of bladder, genital and urinary infections.

Canadian balsam essential oil has been found to be active against human tumor cell lines in breast, colon, lung, prostate and skin cancers. One 2003 study on the prevention of bone loss demonstrated that essential oils in the pine family can be helpful in cases of osteoporosis.

Uses

- When prepared in an ointment, Canadian balsam can be used as a treatment to relieve the swelling and pain of hemorrhoids.
- Canadian balsam reduces inflammation. For example, 4 to 6 drops can be added to a bath to reduce the pain and stiffness of arthritis.
- The antiseptic and pulmonary properties of Canadian balsam indicate that its inclusion in immune-boosting blends can help to loosen mucus and improve lung function in chronic bronchitis.

BALSAM, PERU

Myroxylon balsamum var. *pereirae*

Peru balsam is a native of El Salvador. Every part of this tall, spreading evergreen tree contains a resinous juice from which the oil is extracted. The perfume is deliciously rich and vanilla-like, and the oil blends well with most other oils. Because of its antiseptic and aromatic properties, Peru balsam is used widely as a fixative (see page 38) and fragrance in perfumes and soaps. It is also used in alcoholic beverages and soft drinks. There is evidence to support a delayed allergic reaction to Peru balsam in hypersensitive individuals and those with chronic eczema.

Uses

- Peru balsam oil reduces inflammation and kills bacteria. It can be used to treat skin conditions such as bedsores, dermatitis, eczema, inflammations, rashes, painful nipples and sores. It has a softening and soothing effect on dry, cracked and chapped skin and encourages the growth of new cells.
- Peru balsam oil increases energy and glandular function, raises low blood pressure and eases muscular pains such as those of rheumatism.
- It is a very effective treatment for respiratory problems such as asthma, bronchitis, colds and coughs, as it helps to relieve excess mucus.
- Peru balsam oil softens, comforts and opens a heart that is closed through stress and grief.

Caution

Canadian balsam may cause skin sensitization if it is old or oxidized.

Cautions

- Use of Peru balsam should not exceed 1 drop per 3 tsp (15 mL) carrier oil or lotion for topical applications such as massage or body lotions.
- This oil may be an allergen to sensitive individuals.
- There is a moderate risk of skin sensitization in hypersensitive individuals.
- Do not use on damaged skin.
- Not to be used with children under 2 years old.

BALSAM, TOLU

Myroxylon balsamum

A close relative of Peru balsam, Tolu balsam oil is extracted through V-shaped incisions cut into the sapwood and bark of the snowbell tree. The liquid is collected from these incisions and allowed to solidify, then the essential oil is extracted by steam distillation (a dry distillation method is also used). The oil has a delicious rich floral scent. It blends well with cedarwood, spice oils, sandalwood, neroli, patchouli and most flower oils. It is often used in pharmaceuticals as a flavoring and as an expectorant in cough remedies.

Uses

- Tolu balsam oil is excellent for soothing and healing dry, cracked and chapped skin, eczema and sores (including bedsores) and wounds.

- It has good deodorant properties, as have many of the oils with which it blends.

- Tolu balsam oil has expectorant properties. It is an ingredient in the famous expectorant friar's balsam and is still included in Martindale's *Pharmacopoeia* (a definitive source of information on drugs and complementary treatments, among other agents) as an expectorant. It can be used in inhalants for loosening mucus during chronic bronchitis, laryngitis, coughs and croup.

BASIL

Ocimum basilicum

Few people are unfamiliar with the taste and sweetly spicy aroma of fresh sweet basil. The flowering tops and leaves are distilled to produce the oil, which blends well with bergamot, geranium and hyssop. The Latin name for basil is derived from the Greek for "king," and like a king, this powerful oil needs to be treated with a little respect—1 drop in 4 tsp (20 mL) of blend will be enough.

Basil is one of several plants that produce a variety of chemotypes (see page 29). Each possesses particular therapeutic benefits (and cautions for use) based on its major constituent. Two main chemotypes of *Ocimum basilicum* are sold: estragole (*Ocimum basilicum* ct. estragole) and linalool (*Ocimum basilicum* ct. linalool). The estragole chemotype contains more than 73% estragole and is potentially carcinogenic; it may also inhibit blood clotting. It should be used only by professionally trained aromatherapists. The linalool chemotype is gentler and is recommended for general blending. It is labeled and sold as "basil" and is readily available.

Research has shown that basil oil is highly effective as an antibacterial agent. It combats multidrug-resistant strains of *E. coli*, which makes it a nice addition to liquid hand soaps and kitchen cleaning sprays.

Uses

- The tonic and antiseptic properties of basil are helpful for treating skin problems such as acne and abrasions.

- It is worth including basil oil in blends to ease insect bites and stings, as well as to repel insects.

- Basil oil is a very good hair tonic when blended with oils such as rosemary, lavender and jojoba.

- Basil oil is a popular choice for blends that are used to treat respiratory problems such as bronchitis, colds and influenza; it helps to loosen and remove mucus and reduce fever. Incorporate basil with other oils in blends for inhalation, massage and baths.

- Basil oil has estrogenic-like properties that may help to relieve cramps in the uterus and intestines and encourage menstrual flow. It is contraindicated in breastfeeding.

- Basil is an appetite stimulant. It tones the digestive system, aiding digestion and helping to expel gases from the intestines. It also eases hiccups, heartburn, nausea and gastroenteritis.

- Included in blends with lavender, marjoram and black pepper, basil oil makes an excellent massage and bath oil for overworked muscles and muscular aches and pains.

- Basil oil has a reputation for minimizing uric acid in the blood and may be useful for treating gout.

- Basil oil is an excellent oil for the brain: it stimulates the intellect, clears the mind and aids concentration. It is also useful for easing headaches and migraine. It lifts depression; eases hysteria, mental fatigue, insomnia and anxiety; and provides endurance and stamina.

Caution
Basil ct. estragole (methyl chavicol) should not be used in home aromatherapy.

Cautions

- Use up to 1 drop of West Indian bay in 2 tsp (10 mL) carrier oil for hair preparations.

- We do not recommend the ingestion of essential oils for home aromatherapy use. In the case of West Indian bay oil, negative interactions have been known to occur in individuals taking certain medications. This oil may interact with pethidine, MAOIs or SSRIs and anticoagulant medications. It may also have a negative effect on conditions such as hemophilia and other bleeding disorders, peptic ulcer and recovery from major surgery.

Tip: Children, frail or elderly people, or those who are convalescing require 50% less essential oil than other people.

BAY, WEST INDIAN

Pimenta racemosa

Although one of the synonyms for this tree is "bayberry," it shouldn't be confused with the North American bayberry, or wax myrtle (*Myrcia cerifera*). The leaves of the tropical evergreen West Indian bay tree are distilled with rum to produce the famous bay rum hair tonic, which is fragrant and reputedly reduces oil and stimulates hair growth. West Indian bay oil is used extensively in commercial soaps, perfumes, aftershaves and hair preparations. The aroma of this oil is fresh and balsamic. It blends well with citrus and spice oils, geranium, lavender, rosemary and ylang ylang.

Uses

- The main use of West Indian bay oil is in hair preparations. It is thought to be a scalp stimulant, to restore the appearance of lank and greasy hair, to encourage growth and to help to treat dandruff. It has been suggested that it could be useful for treating muscular pain and problems, but as it is moderately toxic, we feel that there are safer and more effective oils that can be used.

BAY LAUREL

Laurus nobilis

Not to be confused with West Indian bay (*Pimenta racemosa*, above), bay laurel (*Laurus nobilis*), or sweet bay, is a tall, stately tree. It has shiny dark green leaves and is often grown in tubs as an ornamental shrub. The leaves, which are spicily fragrant, are used in cooking or kept with dried foods as a deterrent to weevils. They were woven into wreaths by the ancient Greeks and Romans to crown their victors.

The oil is steam-distilled from the leaves and twigs. It has a spicy, almost medicinal aroma that blends with clary sage, cedarwood, citrus oils, cypress, eucalyptus, ginger, lavender, marjoram, rosemary and all spice oils. Commercially it is used in many products ranging from detergents to cosmetics and perfumes. It is also used in processed foods.

Research shows that bay laurel possesses moderate antioxidant activity. This makes it a mild immune-system booster capable of treating influenza, infectious diseases and bronchitis.

Uses

- As with other spice oils, bay laurel oil helps the digestive system. It has a tonic effect on the liver and gallbladder.
- It can be used in small amounts (1 drop in 2 tsp/10 mL vegetable oil) to massage the abdomen and ease the discomfort of indigestion, flatulence and loss of appetite.
- Bay laurel oil can be included in blends for inhalation and massage to treat fever, infectious diseases and bronchitis.
- Used in a massage oil blend, bay laurel oil can help to relieve lymph congestion and the pain of swollen lymph nodes.

BENZOIN

Styrax benzoin

Benzoin oil is prepared from a crude resin that exudes from the trunk of the styrax (benzoin) tree when it is cut. It is not a true essential oil because the resin is dissolved in alcohol or benzene and then the solvent is removed through a vacuum process. This leaves a "resinoid" with a sticky residue. As the resinoid is not liquid, when adding it to your recipes, it is best to warm the bottle in a bowl of hot water or roll it back and forth between your palms to make it less viscous.

Benzoin has been used in Asia for thousands of years as an ingredient in incense, as the fumes supposedly drive away evil spirits. The perfume has been described as vanilla-like, although there is a resinous undernote. Benzoin blends well with spice oils, bergamot, cypress, juniper, lavender, myrrh, petitgrain and sandalwood.

Uses

- Benzoin oil helps to destroy bacterial and fungal infections of the skin, reduces inflammation and acts as an antioxidant. It is useful in blends to heal skin irritations and ease itching (such as from pruritus and dermatitis) and is excellent when added to creams to soothe and soften cracked and dry or work-worn skin.
- Benzoin oil contracts and tones tissue, stops external bleeding, helps to heal wounds and reduces body odor. It can be used in making ointments, creams and lotions for both its healing and preservative actions. It is also used in perfumes for its fixative properties (see page 38).
- Benzoin oil is a warming oil, and this, combined with its tonic and mucus-loosening properties, gives it a reputation for helping with respiratory problems such as asthma, bronchitis, coughs, colds and laryngitis. It is an ingredient in the world-famous friar's balsam, which is used for inhalations to help ease sore throat and relieve hoarseness and voice loss (benzoin 10%, storax 7.5%, Tolu balsam 2.5%, aloe 2% and alcohol).

Cautions

- Avoid using bay laurel if pregnant or breastfeeding.
- Do not use on damaged skin. Use no more than 1 drop in 2 tsp (10 mL) carrier oil.
- Unsuitable for baths, as it may cause skin irritation.
- Not to be used on children under 2 years old.

Caution

Not for use with children under the age of 2 (there is a low risk of skin sensitization).

- Benzoin oil's warming properties are helpful for arthritis, gout, poor circulation and rheumatism. It also increases the flow of urine, which makes it a good remedy for problems such as cystitis and urinary tract infections.
- This oil gently but powerfully works its way into the subconscious to release hidden resistance and tension. It comforts and eases the grieving, lonely, stressed or mentally exhausted. Benzoin is a communicator: it helps in difficult or uncomfortable situations.

Fixatives and Preservatives

Benzoin oil is used in perfumery for its fixative properties. A **fixative** is a substance that slows the rate of evaporation of volatile substances. Used in perfumery, a fixative is a substance that anchors the scent and improves the stability of the perfume.

A **preservative**, on the other hand, is a substance that is added to a product to extend its shelf life by inhibiting the growth of bacteria. Essential oils such as cinnamon, ginger and clove have preservative properties and are often used in the food-processing industry.

BERGAMOT

Citrus bergamia

Bergamot is a small, delicate tree that is grown mainly in southern Italy; it bears small, round fruits that are similar in appearance to oranges but are pear-shaped. Oil of bergamot is expressed from the skin of the fruit just before it ripens. This is the oil that imparts the unique flavor to Earl Grey tea. The perfume is a delicious combination of citrus and floral aromas. The oil blends well with cypress, geranium, lavender, lemon, neroli, palmarosa, patchouli and ylang ylang.

In Italian folk medicine, bergamot oil was used for fever and to treat intestinal parasites. The oil is useful as a fixative in cosmetic preparations and perfumes and is the most important ingredient in eau de cologne.

Tip: Bergamot FCF (furanocoumarin-free), also known as "bergapten-free," is a rectified essential oil from which the phototoxic components have been removed. However, the aroma of this version is somewhat lacking compared to the whole essential oil.

Uses

- Bergamot oil is excellent for treating many skin complaints, including acne, eczema, psoriasis, scabies, varicose ulcers and seborrhea of the skin and scalp. It also eases skin irritations and softens cracked and dry skin.

- Bergamot oil eases pain by numbing nerves, is antifungal, aids in wound healing and helps to clear skin infections. It is said to inhibit the virus responsible for cold sores if 1 drop is dabbed on the site as soon as the first warning tingle is felt. Added to deodorant blends, it reduces body odor. It is also a very good personal insect repellent.

- A tonic for the digestive system, bergamot oil aids digestion and strengthens the bodily systems. It also relieves cramps and spasms in the intestines and uterus.

- Bergamot oil increases the flow of urine and acts as an antiseptic and disinfectant for the genitourinary system. It is used to treat problems such as the infection and inflammation that characterize cystitis and urethritis.

- Used in inhalations and chest rubs, bergamot oil's antiseptic action helps treat respiratory infections, easing the symptoms of bronchitis, coughs, colds and laryngitis.

- Because of its powerful uplifting and relaxing properties, bergamot oil is one of the most important oils to use in air sprays, diffusers and bath and massage blends to treat tension, anxiety and depression. Its antidepressant qualities make it a favored oil for treating psychological, mental and emotional issues such as depression, fear and anxiety. Use bergamot combined with other uplifting and comforting oils such as rose, Roman chamomile and sandalwood in a personal inhaler or diffuser to stabilize mood.

- A research study of the mind/body effects of bergamot essential oil showed that it has a sedative action. This makes it useful in aromatic inhalers as well as in diffusers to treat agitation and insomnia.

Skin Reactions

Essential oils that contain specific chemical components such as limonene can cause dermal irritation when oxidized. Be sure to store these oils in dark glass bottles in the refrigerator, ensuring that the caps are tightly closed.

Cautions

- Bergamot oil may cause irritation to sensitive skin if it is old or oxidized. Keep the oil in a dark glass bottle in the refrigerator, ensuring that the cap is tightly closed.

- Use only 1% to 2% in blends. Use 1 drop in 3 tsp (15 mL) carrier oil to reduce the potential for phototoxicity (see page 19).

- Avoid using bergamot oil on skin that will be exposed to sunlight or a sunbed within 12 hours of use.

- It is especially important to make sure that bergamot oil is not accidentally ingested. Ingestion should be avoided when taking certain medications; negative interactions have been known to occur.

BIRCH BUD or WHITE BIRCH

Betula pendula syn. *Betula alba*

This is the beautiful silver birch from Europe. Be totally sure of your source when you buy this oil: it's very important not to confuse birch bud (or white birch) oil with black birch (*Betula nigra*) oil or sweet birch (*Betula lenta*) oil, which should be used only by professional aromatherapists. Birch bud essential oil is produced by steam distillation from the buds of the tree. It has an intense, resinous aroma and blends well with the balsams, cajuput, lavender, niaouli and tea tree essential oils. Much research is being done on its properties because it contains a compound called betulinic acid, which in laboratory tests was found to kill melanoma cells transplanted into mice; other compounds were found to inhibit the AIDS virus.

Uses

- Birch bud oil exerts a cleansing and purifying effect on the body, thanks to its diuretic, blood-cleansing and tonic action. It is also an anti-inflammatory and an antiseptic, so it is useful in compresses, creams and ointments for inflamed skin conditions such as chronic eczema, boils, dermatitis, ulcers and psoriasis.
- Birch bud oil's combined actions of increasing the flow of urine and eliminating uric acid are useful when treating cellulitis, edema, cystitis, rheumatism and arthritic conditions.

BITTER ORANGE

See Orange, Bitter (page 90)

BLACK PEPPER

Piper nigrum

Black pepper is a climbing vine that can reach up to 20 feet (6 m) if left unpruned. The black dried fruit is ground as a cooking spice and for steam distillation as an oil. The perfume is warm, spicy and familiar, blending with basil, bergamot, cypress, frankincense, geranium, citrus oils, palmarosa, sandalwood and ylang ylang. It is often used in tiny amounts in perfumery to add a warm, deep and spicy note.

Studies report that black pepper essential oil may prove useful in smoking cessation. Subjects who puffed on a vapor of black pepper essential oil found that their cigarette cravings were significantly reduced; they also felt fewer symptoms of anxiety. The intensity of sensations felt in the chest supports the theory that respiratory tract sensations are important in alleviating smoking-withdrawal symptoms.

Uses

- Black pepper oil is one of the important oils for treating muscular problems. When applied to the skin, it dilates blood vessels and produces localized redness and warmth, which relieves aching, tired muscles. Used in a massage oil prior to intense activity (particularly by runners and dancers), it can reduce strain on muscles by increasing the blood flow to a specific area. In small amounts in bath and massage blends, it may be used to ease arthritis, rheumatism, muscular aches and pains, sprains, strains, poor muscle tone, muscular stiffness, neuralgia, chilblains and poor circulation. It eases pain by numbing nerves.

- Black pepper oil is reported to flush lactic acid from the body after a workout (see Muscle Relief Massage Oil, page 274).

- Black pepper oil tones and stimulates the nervous, circulatory and digestive systems, aiding digestion, relieving cramps, gas and spasms in the intestines and uterus, and easing colic, constipation, diarrhea and nausea. It reputedly counteracts the effects of poison. It also kills bacteria.

- Use black pepper oil in small amounts (3 drops only) in baths to increase perspiration and to cool and reduce fever during colds and influenza. It strengthens the immune system and helps to avoid viral infections.

- This oil warms a cold heart and promotes courage and stamina in adversity.

Cautions

- Black pepper oil may cause skin sensitization if it is old or oxidized. Keep the oil in a cool, dark place, ensuring that the cap is tightly closed.

- Do not use undiluted. This oil should always be diluted in a carrier oil or lotion.

CAJUPUT

Melaleuca leucadendra var. *cajuputi*

Cajuput, a tall, vigorous, robust tree also called weeping paperbark, is found from northern Australia up to eastern Indonesia. It is a member of the *Melaleuca* genus and in the same family as eucalyptus, clove, myrtle, tea tree and niaouli. Like these oils, cajuput has the ability to successfully combat and prevent infection.

The oil is extracted by steam distillation from the buds, leaves and twigs. The perfume is similar to eucalyptus but sweeter. Cajuput blends well with angelica, bergamot, clove, geranium, lavender, niaouli, nutmeg, rosewood and thyme. It is used in pharmaceutical preparations as an antiseptic, and thanks to this property it is also used in manufacturing soaps, detergents and cosmetics.

Cautions

- Do not use with young children. Cajuput may cause distress to a child's nervous system and create breathing problems.

- Do not use cajuput along with homeopathic remedies—the essential oil will neutralize the effect of the homeopathic remedy. This is true of some essential oils that are high in 1.8 cineole and camphor.

Caution

Do not use with young children. Cardamom may cause distress to a child's nervous system and create breathing problems.

Cajuput has been found to be one of the most effective essential oils against a variety of bacteria, including *Escherichia coli*, *Staphyloccocus aureus* and *Streptococcus faecalis*, and *Candida albicans*. This makes it a useful addition to cleaning products and air sprays. A few drops can be added to a vaporizer in a sickroom to provide an antiseptic environment.

Uses

- Cajuput oil is useful for treating insect bites, acne, psoriasis and pimples. It mildly eases pain by numbing nerves and destroys infection-causing bacteria. It is also a valuable insecticide.

- Its similarity to tea tree means that cajuput oil can be used in many of the same situations. However, it is particularly useful for easing rheumatic pains, arthritis, muscular aches and pains and rheumatism. It also relieves cramps and spasms in the intestines and uterus.

- Cajuput oil has expectorant, tonic and antiseptic properties. This makes it a fine respiratory tract treatment for helping to loosen and remove mucus, increase perspiration and cool and reduce fever. Asthma, bronchitis, sinusitis, sore throat, feverish colds, laryngitis and viral infections will all respond to treatments using cajuput oil, including baths, massage, inhalation (except for asthma sufferers) and air sprays.

- Its antiseptic properties also help in the treatment of cystitis and urethritis. It is a mild painkiller for easing toothache.

CARDAMOM

Elettaria cardamomum

Cardamom is a tall shrub with long, silky leaves. It produces flowers as well as the seeds from which the oil is steam-distilled. It is related to ginger; they have several properties in common, particularly their ability to warm and tone the system. Cardamom is a plant that has been used in cooking, medicine, perfume and incense for more than 3,000 years. The aroma is warm and spicy; it blends with other spice oils, frankincense, geranium, juniper, orange, neroli and rosewood.

Uses

- The main use of cardamom oil is for its tonic and digestive action. When used in baths, massages or hot compresses, it will stimulate appetite and ease flatulence, indigestion, nausea and the pains of diarrhea. It may also help to treat bad breath due to poor digestion.

CARROT SEED

Daucus carota

The carrot is a popular and nutritious root vegetable. It was introduced to Europe from Asia about 600 years ago. The essential oil is distilled mainly from the seed of the wild carrot, but oil is contained in the whole plant. The perfume is dry, warm and sweet and has the characteristic smell of carrots. It blends well with bergamot, cedarwood, geranium, juniper, lavender, lemon, lemon verbena, lime, melissa, neroli, orange, petitgrain and rosemary. A cold-pressed "fixed oil" is also produced from the seeds; however, its properties are different from those of the essential oil.

Uses

- This rich golden oil (used discreetly) is wonderful for the skin; it contracts and tones tissue, kills bacteria and adds elasticity, especially with prematurely aging skin. It may also remove or fade age spots and scars. It is exceptionally healing and may be included in small amounts in blends for dermatitis, anal or vaginal itching, eczema, ulcers, boils and psoriasis.

- Carrot seed oil helps to rid the body of toxins, so it is useful added in small amounts to bath and massage blends for treating arthritis, gout and rheumatism.

- Carrot seed oil acts as a powerful tonic for the digestive system, particularly the liver and gallbladder, aiding digestion and helping to expel gas from the intestines.

- Because of its regulating effect on hormone production, carrot seed oil may be employed in blends for all menstrual problems, PMS and menopause symptoms.

- Carrot seed oil is currently being used in the treatment of jaundice, and its diuretic effects are beneficial in cases of bladder infections and kidney stones. It is said to increase the production of red blood corpuscles, so it could be used in conjunction with medical treatment for anemia and other complaints that occasion weakness and lethargy.

- Carrot seed oil has been found to have remarkable antitumor activity in some skin cancers.

Caution
Do not use carrot seed oil during pregnancy or while breastfeeding.

CATNIP

Nepeta cataria

Also known as catmint, catnip is native to Europe and southwestern to central Asia and grows widely throughout the United States. This short-lived perennial plant resembles mint in appearance, with brownish green leaves. Catnip has a herbaceous and slightly minty aroma that some say is reminiscent of freshly cut grass. As an ornamental plant, catnip attracts butterflies, but it is better known for its stimulating effect on the behavior of cats.

Research to date has been on the use of the oil as an insect repellent. Findings show that the nepetalactone chemotype repels mosquitoes 10 times more effectively than DEET, the chemical found in most commercial insect repellents. It has also been said to be effective at repelling bees and other flying insects. Traditionally catnip was used medicinally for nervousness, headache and insomnia, although its medicinal use fell out of favor as new medicines were developed. Today the young leaf shoots are used as a culinary herb and in medicinal teas to help relaxation, ease headaches and promote restful sleep. Catnip is rumored to repel rats.

Uses

- The antispasmodic effect of catnip oil is helpful in massage blends for diarrhea, stomach cramps and intestinal gas. Working in a clockwise motion, massage ½ tsp (2.5 mL) of the blend onto your abdomen.
- Catnip oil is antimicrobial and antiseptic. The addition of 1 to 2 drops of catnip oil along with 1 to 2 drops of cypress or peppermint oil to a vaporizer can help to relieve nasal congestion due to colds or influenza and disinfect a sickroom.
- The inclusion of this oil is a must in natural mosquito-repellent sprays! Be sure to obtain the nepetalactone chemotype. Use 40% to 60% catnip essential oil in your bug-repellent blends.

CEDARWOOD

Cedrus atlantica

Cedarwood comes from a very tall, majestic, pyramid-shaped tree that grows in the Atlas Mountains in Algeria. The tree is prized for its scented wood, which is insect repellent and used for making chests and other furniture for storing precious items. The oil was used in ancient Egypt for embalming bodies for mummification, and the wood was used for sarcophagi—double insurance!

Cedarwood essential oil is steam-distilled from the leaves and sawdust of Atlas cedar trees. Do not confuse cedarwood 'Atlas' with cedarwood 'Virginian' (*Juniperus virginiana*), as the latter tree is actually a juniper. Cedarwood 'Atlas' has a warm, sweet and woody perfume, a little similar to sandalwood. The oil blends well with benzoin, bergamot, cypress, frankincense, juniper, lavender, lemon and rosemary.

Uses

- Cedarwood oil kills bacteria, prevents or destroys fungal infections, and is insecticidal and mildly astringent. These properties make it excellent for adding to oil blends, steams and masks to treat a variety of skin complaints such as acne, eczema, dermatitis, fungal infections, ulcers and psoriasis. It contracts and tones tissue and is a useful treatment for oily skin. Because of its antiseptic and astringent properties, it is a lovely oil to use in aftershaves and other preparations for men, who seem to appreciate its rather masculine perfume. It is nice for insect-repellent blends too.

- Cedarwood oil is a circulatory stimulant and strengthens bodily systems. Include this oil in massage and bath blends for easing arthritis and chronic rheumatism. It is well known for its ability to treat urinary tract infections, as it is a strong antiseptic and also increases the flow of urine.

- A powerful bronchial tract antiseptic and decongestant, it helps to loosen and remove mucus during attacks of bronchitis, coughs, colds, influenza and other congestive conditions.

- Cedarwood soothes the overexcitable and softens and mellows those with selfish, unyielding, stiff-necked attitudes. It relieves mental strain and gently helps those suffering from depression or insomnia caused by stress-related problems.

CELERY SEED

Apium graveolens

Wild celery is a strong-smelling plant, but it has been domesticated for some 2,000 years to produce the popular vegetable widely enjoyed in soups and salads. The oil is produced in France, India and the Netherlands by steam distillation of the seeds of particular varieties. The perfume is spicy and warm, with a long-lasting aroma, and it blends well with angelica, basil, chamomile, grapefruit, lemon, orange, palmarosa and rosemary.

Uses

- Perhaps the best-known benefits of celery seed oil are its abilities to provide a good flow of urine and to remove toxins and excess uric acid from the blood. The oil may be included in massage and bath blends for arthritis, gout, rheumatism and sciatica. The increased flow of urine also helps to ease the symptoms of cystitis and urethritis.

Caution

Do not confuse cedarwood with white cedar, or thuja (*Thuja occidentalis*). Thuja oil has been found to induce seizures.

Cautions

- Celery seed oil may cause skin sensitization if it is old or oxidized. Keep in a cool, dark place, ensuring that the cap is tightly closed.

- Be sure not to use the oil undiluted.

Tip: Combining essential oils with a solubilizer (honey, milk, lotion, liquid soap, vodka, Solubol) will enable them to mix with water.

Caution

It is especially important to make sure that German chamomile essential oil is not accidentally ingested. Ingestion should be avoided when taking a fairly wide range of medications; negative interactions have been known to occur.

- Used in a compress, celery seed oil relieves cramps and spasms in the uterus, encourages and regulates menstrual flow, and increases the production of breast milk.

- Celery seed oil strengthens the digestive system, stimulates and strengthens the liver, aids digestion, relieves cramps and spasms in the intestines, and will help with flatulence, indigestion, liver congestion and jaundice.

- It calms and strengthens the nervous system, reducing stress and creating a feeling of wellbeing.

CHAMOMILE

Roman chamomile: *Chamaemelum nobile* syn. *Anthemis nobilis*

German chamomile: *Matricaria recutita* syn. *M. chamomilla*

The botanical name *Chamaemelum* comes from the Greek, meaning "earth apple." The perfume of chamomile oil is refreshing, pleasant and remarkably apple-like. The appearance and properties of these two chamomiles are very similar, and the essential oil distilled from the flowers of both varieties contains chamazulene, a powerful anti-inflammatory agent. German chamomile oil is a darker blue than the Roman variety and contains a little more chamazulene. Roman chamomile oil becomes yellow as it ages.

Chamomile is an expensive oil. You can substitute with lavender, although it is not as effective at easing dull, aching pain. Chamomile essential oil blends well with geranium, lavender, patchouli and rose. It is widely used in pharmaceutical preparations, the perfume industry and food products.

Uses

- Chamomile essential oil has applications for most skin problems. It prevents or destroys fungal infections, kills bacteria, reduces inflammation, promotes the formation of scar tissue and is widely used to treat skin conditions such as acne, allergies, burns, blisters, cold sores, dermatitis, eczema, inflammations, insect bites, cuts and boils.

- The oil softens and soothes tight, dry and itchy skin. In baths, creams or lotions, the antiallergenic properties of chamomile oil will benefit those who suffer from allergic skin reactions such as dermatitis, hives and eczema.

- Chamomile oil eases pain by numbing nerves and reducing inflammation in tissues, which makes it useful in hot compresses, baths and massage blends to treat the discomfort of arthritis, rheumatism, inflamed joints, sprains, strains, neuralgia, toothache, headaches and migraine. It seems to be particularly beneficial in combination with other oils for massage and bath treatments for lower back pain.

- Chamomile increases the flow of urine, stimulates bile production and aids digestion, stimulates and strengthens the liver, and tones the digestive system. When used in baths, massage or compresses, it will help to treat flatulence, diarrhea, gastritis, colitis, cystitis, peptic ulcer, nausea and other stomach complaints.

- Chamomile oil is popular for treating problems connected with the reproductive system, as it encourages menstrual flow and regulates irregular and painful periods. Its calming effect helps to reduce irritability caused by menopause and PMS.

- Chamomile tea is a classic and popular bedtime anti-insomnia drink. The same effect can be achieved by using the oil in a pre-bedtime bath, shower or massage and also in an air spray in the bedroom. It soothes the overexcitable and relieves mental strain, stress, depression and insomnia.

- When used as directed, this is a safe and gentle oil for babies and children. It eases colic and the pain of teething and soothes restlessness and crankiness.

Other Varieties of Chamomile

Two other chamomiles—Maroc, or wild, chamomile (*Ormenis mixta* syn. *O. multicaulis*) and Cape chamomile (*Eriocephalus punctulatus*)—bear some resemblance to the two better-known varieties. However, they possess different chemical properties.

Caution

While there are no precautions to consider with Roman chamomile oil, German chamomile oil, even when applied topically, can pose an interaction problem with certain drugs, including some analgesic, antiarrhythmic, antipsychotic and antidepressant medications, as well as those containing estrogen or serotonin. When in doubt, use Roman chamomile.

CINNAMON (Bark and Leaf)

Cinnamomum zeylanicum syn. *C. verum*

This species of tree is the main source of the aromatic culinary spice obtained by peeling off its papery bark and letting it dry into "quills." The essential oil is water- or steam-distilled from the crushed bark or leaves. The oil produced from the bark is high in cinnamaldehyde, which is irritating to the skin and should be used with care (see Cautions, page 48). The essential oil produced from the leaf is high in eugenol, an analgesic, and provides pain relief. The perfumes of both are fragrant and spicy and blend well with benzoin, frankincense, ginger, grapefruit, lavender, mandarin, orange, pine, rosemary, thyme and ylang ylang.

Cinnamon is an ancient remedy that has been used for thousands of years to treat a wide range of complaints. Cinnamaldehyde, often used in chewing gums, is a strong antimicrobial and has been found to prevent oral bacterial growth. As an anti-cancer agent, cinnamaldehyde has been found to inhibit the spread and growth of tumors in cases of prostate, lung and breast cancer.

- Use no more than 0.05% (bark oil) and 0.5% (leaf oil) in blends. Cinnamon oil may cause a severe skin reaction, including a burning sensation and some blistering, if used above the recommended amount. Do not use undiluted on your skin.

- Avoid using if pregnant or breastfeeding.

- It is especially important to make sure that neither cinnamon bark nor cinnamon leaf essential oil is accidentally ingested. Ingestion should be avoided when taking certain medications; negative interactions have been known to occur.

Uses

- Insect bites, head lice, scabies, warts and wasp stings all seem to respond to treatment with cinnamon oil. It is mildly astringent. With its spicy note, it is especially appealing in aftershave preparations for men.

- Cinnamon is very strongly insecticidal and antiseptic. It resists viruses and kills bacteria and is also reputed to be an antidote to poisons.

- It slightly raises the body temperature, and its antiseptic and tonic action helps to ease colds, influenza and infectious and viral diseases.

- Cinnamon tones the digestive system and can be used to treat colic, indigestion, diarrhea, nausea and vomiting; to expel gas from the intestines; to calm spasms of the stomach and intestines; and to stimulate the production of gastric juices. It promotes appetite and helps digestion, so it could be useful in bath and massage blends to treat anorexia, colitis, nausea, flatulence and diarrhea.

- Cinnamon has a stimulant action that increases energy and speeds up the function of the glandular, circulatory and respiratory systems. This indicates its usefulness in poor circulation, breathlessness, scanty periods (helping to encourage and regulate menstrual flow) and menstrual pains.

- It is also useful for arthritis, neuralgia and rheumatism.

- Cinnamon increases awareness of spirituality and eases stress-related weak and exhausted conditions.

- In synergy with lavender, cinnamon has been shown to be effective against candida (see Candidiasis, page 195).

CISTUS

Cistus ladaniferus syn. *C. ladanifer*

Also known as labdanum (the substance produced by the gum) and rock rose, cistus is one of the earliest aromatics used by ancient cultures (myrrh, which is referred to in parts of the Bible, has been more accurately identified as labdanum). A small shrub that grows to just over 8 feet high (about 3 m), the cistus plant has dark green leaves with a lighter furry underside. The entire shrub is sticky because of its resinous discharge. Traditionally the gum, obtained by boiling the plant in water, was used to dispel mucus and diarrhea. This oleoresin is used in perfumery as a fixative, to anchor the scent (see page 38).

Cistus essential oil is used to support the immune system and in the treatment of respiratory complaints, including bronchitis and coughs. It is often used in meat products to protect against oxidation.

The essential oil is obtained through distillation of the whole plant, including its extremely fragrant papery white flowers; it can be a pale yellow to olive green in color. It has a heady, warm, herbaceous yet spicy aroma and is often used in perfumes that have what is described as an "oriental" profile. It blends well with oils in the pine family and heavier-scented oils such as patchouli, sandalwood and vetiver.

The antimicrobial property of various extracts of cistus was found to be beneficial against candida and several strains of bacteria, including MRSA and ulcer-causing bacteria in the gastrointestinal tract. This makes it an important ingredient for the treatment or prevention of several infections.

Uses

- Cistus essential oil is often added to skincare products for mature skin, to diminish wrinkles. It is also helpful in diminishing scars and soothing inflamed skin.

- Because cistus oil has antiviral and anti-infectious properties, adding a few drops to a vaporizer in a sickroom can help to combat childhood ailments, including chicken pox, measles and whooping cough.

- Cistus oil is sedative to the nervous system; it can be added to blends for chronic fatigue syndrome or fibromyalgia, anxiety and insomnia. Blend with lavender, sandalwood and vetiver for a calming effect; add the blend to a warm bath at the end of the day.

CITRONELLA

Cymbopogon nardus

Cymbopogon is a genus of some 50 species of grasses, including a number with aromatic foliage that are of considerable economic importance for their oils. These include lemongrass (*C. citratus*) and palmarosa (*C. martinii* var. *martini*). The oil is distilled from all parts of the plant. Citronella is used extensively throughout the world in soaps, candles, perfumes and flavoring.

In the United States, the most popular use for the essential oil is in insect repellents, although it is no longer used in these preparations in Canada and the European Union—but not because of safety concerns. In Canada, manufacturers did not submit enough data regarding human health risk assessments. In the EU, citronella was not registered as an insect repellent in time for the deadline imposed by the Biocide Products Directive.

Citronella has been found to be a useful component in the treatment of head lice. The perfume is clean, powerful and lemony. It blends well with bergamot, eucalyptus, geranium, lavender, neroli, peppermint, petitgrain and ylang ylang.

Cautions

- Cistus oil may cause skin sensitization if it is old or oxidized. Keep the oil in a cool, dark place, ensuring that the cap is tightly closed.

- Do not use undiluted. This oil should always be diluted in a carrier oil or lotion.

Uses

- Citronella oil is mainly used in air sprays and body rubs as an insect repellent (particularly against mosquitoes) for both humans and animals. Added to an unscented shampoo, citronella can help repel and mitigate the presence of head lice. It can be used in deodorant blends for excessive perspiration, but cautiously, as the scent is quite distinctive and overpowering.

- Citronella encourages perspiration, increases energy and quickens the function of glands, making it quite useful in bath and massage blends to treat colds, influenza and other infections.

- Citronella helps to ease depression and to stimulate and clear the mind of depressing thoughts.

CLARY SAGE

Salvia sclarea

Clary sage, with its greenish white spikes tinged with purple flowers, is a native of southern Europe. The essential oil is distilled from the flowering tops and leaves of the plant. It is a natural antidepressant and also one of the most powerful relaxants in the essential oil pharmacy. It is used in preference to other varieties of sage because its toxicity levels are much lower. Its perfume is intoxicating—sweet, floral and fixative, blending well with cedarwood, geranium, juniper, lavender and sandalwood.

   A study conducted in Greece to investigate the anticancer potential of clary sage essential oil found that two of its components were effective in inducing cell death in leukemia cancer cells. Other studies show components in clary sage oil to be effective in reducing cancer cells in breast cancer. Clary sage oil is often referred to as being estrogenic and best avoided in pregnancy; however, further research indicates that clary sage oil has not been found to have estrogen-like activity.

Uses

- Clary sage's antiseptic and sebum-regulating action is useful in the treatment of acne, boils and inflammation of the skin. It has a reputation for combating hair loss and dandruff. Use the oil in blends for care of mature, dry skin and also as a deodorant.

- Clary sage is a soothing and powerful muscle-relaxing oil that will help to ease muscular aches and pains, whooping cough and asthma attacks.

- Its tonic and hormonal properties help to regulate and encourage labor (but it should not be used until after labor has begun); tone, strengthen and relieve cramps and spasms in the uterus; ease menstrual pain and encourage and regulate menstrual flow; and ease premenstrual problems.

- Clary sage may be used in compresses and massage and bath blends to help tone the digestive system, aid digestion, expel gas from the intestines and treat colic, cramps and flatulence.

- The warming and spasm-relieving properties of clary sage can be employed in compresses and/or gentle massage when dealing with colic and stomach or intestinal cramps. Clary sage may also be used to reduce sweating.

- Its tonic and antidepressant properties are useful when people are recovering from illness and may feel weak and depressed. It strengthens the nervous system, calms, and reduces stress and high blood pressure. In small doses it can alleviate hysteria and paranoia. It is reputed to have aphrodisiac properties.

CLOVE

Syzygium aromaticum syn. *Eugenia caryophyllata*

The warming aromatic cloves you use in cooking are the unexpanded dried flower buds from a tree—a native of the Moluccas. The essential oil is distilled from the flower and has a pungent and spicy aroma. Clove essential oil is often used in toothpastes and other dental preparations and in commercial foods and drinks.

Clove oil can also be produced by distilling the leaves and the stem. While the chemical composition may be somewhat similar, there are some differences that make each type smell different. The oil used most often is produced from the flower buds.

Uses

- Clove oil is very good in blends for treating infectious sores, leg ulcers, acne, athlete's foot, bruises and burns, as well as in insect repellents.

- Cloves and their oil are well known for their power to ease toothache by numbing the nerve and causing loss of sensation. This pain-numbing property may also be used to ease mouth ulcers, neuralgia, arthritis and rheumatism.

- Clove oil's other claim to fame is the benefits it bestows on the digestive system. Used in compresses, baths, massages and mouthwashes, it tones the digestive system, relieves cramps and spasms in the intestines, helps to control vomiting and nausea, expels gas from the intestines, aids digestion and sweetens bad breath due to fermentation in the stomach.

- Clove oil has the power to increase energy and quicken the function of the glands. It is often included in chest massage blends to relieve asthma and bronchitis.

- Clove oil was investigated for its antibacterial properties and found to be effective against several strains of bacteria, including those that cause skin and urinary tract infections and respiratory infections such as sinusitis and pneumonia,

Cautions

- Never use clove oil undiluted or in a high concentration in skin preparations. One drop in 2 tsp (10 mL) carrier oil or lotion is a safe amount for skin preparations. It should not be used on damaged or sensitive skin.

- Not for use with children under the age of 2.

- It is especially important to make sure that clove essential oil is not accidentally ingested. Clove oil can cause a drug interaction when used topically with certain drugs that are metabolized by CYP2B6. These include but are not limited to opioid analgesics, anesthetics, anticonvulsants, antidepressants, chemo-therapeutic drugs, estrogen receptor antagonists, nervous system stimulants and reverse-transcriptase inhibitors.

as well as food poisoning and intestinal infections. Clove is a wonderful addition to blends used to keep your kitchen clean, including surfaces, sinks and cutting boards.

CUBEB

Piper cubeba

Cubeb, also called Java pepper, is an evergreen climbing vine similar to the black pepper plant. It produces a fruit that is dried, ground and used as a spice in Indonesian cooking. The essential oil is extracted by steam distillation from the fully grown but unripe berries. It has a warm, pungent, spicy odor that blends well with other spice oils, especially lavender, rosemary and ylang ylang. Commercial cubeb oil is often altered by mixing with other pepper oils.

Uses

- The diuretic and antiseptic properties of cubeb oil make it a good choice for treating cystitis, urethritis and leukorrhea.
- Its combined antiseptic and expectorant actions are helpful for bronchitis, congestion, coughs, mucus, sinusitis and throat infections.
- It is certainly useful for easing digestive upsets such as flatulence. Its carminative activity makes cubeb a good choice for aiding sluggish digestion and relieving indigestion.

CYPRESS

Cupressus sempervirens

The cypress tree is a familiar sight in the landscapes of Italy, France and Spain. It is long known for its medicinal properties. Cypress, one of the safest and gentlest oils, is distilled from leaves, twigs and needles. The perfume is clean and woody and blends well with juniper, lavender, pine, rosemary and sandalwood.

Uses

- Cypress oil is a tonic and a sebum balancer for oily skin. It tones tissue and causes small blood vessels to contract, which helps to reduce the appearance of broken capillaries.
- Cypress oil has a notable astringent action. Its woody, masculine aroma makes it an excellent choice for inclusion in aftershave.
- You can add it to deodorant and insect-repellent blends or use it in a mouthwash to treat pyorrhea.
- Cypress is a good wound oil, as it stops or reduces external bleeding.

- The circulation-stimulating properties of cypress oil increase energy, warm cold hands and feet, and ease muscle cramps and rheumatism.
- Used in hot compresses, baths and massage blends, it relieves painful cramps and spasms in the uterus, regulates the menstrual cycle and reduces heavy blood loss. It can be a helpful oil to treat PMS and the unpleasant symptoms of menopause.
- A cypress inhalation and chest rub will help the spasms of asthma, coughs, bronchitis and whooping cough.
- The strongly astringent and circulatory tonic properties of cypress oil will be of value wherever there is an excess of fluid or poor circulation, such as in edema, heavy sweating, hemorrhoids, vomiting or heavy periods. The astringency also helps in the treatment of pyorrhea. Cold compresses using this oil will help to soothe and reduce hemorrhoids and varicose veins.
- Cypress is very helpful with problems of the reproductive system, and in particular with menstrual and menopausal problems. It removes excess liquid from the body, thus reducing edema. By increasing the flow of urine it can ease the symptoms of cystitis and urethritis.
- Cypress reduces stress and tension and calms the nervous system. It eases the pain of loss or separation and allows us to "let go" with love. It lightens the burden of introspection.

Preventing Oxidation

Essential oils oxidize when they are not stored properly, and so should be kept in a cool, dark place with the cap securely tightened. Be sure to recap your bottles immediately after dispensing—leaving them open allows more time for the oils to react with oxygen. As you use your oils, you should decant them into smaller bottles to reduce the amount of oxygen in the bottle. Some essential oils are more reactive than others. Using oxidized essential oils on the skin can lead to skin sensitization.

EUCALYPTUS

Eucalyptus globulus

Eucalyptus is one of the most powerful natural antiseptic oils. Eucalyptus essential oil is distilled principally from the fresh leaves and twigs of *Eucalyptus globulus*, the well-loved tall and handsome Tasmanian evergreen blue gum tree. It has a clean, camphoric and cleansing perfume that blends well with lavender, pine and rosemary. Eucalyptus is a very powerful essential oil, so use it with care. If a recipe says 1 drop, then that's all you require!

E. globulus contains approximately 75% oxides, which are stimulating to body systems. It provides relief in cold and flu season, as it is antiviral, decongestant and mucolytic.

While *E. globulus* is perhaps the most popular of the eucalyptuses, do not discount the benefits of the others. A closer look at the differences in chemistry can help you to determine which eucalyptus is most suitable for the condition you hope to mitigate.

Other Varieties of Eucalyptus

The oils of several other varieties of eucalyptus are also used in aromatherapy, notably

- the lemon-scented gum *E. citriodora* (syn. *Corymbia citriodora*);
- cooling peppermint gum (*E. dives*), which is used as an expectorant;
- *E. radiata*, which has a softer aroma;
- *E. smithii*, which is gentler and more suitable for use with children; and
- lemon-scented ironbark (*E. staigeriana*), which has a more balanced chemistry and is excellent for women's problems.

Eucalyptus citriodora is approximately 80% aldehydes, which makes the oil more relaxing for the body systems, as it is calming to the nervous and respiratory systems and may lower blood pressure. In addition, the synergism of the bacteriostatic components of the essential oil of *E. citriodora* make it an excellent addition to natural cleaning products.

The chemical makeup of *Eucalyptus dives*, or broad-leaf peppermint, is different from the others. Containing mostly ketones and monoterpenes, *E. dives* has a camphoraceous and minty aroma suitable for calming the respiratory system. It lends itself to sport blends and those used to treat arthritis, rheumatism, muscular aches and pains, and sprains.

Eucalyptus radiata contains less 1,8-cineole and is considered gentler than the well-known blue gum, *E. globulus*. *E. radiata* is similarly warming and aids respiratory ailments, but is less harsh. *E. smithii*, which contains a high level of 1,8-cineole, was previously thought to be more suitable for use with children. This belief was based on empirical evidence and the idea that some sort of antagonism occurs naturally in the whole oil making it gentler than *E. globulus*, however there is no research to support this.

Eucalyptus staigeriana has a pleasant lighter, somewhat faint lemony scent. Possessing a more varied composition of the various chemical families, *E. staigeriana* is a well-balanced oil. It is a gentle decongestant, calming to digestive complaints and stress in general. It also stimulates the immune system. It is a gentle oil for use with the elderly and young children.

Cautions

- Do not use *E. globulus*, *E. radiata* or *E. smithii* on or near the face of infants or children under the age of 10.

- People with dermatitis are advised to use no more than 1 drop of *E. globulus*, *E. radiata* or *E. smithii* per 1 tsp (5 mL) carrier oil or lotion for topical applications such as massage or body lotions, because of its 1,8-cineole content. Consider using *E. staigeriana*, *E. dives* or *E. citriodora* instead.

Tip: A few drops of eucalyptus on a tissue placed on the bedside table will help to clear a stuffy nose and allow you to sleep.

Uses

- *E. globulus* oil is used in the treatment of burns, blisters, cuts, herpes outbreaks, wounds and sores because it prevents bacterial growth, inhibits the growth of viruses in damaged tissue, and eases pain by numbing nerves. It is one of the best oils to use in blends to kill head lice and ease insect bites. It also acts as an insect repellent. It is used in low concentrations in creams for cold sores and for genital herpes.

- Added to baths and massage oils or creams, *E. globulus* oil will ease the pains of sore muscles, body aches, rheumatism and rheumatoid arthritis.

- Eucalyptus has long been respected for its ability to lower temperature and help the respiratory tract by loosening and removing mucus during attacks of bronchitis, coughs, influenza, sinusitis and throat infections. *E. radiata* is said to be a powerful expectorant, especially when blended with *E. smithii*.

- Added to a footbath, it is a prime remedy during feverish attacks.

- Use in inhalations and air sprays during outbreaks of disease such as those mentioned above, chicken pox or measles. Its antiviral and antibacterial action will deter further growth of the bacteria or viruses. At the same time it will also give some protection to other members of the family. Used in an air spray, its antibacterial and antiviral properties will help to prevent the spread of epidemics and diseases. A researcher has found that as little as 2% eucalyptus oil in a room spray can kill as much as 70% of *Staphylococcus* bacteria in the air.

- A hot compress containing eucalyptus will increase the flow of urine; combined with its other properties, this will help to ease cystitis and urethritis.

- Another useful and interesting property of eucalyptus oil is that it removes many stains and grease marks from clothes. Be sure to wash well with hot water and air dry (see Caution, page 189).

- Eucalyptus is definitely a brain cleanser, crystallizing the mind like a breath of fresh air and aiding concentration.

Cautions

- Do not store near homeopathic remedies or use in conjunction with them—it might act as an antidote.

- We do not recommend the ingestion of essential oils for home use. This is especially important in the case of *E. staigeriana* essential oil. Even when used topically, negative interactions have been known to occur with certain opioid analgesics, anesthetics, anticonvulsants, antidepressants, chemo-therapeutic drugs, estrogen receptor antagonists, nervous system stimulants and reverse-transcriptase inhibitors.

FENNEL

Foeniculum vulgare

Graceful perennial fennel is a popular culinary herb: the seeds are used in curries and spicy dishes and the leaves are delicious with fish and seafood. It has well-established healing properties—it is said that Charlemagne decreed fennel essential in every imperial garden! Sweet fennel (*Foeniculum vulgare* var. *dulce*) is the variety used in aromatherapy, as it is less sensitizing. The seeds are crushed and distilled to produce an essential oil that has a perfume similar to anise seed; it blends well with frankincense, geranium, lavender, rose and rosemary. Florence fennel (*F. azoricum*) is closely related but is used only as a vegetable.

Uses

- Fennel is a cleansing tonic for oily skin. It has a reputation for retarding the appearance of wrinkles (perhaps because of its estrogen-like properties).
- Fennel is best known for its tonic, antispasmodic and cleansing actions on the digestive system. It acts as a liver cleanser and eases digestive problems from indigestion to constipation, cramps and spasms, colic, nausea, flatulence and hiccups.
- Fennel is an effective antioxidant and scavenger of damaged cells that lead to disease. It is the most important oil in the treatment of alcoholism. It increases energy and quickens the function of glands, having a tonic action on the liver, kidneys, spleen and digestive system, and it is also helpful for clearing out poisonous toxins. However, it should not be used by those with peptic ulcers.
- Fennel works well on the reproductive system, where its estrogen-like and antispasmodic properties are helpful for relieving symptoms such as cramps and spasms in the uterus, scanty and irregular menstrual flow, PMS and water retention. It stimulates the adrenal glands to produce estrogen after the ovaries have stopped working, and in doing so helps to correct menopausal irregularities due to fluctuating hormones. Its hormone activity also increases the production of milk in nursing mothers.
- Fennel cheers and consoles and bestows the courage to make changes.

Caution

We do not recommend the ingestion of essential oils for home use. This is especially important in the case of fennel essential oil. Negative interactions have been known to occur in individuals taking certain medications. Fennel essential oil may interact with diabetes and anticoagulant medications and may create problems with conditions such as recovery from major surgery, peptic ulcer, hemophilia or other bleeding disorders.

Cautions

- Fennel oil may cause skin sensitization if it is old or oxidized. Keep the oil in a cool, dark place, ensuring that the cap is tightly closed.

- Do not use undiluted. This oil should always be diluted in a carrier oil or lotion.

- Avoid use if pregnant or breastfeeding or in cases of estrogen-dependent cancer, endometriosis or a blood-clotting disorder.

- Avoid fennel if you suffer from epilepsy. Do not use it in blends for children under 5 years old.

Fennel was one of the nine sacred herbs of the Anglo-Saxons of Britain. It was used in purification ceremonies.

FIR, DOUGLAS

Pseudotsuga menziesii

Also known as Oregon pine or hemlock spruce, the Douglas fir is native to western North America and can also be found in northern Europe. The name is misleading: it is a member of the pine family, not a true fir. The trees usually grow 200 to 250 feet (60 to 75 m) tall, although some have reached almost 400 feet (120 m).

The oil is obtained by distillation of the needles and twigs. Pale yellow in color, it has a slightly sweet, pine-like aroma with other floral notes mixed in. Imagine walking into a florist's shop at Christmas and inhaling the collective aroma of the pine boughs on display along with all the flowers—that's Douglas fir. It blends well with other oils in the pine family, such as cedarwood, bergamot and lime.

Traditionally Douglas fir is used to treat diarrhea, cystitis and colitis and for skincare. Its chemical composition suggests that it is antioxidant, anti-inflammatory and antispasmodic and may prevent bone loss. Research indicates that the oil has antimicrobial activity. It is cleansing and refreshing for the mind and balancing for the body.

Uses

- A natural deodorizer, Douglas fir oil in a room spray or diffuser can help to neutralize unpleasant odors. It says "Happy Holidays" to your houseguests.

- Blended with essential oils of manuka, cypress and lemon and used during the cold and flu season, Douglas fir oil is antiviral, helps to fight infection, and aids in reducing and expelling mucus.

- Its pleasant and refreshing aroma will lift your spirits.

FIR, SILVER

Abies alba

Silver fir, often associated with Christmas, is a coniferous tree with flat dark green needles and white bark. The essential oil is distilled from the needles and twigs and has a warming balsamic aroma with a slight fresh green scent. It is often used in perfumes, bath products and deodorizing air sprays.

A valued essential oil in eastern Europe, silver fir is used to treat respiratory issues, fever and muscular aches and pains. It is moderately antibacterial and its antiseptic activity can help fight sinus and respiratory tract infections. Its aroma is uplifting to those with the winter blues. Silver fir oil blends well with other pine oils, lavender, sandalwood and sweet orange.

Cautions

- Douglas fir oil may cause skin sensitization if it is old or oxidized. Keep the oil in a cool, dark place, ensuring that the cap is tightly closed.

- Do not use undiluted. This oil should always be diluted in a carrier oil or lotion.

Cautions

- Silver fir oil may cause skin sensitization if it is old or oxidized. Keep the oil in a cool, dark place, ensuring that the cap is tightly closed.

- Do not use undiluted. This oil should always be diluted in a carrier oil or lotion.

Uses

- Add silver fir oil to blends for colds, to help reduce inflammation of the bronchial passages and mucus (lung congestion) in chesty coughs.
- Adding 4 to 5 drops to a diffuser can lift the spirits of those who are withdrawn and suffering from seasonal affective disorder (SAD).

FRAGONIA™

Taxandria fragrans syn. *Agonis fragrans*

By comparison with other oils that have many years of documented use, *Taxandria fragrans* is a relatively new oil that is steam-distilled from a plant first described botanically in 2001, under the name *Agonis fragrans*. Based on its chemical properties, a specific cultivar of this plant is considered by some experts to produce a perfectly balanced essential oil. This particular oil can be found under the trademarked name "Fragonia."

Taxandria fragrans, the cultivar from which this oil is produced, grows to almost 8 feet (2.4 m) high, with solid foliage and large clusters of light pink and white flowers. Fragonia has a clean, fresh aroma that resembles the somewhat medicinal-smelling tea tree oil but with a mild fruitiness layered throughout.

Because this is a newer essential oil, little published research is available. However, there is a growing number of reports regarding its clinical use. In one study, the antimicrobial and anti-inflammatory properties of *Taxandria fragrans* were found to be comparable to tea tree oil. Aromatherapy practitioners report that the oil has a positive effect on regulating mental and emotional states, including anger, depression, anxiety, stress and sleeplessness, and there are reports of individuals having more vivid dreams.

On the physical side, Fragonia has been found to stimulate the immune system and balance hormones. It is also antifungal, pain relieving and useful in reducing respiratory congestion.

Uses

- Add Fragonia to massage oil blends to ease muscle stiffness, soreness and cramping. The oil will also soothe pain and inflammation from sprains and joint problems.
- Blend 1 drop into 1 tsp (5 mL) honey and add to tea to soothe a sore throat or use in a throat gargle recipe.
- Inhalation of Fragonia oil has reportedly shown the ability to help open blocked emotions and release deeply rooted grief and psychological trauma. Blend with sandalwood, mandarin, geranium and vetiver for a soothing bedtime blend, or add to a personal spray to scent your meditation or yoga space.

Cautions

- Fragonia oil may cause skin sensitization if it is old or oxidized. Keep in a cool, dark place, ensuring that the cap is tightly closed.
- Do not use undiluted. This oil should always be diluted in a carrier oil or lotion.

FRANKINCENSE

Boswellia carteri syn. *B. sacra*

This ancient and spiritual essential oil comes from a small tree native to North Africa, but its cultivation is widespread. Frankincense, also called olibanum, is tapped from *Boswellia* trees, which grow on lands around the Red Sea and the Arabian Sea and are also found in the Horn of Africa, on the coasts of Yemen and the emirates. The tapped trees exude a white sap, which is allowed to harden into "tears." The tears are then dried and powdered to be used in incense or distilled to produce the essential oil.

In ancient times wine was fortified with frankincense resin to aid digestion. It has a perfume that is spicy, woody and sweet and blends well with basil, citrus, cypress, lavender, patchouli, pine and sandalwood. The essential oil is used in perfumery, for soap making and in cosmetics as a fixative (see page 38) and fragrance.

Uses

- Frankincense oil helps to destroy infection-causing bacteria. It is a good cleanser for boils, wounds and ulcers.

- Frankincense oil contracts and tones tissue. A gentle "balancer" for oily skin, it helps to regenerate aging skin, keeps wrinkles at bay and may smooth out some existing ones!

- This oil is particularly valuable for congestive lung problems, as it helps to loosen and remove mucus from the lungs and is a pulmonary antiseptic. Used in a chest massage, it slows down the breathing, which is helpful during attacks of asthma. Also use as an inhalation or massage oil to ease coughs, chronic bronchitis, laryngitis and shortness of breath.

- Frankincense tones and strengthens the uterus, particularly during labor. It regulates heavy menstrual flow, helps to expel gas from the intestines and generally aids digestion.

- Its diuretic and antiseptic properties help with urinary tract and genital infections such as cystitis, urethritis and leukorrhea.

- Frankincense subdues those who gush nervously, reduces stress and calms the nervous system. While we should cherish the past, we need to live in the present, and this ancient and spiritual oil enables us to "be here now."

Cautions

- Frankincense oil may cause skin sensitization if it is old or oxidized. Keep the oil in a cool, dark place, ensuring that the cap is tightly closed.

- Do not use undiluted. This oil should always be diluted in a carrier oil or lotion.

GALBANUM

Ferula galbaniflua communis

Galbanum is a shrub native to the Mediterranean region that produces a gum or oleoresin from which the essential oil is distilled. Galbanum—sometimes called "giant fennel" but no relation to the culinary herb—has been used since ancient times in incense and holy oil. In Egypt it was an important ingredient in the embalming process, as it has powerful preservative properties. The perfume is smoky and woody and blends well with floral and tree essential oils.

Uses

- Its wound-healing, anti-inflammatory and antiseptic properties make galbanum oil useful for treating skin problems such as abscesses, acne, boils, inflammations and wounds. Added to other blends, it may help to tone mature skin.

- Galbanum is often used as a tonic for the respiratory system, where it will loosen and remove excessive mucus, ease asthma and calm bronchial spasm and chronic coughs.

- Its analgesic and anti-inflammatory actions make galbanum suitable for use in lotions and massage blends to aid muscular aches and pains.

- Massaged onto the abdomen, it can provide relief for indigestion, flatulence and stomach cramps.

GERANIUM

Pelargonium x *asperum* syn. *P. graveolens, P. capitatum, P. odoratissimum*

There is a lot of confusion over the types of geranium used to produce essential oils. With more than 250 species of geranium, it's no wonder. Geraniums are grown all over the world, including but not limited to Egypt, Morocco, China, the Middle East, Madagascar, Ukraine and South Africa. Once called "rose geranium," the variety known as "Bourbon" from Réunion Island was often found on essential oil distributors' lists, but production is now limited. Oftentimes when you see "rose geranium" now, it is actually an essential oil that has been co-distilled from rose petals and geranium leaves to produce a gorgeous rose-scented geranium essential oil.

The name used most often on commercial geranium essential oil is *Pelargonium graveolens*; however, that is unlikely to be the true botanical source. Botanists have identified *Pelargonium* x

Cautions

- Galbanum oil may cause skin sensitization if it is old or oxidized. Keep the oil in a cool, dark place, ensuring that the cap is tightly closed.

- Do not use undiluted. This oil should always be diluted in a carrier oil or lotion.

asperum as a cross between two other rose geranium species, *P. capitatum* and *P. radens*. Yet another geranium oil can be found, albeit rare, named *Pelargonium odoratissimum*, which is from the apple geranium.

Regardless of which oil is in your bottle, geranium essential oil, with its heady, languorous and relaxing aroma, is much used in the perfume industry. It blends well with most other oils and harmonizes and balances other scents.

Uses

- Historically, geranium was considered a powerful wound cure, as it encourages speedy healing, can help to stop bleeding and is an antiseptic, which makes it a valuable oil to use for wounds and cuts.

- Geranium can also be used to treat acne, bruises, minor burns and scalds, dermatitis, eczema, ulcers and hemorrhoids. Head lice and ringworm also respond to this oil. It is a good essential oil for all skin types, as it balances the production of sebum (the oily secretion from the sebaceous glands that helps to keep skin supple) and stimulates both dry and oily sluggish skin.

- Geranium eases pain by numbing nerves, so use it in gargles and mouthwashes for sore throat, tonsillitis and mouth infections and inflammation (remember to spit out the gargle). However, it has been reported to cause contact dermatitis and inflammation of the lips in some sensitive individuals.

- It exerts a tonic and diuretic action on the urinary system and the liver, which helps to rid the body of toxins.

- Studies indicate that geranium essential oil is an effective insecticide against dust mites and a fumigant against some species of termites and beetles. In a 2 oz (60 mL) spray bottle, combine 18 drops geranium essential oil and 1 tsp (5 mL) vegetable glycerin; shake to blend. Fill the remainder of the bottle with water, seal and shake to combine well. Spray carpets and bed linens to deter dust mites. (*Eucalyptus globulus* is also effective against dust mites.)

- Sometimes geranium is called the "woman's oil" because of its regulatory action on the hormones secreted by the adrenal cortex. This property makes geranium an appropriate and valuable remedy for problems caused by fluctuating hormone balance. These include engorged breasts, menopausal problems and PMS. While there is no research to support this use, extensive anecdotal data suggests that the assertion has validity.

- Geranium is the gentle bringer of grace and harmony, and its uplifting and calming perfume is particularly useful for women. It also helps to ease depression and nervous tension for those moving through menopause.

Cautions

- Geranium oil may cause irritation to sensitive skin.

- It is especially important to make sure that geranium essential oil is not accidentally ingested, especially when taking certain medications. Negative interactions have been known to occur.

The healing power of ginger was mentioned by Confucius around 500 BCE.

GINGER

Zingiber officinale

Gingerroot (fresh or dried and powdered) has been used in cooking and medicine since ancient times. It is also used as a herbal remedy for queasy stomach and loss of appetite (it stimulates salivation). In southern Asia, where it originated, its aroma was once thought to guard against marauding tigers! The essential oil is distilled from the rhizome and produces a perfume that is rich and spicy, blending well with lavender, lemon, orange and petitgrain.

Ginger is still being studied for its benefits to cancer patients. According to the American Cancer Society, many studies have been conducted on the efficacy of ginger for postoperative nausea, but the results vary depending on whether or not it is taken before or immediately after surgery. Studies did find that ginger essential oil was cytotoxic (toxic to cells) in prostate and lung cancers, but not in breast cancer.

Uses

- According to the "doctrine of signatures," an ancient theory that linked the shapes of various herbs with their efficacy for treating specific parts of the body, ginger's shape shows an affinity with the digestive system. Ginger indeed tones the digestive system and stimulates production of gastric juices. It increases appetite, aids digestion and relieves cramps and spasms in the intestines and uterus. It will help ease diarrhea, colic and flatulence. It calms morning sickness and is an excellent remedy for travel sickness when taken in powder or capsule form an hour before setting off, followed by sniffing the oil every half-hour during the journey.

- The pain-relieving and warming properties of ginger make it a good choice for blends to treat arthritis, rheumatism, muscular aches and pains, poor circulation, sprains and strains. It should be used in concentrations of no more than 1% to 1.5% in warm compresses and massage oils.

- Catarrh (excess mucus), colds, coughs, fever, influenza, sinusitis and sore throat are all helped by ginger essential oil. It reduces fever by increasing sweating.

- This oil is very sexually arousing, builds physical courage and confidence in one's capabilities to survive, and creates a store of vibrant energy that dispels nervous exhaustion.

GRAPEFRUIT

Citrus x paradisi

Grapefruit—the whole fruit or the juice—plays a vital part in a healthy diet. It is high in vitamin C and is a popular breakfast item. The best essential oil is expressed from the peel of fresh ripe grapefruit, while the distilled oil is inferior. The perfume of the expressed oil is a fresh, sweet citrus aroma that instills feelings of happiness. It blends well with basil, bergamot, cedarwood, chamomile, frankincense, geranium, palmarosa, rosewood and ylang ylang.

Unlike some other citrus oils (bergamot, lemon, lime, bitter orange and sweet orange, if expressed from the peel), grapefruit presents a low risk of phototoxicity; it may be substituted for them up to 4% in skincare preparations if the skin is to be exposed to sunlight. However, because grapefruit oil oxidizes quickly, it should be bought in very small amounts and used within a short time.

A study found that grapefruit essential oil shows promise against hospital-acquired infections and antibiotic-resistant bacteria. This suggests that essential oil of grapefruit is an effective topical antiseptic treatment option, even for antibiotic-resistant strains such as MRSA and antimycotic-resistant *Candida* species.

Uses

- Grapefruit oil contracts and tones tissue and is a useful oil in blends for oily skin and acne.
- It is said to disperse lactic acid in hard-worked muscles, thus easing stiffness, soreness and fatigue. It is also an excellent oil for a bath or shower blend to relieve travel fatigue and jet lag.
- Grapefruit balances and tones the digestive system and has a cleansing effect on the kidneys, liver and gallbladder and the lymphatic system, which in turn helps to rid the body of excess toxins.
- This is essentially a happy oil that lifts lethargy and depression, eases nervous exhaustion and improves memory.

Avoiding Grapefruit

Grapefruit juice is to be avoided by those taking certain medications, as the juice contains dihydroxybergamottin, a chemical that interferes with many medications. Dihydroxybergamottin is not contained in the expressed essential oil, so it is safe to use in aromatherapy for individuals who would need to avoid grapefruit juice.

Cautions

- Grapefruit oil may cause skin sensitization if it is old or oxidized. Keep the oil in a cool, dark place, ensuring that the cap is tightly closed.
- Do not use undiluted. This oil should always be diluted in a carrier oil or lotion.

HELICHRYSUM

Helichrysum italicum syn. *H. angustifolium*

Helichrysum has strongly aromatic daisy-like flowers that become dry as the plant matures but retain their color and perfume. The oil is extracted by steam distillation from the fresh flowers before they dry.

There are many varieties of helichrysum, each with very different therapeutic properties, but only one—a perennial herb from the Mediterranean (*H. italicum*)—is used for making the essential oil. It has a honey-sweet perfume that blends well with chamomile, citrus oils, clary sage, clove, frankincense, geranium and lavender. Therapeutically, helichrysum is best used synergistically with other essential oils having the same properties. The distillate water, or hydrolat, that remains after distillation is called "immortelle" and possesses antioxidant and anti-inflammatory properties (see Hydrolats, page 118).

Another helichrysum worth mentioning is *H. gymnocephalum*. Grown primarily in Madagascar, this variety is sweet and herbaceous yet camphoraceous; it has a eucalyptus-like aroma and is useful in treating respiratory conditions as an effective decongestant. It is also helpful for treating infections and relieving rheumatic pain. It is traditionally used as an ingredient in toothpaste and deodorant, because of its antibacterial benefits, and in the treatment of mouth sores and gingivitis. However, care should be taken with *H. gymnocephalum*, as its chemical composition makes it susceptible to oxidation, which could lead to sensitization if used on the skin.

Uses

- Helichrysum oil has antiallergenic, anti-inflammatory and antiseptic properties, all of which make it ideal to use in blends to treat conditions such as acne, allergic reactions such as hives, dermatitis, eczema, inflammations, psoriasis and wounds. It promotes cell growth, making it valuable in skincare preparations.

- Blended with lavender and mandarin, helichrysum makes a lovely safe, sweetly perfumed oil that can be used on babies and children to help treat asthma, bronchitis and coughs and to ease the distressing "whoop" of whooping cough.

- Helichrysum boosts the immune system, helping the body to fight infections and allergies. It can be used to prevent or treat colds, influenza or any problem that is caused by a compromised immune system.

- Use in baths and massage oils for rheumatism, muscular aches and pains, sprains and strains.

- Helichrysum brings a ray of hope to those who feel that life is not worth living. Its antidepressant properties are helpful for those experiencing shock, phobias, lethargy or stress.

HYSSOP

Hyssopus officinalis

Hyssop is a bushy perennial aromatic and culinary herb with slightly bitter leaves that are sometimes added to salads or to legumes or meats during cooking. The essential oil is used to flavor the liqueurs Benedictine and Grande Charteuse. The essential oil is distilled from the leaves and flowers, which are also very popular with butterflies and bees. The perfume is warm, herbaceous and penetrating, and difficult to describe—a combination of camphor and spice. It blends well with citrus, geranium, lavender, rosemary and sage.

Hyssop is a questionable oil to use because the pinocamphone chemotype also contains thujone, which makes it fairly neurotoxic. It should definitely be avoided if pregnant or breastfeeding and not used on children under the age of 2. In blends it is safe to use 1 drop per 4 tsp (20 mL) carrier oil or lotion. Note that *Hyssopus officinalis* ct. pinocamphone may cause convulsions if not used with care; it should be avoided by those with epilepsy and high blood pressure. However, the chemotype *H. officinalis* ct. linolool (*H. officinalis* ct. decumbens) is a safe and gentle alternative with no known contraindications.

Uses

- Hyssop contracts and tones tissue and is quite useful for bruises, cuts, eczema and wound healing.

- Hyssop has a normalizing effect on the circulation, helping to raise low blood pressure.

- Hyssop strengthens bodily systems, tones the digestive system and aids digestion; it helps to expel gas from the intestines and eases mild constipation and gastroenteritis.

- It is a well-known expectorant—Hippocrates prescribed it for bronchitis and pleurisy. It cools and reduces fever by increasing perspiration and helps to thin, loosen and remove mucus. Hyssop may be of use for asthma, bronchitis, coughs, emphysema, catarrh, sore throat and tonsillitis. When hyssop oil is blended with *Eucalyptus globulus*, *Ravensara aromatica* and niaouli essential oils, it makes an effective blend for respiratory complaints.

- It is beneficial for menstrual problems such as cramps and spasms in the uterus, encourages and regulates menstrual flow, and increases the flow of urine.

- Overall, hyssop essential oil gives quickness and clarity to the mind, strengthens the nervous system, reduces stress and brings relaxation.

Cautions

All cautions are for *Hyssopus officinalis* ct. pinocamphone. The linalool chemotype (*H. officinalis* ct. decumbens) has no restrictions.

- Toxic in large doses.

- Avoid if pregnant or breastfeeding.

- Avoid if you suffer from epilepsy.

- Avoid if you suffer from high blood pressure.

- Do not use on children under 2 years of age.

- Use only in conjunction with other oils, and not in excess of 0.25% total essential oil content.

Cautions

- Jasmine oil may cause skin sensitization in some individuals. Long-term use is not recommended.
- Avoid use if pregnant or breastfeeding.
- Overuse can cause headaches or nausea.
- Unsuitable for children under the age of 3.
- The absolute must never be ingested.

JASMINE

Jasminum officinale var. *grandiflorum* syn. *J. grandiflorum*

For most people, jasmine is absolutely synonymous with a sweet and heady fragrance. The plant's essential oil, sometimes called "the king of the oils," is one of the most expensive, as its extraction is a lengthy business involving several different processes. Only the flowers are used for extracting the essential oil, and they have to be picked at night, when the perfume is most intense! It takes approximately 2,000 lbs (907 kg) of jasmine flowers to produce just 1 lb (500 g) essential oil. For this reason, jasmine is considered a "luxury" essential oil; it is often sold pre-diluted at 3% to 5% in jojoba oil to achieve a reasonable price. (Substituting ylang ylang will give almost the same effect in recipes and blends.) Jasmine's exotic, sensual and relaxing perfume blends well with most other oils, especially citrus oils and rose. It is one of the most important oils in high-quality perfumery.

Working with Absolutes

Jasmine is available as an essential oil or as an "absolute." The absolute is unlike the essential oil in that it is a thick and sticky substance used primarily in perfumery (see Absolute vs. Essential Oil, page 67). However, the absolute is easier to find and typically costs less. To use the absolute you need to warm it gently to make it pourable. Place the opened bottle (to allow for expansion when warmed) in a shallow bowl of warm water for 15 to 20 minutes (longer if necessary), replacing the water as needed until the absolute becomes the desired consistency (take care not to get any water in the bottle). Start with just 1 drop added to your blend, as sometimes that is all you really need—absolutes have a very strong scent. If making a lotion, once you have made your blend, you can add a little vodka (just ¼ teaspoon/1 mL or so) to dilute the absolute further before adding to your lotion.

Uses

- Jasmine softens and smooths dry, irritated skin and balances the production of sebum, thus making it useful for most skin types. It is said to encourage a glorious head of hair when used in shampoos and hair tonics.

- Jasmine strengthens and tones the uterus, particularly after childbirth, and relieves cramps and muscular spasms of the uterus during painful periods.

- Jasmine can be used to great effect when the heart is beating rapidly and breathlessness is caused by shock or anxiety. It will also help to reduce high blood pressure.

- This beautiful, uplifting and transforming oil will raise and lighten the listless spirit. The scent of jasmine is best known for its ability to stimulate our responses and to create and increase sexual desire. It is one of the most important oils for helping to ease depression.

Absolute vs. Essential Oil

The flowers of jasmine and rose are very delicate and cannot withstand the heat of the steam-distillation process used to extract essential oils. As a result, they are either hydro-distilled or made into an absolute. The process of making an absolute begins with making what is called a "concrete." The process depends on the plant material used; in some cases it is left to dry, spread in a thin layer and "washed over" with a hydrocarbon solvent such as benzene or hexane. When the solvent evaporates, the remaining waxy, aromatic residue is the concrete. Concretes can also be obtained through a process called "enfleurage," in which the plant material is layered with tallow or another fat. The plant material is replaced continually until the fat becomes saturated with the aromatic oils; it is then used to make another type of concrete, called a "pomade."

In either case, the concrete or pomade is then warmed with an alcohol (usually ethanol), which extracts the volatile aromatic molecules from the wax or fat. The liquid is then filtered to remove any remaining plant material and the alcohol evaporates, leaving behind a sticky substance called an absolute. In enfleurage the remaining fat is strained and may be used to make fragrant soaps. Many aromatherapists prefer not to use absolutes in aromatherapy treatment because they contain traces of the solvents used in the process. However, in perfumery the absolutes are preferred, as the aromas are stronger and fresher smelling, more like the plant material.

Caution

It is especially important to make sure that jasmine sambac absolute is not accidentally ingested. Negative interactions have been known to occur in individuals taking certain medications, including acetyl-cholinesterase inhibitors, adrenalin β-receptor antagonists, opioid and non-opioid analgesics, antiarrhythmic drugs, anti-depressants, antipsychotics, dopamine receptor antagonists, estrogen receptor antagonists, histamine H1–receptor antagonists, nervous system stimulants, seratonin 5-HT3–receptor anagonists and SSRIs.

Other Varieties of Jasmine

Another species of jasmine frequently found on the market is jasmine sambac, from India. This essential oil has a different chemical composition from *Jasminum grandiflorum*, and the absolute is safe to use in skin products (up to 4% in lotion or carrier oil). Avoid during breastfeeding, as research has found that jasmine sambac supresses lactation.

JUNIPER

Juniperus communis

Users of this oil should be aware that its powerful detoxifying action may produce a "healing crisis"—the condition may appear to worsen before it begins to improve. Juniper was once considered an oil not to be used during pregnancy and by those with kidney disease; however, further investigation discovered these concerns to be unfounded. The best essential oil is steam-distilled from the ripe berries. The oil can also be distilled from the needles and twigs, but that is thought to produce an inferior oil.

The aroma is sharp and stimulating and blends well with citrus oils, cypress, lavender and pine. Its perfume and properties make it ideal to use in air sprays and oil burners to purify the air in sickrooms. The berries, which take a couple of years to ripen, are also used to flavor liquors such as gin.

Uses

- Juniper oil's detoxifying action is indicated for treating the possible causes of acne, dermatitis, psoriasis and eczema. Juniper is one of the most useful oils for clearing oily skin and scalp. It can be added to gel or oil (no more than 1%) for external application to hemorrhoids. It is also useful to include in personal insect-repellent blends for humans as well as dogs, where it may be used to deter ticks and fleas.

- Probably the best-known health fact about juniper is its ability to increase the flow of urine in fluid retention, enlarged prostate gland (after medical opinion has been sought) and kidney stones. It also acts as an antiseptic for relieving cystitis and urethritis.

Caution

Some research reports indicate that juniper is highly toxic. However, they do not name *Juniperus communis* specifically and are likely referring to another variety, known as savin (*Juniperus sabina*), which is toxic. While other juniper oils exist, they are not normally available to the general consumer. For everyday aromatherapy, use *Juniperus communis* that is distilled from the berries.

- Juniper is a very useful tonic for the digestive system and liver. It is a powerful detoxifier that is useful for such conditions as food poisoning, excessive consumption of rich food or alcohol, gout and rheumatism. These actions, combined with its ability to increase perspiration and reduce temperature, make it suitable for feverish conditions such as colds, influenza and infectious diseases. Blend with rosemary for a deodorizing room spray or vaporizer blend for sickrooms.

- Juniper increases energy and quickens the function of the lymphatic system; it can be beneficial for those recovering from severe or prolonged illness.

- Juniper produces localized redness and warmth when applied to the skin, which eases muscular pain. It also works well on the reproductive system, where it relieves cramps and spasms in the uterus and encourages and regulates menstrual flow.

- This vital oil will dispel the anxiety, nervous tension and stress created by too much "busy-ness." It creates a calm, clear flow to the brain and psyche and strengthens the nervous system. It is reputed to increase sexual desire.

Juniper and Toxicity

There are many different species of juniper; some are toxic and some are not. Some oils are distilled from the needles and some from the berries. Most common on the market is *Juniperus communis* (common juniper), which is distilled from the berries or the needles. The oil from the needles smells more wood-like, with camphor notes; the berry is a little fruitier in aroma. In the world of essential oil research, sometimes a non-aromatherapist or non-botanist will conduct a study and publish findings that discuss "juniper" essential oil without providing a Latin name to clarify, so the type of juniper used isn't known, nor whether it was oil from the twigs/needles or the berries. The research that does distinguish the oils by name shows that common juniper (*Juniperus communis*) is not toxic, whereas *Juniperus sabina* (also known as savin juniper) is highly toxic. It is generally understood that when the Latin name is not given and the research indicates high levels of toxins, the information refers to savin, which should not be used in aromatherapy.

Cautions

- Juniper oil may cause skin sensitization if it is old or oxidized. Keep the oil in a cool, dark place, ensuring that the cap is tightly closed.

- Do not use undiluted. This oil should always be diluted in a carrier oil or lotion.

Until fairly recently, sprigs of juniper and rosemary were burned in hospital wards in France to prevent the spread of infection.

KANUKA

Kunzea ericoides

Also known as white tea tree, kanuka is indigenous to New Zealand but is also grown in Australia. It is a relatively new essential oil and most of the data on it is empirical. The chemical composition can vary greatly, depending on where the plant was grown and how old the tree was when the branches and leaves were harvested for distillation of the essential oil. When purchasing the oil, however, you will find that specific chemotypes (see page 29) are not given on the label.

Current evaluations of the chemical composition of the oil suggest that it is beneficial for colds and flu; however, there is little documentation with regard to clinical use. Traditionally the leaves (which contain the essential oil) are used in vapor baths for colds and flu and to reduce fever; it is thought to ease coughs, especially in cases of bronchitis. As an antimicrobial, it is effective for urinary and intestinal complaints, and it has a moderate action against ringworm. It is used in mouthwashes and gargles for gum disease.

Uses

- Because of its strong anti-inflammatory effects, kanuka would be an effective essential oil to use for chronic inflammatory conditions such as rheumatoid arthritis and fibromyalgia.

- Kanuka oil is an effective analgesic; combined with its anti-inflammatory benefit, this may make it useful for sore muscles and strains after a workout.

- Kanuka can relieve the pain from scalds and burns, as well as ease back pain.

- Kanuka can provide relief for intestinal complaints such as irritable bowel syndrome, bloating, constipation and diarrhea.

- The oil is high in alpha-pinenes, which research suggests may inhibit bone loss, making it a preventative for osteoporosis.

Cautions

- Kanuka oil may cause skin sensitization if it is old or oxidized. Keep the oil in a cool, dark place, ensuring that the cap is tightly closed.

- Do not use undiluted. This oil should always be diluted in a carrier oil or lotion.

LAVANDIN

Lavandula x *intermedia* syn. *L. hybrida*

Lavandin is often mistaken for lavender, but they are different plants. Lavandin is actually a hybrid of true lavender (*Lavandula angustifolia*) and spike lavender (*Lavandula latifolia*). When you see splendid images of "lavender fields" with impeccable rows of perfectly rounded vivid purple plants, often those plants are lavandin (true lavender is less perfectly shaped, and the flowers are purplish gray).

There are many cultivars of lavandin, among them 'Abrialis', 'Grosso' and 'Super'. Each one is similar yet different: they possess most of the same chemicals but in different concentrations. The name of the cultivar should be indicated on the bottle, in single quotation marks, for example, *Lavandula* x *intermedia* 'Super'. All lavandins have a floral aroma; however, lavandin 'Grosso' is more camphoraceous, while lavandin 'Abrialis' has a touch of spice. 'Super' is the sweetest and has a hint of fruitiness in its aroma.

Lavandin can be used in much the same way as lavender (see below). It blends well with pine-scented oils such as rosemary, and clary sage and patchouli.

Uses

- Lavandin is anti-catarrhal, antiviral and an expectorant, making it effective in conditions such as asthma, bronchitis, throat infections and bad breath.
- As an antifungal it can be used in blends to treat candida and athlete's foot.
- Use lavandin in circulatory blends and for muscular pains, backache, sprains and rheumatism.
- A hospital study investigated the use of lavandin essential oil as a means to reduce anxiety in patients prior to surgery. They found it to be an effective low-cost and low-risk alternative to anxiety medication to reduce preoperative stress.

LAVENDER

Lavandula angustifolia syns. *L. officinalis, L. vera*

Lavandula latifolia syn. *L. spica* (spike lavender);
Lavandula stoechas (Spanish lavender)

Lavender has been appreciated for thousands of years and today must be the most loved—and used—essential oil. It is probably the oil with the widest and most impressive list of applications. If you can afford only one oil, choose lavender; it is very safe, versatile and gentle. It may even be used undiluted over small areas. Everyday common lavender is sold under different names—*Lavandula angustifolia, L. officinalis, L. vera* ("true lavender")—but they are all the same oil.

The essential oil is steam-distilled from the plant's flowering tops and aromatic leaves. Lavender essential oil, with its balancing qualities, is primarily thought of as calming and relaxing, but it is also anti-inflammatory, antibacterial, antispasmodic, stimulating to the immune system and somewhat analgesic. Sometimes it is sold as "lavender 40/42" or "lavender 50/52," also known as "high-altitude" lavender. Again, despite the different terms, these are the same oil. The difference is the quantity of esters within the

Caution

It is especially important to make sure that lavandin essential oil is not accidentally ingested. In the case of lavandin absolute, negative interactions have been known to occur in individuals taking Aspirin and anticoagulant medications.

essential oil: the 50/52 contains 50% to 52% esters, whereas the other version has fewer. The esters are responsible for the calming and sedating action of the oil, and lavender grown at high altitudes typically yields more esters. These are particularly beneficial when the oil is used in cases of insomnia and to reduce anxiety and excessive stress.

Lavandula angustifolia, *L. officinalis* and *L. vera*, whether high-altitude or not, have a floral, herbaceous and slightly sweet scent with some earthy, woody notes. These "true lavenders" blend well with most oils, but particularly with citrus oils, clary sage, pine, rosemary and geranium.

Spike lavender (*Lavandula latifolia* syn. *L. spica*), a different variety, is used for medicinal purposes. Spike lavender is less relaxing and has a more medicinal scent than other varieties because of its chemical composition. It is more analgesic and antiseptic, which makes it useful for muscle aches and pains, rheumatism and cuts and scrapes. It is also wonderful for colds and flu, helping to ease coughs and loosen and expel mucus. Use spike lavender in hand soaps for preventive care. The scent of spike lavender is slightly harsh and camphoraceous but pleasant, as it still retains much of its lavender aroma. It blends well with true lavender and spicy oils such as cedarwood, eucalyptus, patchouli, petitgrain, pine and rosewood.

Spanish lavender (*Lavandula stoechas*) is another type of lavender often used in aromatherapy. Often identified as "lavender stoechas," it is more camphoraceous than spike lavender. Spanish lavender is useful for relieving aches and pains and helps to suppress coughing and loosen mucus. It is stimulating to the central nervous system and can help with fatigue and mental exhaustion. It blends well with clary sage, geranium, lemon and sandalwood.

Current research suggests that lavender stoechas may be effective in the treatment of hyperglycemia. A study conducted on diabetic rats concluded that, in part, the antioxidant properties of lavender stoechas essential oil protect against diabetes and oxidative stress. One study found that the synergy of lavender with lavender stoechas produced a greater antimicrobial effect against MSSA and MRSA than the individual oils.

Uses

- Lavender is one of the most valuable oils for skincare and skin conditions. It stimulates the growth of new cells, kills bacteria, is antibiotic and antiviral, prevents scarring and eases pain. Use it to treat abscesses, acne, allergies, athlete's foot, boils, bruises, inflammations, dermatitis, eczema, insect bites and stings (and as an insect repellent), psoriasis, scabies, sunburn, minor burns and scalds, sores, pimples and wounds. Include it in deodorants too—it reduces body odor.

Cautions

- Spike lavender may be mildly neurotoxic.
- Spanish lavender may be mildly neurotoxic.
- Spanish lavender is not recommended for use when pregnant or breastfeeding.
- Spanish lavender is not recommended for use with babies or children.

- Lavender increases energy, quickens the function of glands and strengthens bodily systems. It eases problems with the digestive, respiratory and urinary systems, relieves cramps and spasms in the intestines and uterus, and stimulates bile production. It will help to expel gas from the intestines and encourage and regulate menstrual flow.

- Lavender's antiseptic, antiviral and antibiotic properties, combined with its ability to loosen and expel mucus, make it an ideal oil to use as an inhalation and chest rub for bronchitis, coughs, colds, laryngitis, excess mucus and throat infections.

- Lavender is renowned for its effective relief of the pain and inflammation caused by arthritis, lumbago, muscular aches and pains, rheumatism, sciatica and muscular pain arising from tension. The best way of utilizing lavender oil for these problems is in a synergistic massage or bath blend with other oils, where it will strengthen their properties. One study, conducted on 48 patients, revealed that inhalation of lavender essential oil reduced the need for analgesic medications in children aged 6 to 12 after a tonsillectomy.

- When researchers investigated the protective effect of lavender oil against brain swelling due to stroke, the oil was found to offer neuroprotection. It increased the blood supply to the brain by clearing obstructions in blood vessels.

- Beautiful lavender is the great leveler. It can create calm and order from mental chaos to harmonize and balance every aspect of our bodies and minds. It reduces stress and calms the nervous system, lifts depression and eases headaches and insomnia.

Tips

- Always check the Latin name when buying lavender oil to ensure that you have the one you need.

- There is an old belief that if you want to stay chaste and virginal, you must dry lavender flowers and sprinkle them on your head. However, it's definitely easier to use the essential oil if chaste and virginal is what you desire!

- Remember that, in an emergency, lavender fixes almost everything.

Distillation Time Matters

Longer distillation times can extract more of the chemical components desirable in an essential oil. Most commercial lavender essential oils are moderately priced because they have been distilled for only 40 minutes. Lavender essential oil allowed to distill for more than an hour (78 minutes produces maximum results) will have more beneficial components than are found in some commercially produced essential oils.

LEMON

Citrus limon

Lemons are an amazing and versatile fruit with a deliciously clean, sharp, fresh fragrance. Rich in vitamin C, they have abundant culinary, medicinal and cosmetic uses in and around the home. The essential oil, like other citrus oils, can be obtained either through cold expression from the fruit peel or by distilling the whole fruit. The oil expressed from the peel has a strong, fresh scent but is phototoxic. Oil distilled from the fruit does not promote phototoxicity, but it has a harsh, bittersweet aroma caused by chemical breakdown of the citral content, from the heat used in the process.

Lemon essential oil is used widely by the food and perfume industries. It blends well with benzoin, chamomile, eucalyptus, frankincense, grapefruit, lavender, orange, rosemary, sandalwood and ylang ylang.

Citrus Oils and Phototoxicity

Although an essential oil can be distilled from citrus leaves, the result has very different chemical properties from that produced from the fruit. It is not widely available because there are many contraindications regarding its use. Citrus oils purchased for use in aromatherapy will be either expressed from the peel or distilled from the whole fruit. Oils expressed from the peel are more complete therapeutically, but they are also likely to promote phototoxicity. On the other hand, those distilled from the whole fruit are not likely to promote phototoxicity but lack aroma and robustness in terms of their general efficacy. When purchasing a citrus essential oil, look on the label for how the oil was obtained—by steam distillation of the whole fruit or expressed from the peel. If the method is not indicated, ask before purchasing.

Uses

- Lemon oil smooths the skin and contracts and tones tissue; it can be used to treat dull, oily skin through its mild bleaching action. It is successful in removing warts and soothes and prevents infection when used on insect bites and stings.

- Lemon oil helps to stop external bleeding such as from nosebleeds and wounds and after tooth extraction. When using in the mouth, dip a cotton swab in a little carrier oil or water, then add a drop of lemon oil. Rub onto the area where the tooth was extracted.

- Lemon essential oil supports the regeneration of white blood cells, stimulates the production of red blood cells and purifies the blood; in Europe it has been used successfully by medically qualified aromatherapists to treat some serious illnesses. This property, combined with its antibacterial and fever-lowering action, makes it an extremely valuable oil for treatment of sore throats, bronchitis, coughs, throat infections, colds and influenza. To cool a fever, combine 4 to 6 drops lemon essential oil and 1 tsp (5 mL) liquid honey, then add to a tepid bath.

- The monoterpene d-limonene, a major chemical component in lemon essential oil, has been found to be effective in the prevention and treatment of cancer. In cases where a tumor is present, the monoterpene can effect reversal of tumor growth in multiple ways.

- Lemon oil lifts feelings of sluggishness and apathy—it brightens your outlook, leaving the mind alert and clear.

Lemon for Digestion

Lemon creates alkalinity in the body and improves the function of the pancreas, gallbladder and liver. It is an essential oil that with great care may be ingested in home aromatherapy use. In cases of unbearable pain, combine 2 to 3 drops lemon essential oil and 4 drops olive oil in a cellulose capsule and mix with a toothpick. Close the capsule and swallow with a small glass of water. Ingest to ease indigestion, stomach acidity and acid reflux and to expel painful gas from the intestines. The pain typically subsides within 20 minutes. *This remedy is not intended for ongoing use.*

LEMON BALM
See Melissa (page 83)

LEMONGRASS

Cymbopogon citratus (West Indian lemongrass);
C. flexuosus (East Indian lemongrass)

The fleshy white base of the stems of lemongrass is widely used in Southeast Asian cookery. The leaves themselves are tough and virtually inedible, but it is from those leaves, with their strong, fresh lemony fragrance when crushed or bruised, that the essential oil is distilled. It is used extensively in the flavor and fragrance industries. Lemongrass oil blends well with cedarwood, geranium, jasmine, lavender, neroli, palmarosa, rosemary and tea tree.

Cautions

- Lemon oil may cause skin sensitization if it is old or oxidized. Store in a dark bottle in the refrigerator, ensuring that the cap is tightly closed. Citrus fruit oils have a shelf life of 1 to 2 years.

- Be particularly cautious not to use undiluted.

- Avoid using an expressed lemon oil on skin that will be exposed to sunlight or a sunbed within 12 hours of use.

- To avoid phototoxicity (see page 19), use only 1% to 2% in blends or 1 drop in 3 tsp (15 mL) carrier oil or lotion, or use oil that has been distilled from the whole fruit.

Uses

- Lemongrass essential oil is a refreshing, cleansing and stimulating tonic for the skin and also has very powerful antiseptic properties for skin tissues. It is useful in deodorants. A good insect repellent, it protects animals and humans from fleas, lice and ticks. Added to shampoos, it gives shine to the hair.

- Lemongrass kills bacterial and fungal infections. It is a good oil to include in blends to treat athlete's foot (or any fungal condition), where its deodorant and antifungal properties are of help.

- It cools and reduces fever and strengthens the bodily systems, making it a useful oil in the prevention and treatment of infectious diseases and during convalescence.

- It stimulates the circulation and helps to eliminate lactic acid, easing muscular aches and pains and aching feet.

- Lemongrass helps to ease depression, reduces stress and calms the nervous system. It lifts and revives the spirits when they are flagging from nervous exhaustion.

Cautions

- It is especially important to make sure that lemongrass essential oil is not accidentally ingested. Ingestion should be avoided if pregnant or diabetic and when taking certain medications; negative interactions have been known to occur.

- Lemongrass can pose a drug interaction problem with some analgesic, anticonvulsant and antidepressant medications, some chemotherapy drugs and some forms of estrogen and nicotine in the form of treatments such as patches, as well as reverse-transcriptase inhibitor medications. If you are taking any of these drugs, do not use lemongrass oil; consider using *Eucalyptus citriodora* instead.

LIME

Citrus aurantifolia

Citrus hystrix (kaffir lime); *C. medica* (limbu or Indian lime)

Limes have a stronger flavor and greater acidity than lemons, but their essential oil has a similar fragrance and the same properties and can be used in the same way. Like other citrus oils, lime oil for aromatherapy purposes can be obtained either through cold expression of the fruit peel or by distilling the whole fruit. The expressed oil has a strong, fresh scent but is phototoxic. Lime oil distilled from the whole fruit has a harsh, bittersweet aroma caused by chemical breakdown of the citral content, from the heat used in the process, but it is not phototoxic.

Cautions

- Lemongrass oil may cause irritation to sensitive or damaged skin. There is a slight risk of allergic reaction in a small percentage of the population.

- Use 3 drops only in a bath, and no more than 1 drop in 4 tsp (20 mL) carrier oil or lotion.

- Not suitable for babies or toddlers under the age of 2.

The perfume of lime essential oil is fresh and sharp and smells of fresh limes. It blends well with angelica, bergamot, citronella, clary sage, geranium, lavender, neroli, palmarosa, rose, rosemary and ylang ylang.

Lime essential oil is also produced from two other varieties of lime: kaffir and limbu. The oil expressed from the rind of **kaffir lime** (*Citrus hystrix*) has been described as having a fresh, sweet citrus-peel odor. It is used in aromatherapy for fever, infections, colds, flu and sore throat. Because this essential oil is carminative, it is useful in cases of indigestion. Traditionally kaffir lime oil is used as a natural cleanser, often in shampoos to encourage healthy hair and to fight dandruff. Essential oils from both the leaves and the peel have been studied. It was found that when used in mouthwashes, the oil can prevent periodontal disease. Kaffir lime oil blends well with citrus oils, citronella, clary sage, lavandin, lavender, neroli and rosemary.

The **limbu**, or Indian lime (*Citrus medica*), has an extremely delicious and exotic aroma. It invigorates the senses and inspires a lively and uplifting feeling. Being astringent in nature, it helps to tone, rejuvenate and cleanse the skin. Research shows that *C. medica* is an effective anti-inflammatory agent against septic shock and meningococcal disease. It is a great oil to open the mind and energize the body; limbu oil is widely used in Ayurvedic aromatherapy to balance all three doshas, or humors, that govern the body's health.

Lime Oil from the Leaves

The pungent leafy-green, lemon-lime aroma in combava essential oil is distilled from the leaves of *Citrus hystrix*. Combava leaf (or kaffir lime petitgrain) oil will stimulate the senses and support the immune system. It is calming and relaxing for depressive states and anxiety. The leaf oil is also perfect for household cleaning and in room sprays.

The fruit and leaf oils of citrus have different chemical compositions and are used differently therapeutically. In general, fruit oils are diuretic and carminative—useful for the digestive and urinary systems. Leaf oil contains a large amount of citronellol, making it more useful in insect repellents and as an antifungal.

Uses

- Like lemon essential oil, lime smooths the skin and contracts and tones tissue. It can be used to treat dull, oily skin through its mild bleaching action. It is successful at removing warts and soothes and prevents infection when used on insect bites and stings.

Tips: The term *kaffir* may be offensive to some people. However, we have used it here because that is how this variety of lime essential oil is identified in aromatherapy. The alternative, *makrut*, is rarely, if ever, used; on the rare occasions where it is noted, it is defined as a synonym.

Spraying an outdoor table with lemongrass and catnip will help to deter flies and mosquitoes.

- Lime oil may cause irritation to sensitive skin.

- This oil may cause skin sensitization if it is old or oxidized. Keep the oil in a dark bottle in the refrigerator, ensuring that the cap is tightly closed. Citrus fruit oils have a shelf life of 1 to 2 years.

- Do not use undiluted. This oil should always be diluted in a carrier oil or lotion.

- Lime essential oil helps to stop external bleeding such as from nosebleeds and wounds and after tooth extraction.

- Lime stimulates the production of white corpuscles. Combined with its antibacterial and fever-lowering action, this makes it an extremely valuable oil in the treatment of sore throat, bronchitis, coughs, throat infections, colds and influenza.

- Lime improves the function of the pancreas, gallbladder and liver. It eases indigestion, expels gas from the intestines and purifies the blood.

- Lime will lighten your outlook, leaving the mind alert and clear.

Cautions

- Use no more than 3 drops in a bath.

- Use only 1% to 2% in blends. Use 1 drop in 3 tsp (15 mL) carrier oil or lotion to avoid phototoxicity (see page 74), or use oil that has been distilled from the whole fruit.

- If using oil that has been expressed from peel, avoid skin that will be exposed to sunlight or a sunbed within 12 hours of use.

- The leaf oil is not phototoxic or sensitizing.

LITSEA CUBEBA
....

Litsea cubeba

Litsea cubeba is a small tropical tree, native to China and other regions in East Asia, that has scented flowers and foliage and small berries shaped like peppers, from which it derives its name. The essential oil (sometimes called "may chang") is produced by steam distillation from the fruits; it has an intense lemony perfume similar to that of lemongrass. The oil blends well with basil, geranium, jasmine, lavender, lemongrass, neroli, orange, petitgrain, rose, rosemary, rosewood and ylang ylang.

Uses

- The main benefits of this essential oil are its usefulness in dealing with skin problems. Use it in blends to treat acne, dermatitis, pimples and greasy skin, and in deodorants, where it will help to control perspiration. We have heard that it can be used as a substitute for bergamot. As there are no photosensitivity effects with *Litsea cubeba*, it can be used in preparations for skin that will be exposed to sunlight.

- The oil has digestive properties and may be added to warm compresses or massage blends to ease indigestion and flatulence.

- *Litsea cubeba* has a strengthening and tonic action on bodily systems, particularly the immune system and the heart, and is useful during convalescence to lift low energy.
- It has been found to significantly repel mosquitoes; its lemony scent can make an insect-repellent spray smell pleasant.
- The essential oil has been investigated for its anticancer activity and was found to be cytotoxic against lung, liver and oral cancer cells.

Cautions

- *Litsea cubeba* may cause irritation to sensitive skin. There is a slight risk of allergic reaction in a small percentage of the population. Use 1 drop in 3 tsp (15 mL) carrier oil or lotion to avoid skin sensitization.
- Do not use with children under the age of 2.
- *Litsea cubeba* can pose a drug interaction problem when used topically with certain drugs, including some analgesic, anticonvulsant and antidepressant medications, some chemotherapy drugs and some forms of estrogen and nicotine in the form of treatments such as patches, as well as reverse-transcriptase inhibitor medications.
- It is especially important to make sure that *Litsea cubeba* essential oil is not accidentally ingested. Ingestion should be avoided if pregnant or diabetic and when taking certain medications; negative interactions have been known to occur.

MANDARIN

Citrus reticulata

The names *mandarin* and *tangerine* are often used to describe the same oil, but they are in fact different cultivars within the same family, and the oils have slightly different properties. The mandarin tree has heavily perfumed flowers. Mandarin is a delicate oil, safe to use with children and the elderly and during pregnancy. It is a terrific pick-me-up for those recovering from illness. The perfume is intense: a deliciously sweet, citrus floral that blends well with basil, bergamot, black pepper, chamomile, grapefruit, lavender, lemon, lime, neroli, orange, palmarosa, petitgrain and rose.

Uses

- Mandarin is a lovely oil to use in blends to prevent or treat stretch marks and scars. It is excellent for aging and mature skin.
- One of the main applications of this delicious-smelling oil is as a digestive tonic. It relieves cramps and spasms and helps to expel gas from the intestines. It also relieves constipation. Mandarin stimulates bile production, aids digestion and hiccups and encourages the appetite. It is particularly good

Cautions

- Mandarin oil may cause skin sensitization if it is old or oxidized. Keep the oil in a dark bottle in the refrigerator, ensuring that the cap is tightly closed. Citrus fruit oils have a shelf life of 1 to 2 years.
- Do not use undiluted. This oil should always be diluted in a carrier oil or lotion.
- Mandarin oil is not a photo-sensitizer itself, but combination with other citrus oils can synergize its phototoxic potential.

for babies suffering from the miseries and pain of colic, as the digestive properties relieve cramps and the sedative action helps calm the fretfulness.

- As a mild diuretic, mandarin also helps with fluid retention and obesity.
- Mandarin oil cheers the psyche, relieves insomnia and nervous tension, reduces stress and calms the nervous system.

Variety vs. Cultivar

Varieties often occur in nature, and most varieties are "true to type." This means that the seedlings grown from a variety will have the same unique characteristics as the parent plant. Sweet basil and Thai basil are examples of different varieties of the same plant.

Unlike varieties, cultivars do not occur naturally; they are, as the term implies, cultivated. A **cultivar** is bred with human intervention from a naturally occurring plant to develop specific characteristics that are deemed desirable. The resulting hybrid is maintained under cultivation. Additional cultivars may subsequently be developed from the hybrids, based on similar principles of selection. When a cultivar is identified by its full scientific name, the fact that it is a cultivar is identified by single quotation marks. For example, lavandin is a **variety** of lavender that is a naturally occurring hybrid of true lavender (*Lavandula angustifolia*) and spike lavender (*L. latifolia*). Its name is written *Lavandula* x *intermedia* or *Lavandula hybridia*. A specific cultivar of lavandin is lavandin 'Grosso', written *Lavandula* x *intermedia* cv. 'Grosso', or sometimes *Lavandula hybridia* 'Grosso'.

MANUKA

Leptospermum scoparium

Manuka, commonly known as New Zealand tea tree, is part of the myrtle family. It really has nothing to do with tea (*Camellia sinensis*). The story goes that Captain Cook used the aromatic leaves for making a tea while his expedition was charting the New Zealand coastline. Bees that feed from manuka flowers produce a type of honey that is very highly valued for its antibiotic qualities. Today manuka leaves are used to produce a lovely and powerful essential oil that is often preferred over tea tree, as it has a softer, honey-like smell.

The chemical composition of the oil can vary greatly, depending on where the plant was grown and how old the tree was when the branches and leaves were harvested. When purchasing the oil, however, you will find that specific chemotypes are not given on the label. The perfume of manuka oil is sweet and soft; it blends well with cinnamon, clary sage, clove, cypress, eucalyptus, geranium, ginger, lavender, lemon, lemongrass, mandarin, marjoram, rosemary and thyme.

Uses

- Powerfully antiseptic, antibacterial, antiviral and antifungal, manuka oil can be used to treat abscesses, ringworm, corns, mouth ulcers, blisters, warts and cold sores. Add to baths and footbaths to treat athlete's foot, wounds, sunburn and minor burns and scalds.

- Manuka oil can be used as a mouthwash or gargle to treat bad breath, gingivitis and tonsillitis. Just be sure to dilute it properly (see page 17) and spit it all out.

- Manuka oil has the capacity to loosen and remove mucus. This, combined with its other properties, makes it a valuable remedy to use in baths, massage oils and inhalations to treat bronchitis, catarrh, colds, influenza, fevers, coughs, sinusitis, tuberculosis and whooping cough.

- When used in a diffuser or air spray, manuka oil will help to prevent the spread of infectious diseases.

- The antihistamine action of manuka is useful for treating insect bites and stings and allergic reactions such as hives.

- Diaper rash can be avoided or healed if you add manuka oil to the cream or powder used on your baby's bottom.

- It can be used to treat urinary tract infections such as urethritis and cystitis, vaginal trichomonas, candida, thrush, herpes and vaginitis.

MARJORAM, SWEET

Origanum majorana

Sweet marjoram is a very aromatic herb long used for both cooking and herbal medicine. Its leaves are used fresh or dried in many Mediterranean dishes, giving them their distinctive flavor. The essential oil is steam-distilled from both the leaves and flowers. The perfume is gently pungent and warm; it blends well with bergamot, black pepper, cedarwood, chamomile, clary sage, cypress, eucalyptus, juniper, lavender, mandarin, nutmeg, patchouli, peppermint, petitgrain, rosemary and tea tree.

Uses

- Sweet marjoram strengthens the immune system, is a warming and relaxing oil and has painkilling properties. It helps to loosen and remove mucus and increases perspiration, making it useful in air sprays, inhalations, baths and massage oils to ease

respiratory complaints and fevers such as asthma, bronchitis, coughs, colds, influenza and sinusitis.

- Marjoram dilates arteries and small blood vessels, making it an ideal massage oil for treating arthritis, lumbago, sprains, bruises, rheumatism and joint and muscle pain. This same property will help with fainting, headache, migraine and high blood pressure.

- As with several other culinary herbs, marjoram is an excellent toner for the digestive system and may be used to treat intestinal cramps, flatulence, diarrhea, indigestion and constipation. Menstrual cramping, scantiness and irregularity can also be eased by laying a hot marjoram compress over the lower abdomen. A research study found that a blend (at 3% dilution) of essential oils—comprising 2 parts lavender, 1 part clary sage and 1 part marjoram—added to an unscented cream provided significant relief and reduced the duration of menstrual pain in the 24 women studied.

- Research conducted on the use of marjoram essential oil on mice with liver damage from mosquito insecticide revealed the liver-protective activity of this essential oil, suggesting that using it may be an economical way to protect humans exposed to household pesticides and their toxic effects.

- Sweet marjoram oil has powerful sedative properties that can "stupefy" if used to excess. Combined with lavender and mandarin in a bath or massage before bedtime (especially for children: see Monster Spray, page 174), it calms the nervous system and makes a good remedy for insomnia (particularly if the sleeplessness is caused by stress), hyperactivity or PMS.

- It encourages tender, gentle feelings, consoles a grief-stricken heart and brings peace.

MARJORAM, SPANISH

Thymus mastichina

Spanish marjoram, despite the name, is actually a member of the thyme family and has little similarity to sweet marjoram. It has a spicy, herbaceous odor and is more camphoraceous than sweet marjoram. Distilled mostly from wild-growing plants in Portugal and Spain, it can be used as a decongestant, antiseptic or antispasmodic. It is antibacterial (found to be effective against *M. tuberculosis*) and antifungal against a variety of *Candida* species. More recently it has been investigated for its cytotoxic activity in colon cancer.

Add it to your blends for sore, tired and achy muscles. The essential oil can be relaxing or sedative, providing comfort and warmth. However, because it is distilled from wild-growing plants, its chemical composition may vary.

MASTIC

Pistacia lentiscus

Mastic is a slow-growing evergreen shrub native to the Mediterranean. Today most mastic is produced on the Greek island of Chios, where the gum mastic they produce is recognized as a Protected Designation of Origin (PDO) product. To harvest the gum, the trees are scored and resin exudes from the wounds, forming droplets that fall to the ground, where they glisten like diamonds. Mastic is used in perfumes and cosmetics, in Mediterranean cooking and confections, and to flavor ouzo.

The resin "tears" are distilled to produce an essential oil with a unique aroma of musk, incense, pine and wood. It blends well with lavender, citrus and floral oils. Research has shown that this oil has therapeutic potential in the treatment of prostate cancer, stomachaches and pains and peptic ulcer, and it modulates the immune system.

Uses

- Mastic essential oil can be used as an insect repellent or in sprays to deter fleas and other bugs. Add to preparations to control head lice, scabies and ringworm.

- Mastic is antiseptic, antispasmodic, anti-inflammatory and an expectorant, making it useful in treating respiratory complaints and congestion, including bronchitis, catarrh and whooping cough, and soothing the inflammation associated with asthma.

- Mastic is used in preparations such as toothpaste and mouthwash to reduce plaque and combat foul mouth odor.

- Add 2 drops to a 1 tsp (5 mL) sweet almond oil and massage onto the abdomen to relieve indigestion.

MAY CHANG

See *Litsea cubeba* (page 78)

See *Litsea cubeba* (page 78)

MELISSA (Lemon Balm)

Melissa officinalis

The herb called lemon balm has long been known for its healing properties, especially for children. It is one of the earliest recorded medicinal herbs; Paracelsus called it "the elixir of life." With its sweet, soft and lemony-smelling flowers, leaves and abundant nectar, lemon balm brings bees to the garden—hence its other name, bee balm (*Melissa* comes from the Greek word for "bee"). The oil is extracted by steam distillation from the leaves and

Cautions

- Mastic oil may cause skin sensitization if it is old or oxidized. Keep the oil in a dark bottle in the refrigerator, ensuring that the cap is tightly closed.

- Do not use undiluted, as oxidized essential oils containing the naturally occurring chemical α-pinene can cause skin sensitization.

- Melissa oil may cause irritation to sensitive skin.

- Use only 3 drops in a bath and no more than 0.9% in a carrier oil or lotion.

- Do not use with children under the age of 2.

- We do not recommend the ingestion of essential oils for home aromatherapy use. It is especially important in the case of melissa. Negative interactions have been known to occur in individuals who are pregnant or who are taking diabetes or other medications, particularly certain opioid analgesics, anesthetics, anticonvulsants, antidepressants, chemo-therapeutic drugs, estrogen receptor antagonists, nervous system stimulants or reverse-transcriptase inhibitors.

flowering tops, and as there is very little oil in those parts of the plant, melissa is very expensive to extract and thus to buy. A blend of lemon and petitgrain essential oils will give an approximation of its properties and scent.

Melissa blends well with basil, chamomile, frankincense, geranium, ginger, lavender, petitgrain, rosemary and ylang ylang. In recent years it has been investigated for its use with the aged, in particular for its therapeutic benefit with dementia patients. At low doses, melissa essential oil was found to enhance glucose uptake and metabolism in the liver and adipose tissue. It also inhibited the formation of glucose through breakdown of glycogen in the liver, which makes it an efficient hypoglycemic agent.

Uses

- The words that spring to mind when thinking about melissa are *calming* and *soothing*. These are the properties that this oil brings to bear on both body and mind, making it especially useful in cases of agitation, nervousness, anxiety and melancholy.

- Skin allergies respond well to melissa. It can be used to treat various diseases associated with inflammation, pain, acne, eczema and even bee stings. It is also useful as an insect repellent.

- Melissa was tested against the herpes virus and found to have a direct effect on it. It may be added to a carrier oil or made into an ointment for topical treatment of cold sores and genital herpes.

- No matter whether the problems are in the reproductive, digestive or circulatory system, melissa will relieve cramps and spasms of the intestines and uterus. It will cool and reduce fevers and tone and calm the heart, slowing palpitations, lowering blood pressure and easing headaches and migraine. It exerts the same calming effect on persistent coughs.

- Melissa is one of the best oils for treating allergies of both the skin and the respiratory system. It can be used to relieve allergic skin reactions as well as hay fever and asthma.

- Melissa creates a secure and loving aura around us. Within this safe golden light we feel protected from the vicissitudes of life. Its loving protection helps us to come to terms with grief, depression and sadness. It reduces stress and gently calms the nervous system.

MYRRH

Commiphora myrrha

Myrrh was widely used in ancient times throughout the Middle East. It was especially esteemed in Egypt, where it was valued for its rejuvenating properties and as an ingredient in the embalming process. Today the oil is obtained by steam distillation from the crude myrrh oleoresin that exudes from the trunk of the tree. It is often included in products to treat pain, skin infections, inflammatory conditions, diarrhea and periodontal diseases. Current research now points to this essential oil's having significant antiseptic, anesthetic and antitumor properties. The perfume is smoky, musky and slightly acrid and blends well with benzoin, frankincense, galbanum, lavender, patchouli and sandalwood.

Uses

- The cooling action of myrrh oil reduces inflammation and helps to heal boils, ulcers, weeping eczema and infected wounds. It has antifungal properties, which are helpful when treating athlete's foot.

- Add a few drops of myrrh oil to skincare blends created for mature or prematurely aging skin or to treat chapped skin on lips or hands and rough, cracked skin on heels.

- The tincture and oil are used in dental and pharmaceutical products such as toothpaste and mouthwashes—myrrh is possibly the best remedy for healing mouth ulcers, gum infections, gingivitis and sore throat. The best way of using myrrh in the mouth is either to buy tincture of myrrh from a pharmacy or to make a 3% essence: dissolve 40 drops of myrrh oil in 1/4 cup (60 mL) high-proof vodka or brandy. The essence or tincture may be dabbed undiluted on mouth ulcers or used to make a gargle or mouth rinse by combining 1 tsp (5 mL) with 4 tsp (20 mL) water.

- Myrrh is a powerful treatment for respiratory infections. Its cleansing and drying properties help to kill infection and loosen and remove mucus during attacks of asthma, bronchitis, coughs and colds.

- Used in massage oil or hot compresses applied to the abdomen, myrrh acts as a tonic and strengthener for the digestive system, easing diarrhea, indigestion and flatulence. Add to ointments or oil for treating hemorrhoids.

- Myrrh's antifungal action can be employed successfully to treat thrush, leukorrhea and itching.

- Use myrrh to ease the anguish of grief when someone close has passed away. It also creates a bridge between this world and the next, making the transition less painful for both the person who is dying and those who are being left behind.

"From the days of Moses to the time of Christ and since then to the 20th century, myrrh has proven over and over again to be one of the finest antibacterial and antiviral agents placed on earth."
John Heinerman, The Science of Herbal Medicine, 1978

Tip: When purchasing myrtle, be sure to check the Latin name of the oil. There are "myrtle" oils on the market that are produced from different plants in the same family. They have different chemical compositions and are not interchangeable with true myrtle.

Cautions

- Use no more than 1.9% true myrtle in blends.

- It is especially important to make sure that myrtle essential oil is not accidentally ingested. Ingestion should be avoided when taking certain medications; negative interactions have been known to occur.

MYRTLE

Myrtus communis

Myrtle (or "true myrtle," as it is also known) is a large shrub native to North Africa. It now grows wild over the entire Mediterranean region. Both the flowers and leaves are highly perfumed, but the essential oil is steam-distilled mainly from the leaves and twigs. The oil has a clear, herbaceous perfume and blends well with bergamot, cedarwood, clary sage, cypress, hyssop, lavender, lemon, lime, pine, rosemary, spice oils, thyme and tea tree.

True myrtle, also known as green or orange myrtle, is the variety most commonly used in aromatherapy. The oil is composed predominantly of pinenes, which are anti-inflammatory, antibacterial, antifungal, antispasmodic and antiviral, which makes it useful in cases of asthma, candida and other fungal infections, for reducing coughs and as a skin tonic. In addition to true myrtle, there are other varieties. **Red myrtle** is higher in 1,8-cineole, which is antimicrobial, anti-inflammatory, antibacterial, antispasmodic, antiviral and mycolytic, making it great in sprays as an airborne antimicrobial agent. It is a useful analgesic and can help to thin and expel mucus. Green (orange) myrtle is high in myrtenyl acetate and linalool, giving it a gentler chemical composition that is calming to the various systems of the body.

Uses for Myrtle

- "True myrtle" oil helps to destroy infection-causing bacteria and contracts and tones tissue. It can be used in blends to treat acne, bruises, hemorrhoids, oily skin and psoriasis.

- A gentle oil, it is particularly effective for respiratory problems and suitable for use with very young and elderly people. It helps to loosen and remove mucus, and that, combined with its antiseptic properties, helps to treat asthma, bronchitis, catarrh, colds and coughs. Its antioxidant and anti-inflammatory activity also helps to prevent infectious diseases. This makes it a good choice to use in blends for air sprays during epidemics.

- The antiseptic action will be found useful for clearing cystitis and urethritis. It is also thought to be of use to ease hemorrhoids, diarrhea and dysentery.

- Myrtle calms an angry mind and promotes restful sleep.

Other Myrtle Oils

When purchasing myrtle, check the Latin name of the oil to make sure you are buying "true" myrtle. There are other so-called myrtle oils on the market that are produced from other plant species and thus possess different chemical compositions. The following are *not* interchangeable with true myrtle.

Anise Myrtle (*Syzygium anisatum* syn. *Backhousia anisata*)
Anise myrtle has an intense, spicy, licorice-like aroma and is widely used in the flavoring and fragrance industries. Its major chemical components are trans-anethole and methyl chavicol, which contribute to this oil's antibacterial, antifungal (against *Candida*), sedative, carminative (relief of intestinal gas) and insect-repellent activities.

Lemon Myrtle (*Backhousia citriodora*)
Lemon myrtle essential oil is calming and uplifting on your moodiest of days. As effective as tea tree and eucalyptus as an antibacterial, this lemony essential oil can be used in cleaning products without adding a medicinal aroma. Add it to air sprays to cut through foul odors and freshen any space, as well as to support your immune system through the cold and flu season. Blend into ointments for herpes viruses such as cold sores and genital herpes. Add it to your natural mosquito spray to keep the bugs at bay. It blends well with citrus oils, bay laurel, eucalyptus, pine, rosemary and thyme.

Honey Myrtle (*Melaleuca teretifolia*)
The sweet and soft aroma of honey myrtle is reminiscent of a soothing cup of lemon tea with honey. It increases cerebral blood flow yet is calming and sedative. It can help to relieve fatigue, muscle spasms and cramps and a stuffy head. It is highly antimicrobial, and its pleasant aroma makes it a nice addition to diffuser blends and inhalers to ward off infection.

Cautions for lemon myrtle and honey myrtle:

- May cause irritation in some sensitive individuals. Use no more than 1 drop in 2 tsp (10 mL) carrier oil.

- Not for use with children under the age of 2.

- Lemon and honey myrtle can pose a drug interaction problem even when applied topically. This applies to some analgesic, anticonvulsant and antidepressant medications, some chemotherapy drugs, some forms of estrogen and nicotine in the form of treatments such as patches, and reverse-transcriptase inhibitor medications.

- It is especially important to make sure that lemon and honey myrtle essential oils are not accidentally ingested. Ingestion should be avoided when taking certain medications; negative interactions have been known to occur.

Tip: For painful gas, pour a small amount of diluted anise myrtle or another carminative essential oil (see page 25) into your hand and massage onto the abdomen in a clockwise direction.

Cautions for anise myrtle:

- Avoid using anise myrtle if pregnant or breastfeeding.

- Avoid in cases of endometriosis and estrogen-dependent cancers.

- Not for use with children under the age of 5.

- May cause irritation in some sensitive individuals. Use no more than 2 drops in 1 tsp (5 mL) carrier oil.

- It is especially important to make sure that anise myrtle essential oil is not accidentally ingested. Ingestion should be avoided when taking certain medications; negative interactions have been known to occur.

NEROLI (Orange Blossom)

Citrus aurantium var. *amara flos*

Neroli essential oil is extracted from the flowers of the Seville (bitter) orange tree by either steam distillation or the time-consuming and labor-intensive method known as enfleurage, which extracts the oils from fats. This generously fruiting tree also produces the ideal oranges for making marmalade. Neroli is one of the most widely used floral oils in perfumery; the aroma is sweet and ultra-feminine and blends well with most other oils. Neroli's exquisite scent isn't immediately apparent in the undiluted oil (in fact, when smelled in the bottle it can be quite unappealing), but when added to a carrier oil or other base, the true aroma appears—that is when you understand why it is used in the best and most expensive perfumes in the world. For therapeutic purposes, substituting for neroli with equal parts mandarin and petitgrain will give almost the same effect, but if you are making a top-quality perfume, there is no substitute.

Uses

- Neroli is an excellent skincare oil. It has a reputation for regenerating skin cells and maintaining or restoring elasticity, particularly in mature, prematurely aged or sensitive skin. It helps to prevent wrinkles, remove scars and stretch marks and lessen thread veins.

- Neroli relieves cramps and spasms and helps to expel gas from the intestines. It will ease diarrhea and indigestion related to shock or nerves. It also relieves cramps and spasms in the uterus.

- Neroli is a very tranquilizing oil. It is one of the major oils for treating long-term anxiety, calming nerves, easing depression and palpitations and soothing the spirit. It is also useful for easing those turbulent emotions that often accompany PMS and menopause.

- Neroli is a tender and sensitive oil that increases sexual desire. Orange blossoms (from which the oil is distilled) are traditionally used in wedding bouquets to ease "first-night nerves."

- In research studies, neroli oil displayed notable activity against bacteria that cause respiratory and urinary infections prevalent among people with compromised immune systems. Neroli oil has a very strong antifungal activity compared to traditional antibiotics; it is very useful with yeast infections such as candida.

NIAOULI

Melaleuca quinquenervia

Niaouli essential oil is extracted by steam distillation from the leaves and young twigs of the broad-leafed paperbark tree, a native of Australia's tropical north. Its bottlebrush flowers provide food for bats and insect-eating birds, and its natural antiseptic qualities make it ideal for the medicine cabinet. There are several chemotypes (see page 29) of this essential oil. Most of the chemotypes—linalool, nerolidol and viridiflorol—are nonhazardous and nonsensitizing (the linalool chemotype is also referred to as *nerolina*). The most commercially available naouli essential oil is the cineole chemotype, which is very high in 1,8-cineole and needs to be used with care (see Caution, right).

The perfume is strong, camphor-like and clean, blending well with juniper, lavender, lemon, lemongrass, lime, orange, peppermint, pine and rosemary. It is used in commercial preparations such as gargles, toothpaste and breath fresheners.

Uses

- Although niaouli and cajuput oils are closely related, niaouli is a better choice for using on the skin, because it is less likely to irritate. Acne, boils, cuts and minor burns, grazes, insect bites, sores, pimples and wounds will all be helped to heal by application of the diluted oil, which eases pain by numbing nerves while killing bacteria.

- Used in a mouthwash, niaouli will help to sweeten bad breath caused by gum disease or bad teeth. (Obviously, a visit to a dentist is also recommended.)

- Included in a bath or massage blend, niaouli will help to ease muscular aches and pains, rheumatism, poor circulation and neuralgia.

- It has a powerful effect on the respiratory system. Inhalations will loosen and remove mucus. Because niaouli also cools and reduces fever, it may be used with good effect to treat bronchitis, coughs, colds, sinusitis, laryngitis, influenza and whooping cough.

- Niaouli reputedly increases white blood cells, strengthens the immune system and increases antibody activity.

- Niaouli sweeps the cobwebs from the brain and helps concentration.

Caution

Do not use niaouli oil with young children. Niaouli ct. cineole may cause distress to a child's nervous system and create breathing concerns. Use nerolina (niaouli ct. linalool) in its place.

- Nutmeg oil is potentially carcinogenic and can be psychotropic in high doses. Do not ingest.

- Do not use in large doses or for prolonged periods of time. Use only 1% in blends and only 3 drops in inhalations, compresses and baths.

Cautions

- Bitter orange oil may cause irritation to sensitive skin.

- This oil may cause skin sensitization if old or oxidized. Keep the bottle in the refrigerator, ensuring that the cap is tightly closed. Citrus oils have a shelf life of 1 to 2 years.

- Avoid using bitter orange essential oil on skin that will be exposed to sunlight within 12 hours of use.

- Use 1 drop in 1 tsp (5 mL) carrier oil to reduce the potential for phototoxicity (see page 19).

NUTMEG

Myristica fragrans

The fruit of the nutmeg tree has many culinary and medicinal uses. The dried kernel is grated and used to flavor sweet and savory dishes, especially those with cheese or milk (just imagine rice pudding without a thick sprinkling of nutmeg on top!). Its outer "jacket" is harvested for mace. The perfume is sweet-spicy and blends well with black pepper, clary sage, cypress, frankincense, geranium, lavender, lemon, lime, orange, patchouli, petitgrain and rosemary. It is widely used by the pharmaceutical industry in analgesic and tonic preparations, and also as a flavoring in many commercially prepared foods.

Uses

- Nutmeg oil is beneficial to the hair when added to hair tonics and shampoos.

- The most powerful use of nutmeg oil is its toning action on the digestive system. It will help to control vomiting and nausea, relieve cramps and spasms in the intestines, help to expel gas from the intestines, and ease indigestion, diarrhea, vomiting, nausea, parasites and poor digestion.

- In animal studies, nutmeg has been shown to protect the liver and maintain blood glucose levels. It stimulates the appetite and helps in digesting fatty foods, making it useful in cases of anorexia.

- A massage blend containing warming and pain-relieving nutmeg oil will be very soothing and comforting for muscular aches and pains, arthritis, gout, poor circulation and rheumatism. It can also be used in a bath to ease these problems, but use only 3 drops (no more!) dissolved in a little vegetable oil; otherwise it may irritate the skin. A hot compress, again using only 3 drops of the oil, will help with the pain of neuralgia.

- Nutmeg is invigorating and strengthens the mind. It has an aphrodisiac quality that can help to stimulate low sex drive.

ORANGE, BITTER

Citrus aurantium var. *amara*

Although bitter orange and sweet orange can be used interchangeably in aromatherapy, the oils are obtained from different species. Some experts believe the bitter orange to be a hybrid of mandarin (*Citrus reticulata*) and pomelo (*C. maxima*), which is similarly in flavor to the grapefruit. The bitter orange is smaller and darker than the sweet orange, and the essential oil has a fresher and greener aroma, which makes it very nice for blending. It is used in commercial laxatives and digestive products. Bitter orange has also been investigated as an antihistamine and for its effects in reducing swelling (edema).

ORANGE, SWEET

Citrus sinensis

Originally from China, the orange tree is now grown in many nontropical climates. Glowing and sunny, fresh oranges and orange juice are rich in vitamin C and among the most popular fruits and juices. Orange oil is obtained from the peel through cold expression. The perfume is happy and citrusy and blends well with angelica, benzoin, cinnamon, cypress, frankincense, lavender, neroli, nutmeg, petitgrain, rose and rosewood. It is widely used as a fragrance in soaps, cosmetics, colognes and perfumes, but it is most often used as a flavoring component in liqueurs, soft drinks and food.

Blood orange is a variety of sweet orange. Its aroma has a certain richness that is not found in sweet orange. Unlike other citrus oils, its essential oil (also obtained by cold expression of the rind) is not phototoxic.

Uses

- Orange oil is a good tonic for all skin types. It stimulates and brightens oily skin but is also useful for dry and normal skin.

- In blends with other oils, it is useful for treating fungal infections and killing bacteria.

- Orange oil has a toning effect on the digestive system. It relieves gas, cramps and spasms in the intestines, settles a nervous stomach and eases indigestion. Orange oil also increases energy and quickens the function of glands, boosts the immune system and reduces fever during colds and influenza.

- Lavender in synergy with orange has been shown to have enhanced effectiveness against respiratory infections.

- Orange oil is one of the essential oils preferred by children and has been shown to help them overcome fear and reduce anxiety.

- This is a cheerful oil that helps to ease depression and encourages us to be joyful. Glowing and sunny but still soft, it reminds us to enjoy life and not take ourselves quite so seriously!

Cautions

- Sweet orange oil may cause skin sensitization if it is old or oxidized. Keep the oil in a dark bottle in the refrigerator, ensuring that the cap is tightly closed.

- Do not use undiluted. This oil should always be diluted in a carrier oil or lotion.

One Tree, Three Oils

The orange tree is one of the few plants that yields multiple essential oils. We obtain orange essential oil from the fruit and rind, neroli essential oil from the flowers, and petitgrain essential oil from the leaves. Each is distinctly different in aroma, despite being produced by the same plant. Orange oil is the essential oil that is most plentiful in terms of production. Citrus oils have a shelf life of 1 to 2 years.

PALMAROSA

Cymbopogon martinii var. *motia*

Palmarosa essential oil is steam- or water-distilled from the whole plant, which is part of the same aromatic family as lemongrass and citronella. Palmarosa is the finest essential oil for all skin types, because it moisturizes, stimulates cell regeneration, encourages elasticity and regulates the production of sebum. It is also widely used for making soap because, unlike other oils, it retains its perfume. It is also used to flavor tobacco.

The perfume is sweet, grassy, rose-like and floral and blends well with bergamot, cedar, citronella, geranium, jasmine, lavender, orange, petitgrain, sandalwood and ylang ylang.

Uses

- Few people seem to be aware of the wonderful skincare properties of this oil, which is great for all skin types. Include it in preparations to restore and maintain correct water balance, moisturize, stimulate cell regeneration and regulate the production of sebum. If used regularly, it will help to smooth and tone wrinkles and rough skin. Its antibacterial action adds to the impressive list of its skin-enhancing qualities, making palmarosa a first-rate treatment for problems such as acne, dermatitis, eczema, psoriasis, rosacea, scars, sores, skin infections and (possibly) wrinkles.

- It kills bacteria, particularly those of the digestive system, and is excellent for combating intestinal infections and easing the pain of stomach cramps. It can be used in the treatment of anorexia because it stimulates appetite.

- Mix palmarosa into your massage blends to ease the aches and pains of arthritis and rheumatic conditions, as well as general muscular aches. It is also beneficial for cramps and gastric conditions.

- It is uplifting and steadying to the emotions and helps to reduce stress, nervous exhaustion and anxiety.

PALO SANTO

Bursera graveolens

Palo santo, also known as "holy wood" or "sacred wood," is a newer essential oil on the market. It is obtained through distillation of wood from the wild-growing palo santo tree, which is found primarily in Mexico and South America. However, the oil is produced mainly in Peru and Ecuador, where the tree is considered endangered. The warm, somewhat citrusy aroma of the oil is very strong and penetrating, with notes of frankincense.

Cautions

- Use no more than 6% palmarosa oil in your preparations, to avoid skin sensitization.

- It is especially important to make sure that palmarosa essential oil is not accidentally ingested. Negative interactions can occur in individuals taking certain opioid analgesics, anesthetics, anticonvulsants, antidepressents, chemo-therapeutic drugs, estrogen receptor antagonists, nervous system stimulants and reverse-transcriptase inhibitors.

Its smell is considered by some to be an acquired taste. It is used most often to relieve the symptoms of colds and flu, as well as respiratory problems such as asthma and bronchitis. It blends well with citrus oils, frankincense, myrrh and other wood oils.

Uses

- Use in blends for joint pain and inflammation, as well as for general aches and pains, arthritis, headaches, allergies and migraine.

- Relaxing to the mind and body, palo santo can be used in personal inhalers and massage blends to relieve stress, anxiety, panic, dizziness and nervousness, and to help with concentration.

- A few drops of palo santo added to a diffuser can help to boost the immune system and clear respiratory infections and bad karma from the home.

- Palo santo is reported to be chemopreventive in liver, lung and skin cancer. In a recent study the essential oil was shown to inhibit the growth of breast tumor cells, making it a promising ingredient for cancer medications.

- Palo santo stimulates circulation and revives energy in fatigued states. It is considered a spiritual oil and enhances meditation.

PARSLEY

Petroselinum crispum

Parsley is one of the most popular culinary herbs, and it has been cultivated for thousands of years. The Greeks believed it came from the blood of heroes, and this led to the notion that it could be used medicinally; it is thought that the Romans were the first to eat it. The essential oil is steam-distilled from the leaves, the root and (mainly) the seed. The perfume is warm and spicy and blends well with clary sage, lavender, lime, marjoram, orange, rosemary and tea tree.

Uses

- Parsley helps to shrink small blood vessels and can be used to treat hemorrhoids, bruising and thread veins. But possibly the main benefit to be gained from parsley oil is through its diuretic action. It increases the flow of urine and reduces water retention during menstruation or in other conditions where edema is a problem, such as swollen ankles and PMS. The increased flow of urine and parsley's antiseptic action can also be used to treat cystitis and urethritis. However, parsley must not be used when there is kidney disease or inflammation, or during pregnancy, because it stimulates muscle contractions in the uterus. Its use is also contraindicated when periods are painful, as it could cause cramping.

Cautions

- Palo santo oil may cause skin sensitization if it is old or oxidized. Keep the oil in a cool, dark place, ensuring that the cap is tightly closed.

- Do not use undiluted. This oil should always be diluted in a carrier oil or lotion.

- Use no more than 3% in your preparations.

- Not for prolonged use, as the oil can be toxic to the liver over longer periods of time.

Cautions

- Use only 0.5% parsley seed oil in blends.

- Avoid use if pregnant or breastfeeding or during painful menstruation.

- A good digestive aid, parsley stimulates the appetite, helps in digesting food (eat the parsley that decorates your food in restaurants—it may be the healthiest thing on your plate) and eases nausea and gas. It is used in some pharmaceutical digestive remedies and also by the perfume industry. Parsley relieves cramps and spasms and expels gas from the intestines. It also eases colic, indigestion and nausea.

PATCHOULI

Pogostemon cablin

The patchouli plants of tropical East and Southeast Asia are renowned for their aromatic oils. *Pogostemon cablin* is widely used in perfumery to provide a sensuous, earthy base note. The essential oil is steam-distilled from the leaves, and there is a definite hint of laughter from the great god Pan in this musky perfume! Its earthy aroma is reputed to balance the emotions, but that probably depends on whether or not you can tolerate the smell. Unlike many essential oils, the hot, heavy perfume improves with age, and if used in very discreet amounts, it blends well with most other scents. Patchouli is one of the best perfume fixatives. Many people find the smell unpleasant, but if a small amount is included in a blend, its powerful aroma is somewhat neutralized.

Uses

- Patchouli oil reduces inflammation, kills bacteria and prevents or destroys fungal infections. It is also a cell regenerator. This impressive list of properties makes it a valuable oil for skincare products and the treatment of skin problems. Use it to treat acne, athlete's foot, cracked and chapped skin, dermatitis, weeping eczema, fungal infections and insect bites. The astringent action helps to tighten loose skin. It increases the flow of urine, making it useful against fluid retention and possibly helpful for cystitis and urethritis.

- Patchouli is used in the treatment of digestive complaints such as indigestion, colitis and constipation.

- An effective antimicrobial, patchouli is effective for treating vaginal infections, oral thrush and herpes.

- Patchouli essential oil has been found to be a viable alternative to conventional insecticides in repelling ants.

- The quality of this oil can be likened to harvest time: it is rich, fruitful and abundant. It can rekindle desire in relationships that have become jaded through familiarity.

Tip: In India, patchouli leaves and flowers are laid between clothes and linens to protect them against insects.

PEPPERMINT

Mentha x piperita

Refreshing peppermint is a spreading perennial herb grown for its aromatic foliage, which has a variety of culinary uses. It is one of the most popular of the herbal teas, and the leaves add a delicious tang to cool drinks. Its clean, refreshing flavor and therapeutic qualities ensure that peppermint is widely used in the food and pharmaceutical industries.

Peppermint's most important chemical component is menthol, from which menthol crystals are formed. The oil is extracted from the leaves by steam distillation and is refreshing, cooling and warming. The perfume is highly penetrating and minty; it blends well with benzoin, eucalyptus, lavender, lemon, marjoram, rosemary and other mints. Peppermint and lavender oils have an affinity for each other and work in a complementary and synergistic way. Peppermint oil is widely used.

Uses

- Two or three drops of peppermint oil used in a facial steam help to cleanse congested skin and kill bacteria. This makes it helpful for treating acne, dermatitis, itching, ringworm and scabies.

- Peppermint oil is a very good deterrent to insects and rodents, who all seem to detest its smell.

- It is one of the most important oils for treating problems of the digestive system; it also encourages bile production and stimulates and strengthens the liver.

- Peppermint oil helps to expel gas from the stomach and intestines, easing nausea, stomach cramps and indigestion. For indigestion after a meal, mix 1 drop only of peppermint oil with a little honey in a glass. Add warm water (at least ½ cup/125 mL), stir and enjoy. The burping that follows is almost immediate and most satisfactory! The same treatment can be used to ease nausea or vomiting caused by food or travel sickness.

- A hot bath containing 3 drops peppermint oil, 3 drops marjoram oil and 4 drops lavender oil in 1 tsp (5 mL) vegetable oil will warm and stimulate and will often avert a cold or influenza. Drink a cup of peppermint and lemon tea while in the bath, to encourage perspiration and to help kill viruses and bacteria. If an infection such as a feverish cold, bronchitis or influenza has already struck, peppermint oil will help to loosen mucus and cool and reduce the fever.

- The cooling and pain-relieving action of peppermint is immensely soothing to hot, tired and aching feet and legs. Use 1% oil in a spray or gel to apply to the legs and feet (it shouldn't be rubbed in but allowed to dry naturally on the skin).

Tip: Enteric-coated peppermint capsules are available from pharmacies. These capsules don't release the peppermint oil until they have reached the intestine, where they will relieve the symptoms of painful colic and irritable bowel syndrome.

Cautions

- Do not use in conjunction with homeopathic remedies. Store separately too, as peppermint can act as an antidote to them.

- Do not use more than 5% in a preparation.

- Do not apply peppermint oil on or near the face of babies and children. The essential oil can be a mucous membrane irritant, although the risk is low.

- Avoid using if you have irregular heartbeat or glucose-6-phosphate dehydrogenase deficiency (G6PD).

- It is especially important to make sure that peppermint essential oil is not accidentally ingested. Ingestion should be avoided if you have cholestasis or gastro-esophageal disease (GERD); negative inter-actions have been known to occur.

Peppermint oil will constrict capillaries at first, which leads to a cooling sensation. This will be followed by a rubifacient effect, which brings a warming sensation.

- Headaches, mental fatigue, nervous stress, palpitations, vertigo, dizziness and fainting attacks can be treated by applying cold peppermint oil compresses to the forehead, smelling the oil directly from the bottle, or by using it in a diffuser or, where appropriate, in an air spray.

- A mental stimulant, peppermint promotes mental clarity, rouses the conscious mind, encourages positivity and enables one to overcome negative thoughts.

- Peppermint relieves palpitations and the symptoms of shock and hysteria.

- Peppermint was investigated for its anticonvulsant activity and found to be very promising for the treatment of epilepsy, because it reduced seizure activity.

- Peppermint-soaked cloths plugged into holes in walls can keep rats and mice away, as they are repelled by the scent.

PETITGRAIN

Citrus aurantium var. *amara fol* syn. *C. aurantium* var. *bigardia*

Petitgrain (bigarade) essential oil is distilled from the same Seville orange tree as neroli, but it is extracted from the leaves and twigs rather than the flowers. It can be used as a less expensive substitute for neroli because it has similar qualities. However, the perfume is not as subtle and the therapeutic properties are not as profound. Prior to this century, the tiny green unripe fruits of the tree were used to obtain the oil, giving it the name *petit grain*, or "little berry." Petitgrain's perfume is sweet and green, with sharper undernotes of citrus. It blends well with benzoin, bergamot, clary sage, geranium, lavender, neroli and palmarosa.

Not the Same Oil

Petitgrain from Paraguay is produced from a different variety of orange tree and has a different chemical composition from bigarade. Be sure to check the label on your oil when purchasing.

Uses

- Petitgrain is an antiseptic tonic and sebum regulator for oily skin and hair; it is particularly beneficial for oily dandruff and acne.

- It is lovely to use in baths and blends as an antiperspirant and deodorant.

- Petitgrain is useful in perfume blends to add a fresh citrus note and to act as a middle-note moderator, balancing the top and base notes.

- Petitgrain is helpful to people recovering from severe or long illness, as it has a mildly stimulating effect on the immune system, lifts the spirits and eases nervous indigestion and flatulence.

- It changes the feeling of wanting to be alone to one of sociability. Petitgrain clears the conscious mind and leaves it bright, cheerful and aware. It has a gentle sedative effect that soothes anger and panic.

Tip: Try a blend of petitgrain, orange and neroli essential oils for the ultimate orange experience. The effect on the emotions is that of a broad ray of sunshine breaking through dark clouds on a winter's day.

A Great Aroma

For a wonderful aromatic lift, try petitgrain sur fleurs ("petitgrain on flowers"). This essential oil is distilled from the flowers and the leaves, which brings the best of both aromas together in a heady and engaging fragrance.

PIMENTO

Pimenta dioica syn. *P. officinalis*

Pimento, a native of the West Indies, is commonly called Jamaica pepper or allspice. It should not be confused with a variety of capsicum pepper known as pimiento. It is an evergreen tree that bears white flowers, which become the peppery-flavored berries used in cooking and as a scent for potpourri. The spicy aromatic oil is distilled from the leaves and berries; however, the oil from the berries is preferred to the leaf oil. This oil blends well with other spice oils, frankincense, lemon, orange and pine.

Caution

It is especially important to make sure that pimento (allspice) essential oil is not accidentally ingested. Ingestion should be avoided when taking certain medications; negative interactions have been known to occur.

Uses

- Pimento is a very warming oil that quickly stimulates the circulation. It is best used for massaging small areas of the body that are cold rather than for a complete body massage. One drop of the essential oil in 4 tsp (20 mL) carrier oil or lotion will be sufficient. The areas to massage include the chest during infections such as persistent coughs, colds and influenza; the abdomen (in a clockwise direction) during attacks of colic, flatulence, vomiting or intestinal cramps; and the legs when there are cramps and muscle pain, especially due to tension. If using the essential oil from the leaf, you may use 2 drops in 4 tsp (20 mL) carrier oil.

- Blend with other carminative oils to make an inhaler for nausea, stomach cramps, gas and indigestion.

PINE

Pinus sylvestris

The Scots pine is the only one indigenous to the United Kingdom and is also the most common pine found throughout Europe. Pine essential oil is steam-distilled from the needles; the chemical composition may vary among different varieties of the tree. Its refreshing, clean perfume makes pine one of the most commercial of the oils—its aroma is in demand for products ranging from perfumes to household disinfectants, detergents and insecticides. Pine oil blends well with cedarwood, clary sage, eucalyptus, rosemary and tea tree. Note that there are other species of pine essential oil, but they are limited in availability. The oil from the dwarf Swiss mountain pine (*Pinus mugo* var. *pumilo*) can cause contact dermatitis if it has been left to oxidize.

Uses

- Pine oil is one of the best oils for treating scabies, cuts, head lice and sores.

- Pine is a strong pulmonary antiseptic. It has a particularly powerful effect on the respiratory system: when used in baths, massage oil or inhalations and air sprays, it kills bacteria, helps to loosen and remove mucus, increases perspiration and acts as a restorative. It can be used to great advantage in the treatment of bronchitis, catarrh, coughs, sinusitis, sore throat, colds and influenza.

- It is a warming and soothing treatment for tired, sore muscles.

- Add pine oil to the bath either on its own or in a blend, in 1 tsp (5 mL) milk or mixed with Epsom salts. Those who suffer from arthritis, rheumatism, muscular aches and pains, poor circulation, gout, fatigue and nervous exhaustion will benefit from this mentally and physically restorative bath. It also works to soothe achy, tired and grumpy children—just pop them in a bath with Epsom salts that smell of pine forests.

- Cystitis, urethritis and other urinary infections may be eased by the diuretic and antiseptic properties of pine.

- Pine comforts and strengthens us when we are feeling unworthy, weak or unsure of ourselves. It tells us that we are unique and helps us to tap into our inner power.

PLAI

Zingiber cassumunar syn. *Z. montanum*

In the same family as ginger, plai has a similarly spicy aroma. It is a favorite among Thai massage therapists for its curative properties. The plant grows wild in Thailand and the essential oil is steam-distilled from the rhizome. The aroma is reminiscent of eucalyptus and green pepper, with soft notes of ginger and bitter citrus. Blend with bergamot, black pepper, citrus oils, ginger, helichrysum, lavender, marjoram or nutmeg, depending on the effect desired for your blend.

Uses

- Use in massage blends to relieve aches and pains, joint problems, muscle spasms, rheumatism, inflammation, arthritis, sciatica, sprains and strains, torn muscles and sore ligaments and tendons.

- Plai, with its cooling anti-inflammatory action, is reported to be a natural antihistamine. It may reduce the severity of asthma attacks and aid with respiratory problems.

- Plai essential oil is antimicrobial and antiviral. It is stimulating to the immune system and can be considered a general tonic to support the body.

- Use to reduce the pain and discomfort of menstrual cramps, lift your spirits and calm your nerves.

- Use in a vaporizer or diffuser during cold and flu season to take advantage of this oil's anti-infection benefits.

- The oil is used traditionally for treatment of digestive complaints and gas.

RAVENSARA

Ravensara aromatica

There is much confusion between ravensara and ravintsara (*Cinnamonum camphora*; see page 101) essential oils because of the similarity in names. To add to the uncertainty, *Ravensara aromatica* is distilled from both the bark and the leaf, and there are differences between the two types of oils. It is extremely important to know the difference between them: the bark oil is much higher in methyl chavicol, or estragole (90% to 95%); the leaf oil contains far less of this substance (2.4% to 12%).

The leaf oil is more readily available. Although it contains less estragole, any amount in an oil is of concern because methyl chavicol is potentially carcinogenic. Great care must be taken with this essential oil. *Ravensara aromatica* oil distilled from the bark alone is used mainly by professional aromatherapists for respiratory and circulatory conditions.

The aroma of ravensara oil is camphoraceous, with notes of spice and wood.

Uses

- Make good use of the immunostimulant and virus-inhibiting properties of ravensara to protect the body during epidemics of influenza or other viral infections. If you have already been infected by a virus, a bath followed by a massage containing the oil or the use of an air spray along with inhalation will dispel the virus very rapidly.

- Use ravensara to treat all respiratory tract infections, such as bronchitis, catarrh, sinusitis, colds and coughs. Its combination of antiseptic, antibacterial and strongly antiviral properties will loosen and remove mucus.

- As it is powerfully antiviral, ravensara can be used for cold sores, genital herpes and shingles. Blend it with oils such as lavender or chamomile to ease pain. Used in air sprays, it will help to prevent the spread of diseases such as chicken pox and measles.

- Arthritis, rheumatism, sore joints and tight, tense muscles will all benefit from the muscle-relaxant effect and pain relief offered by this oil.

Ravensara

Ravensara is a Latinization of the Malagasy word *ravintsara*. It was generally applied to the oil distilled from either *Ravensara aromatica* or *Cinnamonum camphora*.

Cautions

- Ravensara oil is potentially carcinogenic.

- The bark oil may inhibit blood clotting.

- Do not use undiluted. This oil should always be diluted in a carrier oil.

- Use only 1 drop bark oil in 10 tsp (50 mL) carrier oil.

- Use 1 drop leaf oil in 1 tsp (5 mL) carrier oil. The leaf oil may cause skin sensitization if it is old or oxidized. Keep it in a cool, dark place, ensuring that the cap is tightly closed.

- It is especially important to make sure that ravensara essential oil is not accidentally ingested. Ingestion should be avoided when taking certain medications; negative interactions have been known to occur.

RAVINTSARA

Cinnamomum camphora syn. *Ravintsara aromatica,*
R. camphora

Ravintsara oil, also referred to as "ho leaf" and "white camphor,"
is extracted by steam distillation from the leaves of *Cinnamomum camphora*. It has a fresh, slightly sweet, earthy aroma with green
notes, similar to rosemary. The main chemical component of this
oil is 1,8-cineole; its chemical composition indicates that the
essential oil is antimicrobial, analgesic, antibacterial, antifungal
and neurotonic.

Uses

- Ravintsara is a good choice to include in the treatment of
  respiratory concerns, including colds and flu, coughs, bronchitis
  and asthma, because the oil can help to loosen mucus and
  clear the sinuses.

- Include ravintsara in your blends to stimulate and support the
  immune system.

- Combined with melissa essential oil and tamanu vegetable oil,
  ravintsara is reported to be effective in treating viral and fungal
  infections such as herpes simplex, shingles and athlete's foot.

- Use for stress-related conditions, including chronic anxiety,
  paralyzing fear and restlessness—the oil helps to calm the
  nerves and encourages self-esteem.

- Ravintsara soothes tired, achy muscles and relieves the pain
  of arthritis.

Cautions

- Do not use with children under the age of 10, as *Cinnamomum camphora* may cause distress to a child's nervous system and
  create breathing concerns.

- It is especially important to make sure that ravintsara essential oil
  is not accidentally ingested. Ingestion should be avoided when
  taking certain medications; negative interactions have been
  known to occur.

- Ravintsara oil may be known as "white camphor." It should not
  be confused with yellow, brown or red camphor essential oil.
  These oils are potentially carcinogenic and not suitable for use
  in aromatherapy.

- Care must be taken when using with people who are asthmatic.

- This oil may act as an antidote with homeopathic remedies.

Cautions

- Ravintsara oil
  may cause skin
  sensitization
  if it is old or
  oxidized. Keep
  the oil in a cool,
  dark place,
  ensuring that
  the cap is tightly
  closed.

- Do not use
  undiluted. This
  oil should always
  be diluted in
  a carrier oil or
  lotion.

- People with
  dermatitis are
  advised to use
  no more than
  3 drops per
  2 tsp (10 mL)
  carrier oil or
  lotion for topical
  applications
  such as massage
  or body lotions,
  because of its
  1,8-cineole
  content.

Tip: Buy essential oils one at a time and learn as much as you can about each one before buying more.

ROSE

Rosa centifolia (cabbage rose), *R. damascena* (damask rose), *R. gallica* (French rose)

The rose has been prized for its beauty and perfume for such a long time that it is hard to imagine that in centuries past it was more highly regarded for its gentle medicinal qualities. In medieval Europe, "rose juice" seems to have been something of a cure-all for every imaginable ailment. The flower has long been a symbol of love and purity, and at weddings rose petals are still often strewn in the path of the bride and groom.

Rose "otto" essential oil is distilled from the plant, but the main method of extraction is by enfleurage, a labor-intensive (and thus expensive) method that requires a huge quantity of petals to yield a small amount of a sticky substance known as an absolute (see page 67). The distilled rose oil ("rose otto") costs twice as much the absolute, but aromatherapists prefer to use it for treatments because the absolute can contain trace amounts of solvents. The perfume of rose essential oil is sweet, sensual and romantic and blends with almost all other oils. Rose water, which is used in skin- and hair-care products, is a byproduct of steam distillation (see page 125).

Rose essential oil and rose water are produced in several parts of the world. The best and most popular products are from Bulgaria and Turkey. Bulgarian rose essential oil smells like a sweet, fresh bouquet of flowers, whereas the Turkish version has a hint of green or a slight musty note.

The absolute is preferred for perfume making because the aroma is sweeter and more lasting than that of the essential oil. It appears that the scent of the absolute works like a reverse version of the plant's life cycle: its aroma starts out a little musty, like week-old roses, but develops over time into a sweet and lively floral perfume like that of fresh flowers.

Uses

- Rose is good for all skin types, especially dry, mature and sensitive skin. It soothes inflammation and constricts capillaries, making it useful for those suffering from thread veins. It can be used to treat eczema and herpes.

- Rose is considered a "woman's oil," partly because of its perfume but largely because of its affinity with the female reproductive system. It tones the uterus, encourages and regulates menstrual flow, and eases problems such as menstrual irregularity and excessive menstrual loss. It soothes cramps and spasms in the intestines and uterus, postpartum depression and leukorrhea. Despite its seemingly "female only" uses, it also has a reputation for increasing the production of semen.

- Rose tones the digestive system, stimulates and strengthens the liver, stimulates the secretion of bile and relieves liver congestion. This makes it useful in blends as a digestive and to ease nausea and vomiting. It has a tonic action on the heart, easing palpitations and stimulating circulation.

- Research shows that use of rose essential oil can delay the onset and duration of seizures. Studies of the effects of rose essential oil as a complementary treatment for children with refractory seizures showed that patients who used the oil displayed a significant reduction in the frequency of attacks.

- Sensual but never sensuous, rose teaches us to be loving, caring and compassionate, both to ourselves and to others. Warmly relaxing and gentle, this oil reduces stress and tension, calms the nervous system and lifts our spirits from gloomy introspection and depression. Rose is a calming hug when you most need it, especially for sad and anxious children.

Attars

An attar is a natural perfume made from delicate flower petals and sandalwood essential oil. The flower petals are distilled using low heat and low pressure. The aromatic molecules rise with the steam and then drop when cooled into a copper receptacle filled with sandalwood oil. The water is then poured off. New petals are placed in the still and the process starts again, to be repeated over several days until the sandalwood oil is saturated with the scent of the flower's essential oil. This creates a beautiful natural perfume, free of chemicals and alcohol. It is, however, not intended for therapeutic use.

ROSEMARY

Rosmarinus officinalis

Rosemary has long been valued for its culinary and medicinal uses and is widely used in the food industry as a flavoring and an antioxidant. The best essential oil is distilled from the flowering tips and leaves. The perfume is sharp, penetrating, fresh and enlivening. It blends well with basil, bergamot, cedarwood, all citrus oils (especially grapefruit), lavender and peppermint.

Uses

- A strong astringent, rosemary is useful for tightening and toning skin that is loose and sagging. It kills bacteria and is a good oil to use for treating acne, dermatitis, eczema, athlete's foot and scabies.

Cautions

- Use only low doses of rosemary oil during pregnancy. To be safe, avoid the bornyl acetate and verbenone chemotypes, as they have not been studied for use in pregnancy.

- Depending on their camphor content, some rosemary oils may be neurotoxic and should be used with care.

- When using *Rosmarinus officinalis* ct. cineole, do not apply on or near the face of babies or children.

- Encouraging research shows that rosemary essential oil is effective against multidrug-resistant strains of bacteria found in the respiratory tract, abdomen, urinary tract and skin, as well as on medical equipment in a hospital setting.

- Rosemary is an excellent hair and scalp treatment; it is said to promote hair growth, which is why it's a good idea to include rosemary in shampoos, rinses and hair tonics. It will also control dandruff, greasy hair and oily scalp.

- A restorative oil, rosemary strengthens bodily systems, increases energy and quickens the function of glands.

- It is a good tonic for the heart, liver and gallbladder, normalizing blood pressure, easing palpitations and improving circulation. Rosemary essential oil was found to be clinically significant in improving the quality of life for patients with low blood pressure.

- Rosemary improves digestive problems such as indigestion and flatulence. It also eases cramps and spasms in the intestines and symptoms of colitis.

- A powerful stimulant and strengthener of the nervous system, rosemary has the effect of sharpening the memory and restoring a lost sense of smell. As little as a drop or two of rosemary can be beneficial in an inhalation blend.

- Rosemary has a reputation for a tonic effect on the lungs, which is useful when treating asthma, bronchitis, colds, coughs and whooping cough.

- Rosemary eases pain by numbing nerves. It produces localized redness and warmth when applied to the skin, which makes it a good choice for baths and massage oils for treating arthritis, rheumatism, stiff and sore muscles and gout.

- Rosemary is the practical teacher, lending strength and power to our thinking, clearing the fog from our minds, and easing symptoms of nervous exhaustion.

Rosemary Chemotypes

There are many chemotypes (see page 29) of rosemary essential oil. Unfortunately, most research papers do not identify which chemotype of the oil was used in a particular study. Here are the therapeutic benefits of each chemotype:

Rosmarinus officinalis ct. cineole is a strong expectorant. It increases bile in the liver and stimulates the digestive system, helping to expel gas. It strengthens the heart and nerves and calms muscle spasms. It is antibacterial and mildly anesthetic.

R. officinalis ct. verbenone is particularly effective for clearing thick mucus. It is antibacterial and promotes skin healing through the formation of scar tissue. It is good as a general tonic because it is hormone-balancing and regulates the endocrine system. It regulates the hypothalamus and is calming and lifts depression. Verbenone is considered safe and nonirritating and is acceptable for use with children over the age of 2.

R. officinalis ct. **camphor** stimulates circulation and promotes elimination from the liver and kidneys. It eases the aches and pains of overworked and sore muscles and aches due to colds and flu. It can help to improve circulation in rheumatic conditions and ease respiratory complaints, such as those experienced with cold and flu. It is useful with chronic bladder infections and gallstones, as well as menstrual irregularities, including lack of menstruation, cramping and heavy or long periods. It clears a foggy brain.

R. officinalis ct. **bornyl acetate**. This chemotype is especially good for aches and pains, arthritis and rheumatism. It has a sedative effect and calms anxiety and stress. It is antifungal, anti-inflammatory and analgesic. It soothes rashes, promotes regeneration of skin cells and promotes healing through the formation of scar tissue. It helps to relieve the symptoms of bronchitis and make breathing easier.

ROSEWOOD

Aniba rosaeodora

The rosewood tree is a native of the Amazon Basin. Its fragrant heartwood is used to make very fine and expensive furniture. The essential oil is steam-distilled from heartwood chips; its perfume is a pleasant blend of wood and flower with spicy undertones that blends well with most other essential oils. It is sometimes sold as *"bois de rose."*

Rosewood is an endangered species, and in 2010 it was placed on the CITES II (Convention on International Trade in Endangered Species of Wild Fauna and Flora) list to protect existing plants. Although the oil can now be sold with a special permit, sales and trading have declined drastically. Essential oil producers are now (perhaps too late) successfully cultivating the trees, although large-scale plantings do not yet exist. Before purchasing rosewood essential oil, inquire as to where the wood was obtained and how the oil was produced, to learn if it was ethically harvested and manufactured.

Uses

- Rosewood oil assists in cell stimulation and regeneration. It is antiseptic and can help to treat acne, cuts, dermatitis, eczema, scars and wounds. It is a good oil to use in skincare blends to treat dry, sensitive and wrinkled skin. It is also a good deodorant and insect repellent.

- Rosewood is an excellent immune system booster. It would be the obvious choice to use in baths and massages to treat chronic fatigue syndrome, glandular fever (mononucleosis), influenza and other conditions where the immune system is weakened.

- Rosewood has a calming effect on the nerves and brain, which, combined with its modest painkilling ability, makes it a good oil to use in blends for headaches, jet lag, female sexual dysfunction or other times when the brain and nerves are strained or stressed.

- Rosewood lifts and soothes a tired, stressed mind that is beset by too many problems. It is also reputed to be an aphrodisiac.

SAGE

Salvia officinalis

This fragrant herb is originally from the Mediterranean. Prized for its use in both culinary applications and medicines since ancient Rome, sage was used for a wide range of disorders, including respiratory infections, digestive problems and menstrual discomfort. It was even used to increase a woman's fertility. Sage is not as widely used in aromatherapy because it is reputedly highly toxic and extremely stimulating to the nervous system. However, used with care, sage oil can fight fever, aid in digestive complaints and encourage menstruation. This essential oil has been studied for its benefit with Alzheimer's disease and has been found effective in managing the symptoms of mild to moderate dementia. It is suspected that it may also reduce agitation in Alzheimer's patients.

Since sage is moderately toxic, we feel that safer and more effective oils can be used instead. Sage oil blends well with citrus oils, hyssop, lavender, rosemary and rosewood.

SAGE, SPANISH (Lavender Sage)

Salvia lavandulaefolia

In Spain, Spanish sage was considered a panacea. It was thought to protect against even the deadliest infections, aid fertility and promote longevity. Use of this essential oil was preferred over that of common sage because it combines the lovely floral scent of lavender with the fresh, camphoraceous aroma of sage, and it is considered a safer alternative. It is used largely in food and beverages and as a fragrant ingredient in cosmetics and soaps. It blends well with clary sage, cypress, geranium, lavender and rosemary.

Uses

- Spanish sage essential oil is considered a general nerve tonic and can be useful in an inhaler for headaches, fatigue, nervous exhaustion and general stress. It aids circulation and brings relief for arthritis, fluid retention, painful menstruation and general malaise.

Cautions

- Avoid use if pregnant or while breastfeeding.

- Sage oil is neurotoxic. Use no more than 1 drop in 2 tsp (10 mL) carrier oil or lotion.

- It is especially important to make sure that sage essential oil is not accidentally ingested. Ingestion can cause seizures, coma and even death, depending on the dose.

- Used in personal care, the essential oil can be used in hair preparations to combat hair loss and dandruff. As a natural antiperspirant, it also helps to reduce sweating. It is used in mouthwash to treat sore and infected gums (be sure to spit it all out) and also soothes skin affected by dermatitis and eczema and helps to fight acne.

- This oil has value as an immune enhancer. Use it in a diffuser or vaporizer to fight colds and flu, or in cool compresses to reduce fever.

- Spanish sage is detoxifying to the blood. It unclogs a congested liver and supports the gallbladder and bile ducts.

SANDALWOOD

Santalum album

Sandalwood is a small parasitic tree that feeds through suckers attached to the roots of other trees. The oil is steam-distilled from the heartwood of trees that are at least 25 years old (and as old as 40), depending on the species. Although there is a high demand for the oil, today sandalwood is in a critical situation because overharvesting has severely depleted the legal supplies. As of this writing, it is estimated that 90% of India's and 20% of Australia's annual supply have been subject to poaching.

India has been replaced by Australia as the leading grower of sandalwood. Australia provides essential oil from two species: cultivated *Santalum album* and wild-grown S. *spicatum*. Although there are differences between the two, S. *spicatum* is a reasonable alternative to S. *album*; this species, which is sustainable, accounts for about 60% of the world's supply. However, S. *spicatum* is obtained through various methods that include solvent extraction, in which case trace amounts of the solvent can remain in the essential oil. If you are concerned about this, look for oil that is steam-distilled. Hawaiian sandalwood (S. *paniculatum*) essential oil is very close to the Indian versions in terms of aroma. It has a beautiful rich, woody aroma; however, the yield is not sustainable and it has been recommended that the tree be listed as an endangered species.

A gorgeous sandalwood grown in the South Pacific region, S. *austrocaledonicum*, is similar in aroma and composition to S. *album*. The essential oil is produced from trees native to New Caledonia and Vanuatu. However, because of excessive logging and faulty reforestation practices, these trees are in very short supply. The growing areas are reforesting naturally, but the process is very slow. Because of the high demand and an inadequate supply to meet that demand, all the species of sandalwood that are wild-harvested for oil production are becoming increasingly rare and more difficult to find.

Renowned for its spiritual and uplifting qualities, sandalwood incense and oil were (and still are) used in temples to aid and deepen meditation. Today those distinctive mysterious, sweet, woody characteristics are used as a fixative and fragrance in the manufacture of perfumes, cosmetics and toiletries such as soap and aftershave. It blends well with most other essential oils, but especially benzoin, neroli, petitgrain and rose.

Uses

- Sandalwood is a lovely oil to use in blends for all skin types, but it is particularly beneficial for dry, thin, aging skin and cracked, chapped skin. It is a good oil to include in aftershave preparations, as it prevents inflammation and has an aroma that is very acceptable to men. Use in compresses or creams to heal dry eczema and acne and to cool inflammations.

- Sandalwood is a pulmonary antiseptic; it also helps to loosen and remove mucus. Use in inhalations and chest and throat rubs, where it will ease chronic bronchitis, excess mucus, dry, irritating cough and sore throat.

- Sandalwood acts as a urinary system cleanser, increases the flow of urine and is antiseptic. It can be used with warm compresses and massage to ease cystitis and urethritis.

- Sandalwood oil can help us to move deeper into meditation by allaying the fears that are sometimes present when we begin to explore our psyche. It is also recognized as one of the few true aphrodisiacs and can help to promote sexuality in those who suffer from sexual dysfunction. Its warm and comforting aroma soothes nervous tension, lifts depression, calms hyperactivity and can help to encourage sound sleep.

SARO

Cinnamosma fragrans

Saro may not be as well known as other essential oils, but it packs a punch! The oil is distilled from the small, tough leaves of a plant that grows in Madagascar, in tropical gorges and on rocks along riversides. Distillation is done in partnership with local villagers and nongovernmental organizations, who work together to ensure sustainability of the plants.

Saro covers a broad spectrum of ailments. It is antiviral, tonic and expectorant. Its aroma is described as subtle, pleasant, green and warm. Because of its chemical composition, the oil is wonderful for fighting germs and infection—it is balancing to the immune system.

Cautions

- Sandalwood has a very penetrating and long-lasting perfume.

- Use up to 2% in blends. *Santalum album* has been known to cause adverse skin reactions, but that is very rare. No adverse reactions have been reported with *S. austro-caledonicum* or *S. spicatum*.

- It is especially important to make sure that *Santalum spicatum* (West Australian sandalwood) essential oil is not accidentally ingested. Ingestion should be avoided when taking certain medications; negative interactions have been known to occur.

Uses

- Saro is a wonderful essential oil that benefits ears, nose and throat complaints. It helps to relieve congestion and thin and expel mucus. Used in inhaler blends, diffusers and vaporizers, it helps to relieve the pressure and pain of sinusitis, reduce inflammation in bronchitis and asthma (in small doses), and encourage a productive cough.

- The oil supports the immune system, relieves sore throats and fights viral infections such as chicken pox, measles, herpes simplex 1 and 2, and shingles.

- The essential oil is restorative to the liver and kidneys, helping them to perform their many functions affiliated with digestion, metabolism, immunity and maintaining the storehouses that supply nutrients to the body.

- Used in massage oil, saro has a pleasant aroma that will lift your mood and ease physical and mental exhaustion.

SPEARMINT

Mentha spicata

Spearmint is a popular culinary herb. Its dark, crinkly leaves and flowering tops are steam-distilled to produce an essential oil that is gentler than peppermint, making it more suitable for children, pregnant women, elderly people and those who are convalescing. The perfume is sweet and minty; it blends well with basil, benzoin, grapefruit, lavender, marjoram, peppermint and rosemary.

Uses

- Two or three drops of spearmint oil used in a facial steam help to cleanse congested skin and kill bacteria, which makes it helpful for treating acne, dermatitis, itching, ringworm and scabies.

- Like peppermint, spearmint oil is one of the most important oils for treating problems of the digestive system; it encourages bile production and stimulates and strengthens the liver. It helps to expel gas from the stomach and intestines and eases nausea, stomach cramps and indigestion.

- If an infection such as a feverish cold, bronchitis or influenza has already struck, spearmint oil will help to loosen and remove mucus and cool and reduce the fever.

- The cooling and pain-relieving action of spearmint is immensely soothing to hot, tired and aching feet and legs. A 1% dilution can be used in a spray or gel to apply to the legs and feet (don't rub it in; let it dry naturally on the skin).

Cautions

- Do not apply saro oil on or near the face of children.

- Do not use with children under the age of 5, as saro may cause distress to a child's nervous system and create breathing concerns.

- Saro may cause skin sensitization if it is old or oxidized. Keep the oil in a cool, dark place, ensuring that the cap is tightly closed.

- Do not use undiluted. This oil should always be diluted in a carrier oil or lotion.

- Headaches, mental fatigue, nervous stress, shock, palpitations, vertigo, dizziness and fainting attacks can be treated by applying cold compresses to the forehead, smelling a drop of the oil on a tissue, or by using in a diffuser or, where appropriate, an air spray.

- A mental stimulant, spearmint promotes mental clarity, encourages positivity and enables one to overcome negative thoughts. It relieves the symptoms of shock, hysteria and palpitations.

SPIKENARD

Nardostachys jatamansi syn. *N. grandiflora*

Spikenard was one of the earliest aromatic plants used for medicine, in religious practices and to make perfume. There are many biblical references to spikenard; it is, for instance, mentioned in the Song of Solomon. Medieval Europeans used it as a flavoring in spiced wines and beer. The essential oil is distilled from the roots and rhizome of the plant. It is part of the valerian family and, like valerian, is used in applications that help to relieve tension, nervous indigestion, insomnia and inflammation of the skin. The aroma is strong, sweet and earthy, with an animal-like quality. It blends well with cistus, clary sage, cypress, frankincense, geranium, lavender, lemon, myrrh, patchouli, pine, rose, spice oils and vetiver.

Uses

- Add spikenard to a cool compress to help reduce fever or skin rashes. Blend into creams and lotions to rejuvenate mature skin.

- Use in massage blends to aid sleep (especially in cases of insomnia) and relax the body and mind in traumatic and stressful times.

- Massage into the abdomen and lower back to aid heavy and painful menstruation and cramping. Combine with lavender to make an inhaler for headaches and migraine.

STAR ANISE
See Anise, Star (page 32)

SWEET ORANGE
See Orange, Sweet (page 91)

Cautions

- Use spikenard in small quantities— 0.5% to 1% is plenty in any blend.

- There is a low risk that this oil may be sensitizing to the skin or irritating to mucous membranes in some individuals.

- Do not use in conjunction with homeopathic remedies. Store separately, as the oil may act as an antidote with them.

TANSY

Tanacetum vulgare

Tansy has a long history, from the ancient Greeks to the eighth century CE, when it was used by Benedictine monks as medicine to prevent intestinal worms, relieve rheumatic conditions and digestive complaints, reduce fevers, treat sores and "bring out" measles. The leaves were once used as a preservative for meat. Tansy is used as a companion planting for pest control, so it's not surprising that the essential oil is used in blends to repel insects. Not only can it deter flies, it is also used to keep rodents away. Traditionally used for digestive problems, fevers and wound healing, the oil can be soothing to the skin.

Today tansy seems to be gaining popularity, along with another species called blue tansy (*Tanacetum annum*); both oils are used to fight and prevent the flu, colds and infections—a fad that is dangerous. Regular tansy (*T. vulgare*) contains a large amount of thujone. This compound is neurotoxic and can cause convulsions, irregular heartbeat, gastrointestinal distress and loss of consciousness, depending on the amount used. Because of its thujone content, *T. vulgare* is rarely employed by professional aromatherapists.

Blue tansy (*T. annuum*) is considered the lesser of two evils. However, little research has been done with regard to its use and safety. It is reputed that blue tansy essential oil possesses a powerful antihistamine and anti-inflammatory action. Research has shown it to have strong antifungal activity against a number of fungi. This oil is considered by some to be nontoxic and nonirritating and suitable for healing the skin and preventing inflammation, sore muscles and joints. However, blue tansy contains camphor, a ketone that can build up in the body over time, and a large amount of chamazulene, which presents a risk of drug interaction with several types of medications. If used at all, it should be only in minimal doses and for a short period of time.

Regular tansy (*T. vulgare*) should not be used in home aromatherapy. Blue tansy (*T. annuum*) can be used with care.

Cautions

- Blue tansy (*Tanacetum annuum*) can pose a drug interaction problem with certain drugs, including some analgesic, antiarrhythmic, antipsychotic and anti-depressant medications, as well as those containing estrogen and serotonin.

- It is especially important to make sure that all types of tansy essential oil are not accidentally ingested. Ingestion should be avoided when taking certain medications, as negative interactions have been known to occur.

TEA TREE

Melaleuca alternifolia

There is no doubt about it: tea tree (or ti-tree, as it is sometimes spelled) is tops when it comes to healing oils. It is an excellent antifungal and antimicrobial essential oil. Tea tree is closely related to cajuput (*Melaleuca leucadendra*) and niaouli (*M. quinquenervia*) but is more powerful than both. It is grown on commercial plantations in Australia. The steam-distilled essential oil is widely used in household and personal toiletries and cleansers as well as in natural remedies. The perfume is resinous and slightly musty; it blends well with cinnamon, clary sage, clove, cypress, eucalyptus, geranium, ginger, lavender, lemon, lemongrass, mandarin, marjoram, rosemary and thyme.

Uses

- Tea tree oil is a "first aid in a bottle" treatment for abscesses, acne, athlete's foot, blisters, boils, minor burns and scalds, rashes, gingivitis, mouth ulcers, insect bites, lice, diaper rash, ringworm and infected wounds.

- It may be used undiluted on small areas of skin. One drop of undiluted tea tree oil applied to a cold sore will often prevent it from getting worse. Corns and plantar warts can also be treated this way (use the oil directly on the corn or wart and cover it with a bandage), but they take a little longer to heal. Pimples will often respond to the "one-drop treatment" as well. However, in our experience it is best to dilute the essential oil in a couple of drops of jojoba oil. Sometimes undiluted use will "harden" the pimple because it is very drying, and then it can take almost 2 weeks for the bump to disappear.

- Tea tree has many outstanding properties. It is best known for its capacity to stimulate the immune system, inhibit the growth of viruses, prevent or destroy fungal infections and kill bacteria.

- Tea tree helps to loosen and remove mucus. Because it has the ability to stimulate heavy sweating, it also reduces fever. In conjunction with its antiviral, antibacterial and antifungal qualities, these capacities make it one of the most important oils to use in gargles, baths, massage blends, air sprays and diffusers to treat respiratory tract infections such as bronchitis, catarrh, colds, coughs, influenza, fevers, sinusitis, tonsillitis, tuberculosis and whooping cough. Add it to air sprays and diffusers to prevent infectious diseases from spreading.

- Under the guidance of a qualified health-care provider, tea tree oil is often recommended for use in sitz baths and other treatments for genital conditions, including vaginal trichomonas, candida, thrush, pruritus (itching of the anus and genital area) and genital herpes.

- Use its ability to boost the immune system in baths and massages prior to and after surgery, to strengthen the system.

Cautions

- Tea tree oil may cause skin sensitization if it is old or oxidized.

- Although many books and practitioners will tell you it is okay to use tea tree essential oil undiluted, we recommend that it always be diluted. The oil has the potential to oxidize quickly, and dilution helps to avoid possible dermal irritation.

- Keep the oil in a cool, dark place, ensuring that the cap is tightly closed.

THYME

Thymus vulgaris

Aromatic thyme, a perennial herb with culinary, medicinal and cosmetic uses, has long been associated with strength and wellbeing. Thyme is a powerful essential oil distilled from the leaves and flowering tops. There are several chemotypes (see page 29) of thyme, each with its own risks and enhanced benefits. Two types are predominant in the market: the thymol chemotype (*Thymus vulgaris* ct. thymol) and the linalool chemotype (*T. vulgaris* ct. linalool). The linalool oil contains fewer toxic phenols and is safer to use, particularly for the skin and in blends for children. Thyme has a perfume that is warmly, sweetly pungent and blends well with bergamot, cedarwood, chamomile, juniper, lemon, mandarin, niaouli, petitgrain and rosemary.

Uses

- Thyme oil is a powerful healer for all types of skin infections; it is strongly antibacterial and stimulates the production of white blood corpuscles, prevents or destroys fungal infections, and promotes the formation of scar tissue in wound healing. This makes it suitable for treating a wide range of problems, including abscesses, acne, boils and carbuncles, bruises, minor burns and scalds, cold sores, dermatitis, eczema and insect bites. Thyme oil must always be well diluted, as it can sting and cause irritation.

- Thyme oil is the reviver—it has a stimulant action on the immune system and a strengthening and tonic action on the circulation system and the mind. It increases energy and quickens the function of glands.

- Thyme also stimulates the digestive system, acting as an intestinal antiseptic, aiding digestion, relieving cramps and spasms in the intestines and easing flatulence and gastric infections.

Cautions

- Thyme is very powerful—use a maximum of 1% in blends.

- Do not use undiluted. This oil should always be diluted in a carrier oil or lotion.

- There is a low risk of skin irritation and a moderate risk of mucous membrane irritation with the thymol and carvacrol chemotypes.

- It increases the flow of urine, and this, combined with its antiseptic action, makes it useful in abdominal compresses to treat cystitis and urethritis (use only 3 drops, dissolved in 4 tsp/20 mL whole milk). The diuretic action helps to remove uric acid, making it useful in blends for easing arthritis, gout, rheumatism and sciatica.

- Thyme is a respiratory tract disinfectant; it also helps to loosen and remove mucus and increase perspiration. In chest rubs or used in a diffuser, it will ease the symptoms of asthma. Used in massage blends or in an inhaler (use 3 drops), it can help to treat bronchitis, catarrh, colds, coughs, croup, emphysema, sinusitis and whooping cough.

- Thyme oil encourages and regulates menstrual flow.

- Thyme gives courage and strengthens the will and the nervous system. It is useful in treating insomnia, headaches, nervous debility and stress.

VALERIAN

Valeriana officinalis

Held in high regard since medieval times as a cure-all, valerian is used for all manner of nervous tension and agitation. The essential oil has been shown to have moderate antifungal activity against candida and moderate antioxidant benefit. Although used in different cultures for a variety of ailments ranging from cholera to backache, valerian appears to be most effective for use in conditions relating to the nervous system. The essential oil is distilled from the rhizome and has a strong warm, woody, earthy, musky aroma. It blends well with cedarwood, lavender, patchouli, petitgrain, pine and rosemary.

Uses

- Blend with vetiver, sandalwood and rose to calm restlessness and encourage good-quality sleep. Add a couple of drops to a tissue and slip inside the pillowcase.

- Use in massage blends to melt away tension and stress. Massage into the abdomen to calm a nervous stomach.

- Combine with star anise, lavender and rosemary to make an inhaler for migraine.

VETIVER

Vetiveria zizanoides

Vetiver is a scented wild grass that originated in South Asia. The essential oil is steam-distilled from its roots. The thick dark brown oil has an earthy aroma with musty undertones. It can be used as a fixative (see page 38) and to add depth to perfumes. It blends well with benzoin, clary sage, frankincense, geranium, jasmine, lavender, patchouli, violet and ylang ylang. It is widely used as a fragrance and fixative in soaps, perfumes and cosmetics, and in the food industry as a preservative.

Uses

- By far the most important attribute of this mysterious oil is its ability to strengthen the nervous and immune systems. This helps to reduce the risk of becoming sick because of lowered defenses.

- Vetiver is sometimes known as the "oil of tranquility," and certainly that property has been made use of for centuries. It is a deeply relaxing, balancing and healing oil for those who feel depressed, isolated and rootless. Use vetiver in baths that are wonderfully relaxing. It is useful in massage oil, particularly when you are nervous about future events or depressed because of the past. It helps to ease stress, calm the nerves and relieve insomnia.

- Vetiver is very grounding, useful in blends to help quiet hyperactive children and to encourage restful sleep.

- Vetiver's antiseptic properties help to heal acne, cuts and infected wounds.

- It is sometimes used in massage blends for arthritis, muscular aches and pains and rheumatism, as it increases the blood flow to a localized area.

Caution

Some vetiver essential oils contain isoeugenol, a known skin sensitizer. If you don't know whether isoeugenol is present in your essential oil, it is best to use no more than 1 drop in 4 tsp (20 mL) carrier oil or lotion.

VIOLET LEAF

Viola odorata

The heart-shaped leaves, delicate purple flowers and sweet perfume of the violet are well known to anyone who has walked in the damp and shady woodlands of Europe. This flower is now cultivated in gardens worldwide. Crystallized violet flowers are used as pretty and delicious decorations for cakes and desserts. Though the essential oil does exist, it is rare and difficult to find. Violet leaf is more commonly sold as an absolute (see page 67) that smells sweet, rich and floral. Obtained from the leaves and flowers, it blends with benzoin, citrus oils, frankincense, lavender, rose and sandalwood.

Uses

- Violet oil has antiseptic and healing properties that make it especially useful for treating skin problems such as acne, bruises and eczema, as well as swellings and wounds of all kinds.

- It has been found to be useful for treating a wide variety of problems ranging from rheumatism and fibromyalgia to poor circulation, headaches and excessive mucus.

- Violet leaf essential oil has been explored as an adjunct to medical treatment for breast cancer, having displayed its antitumor effect in research studies.

- From an emotional standpoint, those who experience a sense of loneliness because they feel out of sync with the world around them may take comfort in the aroma of violet leaf, as it provides deep emotional support for the individual.

YARROW

Achillea millefolium

As a traditional herbal medicine, yarrow was used for an array of conditions from respiratory infections and fever to digestive disorders and wound care. It is used as a flavoring ingredient in vermouths and bitters. The essential oil is steam-distilled from the flowers to produce a beautiful blue oil that has a sweet, fresh, green aroma. Yarrow blends well with black pepper, cedarwood, chamomile, citrus oils, clary sage, juniper, lavender, manuka, marjoram and ylang ylang.

Uses

- Use in creams to reduce inflammation and itching from eczema and rashes and hemorrhoids. Blend with aloe vera gel or calendula oil to tone the skin and heal wounds.

- Add to a carrier oil and massage on the abdomen to stimulate the liver and to relieve cramps, diarrhea, constipation and indigestion.

- Blend with manuka, lemon and cypress oils and use in a chest rub or diffuser to reduce fever, fight viral infections and soothe inflamed mucous membranes and sinuses.

- Combine yarrow with other essential oils such as juniper berry, *Eucalyptus citriodora*, helichrysum and lavender in a carrier oil for massage to improve circulation and provide relief for arthritis, thrombosis and arteriosclerosis and to lower blood pressure.

Cautions

- Yarrow can pose a drug interaction problem (even in topical applications) with certain drugs, including some analgesic, antiarrhythmic, antipsychotic, antidepressant, estrogen and serotonin drugs. When in doubt, use Roman chamomile.

- It is especially important to make sure that yarrow essential oil is not accidentally ingested. Ingestion should be avoided when taking certain medications; negative interactions have been known to occur.

YLANG YLANG

Cananga odorata

Ylang ylang (its Malay name) means "flower of flowers," or maybe the name is derived from *alang-ilang*, for the way in which the flowers hang. It is prized for its extraordinarily fragrant blossoms of pink, mauve and yellow. It is from these flowers (mainly the yellow ones) that the essential oil is steam-distilled.

Ylang ylang has a reputation for being an aphrodisiac; this is supported by the Indonesian practice of sprinkling a marriage bed with its flowers on the wedding night. No doubt the sweet, sensual and exotic perfume ensures a perfect union. Ylang ylang blends well with bergamot, jasmine, lemon, neroli, rose, rosewood and sandalwood. However, be aware that this oil can be overpoweringly sweet (to the point of nausea) unless blended with sharper citrus oils. It is one of the most used fragrances and fixatives in perfumes, colognes, cosmetics and soaps. Affordable ylang ylang is often used as a substitute for expensive jasmine essential oil, as its properties and perfume are similar.

Uses

- Ylang ylang has a sebum-balancing effect, making it useful for all skin types. It has been used for years in oils and tonics to encourage hair growth and shine.

- It is said to help sexual dysfunction because of its powerful relaxing properties.

- The most important property of ylang ylang is the deeply tranquilizing and strengthening effect it exerts on the nervous system. If used quickly as the situation arises, it will lower raised blood pressure and slow rapid breathing or palpitations that are due to shock, anger or fright. (If these physical symptoms have not been caused by sudden emotional trauma, or if they don't respond quickly, a health professional should be consulted.)

- This oil can create a calming environment in which to tackle unpleasant jobs or issues.

Cautions

- Ylang ylang oil may cause irritation to sensitive or damaged skin.

- Use no more than 1 drop in 4 tsp (20 mL) carrier oil or lotion.

- Do not use with children under the age of 2.

HYDROLATS

Tip: Not all hydrolats have the same aroma as the essential oil. Lavender, for example, smells more like wildflowers or weeds; it doesn't have the characteristic lavender aroma. Neroli (orange flower) is strong and heady and very perfume-like. Hydrolats can be mixed together to make the aroma more pleasing or to combine the therapeutic effect.

Hydrolats, also called hydrosols, were once simply a byproduct of essential oil distillation. Hydrolats are softer in aroma and gentler to use than essential oils. They contain the water-soluble molecules of the essential oil in trace amounts as well as other water-soluble components of the plant. There are some plants, such as witch hazel and cucumber, that do not yield an essential oil but are distilled solely for the hydrolat. Hydrolats possess therapeutic benefits and are a complementary addition to aromatherapy.

In the 16th century many affluent homes had what was known as a "stillroom"—a space that housed the woman's area of expertise. It wasn't unusual for a home to have a medicinal garden. Herbs and flowers picked from the garden would be distilled to produce both the essential oil and the hydrolat. The hydrolat was used as a flavoring in cooking, as a toilet water for personal hygiene and as medicine. In the beginning of the 18th century, as essential oils began to be more commercially produced, the manufacture and use of hydrolats began to diminish.

Today the art of making hydrolats is being revived by artisans who distill specifically for the hydrolat rather than for the essential oil. Hydrolats are being used once again, this time by aromatherapists, who substitute them for water in remedies and other uses, where they add value in the form of a therapeutic contribution. Many natural shampoos, lotions and creams available at your local natural foods store contain hydrolats as a main ingredient.

Don't Be Confused

Hydrolats are often referred to as "hydrosols." This has been a common practice for years but it is technically incorrect. *Hydrosol* is a generic term that is not specific to distilled plant waters. It can mean anything from a bleaching or cleaning agent employed in industrial use to a water-soluble fertilizer. *Hydrolat* refers specifically to distilled plant waters.

Buying and Storing Hydrolats

Be sure to check the label of any product containing a hydrolat, because some companies add 15% ethanol as a preservative. This can be drying to the skin and will sting if applied to wounds. Look for hydrolats that are alcohol-free and have been pH-tested. Many essential-oil companies sell hydrolats without added alcohol.

When ingesting a hydrolat, be sure that it is clean and fresh. As they age, hydrolats can "bloom," or develop a cloudy mold that appears suspended near the bottom of the bottle. Although

Hydrolats vs. Floral Waters

Hydrolats are achieved through the distillation of plant material. Floral waters are hydrosols, and they also have a variety of uses in aromatherapy. Although there are a number of processes for making these products, at their simplest, floral waters can be made by steeping plant materials in alcohol, then following with steam distillation and then a second distillation. The result is a concentrated distilled water. While they produce a lightly fragrant water, these processes do not yield a true hydrolat—they lack some of the hydrophilic compounds.

Floral waters can be found on the shelves of your local grocery store and pharmacy. Orange flower water is often used to flavor cakes and confectionery items. Rose water is another common one. For therapeutic purposes, hydrolats, obtained through distillation of plant material without the use of alcohol, are preferred.

Tip: When purchasing hydrolats, look for the date of distillation on the label. Check the country of origin and purchase a domestic product. The fresher it is and the fewer hands that have been on the product, the better. Look for organic! Hydrolats are best kept in glass bottles.

the mold can be filtered out with unbleached coffee filters, the product is no longer safe for ingestion. Use older hydrolats in footbaths and room sprays.

The shelf life of a hydrolat is normally one year, so it is best to buy them in smaller sizes and to use them quickly. They keep well under constant temperature in a cool, dark place. They can be refrigerated, in which case return them to the refrigerator immediately after use, to maintain a constant temperature. As you use the hydrolat, it's a good idea to decant it into smaller sterile bottles to minimize the amount of oxygen in the bottle. Close the bottle immediately after dispensing to minimize oxidation. Keep out of direct sunlight. Do not put anything, such as fingers or a spoon, into the hydrolat. Keep it sterile!

Uses

- in place of water in recipes for room, nasal and body sprays
- added to steamers for inhalation
- in a nasal wash using a neti pot
- in compresses and poultices (for children, dilute 50:50 with water)
- as a topical application when treating skin disorders such as bruises, burns, rashes and sores
- as an aftershave
- in hydrotherapy: add 1 cup (250 mL) to a sitz bath or $\frac{1}{4}$ to $\frac{1}{2}$ cup (60 to 125 mL) to a foot or hand bath
- in place of water when making lotions and creams
- as a wetting agent for clay facial masks
- for first aid such as cleaning wounds
- in cooking (for example, baking and making flavored waters)

Distillation

When making essential oils and hydrolats, similar methods of distillation are used, depending on the plant material. Generally plant material is placed on a mesh screen set above water in a still. The water is heated, which causes steam to rise through the plant material. This releases essential oils into the rising steam. That steam is channeled through a tube that passes through a condenser, where it cools and becomes liquid. The liquid travels through a spout into a collection vessel. At this point the oil and water separate, with the oil rising to the top. Each component—essential oil and hydrolat—is collected separately. Another popular method is "hydrodistillation," in which the plant material is placed directly in the water and allowed to boil.

More than 60 hydrolats are available in most markets. Artisan distillers usually offer different varieties, as they are likely to use plants indigenous to their region. The following are some common hydrolats that are commercially available in most countries.

CHAMOMILE HYDROLAT

Roman chamomile (*Chamaemelum nobile* syn. *Anthemis nobilis*)

The flavor is described as sweet and honey-like, with hints of green apple. It is anti-infectious, anti-inflammatory, antispasmodic, antiviral, calming and cicatrizant (healing scars).

Uses

- Dilute 1 tsp (5 mL) in water and use in a compress for conjunctivitis and tired eyes. Do not put directly into the eyes.
- Saturate a cotton ball and apply to skin to calm inflamed and irritated skin from burns and from rashes such as rosacea and sunburn. Use in the short term as a skin tonic; if overused, it may become drying.
- Add 1 tsp (5 mL) to a drink to calm diarrhea or before bed to aid sleep.
- Add 1 tsp (5 mL) to baby's bath to quiet and prepare for bed.
- Saturate a cotton swab and apply to sore gums to relieve teething pain.
- Saturate a cotton ball and apply to soothe baby's bottom.
- Spray bed linens to relax and encourage sleep.
- Spritz over anxious dogs during a thunderstorm.

German chamomile (*Matricaria recutita* syn. *M. chamomilla*)

This hydrolat is antifungal, anti-infectious, anti-inflammatory, antispasmodic, calming and cicatrizant.

Uses

- Use in the treatment of candida and thrush: add to a sitz bath or drink 1 tsp (5 mL) of the hydrolat.
- Ingest 1 tsp (5 mL) for urinary tract infections or to soothe intestinal spasms.
- Saturate a cotton ball and apply topically for varicose veins or hemorrhoids.
- Mix with geranium hydrolat to calm rosacea.
- Calm skin rashes and itching by using in a compress or lotion.
- Saturate a cotton ball and apply as a facial toner to cleanse skin affected by acne or to soothe itching from eczema or psoriasis.
- Use to reduce inflammation on baby's bottom.
- Spray on sunburn to cool and soothe the skin.

GERANIUM HYDROLAT

Pelargonium asperum, P. graveolens, P. capitatum

Geranium hydrolat has a sweet floral aroma and taste, with hints of rose. It is anti-inflammatory, tissue-regenerating (healing scars), digestive and stimulating.

Uses

- Use geranium hydrolat in a spray to cool hot flashes, ease hormonal imbalances and lift the spirits.
- Saturate a cotton ball and apply topically as a facial tonic to balance sebum production on the face and scalp and to calm rosacea. It is good for acne and both oily and dry skin types.
- Use to soothe rashes, insect bites and sunburn. It can be used to soften rough skin and calluses.
- Use as the wetting agent in a clay facial mask. Replace the water in your lotion and foaming handwash recipes with the hydrolat.
- Add 1 cup (250 mL) to a bath to lift the spirits and alleviate PMS and menstrual cramps. It may be combined with lavender to enhance the effects.
- Replace 1 tsp (5 mL) of the water or milk in your baking recipes to give an aromatic lift to pastries and cakes. Drizzle or spritz over fruit. Add ½ tsp (2.5 mL) to lemonade for a refreshing summer drink.

IMMORTELLE HYDROLAT
(Helichrysum, Everlasting)

Helichrysum italicum syn. *H. angustifolium*

This hydrolat has a strongly bitter flavor and a unique herbaceous aroma. It is useful as a sedative, relieves itching and is anti-inflammatory, digestive, antidiabetic and a mild analgesic.

Uses

- Immortelle hydrolat has been recommended for diabetes, upset stomach and nervous depression. Add 1 tsp (5 mL) to a small glass of water and drink.

- It is reputed to be purifying to the lungs and the heart. Add 1 tsp (5 mL) to a small glass of water and drink. Use instead of water in your cool-mist diffuser.

- Use undiluted on a compress for bruises, abscesses and post-workout aches.

- It is an effective mouthwash and gargle for gum diseases or sore throat, and to relieve the pain from dental work.

- It soothes skin irritated by poison ivy or poison oak or other inflammatory conditions such as rosacea. Use in a lotion or spray a mist directly onto skin.

LAVENDER HYDROLAT

Lavandula angustifolia

The scent of lavender hydrolat is similar to that of the flowers, but more "weedy," and it has a soapy perfume taste. It can be sweetened when added to beverages. It is analgesic, anti-inflammatory, bactericidal, calming and cicatrizant (healing scars).

Uses

- Saturate a cotton ball with lavender hydrolat and apply to clean wounds, soothe burns or relieve itching from insect bites. Use to relieve inflammation from shaving or waxing.

- Use undiluted in a compress to reduce stress or in a spray to reduce jet lag and mental fatigue.

- Add 1 tsp (5 mL) to a baby's bath or 1 cup (250 mL) to a child's bath to ease overstimulation and to quiet and prepare for bed.

- Saturate a cotton ball and apply to soothe baby's bottom. It may be combined with Roman chamomile to soothe diaper rash.

- As a toner, saturate a cotton ball and apply to skin for acne, oily skin or eczema.
- Use as a wetting agent in facial masks.
- Make a room spray to scare away monsters by adding 5 drops each of lavender, Roman chamomile and sweet marjoram essential oils to 2 oz (60 mL) hydrolat.
- Use in a rinse to strengthen hair.
- Use 1 tsp (5 mL) to flavor lemonade or sparkling water. Replace 1 tsp (5 mL) of the milk in recipes to flavor cakes and cookies.

MELISSA HYDROLAT
(Lemon Balm)

Melissa officinalis

Melissa contains many hydrophilic molecules that saturate the hydrolat and give it a fresh, light floral scent and a slightly bitter lemon flavor. It is analgesic, anti-infectious, anti-inflammatory, antiviral, calming, antispasmodic, sedative and tonic.

Uses

- Use melissa hydrolat undiluted in a compress to aid the symptoms of PMS, cramping, headaches and irregular menstruation.
- Take 1 tsp (5 mL) to calm intestinal spasms and inflammation. It can also be taken as a digestive or laxative, eases morning sickness and helps relieve water retention.
- Add 1 cup (250 mL) to a bath to lift the spirits in times of emotional upset, to help cope with children's temper tantrums, and to induce relaxation and encourage sleep when overstressed.
- Take 1 tsp (5 mL) to relieve headaches, migraine and internal pains.
- Saturate a cotton ball and apply to baby's scalp after treating for cradle cap (see page 166). Use to soothe skin irritated by stings, bites, acne and diaper rash.
- Melissa hydrolat is good for all skin types. Saturate a cotton ball and apply to the face as a toner. Include it as an ingredient in lotions for sunburn care and in anti-aging creams.
- Add 1 tsp (5 mL) to beverages to give them a lemony lift. Use as the steaming liquid for vegetables or fish. Kick up your cocktails a notch with the addition of a little of this hydrolat.

NEROLI HYDROLAT
(Orange Blossom)

Citrus aurantium var. *amara flos*

Orange flower water has a heady floral aroma very similar to that of the essential oil. This hydrolat is calming, uplifting, aphrodisiac and astringent.

Uses

- Add 1 tsp (5 mL) to a glass of water to soothe emotional upset and digestive complaints, or to a cup of coffee to counteract the effects of caffeine.
- Replace 1 tsp (5 mL) of the water or milk in your baking recipes to provide an aromatic lift to pastries and cakes.
- Saturate a cotton ball and apply as a facial toner to clear oil from the pores, soothe irritation and hydrate dry skin.
- Add 1 cup (250 mL) to a bath to lift the spirits and encourage sleep.

PEPPERMINT HYDROLAT

Mentha x *piperita*

The hydrolat has a softer aroma and flavor than fresh peppermint. It is anti-inflammatory, digestive and stimulating.

Uses

- Add 1 tsp (5 mL) to a glass of water for a refreshing drink with digestive properties. It can help relieve indigestion, acid reflux, heartburn and irritable bowel syndrome.
- Store in the refrigerator and spray a mist all over the skin to refresh and invigorate body and mind or to cool hot flashes. Spritz over the face to relieve the pain of a headache. Use in travel to help with jet lag and travel sickness. Use as a "study buddy" to calm anxiety and aid concentration.
- Use as a mouthwash and to freshen the breath.
- Saturate a cotton ball and apply topically to treat acne, to soothe rashes and as an aftershave.
- Add 1 cup (250 mL) to a bath or use in a compress for stiff muscles, sprains, aches and pains and to invigorate the body and stimulate the mind.
- Replace 2 tsp (10 mL) of the liquid in a recipe to flavor rice or couscous.

Caution

Do not use with children under 3 years of age.

ROSE HYDROLAT

Rosa damascena

Before use, be sure to check your rose water to make sure it is a hydrolat. Many commercially prepared waters are not true hydrolats; they may contain synthetic fragrance or alcohol and are not suitable for therapeutic purposes and ingestion. Rose hydrolat is widely used for many ailments and in cooking. It is anti-infectious, anti-inflammatory, antispasmodic, bactericidal, calming, decongestant, tissue-regenerating (healing scars), stimulating and uplifting.

Uses

- Use rose hydrolat in a spray to refresh the mind, ease nervousness and lift the spirits.

- Saturate a cotton ball and apply topically as a facial tonic for normal, dry, sensitive and mature skin types. Use to soothe rashes, dermatitis and sunburn.

- Use as the wetting agent in a clay facial mask. Use to replace the water in lotions and foaming handwashes.

- This hydrolat is an effective gargle or spray for sore throat and for mouth and throat infections.

- Dilute 1 tsp (5 mL) in water and use in a compress for conjunctivitis and tired eyes. Do not put directly into eyes.

- Take 1 tsp (5 mL) for nausea, vomiting and congested liver.

- Add 1 cup (250 mL) to a bath to lift the spirits and reduce mental strain and to relieve tension, low libido and mood swings. It helps keep hormones balanced and eases PMS symptoms, menstrual cramps and anxiety. Use in a sitz bath for postpartum healing.

- Replace 1 tsp (5 mL) of the water or milk in baking recipes to provide an aromatic lift to pastries and cakes. Marinate sliced strawberries in 1 to 2 tsp (5 to 10 mL) hydrolat and a little sugar for a sweet dessert. Inject a lychee fruit with hydrolat and drop into a glass of champagne for an elegant cocktail.

Is My Rose Water a Hydrolat?

Alcohol is often added to hydrolats. When purchasing from a small distiller or distributor, you can ask how the hydrolat was obtained (often this information is in their price list or literature). If you are shopping at a grocery or natural foods store, the purity of the product may be unclear, in which case you should check the manufacturer's website. Rose water sold in a grocery store is undoubtedly *not* a hydrolat. Natural foods stores may be a better choice; however, it is worth checking. In addition to artisan distillers, many essential oil suppliers sell hydrolats (see Resources, page 459).

ROSEMARY HYDROLAT

Rosmarinus officinalis

This hydrolat has a strong flavor of rosemary essential oil, but the scent is far less appealing. You might consider adding another hydrolat to balance out the aroma. It is analgesic, anti-inflammatory, digestive and tissue-regenerating (healing scars).

Uses

Caution

Avoid rosemary hydrolat if pregnant or breastfeeding or if you have high blood pressure.

- Ingest 1 tsp (5 mL) to cleanse the bladder and stimulate the liver and gallbladder. Rosemary hydrolat is mildly diuretic and can be used as a digestive, to curb hunger and to facilitate detoxification.
- Add 1 cup (250 mL) to a bath to stimulate circulation, relieve the pain and stiffness of rheumatism and gout, and promote menstruation.
- Use in a spray to stimulate and restore the mind and body, increase mental alertness and refresh tired feet (you can also use it in a foot soak).
- Use in place of water in a cool-mist diffuser to aid breathing during allergy season.
- Use as the wetting agent in a clay mask for acne or combination and oily skin.
- Saturate a cotton ball and apply topically as a facial tonic to treat blemishes and restore elasticity.
- Spritz over your face as a revitalizing spray, or over the body after a workout.
- Add to a shampoo, conditioner or rinse for soft, shiny hair.
- Use in meat dishes and sauces, or sprinkle over vegetables or fruit.
- Add 1 tsp (5 mL) to water along with lemon to make a refreshing drink.

TEA TREE HYDROLAT

Melaleuca alternifolia

Tea tree hydrolat has a sharp medicinal smell and a pungent taste. It is anti-infectious, antifungal, bactericidal and antiviral.

Uses

- Saturate a cotton ball and apply to clean wounds or scrapes and to soothe irritated or infected skin.

- Tea tree hydrolat is helpful in cases of fungal ailments such as thrush, infected nail beds and vaginal infections. Saturate a cotton ball and apply to the affected area. For oral thrush, use as a mouthwash or gargle. For vaginal thrush, use in a sitz, foot or sponge bath.
- Use as a gargle for cough, sore throat, inflamed gums and mouth infections.
- Use as a nasal spray for sinus congestion and allergy relief.

WITCH HAZEL HYDROLAT

Hamamelis virginiana

Witch hazel often has a strong herbaceous aroma. Distilled solely for its hydrolat, witch hazel is widely used as an astringent. However, the commercial preparations found in pharmacies contain 15% to 30% ethanol. Neither commercially produced nor artisanal versions of the hydrolat are recommended for ingestion. It is mildly astringent, anti-inflammatory, antibacterial, antiseptic and antifungal. It is a strong antioxidant, cooling and styptic (helps to stop bleeding).

Uses

- Saturate a cotton ball and apply to soothe minor burns, sunburn, itching, swelling, insect bites and stings.
- Stop the bleeding of minor cuts and scrapes by saturating a cotton ball and applying directly to the affected area. For nosebleeds, insert a saturated cotton ball in the nostril.
- Dilute 1 tsp (5 mL) in water and use in a compress for conjunctivitis and tired eyes. Do not put directly into the eyes.
- Use 1 tsp (5 mL) in a sitz bath to relieve the pain and itching of hemorrhoids.
- For varicose veins, use undiluted in a compress: place on leg and cover with plastic wrap to keep moist. Use undiluted on the area when a vein bleeds under the skin: saturate a cotton ball and apply directly to stop the bleeding.
- Use as a toner to refresh and clear congested skin or as an aftershave. Witch hazel can be combined with other hydrolats to adjust its scent. Mix with rose hydrolat for dry or aging skin.

Caution

Avoid commercially prepared witch hazel products—they are very high in alcohol and preservatives.

FIXED (CARRIER) OILS AND BUTTERS

Fixed, or carrier, oils are the nutritive natural oils found in seeds, kernels, beans and so on. They are extracted by pressing, chemicals or heat. Sometimes known as base oils, they form the basis for making blends such as those used in Part 2 of this book, as well as for healing or cosmetic lotions and creams.

Fixed oils are fats that are liquid at room temperature. They should not be confused with aromatic or essential oils. Fixed oils are usually nonvolatile, meaning they don't evaporate, unlike essential oils, which evaporate at room temperature. Most fixed oils have little aroma.

The following information will help you choose the best oil for making your own natural healing and skincare products. There are many more fixed oils than those we have listed below, but the following are our favorites. They have been tried and tested over decades.

Cold-Pressed Oils

For therapeutic purposes, always look for organic cold-pressed oils or extra virgin olive oil. Cheaper refined oils have gone through additional processes to deodorize, remove color and lengthen shelf life, which also removes some of their therapeutic components.

ALMOND OIL (Sweet)

Prunus dulcis

Sweet almond oil is a fine, emollient, non-drying fixed oil expressed from the kernels of sweet almonds. It is an excellent oil to use in creams, lotions and massage oils formulated for dry, normal or combination skins. It helps to reduce itching, cracking and inflammation. It is difficult to find a truly pure cold-pressed sweet almond oil; it is often partially refined and often adulterated with sunflower, hazelnut or some other fixed oil. The oil may be used 100% as a carrier oil. Its average shelf life is 1 year, or 2 years if refined. (Shelf life depends on what proportion of the oil is refined; the more refined, the longer the shelf life.)

Caution

People with nut allergies should avoid using sweet almond oil.

APRICOT KERNEL OIL

Prunus armeniaca

A fine, light, pale yellow oil obtained from the kernels of apricots, apricot kernel oil is similar to sweet almond oil in that it is easily absorbed. It is suitable for all skin types, especially mature, sensitive and dry. It is useful for sensitive skin and can relieve the itching caused by eczema. The oil may be used 100% as a carrier oil. Its shelf life is 2 years.

AVOCADO OIL

Persea gratissima

A beautiful thick, dark green oil that contains vitamins A, B_1, B_2, D and E, avocado oil is rich, nourishing, deeply penetrating and invaluable in moisture creams and lotions, particularly for sensitive, dehydrated or sunburned skin. It is reputed to be beneficial for reducing scars and fading age spots, as well as being highly moisturizing. The vitamin E content helps to preserve other oils in blends.

One of the favorites of the cosmetic industry, most avocado oils have been heavily refined and are a pale yellow color. Look for the darker green unrefined oil for therapeutic use in aromatherapy. Because of its thick consistency, it is best to use no more than 5% to 10% in massage and face oils. Do not store in the refrigerator, as cold can harm some of the beneficial components of the oil. We recommend purchasing avocado oil in small quantities to be used quickly; its shelf life is 1 to 2 years.

BORAGE SEED OIL

Borago officinalis

Borage seed oil is cold-pressed and is the richest source of gamma linolenic acid (GLA) of all the oils. Because of the fragility of GLA, the bottle needs to be tightly sealed and stored in a cool, dark place away from light, heat and humidity. The oil is emollient and used for mature skin, as it is reputed to prevent wrinkles. It soothes injured, irritated or inflamed skin. Use 5% to 10% in blends to treat skin problems such as eczema and psoriasis. Borage seed oil has a shelf life of 6 to 12 months. Store in the refrigerator.

> ## Rapeseed and Canola Oil
>
> Rapeseed oil is extracted from the seeds of *Brassica napus*, whose yellow flowers can be seen all over the English countryside. Canola oil is made from modified rape seed. It was developed in Canada, hence the first three letters of the name. Both oils are usually highly refined and have no meaningful therapeutic benefit in aromatherapy. Canola oil may contain erucic acid, which can cause heart damage and cancer. Unless the source is identified as organic, plants used to make rapeseed oil for human ingestion have been genetically altered and do not contain much, if any, erucic acid. Besides their use in cooking, rapeseed oils are used to make plastics and detergents and as a lubricant for machinery.

CARROT SEED OIL

Daucus carota var. *sativa* (wild carrot, Queen Anne's lace)

Not to be confused with the essential oil, carrot seed fixed oil is cold-pressed from the seeds. This oil is absorbed quickly, is rich in antioxidants and is valued for being nutritive and rejuvenating to aging skin. It noticeably improves skin tone and elasticity, slows the progression of wrinkles and helps to heal dry, chapped or cracked skin. Carrot seed oil is appropriate for all skin types. Use up to 10% in hair and skin preparations. Store in a cool, dark place. It has a shelf life of 2 years.

COCOA BUTTER

Theobroma cacao

Cocoa butter is a solid fat, rich in antioxidants and vitamin E. Used widely in ointments, body butters and "massage lotion" bars, it softens and moisturizes very dry and dehydrated skin. It is reputed to fade the appearance of scars. It has the aroma of chocolate, and who doesn't love that? It is very stable because of its antioxidant content, with a shelf life of 2 to 5 years.

COCONUT OIL

Cocos nucifera

Coconut oil is a semisolid saturated fat extracted from the white meat of coconuts. It is easily absorbed, leaving the skin feeling soft but not greasy. A wonderful lubricant and moisturizer, it is suitable for the delicate eye and throat areas. If used very discreetly, it lubricates and gives shine and condition to hair. Coconut oil is the number one oil used as a surfactant in soap making, because it produces a nice luxuriant lather. It has a sweet coconut aroma. Rich in antioxidants, coconut oil is slow to oxidize and has a shelf life of at least 3 years.

"Fractionated coconut oil" has been put through a physical (not chemical) process that separates out the fatty acid triglycerides, which leaves a liquid oil that doesn't go rancid. It is great for massage because it is not greasy and doesn't stain the sheets. It is perfect for use in natural perfume roll-ons because it is odorless. A great substitute for sweet almond oil, it has an indefinite shelf life.

Caution
Coconut oil has been known to cause allergic skin rashes in some individuals.

EVENING PRIMROSE OIL

Oenothera biennis

Evening primrose oil is a relatively expensive oil expressed from the seeds of evening primrose. This oil is a natural antioxidant, which makes it ideal to add to other oils to retard rancidity. Evening primrose oil is high in essential fatty acids (EFAs) and gamma linoleic acid (GLA). The oil is emollient and used for mature skins; used at up to 20% in preparations, it is reputed to prevent wrinkles. It is a soothing oil when added to creams and blends to aid in the healing of acne, eczema, psoriasis and other inflammatory skin conditions. It penetrates deeply, counteracts free-radical damage, is a skin rejuvenator and accelerates wound healing, so it is well worth including in small amounts (such as 5%) in preparations. In hair care, the addition of evening primrose can help with dry scalp and dandruff. Because of the fragility of GLA, the bottle should be tightly sealed and stored in a cool, dark place away from light, heat and humidity.

GRAPESEED OIL

Vitis vinifera

As the name suggests, this oil is produced from grape seeds (from spent grapes after winemaking). They are washed, crushed and then pressed, using low heat because there is not much oil remaining in the seed. The extracted oil may be further refined or it may be obtained through another process that uses chemical solvents. Cold-pressed oils are not easily found. The result is a light, fine oil that is not greasy and is slightly astringent, suitable for most skin types. It is a very good basic carrier oil—it is light, clear, penetrates the skin quickly and has no smell. It is often used in hypoallergenic products, as it doesn't tend to cause allergic reactions. Add 5% to 10% wheat germ oil to help prevent rancidity (see Caution, page 138). It has a shelf life of 1 year.

JOJOBA WAX

Simmondsia sinensis

Not an oil at all, jojoba wax is a liquid wax pressed from beans of the desert plant. Jojoba is most like our own skin's sebum (the natural moisturizer produced by our bodies) and is suitable for all skin types. It is nongreasy and keeps skin smooth and supple. Jojoba is an amazing balancer: it is deeply penetrating and has the capacity to moisturize dry skin, but it can also unclog pores in oily skin and restore the natural pH balance. It is useful for treating acne, eczema, psoriasis and inflammatory conditions such as diaper rash, chapped skin and sunburn. It visibly reduces shallow lines and wrinkles. Add 10% to creams, massage oils and other preparations. Jojoba has a shelf life of up to 25 years. It is considered hypoallergenic for external use.

A Less Expensive Alternative

Jojoba oil is virtually odorless. Use it to extend more expensive essential oils when blending lotions and creams. Add 5 drops of rose, melissa, jasmine or sandalwood essential oil to a $\frac{1}{6}$ oz (5 mL) bottle with orifice reducer; fill the remainder of the bottle with jojoba oil, replace the cap and shake well. Use this mix for blending facial products when rose, melissa, jasmine or sandalwood oil is called for, or use it as a lovely facial serum.

KUKUI NUT OIL

Aleurites moluccana

Kukui oil is expeller-pressed from the roasted nut. It is used by Hawaiians to protect and heal skin that has been damaged by sun, saltwater and dry winds. The oil is penetrating without clogging pores. It is used for acne, psoriasis, eczema, dry or wrinkled skin, sunburn and hemorrhoids. It has a light, pleasant tropical scent. Its shelf life is 6 to 8 months when kept in a cool, dark place.

Caution

People with nut allergies should avoid use of kukui nut oil.

MACADAMIA NUT OIL

Macadamia ternifolia syn. *M. integrifolia*

This cold-pressed oil is obtained from cultivated hybrids of the original macadamia nut tree. The oil is available refined or unrefined; however, no solvents are used in either process and both versions retain their natural therapeutic properties. As a skin lubricant, the oil is easily and quickly absorbed, leaving the skin supple and not greasy. Some anecdotal reports indicate that the oil is useful for reducing scarring after surgery and that it has an ability to slow the aging process of the skin. It is useful as a massage oil because it is deeply penetrating, thereby offering quick delivery of the essential oils used. It is often used in hot-oil conditioning treatments for hair. It has a shelf life of 1 year.

Macadamia Nuts

Macadamia nuts contain a large amount of palmitoleic acid, which, when massaged on the body, penetrates quickly and deeply. It can lead to improvement of insulin resistance and atherosclerosis and holds promise as a possible cure for metabolic syndrome.

MEADOWFOAM OIL

Limnanthes alba

Meadowfoam oil is rich in antioxidants, extremely emollient, deeply penetrating and not greasy. Include it in blends intended to help heal bruises or delay the signs of aging. It can be used in natural sunscreens and facial creams because it offers some UV (ultraviolet) protection. It is a very stable oil; when added to other, less stable oils, it can extend their shelf life. Meadowfoam oil helps to repair damage and add shine to hair; use as a deep conditioner for hair and scalp. As a massage oil it has a nice amount of "slip" and helps the skin retain moisture by forming a protective barrier.

Aromatherapists like meadowfoam because the refined oil, which is expeller-pressed, is nearly odorless and possesses fixative qualities when combined with essential oils. This means it really holds on to the scent, allowing it to linger longer. It is available as a filtered cold-pressed oil; however, that oil is a deep orange color and has a strong grassy odor that is difficult (but not impossible) to mask. Meadowfoam can be obtained through cold (expeller) pressing or solvent extraction. Sometimes it is further refined to remove the color and odor. It is easily purchased online, and the manufacturer almost always indicates how it was obtained. If that information isn't given, just ask! It has a shelf life of 2 years.

NEEM OIL

Azadirachta indica

Neem oil is cold-pressed from the seed. It has a dark greenish brown color and a very strong, unpleasant odor. The oil is antifungal, regenerating and restoring. It is suitable for sensitive and allergic skin. While it is useful in healing a wide variety of skin disorders, including psoriasis, itching, herpes and sunburn, it is used only in small amounts because of the smell. Neem oil is most notably used in insecticides, as that is where it excels. It has a shelf life of 2 years.

OLIVE OIL

Olea europaea

Olive oil is a calming, skin-softening and emollient oil expressed from ripe olives. Cold-pressed (extra virgin) oil, which is from the first pressing, contains the highest amount of minerals and vitamins; however, it is very green and strongly aromatic, which is great for flavor in culinary use but less desirable for aromatherapy. If you don't like the smell, try one of the lighter olive oils from later pressings, or blend at 20% with lighter oils such as sunflower or grapeseed. Olive oil is too rich for oily skins but excellent for massage oils, soaps and lotions for dry and normal skins. The oil has wonderful therapeutic properties. It is effective in relieving itchy skin, including from insect bites, is somewhat astringent and antiseptic, and is helpful in healing sprains, strains and bruises. It is a nice oil to use for lifting cradle cap on babies. Its shelf life is 18 to 24 months.

PEANUT OIL

Arachis hypogea

This expressed oil (it is almost always refined) is used as a less expensive version of sweet almond oil. It has a very oily consistency and characteristic nutty aroma; consequently, it is not the first oil of choice for the massage therapist. However, in aromatherapy, the chemical composition of peanut oil makes it an excellent choice for treating arthritis and rheumatic conditions. It is used in commercial preparations as an emollient ingredient in hair-care products, soaps and skin creams. Stored in a cool, dark place, its shelf life is about 9 months.

Cautions

- Olive oil has been known to cause allergic reactions when applied topically to sensitive skin or dry scalp. It can make dandruff worse.

- Be careful not to splash into the eyes, as it can sting.

Caution

People with nut allergies should avoid using peanut oil.

ROSEHIP SEED OIL

Rosa mosqueta syn. *R. rubingosa, R. canina*

This valued oil is expressed from the hips, or fruit, of the rose bush, which produce a golden reddish oil particularly high in vitamin C (about 20 times more than oranges). It is rejuvenating and healing to skin, which makes it a good choice for blends to treat wounds and burns. Rosehip seed oil is absorbed quickly and is useful for improving dry and aging skin and eczema, reducing scarring, and healing damaged tissue. It is reputed to help in healing radiation burns from cancer treatments. For acne, use a drop or two on the eruption; however, be careful not to overuse this oil undiluted, as it may cause irritation. Use up to 10% in blends. The oil is fragile and should be stored in the refrigerator. It will keep for up to 6 months.

SAFFLOWER OIL

Carthamus tinctorius

Two different types of safflower oils are produced. The oil obtained from cultivated safflower is high in oleic acid (72% to 79%), a monounsaturated fatty acid. This oil has a higher oxidative stability, which means it is heat stable; it is used as a cooking oil for foods such as french fries. The other oil is obtained from "wild" safflower seeds. It is higher in linoleic acid (75% to 77%), a polyunsaturated fatty acid, which is by definition less stable than a monounsaturated fat. It is used in salad dressings and for therapeutic purposes.

While both types of safflower oil can be obtained through chemical processes (refined) or by expeller pressing, for therapeutic use look for 100% expeller-pressed high-linoleic safflower oil. It may be used in soaps, creams and lotions, bath oils, massage oils, hair conditioners and makeup. It is helpful in treating eczema and smoothing rough, dry skin. Expeller-pressed safflower oil is very unstable and needs to be refrigerated. Whether refined or expeller-pressed, the high–oleic fatty acid type has a shelf life of 2 years if properly stored. The shelf life of the high–linoleic fatty acid type is 12 months.

SESAME OIL

Sesamum indicum

Sesame oil is pressed from the white seeds of the sesame plant. Use the light-colored oil from unroasted seeds. It is a light oil that contains small amounts of vitamins B_6, K and E and the minerals calcium, copper, magnesium and zinc. It is useful at 10% in moisturizing creams and lotions to prevent drying and to soften the skin. Sesame oil is highly valued in Ayurvedic treatments and Ayurvedic aromatherapy. Blend at 20% into massage oils to benefit rheumatic disorders and skin conditions such as psoriasis, dry eczema and broken veins. The oil possesses components that are beneficial in eradicating head lice (see Head Lice Oil Treatment, page 247). Sesame seed oil absorbs ultraviolet (UV) rays and is reputed to have a sunscreen effect of SPF4. It has a shelf life of 1 year.

Caution

Sesame oil may cause contact dermatitis in hypersensitive individuals.

SHEA BUTTER

(Vitellaria paradoxa)

Shea butter is a natural fat obtained by beating the dried fruits of the shea tree and then boiling them until the fat rises to the top. Unrefined shea butter is light green in color; it is anti-inflammatory and wonderful for skin regeneration, making it a good choice for creams for wounds, burns, rashes and skinned knees. It is humectant, bringing moisture from the air to the skin, which is helpful when dealing with aging, dry or irritated skin, as well as eczema. It is often included in skin creams because it improves circulation in the capillaries. It can soften and reduce the appearance of stretch marks and scars and soothes sore, achy muscles. It is also used in sunscreens because it helps protect the skin from the sun's harmful UV (ultraviolet) rays. It has a shelf life of 1 year.

Cautions

- Shea butter may trigger an allergic reaction in people who have a latex allergy.
- People with nut allergies should avoid use of shea butter.

Refined Shea Butter

Shea butter can be obtained through solvent extraction, then boiled to remove the solvent, refined, bleached and deodorized (again using chemicals). Finally, antioxidants are added to preserve the rich white butter. Refined shea butter is less desirable than the unrefined version, as most of the therapeutic components are lost in the rigorous process; however, it is more readily available commercially.

SUNFLOWER OIL

Helianthus annuus

Organic sunflower oil is cold-pressed. If sunflower oil is not identified as organic, it was likely obtained through solvent extraction. Cold-pressed sunflower oil is high in vitamin E, linoleic acid and other essential fatty acids. Used topically, the oil forms a protective yet breathable barrier that retains moisture and softens the skin. It is used for bruises, acne, hemorrhoids and sinusitis. It is a wonderful cost-effective oil to include in base massage oils (see Basic Base Oil Blends, page 139). It has a shelf life of 1 year.

TAMANU OIL

Calophyllum inophyllum

Tamanu oil comes from cold expression of the sun-dried fruits and seeds of an evergreen tree of the same name, found in Africa and along the coast in Australia and India. It is cultivated in other tropical areas. The dark greenish brown oil is an excellent anti-inflammatory that is useful in cases of eczema, psoriasis, scars and acne. When combined with *Ravensara aromatica* essential oil, it makes a very effective preparation for the treatment of shingles. It is reported to have pain-relieving properties, which makes it a good addition to massage oils for rheumatic conditions and nerve pain such as sciatica and trigeminal neuralgia. It is blended into ointments for cracked nipples, anal fissures and other severely cracked and dry skin. It has a shelf life of 1 year.

VITAMIN E OIL

Vitamin E is found in many vegetable oils; however, it is most plentiful in wheat germ oil, followed by safflower and sunflower oils. Vitamin E oil is an antioxidant oil produced by distillation of various vegetable oils. Adding as little as 2% will help to prevent oil blends from oxidizing. It offers protection to skin cells from ultraviolet radiation and other factors that produce cell-damaging free radicals, including pollution and medications. Vitamin E oil rejuvenates aging skin, helps to reduce the appearance of fine lines and wrinkles, reduces the appearance of stretch marks, stops the appearance of age spots and supports the skin's barrier function.

WHEAT GERM OIL

Triticum vulgare

Wheat germ oil is extracted from the germ of wheat kernels by cold pressing and then put through a process to make the oil more stable yet still unrefined. This yields a superior oil for therapeutic use, but it is limited in availability. The germ yields so little oil that other methods are employed to obtain the most oil possible, including maceration, solvent extraction and heat pressing. Cold-pressed wheat germ oil is a richly nourishing, healing oil. It contains small amounts of vitamins A, B_1, B_2, B_3 and B_6 and is significantly higher in vitamin E than other oils. It also contains a range of minerals.

Wheat germ oil's vitamin E content makes it useful for most skins, especially dry, prematurely aged skin, or for skin problems such as eczema, psoriasis and dermatitis. It is good in anti–stretch mark blends. Its high levels of vitamin E, a natural antioxidant, help to preserve other oils; 10% to 25% wheat germ oil is a valuable addition to creams and lotions, massage oils and soaps. It has a shelf life of 1 year.

Caution

People with a wheat or gluten allergy should avoid using wheat germ oil.

Allergies and Certain Oils

The use of nut and wheat germ oils raises concerns about the potential for allergic reactions in people who are allergic to nuts, wheat or gluten. Potential reactions depend on whether or not the fixed oil contains any protein. Refined oils typically do not contain proteins; however, for aromatherapy purposes we recommend using organic cold-pressed oils, which could be problematic. The amount of protein in a cold-pressed oil can vary with the batch, who produced it and how it was produced. When proteins are present, even in trace amounts, there is a slight risk of allergic reaction and the oil should be avoided.

Basic Massage Oil Blends and Treatment Bases

The following are base carrier oil blends for use in massage and treatments. Select the base that is best suited to you and prepare a suitable quantity to keep on hand for when you need to make a quick preparation.

Basic Base Oil Blends

Recipe 1

This blend is suitable for people who don't have nut or wheat allergies.

30%	sweet almond oil
30%	sunflower oil
30%	apricot seed oil
10%	wheat germ oil

In a glass bottle, combine sweet almond, sunflower, apricot seed and wheat germ oils. Shake to blend. Will keep for up to 15 months in a cool, dark place.

Recipe 2

This blend is not suitable for people who have nut allergies.

33%	sweet almond oil
33%	sunflower oil
33%	apricot seed oil
1%	vitamin E oil

In a glass bottle, combine sweet almond, sunflower, apricot seed and vitamin E oils. Shake to blend. Will keep for up to 15 months in a cool, dark place.

Recipe 3

This blend is not suitable for people who have a wheat or gluten allergy.

30%	grapeseed oil
30%	sunflower oil
30%	apricot seed oil
10%	wheat germ oil

In a glass bottle, combine grapeseed, sunflower, apricot seed and wheat germ oils. Shake to blend. Will keep for up to 15 months in a cool, dark place.

Hypoallergenic Blend

This blend is suitable for most people.

33%	grapeseed oil
33%	sunflower oil
33%	apricot seed oil
1%	vitamin E oil

In a glass bottle, combine grapeseed, sunflower, apricot seed and vitamin E oils. Shake to blend. Will keep for up to 15 months in a cool, dark place.

Mineral Oil and Petroleum Jelly

Mineral oil and petroleum products such as Vaseline are byproducts of the distillation of crude oil to make gasoline. Petroleum jelly provides a barrier to keep moisture in, but it doesn't allow moisture out either. This disruption of the natural water-exchange cycle leads to extreme dryness and rough, often chapped skin. If you don't want to put anything on your skin that you aren't willing to ingest, would you really consider using a petroleum-based product?

INFUSED OILS

Infused oils are produced by soaking a whole piece of a plant (leaves, stems and flowers) in oil over a long period of time. Infusing is probably the oldest method of extraction; it was used for thousands of years before distillation and other methods were devised. Infused oils have many of the properties of essential oils, and they also have the benefits of other plant substances not present in essential oils. The resulting oil isn't as strong as an essential oil and can usually be used safely without further dilution. One of the main advantages of this method is that it makes it possible to utilize many plants that yield very little or no essential oil but are immensely useful in aromatherapy.

The infused oils included here are relatively easy to purchase (see Resources, page 459). If purchased from a reliable supplier, they are likely to have been properly prepared and stored. However, if good-quality plant material is available, you can certainly make your own (see page 145).

Tip: To make your own infused oil for massage, combine 1 part flowers to 10 parts carrier oil.

ARNICA-INFUSED OIL

Arnica montana

Essential arnica oil contains a high percentage of toxic constituents. However, arnica-infused oil or a homeopathic tincture or ointment is a valuable addition to any home first-aid box. When applied externally, arnica-infused oil stimulates the peripheral blood supply, making it one of the best remedies for sports massage, sprains, strains, bruises, wounds, diaper rash and sunburn. It may also be used in blends to relieve rheumatism and other inflammatory conditions. Purchase this infused oil or make it yourself (see Tip, above right). Arnica flowers are available for sale in bulk.

Cautions
- Never use arnica-infused oil on broken skin.
- Arnica-infused oil can cause an allergic reaction in some individuals.
- Avoid if pregnant or breastfeeding.

CALENDULA-INFUSED OIL

Calendula officinalis

Calendula-infused oil has powerful skin-healing properties. This makes it useful as the main oil in creams and ointments for cracked skin, burns, bruises, cuts, eczema, inflammations, rashes, work-roughened hands, diaper rash, grazes and wounds. It is an excellent treatment for sore nipples—use the oil alone rather than a cream. It also helps to fade old scars and can be used in the treatment of skin ulcers and varicose veins. Although this oil can easily be purchased, it is pricy and therefore a nice oil to make yourself (see page 145).

Tip: Because calendula-infused oil can be pricy, it is often used at 25%, with 75% other fixed oils, in carrier oil blends.

Be sure that you are using an infused oil made from true calendula flowers (marigold, *Calendula officinalis*), as they are often confused with African marigold (*Tagetes erecta*) and French marigold (*Tagetes patula*). If you are making your own oil, be sure that you are using whole dried *C. officinalis* flowers, which can be purchased in bulk. The other varieties don't have the same properties and aren't suitable for therapeutic use.

COMFREY-INFUSED OIL

Symphytum officinale

Comfrey is known variously as knitbone, boneset, bruisewort and other very descriptive names. Comfrey-infused oil is impressive in its healing powers for wounds, skin ulcers, strains, sprains, muscular injuries and fractures. It may also be used to good effect on dry eczema, itchy skin and rough skin. You can easily make this oil yourself (see page 145), as dried comfrey is readily available.

ECHINACEA-INFUSED OIL

Echinacea purpurea

Already very well known as an internal treatment, echinacea also makes a valuable infused oil that is useful for healing skin conditions of all types and cosmetically softening wrinkles, stretch marks and scars. This is a nice oil to make (see page 145) if you live in central or eastern North America, where the plant is readily available. Dried echinacea is available through online bulk herb suppliers.

ELDERFLOWER-INFUSED OIL

Sambucus nigra

Keep a good supply of this infused oil on hand for blending with calendula-infused oil to make moisture lotions and creams. The resulting blend is softening, anti-inflammatory, healing and good for all skin types. This is a nice oil to make (see page 145) if you live in the warmer parts of Europe and North America, as well as western Asia, where the aromatic flowers are frequently found. The dried flowers are available for purchase through online bulk herb suppliers.

MULLEIN-INFUSED OIL

Verbascum thapsus

The yellow flowers of mullein plus olive oil make a very valuable infused oil for the treatment of simple earache (prolonged or severe earache needs urgent professional treatment). Use also for painful and inflamed conditions such as wounds and hemorrhoids. If you want to make your own infused oil (see page 145), use fresh mullein flowers. If your aim, however, is to relieve muscle aches and pains, dried mullein leaves are a better choice.

PASSION FLOWER–INFUSED OIL

Passiflora incarnata

To make this infused oil, these beautiful, exotic-looking purple and white flowers are typically macerated in organic sunflower oil. Passion flower oil is especially useful to aromatherapists, as it is particularly skin-soothing and pain-relieving. Passion flower is a great oil to use in massage because it is anti-inflammatory and deeply relaxing, which makes it very helpful for those with insomnia and extreme nervousness. It is neurosedative and antispasmodic, which helps to alleviate agitation and anxiety. Passion flower oil is readily available, but it is nice to make your own (see page 145). The cut and dried herb is available for purchase through online bulk suppliers. The dried herb can also be used in bath teas and eye pillows.

SEA BUCKTHORN–INFUSED OIL

Hippophae rhamnoides

Sea buckthorn is a thorny shrub that tends to grow along the seacoast, although there are species that grow in semi-desert areas in some Asian countries. It should not be confused with buckthorn from the Rhamnaceae family—they are quite different. To make an infused oil, the berries are usually macerated in olive oil, although sometimes almond or apricot seed oil is used. Sea buckthorn oil is most often used in skincare preparations; the oil is easily absorbed and contains a large amount of essential fatty acids that rejuvenate and are said to have an anti-aging effect, reducing wrinkles. The oil promotes healing of wounds and burns, including skin lesions and ulcers, bedsores, sunburn and dry skin and eczema. It has a strong color and odor and should be used at 10%, blended with other fixed oil(s). It has a longer shelf life than

most infused oils because it is high in antioxidants. Stored in the refrigerator, it will keep for up to 3 years. Sea buckthorn–infused oil is easily purchased, but if the dried berries are available you can make your own (see page 145).

ST. JOHN'S WORT–INFUSED OIL

Hypericum perforatum

This oil is also known as hypericum-infused oil. When steeped in warm (preferably olive) oil, the yellow flowers of St. John's wort release a rich ruby-red oil with analgesic, astringent and antiseptic properties. It is excellent for easing the pain of minor burns, including sunburn, muscle and joint inflammation, gout, rheumatism and hemorrhoids, as well as nerve-related pain such as neuralgia and fibromyalgia and wounds. Use a 50:50 blend of St. John's wort and calendula-infused oils to treat bruises and swelling. For massage it is best used at 25%, blended with other fixed oils. The infused oil is available in most good health-food stores, although it is a bit expensive.

It is exciting to make this oil yourself. If you can find the plant in flower, it is best to use the fresh flowering tops (ideally mostly in bud). Follow the method on page 145, but set the jar in the sun. Although infusing oils in the sun usually destroys some of a plant's properties, with this herb the method has a long tradition. St. John's wort contains hypericin, known for its effects on mild to moderate depression; however, in larger amounts this constituent can have negative side effects. Infusing in the sun alters the hypericin content and some of the other components, which makes it safer and more beneficial.

A Cost-Effective Oil

Neroli, rose, chamomile, jasmine and melissa are all very expensive essential oils. Beautiful, effective and inexpensive massage oils can be made from these plants by using the infusion method. Here are the parts to use when making an infused oil:

- neroli: flowers
- rose: petals
- chamomile: flowers
- jasmine: flowers
- melissa: leaves and flowers

Making an Infused/Macerated Oil

Infused or macerated oils can be made by using either dried or fresh plant material. Dried plant material is relatively easy to find (good natural foods shops stock many dried herbs) or they can be ordered online from herb and spice companies. Making your own can be fun and rewarding if herbs and flowers are available. Use the method appropriate to the type of plant material.

Method for Using Dried Plant Material

1. Fill a sterilized 16 oz (500 mL) jar halfway with finely chopped dried plant material. Top with good-quality oil—a blend of organic extra virgin olive (20%), almond (40%) and sunflower (40%) oils would be excellent—leaving about 2 inches (5 cm) headspace (all the plant material should be covered in oil). Add 5% wheat germ oil as a preservative to keep the oil from going rancid (if you have a wheat or gluten allergy, substitute 1% vitamin E oil with mixed tocopherols).

2. Seal the jar tightly, shake to combine and store in a cool, dark place. Shake the jar once a day for several days or up to 3 weeks. (The longer it is left to infuse, the stronger the aroma and color will be.)

3. Place coarse muslin or a coarsely woven tea towel in a strainer set over a nonreactive bowl. Strain the oil into the bowl, squeezing the fabric to extract as much oil as possible.

4. Place another cloth, with the finest weave available, in strainer and strain the oil again, this time into a sterilized dark glass jar.

5. Seal tightly and store in the refrigerator for up to 2 years.

Tip: For stronger saturation, repeat Steps 1 to 4 one more time, replacing the original plant material with new material.

Method for Using Fresh Plant Material

1. Fill a sterilized 16 oz (500 mL) jar about three-quarters full with finely chopped fresh plant material. Top with good-quality oil—a blend of organic extra virgin olive, almond and sunflower oils would be excellent—leaving about 2 inches (5 cm) headspace (all the plant material should be covered in oil). Cover the opening of the jar with two layers of cheesecloth or a small piece of muslin; secure with a rubber band around the neck of the jar. (This allows moisture from the plant material to evaporate. Do not cap the jar, as the mixture needs to breathe to avoid bacterial growth.)

While the oil is infusing, it is important to keep the mixture in a cool, dark place. If it is placed in the sun, the properties of the plant will be destroyed and the potential for bacterial growth is increased. The only exception to this is St. John's wort, which has always been made in the sun (see page 144).

2. Place in a cool, dark place for 4 to 6 weeks, checking daily to ensure that the plant material is completely covered by oil (top up with more oil if necessary to prevent bacterial growth). Spoon off any water that rises to the surface with a sterilized spoon. You will know your oil is ready when it takes on the scent and color of the plant material that was used.

3. Place coarse muslin or a coarsely woven tea towel in a strainer set over a nonreactive bowl. Strain the oil into the bowl, squeezing the fabric to extract as much oil as possible.

4. Place another cloth, with the finest weave available, in strainer and strain the oil again, this time into a sterilized dark glass jar. Add 5% wheat germ oil as a preservative to keep the oil from going rancid (if you have a wheat or gluten allergy, substitute 1% vitamin E oil with mixed tocopherols).

5. Seal tightly and store in the refrigerator for up to 2 years.

Store Infused Oils in the Refrigerator

All infused oils should be stored in the refrigerator to extend their life. If they are used often, as in the case of body and face oils, decant a small amount into another bottle to leave out. In general, infused oils should not be used after 1 year. If refrigerated they may last for up to 2 years. As long as there are no signs of mold, they are safe to use.

Heat Infusion Method

Consider using a heat infusion method with fresh plant material to ensure that all the moisture is evaporated. (This method should not be used for St. John's wort, which is sun-infused.) There are three ways to make a heat-infused oil.

Pan method

1. Follow the directions for making an infused oil on page 145, placing the plant material and oil in a jar. Once the jar is filled, place it, uncapped, in a saucepan filled two-thirds with water. Turn heat to very low and allow the water to heat the oil until small bubbles form on the bottom of the jar (do not boil). Continue for several hours to all day, stirring occasionally. Check the jar regularly to make sure the water is not too hot, or you will burn the oil. (If you are concerned about too high a heat level, use a heat diffuser under the pot or place a ring from the lid of a Mason jar inside the pan and set the jar on top of it.)

2. When you are satisfied with the color and scent of the oil, strain as indicated for the methods on page 145 and transfer to a sterilized glass jar. Add vitamin E or wheat germ oil as a preservative (see page 137).

3. Seal tightly, set aside to cool completely, and store in the refrigerator for up to 2 years.

Double boiler method

1. In a nonreactive bowl, cover your fresh plant material with oil. Set over a pan of simmering water (the bowl should not touch the water). Check regularly to make sure the water in the pan doesn't evaporate.

2. When you are satisfied with the color and scent of the oil, strain as indicated for the methods on page 145 and transfer to a sterilized glass jar. Add vitamin E or wheat germ oil as a preservative (see pages 137 and 138).

3. Seal tightly, set aside to cool completely, and store in the refrigerator for up to 2 years.

Slow cooker method

1. Place your plant material in the insert of a slow cooker and cover with oil. Do not cover slow cooker with lid. Heat on the lowest setting, stirring regularly, for 12 to 24 hours.

2. When you are satisfied with the color and scent of the oil, strain as indicated as indicated for the methods on page 145 and transfer to a sterilized glass jar. Add vitamin E or wheat germ oil as a preservative (see pages 137 and 138).

3. Seal tightly, set aside to cool completely, and store in the refrigerator for up to 2 years.

Tip: Even the lowest temperature on some slow cookers is too hot and can burn your oil. You want the temperature to be 100°F (38°C). If you place a drop of oil on the inside of your wrist, it should feel slightly warmer than your body temperature.

Part 2
Remedies

Conditions and Remedies

Abrasions 153

Abscesses 154

Allergies 155

Anemia 156

Anal Fistula 157

Angina Pectoris 158

Anorexia Nervosa 159

Arteriosclerosis 160

Arthritis 160

Atherosclerosis 162

Babies and Children 163

   Babies *163*

      Bathing Baby *163*

      Baby Massage *164*

      Colic *166*

      Coughs and Colds *166*

      Diaper Rash *167*

      Insect Bites *168*

      Overexcitement *168*

      Teething *168*

   Toddlers and Older Children . . . *169*

      Chicken Pox *169*

      Coughs and Colds *170*

      Croup *171*

      Cuts and Abrasions *172*

      Earache *172*

      Fevers *172*

      Insomnia *173*

      Overexcitement *175*

      Whooping Cough *175*

   Children with Special Needs . . . *177*

Back Pain 181

   Lumbago *182*

   Sciatica *183*

Bites and Stings 184

   Bee Stings *184*

   Dog Bites *184*

   Insect Bites *185*

   Spider Bites *185*

   Wasp Stings *185*

Black Eye 186

Bleeding, External (Minor) 186

Blisters 186

Blood Pressure 187

   High Blood Pressure
      (Hypertension) *187*

   Low Blood Pressure
      (Hypotension) *188*

Boils and Carbuncles 189

Breath, Bad 190

Bruises 191

Burns and Scalds (Minor) 192

Bursitis 192

Cancer 194

Candidiasis 195

Carpal Tunnel Syndrome 196

Cellulite 197

Cerebral Palsy 198

Chronic Fatigue Syndrome 199

Circulation 202

Common Cold and Influenza 203

Conjunctivitis 208

Convalescence 208

Cramp 210

Cuts and Wounds 211

Cystic Fibrosis 211

Cystitis 213

Debility (Physical) 214

Digestive Problems 216

   Constipation *216*

   Diarrhea *216*

   Heartburn *217*

   Indigestion *217*

   Intestinal Gas *218*

   Diverticulitis *218*

Earache 219
Edema 220
Emphysema 221
Exhaustion 222
Fainting 223
Fatigue 224
Feet 226
   Aching Feet *226*
   Athlete's Foot *228*
   Bunions *229*
   Corns *229*
   Smelly Feet *230*
   Swollen Feet and Ankles *230*
Fever 231
Fibromyalgia (Fibrositis) 232
First Aid 234
   The Essential Oil First Aid Box . . . *235*
   First Aid Treatment with
     Essential Oils *236*
   Procedures for Essential Oil
     Poisoning or Adverse
     Reaction *238*
Gout 240
Hemorrhoids 241
Hangover 242
Hay Fever 243
Headaches 244
   Tension Headaches *244*
   Gastric Headaches *246*
Head Lice 247
Heat Rash (Prickly Heat) 248
Herpes 249
Hiccups 252
Immune System 252
Inflammation 253
Insect Repellent 254
Insomnia 255
Intertrigo 256
Irritable Bowel Syndrome 257

Itching (Pruritis) 258
Kidneys 259
Liver 260
   Hepatitis *261*
Lymphatic System 261
Maturity and Old Age 262
Measles 264
Memory (Loss) 265
Men's Health 266
   Impotence *267*
   Jock Itch *268*
   Prostatitis *268*
Migraine 270
Mononucleosis (Infectious) 271
Mouth Ulcers 272
Multiple Sclerosis 272
Mumps 273
Muscles 274
Nausea 275
Neuralgia 276
Nose (Blocked) 277
Obesity 278
Paraplegia, Quadriplegia
  and Hemiplegia 279
Poison Ivy, Oak and Sumac 281
Pregnancy and Birth 282
   Pregnancy *283*
     Morning Sickness *283*
     Stretch Marks *283*
     Nipples *284*
     Aching Back *285*
     Varicose Veins *285*
     Anxiety and Depression *286*
   The Birth *286*
   After the Birth *288*
     Breastfeeding *288*
     Breast Abscesses *288*
     Sore Perineum *289*
     Postnatal Depression *290*

Raynaud's Disease 291
Repetitive Strain Injury 293
Respiratory Problems 293
  Asthma. 293
  Bronchitis 294
  Catarrh 295
  Coughs. 296
  Laryngitis 297
  Sinusitis 298
  Tonsillitis. 299
Restless Legs Syndrome. 300
Rheumatism (Muscular) 300
Ringworm 302
Rubella 303
Scabies 304
Scar Tissue 305
Shock 306
Sports 306
  Pre-sport Treatment. 306
  After-Sport Treatment 307
  Achilles Tendonitis. 307
  Cartilage Injury (Knee). 308
  Strains and Sprains 309
  Sports Stress 310
Stress and Emotional Problems . . . 310
Sunburn. 314
Sunstroke and Heatstroke 315
Teeth and Gum Problems 316
  Abscess, Dental. 316
  Gingivitis 317
  Gum Infections 317
  Toothache 318
Throat (Sore) 318
Travel. 320
  Airplane Travel. 320
  Motion Sickness. 324
  Dysentery. 325
Urethritis 326
Urticaria (Hives). 326

Viral Infections 327
Vomiting 327
Warts. 328
Water Warts 328
West Nile Virus 329
Whitlow. 329
Women's Health 330
  Cervical Dysplasia 330
  Endometriosis 330
  Fibrocystic Breast Disease 331
  Leukorrhea. 332
  Menopause 333
    Hot Flashes 334
    Depression. 335
    Mood Swings and Anxiety 336
  Menstruation 337
    Amenorrhea 337
    Dysmenorrhea 338
  Premenstrual Syndrome (PMS). . . 339
Workplace (and School) Stress . . . 341
  Commuting 344
  Environmental and Physical
    Stresses. 344
  Burnout 348

Glass Euro dropper bottles (⅙ oz/5 mL), which accommodate up to 100 drops of essential oils are ideal for making most of these blends. Do not use bottles with eyedropper screw tops—the essential oils will degrade the rubber and spoil your blend.

Conditions and Remedies

The remedies in this section are based on our collective experience learning about and using essential oils. The recipes are not difficult—they don't take long to make and most of the ingredients are relatively inexpensive. However, they are not intended to replace the advice of your health-care practitioner. Please remember that even seemingly simple symptoms can mask serious conditions. If symptoms are severe or persist longer than a few days, seek assessment and treatment by a health professional.

The real value of essential oils is their ability to assist the body with healing itself. Essential oils can help you:

- heal everyday ailments, such as minor cuts and abrasions, burns, headaches, sleeplessness, fatigue and anxiety;
- strengthen your immune system, organs and glands to fight bacteria, fungi and viruses such as *Candida albicans*, *E. coli*, *Listeria*, *Norovirus* and *Staphylococcus*;
- lower your stress level; and
- tone and relax your muscles.

Using the Oils

Whenever possible, use all of the recommended oils listed for each remedy. If you don't have some of the oils called for, you can substitute others that share the same properties (see Key Essential Oils and Their Properties, pages 24 to 27) or those listed under Essential Oils for each condition.

Quantity and ratio are important. When preparing remedies, pay close attention to the quantities of oils called for. Whether you use 1 or 2 drops may greatly affect the efficacy of the result. Always use the appropriate proportions of essential oils and carrier oil. The total amount of essential oils used should rarely exceed 4% of the total remedy, and some oils should be added in far smaller amounts. Most of the recipes in this section have a 2% to 3% dilution. In select cases where a different dilution is more beneficial or safer for its intended use, the recipes have been adjusted. If making up a lotion or massage oil for daily use, you should use a 1.5% dilution—40 to 50 drops per 4 oz (125 mL) carrier oil or lotion.

If you have time, you can set the blends aside for 4 days to ensure that they combine well. Some practitioners believe this creates synergy (see page 21) among the ingredients and allows the fragrance of each blend to fully develop.

People with more serious conditions can also benefit from using essential oils. Where appropriate, essential oils can be used to complement medical treatments. Of course, it is important to discuss complementary treatments with your health-care practitioner first.

Abrasions

While abrasions are generally not serious, they can be very painful because nerve endings have been injured. Usually they require only careful cleansing. Cleansing with a solution containing essential oils can help speed the healing process.

Essential Oils

Helichrysum, lavender, manuka, tea tree

Treatments

Topical application: Using a cotton ball, thoroughly clean affected area with Antiseptic Wound Wash. Leave wound uncovered if possible. If a bandage is required, apply 1 drop lavender, tea tree or manuka essential oil to the gauze (see Tip, right). When changing the bandage, repeat as necessary until wound appears "closed." Once closed, leave wound uncovered to dry and scab.

In a small glass bottle, combine 2 drops lavender essential oil and 1 tsp (5 mL) jojoba oil; shake to blend. Using a cotton ball, apply to drying wound after cleansing/showering, until the scab heals.

Abscesses

An abscess is a localized pus-filled cavity created by bacterial invasion. Frequent abscesses could indicate a compromised immune system (see Immune System, page 252), in which case you should take steps to boost your immunity. Consult your health-care practitioner.

Essential Oils

Chamomile, lavender, tea tree

Hot Compress for Abscesses

½ cup (125 mL)	hot water
4 drops	tea tree essential oil
3 drops	lavender essential oil
3 drops	chamomile essential oil

1. *In a small non-reactive bowl, combine water and tea tree, lavender and chamomile essential oils. Stir well to disperse oils. Submerge a cloth just large enough to absorb all the liquid without dripping.*

2. *Apply compress to affected area every 2 hours.*

Variation

For an even more effective compress, in a small non-reactive bowl, combine 2 drops tea tree oil, 2 drops lavender oil, 1 drop chamomile oil and ½ tsp (2.5 mL) grapeseed or sweet almond oil. Using a cotton ball, apply to affected area. Cover with a bandage or plastic wrap. Place a hot towel overtop and leave for up to 30 minutes. Repeat as necessary.

Abscesses, Breast
See Pregnancy and Birth (page 288)

Abscesses, Dental
See Teeth and Gum Problems (page 316)

Acne
See Skin Problems (page 375)

Caution

People with nut allergies should avoid using sweet almond oil. Substitute an equal amount of grapeseed oil.

Compresses

A **cold compress** is used to reduce inflammation by drawing heat away from the area, easing swelling and pain. To make a cold compress, combine ½ cup (125 mL) cold water and essential oil(s) as directed in the recipe; stir well to disperse the oils. Soak a soft cloth in the water. Wring out the cloth to distribute the oils evenly, leaving enough liquid so that it is very moist but does not drip. Apply the cloth to the injured area and replace it when it becomes warm.

A **warm** or **hot compress** brings increased blood flow to the area. It eases pain, relaxes spasms, draws pus and relieves congestion. Warm or hot compresses are made in the same way as cold compresses, substituting hot water for cold. Work quickly after adding the oils, or they will evaporate and be lost. When preparing a warm or hot compress, always test its temperature on the inside of your wrist before applying to a sore area. Make it as hot as comfortable. Cover it with plastic wrap or a towel to keep the heat in, and reapply every 2 hours until relief is obtained.

Caution
Before using any essential oil, consult the relevant entry in Part 1: Essential Oils (A to Y), pages 28 to 117, taking careful note of any cautions.

Allergies

Many conditions such as hay fever, fatigue, hyperactivity, ear infection, headache and migraine are now thought to be allergy-related. Allergies are caused by proteins that the body does not recognize and tries to remove. Most allergic reactions are exacerbated by stress, which calming oils such as chamomile, lavender and melissa can help alleviate.

The following oils are good for general uses related to allergies, such as purifying the air, controlling airborne bacteria and viruses, and promoting relaxation. Most are anti-infectious and antiviral, while some are also stimulating to the adrenal and immune systems, as well as being relaxing in general. German chamomile in particular has been shown to be antiallergenic, antispasmodic and anti-inflammatory. To treat specific allergy symptoms such as excessive mucus, consult the relevant entries in this section.

Essential Oils

Bergamot, chamomile (German), cinnamon, clove (bud), eucalyptus (*dives, radiata, globulus, smithii*), helichrysum, juniper (needle), lavender, lemon, niaouli, peppermint, ravensara, rosemary ct. cineole, rosewood, tea tree

Caution
If someone has a known allergy to a specific essential oil, it should be completely avoided. Patch tests are somewhat controversial, and whether to use them is an individual decision (see page 13).

Allergy Blend

30 drops	bergamot essential oil
20 drops	lavender essential oil
20 drops	juniper essential oil
10 drops	peppermint essential oil

In a $\frac{1}{6}$ oz (5 mL) glass dropper bottle, combine bergamot, lavender, juniper and peppermint essential oils. Shake to blend.

Tips

If you prefer, when making an air spray, substitute Solubol for the vodka called for, in a ratio of 4 drops Solubol for every 1 drop essential oil. Solubol is a natural product that allows essential oils to disperse in liquid.

When making air sprays, be sure to add the essential oils to the bottle first, followed by the chosen dispersant (vodka or Solubol), to ensure that the essential oils disperse properly (they will not mix directly with water).

Caution

Before using any essential oil, consult the relevant entry in Part 1: Essential Oils (A to Y), pages 28 to 117, taking careful note of any cautions.

Treatments

Air spray: In a 4 oz (125 mL) PET plastic spray bottle, combine 75 drops Allergy Blend and 1 tsp (5 mL) vodka. Add ½ cup (125 mL) distilled or filtered water (see Tips, left). Shake vigorously before each use. Spray as desired.

Bath: Fill tub with warm water. Meanwhile, in a small non-reactive bowl, combine 1 tsp (5 mL) milk and 4 to 6 drops Allergy Blend. Add to water, agitate to disperse oil, then soak for 30 minutes, massaging any floating droplets of oil into your skin.

Hand/foot/sitz bath: Combine 1 tsp (5 mL) milk and 4 drops Allergy Blend. Add to a basin of warm water, agitate to disperse oil, then soak desired area for 10 minutes, massaging any floating droplets of oil into your skin.

Massage: In a small non-reactive bowl, combine 4 tsp (20 mL) grapeseed or sweet almond oil and 8 drops Allergy Blend. Mix well and massage over your body.

Anemia

People with anemia have a pale complexion and feel weak and lethargic. They tend to tire easily because their blood is deficient in red blood cells, or hemoglobin. The most common cause of anemia is iron deficiency. Children under 2 years of age, teenagers, pregnant women and women who are breastfeeding, the elderly and some vegetarians are most at risk for anemia.

A proper diet, including supplementation with vitamins and minerals, is essential in managing this condition. See your health-care practitioner if you think you may be anemic. You will need to have the appropriate blood tests done before initiating any dietary or nutritional changes.

The following blend is for home treatment after testing has confirmed anemia. It is meant to be used as an adjunct to medical treatment.

Essential Oils

Black pepper, chamomile, lemon, peppermint, spikenard, thyme

Anemia Blend

10 drops	chamomile essential oil
3 drops	lemon or peppermint essential oil
3 drops	black pepper or thyme ct. linalool essential oil

In a $\frac{1}{6}$ oz (5 mL) glass bottle, combine chamomile, lemon and black pepper essential oils. Shake to blend.

Treatments

Air spray: In a 4 oz (125 mL) PET plastic spray bottle, combine 75 drops Anemia Blend and 1 tsp (5 mL) vodka. Add $\frac{1}{2}$ cup (125 mL) water (see Tips, page 156).

Bath: Fill tub with warm water. Meanwhile, in a small non-reactive bowl, combine 1 tsp (5 mL) milk and 4 to 6 drops Anemia Blend (see Tips, right). Add to tub and agitate to disperse oil, then soak for 30 minutes, massaging any floating droplets of oil into your skin.

Hand/foot/sitz bath: In a small non-reactive bowl, combine 1 tsp (5 mL) milk and 4 drops Anemia Blend. Add to a basin of warm water, agitate to disperse oil, then soak desired area for 30 minutes, massaging any floating droplets of oil into your skin.

Massage: In a small non-reactive bowl, combine 4 tsp (20 mL) grapeseed or sweet almond oil and 8 drops Anemia Blend. Mix well and massage over your body.

Anal Fistula

Anal fistula is the medical term for an infected tunnel that develops between the skin and the muscular opening at the end of the digestive tract (the anus). Most anal fistulas are the result of an infection in an anal gland that spreads to the skin. Surgery is usually needed to treat a fistula.

Essential Oils

Geranium, lavender, tea tree

Tips

Do not add essential oils to the tub while the water is running, as some of the precious essences may evaporate, depriving you of the full benefits.

If you prefer, substitute an equal quantity of liquid castile soap for the milk called for in any bath recipe.

If you are using a blend around bath/shower time, you can enhance the benefit by combining the essential oils with a carrier oil and rub it into your skin *before* getting into the shower or bath. This enables the essential oils to be absorbed and work their way into the bloodstream. The heat of the water encourages the essential oil vapors to rise, allowing you to inhale the aromas more easily and thus creating a dual application.

Tip

For more potent treatments, substitute cold-pressed tamanu oil for grapeseed or sweet almond oil. Tamanu oil is nonirritating and anti-inflammatory, making it a good choice to be used on sensitive areas.

Anal Fistula Massage Gel or Oil

4 tsp (20 mL)	aloe vera gel, grapeseed oil or tamanu oil
5 drops	lavender essential oil
4 drops	geranium essential oil
3 drops	tea tree essential oil

In a small non-reactive bowl, combine gel (or oil) and lavender, geranium and tea tree essential oils. Mix thoroughly.

Treatment

Wash: In a small non-reactive bowl, combine 3 drops tea tree oil and ½ tsp (2.5 mL) unpasteurized liquid honey. Mix thoroughly. Add 1 cup (250 mL) warm water and stir well. Using a cotton ball, bathe affected area with mixture. Pat dry and massage area with Anal Fistula Massage Gel or Oil. Apply twice daily.

Angina Pectoris

Angina is usually experienced as a sharp pain radiating down either arm, into the jaw and across the chest, or it may feel like a squeezing pain in the chest. The feeling usually lasts for up to 15 minutes and may be worse when lying down. Consult your doctor immediately if you experience these symptoms. Angina occurs when an adequate supply of oxygenated blood fails to reach the heart muscle because of clogged or hardening arteries. Attacks can be brought on by physical exertion, overeating or emotional stress. Essential oil treatment is used as an adjunct to medical treatment. (See also Stress and Emotional Problems, page 310.)

Essential Oils

Bergamot, black pepper, ginger, lemon, melissa, rosemary ct. verbenone, sage, thyme

---

Angina Blend

15 drops	bergamot essential oil
6 drops	ginger or lemon essential oil
3 drops	black pepper or thyme essential oil

In a ⅙ oz (5 mL) glass dropper bottle, combine bergamot, ginger and black pepper essential oils. Shake to blend.

Treatments

Bath: Fill tub with warm water. Meanwhile, in a small non-reactive bowl, combine 1 tsp (5 mL) milk and 4 to 6 drops Angina Blend. Add to tub and agitate to disperse oil, then soak for 30 minutes, massaging any floating droplets of oil into your skin.

Inhaler: Place Angina Blend in a small non-reactive bowl. Place the inhaler wick in the bowl and allow it to absorb the entire amount. Insert the wick in the inhaler tube and tightly cap the bottom of the inhaler with the plug. Place the inhaler tube inside its cover and screw tightly to close.

Massage: In a small non-reactive bowl, combine 4 tsp (20 mL) grapeseed or sweet almond oil and 8 drops Angina Blend. Mix well and massage over your body.

Anorexia Nervosa

Aromatherapy is a useful part of a treatment plan for anorexia nervosa that includes other approaches such as counseling. Massage can help increase a person's sense of self-worth, reduce stress and encourage a positive body image. Some of the oils soothe, others act as antidepressants and some stimulate appetite. Avoid patchouli in cases of anorexia, as it can decrease appetite.

Essential Oils

Angelica, bergamot, clary sage, lavender, rose, ylang ylang

Anorexia Blend

A professional massage using this blend is ideal, but self-massage or bathing with the oils works well too.

9 drops	bergamot essential oil
9 drops	lavender or ylang ylang essential oil
3 drops	clary sage essential oil

In a ⅙ oz (5 mL) glass dropper bottle, combine bergamot, clary sage and lavender essential oils. Shake to blend.

Treatments

Air spray: In a 4 oz (125 mL) PET plastic spray bottle, combine 75 drops Anorexia Blend and 1 tsp (5 mL) vodka. Add ½ cup (125 mL) distilled or filtered water (see Tips, page 160).

Tips

Do not add essential oils to the tub while the water is running, as some of the precious essences may evaporate, depriving you of the full benefits.

If you prefer, substitute an equal quantity of liquid castile soap for the milk called for in any bath recipe.

If you are using a blend around bath/shower time, you can enhance the benefit by combining the essential oils with a carrier oil and rub it into your skin *before* getting into the shower or bath. This enables the essential oils to be absorbed and work their way into the bloodstream. The heat of the water encourages the essential oil vapors to rise, allowing you to inhale the aromas more easily and thus creating a dual application.

If you prefer, when making an air spray, substitute Solubol for the vodka called for, in a ratio of 4 drops Solubol for every 1 drop essential oil. Solubol is a natural product that allows essential oils to disperse in liquid.

When making air sprays, be sure to add the oils to the bottle first, followed by the chosen dispersant (vodka or Solubol), to ensure that the essential oils disperse properly (they will not mix directly with water).

Do not add essential oils to the tub while the water is running, as some of the precious essences may evaporate, depriving you of the full benefits.

If you prefer, substitute an equal quantity of liquid castile soap for the milk called for in any bath recipe.

Bath: Fill tub with warm water. Meanwhile, in a small non-reactive bowl, combine 1 tsp (5 mL) milk and 4 to 6 drops Anorexia Blend. Add to tub and agitate to disperse oil, then soak for 30 minutes, massaging any floating droplets of oil into your skin.

Inhaler: Place Anorexia Blend in a small non-reactive bowl. Place inhaler wick in the bowl and allow it to absorb the entire amount. Insert the wick in the inhaler tube and tightly cap the bottom of the inhaler with the plug. Place the inhaler tube inside its cover and screw tightly to close.

Massage: In a small non-reactive bowl, combine 4 tsp (20 mL) grapeseed or sweet almond oil and 8 drops Anorexia Blend. Mix well and massage over your body.

Anxiety
See Stress and Emotional Problems (page 310)

Arteriosclerosis

Arteriosclerosis describes the thickening of artery walls. Almost everyone develops some arterial thickening as they grow older. Narrowing of the coronary arteries means that the heart receives insufficient blood and is deprived of oxygen and nutrients. (See also Atherosclerosis, page 162.)

Arthritis

Both osteoarthritis and rheumatoid arthritis are characterized by pain, stiffness and inflammation. Being overweight puts an extra load on joints and worsens symptoms. *Osteoarthritis* is known as a "wear and tear" disease that usually occurs with aging. It mainly affects weight-bearing joints (knees, hips, lower back, neck) and hands (fingers and thumbs), but it may also affect a shoulder, or even a big toe! *Rheumatoid arthritis* is an autoimmune disease that is distinct from osteoarthritis, although the symptoms may appear similar. The treatments included here are suitable for both types of arthritis. However, rheumatoid arthritis sufferers should seek professional advice in addition to using natural therapies.

Essential Oils

Angelica, Canadian balsam, bay laurel, bergamot, benzoin, black pepper, eucalyptus, silver fir, frankincense, ginger, helichrysum, juniper, marjoram, plai, rosemary

Arthritis Oil Blend

10 drops	German chamomile (*Matricaria recutita*) essential oil
7 drops	geranium essential oil
5 drops	birch essential oil
5 drops	rosemary (*Rosmarinus officinalis* ct. verbenone) or plai essential oil

In a ⅙ oz (5 mL) glass dropper bottle, combine German chamomile, geranium, birch and rosemary essential oils. Shake to blend.

Variation

For a more potent treatment, if nut allergies are not a concern, substitute cold-pressed organic peanut oil for the grapeseed or sweet almond oil. Peanut oil is effective in cases of arthritis and rheumatism, as it contains a significant amount of vitamin E, which can help to reduce inflammation. Peanut oil, like most cold-pressed oils, needs to be kept cold, so store this blend in the refrigerator. Cold-pressed peanut oil has a shelf life of 9 months.

Treatments

Massage: In a small non-reactive bowl, combine 4 tsp (20 mL) grapeseed or sweet almond oil and 12 drops Arthritis Oil Blend. Mix well and massage over your body.

Bath: Fill tub with warm water. Meanwhile, in a small non-reactive bowl, combine 10 drops Arthritis Oil Blend and 1 tsp (5 mL) grapeseed or sweet almond oil. Mix well. Add 1 cup (250 mL) Epsom salts and stir well. Add to bath. Agitate to disperse, then soak for at least 20 minutes, massaging your limbs gently with any floating droplets of oil.

Hot compress: In a small non-reactive bowl, combine ½ cup (125 mL) very hot water and 10 drops Arthritis Oil Blend. Stir well to disperse oils. Submerge a cloth just large enough to absorb all the liquid without dripping. Lay the cloth on the affected area and secure by placing a sock or glove over the compress. For larger areas, place plastic wrap over the damp cloth and around the area. Leave compress on for 1 hour.

Variation

For a more effective compress, in a small non-reactive bowl, combine ½ tsp (2.5 mL) grapeseed or sweet almond oil and 4 to 6 drops Arthritis Oil Blend. Using a cotton ball, apply to affected area. Cover with plastic wrap and place a hot towel overtop. Leave for up to 30 minutes.

Cautions

Before using any essential oil, consult the relevant entry in Part 1: Essential Oils (A to Y), pages 28 to 117, taking careful note of any cautions.

People with nut allergies should avoid using sweet almond or peanut oil. Substitute an equal amount of grapeseed oil.

Tip

If you are using a blend around bath/shower time, you can enhance the benefit by combining the essential oils with a carrier oil and rub it into your skin *before* getting into the shower or bath. This enables the essential oils to be absorbed and work their way into the bloodstream. The heat of the water encourages the essential oil vapors to rise, allowing you to inhale the aromas more easily and thus creating a dual application.

Asthma
See Respiratory Problems (page 293)

Atherosclerosis

Atherosclerosis is a condition that develops slowly. Over the years, the arteries harden and fatty deposits (atheroma) begin lining the artery walls. Numerous risks are associated with this condition, including angina and other forms of heart disease and stroke.

Essential Oils

Basil ct. linalool, black pepper, ginger, juniper, lemon, niaouli, rosemary ct. cineole

---

Atherosclerosis Oil

20 drops	rosemary essential oil
15 drops	juniper essential oil
15 drops	lemon essential oil
10 drops	black pepper essential oil
5 drops	ginger essential oil

In a $\frac{1}{6}$ oz (5 mL) glass dropper bottle, combine rosemary, juniper, lemon, black pepper and ginger essential oils. Shake to blend.

Treatments

Massage: In a small non-reactive bowl, combine 4 tsp (20 mL) grapeseed or sweet almond oil and 8 drops Atherosclerosis Oil. Mix well and massage over your body.

Bath: Fill tub with warm water. Meanwhile, in a small non-reactive bowl, combine 1 tsp (5 mL) milk and 4 to 6 drops Atherosclerosis Oil. Add to tub and agitate to disperse oil, then soak for 30 minutes, massaging any floating droplets of oil into your skin.

Athlete's Foot See Feet (page 228)

Tips

Do not add essential oils to the tub while the water is running, as some of the precious essences may evaporate, depriving you of the full benefits.

If you are using a blend around bath/shower time, you can enhance the benefit by combining the essential oils with a carrier oil and rub it into your skin *before* getting into the shower or bath. This enables the essential oils to be absorbed and work their way into the bloodstream. The heat of the water encourages the essential oil vapors to rise, allowing you to inhale the aromas more easily and thus creating a dual application.

Babies and Children

Our children deserve the best. By using pure, natural oils on their bodies you are giving them just that. The following table specifies the amounts of oils to use in preparations for babies and children. Most essential oils are too powerful to use on the skin of newborn babies and should not be used until the baby is at least 3 months old. However, the gentle nature of Roman chamomile and lavender essential oils, when properly diluted in a pure unscented lotion, makes them suitable for use with children under 2 months old. A safe dilution is 6 drops in $\frac{1}{2}$ cup (125 mL) sweet almond oil.

Age-Appropriate Essential Oils

3 days to 3 months	Roman chamomile, lavender, mandarin
3 months to 5 years	The above, plus bergamot, cedarwood, frankincense, geranium, ginger, lemon, sweet marjoram, sweet orange, rose, rosemary, sandalwood, tea tree, thyme ct. linalool, ylang ylang
5 years to puberty	All oils considered safe for adults, but used in smaller amounts

BABIES

Bathing Baby

Bathing baby in an essential oil bath can be an enjoyable experience for both parent and child. Inhaling the essential oil as baby is being bathed can be very relaxing. Therapeutically, using an essential oil in the bath can aid skin conditions and soothe minor aches and pains—just be sure to use age-appropriate oils (see page 164).

Baby's First Year

When a baby is 3 days old, Roman chamomile, lavender and mandarin essential oils may be introduced. They help to calm the nervous system and boost immunity; they are also antibacterial and mildly antiviral. You can use these oils to soothe babies who are restless, scratching themselves or suffering from a cold. A drop of lavender or Roman chamomile in a diffuser or floating in a bowl of warm water near baby's crib should help to ensure that restful sleep. Mandarin can help to ease painful gas and anxiety.

Once your baby is more than 3 months old, you can extend the range of essential oils you use and carefully increase the amounts. However, do not exceed the quantity of oils called for in the recipes.

Cautions

- Before using any essential oil, consult the relevant entry in Part 1: Essential Oils (A to Y), pages 28 to 117, taking careful note of any cautions.

- Do not use *Eucalyptus smithii* or rosemary essential oil on or near the face of infants and children under the age of 10.

Blends for Baby's Bath

Fill the tub, add the age-appropriate bath blend and agitate to disperse it in the water.

3 days to 3 months	1 drop Roman chamomile, lavender or mandarin essential oil mixed thoroughly with 1 tsp (5 mL) milk, sweet almond oil or liquid castile soap
3 months to 3 years	1 drop age-appropriate essential oil (see page 163) mixed thoroughly with 1 tsp (5 mL) milk, sweet almond oil or liquid castile soap
3 to 7 years	2 drops age-appropriate essential oil mixed thoroughly with 1 tsp (5 mL) milk, sweet almond oil or liquid castile soap
7 to 10 years	3 to 5 drops age-appropriate essential oil mixed thoroughly with 1 tsp (5 mL) milk, sweet almond oil or liquid castile soap
10 years through puberty	4 to 6 drops age-appropriate essential oil mixed thoroughly with 1 tsp (5 mL) milk, sweet almond oil or liquid castile soap

Tip

To extend the shelf life of your massage oil, consider using a blend of sweet almond oil and 5% to 10% unrefined wheat germ oil. Wheat germ oil is a natural preservative, rich in antioxidants and vitamin E. It should be kept in the refrigerator and should not be used by those with gluten or wheat allergies. If you prefer, simply split open a capsule of vitamin E and add to your massage oil. Many variables can affect the shelf life of your product, including the age of any of the oils used. That said, the addition of wheat germ oil (5% to 10%) or vitamin E (0.5% to 1.5%) should add 3 to 6 months to its life.

Baby Massage

All babies love to be massaged. It's good for bonding and has a calming effect if a baby is suffering from colic or is restless or generally unhappy. Just be sure to use age-appropriate essential oils (see page 163). The recommended carrier oil for newborn babies is sweet almond oil—it is emollient, nourishing to dry skin, relieves itching and can be used to soothe general irritation on baby's bottom as well as cradle cap, if it's a problem. Meadowfoam oil is also a good choice for babies, as it is emollient and penetrating. Meadowfoam and sweet almond oils can be combined or used alone during the first 2 days of baby's life.

Gentle Baby Oil

Babies and children from 2 to 24 months: *In a small glass bottle, combine 6 drops Gentle Baby Blend (page 165) and* $^1/_4$ *cup (60 mL) sweet almond oil.*

Children age 2 to 12 years: *In a 2 oz (60 mL) glass bottle, combine 9 drops Gentle Baby Blend and* $^1/_4$ *cup (60 mL) sweet almond oil.*

This oil is good for multiple uses. Store in a cool, dark place. It will keep in the refrigerator for up to 1 year.

Basic Massage Oil for Babies and Children

Makes about ½ cup (125 mL)

3 days to 12 months	6 drops (total) age-appropriate mixed or single essential oils
1 to 12 years	9 drops (total) age-appropriate mixed or single essential oils
13 years and older	18 drops (total) mixed or single essential oils (adult dose)

Place ½ cup (125 mL) sweet almond oil in a 4 oz (125 mL) glass bottle. Add essential oil(s) (see page 163) and shake to blend. Store in a cool, dark place for up to 12 months. Shake well before using.

Variation

If you prefer, use half meadowfoam and half sweet almond oil.

Gentle Baby Blend

We recommend that you make a small bottle of this blend, as it is used frequently in many of the recipes in this section. When blended into oil for massage, it will help to ease various symptoms from colic to restlessness. It is also useful for general skin care, such as loosening cradle cap, or as an after-bath oil. You can add it to baby's bathwater too (see page 164 for quantities).

48 drops	lavender essential oil
30 drops	chamomile essential oil

In a ⅙ oz (5 mL) glass dropper bottle, combine essential oils. Shake to blend.

Cautions

- Essential oils must never be taken internally and must always be correctly diluted before use. This is particularly important for babies and children.

- Essential oils, whether diluted or not, can cause permanent damage to the eyes upon contact. If essential oil gets into the eyes, immediately flush with cold milk or vegetable oil to dilute. If stinging persists, seek medical attention.

- If you are concerned your baby may have nut allergies, substitute an equal amount of meadowfoam oil for any almond oil called for in the treatments.

Treatments

Diaper change: Sprinkle Gentle Baby Oil (page 164) on a baby wipe and use to clean baby during a diaper change.

Massage: After bathing, massage baby with Gentle Baby Oil to moisturize the skin and to induce relaxation. Avoid the genitals and eyes when massaging, and pay particular attention to the feet.

Cradle cap (for babies at least 3 months old): To lift cradle cap, in a non-reactive bowl, combine 4 drops Gentle Baby Blend, 2 drops cedarwood or sandalwood essential oil, and ¼ cup (60 mL) sweet almond oil. Gently massage onto baby's scalp. Leave on overnight and shampoo off in the morning. Be sure to shampoo and rinse well—not doing so could worsen the condition. Repeat as often as necessary.

Colic

If your baby has colic, it is very distressing for you as well as for the infant. Calming essential oils such as lavender will help to improve the situation.

Essential Oils

Chamomile, ginger, lavender, mandarin

Treatment

Massage (for babies at least 3 months old): In a 2 oz (60 mL) glass bottle, combine 4 drops Gentle Baby Blend (page 165), 1 drop each ginger and mandarin essential oils, and ¼ cup (60 mL) sweet almond oil. Using a clockwise motion and avoiding the genitals, gently massage baby's abdomen.

Coughs and Colds

Essential Oils

Lavender, lemon, tea tree

Treatments

Diffuser/vaporizer: For babies older than 3 months, add 2 drops tea tree essential oil to a diffuser, following the manufacturer's instructions, or 3 drops to a vaporizer. Place near baby's crib or bed to aid breathing. If baby is younger than 3 months, use *Eucalyptus staigeriana*.

Massage (for babies at least 3 months old): In a small non-reactive bowl, combine 1 drop each lavender, lemon and tea tree essential oils and 6 tsp (30 mL) unscented baby lotion or sweet almond oil. Use for a chest and back massage.

Diaper Rash

Essential Oils

Chamomile, lavender, tea tree

Healing Bottom Lotion

This is a soothing lotion that can be used regularly when changing diapers.

Makes about ½ cup (125 mL)

4 tsp (20 mL)	calendula oil
4 tsp (20 mL)	sweet almond oil
8 drops	Gentle Baby Blend (see page 165)
2 drops	frankincense essential oil
2 drops	geranium essential oil
¼ cup + 4 tsp (80 mL)	unscented baby lotion

In a 4 oz (125 mL) PET plastic bottle, combine calendula and sweet almond oils, Gentle Baby Blend, and frankincense and geranium essential oils. Shake to combine. Add lotion and shake vigorously to mix thoroughly.

Diaper Rash Powder

This powder is excellent for preventing diaper rash.

Makes about 2 cups (500 mL)

2 cups (500 mL)	cornstarch
8 tsp (40 mL)	zinc oxide powder (see Resources, page 459)
20 drops	lavender essential oil

1. *In a small non-reactive bowl, thoroughly combine cornstarch and zinc oxide powder. Add lavender oil 1 drop at a time, stirring constantly to prevent lumps forming.*

2. *Cover with plastic wrap and set aside for 4 days to allow the essential oil to permeate the dry ingredients. Transfer to an airtight container and store at room temperature for up to 1 year. Shake well before using.*

3. *Sprinkle over baby's bottom at change time. Use sparingly—a light dusting helps keep creases dry.*

Tip

Avoid baby lotions that contain perfumes and use only those with natural organic preservatives. The health and beauty section of a trusted natural foods store is a good place to look for appropriate products.

Tips

If a fungal rash exists, substitute arrowroot powder for cornstarch.

Dispense the finished powder into small powder shakers for convenient use (see Resources, page 459).

Tip

Avoid baby lotions that contain perfumes and use only those with natural organic preservatives. The health and beauty section of a trusted natural foods store is a good place to look for appropriate products.

Soothing Wash for Diaper Rash

1 tsp (5 mL)	liquid castile soap
2 drops	tea tree essential oil
2 cups (500 mL)	warm water

In a non-reactive bowl, combine liquid castile soap and tea tree essential oil; mix well. Stir in warm water.

Use to wash baby's bottom. Dry skin gently and follow with either Diaper Rash Powder or Healing Bottom Lotion (page 167).

Insect Bites

Insect Bite Paste

1 tsp (5 mL)	baking soda
1 drop	lavender essential oil
	Distilled or filtered water

In a small non-reactive bowl, combine baking soda and lavender essential oil. Mix well, adding just enough distilled or filtered water to make a soft paste. Dab frequently on bites.

Variation
Substitute lavender or immortelle hydrolat for the water to enhance the benefit of the insect bite paste.

Overexcitement

For babies at least 3 months old: Bathe baby using a mixture of mandarin and lavender essential oils. Fill tub with warm water. Meanwhile, in a small non-reactive bowl, combine the number of drops of oil appropriate for baby's age (see page 164) and 1 tsp (5 mL) milk or liquid castile soap. Mix thoroughly. Add to tub and agitate to disperse, then bathe baby.

Teething

Facial massage: In a small non-reactive bowl, combine 1 drop chamomile essential oil and 1 tsp (5 mL) sweet almond oil. Massage baby's cheeks and jaw gently, carefully avoiding the eye area.

Even if your baby has just graduated to the advanced age of 1, he or she still needs smaller amounts of essential oils than an older child.

Chicken Pox

Chicken pox is a highly infectious viral disease. It starts off as a feverish cold before the spotty red rash that looks like insect bites appears. The spots then develop into blisters that are often intensely itchy. Essential oils are useful for soothing the itchy spots—and the child!

Essential Oils

Roman chamomile, frankincense, geranium, lavender, lemon, ravensara, tea tree

---

Chicken Pox Blend

2 cups (500 mL)	baking soda
10 drops	Roman chamomile essential oil
5 drops	geranium essential oil
5 drops	lavender essential oil

Place baking soda in a non-reactive bowl. Add Roman chamomile, geranium and lavender essential oils 1 drop at a time (to prevent lumping). Mix thoroughly and store in an airtight container in a cool, dry place.

Treatments

Lotion: In a non-reactive bowl, combine 1 to 2 tsp (5 to 10 mL) Chicken Pox Blend with enough cold water to make a milky lotion. Using a cotton ball, dab the lotion on the affected areas up to 3 times daily to relieve itching.

Spray: In a non-reactive bowl, combine 1 to 2 tsp (5 to 10 mL) Chicken Pox Blend with enough cold water to make a very thin lotion. Pour the mixture into a 1 oz (30 mL) PET plastic spray bottle and spray the affected areas as often as needed. Shake well before using.

Chicken Pox Bath

This bath will soothe the itching and has the added advantage of making the patient feel calmer. Use for children with rubella (German measles) too.

Fill tub with warm water. Meanwhile, in a non-reactive bowl, combine 2 drops lavender essential oil, 2 drops tea tree oil and $\frac{1}{2}$ cup (125 mL) baking soda. Mix thoroughly. Add to tub and agitate to disperse mixture, then bathe child for 30 minutes, massaging any floating droplets of oil into the skin. Repeat daily until the itching subsides and the pocks begin to heal.

Coughs and Colds

Essential Oils

Bergamot, lavender, lemon, rosemary, tea tree, thyme ct. linalool

Add 1 drop each tea tree and thyme ct. linalool essential oils to a diffuser, following the manufacturer's instructions, or 3 drops (total) to a vaporizer. To aid breathing, diffuse the oils for about 30 minutes prior to bedtime.

Treatments

Bath: Fill tub with warm water. Meanwhile, in a small non-reactive bowl, combine 1 tsp (5 mL) liquid castile soap or milk and 1 to 2 drops each (as age-appropriate; see page 164) lavender, rosemary and tea tree essential oils. Add to tub and agitate to disperse, then bathe child.

Massage: In a small non-reactive bowl, combine 1 drop each lavender, lemon or bergamot, and tea tree essential oils with 4 tsp (20 mL) unscented lotion or sweet almond oil. Use for a chest and back massage.

Croup

Most cases of croup are benign but disturbing, as the harsh, barking cough can be quite frightening. Breathing difficulties and shortness of breath can occur in more serious cases of croup. Using essential oils that fight the infection and simultaneously calm the child are best. Thyme ct. linalool and sweet marjoram are effective in cases of infection and breathing difficulties, while rose provides a comforting hug for anxiety and crying.

Essential Oils

Sweet marjoram, rose, thyme ct. linalool

Croup Blend

10 drops	sweet marjoram essential oil
10 drops	thyme ct. linalool essential oil
2 drops	rose essential oil

In a ⅙ oz (5 mL) glass dropper bottle, combine sweet marjoram, thyme and rose essential oils. Shake to blend.

Variation
For children with asthma, add 3 to 5 drops of the blend to a cool-mist diffuser and have the child sit near it for 10 minutes.

Treatments

Massage: In a small non-reactive bowl, combine 1 tsp (5 mL) unscented lotion or sweet almond oil and 3 drops Croup Blend. Massage over child's torso, avoiding the face and neck. Sit child in an enclosed bathroom with a hot shower running so he or she can breathe in the steam for 10 minutes. For children with asthma, use as a chest rub instead, as steaming may not be appropriate (also see Variation, above).

Vaporizer: Add 3 to 5 drops Croup Blend to a vaporizer in child's bedroom. Diffuse the oils for about 30 minutes prior to bedtime.

Cuts and Abrasions

Once children start moving around independently, they enter a phase when their legs and arms are usually covered with abrasions, cuts and bruises. Cuts and abrasions should be washed with Antiseptic Wound Wash and covered with a bandage.

Treatment

Wash: Swab the wound clean, using Antiseptic Wound Wash (page 153). If child is resuming play, cover the wound to protect it from further injury or infection—add a drop of lavender or tea tree oil to the bandage pad before applying. Leave shallow or superficial wounds uncovered overnight. If the wound is more serious than a minor cut or scrape and skin is missing, you might consider following up with Basic Healing Ointment (page 234).

Diaper Rash
See Babies (page 167)

Earache

It is not advisable to use essential oils in the ears. Mullein garlic drops (an extract available from Herb Pharm) may be used as directed.

Earache can be a warning of more severe problems such as sinus congestion, mumps, measles or a toothache. It can lead to serious infections or other major complaints, so it should never be ignored.

Fevers

A fever is the body's response to infection. Children can run alarmingly high fevers very quickly, but usually their temperature drops just as fast. Fevers are an important part of the healing process, but if they get too high it is important to reduce the child's temperature promptly to lessen the chance of complications. Using essential oils that promote sweating can help to manage this process.

Essential Oils

Roman chamomile, ginger, lavender, lemon

Treatments

Cool compress: Pour 2 cups (500 mL) cool (not icy) water into a non-reactive bowl and add 2 to 3 drops (as age-appropriate; see page 163) Roman chamomile, ginger, lavender or lemon essential oil. Stir well to disperse oil. Soak a cloth and wring out enough water so cloth doesn't drip. Place on child's forehead, repeating often. Follow with a bath (below).

Bath: Fill tub with cool to lukewarm water, deep enough to cover as much of the child's body as possible. Meanwhile, in a small non-reactive bowl, combine 1 tsp (5 mL) liquid castile soap and 1 to 2 drops (as age-appropriate; see page 164) Roman chamomile, ginger, lavender or lemon essential oil. Add to tub along with a few slices of lemon and agitate to disperse. Bathe child for 20 to 30 minutes, if possible.

Tip

Do not add essential oils to the tub while the water is running, as some of the precious essences may evaporate, depriving you of the full benefits.

Insomnia

Children suffer from insomnia if they are overtired, fearful or worried about an event, or sometimes for no apparent reason. Try to work out why your child is having trouble sleeping and follow one of the suggestions that follow.

Essential Oils

Chamomile, geranium, lavender, mandarin

Overtired and Strung-Out Blend

The lavender and chamomile oils combine to soothe on many different levels.

2 tsp (10 mL)	sweet almond oil
1 drop	lavender essential oil
1 drop	Roman chamomile essential oil

In a ⅓ oz (10 mL) glass dropper bottle, combine sweet almond oil and Roman chamomile and lavender essential oils. Shake to blend.

Treatment

Massage and bath: Massage half of the Overtired Blend into child's skin. Then give child a warm bath. After the bath, put the little one to bed in a dimly lit room and massage remainder of oil into his or her arms and torso. See also Overexcitement (page 175).

Tip

Using a natural
product like Solubol
is a great way to
disperse essential
oils when they are
mixed with water.

Monster Spray

The oils in this spray will help to allay fears and assist in
bringing sound sleep. Sweet marjoram is effective for
anxiety, agitation and insomnia. Roman chamomile and
lavender are soothing and comforting for the nerves.
Mandarin's sweet floral aroma is uplifting and has a tonic
effect on the digestive system.

1 tsp (5 mL)	lavender hydrolat (see page 122)
4 drops	lavender essential oil
4 drops	mandarin essential oil
2 drops	Roman chamomile essential oil
2 drops	sweet marjoram essential oil
	Distilled or filtered water

*In a 4 oz (125 mL) PET plastic spray bottle, combine
lavender hydrolat and lavender, mandarin, Roman
chamomile and sweet marjoram essential oils. Fill bottle
with water. Shake well before using.*

Variation
*In a 4 oz (125 mL) PET plastic spray bottle, combine
48 drops Solubol (see Resources, page 459) and Monster
Spray blend. Once they are mixed, fill the bottle with
distilled or filtered water.*

Treatment
Surface spray: Lightly spray your child's pillow and the floor
around the bed or closet (wherever the monsters hide). While you
are spraying, tell the child that this spray gets rid of monsters.

Achy and Grumpy Blend

This blend is for children over 5 years of age who have
overextended themselves emotionally and physically and
may need to calm down before bedtime.

5 drops	lavender essential oil
5 drops	mandarin essential oil
3 drops	rosemary essential oil
2 drops	Roman chamomile essential oil

*In a ⅙ oz (5 mL) glass dropper bottle, combine lavender,
mandarin, rosemary and Roman chamomile essential
oils. Shake to blend.*

Treatments

Bath: Fill tub with warm water. Meanwhile, in a small non-reactive bowl, combine the age-appropriate number of drops of Achy and Grumpy Blend (see page 164) and 1 tsp (5 mL) milk or liquid castile soap. Add to tub and agitate to disperse. Place child in the bath to soak for 10 to 15 minutes while you massage his or her limbs. Try to keep child calm.

Massage: In a small non-reactive bowl, combine the age-appropriate number of drops of Achy and Grumpy Blend (see page 164) and 1 tsp (5 mL) sweet almond oil. Mix well. Pour a little of the mixture into the palm of your hand and massage over child's body after showering or bathing. Massage child's back, legs or whatever aches the most!

Overexcitement

Sometimes a child can be overstimulated or hyperactive. A warm bath can help to start the relaxation process necessary for sound sleep.

Essential Oils

Cedarwood, frankincense, sweet orange, rose, sandalwood, ylang ylang

Treatment

Bath: Fill tub with warm water. Meanwhile, in a small non-reactive bowl, combine 1 tsp (5 mL) grapeseed or sweet almond oil and the age-appropriate number of drops (see page 163)—in any combination—of sandalwood, rose, frankincense, sweet orange and/or ylang ylang essential oils. Add to tub and agitate to disperse, then place child in the bath to soak quietly (under supervision) for 10 to 15 minutes. Try to keep child calm.

Whooping Cough

Whooping cough, with its violent and distressing spasms of coughing, is a highly infectious and serious bacterial disease. Professional help is always needed. The inhalation blends here are an adjunct to professional treatment and can help to reduce the severity and discomfort of the disease. Alternating sitting in a steamy bathroom (run a hot shower while the child sits on the toilet) and breathing fresh, cool air (from an open window) can help. Keep the bedroom airy but humid with a bowl of steaming water, a cool-mist diffuser or a vaporizer.

Essential Oils

Cypress, helichrysum, lavender, ravensara, rosemary (ct. cineole and ct. camphor), tea tree, thyme

---

Whooping Cough Inhalation Blend

7 drops	marjoram essential oil
7 drops	lavender essential oil
7 drops	cypress essential oil

In a small non-reactive bowl, combine marjoram, lavender and cypress essential oils and mix well. Place inhaler wick in the bowl and allow it to absorb the entire amount. Insert the wick inside the inhaler tube and tightly cap the bottom of the inhaler with the plug. Place the inhaler tube inside its cover and screw tightly to close.

Treatment

For children over 3 years old: Inhale from the tube as needed.

Whooping Cough Massage Blend

24 drops	cypress essential oil
12 drops	marjoram essential oil
12 drops	lavender essential oil

In a $^1/_6$ oz (5 mL) glass bottle, combine cypress, marjoram and lavender essential oils. Shake to blend.

Treatments

Bath: Fill tub with warm water. In a small non-reactive bowl, combine 1 tsp (5 mL) milk and 2 to 4 drops Whooping Cough Massage Blend (for children aged 3 to 12); use 4 to 6 drops for children age 13 and up. Add to tub and agitate to disperse oil. Soak child for 20 minutes, massaging any floating droplets of oil into skin of chest, back and throat.

Massage for children 1 to 3 years old: In a small non-reactive bowl, combine 2 tsp (10 mL) grapeseed or meadowfoam oil and 1 to 2 drops Whooping Cough Massage Blend. Mix thoroughly. Massage over child's chest and back.

Massage for children 3 to 12 years old: In a small non-reactive bowl, combine 4 tsp (20 mL) grapeseed or meadowfoam oil and 4 drops Whooping Cough Massage Blend. Massage over child's chest and back.

Massage for children 13 years old and up: In a small non-reactive bowl, combine 4 tsp (20 mL) grapeseed or meadowfoam oil and 8 drops Whooping Cough Massage Blend. Massage over child's chest and back.

CHILDREN with SPECIAL NEEDS

While it is not within the scope of this book to address the many different types of special needs of children, the following blends may assist in providing some relief for anxiety, lack of attention or focus, hyperactivity and sluggishness.

> ### *Anxiety Blend*
>
> | | |
> |---|---|
> | 8 drops | frankincense essential oil |
> | 8 drops | rose essential oil |
> | 4 drops | sandalwood or cedarwood essential oil |
> | 4 drops | sweet marjoram essential oil |
>
> *In a small glass dropper bottle, combine frankincense, rose, sandalwood and sweet marjoram essential oils. Shake to blend.*

Treatments

Bath: Fill tub with warm water. Meanwhile, in a small non-reactive bowl, combine 1 tsp (5 mL) milk and 2 to 6 drops (as age-appropriate; see page 163) Anxiety Blend. Add to tub and agitate to disperse oil. Soak child for 20 minutes, massaging any floating droplets of oil into the skin.

Roll-on: In a ⅓ oz (10 mL) glass bottle with roller ball, combine 15 drops Anxiety Blend and fractionated coconut oil to top up (be careful not to overfill). Insert the ball holder, then the ball, and screw on the top. Shake to blend. Roll onto temples, wrists and collarbones, as needed.

Cautions

- Before using any essential oil, consult the relevant entry in Part 1: Essential Oils (A to Y), pages 28 to 117, taking careful note of any cautions. Of particular note: do not use *Eucalyptus smithii* or rosemary essential oil on or near the face of infants or children under the age of 10.

- As a parent of a child with special needs, you know that medications and brain chemistry can affect the results of any treatment. If your child does not respond in a positive way to the remedies in this section, discontinue immediately.

Attention (Calming) Blend

When it comes to attention and focus, the question you should ask is, what is suppressing your child's focus and attention? Is it overstimulation and a need to relax, or is it lack of attention that requires stimulation?

16 drops	lavender essential oil
16 drops	frankincense essential oil
11 drops	cedarwood essential oil
8 drops	vetiver essential oil

In a ¹⁄₆ oz (5 mL) glass dropper bottle, combine lavender, frankincense, cedarwood and vetiver essential oils. Shake to blend.

Treatment

Inhaler: Place 15 drops Attention Blend in a small non-reactive bowl. Place inhaler wick in the bowl and allow it to absorb the entire amount. Insert the wick inside the inhaler tube and tightly cap the bottom of the inhaler with the plug. Place the inhaler tube inside its cover and screw tightly to close. From a few inches away, wave under the child's nose for 15 to 20 seconds. Use 20 minutes before any activity that requires focus. Do not place inside the child's nose or mouth.

Mental Alertness (Stimulating) Blend

20 drops	basil essential oil
15 drops	rosemary essential oil
9 drops	black pepper essential oil
3 drops	melissa essential oil
1 drop	rose essential oil

In a ¹⁄₆ oz (5 mL) glass dropper bottle, combine basil, rosemary, black pepper, melissa and rose essential oils. Shake to blend.

Treatment

Inhaler: Place 15 drops Mental Alertness Blend in a small non-reactive bowl. Place inhaler wick in the bowl and allow it to absorb the entire amount. Insert the wick inside the inhaler tube and tightly cap the bottom of the inhaler with the plug. Place the inhaler tube inside its cover and screw tightly to close. From a few inches away, wave under the child's nose for 15 to 20 seconds. Use 20 minutes before any activity that requires focus. Do not place inside the child's nose or mouth.

Calm Way Down Blend
(for Hyperactivity)

20 drops	vetiver essential oil
12 drops	sandalwood or cedarwood essential oil
10 drops	patchouli essential oil
10 drops	ylang ylang essential oil
6 drops	co-distilled rose and geranium essential oils

In a ⅙ oz (5 mL) glass dropper bottle, combine vetiver, sandalwood, patchouli, ylang ylang and rose/geranium essential oils. Shake to blend.

Treatments

Air spray: In a 4 oz (125 mL) PET plastic spray bottle, combine 75 drops Calm Way Down Blend and 1 tsp (5 mL) vodka. Fill bottle with distilled or filtered water (see Tips, page 180). Spray into the air above the child and have him or her walk through the falling mist. At bedtime, spritz over the pillow and on bed linens.

Bath: Fill tub with warm water. Meanwhile, in a small non-reactive bowl, combine 1 tsp (5 mL) milk and 2 to 6 drops (as age-appropriate; see page 164) Calm Way Down Blend. Add to tub and agitate to disperse oil. Soak child for 20 minutes, massaging any floating droplets of oil into the skin.

Diffuser: Add 3 to 5 drops Calm Way Down Blend to a diffuser, according to the manufacturer's instructions. Diffuse for 20 minutes before bed. (See Supplies and Equipment, page 459.)

Inhaler: Add 21 drops Calm Way Down Blend to a small non-reactive bowl. Place inhaler wick in the bowl and allow it to absorb the entire amount. Insert the wick inside the inhaler tube and tightly cap the bottom of the inhaler with the plug. Place the inhaler tube inside its cover and screw tightly to close.

Massage: In a small non-reactive bowl, combine 2 tsp (10 mL) grapeseed oil and 2 to 6 drops (as age-appropriate; see page 164) Calm Way Down Blend. Mix well and massage over child's body (see Tip, right).

Roll-on: In a ⅓ oz (10 mL) glass bottle with roller ball, combine 15 drops Calm Way Down Blend and fractionated coconut oil to top up (be careful not to overfill). Insert the ball holder, then the ball, and screw on the top. Shake to blend. Roll onto temples, wrists and collarbones, as needed.

Tip

For a more potent treatment, substitute passion flower-infused oil for the grapeseed oil. This oil is neurosedative and antispasmodic, which helps to alleviate extreme agitation and anxiety.

Sunshine Blend

Children who have a sluggish demeanor may be suffering from a range of issues, including digestive problems, a toxic liver caused by medication, anxiety or trouble sleeping. This blend clears the mind and aids relaxation, concentration and digestion. It has been adapted here for air dispersion and inhalation; it is not recommended for topical use with children.

22 drops	sweet orange essential oil
9 drops	bergamot essential oil
9 drops	lemon essential oil
5 drops	basil essential oil
2 drops	fennel essential oil
2 drops	co-distilled petitgrain sur fleurs or petitgrain essential oil
1 drop	lavender essential oil

In a $\frac{1}{6}$ oz (5 mL) glass dropper bottle, combine sweet orange, bergamot, lemon, basil, fennel, petitgrain and lavender essential oils. Shake to blend.

Tips

If you prefer, when making an air spray, substitute Solubol for the vodka called for, in a ratio of 4 drops Solubol for every 1 drop essential oil. Solubol is a natural product that allows essential oils to disperse in liquid.

When making air sprays, be sure to add the oils to the bottle first, followed by the chosen dispersant (vodka or Solubol), to ensure that the essential oils disperse properly (they will not mix directly with water).

Treatments

Air spray: In a 4 oz (125 mL) PET plastic spray bottle, combine 75 drops Sunshine Blend and 1 tsp (5 mL) vodka. Fill bottle with distilled or filtered water (see Tips, left). Spray into the air where the child is active.

Diffuser: Add 3 to 5 drops Sunshine Blend to a diffuser, according to the manufacturer's instructions. Diffuse for 20 minutes. (See Supplies and Equipment, page 459.)

Inhaler: Place 21 drops Sunshine Blend in a small non-reactive bowl. Place inhaler wick in the bowl and allow it to absorb the entire amount. Insert the wick inside the inhaler tube and tightly cap the bottom of the inhaler with the plug. Place the inhaler tube inside its cover and screw tightly to close.

Back Pain

After a day in the garden or some other manual labor, our bodies often ache, reminding us of the good work we've done and that we are entitled to a soak in the bath and, with luck, a massage afterward.

Essential Oils

Anise, Canadian balsam, basil ct. linalool, clove (bud), cypress, *Eucalyptus citriodora*, fennel, geranium, ginger, lavender, niaouli, nutmeg, peppermint, rosemary

---

Backache Bath Blend

4 drops	geranium or lavender essential oil
2 drops	eucalyptus or cypress essential oil
2 drops	peppermint essential oil
2 drops	nutmeg or ginger essential oil

In a ⅙ oz (5 mL) glass dropper bottle, combine geranium, eucalyptus, peppermint and nutmeg essential oils. Shake to blend.

Treatment

Bath: Fill tub with warm water. Meanwhile, in a small non-reactive bowl, combine 1 tsp (5 mL) milk and 4 to 6 drops Backache Bath Blend. Mix thoroughly. Add to tub and agitate to disperse oil, then soak for 30 minutes, massaging any floating droplets of oil into your skin.

Backache Oil

2 drops	rosemary or plai essential oil
1 drop	black pepper essential oil
1 drop	eucalyptus essential oil

In a ⅙ oz (5 mL) glass dropper bottle, combine rosemary, black pepper and eucalyptus essential oils. Shake to blend.

Treatment

Massage: In a small non-reactive bowl, combine Backache Oil blend with 1 tsp (5 mL) sweet almond or peanut oil. Mix well and have someone massage it over your back.

Caution

Before using any essential oil, consult the relevant entry in Part 1: Essential Oils (A to Y), pages 28 to 117, taking careful note of any cautions.

Tip

Do not add essential oils to the tub while the water is running, as some of the precious essences may evaporate, depriving you of the full benefits.

Lumbago

Lumbago is a painful condition of the lower back caused by a slipped disk or muscle strain.

Essential Oils

Ginger, lavender, marjoram, rosemary

> ### *Lumbago Bath and Massage Blend*
>
> | 10 drops | lavender essential oil |
> |---|---|
> | 10 drops | ginger essential oil |
> | 5 drops | marjoram essential oil |
> | 5 drops | rosemary essential oil |
>
> *In a ¹⁄₆ (5 mL) glass dropper bottle, combine lavender, ginger, marjoram and rosemary essential oils. Shake to blend.*

Treatments

Bath: Fill tub with warm water. Meanwhile, in a small non-reactive bowl, combine 1 tsp (5 mL) milk and 4 to 6 drops Lumbago Bath and Massage Blend. Add to tub and agitate to disperse oil, then soak for 20 minutes, massaging any floating droplets of oil into your skin.

Cool compress: In a small non-reactive bowl, combine 2 cups (500 mL) cool (not icy) water and 12 drops Lumbago Bath and Massage Blend. Stir well to disperse oils. Soak a cloth and wring out enough water so cloth doesn't drip. Apply compress to affected area every 2 hours, until pain subsides. Apply cold packs in between compresses.

Massage: In a small non-reactive bowl, combine 4 tsp (20 mL) grapeseed or sweet almond oil and 8 drops Lumbago Bath and Massage Blend. Mix well and massage over your back after inflammation has receded.

Tips

Do not add essential oils to the tub while the water is running, as some of the precious essences may evaporate, depriving you of the full benefits.

If you prefer, substitute an equal quantity of liquid castile soap for the milk called for in any bath recipe.

Sciatica

Sciatica means a pain at any point along the sciatic nerve. It may be felt in the buttocks, behind the hip joint, down the back (sometimes the front) of the thigh, down the calf and into the foot. The cause of sciatica—often poor sitting posture or pressure on a disk—needs to be found before a cure can be effected. A visit to a chiropractor is usually beneficial.

When the pain is severe, there may be inflammation, and massage is not recommended. Cold packs and lavender and chamomile compresses (see page 186) will help reduce the inflammation.

Essential Oils

Anise, cedarwood, chamomile, lavender, marjoram, peppermint, rosemary, sandalwood, thyme (ct. thymol or ct. carvacrol)

Sciatica Massage Blend

12 drops	lavender essential oil
10 drops	rosemary essential oil
10 drops	marjoram essential oil

In a ¹⁄₆ oz (5 mL) glass dropper bottle, combine lavender, rosemary and marjoram essential oils. Shake to blend.

Treatments

Bath: Fill tub with warm water. Meanwhile, in a small non-reactive bowl, combine 1 tsp (5 mL) milk and 4 to 6 drops Sciatica Massage Blend. Add to tub and agitate to disperse oil, then soak for 20 minutes, massaging any floating droplets of oil into painful areas.

Massage: In a small non-reactive bowl, combine 4 tsp (20 mL) grapeseed or calendula-infused oil and 12 drops Sciatica Massage Blend. Mix well and massage over your back after the inflammation has gone.

If you are using a blend around bath/shower time, you can enhance the benefit by combining the essential oils with a carrier oil and rub it into your skin *before* getting into the shower or bath. This enables the essential oils to be absorbed and work their way into the bloodstream. The heat of the water encourages the essential oil vapors to rise, allowing you to inhale the aromas more easily and thus creating a dual application.

Bad Breath
See Breath, Bad (page 190)

Birth
See Pregnancy and Birth (page 282)

Bites and Stings

Essential oils are a quick and easy way of dealing with insect bites and stings. Keep a small bottle of lavender oil handy when walking, hiking or swimming.

Essential Oils

Chamomile, lavender, lemon, niaouli, sage, tea tree

Bee Stings

Bee Sting Paste

1 tsp (5 mL)	baking soda
1 drop	chamomile essential oil
1 drop	lavender essential oil
	Distilled or filtered water

In a non-reactive bowl, combine baking soda, chamomile and lavender essential oils and just enough water to make a soft paste (the baking soda counteracts the acidity of the sting). Mix thoroughly.

Treatment
Topical application: Using the tip of a sterilized sharp blade or pin in a sideways motion, carefully scrape the stinger out of your skin—don't pull it out, as it can release additional venom into the area. If an allergy is known or suspected, seek immediate medical attention. Apply paste to the affected area hourly until the stinging subsides (or on the way to hospital, in the case of allergy).

Dog Bites

Treatment
Topical application: In a small non-reactive bowl, combine 4 drops (total) tea tree and/or lavender essential oils, ½ tsp (2.5 mL) unpasteurized liquid honey, and ½ cup (125 mL)

water. Using a cloth, wash the area of the bite with the mixture (even if the skin isn't broken). Using a cotton ball, dab on a little undiluted tea tree essential oil. Apply a dressing, if necessary. If the skin is broken, seek medical attention for further treatment.

Insect Bites

Gnat and fly bites are annoying, but mosquitoes can also carry disease, including West Nile virus, dengue fever and malaria. Here are some ways to avoid being bitten:

- Protect yourself from bites by wearing loose-fitting, long-sleeved clothing when outside in known mosquito areas or in the evening during summer. Avoid dark clothes and perfumed products.
- Avoid being out-of-doors at dusk and dawn.
- Use a personal insect repellent lotion at all times when outdoors.
- If you live in an area that requires it, use mosquito nets around beds at night and screen windows.

Treatment
Topical application: Using a cotton ball, apply undiluted lavender essential oil to the affected area(s). If pain persists, repeat application as necessary.

Spider Bites

Treatment
Topical application: In a small non-reactive bowl, combine 5 drops lavender essential oil and 1 tsp (5 mL) vinegar. Using a cotton ball, dab the affected area hourly.

If you suspect the spider was poisonous, seek immediate medical attention, dabbing the wound constantly with undiluted lavender essential oil until treatment begins. It is important to try to identify the spider.

Wasp Stings

Treatment
Topical application: In a small glass bottle, combine 8 drops lavender essential oil and 1 tsp (5 mL) vinegar. Shake to blend. Using a cotton ball, dab on affected area to counteract the alkaline poison of the sting and reduce pain and swelling. Repeat hourly until pain is relieved.

Black Eye

Essential Oils

Chamomile, lavender

Treatment

Cool compress: In a small nonreactive bowl, combine 1 drop each lavender and chamomile essential oils and 2 tsp (10 mL) immortelle (helichrysum) hydrolat. Mix thoroughly. Drop in 1 ice cube. Stir until ice is melted and oils are well dispersed. Submerge a cloth, then remove and wring out completely, until no longer dripping. Gently apply compress over bruise (see Caution, left). Repeat when the cloth gets warm.

Bleeding, External (Minor)

Essential Oils

Geranium, lemon, rose, yarrow

Treatment

Cool compress: Pour ½ cup (125 mL) cool (not icy) water into a non-reactive bowl and add 25 drops geranium, lemon, rose or yarrow essential oil. Stir well to disperse oil. Soak a cloth and wring out enough water so cloth doesn't drip. Lay the cloth on the affected area and secure firmly, but not too tightly, by wrapping plastic wrap around the area and over the damp cloth. If bleeding doesn't stop, reapply compress and seek medical attention.

Blisters

Essential Oils

Lavender, tea tree

Treatment

Topical application: Using a cotton ball, apply 2 drops lavender or tea tree essential oil to the blister. Pat gently. Don't break the blister unless it's very big. If you have to break the blister, use a needle that has been sterilized in a flame, then press the skin flat. Apply a drop of lavender essential oil and bandage.

Blood Pressure

High Blood Pressure (Hypertension)

High blood pressure needs to be taken seriously. It is important to consult your doctor about treatment. A relaxing massage can help relieve stress and is a useful adjunct to treatment.

Essential Oils

Eucalyptus citriodora, geranium, lavender, lemon, mandarin, marjoram, melissa, neroli, yarrow, ylang ylang

---

Take-the-Pressure-Off Massage Blend

20 drops	marjoram essential oil
10 drops	geranium or ylang ylang essential oil
10 drops	mandarin essential oil
5 drops	lavender (high-altitude) essential oil

In a ¹⁄₆ oz (5 mL) glass dropper bottle, combine marjoram, geranium, mandarin and lavender essential oils. Shake to blend.

Variation
For a more potent treatment, substitute passion flower-infused oil for grapeseed or sweet almond oil. Passion flower oil offers strong relaxant properties.

Treatments

Bath: Fill tub with warm water. Meanwhile, in a small non-reactive bowl, combine 1 tsp (5 mL) milk and 4 to 6 drops Take-the-Pressure-Off Massage Blend. Add to water and agitate to disperse, then soak for 20 minutes, massaging any floating droplets of oil into your skin. Limit use to twice a week only.

Massage: In a small non-reactive bowl, combine 6 drops Take-the-Pressure-Off Massage Blend and 2 tsp (10 mL) grapeseed or sweet almond oil. Mix well and massage over your body.

Tip

If you are using a blend around bath/shower time, you can enhance the benefit by combining the essential oils with a carrier oil and rub it into your skin *before* getting into the shower or bath. This enables the essential oils to be absorbed and work their way into the bloodstream. The heat of the water encourages the essential oil vapors to rise, allowing you to inhale the aromas more easily and thus creating a dual application.

Low Blood Pressure (Hypotension)

Low blood pressure can cause occasional dizziness and fatigue. Exercise is helpful for raising the pressure to a more acceptable level.

Essential Oils

Basil, black pepper, clary sage, hyssop, peppermint, pine, rosemary ct. cineole, sage, thyme ct. linalool

---

Put-the-Pressure-On Massage Blend

25 drops	clary sage essential oil
20 drops	rosemary essential oil
10 drops	black pepper essential oil
10 drops	peppermint essential oil

In a ⅙ oz (5 mL) glass dropper bottle, combine clary sage, rosemary, black pepper and peppermint essential oils. Shake to blend.

Treatments

Bath: Fill tub with warm water. Meanwhile, in a small non-reactive bowl, combine 1 tsp (5 mL) milk and 4 to 6 drops Put-the-Pressure-On Massage Blend (see Tips, left). Add to tub and agitate to disperse, then soak for 30 minutes, massaging any floating droplets of oil into your skin.

Massage: In a small non-reactive bowl, combine 4 tsp (20 mL) grapeseed or sweet almond oil and 4 drops Put-the-Pressure-On Massage Blend. Mix well and massage over your body.

Tips

Do not add essential oils to the tub while the water is running, as some of the precious essences may evaporate, depriving you of the full benefits.

If you prefer, substitute an equal quantity of liquid castile soap for the milk called for in any bath recipe.

Boils and Carbuncles

Boils (and carbuncles) are staphylococcal infections that result in skin abscesses. Treatment aims to bring the boil to a head and allow the pus to escape and the area to heal. If the boil is near your face, spine or anus; if you have diabetes; or if a fever develops or red streaks radiate out from the boil, seek medical attention immediately.

Boils are very contagious. Avoid handling and preparing food while the infection is present. Any clothes in contact with the area should be washed separately. Add a few drops of tea tree or lavender essential oil to the washing and rinsing water. Hang to dry (see Caution, right).

Essential Oils

Bay laurel, bergamot, Roman chamomile, lavender, lemon, niaouli, petitgrain, tea tree, thyme ct. linalool

---

Blend for Boils

¼ cup (60 mL)	warm water
1 tsp (5 mL)	liquid castile soap
3 drops	lavender essential oil
2 drops	bergamot essential oil

In a small non-reactive bowl, combine water, soap and lavender and bergamot essential oils. Using a cotton ball, wash the boil and surrounding area. Wash 3 times daily and follow with a hot compress (see Treatment).

Treatment

Hot compress: In a small non-reactive bowl, combine 2 drops bergamot essential oil, 2 drops niaouli essential oil, and ½ cup (125 mL) very hot water. Stir well to disperse the oils. Submerge a cloth just large enough to absorb all the liquid without dripping. Lay the cloth on the affected area and secure by wrapping plastic wrap around it. Applying a heat pack or waterproof heating pad over the compress can help the boil to open and drain. Leave the compress on for 20 to 30 minutes. Apply 3 to 4 times daily.

You may need to do this for several days or up to 1 week. When the boil begins to drain, continue to clean as directed and cover with a non-stick bandage on which a drop of tea tree essential oil has been placed. To avoid the spread of infection, be sure to keep the draining boil covered and do not share washcloths or towels with others. Change the bandage daily until wound is completely drained.

Caution

Fires have been known to occur in dryers when essential oils (and sometimes vegetable oils too) have not been thoroughly removed from fabrics in the washing machine. To ensure that your detergent can break down the oils during the washing process, be sure to use a wash temperature of at least 104°F (40°C).

Breath, Bad

A dental check is recommended if you have bad breath, as bad teeth are a common source. Stomach upsets and insufficient gastric acids can also cause bad breath. Depending on their formulation, mouthwashes can be used to sweeten the breath, keep bacteria and fungus infections at bay, and ensure healthy gums. Brush the tongue gently with toothpaste when brushing your teeth.

Essential Oils

Cardamom, clove, lavender, lemon, myrrh, peppermint, tea tree, thyme

Quickie Mouthwash

Add 1 drop peppermint or cardamom essential oil to 1 tsp (5 mL) cider vinegar. Mix thoroughly with a toothpick and add to a glass containing 4 oz (125 mL) water. Stir thoroughly to disperse the oil. Swish mixture around mouth several times, then spit it out (do not swallow). Cardamom is especially helpful in severe cases of bad breath caused by halitosis.

Myrrh Mouthwash

Myrrh helps to heal mouth ulcers.
Makes about ½ cup (125 mL)

⅓ cup (75 mL)	sherry or brandy
8 tsp (40 mL)	cider vinegar
1 tsp (5 mL)	unpasteurized liquid honey
1 tsp	vegetable glycerin (5 mL)
10 drops	peppermint essential oil
3 drops	clove essential oil
1 tsp (5 mL)	tincture of myrrh or 5 drops myrrh essential oil

In a 5 oz (150 mL) glass jar with a tight-fitting lid, combine sherry, vinegar, honey, glycerin and peppermint, clove and myrrh essential oils. Seal jar and shake thoroughly. Set aside in a cool, dark place for 1 week, shaking the jar often. Using cheesecloth or a coffee filter, strain mixture into a clean jar. Store in a cool, dark location.

Treatment

Mouthwash: In a glass, combine ¼ cup (60 mL) lukewarm water and 1 tsp (5 mL) Myrrh Mouthwash. Mix thoroughly. Swish mixture around mouth several times, then spit it out (do not swallow).

Lemon and Mint Mouthwash

This mouthwash will keep the mouth healthy and sweet-smelling. It will also help to cure sores or ulcers in the mouth.

½ cup (125 mL)	vodka or brandy
1 tsp (5 mL)	vegetable glycerin
5 drops	lemon essential oil
5 drops	peppermint essential oil
2 drops	lavender essential oil
2 drops	tea tree essential oil
1 drop	thyme essential oil

In a 5 oz (150 mL) glass jar with a tight-fitting lid, combine vodka, glycerin and lemon, peppermint, lavender, tea tree and thyme essential oils. Seal jar and shake thoroughly. Set aside in a cool, dark place for 1 week, shaking the jar often. Using cheesecloth or a coffee filter, strain mixture into a clean jar. Store in a cool, dark location.

Treatment

Mouthwash: In a glass, combine ¼ cup (60 mL) lukewarm water and 1 tsp (5 mL) Lemon and Mint Mouthwash. Mix thoroughly. Swish mixture around mouth several times, then spit it out (do not swallow).

Bronchitis

See Respiratory Problems (page 294)

Bruises

Essential Oils

Roman chamomile, fennel, geranium, helichrysum, lavender, marjoram, rosemary ct. cineole

Treatment

Topical application: Apply an ice pack to the bruised area to reduce swelling. In a small non-reactive bowl, combine 1 tsp (5 mL) grapeseed or sweet almond oil and 4 drops geranium or

lavender essential oil. Mix well and apply to affected area. Repeat hourly until bruise is no longer painful to the touch. Repeat every 2 hours until bruise begins to diminish.

Variation

For a more potent treatment, substitute infused arnica oil for the grapeseed or sweet almond oil. Arnica-infused oil has been shown to reduce swelling and pain, making it an effective treatment for bruises.

Bunions See Feet (page 229)

Burns and Scalds (Minor)

Essential Oils

Bergamot, Roman chamomile, geranium, helichrysum, lavender, niaouli, rosemary ct. cineole

Treatments

Cold compress: For minor burns and scalds over a small area, reduce the pain by holding the burned area under cold water or apply ice-cold compresses of lavender hydrolat for 10 minutes. Then dab lavender essential oil or manuka honey gently on the burn area. Cover with gauze and lightly secure the corners with a bandage or medical tape. Add a drop of lavender essential oil to the center of the gauze every 2 hours over the course of a day.

Topical application: In a small non-reactive bowl, combine 6 drops lavender essential oil, 2 drops Roman chamomile essential oil and 1 tsp (5 mL) aloe vera gel. Using a cotton ball, gently apply 3 to 4 times per day until the burn is healed.

Moderate to severe burns and scalds require urgent medical attention. Do not attempt to remove clothing stuck to a burn.

Bursitis

Bursitis is characterized by severe pain in a joint (usually the shoulder, knee or elbow), especially on movement; skin that is hot to the touch; and swelling. It is often known as "housemaid's knee" or "tennis elbow," indicating that an occupation or sport has caused the joint to be overused. It is sometimes the result of an inflammatory joint disease.

As soon as damage becomes apparent, rest the affected joint. Eliminate as far as possible the cause of the condition. Elevate the joint above the head (where feasible) to keep blood from pooling in the area.

Tip

Squeeze the oil from vitamin E capsules onto the burn area the day after first-aid treatment, to facilitate swift and scar-free healing.

Essential Oils

Chamomile, clary sage, clove, cypress, eucalyptus, hyssop, juniper, rosemary; St. John's wort (hypericum)–infused oil

Caution

Before using any essential oil, consult the relevant entry in Part 1: Essential Oils (A to Y), pages 28 to 117, taking careful note of any cautions.

Bursitis Massage Blend

18 tsp (90 mL)	grapeseed or sweet almond oil
6 tsp (30 mL)	St. John's wort–infused oil
22 drops	rosemary essential oil
16 drops	eucalyptus essential oil
16 drops	chamomile essential oil
16 drops	juniper essential oil

In a 4 oz (125 mL) glass bottle, combine grapeseed oil, St. John's wort–infused oil, and rosemary, eucalyptus, chamomile and juniper essential oils. Shake to blend.

Treatment

Massage: Massage Bursitis Massage Blend gently over the affected area 3 times a day.

Bursitis Compress Blend

50 drops	cypress essential oil
30 drops	clary sage essential oil
20 drops	hyssop essential oil

In a ⅙ oz (5 mL) glass bottle, combine cypress, clary sage and hyssop essential oils. Mix thoroughly.

Treatment

Cool compress: Pour ½ cup (125 mL) cool (not icy) water into a non-reactive bowl and add 4 to 6 drops Bursitis Compress Blend. Stir well to disperse oils. Soak a cloth and wring it out enough that it doesn't drip. Place cloth on affected area. Repeat 3 times a day, as needed.

Cancer

It would be unethical (and illegal) to claim that a treatment can cure cancer. Nevertheless, there are many, many alternative ways in which the immune system can be supported and unpleasant symptoms alleviated while being treated by orthodox methods. It is very important to tell your doctor about alternative treatments you would like to use in conjunction with your medical treatment. Also, you should seek out aromatherapists and massage therapists who specialize in cancer care before complementing your care with aromatherapy. Certain types of cancer do not respond well to some essential oils or to massage therapy.

Essential Oils

Bergamot, cedarwood, frankincense, lavender, mandarin, sweet orange, rose

---

Massage Blend for Cancer Patients

15 drops	cedarwood essential oil
10 drops	lavender essential oil
5 drops	bergamot or mandarin essential oil

In a ⅙ oz (5 mL) glass dropper bottle, combine cedarwood, lavender and bergamot essential oils. Shake to blend.

Treatments

Air spray: In a 4 oz (125 mL) PET plastic spray bottle, combine 75 drops Massage Blend for Cancer Patients and 1 tsp (5 mL) vodka. Fill bottle with distilled or filtered water (see Tips, left).

Bath: Fill tub with warm water. Meanwhile, in a small non-reactive bowl, combine 1 tsp (5 mL) milk and 4 to 6 drops Massage Blend for Cancer Patients. Add to tub and agitate to disperse oil, then soak for 20 minutes, massaging any floating droplets of oil into your skin.

Inhaler: Place 21 drops Massage Blend for Cancer Patients in a small non-reactive bowl. Place the inhaler wick in the bowl and allow it to absorb the entire amount. Insert the wick inside the inhaler tube and tightly cap the bottom of the inhaler with the plug. Place the inhaler tube inside its cover and screw tightly to close.

Massage: In a small non-reactive bowl, combine 4 tsp (20 mL) grapeseed or sweet almond oil and 8 drops Massage Blend for Cancer Patients. Mix well and massage over your body.

Candidiasis

Candida albicans is a harmless yeast (fungus) present in our bodies from birth. Occasionally it grows excessively and causes health problems. Thrush, an infection of the mucous membranes, is the most common symptom. It sometimes affects the mouth (especially in babies) but is more usually found in the vagina. Men can transmit thrush even though they may show no symptoms, so it is important to treat both partners. As well as using the following blends, it is important to eat 3 cups (750 mL) of yogurt and take a multi-B vitamin tablet daily. Thrush in a baby's mouth can be treated with yogurt and gentle swabbing with chamomile tea.

Essential Oils

Cedarwood, *Eucalyptus globulus*, geranium, helichrysum, lavandin, lavender, lemon, manuka, rosemary ct. verbenone, rosewood, tea tree

Treatments

Douche 1: In a non-reactive bowl, combine 2 drops manuka, lavender or tea tree essential oil, 4 tsp (20 mL) plain yogurt and 1 tsp (5 mL) water. Mix thoroughly. Insert into the vagina using a needleless syringe, or roll an unbleached organic cotton tampon in the mixture and insert into the vagina. You can also double the recipe and freeze it in an ice-cube tray that makes small cubes (see Tip, right). Be sure to wear a sanitary pad or panty-liner to catch the discharge. Follow with a shower.

Douche 2: In a non-reactive bowl, combine 1 drop cinnamon leaf oil, 3 drops lavender oil and 1 tsp (5 mL) raw honey. Mix well. Add 2 tsp (10 mL) German chamomile hydrolat and ½ cup (125 mL) distilled or filtered water and stir to combine. Fill a douche bag (available at pharmacies) with the mixture. Sit on the toilet seat, lean back and insert the nozzle of the douche bag into the vagina.

> ### Tip
> You can find ice-cube trays online that make smaller, egg-shaped "cubes" or water-bottle ice sticks.

> ### Caution
> If you are taking medications, avoid topical use of German chamomile (see Caution, page 47).

Douches

Vaginal secretions are unpleasant only if there is an infection or if hygiene is neglected. Douches should be used only when there is a local infection, as unnecessary douching can upset the acid/alkaline balance in the vagina and can destroy natural and necessary secretions. Douche twice a day for up to a week. If the infection hasn't cleared by then, consult a health-care provider. Undiagnosed, untreated vaginal infections can lead to or be indicative of serious problems.

Allow the liquid to bathe the inside of the vagina. If you don't have a douche bag you can mix the oils and water in a jug. Stir the mixture thoroughly, sit in the bathtub, lean as far back as you can and pour from the jug into the vagina. Apply twice a day for up to a week (see Douches, page 195).

Sitz bath: In a basin large enough to sit in, combine $1\frac{1}{3}$ cups (325 mL) baking soda and 16 cups (4 L) warm water. Sit in the basin and, holding the vagina open with one hand, swoosh the water as far inside as possible. Bathe for about 10 minutes.

Carpal Tunnel Syndrome

Carpal tunnel syndrome seems to be most common in middle-aged or pregnant women, arthritis sufferers and those who use a computer keyboard constantly, although the actual cause is often uncertain. Use a wrist and thumb brace to immobilize the area for much of the day.

Essential Oils

Chamomile; arnica-infused oil

Treatment

Massage: In a small non-reactive bowl, combine 3 drops arnica-infused oil (see Tips, left) and 1 tsp (5 mL) grapeseed oil. Mix well and massage into wrist, thumb and forearm up to the elbow. Then, in a clean non-reactive bowl, combine 4 drops chamomile essential oil and 1 tsp (5 mL) grapeseed oil (substitute St. John's wort–infused oil for the grapeseed oil if you have some). Mix well and massage affected areas again. Repeat 4 to 6 times a day until the pain subsides.

Tips

Do not use arnica-infused oil on broken skin.

When the pain lessens, it is important to exercise the hand and fingers regularly until cured. It is also a good idea to continue with these exercises to help prevent the problem recurring. First open your hands right out, then clench to make fists, 10 to 12 times. Stretch out your arms, rotating your hands from the wrist (fingers open) 10 times in one direction and then 10 times the other way.

Cellulite

Cellulite can be caused by a variety of conditions, including poor lymphatic drainage, allergies, toxicity, hormonal changes and fluid retention. Cellulite is a part of your skin and cannot be eliminated; however, with dry brushing and the use of essential oils, you can reduce its appearance. Aromatherapy massage is an important part of an overall treatment.

Essential Oils

Cedarwood, fennel, geranium, grapefruit, juniper, lemongrass, rosemary, sage

---

Cellulite Massage Oil

20 drops	rosemary essential oil
20 drops	fennel essential oil
15 drops	juniper essential oil
15 drops	grapefruit essential oil
5 drops	geranium essential oil

In a ¹/₆ oz (5 mL) glass bottle, combine rosemary, fennel, juniper, grapefruit and geranium essential oils. Shake to blend.

Treatments

Bath: Fill tub with warm water. Meanwhile, in a small non-reactive bowl, combine 1 tsp (5 mL) milk and 4 to 6 drops Cellulite Massage Oil. Add to tub and agitate to disperse oil, then soak for 30 minutes, massaging any floating droplets of oil into your skin.

Dry brushing: Before bathing or showering, sprinkle 1 to 2 drops Cellulite Massage Oil onto a natural-bristle body brush. Using small circular motions, brush the limbs up toward the heart to stimulate and improve circulation.

Massage: In a small non-reactive bowl, combine 4 tsp (20 mL) grapeseed or sweet almond oil and 10 drops Cellulite Massage Oil. Mix well and massage over your body. (If possible, get regular lymphatic massages from a health-care practitioner.)

Tips

Do not add essential oils to the tub while the water is running, as some of the precious essences may evaporate, depriving you of the full benefits.

If you prefer, substitute an equal quantity of liquid castile soap for the milk called for in any bath recipe.

If you are using a blend around bath/ shower time, you can enhance the benefit by combining the essential oils with a carrier oil and rub it into your skin *before* getting into the shower or bath. This enables the essential oils to be absorbed and work their way into the bloodstream. The heat of the water encourages the essential oil vapors to rise, allowing you to inhale the aromas more easily and thus creating a dual application.

Use a natural-bristle body brush before showering or bathing to stimulate circulation and tone the skin. Always brush the limbs up toward the heart, using small circular movements.

Cerebral Palsy

Cerebral palsy is the name given to a condition of spastic paralysis caused when some of the nerve cells in the brain fail to function, resulting in lack of coordination and muscle spasms. The aim of aromatherapy treatment is to strengthen weak muscles and to reduce spasm. The massages need to be continued on a regular basis. After a while, people with this condition may enjoy trying to massage themselves.

Note: If using on babies or children, adjust the amounts of essential oil in each of the following blends to suit the age of the child (see Babies and Children, page 164).

Essential Oils

For muscular spasm: basil ct. linalool, cypress, eucalyptus, geranium, ginger, lavender, lemon, marjoram, nutmeg

For muscular weakness: basil, black pepper, eucalyptus, lemon, rosemary; St. John's wort–infused oil

---

Muscular Spasm Blend

Makes about ½ cup (125 mL)

20 drops	cypress essential oil
20 drops	marjoram essential oil
15 drops	ginger essential oil
15 drops	lavender essential oil
10 drops	eucalyptus essential oil
	Grapeseed or sweet almond oil

In a 4 oz (125 mL) glass bottle, combine cypress, marjoram, ginger, lavender and eucalyptus essential oils. Fill bottle with grapeseed oil and shake to blend. Store in a cool, dark place for up to 12 months. Shake well before using.

Treatment

Massage: Massage Muscular Spasm Blend into limbs and back. Repeat, alternating with Muscular Weakness Blend (page 199), once or twice a day.

Muscular Weakness Blend

Makes about ½ cup (125 mL)

¼ cup + 6 tsp (90 mL)	grapeseed or sweet almond oil
6 tsp (30 mL)	St. John's wort–infused oil
25 drops	lemon essential oil
20 drops	basil essential oil
15 drops	ginger essential oil
15 drops	rosemary essential oil

In a 4 oz (125 mL) glass bottle, combine grapeseed oil, St. John's wort–infused oil and lemon, basil, ginger and rosemary essential oils. Shake to blend. Store in a cool, dark place for up to 12 months. Shake well before using.

Caution
Before using any essential oil, consult the relevant entry in Part 1: Essential Oils (A to Y), pages 28 to 117, taking careful note of any cautions.

Treatment
Massage: Massage Muscular Weakness Blend into limbs and back. Repeat, alternating with Muscular Spasm Blend (page 198), once or twice a day.

Cervical Dysplasia
See Women's Health (page 330)

Children
See Babies and Children (page 163)

Chronic Fatigue Syndrome

Chronic fatigue syndrome is also known as myalgic encephalomyelitis (ME). Whatever you call it, the result is the same: the sufferer is chronically tired. A debilitating and depressing disorder that causes profound weariness and muscle fatigue, it has been recognized by the medical profession only since the 1980s. There is some uncertainty as to its cause; it is thought to be triggered by a number of factors, including post-viral infection, environmental toxins, an immune reaction or perhaps even genetic predisposition. The symptoms last for at least six months and sometimes for years, becoming less acute with the passing of time. Treatment aims largely at improving general health and that of the immune system.

Aromatherapy has a role to play in treating chronic fatigue, by helping ease muscular pain with massage, lifting the spirits when depressed, and helping stimulate the immune system. Make up a bottle of each of the following essential oil blends and use them at appropriate times.

See also Immune System (page 252), Mononucleosis (page 271) and Stress and Emotional Problems (page 310).

Essential Oils

For depression: bergamot, cedarwood, grapefruit, lavender, neroli, petitgrain, ravensara, rose, rosewood, sandalwood, ylang ylang

For muscular pain: bergamot, black pepper, *Eucalyptus smithii*, ginger, lavender, manuka, marjoram, ravensara

Antiviral and immunostimulant: cinnamon, cistus, clove, *Eucalyptus radiata*, marjoram, rosewood, tea tree, thyme ct. linalool, vetiver

Tips

If you prefer, when making an air spray, substitute Solubol for the vodka called for, in a ratio of 4 drops Solubol for every 1 drop essential oil. Solubol is a natural product that allows essential oils to disperse in liquid.

When making air sprays, be sure to add the oils to the bottle first, followed by the chosen dispersant (vodka or Solubol), to ensure that the essential oils disperse properly (they will not mix directly with water).

Chronic Fatigue Spirit Lifter

20 drops	bergamot, *Eucalyptus radiata* or lavender essential oil
15 drops	grapefruit essential oil
15 drops	cistus, ylang ylang, cedarwood or sandalwood essential oil

In a 1/6 *oz (5 mL) glass dropper bottle, combine essential oils. Shake to blend.*

Treatments

Air spray: In a 4 oz (125 mL) PET plastic spray bottle, combine 75 drops Chronic Fatigue Spirit Lifter and 1 tsp (5 mL) vodka. Fill bottle with distilled or filtered water (see Tips, left) and shake to combine.

Bath: Fill tub with warm water. Meanwhile, in a small non-reactive bowl, combine 1 tsp (5 mL) milk and 4 to 6 drops Chronic Fatigue Spirit Lifter. Add to tub and agitate to disperse oil, then soak for 30 minutes, massaging any floating droplets of oil into your skin.

Inhaler: Place 25 drops Chronic Fatigue Spirit Lifter in a small non-reactive bowl. Place inhaler wick in the bowl and allow it to absorb the entire amount. Insert the wick inside the inhaler tube and tightly cap the bottom of the inhaler with the plug. Place the inhaler tube inside its cover and screw tightly to close.

Massage: In a small non-reactive bowl, combine 4 tsp (20 mL) grapeseed or sweet almond oil and 8 drops Chronic Fatigue Spirit Lifter. Mix well and massage over your body.

Chronic Fatigue Muscular Pain Oil

20 drops	bergamot essential oil
15 drops	marjoram essential oil
10 drops	ginger essential oil
5 drops	black pepper essential oil

In a ¹⁄₆ oz (5 mL) glass bottle, combine bergamot, marjoram, ginger and black pepper essential oils. Shake to blend.

Treatments

Bath: Fill tub with warm water. Meanwhile, in a small non-reactive bowl, combine 1 tsp (5 mL) milk and 4 to 6 drops Chronic Fatigue Muscular Pain Oil. Add to tub and agitate to disperse oil, then soak for 30 minutes, massaging any floating droplets of oil into your skin.

Massage: In a small non-reactive bowl, combine 4 tsp (20 mL) grapeseed or sweet almond oil, 20 drops borage seed oil and 8 drops Chronic Fatigue Muscular Pain Oil. Mix well and massage over your body.

Chronic Fatigue Immunostimulant and Antiviral Oil

20 drops	rosewood essential oil
10 drops	thyme essential oil
10 drops	tea tree essential oil
10 drops	cinnamon essential oil

In a ¹⁄₆ oz (5 mL) glass dropper bottle, combine rosewood, thyme, tea tree and cinnamon essential oils. Shake to blend.

Tips

Do not add essential oils to the tub while the water is running, as some of the precious essences may evaporate, depriving you of the full benefits.

If you prefer, substitute an equal quantity of liquid castile soap for the milk called for in any bath recipe.

If you are using a blend around bath/shower time, you can enhance the benefit by combining the essential oils with a carrier oil and rub it into your skin *before* getting into the shower or bath. This enables the essential oils to be absorbed and work their way into the bloodstream. The heat of the water encourages the essential oil vapors to rise, allowing you to inhale the aromas more easily and thus creating a dual application.

Tips

If you prefer, when making an air spray, substitute Solubol for the vodka called for, in a ratio of 4 drops Solubol for every 1 drop essential oil. Solubol is a natural product that allows essential oils to disperse in liquid.

When making air sprays, be sure to add the oils to the bottle first, followed by the chosen dispersant (vodka or Solubol), to ensure that the essential oils disperse properly (they will not mix directly with water).

Treatments

Bath: Fill tub with warm water. Meanwhile, in a small non-reactive bowl, combine 1 tsp (5 mL) milk and 4 to 6 drops Chronic Fatigue Immunostimulant and Antiviral Oil. Add to tub and agitate to disperse oil, then soak for 30 minutes, massaging any floating droplets of oil into your skin.

Air spray: In a 4 oz (125 mL) PET plastic spray bottle, combine 75 drops Chronic Fatigue Immunostimulant and Antiviral Oil and 1 tsp (5 mL) vodka. Fill bottle with distilled or filtered water (see Tips, left) and shake to combine.

Inhaler: Place 25 drops Chronic Fatigue Immunostimulant and Antiviral Oil in a small non-reactive bowl. Place the inhaler wick in the bowl and allow it to absorb the entire amount. Insert the wick inside the inhaler tube and tightly cap the bottom of the inhaler with the plug. Place the inhaler tube inside its cover and screw tightly to close.

Massage: In a small non-reactive bowl, combine 20 drops borage seed oil, 4 tsp (20 mL) grapeseed or sweet almond oil and 8 drops Chronic Fatigue Immunostimulant and Antiviral Oil. Mix well and massage over your body.

Circulation

Walking, swimming or other forms of exercise will improve circulation. The following blend will stimulate circulation to the extremities.

Essential Oils

Black pepper, cypress, eucalyptus, fennel, ginger, juniper, lemon, marjoram, nutmeg, bitter orange, rosemary ct. cineole

---

Circulation Massage Blend

16 drops	lemon essential oil
8 drops	rosemary ct. cineole essential oil
8 drops	black pepper essential oil

In a ⅙ oz (5 mL) glass dropper bottle, combine lemon, rosemary and black pepper essential oils. Shake to blend.

Treatment

Massage: In a small non-reactive bowl, combine 4 tsp (20 mL) grapeseed or sweet almond oil and 12 drops Circulation Massage Blend. Mix well and massage fairly vigorously over your hands or feet, squeezing and moving your fingers and toes to stimulate blood flow. Using the massage oil, knead the palms of your hands and the soles of your feet.

For chilblains (frostbite damage), use Circulation Massage Blend on a daily basis.

Bath Blend for Improving Circulation

1⅓ cups (325 mL)	Epsom salts
1⅓ cups (325 mL)	sea salt
2 tsp (10 mL)	baking soda
3 drops	ginger essential oil
3 drops	grapefruit essential oil
2 drops	eucalyptus essential oil
2 drops	nutmeg essential oil

In a non-reactive bowl, combine Epsom salts, sea salt and baking soda. Very slowly, stirring continuously to avoid lumps, add ginger, grapefruit, eucalyptus and nutmeg essential oils. Stir until well combined.

Treatment

Bath: Fill tub with very warm water. Add Bath Blend for Improving Circulation to tub and agitate to dissolve completely. Soak for 30 minutes, massaging your limbs firmly. After the bath, dry very briskly with a towel to further stimulate circulation.

Common Cold and Influenza

Handling money and shaking hands are easy ways of picking up illness. This is because you transfer the infection or virus to your mouth or nose when you touch your face—and most of us are unaware of how often we do that. Wiping fingers or hands (discreetly) with Anti-infection Blend (page 204) after contact can help protect you from what's going around.

If you take notice of the first subtle symptoms of a cold or influenza and take action, it is possible to alleviate some of the attendant miseries. You should avoid others as much as possible when you have a cold or the flu, to try to prevent the disease spreading. Using an inhaler containing Cold and Cough Blend (page 204) will help keep your head clear.

Tips

Do not add essential oils to the tub while the water is running, as some of the precious essences may evaporate, depriving you of the full benefits.

If you prefer, substitute an equal quantity of liquid castile soap for the milk called for in any bath recipe.

If you are using a blend around bath/shower time, you can enhance the benefit by combining the essential oils with a carrier oil and rub it into your skin *before* getting into the shower or bath. This enables the essential oils to be absorbed and work their way into the bloodstream. The heat of the water encourages the essential oil vapors to rise, allowing you to inhale the aromas more easily and thus creating a dual application.

Essential Oils

Cinnamon bark, eucalyptus (*globulus* and *smithii*), helichrysum, hyssop, lavender, lemon, lime, manuka, Spanish marjoram, myrtle (green or orange), niaouli, bitter orange, pine, rosewood, tea tree, thyme (ct. thymol or ct. carvacrol), thyme ct. linalool, yarrow

Tips

If you prefer, substitute Solubol for the vodka in a ratio of 4 drops Solubol for every 1 drop essential oil.

When making air sprays, be sure to add the oils to the bottle first, followed by the chosen dispersant (vodka or Solubol), to ensure that the essential oils disperse properly (they will not mix directly with water).

In order for your hand sanitizer to be effective, it must contain a minimum of 60% alcohol.

Caution

Keep out of reach of children to avoid accidental ingestion.

Anti-infection Blend

40 drops	lavender or manuka essential oil
30 drops	lemon or lime essential oil
20 drops	tea tree essential oil
10 drops	Spanish marjoram or yarrow essential oil

In a $1/6$ oz (5 mL) glass bottle, combine lavender, lemon, tea tree and marjoram essential oils. Shake to blend.

Treatments

Air spray: In a 4 oz (125 mL) PET plastic spray bottle, combine 75 drops Anti-infection Blend and 1 tsp (5 mL) vodka. Fill bottle with distilled or filtered water (see Tips, left). Shake well to disperse oil.

Hand sanitizer: In a 2 oz (60 mL) PET plastic bottle with a flip-top cap, combine 4 tsp (20 mL) aloe vera gel, 6 tsp (30 mL) isopropyl (rubbing) alcohol and 40 drops Anti-infection Blend. Shake well to combine. Use a small amount to clean hands when needed (after handling money, shaking hands, etc.).

Cold and Cough Blend

An excellent blend for treating colds and coughs, this anti-infection blend is a strong decongestant, helping to thin and expel mucus. The addition of lemon makes it antiviral as well.

80 drops	eucalyptus essential oil
60 drops	tea tree essential oil
45 drops	lemon essential oil
10 drops	thyme ct. thymol essential oil
5 drops	cinnamon essential oil

In a $1/3$ oz (10 mL) glass dropper bottle, combine eucalyptus, tea tree, lemon, thyme and cinnamon essential oils. Shake to blend.

Treatments

Bath: Fill tub with warm water. Meanwhile, in a small non-reactive bowl, combine 1 tsp (5 mL) milk and 4 to 6 drops Cold and Cough Blend. Add to tub and agitate to disperse oil, then soak for 30 minutes, massaging any floating droplets of oil into your skin. While sitting in the bath, drink a glass of piping hot ginger and lemon tea (see Ginger Honey, below).

Massage: In a small non-reactive bowl, combine 4 tsp (20 mL) grapeseed or sweet almond oil and 8 drops Cold and Cough Blend. Mix well and massage over your body, especially your chest.

Ginger Honey

Make a soothing brew with this infused honey when you feel a cold coming on or when you are feeling low and have no appetite.

1½ cups (375 mL)	unpasteurized liquid honey
1 piece	(2 inches/5 cm) fresh gingerroot, cut into paper-thin slices

1. *In a glass jar with an airtight lid, combine honey and ginger. Cover jar loosely with the lid and place in a saucepan of water over medium-low heat. Warm honey (do not boil) for an hour or so to infuse it with the ginger.*

2. *Using a fine-mesh sieve, strain honey into a bowl. Using the back of a spoon, press the ginger to extract as much of its juice and essential oils as possible. Return to the jar and set aside to cool, then cover and store at room temperature.*

3. *Add 1 to 2 tsp (5 to 10 mL) ginger honey and the juice of 1 lemon to a glass of hot water. Drink while relaxing.*

Stuffy Head and Achy Body Blend

Use this blend when you are really down for the count with the aches and pains associated with colds and flu. This blend is a strong decongestant and antiviral.

9 drops	plai essential oil
9 drops	saro essential oil
7 drops	silver fir or mastic essential oil
5 drops	lemon essential oil

In a small glass bottle, combine plai, saro, silver fir and lemon essential oils. Shake to blend.

Treatments

Body lotion: Place 18 drops Stuffy Head and Achy Body Blend in a 2 oz (60 mL) PET plastic bottle. Fill bottle with unscented lotion. Massage into chest and back several times daily to relieve aches and pains associated with the flu.

Diffuser: Place 4 to 6 drops Stuffy Head and Achy Body Blend in a diffuser to clean the air and help to unclog a stuffy head.

Inhaler: Place 21 drops Stuffy Head and Achy Body Blend in a small non-reactive bowl. Place the inhaler wick in the bowl and allow it to absorb the entire amount. Insert the wick inside the inhaler tube and tightly cap the bottom of the inhaler with the plug. Place the inhaler tube inside its cover and screw tightly to close.

Winter Blend for Cold and Flu Prevention

This is an excellent blend to use in a diffuser to ward off the onset of colds and flu. The essential oils used are antiviral and supportive of the respiratory system.

36 drops	Douglas fir essential oil
30 drops	cypress essential oil
15 drops	lemon essential oil
12 drops	manuka essential oil

In a ¹/₆ oz (5 mL) glass bottle, combine Douglas fir, cypress, lemon and manuka essential oils. Shake to blend.

Treatments

Air spray: In a 4 oz (125 mL) PET plastic spray bottle, combine 75 drops Winter Blend for Cold and Flu Prevention and 1 tsp (5 mL) vodka. Fill bottle with distilled or filtered water (see Tips, right). Shake to combine.

Diffuser: Place 4 to 6 drops Winter Blend for Cold and Flu Prevention in a diffuser to clean the air and help to unclog a stuffy head.

If you prefer, when making an air spray, substitute Solubol for the vodka called for, in a ratio of 4 drops Solubol for every 1 drop essential oil. Solubol is a natural product that allows essential oils to disperse in liquid.

When making air sprays, be sure to add the oils to the bottle first, followed by the chosen dispersant (vodka or Solubol), to ensure that the essential oils disperse properly (they will not mix directly with water).

Respiratory Infection Prevention Blend

Use this blend in a steam treatment up to 4 times a day for 3 days to benefit from the mucolytic and expectorant properties of these oils. Add to a carrier oil to use as a chest rub after a hot morning shower.

8 drops	ravintsara essential oil
4 drops	*Eucalyptus globulus* essential oil
2 drops	tea tree essential oil

In a $\frac{1}{6}$ oz (5 mL) glass bottle, combine ravintsara, eucalyptus and tea tree essential oils. Shake to blend.

Treatments

Chest rub: In a small non-reactive bowl, combine 2 drops Respiratory Infection Prevention Blend and 1 tsp (5 mL) grapeseed or sweet almond oil. Massage into chest and inhale deeply.

Inhaler: Place 21 drops Respiratory Infection Prevention Blend in a small non-reactive bowl. Place the inhaler wick in the bowl and allow it to absorb the entire amount. Insert the wick inside the inhaler tube and tightly cap the bottom of the inhaler with the plug. Place the inhaler tube inside its cover and screw tightly to close.

Steam inhalation: In a small non-reactive bowl, combine 2 cups (500 mL) boiling water and 1 drop Respiratory Infection Prevention Blend. Sit comfortably in a chair with the bowl on a table in front of you. Place your face 8 to 12 inches (20 to 30 cm) over the bowl and drape a towel over your head and the bowl, covering the base of your neck. Be sure to hold down the ends of the towel with your forearms as they rest on the table or tuck the ends of the towel around the sides of the bowl to keep the steam from escaping. Breathe in the vapors for a minute or so (as long as is comfortable), then pop your head out for a few moments of fresh air. Repeat for 5 to 10 minutes, if possible. (This may be irritating for people with asthma; see Asthma, page 293.)

Cold Sores
See Herpes (page 249)

Colic
See Babies and Children (page 166)

Conjunctivitis

Essential Oils

Roman chamomile hydrolat, rose hydrolat

Treatment

In a nonreactive bowl, combine 1 tsp (5 mL) Roman chamomile or rose hydrolat and 6 tsp (30 mL) water. Stir well to disperse hydrolat. Soak a cloth and wring out as much liquid as possible. Close eyes and place cloth over them for 10 minutes. Turn the cloth over and place over closed eyes for another 10 minutes.

Constipation
See Digestive Problems (page 216)

Convalescence

Convalescence can range from a few days of feeling weak after a bad cold to weeks of recovery from a serious illness, accident or operation. Aromatherapy can help speed up the recovery process by increasing the body's defenses. The oils will improve appetite, strengthen nerves and generally regenerate bodily systems. Pick-Me-Up Blend (page 209) is tonic, gently stimulating and energy-raising.

Essential Oils

Geranium, ginger, grapefruit, lavender, lemon, rosemary, thyme ct. linalool

---

Cautions
- Do not put essential oils directly into eyes.
- Be sure to use ethanol/alcohol-free hydrolats for eye care.

Pick-Me-Up Blend

20 drops	grapefruit essential oil
10 drops	lavender or geranium essential oil
10 drops	rosemary essential oil
5 drops	lemon essential oil
5 drops	thyme ct. linalool or ginger essential oil

In a ⅙ oz (5 mL) glass dropper bottle, combine grapefruit, lavender, rosemary, lemon and thyme essential oils. Shake to blend.

Treatments

Bath: Fill tub with warm water. Meanwhile, in a small non-reactive bowl, combine 1 tsp (5 mL) milk and 4 to 6 drops Pick-Me-Up Blend. Add to water, agitate to disperse oils, then soak for 30 minutes, massaging any floating droplets of oil into your skin.

Inhaler: Place 21 drops Pick-Me-Up Blend in a small non-reactive bowl. Place inhaler wick in the bowl and allow it to absorb the entire amount. Insert the wick inside the inhaler tube and tightly cap the bottom of the inhaler with the plug. Place the inhaler tube inside its cover and screw tightly to close.

Massage: In a small non-reactive bowl, combine 4 tsp (20 mL) grapeseed or sweet almond oil and 8 drops Pick-Me-Up Blend. Mix well and massage over your body. If you feel too weak for a full massage, a hand, foot and/or back massage may be the best treatment.

Corns
See Feet (page 229)

Coughs
See Respiratory Problems (page 296)

Cradle Cap
See Babies and Children (page 166)

See Feet (page 229)

See Respiratory Problems (page 296)

See Babies and Children (page 166)

Tips

Do not add essential oils to the tub while the water is running, as some of the precious essences may evaporate, depriving you of the full benefits.

If you prefer, substitute an equal quantity of liquid castile soap for the milk called for in any bath recipe.

If you are using a blend around bath/shower time, you can enhance the benefit by combining the essential oils with a carrier oil and rub it into your skin *before* getting into the shower or bath. This enables the essential oils to be absorbed and work their way into the bloodstream. The heat of the water encourages the essential oil vapors to rise, allowing you to inhale the aromas more easily and thus creating a dual application.

Cramp

A cramp is a painful contraction of the muscles, usually in the feet or the calves of the legs. Cramps often occur at night. Keep a bottle of the following blend on your bedside table, ready for emergencies! If such cramps are a regular part of your life, you need to find the cause and/or consult a health-care practitioner.

Caution

Before using any essential oil, consult the relevant entry in Part 1: Essential Oils (A to Y), pages 28 to 117, taking careful note of any cautions.

Essential Oils

Bay laurel, black pepper, geranium, lavender, marjoram, rosemary, valerian, ylang ylang

---

Cramp Massage Oil

Massage a little of this blend into the affected muscle. Walking and stretching the muscle will also help. Sometimes cramps occur at night because your legs and feet are cold. Try wearing woolen socks or sleeping with your lower body in a sleeping bag.

15 drops	geranium or lavender essential oil
15 drops	rosemary essential oil
10 drops	marjoram essential oil
5 drops	black pepper or bay laurel essential oil

In a ⅙ oz (5 mL) glass dropper bottle, combine lavender, rosemary, marjoram and black pepper essential oils. Shake to blend.

Treatment

Massage: In a small non-reactive bowl, combine 3 tsp (15 mL) grapeseed or sweet almond oil, 1 tsp (5 mL) St. John's wort–infused oil and 8 drops Cramp Massage Oil. Mix well and massage into the cramping muscle.

Cuts and Wounds

Tip
When possible, use a waterproof bandage that completely seals around the gauze pad, to prevent the essential oil from evaporating.

Essential Oils

Canadian balsam, bergamot, cedarwood, chamomile, frankincense, geranium, helichrysum, lavender, lemon, niaouli, rose, rosewood, tea tree, yarrow

Treatments

Wash: In a nonreactive bowl, combine 1 tsp (5 mL) liquid castile soap and 1 drop each geranium, lavender and tea tree essential oils. Add ½ cup (125 mL) boiling water and stir well to disperse oils. Using a cotton ball, thoroughly clean the affected area. If a bandage is required, apply 1 drop tea tree essential oil to the gauze (see Tips, right). When changing the bandage, repeat as necessary until wound appears "closed." Then leave wound uncovered to dry and scab.

If the cut requires stitches, dampen a cotton ball with distilled witch hazel and dab on the affected area to cleanse. Place 2 drops tea tree or lavender essential oil on a bandage and use it to apply pressure to the wound, then seek appropriate medical attention.

Cystic Fibrosis

Cystic fibrosis (CF) is a hereditary disease that appears in infancy or childhood. It characterized by symptoms that interfere with digestion (inability to digest fats) and breathing (the lungs constantly produce too much mucus). Medical treatment aims to minimize the effects of the disease and includes massive doses of medication. Parents of children who suffer from this disease are taught physiotherapy methods that are carried out daily to help rid the lungs of excess mucus. Essential oils can help enormously in this area, as well as protecting from lung infections. The essential oils listed below work variously on the pulmonary system, the immune system, the digestive tract and the liver and gallbladder.

The amount of essential oil used in the following blends is 1% and therefore suitable for use on young children. To increase the amount of essential oil for older children, see Babies and Children (page 164).

Caution
When using essential oil treatments for cystic fibrosis, it is particularly important to alternate the blends. Limit the use of each to a 3-week period—during which the essential oils are used for 5 days on and 2 days off—to avoid exposure to the same oils over a long period of time.

Essential Oils

Chamomile, *Eucalyptus globulus*, frankincense, lavender, ravensara, rosemary, tea tree

Cystic Fibrosis Blend 1

30 drops	lavender essential oil
30 drops	chamomile or ravensara essential oil
20 drops	tea tree essential oil
10 drops	rosemary essential oil

In a ⅙ oz (5 mL) glass dropper bottle, combine lavender, chamomile, tea tree and rosemary essential oils. Shake to blend.

Cystic Fibrosis Blend 2

30 drops	frankincense essential oil
30 drops	lavender essential oil
15 drops	eucalyptus essential oil
15 drops	rosemary essential oil

In a ⅙ oz (5 mL) glass dropper bottle, combine frankincense, lavender, eucalyptus and rosemary essential oils. Shake to blend.

Caution

Do not spray directly into child's face.

Tips

If you prefer, when making an air spray, substitute Solubol for the vodka called for, in a ratio of 4 drops Solubol for every 1 drop essential oil. Solubol is a natural product that allows essential oils to disperse in liquid.

When making air sprays, be sure to add the oils to the bottle first, followed by the chosen dispersant (vodka or Solubol), to ensure that the essential oils disperse properly (they will not mix directly with water).

Treatments

Air spray: In a 4 oz (125 mL) PET plastic spray bottle, combine 75 drops Cystic Fibrosis Blend 1 or 2 and 1 tsp (5 mL) vodka. Fill bottle with distilled or filtered water (see Tips, left).

Inhaler: Place 25 drops Cystic Fibrosis Blend 1 or 2 in a small non-reactive bowl. Place inhaler wick in the bowl and allow it to absorb the entire amount. Insert the wick inside the inhaler tube and tightly cap the bottom of the inhaler with the plug. Place the inhaler tube inside its cover and screw tightly to close.

Massage: In a 2 oz (60 mL) bottle, combine 10 tsp (50 mL) sweet almond or cold-pressed safflower oil and 12 drops Cystic Fibrosis Blend 1 or 2. Mix well and massage over the chest and back prior to physiotherapy. If the child is fretful and resists any more back treatment, a foot and/or hand massage is very comforting and valuable. The oils will still enter the bloodstream and do their work.

Cystitis

Cystitis is an inflammation of the bladder caused by a bacterial infection of the urinary tract. The symptoms are a burning or scalding sensation when passing urine, a need to pass urine frequently, a persistent dull ache above the pubic bone, and/ or urine that smells or contains blood or pus. If the attack is accompanied by fever and low back pain, the infection may be in the kidneys as well as the bladder and urethra—you should consult your health-care practitioner.

Essential Oils

Canadian balsam, bergamot, cedarwood, chamomile, eucalyptus (*citriodora* or *globulus*), fennel, juniper, lavender, rosemary ct. cineole, sandalwood, tea tree, thyme ct. linalool

---

Cystitis Blend

6 drops	juniper essential oil
4 drops	sandalwood or parsley essential oil
3 drops	chamomile essential oil
3 drops	*Eucalyptus citriodora* essential oil

In a ¹⁄₆ oz (5 mL) glass dropper bottle, combine juniper, sandalwood, chamomile and eucalyptus essential oils. Shake to blend.

Treatments

Bath: Fill tub with warm water. Meanwhile, in a small non-reactive bowl, combine 1 tsp (5 mL) milk and 4 to 6 drops Cystitis Blend (see Tips, right). Add to tub and agitate to disperse oil, then soak for 15 to 20 minutes, massaging any floating droplets of oil into your skin.

Hot Compress: In a small non-reactive bowl, combine ½ cup (125 mL) very hot water and 10 drops Cystitis Blend. Stir well to disperse oils. Submerge a cloth just large enough to absorb all the liquid without dripping. Lay the cloth on the affected area and secure by wrapping plastic wrap around your body to secure it. Leave compress on for 1 hour.

Caution

Before using any essential oil, consult the relevant entry in Part 1: Essential Oils (A to Y), pages 28 to 117, taking careful note of any cautions.

Tips

Do not add essential oils to the tub while the water is running, as some of the precious essences may evaporate, depriving you of the full benefits.

If you prefer, substitute an equal quantity of liquid castile soap for the milk called for in any bath recipe.

If you are using a blend around bath/ shower time, you can enhance the benefit by combining the essential oils with a carrier oil and rub it into your skin *before* getting into the shower or bath. This enables the essential oils to be absorbed and work their way into the bloodstream. The heat of the water encourages the essential oil vapors to rise, allowing you to inhale the aromas more easily and thus creating a dual application.

Variation

For an even more effective compress, in a small non-reactive bowl, combine 4 to 6 drops Cystitis Blend and ½ tsp (2.5 mL) grapeseed or sweet almond oil. Stir well to disperse oils. Using a cotton ball, apply to lower abdomen (over the bladder). Cover with a bandage or plastic wrap. Place a hot towel overtop and leave for up to 30 minutes. Repeat as necessary.

Massage: Warm ½ tsp (2.5 mL) grapeseed or sweet almond oil and 1 drop Cystitis Blend in a hot spoon (heat the spoon first by dipping it in boiling water or running under the hot-water tap). Stir with a toothpick to disperse the oil. Massage over your lower abdomen.

Dandruff
See Hair Problems (page 396)

Debility (Physical)

Essential Oils

Basil, cypress, geranium, juniper (needle), lavandin, lavender, marjoram, nutmeg, peppermint, pine, rose, rosemary ct. cineole, rosewood, tea tree

Caution

Before using any essential oil, consult the relevant entry in Part 1: Essential Oils (A to Y), pages 28 to 117, taking careful note of any cautions.

> ## *Debility Massage and Bath Oil Blend 1*
>
> | | |
> |---|---|
> | 20 drops | geranium essential oil |
> | 15 drops | rosemary essential oil |
> | 10 drops | peppermint essential oil |
>
> ## *Debility Massage and Bath Oil Blend 2*
>
> | | |
> |---|---|
> | 20 drops | lavandin essential oil |
> | 15 drops | sweet marjoram essential oil |
> | 5 drops | basil essential oil |
>
> *In a ⅙ oz (5 mL) glass bottle, combine essential oils for Debility Massage and Bath Oil Blend 1 or 2. Shake to blend.*

Treatments

Bath: Fill tub with warm water. Meanwhile, in a small non-reactive bowl, combine 1 tsp (5 mL) milk and 4 to 6 drops Debility Massage and Bath Oil Blend 1 or 2. Add to tub and agitate to disperse oil, then soak for 30 minutes, massaging any floating droplets of oil into your skin.

Hand/foot/sitz bath: Combine 1 tsp (5 mL) milk and 4 drops Debility Massage and Bath Oil Blend 1 or 2. Add to a basin of warm water, agitate to disperse oil, then soak desired area for 10 minutes, massaging any floating droplets of oil into your skin.

Massage: In a small non-reactive bowl, combine 2 tsp (10 mL) grapeseed or sweet almond oil and 4 drops Debility Massage and Bath Oil Blend 1 or 2. Mix well and massage over your body. If you don't feel up to a full massage, massage just your hands and/or feet—the oils will still enter the bloodstream to do their work.

Deodorants
See Body Care (page 417)

Depression
See Stress and Emotional Problems (page 310)

Dermatitis
See Skin Problems (page 379)

Tips

Do not add essential oils to the tub while the water is running, as some of the precious essences may evaporate, depriving you of the full benefits.

If you prefer, substitute an equal quantity of liquid castile soap for the milk called for in any bath recipe.

If you are using a blend around bath/shower time, you can enhance the benefit by combining the essential oils with a carrier oil and rub it into your skin *before* getting into the shower or bath. This enables the essential oils to be absorbed and work their way into the bloodstream. The heat of the water encourages the essential oil vapors to rise, allowing you to inhale the aromas more easily and thus creating a dual application.

Tip

Once a day, eat 2 tsp (10 mL) crushed flax seeds or psyllium seeds, sprinkled over cereal or yogurt. Be sure to include lots of fresh fruit and vegetables in your diet.

Tip

One of the dangers of diarrhea is dehydration, so be sure to drink plenty of liquids such as filtered, bottled or mineral water, peppermint tea (excellent!) or diluted fruit juices.

Caution

If using lemon essential oil, do not expose skin to sunlight for 12 hours.

Digestive Problems

Many people believe that the stomach is the source of all illness. When you're experiencing digestive problems, it's easy to believe that's true.

Constipation

Essential Oils

Black pepper, fennel, ginger, grapefruit, mandarin, marjoram, bitter orange, peppermint, rosemary ct. cineole, spearmint

Treatment

Abdominal massage: In a small non-reactive bowl, combine 1 drop black pepper essential oil, 2 drops peppermint essential oil and 1 tsp (5 mL) warmed grapeseed or sweet almond oil. Massage abdomen with this blend in a clockwise direction 2 to 3 times daily.

Diarrhea

The following treatments are for short-term bouts of diarrhea, which may be acute. See your health-care provider if the diarrhea persists.

Massage Oil for Food-Related Diarrhea

1 tsp (5 mL)	grapeseed or sweet almond oil
2 drops	Roman chamomile essential oil
1 drop	marjoram essential oil
1 drop	ginger essential oil

Massage Oil for Virus-Related Diarrhea

1 tsp (5 mL)	grapeseed or sweet almond oil
2 drops	niaouli essential oil
1 drop	lavender essential oil
1 drop	lemon essential oil

Massage Oil for Stress-Related Diarrhea

1 tsp (5 mL)	grapeseed or sweet almond oil
2 drops	chamomile essential oil
1 drop	geranium or spearmint essential oil
1 drop	lavender essential oil

In a small non-reactive bowl, combine grapeseed oil and essential oils. Mix thoroughly.

Essential Oils

Cedarwood, Roman chamomile, cinnamon (bark), clove (bud), geranium, ginger, lavender, lemon, marjoram, niaouli, nutmeg, sandalwood, spearmint

Treatment

Abdominal massage: Massage your whole abdomen in a clockwise direction with the appropriate oil blend, 2 to 3 times a day.

Heartburn

Essential Oils

Cedarwood, Roman chamomile, lemon, peppermint, sandalwood

Treatment

Ingestion: In an 8 oz (250 mL) glass, combine 1 drop peppermint essential oil and 1 tsp (5 mL) unpasteurized liquid honey. Top up with lukewarm water and mix thoroughly. Sip slowly 2 to 3 times per day, as needed.

Indigestion

Essential Oils

Anise, basil ct. linalool, bergamot, Roman chamomile, fennel, ginger, lavender, lemon, mandarin, marjoram, peppermint, rosemary ct. cineole, spearmint, thyme ct. linalool

Treatment

Ingestion: In an 8 oz (250 mL) glass, combine 1 drop lemon or ginger essential oil and 1 tsp (5 mL) unpasteurized liquid honey. Top up with lukewarm water and mix thoroughly. Sip slowly 2 to 3 times per day as needed.

Indigestion Massage Blend

1 tsp (5 mL)	grapeseed or sweet almond oil
2 drops	rosemary ct. cineole essential oil
1 drop	Roman chamomile essential oil
1 drop	marjoram essential oil

In a small non-reactive bowl, combine grapeseed oil and rosemary, chamomile and marjoram essential oils. Mix thoroughly.

Caution

Ingestion of peppermint essential oil should be avoided if you have cholestasis or gastroesophageal reflux disease (GERD). Negative interactions have been known to occur.

Caution

Before using any essential oil, consult the relevant entry in Part 1: Essential Oils (A to Y), pages 28 to 117, taking careful note of any cautions.

Tips

Do not add essential oils to the tub while the water is running, as some of the precious essences may evaporate, depriving you of the full benefits.

If you prefer, substitute an equal quantity of liquid castile soap for the milk called for in any bath recipe.

Treatment

Abdominal massage: Rub Indigestion Massage Blend in a clockwise direction over your stomach and abdomen.

Intestinal Gas

Gas trapped in the intestines can cause pain, flatulence, bloating and belching.

Essential Oils

Angelica, cardamom, Roman chamomile, fennel, ginger, lemon, peppermint, rosemary ct. cineole

---

Intestinal Gas Massage Blend

1 tsp (5 mL)	grapeseed or sweet almond oil
2 drops	Roman chamomile essential oil
1 drop	peppermint or ginger essential oil

In a small non-reactive bowl, combine grapeseed oil and chamomile and peppermint essential oils. Mix thoroughly.

Treatment

Abdominal massage: Massage abdomen with Intestinal Gas Massage Blend in a clockwise direction, as needed. Drink peppermint or ginger tea 3 times daily.

Diverticulitis

The symptoms of diverticulitis are lower abdominal pain and/or discomfort and cramping, flatulence, constipation and/or diarrhea. It seems to be caused by a diet that's low in fiber, lack of exercise, and stress. Massage can ease the discomfort.

Diverticulitis Massage Blend

18 drops	German chamomile essential oil
12 drops	peppermint essential oil
12 drops	rosemary ct. cineole essential oil
6 drops	marjoram essential oil

In a 1/6 oz (5 mL) glass dropper bottle, combine chamomile, peppermint, rosemary and marjoram essential oils. Shake to blend.

Essential Oils

German chamomile, geranium, juniper (berry), melissa, myrrh, niaouli, bitter orange, peppermint, rosemary, marjoram

Treatments

Bath: Fill tub with warm water. Meanwhile, in a small non-reactive bowl, combine 1 tsp (5 mL) milk and 4 to 6 drops Diverticulitis Massage Blend (page 218). Add to water, agitate to disperse oil, then soak for 20 minutes, massaging any floating droplets of oil into your skin.

Hot compress: In a small non-reactive bowl, combine 1/2 cup (125 mL) very hot water and 10 drops Diverticulitis Massage Blend (page 218). Stir well to disperse oils. Submerge a cloth just large enough to absorb all the liquid without dripping. Lay the cloth on the affected area and then wrap plastic wrap around the area and over the damp cloth. Leave compress on for 1 hour.

Massage: In a small non-reactive bowl, combine 3 drops Diverticulitis Massage Blend (page 218) and 1 tsp (5 mL) grapeseed or sweet almond oil. Mix well and massage over your abdomen in a clockwise direction, twice daily.

Dysentery
See Travel (page 325)

Earache

Treat earaches seriously, as any infection can spread to the middle and inner ear. The following suggestions are for simple earaches caused by drafts or a mild infection. See your health-care practitioner if an earache is regular, persistent or severe. Never poke around in the ear.

Essential Oils

Basil, cajuput, Roman chamomile, *Eucalyptus radiata*, lavender, rosemary ct. cineole, tea tree

Treatment

In a 1/6 oz (5 mL) glass dropper bottle, combine 6 drops of your chosen essential oil and 1 tsp (5 mL) extra virgin olive oil. Apply 3 drops of the mixture to a cotton ball and place in the external opening of the ear. Repeat 3 times per day, as needed. Never apply essential oils (diluted or undiluted) directly into the ear.

Tip

If you are using a blend around bath/shower time, you can enhance the benefit by combining the essential oils with a carrier oil and rub it into your skin *before* getting into the shower or bath. This enables the essential oils to be absorbed and work their way into the bloodstream. The heat of the water encourages the essential oil vapors to rise, allowing you to inhale the aromas more easily and thus creating a dual application.

Remember, the smallest thing you should put in your ear is your elbow!

Eczema
See Skin Problems (page 380)

Edema

Edema is a term used to describe swelling of tissues due to fluid retention. There are a number of possible causes. If the edema is generalized, the condition could be a serious one; it might indicate severe kidney or heart problems that require the immediate attention of a health-care practitioner. Some of the simpler causes of temporary edema are sprains, PMS, prolonged standing or sitting, flying, insect bites, hot weather or allergic reactions. Essential oils can be used successfully as a treatment aimed at reducing fluid in the cells. The following treatments target temporary swelling resulting from simple causes.

Treatments
Allergic reactions such as urticaria (hives)

Pour 2 cups (500 mL) ice-cold water into a non-reactive bowl and add 4 to 6 drops of Roman chamomile, melissa, peppermint, vetiver or lavender essential oil. Stir well to disperse oil. Soak a cloth and wring out enough water so cloth doesn't drip. Place cloth on affected area; repeat often.

Sprains and insect bites

Pour 2 cups (500 mL) ice-cold water into a non-reactive bowl and add 8 drops either lavender or chamomile essential oil. Stir well to disperse oil. Soak a cloth and wring out enough water so cloth doesn't drip. Place cloth on affected area; repeat often.

Swollen feet and ankles

In a small non-reactive bowl, combine 1 tsp (5 mL) milk and 6 drops fennel, pine, cypress or lemon essential oil. Add to a basin of warm water, agitate to disperse oil, then soak feet and ankles for 30 minutes, massaging any floating droplets of oil into your skin. After bathing, sit with legs elevated.

Tip

Remember that, in an emergency, lavender can help almost everything!

Emphysema

Chronic severe emphysema causes breathlessness, which is made worse by infections. Some patients become dependent on oxygen. Treatments aim to make breathing easier; sufferers also need to avoid tobacco smoke, do breathing exercises, whistle, and exercise regularly (walking, swimming or cycling). Seek medical help if there is any sign of respiratory failure, such as blue lips or extreme shortness of breath.

Essential Oils

Basil, cedarwood, eucalyptus, hyssop, peppermint, thyme ct. thymol

---

Emphysema Massage Blend

15 drops	cedarwood essential oil
10 drops	eucalyptus essential oil
5 drops	thyme ct. thymol or hyssop essential oil

In a ⅙ oz (5 mL) glass dropper bottle, combine cedarwood, eucalyptus and thyme essential oils. Shake to blend.

Treatments

Air spray: In a 4 oz (125 mL) PET plastic spray bottle, combine 75 drops Emphysema Massage Blend and 1 tsp (5 mL) vodka. Fill bottle with distilled or filtered water (see Tips, right). Shake to disperse oil.

Bath: Fill tub with warm water. Meanwhile, in a small non-reactive bowl, combine 1 tsp (5 mL) milk and 4 to 6 drops Emphysema Massage Blend. Add to tub and agitate to disperse oil, then soak for 20 minutes, massaging any floating droplets of oil into your skin.

Inhaler: Place 21 drops Emphysema Massage Blend in a small non-reactive bowl. Place the inhaler wick in the bowl and allow it to absorb the entire amount. Insert the wick inside the inhaler tube and tightly cap the bottom of the inhaler with the plug. Place the inhaler tube inside its cover and screw tightly to close.

Massage: In a small non-reactive bowl, combine 4 tsp (20 mL) grapeseed or sweet almond oil and 8 drops Emphysema Massage Blend. Mix well and massage over your chest and back.

Tips

If you prefer, when making an air spray, substitute Solubol for the vodka called for, in a ratio of 4 drops Solubol for every 1 drop essential oil. Solubol is a natural product that allows essential oils to disperse in liquid.

When making air sprays, be sure to add the oils to the bottle first, followed by the chosen dispersant (vodka or Solubol), to ensure that the essential oils disperse properly (they will not mix directly with water).

Endometriosis
See Women's Health (page 330)

Exhaustion

Essential Oils

Physical exhaustion: *Eucalyptus radiata*, geranium, ginger, grapefruit, lavender, peppermint, spearmint

Nervous exhaustion: basil ct. linalool, clary sage, frankincense, geranium, peppermint, tea tree, thyme ct. linalool

---

Physical Exhaustion Blend

10 drops	geranium essential oil
3 drops	*Eucalyptus radiata* essential oil
3 drops	spearmint essential oil

In a ¹⁄₆ oz (5 mL) glass bottle, combine geranium, eucalyptus and spearmint essential oils. Shake to blend.

Nervous Exhaustion Blend

10 drops	clary sage essential oil
3 drops	frankincense essential oil
3 drops	peppermint essential oil

In a ¹⁄₆ oz (5 mL) glass bottle, combine clary sage, frankincense and peppermint essential oils. Shake to blend.

Treatments

Massage: In a small non-reactive bowl, combine 2 tsp (10 mL) grapeseed or sweet almond oil and 4 drops Physical or Nervous Exhaustion Blend. Mix well and massage over your body. If you don't feel up to a full massage, just massage your hands and/or feet—the oils will still enter the bloodstream to do their work.

Air spray: In a 4 oz (125 mL) PET plastic spray bottle, combine 75 drops Physical or Nervous Exhaustion Blend and 1 tsp (5 mL) vodka. Fill with distilled or filtered water (see Tips, left). Shake well to disperse oils.

Tips

If you prefer, substitute Solubol for the vodka in a ratio of 4 drops Solubol for every 1 drop essential oil.

When making air sprays, be sure to add the oils to the bottle first, followed by the chosen dispersant (vodka or Solubol), to ensure that the essential oils disperse properly (they will not mix directly with water).

Bath: Fill tub with warm water. Meanwhile, in a small non-reactive bowl, combine 1 tsp (5 mL) milk and 4 to 6 drops Physical or Nervous Exhaustion Blend. Add to tub and agitate to disperse oil, then soak for 20 minutes, massaging any floating droplets of oil into your skin.

Inhaler: Place 21 drops Physical or Nervous Exhaustion Blend in a small non-reactive bowl. Place the inhaler wick in the bowl and allow it to absorb the entire amount. Insert the wick inside the inhaler tube and tightly cap the bottom of the inhaler with the plug. Place the inhaler tube inside its cover and screw tightly to close.

Fainting

Essential Oils

Lavender, marjoram, peppermint, rosemary (ct. cineole and ct. camphor)

Treatments

Inhalation: If someone you are with feels faint or has fainted, place a few drops of lavender, marjoram or peppermint essential oil on a tissue and hold just under their nose, or encourage them to gently inhale the aroma from the oil bottle.

Temple massage: Massage 1 to 2 drops lavender essential oil on the person's temples, keeping the oil well away from the eyes.

Smelling Salts

20 drops	marjoram essential oil
20 drops	lavender essential oil
10 drops	peppermint essential oil
1/3 cup (75 mL)	coarse sea salt

In a small non-reactive bowl, combine marjoram, lavender and peppermint essential oils. Mix thoroughly. Stir in salt until well combined. Transfer mixture to a small (4 oz/125 mL) resealable jar and seal tightly.

Treatment

Inhalation: If feeling faint, sniff Smelling Salts to restore equilibrium. You can also use Smelling Salts to treat tension headaches.

Do not add essential oils to the tub while the water is running, as some of the precious essences may evaporate, depriving you of the full benefits.

If you prefer, substitute an equal quantity of liquid castile soap for the milk called for in any bath recipe.

If you are using a blend around bath/shower time, you can enhance the benefit by combining the essential oils with a carrier oil and rub it into your skin *before* getting into the shower or bath. This enables the essential oils to be absorbed and work their way into the bloodstream. The heat of the water encourages the essential oil vapors to rise, allowing you to inhale the aromas more easily and thus creating a dual application.

Fatigue

Essential Oils

Physical fatigue: clary sage, *Eucalyptus radiata*, geranium, ginger, grapefruit, lavender, lemon, spearmint

Mental fatigue: Angelica, geranium, lavender, peppermint, rosemary (ct. cineole and ct. camphor), spearmint, thyme ct. linalool

---

Physical Fatigue Massage Blend

60 drops	lavender essential oil
18 drops	lemon essential oil
18 drops	clary sage essential oil

In a $1/6$ oz (5 mL) glass dropper bottle, combine lavender, lemon and clary sage essential oils. Shake to blend.

Treatments for Physical Fatigue

Air spray: In a 4 oz (125 mL) PET plastic spray bottle, combine 75 drops Physical Fatigue Massage Blend and 1 tsp (5 mL) vodka. Fill bottle with distilled or filtered water (see Tips, left). Shake to disperse oil.

Bath: Fill bathtub with warm water. Meanwhile, in a small non-reactive bowl, combine 5 drops lavender, 3 drops lemon and 2 drops grapefruit essential oils and mix thoroughly. Add 1 cup (250 mL) Epsom salts and stir to combine well. Add to tub and agitate to disperse oils and dissolve the salts. Soak for 30 minutes, massaging any floating droplets of oil into your skin.

Footbath: In a small non-reactive bowl, combine 1 tsp (5 mL) milk and 6 to 8 drops Physical Fatigue Massage Blend. Add to a basin of warm water, agitate to disperse oil, then soak feet for 10 minutes, massaging any floating droplets of oil into your skin.

Inhaler: Place 25 drops Physical Fatigue Massage Blend in a small non-reactive bowl. Place the inhaler wick in the bowl and allow it to absorb the entire amount. Insert the wick inside the inhaler tube and tightly cap the bottom of the inhaler with the plug. Place the inhaler tube inside its cover and screw tightly to close.

Tips

If you prefer, when making an air spray, substitute Solubol for the vodka called for, in a ratio of 4 drops Solubol for every 1 drop essential oil. Solubol is a natural product that allows essential oils to disperse in liquid.

When making air sprays, be sure to add the oils to the bottle first, followed by the chosen dispersant (vodka or Solubol), to ensure that the essential oils disperse properly (they will not mix directly with water).

Massage: In a small non-reactive bowl, combine 2 tsp (10 mL) grapeseed or sweet almond oil and 4 drops Physical Fatigue Massage Blend. Mix well and massage over your body.

Mental Fatigue Massage Blend

5 drops	geranium essential oil
5 drops	lavender essential oil
3 drops	rosemary essential oil
3 drops	peppermint essential oil

In a $1/6$ oz (5 mL) glass bottle, combine geranium, lavender, rosemary and peppermint essential oils. Shake to blend.

Treatments for Mental Fatigue

Air spray: In a 4 oz (125 mL) PET plastic spray bottle, combine 75 drops Mental Fatigue Massage Blend and 1 tsp (5 mL) vodka. Fill bottle with distilled or filtered water (see Tips, page 224). Shake to disperse oil.

Bath: Fill tub with warm water. Meanwhile, in a small non-reactive bowl, combine 1 tsp (5 mL) milk and 4 to 6 drops Mental Fatigue Massage Blend. Add to tub and agitate to disperse oil, then soak for 30 minutes, massaging any floating droplets of oil into your skin.

Inhaler: Place 21 drops Mental Fatigue Massage Blend in a small non-reactive bowl. Place inhaler wick in the bowl and allow it to absorb the entire amount. Insert the wick inside the inhaler tube and tightly cap the bottom of the inhaler with the plug. Place the inhaler tube inside its cover and screw tightly to close.

Massage: In a small non-reactive bowl, combine 2 tsp (10 mL) grapeseed or sweet almond oil and 4 drops Mental Fatigue Massage Blend. Mix well and massage over your body.

Tips

Do not add essential oils to the tub while the water is running, as some of the precious essences may evaporate, depriving you of the full benefits.

If you prefer, substitute an equal quantity of liquid castile soap for the milk called for in any bath recipe.

If you are using a blend around bath/ shower time, you can enhance the benefit by combining the essential oils with a carrier oil and rub it into your skin *before* getting into the shower or bath. This enables the essential oils to be absorbed and work their way into the bloodstream. The heat of the water encourages the essential oil vapors to rise, allowing you to inhale the aromas more easily and thus creating a dual application.

Feet

Feet are the unsung heroes that carry us, more or less without complaint, on our journey through life. We usually give them attention only if they ache or grow corns. We abuse them with ill-fitting footwear, by cutting toenails incorrectly, weighing too much and standing for too long. Let's give our feet a bit of loving care.

Aching Feet

Essential Oils

Benzoin, cypress, lavender, lemongrass, peppermint, rosemary

Treatments

Foot and leg massage: Pour a little Foot and Leg Gel (below) or Foot-Ease Oil (page 227) into the palm of your hand and massage over your feet and ankles and up to the calves on each leg. Pour a little Soothing Foot Lotion (page 227) into the palm of your hand and massage over your feet.

Footbath: In a non-reactive basin large enough to fit your feet comfortably, combine ½ cup (125 mL) Epsom salts and, 1 drop at a time, 6 drops of your chosen essential oil(s), stirring after each addition to avoid clumping. Fill the basin with warm water and agitate to disperse oil and salts. Soak for 10 minutes. Follow with a foot massage using Foot-Ease Oil (page 227).

Foot and Leg Gel

Because this gel isn't greasy, it can be used anywhere, anytime. Keep a little container of it in your pocket or handbag so you can gently smooth it over tired feet and legs when necessary. It is a lovely soothing treatment for those times when your legs ache but you can't have a footbath and don't want to use an oil.

Makes 1 oz (30 mL)

6 tsp (30 mL)	unscented aloe vera gel
8 drops	peppermint essential oil

In a small non-reactive bowl, combine aloe vera gel and peppermint essential oil. Mix thoroughly. Transfer to a small (1 oz/30 mL) resealable glass jar. Store in a dark, cool place.

Soothing Foot Lotion

If your work involves a lot of standing, your feet are probably aching and swollen when you get home. Make the following lotion and treat your feet daily.

Makes ½ cup (125 mL)

½ cup (125 mL)	unscented lotion
10 drops	grapefruit essential oil
10 drops	lavender essential oil
10 drops	black pepper essential oil
10 drops	rosemary ct. verbenone essential oil
5 drops	thyme ct. linalool essential oil

In a 4 oz (125 mL) PET plastic bottle, combine half of the unscented lotion and the grapefruit, lavender, black pepper, rosemary and thyme essential oils. Shake vigorously to blend. Add the remaining lotion, leaving about ½ inch (1 cm) headspace, and shake vigorously to combine (see Tip, right).

Tip

Decanting unscented lotion into a smaller bottle to blend with essential oils can be a very messy proposition. Using a pump dispenser makes it easy to fill a smaller bottle. Always add a small amount of lotion to your PET plastic bottle at first, then the essential oils, and shake to blend. Then add the remaining lotion and shake again. This helps to disperse the oils more evenly in the lotion.

Foot-Ease Oil

For an exquisitely relaxing experience, use this blend alone or after a footbath (see page 226).

Makes 2 oz (60 mL)

4 tsp (20 mL)	grapeseed or sweet almond oil
2 tsp (10 mL)	avocado oil
2 tsp (10 mL)	jojoba oil
1 tsp (10 mL)	wheat germ oil or 2 capsules vitamin E (250 IU)
1 tsp (5 mL)	vodka
10 drops	rosemary essential oil
10 drops	lavender essential oil
5 drops	benzoin essential oil

In a 2 oz (60 mL) glass bottle, combine grapeseed, avocado, jojoba and wheat germ oils, vodka, and rosemary, lavender and benzoin essential oils. Shake to blend. Store in a dark, cool place. Shake before use.

Caution

Avoid wheat germ oil if you have a wheat or gluten allergy. Substitute vitamin E as indicated in the recipe. Pierce the capsules with a clean, sharp knife and squeeze the oil into the blend. Vitamin E is also available in dropper bottles, in which case add 2 drops.

Tips

If you suffer from athlete's foot, wear cotton socks and non-synthetic or breathable shoes. Be sure to dry your feet very thoroughly after washing. Wash socks and towels separately, using a few drops of tea tree oil in the final rinse cycle to prevent the infection from spreading to others. Hang socks to dry (see Caution below).

Caution

Fires have been known to occur in dryers when essential oils (and sometimes vegetable oils too) have not been thoroughly removed from fabrics in the washing machine. To ensure that your detergent can break down the oils during the washing process, be sure to use a wash temperature of at least 104°F (40°C).

Athlete's Foot

Athlete's foot, or tinea pedis, is caused by an infectious fungus that is rife in gymnasiums and swimming pools. The skin becomes itchy and flaky and the areas between the toes turn spongy and white.

Essential Oils

Cypress, geranium, lavandin, lavender, manuka, rosemary, tea tree

Treatment

Footbath: Fill a basin large enough to fit your feet comfortably with warm water. In a small non-reactive bowl, combine 4 drops tea tree or manuka essential oil, 4 drops lavender essential oil and 1 tsp (5 mL) raw honey or mustard powder. Add to water in basin and agitate to disperse. Soak feet for 10 minutes. Using a clean towel, dry feet gently but well, particularly between the toes. Dust with Herb Oil Foot Powder (below), which is antifungal and a deodorant.

Herb Oil Foot Powder

1 cup (250 mL)	arrowroot powder
6 drops	cypress essential oil
6 drops	tea tree essential oil
6 drops	lavender essential oil
6 drops	rosemary essential oil

Place arrowroot powder in a non-reactive bowl. Very slowly, and stirring constantly to prevent lumps, add cypress, tea tree, lavender and rosemary essential oils. Mix thoroughly. Transfer to an 8 oz (250 mL) resealable glass jar. Store in a dark, cool place.

Treatment

Topical application: Using a cotton ball, apply Herb Oil Foot Powder to your feet, particularly between your toes. Use after bathing and before bed. This foot powder also works well sprinkled inside socks and shoes, especially if you suffer from sweaty or smelly feet.

Bunions

A bunion is a swelling, thickening and deformity of the largest joint of the big toe. Pain and discomfort are created by chafing from shoes.

Essential Oils

Carrot seed, chamomile; calendula-infused oil

Bunion Massage Blend

9 drops	chamomile essential oil
9 drops	carrot seed essential oil
6 tsp (30 mL)	calendula-infused oil

In a 1 oz (30 mL) glass bottle, combine chamomile and carrot essential oils. Fill bottle with calendula-infused oil and shake to blend.

Treatment

Foot massage: Pour a small amount of Bunion Massage Blend into the palm of your hand and gently massage over your whole foot, paying special attention to the bunion. Repeat twice daily.

Corns

Essential Oils

Birch bud (white birch); calendula-infused oil

Treatments

Topical application: After showering, use a pumice stone to remove dead skin from the corn. Using a cotton ball, apply calendula-infused oil to the area. Cover with a bandage or non-stick dressing. Repeat daily until all traces of dead skin have been removed.

Foot soak: If the corn(s) is too painful for the abrasive treatment, try soaking your feet. In a basin large enough to fit the feet comfortably, combine 6 drops birch essential oil and $\frac{1}{2}$ cup (125 mL) Epsom salts. Add warm water to fill basin about halfway; agitate water to dissolve salts and disperse oil. Soak feet for 10 minutes, then dry thoroughly. Using a cotton ball, apply calendula-infused oil to the corn(s). Cover feet with thick socks. Shoes are almost invariably the cause of corns—find the culprits and get rid of them!

Tip

If you suffer from bunions, find shoes that fit and visit a qualified podiatrist, who can make special pads to protect the bunion. Go barefoot as much as possible or find sandals with straps that don't touch the sore area.

Caution

Do not use carrot seed essential oil if pregnant or breastfeeding.

Treating Difficult Corns

Hard, thick corns can be difficult to remove. Aspirin can help! The salicylic acid in Aspirin can soften the corn, making it easier to scrub away the dead skin. Using the back of a spoon, crush 5 Aspirin tablets into a fine powder and transfer to a small non-reactive bowl. Add ½ tsp (2.5 mL) lemon juice and ½ tsp (2.5 mL) distilled or filtered water; stir to form a paste. Apply the paste to the corn and wrap the foot with plastic wrap. Cover the area with a hot dry towel and leave it on for 10 minutes. Rinse the foot under warm running water, then gently scrub with a pumice stone. Follow with a few dabs of calendula-infused oil and cover with a soft bandage.

Smelly Feet

Odorous feet is an embarrassing condition that is often worse during puberty, but it can also be the result of a poor diet, with too many "indulgences." Follow the suggestions for athlete's foot (page 228).

Swollen Feet and Ankles

Feet can swell for many reasons—standing for long periods, arthritis, rheumatism, varicose veins, constipation, hot weather, a long flight—and the swelling caused by most of these conditions is easily treated. If your feet and legs swell often, however, it may indicate a heart or kidney problem; you should seek help from your health-care practitioner. Before massaging or applying any type of lotion to the legs, raise the feet so they are even with the heart and rest for 10 to 15 minutes.

Essential Oils

Cypress, eucalyptus, fennel, lavender

Swollen Feet and Ankles Blend

10 drops	cypress essential oil
5 drops	eucalyptus essential oil
5 drops	lavender essential oil

In a ⅙ oz (5 mL) glass bottle, combine cypress, eucalyptus and lavender essential oils. Shake to blend.

Treatments

Foot massage: In a small non-reactive bowl, combine 1 tsp (5 mL) grapeseed or sweet almond oil, 2 drops cypress, 1 drop eucalyptus or fennel and 1 drop lavender essential oils. Mix thoroughly. Using light, sweeping movements, gently massage over your feet, ankles and calves. Then start at the tops of the calves and work your way down to the ankles, using upward strokes (toward the heart). Repeat several times. Elevate the feet when sitting and avoid sitting or standing without movement for lengthy periods.

Cold compress: In a non-reactive bowl, combine 4 drops Swollen Feet and Ankles Blend and 1 tsp (5 mL) milk. Add 1 cup (250 mL) ice-cold water and stir well to disperse oils. Soak a cloth and wring out enough water so cloth doesn't drip. Place cloth on your ankles and feet. Repeat often and follow with a foot massage (above).

Fever

Fever is one of the ways in which the body reacts to defend itself against infection. Left to run its natural course, fever can heal the body—a temperature of 102° to 104°F (39° to 40°C) can help shorten the infection. If the temperature soars or the fever continues for more than 2 days, contact your health-care practitioner. You may need to reduce it by encouraging sweating or taking cooling tub or sponge baths—this is where aromatherapy helps.

Essential Oils

Cajuput, Roman chamomile, hyssop, lemon, peppermint, spearmint, tea tree

Treatments

Cool compress: Pour 2 cups (500 mL) cool (not icy) water into a non-reactive bowl and add 3 to 4 drops mixed lavender and peppermint essential oils. Stir well to disperse oils. Soak a cloth and wring out enough water so cloth doesn't drip. Place cloth on forehead. Repeat often and follow with a bath (page 232).

Tub bath: Fill tub with warm water. In a small non-reactive bowl, combine 5 to 10 drops mixed Roman chamomile and cajuput essential oils (amount depends on patient's age; see page 163) and 2 tsp (10 mL) unpasteurized liquid honey. Cut 1 lemon into slices. Pour oil blend into bath and add lemon slices to water. Agitate water to disperse oils, then soak for 30 minutes, massaging any floating droplets of oil into the skin.

Sponge bath: Fill a bowl with warm water. In a small non-reactive bowl, combine 2 drops each Roman chamomile and cajuput essential oils and 1 tsp (5 mL) unpasteurized liquid honey. Cut half a lemon into slices. Pour the oil blend into the water and add lemon slices. Agitate to disperse oils and use to give a sponge bath.

Fibromyalgia (Fibrositis)

Fibromyalgia is an inflammation caused by overgrowth of cells of the fibrous white tissue of the musculoskeletal system. It can occur in response to chronic inflammation or hormone dysfunction or as a result of other damage or disease. The condition is also known as fibrositis or myofascial pain syndrome.

Essential Oils

Black pepper, cypress, juniper, lavender, marjoram, peppermint, rosemary

---

Fibromyalgia Blend for Compresses

1 tsp (5 mL)	rosemary essential oil
50 drops	lavender essential oil
50 drops	marjoram essential oil

In a ⅓ oz (10 mL) glass dropper bottle, combine rosemary, lavender and marjoram essential oils. Shake to blend.

Fibromyalgia Blend for Baths

1 tsp (5 mL)	grapeseed or sweet almond oil
2 drops	juniper essential oil
2 drops	cypress essential oil
1 drop	black pepper essential oil

Fibromyalgia Blend for Massage

1 tsp (5 mL)	grapeseed or sweet almond oil
2 drops	lavender essential oil
1 drop	juniper essential oil
1 drop	peppermint essential oil

Treatments

Warm compress: In a non-reactive bowl, combine 1 cup (250 mL) hot water and 10 drops Fibromyalgia Blend for Compresses (page 232). Stir well to disperse oils. Soak a cloth and wring out enough water so cloth doesn't drip. Lay cloth on affected area and secure firmly, but not too tightly, by wrapping plastic wrap around the area and over the damp cloth.

Cold compress: Try the above as a cold treatment to see which gives you the most relief. Treat as often as needed. See also Rheumatism (page 300).

Bath: Fill tub with warm water. Meanwhile, in a small non-reactive bowl, combine ingredients of Fibromyalgia Blend for Baths (page 232). Massage blend into skin before getting into bath. Soak in the tub for 30 minutes.

Massage: In a small non-reactive bowl, combine ingredients of Fibromyalgia Blend for Massage (above). Mix well and massage over your body.

Tips

Do not add essential oils to the tub while the water is running, as some of the precious essences may evaporate, depriving you of the full benefits.

If you prefer, substitute an equal quantity of liquid castile soap for the milk called for in any bath recipe.

If you are using a blend around bath/shower time, you can enhance the benefit by combining the essential oils with a carrier oil and rub it into your skin *before* getting into the shower or bath. This enables the essential oils to be absorbed and work their way into the bloodstream. The heat of the water encourages the essential oil vapors to rise, allowing you to inhale the aromas more easily and thus creating a dual application.

First Aid

Injuries are an unavoidable fact of life. It's important to know what to do in these situations, as early intervention can reduce pain and trauma. It may even save a life! Keep a list of emergency numbers in easily accessible places.

It is beyond the scope of this book to provide basic first aid information. If you haven't taken a first aid course, then make sure to purchase a first aid book (there are many excellent ones) or visit a Red Cross website to locate a class near you.

Tip

The tricky part of ointment making is knowing when to pour it into the jar. If you pour it too soon, the emulsion might break; too late and the mixture will be too thick. Allow the mixture to cool just slightly before pouring it into the jar.

Basic Healing Ointment

Ointments are used to protect raw, irritated or wounded skin from air and moisture while providing antibacterial and/or antifungal healing benefits. This recipe makes a good general-purpose ointment for your first aid needs.

Makes about ¼ cup (60 mL)

¼ oz (7 g)	beeswax prills (pellets)
8 tsp (40 mL)	anhydrous lanolin
4 tsp (20 mL)	cold-pressed olive or grapeseed oil
30 drops	tea tree or manuka essential oil
20 drops	lavender essential oil
20 drops	rosemary essential oil
10 drops	thyme essential oil

1. *In a small saucepan over medium heat, gently melt beeswax, being careful not to overheat. Add lanolin and heat, stirring constantly, until completely melted into the wax. Stirring constantly, slowly pour in olive oil. Remove saucepan from heat and set aside to cool slightly, until just above blood heat (98°F/37°C)—do not allow beeswax to solidify.*

2. *Stirring constantly, 1 drop at a time, add tea tree, lavender, rosemary and thyme essential oils. Stir thoroughly to disperse oils. Transfer mixture to an airtight dark glass jar before it begins to thicken (see Tip, left). Store in a cool, dry place.*

Variations

Substitute calendula- or comfrey-infused oil for the olive oil. Calendula is a prime first aid remedy for wounds, cuts, sores, abrasions, sore nipples, ulcers and sprains, and to reduce inflammation and pain from measles and chicken pox spots. Comfrey is used on bruises, sprains and strains and to accelerate healing of fractures, cuts, ulcers and wounds.

The Essential Oil First Aid Box

Every home and car should have a well-equipped first aid box. Prompt assistance can often prevent excessive pain and trauma and, perhaps, save a life. Here is what you need:

- 2 empty **dropper bottles**, for mixing
- 2 **disposable eyedroppers**, for measuring essential oils
- wooden **applicator sticks**, for taking ointment out of jars
- **cotton balls**, for topical applications and for inhalations
- 1 small bottle of **grapeseed or sweet almond oil**, for making blends
- 1 small bottle of **unscented lotion**
- **Basic Healing Ointment** (page 234)
- **witch hazel hydrolat (alcohol-free)**, to reduce inflammation and the pain of bites and stings (see page 127)
- **chamomile tea bags**, to calm tension, depression and anxiety, insomnia, internal inflammations such as gastritis, diarrhea, cystitis, menstrual pain and PMS
- **chamomile essential oil**, to treat the above problems externally and also to ease dull pain (see page 46)
- **eucalyptus essential oil**, for its anti-inflammatory, antiseptic, antiviral and pain-relieving properties (see page 53)
- **geranium essential oil**, to use with lemon essential oil and witch hazel to stop bleeding, as a nerve tonic or with lemon and lavender essential oils to repel insects (see page 60)
- **ginger essential oil**, for nausea, stomach cramps, muscular pain, travel sickness/jet lag and fatigue (see page 62)
- **grapefruit essential oil**, to combat fatigue, depression and nervous exhaustion (see page 63) or, with geranium essential oil, to counteract muscle stiffness
- **lavender essential oil**, used undiluted for its antibacterial, antiviral and antidepressant properties, especially for headaches and depression (see page 71), or mixed with witch hazel for insect bites (or as an insect repellent), bruises, minor burns and sunburn
- **lemon essential oil** (see page 74), used with geranium essential oil and witch hazel to stop bleeding and prevent bacterial infection of wounds
- **peppermint essential oil**, to ease stomach cramps, travel sickness and nausea (see page 95)
- a small jar of **manuka honey**
- **rosemary essential oil**, to stimulate the central nervous system, to ease colds, coughs and catarrh when inhaled and to ease the pain of tired, stiff muscles (see page 103)
- **tea tree essential oil**, used undiluted to treat abscesses, athlete's foot, cold sores, cuts, grazes, bites, ringworm and sunburn (see page 112)

Tip

Be sure to include gauze, adhesive bandages, 1 small cloth for compresses, tweezers and scissors in your first aid box. You will also need cotton balls for topical applications of oils and ointments.

Remedies **235**

First Aid Treatment with Essential Oils

(For use, see *Key to First Aid Treatment Methods* on page 238)

Condition	Essential Oil	Treatment Method
Bites, animal (page 184)	Lavender, tea tree	Undiluted
Bites, insect (page 185)	Lavender, tea tree	Undiluted
Bleeding (page 186)	Lemon, geranium, witch hazel	Compress
Blisters (page 186)	Geranium, tea tree	Undiluted
Bruises (page 191)	Witch hazel, lavender	Compress
Burns (page 192)	Lavender	Undiluted
Chills and fever (page 231)	Ginger, geranium	Bath, shower, massage
Colds (page 203)	Eucalyptus, ginger	Bath, massage
Cramps, menstrual (page 338)	Geranium	Massage
Cramps, muscular (page 210)	Ginger	Massage
Cuts and abrasions (page 211)	Lavender, tea tree	Wash
Diarrhea, traveler's (page 325)	Ginger, peppermint	Stomach massage
Exhaustion, physical (page 222)	Lavender, peppermint	Bath, shower, massage
Hay fever (page 243)	Chamomile, eucalyptus	Inhalation
Headache (page 244)	Lavender, peppermint	Inhalation, neck massage

Condition	Essential Oil	Treatment Method
Heat rash (page 248)	Geranium, lavender, witch hazel	Lotion
Heatstroke (page 315)	Lavender, eucalyptus, lemon	Cold-water sheet wrap
Indigestion (page 217)	Peppermint, ginger	Drink
Insect repellent (page 254)	Lavender, peppermint	Lotion
Insomnia (page 255)	Chamomile, lavender	Bath, massage
Itching (page 258)	Lavender, eucalyptus	Lotion
Jet lag (page 323)	Lavender, rosemary, grapefruit	Bath, shower, massage
Motion sickness (page 324)	Peppermint, ginger	Inhalation, drink
Muscle aches (page 274)	Lavender, rosemary, ginger	Bath, massage
Sprain or strain (page 309)	Lavender, chamomile, witch hazel	Compress for 4 days
Sunburn (page 314)	Lavender	Bath, undiluted
Sunstroke (page 315)	Lavender, eucalyptus, lemon	Cold-water sheet wrap
Toothache (page 318)	Chamomile (children), clove (adults)	Massage on gum, spit out
Vomiting (page 327)	Peppermint, ginger	Inhalation, drink
Wounds (page 211)	Lavender, tea tree, witch hazel	Lotion

Key to First Aid Treatment Methods

Bath	4 to 6 drops (total) essential oil in 1 tsp (5 mL) grapeseed or sweet almond oil; add to bath
Cold-water sheet wrap	4 to 6 drops essential oil added to a sinkful of water; agitate to disperse oils; submerge large cloth or sheet to absorb water, then wring out; wrap person (or part of body) with sheet
Compress	4 drops (total) essential oil on cold wet cloth; wring to distribute oils
Drink	1 drop essential oil in ½ tsp (2.5 mL) honey, stirred into 1 cup (250 mL) warm water; stir vigorously before drinking
Inhalation	1 to 2 drops on a cotton ball; inhale
Lotion	3 drops (total) essential oil in 1 tsp (5 mL) unscented lotion
Massage	3 drops (total) essential oil in 1 tsp (5 mL) grapeseed or sweet almond oil
Shower	3 drops (total) essential oil in 1 tsp (5 mL) grapeseed or sweet almond oil; rub all over body before showering
Undiluted	1 to 3 drops on cotton ball; apply to affected area
Wash	3 drops (total) essential oils in ½ tsp (2.5 mL) honey; stir into 1 cup (250 mL) witch hazel hydrolat (alcohol-free)

Procedures for Essential Oil Poisoning or Adverse Reaction

The following suggestions are appropriate when essential oils have been swallowed, spilled undiluted on the skin, or gone into the eyes of a child or an adult.

If an essential oil has been ingested:

1. Do not induce vomiting.
2. If the person is not convulsing or unconscious, they should rinse out their mouth with lots of cool water, then spit out the water.
3. If the person is convulsing or unconscious, ensure that the airway is clear and turn them on their side. Do not give anything by mouth!
4. If the adverse reaction was caused by inhalation of an essential oil, move the person to a place where they can breathe fresh air.

5. If the person is not breathing, ensure that the airway is clear and begin mouth-to-mouth resuscitation. Seek medical attention immediately.

6. Try to find someone to stay with the person while you telephone 911. (Keep a list of emergency numbers, including the Poison Control Centre, next to the telephone.)

7. Have the bottle of essential oil with you when you telephone. You will be asked a series of questions that may include the following:
   - Age and weight of patient?
   - What oil has been swallowed?
   - Was the oil undiluted or diluted with another liquid? If diluted, what percentage dilution?
   - How much oil was swallowed?
   - How long ago did the accident happen?
   - What has been done so far in the way of treatment?
   - Are there any symptoms?

If undiluted essential oil has been spilt on the skin:

1. Wash the area with soap and warm running water, continuing to rinse until all traces of the oil have disappeared.

2. Expose the affected skin to the air to allow full evaporation of the oil (avoid direct sunlight).

3. Take a warm bath with ½ cup (125 mL) ground oatmeal, or apply a topical hydrocortisone cream. Oral antihistamines may be used to relieve itching. (*Caution:* Some corticosteroid creams and topical antihistamines can cause allergic contact dermatitis.)

4. If irritation continues, seek medical attention.

If an essential oil has got into the eyes:

1. Flush eyes with cool water for a minimum of 15 minutes. (Contact lens wearers should remove lenses after 5 minutes of flushing with water, then continue.)

2. Seek medical attention if irritation continues.

Caution

Remember that essential oils are potentially lethal if swallowed—even ½ tsp (2.5 mL) could kill a child. There is no such thing as a "child-proof" container; it is merely a child-resistant cap. Children are persistent and will spend time to solve a problem that interests them. Children are also curious and impatient: they rarely smell the contents of a bottle first and they rarely sip—the bottle is simply upended and the contents gulped. Such behavior has led to fatalities.

Flu
See Common Cold and Influenza (page 203)

Fungal Infections
See Athlete's Foot (page 228); Candidiasis (page 195); Itching (page 258); Jock Itch (page 268)

German Measles
See Rubella (page 303)

Gingivitis
See Teeth and Gum Problems (page 317)

Glandular Fever
See Mononucleosis (page 271)

Gout

Gout is caused by an excessive buildup of uric acid in the body; it turns into crystals around the joints, most commonly at the base of the big toe. Attacks are accompanied by extremely painful swelling and inflammation.

Essential Oils

Basil ct. linalool, cajuput, Roman chamomile, cinnamon, cypress, fennel, Fragonia, juniper, lemon, peppermint, pine, rosemary (ct. cineole and ct. camphor), rosewood

---

Gout Blend

15 drops	chamomile essential oil
15 drops	cajuput or Fragonia essential oil
5 drops	peppermint or rosemary ct. verbenone essential oil

In a ¹⁄₆ oz (5 mL) glass dropper bottle, combine chamomile, cajuput and peppermint essential oils. Shake to blend.

Treatments
Footbath: Combine 2 tsp (10 mL) milk and 12 drops Gout Blend. Fill two basins with water—one cool and one warm. Add half of the mixture to each basin and agitate to disperse oil. Soak feet in

warm water for 10 minutes, then transfer to cool water and soak for 10 minutes. Massage any floating droplets of oil into your skin.

Massage: In a small non-reactive bowl, combine 4 tsp (20 mL) grapeseed or sweet almond oil and 12 drops Gout Blend. Mix well and massage affected areas very gently 3 times a day.

Hemorrhoids

Hemorrhoids are varicose veins in the rectum, just above the anus. Caused by straining during bowel movements or while delivering a baby, they can become itchy, swollen and painful.

Essential Oils

Cajuput, cedarwood, Roman chamomile, clary sage, cypress, geranium, juniper, niaouli, patchouli, sandalwood, spikenard, tea tree

---

Hemorrhoid Gel

1 tsp (5 mL)	witch hazel hydrolat (alcohol-free)
2 drops	cypress essential oil
2 drops	juniper essential oil
2 drops	geranium essential oil
8 tsp (40 mL)	unscented aloe vera gel

In a small non-reactive bowl, combine witch hazel and cypress, juniper and geranium essential oils. Mix thoroughly to disperse the oils. Add gel and mix thoroughly to blend. Transfer to a 1 oz (30 mL) resealable glass jar. Store in a dark, cool place. Stir well before each application.

Treatment

Sitz bath: Fill tub or a large basin with just enough warm water to cover your bottom. Meanwhile, in a small non-reactive bowl, combine 1 tsp (5 mL) milk and 2 drops each Roman chamomile, juniper and cedarwood or sandalwood essential oils. Add to water, agitate to disperse oil, and then soak for 10 to 15 minutes. Follow by gently massaging the hemorrhoids with Hemorrhoid Gel. If the blend stings, dilute the mixture with more aloe vera gel.

Caution

Before using any essential oil, consult the relevant entry in Part 1: Essential Oils (A to Y), pages 28 to 117, taking careful note of any cautions.

Soothing Hemorrhoid Cleansing Pads

⅓ cup (75 mL)	witch hazel hydrolat (alcohol-free)
10 drops	Roman chamomile essential oil
5 drops	niaouli essential oil
20 to 25	cotton cosmetic pads

In a 4 oz (125 g) glass jar, combine witch hazel with Roman chamomile and niaouli essential oils. Seal jar and shake well. Place the cotton pads in the jar, carefully submerging them to soak up the liquid (they should be saturated but not dripping). If unabsorbed liquid remains, add a few more pads to the jar.

Treatment
Wash: Use Soothing Hemorrhoid Cleansing Pads to wipe the anus after going to the toilet, or as needed to relieve itching.

Hangover

We don't suppose there are many people reading this book who haven't experienced the pain and misery of a hangover at least once in their lives. A hangover is basically a symptom of poisoning, and the body needs to get rid of the offending toxins as soon as possible.

If you think you're in for a festive night, drink lots of water and eat a slice or two of dry bread before going out. Try to drink one glass of water for every alcoholic drink you consume. When you return home, drink more water (alcohol causes dehydration) and take a 1,000 mg vitamin C tablet and a multi-B vitamin. If you still feel terrible in the morning, repeat the vitamin treatment and take a bath (see below).

Essential Oils

Grapefruit, juniper, rosemary

Treatments
Bath: Fill bathtub with warm water. Meanwhile, in a small non-reactive bowl, combine 1 tsp (5 mL) milk and 2 drops juniper, 2 drops grapefruit and 1 drop rosemary essential oils. Add to water and agitate to disperse oil, then soak for 30 minutes, massaging any floating droplets of oil into your skin.

Alternatively, after showering, sprinkle a wet washcloth with 1 drop each juniper, grapefruit and rosemary essential oils and rub briskly over your entire body. Or, before showering, add 1 drop of each essential oil to a natural-bristle body brush, then brush in small, circular motions, starting at your ankles and wrists and moving slowly upward on the body.

Hay Fever

The majority of people who suffer from hay fever are reacting to grass, flower and tree pollens. They spend months of every year (usually in the spring) in a misery of sneezing, streaming nose, sore throat and itchy eyes. Dust mites, mold spores, chemicals and animal fur are also problems for many people. For maximum relief, alternate using the inhalers below.

Essential Oils

Roman chamomile, eucalyptus, geranium, helichrysum, hyssop, lavender, lemon, myrtle (green or orange), tea tree

Hay Fever Inhaler 1

7 drops	Roman chamomile or helichrysum essential oil
7 drops	eucalyptus essential oil
7 drops	lemon essential oil

Hay Fever Inhaler 2

7 drops	lavender essential oil
7 drops	tea tree or myrtle essential oil
4 drops	geranium essential oil
4 drops	lemon essential oil

In a small non-reactive bowl, combine the essential oils, then place inhaler wick in the bowl and allow it to absorb the entire amount. Place the wick inside the inhaler tube and tightly cap the bottle of the inhaler with the plug. Insert the inhaler tube inside its cover and screw tightly to close.

Hay Fever Blend

10 drops	Roman chamomile essential oil
4 drops	lemon essential oil
2 drops	myrtle essential oil

In a ⅙ oz (5 mL) glass dropper bottle, combine Roman chamomile, lemon and myrtle essential oils. Shake to blend.

Treatments

Massage: In a small non-reactive bowl, combine 4 tsp (20 mL) grapeseed or sweet almond oil and 8 drops Hay Fever Blend. Mix well and massage over your chest and upper back.

Steam inhalation: Pour 2 cups (500 mL) boiling water in a non-reactive bowl. Add 3 drops of any essential oil recommended for hay fever (see page 243). Sit comfortably in a chair with the bowl on a table in front of you. Place your face 8 to 12 inches (20 to 30 cm) above the bowl and drape a towel over your head and the bowl, covering the base of your neck. To keep the steam from escaping, tuck the ends of the towel under your forearms as they rest on the table, or around the sides of the bowl. Breathe in the vapors for a minute or so (as long as is comfortable), then pop your head out for a few moments of fresh air. Repeat for 5 to 10 minutes, if possible.

Headaches

If you suffer from regular and persistent headaches and the cause isn't obvious, see your health-care provider. There can be many causes for headaches, from eyestrain to indigestion and other, more serious conditions. (For migraine headaches, see page 270.)

Tension Headaches

Tension or stress headaches are the most common type of headache. While the pain won't necessarily keep you from performing daily activities, it is really bothersome. Tension headaches may appear periodically when you are under stress, but tension headaches that occur more than 15 days per month are considered chronic. The headache may last for as little as 30 minutes or as long as several days. The methods below can be useful for reducing the frequency and duration of headaches.

Essential Oils

Lavender, marjoram, peppermint

Tension Headache Massage and Bath Blend

48 drops	lavender essential oil
30 drops	marjoram essential oil
18 drops	peppermint essential oil

In a $\frac{1}{6}$ oz (5 mL) glass dropper bottle, combine lavender, marjoram and peppermint essential oils. Shake to blend.

Treatments

Bath: Fill tub with warm water. Meanwhile, in a small non-reactive bowl, combine 1 tsp (5 mL) milk and 4 to 6 drops Tension Headache Massage and Bath Blend. Mix thoroughly. Add to water, agitate to disperse oil, then soak for 30 minutes, inhaling the vapors and massaging any floating droplets of oil into your skin, concentrating on the back of your neck, especially just below the skull.

Air spray: In a 4 oz (125 mL) PET plastic spray bottle, combine 75 drops Tension Headache Massage and Bath Blend and 1 tsp (5 mL) vodka. Fill bottle with filtered or distilled water (see Tips, page 244). Shake vigorously before each use. Spray as desired.

Roll-on: In a ⅓ oz (10 mL) glass bottle with roller ball, place 15 drops Tension Headache Massage and Bath Blend. Top up with fractionated coconut oil (be careful not to overfill). Insert the ball holder, then the ball, and screw on the top. Shake to blend. Roll onto your temples and the back of your neck (be careful not to get any in your eyes). Massage in the oil using your fingertips.

see Tips, page 244

Inhaler for Tension Headaches

12 drops	lavender essential oil
5 drops	rosemary essential oil
4 drops	peppermint essential oil
4 drops	marjoram essential oil

In a small non-reactive bowl, combine lavender, rosemary, peppermint and marjoram essential oils. Place inhaler wick in the bowl and allow it to absorb the entire amount. Insert the wick inside the inhaler tube and tightly cap the bottom of the inhaler with the plug. Place the inhaler tube inside its cover and screw tightly to close.

Inhale as needed to ease headache, clear the brain and lessen tension.

How to Use Inhaler Sticks

With one finger pressing closed your left nostril, inhale from the tube through the right nostril. Then close the right nostril with your finger and inhale through the left. Repeat on each side one more time. Exhale through the mouth, not the nose.

Tips

Do not add essential oils to the tub while the water is running, as some of the precious essences may evaporate, depriving you of the full benefits.

If you prefer, substitute an equal quantity of liquid castile soap for the milk called for in any bath recipe.

If you are using a blend around bath/shower time, you can enhance the benefit by combining the essential oils with a carrier oil and rub it into your skin *before* getting into the shower or bath. This enables the essential oils to be absorbed and work their way into the bloodstream. The heat of the water encourages the essential oil vapors to rise, allowing you to inhale the aromas more easily and thus creating a dual application.

Gastric Headaches

A gastric headache occurs when the digestive system slows, causing a delay in breaking down foods and emptying the contents of the stomach. It is likely to occur on either side of the head and is often accompanied by nausea and/or vomiting. People often seek relief by taking migraine medications, but that can become part of the problem, since the body will have trouble breaking down and using the medication. Inhalation is an effective way to relieve a gastric headache, as the essential oils bypass the digestive system and enter the system in as little as 20 minutes.

Essential Oils

Cardamom, peppermint

Treatments

Bath: Fill tub with warm water. Meanwhile, in a small non-reactive bowl, combine 1 tsp (5 mL) milk and 4 to 6 drops peppermint or cardamom essential oil. Add to tub and agitate to disperse oil, then soak for 30 minutes, massaging any floating droplets of oil into your skin.

Massage: In a small non-reactive bowl, combine 1 tsp (5 mL) grapeseed or sweet almond oil and 3 drops peppermint or cardamom essential oil. Mix well and massage over your stomach and abdomen in a clockwise direction.

Head Lice

Lice have always been and will continue to be a problem among school-age children. Young children are cozy creatures—they get their heads together to share secrets, hats, combs and head lice. Broad-spectrum treatment is needed, because if the nits (eggs) of head lice aren't destroyed, then the problem will recur.

When treating head lice, it is important to wash all bedding and personal clothes in very hot water. Add 2 tsp (10 mL) eucalyptus oil to the rinse cycle. Hang in the sun for a whole day, turning inside out at intervals so that every part of the material (particularly seams and hems) receives air and sun. Nits hatch out at 48-hour intervals, so this treatment of clothes and bedding will need to be carried out every 2 days until the problem no longer exists.

Essential oils are an excellent way of dealing with the problem. You may notice that the percentage of oils is higher than normally used. If there is any burning or discomfort to the skin, dilute with more sesame oil.

Essential Oils

Bergamot, cinnamon (leaf), citronella, clove, eucalyptus, geranium, lavender, rosemary, tea tree, thyme

---

Head Lice Oil Treatment (Adults)

15 drops	tea tree essential oil
15 drops	lavender essential oil
8 drops	citronella essential oil
6 drops	thyme ct. linalool essential oil
4 drops	clove essential oil
1 drop	cinnamon leaf essential oil
1/4 cup (60 mL)	sesame oil

In a 2 oz (60 mL) glass bottle, combine tea tree, lavender, citronella, thyme, clove and cinnamon leaf essential oils. Fill bottle with sesame oil and shake to blend.

Variation
If using on children, increase the quantity of sesame oil to 1/2 cup (125 mL) and use a 4-oz (125 mL) bottle.

Treatment
1. Massage Head Lice Oil Treatment thoroughly into hair and scalp. Cover hair with a shower cap and leave on either all day or all night.

Caution

Fires have been known to occur in dryers when essential oils (and sometimes vegetable oils too) have not been thoroughly removed from fabrics in the washing machine. To ensure that your detergent can break down the oils during the washing process, be sure to use a wash temperature of at least 104°F (40°C).

Tip

For a more effective treatment, substitute palm kernel oil for the sesame oil.

2. Shampoo hair and, while lathering, comb through with a fine-tooth comb, paying particular attention to behind the ears and the back of the neck (this will help to get rid of nits).
3. Rinse hair with water, then use Hair Rinse for Lice (below) as a final rinse.
4. Dry hair and comb through again with a clean fine-toothed comb. Repeat the process every 2 days for 1 week, but no longer.

Hair Rinse for Lice

4 drops	tea tree essential oil
3 tsp (15 mL)	lemon juice or vinegar
2 cups (500 mL)	very warm water

In a medium non-reactive bowl or 2-cup (500 mL) glass measuring cup, combine tea tree essential oil and lemon juice or vinegar. Mix thoroughly to disperse oil. Add water and stir to combine. Leaning over a sink or in the shower, pour over hair after shampooing and rinsing.

Heartburn
See Digestive Problems (page 217)

Heat Exhaustion
See Sunstroke and Heatstroke (page 315)

Heat Rash (Prickly Heat)

Heat rash is an itchy, uncomfortable rash that occurs during hot weather when skin hasn't been able to "breathe" and sweat to evaporate. Wear natural fibers such as cotton, and loose or as little clothing as possible.

Essential Oils

Eucalyptus, lavender

Treatment
Bath: Fill tub with warm water. Meanwhile, in a small non-reactive bowl, combine 8 drops lavender essential oil and 1 cup (250 mL) baking soda. Add to tub and agitate to disperse oil, then soak for 30 minutes, keeping the itchy rash underwater

and massaging any floating droplets of oil into your skin. After bathing, pat rather than rub the skin dry. For children, use the amounts of essential oil recommended in Babies and Children (page 164), and halve the amount of baking soda.

Heat Rash Anti-itch Spray

1 tsp (5 mL)	vodka
40 drops	lavender essential oil
35 drops	*Eucalyptus smithii* essential oil
4 tsp (20 mL)	witch hazel hydrolat (alcohol-free)
	Distilled or filtered water

In a 4 oz (125 mL) PET plastic spray bottle, combine vodka and lavender and eucalyptus essential oils. Add witch hazel and shake to blend. Fill bottle with water and shake again to combine. Shake before each use. Spray the affected areas and allow to air-dry.

Hepatitis
See Liver (page 261)

Herpes

There are numerous viruses in the herpes family. Herpes simplex 1 is responsible for those painful fever blisters and cold sores on the lips. It can be transmitted through contact with any discharge and spread by kissing or sharing toothbrushes.

Herpes simplex 2, generally contracted through sexual contact with an infected person, produces sores on and around the genitals, anus and buttocks; although they are mostly found below the waist, the sores can also be found elsewhere. The disease can be spread even when sores are not present.

Herpes zoster, or shingles, is a painful skin rash caused by the varicella-zoster virus, which is responsible for chicken pox. The virus may lie dormant for years but can recur when triggered by stress, too much sun or minor infections. See Immune System (page 252) for treatments that may help to avoid outbreaks.

Essential Oils

Herpes simplex 1: anise, bergamot, cajuput, cedarwood, chamomile, cypress, *Eucalyptus globulus*, ginger, hyssop, spike lavender, manuka, marjoram, melissa, sandalwood, tea tree, thyme ct. thymol

Tips

If you prefer, when making an air spray, substitute Solubol for the vodka called for, in a ratio of 4 drops Solubol for every 1 drop essential oil. Solubol is a natural product that allows essential oils to disperse in liquid.

Solubol contains glycerin, sunflower and coconut oils and other beneficial extracts.

Herpes simplex 2: cedarwood, chamomile, cypress, *Eucalyptus globulus*, juniper, spike lavender, manuka, marjoram, melissa, sandalwood, tea tree

Herpes zoster: bergamot, *Eucalyptus globulus*, geranium, manuka, melissa, myrrh, niaouli, ravensara, tea tree

---

Herpes Simplex 1 Blend

3 drops	tea tree essential oil
2 drops	bergamot essential oil
1 drop	*Eucalyptus globulus* essential oil
1 tsp (5 mL)	St. John's wort–infused oil

In a small non-reactive bowl, combine tea tree, bergamot and eucalyptus essential oils with St. John's wort–infused oil.

Treatment
Topical application: Using a cotton ball, dab blisters and sores with Herpes Simplex 1 Blend. Repeat twice daily until the sores diminish in size and appear to be dry and healing.

Herpes Simplex 2 Blend

4 drops	bergamot essential oil
4 drops	*Eucalyptus globulus* essential oil
4 drops	melissa essential oil
4 drops	manuka essential oil
4 drops	sandalwood or cedarwood essential oil

In a ⅙ oz (5 mL) glass dropper bottle, combine bergamot, eucalyptus, melissa, manuka and sandalwood essential oils. Shake to blend.

Treatment
Topical application: In a small non-reactive bowl, combine Herpes Simplex 2 Blend and 4 tsp (20 mL) aloe vera gel. Mix thoroughly. Using a cotton ball, gently dab the external lesions. Repeat every 2 hours until the sores diminish in size and appear to be dry and healing (usually within 7 to 10 days).

Shingles Blend 1

60 drops	bergamot essential oil
60 drops	*Eucalyptus globulus* essential oil
60 drops	tea tree essential oil
18 drops	melissa essential oil

In a ⅓ oz (10 mL) glass bottle, combine bergamot, eucalyptus, tea tree and melissa essential oils. Shake to blend.

Treatments

Air and body spray: In a 4 oz (125 mL) PET plastic spray bottle, combine 165 drops (6 mL) Shingles Blend 1 and 1 tsp (5 mL) glycerin. Shake to blend. Fill bottle with filtered or distilled water (see Tips, right). Shake vigorously before each use. Spray as desired.

Bath: Fill tub with warm water. Meanwhile, in a small non-reactive bowl, combine 1 tsp (5 mL) milk and 4 to 6 drops Shingles Blend 1. Mix thoroughly. Add to water, agitate to disperse oil, then soak for 30 minutes, inhaling the vapors and massaging any floating droplets of oil into your skin.

Shingles Blend 2

2 tsp (10 mL)	tamanu oil
6 drops	ravensara essential oil

In a small non-reactive bowl, combine tamanu oil and ravensara essential oil.

Treatment

Topical application: Using a cotton ball, apply Shingles Blend 2 to affected area every 2 hours. Continue for 7 to 10 days, until the bumps are gone and pain has subsided.

Tips

If you prefer, when making an air spray, substitute Solubol for the vodka called for, in a ratio of 4 drops Solubol for every 1 drop essential oil. Solubol is a natural product that allows essential oils to disperse in liquid.

When making air sprays, be sure to add the oils to the bottle first, followed by the chosen dispersant (glycerin or Solubol), to ensure that the essential oils disperse properly (they will not mix directly with water).

Hiccups

There are as many "cures" for hiccups as there are for warts! Give these a try.

Essential Oils

Roman chamomile, lavender, mandarin

Treatments

Ingestion: Add 1 drop mandarin essential oil to either a sugar cube or ½ tsp (2.5 mL) sugar. Suck sugar slowly until dissolved.

Inhalation: Place 1 drop lavender or chamomile essential oil inside a paper bag and hold the bag over your nose and mouth. Breathe in and out slowly until the hiccups stop (give it a few minutes).

Hot Flashes
See Women's Health (page 334)

Hypertension
See Blood Pressure (page 187)

Immune System

A strong and healthy immune system protects us from recurring colds and flu, candidiasis, chronic fatigue and many other disorders. To enhance and strengthen this system, try to stay positive, laugh and hug a lot, eat plenty of good nutritious food, stay active and get enough restful sleep. Immune-boosting natural supplements such as astragalus (*Astragalus membranaceus*), reishi mushroom (*Ganoderma lucidum*) and privet fruit (*Ligustrum lucidum*) are available from health-food stores. If taken in conjunction with aromatherapy treatments they will strengthen the immune system very quickly.

Essential Oils

Eucalyptus radiata, frankincense, lavender, manuka, niaouli, patchouli, tea tree, thyme ct. linalool, vetiver

Tips

If you prefer, when making an air spray, substitute Solubol for the vodka called for, in a ratio of 4 drops Solubol for every 1 drop essential oil. Solubol is a natural product that allows essential oils to disperse in liquid.

When making air sprays, be sure to add the oils to the bottle first, followed by the chosen dispersant (vodka or Solubol), to ensure that the essential oils disperse properly (they will not mix directly with water).

Immune System Booster Blend

1 tsp (5 mL)	lavender essential oil
60 drops	*Eucalyptus radiata* essential oil
20 drops	vetiver essential oil
20 drops	tea tree or manuka essential oil

In a ⅓ oz (10 mL) glass dropper bottle, combine lavender, eucalyptus, vetiver and tea tree essential oils. Shake to blend.

Treatments

Air spray: In a 4 oz (125 mL) PET plastic spray bottle, combine 75 drops Immune System Booster Blend and 1 tsp (5 mL) vodka. Fill bottle with distilled or filtered water (see Tips, page 252).

Bath: Fill tub with warm water. Meanwhile, in a small non-reactive bowl, combine 1 tsp (5 mL) milk and 6 drops Immune System Booster Blend. Add to tub and agitate to disperse oil, then soak for 30 minutes, massaging any floating droplets of oil into your skin.

Inhaler: Place 21 drops Immune System Booster Blend in a small non-reactive bowl. Place inhaler wick in the bowl and allow it to absorb the entire amount. Insert the wick inside the inhaler tube and tightly cap the bottom of the inhaler with the plug. Place the inhaler tube inside its cover and screw tightly to close.

Massage: In a small non-reactive bowl, combine 2 tsp (10 mL) grapeseed or sweet almond oil and 4 drops Immune System Booster Blend. Mix well and massage over your body.

Indigestion
See Digestive Problems (page 217)

Inflammation

Inflammation indicates that the body is responding to cell damage by bringing increased blood supply and heat to the area. It's only necessary to deal with inflammation if the area becomes very painful.

Tips

Do not add essential oils to the tub while the water is running, as some of the precious essences may evaporate, depriving you of the full benefits.

If you prefer, substitute an equal quantity of liquid castile soap for the milk called for in any bath recipe.

If you are using a blend around bath/ shower time, you can enhance the benefit by combining the essential oils with a carrier oil and rub it into your skin *before* getting into the shower or bath. This enables the essential oils to be absorbed and work their way into the bloodstream. The heat of the water encourages the essential oil vapors to rise, allowing you to inhale the aromas more easily and thus creating a dual application.

Essential Oils

Cedarwood, German chamomile, clary sage, *Eucalyptus globulus*, frankincense, geranium, helichrysum, lavender, myrrh, plai, rose, sandalwood, yarrow

Treatment

Cool compress: Pour 1 cup (250 mL) cold water into a non-reactive bowl and add 4 to 6 drops (as age-appropriate; see page 164) chamomile (particularly useful), lavender or myrrh essential oil. Stir well to disperse oil. Soak a cloth and wring out enough water so cloth doesn't drip. Place cloth on affected area. Repeat often.

Influenza

See Common Cold and Influenza (page 203)

Insect Bites

See Bites and Stings (page 185)

Insect Repellent

Essential oils can provide effective protection from mosquitoes and biting flies such as gnats, blackflies and horseflies.

Essential Oils

Catnip, cedarwood, citronella, lemongrass, peppermint

See Common Cold and Influenza (page 203)

See Bites and Stings (page 185)

Tip

The sesame oil in this repellent also offers UV protection in the sun.

Caution

Do not use this insect repellent on children. Cajuput may cause distress to a child's nervous system and breathing problems.

Mosquito and Sandfly Repellent

35 drops	catnip essential oil
15 drops	lemongrass essential oil
10 drops	geranium essential oil
5 drops	cajuput essential oil
5 drops	lemon essential oil
5 drops	mandarin essential oil
3 drops	cedarwood essential oil
½ cup (125 mL)	sesame oil

In a 4 oz (125 mL) PET plastic spray bottle, combine catnip, lemongrass, geranium, cajuput, lemon, mandarin and cedarwood essential oils. Shake to blend. Fill bottle with sesame oil (see Tip). Spray on all exposed areas and massage into the skin, keeping well clear of the eyes. Reapply every 2 to 3 hours.

Insomnia

The occasional sleepless night isn't the same as real insomnia, which involves losing sleep on a regular basis. If you can't sleep, don't lie there tossing and turning. Get up and do something relatively relaxing, like reading a book or having a warm milky drink. Essential oils, used for massage, in the bath or with a diffuser or air spray, are an easy and pleasurable way to enhance your chances of getting a good night's sleep.

Essential Oils

Angelica, bergamot, cedarwood, Roman chamomile, cistus, clary sage, jasmine, lavender, mandarin, marjoram, melissa, sandalwood, spikenard, valerian, vetiver, ylang ylang

---

Deep Sleep Oil

45 drops	vetiver essential oil
20 drops	sandalwood or cedarwood essential oil
15 drops	ylang ylang essential oil

In a $1/6$ oz (5 mL) glass bottle, combine vetiver, sandalwood and ylang ylang essential oils. Shake to blend.

Treatments

For children who can't sleep, see Babies and Children (page 173).

Air spray: In a 4 oz (125 mL) PET plastic spray bottle, combine 75 drops Deep Sleep Oil and 1 tsp (5 mL) vodka. Fill bottle with distilled or filtered water. Shake to blend. Shake well before using.

Bath: Fill tub with warm water. Meanwhile, in a small non-reactive bowl, combine 1 tsp (5 mL) milk and 4 to 6 drops Deep Sleep Oil. Add to tub and agitate to disperse oil, then soak for 30 minutes, massaging any floating droplets of oil into your skin. Sip a cup of chamomile tea while having your bath.

Diffuser: Add 4 to 6 drops Deep Sleep Oil to a diffuser, according to the manufacturer's instructions (see Supplies and Equipment, page 459). Diffuse for 20 minutes before bed.

Tips

Do not add essential oils to the tub while the water is running, as some of the precious essences may evaporate, depriving you of the full benefits.

If you prefer, substitute an equal quantity of liquid castile soap for the milk called for in any bath recipe.

If you are using a blend around bath/shower time, you can enhance the benefit by combining the essential oils with a carrier oil and rub it into your skin *before* getting into the shower or bath. This enables the essential oils to be absorbed and work their way into the bloodstream. The heat of the water encourages the essential oil vapors to rise, allowing you to inhale the aromas more easily and thus creating a dual application.

Inhaler: Place 21 drops Deep Sleep Oil in a small non-reactive bowl. Place inhaler wick in the bowl and allow it to absorb the entire amount. Insert the wick inside the inhaler tube and tightly cap the bottom of the inhaler with the plug. Place the inhaler tube inside its cover and screw tightly to close.

Massage: In a small non-reactive bowl, combine 2 tsp (10 mL) grapeseed or sweet almond oil and 4 drops Deep Sleep Oil. Mix well and massage into your temples and the back of your neck.

Roll-on: Place 16 drops Deep Sleep Oil in a ⅓ oz (10 mL) glass bottle with roller ball. Top up with fractionated coconut oil (be careful not to overfill). Insert the ball holder, then the ball, and screw on the top. Shake to blend. Roll on collarbones and temples before bed.

Intertrigo

Intertrigo is a type of dermatitis caused by a bacterial, fungal or viral infection. It develops in the groin area, under the breasts and in other places where skin is in contact with skin. The infection can be very serious, so it is best to consult a dermatologist. Treatment typically includes compresses using an astringent known as Burow's solution, followed by air-drying the area and using a barrier cream. Natural options include wet teabag compresses and natural powders to keep the area dry.

Essential Oils

Geranium, lavender, rosemary, tea tree

Intertrigo Powder

1 cup (250 mL)	cornstarch
2 tsp (10 mL)	zinc oxide powder
20 drops	tea tree essential oil
20 drops	lavender essential oil
20 drops	rosemary essential oil

In a small non-reactive bowl, combine cornstarch and zinc oxide powder; stir well. A few drops at a time, and stirring constantly to prevent clumping, add tea tree, lavender and rosemary essential oils. Transfer to an airtight container and store in a cool, dark place.

Treatment

Wash and topical application: In a small non-reactive bowl, combine 4 drops tea tree essential oil and 1 tsp (5 mL) vinegar. Add 1 cup (250 mL) lukewarm water and agitate to combine. Using a cotton ball, wash the affected area. Gently pat skin dry with a very soft towel. Using a fresh cotton ball, dust skin lightly with Intertrigo Powder. Repeat 2 to 3 times a day.

Irritable Bowel Syndrome

Irritable bowel syndrome (IBS) has a variety of symptoms, including pain in the lower abdomen, abdominal bloating and cramping, constipation, diarrhea, flatulence and sometimes heartburn. No one knows for sure what causes IBS, which means that you need a professional assessment of possible factors such as diet and stress levels before you begin any home treatment.

Essential Oils

Catnip, chamomile, marjoram, peppermint, sage

IBS Massage Blend

¼ cup (60 mL)	grapeseed or sweet almond oil
12 drops	chamomile essential oil
12 drops	marjoram essential oil
8 drops	peppermint essential oil

In a small glass bottle, combine grapeseed oil and chamomile, marjoram and peppermint essential oils. Shake to blend. Massage over your abdomen in a clockwise direction, 2 to 3 times daily.

Itching (Pruritus)

The most embarrassing and awkward itch is pruritis ani, or itching of the anus (or the vulva), as you can't scratch it in public! Causes can range from inadequate washing or rinsing away of soap to antibiotics, allergic reaction to chemicals in toilet paper and toiletries, or wearing synthetic fabrics. Because the area is warm, dark and moist, it is the perfect breeding ground for fungi and bacteria.

Essential Oils

Bay laurel, bergamot, cedarwood, chamomile, geranium, lavender, myrrh, niaouli, peppermint, tea tree

---

Anti-itch Washing Blend

1 cup (250 mL)	witch hazel hydrolat (alcohol-free) or distilled or filtered water
1 tsp (5 mL)	liquid castile soap or unpasteurized liquid honey
40 drops	lavender essential oil
35 drops	niaouli essential oil

In an 8 oz (250 mL) glass or PET plastic bottle, combine witch hazel hydrolat, castile soap and lavender and niaouli essential oils. Shake to blend. Shake well before using. After using the toilet, moisten a cotton ball with Anti-itch Washing Blend and clean the affected area.

Anti-itch Oil Blend

2 tsp (10 mL)	grapeseed oil or aloe vera gel
3 drops	lavender essential oil
2 drops	chamomile or bergamot essential oil
1 drop	bay laurel or niaouli essential oil

In a ⅓ oz (10 mL) glass bottle, combine grapeseed oil and lavender, chamomile and bay laurel essential oils. Mix thoroughly. Stir well before using. After bathing, showering or washing, use a cotton ball to apply Anti-itch Oil Blend to the affected area.

Jet Lag
See Travel (page 323)

Jock Itch
See Men's Health (page 268)

Kidneys

The kidneys are wonderful, hard-working organs whose vital functions include removing excess water, waste products and toxic chemicals from the blood. If any of their functions are compromised, serious problems can arise. If a problem is suspected (pain in the kidney region, blood in the urine), consult a health-care practitioner immediately.

Essential Oils

Cardamom, cedarwood, German chamomile, cistus, fennel, geranium, ginger, grapefruit, helichrysum, juniper, lemon, lime, marjoram, rosemary ct. cineole, sandalwood, thyme ct. linalool, yarrow

---

Diuretic Oil Blend

12 drops	geranium essential oil
8 drops	fennel essential oil
8 drops	cedarwood essential oil
4 drops	rosemary ct. cineole essential oil

In a ⅙ (5 mL) glass bottle, combine geranium, fennel, cedarwood and rosemary essential oils. Shake to blend.

Treatments
Bath: Fill tub with warm water. Meanwhile, in a small non-reactive bowl, combine 1 tsp (5 mL) milk and 4 to 6 drops Diuretic Oil Blend. Add to tub and agitate to disperse oil, then soak for 30 minutes, massaging any floating droplets of oil into your skin.

Massage: In a small non-reactive bowl, combine 4 tsp (20 mL) grapeseed or sweet almond oil and 8 drops Diuretic Oil Blend. Mix well and massage over your body.

Labor
See Pregnancy and Birth (page 282)

Laryngitis
See Respiratory Problems (page 297)

Liver

The liver has many vital functions and is largely responsible for our health and energy. A few of the innumerable symptoms of a sluggish or otherwise malfunctioning liver are fatigue, allergic reactions, digestive problems, a feeling of being under the weather and PMS. The following massage blend will help to improve general liver health, but it needs to be combined with lifestyle changes as well.

Essential Oils

Basil ct. linalool, black pepper, chamomile, cypress, ginger, helichrysum, lemon, melissa, peppermint, rosemary, thyme

---

Healthy Liver Massage Oil

40 drops	rosemary essential oil
20 drops	chamomile essential oil
20 drops	lemon essential oil
5 drops	peppermint essential oil

In a $1/6$ oz (5 mL) glass bottle, combine rosemary, chamomile, lemon and peppermint essential oils. Shake to blend.

Treatment
Massage: In a small non-reactive bowl, combine 4 tsp (20 mL) grapeseed oil and 8 drops Healthy Liver Massage Oil. Mix well and massage over your body once or twice daily after bathing or showering. A professional lymphatic massage using the blend can be very helpful.

Hepatitis

Hepatitis means inflammation of the liver. There are several types—all contagious and all caused by related viruses; the most common types are hepatitis A, B and C. If you have hepatitis (or think you have), it is essential to consult your health-care practitioner. Symptoms can include fatigue, flulike symptoms, fever, jaundice, loss of appetite and/or nausea and dark urine. Body-brushing twice daily will improve circulation and excretion through the skin, and this in turn relieves the liver of some of its work. See a health-care practitioner for advice regarding diet.

Hepatitis Massage Oil

40 drops	chamomile essential oil
20 drops	basil or rosemary ct. cineole essential oil
20 drops	eucalyptus essential oil
10 drops	cypress essential oil
½ cup (125 mL)	mixed extra virgin olive and avocado oil

In a 4 oz (125 mL) glass bottle, combine chamomile, basil, eucalyptus and cypress essential oils. Add mixed olive and avocado oils and shake to blend. After bathing or showering, while your skin is still damp, pour a little into the palm of your hand and massage over your body.

Lumbago
See Back Pain (page 182)

Lymphatic System

The lymphatic system is the body's second circulatory system (the blood system is the first). Pressure from surrounding muscles keeps the flow of lymph moving around the body, which means that insufficient exercise equals inefficient lymph flow! Lymph is involved in draining body fluids and removing toxic wastes; it plays a key role in immune response and absorption of fat from the small intestine. Specialized lymphatic massage is of benefit to those who suffer from fluid retention, catarrh, headaches or migraine and an under-functioning immune system. (**Note:** Cancer patients should ask a practitioner specializing in manual lymphatic drainage [MLD]; see page 194.)

Do not add essential oils to the tub while the water is running, as some of the precious essences may evaporate, depriving you of the full benefits.

If you prefer, substitute an equal quantity of liquid castile soap for the milk called for in any bath recipe.

If you are using a blend around bath/shower time, you can enhance the benefit by combining the essential oils with a carrier oil and rub it into your skin *before* getting into the shower or bath. This enables the essential oils to be absorbed and work their way into the bloodstream. The heat of the water encourages the essential oil vapors to rise, allowing you to inhale the aromas more easily and thus creating a dual application.

Essential Oils

Black pepper, cedarwood, fennel, geranium, juniper, myrtle (green or orange), pine, rosemary

---

Lymphatic Massage and Bath Blend

15 drops   juniper essential oil
10 drops   rosemary essential oil
8 drops   geranium or black pepper essential oil

In a ¹⁄₆ oz (5 mL) glass bottle, combine juniper, rosemary and geranium essential oils. Shake to blend.

Treatments

Bath: Fill tub with warm water. Meanwhile, in a small non-reactive bowl, combine 1 tsp (5 mL) milk and 4 to 6 drops Lymphatic Massage and Bath Blend (see Tips, left). Add to tub and agitate to disperse oil, then soak for 30 minutes, massaging any floating droplets of oil into your skin.

Massage: In a small non-reactive bowl, combine 4 tsp (20 mL) grapeseed oil and 8 drops Lymphatic Massage and Bath Blend. Mix well and massage over your body. Use movements that travel from the hands up the arms and from the feet up the legs, toward the collarbone, paying special attention to the glands in the groin and armpits and underneath the collarbones.

Maturity and Old Age

Maturity and old age aren't a disease, or a reason to give up on life. In fact, this is the beginning of the "third age," that of the freedom to be yourself and to please yourself. Make getting older an opportunity to do the things you dreamed about during the busy years of earning money, paying the mortgage and raising children. You can now reap the benefits of the wisdom you have acquired over the years. You can travel and experience those places in the world that were once just names on the map. You can read books, write books (or poetry— there are fun weekend courses on these subjects), play golf or go bowling. You can learn to paint, take up swimming or yoga, listen uninterrupted to music, start a new hobby… Do we need to go on?

The way to keep mind and body young is to use them. Challenge yourself with projects that at first seem overly ambitious—you will find that much of what we perceive to be impossible is perfectly achievable. These days, people in their seventies and eighties are skydiving, whitewater rafting, writing first novels, starting new

businesses, and doing all kinds of things that a few years ago would have seemed impossible for the elderly, who were supposed to sink quietly and uncomplainingly into their twilight years.

The trick is to take care of yourself in order to get the maximum mileage out of that classic vintage body you inhabit.

- Swim or walk every day. It doesn't need to be a marathon—a half-hour stroll is fine.
- Do yoga every day. Yoga today will improve balance and allay equilibrium problems tomorrow.
- Eat well. Good, fresh food doesn't have to be time-consuming to prepare, and you need your nutrients in order to stave off serious illness.
- Sleep enough—but not too much.
- Laugh and hug a lot.

Essential oils can become a wonderfully therapeutic and aromatic part of your lifestyle. The blend suggestion below is meant for pleasure—to keep the atmosphere of your home tranquil and welcoming. For specific remedies using essential oils for skin and hair care or health problems, look under the relevant headings throughout the book.

Welcoming Home Blend

40 drops	lavender essential oil
40 drops	geranium essential oil
20 drops	sweet or blood orange essential oil
10 drops	sandalwood or cedarwood essential oil

In a ⅙ oz (5 mL) glass dropper bottle, combine lavender, geranium, orange and sandalwood essential oils. Shake to blend.

Treatments

Air spray: In a 4 oz (125 mL) PET plastic spray bottle, combine 75 drops Welcoming Home Blend and 1 tsp (5 mL) vodka. Add ¼ cup (60 mL) rose hydrolat and shake to combine. Fill bottle with distilled or filtered water.

Inhaler: Place 21 drops Welcoming Home blend in a small non-reactive bowl. Place inhaler wick in the bowl and allow it to absorb the entire amount. Insert the wick inside the inhaler tube and tightly cap the bottom of the inhaler with the plug. Place the inhaler tube inside its cover and screw tightly to close.

Myalgic Encephalomyelitis (ME)
See Chronic Fatigue Syndrome (page 199)

> **Tip**
>
> Using a dispersant such as Solubol (see page 156) will enable essential oils to mix with water.

Measles

Measles should never be treated lightly, as it is potentially a very serious disease that can lead to secondary infections of the eyes, ears and chest. It is best to confine the patient during the contagious period. Complete bed rest is essential to help to avoid complications. Give sponge baths to reduce high temperature. Keep both the bedroom and the rest of the house sprayed with the following blend to help prevent the spread of infection. It is important to consult your doctor if your child has measles, but there are also things you can do to reduce the discomfort of the symptoms.

Essential Oils

Cypress, eucalyptus, geranium, lavender, lemon, rosemary, tea tree

---

Anti-infection Blend for Measles

34 drops	lavender essential oil
17 drops	geranium essential oil
17 drops	rosemary essential oil
17 drops	lemon essential oil

In a $\frac{1}{6}$ oz (5 mL) glass bottle, combine lavender, geranium, rosemary and lemon essential oils. Shake to blend.

Treatments

Air spray: In a 4 oz (125 mL) PET plastic spray bottle, combine 75 drops Anti-infection Blend for Measles and 1 tsp (5 mL) vodka. Fill bottle with distilled or filtered water (see Tips, left).

Bath: This bath will soothe the itching and has the added advantage of making young patients calmer. Fill the tub with warm water. Meanwhile, in a small non-reactive bowl, combine 4 to 6 drops lavender essential oil and $\frac{1}{2}$ cup (125 mL) baking soda. Add to tub and agitate to disperse oil, then soak the patient for 30 minutes, massaging any floating droplets of oil into the skin.

Lotion: In a non-reactive bowl, combine 15 drops lavender and 5 drops niaouli essential oils and $\frac{1}{4}$ cup (60 mL) carrot seed macerated oil (the carrot seed oil helps relieve itching). Pour into a 2 oz (60 mL) PET plastic or glass bottle. Fill the bottle to the shoulder with unscented lotion and shake vigorously to blend. Using a cotton ball, dab the lotion on the itchy spots as often as needed.

Tips

If you prefer, substitute Solubol (see Resources, page 459) for the vodka in a ratio of 4 drops Solubol for every 1 drop essential oil.

When making air sprays, be sure to add the oils to the bottle first, followed by the chosen dispersant (vodka or Solubol), to ensure that the essential oils disperse properly (they will not mix directly with water).

Caution

Do not use carrot seed macerated oil if pregnant.

Memory

Forgetfulness is usually nothing more sinister than a lack of attention, and it affects everyone from the very young to the very old. As we get older, we become more afraid that our simple forgetfulness is a sign of Alzheimer's or senile dementia. This fear can paralyze us and hamper efforts at improving our memories. Remember—use it or lose it! We can do things to keep our brains in optimum condition. The herb known as ginkgo biloba has been shown to improve blood supply to the brain and to increase the rate at which information is transmitted to the brain.

Essential Oils

Basil ct. linalool, black pepper, ginger, grapefruit, lemon, rosemary, sage, Spanish sage

---

Memory Sharpener Blend

30 drops	basil ct. linalool essential oil
30 drops	rosemary or Spanish sage essential oil
18 drops	lemon essential oil
18 drops	black pepper essential oil

In a $^1/_6$ oz (5 mL) glass bottle, combine basil, rosemary, lemon and black pepper essential oils. Shake to blend.

Treatments

Air spray: In a 4 oz (125 mL) PET plastic spray bottle, combine 75 drops Memory Sharpener Blend and 1 tsp (5 mL) vodka. Fill with distilled or filtered water (see Tips, page 264). Shake to blend.

Bath: Fill tub with warm water. Meanwhile, in a small non-reactive bowl, combine 1 tsp (5 mL) milk and 4 to 6 drops Memory Sharpener Blend (see Tips, right). Add to tub and agitate to disperse oil, then soak for 30 minutes, massaging any floating droplets of oil into your skin.

Inhaler: Place 25 drops Memory Sharpener Blend in a small non-reactive bowl. Place inhaler wick in the bowl and allow it to absorb the entire amount. Insert the wick inside the inhaler tube and tightly cap the bottom of the inhaler with the plug. Place the inhaler tube inside its cover and screw tightly to close.

Massage: In a small non-reactive bowl, combine 4 tsp (20 mL) grapeseed or sweet almond oil and 8 drops Memory Sharpener Blend. Mix well and massage over your body.

Tips

Do not add essential oils to the tub while the water is running, as some of the precious essences may evaporate, depriving you of the full benefits.

If you prefer, substitute an equal quantity of liquid castile soap for the milk called for in any bath recipe.

If you are using a blend around bath/ shower time, you can enhance the benefit by combining the essential oils with a carrier oil and rub it into your skin *before* getting into the shower or bath. This enables the essential oils to be absorbed and work their way into the bloodstream. The heat of the water encourages the essential oil vapors to rise, allowing you to inhale the aromas more easily and thus creating a dual application.

Men's Health

Research suggests that men are less likely to engage in even the most basic preventive care, such as cholesterol or blood pressure monitoring. Some experts believe this is because society teaches men to be "tough," which may lead them to brush off the warning signs of serious health problems. A healthy lifestyle, including good nutrition, exercise and reducing stress, can help to lessen the chances of serious illness later. Aromatherapy can help as well.

Essential Oils

To stimulate circulation: black pepper, clary sage, cypress, eucalyptus, fennel, geranium, ginger, hyssop, lemon, marjoram, peppermint, sweet orange, rose, rosemary (ct. cineole or ct. camphor), sage

To reduce stress: Canadian balsam, basil ct. linalool, bergamot, cedarwood, chamomile, clary sage, cypress, frankincense, *Litsea cubeba*, manuka, marjoram, sandalwood

---

Heart's Ease Blend

This recipe will improve circulation, reduce stress and aid in lowering blood pressure.

30 drops	lavender essential oil
30 drops	clary sage essential oil
15 drops	sweet orange essential oil
15 drops	rosemary essential oil
8 drops	marjoram essential oil

In a ⅙ oz (5 mL) glass bottle, combine lavender, clary sage, orange, rosemary and marjoram essential oils. Shake to blend.

Treatments

Air spray: In a 4 oz (125 mL) PET plastic spray bottle, combine 75 drops Heart's Ease Blend and 1 tsp (5 mL) vodka. Fill with distilled or filtered water (see Tips, left). Shake to blend.

Bath: Fill tub with warm water. Meanwhile, in a small non-reactive bowl, combine 1 tsp (5 mL) milk and 4 to 6 drops Heart's Ease Blend (see Tips, page 267). Add to tub and agitate to disperse oil, then soak for 30 minutes, massaging any floating droplets of oil into your skin.

Caution

Before using any essential oil, consult the relevant entry in Part 1: Essential Oils (A to Y), pages 28 to 117, taking careful note of any cautions.

Tips

If you prefer, when making an air spray, substitute Solubol for the vodka called for, in a ratio of 4 drops Solubol for every 1 drop essential oil. Solubol is a natural product that allows essential oils to disperse in liquid.

When making air sprays, be sure to add the oils to the bottle first, followed by the chosen dispersant (vodka or Solubol), to ensure that the essential oils disperse properly (they will not mix directly with water).

Inhaler: Place 21 drops Heart's Ease Blend in a small non-reactive bowl. Place inhaler wick in the bowl and allow it to absorb the entire amount. Insert the wick inside the inhaler tube and tightly cap the bottom of the inhaler with the plug. Place the inhaler tube inside its cover and screw tightly to close.

Massage: In a small non-reactive bowl, combine 4 tsp (20 mL) grapeseed or sweet almond oil and 8 drops Heart's Ease Blend. Mix well and massage over your body.

Impotence

Women these days have such high expectations of sex that men are often completely intimidated and can become impotent because of "performance anxiety." Work stresses and money worries add to the load, until everything becomes too much. Let's see what a little tenderness and sharing can achieve.

Essential Oils

Anise, black pepper, cedarwood, clary sage, clove, ginger, jasmine, neroli, nutmeg, peppermint, pine, rose, rosemary (ct. cineole and ct. camphor), sandalwood, vetiver, ylang ylang

---

Loving Touch Blend

You and your partner can make a pact that for as long as it takes—maybe months—you will give each other lots of TLC without any expectation of intercourse. Take time to enjoy shared sensual experiences without the stress of "performing."

20 drops	sandalwood essential oil
20 drops	cedarwood essential oil
15 drops	clary sage essential oil
10 drops	rosewood essential oil

In a ⅙ oz (5 mL) glass bottle, combine sandalwood, cedarwood, clary sage and rosewood essential oils. Shake to blend.

Treatments

Bath: Fill tub with warm water. Meanwhile, in a small non-reactive bowl, combine 1 tsp (5 mL) milk and 4 to 6 drops Loving Touch Blend. Add to tub and agitate to disperse oil, then soak (sharing the bath, perhaps) for 30 minutes, massaging any floating droplets of oil into your (or each other's) skin.

Tips

Do not add essential oils to the tub while the water is running, as some of the precious essences may evaporate, depriving you of the full benefits.

If you prefer, substitute an equal quantity of liquid castile soap for the milk called for in any bath recipe.

If you are using a blend around bath/ shower time, you can enhance the benefit by combining the essential oils with a carrier oil and rub it into your skin *before* getting into the shower or bath. This enables the essential oils to be absorbed and work their way into the bloodstream. The heat of the water encourages the essential oil vapors to rise, allowing you to inhale the aromas more easily and thus creating a dual application.

Tip

Wear cotton boxer shorts and, if possible, loose-fitting cotton or wool trousers.

Massage: In a small non-reactive bowl, combine 4 tsp (20 mL) grapeseed or sweet almond oil and 8 drops Loving Touch Blend. Mix well and take turns massaging each other's bodies.

Jock Itch

"Jock itch" is a fungal infection of the groin area related to athlete's foot. It is often caused by wearing underpants and/or trousers that are too tight and that are made of synthetic material. The perspiration can't evaporate and the area becomes a perfect breeding ground for the fungus. The condition is typified by small itchy red spots that can become very sore.

Essential Oils

Cedarwood, geranium, lavender, tea tree

Treatments
Massage: In a small non-reactive bowl, combine 2 tsp (10 mL) grapeseed oil and 2 drops each tea tree and lavender essential oils. Mix well and massage over itchy area 2 to 3 times a day.

Wash: In a small non-reactive bowl, combine 4 to 6 drops lavender essential oil, 1 tsp (5 ml) liquid castile soap and $\frac{1}{2}$ cup (125 mL) distilled or filtered water. Using a clean cloth, wash the affected area carefully twice a day. Dry gently but thoroughly.

Prostatitis

Prostatitis is an infection that causes a burning sensation when passing urine, pain and tenderness in the pelvic area and lower back, fever and exhaustion. The suggestions in this section should be followed only after examination by a health-care practitioner has ruled out anything more serious.

Essential Oils

Chamomile, cypress, eucalyptus, lavender, myrrh, myrtle (green or orange), naiouli, pine, yarrow

Prostatitis Bath and Massage Blend

15 drops	cypress essential oil
15 drops	myrtle essential oil
10 drops	lavender or chamomile essential oil
10 drops	myrrh essential oil

In a ¹⁄₆ oz (5 mL) glass bottle, combine cypress, myrtle, lavender and myrrh essential oils. Shake to blend.

Treatments

Bath: Fill tub with warm water. Meanwhile, in a small non-reactive bowl, combine 1 tsp (5 mL) milk and 4 to 6 drops Prostatitis Bath and Massage Blend. Add to tub and agitate to disperse oil, then soak for 30 minutes, massaging any floating droplets of oil into your skin.

Massage: In a small non-reactive bowl, combine 2 tsp (10 mL) grapeseed oil and 4 drops Prostatitis Bath and Massage Blend. Mix well and massage over your abdomen and lower back.

Menopause
See Women's Health (page 333)

Menstruation
See Women's Health (page 337)

See Women's Health (page 333)

See Women's Health (page 337)

Tips

Do not add essential oils to the tub while the water is running, as some of the precious essences may evaporate, depriving you of the full benefits.

If you prefer, substitute an equal quantity of liquid castile soap for the milk called for in any bath recipe.

If you are using a blend around bath/shower time, you can enhance the benefit by combining the essential oils with a carrier oil and rub it into your skin *before* getting into the shower or bath. This enables the essential oils to be absorbed and work their way into the bloodstream. The heat of the water encourages the essential oil vapors to rise, allowing you to inhale the aromas more easily and thus creating a dual application.

Migraine

Migraine is not just a bad headache! There are many triggers, including food allergies and stress. Essential oil treatments are useful, especially as a preventive measure.

Essential Oils

Anise, basil ct. linalool, Roman chamomile, *Eucalyptus globulus*, lavandin, lavender, marjoram, peppermint, rosemary (ct. cineole and ct. camphor)

Treatment

Cold compress: *This treatment may help when the blood vessels are beginning to dilate.* Pour 2 cups (500 mL) cold water into a non-reactive bowl and add 4 to 6 drops lavender and/or peppermint essential oil. Stir well to disperse oils. Soak a cloth and wring out enough water so cloth doesn't drip. Apply compress to forehead every 2 hours. Practice some stress-relieving deep breathing.

Tips

If you suffer from migraines, consult a health-care practitioner regarding food intolerances. Learning stress-management techniques may also be helpful.

Tips

If you prefer, substitute Solubol (see Resources, page 459) for the vodka in a ratio of 4 drops Solubol for every 1 drop essential oil.

When making air sprays, be sure to add the oils to the bottle first, followed by the chosen dispersant (vodka or Solubol), to ensure that the essential oils disperse properly (they will not mix directly with water).

Melting Migraine Blend

This recipe contains numerous essential oils so that the user cannot distinguish any one aroma and associate it with migraines. (Using just one or two essential oils makes it likely that a particular oil will become associated with migraines, triggering undesirable symptoms.)

27 drops	peppermint essential oil
24 drops	*Eucalyptus globulus* essential oil
17 drops	rosemary ct. cineole essential oil
10 drops	Roman chamomile essential oil
10 drops	ginger essential oil
10 drops	melissa essential oil
7 drops	*Eucalyptus staigeriana* essential oil
5 drops	lavender essential oil
4 drops	basil essential oil
3 drops	anise essential oil

In a ¹⁄₆ oz (5 mL) glass bottle, combine peppermint, Eucalyptus globulus, rosemary, chamomile, ginger, melissa, E. staigeriana, lavender, basil and anise essential oils. Shake to blend.

Treatments

Air spray: In a 4 oz (125 mL) PET plastic spray bottle, combine 75 drops Melting Migraine Blend and 1 tsp (5 mL) vodka. Fill bottle with distilled or filtered water (see Tips, page 270).

Bath: Fill tub with warm water. Meanwhile, in a small non-reactive bowl, combine 1 tsp (5 mL) milk and 4 to 6 drops Melting Migraine Blend. Add to tub and agitate to disperse oil, then soak for 30 minutes, massaging any floating droplets of oil into your skin.

Inhaler: Place 25 drops Melting Migraine Blend in a small non-reactive bowl. Place inhaler wick in the bowl and allow it to absorb the entire amount. Insert the wick inside the inhaler tube and tightly cap the bottom of the inhaler with the plug. Place the inhaler tube inside its cover and screw tightly to close. Inhale as needed.

Using Inhaler Sticks

Place inhaler tube under your nose. With one finger pressing closed your left nostril, inhale through the right nostril. Then close the right nostril with your finger and inhale through the left. Repeat on each side one more time. Exhale through the mouth, not the nose.

Mononucleosis (Infectious)

Infectious mononucleosis, also known as glandular fever, most commonly occurs in young adults; it is sometimes called the "kissing disease" or "student flu." The Epstein-Barr virus (a member of the herpes family) is the cause. After the acute phase, its symptoms are typified by extreme lethargy that can last for months. See Chronic Fatigue Syndrome (page 199) for treatment suggestions.

Morning Sickness
See Pregnancy and Birth (page 283)

Do not add essential oils to the tub while the water is running, as some of the precious essences may evaporate, depriving you of the full benefits.

If you prefer, substitute an equal quantity of liquid castile soap for the milk called for in any bath recipe.

If you are using a blend around bath/shower time, you can enhance the benefit by combining the essential oils with a carrier oil and rub it into your skin *before* getting into the shower or bath. This enables the essential oils to be absorbed and work their way into the bloodstream. The heat of the water encourages the essential oil vapors to rise, allowing you to inhale the aromas more easily and thus creating a dual application.

Mouth Ulcers

If you have frequently recurring mouth ulcers, you will continue to be plagued with them until you find the cause. Some of the causes are a poor diet low in vitamins B and C, stress, ill-fitting dentures, a rough edge on a tooth, biting the tongue or the inside of the cheek, and food allergies. Mouth ulcers can also indicate a more serious underlying condition, such as irritable bowel syndrome, celiac disease or some other immune system disorder.

Essential Oils

Clove (bud), geranium, lemon, myrrh, tea tree

Treatment

In a glass, combine 1 cup (250 mL) warm water, 1 drop myrrh oil or $\frac{1}{4}$ tsp (1 mL) tincture of myrrh, 1 tsp (5 mL) baking soda, and a pinch of sea salt. Stir to combine. Rinse your mouth several times with the mixture, swishing it around as vigorously as possible, and then spit it out (do not swallow the mixture). Repeat until the glass is empty.

Multiple Sclerosis

Multiple sclerosis (MS) is a chronic disease that affects twice as many women as men; it usually strikes between the ages of 20 and 50. It can affect muscles, eyesight, speech, and bladder and bowels. Exercise and physiotherapy can reduce the symptoms and maintain joint flexibility and balance. Chronic fatigue is a common problem affecting MS sufferers. Most people with MS take medication by injection, which causes a skin reaction and itching. Essential oils can help relieve the itching and irritation at the injection site.

Treatments

Use the blends recommended for Chronic Fatigue Syndrome (page 199), Muscles (page 214) and Stress and Emotional Problems (page 310), as needed.

Pain and Itch Relief Oil for MS

8 drops	basil essential oil
4 drops	lavender essential oil
3 drops	rosemary essential oil
2 drops	Roman chamomile essential oil
½ tsp (2.5 mL)	calendula-infused oil
½ tsp (2.5 mL)	St. John's wort–infused oil
	Grapeseed or sweet almond oil

In a ⅙ oz (10 mL) bottle with roll-on applicator, combine basil, lavender, rosemary and Roman chamomile essential oils. Shake to blend. Add calendula- and St. John's wort–infused oils and shake again. Top up with grapeseed or sweet almond oil (be careful not to overfill). Insert the ball holder, then the ball, and screw on the top. Shake to blend.

Roll Pain and Itch Relief Oil for MS in a circular pattern around the injection site—not on it—10 minutes before injecting medication.

Mumps

Mumps is a viral infection characterized by swollen glands on one or both sides of the jaw and possibly earache, mild fever and headache. The very uncomfortable stage usually lasts for only a few days, but during this time bed rest is essential to avoid complications. The swollen glands under the ears may make the patient very miserable, as it becomes painful to eat or swallow.

Essential Oils

Lavender, lemon, niaouli, tea tree

Swollen Glands Blend

20 drops	lavender essential oil
20 drops	lemon or niaouli essential oil
10 drops	tea tree essential oil

In a ⅙ oz (5 mL) glass bottle, combine lavender, lemon and tea tree essential oils. Shake to blend.

If you prefer, when making an air spray, substitute Solubol for the vodka called for, in a ratio of 4 drops Solubol for every 1 drop essential oil. Solubol is a natural product that allows essential oils to disperse in liquid.

When making air sprays, be sure to add the oils to the bottle first, followed by the chosen dispersant (vodka or Solubol), to ensure that the essential oils disperse properly (they will not mix directly with water).

Treatments

Air spray: In a 4 oz (125 mL) PET plastic spray bottle, combine 20 drops each tea tree, lavender, lemon and niaouli essential oils and 1 tsp (5 mL) vodka. Fill bottle with distilled or filtered water (see Tips, left).

Cool compress: Pour 2 cups (500 mL) cool (not icy) water into a non-reactive bowl and add 2 to 3 drops Swollen Glands Blend. Stir well to disperse oils. Soak a cloth and wring out enough water so cloth doesn't drip. Place cloth on affected area; repeat often.

Inhaler: Place 21 drops Swollen Glands Blend in a small non-reactive bowl. Place inhaler wick in the bowl and allow it to absorb the entire amount. Insert the wick inside the inhaler tube and tightly cap the bottom of the inhaler with the plug. Place the inhaler tube inside its cover and screw tightly to close.

Massage: In a small non-reactive bowl, combine 6 drops Swollen Glands Blend and 2 tsp (10 mL) grapeseed or sweet almond oil. Massage painful glands and entire neck area. Cover the neck with a scarf or cloth.

Muscles

Muscles that aren't regularly exercised can punish us if we suddenly plunge into vigorous activity. There is a real danger of muscle strain in these situations.

Essential Oils

Black pepper, *Eucalyptus smithii*, juniper, lavender, manuka, marjoram, nutmeg, peppermint, rosemary (ct. cineole and ct. camphor); arnica-infused oil

---

Muscle Relief Massage Oil

If your muscles are extremely sore, don't expect the pain to subside after a single massage. You might have to give yourself the "bath and massage" treatment for 2 to 3 days before your muscles have completely recovered.

15 drops	juniper essential oil
15 drops	marjoram essential oil
10 drops	rosemary essential oil
5 drops	black pepper essential oil

In a ¹⁄₆ oz (5 mL) glass bottle, combine juniper, marjoram, rosemary and black pepper essential oils. Shake to blend.

> ## Sore Muscle Soak
>
> | | |
> |---|---|
> | 1 cup (250 mL) | Epsom salts |
> | 3 drops | lavender essential oil |
> | 3 drops | juniper essential oil |
> | 2 drops | peppermint essential oil |
> | 2 drops | black pepper essential oil |
>
> *Fill tub with warm water. Meanwhile, pour Epsom salts into a small non-reactive bowl. Add, 1 drop at a time and stirring after each addition, lavender, juniper, peppermint and black pepper essential oils. Mix thoroughly. Add to tub and agitate to disperse oils, then soak for 30 minutes, gently massaging your sore muscles under the water.*

Treatments

Massage: In a small non-reactive bowl, combine 4 tsp (20 mL) grapeseed oil and 8 drops Muscle Relief Massage Oil. Mix well and massage over your body.

Alternatively, combine 3 drops Muscle Relief Massage Oil with 1 tsp (5 mL) arnica-infused oil in the palm of your hand. Massage over smaller areas that are particularly sore (but not if the skin is broken).

Nausea

Nausea and that awful feeling of wanting to vomit can be the result of smelling something putrid, seeing something really distressing, overeating or drinking too much, fever, migraine, early pregnancy or motion sickness. See also Motion Sickness (page 324) and Vomiting (page 327).

Essential Oils

Bergamot, cardamom, geranium, grapefruit, lavender, peppermint, spearmint

Treatments

Inhaler: In a small non-reactive bowl, combine 5 drops each bergamot, cardamom, grapefruit and spearmint essential oils and 3 drops geranium essential oil. Place inhaler wick in the bowl and allow it to absorb the entire amount. Insert the wick inside the inhaler tube and tightly cap the bottom of the inhaler with the plug. Place the inhaler tube inside its cover and screw tightly to close.

Inhalation: Place 2 drops peppermint or lavender essential oil inside a paper bag. Secure the open bag over your nose and mouth and inhale deeply. If you don't have a paper bag, put 1 drop peppermint or lavender essential oil on the palm of your hand and rub your hands together. Cup your palms over your nose and mouth and inhale deeply.

Soothing drink: In a glass, combine 1 drop peppermint essential oil, 1 tsp (5 mL) unpasteurized liquid honey (or Ginger Honey, page 205) and 1 cup (250 mL) warm water. Mix thoroughly. Sip slowly. Repeat as needed.

Caution
Do not use with young children.

Neuralgia

Neuralgia is an intense pain caused by triggering of a nerve. It is especially severe when it occurs in the face (known as trigeminal neuralgia).

Essential Oils

Cajuput, chamomile, citronella, clove, geranium, lavender, marjoram, nutmeg, peppermint, rosemary ct. cineole, sandalwood, yarrow; St. John's wort–infused oil

---

Neuralgia Oil Blend

6 drops	lavender essential oil
6 drops	chamomile essential oil
4 drops	rosemary ct. cineole essential oil

In a ⅙ oz (5 mL) glass bottle, combine lavender, chamomile and rosemary essential oils. Shake to blend.

Treatments

Apply either a cool or hot compress, whichever works for you.

Cool compress: Pour 2 cups (500 mL) cool (not icy) water into a non-reactive bowl and add 2 to 3 drops Neuralgia Oil Blend. Stir well to disperse oils. Soak a cloth and wring out enough water so cloth doesn't drip. Place cloth on affected area; repeat often.

Hot compress: In a small non-reactive bowl, combine 2 cups (500 mL) hot water and 3 to 4 drops Neuralgia Oil Blend. Stir well to disperse oils. Submerge a cloth just large enough to absorb all the liquid without dripping. Apply to affected area.

Massage: In a small non-reactive bowl, combine 1 tsp (5 mL) St. John's wort–infused oil, 3 tsp (15 mL) grapeseed or sweet almond oil, and 8 drops Neuralgia Oil Blend. Mix well. Place a few drops in the palm of your hand and massage along the affected nerve.

Nose (Blocked)

Essential Oils

Canadian balsam, cajuput, clove, *Eucalyptus dives*, lavandin, myrrh, niaouli, peppermint, rosemary, tea tree, thyme

Clear Air Blend

25 drops	cajuput essential oil
25 drops	*Eucalyptus dives* essential oil
13 drops	peppermint essential oil
8 drops	clove essential oil
5 drops	thyme essential oil

In a ¹⁄₆ oz (5 mL) glass bottle, combine cajuput, eucalyptus, peppermint, clove and thyme essential oils. Shake to blend.

Treatments

Air spray: In a 4 oz (125 mL) PET plastic spray bottle, combine 75 drops Clear Air Blend and 1 tsp (5 mL) vodka. Fill bottle with distilled or filtered water (see Tips, right).

Inhaler: Place 21 drops Clean Air Blend in a small non-reactive bowl. Place inhaler wick in the bowl and allow it to absorb the entire amount. Insert the wick inside the inhaler tube and tightly cap the bottom of the inhaler with the plug. Place the inhaler tube inside its cover and screw tightly to close. Inhale as needed to relieve stuffy nose.

Cautions

Do not use on or near the face of young children.

Do not use clove essential oil with young children.

Tips

If you prefer, when making an air spray, substitute Solubol for the vodka called for, in a ratio of 4 drops Solubol for every 1 drop essential oil. Solubol is a natural product that allows essential oils to disperse in liquid.

When making air sprays, be sure to add the oils to the bottle first, followed by the chosen dispersant (vodka or Solubol), to ensure that the essential oils disperse properly (they will not mix directly with water).

Tip

Buy essential oils one at a time and learn as much as you can about each before stocking up on more.

Obesity

Aromatherapy treatment can have positive benefits for those wishing to lose weight. It is obviously only part of a complex process, but along with counseling, changes in eating habits and gradual exercise, the use of essential oils can encourage a person to respect and love their body and develop a good self-image. Some overweight people may not want another person to see their body. They need to be assured that an aromatherapist is a practitioner who is trained to help and isn't judgmental. If, however, they prefer not to visit an aromatherapist, the massage section in this book will help a friend or partner learn to give a loving and therapeutic massage. Baths are also a valuable way by which to introduce essential oils into the bloodstream. The essential oils listed have properties that complement each other: they are diuretic, stimulant, tonic and hormone-balancing.

Essential Oils

Cypress, fennel, geranium, grapefruit, juniper, lavender, lemon, rosemary

---

Learn to Love Your Body Massage Oil

15 drops	lavender essential oil
10 drops	lemon essential oil
10 drops	fennel essential oil
5 drops	rosemary essential oil
5 drops	geranium essential oil

In a $^{1}/_{6}$ oz (5 mL) glass bottle, combine lavender, lemon, fennel, rosemary and geranium essential oils. Shake to blend.

Treatment

Massage: In a small non-reactive bowl, combine 4 tsp (20 mL) grapeseed or sweet almond oil and 8 drops Learn to Love Your Body Massage Oil. Mix well and massage over your body using firm kneading movements. Repeat daily.

> ## *Learn to Love Your Body Bath Blend*
>
> | 12 drops | juniper essential oil |
> |---|---|
> | 9 drops | grapefruit essential oil |
> | 9 drops | cypress essential oil |
> | 6 drops | fennel essential oil |
>
> *In a $^1/_6$ oz (5 mL) glass bottle, combine juniper, grapefruit, cypress and fennel essential oils. Mix thoroughly.*

Treatment

Bath: Fill tub with warm water. Meanwhile, in a small non-reactive bowl, combine 1 tsp (5 mL) milk and 4 to 6 drops Learn to Love Your Body Bath Blend. Add to tub and agitate to disperse oil, then soak for 30 minutes, massaging any floating droplets of oil into your skin (knead firmly). Keep as much of your body under the water as possible.

Panic Attack
See Stress and Emotional Problems (page 310)

Paraplegia, Quadriplegia and Hemiplegia

These terms mean that part or most of the body is paralyzed. *Paraplegia* is paralysis of the lower half of the body, *quadriplegia* refers to both the upper and lower body, and *hemiplegia* means that one side of the body is paralyzed.

Massage and essential oils can be of great benefit in improving the tone of wasted muscles. The massage needs to be carried out regularly, and because of this we have given two recipes, to prevent the danger of using any one oil for extended periods. Use the mixtures alternately on a weekly basis.

Essential Oils

Basil, benzoin, black pepper, chamomile, clary sage, grapefruit, lavender, marjoram, orange, peppermint, rosemary

Massage Oil for Limbs 1

10 tsp (50 mL)	grapeseed or sweet almond oil
2 tsp (10 mL)	jojoba oil
10 drops	lavender essential oil
10 drops	grapefruit essential oil
3 drops	rosemary essential oil
3 drops	black pepper or benzoin essential oil

In a 2 oz (60 mL) glass bottle, combine grapeseed oil, jojoba oil and lavender, grapefruit, rosemary and black pepper essential oils. Shake to blend.

Massage Oil for Limbs 2

10 tsp (50 mL)	grapeseed or sweet almond oil
2 tsp (10 mL)	jojoba oil
10 drops	marjoram essential oil
10 drops	orange essential oil
3 drops	chamomile essential oil
3 drops	benzoin essential oil

In a 2 oz (60 mL) glass bottle, combine grapeseed oil, jojoba oil and marjoram, orange, chamomile and benzoin essential oils. Shake to blend.

Treatment

Massage: Using chosen Massage Oil for Limbs, massage limbs in sweeping upward movements, always moving toward the heart. Repeat the massage 1 to 2 times daily, if possible. Alternate use of Massage Oil for Limbs 1 and 2 weekly.

Periods
See Women's Health (page 337)

Piles
See Hemorrhoids (page 241)

Pimples
See Skin Problems (page 375)

Poison Ivy, Oak and Sumac

The leaves of poison ivy, poison oak and poison sumac plants—which contain a colorless, odorless allergen called urushiol—can cause a nasty, itchy dermatitis when they come into contact with skin. The rash can present with red streaks, small bumps (hives) and leaky blisters and usually develops within 8 to 48 hours of contact (it has, however, been known to show up in as little as 5 hours and as long as 15 days). The rash is not contagious or life-threatening, but it can be very uncomfortable. The following treatment may provide some relief.

Poison Ivy Relief Spray

1 tsp (5 mL)	unpasteurized liquid honey
27 drops	lavender essential oil
27 drops	tea tree essential oil
⅓ cup + 5 tsp (100 mL)	immortelle hydrolat

In a 4 oz (125 mL) PET plastic spray bottle, combine honey and lavender and tea tree essential oils. Shake well. Add immortelle hydrolat and shake vigorously to combine.

Treatment

Skin spray: Bathe or shower as soon as possible after contact to wash any remaining plant oils from your skin and avoid spreading the rash. Gently pat the skin dry with a clean cotton towel. Spray Poison Ivy Relief Spray over the affected areas. Spray as needed to relieve itching.

Postnatal Depression
See Pregnancy and Birth (page 290)

Postviral Syndrome
See Chronic Fatigue Syndrome (page 199)

Pregnancy and Birth

There should be no more satisfying and special time in a woman's life than the nine months of pregnancy, but mothers-to-be are often beset by anxiety and discomfort. This is a time to take the ultimate care of yourself to help ensure that you and your baby are as healthy as possible. The use of essential oils during pregnancy and labor and after delivery can help immeasurably, both physically and emotionally. The essential oils will pass through your skin and be experienced by your baby, so don't be tempted to increase or change the recommended oils in any way. Some oils should never be used during pregnancy and while breastfeeding. The recipes here are for external use only.

Essential Oils

During pregnancy: benzoin, Roman (not German) chamomile, cypress, Douglas fir, silver fir, Fragonia, geranium, ginger, grapefruit, juniper (berry), lavender, lemon, mandarin, neroli, sweet orange, palmarosa, patchouli, pine, rose, rosewood, thyme ct. linaool, ylang ylang

During labor: clary sage, geranium, jasmine, lavender, neroli

Postnatal care: Roman chamomile, clary sage, frankincense, geranium, grapefruit, lavender, patchouli, rose

Caution

These oils are UNSAFE to use during pregnancy and while breastfeeding:

- aniseed
- star anise
- basil ct. linalool
- bay laurel
- birch, sweet
- carrot seed
- cinnamon (bark)
- fennel
- hyssop
- jasmine (absolute)
- Spanish lavender (*Lavandula stoechas*)
- lemongrass
- *Litsea cubeba*
- melissa
- myrrh
- myrtle
- parsley
- pennyroyal
- ravintsara
- sage
- Spanish sage
- savin
- tansy
- tea tree, lemon-scented (*Leptospermum petersonii*)
- thuja
- thyme, lemon
- verbena, lemon
- wintergreen
- wormwood
- yarrow

Morning Sickness

The following suggestions should work very quickly to dispel morning sickness. The scent of the spearmint or ginger essential oil will calm your tummy during the night, and you should wake up with no nasty queasiness. Use any or all of the following ideas.

Morning Sickness and Nausea Blend

30 drops	lemon essential oil
30 drops	ginger essential oil
25 drops	spearmint essential oil

In a $\frac{1}{6}$ oz (5 mL) glass dropper bottle, combine lemon, ginger and spearmint essential oils. Shake to blend.

Treatments

Air spray: In a 4 oz (125 mL) PET plastic spray bottle, combine 75 drops Morning Sickness and Nausea Blend and 1 tsp (5 mL) vodka. Fill remainder of bottle with distilled or filtered water (see Tips, right).

Inhaler: Place 21 drops Morning Sickness and Nausea Blend in a small non-reactive bowl. Place inhaler wick in the bowl and allow it to absorb the entire amount. Insert the wick inside the inhaler tube and tightly cap the bottom of the inhaler with the plug. Place the inhaler tube inside its cover and screw tightly to close. Inhale as needed to settle stomach.

Stretch Marks

As soon as pregnancy is confirmed, it's time to start taking extra care of the skin on your tummy, thighs, bottom and breasts. Stretch marks can be largely avoided but not easily cured. The use of these oils morning and night will certainly help to keep your constantly and rapidly stretching skin supple and pliable.

Tips

If you prefer, when making an air spray, substitute Solubol for the vodka called for, in a ratio of 4 drops Solubol for every 1 drop essential oil. Solubol is a natural product that allows essential oils to disperse in liquid.

When making air sprays, be sure to add the oils to the bottle first, followed by the chosen dispersant (vodka or Solubol), to ensure that the essential oils disperse properly (they will not mix directly with water).

Tummy Oil

4	250 IU vitamin E capsules or ⅓ tsp (1.5 mL) vitamin E oil
¼ cup+ 4 tsp (80 mL)	rosehip seed oil
6 tsp (30 mL)	calendula-infused oil
40 drops	lavender essential oil
40 drops	frankincense essential oil
40 drops	rosewood essential oil

Using a clean, sharp knife, pierce the vitamin E capsules and squeeze the oil into a 4 oz (125 mL) glass bottle. Add the rosehip seed oil, calendula-infused oil and lavender, frankincense and rosewood essential oils. Shake to blend.

Massage thoroughly into your breasts and from the waist down to the knees. Use twice daily if possible.

Nipples

It's a good idea to begin to massage the nipples a couple of months before the birth. Massaging will help to avoid the painfully cracked nipples from which so many mothers suffer, and which change the joyful time of breastfeeding into a miserable experience. Make the following oil and begin to use it several weeks before the baby is due. If you prefer, calendula ointment and calendula-infused oil are available in health-food stores. Be sure to wash nipples clean of cream or oil before feeding the baby.

Caution

Avoid wheat germ oil if you have a wheat or gluten allergy. Substitute vitamin E as indicated in the recipe. Pierce the capsules with a clean, sharp knife and squeeze the oil into the blend. Vitamin E is also available in dropper bottles, in which case add 2 drops.

Nipple Oil

8 tsp (40 mL)	calendula-infused or sweet almond oil
1 tsp (5 mL)	wheat germ oil or 2 capsules vitamin E (250 IU)
25 drops	Roman chamomile essential oil

In a 2 oz (60 mL) glass bottle, combine calendula-infused oil, wheat germ oil and chamomile essential oil. Shake to blend.

Massage onto nipples and surrounding area with a firm but gentle squeezing motion. Be sure to thoroughly wash away all traces of oil before breastfeeding your baby.

Aching Back

Toward the end of pregnancy can be a trying time as the body gets heavier and backaches more frequent. This oil is very gentle and will help to alleviate that depressing dragging feeling. If used regularly it may help to prevent backache.

Aching Back Massage Blend

15 drops	lavender essential oil
10 drops	cypress essential oil
5 drops	juniper berry essential oil

In a ¹⁄₆ oz (5 mL) glass bottle, combine lavender, cypress and juniper berry essential oils. Shake to blend.

Treatments

Massage: In a small non-reactive bowl, combine 4 tsp (20 mL) grapeseed or sweet almond oil and 8 drops Aching Back Massage Blend. Mix well. After you have had a bath or shower, ask a friend or your partner to massage your lower back very gently with the blend.

Perineum massage: Massaging the perineum (the area between the vaginal opening and the anus) has been shown to lessen the risk of tearing during delivery. Massage twice daily with a mixture of 4 tsp (20 mL) grapeseed or sweet almond oil, 4 drops lavender essential oil and 2 drops each geranium and juniper essential oils for the 2 months before the birth.

Varicose Veins

Varicose veins are largely hereditary, so if members of your family suffer from them, take precautionary measures as early as possible.

Varicose Massage Blend

4 tsp (20 mL)	grapeseed or sweet almond oil
10 drops	geranium essential oil
10 drops	neroli essential oil
5 drops	cypress essential oil

In a 1 oz (30 mL) glass bottle, combine grapeseed oil and geranium, neroli and cypress essential oils. Shake to blend.
Use about 1 tsp (5 mL) to massage your legs twice daily, starting at the ankles and stroking firmly but gently upward. In the later stages of pregnancy this will be difficult, so you may need a friend or your partner to do it for you.

Caution

If you already have varicose veins, avoid massaging over the veins.

Caution

Before using any essential oil, consult the relevant entry in Part 1: Essential Oils (A to Y), pages 28 to 117, taking careful note of any cautions.

Tip

Choose a time for your bath when other children are at school, or ask a friend or relative to mind young children for half an hour or so. If you don't own a bath pillow, fill a hot-water bottle with warm water and tuck it under your neck (the warmth will help you relax).

Anxiety and Depression

It's very natural for you to feel conflicting emotions during pregnancy. Your body is undergoing immense changes and this, combined with tiredness, can result in tearfulness and the miseries. When it happens, stop what you are doing and have a bath! During pregnancy, taking time for a bath can be quite comforting. The water supports your tummy and removes that heavy feeling, while the warm (not hot) water with essential oils takes away the gloominess.

Prenatal Nerves Bath Blend

20 drops	mandarin or lavender essential oil
20 drops	grapefruit or geranium essential oil
10 drops	ylang ylang essential oil

In a ⅙ oz (5 mL) glass dropper bottle, combine mandarin, grapefruit and ylang ylang essential oils. Shake to blend.

Treatment

Bath: Fill tub with warm water. In a small bowl, combine 4 to 6 drops Prenatal Nerves Bath Blend and 1 tsp (5 mL) milk. Add to tub and agitate to disperse oil, then soak for 30 minutes, massaging any floating droplets of oil into your tummy and breasts. Relax, talk to your baby, and enjoy!

THE BIRTH

This is it! Soon you will see the little person who has been your constant companion for nine months. A few oils can help you welcome your baby into the world. You will be working very hard during the journey baby takes from the womb to the world. Your needs and desires are paramount at this time, so make the most of it! Don't hesitate to say what you want.

The first stages of labor can really drag if you sit around waiting for the next contraction. It's a good idea to go for a walk (near home and accompanied, of course), as this will help to speed things up. If you feel nervous about leaving the house, you can occupy yourself with household jobs.

When the contractions begin to get stronger and closer together, you may enjoy a warm bath to which you have added 6 drops of lavender essential oil. Other comforting things include soft music, a hot-water bottle for a sore lower back, lip salve for dry lips, frozen fruit juice or ice cubes to suck, and diluted apple juice to keep your blood sugar level up. The following massage blend will help to lesson the discomfort, gently speed up contractions, create a calm and tranquil atmosphere, and help to keep you and the surrounding air free of bacteria.

Waiting for Baby Massage Blend

8 tsp (40 mL)	sweet almond oil
5 drops	clary sage essential oil
5 drops	lavender essential oil
3 drops	geranium or frankincense essential oil
3 drops	rose or co-distilled rose/geranium essential oil

In a 2 oz (60 mL) glass bottle, combine sweet almond oil and clary sage, lavender, geranium and rose essential oils. Shake to blend.

During the first stage of labor, massage your abdomen once with the blend, using only the lightest of strokes. Massage your lower back as often and as firmly as desired. Guide the person doing the massage as to the movements and areas that are most comfortable and helpful.

Welcoming Baby Spray

Welcome your child into a room scented with an essential oil. Baby will later associate that scent with loving individuals in her life and find comfort, and it is also relaxing for the mommy-to-be. When the baby is to be held by another family member or a friend, first spray the front of their shirt with the following blend. The baby will associate the aroma with mom and be less likely to cry. This can work well with babysitters to help ease separation anxiety.

1 tsp (5 mL)	glycerin or Solubol
60 drops	lavender essential oil
¼ cup (60 mL)	lavender hydrolat
¼ cup (60 mL)	distilled or filtered water

In a 4 oz (125 mL) PET plastic spray bottle, combine glycerin and lavender essential oil. Shake to blend. Add lavender hydrolat and water and shake well. Shake thoroughly before using.

Tips

If you prefer, substitute Solubol (see Resources, page 459) for the vodka in the ratio of 4 drops Solubol for every 1 drop essential oil.

When making air sprays, be sure to add the oils to the bottle first, followed by the chosen dispersant (glycerin or Solubol), to ensure that the essential oils disperse properly (they will not mix directly with water).

Now you and your baby will be having a wonderful time getting to know each other. This time can be stressful and demanding, however, and essential oils can help you avoid or banish some of the annoying problems that occasionally arise. The choice of oils is still limited, as breastfed babies will receive any oils in the breast milk.

Breastfeeding

It's beyond the scope of this book to discuss breastfeeding in depth, but we urge you—even if you have decided not to breastfeed—to consider it for the first vital days when the baby will receive colostrum. This is a thin, cream-colored fluid that contains constituents important for supporting the baby's immunity to disease.

The most important thing is to keep the new mom relaxed to improve lactation. Drinking plenty of water and the occasional cup of fennel tea, as well as eating oats and getting enough restful sleep, can help.

Treatments

Bath: In a small non-reactive bowl, combine 4 to 6 drops lavender essential oil and 1 tsp (5 mL) milk. Add to tub and agitate to disperse oil, then soak for 30 minutes, massaging any floating droplets of oil into your skin.

Inhaler: Apply 1 drop lavender and 1 drop mandarin essential oil to a tissue and inhale directly for an uplifting yet relaxing pick-me-up.

Breast Abscesses

A breast infection at this time can be very painful and distressing. Consult your health-care practitioner if you have a fever.

Breast Abscess Blend

10 drops	geranium essential oil
15 drops	Roman chamomile essential oil

In a $^1/_6$ oz (5 mL) glass bottle, combine geranium and Roman chamomile essential oils. Shake to blend.

Do not add essential oils to the tub while the water is running, as some of the precious essences may evaporate, depriving you of the full benefits.

If you prefer, substitute an equal quantity of liquid castile soap for the milk called for in any bath recipe.

If you are using a blend around bath/shower time, you can enhance the benefit by combining the essential oils with a carrier oil and rub it into your skin *before* getting into the shower or bath. This enables the essential oils to be absorbed and work their way into the bloodstream. The heat of the water encourages the essential oil vapors to rise, allowing you to inhale the aromas more easily and thus creating a dual application.

Treatments

Massage: In a small non-reactive bowl, combine 4 tsp (20 mL) grapeseed or sweet almond oil and 8 drops Breast Abscess Blend. Mix well and very gently massage over your breasts up to 4 times daily.

Hot compress: Pour 1 cup (250 mL) hot water into a non-reactive bowl and add 4 to 6 drops Breast Abscess Blend. Stir well to disperse oils. Soak a cloth and wring out enough water so cloth doesn't drip. Place cloth on breast, cover with a piece of plastic wrap and keep it in place with your bra. Repeat every 4 hours.

Sore Perineum

Your perineum may be very sore after the birth. Even though you may not have stitches, there are often tiny little tears or sore areas that can be very uncomfortable.

Perineum Massage Oil

9 tsp (45 mL)	macadamia nut or sunflower oil
1 tsp (5 mL)	wheat germ oil or 2 capsules vitamin E (250 IU)
8 drops	lavender essential oil
8 drops	geranium essential oil

In a 2 oz (60 mL) glass bottle, combine macadamia nut and wheat germ oils and lavender and geranium essential oils. Shake to blend.

Caution

Avoid wheat germ oil if you have a wheat or gluten allergy. Substitute vitamin E as indicated in the recipe. Pierce the capsules with a clean, sharp knife and squeeze the oil into the blend. Vitamin E is also available in dropper bottles, in which case add 2 drops.

Treatments

Cool compress: Pour 1 cup (250 mL) cool (not icy) water into a non-reactive bowl and add 5 drops geranium essential oil. Stir well to disperse oil. Soak a cloth and wring out enough water so cloth doesn't drip. Place cloth on perineum. Repeat often.

Massage: Pour a little Perineum Massage Oil into the palm of your hand and massage the perineum for 2 minutes, twice daily.

Sitz Bath for Perineum

8 tsp (40 mL)	sea salt
1 tsp (5 mL)	grapeseed or sweet almond oil
2 drops	tea tree essential oil
2 drops	cypress or geranium essential oil

Fill tub with enough warm water to cover lower hips. Meanwhile, in a small non-reactive bowl, combine sea salt, grapeseed oil and tea tree and cypress essential oils. Add to tub and agitate to disperse oils and dissolve salt. Soak for 10 minutes, massaging any floating droplets of oil into your skin.

Postnatal Depression

Few people understand or sympathize with postnatal depression unless they have suffered it themselves. The depression can range from mild (experienced by most women on the second or third day after the birth) to very severe. Plenty of rest and pampering yourself will help you feel relaxed—you will have more energy and enthusiasm to cope with the baby and household chores. Use the following oils to lift your spirits and give you confidence.

Essential Oils

Bergamot, frankincense, geranium, grapefruit, jasmine, lavender, lemon, mandarin

Postnatal Blues Beater

30 drops	bergamot essential oil
30 drops	lavender essential oil
20 drops	geranium or frankincense essential oil
20 drops	grapefruit or mandarin essential oil

In a 1 oz (30 mL) glass bottle, combine bergamot, lavender, geranium and grapefruit essential oils. Shake to blend.

Tips

If you prefer, when making an air spray, substitute Solubol for the vodka called for, in a ratio of 4 drops Solubol for every 1 drop essential oil. Solubol is a natural product that allows essential oils to disperse in liquid.

When making air sprays, be sure to add the oils to the bottle first, followed by the chosen dispersant (vodka or Solubol), to ensure that the essential oils disperse properly (they will not mix directly with water).

Treatments

Air spray: In a 4 oz (125 mL) PET plastic spray bottle, combine 75 drops Postnatal Blues Beater and 1 tsp (5 mL) vodka. Fill bottle with distilled or filtered water (see Tips, page 290). Shake to blend.

Bath: Fill tub with warm water. Meanwhile, in a small non-reactive bowl, combine 1 tsp (5 mL) milk and 4 to 6 drops Postnatal Blues Beater. Add to tub and agitate to disperse oil, then soak for 30 minutes, massaging any floating droplets of oil into your skin.

Inhaler: Place 21 drops Postnatal Blues Beater in a small non-reactive bowl. Place inhaler wick in the bowl and allow it to absorb the entire amount. Insert the wick inside the inhaler tube and tightly cap the bottom of the inhaler with the plug. Place the inhaler tube inside its cover and screw tightly to close.

Massage: In a small non-reactive bowl, combine 4 tsp (20 mL) grapeseed or sweet almond oil and 8 drops Postnatal Blues Beater. Mix well and massage over your body.

Prostatitis See Men's Health (page 268)

Psoriasis See Skin Problems (page 382)

Pyorrhea See Teeth and Gum Problems (page 316)

Raynaud's Disease

Raynaud's disease is a circulatory system ailment involving small blood vessels. It is caused by a spasm of small arteries, usually during cold weather, that in turn starves the skin of blood. It occurs mainly in the fingers and toes but may involve the whole hand and foot. It is a problem suffered almost exclusively by young women, and there is usually no warning or apparent reason for the attack. Prevention is definitely better than cure; addressing the symptoms quite aggressively with baths, massage and essential oils should ease the problem. Sufferers may have difficulty feeling the bathwater temperature and should use a thermometer to test it. See also Circulation (page 202).

Tips

Do not add essential oils to the tub while the water is running, as some of the precious essences may evaporate, depriving you of the full benefits.

If you prefer, substitute an equal quantity of liquid castile soap for the milk called for in any bath recipe.

If you are using a blend around bath/shower time, you can enhance the benefit by combining the essential oils with a carrier oil and rub it into your skin *before* getting into the shower or bath. This enables the essential oils to be absorbed and work their way into the bloodstream. The heat of the water encourages the essential oil vapors to rise, allowing you to inhale the aromas more easily and thus creating a dual application.

Tips

Do not add essential oils to the tub while the water is running, as some of the precious essences may evaporate, depriving you of the full benefits.

If you prefer, substitute an equal quantity of liquid castile soap for the milk called for in any bath recipe.

If you are using a blend around bath/shower time, you can enhance the benefit by combining the essential oils with a carrier oil and rub it into your skin *before* getting into the shower or bath. This enables the essential oils to be absorbed and work their way into the bloodstream. The heat of the water encourages the essential oil vapors to rise, allowing you to inhale the aromas more easily and thus creating a dual application.

Essential Oils

Basil ct. linalool, Roman chamomile, fennel, rosemary (ct. cineole and ct. camphor), thyme ct. carvacrol

---

Raynaud's Bath Oil

25 drops	black pepper essential oil
15 drops	rosemary ct. cineole or ct. camphor essential oil
10 drops	Roman chamomile essential oil

In a ⅙ oz (5 mL) glass bottle, combine black pepper, rosemary and chamomile essential oils. Shake to blend.

Fill tub with warm to hot water. Add 4 to 6 drops to tub and agitate to disperse oil, then soak for 30 minutes, massaging any floating droplets of oil into your skin (as much as you can reach). Pay special attention to your hands and feet.

Raynaud's Massage Oil

20 drops	rosemary essential oil
10 drops	black pepper essential oil
10 drops	nutmeg essential oil
5 drops	basil or fennel essential oil

In a ⅙ oz (5 mL) glass dropper bottle, combine rosemary, black pepper, nutmeg and basil essential oils. Shake to blend.

Treatments

Bath: Fill tub with warm water. Meanwhile, in a small non-reactive bowl, combine 1 tsp (5 mL) milk and 4 to 6 drops Raynaud's Massage Oil. Add to tub and agitate to disperse oil, then soak for 30 minutes, massaging any floating droplets of oil into your skin.

Footbath: Combine 1 tsp (5 mL) milk and 4 drops Raynaud's Massage Oil. Add to a basin of warm water and agitate to disperse oil. Soak feet or hands for 10 to 20 minutes, massaging any floating droplets of oil into your skin.

Massage: In a small non-reactive bowl, combine 4 tsp (20 mL) grapeseed or sweet almond oil and 8 drops Raynaud's Massage Oil. Mix well and massage over your body.

Relaxation
See Stress and Emotional Problems (page 310)

Repetitive Strain Injury

Repetitive strain injury, or RSI, is a painful and disabling condition that results from using the same muscles over and over again. The condition is similar to bursitis, tendonitis and possibly carpal tunnel syndrome. The joints most usually affected are the wrists, elbows and shoulders. It's important to identify the cause of the problem and to rectify it. Frequent massage of the most used muscles will also help to prevent the problem from occurring. See Carpal Tunnel Syndrome (page 196) for treatment.

Caution

Before using any essential oil, consult the relevant entry in Part 1: Essential Oils (A to Y), pages 28 to 117, taking careful note of any cautions.

Respiratory Problems

Asthma

Asthma is a chronic inflammatory condition that can be brought on by environmental triggers such as dust mites, mold, cigarette smoke, car and other chemical fumes, animal fur or feathers, or certain foods. Asthma is potentially a very serious condition. Aromatherapy treatment should be considered an adjunct to, not a substitute for, professional treatment.

Essential Oils

Canadian balsam, eucalyptus (*globulus and smithii*), helichrysum, hyssop, myrtle (green and orange), pine, rose, thyme ct. thymol

---

Asthma Inhalation and Massage Blend

20 drops	Canadian balsam essential oil
15 drops	pine essential oil
5 drops	rose otto essential oil

In a ⅙ oz (5 mL) glass bottle, combine balsam, pine and rose essential oils. Shake to blend.

Treatments

Cool-mist diffuser: Moist air can help with asthma-related symptoms where steaming may be irritating. Use 2 to 3 drops eucalyptus or hyssop essential oil in a cool-mist diffuser (see Resources, page 459). Sit comfortably in a chair and place the diffuser on a table in front of you. Lean in toward the mist and inhale for 1 minute, then break for 2 minutes. Repeat for a total of 10 minutes.

Note: Steam inhalation isn't recommended for asthma sufferers.

Inhaler: Place 21 drops Asthma Inhalation and Massage Blend in a non-reactive bowl. Place inhaler wick in the bowl and allow it to absorb the entire amount. Insert the wick inside the inhaler tube and tightly cap the bottom of the inhaler with the plug. Place the inhaler tube inside its cover and screw tightly to close. During an attack, sniff the contents of the inhaler.

Massage: In a small non-reactive bowl, combine 4 tsp (20 mL) grapeseed or sweet almond oil and 10 drops Asthma Inhalation and Massage Blend. Mix well and massage over your chest twice daily. Use between, not during, attacks.

Bronchitis

Bronchitis is an acute or chronic inflammation of the lining of the bronchial tubes and needs careful treatment.

Essential Oils

Balsam (Canadian and Peru), benzoin, cedarwood, eucalyptus (*dives*, *globulus*, *radiata* and *smithii*), frankincense, helichrysum, hyssop, lavandin, lemon, marjoram, neroli, niaouli, peppermint, rose, rosemary ct. verbenone

---

Bronchitis Chest Blend

15 drops	*Eucalyptus radiata* essential oil
10 drops	cedarwood essential oil
8 drops	peppermint essential oil

In a ⅙ oz (5 mL) glass bottle, combine eucalyptus, cedarwood and peppermint essential oils. Shake to blend.

Treatments

Air spray: In a 4 oz (125 mL) PET plastic spray bottle, combine 75 drops Bronchitis Chest Blend and 1 tsp (5 mL) vodka. Fill bottle with distilled or filtered water (see Tips, left). Shake to blend.

Tips

If you prefer, when making an air spray, substitute Solubol for the vodka called for, in a ratio of 4 drops Solubol for every 1 drop essential oil. Solubol is a natural product that allows essential oils to disperse in liquid.

When making air sprays, be sure to add the oils to the bottle first, followed by the chosen dispersant (vodka or Solubol), to ensure that the essential oils disperse properly (they will not mix directly with water).

Bath: Fill tub with warm water. Meanwhile, in a small non-reactive bowl, combine 1 tsp (5 mL) milk and 4 to 6 drops Bronchitis Chest Blend. Add to tub and agitate to disperse oil, then soak for 30 minutes, massaging any floating droplets of oil into your skin.

Inhaler: Place 21 drops Bronchitis Chest Blend in a non-reactive bowl. Place inhaler wick in the bowl and allow it to absorb the entire amount. Insert the wick inside the inhaler tube and tightly cap the bottom of the inhaler with the plug. Place the inhaler tube inside its cover and screw tightly to close. Inhale as necessary.

Massage: In a small non-reactive bowl, combine 2 tsp (10 mL) grapeseed or sweet almond oil and 6 drops Bronchitis Chest Blend. Mix well and massage over your throat and chest.

Catarrh

Production of excessive mucus can be caused by an infection, hay fever, food allergies or irritants such as tobacco smoke, chemical fumes, cat fur and pollens.

Essential Oils

Canadian balsam, black pepper, *Eucalyptus dives*, lavandin, marjoram, myrrh, myrtle (green or orange), niaouli, pine, tea tree

---

Catarrh Clearing Blend

48 drops	Scots pine essential oil
32 drops	tea tree or *Eucalyptus dives* essential oil
16 drops	lavandin essential oil

In a ¹⁄₆ oz (5 mL) glass bottle, combine pine, tea tree and lavandin essential oils. Shake to blend.

Treatments

Air spray: In a 4 oz (125 mL) PET plastic spray bottle, combine 75 drops Catarrh Clearing Blend and 1 tsp (5 mL) vodka. Shake well. Fill bottle with distilled or filtered water (see Tips, page 294). Shake to blend.

Tips

Do not add essential oils to the tub while the water is running, as some of the precious essences may evaporate, depriving you of the full benefits.

If you prefer, substitute an equal quantity of liquid castile soap for the milk called for in any bath recipe.

If you are using a blend around bath/shower time, you can enhance the benefit by combining the essential oils with a carrier oil and rub it into your skin *before* getting into the shower or bath. This enables the essential oils to be absorbed and work their way into the bloodstream. The heat of the water encourages the essential oil vapors to rise, allowing you to inhale the aromas more easily and thus creating a dual application.

Inhaler: Place 25 drops Catarrh Clearing blend in a small non-reactive bowl. Place inhaler wick in the bowl and allow it to absorb the entire amount. Insert the wick inside the inhaler tube and tightly cap the bottom of the inhaler with the plug. Place the inhaler tube inside its cover and screw tightly to close.

Massage: Place $\frac{1}{2}$ cup (125 mL) unscented cream in a 4 oz (125 mL) double-walled jar. Add 40 drops Catarrh Clearing Blend and stir until well combined. Scoop a little into the palm of your hand and massage onto your chest and upper back, twice daily.

Coughs

Treatment for coughs is aimed at lessening, loosening and expelling mucus and strengthening the lungs. If a cough persists for a long time, consult a health-care practitioner.

Essential Oils

Balsam (Canadian and Peru), benzoin, cajuput, cedarwood, eucalyptus (*globulus*, *radiata* and *smithii*), helichrysum, hyssop, lavandin, lavender, marjoram, myrtle (green or orange), niaouli, pine, ravensara, rosemary, rosewood

---

Inhalation Blend for Coughs

45 drops   marjoram essential oil
30 drops   benzoin essential oil
15 drops   helichrysum or hyssop essential oil

In a $\frac{1}{6}$ oz (5 mL) glass bottle, combine marjoram, benzoin and helichrysum essential oils. Mix well.

Treatments

Air spray: In a 4 oz (125 mL) PET plastic spray bottle, combine 75 drops Inhalation Blend for Coughs and 1 tsp (5 mL) vodka. Fill bottle with distilled or filtered water (see Tips, left). Shake to blend.

Inhaler: Place 25 drops Inhalation Blend for Coughs in a small non-reactive bowl. Place inhaler wick in the bowl and allow it to absorb the entire amount. Insert the wick inside the inhaler tube and tightly cap the bottom of the inhaler with the plug. Place the inhaler tube inside its cover and screw tightly to close. Inhale as necessary.

Massage Blend for Coughs

36 drops	*Eucalyptus smithii* essential oil
24 drops	cedarwood essential oil
12 drops	pine essential oil
8 drops	myrtle (green or orange) essential oil

In a ⅙ oz (5 mL) glass bottle, combine eucalyptus, cedarwood, pine and myrtle essential oils. Mix well.

Treatments

Air spray: In a 4 oz (125 mL) PET plastic spray bottle, combine 80 drops Massage Blend for Coughs and 1 tsp (5 mL) vodka. Fill bottle with distilled or filtered water (see Tips, page 296). Shake to blend.

Bath: Fill tub with warm water. Meanwhile, in a small non-reactive bowl, combine 1 tsp (5 mL) milk and 4 to 6 drops Massage Blend for Coughs. Add to tub and agitate to disperse oil, then soak for 30 minutes, massaging any floating droplets of oil into your chest and throat.

Inhaler: Place 23 drops Massage Blend for Coughs in a small non-reactive bowl. Place inhaler wick in the bowl and allow it to absorb the entire amount. Insert the wick inside the inhaler tube and tightly cap the bottom of the inhaler with the plug. Place the inhaler tube inside its cover and screw tightly to close.

Massage: In a small non-reactive bowl, combine 4 tsp (20 mL) grapeseed or sweet almond oil and 8 drops Massage Blend for Coughs. Mix well and massage over your chest, throat and back.

Laryngitis

Laryngitis can lead to hoarseness or temporary loss of voice.

Essential Oils

Black pepper, chamomile, cypress, *Eucalyptus globulus*, lavender, lemon, myrrh, peppermint

Laryngitis Inhalation Blend

12 drops	lavender essential oil
6 drops	black pepper essential oil
3 drops	myrrh essential oil

In a ¹⁄₆ oz (5 mL) glass bottle, combine lavender, black pepper and myrrh essential oils. Shake to blend.

Treatment

Inhalation: Place 23 drops Laryngitis Inhalation Blend in a small non-reactive bowl. Place inhaler wick in the bowl and allow it to absorb the entire amount. Insert the wick inside the inhaler tube and tightly cap the bottom of the inhaler with the plug. Place the inhaler tube inside its cover and screw tightly to close.

Place inhaler halfway into your mouth and wrap lips around it. Inhale through your mouth and hold breath for 5 seconds. Breathe normally for a few seconds and then repeat.

Sinusitis

Sinusitis can be either acute or chronic, and both types need attention, as there is a danger that the infection will travel upward, causing meningitis. You will need to persevere with the treatment outlined below for some time, but believe me, your perseverance will be rewarded with a clear, pain-free head.

Essential Oils

Canadian balsam, eucalyptus (*dives* and *globulus*), helichrysum, hyssop, lavender, marjoram (sweet and Spanish), myrtle (green or orange), niaouli, peppermint, pine, ravensara, rosemary (ct. cineole and ct. camphor), tea tree, thyme (ct. linalool and ct. thymol)

Treatments

Inhalation: In a small non-reactive bowl, combine 4 drops each eucalyptus, lavender, peppermint, pine and tea tree essential oils. Place inhaler wick in the bowl and allow it to absorb the entire amount. Insert the wick inside the inhaler tube and tightly cap the bottom of the inhaler with the plug. Place the inhaler tube inside its cover and screw tightly to close. Use inhaler up to 5 times a day.

Warm compress: Pour 1 cup (250 mL) warm water into a non-reactive bowl and add 1 drop each eucalyptus, lavender, peppermint, pine and tea tree essential oils. Stir well to disperse oils. Soak a cloth and wring out enough water so cloth doesn't drip. Place cloth on nose and sinus area. Repeat often, being careful not to get any of the mixture in the eyes.

Tonsillitis

Tonsillitis is an inflammation of the tonsils and is most likely to occur in children and young adults, but sometimes it afflicts older people. (See also Throat (Sore), page 318.)

Essential Oils

Bergamot, cedarwood, eucalyptus, geranium, hyssop, myrrh, myrtle (green or orange), sweet orange, tea tree, thyme (ct. geraniol or ct. linalool)

Throat Oil

4 tsp (20 mL)	grapeseed or sweet almond oil
6 drops	geranium essential oil
4 drops	hyssop or myrrh essential oil
2 drops	sweet orange essential oil

In a 1 oz (30 mL) glass bottle, combine grapeseed oil and geranium, hyssop and orange essential oils. Shake to blend.

Treatments

Gargle: In a glass, combine 1 drop tea tree essential oil and 1 tsp (5 mL) unpasteurized liquid honey. Add 1 cup (250 mL) warm water and stir well. Take a small mouthful of the mixture and gargle several times, then spit it out (do not swallow the mixture). Repeat every 2 hours until symptoms diminish.

Massage: Warm a spoon in very hot (not boiling) water. Pour 1 tsp (5 mL) Throat Oil into spoon to warm the oil. Massage warm oil over your throat, then cover the entire area with a scarf or warm cloth. Repeat every 2 hours until symptoms diminish.

Restless Legs Syndrome

Restless legs syndrome (RLS) is a nervous system disorder that usually starts about an hour after going to bed. Symptoms include involuntarily jerking leg muscles, an irresistible urge to move the legs, muscle contractions, aching legs or feelings of pins and needles or itchiness. The cause is unknown but suspected to be hereditary. It is exacerbated by chronic illness, pregnancy, some medications, alcohol and sleep deprivation. Daily exercise improves circulation to the legs. Minimize or eliminate alcohol, caffeine and smoking. Hot baths and deep leg massage often provide effective treatment.

Essential Oils

Black pepper, ginger, lavender, marjoram, nutmeg, rosemary

Massage Blend for Restless Legs

30 drops	rosemary essential oil
20 drops	marjoram essential oil
10 drops	lavender or nutmeg essential oil
10 drops	black pepper or ginger essential oil

In a ⅙ oz (5 mL) glass bottle, combine rosemary, marjoram, lavender and black pepper essential oils. Shake to blend.

Treatment

Massage: In a small non-reactive bowl, combine 4 tsp (20 mL) grapeseed oil and 12 drops Massage Blend for Restless Legs. Mix well and massage over your legs, using firm upward strokes. Use the oil last thing at night after a hot shower or bath.

Rheumatism (Muscular)

Rheumatism is no longer a recognized medical term, but it is still used to describe an inflammatory disorder that involves pain and inflammation in the joints and connective tissue. It can be localized (between tendon and bone or between muscle and muscle), regional (involving a larger section of the body, such as the legs) or general, which involves many parts and is similar to fibromyalgia. See Arthritis (page 160) and Gout (page 240) for treatment of rheumatism in the joints.

Essential Oils

Basil, cajuput, cypress, ginger, juniper, lavender, sweet marjoram, rosemary (ct. cineole and ct. camphor)

Rheumatism Blend for Compresses

100 drops	rosemary essential oil
50 drops	lavender essential oil
50 drops	sweet marjoram essential oil

In a 2 oz (60 mL) glass bottle, combine rosemary, lavender and marjoram essential oils. Shake to blend.

Treatments

Apply either a cool or hot compress, whichever works for you. Treat as often as needed.

Cool compress: Pour 2 cups (500 mL) cool (not icy) water into a non-reactive bowl and add 5 to 8 drops Rheumatism Blend for Compresses. Stir well to disperse oils. Soak a cloth and wring out enough water so cloth doesn't drip. Place cloth on affected area; repeat often.

Hot compress: In a small non-reactive bowl, combine 1 cup (250 mL) hot water and 5 to 8 drops Rheumatism Blend for Compresses. Stir well to disperse oils. Submerge a cloth just large enough to absorb all the liquid without dripping. Apply to affected area.

Rheumatism Blend for Bath or Massage

24 drops	cypress essential oil
16 drops	rosemary or marjoram essential oil (see Cautions, page 104)
12 drops	juniper essential oil
12 drops	Roman chamomile essential oil

In a ¹⁄₆ oz (5 mL) glass bottle, combine cypress, rosemary, juniper and chamomile essential oils. Shake to blend.

Treatments

Bath: Fill tub with warm water. Meanwhile, in a small non-reactive bowl, combine 1 tsp (5 mL) milk and 4 to 6 drops Rheumatism Blend for Bath or Massage. Add to tub and agitate to disperse oil, then soak for 30 minutes, massaging any floating droplets of oil into your sore muscles.

Massage: In a small non-reactive bowl, combine 4 tsp (20 mL) grapeseed or sweet almond oil and 12 drops Rheumatism Blend for Bath or Massage. Mix well and massage sore muscles.

Ringworm

Ringworm, or tinea, is a highly contagious fungal infection of the skin that exhibits as an itchy rash. There are different types of tinea; it can appear in the shape of a red ring, white scales or tiny white "cotton balls." Observe careful hygiene and do not share clothing and linens.

Essential Oils

Manuka, myrrh, palmarosa, tea tree

Ringworm Blend

16 drops	manuka essential oil
16 drops	palmarosa essential oil
16 drops	sandalwood or cedarwood essential oil
16 drops	tea tree essential oil

In a $1/6$ oz (5 mL) glass dropper bottle, combine manuka, palmarosa, sandalwood and tea tree essential oils. Shake to blend.

Treatments

Topical application: In a small non-reactive bowl, combine 3 drops Ringworm Blend and 1 tsp (5 mL) grapeseed or sweet almond oil. Mix thoroughly. Using a cotton ball, apply to affected area several times daily, for 3 to 4 weeks. Although the ringworm may appear to be healed, it can linger as a hidden infection for several weeks. Continue daily treatment by soaking in Ringworm bath treatment (page 303) and following up with Ringworm lotion (below) for a minimum of 2 months after all signs of ringworm have gone.

Lotion: Fill a 4 oz PET plastic bottle halfway with unscented lotion and add 16 drops Ringworm Blend (**Note:** for children under 13 years old, use 8 drops). Shake vigorously to combine. Add more lotion to fill bottle to the shoulder, leaving $1/2$ inch (1 cm) headspace. Shake vigorously to disperse essential oils evenly. Apply to affected area twice daily.

Bath treatment: In a 4 oz (125 mL) PET plastic bottle, combine 4 oz (125 mL) unscented bath gel/body wash and 32 drops Ringworm Blend (*Note:* for children under 13 years old, use 16 drops). Shake vigorously to combine. Add 3 tsp (15 mL) to warm bathwater and bathe as usual.

Rubella

Rubella, or German measles, is a highly infectious viral disease that produces a slight fever, an itchy rash and swollen glands. Symptoms usually last only a few days. The following treatments will soothe the skin and may help to prevent the spread of infection.

Essential Oils

Chamomile, lavender, tea tree

Treatments

Bath: Fill tub with warm water. Meanwhile, in a small non-reactive bowl, combine 4 drops lavender essential oil and ¼ cup (60 mL) baking soda. Add to tub and agitate to disperse, then allow patient to sit in the bath for half an hour or more (don't leave young children alone in the bath). This bath will soothe the itching and calm the patient.

Lotion: Place 1 cup (250 mL) baking soda in a small non-reactive bowl. One drop at a time (to prevent clumping), add 5 drops each lavender and chamomile essential oils. Stir thoroughly and transfer to a resealable jar. In another small non-reactive bowl, combine 1 to 2 tsp (5 to 10 mL) of the baking soda mixture with enough cold water to make a milky lotion. Using cotton balls, dab the lotion on the itchy spots. Repeat as often as needed.

Variation

Honey has been found to be beneficial in the treatment of rubella. You can blend the essential oils with 3 tsp (15 mL) unpasteurized liquid honey instead of preparing the lotion. Store any unused mixture in a small airtight jar.

Skin spray: In a 4 oz (125 mL) PET plastic spray bottle, combine 16 drops each lavender and chamomile essential oils and 1 tsp (5 mL) unpasteurized liquid honey. Add ¼ cup (60 mL) witch hazel or immortelle hydrolat and shake to combine. Fill the bottle with distilled or filtered water. Shake well to blend. Spray on the spots to ease itching.

Tips

Do not add essential oils to the tub while the water is running, as some of the precious essences may evaporate, depriving you of the full benefits.

If you prefer, substitute an equal quantity of liquid castile soap for the milk called for in any bath recipe.

If you are using a blend around bath/shower time, you can enhance the benefit by combining the essential oils with a carrier oil and rub it into your skin *before* getting into the shower or bath. This enables the essential oils to be absorbed and work their way into the bloodstream. The heat of the water encourages the essential oil vapors to rise, allowing you to inhale the aromas more easily and thus creating a dual application.

Scabies

Scabies is an intensely itchy skin condition caused by a tiny insect that burrows beneath the skin to lay its eggs. It is difficult to treat and you may need to see your health-care practitioner. It is essential to wash all clothing, towels and bedding in very hot water. Add 4 to 6 drops eucalyptus essential oil to the wash and rinse water and dry in the sun (see Cautions, left). Wipe mattresses and pillows with a mixture of tea tree and lavender essential oils and dry in the sun.

Essential Oils

Roman chamomile, lavender, lemongrass, sweet orange, peppermint, rosewood, tea tree, thyme ct. linalool

Cautions

- Fires have been known to occur in dryers when the essential oils (and sometimes vegetable oils too) have not been thoroughly removed from fabrics in the washing machine. To ensure that your detergent can break down the oils during the washing process, be sure to use a wash temperature of at least 104°F (40°C).

- Scabies ointment has a much higher proportion of essential oil than is usual. Apply very frequently, but take care to use only on affected areas of skin.

Scabies Ointment

⅓ cup (75 mL)	extra virgin olive oil
3 tsp (15 mL)	beeswax prills (pellets)
1 tsp (5 mL)	meadowfoam or calendula-infused oil
2	250 IU vitamin E capsules or ¼ tsp (1 mL) vitamin E oil
¾ tsp (3 mL)	tamanu oil
40 drops	lavender essential oil
20 drops	sweet orange or lemongrass essential oil
20 drops	tea tree essential oil
10 drops	thyme ct. linalool essential oil
10 drops	peppermint essential oil

1. *In a glass measuring cup, combine olive oil, beeswax and meadowfoam oil. Microwave on High for 1 minute, then stir. Heat for another 30 seconds and stir. Repeat in 30-second increments until the beeswax is completely melted. (Alternatively, use a double boiler.)*

2. *Pierce the vitamin E capsules with the point of a clean, sharp knife and add to the beeswax mixture. Add tamanu oil and stir to combine. Add lavender, orange, tea tree, thyme and peppermint essential oils and stir well to combine. Pour into a 4 oz (125 mL) double-walled container and set aside to cool completely and harden before replacing lid.*

Treatment

Topical application: Rub Scabies Ointment onto affected areas (see Cautions, left).

Scalds
See Burns and Scalds (page 192)

Scar Tissue

Essential Oils

Benzoin, frankincense, lavender, myrrh

Caution
Before using any essential oil, consult the relevant entry in Part 1: Essential Oils (A to Y), pages 28 to 117, taking careful note of any cautions.

Scar Tissue Oil

2	250 IU capsules vitamin E oil or ⅛ tsp (0.5 mL) vitamin E oil
9 tsp (45 mL)	sweet almond or sunflower oil
1 tsp (5 mL)	rosehip seed oil
30 drops	frankincense essential oil
30 drops	lavender essential oil
30 drops	myrrh essential oil
30 drops	sandalwood or cedarwood essential oil

Using the point of a clean, sharp knife, pierce the vitamin E capsules and squeeze them into a 2 oz (60 mL) glass bottle. Add sweet almond and rosehip seed oils and frankincense, lavender, myrrh and sandalwood essential oils. Shake to blend.

Treatment
Scar massage: Pour a little Scar Tissue Oil into the palm of your hand and massage onto the scar twice daily, for as long as is needed. (Patience will be rewarded with this treatment, as it can take up to 6 months to see results.)

Sciatica
See Back Pain (page 183); Neuralgia (page 276)

Shingles
See Herpes (page 249)

Sinusitis
See Respiratory Problems (page 298)

Tip

In addition to essential oils, every first aid box should have a bottle of Bach Rescue Remedy. It is a blend of five flower essence remedies meant to help you cope in case of emergency or crisis. Flower essences work on a vibrational level to calm and restore balance to body and mind. Place a few drops of Rescue Remedy under the tongue, or massage 2 or 3 drops on the insides of the wrists.

Shock

Shock is a serious, life-threatening condition. Emergency response should be called for right away.

Shock occurs when the body is not getting enough blood flow and oxygen. It can result in low blood pressure, cool skin, weak pulse and shallow, rapid breathing. Trauma, bacterial infection, allergic reaction, heart damage, heatstroke or blood loss can all induce shock. For mild cases of shock (caused by bad news, a highly stressful situation or being shaken up by an accident), relaxing essential oils can help to soothe the nerves.

Essential Oils

Chamomile, lavender, peppermint

Treatment

Inhalation: Sprinkle 2 drops peppermint essential oil onto a tissue and inhale deeply.

Sore Throat
See Throat (page 318)

Sports

Pre-sport Treatment

This massage oil will tone your muscles so that they are ready for the football game, marathon walk, triathlon or whatever. It will also help you to achieve a calm, positive frame of mind.

Up and At 'Em Oil

10 drops	rosemary essential oil
10 drops	cypress essential oil
8 drops	lavender essential oil
5 drops	juniper essential oil
¼ cup (60 mL)	grapeseed or sweet almond oil

In a small glass bottle, combine rosemary, cypress, lavender and juniper essential oils. Add grapeseed oil and shake to blend.

Treatment

Massage: Pour a little Up and At 'Em Oil into the palm of your hand and massage onto muscles before strenuous or competitive sport.

After-Sport Treatment

This oil will help to prevent or ease muscle soreness—and also emotional soreness! Use it as soon as possible after activity.

Hero's Bath and Massage Oil

15 drops	rosemary essential oil
15 drops	lemon essential oil
12 drops	clary sage essential oil (see Cautions, page 50)
6 drops	black pepper or peppermint essential oil
½ cup (125 mL)	grapeseed or sweet almond oil

In a 4 oz (125 mL) glass bottle, combine rosemary, lemon, clary sage and black pepper essential oils. Add grapeseed oil and shake to blend.

Treatments

Massage: Pour 1 to 2 tsp (5 to 10 mL) Hero's Bath and Massage Oil into the palm of your hand and massage onto muscles before bathing or showering.

Bath: Fill tub with warm water. Pour 1 to 2 tsp (5 to 10 mL) Hero's Bath and Massage Oil into water and agitate to disperse oil. Soak for 30 minutes.

Achilles Tendonitis

Inflammation of the Achilles tendon, which is situated behind the ankle, can be caused by overuse or by strains. The area is often hot and painful and has restricted movement. Rest to avoid further injury, elevating the foot above the level of the heart.

Essential Oils

Black pepper, chamomile, ginger, lavender, thyme

Tips

Do not add essential oils to the tub while the water is running, as some of the precious essences may evaporate, depriving you of the full benefits.

If you prefer, substitute an equal quantity of liquid castile soap for the milk called for in any bath recipe.

If you are using a blend around bath/shower time, you can enhance the benefit by combining the essential oils with a carrier oil and rub it into your skin *before* getting into the shower or bath. This enables the essential oils to be absorbed and work their way into the bloodstream. The heat of the water encourages the essential oil vapors to rise, allowing you to inhale the aromas more easily and thus creating a dual application.

> ## *Achilles Tendonitis Massage Oil*
>
> 15 drops   chamomile essential oil
> 12 drops   lavender essential oil
> 12 drops   ginger essential oil
> ¼ cup (60 mL)   grapeseed or sweet almond oil
>
> *In a 2 oz (60 mL) glass bottle, combine chamomile, lavender and ginger essential oils. Top up with grapeseed oil and shake to blend.*

Treatments

Cold compress: Pour 2 cups (500 mL) cold (not icy) water into a non-reactive bowl and add 2 to 3 drops (total) chamomile and lavender essential oils. Stir well to disperse oils. Soak a cloth and wring out enough water so cloth doesn't drip. Place cloth on affected area. Repeat every 30 minutes for 3 hours, then decrease to 4 compresses a day for 2 days.

Massage: Pour a little Achilles Tendonitis Massage Oil into the palm of your hand and massage heel area several times a day. After massage, place a cold pack wrapped in a towel over the affected area. Treatment is often lengthy, but unless you persevere it will be even lengthier!

Cartilage Injury (Knee)

Keep the injured leg elevated. Apply alternating ice packs and towels or cloths wrung out in very hot water. Wear a knee brace or bandage until the damage is repaired. Massage the affected area with the following blend several times a day.

Essential Oils

Black pepper, clove, ginger, juniper, *Eucalyptus smithii*, manuka, tea tree, thyme ct. linalool

Caution
Do not use with children under the age of 2.

> ## *Cartilage Massage Blend*
>
> 16 drops   ginger essential oil
> 10 drops   black pepper essential oil
> 8 drops   clove essential oil
>
> *In a ⅙ oz (5 mL) glass bottle, combine ginger, black pepper and clove essential oils. Shake to blend.*

Treatment

Massage: In a small non-reactive bowl, combine 4 tsp (20 mL) grapeseed or sweet almond oil and 6 drops Cartilage Massage Blend. Mix well and massage over knee 2 to 3 times a day.

Strains and Sprains

Sprains are damage to ligaments that support a joint, while strains are injuries to muscles. The injured area shouldn't be massaged until the initial inflammation and swelling have receded. Apply ice packs to reduce swelling and inflammation.

Essential Oils

Black pepper, Roman chamomile, clove, ginger, lavender, manuka, marjoram, nutmeg, peppermint, rose, rosemary (ct. verbenone and ct. cineole), yarrow

---

Arnica Massage Oil Blend

6 drops	lavender essential oil
6 drops	rosemary ct. cineole or ct. verbenone essential oil
5 drops	Roman chamomile essential oil
4 drops	marjoram essential oil
3 drops	peppermint essential oil
¼ cup (60 ml)	arnica-infused oil

In a 2 oz (60 mL) glass bottle, combine lavender, rosemary, chamomile, marjoram and peppermint essential oils. Add arnica-infused oil and shake well.

Treatments

Cold compress: Pour 2 cups (500 mL) cold (not icy) water into a non-reactive bowl and add 2 to 3 drops each lavender, chamomile and marjoram essential oils. Stir well to disperse oils. Soak a cloth and wring out enough water so cloth doesn't drip. Place cloth on affected area. Repeat every 2 to 3 hours until relief from initial pain is obtained.

Massage: After the cold treatments have done their work and the initial heat and swelling have subsided, massage the affected area twice a day with Arnica Massage Oil Blend (do not use on broken or damaged skin) or Cartilage Massage Blend in a carrier oil (see page 128).

Sports Stress

Never underestimate the stress created by sport, particularly competitive sport. There is pregame stress, with all its worries about being a worthy member of the team, and the unresolved stress after the game if you feel that you have failed or could have achieved more. Here's a plea to parents whose children play sports: remember, games are supposed to be fun! See Stress and Emotional Problems (below).

Stress and Emotional Problems

Stress is the underlying cause of 80% of all disease and is a constant part of our lives. There are two main types of stress—eustress and dystress. *Eustress* ("good stress") is the healthy one that adds sparkle to our lives. We need eustress in order to function and to be alert. It has a beginning, a middle and, most important, an end.

Dystress (distress) is unresolved stress that is emotionally and physically damaging. The chemicals that our bodies produce in these situations, such as adrenalin, are not dispersed and can contribute to a variety of illnesses including high blood pressure, heart problems, digestive problems, diabetes, obesity, migraine, back problems, depression and nervous breakdown.

If you have the following symptoms, your stress and tension levels need to be addressed before you burn out:

- No enthusiasm for work, play, family or friends.
- Finding it difficult to laugh and getting upset and irritable easily.
- A feeling of impending doom.
- Constant backaches, headaches or stomachaches.
- An inability to sleep, or waking up in the morning feeling just as anxious and tired as when you went to bed.

Fortunately, this is where aromatherapy really shines! Essential oils, used in massage, baths and diffusers, can help you to relax. If you do not have one of the essential oils specified, you may substitute another that feels appropriate. Make up your own blends, using the emotions and conditions detailed below as a guide.

It's not always a good idea to use all the essential oils suggested for one condition. Instead, try to choose just one or two for the main problem, along with another one or two that balance the blend. See Properties of Essential Oils (page 21).

Tips

If you prefer, substitute Solubol (see Resources, page 459) for the vodka in a ratio of 4 drops Solubol for every 1 drop essential oil.

When making air sprays, be sure to add the oils to the bottle first, followed by the chosen dispersant (vodka or Solubol), to ensure that the essential oils disperse properly (they will not mix directly with water).

Aromatic baths are an ideal way of using essential oils to alleviate stress. It is very difficult to lie in warm, beautifully scented water and remain tense. Breathe slowly and gently. As you breathe in, feel the aromatic vapors entering every cell of your body, collecting all the negative feelings as a gray mist. As you breathe out, imagine that mist leaving your body. Remain in the bath for at least 30 minutes, topping up with more warm water as necessary. Afterwards, imagine all the tension and negative feelings running down the drain with the bathwater.

Some of the suggestions below may help you to cope until a long-term solution is found. If you suffer from depression, you need the help of a trained therapist, but essential oils can help to raise your spirits during this time. See Essential Oils for Stress and Relaxation, page 312.

Basic Essential Oil Stress Blend

100 drops	mixed essential oils for stress (see pages 312 and 313)

In a ⅙ oz (5 mL) glass dropper bottle, combine chosen essential oils. Shake to blend.

Treatments

Air spray: In a 4 oz (125 mL) PET plastic spray bottle, combine 75 drops Basic Essential Oil Stress Blend and 1 tsp (5 mL) vodka. Shake well. Fill with distilled or filtered water. Shake well.

Bath: Fill tub with warm water. Meanwhile, in a small non-reactive bowl, combine 1 tsp (5 mL) milk and 4 to 6 drops Basic Essential Oil Stress Blend. Add to tub and agitate to disperse oil, then soak for 30 minutes.

Inhaler: Place 21 to 25 drops Basic Essential Oil Stress Blend in a small non-reactive bowl. Place inhaler wick in the bowl and allow it to absorb the entire amount. Insert the wick inside the inhaler tube and tightly cap the bottom of the inhaler with the plug. Place the inhaler tube inside its cover and screw tightly to close.

Massage: Place 24 drops Basic Essential Oil Stress Blend in a 2 oz (60 mL) glass bottle. Top up with about ¼ cup (60 mL) passion flower (best for stress), grapeseed or sweet almond oil. Shake to combine.

Roll-on: In a ⅓ oz (10 mL) glass bottle with roller ball, combine 25 drops Basic Essential Oil Stress Blend and just enough fractionated coconut or passion flower oil to barely fill bottle (be careful not to overfill). Insert the ball holder, then the ball, and screw on the top. Shake to blend. Apply to pulse points as a natural perfume.

Tips

Do not add essential oils to the tub while the water is running, as some of the precious essences may evaporate, depriving you of the full benefits.

If you prefer, substitute an equal quantity of liquid castile soap for the milk called for in any bath recipe.

If you are using a blend around bath/ shower time, you can enhance the benefit by combining the essential oils with a carrier oil and rub it into your skin *before* getting into the shower or bath. This enables the essential oils to be absorbed and work their way into the bloodstream. The heat of the water encourages the essential oil vapors to rise, allowing you to inhale the aromas more easily and thus creating a dual application.

Essential Oils for Stress and Relaxation

Application	Essential Oils
Anger	Bergamot, Roman chamomile, cypress, geranium, lavender, lemon, peppermint, ylang ylang
Anxiety	Bergamot, Roman chamomile, clary sage, cypress, frankincense, geranium, juniper, lavender, mandarin, marjoram, melissa, neroli, bitter orange, rose, ylang ylang
Apathy	Clary sage, ginger, grapefruit, jasmine, juniper, lavender, lemon, marjoram, peppermint, rosemary
Bipolar disorder	Geranium, grapefruit, lavender
Burnout	Grapefruit, jasmine, lavender, lemon, vetiver
Calming	Bergamot, cedarwood, clary sage, frankincense, jasmine, lavender, mandarin, marjoram, ylang ylang
Depression (long-term)	Basil, bergamot, Roman chamomile, Douglas fir, grapefruit, neroli, orange (blood or sweet), petitgrain, rose, spearmint
Excitability	Cedarwood, chamomile, *Eucalyptus smithii*, lavender, mandarin, marjoram, vetiver, ylang ylang
Fainting	Lavender (and spike lavender), marjoram, peppermint, rosemary (ct. cineole and ct. camphor)
Fear	Basil, bergamot, lavender, marjoram, melissa, rosemary, ylang ylang
Frustration	Bergamot, lavender
Grief	Cypress, frankincense, lavender, marjoram, melissa, neroli, rose, sage
Guilt	Chamomile, clary sage, frankincense, lavender, peppermint, rosemary
Hysteria	Clary sage, *Litsea cubeba*, melissa, peppermint, rosemary (ct. cineole and ct. camphor), spikenard
Insomnia	Angelica, basil ct. linalool, cedarwood, Roman chamomile, cistus, lavender, mandarin, marjoram, melissa, valerian, ylang ylang
Irritability	Roman chamomile, cypress, grapefruit
Listlessness	Geranium, jasmine, lavandin 'Super', lavender
Meditation	Cedarwood, frankincense, patchouli, rose, vetiver
Mental dullness	Basil, bergamot, black pepper, fennel, lemon, Spanish marjoram, peppermint, rosemary
Mental stress	Basil, cedarwood, Roman chamomile, rosemary, thyme ct. thymol

Application	Essential Oils
Migraine	Aniseed, basil ct. linalool, Roman chamomile, *Eucalyptus globulus*, grapefruit, lavandin, lavender, marjoram, peppermint, rosemary (ct. cineole and ct. camphor)
Mood balancing	Clary sage, cypress, geranium, jasmine, lavender, marjoram, niaouli, rose
Negative thoughts	Bergamot, Roman chamomile, clary sage, cypress, geranium, lavender, lemon, marjoram, orange, peppermint, rosemary
Nervous exhaustion	Basil, clary sage, clove (bud), geranium, grapefruit, lavender, mandarin, rosemary, tea tree, thyme ct. linalool, ylang ylang
Nervousness (jitters)	Bergamot, frankincense, geranium, lavender, marjoram
Obsessiveness	Frankincense
Panic attack	Basil, bergamot, clary sage, lavender, marjoram, melissa, Rescue Remedy (see page 457), rosemary, ylang ylang
Paranoia	Basil, bergamot, clary sage, lavender (high-altitude), marjoram, melissa, rosemary, ylang ylang
Pre-exam or interview stress	Bergamot, grapefruit, lavender, lemon, rosemary
Pre-operative stress	Chamomile, clary sage, lavender, Rescue Remedy (see page 457), ylang ylang
Post-operative stress	Grapefruit, lavender, mandarin, peppermint, Rescue Remedy (see page 457)
Restlessness	Bergamot, Roman chamomile, mandarin, marjoram, valerian, vetiver, ylang ylang
Sexual dysfunction (female)	Star anise, black pepper, clary sage, nutmeg, rose, ylang ylang
Sexual insecurity	Clary sage, jasmine, rose, rosewood, ylang ylang
Shock	Roman chamomile, lavender, marjoram, peppermint, Rescue Remedy (see page 457)
Sluggishness (mental)	Basil, black pepper, grapefruit, lemon, Spanish marjoram, peppermint, rosemary
Tension headache	Grapefruit, lavender, marjoram, peppermint, rosemary
Trauma	Roman chamomile, lavender, marjoram, Rescue Remedy (see page 457), rose
Vertigo	Basil, lavender, *Litsea cubeba*, marjoram, melissa, orange (blood or sweet), peppermint, rosemary (ct. cineole and ct. camphor), sage

Stretch Marks
See Pregnancy and Birth (page 283)

Sunburn

We should all now be completely aware of the dangers of overexposure to ultraviolet (UV) radiation. We only need to expose our skin to sunshine for 10 minutes a day, in the early morning or late afternoon, to manufacture the necessary amount of vitamin D for our bodies. However, even when we try to be careful, sometimes we end up with a painful, itchy sunburn. Essential oils can help ease the discomfort.

Essential Oils

Moroccan chamomile, geranium, lavender, peppermint

Treatments

Bath: Fill tub with enough cool water to submerge your body up to the neck. Meanwhile, in a small non-reactive bowl, combine 1 tsp (5 mL) milk and 4 to 6 drops either chamomile or lavender essential oil (as age-appropriate; see page 164). Add to tub and agitate to disperse oil, then soak for 15 to 30 minutes, gently massaging any floating droplets of oil into your skin. Pat dry. Smooth Sunburn Blend (below) all over burned area. Be very gentle when applying it, or the skin will feel even more painful!

Cool compress: Pour 2 cups (500 mL) cool (not icy) water into a non-reactive bowl and add 4 to 6 drops lavender or chamomile essential oil. Stir well to disperse oils. Soak a cloth and wring out enough water that cloth doesn't drip. Place cloth on affected areas.

Topical application: Place 8 tsp (40 mL) yogurt or 4 tsp (20 mL) aloe vera gel in a small non-reactive bowl. Add 20 drops lavender essential oil and mix thoroughly. Use a cotton ball to apply mixture to any sunburn-blistered areas.

Sunburn Blend

4 tsp (20 mL)	aloe vera gel or juice
1 tsp (5 mL)	arnica-infused oil (do not use on broken skin) or sea buckthorn oil
20 drops	lavender essential oil

In a 1 oz (30 mL) double-walled jar, combine aloe vera gel, arnica-infused oil and lavender essential oil. Mix thoroughly. Apply with a cotton ball. Stir well before reapplying.

Sunstroke and Heatstroke

Treat sunstroke as an emergency—it means that the body's heat regulation system isn't working. This causes body temperature to rise to dangerous levels. The point of treatment is to cool the patient as quickly as possible.

Essential Oils

Eucalyptus citriodora, lavender, lemon, lemongrass, kaffir lime, palmarosa, peppermint, rose

Treatments

Bath: To reduce temperature, fill tub with enough cool water to submerge your body up to the neck. Meanwhile, in a small non-reactive bowl, combine 1 tsp (5 mL) milk and 4 drops lavender, 2 drops *Eucalyptus citriodora* and 3 drops lemon essential oils. Add to tub and agitate to disperse oils, then soak for 15 to 30 minutes, gently massaging any floating droplets of oil into your skin. Apply cool compresses to head while bathing (see below).

Continue with frequent cool showers or body sponging for up to 48 hours. Restore circulation by rubbing the arms and legs.

Cool compress: In a non-reactive bowl, combine 1 cup (250 mL) cold (not icy) water and 1 cup (250 mL) geranium or peppermint hydrolat. Add 1 drop each lavender, *Eucalyptus citriodora* and lemon essential oils. Stir well to disperse oils. Soak a cloth and wring out just enough water that cloth doesn't drip. Place very wet, cold compresses over the entire head during bathing, changing compresses frequently to keep them cold.

Drink: Electrolytes help to maintain proper functioning of the body's systems. Without proper functioning, the nervous system can shut down. To make your own electrolyte water, combine 4 cups (1 L) cool (not ice-cold) water, $\frac{1}{2}$ tsp (2.5 mL) baking soda, 1 oz (30 mL) agave syrup and $1\frac{1}{2}$ tsp (7.5 mL) pink Himalayan salt. Shake to combine. Drink up to 12 cups (3 L) to replace lost body fluids and electrolytes.

Caution

Avoid exposure to the sun within 12 hours of using lemon essential oil. Or, to avoid phototoxicity, use lemon essential oil distilled from the whole fruit.

Teeth and Gum Problems

Regular dental checkups, brushing with a soft-bristle brush after eating, flossing, and eating foods such as fruit and raw vegetables that exercise teeth and jaws will all help to keep your teeth and gums strong and healthy. The following recipes will help to prevent and treat mouth infections.

Tip

To prevent bacteria growing on toothbrushes, dip them in a solution of 2 drops tea tree essential oil in ½ cup (250 mL) distilled or filtered water. Rinse thoroughly. Always store in a place with good air circulation.

Mint and Lemon Tooth Powder

½ cup (125 mL)	baking soda
¼ cup (60 mL)	finely ground sea salt
4 tsp (20 mL)	dried lemon zest (yellow part only), finely ground to a powder
4 tsp (20 mL)	dried sage leaves, finely ground to a powder
3 drops	lemon essential oil
2 drops	peppermint essential oil

1. *In a non-reactive bowl, combine baking soda, salt, lemon zest and sage. Using the back of a spoon, sift or press through a fine-mesh sieve into a clean non-reactive bowl. A drop at a time, add the lemon and peppermint essential oils, stirring constantly.*

2. *Transfer the mixture to an 8 oz (250 mL) double-walled jar and close tightly. Make a jar for each family member to prevent the spread of mouth infections.*

   To use, dampen a toothbrush and dip into Mint and Lemon Tooth Powder. Brush and rinse teeth (thoroughly) as usual. Be sure to spit out all traces of the tooth powder when rinsing.

Abscess (Dental)

Essential Oils

Roman chamomile, clove, tea tree

Treatment

Topical application: In a non-reactive tablespoon (15 mL), combine 2 to 3 drops extra virgin olive oil and 1 drop either chamomile, clove or tea tree essential oil. Stir using a cotton swab. Using cotton swab, dab onto abscess. It will sting initially, but then it will help to both numb the area and heal the abscess. After applying, swish out the mouth with 6 tsp (30 mL) rose hydrolat, then spit it out.

Gingivitis

Gingivitis is inflammation and bleeding of the gums caused largely by bacterial plaque and poor brushing technique. Check with your dentist if the problem has been long-term. To prevent or treat gingivitis, brush teeth regularly (and properly) with a medium- or soft-bristle toothbrush. Thorough rinsing of the mouth several times a day with Gingivitis Mouthwash can be helpful.

Gingivitis Mouthwash

¼ cup (60 mL)	sherry
8 tsp (40 mL)	brandy
1 tsp (5 mL)	glycerin
6 drops	thyme ct. linalool or sage essential oil
6 drops	peppermint essential oil
4 drops	myrrh essential oil or 1 tsp (5 mL) tincture of myrrh
2 drops	rose essential oil and/or 2 tsp (10 mL) rose hydrolat

In a 4 oz (125 mL) glass jar, combine sherry, brandy, glycerin and thyme, peppermint, myrrh and rose essential oils. Mix thoroughly. Using a coffee filter, strain mixture into a dark glass bottle with a stopper.

Treatment
Mouthwash: Add 1 tsp (5 mL) Gingivitis Mouthwash mixture to ½ cup (125 mL) warm water and mix well. Rinse mouth several times and then spit it out (do not swallow). Repeat several times daily.

Gum Infections

Essential Oils

Myrrh, tea tree

Treatment
Mouthwash: Add 2 drops tea tree or myrrh essential oil (or 1 of each) to a spoon containing 1 tsp (5 mL) unpasteurized liquid honey. Mix with a toothpick and add to ½ cup (125 mL) warm water. Stir well to combine. Rinse mouth several times and then spit it out (do not swallow). Repeat several times daily.

Caution
As noted, essential oils should never be ingested for home use. If using an essential oil in a gargle or mouthwash, be sure to prepare the proper dilution (as specified) and spit it all out when treatment is completed.

Toothache

Essential Oils

Black pepper, Roman chamomile, clove, cinnamon (leaf), ginger, marjoram, nutmeg

Treatments

Massage: Dip a tablespoon in hot (not boiling) water to warm the spoon. Place 1 tsp (5 mL) grapeseed oil in the spoon and stir with a toothpick. Add 5 drops chamomile essential oil and stir well to disperse oil. Using your fingertips, gently massage the oil into your face, focusing on the cheek over the aching tooth and along the jaw. Repeat as necessary for pain.

Topical application: Using a cotton swab, apply 1 drop clove essential oil to the aching tooth and gently massage the gum around the tooth.

Teething
See Babies and Children (page 168)

Throat (Sore)

Many sore throats are bacterial or viral in origin. They can also be the result of what we call irritants—talking too much or too loudly for too long, hay fever, open-mouth breathing, dust, cigarette smoke, airborne chemical fumes or air conditioning. Gargles work well where irritants have caused the sore throat. (See also Respiratory Problems, page 293.)

Essential Oils

Benzoin, clary sage, geranium, lavender, myrtle (green or orange), sweet orange, sage (see Cautions, page 106), thyme (ct. geraniol or ct. linalool)

Treatments

Mouthwash: In a glass, combine 1 to 2 drops clary sage, geranium or lavender essential oil and ½ tsp (5 mL) salt. Mix thoroughly. Add 1 cup (250 mL) warm water and stir well to combine. Rinse mouth several times and then spit it out (do not swallow). Repeat several times daily.

Drink: Place 1 drop cedarwood essential oil on a sugar cube or teabag (chamomile tea works best) and make tea as usual. Alternatively, combine 1 drop cedarwood essential oil and 1 tsp (5 mL) unpasteurized liquid honey. Swallow as is, add to a cup of tea, or mix with 3 tsp (15 mL) very hot water in a small glass and drink.

Topical application: In the palm of your hand, combine 1 drop cedarwood essential oil and ½ tsp (2.5 mL) grapeseed or sweet almond oil. Massage over the throat. Repeat 2 to 3 times per day to relieve pain.

Thrush
See Candidiasis (page 195)

Tinea
See Athlete's Foot (page 228); Jock Itch (page 268); Ringworm (page 302)

Tonsillitis
See Respiratory Problems (page 299)

Tip

When blending fewer than 500 drops (20 mL) of essential oils, use a 1 oz (30 mL) measuring glass or shot glass as your small non-reactive bowl.

Travel

Holiday trips are one of life's great pleasures, but it's all too easy for them to be ruined by health problems that could have been avoided. In addition to taking normal precautions, packing a small but effective selection of essential oils can help to ensure that your trip is not undermined by sickness.

Airplane Travel

Following a few simple rules during a flight can help you arrive feeling as bright as possible and, hopefully, avoid jet lag.

- Drink plenty of water on the plane and try to avoid being tempted to drink alcohol. If you feel nauseated, use your inhaler (page 275).
- Do not eat unless you are really hungry.
- Wear loose shoes, as your feet might swell on a long journey. Take short walks along the aisle to improve circulation.
- Use the Travel Buddy inhaler (see page 323). Place 1 drop Travel Buddy Blend on a small cotton ball and let it rest on the ledge of your ear (don't push it inside).

Pre-flying Nerves Tamer

Many people are nervous about flying, even though statistically it is one of the safest forms of transportation. If this fear is ruining your pre-holiday excitement, use this blend for a week before you leave. This blend will also help children feel calmer.

1 tsp (5 mL)	lavender essential oil
½ tsp (2.5 mL)	bergamot essential oil
½ tsp (2.5 mL)	geranium essential oil
40 drops	sandalwood or cedarwood essential oil
10 drops	chamomile essential oil

In a small glass dropper bottle, combine lavender, bergamot, geranium, sandalwood and chamomile essential oils. Shake to blend.

Treatments

Air spray: In a 4 oz (125 mL) PET plastic spray bottle, combine 75 drops Pre-flying Nerves Tamer and 1 tsp (5 mL) vodka. Fill bottle with distilled or filtered water (see Tips, page 321). Shake to blend.

Tips

Carry hand sanitizer (see page 204) with you, as colds, gastroenteritis, hepatitis, influenza and scabies are just a few of the diseases that can be transmitted via doorknobs, money, handrails, toilet flush handles and many other sources.

With airline restrictions on luggage and carry-ons, bear in mind that it may be easier to pack only very small, well-labeled bottles of essential oils or blends, especially if you plan to carry them in your hand luggage or purse with other toiletries. Ensure that your bottles are sealed tightly, as citrus oils tend to pique the interest of sniffer dogs. Just be sure to have your inhaler and any items that essential oils may have spilled on ready for inspection.

Bath: Fill tub with warm water. Meanwhile, in a small non-reactive bowl, combine 1 tsp (5 mL) milk and 4 to 6 drops Pre-flying Nerves Tamer. Add to tub and agitate to disperse oil, then soak for 30 minutes, massaging any floating droplets of oil into your skin.

Massage: In a small non-reactive bowl, combine 2 tsp (10 mL) grapeseed or sweet almond oil and 4 drops Pre-flying Nerves Tamer. Mix well and massage over your body.

Roll-on: Place 15 drops Pre-flying Nerves Tamer blend in a ⅓ oz (10 mL) glass bottle with roller ball, and fill with fractionated coconut oil (be careful not to overfill). Insert the ball holder, then the ball, and screw on the top. Shake to blend. Roll onto temples, wrists and other pulse points.

Flying High Blend

Use this blend once you are airborne to deal with nerves and exhaustion. The best way to carry it is in a small spray bottle. The blend may be used for adults and children over the age of 2. If using on children, the spray must be very light—just one quick squirt.

30 drops	lavender essential oil
30 drops	geranium essential oil
20 drops	grapefruit essential oil

In a small glass dropper bottle, combine lavender, geranium and grapefruit essential oils. Shake to blend.

Treatments

Air spray: In a 1 oz (30 mL) PET plastic spray bottle, combine 20 drops Flying High Blend and ½ tsp (2.5 mL) vodka. Fill bottle with distilled or filtered water (see Tips, right). Shake to blend.

Inhaler: Place 21 drops Flying High Blend in a small non-reactive bowl. Place inhaler wick in the bowl and allow it to absorb the entire amount. Insert the wick inside the inhaler tube and tightly cap the bottom of the inhaler with the plug. Place the inhaler tube inside its cover and screw tightly to close.

Travel compress: Wring a cloth out in very hot water, spray very lightly with a little Flying High Blend (the equivalent of 1 to 2 drops) and use to wipe face and hands. The heat has a calming effect. Holding the hot cloth on the back of the neck is also soothing and relaxing.

Caution

Before using any essential oil, consult the relevant entry in Part 1: Essential Oils (A to Y), pages 28 to 117, taking careful note of any cautions.

Tips

If you prefer, when making an air spray, substitute Solubol for the vodka called for, in a ratio of 4 drops Solubol for every 1 drop essential oil. Solubol is a natural product that allows essential oils to disperse in liquid.

When making air sprays, be sure to add the oils to the bottle first, followed by the chosen dispersant (vodka or Solubol), to ensure that the essential oils disperse properly (they will not mix directly with water).

For babies less
than 1 year old, use
2 drops chamomile
essential oil in 4 tsp
(20 mL) grapeseed
oil. Massage the
child's arms and
legs, using a gentle
upward movement
toward the heart.

Caution

Not for use on the
plane, as sitting
for long periods of
time constricts the
blood vessels.

Toddler Tamer

Children can get very overexcited, tired and cranky when
traveling. This blend is suitable for children over 1 year old
(see Tip, left).

4 tsp (20 mL)	grapeseed or sweet almond oil
3 drops	chamomile essential oil
2 drops	lavender essential oil

*In a 1 oz (30 mL) glass bottle, combine grapeseed oil and
chamomile and lavender essential oils. Shake to blend.*

Treatment

Inhalation: Apply a little Toddler Tamer to a tissue and encourage
the child to inhale. This will have a calming effect.

Aching, Swollen Legs and Feet Gel

¼ cup (60 mL)	aloe vera gel
24 drops	lavender essential oil
12 drops	peppermint essential oil

*In a small non-reactive bowl, combine aloe vera gel and
lavender and peppermint essential oils. Mix thoroughly.
Transfer to a resealable 1 oz (30 mL) double-walled jar.
Store in a dark, cool place.*

Variation
*If the blend is to be used for children, substitute an equal
amount of spearmint essential oil for the peppermint
essential oil.*

Treatment

Topical application: Pat Aching, Swollen Legs and Feet Gel over
your legs and feet whenever you feel the need. Don't massage
it into the skin—peppermint causes blood vessels to constrict,
which triggers a cooling sensation followed by a warming
sensation. (See Caution, left.)

Travel Buddy Blend

Make up an inhaler of Travel Buddy Blend and use on the descent during air travel and to allay the symptoms of jet lag. The inhaler is most effective when used for 2 days prior to travel and throughout the trip.

30 drops	lavender essential oil
20 drops	grapefruit essential oil
12 drops	peppermint or rosemary essential oil
12 drops	ginger essential oil

In a small glass dropper bottle, combine lavender, grapefruit, peppermint and ginger essential oils. Shake to blend.

Treatments

Bath: Fill tub with warm water. Meanwhile, in a small non-reactive bowl, combine 1 tsp (5 mL) milk and 4 to 6 drops Travel Buddy Blend. Add to tub and agitate to disperse oil, then soak for 30 minutes, massaging any floating droplets of oil into your skin. (See also Sunshine Blend, page 180.)

Inhaler: Place 21 drops Travel Buddy Blend in a small non-reactive bowl. Place inhaler wick in the bowl and allow it to absorb the entire amount. Insert the wick inside the inhaler tube and tightly cap the bottom of the inhaler with the plug. Place the inhaler tube inside its cover and screw tightly to close.

Roll-on: Place 15 drops Travel Buddy Blend in a $1/3$ oz (10 mL) glass bottle with roller ball, and top up with fractionated coconut oil (be careful not to overfill). Insert the ball holder, then the ball, and screw on the top. Shake to blend. Roll onto temples, wrists and collarbones, as needed.

Jet Lag

Flying can get us from one side of the globe to the other in the space of a few hours. The following suggestions can be helpful for overcoming the problems our bodies often experience adjusting to the time change. They can also be used to help you recover from your trip when you return home.

- Don't go to sleep until the local bedtime.
- Drink lots of filtered or bottled water. Avoid alcohol.
- When you go to bed, place 1 drop chamomile and 1 drop lavender essential oil on a tissue and slip it inside your pillowcase to ensure a good sleep. This method will also soothe overexcited and fractious children.

Tips

Do not add essential oils to the tub while the water is running, as some of the precious essences may evaporate, depriving you of the full benefits.

If you prefer, substitute an equal quantity of liquid castile soap for the milk called for in any bath recipe.

If you are using a blend around bath/ shower time, you can enhance the benefit by combining the essential oils with a carrier oil and rub it into your skin *before* getting into the shower or bath. This enables the essential oils to be absorbed and work their way into the bloodstream. The heat of the water encourages the essential oil vapors to rise, allowing you to inhale the aromas more easily and thus creating a dual application.

Sleep Easy Blend

30 drops	lavender essential oil
30 drops	geranium essential oil
30 drops	chamomile essential oil

In a ¹⁄₆ oz (5 mL) glass dropper bottle, combine lavender, geranium and chamomile essential oils. Shake to blend.

Treatments

Bath: Fill tub with warm water. Meanwhile, in a small non-reactive bowl, combine 1 tsp (5 mL) milk and 4 to 6 drops Sleep Easy Blend. Add to tub and agitate to disperse oil, then soak for 30 minutes, massaging any floating droplets of oil into your skin.

Massage: In a small non-reactive bowl, combine 2 tsp (10 mL) grapeseed oil and 4 drops Sleep Easy Blend. Mix well and massage over your body.

Motion Sickness

Car, boat or plane sickness can make you regret ever having left home. But don't let it spoil your trip—there are remedies that can overcome this.

Tip

Thirty minutes to one hour before setting off on a trip, take 2 ginger tablets or capsules (available from pharmacies and health-food stores) or chew crystallized or candied ginger.

Quiet the Queasiness Tonic

In a 16 oz (500 mL) bottle, combine 2 tsp (10 mL) unpasteurized liquid honey and 2 drops peppermint essential oil. Fill bottle with distilled or filtered water and shake well. Store for up to 1 week in the refrigerator to use as needed. Follow these use guidelines:

Children ages 2 to 5	1 tsp (5 mL) tonic in ¼ cup (60 mL) distilled or filtered water
Children ages 5 to 12	2 tsp (10 mL) tonic in ¼ cup (60 mL) distilled or filtered water
Children ages 12 to 16	¼ cup (60 mL) undiluted mixture
Adults	½ cup (125 mL) undiluted mixture

Treatment

Inhalation: When traveling by car, apply 1 drop each peppermint and lavender essential oils to cotton balls and place on the back and front window ledges. These will help prevent nausea and also act as a calmative.

Dysentery

Dysentery, or shigellosis, is a highly infectious disease caused by a bacillus found in contaminated water and food. It is spread mainly by human contact and flies. Seek medical help to treat this condition. Essential oils can be useful to help prevent spread of the disease and to protect the care provider.

Essential Oils

Bergamot, cinnamon (bark), ginger, lavender, thyme ct. linalool

Air spray: In a 4 oz (125 mL) PET plastic spray bottle, combine 36 drops each bergamot and lavender essential oils, 3 drops cinnamon essential oil and 1 tsp (5 mL) vodka. Shake well. Fill bottle with distilled or filtered water (see Tips, right). Shake to blend. Use frequently in the sickroom and throughout the whole house.

Bath: Fill tub with warm water. Meanwhile, in a small non-reactive bowl, combine 1 tsp (5 mL) milk and 3 drops thyme and 2 drops lavender essential oil. Add to tub and agitate to disperse oils, then soak for 30 minutes, massaging any floating droplets of oil into your skin.

Handwash for caregivers: After dealing with the patient (see above), wash your hands with soap and a nailbrush for at least 30 seconds, paying particular attention to around the nails and the wrists. In a medium non-reactive bowl, combine 6 drops thyme and 4 drops lavender essential oil with 1 tsp (5 mL) milk. Fill bowl with water and place next to the washbasin. Rinse hands and lower arms thoroughly in the bowl and dry with paper towels.

Massage: In a small non-reactive bowl, combine 2 tsp (10 mL) grapeseed or sweet almond oil and 2 drops each thyme and lavender essential oils. Mix well and massage over your body.

Tips

If you prefer, when making an air spray, substitute Solubol for the vodka called for, in a ratio of 4 drops Solubol for every 1 drop essential oil. Solubol is a natural product that allows essential oils to disperse in liquid.

When making air sprays, be sure to add the oils to the bottle first, followed by the chosen dispersant (vodka or Solubol), to ensure that the essential oils disperse properly (they will not mix directly with water).

Tips

Do not add essential oils to the tub while the water is running, as some of the precious essences may evaporate, depriving you of the full benefits.

If you prefer, substitute an equal quantity of liquid castile soap for the milk called for in any bath recipe.

If you are using a blend around bath/shower time, you can enhance the benefit by combining the essential oils with a carrier oil and rub it into your skin *before* getting into the shower or bath. This enables the essential oils to be absorbed and work their way into the bloodstream. The heat of the water encourages the essential oil vapors to rise, allowing you to inhale the aromas more easily and thus creating a dual application.

Urethritis

When the urethra becomes infected, the infection usually travels quickly into the bladder, where it causes cystitis. The symptoms of urethritis include frequent and painful urination, a sensation of burning and stinging, and often a feeling of exhaustion. Treatment needs to be prompt to prevent the infection worsening. If the condition worsens or if the attack lasts more than 2 days, consult your health-care practitioner. See Cystitis (page 213) for treatment.

Urticaria (Hives)

Commonly known as hives, urticaria is characterized by angry red raised welts on the skin that are very itchy. It is triggered by an allergic reaction, which releases histamines. The amount of essential oil used in treatments is less than for many other complaints, as the skin is very sensitive and a high percentage of oil could irritate.

Essential Oils

Bergamot, Roman chamomile, lavender, peppermint, vetiver

Treatments

Bath: Fill tub with warm water. Meanwhile, in a small non-reactive bowl, combine 1 tsp (5 mL) milk and 2 drops each vetiver, lavender and chamomile essential oils. Add to tub and agitate to disperse oil, then soak for 30 minutes, massaging any floating droplets of oil into your skin.

Hot compress: *If the rash covers a small area:* In a small non-reactive bowl, combine 1 cup (250 mL) hot water and 4 drops Roman chamomile essential oil. Stir well to disperse oil. Submerge a cloth just large enough to absorb all the liquid without dripping. Apply to the affected area every few hours.

If the rash covers a large area: Fill tub with lukewarm water. Add $\frac{1}{2}$ cup (125 mL) baking soda and 6 drops Roman chamomile essential oil and agitate to dissolve baking soda and disperse oil. Soak for 30 minutes, massaging any floating droplets of oil into your skin.

Topical Application: In a small nonreactive bowl, combine 1 drop each vetiver, lavender and chamomile essential oils and 2 tsp (10 ml) grapeseed oil or St. John's wort–infused oil. Using a cotton ball, apply to affected area.

Alternatively, in a small nonreactive bowl, combine 4 drops lavender essential oil and 2 tsp (10 mL) cider vinegar. Using a cotton ball, apply to affected area to ease itching.

Varicose Veins
See Pregnancy and Birth (page 285)

Verruca
See Warts (page 328)

Viral Infections

Viruses are responsible for most epidemic illnesses. According to aromatherapy experts, the following essential oils have antiviral action: basil, bay laurel, West Indian bay, bergamot, catnip, cinnamon, cistus, clove (bud), eucalyptus (*globulus*, *smithii*, *radiata* and *dives*), helichrysum, lavandin 'Super', lemon, lime, *Litsea cubeba*, manuka, melissa, niaouli, peppermint, ravensara, rosewood, black spruce, tea tree and thyme (ct. linaool and ct. geraniol). For treatment, see Chicken Pox (page 169), Common Cold and Influenza (page 203), Herpes (page 249), Measles (page 264), Mumps (page 273), Rubella (page 303) and West Nile Virus (page 329).

Vomiting

See also Nausea (page 275) for additional treatments for vomiting.

Essential Oils

Digestive upsets: ginger, peppermint

Morning sickness: spearmint

Stress-induced vomiting: anise, Roman chamomile, lavender, peppermint

Treatment
Stomach massage: In a small non-reactive bowl, combine 2 drops total of oils listed above (according to cause of vomiting) and 1 tsp (5 mL) grapeseed oil. Mix thoroughly. Inhale the vapors and gently massage the oil over your stomach and abdomen.

Warts

Warts (medically termed *verrucae*) are caused by a virus. If you suffer from either recurrent or large numbers of warts, your immune system may need help and you should consult a health-care practitioner.

Essential Oils

Cinnamon (bark), lemon, lemon myrtle, tea tree; calendula-infused oil

Treatment

Topical application: Using a cotton swab, apply 1 drop tea tree or lemon essential oil directly to the wart and cover with a bandage. Repeat twice daily until wart has gone. If skin is very dry afterward, massage with a little calendula-infused oil.

Water Warts

"Water warts" is a viral infection of the skin caused by a pox virus (its medical name is *molluscum contagiosum*). It is seen most often in children aged 1 through 10 and is transmitted through skin-to-skin contact or shared items such as towels, clothing or toys. Water warts present as small, raised pearl-like nodules or bumps on the skin that are filled with a cheesy or waxy white substance. They are not painful or itchy and the lesions are not red unless they have been irritated by scratching. Scratching or popping the bumps is discouraged, as it leads to spreading of the virus to adjacent skin or to other people. It is contagious until the bumps are gone, which, if untreated, may take 6 to 18 months. Common medical treatments can be unpleasant and leave scars. An aromatherapeutic approach is effective and non-invasive.

Treatment

Topical application: In a ⅙ oz (5 mL) glass dropper bottle, combine 15 drops lemon myrtle essential oil and 1 tsp (5 ml) organic extra virgin olive oil. Pour 1 to 2 drops on a cotton swab and dab on the affected area. If you need to apply more, add 1 to 2 more drops to the swab (be sure not to touch the used swab with the dropper). Cover treated area with a bandage. Repeat treatment once daily until water warts have gone (in some cases in as little as a month!).

West Nile Virus

West Nile virus is transmitted to humans via infected mosquitoes. The symptoms can easily be confused with chronic fatigue syndrome or some rheumatic diseases, but the illness can be diagnosed by a blood test. See Chronic Fatigue Syndrome (page 199) for suggestions for dealing with fatigue. See Bites and Stings (page 184) and Insect Repellent (page 254) for suggestions on how to avoid being bitten by mosquitoes.

Whitlow

A whitlow is a herpes simplex infection of the fingertip in which pus collects and creates pressure under the skin and sometimes under the fingernail. Untreated, it generally resolves itself within 2 to 3 weeks, but living with it is very painful. The essential oils recommended are useful antivirals as well as providing pain relief.

Essential Oils

Basil ct. linalool, bay laurel, cinnamon, clove (bud), *Eucalyptus smithii*, lavender, niaouli, peppermint, rosemary (ct. cineole and ct. camphor)

Treatment
Soaking and topical application: Place 1 cup (250 mL) boiling water in a small non-reactive bowl and set aside to cool slightly (until it can be tolerated). In another small non-reactive bowl, combine 2 drops each rosemary and lemon essential oils and 1 tsp (5 mL) unpasteurized liquid honey or milk and stir well. Add the essential oil mixture to the water and stir to combine. Immerse the affected finger in the mixture for 2 to 3 minutes, then dry gently with a clean towel. Place 1 drop lavender essential oil on the pad of a breathable bandage and cover the affected finger. Repeat 2 to 3 times a day, as needed for pain.

Whooping Cough
See Babies and Children (page 175)

Women's Health

Cervical Dysplasia

Cervical dysplasia is a precancerous condition of the cervix. It is treatable if diagnosed in its early stages. The following douche treatment is for what are described as Grades 1 and 2 dysplasia (as diagnosed by your doctor). In the case of Grades 3 or 4, the treatment may be carried out alongside conventional treatment.

Essential Oils

Lavender, tea tree

Treatment

Douche: In a non-reactive bowl, combine 2 drops tea tree or lavender essential oil and 2 cups (500 mL) warm water. Mix thoroughly. Pour into a douche bag (available at most pharmacies) and follow manufacturer's directions for use.

Endometriosis

Endometriosis, in which tissue that normally lines the uterus grows elsewhere in the abdomen, can be an acutely painful condition. Its numerous unpleasant symptoms include heavy and painful periods; internal bleeding; pain with sexual intercourse, ovulation and/or bowel movements; constipation; diarrhea; infertility and more. It affects about 10% of all women. Aromatherapy treatment can often ease the pain and discomfort, but lifestyle changes— diet, more exercise, and vitamin and mineral supplements—are also advised.

Essential Oils

Roman chamomile, clary sage, cypress, geranium, juniper, lavender

Treatment

Sitz bath: A daily sitz bath, alternating between hot and cold water, will stimulate the pelvic region. Fill tub with enough hot water to cover your lower abdomen. Fill with cold water a basin big enough to sit in and place on the floor alongside the tub. Meanwhile, in a small non-reactive bowl, combine 2 drops each geranium, clary sage and cypress essential oils and 1 tsp (5 mL) grapeseed oil. Add to tub and agitate to disperse oils, then sit in bath for 10 minutes. Then sit in the cold water (with no essential oils added) for 5 minutes. Repeat.

Treatment

Stomach massage: In a small non-reactive bowl, combine 2 tsp (10 mL) grapeseed or sweet almond oil and 5 drops Massage Blend for Endometriosis. Mix well and massage over your abdomen and lower back once or twice a day.

Fibrocystic Breast Disease

The symptoms of fibrocystic disease (which is not actually a disease but a common condition) are nodules or lumps in the breasts that can change in size and location. Sometimes there is soreness, swelling, pain and tenderness. Lumpy breasts are often associated with PMS, as they appear to be caused by hormonal changes in the body. The lumps usually disappear at menopause (unless you are on a hormone replacement program). See your doctor for a breast examination and, if recommended, a mammogram.

Essential Oils

Roman chamomile, cypress, geranium, lavender, patchouli, petitgrain, rose

Treatments

Massage: Pour a few drops Breast Massage Oil onto your fingers and, using your thumb and first two fingers in a firm rolling movement, massage into nipples and the surrounding area. Massage both breasts twice daily.

Warm compress: In a non-reactive bowl, combine 1 cup (250 mL) warm water and 2 drops each chamomile and lavender essential oils. Stir well to disperse oils. Soak a cloth and wring out enough water so cloth doesn't drip. Place warm cloth on breast. Repeat twice daily.

Leukorrhea

The term *leukorrhea* means simply "white discharge." This normal, non-infectious, colorless to thick white vaginal discharge is often affected by hormonal cycles, sometimes becoming quite heavy.

Essential Oils

Cinnamon (bark), lavender, myrrh, niaouli, rosemary ct. verbenone

---

Sitz Bath Blend

1 tsp (5 mL)	cider vinegar
1 drop	lavender essential oil
1 drop	rosemary essential oil

1. *In a small non-reactive bowl, combine the vinegar and lavender and rosemary essential oils. Mix thoroughly and set aside for 2 to 3 minutes to allow oils to dissolve a little.*

2. *Meanwhile, fill tub with enough warm water to come just below the abdomen. Add the mixture to the bath and agitate to disperse oils. Sit in the bath for 10 to 20 minutes.*

Menopause

Menopause is a normal condition of aging. Symptoms may begin 1 to 3 years before periods and ovulation cease (perimenopause) and may continue for several years afterward. Menopause is one of the biggest changes in a woman's life. When the symptoms—mood swings; hot flashes; night sweats; drying of the skin, mucous membranes and vagina; insomnia; anxiety; loss of libido—are coupled with other major changes, such as children leaving home, it can be a stressful and emotional time. It seems, though, that it doesn't have to be this way. Some or all of the following suggestions may bring relief.

Hormonal Balance Blend

30 drops	borage seed oil
30 drops	clary sage essential oil
30 drops	geranium essential oil
23 drops	bergamot essential oil

In a $^1/_6$ oz (5 mL) glass bottle, combine borage seed oil and Clary sage, geranium and bergamot essential oils. Shake to blend. (Discard any unused blend after 6 months.)

Variation
Air spray: *Omit borage seed oil. In a 4 oz (125 mL) PET plastic spray bottle, combine 75 drops Hormonal Balance Blend and 1 tsp (5 mL) vodka. Fill bottle with distilled or filtered water (see Tips, right).*

Treatments
Bath: Fill tub with warm water. Meanwhile, in a small non-reactive bowl, combine 1 tsp (5 mL) milk and 4 to 6 drops Hormonal Balance Blend. Add to tub and agitate to disperse oil, then soak for 30 minutes, massaging any floating droplets of oil into your skin.

Inhaler: Place 25 drops Hormonal Balance Blend in a small non-reactive bowl. Place inhaler wick in the bowl and allow it to absorb the entire amount. Insert the wick inside the inhaler tube and tightly cap the bottom of the inhaler with the plug. Place the inhaler tube inside its cover and screw tightly to close.

Massage: In a small non-reactive bowl, combine 2 tsp (10 mL) grapeseed or sweet almond oil and 6 drops Hormonal Balance Blend. Mix well and massage over your abdomen and lower back.

Tips

If you prefer, when making an air spray, substitute Solubol for the vodka called for, in a ratio of 4 drops Solubol for every 1 drop essential oil. Solubol is a natural product that allows essential oils to disperse in liquid.

When making air sprays, be sure to add the oils to the bottle first, followed by the chosen dispersant (vodka or Solubol), to ensure that the essential oils disperse properly (they will not mix directly with water).

Tips

If you prefer, substitute Solubol (see Resources, page 459) for the honey in a ratio of 4 drops Solubol for every 1 drop essential oil.

When making body sprays, be sure to add the oils to the bottle first, followed by the chosen dispersant (liquid honey or Solubol), to ensure that the essential oils disperse properly (they will not mix directly with water).

Keep your body spray in the refrigerator for when you need to cool hot flashes.

Keep a small bottle of peppermint hydrolat in the refrigerator and spray liberally around your head, shoulders and torso when experiencing a hot flash.

Hot Flashes
Essential Oils

Clary sage, cypress, geranium, lime, peppermint

Beat Hot Flashes Blend

20 drops	borage seed oil
20 drops	clary sage essential oil
20 drops	geranium essential oil
15 drops	cypress or peppermint essential oil

In a ¹⁄₆ oz (5 mL) glass bottle, combine borage seed oil and clary sage, geranium and cypress essential oils. Shake to blend. (Discard any unused blend after 6 months.)

Treatments

Bath: Fill tub with warm water. Meanwhile, in a small non-reactive bowl, combine 1 tsp (5 mL) milk and 4 to 6 drops Beat Hot Flashes Blend. Add to tub and agitate to disperse oil, then soak for 30 minutes, massaging any floating droplets of oil into your skin.

Massage: In a small non-reactive bowl, combine 2 tsp (10 mL) grapeseed or sweet almond oil and 6 drops Beat Hot Flashes Blend. Mix well and massage over your abdomen, chest, upper arms and lower back.

Body spray: Omit borage seed oil from Beat Hot Flashes Blend. Combine the essential oils in a 4 oz (125 mL) PET plastic spray bottle, then add 1 tsp (5 mL) unpasteurized liquid honey. Add ¼ cup (60 mL) peppermint hydrolat and 6 tsp (30 mL) distilled or filtered water (see Tips, left). Shake to blend. Spray mist over body when experiencing a hot flash. If hot flashes keep you awake at night, spray over body before bed and keep near bedside.

Depression
Essential Oils

Bergamot, clary sage, cypress, geranium, grapefruit, jasmine, lavender, marjoram, neroli, niaouli, sweet orange, petitgrain, rose, ylang ylang

---

Beat the Blues Blend

20 drops	borage seed oil
50 drops	grapefruit essential oil
25 drops	geranium essential oil
15 drops	petitgrain essential oil
1 drop	neroli essential oil

In a $\frac{1}{6}$ oz (5 mL) glass bottle, combine borage seed oil and grapefruit, geranium, petitgrain and neroli essential oils. Shake to blend. (Discard any unused blend after 6 months.)

Treatments

Bath: Fill tub with warm water. Meanwhile, in a small non-reactive bowl, combine 1 tsp (5 mL) milk and 4 to 6 drops Beat the Blues Blend. Add to tub and agitate to disperse oil, then soak for 30 minutes, massaging any floating droplets of oil into your skin.

Massage: In a small non-reactive bowl, combine 2 tsp (10 mL) grapeseed or sweet almond oil and 6 drops Beat the Blues Blend. Mix well and massage over your abdomen and lower back.

Air spray: Omit the borage seed oil from Beat the Blues Blend. Combine essential oils and place 75 drops of the blend in a 4 oz (125 mL) PET plastic spray bottle. Add 1 tsp (5 mL) vodka and shake to blend. Fill bottle with distilled or filtered water (see Tips, page 334). Shake to blend. Spray mist over body as desired.

Inhaler: Omit the borage seed oil from Beat the Blues Blend. Combine essential oils and place 21 drops in a small non-reactive bowl. Place inhaler wick in the bowl and allow it to absorb the entire amount. Insert the wick inside the inhaler tube and tightly cap the bottom of the inhaler with the plug. Place the inhaler tube inside its cover and screw tightly to close.

Tips

Do not add essential oils to the tub while the water is running, as some of the precious essences may evaporate, depriving you of the full benefits.

If you prefer, substitute an equal quantity of liquid castile soap for the milk called for in any bath recipe.

If you are using a blend around bath/shower time, you can enhance the benefit by combining the essential oils with a carrier oil and rub it into your skin *before* getting into the shower or bath. This enables the essential oils to be absorbed and work their way into the bloodstream. The heat of the water encourages the essential oil vapors to rise, allowing you to inhale the aromas more easily and thus creating a dual application.

Mood Swings and Anxiety
Essential Oils

Bergamot, cedarwood, Roman chamomile, clary sage, frankincense, geranium, jasmine, lavender, mandarin, marjoram, sandalwood, ylang ylang

> ## *Calming Blend*
>
> | 40 drops | chamomile essential oil |
> |---|---|
> | 40 drops | lavender essential oil |
> | 30 drops | marjoram essential oil |
>
> *In a $^1/_6$ oz (5 mL) glass bottle, combine chamomile, lavender and marjoram essential oils. Shake to blend.*

Treatments

Air spray: In a 4 oz (125 mL) PET plastic spray bottle, combine 75 drops Calming Blend and 1 tsp (5 mL) vodka. Fill bottle with distilled or filtered water (see Tips, left). Shake to blend.

Bath: Fill tub with warm water. Meanwhile, in a small non-reactive bowl, combine 1 tsp (5 mL) milk and 4 to 6 drops Calming Blend. Add to tub and agitate to disperse oil, then soak for 30 minutes, massaging any floating droplets of oil into your skin.

Inhaler: Place 25 drops Calming Blend in a small non-reactive bowl. Place inhaler wick in the bowl and allow it to absorb the entire amount. Insert the wick inside the inhaler tube and tightly cap the bottom of the inhaler with the plug. Place the inhaler tube inside its cover and screw tightly to close.

Massage: In a small non-reactive bowl, combine 2 tsp (10 mL) grapeseed or sweet almond oil and 6 drops Calming Blend. Mix well and massage over your abdomen and lower back.

Roll-on: Place 12 to 15 drops Calming Blend in a $^1/_6$ oz (10 mL) glass bottle with roller ball. Fill bottle with passion flower oil (best for stress). Insert the ball holder, then the ball, and screw on the top. Shake to blend. Roll onto temples, wrists and collarbones, as needed.

Menstruation

Women begin their approximately 28-day cycle at about 12 years of age and continue (except during pregnancy and some illnesses) until they are around 50. The cycle involves many hormonal changes that culminate in shedding the lining of the uterus; this is referred to as menstruation or "having your period." This cycle affects different women in very different ways. Some scarcely notice any changes and experience no pain or emotional problems. Many others, however, suffer from problems such as bloating, uterine cramps, pelvic pain, constipation, backache, headaches, fatigue and/or other unpleasant and incapacitating symptoms for almost a week. Essential oils are a useful part of treatment that should also include herbal and homeopathic remedies, relaxation and, where necessary, consultation with a health practitioner.

Amenorrhea

Amenorrhea means irregular or absent periods. There are many reasons for scanty periods, including pregnancy and breastfeeding, menopause, severe weight loss, over-exercising, stress and illness. Before using essential oil remedies (these all encourage menstruation), make sure that you aren't pregnant. Consult your doctor if you stop menstruating suddenly.

Essential Oils

Aniseed, chamomile, clary sage, marjoram, myrtle (green or orange), niaouli, rosemary (ct. cineole and ct. camphor), star anise, vetiver, yarrow

---

Menstruation Blend

15 drops	rosemary essential oil
10 drops	marjoram essential oil
10 drops	clary sage essential oil

In a ¹⁄₆ oz (5 mL) glass bottle, combine rosemary, marjoram and clary sage essential oils. Shake to blend.

Treatments

Bath: Fill tub with warm water. Meanwhile, in a small non-reactive bowl, combine 1 tsp (5 mL) milk and 4 to 6 drops Menstruation Blend. Add to tub and agitate to disperse oil, then soak for 30 minutes, massaging any floating droplets of oil into your skin.

Do not add essential oils to the tub while the water is running, as some of the precious essences may evaporate, depriving you of the full benefits.

If you prefer, substitute an equal quantity of liquid castile soap for the milk called for in any bath recipe.

If you are using a blend around bath/shower time, you can enhance the benefit by combining the essential oils with a carrier oil and rub it into your skin *before* getting into the shower or bath. This enables the essential oils to be absorbed and work their way into the bloodstream. The heat of the water encourages the essential oil vapors to rise, allowing you to inhale the aromas more easily and thus creating a dual application.

Tip

For a more effective compress, combine 4 to 6 drops Menstruation Blend with ½ tsp (2.5 mL) grapeseed or sweet almond oil or unscented lotion. Rub into abdomen and/or lower back. Wrap your torso with plastic wrap and cover with a hot towel for 20 to 30 minutes.

Massage: In a small non-reactive bowl, combine 2 tsp (10 mL) grapeseed or sweet almond oil and 6 drops Menstruation Blend. Mix well and massage very firmly over your lower back, abdomen, feet and ankles. Apply twice daily.

Warm compress: Pour 2 cups (500 mL) warm water into a non-reactive bowl. Add 2 drops each rosemary, marjoram and clary sage essential oils. Stir well to disperse oils. Soak a cloth and wring out enough water so cloth doesn't drip. Place warm cloth over the pelvic area, turning it as it begins to cool. (See Tip, left.)

Dysmenorrhea

Dysmenorrhea means painful menstruation, often with disabling cramps. Besides the suggestions here, see also Premenstrual Syndrome (PMS), page 339.

Essential Oils

Angelica, chamomile, clary sage, fennel, geranium, ginger, lavender, marjoram, myrtle (green or orange), rose, tea tree, yarrow

---

Prevent Cramps Blend

15 drops	marjoram essential oil
10 drops	lavender essential oil
5 drops	clary sage essential oil

In a ¹⁄₆ oz (5 mL) glass bottle, combine marjoram, lavender and clary sage essential oils. Shake to blend.

Tip

For a more effective compress, combine 4 to 6 drops Prevent Cramps Blend with ½ tsp (2.5 mL) grapeseed or sweet almond oil or unscented lotion. Rub into abdomen and/or lower back. Wrap your torso with plastic wrap and cover with a hot towel for 20 to 30 minutes. Repeat daily for 10 days prior to period.

Treatments

Bath: Fill tub with warm water. Meanwhile, in a small non-reactive bowl, combine 1 tsp (5 mL) milk and 4 to 6 drops Prevent Cramps Blend. Add to tub and agitate to disperse oil, then soak for 30 minutes, massaging any floating droplets of oil into your skin.

Massage: In a small non-reactive bowl, combine 2 tsp (10 mL) grapeseed or sweet almond oil and 6 drops Prevent Cramps Blend. Mix well and massage very firmly over your lower back, abdomen, feet and ankles. Apply twice daily.

Warm compress: Pour 2 cups (500 mL) warm water into a non-reactive bowl. Add 2 drops each marjoram, clary sage and lavender essential oils. Stir well to disperse oils. Soak a cloth and wring out enough water so cloth doesn't drip. Place warm cloth over the pelvic area. Repeat often. (See Tip, left.)

Premenstrual Syndrome (PMS)

Essential oils are only part of a total strategy for premenstrual syndrome, which has a wide range of symptoms that affect different women very differently (or not at all, in some cases). You may be agreeably surprised by the benefits you receive from using these combinations of essential oils along with appropriate herbal remedies and stress management techniques. Use the bath and massage treatments for 8 to 10 days before your period is due.

PMS Blend

12 drops	mandarin essential oil
10 drops	lavender essential oil
3 drops	geranium essential oil
1 drop	rose essential oil

In a ¹⁄₆ oz (5 mL) glass dropper bottle, combine mandarin, lavender, geranium and rose essential oils. Shake to blend.

Treatments

Bath: Fill tub with warm water. Meanwhile, in a small non-reactive bowl, combine 1 tsp (5 mL) milk and 4 to 6 drops PMS Blend. Add to tub and agitate to disperse oil, then soak for 30 minutes, massaging any floating droplets of oil into your skin.

Massage: In a small non-reactive bowl, combine 4 tsp (20 mL) grapeseed or sweet almond oil and 8 drops PMS Blend. Mix well and massage over your body.

Beat Water Retention Blend

Begin to use this blend on day 21 of your cycle, counting from the first day of the previous period. This blend will help to rid the body of excess fluid and ease that bloated feeling.

15 drops	fennel essential oil
10 drops	juniper essential oil
8 drops	grapefruit essential oil

In a ¹⁄₆ oz (5 mL) glass bottle, combine fennel, juniper and grapefruit essential oils. Shake to blend.

Tips

Do not add essential oils to the tub while the water is running, as some of the precious essences may evaporate, depriving you of the full benefits.

If you prefer, substitute an equal quantity of liquid castile soap for the milk called for in any bath recipe.

If you are using a blend around bath/shower time, you can enhance the benefit by combining the essential oils with a carrier oil and rub it into your skin *before* getting into the shower or bath. This enables the essential oils to be absorbed and work their way into the bloodstream. The heat of the water encourages the essential oil vapors to rise, allowing you to inhale the aromas more easily and thus creating a dual application.

Do not add essential oils to the tub while the water is running, as some of the precious essences may evaporate, depriving you of the full benefits.

If you prefer, substitute an equal quantity of liquid castile soap for the milk called for in any bath recipe.

If you are using a blend around bath/shower time, you can enhance the benefit by combining the essential oils with a carrier oil and rub it into your skin *before* getting into the shower or bath. This enables the essential oils to be absorbed and work their way into the bloodstream. The heat of the water encourages the essential oil vapors to rise, allowing you to inhale the aromas more easily and thus creating a dual application.

Treatments

Bath: Fill tub with warm water. Meanwhile, in a small non-reactive bowl, combine 1 tsp (5 mL) milk and 4 to 6 drops Beat Water Retention Blend. Add to tub and agitate to disperse oil, then soak for 30 minutes, massaging any floating droplets of oil into your skin.

Massage: In a small non-reactive bowl, combine 2 tsp (10 mL) grapeseed or sweet almond oil and 4 drops Beat Water Retention Blend. Mix well and massage over your body.

Depression and Irritability Blend

15 drops   Roman chamomile essential oil
10 drops   bergamot essential oil
10 drops   petitgrain essential oil

In a $^1/_6$ oz (5 mL) glass bottle, combine chamomile, bergamot and petitgrain essential oils. Shake to blend.

Treatments

Bath: Fill tub with warm water. Meanwhile, in a small non-reactive bowl, combine 1 tsp (5 mL) milk and 4 to 6 drops Depression and Irritability Blend. Add to tub and agitate to disperse oil, then soak for 30 minutes, massaging any floating droplets of oil into your skin.

Massage: In a small non-reactive bowl, combine 2 tsp (10 mL) grapeseed oil and 4 drops Depression and Irritability Blend. Mix well and massage over your body.

Roll-on: Place 12 to 15 drops Depression and Irritability Blend in a $^1/_3$ oz (10 mL) glass bottle with roller ball. Top up with fractionated coconut oil (be careful not to overfill). Insert the ball holder, then the ball, and screw on the top. Shake to blend. Roll onto temples, wrists and collarbones, as needed.

Thrush
See Candidiasis (page 195)

Workplace (and School) Stress

The daily demands of the workplace (and school) often create stress—physical, mental and emotional. And, especially if you commute, it's all too likely you'll feel stressed even before you arrive.

Unwinding with a relaxing aromatic shower or bath is a great way to wash away stresses at the end of the day. If you can't wait until then, there are other ways to incorporate aromatherapy into your workday and your commute.

Many facilities now have scent-free policies, which means you cannot wear perfume or use scented sprays and diffusers in the workplace. However, you can take advantage of personal inhalers and aromatic jewelry, both subtle and discreet ways to bring aromatherapy into your day. For the car ride, use aromatic spray mists, or tuck a few scented cotton balls into the air vent or scent stones into the cup-holder. Diffusers for the car have also made their way into the marketplace (see Resources, page 459).

Children have their own stresses to contend with, and essential oils can help to create a productive and happy day at school. It has been our experience that children respond more quickly than adults to essential oils, and they love having their own special blend that they can keep with them. Any of the following recipes may be used by children; however, the strength must be adapted to suit their age (see Babies and Children, page 164). It's probably not wise to give a bottle of oils to a child under the age of 10. Instead, make up a personal inhaler or a small bottle of lotion and slip it into their backpack, pocket or another convenient place for them to use during the day.

Essential Oils

Bergamot, cedarwood, clary sage, geranium, lavender, lemon, peppermint, rosemary

---

Day Break for Girls Blend

1 tsp (5 mL)	lavender essential oil
68 drops	bergamot essential oil
68 drops	geranium essential oil
20 drops	peppermint essential oil
20 drops	clary sage essential oil

In a ½ oz (15 mL) glass dropper bottle, combine lavender, bergamot, geranium, peppermint and clary sage essential oils. Shake to blend. Store in a dark, cool place.

Caution

Before using any essential oil, consult the relevant entry in Part 1: Essential Oils (A to Y), pages 28 to 117, taking careful note of any cautions.

Treatments

Hand and body lotion: In a 2 oz (60 mL) PET plastic bottle, combine a small amount of unscented lotion and 20 drops (30 drops if over age 10) Day Break for Girls Blend (page 341). Shake vigorously to combine. Fill bottle to the shoulder with unscented lotion and shake vigorously to combine.

Inhalation: Apply 2 drops Day Break for Girls Blend on a cotton ball and tuck it into your bra, where the heat of your body will evaporate the oil and waft it to your nose. *Note:* Be careful not to put the oiled side directly against your skin.

Inhaler: Place 21 drops Day Break for Girls Blend in a small non-reactive bowl. Place inhaler wick in the bowl and allow it to absorb the entire amount. Place the wick inside the inhaler tube and tightly cap the bottom of the inhaler with the plug. Place the inhaler tube inside its cover and screw tightly to close.

Using Inhaler Sticks

With one finger pressing closed your left nostril, inhale from the tube through the right nostril. Then close the right nostril with your finger and inhale through the left. Repeat on each side one more time. Exhale through the mouth, not the nose.

Massage: In a small non-reactive bowl, combine 2 tsp (10 mL) grapeseed oil and 3 drops Day Break for Girls Blend. Mix well and massage over your body.

Spray mist: In a 2 oz (60 mL) PET plastic spray bottle, combine 25 drops Day Break for Girls Blend and 1 tsp (5 mL) glycerin. Shake to combine. Fill bottle with distilled or filtered water. Shake well, then spray into the air at arm's length and walk through the falling mist with your eyes closed.

Roll-on: Place 12 drops Day Break for Girls Blend in a $1/3$ oz (10 mL) glass bottle with roller ball. Top up with fractionated coconut oil (be careful not to overfill). Insert the ball holder, then the ball, and screw on the top. Shake to blend. Roll onto temples, wrists and collarbones, as needed.

Day Break for Guys Blend

1 tsp (5 mL)	bergamot essential oil
1 tsp (5 mL)	lemon essential oil
68 drops	rosemary essential oil
68 drops	cedarwood essential oil

In a 1 oz (30 mL) glass dropper bottle, combine bergamot, lemon, rosemary and cedarwood essential oils. Shake to blend. Store in a dark, cool place.

Treatments

Aftershave: In a 2 oz (60 mL) glass bottle, combine 18 drops Day Break for Guys Blend and 1 tsp (5 mL) unpasteurized liquid honey. Fill bottle with peppermint or witch hazel hydrolat (alcohol-free) and shake vigorously to combine. Pour a few drops on a cotton ball and smooth over face after shaving.

Hand and body lotion: In a 2 oz (60 mL) PET plastic bottle, combine a small amount of unscented lotion and 20 drops (30 drops if over age 10) Day Break for Guys Blend. Shake vigorously to combine. Fill bottle to the shoulder with unscented lotion and shake vigorously to combine. (See Tip, right.)

Inhalation: Put 2 to 3 drops Day Break for Guys Blend on a cotton ball or tissue and tuck it in your pocket. Pull out and sniff anytime you need a reviving lift.

Inhaler: Place 21 drops Day Break for Guys Blend in a small non-reactive bowl. Place inhaler wick in the bowl and allow it to absorb the entire amount. Insert the wick inside the inhaler tube and tightly cap the bottom of the inhaler with the plug. Place the inhaler tube inside its cover and screw tightly to close.

Massage: In a small non-reactive bowl, combine 2 tsp (10 mL) grapeseed oil and 3 drops Day Break for Guys Blend. Mix well and massage over your body.

Roll-on: Place 12 drops Day Break for Guys Blend in a ⅙ oz (10 mL) glass bottle with roller ball. Top up with fractionated coconut oil (be careful not to overfill). Insert the ball holder, then the ball, and screw on the top. Shake to blend. Roll onto temples, wrists and collarbones, as needed.

Tip

Decanting lotion into a smaller bottle to blend with essential oils can be a very messy proposition. Using a pump dispenser makes it easy to fill a smaller bottle. Always add a small amount of lotion to your PET plastic bottle first, then the essential oils, and shake to blend. Then add the remaining lotion and shake again. This helps to disperse the oils more evenly in the lotion.

Spray mist: In a 2 oz (60 mL) PET plastic spray bottle, combine 25 drops Day Break for Guys Blend and 1 tsp (5 mL) glycerin. Shake to combine. Fill bottle with distilled or filtered water. Shake well, then spray into the air at arm's length and walk through the falling mist with your eyes closed.

Commuting

Essential Oils

Lavender, mandarin, peppermint

Well, we all know what a drama commuting can be, so we won't dwell on the traumas that can erupt as soon as you leave the house. You can help to avoid stress and create a happy, positive and calm atmosphere with the following suggestions:

- In a small glass dropper bottle, combine 30 drops each peppermint and lavender essential oils or 30 drops each lavender and mandarin essential oils. Store in a little box or bag in the glove compartment with some cotton balls. Apply a drop or two of this blend to a cotton ball and tuck it into an air vent, onto the rear window ledge, on top of a sun visor, or under or beside a seat.
- When you are waiting at traffic lights or in a traffic jam and things are getting tense in spite of the oils, encourage everyone in the car (including yourself) to slowly lift up their shoulders toward their ears while breathing in. Then let the shoulders drop and relax as the breath leaves the mouth in a long sigh. Kids find this good fun without realizing that they are being de-stressed.
- Clenching the teeth and jaw on the in-breath and then relaxing on the out-breath is another good method of releasing tension.

Environmental and Physical Stresses

It is quite likely that your school or workplace has air conditioning, computers, synthetic carpets and furnishings and veneered furniture. These are sources of just a few of the chemical stresses with which we are confronted every day. They are potentially very hazardous to our health, but fortunately there is quite a lot we can do to counteract them.

Physical stresses result from sitting or standing for long periods of time, using machinery or a computer, and being exposed to other people's airborne germs. Take a minute or two to stretch your muscles at least every 15 to 20 minutes. And make sure you are adequately protected by Antibacterial Blend if sick people are thoughtless enough to come to work and breathe all over their colleagues.

Essential Oils

Bergamot, cedarwood, cypress, eucalyptus, grapefruit, lavender, lemon, pine, rosemary

---

Antibacterial Blend

1 tsp (5 mL)	lavender essential oil
68 drops	cypress essential oil
68 drops	rosemary essential oil
68 drops	eucalyptus essential oil

In a ¹/₂ oz (15 mL) glass dropper bottle, combine lavender, cypress, rosemary and eucalyptus essential oils. Shake to blend. Store in a dark, cool place.

Treatments

Air and surface spray: In a 4 oz (125 mL) PET plastic spray bottle, combine 75 drops Antibacterial Blend and 1 tsp (5 mL) vodka. Fill bottle with distilled or filtered water (see Tips, right). Spray above your desk or near your workstation.

Inhaler: Place 21 drops Antibacterial Blend in a small non-reactive bowl. Place inhaler wick in the bowl and allow it to absorb the entire amount. Insert the wick inside the inhaler tube and tightly cap the bottom of the inhaler with the plug. Place the inhaler tube inside its cover and screw tightly to close.

Stale Air Reviver

Adjust the types and amounts of essential oils in this blend until it suits everyone in your environment.

1 tsp (5 mL)	lemon essential oil
68 drops	lavender essential oil
68 drops	grapefruit essential oil
68 drops	cypress essential oil

In a ¹/₂ oz (15 mL) glass dropper bottle, combine lemon, lavender, grapefruit and cypress essential oils. Shake to blend. Store in a dark, cool place.

Tips

If you prefer, when making an air spray, substitute Solubol for the vodka called for, in a ratio of 4 drops Solubol for every 1 drop essential oil. Solubol is a natural product that allows essential oils to disperse in liquid.

When making air sprays, be sure to add the oils to the bottle first, followed by the chosen dispersant (vodka or Solubol), to ensure that the essential oils disperse properly (they will not mix directly with water).

Treatments

Air spray: In a 4 oz (125 mL) PET plastic spray bottle, combine 75 drops Stale Air Reviver and 1 tsp (5 mL) vodka. Fill bottle with distilled or filtered water (see Tips, left). Shake to blend. Spray over your desk or near your workstation.

Inhaler: Place 21 drops Stale Air Reviver in a small non-reactive bowl. Place inhaler wick in the bowl and allow it to absorb the entire amount. Insert the wick inside the inhaler tube and tightly cap the bottom of the inhaler with the plug. Place the inhaler tube inside its cover and screw tightly to close.

Tips

If you prefer, when making an air spray, substitute Solubol for the vodka called for, in a ratio of 4 drops Solubol for every 1 drop essential oil. Solubol is a natural product that allows essential oils to disperse in liquid.

When making air sprays, be sure to add the oils to the bottle first, followed by the chosen dispersant (vodka or Solubol), to ensure that the essential oils disperse properly (they will not mix directly with water).

Brain Fatigue Blend

10 drops	bergamot essential oil
10 drops	lemon essential oil
10 drops	rosemary essential oil

In a $\frac{1}{6}$ oz (5 mL) glass bottle, combine bergamot, lemon and rosemary essential oils. Shake to blend.

Treatments

Inhaler: Place 21 drops Brain Fatigue Blend in a small non-reactive bowl. Place inhaler wick in the bowl and allow it to absorb the entire amount. Insert the wick inside the inhaler tube and tightly cap the bottom of the inhaler with the plug. Place the inhaler tube inside its cover and screw tightly to close.

Using Inhaler Sticks

With one finger pressing closed your left nostril, inhale from the tube through the right nostril. Then close the right nostril with your finger and inhale through the left. Repeat on each side one more time. Exhale through the mouth, not the nose.

Roll-on: Place 12 drops Brain Fatigue Blend in a $\frac{1}{3}$ oz (10 mL) glass bottle with roller ball. Top up with fractionated coconut oil (be careful not to overfill). Insert the ball holder, then the ball, and screw on the top. Shake to blend. Roll onto temples, wrists and collarbones, as needed.

Spray mist: In a 4 oz (125 mL) PET plastic spray bottle, combine 75 drops Brain Fatigue Blend and 1 tsp (5 mL) vodka. Fill bottle with distilled or filtered water. Spray into air at arm's length and walk through the falling mist with your eyes closed.

Productive Day Blend

Lemon essential oil has been shown to lift the spirits and increase the productivity of employees while decreasing errors. In Japan it has also been shown to increase sales in retail shops where the essential oil is diffused through the central air system; this creates a happy environment, and happy shoppers tend to linger and spend more money.

2 tsp (10 mL)	lemon essential oil
1 tsp (5 mL)	cypress essential oil
1 tsp (5 mL)	cedarwood essential oil
1 tsp (5 mL)	pine essential oil

In a 1 oz (30 mL) glass bottle, combine lemon, cypress, cedarwood and pine essential oils. Shake to blend.

Treatments

Air spray: In a 4 oz (125 mL) PET plastic spray bottle, combine 75 drops Productive Day Blend and 1 tsp (5 mL) vodka. Fill bottle with distilled or filtered water (see Tips, right). Spray into the air.

Diffuser: Pour 3 to 5 drops Productive Day Blend into a diffuser, according to manufacturer's instructions; diffuse for 20 minutes. (See Resources, page 459.)

Inhaler: Place 21 drops Productive Day Blend in a small non-reactive bowl. Place inhaler wick in the bowl and allow it to absorb the entire amount. Insert the wick inside the inhaler tube and tightly cap the bottom of the inhaler with the plug. Place the inhaler tube inside its cover and screw tightly to close.

Afternoon Blend for Brain Fatigue

This blend is ideal for chasing away the cobwebs after lunch or later in the afternoon, when you start to feel drowsy! (See also Fatigue, page 224.)

36 drops	rosemary essential oil
24 drops	lemongrass essential oil
12 drops	basil essential oil

In a 1/6 oz (5 mL) glass dropper bottle, combine rosemary, lemongrass and basil essential oils. Shake to blend.

If you prefer, when making an air spray, substitute Solubol for the vodka called for, in a ratio of 4 drops Solubol for every 1 drop essential oil. Solubol is a natural product that allows essential oils to disperse in liquid.

When making air sprays, be sure to add the oils to the bottle first, followed by the chosen dispersant (vodka or Solubol), to ensure that the essential oils disperse properly (they will not mix directly with water).

Treatments

Inhaler: Place 21 drops Afternoon Blend for Brain Fatigue in a small non-reactive bowl. Place inhaler wick in the bowl and allow it to absorb the entire amount. Insert the wick inside the inhaler tube and tightly cap the bottom of the inhaler with the plug. Place the inhaler tube inside its cover and screw tightly to close.

Roll-on: Place 12 drops Afternoon Blend for Brain Fatigue in a $\frac{1}{3}$ oz (10 mL) glass bottle with roller ball. Top up with fractionated coconut oil (be careful not to overfill). Insert the ball holder, then the ball, and screw on the top. Shake to blend. Roll onto temples, wrists and collarbones, as needed.

Using Inhaler Sticks

With one finger pressing closed your left nostril, inhale from the tube through the right nostril. Then close the right nostril with your finger and inhale through the left. Repeat on each side one more time. Exhale through the mouth, not the nose.

Burnout

Your family and friends have been telling you for weeks, even months, to slow down. However, you felt invincible—or at least that if you did not do all the work yourself the whole universe would grind to a halt! And now? You're so mentally and physically exhausted that you have scarcely enough energy to get up in the morning. It is not too late to begin to start taking care of yourself, but in addition to using aromatherapy, quite a lot of lifestyle changes will be needed. Here are some tips for managing burnout:

- Lessen your workload.
- Eat plenty of fresh, unprocessed foods, but do not eat if you are upset or overtired. Wait until you are calmer, or your body will not be able to cope with digesting the food.
- Get a minimum of 8 hours' sleep every night.
- Avoid negative people and situations. Take a rest from reading or watching the news—it will all continue to happen even if you are not monitoring it!
- Allow yourself time to be alone, with no demands being made on your time or energy.
- Take some sort of exercise every day, such as walking or swimming or whatever you enjoy most.
- Do not be embarrassed or afraid to ask for help.
- Learn to meditate.

Tips

If you prefer, when making an air spray, substitute Solubol for the vodka called for, in a ratio of 4 drops Solubol for every 1 drop essential oil. Solubol is a natural product that allows essential oils to disperse in liquid.

When making air sprays, be sure to add the oils to the bottle first, followed by the chosen dispersant (vodka or Solubol), to ensure that the essential oils disperse properly (they will not mix directly with water).

- Arrange to have a massage once or twice a week, using Burnout Blend (below) in the massage oil. If you cannot afford professional massage, you can trade with a partner or friend. It is almost as rewarding to give a massage as it is to receive one!

Essential Oils

Cedarwood, grapefruit, lavender, lemon, sandalwood, vetiver

Burnout Blend

1 tsp (5 mL)	lavender essential oil
68 drops	grapefruit essential oil
68 drops	lemon essential oil
68 drops	sandalwood or vetiver essential oil

In a ½ oz (15 mL) glass dropper bottle, combine lavender, grapefruit, lemon and sandalwood essential oils. Shake to blend.

Treatments

Air spray: In a 4 oz (125 mL) PET plastic spray bottle, combine 75 drops Burnout Blend and 1 tsp (5 mL) vodka. Fill bottle with distilled or filtered water (see Tips, page 348). Shake to blend.

Bath: Fill tub with warm water. Meanwhile, in a small non-reactive bowl, combine 1 tsp (5 mL) milk and 4 to 6 drops Burnout Blend. Add to tub and agitate to disperse oil, then soak for 30 minutes, massaging any floating droplets of oil into your skin.

Inhaler: Place 21 drops Burnout Blend in a small non-reactive bowl. Place inhaler wick in the bowl and allow it to absorb the entire amount. Insert the wick inside the inhaler tube and tightly cap the bottom of the inhaler with the plug. Place the inhaler tube inside its cover and screw tightly to close.

Massage: In a small non-reactive bowl, combine 2 tsp (10 mL) grapeseed or passion flower oil and 4 drops Burnout Blend. Mix well and massage over your body.

Tips

Do not add essential oils to the tub while the water is running, as some of the precious essences may evaporate, depriving you of the full benefits.

If you prefer, substitute an equal quantity of liquid castile soap for the milk called for in any bath recipe.

If you are using a blend around bath/ shower time, you can enhance the benefit by combining the essential oils with a carrier oil and rub it into your skin *before* getting into the shower or bath. This enables the essential oils to be absorbed and work their way into the bloodstream. The heat of the water encourages the essential oil vapors to rise, allowing you to inhale the aromas more easily and thus creating a dual application.

Caution

Before using any essential oil, consult the relevant entry in Part 1: Essential Oils (A to Y), pages 28 to 117, taking careful note of any cautions.

Tips

If you prefer, when making an air spray, substitute Solubol for the vodka called for, in a ratio of 4 drops Solubol for every 1 drop essential oil. Solubol is a natural product that allows essential oils to disperse in liquid.

When making air sprays, be sure to add the oils to the bottle first, followed by the chosen dispersant (vodka or Solubol), to ensure that the essential oils disperse properly (they will not mix directly with water).

Adrenal Support Blend

Adrenal burnout is nothing to mess with. When overstressed for long periods, your body begins to shut down, which compromises your immune system and lowers your metabolism. It also drains your energy and affects your ability to fall asleep and stay asleep. Using this earthy and grounding blend can help you to relax, decompress and gain a restful night's sleep, thus beginning the process of healing.

20 drops	vetiver essential oil
12 drops	sandalwood or cedarwood essential oil
12 drops	patchouli essential oil
10 drops	ylang ylang essential oil
8 drops	geranium essential oil

In a small glass dropper bottle, combine vetiver, sandalwood, patchouli, ylang ylang and geranium essential oils. Shake to blend.

Treatments

Air spray: In a 4 oz (125 mL) PET plastic spray bottle, combine 75 drops Adrenal Support Blend and 1 tsp (5 mL) vodka. Fill bottle with distilled or filtered water (see Tips, left). Shake to blend. Spritz over pillow and bed linens before bed.

Bath: Fill tub with warm water. Meanwhile, in a small non-reactive bowl, combine 1 tsp (5 mL) milk and 4 to 6 drops Adrenal Support Blend. Add to tub and agitate to disperse oil, then soak for 30 minutes, massaging any floating droplets of oil into your skin.

Diffuser: Pour 3 to 5 drops Adrenal Support Blend into a diffuser, according to manufacturer's instructions. Diffuse for 20 minutes before bed.

Inhaler: Place 21 drops Adrenal Support Blend in a small non-reactive bowl. Place inhaler wick in the bowl and allow it to absorb the entire amount. Insert the wick inside the inhaler tube and tightly cap the bottom of the inhaler with the plug. Place the inhaler tube inside its cover and screw tightly to close.

Massage: In a small non-reactive bowl, combine 2 tsp (10 mL) passion flower oil and 4 drops Adrenal Support Blend. Mix well and massage over your body.

Roll-on: Place 12 drops Adrenal Support Blend in a $\frac{1}{3}$ oz (10 mL) glass bottle with roller ball. Top up with fractionated coconut oil (be careful not to overfill). Insert the ball holder, then the ball, and screw on the top. Shake to blend. Roll onto temples, wrists and collarbones, as needed.

Tips

Do not add essential oils to the tub while the water is running, as some of the precious essences may evaporate, depriving you of the full benefits.

If you prefer, substitute an equal quantity of liquid castile soap for the milk called for in any bath recipe.

If you are using a blend around bath/ shower time, you can enhance the benefit by combining the essential oils with a carrier oil and rub it into your skin *before* getting into the shower or bath. This enables the essential oils to be absorbed and work their way into the bloodstream. The heat of the water encourages the essential oil vapors to rise, allowing you to inhale the aromas more easily and thus creating a dual application.

Part 3
Aromatherapy for Daily Living

Aromatherapy for Personal Care

In this section we put everyday living experiences into aromatic perspective. You'll discover how easy it is to integrate aromatherapy into even the simplest activities. Homemade products using natural ingredients and pure essential oils are pleasing to the sense of smell and will also benefit your body. Once you begin using essential oils, they'll fast become a daily delight and their therapeutic benefits will become obvious.

Caution

Before using any essential oil, consult the relevant entry in Part 1: Essential Oils (A to Y), pages 28 to 117, taking careful note of any cautions.

Skincare

As babies, we usually have perfect skin—smooth, moist and with enough oil to protect without causing problems. As we get older, hormonal changes, heredity and the aging process begin to change the texture of our skin. We need to consider our individual skin type and take care of it in order to keep it at its best for as long as possible. In this section we provide recipes and treatments for every type of skin. The recipes are suitable for both men and women; we do suggest different oils for men, as the aroma of some may be perceived as too feminine.

Proportions

Essential oils are immensely powerful and must be measured accurately. If a recipe says to use 2 drops, then 4 drops is certainly not better! You can purchase droppers or syringes and glass or plastic measures from pharmacies and online (see Resources, page 459). The table on page 355 is a guide to essential oils for various skin conditions. Choose a blend of oils suited to your skin type.

Use the Tables

If you do not have an essential oil called for in a recipe, you may substitute another oil that has similar properties. Use the Essential Oils for Skin tables to find appropriate substitutes.

Essential Oils for Skin

Skin Type	Appropriate Essential Oils
All skin types	Geranium, jasmine, lavender, neroli, palmarosa, rose, rosewood
Dry skin	Balsam (Peru and Tolu), benzoin, bergamot, carrot seed, chamomile (German and Roman), geranium, jasmine, lavender, neroli, palmarosa, petitgrain, rose, rosemary ct. verbenone, rosewood, sandalwood
Normal skin	Geranium, jasmine, lavender, neroli, palmarosa, rose, rosewood, ylang ylang
Oily skin	Basil ct. linalool, cedarwood, cypress, fennel, geranium, grapefruit, juniper, spike lavender, lemon, lime, sweet orange, petitgrain, ylang ylang
Sensitive skin	Chamomile, jasmine, neroli, rose

Skincare Benefit	Essential Oils
Antiseptic	All essential oils to some degree, but especially Canadian balsam, benzoin, cedarwood, *Eucalyptus globulus*, fennel, geranium, juniper, lavender, mandarin, myrtle (green or red), sweet orange, patchouli, rosewood, yarrow, ylang ylang
Astringent	Cypress, geranium, juniper, lemon, limbu, peppermint, sandalwood
Balancer	Cypress, geranium, palmarosa, ylang ylang
Cell growth stimulator	Peru balsam, carrot seed, frankincense, geranium, helichrysum, lavender, neroli, palmarosa
Elasticity enhancer	Carrot seed, neroli, palmarosa
Fixative (for perfume)	Amyris, Peru balsam, benzoin, cistus, clary sage, frankincense, patchouli, sandalwood, vetiver, ylang ylang
Sebum regulator	Basil, cedarwood, cypress, spike lavender, lemongrass, palmarosa, ylang ylang

Skin Problem	Appropriate Essential Oils
Acne	Basil ct. linalool, bergamot, cajuput, cedarwood, chamomile, clary sage, galbanum, geranium, helichrysum, juniper, lavender, melissa, green myrtle, palmarosa, patchouli, petitgrain, rosemary, Spanish sage, spearmint, tea tree, thyme
Aging skin	Amyris, carrot seed, cistus, fennel, frankincense, galbanum, geranium, mandarin, myrrh, neroli, palmarosa, rose, rosewood, spikenard
Allergies	German chamomile, helichrysum, hyssop, manuka, melissa, plai
Cellulite	Cedarwood, fennel, grapefruit, lemongrass, sage
Cracked, dry skin	Balsam (Peru and Tolu), benzoin, bergamot, German chamomile, myrrh, palmarosa, patchouli, sandalwood
Dermatitis	Peru balsam, benzoin, birch bud, carrot seed, chamomile, geranium, helichrysum, juniper, lavender, palmarosa, patchouli, rosewood, Spanish sage, spearmint, thyme
Eczema	Balsam (Peru and Tolu), bergamot, birch bud, carrot seed, cedarwood, chamomile, geranium, helichrysum, hyssop, juniper, lavender, melissa, myrrh, palmarosa, rose, rosemary, rosewood
Fungal infections	Benzoin, German chamomile, geranium, helichrysum, lavandin 'Super', lavender, mandarin, manuka, sweet orange, rosemary ct. cineole, rosewood, spikenard, tea tree
Inflammation/irritation	Chamomile, Fragonia, lavender, myrrh, rose, tea tree, yarrow
Rosacea	Chamomile (Roman and German), helichrysum, lavender, neroli, palmarosa, rose
Scars	Carrot seed, cedarwood, frankincense, geranium, hyssop, juniper, lavender, myrrh, patchouli, rosewood
Thread veins	Chamomile (German and Roman), cypress, frankincense, lavender, lemon, neroli, sweet orange, patchouli, peppermint, rose, rosewood
Wrinkles	Carrot seed, fennel, frankincense, lavender, neroli, palmarosa, patchouli, rose, rosewood

Caring for Your Face

Normal Skin

Normal skin is fine-textured, smooth and soft, with no apparent large pores, blackheads, blemishes, flaking or broken veins. If you press a tissue to your face immediately after waking, only a trace of oil will show. If you are blessed with this type of skin, you are fortunate and should protect it from environmental irritants by using light and gentle moisturizers, cleansers and toners.

Oily Skin

You will know you have oily skin if you press a tissue to your face first thing in the morning and it captures quite a lot of oil. Because the pores become blocked with excessive sebum, oily skin is coarsely textured, with visible large pores. It has a tendency toward blackheads and blemishes. The upside of having oily skin is that it is less prone to wrinkles than dry or normal skin; also, it will become less oily as you get older.

   If you have oily skin, it is a mistake to use harsh soaps and strong, alcohol-heavy astringents to try to control excessive oiliness. These products tend to stimulate the skin to produce more sebum, so over the long term, they will likely make matters worse. In general oily skin needs an oil-free moisturizer, except around the eyes, lips and throat, where richer moisturizing is required. Oily skin benefits from regular masks and steams to unblock pores and prevent blackheads from forming.

Combination Skin

Combination skin is a mixture of normal or dry and oily skin. If you press a tissue to your face first thing in the morning, it will show a greasy T-shape. You may have a tendency toward blackheads around your nose and pimples on your forehead or chin. There are often small oily areas along the jawline as well. A skincare program for this type should combine remedies for both oily and normal or oily and dry skin, depending on your particular combination.

Dry Skin

Dry skin is fine-textured, delicate and thin, with a tendency to line easily. For many people with dry skin, washing with soap and water makes their face feel as though it is going to crack. Cleansing creams and lotions are preferable alternatives. If you have dry skin, use masks and steams with great care, as they may encourage broken veins, to which dry skin can be prone. Neroli and rose hydrolats are excellent toners for dry skin.

Rosacea

Rosacea can affect both men and women. The onset of symptoms, sometimes with accompanying acne, usually occurs around the age of 30 or more. Rosacea can be exacerbated by heat, chocolate, spicy foods, emotional distress, alcohol consumption and some skincare products. People with rosacea should follow a gentle cleansing routine, using a mild, nonabrasive cleanser and lukewarm water; moisturize with jojoba oil.

Facial Steaming

By causing the skin to perspire and "breathe," facial steaming helps to loosen grime, dead skin cells and hardened sebum. The heat increases the blood supply to the skin's surface while hydrating its deeper layers. Well-selected essential oils encourage revitalization and promote necessary healing. The result is softer, more youthful-looking skin and a clearer, brighter complexion. People with normal, oily and combination skin types may use facial steaming as often as twice a week. Those with more sensitive skin or rosacea should avoid facial steaming or use it less frequently.

Using Facial Steams

Before you begin, put on a shower cap and cleanse your face thoroughly. You'll also need a large towel. Place a large bowl on a heatproof non-slip pad on a table, positioned where you can sit comfortably. Fill with 2 quarts (2 L) boiling water. Sprinkle 1 tsp (5 mL) of the appropriate steaming blend over the surface of the water. Using the towel, create a tent over the bowl and your head, keeping your face at least 12 inches (30 cm) from the surface (if you have sensitive skin, up to 16 inches/40 cm away; see sidebar). Keep your eyes closed to prevent the essential oils from irritating them, and relax and enjoy for 5 to 10 minutes. When you have finished, splash your face with cool (not cold) water and complete the cleansing process with a toner and the appropriate moisturizer. For a special treat, enjoy a facial mask (see pages 361 to 364) before toning and moisturizing.

Non-chlorinated Water

If your tap water is chlorinated, it's wise to use either rainwater (if you live in a rural area where pollution isn't a concern) or filtered water for steaming. Failing this, you can expose a bowl of tap water to the air for 24 hours to evaporate the chlorine. The steam from chlorinated water contains chlorine gas, which can be harmful to your skin. Adding green herbs and citrus peel can help to remove the chlorine from your water.

Sensitive Skin Alert

If you have broken capillaries or extremely sensitive skin or if you suffer from rosacea, be very careful when steaming. Apply a thick layer of moisturizer or night cream over veined areas, and keep your face at least 16 inches (40 cm) from the steam source. Do not steam your face more than once every 10 days.

Facial Steam for Normal and Combination Skin

Steaming is an excellent way to unclog pores by softening the sebum and helping to clean and moisturize the skin. When essential oils are added to the water, the steam helps to carry them to the face. Geranium, lavender and ylang ylang essential oils are good for combination skin.

Makes enough for 12 steams

¼ cup (60 mL)	grapeseed or sweet almond oil
8 drops	geranium essential oil
6 drops	lavender essential oil
6 drops	ylang ylang essential oil

In a 2 oz (60 mL) glass bottle, combine grapeseed oil and geranium, lavender and ylang ylang essential oils. Shake to blend. Store in a cool, dark place for up to 12 months. Shake well before using (see Using Facial Steams, page 357).

Facial Steam for Dry Skin

Dry skin is at the mercy of environmental factors such as wind, sun and cold temperatures, which can inhibit sebum production. A facial steam can help to moisturize and bring healing essential oils to the skin. However, dry skin is usually sensitive, so don't steam for too long—5 minutes will do the job.

Makes enough for 12 steams

¼ cup (60 mL)	grapeseed or sweet almond oil
8 drops	palmarosa essential oil
4 drops	rose or lavender essential oil
4 drops	neroli essential oil
4 drops	carrot seed essential oil

In a 2 oz (60 mL) glass bottle, combine grapeseed oil and palmarosa, rose, neroli and carrot seed essential oils. Shake to blend. Store in a cool, dark place for up to 12 months. Shake well before using (see Using Facial Steams, page 357).

Facial Steam for Oily Skin

Excess oil attracts dirt and collects in the large pores normally associated with oily skin. Dirt in pores can breed bacteria and create an environment for infection. Oily skin can benefit from steaming with essential oils such as spike lavender and lemongrass, which can help to reduce sebum production. Essential oils that possess bactericidal properties can reduce the possibility of infection.

Makes enough for 12 steams

¼ cup (60 mL)	grapeseed or sweet almond oil
8 drops	lemongrass essential oil
4 drops	spike lavender essential oil
4 drops	patchouli essential oil
4 drops	sandalwood or cedarwood essential oil

In a 2 oz (60 mL) glass bottle, combine grapeseed oil and lemongrass, spike lavender, patchouli and sandalwood essential oils. Store in a cool, dark place for up to 12 months. Shake well before using (see Using Facial Steams, page 357).

(see Using Facial Steams, page 357).

Treating Acne

Suffering from acne? Follow your steam with a sweep of geranium hydrolat on a cotton ball. Long used for acneic conditions, geranium hydrolat is antiseptic and antimicrobial. Not only can it help to treat acne, it also works to fade the scarring left behind. It is a gentle alternative to chemical-laden commercial toners. Always use an oil-free moisturizer.

Facial Steam for Mature Skin

As we get older our skin begins to thin and production of the "anti-aging" hormones responsible for creating collagen and elastin begins to decline. The presence of free radicals also leads to wrinkles. Since aging skin lacks the necessary moisturizing oils, facial steaming helps to moisturize it by bringing the oils necessary to rejuvenate skin cells to the surface.

Makes enough for 12 steams

¼ cup (60 mL)	grapeseed or sweet almond oil
12 drops	clary sage essential oil
6 drops	frankincense essential oil
2 drops	lavender or rose essential oil

In a 2 oz (60 mL) glass bottle, combine grapeseed oil and clary sage, frankincense and lavender essential oils. Store in a cool, dark place for up to 12 months. Shake well before using (see Using Facial Steams, page 357).

(see Using Facial Steams, page 357).

Scrubs

Scrubs may be used by people of all ages. They exfoliate the skin, which means they clear excessive oiliness, deep-clean pores, improve circulation and generally nourish, leaving the skin looking fresh and rosy. The frequency with which you use scrubs and masks depends entirely on your skin type. If you have oily, blemished skin you will be able to use these preparations twice a week, but if your skin is fine and dry, choose only the gentlest treatment and use it no more than once every 10 days. Scrubs should never be used on thread veins, as they stimulate and can possibly aggravate the condition.

Almond and Rosewood Scrub

This scrub is suitable for all skin types (see Variation, below). It is gentle enough to use often, as long as the almonds are finely ground.

Makes 1 treatment

2 tsp (10 mL)	sweet almond oil
4 tsp (20 mL)	finely ground almond meal
1 tsp (5 mL)	cider vinegar
2 drops	rosewood essential oil

In a small non-reactive bowl, combine sweet almond oil, ground almonds, vinegar and rosewood essential oil to form a paste. Using your fingertips, massage gently over your face and throat. Rinse well with lukewarm water and pat dry. Apply moisturizing cream or lotion.

Variation
To make this blend suitable for dry skin, substitute an equal quantity of orange juice for the cider vinegar and add 1 tsp (5 mL) unpasteurized liquid honey to the mixture.

Yeast and Yogurt Scrub

This scrub is suitable for oily, normal or combination skin.

Makes 1 treatment

4 tsp (20 mL)	yogurt
2 tsp (10 mL)	finely ground almond meal
1 tsp (5 mL)	brewer's yeast
1 tsp (5 mL)	unpasteurized liquid honey
2 drops	lavender essential oil

In a small non-reactive bowl, combine yogurt, almond meal, brewer's yeast, honey and lavender essential oil to form a paste. Using your fingertips, massage gently over face and throat. Rinse well with lukewarm water and pat dry. Apply moisturizing cream or lotion. (See Tip, right.)

Facial Masks

Masks are very beneficial for all skins. They can improve color and texture, deep-cleanse, remove dead cells from the surface and bring fresh color and life to sallow skin.

Basic Mask

This mask is suitable for all skin types. It may be made in advance and stored in the freezer.

Makes enough for 10 applications

⅓ cup (75 mL)	fuller's earth or kaolin clay
8 tsp (40 mL)	cornstarch
4 tsp (20 mL)	finely ground rolled oats (see Tip, right)
4 tsp (20 mL)	finely ground almond meal
20 drops	essential oils suitable for your skin type (see page 354)

In a small non-reactive bowl, combine fuller's earth, cornstarch, ground oats and almond meal. Mix well. A drop at a time, add essential oils, stirring well to prevent clumping. Mix well and store in an airtight container in the freezer for up to 3 months.

In a small non-reactive bowl, combine 3 tsp (15 mL) Basic Mask and enough wetting agent to make a soft paste (see Mixing Face Masks for Different Skin Types, page 362). Follow instructions in Using a Face Mask, page 362.

Tips

The ingredients in this scrub have many beneficial qualities. Yeast stimulates the circulation, bringing blood to the surface of the skin, and yogurt cleanses and balances pH. Almond meal softens and exfoliates, while honey deep-cleanses, hydrates and has a natural antibacterial action.

When using Yeast and Yogurt Scrub, be very careful not to overstimulate the cheeks, where the capillaries are delicate and near the surface. If you have thread veins, avoid using this scrub.

Tip

When making the Basic Mask, use a blender or food processor fitted with the metal blade to grind the rolled oats finely until flourlike in consistency.

Using a Face Mask

Spread the mask over your face and neck (if you have dry skin or broken veins be very careful, as masks may be overstimulating). Relax on your bed or in the bath with cotton balls soaked (not dripping) in witch hazel (alcohol-free) or cucumber slices placed on your closed eyelids. Settle in and let your mind drift for 15 to 20 minutes. Rinse face thoroughly in lukewarm water, followed by a splash of cool water.

Mixing Face Masks for Different Skin Types

When adding a liquid to a dry mix, add just enough to make a soft paste. Choose a wetting agent that suits your skin type from the lists below.

Dry skin: cream, rose or geranium hydrolat, unpasteurized liquid honey (healing), cider vinegar (restores pH after using drying soaps)

Normal skin: water, milk, melissa or neroli hydrolat, egg white (firming)

Combination skin: milk, lavender or witch hazel hydrolat (alcohol-free), egg white (firming), yogurt (astringent), unpasteurized liquid honey (healing), fruit juice

Oily skin: skim milk, water, lavender or geranium hydrolat, egg white (firming), yogurt (astringent), fruit juice or pulp

Milk and Orange Mask

Although this mask is suitable for normal skin, the rosewood oil has antiseptic qualities and also benefits dry and sensitive skin.

Makes 1 treatment

1	egg, beaten
2 tsp (10 mL)	orange juice
1 tsp (5 ml)	olive oil
1 tsp (5 mL)	unpasteurized liquid honey
1 drop	rose or geranium essential oil
1 drop	rosewood or jasmine essential oil
	Dried milk powder

In a small nonreactive bowl, combine egg, orange juice, olive oil, honey and rose and rosewood essential oils. Mix well, adding just enough milk powder to make a smooth paste. Use immediately. Follow instructions in Using a Face Mask, left.

Golden Glow Mask

This mask is suitable for dry skin. The optional carrot seed oil is particularly beneficial for aging skin.

Makes 1 treatment

1	egg yolk, beaten
2 tsp (10 mL)	orange juice
1 tsp (5 mL)	olive oil
1 tsp (5 mL)	unpasteurized liquid honey
2 drops	neroli or geranium essential oil
1 drop	carrot seed essential oil, optional
	Dried milk powder

In a small non-reactive bowl, combine egg yolk, orange juice, olive oil, honey and neroli and carrot seed (if using) essential oils. Mix well, adding just enough milk powder to make a smooth paste. Use immediately. Follow instructions in Using a Face Mask, page 362.

page 362.

Caution

Avoid using carrot seed essential oil during pregnancy or while breastfeeding.

Yeast and Yogurt Mask

This mask is suitable for oily and combination skin. Lemon oil has a mild bleaching action that refreshes dull, oily skin.

Makes 1 treatment

4 tsp (20 mL)	brewer's yeast
1½ tsp (7.5 mL)	yogurt
1 tsp (5 mL)	witch hazel hydrolat (alcohol-free)
1 tsp (5 mL)	olive oil
1 tsp (5 mL)	wheat germ oil or 2 capsules vitamin E (250 IU)
1 drop	palmarosa essential oil
1 drop	lemon essential oil
	Finely ground rolled oats or kaolin clay powder (see Tip, right)

In a small non-reactive bowl, combine brewer's yeast, yogurt, witch hazel, olive and wheat germ oils and palmarosa and lemon essential oils. Mix well, adding just enough ground oats to make a soft paste. Use immediately. Follow instructions in Using a Face Mask, page 362.

Tip

Use a blender or food processor fitted with the metal blade to finely grind the rolled oats until flourlike in consistency.

Caution

Avoid wheat germ oil if you have a wheat or gluten allergy. Substitute vitamin E as indicated in the recipe. Pierce the capsules with a clean, sharp knife and squeeze the oil into your blend. Vitamin E is also available in dropper bottles, in which case add 2 drops.

Caution

Avoid using carrot seed essential oil during pregnancy or while breastfeeding.

Egg and Almond Mask

This mask is suitable for sensitive skin. Chamomile is one of the gentlest essential oils, and its anti-inflammatory properties will help to counteract redness.

Makes 1 treatment

1	egg yolk, beaten
1 tsp (5 mL)	jojoba oil
½ tsp (2.5 mL)	unpasteurized liquid honey
1 drop	chamomile essential oil
1 drop	carrot seed essential oil
1 tsp (5 mL)	milk powder or cornstarch
	Filtered or distilled water or rose water

In a small non-reactive bowl, combine egg yolk, jojoba oil, honey and chamomile and carrot seed essential oils. Mix well. Add milk powder and mix well. Add enough water to make a smooth paste. Use immediately. Follow instructions in Using a Face Mask, page 362.

Cleansers

Daily cleansing is possibly the most important part of your skincare routine. Every day your face is subjected to environmental irritants that clog your pores and make your skin look dull and lifeless. The recipes in this section include a special wash for sensitive skin, a cleansing cream for dry, aging or sensitive skin, and a soap for normal or oily skin.

Tip

Vegetable glycerin is a natural humectant, which means that it brings moisture from the air to your skin. For dry skin, or if you live at a higher altitude, use as much as ½ tsp (2.5 mL) glycerin.

Washing Water

This wash is excellent for cleansing your face if you have very sensitive skin or if you have acne or other skin problems.

Makes about 3½ oz (105 mL)

¼ cup (60 mL)	filtered or distilled water
8 tsp (40 mL)	rose hydrolat
¼ tsp (1 mL)	vegetable glycerin (see Tip, left)
6 drops	essential oil suitable for your skin type (see page 354)

In a 4 oz (125 mL) glass bottle, combine water, rose hydrolat, glycerin and essential oil. Shake to blend. The mixture will keep for up to 3 months in a cool, dark place. Shake well before using.

Treatment

Topical application: Dip a large cotton ball in warm water and squeeze out well. Flatten into a pad, sprinkle with Washing Water and use to cleanse throat and face. Repeat if necessary.

Tip

Adjust the consistency of this cream to suit your preference by increasing or decreasing the amount of olive oil.

Cleansing Cream

This cream is suitable for dry, aging or sensitive skin that needs a gentle cleanser. These types of skin usually feel uncomfortable after being washed with soap and water. Unless the weather is hot (over 75°F/24°C), this cream should not be refrigerated. It will need to be made fresh every 2 weeks or so.

Makes about 3 oz (90 mL)

⅓ cup (75 mL)	coconut or palm kernel oil
4 tsp (20 mL)	olive oil (see Tip, right)
10 drops	rosewood essential oil
10 drops	palmarosa essential oil
1 drop	benzoin essential oil, optional

In a small non-reactive bowl set over a pan of boiling water, combine coconut and olive oils and stir until coconut oil melts. Remove from heat and stir until mixture has cooled to room temperature. Add rosewood, palmarosa and benzoin (if using) essential oils and whisk until incorporated. Transfer to a clean 4 oz (125 mL) glass jar. Store in a cool, dark place for up to 2 weeks.

Variation

Cleansing Cream for Men: This is a good cleanser for men as well as women. Substitute an equal quantity of sandalwood essential oil for the palmarosa.

Tip

You can find melt-and-pour soap bases and soap molds in craft supply stores. There are some excellent ones available online as well (see Resources, page 459).

Glycerin and Honey Soap

If you have normal, combination or oily skin, you may prefer to use soap to cleanse your face and neck. This soap is simple to make and provides the benefits of essential oils, glycerin and honey. The glycerin and honey are both humectants, which means they attract moisture to the skin and hold it there.

Makes about 10 bars
Soap molds (see Tip, left)

4½ cups (1.125 L)	finely grated pure soap (unscented, if possible, such as Ivory, Dr. Bronner's or Lux; see Tip, left)
8 to 12 tsp (40 to 60 mL)	filtered or distilled water
2 tsp (10 mL)	vegetable glycerin
2 tsp (10 mL)	unpasteurized liquid honey
30 drops	rosemary essential oil
10 drops	lavender essential oil

In a small non-reactive bowl set over a pan of boiling water, combine soap flakes and 8 tsp (40 mL) water and stir until soap melts and water is incorporated. Scrape down sides of bowl and stir well. If mixture seems too thick, add more water. Heat until bubbly, 1 to 2 minutes. Remove from heat and add glycerin and honey, stirring well until completely incorporated. Set aside to cool slightly—it should be runny enough to stir but cool enough to touch. Stir in rosemary and lavender essential oils. Press into individual soap molds and set aside in an airy place for 7 to 10 days, until dry.

Toners and Astringents

Toners and astringents remove surplus oil from your skin, restore its pH level and leave it feeling fresh and clean. Toners that contain alcohol or a large amount of witch hazel hydrolat are called astringents. They are more robust than toners and should not be used on dry, sensitive or aging skin. Even if you have very oily skin you shouldn't use astringents that contain a significant amount of alcohol too often, because it will stimulate your oil glands. Toners perform the same functions as astringents but in a less assertive fashion. Both may be used to remove makeup or as a freshener during the day, as well as after cleansing. Men may use them as an aftershave.

To apply, dampen a cotton ball with water and squeeze it dry (this prevents waste by preventing the cotton ball from absorbing too much lotion). Sprinkle cotton ball with a few drops of lotion and gently stroke upward over your throat and face.

Top of the Mornin' Astringent

This lotion is excellent for oily and combination skin. It can also be used as an aftershave.

Makes about 7 oz (210 mL)

½ cup (125 mL)	witch hazel hydrolat (alcohol-free)
¼ cup (60 mL)	filtered or distilled water
4 tsp (20 mL)	cider vinegar
5 drops	cedarwood or sandalwood essential oil
3 drops	benzoin essential oil
2 drops	spearmint essential oil
¼ to ½ tsp (1 to 2.5 mL)	vegetable glycerin

In an 8 oz (250 mL) glass bottle, combine witch hazel, water, vinegar, cedarwood, benzoin and spearmint essential oils and ¼ tsp (1 mL) glycerin. (For dry skin, higher altitudes or drier climates, add an additional ¼ tsp/1 mL glycerin.) Shake to blend. Store in a dark, cool place for up to 1 year. Shake well before using.

Gentle Rose Toner

This toner is perfect for dry or aging skin because it is made with rose hydrolat, one of the gentlest skin tonics.

Makes about 8 oz (250 mL)

¾ cup (175 mL)	rose hydrolat
¼ cup (60 mL)	filtered or distilled water
3 drops	rosewood or rose essential oil
3 drops	palmarosa essential oil
½ tsp (2.5 mL)	vegetable glycerin

In an 8 oz (250 mL) glass bottle, combine rose hydrolat, water, rosewood and palmarosa essential oils and glycerin. Shake to blend. Store in a dark, cool place for up to 1 year. Shake well before using.

Variation

If you have normal or combination skin, substitute an equal quantity of witch hazel hydrolat (alcohol-free) for the water.

Lemon Balm and Witch Hazel Toner

This is a soothing and refreshing toner for all skin types.

Makes about 7 oz (210 mL)

½ cup (125 mL)	lemon balm hydrolat
¼ cup (60 mL)	witch hazel hydrolat (alcohol-free)
6 tsp (30 mL)	filtered or distilled water
10 drops	lavender essential oil
¼ tsp (1 mL)	vegetable glycerin

In an 8 oz (250 mL) glass bottle, combine lemon balm hydrolat, witch hazel, water, lavender essential oil and glycerin. Shake to blend. Store in a dark, cool place for up to 1 year. Shake well before using.

Sunrise Aftershave

Use this gentle but bracing aftershave to help contract your skin after shaving. It won't dry it out and is perfect for normal and combination skin.

Makes about 8 oz (250 mL)

¾ cup (175 mL)	witch hazel hydrolat (alcohol-free)
¼ cup (60 mL)	filtered or distilled water
5 drops	sandalwood or cedarwood essential oil
3 drops	benzoin essential oil
2 drops	rosemary essential oil
¼ tsp (1 mL)	vegetable glycerin

In an 8 oz (250 mL) glass bottle, combine witch hazel, water, sandalwood, benzoin and rosemary essential oils and glycerin. Shake to blend. Store in a cool, dark place for up to 1 year. Shake well before using.

Mint Zinger Aftershave

This is another blend for men that can be used as an aftershave or a toner. Both peppermint and spearmint have antibacterial qualities, in addition to being very refreshing. This toner will leave your face feeling cool and clean.

Makes about 8 oz (250 mL)

½ cup (125 mL)	filtered or distilled water
¼ cup (60 mL)	witch hazel hydrolat (alcohol-free)
¼ cup (60 mL)	peppermint hydrolat
3 drops	peppermint essential oil
2 drops	spearmint essential oil
2 drops	lemon essential oil
2 drops	lavender essential oil
2 drops	clove essential oil
1 tsp (5 mL)	vegetable glycerin
¼ tsp (1 mL)	tincture of benzoin or friar's balsam (see Tip, right)

In an 8 oz (250 mL) glass bottle, combine water, witch hazel, peppermint hydrolat, peppermint, spearmint, lemon, lavender and clove essential oils, glycerin and benzoin. Shake to blend. Set aside in a cool, dark place for 1 week, shaking once a day. Strain through a paper coffee filter before transferring to a sterilized dark glass bottle. Shake well before using.

Tip

Tincture of benzoin is a compound extract of benzoin, Tolu balsam and storax, with added aloe and some alcohol. Friar's balsam is a compound extract of benzoin, Tolu and Peru balsam, storax, myrrh and angelica in an alcohol base. Both are highly antiseptic and useful for cuts and abrasions. They also possess expectorant properties, making them useful for colds or the flu.

Moisturizing Oils

Adding moisture to your skin requires both oil and water. Used alone, water evaporates. Oil, when used as part of a skincare regime, seals the water into the skin, where it is held until completely absorbed. The following range of moisturizing oils includes something for all skin types.

Primrose Path Moisturizing Oil

This oil is particularly beneficial for dry skin. Use it as a daily moisturizer or in the evening as a nighttime facial serum. If you are making it for a man, he may wish you to substitute for some of the essentials oils, as noted.

Makes about 3 oz (90 mL)

8 tsp (40 mL)	grapeseed or sweet almond oil
8 tsp (40 mL)	olive oil
1 tsp (5 mL)	avocado or carrot seed carrier oil
1 tsp (5 mL)	wheat germ oil or 2 capsules vitamin E (250 IU)
60 drops	evening primrose oil
20 drops	borage seed oil
10 drops	jojoba oil
10 drops	palmarosa essential oil (sandalwood for men)
5 drops	carrot seed essential oil
5 drops	rosewood essential oil
5 drops	lavender essential oil
2 drops	cedarwood or sandalwood essential oil (benzoin for men)
2 drops	patchouli essential oil (neroli or frankincense for men)

In a 4 oz (125 mL) resealable glass jar, combine grapeseed, olive, avocado, wheat germ, evening primrose, borage seed and jojoba oils and palmarosa, carrot seed, rosewood, lavender, cedarwood and patchouli essential oils. Shake to blend. Store in a dark, cool place for up to 1 year. Shake well before using.

Dew Drops Moisturizing Oil

This oil is excellent for normal or combination skin. Men will enjoy it too, with the appropriate substitutions, as noted.

Makes about 3 oz (90 mL)

⅓ cup (75 mL)	grapeseed or sweet almond oil
1 tsp (5 mL)	avocado oil
1 tsp (5 mL)	wheat germ oil or 2 capsules vitamin E (250 IU)
30 drops	evening primrose oil
30 drops	jojoba oil
10 drops	palmarosa essential oil (sandalwood for men)
5 drops	carrot seed essential oil
5 drops	rosewood essential oil
5 drops	geranium essential oil (benzoin for men)
5 drops	ylang ylang essential oil (neroli or frankincense for men)

In a 4 oz (125 mL) glass bottle, combine grapeseed, avocado, wheat germ, evening primrose and jojoba oils and palmarosa, carrot seed, rosewood, geranium and ylang ylang essential oils. Shake to blend. Store in a cool, dark place up to 1 year. Shake well before using.

Cautions

People with nut allergies should avoid using sweet almond oil. Substitute an equal amount of grapeseed oil.

Avoid wheat germ oil if you have a wheat or gluten allergy. Substitute vitamin E as indicated in the recipe. Pierce the capsules with a clean, sharp knife and squeeze the oil into your blend. Vitamin E is also available in dropper bottles, in which case add 2 drops.

Avoid using carrot seed essential oil during pregnancy or while breastfeeding.

Satin Skin Gel

This gel is ideal for oily, combination or normal skin. The aloe vera is very soothing and helps to restore the skin's pH. The essential oils used in this blend rejuvenate skin balance, encourage cell growth and aid healing for all skin types. The aloe vera is readily absorbed.

Makes ½ cup (125 mL)

½ cup (125 mL)	aloe vera gel
25 drops	mixed essential oils (see Silky Skin and Hair Moisturizing Oil, page 372)

In a small non-reactive bowl, combine gel and essential oils. Stir well to combine—blending may take a little time but must be done very thoroughly. Transfer to a 4 oz (125 mL) PET plastic or glass jar. Store in a cool, dark place for up to 1 year.

Caution

Avoid using carrot seed essential oil during pregnancy or while breastfeeding.

Silky Skin and Hair Moisturizing Oil

Juniper oil is one of the most effective oils for freshening oily skin. Use this oil on your throat and around your eyes and lips. You can also use it as a night serum: apply thinly over face before going to bed. To use as a hair serum, pour a small amount (3 drops to ¼ tsp/2.5 mL, depending on hair length) into the palm of your hand, rub palms together and then run your hands through damp (towel-dried) hair from the roots to the ends.

Makes about 3 oz (90 mL)

⅓ cup (75 mL)	grapeseed oil
30 drops	evening primrose oil
20 drops	jojoba oil
10 drops	carrot seed essential oil
10 drops	lemon essential oil
10 drops	lavender essential oil
5 drops	juniper essential oil

In a 4 oz (125 mL) glass bottle, combine grapeseed, evening primrose and jojoba oils and carrot seed, lemon, lavender and juniper essential oils. Shake to blend. Store in a cool, dark place for up to 1 year. Shake well before using.

Caution

Avoid wheat germ oil if you have a wheat or gluten allergy. Substitute vitamin E as indicated in the recipe. Pierce the capsules with a clean, sharp knife and squeeze the oil into your blend. Vitamin E is also available in dropper bottles, in which case add 2 drops.

Apricot and Avocado Moisturizing Oil

This oil is excellent for sensitive skin. Use as part of your skincare regime, as a nourishing moisturizer after cleansing. Place a few drops on your fingertips and dot all over your face and throat, then gently smooth over the skin.

Makes about 3 oz (90 mL)

⅓ cup (75 mL)	apricot kernel oil
2 tsp (10 mL)	borage seed oil
45 drops	evening primrose oil
40 drops	wheat germ oil or 2 capsules vitamin E (250 IU)
15 drops	carrot seed carrier oil
5 drops	chamomile essential oil
5 drops	rosewood or rose essential oil
2 drops	lavender or neroli essential oil

In a 4 oz (125 mL) glass bottle, combine apricot kernel, borage seed, evening primrose, wheat germ and carrot seed oils and chamomile, rosewood and lavender essential oils. Shake to blend. Store in a cool, dark place. Shake well before using.

Eye Area

The skin around the eyes shows early lines in the same way as the neck does. Although laugh lines are a positive development, crow's feet, bags and dark circles can be demoralizing. The following natural treatments will help to keep this delicate area in good shape.

Gentle Treatment Required

The skin around your eyes is very fragile and can easily be damaged if you are heavy-handed. Here's a basic method for caring for this area: Using a damp cotton ball, moisten the skin around your eyes. Then pat a few drops of your chosen oil onto the area. Using your middle finger—because it is the weakest finger, so it exerts the least pressure—gently pat to assist absorption. Leave for 20 minutes, then blot off any surplus oil. Do not allow any oil to get into your eyes, as it could sting and/or cause puffiness.

Under-Eye Oil

This blend will soothe and thwart wrinkles for all skin types.

Makes about 1½ oz (45 mL)

8 tsp (40 mL)	apricot kernel oil
15 drops	borage or evening primrose oil
15 drops	carrot seed carrier oil
10 drops	lavender essential oil
5 drops	carrot seed essential oil
5 drops	neroli or lemon essential oil
2	250 IU capsules vitamin E

In a small non-reactive bowl, combine apricot kernel, borage and carrot seed oils and lavender, carrot seed and neroli essential oils. Stir well. Puncture vitamin E capsules and squeeze into bowl. Mix thoroughly. Transfer to a 2 oz (60 mL) bottle. Shake well.

At night, using your fingertips, apply no more than 1 drop under each eye. Leave for 10 minutes and then, using a tissue, carefully blot the excess. Avoid getting this oil into the eye itself, as it will sting and could be harmful.

Caution
Avoid using carrot seed essential oil during pregnancy or while breastfeeding.

Precious Night Oil

This extremely rich and luxurious oil is suitable for all skin types. The essential oils help to regulate and balance sebum and to smooth, soothe and soften the skin. Spray or splash the skin lightly with water or rose hydrolat, then apply a few drops of this oil.

Makes about 2 oz (60 mL)

2 tsp (10 mL)	grapeseed or sweet almond oil
1½ tsp (7.5 mL)	apricot kernel oil
1½ tsp (7.5 mL)	olive oil
1 tsp (5 mL)	hazelnut or grapeseed oil
1 tsp (5 mL)	borage seed oil
1 tsp (5 mL)	jojoba oil
1 tsp (5 mL)	avocado or carrot seed carrier oil
1 tsp (5 mL)	wheat germ oil or 2 capsules vitamin E (250 IU)
5 drops	evening primrose oil
5 drops	carrot seed essential oil
5 drops	palmarosa essential oil
5 drops	rosewood or rose essential oil
5 drops	geranium essential oil
5 drops	ylang ylang or jasmine essential oil

In a 2 oz (60 mL) glass bottle, combine grapeseed, apricot kernel, olive, hazelnut, borage seed, jojoba, avocado, wheat germ and evening primrose oils and carrot seed, palmarosa, rosewood, geranium and ylang ylang essential oils. Shake to blend. Store in a cool, dark place. Shake well before using.

Skin Problems

Acne

This distressing complaint is mainly a concern for teenagers but can occur in adults as well. Teenage acne usually starts at puberty, when many hormonal changes are happening within the body. As with most skin conditions, acne needs to be treated both internally and externally. Here are some choices you can make for a healthy body and healthy skin:

- Wash face 3 times a day using very mild soap that contains vegetable glycerin. Rinse well with lukewarm water and pat dry (if there are any weeping spots, use a fresh towel each time).
- Try to avoid using makeup or concealer, to aid healing.
- Use only Herbal Healing Day Oil and Herbal Healing Night Oil on your skin.
- Steam your face once or twice a week using Cleansing Facial Steam (page 377).
- Never be tempted to squeeze a pimple. The result will be scarring and spread of infection.

Acne Wash

Cleanse face twice daily with this wash and follow with Magic Three Toner (page 376). This blend is antiseptic, kills bacteria, heals skin eruptions and balances the skin's sebum.

Makes about 4 oz (125 mL)

6 tsp (30 mL)	unpasteurized liquid honey
10 drops	geranium essential oil
6 drops	lavender essential oil
3 drops	niaouli essential oil
¼ cup (60 mL)	geranium or lavender hydrolat (or distilled or filtered water)
6 tsp (30 mL)	liquid castile soap

In a 4 oz (125 mL) PET plastic bottle, combine honey and geranium, lavender and niaouli essential oils. Shake to combine. Add geranium hydrolat and liquid soap. Shake well to combine. Cleanse the face with a small amount of this wash and rinse well.

Magic Three Toner

Use this toner after cleansing with Acne Wash. The apple cider vinegar is antifungal, antiseptic and a restorative tonic for the face. The glycerin helps to bring moisture to the skin.

Makes about 6½ oz (190 mL)

½ cup (125 mL)	geranium or lavender hydrolat
¼ cup (60 mL)	distilled or filtered water
1 tsp (5 mL)	cider vinegar
¼ to ½ tsp (1 to 2.5 mL)	vegetable glycerin
5 drops	geranium essential oil
3 drops	lavender essential oil
2 drops	niaouli essential oil

In a 8 oz (250 mL) glass bottle, combine geranium hydrolat, water, vinegar, glycerin and geranium, lavender and niaouli essential oils. Shake to blend. Store in a cool, dark place. Shake well before using.

Pour a little Magic Three Toner on a dampened cotton ball and use twice daily to freshen skin.

Caution

Avoid using carrot seed essential oil during pregnancy or while breastfeeding.

Herbal Healing Day Oil

This gentle but powerful oil is for daytime treatment of acne or otherwise infected skin. Use morning and midday.

Makes about 1½ oz (45 mL)

8 tsp (40 mL)	jojoba oil
10 drops	carrot seed essential oil
10 drops	palmarosa essential oil
5 drops	tea tree essential oil
5 drops	geranium essential oil

In a 2 oz (60 mL) glass dropper bottle, combine jojoba oil and carrot seed, palmarosa, tea tree and geranium essential oils. Shake to blend. Shake well before using.

Place 3 to 4 drops Herbal Healing Day Oil on your fingertips and dot over your face. Using your fingers, gently smooth over your face. Don't get any in your eyes, as it will sting. Leave on for 5 to 10 minutes, then, using a tissue, blot off surplus.

Herbal Healing Night Oil

This blend feels a little oilier than its daytime companion, but don't worry—the oils will heal and regenerate your skin while you sleep.

Makes about 2 oz (60 mL)

20 drops	evening primrose or rosehip seed oil
10 drops	carrot seed essential oil
5 drops	tea tree essential oil
5 drops	palmarosa essential oil
¼ cup (60 mL)	kukui nut oil

In a 2 oz (60 mL) glass dropper bottle, combine evening primrose oil and carrot seed, tea tree and palmarosa essential oils. Fill remainder of bottle with kukui nut oil. Shake to blend. Shake well before using.

Place 3 to 4 drops Herbal Healing Night Oil on your fingertips and gently smooth over your face. Don't get any in your eyes, as it will sting. Leave on for 5 to 10 minutes, then, using a tissue, blot off surplus.

Tip

For acne, apply a drop or two of Herbal Healing Night Oil on eruptions. However, be careful not to overuse it undiluted, as it may cause irritation.

Cautions

People with nut allergies should avoid using kukui nut oil. Substitute an equal amount of grapeseed oil.

Avoid using carrot seed essential oil during pregnancy or while breastfeeding.

Cleansing Facial Steam

The antibacterial action of this treatment, combined with the heat from the steam, will draw impurities to the surface, so don't use it before a big date!

Makes about ½ oz (15 mL)

1 tsp (5 mL)	palmarosa essential oil
1 tsp (5 mL)	lavender essential oil
½ tsp (2.5 mL)	tea tree essential oil
30 drops	geranium essential oil
20 drops	thyme essential oil

In a ½ oz (15 mL) glass dropper bottle, combine palmarosa, lavender, tea tree, geranium and thyme essential oils. Shake to blend. Shake well before using.

Treatment

In a small non-reactive bowl, combine 4 cups (1 L) boiling water and 5 to 10 drops Cleansing Facial Steam. Follow instructions in Using Facial Steams, page 357.

Healing Mask for Acne, Eczema and Other Skin Problems

This mask is for sensitive and problem skin. Kaolin clay is a gentle cleanser and exfoliant, while the almond meal provides vitamins necessary for proper skin function and stimulates circulation. Moisturizing honey is a natural healing ingredient; its antibacterial properties make it a wonderful addition to any facial treatment.

Makes 1 application

4 tsp (20 mL)	finely ground almond meal
2 tsp (10 mL)	kaolin clay
1 tsp (5 mL)	unpasteurized liquid honey
1 drop	juniper essential oil
1 drop	chamomile essential oil
1 drop	lavender essential oil
	Distilled or filtered water

In a small non-reactive bowl, combine ground almonds, clay, honey and juniper, chamomile and lavender essential oils. Add just enough water to form a soft paste.

Using your fingertips, gently spread Healing Mask over your face and neck, keeping it away from your eyes. Lie down for 10 to 15 minutes, with cotton pads soaked in witch hazel hydrolat (alcohol-free) or cooled chamomile tea over your eyes. Wash off mask in lukewarm water, followed by a splash of cool water.

Blackheads

When the sebaceous glands over-secrete and the excess sebum doesn't move out of the duct, a blackhead results. This can become a problem if not dealt with carefully; the pore can become infected if the blackhead is removed roughly and the area isn't disinfected. Facial scrubs are useful for preventing the formation of blackheads.

The safest way to remove blackheads is to steam the skin, using boiling water and antiseptic oil to prevent infection. This loosens the sebum and relaxes the pores. Here is a basic steam procedure for removing blackheads:

1. Fill a bowl three-quarters full of boiling water. Float 1 drop tea tree essential oil and 2 drops geranium essential oil on the water.

2. Cover your head with a towel, forming a tent around the bowl and your head. Steam face for about 10 minutes, keeping it about 12 inches (30 cm) away from the water.

3. Pat your skin dry with a clean, soft towel.

4. With cotton balls wrapped around your fingernails, use your fingers to gently press the skin on either side of the blackhead until it pops out. Alternatively, use a special tool for extracting blackheads, available from cosmetic counters or pharmacies.

5. Splash the skin with Astringent Toner (below), which will help to disinfect the pore.

Astringent Toner

Using an astringent toner after cleansing helps to remove any left-behind traces of dirt or makeup and tightens the pores, leaving your skin healthy-looking.

Makes about 2 oz (60 mL)

½ tsp (2.5 mL)	unpasteurized liquid honey
2 drops	cypress essential oil
1 drop	palmarosa essential oil
8 tsp (40 mL)	distilled or filtered water
3 tsp (15 mL)	witch hazel hydrolat (alcohol-free)

In a 2 oz (60 mL) glass bottle, combine honey and cypress and palmarosa essential oils. Agitate to mix. Add water and witch hazel and shake to blend.

Pour a little Astringent Toner on a damp cotton pad. Pat over the skin after steaming or cleansing.

Dermatitis

Dermatitis is an inflammation and/or irritation of the skin. Chronic dermatitis is more commonly referred to as eczema; it is usually caused by sensitivity to a substance or substances with which the skin has come in contact. Bartenders, cleaning professionals and hairdressers often suffer from dermatitis because of daily skin contact with alcohol, harsh cleaners or the chemicals used in hairdressing. Obviously the condition won't clear up until the irritant is removed (in extreme circumstances, this can mean giving up your occupation). Stress is another factor that can aggravate the condition. The following eczema treatment is appropriate for other types of dermatitis as well.

Eczema

Eczema is an inflammatory condition of the skin that manifests variously as itching, inflammation, dry, thickened skin and/or tiny blisters that burst, weep and can become infected. It is a very difficult problem to treat—particularly if the cause isn't found. Look for causes among allergies, low stomach acid, stress, poor or inadequate diet, a dysfunctional immune system or a buildup of toxins. Initially the aims of aromatherapy treatment are to lower stress, ease the itching and thus prevent scratching, and promote healthy new skin tissue. Various oils should be tried until suitable ones are found. Choose one or two from each of the functions in the following table to use in blends.

Function	Oils
Anti-stress	Bergamot, cedarwood, chamomile, cypress, geranium, juniper, lavender
Detoxifying	Clary sage, juniper, rosemary
Anti-inflammatory	Chamomile, helichrysum, lavender, lemon, myrrh
Healing (carrier oils)	Calendula-infused, carrot seed, rosehip

Compress Blend

Use this comforting and healing compress to decrease the inflammation and itching associated with eczema.

Makes 1 application

2 drops	geranium or lavender essential oil
2 drops	lemon or myrrh essential oil
1 drop	chamomile or cypress essential oil
2 cups (500 mL)	cold water

Place geranium, lemon and chamomile essential oils in a medium-size non-reactive bowl; agitate to combine. Pour 2 cups (500 mL) cool (not icy) water into bowl and stir well to disperse oils. Soak a cloth and wring out enough water so cloth doesn't drip. Place cloth on affected area. Repeat twice daily.

Oil Blend for Dry Eczema

People with dry eczema are advised to take short, warm (not hot) showers and to use mild soaps to avoid excessive drying of the skin. A deficiency in omega-3 fatty acids may contribute to the condition. Keep the skin moisturized and consult with your doctor to determine the diet that is best for you.

Makes about 1⅓ oz (40 mL)

8 tsp (40 mL)	grapeseed or sweet almond oil
10 drops	evening primrose oil
10 drops	chamomile essential oil
5 drops	myrrh essential oil
5 drops	lavender essential oil

In a 2 oz (60 mL) glass dropper bottle, combine grapeseed and evening primrose oils and chamomile, myrrh and lavender essential oils. Shake to blend.

Variation
Hemp seed oil is high in essential fatty acids, with flaxseed oil coming in a close second. Consider using hemp seed oil instead of grapeseed oil for a more beneficial blend.

Treatment
Using your fingertips, smooth gently over affected areas.

Cream Blend for Weeping Eczema

Makes about ¼ cup (60 mL)

¼ cup (60 mL)	shea butter
15 drops	lavender essential oil
15 drops	frankincense essential oil
15 drops	myrrh essential oil
10 drops	chamomile essential oil
2	250 IU capsules vitamin E oil

In a small non-reactive bowl set over a pot of simmering water, carefully melt shea butter. Allow to cool slightly (it should still be liquid). Add lavender, frankincense, myrrh and chamomile essential oils. Mix well. With the tip of a clean, sharp knife, pierce the vitamin E capsules and squeeze the oil into the mixture. Stir to combine. Pour into a 2 oz (60 mL) double-walled jar (see Resources, page 459). Allow to cool completely, then seal tightly with lid. Store in a cool, dry place.

Treatment
Using your fingertips, smooth gently over affected areas.

Weeping Eczema

Weeping eczema begins with itchy red skin, but as time progresses the irritated skin can tear and bleed. As this continues, pus may develop and exude from the dry, cracked skin. Healing eczema like this starts from the inside out. Drinking plenty of water and making dietary changes can help.

Keeping the skin moisturized is a key factor in treatment. Unrefined shea butter is anti-inflammatory and wonderful for skin regeneration, making it a good choice for treatment of eczema. It is a humectant, bringing moisture from the air to the skin, which is helpful when dealing with, dry, irritated skin and eczema. Included in skin creams, it improves circulation in the capillaries and can soften and reduce the appearance of scars caused by cracked skin and scratching.

Psoriasis

Psoriasis is a chronic inflammatory skin condition characterized by thick pink patches with overlapping silvery scales. It usually appears on the scalp, backs of the wrists, elbows, knees and ankles. The condition is difficult to treat and patience may be needed. Environmental factors, heredity, stress or an under-functioning liver may be the cause, and until the cause is found and addressed, there will be no permanent cure. The following suggestions will certainly help, but it is advised to use aromatherapy in conjunction with a stress-management course and a liver-cleansing program. Vitamin D has been shown to be helpful, taken either as a vitamin supplement or simply by getting outside in the sunlight.

Psoriasis Massage Oil Blend

The goal of treatment is to control the symptoms and prevent infection. Taking a daily shower or oatmeal bath can help to keep your skin clean and to soothe and loosen scales.

Makes about ½ cup (125 mL)

30 drops	borage seed oil
30 drops	evening primrose oil
15 drops	manuka essential oil
10 drops	bergamot essential oil
10 drops	thyme ct. linalool essential oil
10 drops	cajuput or niaouli essential oil
½ cup (125 mL)	grapeseed or sweet almond oil

In a 2 oz (125 mL) glass bottle, combine borage seed and evening primrose oils and manuka, bergamot, thyme and cajuput essential oils. Top up with grapeseed oil. Shake to blend.

Treatments

Bath: Fill tub with warm water. Meanwhile, in a small non-reactive bowl, combine 1 tsp (5 mL) Psoriasis Massage Oil Blend and 1 cup (250 mL) finely ground rolled oats. Add to tub and agitate to disperse. Soak for 30 minutes, massaging any floating droplets of oil into your skin. Do not scrub the affected areas, as that can irritate the skin.

Hand/footbath: Add 1 tsp (5 mL) Psoriasis Massage Oil Blend to a basin of warm water, agitate to disperse oil, then soak desired area for 10 to 20 minutes, massaging any floating droplets of oil into your skin.

Massage: Massage Psoriasis Massage Oil Blend all over your body or just on the affected areas. After showering, while your skin is still damp, pour a little of the blend into the palm of your hand and massage over your body.

Topical application: Using your fingertips, smooth blend gently over affected areas several times a day. If it causes any discomfort, increase the amount of grapeseed oil.

Neck

The skin on the neck is usually much drier than that on our faces, and it is also often neglected, resulting in a dry, crepey texture. The following oil blend is gentle and rich. If used regularly, it can help to keep wrinkles at bay and to soften and smooth those that have already appeared.

Special Neck Blend

Makes about 1 oz (30 mL)

2 tsp (10 mL)	jojoba oil
1 tsp (5 mL)	avocado oil
1 tsp (5 mL)	wheat germ oil or 2 capsules vitamin E (250 IU)
½ tsp (2.5 mL)	evening primrose oil
5 drops	carrot seed essential oil
5 drops	lavender essential oil
5 drops	palmarosa essential oil
5 drops	rosewood essential oil
2	250 IU capsules vitamin E

In a 1 oz (30 mL) glass bottle, combine jojoba, avocado, wheat germ and evening primrose oils and carrot seed, lavender, palmarosa and rosewood essential oils. Pierce vitamin E capsules and add to bottle. Shake to blend. Store in a cool, dark place. Shake well before use.

Cautions

Avoid wheat germ oil if you have a wheat or gluten allergy. Substitute vitamin E, as indicated in the recipe. Pierce the capsules with a clean, sharp knife and squeeze the oil into your blend. Vitamin E is also available in dropper bottles, in which case add 2 drops.

Avoid using carrot seed essential oil during pregnancy or while breastfeeding.

Treatment

Neck massage: Spray or splash a little water on your throat. Sprinkle a few drops of Special Neck Blend into the palm of your hand and massage neck gently in an upward direction until oil has been absorbed.

Hands

It is very common to spend a great deal of time and money on our hair and faces and to neglect our poor hands. They are exposed to the weather just as our faces are, and they also have to contend with gardening, washing floors and dishes and all those other jobs that are so hard on skin. Essential oils are particularly good for hands, as they work very quickly and are readily absorbed without leaving a greasy feeling. These hardworking parts of our bodies need all the love and care we can give them. The following oil is a luxurious treat for the tools we use most often and usually appreciate the least.

Lemon and Lavender Hand Softener

This is a cream for dry, rough, work-worn hands. Massage it into the hands before doing dirty jobs. If your hands are really rough, use this rich cream during the evening while talking or watching television, or massage on a generous amount before bedtime and cover the hands with cotton gloves to protect the bedclothes.

Makes about 1 cup (250 mL)

8 tsp (40 mL)	beeswax prills (pellets)
½ cup (125 mL)	olive oil
⅓ cup (75 mL)	grapeseed or sweet almond oil
8 tsp (40 mL)	vegetable glycerin
2 drops	lemon essential oil
2 drops	lavender essential oil

In a small bowl set over a simmering pan of water, melt beeswax. Add olive and grapeseed oils and stir to combine. Stir in glycerin until completely blended. Remove from heat and set aside to cool slightly. Add essential oils 1 drop at a time, stirring well. Transfer to an 8 oz (250 mL) resealable glass jar. Store in a cool, dark place for up to 1 year.

Lavender Barrier Cream

Massage cream well into hands before doing dirty jobs.

Makes about ½ cup (125 mL)

8 tsp (40 mL)	olive oil
8 tsp (40 mL)	kaolin clay
4 tsp (20 mL)	lavender hydrolat or distilled or filtered water
10 drops	lavender essential oil

In a small non-reactive bowl, combine olive oil, kaolin clay, lavender hydrolat and lavender essential oil. Mix thoroughly. Transfer to a 4 oz (125 mL) sterilized resealable glass jar. Store in a cool, dark place for up to 6 months.

Healing Hand Cream

If you do not have the time or energy to make a cream from scratch, this blend is for you. Buy aloe cream, not aloe ointment, from a health-food store, making sure you get one with the largest amount possible of aloe. This combination of aloe cream and essential oils will heal and soften sore, dry or cracked skin. Use it after washing your hands and at bedtime.

Makes about ¼ cup (60 mL)

¼ cup (60 mL)	aloe cream
½ tsp (2.5 mL)	benzoin tincture or 5 drops benzoin essential oil
10 drops	sandalwood essential oil
10 drops	palmarosa or lavender essential oil
10 drops	lavender essential oil

Place aloe cream in a small non-reactive bowl. In another small non-reactive bowl, combine benzoin and sandalwood, palmarosa and lavender essential oils. Add essential oil mixture 1 drop at a time to the cream, stirring constantly. Transfer to a sterilized resealable glass jar. Store in a cool, dark place.

Tip

The skin on the hands contains very little oil. Use suitable gloves for gardening, housework and the like, and use a rich hand cream whenever possible.

Hand and Nail Oil

Our hands are always in use and can show visible signs of wear and tear. Take care to keep them in good condition by cleansing and moisturizing.

Makes about ⅓ cup (75 mL)

8 tsp (40 mL)	avocado oil
4 tsp (20 mL)	grapeseed or sweet almond oil
2 tsp (10 mL)	olive oil
1 tsp (5 mL)	jojoba oil
20 drops	evening primrose oil
10 drops	lavender essential oil
10 drops	lemon or tea tree essential oil
5 drops	geranium essential oil
5	250 IU capsules vitamin E

In a 2 oz (125 mL) glass bottle, combine avocado, grapeseed, olive, jojoba and evening primrose oils and lavender, lemon and geranium essential oils. Prick vitamin E capsules and squeeze contents into bottle. Shake to blend.

Treatments

Nail treatment: Pour 1 to 2 drops Hand and Nail Oil onto a cotton swab and massage oil into the skin around the nail bed until absorbed.

Hand treatment: Pour 8 to 10 drops into the palm of your hand and massage well into your hands. Wear cotton gloves for the next couple of hours or overnight.

Hair Care

Your hair type is largely genetically predetermined. If you have hair that is fine and limp or prematurely thinning, it probably came from your parents. Some people have thick hair, others thin; some have shiny hair, others dull. Despite the fact that we regularly use shampoos and conditioners, only one person in a thousand will have hair that looks like the hair in television commercials.

Many years ago, most people's hair was considerably stronger and in better condition than it is today. Contemporary lifestyles, including various environmental irritants, can rob hair of luster. Commercial shampoos and conditioners contain chemicals and detergents that build up on hair and rob it of nutrients. Those you make at home with pure natural ingredients are infinitely superior to commercial products. (Most commercial manufacturers scrimp on the ingredients and spend their money on expensive packaging and advertising campaigns.)

Essential oils can help to repair damage and keep bleached, colored or processed hair in good condition. Use the following oils in shampoos, rinses, vinegar rinses and tonics, but never use at a greater concentration than 1%—20 drops in just under ½ cup (125 mL) of fluid. Use half this amount of essential oil in shampoos for children ages 5 to 12, and only 2 drops for preschoolers (ages 2 to 5).

Read the Label

Cosmetic labels list contents in order of quantity, from most to least. If you examine the label of an average bottle of mass-market herbal shampoo, for instance, you'll likely discover that its herbal content comes last on the list. Even if it contains a mere 0.0001% herbal extract, the product can legally be called "herbal" shampoo. Wouldn't you prefer to know the exact quantity of beneficial ingredients in your shampoo? It's easy—just make your own.

Pay Attention to Your Hair

It is worth remembering that hair and nails are very useful barometers of health. They are frequently the first parts of our body to warn of a health problem. If your hair becomes thin, dull and lifeless or your nails become brittle, with ridges and possibly white spots, your body may be telling you there is an issue that needs to be addressed, from environmental stress or nutrient deficiencies to more serious problems.

Hair Types

Fine Hair

Fine hair may be limp and lack body, but it can look and feel lovely if it is treated with natural pre-shampoo and after-shampoo conditioners, which give added thickness and body to the strands. Fine hair needs to be treated very gently. Use a soft bristle brush with rounded ends on the bristles. Don't expose it to too much wind or strong sunlight. Don't over-color, perm or bleach fine hair,

Tip

If buying a commercial shampoo, choose the most natural one you can find in a natural foods store, or purchase a good unscented base shampoo from a wholesaler and scent it yourself (see Resources, page 459). You can easily improve shampoos by adding essential oils appropriate to your hair type (see page 389).

as it will become brittle and break easily. Avoid frequent use of rollers, styles where the hair is pulled back tightly, and elastic bands: these can stress the delicate structure of the hair.

Thin Hair

Thin hair is often fine as well (see above). Treat it gently, never use harsh shampoos and avoid over-coloring or perming. Don't brush excessively, and use a soft brush with rounded ends on the bristles. Use pre-shampoo and after-shampoo treatments that contain protein, such as egg and milk, to add fullness.

Coarse hair

Be happy if you have coarse hair. Thick, strong and wiry, this hair will take a lot of abuse without splitting or breaking. You may not need to condition coarse hair, but if it's not as shiny as you would like, an after-shampoo conditioner and/or between-shampoo hair dressing can help.

Oily hair

Overactive sebaceous glands are responsible for excessively oily hair. Shampooing every day can aggravate the problem, because the glands become even more active in response to the constant stimulation. Dry shampoos are a good compromise because they remove the oil between shampoos. Don't brush too hard or for too long. Twenty to 30 strokes are sufficient to distribute oil evenly along the hair shaft. Don't use very hot water for shampooing or rinsing, because the heat will encourage the production of more oil. A vinegar rinse will help strip excessive oil and leave the hair shining and manageable.

Dry hair

Dry hair is dull, has a tendency to split and break, and is difficult to style. Any type of hair may be afflicted with dryness under certain circumstances. Dryness may be the result of ill health, harsh shampoos, overuse of hot hairstyling tools, or too much exposure to sun and wind, among other causes. Treatment for dry hair should begin with an analysis of the cause of the problem; once that is established, one of the remedies outlined in this section may be used to restore your hair to a healthy condition.

Essential Oils for Hair

Condition/Function	Appropriate Essential Oils
Aging hair	Carrot seed, frankincense, galbanum, geranium, lavender, neroli, palmarosa, rose, ylang ylang
Alopecia	Carrot seed, clary sage, lavender, rosemary, thyme
Dandruff	Bay (laurel and West Indian), bergamot, cedarwood, clary sage, lavender, rosemary, sage, sandalwood, tea tree
Dry hair	Geranium, lavender, palmarosa, rosemary, rosewood, sandalwood
Fragile hair	Chamomile, clary sage, lavender, sandalwood
General hair care	Carrot seed, cedarwood, Roman chamomile, clary sage, geranium, lavender, rosemary, ylang ylang
Hair loss	West Indian bay, clary sage, lavender, rosemary, sage, thyme, ylang ylang
Normal hair	Carrot seed, Roman chamomile, lavender, lemon, geranium, rosemary
Oily hair	Bay (laurel and West Indian), clary sage, cypress, lavender, lemon, rosemary
Scalp tonic	West Indian bay, carrot seed, cedarwood
Split ends	Rosewood, sandalwood

Pre-shampoo Treatments

If your hair is dry, both hair and scalp will benefit from a hot oil treatment.

Hot Oil Treatment

Makes 1 treatment

4 tsp (20 mL)	jojoba oil
5 drops	lavender essential oil
3 drops	clary sage essential oil
2 drops	cedarwood or sandalwood essential oil

In a small non-reactive bowl, combine jojoba oil and lavender, clary sage and cedarwood essential oils. Stir well to disperse oils.

Tip

Double the quantities if your hair is very thick or long.

Treatment

Using your fingers, massage 1 to 2 tsp (5 to 10 mL) Hot Oil Treatment into your hair and scalp (adjust amount depending on hair length). Soak a hand towel in water and wring it out so it isn't dripping. Heat towel in a microwave oven for 30 to 50 seconds. (If you don't have a microwave, place towel in a large glass bowl and pour boiling water over it. Use just enough water that it's all absorbed.) When towel is cool enough to handle, wring out excess water. Wrap hair in hot, damp towel. Reheat towel and repeat 2 or 3 times. Do not shampoo for at least an hour. Follow with a herbal shampoo.

Egg and Honey Treatment for Dry, Damaged or Fine Hair

Dry, damaged and fine hair require conditioning that adds moisture and provides volume. Raw egg is a great conditioner and provides body and shine, while honey is restorative and adds moisture, as well as shine, to your hair.

Makes 1 treatment

1	egg yolk, beaten
2 tsp (10 mL)	grapeseed oil
1 tsp (5 mL)	unpasteurized liquid honey
2 drops	cedarwood or sandalwood essential oil
2 drops	clary sage essential oil
	Dried milk powder

In a small non-reactive bowl, combine egg yolk, grapeseed oil and honey. Add cedarwood and clary sage essential oils and mix well. Add just enough dried milk powder to form a very soft paste. Mix thoroughly.

Treatment

Using fingers, massage Egg and Honey Treatment thoroughly into hair and scalp. Cover hair with a shower cap. Soak a hand towel in water and wring it out so it isn't dripping. Heat in a microwave oven for 30 to 50 seconds. (If you don't have a microwave, place towel in a large glass bowl and pour boiling water over it. Use just enough water that it's all absorbed.) When towel is cool enough to handle, wring out excess water and wrap head with it. Leave on for 20 minutes. Shampoo with a mild herbal shampoo.

"Real" Shampoos and Rinses

Commercial shampoos have basically the same formula as carpet shampoo. A foaming agent is one of the main ingredients. We believe that plenty of foam means the product is cleaning well, when in fact foam has nothing to do with the product's cleaning capacity.

Detergent-based shampoos strip the hair of its natural oil, which is why wax conditioners are needed. The following recipes are for natural herbal shampoos based on soap. Soap-based shampoos will not strip your hair of its natural oils, but you will need to use an acid rinse afterward, as soap is alkaline.

Basic Herbal Shampoo

This shampoo will be runny and not full of lather, but it will clean your hair thoroughly. However, it will end up very tangled, so it is important to follow up with an acidic rinse. Use After-Shampoo Rinse (page 392) to smooth the hair cuticles.

Makes about 1 cup (250 mL)

½ cup (125 mL)	liquid castile soap
½ cup (125 mL)	distilled or filtered water, divided
4 tsp (20 mL)	coconut, macadamia or meadowfoam oil
25 drops	essential oils (see page 389)

In a glass measuring cup, combine castile soap and half of the water. Stir to combine. Add coconut oil (omit if hair tends to be oily) and stir. Pour into an 8 oz (250 mL) PET plastic bottle and add chosen essential oils. Top up with additional water. Shake to combine.

Variations

For a creamy, moisturizing lather: Add ½ cup (125 mL) coconut milk, preferably the milkier part, not the heavy cream found at the top of the can.

For dry hair: Add 6 tsp (30 mL) vegetable glycerin, which acts as a natural humectant.

To lighten or add highlights to hair: Steep 3 chamomile teabags in ½ cup (125 mL) boiling water for 6 minutes. Remove teabags and add enough distilled or filtered water to equal ½ cup (125 mL). Use in place of water in the recipe and add 2 tsp (10 mL) lemon juice.

Tip

At first Basic Herbal Shampoo may feel completely different from your regular brands. After about three weeks—it takes that long to get rid of the residues of previously used wax conditioners, fillers and other chemical ingredients in the hair shaft—you will begin to appreciate your new hair treatment.

Liquid Castile Soap

Liquid castile soap is readily available in health-food stores. It is a liquid soap derived purely from vegetable oils (usually olive oil) and not animal fat, or tallow. It does not contain any harsh detergents and is not harmful to the environment (see Resources, page 459).

Tips

One of the best ways to ensure thick, healthy hair is to use only lukewarm water to shampoo, and cold water (or herbal vinegar in cold water) for the final rinse.

Some online stores specialize in unscented natural bases for shampoos, conditioners and shower/bath gels. See Resources, page 459.

Be extra careful when handling wet hair. After shampooing, towel lightly and run your fingers through to arrange it. Wet hair is very elastic and can be badly damaged if brushed or combed roughly.

Quickie Shampoo

If you don't have the time or the inclination to make your own shampoo, buy one that claims to be mild. To 1 cup (250 mL) shampoo, add 12 to 50 drops single or mixed essential oils suitable for your hair type (see page 389). Use 10 drops of essential oil for children ages 5 to 10 and only 5 drops for children ages 2 to 5. Mix thoroughly.

When adding essential oils, start with 12 drops in 1 cup (250 mL) shampoo. Add more a little at a time until you reach the strength of aroma you are seeking—some essential oils have a stronger scent than others. You can use up to 50 drops.

After-Shampoo Rinse

Makes enough for about 33 rinses

2 cups (500 mL)	apple cider vinegar
1 tsp (5 mL)	mixed or single essential oil (see page 389)

In a 2-cup (500 mL) capacity bottle, combine vinegar and essential oil(s). Shake to blend.

In a non-reactive bowl, combine 3 tsp (15 mL) After-Shampoo Rinse and 2 cups (500 mL) warm water. Pour over your hair to rinse, using a bowl to catch the drips. Repeat once more.

Conditioners

You may find that after using the shampoo and vinegar rinse your hair doesn't need a conditioner. If, however, you have very fine, limp hair or if your hair has been overpermed, colored or otherwise abused, you may need a protein conditioner. Leave the conditioner on for at least 10 minutes after shampooing, rinse off and finish with a vinegar rinse or spray.

The following conditioners don't add layers of silicone to the hair shaft, and they will leave your hair full-bodied, soft and glossy.

Rosemary Conditioner

For all hair types except oily.

Makes 1 treatment

1	egg, beaten
1 tsp (5 mL)	vegetable glycerin
2 drops	meadowfoam, coconut or macadamia nut oil
2 drops	rosemary essential oil
2 drops	lavender essential oil
	Skim milk powder

In a small non-reactive bowl, combine egg, glycerin, meadowfoam oil and rosemary and lavender essential oils. Add just enough skim milk powder to form a very soft paste. Mix thoroughly.

Using your fingers, massage Rosemary Conditioner into your hair after shampooing. Leave on for at least 10 minutes, then rinse hair lightly with lukewarm water.

Brandy Lemon Conditioner

For oily hair.

Makes 1 treatment

1/3 cup (75 mL)	brandy
1 tsp (5 mL)	unpasteurized liquid honey
1	egg, beaten
2 drops	lemongrass essential oil
2 drops	West Indian bay essential oil
1 drop	rosemary essential oil
	Skim milk powder

In a small non-reactive bowl, combine brandy, honey, egg and lemongrass, West Indian bay and rosemary essential oils. Add just enough skim milk powder to form a very soft paste. Mix thoroughly.

Using your fingers, massage conditioner into hair after shampooing. Leave on for a few minutes, then rinse lightly with lukewarm water.

Tips

Use a wide-toothed comb. Teeth that are too close together can pull out a lot of hair. Start by combing through the ends and work your way up to your scalp to avoid damaging your hair.

Rinse your hair immediately after swimming, and shampoo it as soon as possible, using a conditioning treatment before and after shampooing. Chlorinated water and seawater are both very damaging to hair.

Tip

Scalp massage is of great benefit in treating alopecia, as it increases blood supply to the hair follicles. Use in conjunction with the vinegar rinse on page 395.

Hair Serum

This treatment can be used as often as you like. Hair dressings are used between shampoos to keep hair glossy, smooth and healthy. The non-greasy essential oils are absorbed into the hair shaft, making it suitable for all hair types.

Makes about 1 oz (30 mL)

15 drops	essential oils (see chart page 389)
6 tsp (30 mL)	jojoba or meadowfoam oil

In a 1 oz (30 mL) glass bottle, combine chosen essential oils and jojoba or meadowfoam oil. Shake to blend.

Treatment

Put a few drops Hair Serum in the palm of one hand and then rub your hands together. Rub your palms through your hair. Alternatively, sprinkle 2 to 3 drops on a natural-bristle hairbrush and brush through the hair.

Hair Problems
Alopecia

Alopecia (baldness) can be the result of illness, thyroid or pituitary deficiency, poorly functioning ovaries or stress; it can be temporary or permanent. The loss is usually gradual, but sudden hair loss has been known to occur after a traumatic shock. Alopecia can often be helped considerably by treatment with essential oils, but it is also necessary to visit a health-care practitioner, who can run tests to determine the reason for the condition.

Essential Oils

West Indian bay, clary sage, lavender, rosemary, thyme ct. linalool

Alopecia Scalp Massage Oil

Makes about 1⅓ oz (40 mL)

4 tsp (20 mL)	jojoba oil
4 tsp (20 mL)	meadowfoam or coconut oil
10 drops	lavender essential oil
5 drops	rosemary essential oil
5 drops	clary sage essential oil

In a 2 oz (60 mL) glass bottle, combine jojoba and meadowfoam oils and lavender, rosemary and clary sage essential oils. Shake to mix thoroughly.

Treatment

1. Pour ½ tsp (2.5 mL) Alopecia Scalp Massage Oil into the palm of your hand. Rub your palms together and gently apply to your scalp. Locking your fingertips onto your scalp, massage by moving the skin over your skull in small circular motions. Massage the entire scalp.

2. Soak a small hand towel in very hot water, wring out well and wrap over hair. Cover with a shower cap or dry towel. Rest with head covered for 30 minutes. Do not shampoo for at least an hour. Follow with Alopecia Shampoo.

Tip

If you wear your hair pulled back tightly for long periods, you can develop a condition called traction alopecia. In other words, you are losing your hair because you are pulling it out!

Alopecia Shampoo

Makes about 4 oz (125 mL)

½ cup (125 mL)	Basic Herbal Shampoo (page 391)
14 drops	jojoba oil
10 drops	lavender essential oil
4 drops	rosemary essential oil

In a 4 oz (125 mL) PET plastic bottle, combine shampoo, jojoba oil and lavender and rosemary essential oils. Mix thoroughly.

Alopecia Vinegar Rinse

Makes about 4 oz (125 mL)

½ cup (125 mL)	cider vinegar
50 drops	mixed or single essential oil (see page 389)

In a 4 oz (125 mL) PET plastic bottle, combine vinegar and essential oil(s). Shake to blend.

Treatment

In a non-reactive bowl, combine 3 tsp (15 mL) Alopecia Vinegar Rinse and 2 cups (500 mL) warm water. Pour over your hair to rinse, using a bowl to catch the drips. Repeat once. Rinse with plain water.

Hair Loss

There are many reasons (other than alopecia) why hair begins to fall out at a faster than usual rate. The following drugs can cause mild to major hair loss: two or more Aspirins a day, birth control pills (see your health-care provider for a change of pills if you notice your hair falling out), diet pills, cortisone (this can make hair grow on your face and fall out on your head!), anticoagulants, amphetamines and chemotherapy. Major trauma such as a serious accident, stress such as the death of someone close, divorce, prolonged illness and liver disease caused by years of heavy drinking can all cause hair loss. If the situation is remedied and the stress brought under control, the hair loss is not usually permanent; the follicles will usually begin to grow hair again within a few weeks.

If you are pregnant or a new mother, the emotional and nutritional demands on your body are heavy; hair loss may result from a combination of stress and nutritional deficiencies such as iron. Very heavy menstrual periods can also cause iron deficiency and accompanying hair loss. A blood test is indicated in these cases if the hair loss is great and you feel very tired. Hypo- and hyperthyroidism are other conditions in which hair loss can be considerable and a blood test is indicated.

Take heart. Unless the hair loss is genetically determined, your hair will slowly grow again when the cause has been eliminated. Use the oils and treatments for Alopecia (page 394).

Dandruff

Dandruff (seborrheic dermatitis) is a common and miserable complaint that causes embarrassment to the sufferer. The creamy white flakes shed from the scalp can ruin the appearance of an outfit. The scalp is sometimes sore or itchy, which causes the sufferer to scratch, and this in turn loosens more flakes. Dandruff is a form of eczema, but it can also be caused by an overgrowth of fungus. The skin cells of the scalp mature and are shed quickly, leaving an abundance of flakes. A combination of Exfoliating Dandruff Treatment (page 397) and Anti-dandruff Vinegar Rinse (page 398) is excellent, as the baking soda gently removes the flakes while the vinegar attacks the fungus.

Here are some tips for treating dandruff:

- Eat plenty of fruit and vegetables daily. Start the day with the juice of a lemon in a glass of water.
- Hats and other head coverings encourage dandruff. Keep the head exposed as much as possible when out of the sun.
- Take zinc and a B-complex vitamin daily.
- Use Hot Oil Treatment (page 390) once every two weeks until the problem is relieved.

Exfoliating Dandruff Treatment

Makes 1 application

1 cup (250 mL)	distilled water
3 tsp (15 mL)	baking soda
3 drops	rosemary or West Indian bay essential oil

In an 8 oz (250 mL) PET plastic bottle, combine water, baking soda and rosemary essential oil. Shake vigorously. Pour onto hair and scalp and gently massage scalp. Repeat until mixture is completely used up. Follow with Anti-dandruff Vinegar Rinse (page 398). Use twice a week.

Dandruff Shampoo

This shampoo will be runny and not full of lather, but remember, lather is not necessarily a sign of good cleansing!

Makes 8 oz (250 mL)

½ cup (125 mL)	liquid castile soap
½ cup (125 mL)	distilled water, divided
4 tsp (20 mL)	coconut, macadamia or meadowfoam oil
25 drops	essential oil (see page 389)

In a glass measuring cup, combine castile soap and half the distilled water. Stir to mix. Add coconut oil (omit if hair tends to be oily) and stir. Pour into an 8 oz (250 mL) PET plastic bottle and add chosen essential oil(s). Shake to combine. Fill bottle with remaining water and shake again.

Treatment

Shampoo: In a small non-reactive container, combine a small amount of Dandruff Shampoo (as you would use for normal shampooing) and 1 tsp (5 mL) baking soda. Stir to mix well, then shampoo with mixture as normal. Follow with Anti-dandruff Vinegar Rinse (page 398). Use 3 to 4 times per week.

Anti-dandruff Treatment

Makes 4 oz (250 mL)

½ cup (125 mL)	distilled water
½ cup (125 mL)	apple cider vinegar
8 drops	lavender essential oil
8 drops	bay laurel or tea tree essential oil

In a 4 oz (250 mL) PET plastic bottle, combine water, vinegar and lavender and bay laurel essential oils. Shake to combine.

Treatment

Scalp massage: Pour a small amount of Anti-dandruff Treatment into palm and apply to hair and scalp. Gently massage into scalp and leave for 5 minutes. Rinse with water. Do not shampoo! The aroma will be strong afterward but will dissipate within an hour or two. Use once a week.

Anti-dandruff Vinegar Rinse

Makes about 4 oz (250 mL)

½ cup (125 mL)	apple cider vinegar
25 drops	lavender essential oil
25 drops	tea tree essential oil

In a 4 oz (125 mL) PET plastic bottle, combine vinegar and lavender and tea tree essential oils. Shake to blend.

Treatment

Hair rinse: In a non-reactive bowl, combine 3 tsp (15 mL) Anti-dandruff Vinegar Rinse and 2 cups (500 mL) warm water. After shampooing, pour over hair to rinse, using a bowl to catch the drips. Repeat once and rinse with warm water.

Body Care

Baths

Quiet, warm, scented, peaceful... these words describe the ideal conditions for a perfect bath. Beautifully fragrant essential oils, candles and a bath pillow (or a hot water bottle full of warm water) on which to rest your head complete the scene. The rest is up to you—music, books, a drink and big, fluffy towels will all enhance the experience. Don't forget a "Do not disturb" sign to hang on the door! (If you've been doing dirty work such as gardening, taking a quick shower to remove the grime is probably a good idea before settling in for a good soak.)

A variety of baths can be used therapeutically, and each type is described below. Warm baths are wonderful for relaxing a stressed mind and body.

Therapeutic Baths

Fill tub with water. Meanwhile, in a small non-reactive bowl, combine chosen essential oils and 1 tsp (5 mL) milk and stir to combine well. Add to tub and agitate to disperse oils, then soak as indicated, massaging any floating droplets of oil into your skin.

Hot Bath

Temperature: 100° to 104°F (38° to 40°C) for 10 to 15 minutes only
A hot bath helps to break a dry fever by increasing perspiration and respiration rates, reducing fever and eliminating toxins from the body. Adult patients should remain in a hot bath for only about 10 minutes, under constant supervision. After the bath, they should be wrapped in warm towels, dried and helped into warm nightwear and then a warm bed. Give them an appropriate herb tea, such as peppermint or yarrow, to drink during and after the bath.

People with high blood pressure, heart problems, diabetes, multiple sclerosis or seizure disorders, children, pregnant women, the elderly and the obese should never have baths this hot unless under professional supervision.

Warm Bath

Temperature: 92° to 100°F (33° to 38°C) for 20 to 60 minutes
A warm bath calms and relaxes. Keep lighting in the bathroom dim to help relieve stress. Indulge for 20 minutes or until...
Who knows how long?

If you prefer, substitute an equal quantity of liquid castile soap for the milk called for in any bath recipe.

Do not add essential oils to the tub while the water is running, as some of the precious essences may evaporate, depriving you of the full benefits.

Tepid Bath

Temperature: 80° to 92°F (27° to 34°C) for 20 to 60 minutes
A tepid bath rejuvenates and cools inflammation. Relax for
20 minutes to soothe the pain and inflammation of arthritis and
rheumatism.

Cold Bath

Temperature: 70° to 80°F (21° to 27°C) for 2 to 5 minutes only
A cold bath—enjoyed by some Spartan characters!—improves
breathing and muscle tone, decreases fatigue, improves thyroid
function and skin tone, and relieves constipation. Avoid prolonged
soaking, as there is a danger of hypothermia.

Epsom Salts Bath

When you're feeling sore and tired, use this bath and feel your
aches and pains melt away!

*Fill tub with warm water. Meanwhile, in a small non-reactive
bowl, combine 4 to 6 drops of your favorite essential oil(s) and
1 cup (250 mL) Epsom salts. Mix thoroughly. Sprinkle into
a warm bath while the water is running. Agitate the water
to dissolve the salts, then soak for at least 20 to 30 minutes,
massaging any floating droplets of oil into your skin. (See also
Basic Epsom Salts Bath, page 413.)*

Herb Bath

Herb baths are most often used for soothing, hydrating, healing
and stimulating the body and skin.

*Fill a little muslin bag with dried herbs and add the bag to the
bath while the water is running. For added therapeutic benefit,
combine 6 drops essential oil(s) and 1 tsp (5 mL) milk in a small
non-reactive bowl and add to the bathwater.*

Milk Bath

Milk baths help to make the skin soft and silky. You can use fresh
or powdered milk. For a mildly acidic bath for oily skin or to
combat fungal skin infections, use buttermilk or yogurt.

*Fill tub with warm water. Meanwhile, in a small non-reactive
bowl, combine 4 to 6 drops essential oil(s) with the desired
properties (see pages 24 to 27) and 1 tsp (5 mL) milk. Mix
thoroughly. Add to tub and agitate to disperse oil, then soak for
30 minutes, massaging any floating droplets of oil into your skin.*

Tip

Use fat-free
powdered milk—it
leaves no bathtub
ring!

Honey Bath

Honey baths are an age-old treatment used to soften the skin and to treat insomnia.

Fill tub with warm water. Meanwhile, in a small non-reactive bowl, combine 3 tsp (15 mL) liquid honey and a few drops of relaxing essential oil(s) (see page 312). Add ¼ cup (60 mL) warm water and stir thoroughly to make a runny mixture. Add to tub and agitate to disperse oil, then soak for 30 minutes, massaging any floating droplets of oil into your skin.

Vinegar Bath

An old remedy for itchy skin is a soothing vinegar bath.

Fill tub with warm water. Meanwhile, in a small non-reactive bowl, combine 8 tsp (40 mL) cider vinegar and 6 drops soothing essential oil(s) (see page 258 for oils that ease itching). Add to tub and agitate to disperse oil, then soak for 30 minutes, massaging any floating droplets of oil into your skin. Alternatively, use a bath vinegar (see page 410).

Sitz Bath

Its name originated from the German *sitzen*, meaning "to sit," and it's very descriptive of what you do—you sit in water that covers only the legs, hips and lower abdomen. You can use a baby bathtub, a large, deep basin or an ordinary tub. Sitz baths are used for hemorrhoids and after giving birth, and for other conditions.

Skin: A Great Detoxifier

Given optimum conditions, your skin can be responsible for excreting as much as one-third of the waste matter your body produces. This relieves your liver, kidneys and lungs of quite a bit of work. However, in order to work efficiently, your skin needs to be clean and free from dead cells, which can block the pores. Using a body brush before bathing or showering helps to get rid of those dead cells.

Footbaths

Soaking the feet in hot water is an excellent treatment for staving off a cold or a bout of influenza, but it must be done as soon as symptoms appear, to gain the full benefits. Footbaths also soothe tired, aching or sports-worn feet. Alternating hot and cold footbaths can help to relieve a tension headache.

Hot Footbath

Fill a basin large enough for both feet with water as hot as can be tolerated. In a small non-reactive bowl, combine 6 to 8 drops appropriate essential oil(s) (see page 226) with 1 tsp (5 mL) milk. Add to the water, mix thoroughly to disperse oils and then immerse feet. Soak for 10 minutes, topping up with more hot water as the temperature cools. (Take your feet out of the basin before adding the water so you don't scald yourself.)

If you don't have a suitable basin, you can fill the bathtub with enough water to cover your feet and sit on the edge with your feet immersed in the water. After the bath, briskly rub your feet dry and put on some cozy footwear.

Hot-and-Cold Footbath

Fill two basins (each large enough for both feet), one with cold water and one with water as hot as can be tolerated. In a small non-reactive bowl, combine 6 to 8 drops appropriate essential oil(s) (see page 226) with 1 tsp (5 mL) milk. Add to the hot water and mix well to disperse the oils. First soak your feet for a few minutes in the hot footbath, then transfer them to the cold basin and soak for a few minutes. Repeat this process for about 15 minutes.

Hand Bath

This is a useful treatment for problems such as Raynaud's disease (see page 291) and arthritic pain (see page 160). Many herbalists in Europe use hand baths as the main therapeutic treatment for most problems.

Fill a basin or bowl large enough to hold both hands with water as hot as can be tolerated. In a small non-reactive bowl, combine 6 to 8 drops appropriate essential oil(s) (see pages 24 to 27) with 1 tsp (5 mL) milk. Add to the water, mix thoroughly to disperse oils and then immerse hands. Soak for 10 minutes, topping up with more hot water as the temperature cools. (Take both hands out of the basin before adding the water, so you don't scald yourself.) Dry hands and apply a moisturizing lotion or cream.

Bath Oil Blends

The following oil blends are for adults. For oils suitable for children, see Babies and Children (pages 163 and 164).

Antibacterial Bath Oil Blend

This bath blend is suitable for coughs, colds or the flu, and for after a full day of work outside in the garden.

1 tsp (5 mL)	grapeseed or sweet almond oil
2 drops	tea tree essential oil
2 drops	eucalyptus essential oil
1 drops	thyme essential oil
1 drop	lemon essential oil

Fill tub with warm water. Meanwhile, in a small non-reactive bowl, combine grapeseed oil and tea tree, eucalyptus, thyme and lemon essential oils. Stir well. Add to tub and agitate to thoroughly disperse oils, then soak for 30 minutes, massaging any floating droplets of oil into your skin.

Antiviral Bath Oil Blend

Use for colds or the flu, other viral infections and respiratory problems such as congestion and catarrh.

1 tsp (5 mL)	grapeseed or sweet almond oil
2 drops	tea tree or manuka essential oil
2 drops	eucalyptus essential oil
2 drops	lavender essential oil
1 drop	thyme essential oil

Fill tub with warm water. Meanwhile, in a small non-reactive bowl, combine grapeseed oil and tea tree, eucalyptus, lavender and thyme essential oils. Stir well. Add to tub and agitate to thoroughly disperse oils, then soak for 30 minutes, massaging any floating droplets of oil into your skin.

Tips

Do not add essential oils to the tub while the water is running. Some the precious essences may evaporate, depriving you of their full benefit.

If you prefer, substitute an equal quantity of liquid castile soap or milk for the grapeseed or sweet almond oil called for in any bath recipe.

Caution

People with nut allergies should avoid using sweet almond oil. Substitute an equal amount of grapeseed oil.

Deodorizing Bath Oil Blend

After a workout or run, cool and refresh yourself with this fragrant bath.

1 tsp (5 mL)	grapeseed or sweet almond oil
2 drops	clary sage essential oil
1 drop	eucalyptus essential oil
1 drop	patchouli essential oil
1 drop	peppermint essential oil

Fill tub with warm water. Meanwhile, in a small non-reactive bowl, combine grapeseed oil and clary sage, eucalyptus, patchouli and peppermint essential oils. Stir well. Add to tub and agitate to thoroughly disperse oils, then soak for 30 minutes, massaging any floating droplets of oil into your skin.

Caution

People with nut allergies should avoid using sweet almond oil. Substitute an equal amount of grapeseed oil.

Dry Skin Bath Oil Blend

This blend is nice for those who live in an arid climate or at high altitudes, where the skin is frequently dry.

1 tsp (5 mL)	grapeseed or sweet almond oil
2 drops	chamomile essential oil
2 drops	palmarosa essential oil
1 drop	patchouli essential oil

Fill tub with warm water. Meanwhile, in a small non-reactive bowl, combine grapeseed oil and chamomile, palmarosa and patchouli essential oils. Stir well. Add to tub and agitate to thoroughly disperse oils, then soak for 30 minutes, massaging any floating droplets of oil into your skin.

Oily Skin Bath Oil Blend 1

Oily skin can result in people who are producing high levels of growth hormones or who are insulin resistant. This blend can also be used for acne that has spread to the chest and back.

1 tsp (5 mL)	grapeseed or sweet almond oil
4 drops	lemon essential oil
2 drops	ylang ylang essential oil

Fill tub with warm water. Meanwhile, in a small non-reactive bowl, combine grapeseed oil and lemon and ylang ylang essential oils. Stir well. Add to tub and agitate to thoroughly disperse oils, then soak for 30 minutes, massaging any floating droplets of oil into your skin.

Oily Skin Bath Oil Blend 2

Use this bath blend to treat oily skin, including back acne. The essential oils in the blend can help to balance oil production, leaving skin smooth and supple.

1 tsp (5 mL)	grapeseed or sweet almond oil
2 drops	juniper essential oil
2 drops	lemon essential oil
2 drops	patchouli essential oil

Fill tub with warm water. Meanwhile, in a small non-reactive bowl, combine grapeseed oil and juniper, lemon and patchouli essential oils. Stir well. Add to tub and agitate to thoroughly disperse oils, then soak for 30 minutes, massaging any floating droplets of oil into your skin.

Spotty Skin Bath Oil Blend

This bath oil blend is suitable for skin affected by acne (blackheads and whiteheads) and for rashes.

1 tsp (5 mL)	grapeseed or sweet almond oil
2 drops	lavender essential oil
1 drop	eucalyptus essential oil
1 drop	thyme ct. linalool essential oil
1 drop	chamomile essential oil

Fill tub with warm water. Meanwhile, in a small non-reactive bowl, combine grapeseed oil and lavender, eucalyptus, thyme and chamomile essential oils. Stir well. Add to tub and agitate to thoroughly disperse oils, then soak for 30 minutes, massaging any floating droplets of oil into your skin.

Caution

People with nut allergies should avoid using sweet almond oil. Substitute an equal amount of grapeseed oil.

Caution

People with nut allergies should avoid using sweet almond oil. Substitute an equal amount of grapeseed oil.

Head-Clearing Bath Oil Blend

Here's a blend for when you need to recover from your day and refresh your senses.

1 tsp (5 mL)	grapeseed or sweet almond oil
2 drops	rosemary essential oil
1 drop	peppermint essential oil
1 drop	lemon essential oil
1 drop	thyme essential oil
1 drop	lavender essential oil

Fill tub with warm water. Meanwhile, in a small non-reactive bowl, combine grapeseed oil and rosemary, peppermint, lemon, thyme and lavender essential oils. Stir well. Add to tub and agitate to thoroughly disperse oils, then soak for 30 minutes, massaging any floating droplets of oil into your skin.

Dry Skin Bath Oil Blend

Dry skin can be itchy and irritating. Using this bath oil blend will help to retain moisture and leave skin soft and glowing.

1 tsp (5 mL)	grapeseed or sweet almond oil
2 drops	lavender essential oil
2 drops	rosewood or rose essential oil
2 drops	palmarosa essential oil

Fill tub with warm water. Meanwhile, in a small non-reactive bowl, combine grapeseed oil and lavender, rosewood and palmarosa essential oils. Stir well. Add to tub and agitate to thoroughly disperse oils, then soak for 30 minutes, massaging any floating droplets of oil into your skin.

Hydrating Bath Oil Blend

This blend is suitable for dry skin and may help to improve skin tone.

1 tsp (5 mL)	grapeseed or sweet almond oil
1 drop	Roman chamomile essential oil
1 drop	lavender essential oil
1 drop	carrot seed essential oil
1 drop	geranium essential oil
1 drop	rose essential oil, optional

Fill tub with warm water. Meanwhile, in a small non-reactive bowl, combine grapeseed oil and chamomile, lavender, carrot seed, geranium and rose (if using) essential oils. Stir well. Add to tub and agitate to thoroughly disperse oils, then soak for 30 minutes, massaging any floating droplets of oil into your skin.

Just "Ahhh!" Bath Oil Blend

This aromatic blend will lift your mood and awaken your spirit.

1 tsp (5 mL)	grapeseed or sweet almond oil
2 drops	grapefruit essential oil
1 drop	lavender essential oil
1 drop	geranium essential oil
1 drop	ylang ylang essential oil
1 drop	patchouli essential oil

Fill tub with warm water. Meanwhile, in a small non-reactive bowl, combine grapeseed oil and grapefruit, lavender, geranium, ylang ylang and patchouli essential oils. Stir well. Add to tub and agitate to thoroughly disperse oils, then soak for 30 minutes, massaging any floating droplets of oil into your skin.

Cautions

People with nut allergies should avoid using sweet almond oil. Substitute an equal amount of grapeseed oil.

Avoid using carrot seed essential oil during pregnancy or while breastfeeding.

Rejuvenating Bath Oil Blend

This revitalizing bath blend will make you feel new again.

1 tsp (5 mL)	grapeseed or sweet almond oil
4 drops	lavender essential oil
3 drops	rosemary essential oil
2 drops	peppermint essential oil

Fill tub with warm water. Meanwhile, in a small non-reactive bowl, combine grapeseed oil and lavender, rosemary and peppermint essential oils. Stir well. Add to tub and agitate to thoroughly disperse oils, then soak for 30 minutes, massaging any floating droplets of oil into your skin.

Relaxing Bath Oil Blend

Here's a euphoric blend to help you wind down after a stressful time.

1 tsp (5 mL)	grapeseed or sweet almond oil
2 drops	Roman chamomile essential oil
2 drops	lavender essential oil
2 drops	ylang ylang essential oil

Fill tub with warm water. Meanwhile, in a small non-reactive bowl, combine grapeseed oil and chamomile, lavender and ylang ylang essential oils. Stir well. Add to tub and agitate to thoroughly disperse oils, then soak for 30 minutes, massaging any floating droplets of oil into your skin.

Rise and Shine Bath Oil Blend

Sometimes you need a stimulating blend to get you going in the morning.

1 tsp (5 mL)	grapeseed or sweet almond oil
2 drops	bergamot essential oil
2 drops	lemon essential oil
1 drop	orange essential oil
1 drop	rosemary essential oil

Fill tub with warm water. Meanwhile, in a small non-reactive bowl, combine grapeseed oil and bergamot, lemon, orange and rosemary essential oils. Stir well. Add to tub and agitate to thoroughly disperse oils, then soak for 30 minutes, massaging any floating droplets of oil into your skin.

Sleep Well Bath Oil

This blend has a relaxing fragrance and sedative properties that will help you enjoy a restful sleep.

1 tsp (5 mL)	grapeseed or sweet almond oil
2 drops	Roman chamomile essential oil
1 drop	lavender essential oil
1 drop	marjoram essential oil
1 drop	sandalwood or cedarwood essential oil

Fill tub with warm water. Meanwhile, in a small non-reactive bowl, combine grapeseed oil and chamomile, lavender, marjoram and sandalwood essential oils. Stir well. Add to tub and agitate to thoroughly disperse oils, then soak for 30 minutes, massaging any floating droplets of oil into your skin.

Caution

People with nut allergies should avoid using sweet almond oil. Substitute an equal amount of grapeseed oil.

Floral Bath Oil

Indulge your senses with this floral bath blend.

1 tsp (5 mL)	grapeseed or sweet almond oil
2 drops	geranium essential oil
2 drops	rosewood or rose essential oil
2 drops	ylang ylang essential oil

Fill tub with warm water. Meanwhile, in a small non-reactive bowl, combine grapeseed oil and geranium, rosewood and ylang ylang essential oils. Stir well. Add to tub and agitate to thoroughly disperse oils, then soak for 30 minutes, massaging any floating droplets of oil into your skin.

Bath Vinegars

Bath vinegars are useful for oily skin, as they restore the acid mantle to the skin. They can also relieve muscle pain and the dryness, itching and pain of sunburn and poison ivy. Bath vinegars are used to treat fungal infections of the skin (and vagina). Cider vinegar seems to have the most therapeutic properties, but any good-quality white wine vinegar can also be used.

In a small non-reactive bowl, combine 1 oz (30 mL) cider or white wine vinegar with 6 drops mixed or single essential oil. Add to a full bath. Alternatively, make up a large bottle of one of the following blends and add 6 tsp (30 mL) to a full bath. Bath vinegar is self-preserving, so it can be kept near the bathtub.

Lavender Vinegar

Makes enough for 8 baths

1 cup (250 mL)	cider or white wine vinegar
50 drops	lavender essential oil

In an 8 oz (250 mL) bottle, combine vinegar and lavender essential oil. Shake to combine. Shake well before each use.

Treatment

Fill tub with warm water. Add 6 tsp (30 mL) Lavender Vinegar to tub and agitate water to disperse oil. Soak for 30 minutes, massaging any floating droplets of oil into your skin.

Citrus Sensation Vinegar

Makes enough for 8 baths

1 cup (250 mL)	cider or white wine vinegar
15 drops	lemon essential oil
13 drops	petitgrain essential oil
10 drops	bergamot essential oil
10 drops	orange essential oil
2 drops	clove essential oil

In an 8 oz bottle (250 mL), combine vinegar and lemon, petitgrain, bergamot, orange and clove essential oils. Shake to combine. Shake well before each use.

Treatment

Fill tub with warm water. Add 6 tsp (30 mL) Citrus Sensation Vinegar to tub and agitate water to disperse oils. Soak for 30 minutes, massaging any floating droplets of oil into your skin.

Mint Tang Vinegar

Makes enough for 8 baths

1 cup (250 mL)	cider or white wine vinegar
20 drops	peppermint essential oil
20 drops	spearmint essential oil
8 drops	lavender essential oil
2 drops	clove essential oil

In an 8 oz bottle (250 mL), combine vinegar and peppermint, spearmint, lavender and clove essential oils. Shake to combine. Shake well before each use.

Treatment

Fill tub with warm water. Add 6 tsp (30 mL) Mint Tang Vinegar to tub and agitate water to disperse oils. Soak for 30 minutes, massaging any floating droplets of oil into your skin.

Forest Fantasy Vinegar

Makes enough for 8 baths

1 cup (250 mL)	cider or white wine vinegar
20 drops	pine essential oil
10 drops	hyssop essential oil
10 drops	lemon essential oil
5 drops	cypress essential oil
5 drops	peppermint essential oil

In an 8 oz bottle (250 mL), combine vinegar and pine, hyssop, lemon, cypress and peppermint essential oils. Shake to combine. Shake well before each use.

Treatment

Fill tub with warm water. Add 6 tsp (30 mL) Forest Fantasy Vinegar to tub and agitate water to disperse oils. Soak for 30 minutes, massaging any floating droplets of oil into your skin.

Shower Gel

For those who prefer the convenience of a shower, you can purchase unscented natural shower gel bases online (see Resources, page 459).

To make shower gel: In an 8 oz (250 mL) PET plastic bottle, combine ¼ cup (60 mL) unscented shower gel base and 12 to 40 drops essential oil(s). Shake well to combine. Fill bottle with additional gel until almost full (allow 1 inch/2.5 cm headspace) and shake again. For a stronger scent, add up to another 10 drops essential oil.

When scenting your own natural shower gel base, start by using a smaller amount of essential oil—0.25%, or 3 to 12 drops per 1 cup (250 mL)—and work your way up to no more than 1%, or 12 to 50 drops per 1 cup (250 mL).

Bubble Bath

Love a bubble bath? You can purchase unscented natural bubble bath gel bases online (see Resources, page 459).

To make bubble bath: In a 8 oz (250 mL) PET plastic bottle, combine ¼ cup (60 mL) unscented bubble bath gel base and 12 to 40 drops essential oil(s). Shake well to combine. Fill bottle with additional gel until almost full (allow 1 inch/2.5 cm headspace) and shake again. For a stronger scent, add up to another 10 drops essential oil.

When scenting your own natural bubble bath gel base, start by using a smaller amount of essential oil—0.25%, or 3 to 12 drops per 1 cup (250 mL)—and work your way up to no more than 1%, or 12 to 50 drops per 1 cup (250 mL).

Bath Salts

Bath salts are used primarily to soften hard water. However, they may contain essential oils that perfume the water and add therapeutic properties.

Basic Epsom Salts Bath

Epsom salts baths are a nice way to soothe painful muscles and joints, calm nerve pain, soothe and tighten skin, improve circulation in arthritis, detoxify the body of harsh chemicals and heavy metals, and aid restful sleep in insomnia. The added baking soda helps to soothe eczema and itchy, irritated and dry skin, as well as to aid detoxification of congested skin.

Makes enough for 4 baths

1 cup (250 mL)	baking soda
1 cup (250 mL)	Epsom salts
25 drops	essential oil(s)

In a small non-reactive bowl, combine baking soda and Epsom salts. Add essential oil(s) 5 drops at a time, stirring to combine well after each addition.

Fill tub with warm water. Add $\frac{1}{2}$ cup (125 mL) bath salts to tub and agitate thoroughly to disperse oils. Soak for 30 minutes, massaging any floating droplets of oil into your skin.

Basic Sea Salt Bath

Sea salts contain high concentrations of minerals and trace elements. They help to soften water, draw out toxins and revitalize the skin. Soaking in a sea salt bath can help replace depleted minerals in the body, as well as treat skin disorders and arthritis and help to boost immunity.

Makes enough for 4 baths

1 cup (250 mL)	baking soda
1 cup (250 mL)	sea salt
25 drops	essential oil(s)

In a small non-reactive bowl, combine baking soda and sea salt. Add essential oil(s) 5 drops at a time, stirring to combine well after each addition.

Fill tub with warm water. Add $\frac{1}{2}$ cup (125 mL) bath salts to tub and agitate to thoroughly disperse oils. Soak for 30 minutes, massaging any floating droplets of oil into your skin.

Tip

Dead Sea salt contains a particularly high concentration of minerals.

Girl's Night In Bath Salts

This is a relaxing blend for a quiet evening at home.

Makes enough for 5 baths

1 cup (250 mL)	tartaric acid or sea salt
1 cup (250 mL)	baking soda
1/2 cup (125 mL)	arrowroot powder
15 drops	lavender essential oil
15 drops	sandalwood or cedarwood essential oil
3 drops	clove essential oil

In a non-reactive bowl, combine tartaric acid, baking soda and arrowroot powder. Mix well. One drop at a time, add lavender, sandalwood and clove essential oils, stirring constantly to prevent clumping. Transfer mixture to an airtight jar and seal. Shake daily for 4 days. Store in a cool, dark place for up to 3 months.

Fill tub with warm water. While water is running, sprinkle 1/2 cup (125 mL) Girl's Night In Bath Salts into tub and agitate to thoroughly disperse oils. Soak for 30 minutes, massaging any floating droplets of oil into your skin.

Colognes

The main difference between a perfume, an eau de toilette and a cologne is the ratio of essential or fragrance oils to alcohol. Perfume contains 18% to 25% essential oils, whereas eau de toilette contains 8% to 14%. Cologne contains 3% to 8% essential oils and thus far more alcohol than a perfume or eau de toilette. In many ways colognes are more pleasurable to use than concentrated perfumes, as they can be sprayed or splashed onto the body to create an aura of scent without being overpowering. Use liberally after a bath or shower to keep the skin cool, dry and delightfully fragrant.

Measuring Larger Quantities of Essential Oils

Essential oils are sold with orifice reducers. You can either count quantities by drops or remove the orifice reducer and use a pipette (see Resources, page 459) to measure in milliliters (mL). Use the following measurements as a guide (amounts are approximate):

54 drops = 2 mL	135 drops = 5 mL
65 drops = 2.5 mL	200 drops = 7.5 mL

Basic Cologne Formula

Use this formula with any of the essential oil blends that follow.

Makes 2 oz (60 mL) cologne

2 oz (60 mL)	alcohol
65 to 135 drops	essential oil blend (page 416)

Combine alcohol and essential oils in a 2 oz (60 mL) glass bottle with spray top. Shake bottle thoroughly to blend. Store in a cool, dark place for 2 to 24 weeks. Check weekly, as the fragrance will mature over time. Begin using when you are happy with the aroma.

Variation
To make 4 oz (125 mL) cologne: In a 4 oz (125 mL) glass bottle with spray top, combine 135 drops to 270 drops essential oil blend and 4 oz (125 mL) alcohol.

Tips

Perfumer's alcohol (made from grape spirits) is ideal for the base but often hard to find in smaller quantities. You can substitute vodka made from grape spirits (see Tip, below) or, failing that, pure grain alcohol (190 proof/95% alcohol by volume). However, grain alcohol may alter the aroma of the essential oils. For an alcohol-free perfume or cologne, substitute jojoba oil.

Ciroc vodka is made from grapes, so it is a good substitute for perfumer's alcohol.

Fragrance Blends

Here are a few fragrance recipes to get you started.

Flower Garden Cologne

65 drops	bergamot essential oil
65 drops	geranium essential oil
20 drops	petitgrain or neroli essential oil
20 drops	palmarosa essential oil
2 drops	sandalwood essential oil

Sweetheart Cologne

135 drops	rosewood essential oil
20 drops	ylang ylang essential oil
10 drops	jasmine essential oil
10 drops	bergamot essential oil

Enticement Cologne

135 drops	ylang ylang essential oil
15 drops	patchouli essential oil
15 drops	sandalwood essential oil
5 drops	jasmine essential oil
5 drops	rose essential oil

Lavender Lady Cologne

200 drops	lavender essential oil
10 drops	lemon essential oil
10 drops	palmarosa essential oil

Macho Man Cologne

135 drops	sandalwood essential oil
30 drops	cedarwood essential oil
10 drops	rosewood essential oil
5 drops	lemon essential oil

In a $\frac{1}{6}$ oz (5 mL) glass dropper bottle, combine the essential oils in any of the above recipes and shake. Use to fragrance your cologne as indicated above.

Deodorants

Deodorants (unlike antiperspirants) do not stop perspiration; rather, they control the unpleasant odor. Sweating is a natural and necessary function of the body. With a proper healthy diet, perspiration has no odor. The following basic deodorant recipe includes zinc oxide powder to neutralize odor, aloe vera juice to moisturize the skin, and witch hazel to inhibit perspiration. The added essential oils help to stop proliferation of odor-causing bacteria.

Basic Underarm Deodorant

Makes 6½ oz (190 mL)

⅔ cup (150 mL)	witch hazel hydrolat (alcohol-free)
6 tsp (30 mL)	aloe vera juice
2 tsp (10 mL)	zinc oxide powder
30 drops	rose geranium essential oil

In an 8 oz (250 mL) dark glass spray bottle, combine witch hazel, aloe vera juice, zinc oxide powder and rose geranium essential oil. Shake vigorously to mix well.

To use, apply Basic Underarm Deodorant to clean, dry armpits. Allow to dry completely before dressing, to avoid white marks on clothing. While this may seem a bit tedious, the spray is quite effective and all natural, not to mention good for your skin!

Variations

For heavy sweating: *Replace rose geranium essential oil with sage essential oil.*

For sensitive skin: *Replace rose geranium essential oil with 30 drops calendula CO_2 extract and 10 drops lavender essential oil.*

Tips

Zinc oxide powder is not completely water soluble and will separate. You must shake the bottle before each use.

Apply to freshly washed and dried skin to help the deodorant perform at its best.

CO_2 Extracts

CO_2 extracts are plant extracts that have been produced using CO_2 (carbon dioxide) rather than steam distillation to extract the essential oil components. Because the oils are not exposed to heat, they are closer in aroma to the originating plant. CO_2 extracts are slightly thicker than essential oils and contain plant compounds not commonly found in distilled essential oils. All trace amounts of CO_2 are removed during processing, making the oils suitable for use in aromatherapy.

Tip

If you find the aroma of cider vinegar unappealing, substitute grape spirits or perfumer's alcohol.

Fresh-as-a-Daisy Deodorant Body Spray

The following recipe makes a light deodorant, suitable for women, that is very pleasant and safe to use. The vinegar smell vanishes in a very short time, leaving only the scent of the essential oils.

Makes 8 oz (250 mL)

½ cup (125 mL)	cider vinegar
½ cup (125 mL)	witch hazel hydrolat (alcohol-free)
20 drops	bergamot essential oil
20 drops	lavender essential oil
10 drops	patchouli essential oil
10 drops	rosewood essential oil
10 drops	benzoin essential oil
½ tsp (2.5 mL)	vegetable glycerin

In an 8 oz (250 mL) PET plastic spray bottle, combine vinegar, witch hazel, bergamot, lavender, patchouli, rosewood and benzoin essential oils and glycerin. Shake well. Store in a dark, cool, dry place for up to 1 year.

To use, spray or splash on after showering and as needed.

Forest Fantasy Deodorant Body Spray

This deodorant is scented to appeal to men.

Makes 8 oz (250 mL)

½ cup (125 mL)	cider vinegar
½ cup (125 mL)	witch hazel hydrolat (alcohol-free)
20 drops	benzoin essential oil
20 drops	bergamot essential oil
20 drops	cypress essential oil
10 drops	eucalyptus essential oil
5 drops	rosewood essential oil
½ tsp (2.5 mL)	vegetable glycerin

In an 8 oz (250 mL) PET plastic spray bottle, combine vinegar, witch hazel, benzoin, bergamot, cypress, eucalyptus and rosewood essential oils and glycerin. Shake well. Store in a dark, cool, dry place for up to 1 year.

To use, spray or splash on after showering and as needed.

Deodorant Powder

Deodorant powders are used where excessive odor-causing moisture can be a problem, such as the genital area, chest or back, especially in the summertime.

Makes 1 cup (250 mL)

½ cup (125 mL)	arrowroot powder
½ cup (125 mL)	cornstarch
20 drops	lavender essential oil
20 drops	myrrh essential oil
10 drops	patchouli essential oil
5 drops	lemon essential oil

In a small non-reactive bowl, sift together the arrowroot powder and cornstarch. In another small non-reactive bowl, combine lavender, myrrh, patchouli and lemon essential oils. One drop at a time, add essential oil mixture to powder mixture, stirring constantly to prevent powder from clumping. Set aside in an airtight container for a few days. Shake container every day to allow essential oils to permeate powder. Powder will keep in a cool, dark place for up to 6 months.

To use, apply Deodorant Powder to chest and back before putting on clothing. The powder can also be used in undergarments to reduce chafing caused by moisture in skin folds and around the genitals.

Tip

Traditional powder canisters make deodorant powder easier to store and use. They can be purchased online (see Resources, page 459).

Mouth and Tooth Care

When we are young, we feel invincible. We are confident that we will have our teeth until the day we die. We use them to crack nuts, remove bottle caps and break tough cotton thread. We forget to floss, eat sweets between meals and generally treat them in a very cavalier fashion. However, it is never too late to change our ways. The following recipes will help to ensure the health of teeth, gums and lips. (The tooth powder recipe is also good for cleaning dentures—you still need to care for them, and for your gums.)

Tip

If the recipe says "1 drop," 2 drops will not be better!

Tooth Powder

Tooth powder is an alternative to commercial toothpaste for keeping your teeth clean and your mouth healthy.

Makes 1 cup (250 mL)

½ cup (125 mL)	fine sea salt
½ cup (125 mL)	baking soda
8 drops	peppermint essential oil
5 drops	lemon essential oil
2 drops	myrrh essential oil

In a small non-reactive bowl, combine sea salt and baking soda. In another small non-reactive bowl, combine peppermint, lemon and myrrh essential oils. Very slowly, 1 drop at a time, add essential oil mixture to powder mixture, stirring constantly to prevent powder from clumping. Store in an airtight container for up to 6 months.

To use, place ¼ tsp (1 mL) Tooth Powder in the palm of your hand. Wet toothbrush, dip into powder and brush teeth (or dentures) to clean, disinfect and deodorize. Rinse well and spit out. Repeat rinsing.

Peppermint and Myrrh Mouthwash

A mouthwash helps to sweeten the breath and heal sores, ulcers and inflamed gums. If bad breath is an ongoing problem, it would be wise to look for its source. A visit to the dentist may be needed. If the cause is digestive, eat 1 to 2 cups (250 to 500 mL) daily of yogurt that contains both acidophilus and bifidus cultures, which will create a healthier digestive system. The myrrh essential oil in this recipe helps to heal mouth ulcers.

Makes about 4 oz (125 mL)

⅓ cup (75 mL)	cider vinegar
4 tsp (20 mL)	brandy or tea tree hydrolat
1 tsp	vegetable glycerin (5 mL)
10 drops	peppermint essential oil
10 drops	lemon essential oil
5 drops	myrrh essential oil

In a sterilized resealable 4 oz (125 mL) glass jar, combine vinegar, brandy, glycerin and peppermint, lemon and myrrh essential oils. Seal and shake well. Set aside in a cool, dark place for 4 days, shaking occasionally. Strain through a fine-mesh sieve into another sterilized resealable jar. Store in a dark cupboard for 12 to 18 months.

To use, in a glass, combine 1 tsp (5 mL) Peppermint and Myrrh Mouthwash and ¼ cup (60 mL) warm water. Rinse mouth thoroughly with mixture, then spit it out (do not swallow).

Quickie Mouthwash

For a quick way to freshen the mouth, combine 1 tsp (5 mL) cider vinegar and 1 drop peppermint essential oil in a glass of water. Rinse mouth and spit out (don't swallow).

Tip

To speed up the cooling process, place the lip balms on a small baking pan and put them in the refrigerator or freezer for 10 minutes. Remove and cap tightly.

Lemon Lip Salve

Lips have much thinner, drier skin than the rest of the face. Dry, cracked lips can be painful and unsightly. Regular use of this lip salve will help to keep them soft and moist. If you don't use lipstick, carry a little container of the salve in your pocket or purse and use it often during the day.

Makes about 2 oz (60 mL)

3 tsp (15 mL)	beeswax prills (pellets)
6 tsp (30 mL)	extra virgin olive oil
3 tsp (15 mL)	honey
3	250 IU capsules vitamin E oil
30 drops	lemon essential oil

In a double boiler over low heat, gently melt beeswax. Stir in olive oil and honey. Remove from heat. Pierce vitamin E capsules with the tip of a clean, sharp knife and squeeze oil into mixture (discard capsules). Add lemon essential oil and stir until completely incorporated. Transfer to small lip balm or ointment tins (see Resources, page 459) and set aside to cool completely. Replace lids when completely cooled. (See Tip, left.)

Variation

If you have a microwave oven, place beeswax, olive oil and honey in a glass bowl and microwave on High for 1 minute. Remove and stir. Repeat two more times. Complete recipe as above.

Aromatherapy for the Home

● ●

You can use essential oils to make your home a calm and loving place. Aromatherapy helps to create a haven where you can let go of anxieties and replenish your strength. Everyone benefits from such a positive environment.

Essential oils can be used to enhance a wide variety of homecare products, from air fresheners and furniture polish to kitchen cleansers and bathroom disinfectants. Essential oils can be blended to ensure that the fragrances used in every area of your home will harmonize. Every breath you and yours take will enhance your physical and mental wellbeing.

Air Fresheners

● ●

Commercial disinfectants, air fresheners, carpet cleaners and other household products are almost exclusively synthetic and can possibly do more harm than good for the people who use them (particularly those who suffer from allergies). The perfumes of these products are often very strong and clash with one another. They contain few therapeutic qualities other than the germicidal capacity of disinfectants, and even that function can be performed by essential oils. The other advantage to be gained from the following suggestions and recipes is that they are environmentally friendly, the contents are largely natural and inexpensive—and they work!

It may be advisable to make and try small amounts of the blends first to ensure that you like the aroma. They are easy to make and are ideal for use in an air spray or diffuser (don't spray them on polished furniture or delicate fabrics).

Measuring Larger Quantities of Essential Oils

Essential oils are sold with orifice reducers. You can either count quantities by drops or remove the orifice reducer and use a pipette (see Resources, page 459) to measure in milliliters (mL). Use the following measurements as a guide (amounts are approximate):

54 drops = 2 mL	135 drops = 5 mL
65 drops = 2.5 mL	200 drops = 7.5 mL

If you prefer, when making an air spray, substitute Solubol for the vodka called for, in a ratio of 4 drops Solubol for every 1 drop essential oil. Solubol is a natural product that allows essential oils to disperse in liquid.

When making air sprays, be sure to add the oils to the bottle first, followed by the chosen dispersant (vodka or Solubol), to ensure that the essential oils disperse properly (they will not mix directly with water).

Welcome Home Blend

Use this blend to create a happy, restful atmosphere in the living room and dining room. The aroma will offer a cheerful welcome to family and friends—but not to any bacteria and viruses they may be carrying!

135 drops	bergamot essential oil
135 drops	geranium essential oil
135 drops	lavender essential oil
135 drops	lemon essential oil
50 drops	cinnamon essential oil
20 drops	clove essential oil

In a 1 oz (30 mL) glass bottle, combine bergamot, geranium, lavender, lemon, cinnamon and clove essential oils. Shake to blend.

Air spray: In a 4 oz (125 mL) PET plastic spray bottle, combine 75 drops Welcome Home Blend and 1 tsp (5 mL) vodka or vegetable glycerin. Shake well. Fill bottle with filtered or distilled water and shake again. Shake well before each use.

Happy Families Blend

This blend is joyful and uplifting and useful for countering family stress.

270 drops	lavender essential oil
270 drops	grapefruit essential oil
65 drops	bergamot essential oil
55 drops	cedarwood or sandalwood essential oil

In a 1 oz (30 mL) glass bottle, combine lavender, grapefruit, bergamot and cedarwood essential oils. Shake to blend.

Air spray: In a 4 oz (125 mL) PET plastic spray bottle, combine 75 drops Happy Families Blend and 1 tsp (5 mL) vodka or vegetable glycerin. Shake well. Fill bottle with filtered or distilled water and shake again. Shake well before each use.

Anti-virus Blend

There will be times when visitors or (heaven forbid!) the family have coughs, colds, influenza or other contagious diseases. You can help protect yourself by using this blend.

135 drops	eucalyptus essential oil
135 drops	tea tree essential oil
135 drops	lavender essential oil
135 drops	pine essential oil
65 drops	thyme essential oil
65 drops	cinnamon or clove essential oil

In a 1 oz (30 mL) glass bottle, combine eucalyptus, tea tree, lavender, pine, thyme and cinnamon essential oils. Shake to blend.

Room spray: In a 4 oz (125 mL) PET plastic spray bottle, combine 75 drops Anti-virus Blend and 1 tsp (5 mL) vodka or vegetable glycerin. Shake well. Fill bottle with filtered or distilled water and shake again. Shake well before each use.

Inhaler: Place 25 drops Anti-virus Blend in a small non-reactive bowl. Place inhaler wick in the bowl and allow it to absorb the entire amount. Insert the wick inside the inhaler tube and tightly cap the bottom of the inhaler with the plug. Place the inhaler tube inside its cover and screw tightly to close.

Housekeeping Helpers

Carpets and Rugs

Carpet Freshener

This powder is for all types of carpets and rugs. People with pets will particularly appreciate its deodorant and disinfectant properties.

Makes 2½ cups (625 mL)

2 cups (500 mL)	baking soda
¼ cup (60 mL)	cornstarch
¼ cup (60 mL)	borax
30 drops	lemon essential oil
20 drops	lavender essential oil
10 drops	cinnamon essential oil
10 drops	pine essential oil

In a medium non-reactive bowl, sift together baking soda, cornstarch and borax. In a 2 oz (5 mL) glass dropper bottle, combine lemon, lavender, cinnamon and pine essential oils; shake to blend. One drop at a time, stirring thoroughly to prevent clumping, add essential oil mixture to powder mixture. Transfer to a sterilized glass jar or container with a shaker lid. Set aside for 3 days, stirring twice a day.

To use, sprinkle Carpet Freshener lightly over the carpet. Leave for a few hours, or overnight if possible, then vacuum.

Vacuum Cleaners

The oils used in the air fresheners (pages 423 to 425) and Carpet Freshener (above) may also be used to get rid of that horrible dusty smell that seems to build up in vacuum cleaners. Sprinkle the oils on the cloth bag or place some on a cotton ball and tuck inside the collection basket or disposable bag. You can also apply 5 drops of essential oil to a tissue and allow the vacuum cleaner to suck it up. The fan on the vacuum will then release a fresh scent.

Humidifying Rooms

The air in some rooms of the house can get very dry during the colder months, when the heat is on, which in turn can dry the skin. Humidify and freshen the air by putting a few drops of your favorite essential oil or blend in a small bowl of water. Place the bowl near a heat source (ensure that it won't get spilled accidentally).

Furniture

Lemon Furniture Polish

This polish gives a lovely gloss to varnished wooden furniture. Just put very little on a soft cloth and apply with gusto to the woodwork. Use only about once every 2 weeks.

Makes ½ cup (125 mL)

¼ cup (60 mL)	olive oil
¼ cup (60 mL)	freshly squeezed lemon juice, strained
1 tsp (5 mL)	lemon or sweet orange essential oil

In a 4 oz (125 mL) PET plastic spray bottle, combine olive oil, lemon juice and lemon essential oil. Shake to blend. Use sparingly.

Natural Glass and Mirror Cleaner

The next time you run out of window cleaner, make your own! Rinse out the old bottle and add 1 cup (250 mL) white vinegar and 10 drops lemon essential oil. Shake to mix. Fill the bottle with distilled or filtered water to about three-quarters full. Shake again. Spray glass surface and wipe clean with paper towels, newspaper or a lint-free cloth. Shake well before each use.

Heaven Scent

Bookmarks: Add to the pleasure of reading a good book by using a scented bookmark. Apply a couple of drops of your favorite essential oil or blend to a store-bought or homemade paper bookmark, or purchase a strip of leather to add scent to. This makes a great gift for the avid readers in your life.

Notepaper: Scented letters are a pleasure to receive and also make a gracious present. The essential oil should reflect the personality of the recipient, and be careful not to make it overpowering. Choose a suitable essential oil or blend from this book and place a few drops on pieces of blotting paper or thin cloth. Interleave them between the writing paper and the envelopes. Leave for a week or so for the scent to permeate.

Table linens: A few drops of essential oil can be placed on the underside of cloth placemats or tablecloths, where the heat of the plates will release the perfume. Choose essential oils that won't clash with or overpower the scent of the food. Citrus and spice oils are most suitable.

Toilet rolls: Place 3 to 5 drops of essential oil inside the cardboard tube of a roll of toilet paper. The scent will fragrance the bathroom with every turn.

Bedroom

The bedroom is the place where we spend about a third of our lives: sleeping, dreaming, talking, reading and making love. All too often, unfortunately, the bedroom can become a battleground, as parents often wait until they are together in private to air their grievances. Confine your disagreements to the car (parked only, please) or the back of the garden, not in the bedroom.

Make sure that oils used in different areas of the bedroom have the same type of fragrance. It would be disturbing to have a heavy, musky scent in competition with a citrus or floral blend. Try making tiny amounts of the following blends until you find what works best for you.

Here are some ways to use the blends:

- Use in an air spray or diffuser a few minutes before retiring (see Tips, page 429), or apply directly to the bed linens.
- Sprinkle a few drops on cotton balls and tuck under the bed.
- Make a flat sachet out of two handkerchiefs or cloth squares sewn together on three sides. Sprinkle a few cotton balls with 1 to 3 drops of the blend and stuff into the sachet. Set on top of the nightstand or on a nearby shelf.

- Sprinkle a few drops on cotton balls and place them between linens in drawers and cupboards.
- Add a few drops to the washing water when cleaning woodwork and windows in bedroom.

Romantic Nights

Let this warm and exotic blend whisk you and your partner away for the evening.

135 drops	ylang ylang essential oil
65 drops	lime essential oil
65 drops	petitgrain essential oil
20 drops	sandalwood or cedarwood essential oil
15 drops	patchouli essential oil
5 drops	clove essential oil

In a ¹/₂ oz (15 mL) glass dropper bottle, combine ylang ylang, lime, petitgrain, sandalwood, patchouli and clove essential oils. Shake to blend. Store in a cool, dark place. Shake well before using.

Sleep Time

This blend will help when, for no particular reason, it's difficult to get to sleep.

65 drops	chamomile essential oil
65 drops	lavender essential oil
20 drops	marjoram essential oil
20 drops	neroli or clary sage essential oil

In a ¹/₃ oz (10 mL) glass dropper bottle, combine chamomile, lavender, marjoram and neroli essential oils. Shake to blend. Store in a cool, dark place. Shake well before using.

Mind Soother

This blend will help chase away the anxieties and stresses of the day, leaving your mind calm and ready for sleep.

135 drops	bergamot essential oil
65 drops	lavender essential oil
20 drops	mandarin essential oil
20 drops	cedarwood essential oil
20 drops	sandalwood, peppermint or juniper essential oil

In a ¹/₃ oz (10 mL) glass dropper bottle, combine bergamot, lavender, mandarin, cedarwood and sandalwood essential oils. Shake to blend. Store in a cool, dark place. Shake well before using.

The Feminine Touch

This is a sweet, feminine floral blend with a touch of spice to lift your day.

135 drops	rose geranium essential oil
135 drops	sweet orange or mandarin essential oil
65 drops	geranium essential oil
20 drops	petitgrain essential oil
10 drops	patchouli essential oil
10 drops	cinnamon essential oil

In a ¹⁄₂ oz (15 mL) glass dropper bottle, combine rose geranium, orange, geranium, petitgrain, patchouli and cinnamon essential oils. Shake to blend. Store in a cool, dark place. Shake well before using.

Anti-moth Blend

Most commercial moth repellents smell bad enough to repel humans as well. This blend will keep closets and drawers fresh and free from insects and moths, without interfering with your daytime perfume or aftershave or clashing with your chosen bedroom blend.

135 drops	lavender essential oil
135 drops	rosemary essential oil
135 drops	lemon essential oil

In a ¹⁄₂ oz (15 mL) glass dropper bottle, combine lavender, rosemary and lemon essential oils. Shake to blend. Store in a cool, dark place. Shake well before using.

Closets: Sprinkle 2 to 3 drops Anti-moth Blend on a padded coat hanger. Combine 2 to 3 drops Anti-moth Blend and 2 cups (500 mL) water to use when washing the insides of closets and cupboards.

Drawers: Sprinkle 2 to 3 drops Anti-moth Blend on the lining paper of drawers containing underwear, woolens or sports clothes, or put a few drops on several cotton balls and place between the clothes.

Children's Bedrooms

Adults often imagine that they have a monopoly on worry and that children are (or should be) completely carefree. Examination nerves, performance-related sports stress, fear of bogeymen, overstimulating movies, peer group pressures, and skin problems, along with many other real or imagined fears, can make life very difficult for young people. Try to make the last half-hour before bedtime as calm as possible, with maybe a warm bath, a glass of warm milk or chamomile tea, and a cuddle while reading a bedtime story.

Children's Blend

Children need to feel secure in the privacy of their bedroom. This blend will help to create a bedroom oasis.

135 drops	lavender essential oil
135 drops	chamomile essential oil
135 drops	mandarin essential oil

In a ½ oz (15 mL) glass dropper bottle, combine lavender, chamomile and mandarin essential oils. Shake to blend. Store in a cool, dark place. Shake well before using.

When using Children's Blend, follow the suggestions for adult bedrooms (page 428). See Babies and Children (page 163) for a guide to safe quantities of essential oils.

Kitchen

The kitchen can be both a health and a smell hazard, as many of its odors are less than pleasant: onions and garlic, boiled cabbage, fried or grilled meat and fish, trash and drains, to name a few. Kitchens can also be a breeding ground for bacteria; 30% of food-borne illnesses, such as *E. coli*, listeria and salmonella, are found in kitchens. The essential oils we use in the kitchen need to be powerful bacteria inhibitors, but they should also smell fresh and clean.

Tips

If you prefer, substitute Solubol (see Resources, page 459) for the vodka in a ratio of 4 drops Solubol for every 1 drop essential oil.

When making air sprays, be sure to add the oils to the bottle first, followed by the chosen dispersant (vodka or Solubol), to ensure that the essential oils disperse properly (they will not mix directly with water).

Citrus Fresh

Use this blend for a calm, confident, cheerful atmosphere in which to prepare food.

135 drops	lemon essential oil
65 drops	bergamot essential oil
65 drops	grapefruit essential oil
25 drops	sandalwood essential oil
30 drops	vanilla essence or Peru balsam essential oil

In a ½ oz (15 mL) glass dropper bottle, combine lemon, bergamot, grapefruit and sandalwood essential oils and vanilla essence. Shake to blend. Store in a cool, dark place. Shake well before using.

Spray mist: In a 4 oz (125 mL) PET plastic spray bottle, combine 75 drops Citrus Fresh blend and 1 tsp (5 mL) vodka. Fill bottle with distilled or filtered water (see Tips, left) and shake vigorously to combine. Mist into the air. Shake well before each use.

Deodorizing Room Spray

Makes 2 oz (60 mL)

1 tsp (5 mL)	vodka
10 drops	lemon essential oil
5 drops	rosemary essential oil
5 drops	peppermint essential oil
	Distilled or filtered water

In a 2 oz (60 mL) PET plastic spray bottle, combine vodka and lemon, rosemary and peppermint essential oils. Shake to blend. Fill bottle with water and shake vigorously to combine. Mist into the air. Shake well before each use.

Disinfecting Cleaning Spray

You can use this disinfecting spray to clean kitchen counters, door and drawer handles, sinks, plastic cutting boards and refrigerator shelves.

Makes 8 oz (250 mL)

3 tsp (15 mL)	liquid castile soap
3 tsp (15 mL)	white vinegar
40 drops	lemon essential oil
37 drops	pine essential oil
3 drops	cinnamon essential oil
	Distilled or filtered water

In an 8 oz (250 mL) PET plastic spray bottle, combine castile soap, vinegar and lemon, pine and cinnamon essential oils. Shake gently to mix. Fill bottle with water and shake to combine. Shake before each use.

Disinfectant Cleaning Concentrate

This concentrated blend can be added to water for washing larger areas.

Makes about 16 oz (500 mL)

½ cup (125 mL)	biodegradable phosphate-free laundry soap
1 tsp (5 mL)	white vinegar
1⅓ cups (325 mL)	water
80 drops	lemon essential oil
64 drops	pine essential oil
6 drops	cinnamon essential oil

In a 16 oz (500 mL) PET plastic bottle, combine soap, vinegar, water and lemon, pine and cinnamon essential oils. Shake to combine. Store in a cool, dark place.

Tip

Sprinkle a few drops of lemon, lavender or orange essential oil on a sponge. Place in the top rack of the dishwasher to disinfect the sponge and leave a fresh scent.

Kill Germs Where They Breed!

One of the worst contributors to the spread of nasty microbial intruders is the kitchen sponge or dishcloth. After repeated use, cleaning up everything from milk spills to raw meat juices and leaky food packages, how clean is yours? Wash sponges and cloths in hot, soapy water after each use and rinse well. Sprinkle with a few drops of lemon essential oil to freshen and to kill any remaining bacteria.

Natural Soft Cleaning Scrub

Use this mixture to gently scrub your sink, stovetop or any place where a mildly abrasive cleanser is needed.

Makes about 11 oz (330 mL)

1 cup (250 mL)	baking soda
¼ cup (60 mL)	liquid castile soap
4 tsp (20 mL)	white vinegar
25 drops	lemon essential oil
15 drops	tea tree essential oil
10 drops	lavender or thyme essential oil

In a 16 oz (500 mL) PET plastic or glass jar, combine baking soda and castile soap. Stir to blend, then add vinegar and mix well. Add lemon, tea tree and rosemary essential oils and stir to combine. The mixture will have the consistency of a soft, smooth paste.

Bacteria-Buster Blend

This is an effective blend for eliminating bacteria and odor-causing germs. Use it to scent your cleaning products, as indicated in the chart on page 435.

270 drops	lemon essential oil
200 drops	pine or thyme essential oil
54 drops	cinnamon essential oil
14 drops	tea tree essential oil

In a 1 oz (30 mL) glass dropper bottle, combine lemon, pine, cinnamon and tea tree essential oils. Shake to blend.

Cleaning Kitchen Trouble Spots

Trouble Spot	Cleaning Method
Work surfaces	Use Disinfecting Cleaning Spray (page 433).
Cupboards	Wipe with 8 drops Bacteria-Buster Blend (page 434) or 1 to 2 tsp (5 to 10 mL) Disinfectant Cleaning Concentrate (page 433) in 4 cups (1 L) warm water. Or use Disinfecting Cleaning Spray (page 433).
Drains	Sprinkle 4 to 6 drops Bacteria-Buster Blend (page 434) or citrus essential oil down the drain after washing dishes, to sweeten and disinfect.
Garbage bins	*Small bins:* Use Disinfecting Cleaning Spray (page 433) and wipe clean. Sprinkle 4 drops Bacteria-Buster Blend (page 434) in bin. *Larger bins:* Use 1 to 2 tsp (5 to 10 mL) Disinfectant Cleaning Concentrate (page 433) in 4 cups (1 L) warm water.
Floors	Use 32 drops Bacteria-Buster Blend (page 434) or 4 to 8 tsp (20 to 40 mL) Disinfectant Cleaning Concentrate (page 433) in 16 cups (4 L) warm water.
Sinks	Use Natural Soft Cleaning Scrub (page 434).
Cutting boards	Clean well with hot water and castile soap. Pour 5 drops lemon essential oil on a sponge and vigorously rub entire surface of cutting board.
Dishwashing	Add 1 tsp (5 mL) Disinfectant Cleaning Concentrate (page 433) to wash water in sink.
Dishwasher	Add 2 drops Bacteria-Buster Blend (page 434) or lemon or lavender essential oil to dishwasher detergent in compartment.
Air spray	In a 4 oz (125 mL) PET plastic spray bottle, combine 75 drops Bacteria-Buster Blend (page 434) and 1 tsp (5 mL) vodka. Fill remainder of bottle with filtered or distilled water and shake to blend. Shake well before use.

Bathroom

Bacteria love bathrooms. In particular, bacteria and molds love shower compartments; many diseases (such as tinea) can be transmitted from person to person via the warm, moist, bacteria- and fungus-laden floor of the shower. No matter how often the shower or bathtub surround is cleaned, it can harbor undesirable microbes unless the appropriate cleaning methods are used.

Bathroom Oil Blend

This blend contains both antibacterial and antifungal oils. Keep cleaning materials in the bathroom and encourage the family to spray the shower and the air before leaving the room.

200 drops	lemon essential oil
135 drops	bergamot essential oil
135 drops	pine essential oil
65 drops	citronella essential oil
65 drops	thyme essential oil
65 drops	tea tree essential oil

In a 1 oz (30 mL) glass dropper bottle, combine lemon, bergamot, pine, citronella, thyme and tea tree essential oils. Shake to blend.

Bathroom Cleaner

This cleaning blend works wonderfully in the bathroom. It cleans wall and floor tiles, baths, showers, washbasins and their surrounds. If extra cleaning power is needed on stubborn stains, use 50 drops Bathroom Oil Blend in place of the essential oils in Natural Soft Cleaning Scrub (page 434) as an abrasive.

Makes 8 oz (250 mL)

3 tsp (15 mL)	liquid castile soap
3 tsp (15 mL)	white vinegar
80 drops	Bathroom Oil Blend (above)
	Distilled or filtered water

In an 8 oz (250 mL) PET plastic spray bottle, combine castile soap, vinegar and Bathroom Oil Blend. Shake gently to mix. Fill bottle with filtered or distilled water and shake to combine. Shake before each use.

Cleaning Bathroom Trouble Spots

Bath and washbasin: Spray with Bathroom Cleaner and leave for a minute or two before wiping.

Vanity: Spray with Bathroom Cleaner and leave for a minute or two before wiping.

Shower: In a 4 oz (125 mL) PET plastic spray bottle, combine 135 drops (5 mL) Bathroom Oil Blend (page 436) and ⅓ cup + 5 tsp (100 mL) vinegar. Shake to blend. Add 4 tsp (20 mL) filtered or distilled water and shake to mix. Spray shower after use. Use as often as needed.

Floor and tiles: Combine 2 tsp (10 mL) Disinfectant Cleaning Concentrate (page 433) and 4 cups (1 L) warm water. Wash floor and tiles weekly.

Air spray: In a 4 oz (125 mL) PET plastic spray bottle, combine 75 drops Bathroom Oil Blend (page 436) and 1 tsp (5 mL) vodka. Fill bottle with filtered or distilled water and shake to blend. Shake well before use.

Tips

If you prefer, substitute Solubol (see Resources, page 459) for the vodka in a ratio of 4 drops Solubol for every 1 drop essential oil.

When making air sprays, be sure to add the oils to the bottle first, followed by the chosen dispersant (vodka or Solubol), to ensure that the essential oils disperse properly (they will not mix directly with water).

Toilets

In the toilet area the two main concerns are bacteria and smells. An essential oil blend can take care of both those problems. It's all very well telling children to wash their hands after going to the toilet (as adults I'm sure we do this automatically), but the very actions of flushing the toilet and then turning on the tap or opening the door are going to spread bacteria from as-yet-unwashed hands to many other people. The use of a combined antibacterial and air-freshening spray means that the toilet seat, flush handle and other surfaces are all being cleansed and the air sweetened every time the spray is used.

Toilet Blend

400 drops	tea tree essential oil
200 drops	lavender essential oil
60 drops	lemon essential oil
60 drops	pine essential oil
60 drops	lemongrass essential oil

In a 1 oz (30 mL) glass dropper bottle, combine tea tree, lavender, lemon, pine and lemongrass essential oils. Shake to blend. Store in a cool, dark place.

Room spray: In a 4 oz (125 mL) PET plastic spray bottle, combine 75 drops Toilet Blend and 4 tsp (20 mL) vodka. Shake well. Fill bottle with distilled or filtered water and shake to blend. Label clearly with the following instructions: "After flushing the toilet, shake this bottle and spray up toward the ceiling so the mist falls on toilet, sink, door handle and this container."

Cleaning the Toilet Area

Toilet: Sprinkle 10 drops Toilet Blend (page 437) in the toilet bowl after cleaning, then scrub thoroughly.

Toilet seat and nearby woodwork: In a non-reactive bowl, combine 1 to 2 tsp (5 to 10 mL) Disinfectant Cleaning Concentrate (page 433), 5 drops eucalyptus or tea tree essential oil and 2 cups (500 mL) water. Wipe surfaces with mixture.

Floor around toilet: Combine 2 to 3 tsp (10 to 15 mL) Disinfectant Cleaning Concentrate (page 433), 10 drops eucalyptus essential oil and 8 cups (2 L) water. Wash floor with mixture.

Laundry

The laundry area is often a multipurpose space. It may be a repository for gardening and sports shoes and equipment; dirty laundry hampers; mops, brooms and other cleaning supplies; damp towels and swimsuits; and dog or cat beds. The smells that can build up and become "interesting" are often not ones with which you want your home associated! The quality to be aimed at is "fresh and clean," so the oils to use are ones that are antibacterial, antifungal and deodorant.

Laundry Blend

This blend will leave your washing fresh and lightly fragrant.

120 drops	lavender essential oil
60 drops	rosemary essential oil
60 drops	lemon essential oil
15 drops	pine essential oil
15 drops	lemongrass essential oil

In a ⅓ oz (10 mL) glass dropper bottle, combine lavender, rosemary, lemon, pine and lemongrass essential oils. Shake to blend. Store in a cool, dark place.

Presoak: If there is a contagious or infectious illness in the house, presoak bed linens, nightwear and any other likely garments in water to which you have added 10 drops of eucalyptus essential oil.

Washing: Add 4 to 5 drops Laundry Blend to the regular wash cycle of your washing machine. (See Tip, right.)

Cleaning the Laundry Area

Floors, cupboards and sinks: Clean with Disinfecting Cleaning Spray (page 433).

Air spray: To ensure a sweet and safe environment, spray the air and the insides of cupboards and laundry hampers with Anti-virus Blend (page 425).

Ironing: Place 2 drops Laundry Blend (page 438) in a 4 oz (125 mL) PET plastic spray bottle and fill bottle with distilled or filtered water. Shake well before using. If concerned about staining, test on the inside of a hem. Never put essential oils in the iron.

Smelly Shoes

If you store shoes in the closet or a cupboard, it can create a less than pleasant ambience! Make up a quantity of Carpet Freshener (page 426). Sprinkle a little in the shoes, shaking to spread it around, leave overnight and then shake it out in the morning. Alternatively, pour a few spoonfuls of the powder into the feet of a pair of stockings or pantyhose, tie a knot in the top and slip the "sock" into the shoe. These socks can be used for some time before more oils are needed to refresh them.

Tip

Be sure to rinse in hot water (104°F/40°C) to help break down the essential oils used in the wash cycle. If rinsing in cooler water, hang the clothes to dry (see Caution, below).

Caution

Dryer fires have been known to occur as result of essential oils not being broken down completely by the laundry detergent and rinsed away. To avoid a potential fire in your dryer, be sure the rinse water is hot (at least 104°F/40°C) and the lint screen is cleaned before each use. In nicer weather, hang the clothes out to dry in the sunshine!

Aromatherapy for Massage

•••

Massage has been used as a therapy for centuries. It has many benefits, not only for the body but also on a psychological level. Properly done, massage promotes a wonderful feeling of wellbeing and lightness.

Why Massage Is Beneficial

The feeling of wellbeing and relaxation you experience after a massage is due in part to its soothing and stimulating effect on nerve endings. The many systems within the body respond to therapeutic massage. It helps to improve blood circulation while increasing the elimination of toxins and waste materials. Massage promotes skin regeneration and repair, as well as improved muscle tone and general appearance. Being physically touched also has a comforting effect on the mind.

Because muscles respond rapidly to massage, it is excellent in sport situations. It helps to stretch muscles, thereby reducing aches and spasms; it also helps to speed the healing of strains and sprains. Massage can smooth away knots of tension, leaving the area around the shoulders, upper back and neck, which is particularly prone to aches and stiffness, feeling lighter. Many situations can stress this area, causing spasms that may lead to headaches or a feeling of tightness or pressure around the head. Abdominal massage improves digestion; it is beneficial for many digestive disorders such as constipation and flatulence.

To make sure that you, your family and your friends enjoy the wonderful benefits of massage with these aromatherapy recipes, we recommend that you learn the proper techniques. There are a number of excellent books that give step-by-step instructions, and many places offer courses.

Essential Oils Enhance Massage

There are few more pleasurable or healing experiences than receiving a massage, but the experience is immeasurably enhanced when essential oils are incorporated into the process.

Tip

Babies who are massaged daily gain weight 47% faster than babies who go without massage.

By adding the appropriate essential oils it's very easy to transform a massage oil, cream or lotion into a powerful therapeutic tool. Studies have shown that including essential oils with massage can enhance its benefits by as much as 50%!

Essential oils have such a potent effect because their molecules are small enough to pass through the skin. There they dissolve readily in body fat, are absorbed into the bloodstream and are carried to all the systems of the body. Moreover, during a massage their aroma is inhaled. This affects the limbic portion of the brain, which controls emotion, memory, breathing and blood circulation, and stimulates the hypothalamus, which in turn regulates hormones. The oils are also absorbed into the body through the lungs as you inhale the aroma during the massage. Skin problems, poor circulation, muscular and joint problems, or problems associated with the digestive, endocrine, immune or nervous system may all be alleviated or healed through the use of essential oils.

Caution

Before using any essential oil, consult the relevant entry in Part 1: Essential Oils (A to Y), pages 28 to 117, taking careful note of any cautions.

Choosing the Most Effective Oils for Massage

The list on page 442 contains only the most effective oils for relieving particular conditions. While there are more oils with similar properties, we didn't want the list to become confusing! For complete profiles of the various oils, see Essential Oils (A to Y), pages 28 to 117.

Massage Oils

Once you have made up your massage oil base from one of the following blends, choose the appropriate essential oils from the list on page 442. It is a good idea to make up ½ cup (125 mL) of the base oil. Then it can be divided into two separate 2 oz (60 mL) PET plastic bottles and essential oils for different purposes can be added to each one.

Add 24 drops of essential oil(s) to each 2 oz (60 mL) bottle. Use only 12 drops if the massage oil is to be used on the elderly or infirm (for children, see the chart on page 164). The added wheat germ oil or vitamin E acts as a natural preservative for your massage oil.

Which Oil to Choose for Massage

Condition	Essential Oils
Arthritis or rheumatism	Canadian balsam, black pepper, cajuput, cedarwood, chamomile, eucalyptus, silver fir, ginger, juniper, sweet marjoram, rosemary, thyme
Asthma	Anise, cajuput, Roman chamomile, eucalyptus, frankincense, hyssop, lavender, thyme
Bronchitis, coughs and catarrh	Canadian balsam, cedarwood, eucalyptus, helichrysum, hyssop, lavandin 'Grosso', sweet marjoram, myrtle, niaouli, pine, rosemary
Circulation and muscle tone	Black pepper, cypress, eucalyptus, ginger, lemon, bitter orange, rosemary ct. cineole
Colic (intestinal gas)	Angelica, cardamom, Roman chamomile, fennel, ginger, lemon, peppermint, rosemary ct. cineole
Constipation	Black pepper, fennel, ginger, bitter orange, rosemary, spearmint
Fluid retention	Cedarwood, cypress, fennel, geranium, grapefruit, juniper, rosemary
Immune system	*Eucalyptus radiata*, Fragonia, frankincense, helichrysum, manuka, lemon myrtle, niaouli, palo santo, ravensara, rosewood, tea tree
Indigestion or flatulence	Anise, basil ct. linalool, fennel, ginger, lemon, mandarin, peppermint
Muscle aches, pains and stiffness	Black pepper, *Eucalyptus smithii*, ginger, juniper, lavender, marjoram, ravensara, rosemary
Muscle cramps	Bay laurel, black pepper, lavender, marjoram, rosemary
Pain	Cajuput, *Eucalyptus smithii*, silver fir, frankincense, lavandin 'Grosso', spike lavender, marjoram, peppermint, rosemary ct. cineole, tea tree
Sexual dysfunction	Anise, black pepper, jasmine, nutmeg, rose, rosewood, sandalwood, ylang ylang
Slack skin with poor tone	Black pepper, cinnamon, clary sage, grapefruit, marjoram, ravensara, rosemary
Sprains and strains	Black pepper, chamomile, lavender, manuka, marjoram, rose, yarrow
Stress and tension	Bergamot, cedarwood, chamomile, cypress, geranium, juniper, lavender, mandarin, peppermint, rosemary
Toxin buildup	Angelica, black pepper, fennel, grapefruit, juniper, lemon
Urinary tract problems	Canadian balsam, bergamot, chamomile, *Eucalyptus citriodora*, juniper, lavender, sandalwood

Massage Oil Base Blends

Recipe 1 (not suitable for people with nut or wheat allergies)

30%	sweet almond oil
30%	sunflower oil
30%	apricot seed oil
10%	wheat germ oil

In a glass bottle, combine sweet almond, sunflower, apricot seed and wheat germ oils. Shake to blend. The blend will keep for up to 15 months in a cool, dark place.

Recipe 2 (not suitable for people with nut allergies)

33%	sweet almond oil
33%	sunflower oil
33%	apricot seed oil
1%	vitamin E oil

In a glass bottle, combine sweet almond, sunflower, apricot seed and vitamin E oils. Shake to blend. The blend will keep for up to 15 months in a cool, dark place.

Recipe 3 (not suitable for people with wheat allergy)

30%	grapeseed oil
30%	sunflower oil
30%	apricot seed oil
10%	wheat germ oil

In a glass bottle, combine grapeseed, sunflower, apricot seed and wheat germ oils. Shake to blend. The blend will keep for up to 15 months in a cool, dark place.

Recipe 4 (hypoallergenic)

33%	grapeseed oil
33%	sunflower oil
33%	apricot seed oil
1%	vitamin E oil

In a glass bottle, combine grapeseed, sunflower, apricot seed and vitamin E oils. Shake to blend. The blend will keep for up to 15 months in a cool, dark place.

Tips

For those who prefer a massage lotion rather than an oil, there are several online sources for unscented natural bases (see Resources, page 459).

When blending for a specific therapeutic benefit, such as rheumatism or stress, substitute an infused or other carrier oil for the apricot seed oil. See Part 1, pages 128 to 138, for an explanation of the benefits of each type of carrier oil.

Setting Up for Massage

A massage can be done on a massage table, a sturdy dining table or a spongy mat on the floor. It is easier to use a massage table, although the dining table and floor are both more than adequate. When choosing a massage table, make sure it is well padded and set at a good height to work on; if it is too low, you, the masseur, could end up with a backache. If you are using a dining table or the floor, it is important to lay down a thick padded surface such as a covered foam mattress, a folded thick duvet or quilt, or several folded blankets. You will also need something soft to kneel on if you are using the floor.

The person receiving the massage should feel as comfortable and as warm as possible. You will need several thick towels and one or two flat pillows. You will find that the person being massaged will feel much cooler than you. If the weather is cold, warm the room first, and always ask during the massage if the person is warm enough. Keep the parts you aren't working on covered at all times with the towels.

The atmosphere of the room is another point to consider. Soft lighting, soothing music and a blend of relaxing essential oils in a diffuser will help make it a haven where relaxation is inevitable.

Giving a Massage

Once you are set up for the massage, you will need to consider several points for your own enjoyment and wellbeing. Your posture during the massage is of prime importance, and you should assess it regularly. Keep a straight back; if you need to get lower, bend your knees, not your back. If you need to apply firm pressure, put your body weight behind your hands and the movement instead of relying on your arm and shoulder muscles to do all the work. Keep your shoulders relaxed and hold in your stomach muscles to help support your back. This advice may seem a lot to remember at first, but once you have practiced it comes naturally. Any aches or stiffness in your own back are signals that your posture has not been correct.

It helps to wear comfortable, loose clothing, and non-slip shoes if you are working on a bare floor. Your freedom of movement is important for your own comfort. Remove your jewelry and make sure your fingernails are short.

Try to avoid any interruptions. Alert other occupants of the house that you cannot be disturbed and, if necessary, switch off the ringer on your telephone.

Consider your own state of mind: if you are tense or anxious or angry, there will not be a flow of positive energy between you and the recipient of the massage. They will sense these emotions and will also become tense. Do not underestimate this flow of energy—although it is subtle, it can make the difference between an ordinary massage and a wonderful one.

Some Cautions about Massage

In some instances it is wise not to give a massage, and there are some problem areas on the body that should not be massaged.

- If the person has a fever or raised body temperature, it is best not to massage their body. However, you can massage their hands and feet, as this is quite comforting.
- Avoid massaging when acute inflammatory conditions such as arthritis are present, or if there are any red, swollen wounds, swelling or bruising. You can lightly massage areas that are not affected, but avoid anywhere below the swollen area. For instance, avoid giving a foot massage if the lower leg is swollen.
- If pus is present, such as with skin ulcers, boils or infected wounds, avoid massage altogether.
- Any skin with conditions such as burns, sores, scabies, ringworm or impetigo should not be massaged. However, some oils are particularly useful for treating psoriasis and eczema (see pages 380 to 382).
- If the person has varicose veins, massage above the veins only. Gentle foot massage and light strokes are acceptable, but any firm massage below the veins will cause more pressure and could lead to complications or further inflammation.
- If a person has been bitten by a snake or spider, any form of massage will increase the flow of poison through the body. It is best to bandage the area firmly and keep it immobile until the person can see a doctor.
- After a recent incident of internal bleeding, such as in the brain, stomach, lungs or bladder, it is best to avoid massage until the patient has the consent of their doctor.
- A person with thrombosis should not be massaged at all. People with severe heart problems should avoid any firm massage that increases circulation.
- Avoid massage if an internal organ or body part is inflamed, such as occurs in pancreatitis, meningitis, gastritis and appendicitis.
- If the person has cancer or tuberculosis, massage should only be performed with a doctor's permission by a qualified practitioner. However, comforting foot, hand and head massages are usually safe if those areas are not affected.

Tip

To center and relax yourself, add a few drops of a relaxing essential oil blend to a diffuser and turn it on while you are setting up the massage area. Then sit still for a few minutes and concentrate on breathing deeply, releasing tension from your body with every out-breath. Put aside any problems you have on your mind to be dealt with afterward. Stand and stretch from toes to fingertips, and then you will feel peaceful and ready to give the massage. You will find that this self-preparation helps immeasurably, not only for the recipient's enjoyment but also for your own.

- Take care when massaging a woman within the first three months of pregnancy, taking into consideration her medical history. Use only very light massage on the abdomen and lower back (see Massage and Pregnancy, below).

Massage and Pregnancy

Massage during pregnancy helps to promote circulation, thus reducing the incidence of varicose veins, fluid retention and muscle cramps. A gentle abdomen massage—omitting deep rubbing or kneading—can be performed. This helps to ease constipation and indigestion, and it also reduces stretch marks by promoting circulation of blood to the skin, while the oils make the skin soft and supple.

Using gentle effleurage (see page 447) around the lower back area will help the muscles relax, and this helps to relieve lower back pain. Further into the pregnancy, some firm effleurage and kneading of the lower back will be beneficial. During labor, back massage and firm foot massage help ease discomfort and provide a source of relief.

The first three months of pregnancy are when the most care must be taken with essential oils and massage.

- Never use tapotement strokes (cupping, hacking and pounding) during pregnancy.
- Do not use deep rubbing or kneading or deep strokes of any kind around the lower back or abdomen during the early months.
- Avoid any firm massage of the feet, as there are acupressure points on the feet that are used to induce labor.
- Use a smaller percentage of safe essential oils in the massage oil blend.

Massage for Pregnant Women and Children
Pregnant Women

To massage a pregnant woman's back, it may be more comfortable for her to lie on her side or to sit on a chair facing backward, with a soft pillow between her abdomen and the chair back.

When she is lying on her back at any stage during the massage, place a couple of pillows under her knees to provide support. Make sure she is comfortable before you begin.

Massage her full body, omitting any deep rubbing on the feet, abdomen and lower back. Omit any cupping, pounding or hacking. Use gentle kneading and rubbing around the upper back, legs, arms and head.

Caution
Oils that are unsafe to use during pregnancy and breastfeeding: aniseed, star anise, bay laurel, sweet birch, carrot seed (both the essential and carrier oils), chaste tree, cinnamon (bark), fennel, hyssop, jasmine absolute, lavender (*L. stoechas*), lemongrass, *Litsea cubeba*, melissa, myrrh, myrtle (anise, honey and lemon), parsley, pennyroyal, ravintsara

Babies and Children

Babies respond to touch naturally: they have not had time to develop any inhibitions about touching. Massaging will help to create a bond between the mother and father and the baby. If the baby is restless and colicky, massage will soothe and comfort and create a more peaceful baby.

Children can be massaged in the same manner as adults, except with less pressure and not such deep strokes. Remember to be gentler with the tapotement strokes of cupping, hacking and pounding too.

Children can also build up muscle tension from sports, bad posture or bending over a desk doing homework. Teach your children the correct posture for sitting at a desk and also while watching television. Bad posture overtaxes the muscles, creating spasms and aches. Make sure that if the child is doing physical activities or sports, the instructor or coach teaches them to stretch their muscles before and afterward to reduce muscle pain.

Basic Strokes

The following strokes are probably the best techniques for beginners to use. They are therapeutic, pleasurable and, if the above cautions are observed, safe to use. We suggest that before working on someone else, you treat yourself to a professional massage; this will give you some idea of what the various strokes feel like.

Effleurage

Effleurage involves stroking—either gently or firmly—in long, uninterrupted movements in an upward direction, toward the heart. As they move back downward, the hands should just brush the flesh. Keep hands in contact with the body at all times. Avoid pressure over the spine. It's good to begin and end a massage with effleurage, finishing with the lightest possible touch.

Kneading

Kneading is usually performed on the fleshy areas of the body, such as the buttocks, calves, thighs and shoulder muscles. Put your hands next to each other on the muscle you want to work on. Pick up the flesh with one whole hand, including the palm. Squeeze and press, firmly but gently, with the fingers while sliding the thumb over the area; alternate the action between thumb and fingers. As you are finishing with one hand, begin the same movements with the other, so that it becomes one continuous rhythmic and fluid movement. There should never be a time when both hands are not in contact with the body.

Part 4
Practicalities

Equipment

Your blends are only as good as the ingredients and equipment you use. The following tips will help you with preparations.

- Organize and store ingredients and equipment in a separate box or cupboard so everything is readily at hand when you need it. If you have small children, keep essential oils locked away for safety.
- Dedicate the equipment you use for making the recipes, as the powerful perfumes of essential oils are absorbed by wooden spoons and utensils and would ruin food with their strong scents, and beeswax and lanolin are difficult to clean off pans and dishes.
- Many of the recipes in this book require the use of a double boiler, which is simply a saucepan or heatproof bowl set overtop—but not touching—water simmering in a pan on the stove. The ingredients are placed in the top pan or bowl so they may be heated or melted gently, which helps to prevent burning.
- Make sure that your equipment is scrupulously clean before you begin. The cleaner your equipment and storage containers, the longer your aromatic products will stay fresh and uncontaminated.
- All glass containers should be sterilized before using—wash them in hot soapy water, rinse well and dry in an oven set on Warm. Alternatively, boil bottles or jars in water for 20 minutes before drying them in the oven (place a folded cloth in the bottom of the pot to keep the jars from bouncing around). Some dishwashers have a Steam or Sanitize option that also works well for sterilizing, or you can use a microwave steamer.
- If you are preparing a very small quantity of cream or lotion, you can make it in the jar in which it will be stored.

Tip

Try to avoid using your cooking implements for making remedies. Tea tree–flavored cheesecake may be a novelty, but gourmet it's not!

Equipment List

- electric blender, food processor or whisk
- mortar and pestle or coffee grinder
- kitchen scales that measure as little as 1 gram (0.04 ounce)
- preserving, candy-making or laboratory thermometers (two if possible)
- large and small saucepans (not aluminum)
- double boiler (not aluminum)
- 2 or 3 glass measuring cups with pouring spouts
- set of measuring cups

- set of measuring spoons
- 25 mL glass beaker (ideal, as these have a pouring spout and measuring lines)
- 2 or 3 mixing bowls
- small non-reactive bowls (glass shot glasses and heatproof condiment serving bowls are great for blending small amounts of ingredients)
- soap molds (trays)
- large and small funnels
- coarse-, medium- and fine-mesh sieves
- paper coffee filters
- cheesecloth or muslin (both coarse and finely woven) for fine straining
- disposable eyedroppers or pipettes
- glass stirring rods (for mixing essential oils)
- wooden spoons
- rubber spatulas
- large and small sharp knives
- scissors
- resealable (airtight) jars and bottles of assorted sizes
- labels for jars and bottles
- fine-tip waterproof marking pen
- kitchen towels

Measuring and Storing Essential Oils

Measurement Guide

It's important to measure essential oils carefully. If a recipe says 2 drops of oil, then 4 drops will not be better! For precise measuring, you can purchase graduated droppers from pharmacies or disposable pipettes from online stores (see Resources, page 459). The following is a general guide to standard quantities for treatments. Refer to Part 2: Remedies (pages 148 to 351) for exact measures to treat specific ailments.

You may notice that in Part 2 the recipes sometimes use more or less than the following recommendations. We do this because some conditions require less or more than the standard amounts of essential oils. When you become conversant with the essential oils, you will be able to gauge safe quantities for yourself, but at first it's best to be guided by the guidelines that follow. See Part 1: The Oils (pages 20 to 147) for maximum safe quantities of specific essential oils.

Massage oils and lotions

- **Full body:** 4 drops essential oil or blend per 2 tsp (10 mL) carrier oil or lotion (2%)
- **Localized application:** 6 drops essential oil or blend per 2 tsp (10 mL) carrier oil or lotion (3%)

Compresses

- 4 to 6 drops essential oil or blend in water (regardless of size of compress)
- 4 to 6 drops essential oil or blend in 1 tsp (5 mL) carrier oil or lotion

Ointments

- 3 to 4 drops essential oil or blend per 1 tsp (5 mL) base (3–4%)

Lotions

- 30 to 40 drops essential oil or blend per 20 tsp (100 mL) lotion (1.5–2%)

Facial/sinus creams

- 1 drop essential oil or blend per 2 tsp (10 mL) cream (0.5%)

Facial steams

- 1 to 2 drops essential oil or blend in 3 to 4 cups (750 mL to 1 L) water

Baths

- 4 to 6 drops essential oil or blend (depending on age) in 1 tsp (5 mL) milk, honey or liquid castile soap

Gargle or mouthwash

- 2 to 3 drops essential oil or blend in 1 cup (125 mL) water

Hand/footbaths

- 6 to 8 drops essential oil or blend, depending on age (see page 163)

Sitz baths

- 3 to 4 drops essential oil or blend in 1 tsp (5 mL) carrier oil

Air sprays

- 75 drops essential oil or blend in 1 tsp (5 mL) vodka or vegetable glycerin plus 1 cup (250 mL) filtered or distilled water (3%)
- If using Solubol, add 300 drops (3 tsp/15 mL) to the essential oils and fill remainder of bottle with filtered or distilled water.

Inhalations

- 1 to 2 drops essential oil or blend on a tissue (depending on age; see page 163)
- 3 to 5 drops essential oil or blend in a diffuser or tabletop vaporizer
- 5 to 8 drops essential oil or blend in a large room vaporizer

Personal inhaler sticks

- 21 drops essential oil or blend

Insect repellents

- 4 to 5 drops essential oil or blend per 2 tsp (10 mL) base (2–2.5%)

Shampoos, conditioners, shower gels and bubble baths

- 12 to 50 drops essential oil or blend per 1 cup (250 mL) base (0.25–1%).
- Start with lower quantities of oil, then increase the quantity as you get used to it.

Floor and furniture cleaners

- 4 tsp (20 mL) essential oil or blend (or whatever smells good!) per 4 cups (1 L) base (2%)

How to Store Essential Oils

- Store essential oils in dark-colored bottles to protect them from damaging light. Blue or amber bottles work well.
- Keep the bottles as full as possible, because air can cause spoilage. After you use an essential oil, decant the remainder into a smaller bottle to reduce the amount of air to which it is exposed.
- Label the bottles carefully, as some essential oils smell very similar.
- Store essential oils in a box in a cool, dry, dark place.

Glossary

Acidity and Alkalinity

Skin has a liquid film on its surface known as the acid mantle, which is the body's first line of defense against invading bacteria. The pH scale goes from strongly acidic (0) to strongly alkaline (14); distilled water is neutral (7). The pH of the acid mantle ranges between 5.5 and 6.2. Being mildly acidic, it creates an environment in which bacteria cannot grow, thus helping to protect the skin from infection and toxins. It is important to balance the pH of the skin so the acid mantle can do its job more effectively. Most soaps are drying and leave the skin in an alkaline condition, which limits its protective function. The skin will readjust its balance but, depending on other factors, this may take from 30 minutes to 2 hours, during which time it is at risk. Using a mildly acidic toner will restore the balance immediately.

Alcohol

Ethanol is a 95% alcohol that is used at various dilutions for making tinctures and astringents and for dissolving essential oils. If you can't find any, it's perfectly fine (albeit expensive) to use the highest-proof drinking alcohol you can find. Unflavored vodka, brandy, gin and similar spirits are suitable—you can find some as high as 80 proof (40% alcohol).

Allergen

Any substance that causes an allergic reaction is called an allergen. There isn't a substance on this earth that won't cause someone to have an allergic reaction, but some substances are more likely than others to cause a problem. If you are allergy-prone or have sensitive skin, it would be wise to patch-test (see below) untried substances before including them in products and using them on your body.

To perform a patch test, add 1 drop of the essential oil you wish to test to 1 tsp (5 mL) carrier oil and, using a toothpick, stir to combine. Massage a little of the blend on the inside of your elbow. Cover with an adhesive bandage and leave for 24 hours. If there is no soreness, itching or redness you can safely use the oil. You can test other substances in the same way (see Patch Testing, page 13).

Baking soda

Also known as bicarbonate of soda, baking soda is an alkali often used as a leavener in baking. Combined with salt, it makes an excellent tooth cleaner. Combined with water or vinegar and essential oils, it makes a paste that quickly eases the pain of insect bites or stings.

Beeswax

Beeswax is a natural wax made by honeybees and harvested from the cell walls of their honeycombs. Beeswax is an ideal wax to use in ointments and creams, as it forms a protective but breathable barrier that softens the skin. In addition, beeswax helps to relieve inflammation and is antiviral and antibacterial. (See page 234 for preparation.)

Benzoin

See *Tincture of benzoin* (page 458).

Borax

Borax is an alkaline mineral salt that forms when saline lake water evaporates. Borax can be used effectively as an exfoliant in acne washes and as a skin softener in cold creams. (Do not take borax internally or use on broken skin or on babies.)

Emulsion

An emulsion is a mixture of oil and water that, after being combined, doesn't separate.

Epsom salts

Epsom salts, or magnesium sulfate, is not salt but rather a naturally occurring pure compound of magnesium, sulfur and oxygen. Named after its origin in saline springs at Epsom, England, the salt is an excellent addition to baths, where it eases tired bodies and aching muscles. It's also therapeutic when added to footbaths, for those times when your feet are killing you.

Fuller's earth

Fuller's earth is a naturally occurring fine mineral clay that ranges in color from white to gray-green. Originally used by fullers (textile workers) to clean raw wool, it is used as an oil-absorbing, cleansing and thickening agent in soaps and in facial masks (mainly for oily skin). Its absorbent properties make it a useful dry shampoo for oily hair and a powder for sweaty feet.

Glycerin

Glycerin is a natural component of both animal and vegetable fats and is most often obtained as a byproduct of soap making. Use only vegetable glycerin in your products, as other types contain harsh chemicals. Glycerin is syrupy in consistency, colorless, odorless, sticky and sweet. If used in small proportions in lotions, creams and toners, it acts as an antibacterial, softener, lubricant and humectant (holding moisture in the skin). However, if more than 20% glycerin is used in any recipe, it will have the opposite effect and draw water from the skin. When combined with benzoin (4 drops tincture of benzoin in 1 tsp/5 mL glycerin), it acts as a mild preservative as well.

Humectant

A humectant is a substance that helps to attract and retain moisture. Glycerin and honey are humectants often used in skincare products.

Hyperpigmentation

Hyperpigmentation is a darkening of the skin, often in small patches, caused by overexposure to the sun or by using plants or oils that cause photosensitivity (for example, bergamot oil).

Kaolin

Kaolin (also called china clay) is a very fine white clay powder valued for its absorption properties. Kaolin is used in industrial processes to make porcelain, soap, paint and paper. It is used cosmetically as a base for masks and packs, particularly for oily or combination skin, as it will absorb the grease.

Lanolin

Also known as wool fat, lanolin is a sticky yellow grease extracted from the shorn wool of sheep and other wool-bearing animals. In the past, the chemicals used in raising sheep and processing their wool affected the purity of lanolin. Although newer farming methods have resulted in purer lanolin, pesticide residue can be detected in the wool fat of sheep that have grazed on pastures treated with organophosphates.

Healthwise, lanolin is a safer choice than petroleum jelly, but we recommend that nursing mothers use cocoa butter or coconut oil in nipple creams instead of lanolin.

Lanolin is often sold as *hydrous lanolin*, which means that water has been beaten into it to make it more spreadable. All the recipes in this book contain *anhydrous lanolin* (no water added) unless otherwise stated. Lanolin can cause an allergic reaction in some individuals who are allergic to wool.

Moisturizer

Any liquid, lotion, cream or other agent that adds moisture to the skin or helps skin to retain moisture is referred to as a moisturizer.

Oats

Oats are a hardy cereal grain. When added to baths, they will soften the water and help to soothe and smooth dry and itchy skin. As an anti-inflammatory, oats can soothe irritated skin and reduce redness. Oats are also a useful ingredient in masks, scrubs, soaps and hand preparations, as they are both cleansing and provide gentle exfoliation.

Orris root

Orris root (*Iris florentina*) is the violet-scented dried two-year-old rhizome of the Florentine iris, which has a bearded purple flower. The powdered root is used as a fixative to hold the scent in potpourris, bath powders, soaps and perfumes. Many people are allergic to orris root, so it is wise to perform a patch test before using (see page 13).

Photosensitivity

Photosensitivity of the skin is an oversensitivity to sunlight that can be caused by applying certain essential oils such as bergamot, lemon, patchouli and angelica. The skin may develop rashes, swelling, redness or hyperpigmentation.

Rescue Remedy™

Rescue Remedy is a blend of flower essences created by Dr. Edward Bach to calm and strengthen during trauma, anguish, bereavement or terror. The remedy is safe to use during pregnancy and childbirth and for young babies, the very old and animals. It is made up of the following Bach flower remedies:

- Rock Rose (*Helianthemum nummularium*) for terror, panic and fear
- Clematis (*Clematis vitalba*) for unconsciousness, faintness and disorientation
- Impatiens (*Impatiens glandulifera*) for stress and agitation leading to muscle tension and pain
- Cherry Plum (*Prunus cerasifera*) for hysteria and fear of being "out of control"
- Star of Bethlehem (*Ornithogalum umbellatum*) for shock and mental and physical trauma

Salve

A salve is a soothing, softening and healing ointment.

Sebum

Sebum is an oily substance secreted by the sebaceous glands in our skin that lubricates the hair and skin.

Storax

Also known as styrax, storax is a balsam harvested from the bark of the tree *Liquidambar orientalis*. The bark is collected, peeled and boiled to obtain raw storax, which is then purified into a syrupy, delicately perfumed resin used in perfumes as a fixative and in soaps, creams and lotions for its scent.

Tincture of benzoin

Tincture of benzoin is derived from resin extracted from the bark of the *Styrax benzoin* tree, which is native to Indonesia. The tincture may be used as a preservative in creams, lotions and ointments. As it is antibacterial, antiseptic and antifungal, it may also be used as a topical application for eczema, blackheads, boils, pimples and itching. When buying the tincture from a pharmacy, be sure to specify *simple tincture of benzoin*. Compound tincture of benzoin (also known as friar's balsam) has additives that may be harmful if it is used incorrectly.

Unguent

Unguent is another word for ointment.

Water

Because water is a good medium for the growth of bacteria, it's necessary to use filtered or distilled water in preparations to help extend their shelf life.

Wool fat

See *Lanolin* (page 456).

Resources

· ·

Supplies and Equipment

Below is a list of suggested suppliers. This list is by no means comprehensive but is a guide to get you started. An online search can help you discover more suppliers in your area.

Australia

Auroma (essential oils)
www.auroma.com

Cospak Queensland (bottles and jars)
www.cospak.com.au

In Essence Aromatherapy (essential oils, diffusers)
www.inessence.com.au

New Directions (essential oils, carrier oils, beeswax, glycerin, honey, clays, tinctures, bottles and jars, equipment)
www.newdirections.com.au

The Paperbark Company (essential oils)
www.paperbarkoils.com.au

The Pharmaceutical Plant Company (herbal medicines)
www.ppcherbs.com.au

Plasdene Glass-Pak (bottles and jars)
www.plasdene.com.au

Southern Light Herbs (organic dried herbs)
www.southernlightherbs.com.au

Springfields (essential oils, carrier oils)
www.springfieldsaroma.com

Sydney Essential Oil Company (essential oils, carrier oils, hydrolats, salts, butters, cosmetic bases, bottles and jars, diffusers, equipment)
www.seoc.com.au

Canada

CoopCoco (essential oils, waxes, butters, Solubol, botanicals, containers, packaging)
www.coopcoco.ca

Green Valley Aromatherapy (essential oils, carrier oils, hydrolats, butters, cosmetic bases, bottles and jars, diffusers)
www.57aromas.com

New Directions (essential oils, carrier oils, beeswax, glycerin, honey, clays, tinctures, bottles and jars, equipment)
www.newdirections.ca

Prime Ingredients (essential oils, carrier oils, hydrolats, butters, salts, cosmetic bases)
www.primeingredients.ca

Rae Dunphy Aromatics (essential oils, carrier oils, hydrolats, butters, clays, salts)
www.raedunphy.ca

France

Florial France (absolutes, essential oils, carrier oils, hydrolats, diffusers)
www.florihana.com

United Kingdom

Avicenna Herbs (hydrolats, carrier oils, bulk herbs, tinctures, plant extracts)
www.avicennaherbs.co.uk

G. Baldwin & Co. (essential oils, carrier oils, floral waters, cosmetic bases, bottles and jars, herbs, tinctures, bulk herbs, supplements, flower essences)
www.baldwins.co.uk

Base Formula (essential oils, hydrolats, carrier oils, cosmetic bases, salts, butters, natural dried flowers, diffusers, inhalers, bottles and jars, equipment)
www.baseformula.com

Materia Aromatica (essential oils, floral waters, Solubol, base products)
www.materiaaromatica.com

Neal's Yard Remedies (essential oils, carrier oils, tinctures, flower essences, teas)
www.nealsyardremedies.com

The Organic Herb Trading Company (essential oils, bulk herbs, hydrolats, carrier oils, tinctures, aloe, butters, salts, clays)
www.organicherbtrading.com

Penny Price Aromatherapy (essential oils, carrier oils, hydrolats, beeswax, bottles and jars, diffusers, equipment, aromatherapy jewelry)
www.penny-price.com

Quinessence Aromatherapy (essential oils, carrier oils, hydrolats, cosmetic bases, bottles and jars, diffusers)
www.quinessence.com

United States

Appalachian Valley Natural Products (essential oils, carrier oils, hydrolats)
www.av-at.com

Aromatics International (essential oils, carrier oils, hydrolats, Solubol, lip balm tubes, inhaler sticks, clays, salts, butters, pipettes, some equipment)
www.aromaticsinternational.com

Creating Perfume (perfumer's alcohol)
www.creatingperfume.com

Earth Solutions (car diffusers, aromatherapy jewelry, aromatherapy inhalers)
www.earthsolutions.com

Essential Wholesale (cosmetic bases, lotions, creams, gels, melt 'n' pour soap base, shampoo, hydrolats, carrier oils, clays, butters, salts, beeswax prills, zinc oxide powder)
www.essentialwholesale.com

Liberty Natural (perfume blotters, pipettes, jars, room and car diffusers, aromatic jewelry)
www.libertynatural.com

Marion Farms (grape alcohol)
www.marionfarmsbiodynamic.com

Morning Myst Botanics (artisan hydrolats)
www.morningmystbotanics.com

Mountain Rose Herbs (bulk herbs, teas, essential oils)
www.mountainroseherbs.com

Nature's Gift (essential oils, carrier oils, salts, beeswax, inhalers, pipettes, bottles and jars, aromatherapy jewelry)
www.naturesgift.com

SKS (bottles, jars, powder containers, inhalers, equipment)
www.sks-bottle.com

Specialty Bottle (bottles and jars)
www.specialtybottle.com

Stillpoint Aromatics (essential oils, hydrolats, carrier oils, salts, beeswax, Trauma Oil, blank inhalers, diffusers)
www.stillpointaromatics.com

Vitacost (unscented lotions, supplements)
www.vitacost.com

Available in most pharmacies or health-food stores

Aloe vera juice
Flower essences
Friar's balsam

Liquid castile soap
Mullein garlic drops

Organizations

The following organizations can provide helpful information on how to use essential oils, where to source quality materials, and how to find reputable schools.

International

Alliance of International Aromatherapists
www.alliance-aromatherapists.org

Aroma Forum International eV
www.aroma-forum-international.de

International Federation of Aromatherapy (IFA)
www.ifaroma.org

International Federation of Professional Aromatherapists (IFPA)
www.ifparoma.org

Australia

International Aromatherapy and Aromatic Medicine Association (IAAMA)
www.iaama.org.au

Austria

Austrian Society for Scientific Aromatherapy and Aromatic Care (ÖGwA)
www.oegwa.at

Aroma Forum Österreich
www.aromaforum-oesterreich.at

Brazil

Brazilian Association of Aromatherapy and Aromatology (ABRAROMA)
www.aromaterapia.org.br

Canada

Canadian Federation of Aromatherapists (CFA)
www.cfacanada.com

British Columbia Alliance of Aromatherapy (BCAOA)
www.bcaoa.org

British Columbia Association of Practicing Aromatherapists
(BCAPA)
www.bcapa.org

Czech Republic

Association of Czech Aromatherapists (ACA)
www.aromaterapie.cz

Germany

Aroma Forum International eV
www.aroma-forum-international.de

Natural Oils Research Association (NORA)
www.nora-international.de

Greece

Hellenic Association of Aromatherapists (HAA)
www.aromatotherapeia.eu

Japan

Aroma Environment Association of Japan
www.aromakankyo.or.jp/english/aeaj.html

Japanese Society of Aromatherapy
www.aroma-jsa.jp

Korea

Korean Aromatherapy Association (KAA)
Email: oharoma@nate.com

Korean Aroma Society (KAS)
Email: sjcho@choaroma.co.kr

Mexico

Asociación mexicana de investigación y práctica de
aromatología y aromaterapía (AMIPAA)
www.amipaa.org.mx

Netherlands

Federatie voor Additief Geneeskundig Therapeuten (FAGT)
www.fagt.org

New Zealand

New Zealand Register of Holistic Aromatherapists (NZROHA)
www.aromatherapy.org.nz

Norway

Norwegian Association of Natural Medicine (NNH)
www.nnh.no

Taiwan

Taiwan Association of Aromatherapy
www.tw-aa.org

United Kingdom

International Federation of Aromatherapy (IFA)
www.ifaroma.org

International Federation of Professional Aromatherapists (IFPA)
www.ifparoma.org

United States

Alliance of International Aromatherapists
www.alliance-aromatherapists.org

Aromatherapy Registration Council (ARC)
www.aromatherapycouncil.org

National Association for Holistic Aromatherapy
www.naha.org

Publications

Aromatherapy on the Record, Canada (newsletter of the CFA)
Aromatherapy Today, Australia
Aromatherapy Thymes, United States
Aromatika, Hungary (in Hungarian)
In Essence, United Kingdom (journal of the IFPA)
International Journal of Clinical Aromatherapy, France (in English)
International Journal of Professional Holistic Aromatherapy, United States
NAHA Aromatherapy Journal, United States (journal of the NAHA)
Phytothérapie, France (in French)

Bibliography

Akhondzadeh, S., M. Noroozian, M. Mohammadi et al. 2003. Salvia officinalis extract in the treatment of patients with mild to moderate Alzheimer's disease: A double blind, randomized and placebo-controlled trial. *Journal of Clinical Pharmacy and Therapeutics* 28, no. 1: 53–59.

Albuquerque, E.L., J.K. Lima, F.H. Souza et al. 2013. Insecticidal and repellence activity of the essential oil of *Pogostemon cablin* against urban ants species. *Acta Tropica* 127, no. 3: 181–86.

American Chemical Society. 2001. Catnip repels mosquitoes more effectively than DEET. ScienceDaily, August 28. http://www.sciencedaily.com/releases/2001/08/010828075659.htm.

American College of Healthcare Sciences. 2002. *Certificate in Aromatherapy Textbook*. Portland, OR: ACHS.

Ammar, A.H., J. Bouajila, A. Lebrihi et al. 2012. Chemical composition and in vitro antimicrobial and antioxidant activities of *Citrus aurantium* L. flowers essential oil (neroli oil). *Pakistan Journal of Biological Sciences* 15, no. 21: 1034–40.

Ballard, C.G., J.T. O'Brien, K. Reichelt and E.K. Perry. 2002. Aromatherapy as a safe and effective treatment for the management of agitation in severe dementia: The results of a double-blind, placebo-controlled trial with *Melissa*. *Journal of Clinical Psychiatry* 63, no. 7: 553–58.

Blakely, T. 2012. International Sandalwood Symposium (Honolulu, Hawaii). *International Journal of Professional Holistic Aromatherapy* 1, no. 3 (October): 47–48.

———. 2013. Essential oil sustainability update: Sandalwood and rosewood. *International Journal of Professional Holistic Aromatherapy* 2, no. 3: 59–61.

Boskabady, M.H., M.N. Shafei, Z. Saberi and S. Amini. 2011. Pharmacological effects of *Rosa damascena*. *Iranian Journal of Basic Medical Sciences* 14, no. 4: 295–307.

Bounihi, A., G. Hajjaj, R. Alnamer et al. 2013. In vivo potential anti-inflammatory activity of *Melissa officinalis* L. essential oil. *Advances in Pharmacological Sciences* 2013: 101759.

Bouzenna, H., and L. Krichen. 2012. *Pelargonium graveolens* L'Her. and *Artemisia arborescens* L. essential oils: Chemical composition, antifungal activity against *Rhizoctonia solani* and insecticidal activity against *Rhysopertha dominica*. *Natural Product Research* 27, no. 9: 841–46.

Braden, R., S. Reichow and M.A. Halm. 2009. The use of the essential oil lavandin to reduce preoperative anxiety in surgical patients. *Journal of PeriAnesthesia Nursing* 24, no. 6: 348–55.

British Herbal Medicine Association. 1983. *British Herbal Pharmacopoeia*. Surrey: British Herbal Medicine Association.

Brudnak, M. 2013. Cancer-preventing properties of essential oil monoterpenes d-limonene and perillyl alcohol. *International Journal of Professional Holistic Aromatherapy* 1, no. 4: 31–35.

Butje, A., and L. Byington. 2013. Natural spring cleaning. *International Journal of Professional Holistic Aromatherapy* 1, no. 4: 42–44.

Cantele, L. 2012. Improving quality of life for children with life-limiting illnesses. *Journal of the Japanese Society of Aromatherapy* 11 (Suppl.).

Carroll, J.F., G. Paluch, J. Coats and M. Kramer. 2010. Elemol and amyris oil repel the ticks *Ixodes scapularis* and *Amblyomma americanum* (Acari: Ixodidae) in laboratory bioassays. *Experimental and Applied Acarology* 51, no. 4: 383–92.

Catty, S. 2001. *Hydrosols: The Next Aromatherapy*. Rochester, VT: Healing Arts Press.

Chaiyana, W., and S. Okonogi. 2012. Inhibition of cholinesterase by essential oil from food plant. *Phytomedicine* 19, no. 8/9: 836–39.

Chung, M.J., S.Y. Cho, M.J. Bhuiyan et al. 2010. Anti-diabetic effects of lemon balm (*Melissa officinalis*) essential oil on glucose- and lipid-regulating enzymes in type 2 diabetic mice. *British Journal of Nutrition* 104, no. 2: 180–88.

Cooksley, V.G. *Aromatherapy*. 1996. New York: Prentice Hall.

Cribb, A.B., and J.W. Cribb. 1982. *Useful Wild Plants in Australia*. Sydney: Collins (Fontana).

Culpeper, N. 1652 (reprint 1952). *Culpeper's Complete Herbal*. London: W. Foulsham.

Cummings, S., and D. Ullman. 1986. *Everybody's Guide to Homeopathic Medicines*. London: Gollancz.

Davies, S., and A. Stewart. 1987. *Nutritional Medicine*. London: Pan Books.

Davis, P. 1988. *Aromatherapy: An A–Z*. London: C.W. Daniel.

de Rapper, S., G. Kamatou, A. Viljoen and S. van Vuuren. 2013. The in vitro antimicrobial activity of *Lavandula angustifolia* essential oil in combination with other aroma-therapeutic oils. *Evidence-Based Complementary and Alternative Medicine* 2013: 852049.

Dimas, K., D. Kokkinopoulos, C. Demetzos et al. 1999. The effect of sclareol on growth and cell cycle progression of human leukemic cell lines. *Leukemia Research* 23, no. 3: 217–34.

Fernández, L.F., O.M. Palomino and G. Frutos. 2014. Effectiveness of *Rosmarinus officinalis* essential oil as antihypotensive agent in primary hypotensive patients and its influence on health-related quality of life. *Journal of Ethnopharmacology* 151, no. 1: 509–16.

Ferreira, A., C. Proença, M.L. Serralheiro and M.E. Araújo. 2006. The in vitro screening for acetylcholinesterase inhibition and antioxidant activity of medicinal plants from Portugal. *Journal of Ethnopharmacology* 108, no. 1: 31–37.

Ferreira, S., J. Santos, A. Duarte et al. 2012. Screening of antimicrobial activity of *Cistus ladanifer* and *Arbutus unedo* extracts. *Natural Product Research* 26, no. 16: 1558–60.

Fulcher, L. 2012. Case study: The effects of *Cymbopogon martinii* on rosacea. *International Journal of Professional Holistic Aromatherapy* 1, no. 1: 9–11.

Gerlach, S.L., R. Rathinakumar, G. Chakravarty et al. 2010. Anticancer and chemosensitizing abilities of cycloviolacin 02 from *Viola odorata* and psyle cyclotides from *Psychotria leptothyrsa*. *Biopolymers* 94, no. 5: 617–25.

Gladman, A.C. 2006. Toxicodendron dermatitis: Poison ivy, oak, and sumac. *Wilderness Environmental Medicine* 17, no. 2: 120–28.

Goëb, P. 2012. Essential oil profile: Saro. *International Journal of Professional Holistic Aromatherapy* 1, no. 3: 19–24.

Gordo, J., P. Máximo, E. Cabrita et al. 2012. *Thymus mastichina*: Chemical constituents and their anti-cancer activity. *Natural Product Communications* 7, no. 11: 1491–94.

Greche, H., N. Hajjaji, M. Ismaili-Alaoui et al. 2011. Chemical composition and antifungal properties of the essential oil of *Tanacetum annuum*. *Journal of Essential Oil Research* 12, no. 1: 122–24.

Grieve, M.A. 1983. *Modern Herbal*. London: Penguin.

Ho, C.L., O. Jie-Pinge, Y.C. Liu et al. 2010. Compositions and in vitro anticancer activities of the leaf and fruit oils of *Litsea cubeba* from Taiwan. *Natural Product Communications* 5, no. 4: 617–20.

Hoffman, D.L. 1991. *Thorson's Guide to Medical Herbalism*. Scarborough, ON: HarperCollins.

Jafarzadeh, M., S. Arman and F.F. Pour. 2013. Effect of aromatherapy with orange essential oil on salivary cortisol and pulse rate in children during dental treatment: A randomized controlled clinical trial. *Advanced Biomedical Research* 2: 10.

Jeon, J.H., H.W. Kim, M.G. Kim and H.S. Lee. 2008. Mite-control activities of active constituents isolated from *Pelargonium graveolens* against house dust mites. *Journal of Microbiology and Biotechnology* 18, no. 10: 1666–71.

Johnston, W.H., J.J. Karchesy, G.H. Constantine and A.M. Craig. 2001. Antimicrobial activity of some Pacific Northwest woods against anaerobic bacteria and yeast. *Phytotherapy Research* 15, no. 7: 586–88.

Kennedy, D.O., and A.B. Scholey. 2006. The psychopharmacology of European herbs with cognition-enhancing properties. *Current Pharmaceutical Design* 12, no. 35: 4613–23.

Kim, K.N., Y.J. Ko, H.M. Yang et al. 2013. Anti-inflammatory effect of essential oil and its constituents from fingered citron (*Citrus medica* L. var. *sarcodactylis*) through blocking JNK, ERK and NF-κB signaling pathways in LPS-activated RAW 264.7 cells. *Food and Chemical Toxicology* 57: 126–31.

Koutroumanidou, E., A. Kimbaris, A. Kortsaris et al. 2013. Increased seizure latency and decreased severity of pentylenetetrazol-induced seizures in mice after essential oil administration. *Epilepsy Research and Treatment* 2013: 532657.

Lassak, E.V., and T. McCarthy. 1983. *Australian Medicinal Plants*. Sydney: Methuen Australia.

Lawless, J. 1992. *The Encyclopaedia of Essential Oils*. Dorset, UK: Element Books.

Legault, J. 2003. Antitumor activity of balsam fir oil: Production of reactive oxygen species induced by alpha-humulene as possible mechanism of action. *Planta Medica* 69, no. 5: 402–7.

Low, D., B.D. Rawal and W. J. Griffin. 1974. Antibacterial action of the essential oils of some Australian Myrtaceae with special references to the activity of chromatographic fractions of oil of *Eucalyptus citriodora*. *Planta Medica* 26, no. 2: 184–85.

Lust, J. 1987. *The Herb Book*. New York: Bantam.

Lyth, G. 2012. Palmarosa essential oil: Versatile or undervalued? *International Journal of Professional Holistic Aromatherapy* 1, no. 1: 5–7.

Maddocks-Jennings, W., J.M. Wilkinson, D. Shillington and H. Cavanagh. 2005. A fresh look at manuka and kanuka essential oils from New Zealand. *International Journal of Aromatherapy* 15, no. 3: 141–46.

Manley, C.H. 1993. Psychological effect of odor. *Critical Reviews in Food Science and Nutrition* 33: 57–62.

Maury, M. 1989. *Marguerite Maury's Guide to Aromatherapy*. London: C.W. Daniel.

Maycock, P., and P. Mackereth. 2010. Going smoke-free: Can aromatherapy help? *In Essence* 8, no. 4: 9–12.

Mencherini, T., L. Campone, A.L. Piccinelli et al. 2013. HPLC-PDA-MS and NMR characterization of a hydroalcoholic extract of *Citrus aurantium* L. var. *amara* peel with antiedematogenic activity. *Journal of Agricultural and Food Chemistry* 61, no. 8: 1686–93.

Mindell, E. 1995. *The Vitamin Bible*. London: Arlington.

Mojay, G. 1996. *Aromatherapy for Healing the Spirit*. London: Hodder & Stoughton.

Monzote, L., G.M. Hill, A. Cuellar et al. 2012. Chemical composition and anti-proliferative properties of *Bursera graveolens* essential oil. *Natural Product Communications* 7, no. 11: 1531–34.

Morita, T., K. Jinno, H. Kawagishi et al. 2003. Hepatoprotective effect of myristicin from nutmeg (*Myristica fragrans*) on lipopolysaccharide/d-galactosamine-induced liver injury. *Journal of Agricultural and Food Chemistry* 51, no. 6: 1560–65.

Mossa, A.T., A.A. Refaie, A. Ramadan and J. Bouajila. 2013. Amelioration of prallethrin-induced oxidative stress and hepatotoxicity in rat by the administration of *Origanum majorana* essential oil. *BioMed Research International* 2013: 859085.

Mühlbauer, R.C., A. Lozano, S. Palacio et al. 2003. Common herbs, essential oils, and monoterpenes potently modulate bone metabolism. *Bone* 32, no. 4: 372–80.

Mumcuoglu, K.Y., S. Magdassi, J. Miller et al. 2004. Repellency of citronella for head lice: Double-blind randomized trial of efficacy and safety. *Israel Medical Association Journal* 6, no. 12: 756–59.

Murray, M., and J. Pizzorno. 1994. *Encyclopaedia of Natural Medicine*. London: Optima.

Ou, M.C., T.F. Hsu, A.C. Lai et al. 2012. Pain relief assessment by aromatic essential oil massage on outpatients with primary dysmenorrhea: A randomized, double-blind clinical trial. *Journal of Obstetrics and Gynaecology Research* 38, no. 5: 817–22.

Patil, S.B., V.A. Ghadyale, S.S. Taklikar et al. 2011. Insulin secretagogue, alpha-glucosidase and antioxidant activity of some selected spices in streptozotocin-induced diabetic rats. *Plant Foods for Human Nutrition* 66, no. 1: 85–90.

Petersen, D. 2013. Mastic: An aromatic journey in the eastern Mediterranean. *International Journal of Professional Holistic Aromatherapy* 2, no. 3: 17–22.

Pfützner, W., A. Niedermeier, P. Thomas and B. Przybilla. 2003. Systemic contact eczema against balsam of Peru. *Journal der Deutschen Dermatologischen Gesellschaft* [Journal of the German Society of Dermatology] 1, no. 9: 719–21.

Price, L., and S. Price. 2004. *Understanding Hydrolats: The Specific Hydrosols for Aromatherapy—A Guide for Professionals.* London: Churchill Livingstone.

———. 2007. *Aromatherapy for Health Professionals.* 3rd ed. London: Churchill Livingstone.

———. 2012. *Aromatherapy for Health Professionals.* 4th ed. London: Churchill Livingstone.

Reynolds., J.E.F., and A.B. Prasad, eds. 1982. *Martindale: The Extra Pharmacopoeia.* 28th ed. London: Pharmaceopeial Press.

Roller, S., N. Ernest and J. Buckle. 2009. The antimicrobial activity of high-necrodane and other lavender oils on methicillin-sensitive and -resistant *Staphylococcus aureus* (MSSA and MRSA). *Journal of Alternative and Complementary Medicine* 15, no. 3: 275–79.

Rose, J.E., and F.M. Behm. 1994. Inhalation of vapor from black pepper extract reduces smoking withdrawal symptoms. *Drug and Alcohol Dependence* 34, no. 3: 225–29.

Sakaue, M., K. Maeda, Y. Koga et al. 2012. Absorption of lipid components in macadamia nut oil. *International Journal of Professional Holistic Aromatherapy* 1, no. 3: 29–34.

Schauenberg, P., and F. Paris. 1977. *Guide to Medicinal Plants.* London: Lutterworth Press.

Schnitzler, P., et al. 2008. *Melissa officinalis* oil affects infectivity of enveloped herpesviruses. *Phytomedicine* 15, no. 9: 734–40.

Sebai, H., S. Selmi, K. Rtibi et al. 2013. Lavender (*Lavandula stoechas* L.) essential oils attenuate hyperglycemia and protect against oxidative stress in alloxan-induced diabetic rats. *Lipids in Health and Disease* 12, no. 1: 189.

Sellar, W. 1993. *The Directory of Essential Oils.* London: C.W. Daniel.

Seo, S.M., J. Kim, S.G. Lee et al. 2009. Fumigant antitermitic activity of plant essential oils and components from ajowan (*Trachyspermum ammi*), allspice (*Pimenta dioica*), caraway (*Carum carvi*), dill (*Anethum graveolens*), geranium (*Pelargonium graveolens*), and litsea (*Litsea cubeba*) oils against Japanese termite (*Reticulitermes speratus* Kolbe). *Journal of Agricultural and Food Chemistry* 57, no. 15: 6596–602.

Sienkiewicz, M., et al. 2013. The potential use of basil and rosemary essential oils as effective antibacterial agents. *Molecules* 18, no. 8: 9334–51.

Solowey, E. 2013. Ancient fragrant trees of Israel. *International Journal of Professional Holistic Aromatherapy* 2, no. 3: 37–43.

Soltani, R., S. Soheilipour, V. Hajhashemi et al. 2013. Evaluation of the effect of aromatherapy with lavender essential oil on post-tonsillectomy pain in pediatric patients: A randomized controlled trial. *International Journal of Pediatric Otorhinolaryngology* 77, no. 9: 1579–81.

Stanton, R. 1989. *Complete Book of Food and Nutrition.* Toronto: Simon & Schuster.

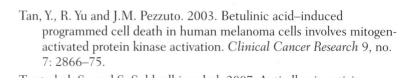

Tan, Y., R. Yu and J.M. Pezzuto. 2003. Betulinic acid–induced programmed cell death in human melanoma cells involves mitogen-activated protein kinase activation. *Clinical Cancer Research* 9, no. 7: 2866–75.

Tewtrakul, S., and S. Subhadhirasakul. 2007. Anti-allergic activity of some selected plants in the Zingiberaceae family. *Journal of Ethnopharmacology* 109, no. 3: 535–38.

Tisserand, R. 1979. *Aromatherapy*. London: Granada.

Tisserand, R., and T. Balacs. 1996. *Essential Oil Safety*. London: Churchill Livingstone.

Tisserand, R., and R. Young. 2013. Clary sage. In *Essential Oil Safety*. 2nd ed. London: Churchill Livingstone.

Valnet, J., et al. 1978. New results and interpretations of 268 clinical tests using an aromatogram. *Plantes médicinales et phytothérapie* 12, no. 1: 43–52.

Vongsombath, C., K. Pålsson, L. Björk et al. 2012. Mosquito (Diptera: Culicidae) repellency field tests of essential oils from plants traditionally used in Laos. *Journal of Medical Entomology* 49, no. 6: 1398–404.

Wang, J., J. Zhao, H. Liu et al. 2010. Chemical analysis and biological activity of the essential oils of two valerianaceous species from China: *Nardostachys chinensis* and *Valeriana officinalis*. *Molecules* 15, no. 9: 6411–22.

Warnke, P.H., S.T. Becker, R. Podschun et al. 2009. The battle against multi-resistant strains: Renaissance of antimicrobial essential oils as a promising force to fight hospital-acquired infections. *Journal of Craniomaxillofacial Surgery* 37, no. 7: 392–97.

Weil, A. 1995a. *Natural Health, Natural Medicine*. New York: Warner.

———. 1995b. *Spontaneous Healing*. New York: Warner.

Williams, K. 2013. Essential oil profile: *Helichrysum gymnocephalum*. *International Journal of Professional Holistic Aromatherapy* 1, no. 3: 38–41.

Worwood, V.A. 1990. *The Fragrant Pharmacy*. London: Macmillan.

Wren, R.C. 1998. *Potter's New Cyclopaedia of Botanical Drugs and Preparations*. London: C.W. Daniel.

Zeinab, R.A., M. Mroueh, M. Diab-Assaf et al. 2011. Chemopreventive effects of wild carrot oil against 7,12-dimethyl benz(a)anthracene-induced squamous cell carcinoma in mice. *Pharmaceutical Biology* 49, no. 9: 955–61.

Internet Resources

Center for Integrative Botanical Studies (CIBS). www.integrativebotanical.com.

Circle H Institute. www.circlehinstitute.com.

Institute of Traditional Herbal Medicine and Aromatherapy (ITHMA). www.aromatherapy-studies.com.

Morning Myst Botanics. www.morningmystbotanics.com

Library and Archives Canada Cataloguing in Publication

Purchon, Nerys, author
    The complete aromatherapy & essential oils handbook for everyday wellness /
Nerys Purchon and Lora Cantele.

Includes index.
"Includes 109 essential oils & more than 450 remedies and uses"— Cover.
"Based on Nerys Purchon's Handbook of aromatherapy published in 1999 by Hodder Headline
Australia Pty Limited, Sydney, Australia"— Title page verso.
ISBN 978-0-7788-0486-4 (pbk.)

    1. Aromatherapy. 2. Essences and essential oils. I. Cantele, Lora, 1964-, author
II. Title. III. Title: Complete aromatherapy and essential oils handbook for everyday wellness.
IV. Title: Aromatherapy & essential oils.

RM666.A68P87 2014   615.3'21   C2014-904364-3

Index

A

abrasions, 153, 172, 236
abscesses, 154
    breast, 288–89
    dental, 316
absolutes, 66, 67, 102
Achilles tendonitis, 307–8
Aching, Swollen Legs and Feet Gel, 322
Aching Back Massage Blend, 285
Achy and Grumpy Blend, 174
acidity, 454
acne, 355, 359, 375–78, 405
Acne Wash, 375
Adrenal Support Blend, 350
African marigold (*Tagetes erecta*), 22, 142
Afternoon Blend for Brain Fatigue, 347
After-Shampoo Rinse, 392
aftershaves, 369. *See also* toners and astringents
air fresheners, 423–25. *See also* room sprays
airplane travel, 320–21
alcohol, 415, 454. *See also* hangover
alkalinity, 454
allergies, 155–56, 355, 454. *See also* sensitization; *specific allergic reactions*
    carrier oils and, 138
    to essential oils, 14, 19
Allergy Blend, 156
allspice. *See* pimento
almond, bitter (*Prunus amygdalus*), 18
Almond and Rosewood Scrub, 360
almond oil, sweet (*Prunus dulcis*), 128
alopecia, 389, 394–95. *See also* hair, loss of
amenorrhea (scanty periods), 337–38
amyris (*Amyris balsamifera*), 30
anal fistula, 157–58
analgesic oils, 24
anemia, 156–57
angelica (*Angelica archangelica*), 30–31

anger, 312
angina pectoris, 158–59
animal bites, 184–85, 236
anise, star (*Illicium verum*), 32
aniseed (*Pimpinella anisum*), 32
anise myrtle (*Syzygium anisatum*; *Backhousia anisata*), 87
anorexia nervosa, 159–60
antagonism, 21
Antibacterial Bath Oil Blend, 403
Antibacterial Blend, 345
Anti-moth Blend, 430
antioxidants, 14, 137
antiseptic oils, 25
Antiseptic Wound Wash, 153
antitoxins, 25
anxiety, 286, 312, 313, 336, 429
Anxiety Blend, 177
apathy, 312
aphrodisiacs, 25, 90, 108, 117, 124, 429
apple geranium (*Pelargonium odoratissimum*), 61
Apricot and Avocado Moisturizing Oil, 372
apricot kernel oil (*Prunus armeniaca*), 129
armoise (*Artemisia herba-alba*), 18
arnica (*Arnica montana*), 18
    oil infused with, 141
Arnica Massage Oil Blend, 309
aromatherapy. *See also* essential oils
    equipment, 449–50, 459–62
    organizations, 462–64
    publications, 464
    supplies, 459–62
arteriosclerosis, 160
arthritis, 160–62, 442
asthma, 293–94, 442
astringents, 25, 367, 369
Astringent Toner, 379
atherosclerosis, 162
athlete's foot, 228
Atlas cedar (*Cedrus atlantica*), 22. *See also* cedarwood
attars, 102, 103
Attention (Calming) Blend, 178
avocado oil (*Persea gratissima*), 129

B

babies and children, 163–80. *See also specific childhood conditions*
    babies, 163–68
    bathing, 163–64
    common cold and influenza in, 166, 170
    coughs in, 170, 171, 175–77
    massage for, 164–65, 447
    oils for, 163, 431
    special needs, 177–80
    toddlers and older children, 169–77, 322, 431
Bach Rescue Remedy, 457
back pain, 181–83, 285
bacteria, 24
    blends for fighting, 345, 403, 434
bad breath, 190
baking soda, 455
balsam
    Canadian (*Abies balsamea*), 32–33
    Peru (*Myroxylon balsamum var. pereirae*), 33
    Tolu (*Myroxylon balsamum*), 34
barrier creams, 384–85
base oils. *See* fixed (carrier) oils
Basic Cologne Formula, 415
Basic Epsom Salts Bath, 413
Basic Essential Oil Stress Blend, 311
Basic Healing Ointment, 234
Basic Herbal Shampoo, 391
Basic Mask, 361
Basic Sea Salt Bath, 413
Basic Underarm Deodorant, 417
basil (*Ocimum basilicum*), 34–35
bathrooms, 436–38
baths, 399–414. *See also* footbaths; sitz baths
    bubble, 412, 452
    cold, 400, 402
    herbal, 400
    hot, 399, 402
    oils for, 403–9, 451
    salts for, 413–14
    vinegars for, 410–11
bay, West Indian (*Pimenta racemosa*), 36

bayberry (*Myrcia cerifera*), 36
bay laurel (*Laurus nobilis*), 36–37
Beat Hot Flashes Blend, 334
Beat the Blues Blend, 335
Beat Water Retention Blend, 339
bedrooms, 428–31
bee stings, 184
beeswax, 455
benzoin (*Styrax benzoin*), 37–38
benzoin, tincture of, 369, 458
bergamot (*Citrus bergamia*), 38–39
bigarade. *See* petitgrain
bipolar disorder, 312
birch (*Betula* spp.). *See also* birch bud
  black (*B. nigra*), 40
  sweet (*B. lenta*), 13, 18, 40
birch bud (*Betula pendula; B. alba*), 38–39
bites and stings. *See also* insects
  from animals, 184–85, 236
  from insects, 168, 185, 220, 236
bitter almond (*Prunus amygdalus*), 18
bitter orange (*Citrus aurantium* var. *amara*), 90. *See also* neroli
black eye, 186
blackheads, 378–79. *See also* acne
black pepper (*Piper nigrum*), 40–41
bleeding (minor), 26, 186, 236
blisters, 186, 236
blood orange (*Citrus sinensis*), 91
blood pressure, 187–88
blue gum. *See* eucalyptus
blue tansy (*Tanacetum annuum*), 111
body care, 399–422. *See also* hair; mouth and teeth; skin
  baths, 399–414
  colognes, 415–16
  deodorants, 417–19
boils and carbuncles, 189
bois de rose. See rosewood
borage seed oil (*Borago officinalis*), 129
borax, 455
botanical names, 22–23, 29
Brain Fatigue Blend, 346
Brandy Lemon Conditioner, 393

breastfeeding, 26, 288
breasts. *See also* breastfeeding
  abscesses, 288–89
  fibrocystic breast disease, 331–32
  nipples, 284
breath, bad, 190
bronchitis, 294–95, 442
bruises, 191–92, 236. *See also* black eye
bubble baths, 412, 452
buchu (*Agothosma betulina*), 18
buckthorn. *See* sea buckthorn–infused oil
bunions, 229
burnout, 312, 348–51
burns and scalds, 192, 236
bursitis, 192–93

C

cabbage rose (*Rosa centifolia*). *See* rose
cajuput (*Melaleuca leucadendra* var. *cajuputi*), 41–42
calamus (*Acorus calamus*), 18
calendula (*Calendula officinalis*), 22
  oil infused with, 141–42
calming oils, 174, 178, 179, 312, 336, 429
camphor (*Cinnamomum camphora*), 18, 101
Canadian balsam (*Abies balsamea*), 32–33
cancer, 194
candidiasis, 195
canola oil, 130
Cape chamomile (*Eriocephalus punctulatus*), 47
carbon dioxide (CO_2) extracts, 417
cardamom (*Elettaria cardamomum*), 42
carminative oils, 25
carpal tunnel syndrome, 196
Carpet Freshener, 426
carrier (fixed) oils, 16, 128–38, 380
carrot seed (*Daucus carota*), 43
carrot seed oil (*Daucus carota* var. *sativa*), 130
cartilage injury (knee), 308–9
cassia (*Cinnamomum cassia*), 18
castile soap (liquid), 391

catarrh, 295, 442
catnip (*Nepeta cataria*), 44
cedar
  red (*Juniperus virginiana*), 44–45
  white (*Thuja occidentalis*), 18, 22, 45
cedarwood (*Cedrus atlantica*), 22, 44–45
celery seed (*Apium graveolens*), 45–46
cellulite, 197, 355
cerebral palsy, 198–99
cervical dysplasia, 330
chamomile, 235
  German (*Matricaria recutita; M. chamomilla*), 46–47
  hydrolats of, 120, 121
  Maroc/wild (*Ormenis mixta; O. multicaulis*), 47
  Roman (*Chamaemelum nobile; Anthemis nobilis*), 21, 46–47
chemotypes, 29
chicken pox, 169–70
children. *See* babies and children
Children's Blend, 431
cholagogue oils, 25
chronic fatigue syndrome, 199–202. *See also* exhaustion; fatigue
cicatrizant oils, 25
cinnamon (*Cinnamomum zeylanicum; C. verum*), 47–48
circulation, 202–3, 442
cistus (*Cistus ladaniferus; C. ladanifer*), 48–49
citronella (*Cymbopogon nardus*), 49–50
Citrus Fresh, 432
citrus oils, 38–39, 63, 74–75, 76–78, 90–91
Citrus Sensation Vinegar, 410
clary sage (*Salvia sclarea*), 50–51
cleansers (facial), 364–66
Cleansing Facial Steam, 377
Clear Air Blend, 277
clove (*Syzygium aromaticum; Eugenia caryophyllata*), 51–52
cocoa butter (*Theobroma cacao*), 130
coconut oil (*Cocos nucifera*), 130–31

CO₂ (carbon dioxide) extracts, 417
Cold and Cough Blend, 204
colds. *See* common cold and influenza
colic, 166, 442
colognes, 415–16
combava (*Citrus hystrix*), 77
comfrey-infused oil (*Symphytum officinale*), 142
common cold and influenza, 203–7, 236
  in children, 166, 170
commuting, 341, 344
Compress Blend (for eczema), 380
compresses, 155, 451
conditioners (hair), 387, 392–94, 452
conjunctivitis, 208
constipation, 216, 442
convalescence, 208
corns, 229–30
costus (*Saussurea costus*), 18
coughs, 296–97, 442. *See also specific respiratory problems*
  in children, 170, 171, 175–77
cradle cap, 166
cramps, 25
  menstrual, 236
  muscular, 210, 236, 442
croup, 171
cubeb (*Piper cubeba*), 52
cultivars, 80
cuts, 172, 211, 236
cypress (*Cupressus sempervirens*), 52–53
cystic fibrosis, 211–12
cystitis, 213–14

D

damask rose (*Rosa damascena*). *See* rose
dandruff, 389, 396–98
Day Break for Girls Blend, 341
Day Break for Guys Blend, 343
debility, 214, 312. *See also* exhaustion; fatigue
Deep Sleep Oil, 255
deodorants, 25, 417–19
Deodorizing Bath Oil Blend, 404
Deodorizing Room Spray, 432
depression, 200–201, 286, 290–91, 335
  oils for, 24, 312

Depression and Irritability Blend, 340
depurative oils, 25
dermatitis, 256–57, 281, 355, 379. *See also* dandruff; eczema; itching
detoxification, 380, 442
Dew Drops Moisturizing Oil, 371
diaper rash, 167–68
diarrhea, 216–17, 236, 325
digestive problems, 26, 27, 75, 216–18. *See also specific problems*
Disinfectant Cleaning Concentrate, 433
Disinfecting Cleaning Spray, 433
distillation, 73, 120
  by enfleurage, 67, 102
  by hydrodistillation, 120
Diuretic Oil Blend, 259
diuretic oils, 26
diverticulitis, 218–19
dog bites, 184–85
dong quai (*Angelica sinensis*), 31
douches, 195–96, 330
Douglas fir (*Pseudotsuga menziesii*), 57
Dry Skin Bath Oil Blend, 404, 406
dwarf Swiss mountain pine (*Pinus mugo* var. *pumilo*), 98
dysentery, 325
dysmenorrhea (painful periods), 338

E

earache, 172, 219
East Indian lemongrass (*Cymbopogon flexuosus*), 75–76
eau de toilette, 415. *See also* colognes
echinacea-infused oil (*Echinacea purpurea*), 142
eczema, 355, 380–81. *See also* dermatitis
edema, 220, 230–31, 322
effleurage, 447
Egg and Almond Mask, 364
Egg and Honey Treatment for Dry, Damaged or Fine Hair, 390

elderflower-infused oil (*Sambucus nigra*), 142
elecampane (*Inula helenium*), 18
emotional problems. *See* stress and emotional problems
emphysema, 221
emulsions, 455
endometriosis, 330–31
enfleurage, 67, 102
Enticement Cologne, 416
Epsom salts baths, 400, 413, 455
Epstein-Barr virus. *See* mononucleosis
essential oils, 12, 13, 28. *See also* aromatherapy; *specific oils and uses*
  blending, 21
  botanical names, 22–23, 29
  buying, 15, 16–17, 18
  chemotypes, 29
  extraction of, 67, 73, 102, 120, 417
  ingestion of, 17, 238–39
  inhalation of, 14
  as irritants, 14, 19, 39
  in luggage, 320
  measuring, 423, 450–52
  mixing/dilution ratios, 16, 152, 353, 453
  oxidation of, 39, 53
  for professional use, 18
  properties, 24–27
  responses to, 14, 15, 19
  safety with, 16–17, 22, 238–39
  sources, 18
  storing, 453
  substituting for, 15
  troubleshooting, 19, 238–39
  using, 14, 15, 16–17, 22
estragole, 34–35, 100
eucalyptus (*Eucalyptus* spp.), 53–55, 235
evening primrose oil (*Oenothera biennis*), 131
everlasting. *See* helichrysum
excitability, 312. *See also* calming oils
Exfoliating Dandruff Treatment, 397
exhaustion, 222, 224, 236, 313. *See also* debility; fatigue
expectorant oils, 26
eyes, 208, 239, 373–74

F

fainting, 223, 312
fatigue, 224–25. *See also*
     debility; exhaustion
   chronic, 199–202
   mental, 225, 346, 347
   physical, 224, 236
fear, 312, 313
feet, 226–31. *See also* footbaths;
     Raynaud's disease
   aching, 226–27
   smelly, 228, 230, 439
   swollen, 220, 230–31, 322
The Feminine Touch, 430
fennel, sweet (*Foeniculum
     vulgare* var. *dulce*), 56
fever, 26, 172–73, 231–32, 236
fibrocystic breast disease,
     331–32
fibromyalgia, 232–33
fir
   Douglas (*Pseudotsuga
     menziesii*), 57
   silver (*Abies alba*), 57–58
first aid, 234–39
   essential oils for, 235
   treatment methods, 238
fistula (anal), 157–58
fixatives, 38
fixed (carrier) oils, 16, 128–38,
     380
flatulence. *See* intestinal gas
Floral Bath Oil, 409
floral waters, 119
Flower Garden Cologne, 416
flu. *See* common cold and
     influenza
fluid retention, 339, 442. *See
     also* edema
Flying High Blend, 321
footbaths, 402–3, 452
Forest Fantasy Deodorant Body
     Spray, 418
Forest Fantasy Vinegar, 411
Fragonia (*Taxandria fragrans;
     Agonis fragrans*), 58
frankincense (*Boswellia carteri;
     B. sacra*), 59
French marigold (*Tagetes patula*),
     22, 142
French rose (*Rosa gallica*). *See*
     rose
Fresh-as-a-Daisy Deodorant
     Body Spray, 418
friar's balsam, 34, 37, 369

frustration, 312
fuller's earth, 361, 455
fungal infections. *See also*
     athlete's foot; candidiasis;
     jock itch; ringworm
   bath vinegars for, 410–11
   oils for, 26, 355
furniture polish, 427

G

galbanum (*Ferula galbaniflua
     communis*), 60
gargles. *See* mouthwashes
gas, intestinal, 218, 442
gastric headaches, 246
Gentle Baby Blend, 165
Gentle Baby Oil, 164, 165
Gentle Rose Toner, 368
geranium (*Pelargonium* x *asperum;
     P. graveolens; P. capitatum; P.
     odoratissimum*), 21, 60–61,
     235
   hydrolat of, 121
German chamomile (*Matricaria
     recutita; M. chamomilla*),
     46–47
   hydrolat of, 121
German measles (rubella), 303
germ-proofing, 345, 403, 433,
     434
ginger (*Zingiber officinale*), 62,
     235
Ginger Honey, 205
gingivitis, 317
Girl's Night In Bath Salts, 414
glandular fever. *See*
     mononucleosis
glass cleaner, 427
glycerin, 364, 456
Glycerin and Honey Soap, 366
Golden Glow Mask, 363
gout, 240–41
grapefruit (*Citrus* x *paradisi*), 63,
     235
grapeseed oil (*Vitis vinifera*), 131
green myrtle. *See* myrtle, true
grief, 33, 58, 82, 84, 85, 312
guilt, 312
gums, 317

H

hair, 387–98. *See also* head lice
   conditioners for, 387, 392–94,
     452
   damaged/fragile, 389, 390

dry, 388, 389, 390
fine, 387–88, 390
loss of, 389, 394–95, 396
mature, 389
moisturizers for, 371
oils for, 389
oily, 388, 389, 393
pre-shampoo treatments,
     389–90
problems with, 394–98
shampoos and rinses, 391–92,
     395, 397–98
thin, 388
hands, 384–86. *See also*
     Raynaud's disease
   barrier creams for, 384–85
   baths for, 402, 451
   sanitizer for, 320
hangover, 242–43
Happy Families Blend, 424
Hawaiian sandalwood (*Santalum
     paniculatum*), 107
hay fever, 236, 243–44. *See also*
     allergies
headaches, 237, 244–46
   gastric, 246
   migraine, 270–71, 313
   tension, 244–45, 313
Head-Clearing Bath Oil Blend,
     406
head lice, 247–48
healing blends, 234
   for diaper rash, 167
   for hands, 385
   for skin problems, 376–78
heartburn, 217
Heart's Ease Blend, 266
heat rash (prickly heat), 237,
     248–49
heatstroke, 237, 315
helichrysum (*Helichrysum
     italicum; H. angustifolium*),
     64. *See also* immortelle
hemiplegia, 279–80
hemlock spruce. *See* Douglas fir
hemorrhoids, 241–42. *See also*
     varicose veins
hepatitis, 261
Herbal Healing Day Oil, 376
Herbal Healing Night Oil, 377
Herb Oil Foot Powder, 228
Hero's Bath and Massage Oil,
     307
herpes, 249–51, 329
hiccups, 252

high blood pressure
(hypertension), 187
hives (urticaria), 220, 326–27
ho leaf. *See* ravintsara
home
cleaners, 426–27, 433–35,
452
cleaning methods, 433–38,
439
germ-proofing, 433, 434
room sprays, 424–25, 432,
435, 452
scent blends, 263, 428–31
honey, 205, 235, 401
honey myrtle (*Melaleuca
teretifolia*), 87
Hormonal Balance Blend, 333
horseradish (*Armoracia
rusticana*), 18
Hot Compress for Abscesses,
154
hot flashes, 334
Hot Oil Treatment (for hair),
390
humectants, 456. *See also*
glycerin; honey; shea butter
Hydrating Bath Oil Blend, 407
hydrolats, 118–27
buying and storing, 118–19
uses, 119
hydrosols, 118, 119
hyperactivity, 178–79. *See also*
calming oils
hypericin, 144
hypericum-infused oil. *See*
St. John's wort–infused oil
hyperpigmentation, 456
hypertension (high blood
pressure), 26, 187
hypotension (low blood
pressure), 26, 188
hyssop (*Hyssopus officinalis*), 65
hysteria, 312. *See also*
overexcitement

I

immortelle (helichrysum
hydrolat), 122. *See also*
helichrysum
immune system, 26, 201, 252–
53, 442. *See also* lymphatic
system
impotence, 267–68
Indian lime (*Citrus medica*), 77
indigestion, 217, 237

infections (blends for), 204, 264.
See also specific conditions
inflammation, 253–54, 355
oils for, 24, 380
influenza. *See* common cold
and influenza
infused oils, 141–47
making, 144, 145–47
storing, 146
Inhalation Blend for Coughs,
296
inhalations, 452
inhalers (personal), 341, 342,
452
insects
bites from, 168, 185, 220, 236
repellents for, 237, 254, 430,
452
insomnia, 237, 254, 255, 312.
See also sleep
in children, 173–75, 431
intertrigo, 256–57
intestinal gas, 218, 442
irritability, 312, 340
irritable bowel syndrome (IBS),
257
itching. *See also* dermatitis;
rashes
bath vinegars for, 410–11
oils for, 237, 258, 273
spray for, 249

J

Jamaica pepper. *See* pimento
jasmine (*Jasminum officinale
var. grandiflorum;
J. grandiflorum*), 66–68
jasmine sambac, 68
Java pepper. *See* cubeb
jet lag, 237
jewelry (aromatic), 15, 341
jock itch, 268
jojoba wax (*Simmondsia sinensis*),
132
juniper (*Juniperus communis*),
68–69
Just "Ahhh!" Bath Oil Blend, 407

K

kaffir lime (*Citrus hystrix*), 77
kanuka (*Kunzea ericoides*), 70
kaolin (china clay), 361, 363,
378, 385, 456
kidneys, 259. *See also* urinary
tract

kitchens, 432–35
kneading (massage), 447
knee injury, 308–9
kukui nut oil (*Aleurites
moluccana*), 132

L

labdanum. *See* cistus
labels, 17, 387
lanolin, 456
laryngitis, 297–98
laundry, 438–39
lavandin (*Lavandula* x
intermedia; L. hybrida),
70–71, 80
lavender (*Lavandula* spp.)
hydrolat of, 122–23
Spanish (*L. stoechas*), 72
spike (*L. latifolia; L. spica*), 72
true (*L. angustifolia;
L. officinalis; L. vera*), 21,
71–73, 235
Lavender Barrier Cream, 385
Lavender Lady Cologne, 416
lavender sage. *See* Spanish sage
Lavender Vinegar, 410
Learn to Love Your Body Bath
Blend, 279
Learn to Love Your Body
Massage Oil, 278
legs. *See also* feet; strains and
sprains
cramps in, 210, 236, 442
swollen, 220
tendonitis, 307–8
lemon (*Citrus limon*), 21, 74–75,
235
Lemon and Lavender Hand
Softener, 384
Lemon and Mint Mouthwash,
191
lemon balm (*Melissa officinalis*),
23, 83–84
hydrolat of, 123
Lemon Balm and Witch Hazel
Toner, 368
Lemon Furniture Polish, 427
lemongrass (*Cymbopogon
citratus; C. flexuosus*), 49,
75–76
Lemon Lip Salve, 422
lemon myrtle (*Backhousia
citriodora*), 87
lemon verbena (*Aloysia tryphilla*),
18, 23

leukorrhea (vaginal discharge), 332

lice (head), 247–48

lime (*Citrus aurantifolia*), 76–78

  kaffir/combava leaf (C. hystrix), 77

  limbu (*C. medica*), 77

linalool, 66

Lip Salve, Lemon, 422

listlessness, 312. *See also* fatigue

Litsea cubeba, 78–79

liver, 26, 260–61

lotions, 16, 152, 451

Loving Touch Blend, 267

low blood pressure (hypotension), 188

lumbago, 182

lymphatic system, 261–62. *See also* immune system

M

macadamia nut oil (*Macadamia ternifolia*; *M. integrifolia*), 133

Macho Man Cologne, 416

Magic Three Toner, 376

mandarin (*Citrus reticulata*), 79–80

manuka (*Leptospermum scoparium*), 80–81

marigold (*Tagetes* spp.), 22, 142. *See also* calendula

marjoram

  Spanish (*Thymus mastichina*), 82

  sweet (*Origanum majorana*), 81–82

Maroc (wild) chamomile (*Ormenis mixta*; *O. multicaulis*), 47

masks (facial), 361–64, 378

massage, 440–47

  for babies and children, 165

  benefits, 440

  cautions, 445–46

  giving, 444–45, 447

  oils for, 165, 440–43, 451

  for pregnant women, 446

Massage Oil Base Blends, 443

mastic (*Pistacia lentiscus*), 83

maturity and old age, 262–63, 355. *See also* hair; menopause; skin

may chang. *See Litsea cubeba*

meadowfoam oil (*Limnanthes alba*), 133

measles, 264

measles, German (rubella), 303

medication cautions, 16, 22

meditation, 312

melissa (*Melissa officinalis*), 23, 83–84

  hydrolat of, 123

Melting Migraine Blend, 270

memory loss, 265. *See also* mental alertness blends

menopause, 333–36. *See also* maturity and old age

men's health, 266–69, 343

menstruation, 26, 337–38. *See also* menopause; premenstrual syndrome

mental alertness blends, 178, 225, 312, 406

migraine, 270–71, 313. *See also* headaches

Milk and Orange Mask, 362

milk baths, 400

Mind Soother, 429

mineral oil, 140

mint (*Mentha* spp.)

  pennyroyal (*M. pulegium*), 18

  peppermint (*M.* x *piperita*), 95–96, 124, 235

  spearmint (*M. spicata*), 109–10

Mint and Lemon Tooth Powder, 316

Mint Tang Vinegar, 411

Mint Zinger Aftershave, 369

moisturizers

  for hair, 371, 372

  for skin, 370–72, 457

molluscum contagiosum ("water warts"), 328

mononucleosis (infectious), 271

Monster Spray, 174

mood swings, 313, 336

morning sickness, 283

motion sickness, 237, 324–25

mouth and teeth, 272, 316–18, 420–22

mouthwashes, 190–91, 451

mugwort (*Artemisia herba-alba*), 18

mullein-infused oil (*Verbascum thapsus*), 143

multiple sclerosis (MS), 272–73

mumps, 273

muscles, 210, 237, 274–75, 300–302, 442

  bath vinegars for, 410–11

  blends for, 198, 199, 274, 275

mustard (*Brassica nigra*), 18

myalgic encephalomyelitis (ME). *See* chronic fatigue syndrome

myrrh (*Commiphora myrrha*), 85

Myrrh Mouthwash, 190

myrtle. *See also* myrtle, true

  anise (*Syzygium anisatum*; *Backhousia anisata*), 87

  honey (*Melaleuca teretifolia*), 87

  lemon (*Backhousia citriodora*), 87

  red, 86

  wax (*Myrcia cerifera*), 36

myrtle, true (*Myrtus communis*), 86–87

N

Natural Soft Cleaning Scrub, 434

nausea, 24, 275–76. *See also* vomiting

  morning sickness, 283

  motion sickness, 237, 324–25

neck, 383. *See also* throat

neem oil (*Azadirachta indica*), 134

negativity, 313. *See also* depression

neroli (*Citrus aurantium* var. *amara flos*), 88. *See also* bitter orange

  hydrolat of, 124

nerolina. *See* niaouli

Nervous Exhaustion Blend, 222

nervousness, 313

nervous system, 26

neuralgia, 276–77

New Zealand tea tree. *See* manuka

niaouli (*Melaleuca quinquenervia*), 89

Nipple Oil, 284

nose (blocked), 277

nutmeg (*Myristica fragrans*), 90

O

oakmoss (*Evernia prunastri*), 18

oats, 361, 363, 457

obesity, 278–79

obsessiveness, 313

oils. *See also* essential oils
  carrier (fixed), 128–38
  infused, 141–47
Oily Skin Bath Oil Blends, 405
ointments, 451, 458
old age. *See* maturity and old age
olibanum. *See* frankincense
olive oil (*Olea europaea*), 134
orange (*Citrus* spp.). *See also*
  bergamot; mandarin; neroli;
  petitgrain
  bitter (*C. aurantium* var.
    amara), 90
  sweet (*C. sinensis*), 91
orange flower water, 119, 124
orange myrtle. *See* myrtle, true
Oregon pine. *See* Douglas fir
orris root (*Iris florentina*), 457
osteoarthritis. *See* arthritis
overexcitement, 168, 175. *See
  also* calming oils
Overtired and Strung-Out Blend,
  174
oxidation, 39, 53

P

pain, 442
Pain and Itch Relief Oil for MS,
  273
palmarosa (*Cymbopogon martinii*
  var. *motia*), 49, 92
palmitoleic acid, 133
palo santo (*Bursera graveolens*),
  92–93
panic attacks, 312, 313. *See also*
  calming oils
paperbark. *See* cajuput
paralysis, 279–80
paranoia, 313
parsley (*Petroselinum crispum*),
  93–94
passion flower–infused oil
  (*Passiflora incarnata*), 143
patchouli (*Pogostemon cablin*), 94
patch testing, 13, 19, 454
peanut oil (*Arachis hypogea*), 134
pennyroyal (*Mentha pulegium*),
  18
pepper, black (*Piper nigrum*),
  40–41
peppermint (*Mentha* x *piperita*),
  95–96, 235
  hydrolat of, 124
Peppermint and Myrrh
  Mouthwash, 421

perfumer's alcohol, 415
perfumes, 415. *See also* colognes
perineum (sore), 289–90
Peru balsam (*Myroxylon
  balsamum* var. *pereirae*), 33
petitgrain (*Citrus aurantium* var.
  amara flos; *C. aurantium* var.
  bigardia), 96–97
petroleum jelly, 140
phototoxicity, 19, 74, 457. *See
  also* hyperpigmentation
pH scale, 454
Physical Exhaustion Blend, 222
Physical Fatigue Massage Blend,
  224
Pick-Me-Up Blend, 209
pimento (*Pimenta dioica*;
  P. officinalis), 97–98
pine (*Pinus* spp.). *See also*
  Douglas fir
  dwarf Swiss mountain
    (*P. mugo* var. *pumilo*), 98
  Scots (*P. sylvestris*), 98–99
plai (*Zingiber cassumunar*;
  Z. montanum), 99
PMS Blend, 339
poison ivy, oak and sumac, 281,
  410–11
Postnatal Blues Beater, 290
Precious Night Oil, 374
Pre-flying Nerves Tamer, 320
pregnancy and birth, 282–91
  pregnancy, 282, 283–86, 446
  labor, 282, 286–87
  birth, 286–87
  postnatal care, 282, 288–91
premenstrual syndrome (PMS),
  339–40
Prenatal Nerves Bath Blend, 286
preservatives, 38
Prevent Cramps Blend, 338
prickly heat (heat rash), 237,
  248–49
Primrose Path Moisturizing Oil,
  370
Productive Day Blend, 347
prostatitis, 268–69
pruritis. *See* itching
psoriasis, 382–83
Put-the-Pressure-On Massage
  Blend, 188

Q

quadriplegia, 279–80
Quickie Mouthwash, 190, 421

Quickie Shampoo, 392
Quiet the Queasiness Tonic, 324

R

rapeseed oil (*Brassica napu*), 130
rashes, 281, 405. *See also*
  dermatitis; itching
  hives, 220, 326–27
  prickly heat, 237, 248–49
ravensara (*Ravensara aromatica*),
  100
ravintsara (*Cinnamomum
  camphora*; *Ravintsara
  aromatica*; *R. camphora*),
  101
Raynaud's disease, 291–92
red cedar (*Juniperus virginiana*),
  44–45
red myrtle, 86
rejuvenating blends, 406–8. *See
  also* stimulating blends
relaxing blends, 407, 408–9,
  414, 429
repetitive strain injury, 293
Rescue Remedy (Bach), 457
Respiratory Infection Prevention
  Blend, 207
respiratory problems, 221, 277,
  293–99. *See also* common
  cold and influenza; coughs
restless legs syndrome (RLS),
  300
restlessness, 313
rheumatism, 300–302, 442
rheumatoid arthritis. *See* arthritis
ringworm, 302–3
rinses. *See* shampoos and rinses
Rise and Shine Bath Oil Blend,
  408
rock rose. *See* cistus
Roman chamomile
  (*Chamaemelum nobile*;
  Anthemis nobilis), 21, 46–47
  hydrolat of, 120
Romantic Nights, 429
room sprays, 424–25, 432, 435,
  452
rosacea, 355, 356, 357
rose (*Rosa centifolia*;
  R. damascena; *R. gallica*),
  102–3. *See also* rosehip seed
  oil
  hydrolat of (rose water), 102,
  119, 125
  "otto" (attar) of, 102

rose geranium. *See* geranium

rosehip seed oil (*Rosa mosqueta*; *R. rubingosa*; *R. canina*), 135

rosemary (*Rosmarinus officinalis*), 103–5, 235
  hydrolat of, 126

Rosemary Conditioner, 393

rosewood (*Aniba rosaeodora*), 105–6

rubefacient oils, 27

rubella (German measles), 303

S

safflower oil (*Carthamus tinctorius*), 135

sage (*Salvia officinalis*), 106
  clary (*S. sclarea*), 50–51
  Spanish (*S. lavandulaefolia*), 106–7

salves, 451, 458

sandalwood (*Santalum album*), 103, 107–8

saro (*Cinnamosma fragrans*), 108–9

sassafras (*Sassafras albidum*), 18

Satin Skin Gel, 371

savin (*Juniperus sabina*), 18, 68, 69

savory (*Satureia hortensis*), 18

scabies, 304–5

scalp tonics, 389

scar tissue, 25, 305, 355

scent-free policies, 341

school stress, 341–51

sciatica, 183

Scots pine (*Pinus sylvestris*), 98–99

scrubs
  facial, 360–61
  household, 434

sea buckthorn–infused oil (*Hippophae rhamnoides*), 143–44

Sea Salt Bath, Basic, 413

seborrheic dermatitis. *See* dandruff

sebum, 458

sedative oils, 27

sensitization, 14, 19, 113. *See also* allergies

sesame oil (*Sesamum indicum*), 136

sexual dysfunction, 267–68, 313, 442

shampoos and rinses, 387, 391–92, 452
  for alopecia, 395
  commercial, 387, 388, 391
  for dandruff, 397, 398
  pre-treatments, 389–90

shea butter (*Vitellaria paradoxa*), 136, 381

shigellosis (dysentery), 325

shingles (herpes zoster), 251

shock, 306, 313

shoes (smelly), 230, 439

shower gels, 412, 452

Silky Skin and Hair Moisturizing Oil, 372

silver fir (*Abies alba*), 57–58

sinusitis, 298–99

sitz baths, 290, 332, 402, 452

skin, 353–86, 401, 451. *See also* body care; *specific skin types (below)*
  eye area, 373–74
  face, 353–72
  of hands, 384–86
  mature, 355, 359, 363, 364, 368
  neck, 383
  oils for, 354–55, 442
  problems with, 197, 375–83
  scarred, 305, 355
  stretch marks on, 283–84

skin, dry, 354, 355, 356
  baths for, 404, 406–7
  cleansers for, 364
  masks for, 358
  moisturizers for, 370
  steams for, 362, 363
  toners and astringents for, 368

skin, oily, 354, 356, 378–79
  baths for, 405, 410–11
  masks for, 363
  moisturizers for, 371
  steams for, 359
  toners and astringents for, 367, 379

skin, sensitive, 354, 356
  cleansers for, 364, 365
  masks for, 362, 364
  moisturizers for, 372

sleep, 429, 431. *See also* insomnia
  blends for, 255, 324, 409, 429

sluggishness, 75, 180, 313. *See also* rejuvenating blends; stimulating blends

Smelling Salts, 223

soaps, 366, 391

Solubol, 156, 249

Soothing Foot Lotion, 227

Soothing Wash for Diaper Rash, 168

Sore Muscle Soak, 275

sore throat, 297–99, 318–19

South Pacific sandalwood (*Santalum austrocaledonicum*), 107

Spanish lavender (*Lavandula stoechas*), 72

Spanish marjoram (*Thymus mastichina*), 82

Spanish sage (*Salvia lavandulaefolia*), 106–7

spearmint (*Mentha spicata*), 109–10

spider bites, 185

spike lavender (*Lavandula latifolia*; *L. spica*), 72

spikenard (*Nardostachys jatamansi*; *N. grandiflora*), 110

sports, 306–10

Spotty Skin Bath Oil Blend, 405

sprains, 220, 237, 442

St. John's wort–infused oil (*Hypericum perforatum*), 144

Stale Air Reviver, 345

star anise (*Illicium verum*), 32

steams
  facial, 357, 358–59, 377, 378–79, 451
  for respiratory problems, 171, 207, 244

stimulating blends, 27, 408. *See also* mental alertness blends; rejuvenating blends

storax, 458

strains and sprains, 237, 309, 442

stress and emotional problems, 310–13, 341–51
  diarrhea caused by, 216
  essential oils for, 311–13, 380, 429, 442

Stress Blend, Basic Essential Oil, 311

stretch marks, 283–84

Stuffy Head and Achy Body Blend, 206

styptic oils, 27

styrax. *See* benzoin

sunburn, 237, 314, 410–11
sunflower oil (*Helianthus annuus*), 137
Sunrise Aftershave, 369
Sunshine Blend, 180
sunstroke, 237, 315
sweating, 25, 27. *See also* deodorants
sweet almond oil (*Prunus dulcis*), 128
sweet birch (*Betula lenta*), 13, 18, 40
sweet fennel (*Foeniculum vulgare* var. *dulce*), 56
Sweetheart Cologne, 416
sweet marjoram (*Origanum majorana*), 81–82
sweet orange (*Citrus sinensis*), 91
Swollen Feet and Ankles Blend, 230
Swollen Glands Blend, 273
synergy, 21, 152

T

Take-the-Pressure-Off Massage Blend, 187
tamanu oil (*Calophyllum inophyllum*), 137
tansy (*Tanacetum vulgare*; *T. annuum*), 111
tarragon (*Artemisia dracunculus*), 18
tea tree (*Melaleuca alternifolia*), 21, 112–13, 235. *See also* kanuka; manuka
hydrolat of, 126–27
teeth and gums, 316–18, 420
teething, 168
tendonitis, Achilles, 307–8
tension. *See* anxiety; stress and emotional problems
throat, 297–98, 299, 318–19. *See also* neck
Throat Oil, 299
thrush. *See* candidiasis
thuja (*Thuja occidentalis*), 18, 22
thujone, 65
thyme (*Thymus vulgaris*), 113–14
ti-tree. *See* tea tree
Toddler Tamer, 322
toilets, 437–38
Tolu balsam (*Myroxylon balsamum*), 34
toners and astringents, 367–69, 376, 379

tonic oils, 27
tonsillitis, 299
Tooth Powder, 420
Top of the Mornin' Astringent, 367
travel, 320–25
by airplane, 320–21
by car, 325, 341, 344
diarrhea during, 32
Travel Buddy Blend, 323
Tummy Oil, 284

U

ulcers (mouth), 272
Under-Eye Oil, 373
unguents, 451, 458
Up and At 'Em Oil, 306
urinary tract, 213–14, 268–69, 326. *See also* kidneys
urticaria (hives), 220, 326–27
uterus, 27. *See also* menstruation; pregnancy and birth

V

vacuum cleaners, 426
vaginal discharge (leukorrhea), 332
valerian (*Valeriana officinalis*), 114
valerianol, 30
varicose veins, 285. *See also* hemorrhoids
varieties (of plants), 80
vehicles. *See* travel
veins, 27, 285, 355
verrucae (warts), 328
vertigo, 313
vetiver (*Vetiveria zizanoides*), 115
vinegar baths, 401, 410–11
violet leaf (*Viola odorata*), 115–16
viral infections, 25, 249–51, 327, 328–29
blends for fighting, 403, 425
diarrhea caused by, 216
vitamin E oil, 14, 137
vodka, 415, 454
vomiting, 237, 327. *See also* nausea

W

Waiting for Baby Massage Blend, 287
warts (verrucae), 328

Washing Water, 364
wasp stings, 185
water, 458
water retention, 339, 442. *See also* edema
wax myrtle (*Myrcia cerifera*), 36
Welcome Home Blend, 424
Welcoming Baby Spray, 287
Welcoming Home Blend, 263
West Australian sandalwood (*Santalum spicatum*), 107, 108
western red cedar (*Thuja plicata*), 18
West Indian bay (*Pimenta racemosa*), 36
West Indian lemongrass (*Cymbopogon citratus*), 49, 75–76
West Indian sandalwood. *See* amyris
West Nile virus, 329
wheat germ oil (*Triticum vulgare*), 138, 164
white birch. *See* birch bud
white camphor. *See* ravintsara
white cedar (*Thuja occidentalis*), 18, 22, 45
white tea tree. *See* kanuka
whitlow, 329
whooping cough, 175–77
Winter Blend for Cold and Flu Prevention, 206
wintergreen (*Gaultheria procumbens*), 13, 18
witch hazel hydrolat (Hamamelis virginiana), 127, 235
women's health, 330–40, 341. *See also specific conditions*
workplace stress, 341–51
wormseed (*Chenopodium ambrosioides*), 18
wormwood (*Artemisia absinthium*), 18
wounds, 27, 237. *See also* abrasions; cuts
wrinkles. *See* skin, mature

Y

yarrow (*Achillea millefolium*), 116
Yeast and Yogurt Mask, 363
Yeast and Yogurt Scrub, 361
ylang ylang (*Cananga odorata*), 117